MODERN
Continental
DRAMAS

Edited by Harlan Hatcher

PROFESSOR OF ENGLISH, OHIO STATE UNIVERSITY

HARCOURT, BRACE & WORLD, INC.

NEW YORK AND BURLINGAME

CONTENTS

CONTENTS

MODERN CONTINENTAL DRAMA

THE drama is a serious rival of the novel as a medium of expression for the genius of our time. Ibsen, Chekhov, Gorky, Strindberg, Hauptmann, Shaw, O'Neill are dominant names among the great literary figures of the world of the last seventy-five years. Viewed solely from the point of view of literature few modern novelists equal or surpass these dramatists. Of the thirty-eight writers in all the forms of literature to receive the Nobel prize since 1901, nine have been dramatists.

Many causes have contributed to the elevation and extension of the drama in the modern period. The number of theatres throughout the world has increased remarkably in response to the renewal of interest in drama, and these theatres have in turn stimulated the writing and production of plays. Architects have designed more interesting and more plastic stages in the modern period; producers have developed more versatile methods, and directors have utilized the attendant advances in the art of scene designing, mounting, lighting and acting to heighten their effects. The theatres have become physically more comfortable. Of even greater importance, they have become respectable; and in the twentieth century an upright citizen may go to a theatre as freely as to a church without besmirching his character. Plays have been made more available to more people. And with the growth, or the revival, of the practice of printing dramas to be read as novels, poems, and biographies are read, the handicaps under which dramatists work as men of letters have been to a large degree removed. While writing primarily for production on stage, they have also reached the wider audience of thoughtful readers, including those in college courses in modern drama.

The activity within the theatres in the modern period has been enormous, and the number of plays written and produced is vast. A moment's calculation will show that if we merely considered the ten best plays of each year throughout the world we would have before us 750 plays since Ibsen's *Brand* and *Peer Gynt*. (Incidentally, Burns Mantle finds ten best plays each season in New York alone.)

The nature of modern drama, however, and the course of its historical development in Europe, Britain, and America help to resolve some of the difficulties. The national characteristics of the dramas have been, in general, clearly marked. French drama is French, not German; Russian drama is Russian, not English. Modern drama may be profitably studied from the point of view of its national development. At the same time, from a more exalted point of view it has been knit into an international unit by a common bond of interest in subject matter and technique. Speaking in broad, general terms, but not inaccurately, French drama has gone through the same cycles as the English, the German, and the Russian. No other form of literary expression reflects so immediately, so accurately, and so fully the international ideas and the interests of the modern period. The intellectual, social, and emotional history of our times could be written from the materials furnished by the plays of the world since Ibsen's *The League of Youth*.

The story of the rise of the modern drama divides itself conveniently into periods. The edges of these periods blur and dissolve into each other, of course, but they remain sufficiently well-marked to impose enough order upon the mass of dramatic writing to permit us to think of it as a whole and to study its characteristics. The drama is also obliging in that its forms are as distinct as the time periods, and correspond roughly to them. With the aid of these two categories of time sequence and technical form we can make our way through the huge output of the modern theatre.

Chronologically the phenomenon that we now call modern drama emerged in the 1870's from the romantic and poetic dramas of the early nineteenth century. By the year 1880 it was emphatic enough to be recognizable as something new. Björnson, Ibsen, Strindberg, Becque, Tolstoy, and Zola were the leading pioneers in the new movement during the 1880's. They took pride in the creed of Realism which they embraced. According to this faith, all aspects of life, especially the ugly, miserable, lowly, and wretched, should be exhibited by the dramatist. He should maintain the detached objectivity of the scientist and report exactly what he saw. He should not falsify by rearranging or softening the harshness of life itself. He should reproduce it visually on the stage through the medium of drama. He should make as few concessions as possible to plot and the artificiality of the theatre.

The second phase of the movement began at the close of the 1880's and reached its climax in the 1890's, though many characteristics of the drama of that period continue with only slight modifications to this day in plays like *Tobacco Road, Dead End, Love on the Dole,* and *The Little Foxes.* The period is a complicated tangle of antagonistic creeds and factions, of movements and reactions. It is the period of Naturalism, Symbolism, and the thesis play; of the rise of the new theatres, and the modification of the old. It is the period of Chekhov and Gorky in Russia; of Hauptmann, Sudermann, Wedekind, von Hofmannstahl, and Halbe in Germany; of Schnitzler in Austria; of Porto-Riche, de Curel, Brieux, Hervieu, of Lemaître, Rostand, and Maeterlinck in France; of Wilde, Jones, Pinero, and Shaw in England; of Echegaray and Benavente in Spain; of Galdós and D'Annunzio in Italy. The burst of creative activity was furious and of a high order.

The Naturalists, like Strindberg and Hauptmann, were closely related to the Realists. As a matter of fact, the two terms are confused; they were often used interchangeably in the eighties and nineties. Later criticism has been more specific. The term Realism is now generally used to denote a method of approach, and the ideal of objective and disinterested accuracy. Naturalism implies an attitude toward the *meaning* of the spectacle, a philosophy of interpretation. In practice it means scientific materialism, a preoccupation with the animality of man, not with his spiritual nature or potentialities. Realism and Naturalism, both well represented by appropriate plays in this volume, have been analysed in some detail in the individual critical introductions.

Symbolism came in as a protest and a reaction against the wave of Naturalism that engulfed the theatre in the 1890's. It attempted, with considerable success, to suggest wider reaches of the human spirit than Naturalism had presented. It called upon symbols and their associations and suggestive values to enlarge the scope of drama beyond the narrow confines of objective, unimaginative reporting, as shown for example in the work of Maeterlinck. It was only a step from symbolistic drama into the world of Romance, as cultivated by Rostand.

The thesis play, employed with notable effect by Pinero, Shaw, Brieux, and many others, was simply the application of the realistic methods for the purpose of discussing an important issue or advocating reform. The emancipation of woman, the evils in the church, social diseases, individual maladjustments, and a score of other controversial problems, all came in for treatment in the thesis plays of "the useful theatre," and continue unabated.

The period from 1900 through the First World War saw an extension and refinement of the advances made in the preceding decade. The one new development was Expressionism. It was a method invented by Strindberg, Wedekind, and others to deal more fluidly with modern psychological phenomena. It made free use of symbolism to break down the rigid pattern of objective experience. It sought to isolate qualities of mind or abstract essences of experience, to cast them into visual form, and to fling them into action on stage. The term itself is unsatisfactory. The best way to give it content is simply to study *The Ghost Sonata*, *The Adding Machine*, *R. U. R.*, and *Transfiguration*. Whatever these plays are—that is Expressionism. Greatly reinforced by the brilliant work of directors and designers such as Craig, Reinhardt, Piscator, Meyerhold, and Kommisarzhevsky, it has continued to the present day.

Symbolism was also extended into the twentieth century in Claudel's *The Tidings Brought to Mary*, and other plays. It is still frequently employed by modern playwrights.

The period from 1920 to the present day has been even more complicated than that of the 1890's. The cycles or vogues have been speeded up until they succeed one another, season by season, with bewildering rapidity. All known methods of dramaturgy are employed, and all subjects of interest or concern to modern man are given dramatic expression. Activity has continued intensively in most of the theatrical centers of the world. The rise of the new drama in America and in Russia increased the interest and the tempo. The stage became more than ever before an international institution. Except for recent restrictions set up by totalitarian countries, the plays of the different nations have crossed all borders and have been performed in nearly every other nation. This free trade, together with the alert spirit of experimentation that continues in most of the world, has helped to keep the modern drama vigorously alive and advancing. Thesis plays, symbolistic plays, naturalistic plays, expressionistic plays; religious, political, industrial, sociological, psychological, romantic plays, all flourish side by side in the contemporary theatre.

It is quite impossible to mention all the interesting and important dramatists in a collection of thirty-one plays, or even in a college course on contemporary drama. It is with reluctance that we omit such figures as Kaiser, Schnitzler, D'Annunzio, Chlumberg, the Quinteros, Vildrac, Giraudoux, Bernard, Brieux, et cetera. But, individual as these dramatists are, they are also a part of a movement or a phenomenon larger than any single figure. Their work may easily be fitted into the study of modern drama as outlined in, and represented by, this collection. The dramas finally chosen for inclusion were selected for their dramatic and literary distinction, for their intrinsic interest, for their representative qualities, or because for one reason or another they are indispensable to an understanding of modern drama. The dramatists represented here are central figures whose works embody almost every dramatic phenomenon of interest to our times.

HENRIK IBSEN

HENRIK IBSEN is for the historians one of the most convenient figures in literature. He is a landmark. Without controversy, and with a minimum of explanatory defense, two sweeping observations can be made about him: that what we now call modern drama began with Ibsen; and that he is the overshadowing giant among the playwrights of the modern theatre. He not only created the vogue of the modern problem play which has dominated the theatre for six decades, but he illustrated in his long career of fifty years, from *Catiline* in 1849 to *When We Dead Awaken* in 1899, almost every aspect of the drama that has interested our times.

Ibsen's life was not colorful. His plays are much more interesting than his biography. But he had the genius to extract the qualities of universal import from the experiences that did befall him, and to transform casual episodes into stirring drama. He was born on March 20, 1828, in Skien, a small coastal town fifty miles up the beautiful Lourvik Fjord off the Skagerrak. It lies at the base of the rugged and legend-haunted mountains of southern Norway which Ibsen described with such spirited enchantment in *Peer Gynt*. In Ibsen's youth the town was flourishing and socially active in a provincial way. At the time of Ibsen's birth, and for the next seven years, his family belonged to the prosperous merchant class. The Stockman house, as their home was called, faced the large public square of Skien. In the center of the square was the church, and around it were the Latin and grammar schools, the town pillory, the madhouse, and the jail. That grim arrangement certainly presented to the eyes of Ibsen a microcosm of the heights and the abysses of man's reach in his institutions of worship, education, punishment, and asylum. Following his own lead and symbolic method in the later plays like *The Wild Duck* and *Rosmersholm*, we may be permitted to speculate upon the significance of this early scene and its effect upon Ibsen's temperament and his mature view of life and human destiny.

At the end of the seven good years in Henrik's life, the Ibsens lost their money and their social station. Their property was liquidated to satisfy their creditors, and they were forced down to a meager existence in a wretched little farmhouse outside Skien which they were able to save from the wreckage. Such bitter family experiences left a deep and ineradicable scar in the developing mindset of this ruminative child. He learned early how to brood through the long gloomy days over human mutability, over the hypocrisy of the professed friends of his family who deserted them in their misfortune, and over the materialistic values that corroded the lives of these pillars of society. Memories of this reversal, of its disastrous effect upon his father who immediately deteriorated, and of the harsh struggle of his mother, come poignantly through the romantic fabric of the first scenes of *Peer Gynt*. Ibsen himself said, "This poem contains much that has its origin in the circumstances of my own youth. My

1

own mother—with the necessary exaggeration—served as the model for Ase."

The effects of these first conscious experiences were not mitigated but only deepened by the years of struggle that preceded his first success. His portraits are all worthy of study. Stern purpose burns through his eyes; the corners of his mouth dip and snap into a pose of stubborn aggressiveness; the forelock above the massive curve of his skull is a plume of confidence; and his flowing beard completes the halo of the zealous and successful champion of reform. But that highly individual countenance was moulded only after years of determined self-discipline, and of persistent achievement. By his own blazing energy he triumphed over all the barriers that lie between a penniless young son of a bankrupt and broken father in an obscure mountain valley and the place of supreme eminence among the poets and dramatists of his age.

During the eight years on the barren farm Ibsen felt his ambitions stirring toward the art of painting, for which he had talent but no means, and toward literature and the theatre about which, shut away by himself, he gloomily daydreamed. Those avenues seemed closed. When he was fifteen, he got a place first as apprentice and then as assistant to a druggist at Grimstad. In this commonplace, provincial, and puritanic community Ibsen shrewdly observed many details of character in men like his Parson Brand in *Brand* and Pastor Manders in *Ghosts*. He also learned a great deal about the human spirit from his own lonely, subordinate, discouraged, and distressed days in this cluster of red houses, on a melancholy sea coast whose isolation, except as a port of call for certain boats, was absolute. He was caged in Grimstad from 1844 to the end

of 1849. His morose rebellion was softened a little during the last years by some progress in his trade, by the solace of writing poetry and dramatic verse, and by a hope of studying medicine. With the questioning spirit appropriate to youth, he was stirred by the radicalism of his day as reflected in the hopeful events of 1848. Remnants of this period of "radical" stirrings lie like dead wood in several of his plays, notably in the sub-plot of *Rosmersholm*.

By 1850, Ibsen's growing sense of need and power could no longer be constrained by Grimstad. He went to Christiania to enter the university, intending to study medicine. But his modest success with *Catiline*, published that year, switched him toward philosophy, literature, and social issues, and then into the theatre. Ole Bull, the Norwegian violinist who made several triumphant tours of America, established the Norwegian Theatre at Bergen in 1850, and had Ibsen appointed as its dramatist in November, 1851, and later as manager. The next April the directors paid Ibsen's traveling expenses on a tour of inspection and study of the theatres in Copenhagen, Hamburg, Dresden, and Berlin. Ibsen wished, he said, to acquaint himself "with the technique of dramatic art, the principles of its practice in the different places and in its various forms, together with everything pertaining to the management of theatres." He was especially well-received by the Theatre Royal at Copenhagen. The experience must have been tremendous for the rising young dramatist from Grimstad; it confirmed him in his bent toward playwriting and the theatre.

In the summer of 1857, after nearly six years of hard training at the theatre in Bergen, Ibsen left to become "artistic director" of the Norwegian Theatre of Christiania. He held that post, working at all hours writing for himself, polishing and presenting old plays, until the theatre failed in the summer of 1862. He had already applied for state aid without success. Now, in desperation, he appealed to the king for the second time for a pension "to enable me to continue labours in the service of literature which I have reason to believe the public does not wish to see interrupted." His appeal was again rejected. Finally, on a third petition the next year, in which he reminded his king "that similar travelling allowances have been granted to all the Norwegian writers except myself," he was given a pension of 400 specie-dollars ($450); and in the spring of 1864, aged thirty-six, with fifteen years apprenticeship behind him, he left Norway for Berlin and Rome, fired with ambition and bubbling with ideas and plans for the future.

The next few years were richly productive. Besides some minor work, he wrote *Brand*, which was published in Copenhagen on March 15, 1866, and *Peer Gynt*, which appeared on November 14, 1867. Ibsen's fame and success were never again in doubt. Except for brief vacation visits back to Norway, he lived abroad for the next twenty-seven years chiefly in Rome, Dresden, and Munich, and wrote in voluntary exile all the famous plays from *Brand* to *Hedda Gabler*. Then in July, 1891, at the age of sixty-three, with most of his great work completed, he returned to Christiania to live the rest of his life as a world celebrity. His active career was practically over when the English speaking world began to take him up. He died in 1906 and was buried at Oslo.

The course of Ibsen's career reflects quite accurately and conveniently the fashions current in the theatre. Modern drama has revolved around three axes—romance in the traditional style; naturalism with an implication of the need if not a direct appeal for reform; and symbolism, sometimes in dramatic verse, sometimes imposed upon a realistic pattern in an attempt to correct the perspective and supply some of the omissions that falsified the naturalistic plays. These included nine important apprenticeship plays, as well as his journeyman's successes, *Brand* and *Peer Gynt*. The pretentious prose drama *Emperor and Galilean* (1873), which cost him several years labor and was more to his satisfaction than any of his earlier works, may also be included in this group. All of Ibsen's early plays were in the hallowed and moribund mold of early nineteenth century romantic drama. Within their circumscribed themes and forms, and for their period, these were remarkable plays. *Peer Gynt* in particular has been continuously and almost universally admired. But after these dramas have been duly praised, we are still confronted with the historical fact that they were the end of an old era, not the beginning of a new one.

The plays that made Ibsen the founder of "modern" drama were not the early romantic dramas but the social problem plays in contemporary settings realistically handled. These plays, with the single exception of his experimental *The League of Youth* (1869), were all written after *Emperor and Galilean* and were concentrated within a period of a dozen years. *The Pillars of Society* came in 1877, *A Doll's House* in 1879, *Ghosts* in 1881, *An Enemy of the People* in 1882, *The Wild Duck* in 1884, *Rosmersholm* in 1886, *The Lady from the Sea* in 1888, and *Hedda Gabler* in 1890.

These plays aroused the Europe of the

eighties and nineties, largely because the time was ripe for them. All sorts of problems kept pressing in upon the complacency of the prosperous mercantile world of Ibsen's day. How long could Society go on under the jungle precept of the survival of the fittest in an era of unrestricted commerce? Was there no moral law higher than the doctrine of laissez-faire in a system of machines, their owners, and their attendants? Even more dramatic were the upheavals caused by the rise of the feminist movement, and the agitation for the emancipation of woman from her state of inferiority. This campaign not only threatened the masculine dominion over the world of property, but it raised the more far-reaching question of just what rights and personal freedom an individual might reserve strictly unto himself, and to what degree he might ignore or defy the conventions and opinions of society.

Ibsen had strong convictions on these issues and on other questions of concern to his age. He had reached the period of ripe middle age sustained by the confidence inspired by his success. He was in his vigorous fifties, famous, and still growing in his mastery of dramatic form. He was in close touch with the swift-flowing currents of contemporary thought, and he had the genius to dramatize ideas in the medium of solidly created character.

The ideas in the plays may have been "no more than the common culture of the day," as Somerset Maugham has charged, but Ibsen was still far enough in advance of the literate, play-reading, theatre-going public to startle it with these ideas and to become the center and the figurehead of a movement.

In *The Pillars of Society* Ibsen dramatized the more general problems raised in the idealistic mind by the spectacle of dishonest, scheming, corrupt, and two-faced men becoming wealthy and powerful leaders of society. In *An Enemy of the People* he presented the obverse phenomenon in which an upright man of highest integrity, who tries disinterestedly to serve his community, as did Ibsen himself, is misunderstood and reviled by the very people whom he is trying to help. He did permit the villain to reform in *The Pillars of Society;* and he ended the play with a little sermon summed up in the tag lines of Bernick and Lona:

BERNICK. . . . I have learnt *this* too, in these last few days; it is you women that are the pillars of society.

LONA. You have learnt a poor sort of wisdom, then, brother-in-law. No, my friend; the spirit of truth and the spirit of freedom—they are the pillars of society.

It was Ibsen's attack on the feminist question in *A Doll's House* that first elevated him into an international figure. That drama was so intimately enmeshed with its time that it did more than any other play to make the modern theatre a platform for the discussion of social problems. It was perfectly timed to become a manifesto for the moderns. By law and custom, if not always in practice, women were inferior and under subjection to their men. Their education was limited, their activities narrowly circumscribed. Until the Married Women's Property Act of 1882 and 1893 in England, the husband controlled his wife's property. But women were getting restive and defiant in the 1880's. They took up mixed tennis (the gentlemen played with coats on) and bicycling, even golf, shooting, hunting, and hiking. They demanded votes and equal opportunities for education and entrance into the professions. Their assault on man's authority and their rebellion against the time-honored conventions that held them in their dolls' houses were shocking. Ibsen's play on the subject was first performed in this surcharged atmosphere; to this day it stands as a venerable landmark in modern social history. It was so squarely at the front and center of this world movement, which was not completed until after the World War, that the play seemed actually to be thought of as the cause of the agitation rather than just another manifestation of it.

A Doll's House is still a fairly lively play, though we may now smile indulgently at its dated technique and at the furor aroused by its thesis. A present day Nora might easily find herself married and in subjection to a Torvald who called her his little skylark, his little squirrel, and stultified her personality by requiring her to act like a silly, wayward, and irresponsible doll; but she would also find herself in a world where the problem was no longer a general one involving the entire social climate but an individual issue which she might settle at her pleasure whenever she wished to become an adult woman.

Ghosts was a quick follow up and a much better play. It dates only in its few passages of "advanced" conversation, and in its self-conscious sense of daring in discussing the hereditary effects of syphilis in paresis. As a play it is tight and firm, and the action unfolds with constantly mounting tension and suspense. Its sermon on the sad limitations of parish-minded Pastor Manders's code as a guide to life, on the ghost-ridden lives of men and women, and on the tragic price paid by Mrs. Alving for violating her personality and living on in apparent respectability with her infected husband to save appearances instead of walking out like Nora, is still powerful and moving long after the removal of the conditions that made it shocking.

These two plays became standard in the new theatres that were organized in the late eighties and nineties in most of the theatrical capitals of Europe. They reached England at the end of the eighties, just as Pinero and Shaw were getting under way. It is hardly possible to exaggerate their place in the modern drama and in the history of social attitudes. They were followed by three plays of considerable strength and occasional beauty—*The Wild Duck, Rosmersholm*, and *The Lady from the Sea*, each distinguished by Ibsen's genius for creating moving and convincing characters, each with its sermonic core, and each invested with a symbol presumably to deepen and heighten the mystery of human experience. *The Wild Duck* has been greatly admired because of the poignant and tender portrayal of the beautiful spirit of the fourteen-year-old Hedvig and of her grandfather Ekdal who has a playhouse forest in the attic of their house. Their lives are wrecked by a nosey, self-righteous reformer who thinks he must drag into the open the scandal behind their lives —as a clever dog dives to the bottom of a pond to drag out from the tangle and seaweed, "and all the devil's own mess that grows down there," the wounded duck that dived and hid from its pursuing enemy.

Rosmersholm created the character of the "emancipated" woman, Rebecca West. Her complex mixture of modernity, hard selfishness, and a mysticism which led her to seek redemption through self-abnegation by suicide with Rosmer, nearly got lost, however, in the tiresome talk about contemporary liberalism and in the spooky whispers of the housekeeper about the White Horses and "the dead that cling to Rosmersholm." *The Lady from the Sea* has moments of poetic beauty, and its central dramatic issue is psychologically sound if not very interesting or important. The sea symbolizes romance and freedom to Ellida, now married and cared for almost to parasitism by her physician husband. She remembers with longing her lost sailor lover and her girlish romance. When she is given complete freedom to choose between her husband and her returned lover, she chooses her husband—and is thereby purged of her neurotic phantasms.

All of the plays, including these three attempts at symbolism, make use of the old device of the confidante to get the exposition out of the way and the plot unfolding. The confidante is usually a long-lost friend who must be brought up to date on the news of the heroine and her family. The villains are conventional and not incapable of reform. In fact, Maugham was not entirely wrong when he summed up the case sardonically in these words: "Ibsen as we know had a meagre power of invention; his characters under different names are very dully repeated and his intrigues from play to play little varied. It is not a gross exaggeration to say that his only gambit is the sudden arrival of a stranger who comes into a stuffy room and opens the windows; whereupon the people who were sitting there catch their death of cold and everything ends unhappily."

Hedda Gabler is in many respects the most perfect of his plays, both in character study and in form. It was an instantaneous international success, despite the critical opinion of its day that to common-sense people it had no motive and the heroine was devoid of any redeeming feature. The first production was at Munich, January 31, 1891. Ibsen was there. In the following April it was played at the Vaudeville Theatre in London by Elizabeth Robins and Marion Lee. It has been interpreted by some of the greatest modern actresses: Duse, Mrs. Patrick Campbell, Mrs. Fiske, Nance O'Neill, Alla Nazimova. It was published at Copenhagen December 16, 1890, with English and American translations made from the proof sheets. Edmund Gosse's translation appeared in 1891.

Hedda Gabler has lost little with the passing of a half century of bewildering change. It is compact, firm, and stripped of irrelevancies. The studied and selected details are arranged into an artistic pattern unexcelled in Ibsen's work. The first act with its six sharp episodes, each designed for a specific purpose, is a model of compression. The play must be seen against the back-drop of the dramas that immediately preceded it. Those thesis dramas, centering around the feminist movement, are now only mildly interesting. *Ghosts* excites admiration not for its daring theme but for its structural beauty; the door in *A Doll's House* now closes quietly without slamming; and both plays depend for survival largely upon their historical importance and the unmistakable timbre of Ibsen's endowed workmanship and character creation. *Hedda Gabler* was not burdened with extraneous essays or sermonic passages. It is a concentrated study of character. Hedda stands before us in all her human perversities and confronted with her own destiny—a phenomenon as sternly natural as arthritis or cancer. She never says that one must accept life whole-heartedly; that one must love, marry, raise a better generation, and have joy in the process—or die a neurotic. She says only indirectly and without emphasis that individualism, cultivated solely for itself, and without relation to other individuals with whom one is inextricably involved for a common end, is as disastrous as Mrs. Alving's denial of her personality in surrender to provincial respectability; or the stultification of a potentially strong character like Nora by playing up to her ninny of a husband.

These themes are not preached, as in *A Doll's House* and *Ghosts;* they must be deduced from the unity of events in the play precisely as moral wisdom must be drawn from a study of the endless flow of life itself. For Hedda is, as all great characters must be, a lump of life hewed out of the great block of humanity. She *is*. Her drama is not bogged down by the self-conscious, unassimilated symbolism of the three preceding plays (and others that followed it) that evidently didn't come quite clear even to Ibsen himself. Symbolism was in accord with the delicate genius of Maeterlinck, but it was too fragile and wanton for the masculine hand of Ibsen. Even in *The Master Builder* (1892) and *When We Dead Awaken* (1899), where the symbolism is more nearly absorbed into the texture of the play, the result is not entirely satisfying.

Hedda Gabler—not Hedda Tesman, we note—is a realistic study in maladjustment. Hedda is neurotic, unemotional, completely self-centered and selfish. Now that the honeymoon journey is over, she is irritated by her pedantic and assinine husband; she is bored to melancholy at the prospect of the years ahead as his wife; and she is overwrought and rebellious against her pregnancy. She dreads motherhood more than the unexpected threat of poverty, and fears scandal more than either. She is trapped by circumstances that are repugnant to her, and she lacks the will to face them. They fail to challenge her luxury-loving, uncourageous, irresponsible nature. She can be roused from her snippish boredom only by the prospect of vanquishing her mousy rival, Mrs. Elvsted, and dominating the brilliant but erratic Lövborg, rival to her stupid husband.

MRS. ELVSTED. You have some hidden motive in this, Hedda!

HEDDA. Yes, I have. I want for once in my life to have power to mould a human destiny.

She moulds it to destruction, however; she is even denied the satisfaction of directing an artistic suicide for him. She urged him "to do it beautifully," but he bungled it. Hedda herself did it beautifully, renouncing not the stuffy existence of Tesman's house, but the futility of life itself. She became the prototype of the inverted Freudian heroine of the 1920's, who haunted the offices of psychoanalysts and peopled the novels and the plays of the post-war world. *Hedda Gabler* best represents the obstinate genius of Ibsen upon whose tomb at Oslo was carved not a blue bird but a symbolic hammer.

HEDDA GABLER

CHARACTERS

GEORGE TESMAN
HEDDA TESMAN, *his wife*
MISS JULIANA TESMAN, *his aunt*
MRS. ELVSTED

JUDGE BRACK
EILERT LÖVBORG
BERTA, *servant at the Tesman's*

The scene of the action is Tesman's villa, in the west end of Christiania.

ACT I

A spacious, handsome, and tastefully furnished drawing-room, decorated in dark colors. In the back, a wide doorway with curtains drawn back, leading into a smaller room decorated in the same style as the drawing-room. In the right-hand wall of the front room, a folding door leading out to the hall. In the opposite wall, on the left, a glass door, also with curtains drawn back. Through the panes can be seen part of a verandah outside, and trees covered with autumn foliage. An oval table, with a cover on it, and surrounded by chairs, stands well forward. In front, by the wall on the right, a wide stove of dark porcelain, a high-backed arm-chair, a cushioned foot-rest, and two foot-stools. A settee, with a small round table in front of it, fills the upper right-hand corner. In front, on the left, a little way from the wall, a sofa. Farther back than the glass door, a piano. On either side of the doorway at the back a whatnot with terra-cotta and majolica ornaments.— Against the back wall of the inner room a sofa, with a table, and one or two chairs. Over the sofa hangs the portrait of a handsome elderly man in a General's uniform. Over the table a hanging lamp, with an opal glass shade.—A number of bouquets are arranged about the drawing-room, in vases and glasses. Others lie upon the tables. The floors in both rooms are covered with thick carpets.—Morning light. The sun shines in through the glass door.

MISS JULIANA TESMAN, with her bonnet on and carrying a parasol, comes in from the hall, followed by BERTA, who carries a bouquet wrapped in paper. MISS TESMAN is a comely and pleasant-looking lady of about sixty-five. She is nicely but simply dressed in a gray walking-costume. BERTA is a middle-aged woman of plain and rather countrified appearance.

MISS TESMAN (*stops close to the door, listens, and says softly*). Upon my word, I don't believe they are stirring yet!

BERTA (*also softly*). I told you so, Miss. Remember how late the steamboat got in last night. And then, when they got home!—good Lord, what a lot the young mistress had to unpack before she could get to bed.

MISS TESMAN. Well, well—let them have their sleep out. But let us see that they get a good breath of the fresh morning air when they do appear. (*She goes to the glass door and throws it open.*)

BERTA (*beside the table, at a loss what to do with the bouquet in her hand*). I declare there isn't a bit of room left. I think I'll put it down here, Miss. (*She places it on the piano.*)

MISS TESMAN. So you've got a new mistress now, my dear Berta. Heaven knows it was a wrench to me to part with you.

BERTA (*on the point of weeping*). And do you think it wasn't hard for me too, Miss? After all the blessed years I've been with you and Miss Rina.

MISS TESMAN. We must make the best of it, Berta. There was nothing else to be done. George can't do without you, you see—he absolutely can't. He has had you to look after him ever since he was a little boy.

BERTA. Ah, but, Miss Julia, I can't help thinking of Miss Rina lying helpless at home there, poor thing. And with only that new girl, too! She'll never learn to take proper care of an invalid.

MISS TESMAN. Oh, I shall manage to train her. And of course, you know, I shall take most of it upon myself. You needn't be uneasy about my poor sister, my dear Berta.

BERTA Well, but there's another thing, Miss. I'm so mortally afraid I shan't be able to suit the young mistress.

MISS TESMAN. Oh, well—just at first there may be one or two things——

BERTA. Most like she'll be terrible grand in her ways.

MISS TESMAN. Well, you can't wonder at that—General Gabler's daughter! Think of the sort of life she was accustomed to in her father's time. Don't you remember how we used to see her riding down the road along with the General? In that long black habit—and with feathers in her hat?

BERTA. Yes, indeed—I remember well enough—! But good Lord, I should never have dreamt in those days that she and Master George would make a match of it.

MISS TESMAN. Nor I.—But, by-the-bye, Berta—while I think of it: in future you mustn't say Master George. You must say Dr. Tesman.

BERTA. Yes, the young mistress spoke of that too—last night—the moment they set foot in the house. Is it true, then, Miss?

MISS TESMAN. Yes, indeed it is. Only think, Berta—some foreign university has made him a doctor—while he has been abroad, you understand. I hadn't heard a word about it, until he told me himself upon the pier.

BERTA. Well, well, he's clever enough for anything, he is. But I didn't think he'd have gone in for doctoring people too.

MISS TESMAN. No, no, it's not that sort of doctor he is. (*Nods significantly.*) But let me tell you, we may have to call him something still grander before long.

BERTA. You don't say so! What can that be, Miss?

MISS TESMAN (*smiling*). H'm—wouldn't you like to know! (*With emotion.*) Ah, dear, dear—if my poor brother could only look up from his grave now, and see what his little boy has grown into! (*Looks around.*) But bless me, Berta—why have you done this? Taken the chintz covers off all the furniture?

BERTA. The mistress told me to. She can't abide covers on the chairs, she says.

MISS TESMAN. Are they going to make this their everyday sitting-room then?

BERTA. Yes, that's what I understood—from the mistress. Master George—the doctor—he said nothing.

[GEORGE TESMAN *comes from the right into the inner room, humming to himself, and carrying an unstrapped empty portmanteau.*

He is a middle-sized, young-looking man of thirty-three, rather stout, with a round, open, cheerful face, fair hair and beard. He wears spectacles, and is somewhat carelessly dressed in comfortable indoor clothes.]

MISS TESMAN. Good morning, good morning, George.

TESMAN (*in the doorway between the rooms*). Aunt Julia! Dear Aunt Julia! (*Goes up to her and shakes hands warmly.*) Come all this way—so early! Eh?

MISS TESMAN. Why of course I had to come and see how you were getting on.

TESMAN. In spite of your having had no proper night's rest?

MISS TESMAN. Oh, that makes no difference to me.

TESMAN. Well, I suppose you got home all right from the pier? Eh?

MISS TESMAN. Yes, quite safely, thank goodness. Judge Brack was good enough to see me right to my door.

TESMAN. We were so sorry we couldn't give you a seat in the carriage. But you saw what a pile of boxes Hedda had to bring with her.

MISS TESMAN. Yes, she had certainly plenty of boxes.

BERTA (*to* TESMAN). Shall I go in and see if there's anything I can do for the mistress?

TESMAN. No, thank you, Berta—you needn't. She said she would ring if she wanted anything.

BERTA (*going towards the right*). Very well.

TESMAN. But look here—take this portmanteau with you.

BERTA (*taking it*). I'll put it in the attic. (*She goes out by the hall door.*)

TESMAN. Fancy, Aunty—I had the whole of that portmanteau chock full of copies of documents. You wouldn't believe how much I have picked up from all the archives I have been examining—curious old details that no one has had any idea of——

MISS TESMAN. Yes, you don't seem to have wasted your time on your wedding trip, George.

TESMAN. No, that I haven't. But do take off your bonnet, Auntie. Look here! Let me untie the strings—eh?

MISS TESMAN (*while he does so*). Well, well —this is just as if you were still at home with us.

TESMAN (*with the bonnet in his hand, looks at it from all sides*). Why, what a gorgeous bonnet you've been investing in!

MISS TESMAN. I bought it on Hedda's account.

TESMAN. On Hedda's account? Eh?

MISS TESMAN. Yes, so that Hedda needn't be ashamed of me if we happened to go out together.

TESMAN (*patting her cheek*). You always think of everything, Aunt Julia. (*Lays the bonnet on a chair beside the table.*) And now, look here—suppose we sit comfortably on the sofa and have a little chat, till Hedda comes.

[*They seat themselves. She places her parasol in the corner of the sofa.*]

MISS TESMAN (*takes both his hands and looks at him*). What a delight it is to have you again, as large as life, before my very eyes, George! My George—my poor brother's own boy!

TESMAN. And it's a delight for me, too, to see you again, Aunt Julia! You, who have been father and mother in one to me.

MISS TESMAN. Oh, yes, I know you will always keep a place in your heart for your old aunts.

TESMAN. And what about Aunt Rina? No improvement—eh!

MISS TESMAN. Oh, no—we can scarcely look for any improvement in her case, poor thing. There she lies, helpless, as she has lain for all these years. But heaven grant I may not lose her yet awhile! For if I did, I don't know what I should make of my life, George—especially now that I haven't you to look after any more.

TESMAN (*patting her back*). There, there, there——!

MISS TESMAN (*suddenly changing her tone*). And to think that here you are a married man, George!—And that you should be the one to carry off Hedda Gabler, the beautiful Hedda Gabler! Only think of it—she, that was so beset with admirers!

TESMAN (*hums a little and smiles complacently*). Yes, I fancy I have several good friends about town who would like to stand in my shoes—eh?

MISS TESMAN. And then this fine long wedding-tour you have had! More than five—nearly six months——

TESMAN. Well, for me it has been a sort of tour of research as well. I have had to do so much grubbing among old records—and to read no end of books too, Auntie.

MISS TESMAN. Oh, yes, I suppose so. (*More confidentially, and lowering her voice a little.*) But listen now, George—have you nothing—nothing special to tell me?

TESMAN. As to our journey?

MISS TESMAN. Yes.

TESMAN. No, I don't know of anything except what I have told you in my letters. I had a doctor's degree conferred on me—but that I told you yesterday.

MISS TESMAN. Yes, yes, you did. But what I mean is—haven't you any—any—expectations——?

TESMAN. Expectations?

MISS TESMAN. Why, you know, George—I'm your old auntie!

TESMAN. Why, of course I have expectations.

MISS TESMAN. Ah!

TESMAN. I have every expectation of being a professor one of these days.

MISS TESMAN. Oh, yes, a professor——

TESMAN. Indeed, I may say I am certain of it. But my dear Auntie—you know all about that already!

MISS TESMAN (*laughing to herself*). Yes, of course I do. You are quite right there. (*Changing the subject.*) But we were talking about your journey. It must have cost a great deal of money, George?

TESMAN. Well, you see—my handsome traveling-scholarship went a good way.

MISS TESMAN. But I can't understand how you can have made it go far enough for two.

TESMAN. No, that's not so easy to understand—eh?

MISS TESMAN. And especially traveling with a lady—they tell me that makes it ever so much more expensive.

TESMAN. Yes, of course—it makes it a little more expensive. But Hedda had to have this trip, Auntie! She really had to. Nothing else would have done.

MISS TESMAN. No, no, I suppose not. A wedding-tour seems to be quite indispensable nowadays.—But tell me now—have you gone thoroughly over the house yet?

TESMAN. Yes, you may be sure I have. I have been afoot ever since daylight.

MISS TESMAN. And what do you think of it all?

TESMAN. I'm delighted! Quite delighted! Only I can't think what we are to do with the two empty rooms between this inner parlor and Hedda's bedroom.

MISS TESMAN (*laughing*). Oh, my dear George, I dare say you may find some use for them—in the course of time.

TESMAN. Why of course you are quite right, Aunt Julia! You mean as **my** library increases—eh?

MISS TESMAN. Yes, quite so, my dear boy. It was your library I was thinking of.

TESMAN. I am specially pleased on Hedda's account. Often and often, before we were engaged, she said that she would never care to live anywhere but in Secretary Falk's villa.

MISS TESMAN. Yes, it was lucky that this very house should come into the market, just after you had started. 10

TESMAN. Yes, Aunt Julia, the luck was on our side, wasn't it—eh?

MISS TESMAN. But the expense, my dear George! You will find it very expensive, all this.

TESMAN (*looks at her, a little cast down*). Yes, I suppose I shall, Aunt!

MISS TESMAN. Oh, frightfully!

TESMAN. How much do you think? In round numbers?—Eh? 20

MISS TESMAN. Oh, I can't even guess until all the accounts come in.

TESMAN. Well, fortunately, Judge Brack has secured the most favorable terms for me,—so he said in a letter to Hedda.

MISS TESMAN. Yes, don't be uneasy, my dear boy.—Besides, I have given security for the furniture and all the carpets. 30

TESMAN. Security? You? My dear Aunt Julia—what sort of security could you give?

MISS TESMAN. I have given a mortgage on our annuity.

TESMAN (*jumps up*). What! On your—and Aunt Rina's annuity!

MISS TESMAN. Yes, I knew of no other plan, you see.

TESMAN (*placing himself before her*). Have 40 you gone out of your senses, Auntie! Your annuity—it's all that you and Aunt Rina have to live upon.

MISS TESMAN. Well, well, don't get so excited about it. It's only a matter of form you know—Judge Brack assured

me of that. It was he that was kind enough to arrange the whole affair for me. A mere matter of form, he said.

TESMAN. Yes, that may be all very well. But nevertheless——

MISS TESMAN. You will have your own salary to depend upon now. And, good heavens, even if we did have to pay up a little——! To eke things out a bit at the start——! Why, it would be nothing but a pleasure to us.

TESMAN. Oh, Auntie—will you never be tired of making sacrifices for me!

MISS TESMAN (*rises and lays her hands on his shoulders*). Have I had any other happiness in this world except to smooth your way for you, my dear boy? You, who have had neither father nor mother to depend on. And now we have reached the goal, George! Things have looked black enough for us, sometimes; but, thank heaven, now you have nothing to fear.

TESMAN. Yes, it is really marvelous how everything has turned out for the best.

MISS TESMAN. And the people who opposed you—who wanted to bar the way for you—now you have them at your feet. They have fallen, George. Your most dangerous rival—his fall was the worst.—And now he has to lie on the bed he has made for himself—poor misguided creature.

TESMAN. Have you heard anything of Eilert? Since I went away, I mean.

MISS TESMAN. Only that he is said to have published a new book.

TESMAN. What! Eilert Lövborg! Recently—eh?

MISS TESMAN. Yes, so they say. Heaven knows whether it can be worth anything! Ah, when your new book appears—that will be another story George! What is it to be about?

TESMAN. It will deal with the domestic industries of Brabant during the Middle Ages.

MISS TESMAN. Fancy—to be able to write on such a subject as that.

TESMAN. However, it may be some time before the book is ready. I have all these collections to arrange first, you see.

MISS TESMAN. Yes, collecting and arranging—no one can beat you at that. There you are my poor brother's own son.

TESMAN. I am looking forward eagerly to setting to work at it; especially now that I have my own delightful home to work in.

MISS TESMAN. And, most of all, now that you have got the wife of your heart, my dear George.

TESMAN (*embracing her*). Oh, yes, yes, Aunt Julia. Hedda—she is the best part of all! (*Looks towards the doorway.*) I believe I hear her coming—eh?

[HEDDA *enters from the left through the inner room. She is a woman of nine-and-twenty. Her face and figure show refinement and distinction. Her complexion is pale and opaque. Her steel-gray eyes express a cold, unruffled repose. Her hair is of an agreeable medium brown, but not particularly abundant. She is dressed in a tasteful, somewhat loose-fitting morning-gown.*]

MISS TESMAN (*going to meet* HEDDA). Good morning, my dear Hedda! Good morning, and a hearty welcome.

HEDDA (*holds out her hand*). Good morning, dear Miss Tesman! So early a call! That is kind of you.

MISS TESMAN (*with some embarrassment*). Well—has the bride slept well in her new home?

HEDDA. Oh yes, thanks. Passably.

TESMAN (*laughing*). Passably! Come, that's good, Hedda! You were sleeping like a stone when I got up.

HEDDA. Fortunately. Of course one has always to accustom one's self to new surroundings, Miss Tesman—little by little. (*Looking towards the left.*) Oh—there the servant has gone and opened the verandah door, and let in a whole flood of sunshine.

MISS TESMAN (*going towards the door*). Well, then, we will shut it.

HEDDA. No, no, not that! Tesman, please draw the curtains. That will give a softer light.

TESMAN (*at the door*). All right—all right. There now, Hedda, now you have both shade and fresh air.

HEDDA. Yes, fresh air we certainly must have, with all these stacks of flowers—— But—won't you sit down, Miss Tesman?

MISS TESMAN. No, thank you. Now that I have seen that everything is all right here—thank heaven!—I must be getting home again. My sister is lying longing for me, poor thing.

TESMAN. Give her my very best love, Auntie; and say I shall look in and see her later in the day.

MISS TESMAN. Yes, yes, I'll be sure to tell her. But by-the-bye, George—(*feeling in her dress pocket*)—I have almost forgotten—I have something for you here.

TESMAN. What is it, Auntie? Eh?

MISS TESMAN (*produces a flat parcel wrapped in newspaper and hands it to him*). Look here, my dear boy.

TESMAN (*opening the parcel*). Well, I declare!—Have you really saved them for me, Aunt Julia! Hedda! isn't this touching—eh?

HEDDA (*beside the whatnot on the right*). Well, what is it?

TESMAN. My old morning-shoes! My slippers.

HEDDA. Indeed. I remember you often spoke of them while we were abroad.

TESMAN. Yes, I missed them terribly. (*Goes up to her*). Now you shall see them, Hedda!

HEDDA (*going towards the stove*). Thanks, I really don't care about it.

TESMAN (*following her*). Only think—ill as she was, Aunt Rina embroidered these for me. Oh you can't think how many associations cling to them.

HEDDA (*at the table*). Scarcely for me.

MISS TESMAN. Of course not for Hedda, George.

TESMAN. Well, but now that she belongs to the family, I thought——

HEDDA (*interrupting*). We shall never get on with this servant, Tesman.

MISS TESMAN. Not get on with Berta?

TESMAN. Why, dear, what puts that in your head? Eh?

HEDDA (*pointing*). Look there! She has left her old bonnet lying about on a chair.

TESMAN (*in consternation, drops the slippers on the floor*). Why, Hedda——

HEDDA. Just fancy, if any one should come in and see it.

TESMAN. But Hedda—that's Aunt Julia's bonnet.

HEDDA. Is it!

MISS TESMAN (*taking up the bonnet*). Yes, indeed it's mine. And what's more, it's not old, Madame Hedda.

HEDDA. I really did not look closely at it, Miss Tesman.

MISS TESMAN (*trying on the bonnet*). Let me tell you it's the first time I have worn it—the very first time.

TESMAN. And a very nice bonnet it is too —quite a beauty!

MISS TESMAN. Oh, it's no such great things, George. (*Looks around her.*) My parasol——? Ah, here. (*Takes it.*) For this is mine too—(*mutters*)—not Berta's.

TESMAN. A new bonnet and a new parasol! Only think, Hedda!

HEDDA. Very handsome indeed.

TESMAN. Yes, isn't it? But Auntie, take a good look at Hedda before you go! See how handsome she is!

MISS TESMAN. Oh, my dear boy, there's nothing new in that. Hedda was always lovely. (*She nods and goes towards the right.*)

TESMAN (*following*). Yes, but have you noticed what splendid condition she is in? How she has filled out on the journey?

HEDDA (*crossing the room*). Oh, do be quiet——!

MISS TESMAN (*who has stopped and turned*). Filled out?

TESMAN. Of course you don't notice it so much now that she has that dress on. But I, who can see——

HEDDA (*at the glass door, impatiently*). Oh, you can't see anything.

TESMAN. It must be the mountain air in the Tyrol——

HEDDA (*curtly, interrupting*). I am exactly as I was when I started.

TESMAN. So you insist; but I'm quite certain you are not. Don't you agree with me, Auntie?

MISS TESMAN (*who has been gazing at her with folded hands*). Hedda is lovely— lovely—lovely. (*Goes up to her, takes her head between both hands, draws it downwards, and kisses her hair*). God bless and preserve Hedda Tesman— for George's sake.

HEDDA (*gently freeing herself*). Oh—! Let me go.

MISS TESMAN (*in quiet emotion*). I shall not let a day pass without coming to see you.

TESMAN. No you won't, will you, Auntie? Eh?

MISS TESMAN. Good-bye—good-bye!

[*She goes out by the hall door.* TESMAN *accompanies her. The door remains half open.* TESMAN *can be heard repeating his*

*message to Aunt Rina and his thanks for
the slippers.*

[*In the meantime,* HEDDA *walks about the
room raising her arms and clenching her
hands as if in desperation. Then she flings
back the curtains from the glass door, and
stands there looking out.*

[*Presently* TESMAN *returns and closes the door
behind him.*]

TESMAN (*picks up the slippers from the floor*).
What are you looking at, Hedda?

HEDDA (*once more calm and mistress of herself*). I am only looking at the leaves.
They are so yellow—so withered.

TESMAN (*wraps up the slippers and lays them
on the table*). Well you see, we are well
into September now.

HEDDA (*again restless*). Yes, to think of it!
—Already in—in September.

TESMAN. Don't you think Aunt Julia's
manner was strange, dear? Almost
solemn? Can you imagine what was
the matter with her? Eh?

HEDDA. I scarcely know her, you see. Is
she often like that?

TESMAN. No, not as she was to-day.

HEDDA (*leaving the glass door*). Do you
think she was annoyed about the
bonnet?

TESMAN. Oh, scarcely at all. Perhaps a
little, just at the moment——

HEDDA. But what an idea, to pitch her
bonnet about in the drawing-room!
No one does that sort of thing.

TESMAN. Well you may be sure Aunt
Julia won't do it again.

HEDDA. In any case, I shall manage to
make my peace with her.

TESMAN. Yes, my dear, good Hedda, if
you only would.

HEDDA. When you call this afternoon,
you might invite her to spend the
evening here.

TESMAN. Yes, that I will. And there's one
thing more you could do that would
delight her heart.

HEDDA. What is it?

TESMAN. If you could only prevail on
yourself to say *du* [1] to her. For my
sake, Hedda? Eh?

HEDDA. No, no, Tesman—you really
musn't ask that of me. I have told you
so already. I shall try to call her
"Aunt"; and you must be satisfied
with that.

TESMAN. Well, well. Only I think now
that you belong to the family, you——

HEDDA. H'm—I can't in the least see
why——

[*She goes up towards the middle doorway.*]

TESMAN (*after a pause*). Is there anything
the matter with you, Hedda? Eh?

HEDDA. I'm only looking at my old piano. It doesn't go at all well with all
the other things.

TESMAN. The first time I draw my
salary, we'll see about exchanging
it.

HEDDA. No, no—no exchanging. I don't
want to part with it. Suppose we put
it there in the inner room, and then
get another here in its place. When
it's convenient, I mean.

TESMAN (*a little taken aback*). Yes—of
course we could do that.

HEDDA (*takes up the bouquet from the piano*).
These flowers were not here last night
when we arrived.

TESMAN. Aunt Julia must have brought
them for you.

HEDDA (*examining the bouquet*). A visiting-
card. (*Takes it out and reads.*) "Shall
return later in the day." Can you
guess whose card it is?

TESMAN. No. Whose? Eh?

HEDDA. The name is "Mrs. Elvsted."

TESMAN. Is it really? Sheriff Elvsted's
wife? Miss Rysing that was.

HEDDA. Exactly. The girl with the irritating hair, that she was always show-

---

[1] *Du*—thou; Tesman means, "If you could
persuade yourself to *tutoyer* her."

ing off. An old flame of yours, I've been told.

TESMAN (*laughing*). Oh, that didn't last long; and it was before I knew you, Hedda. But fancy her being in town!

HEDDA. It's odd that she should call upon us. I have scarcely seen her since we left school.

TESMAN. I haven't seen her either for—heaven knows how long. I wonder how she can endure to live in such an out-of-the-way hole—eh?

HEDDA (*after a moment's thought says suddenly*). Tell me, Tesman—isn't it somewhere near there that he—that —Eilert Lövborg is living?

TESMAN. Yes, he is somewhere in that part of the country.

[BERTA *enters by the hall door.*]

BERTA. That lady, ma'am, that brought some flowers a little while ago, is here again. (*Pointing.*) The flowers you have in your hand, ma'am.

HEDDA. Ah, is she? Well, please show her in.

[BERTA *opens the door for* MRS. ELVSTED, *and goes out herself.*—MRS. ELVSTED *is a woman of fragile figure, with pretty, soft features. Her eyes are light blue, large, round, and somewhat prominent, with a startled, inquiring expression. Her hair is remarkably light, almost flaxen, and unusually abundant and wavy. She is a couple of years younger than* HEDDA. *She wears a dark visiting dress, tasteful, but not quite in the latest fashion.*]

HEDDA (*receives her warmly*). How do you do, my dear Mrs. Elvsted? It's delightful to see you again.

MRS ELVSTED (*nervously, struggling for self-control*). Yes, it's a very long time since we met.

TESMAN (*gives her his hand*). And we too—eh?

HEDDA. Thanks for your lovely flowers—

MRS. ELVSTED. Oh, not at all—— I would have come straight here yesterday afternoon; but I heard that you were away——

TESMAN. Have you just come to town? Eh?

MRS. ELVSTED. I arrived yesterday, about midday. Oh, I was quite in despair when I heard that you were not at home.

HEDDA. In despair! How so?

TESMAN. Why, my dear Mrs. Rysing—I mean Mrs. Elvsted——

HEDDA. I hope that you are not in any trouble?

MRS. ELVSTED. Yes, I am. And I don't know another living creature here that I can turn to.

HEDDA (*laying the bouquet on the table*). Come—let us sit here on the sofa——

MRS. ELVSTED. Oh, I am too restless to sit down.

HEDDA. Oh no, you're not. Come here. (*She draws* MRS. ELVSTED *down upon the sofa and sits at her side.*)

TESMAN. Well? What is it, Mrs. Elvsted?

HEDDA. Has anything particular happened to you at home?

MRS. ELVSTED. Yes—and no. Oh—I am so anxious you should not misunderstand me——

HEDDA. Then your best plan is to tell us the whole story, Mrs. Elvsted.

TESMAN. I suppose that's what you have come for—eh?

MRS. ELVSTED. Yes, yes—of course it is. Well then, I must tell you—if you don't already know—that Eilert Lövborg is in town, too.

HEDDA. Lövborg——!

TESMAN. What! Has Eilert Lövborg come back? Fancy that, Hedda!

HEDDA. Well, well—I hear it.

MRS. ELVSTED. He has been here a week already. Just fancy—a whole week! In this terrible town, alone!

With so many temptations on all sides.

HEDDA. But my dear Mrs. Elvsted—how does he concern you so much?

MRS. ELVSTED (*looks at her with a startled air, and says rapidly*). He was the children's tutor.

HEDDA. Your children's?

MRS. ELVSTED. My husband's. I have none.

HEDDA. Your step-children's, then?

MRS. ELVSTED. Yes.

TESMAN (*somewhat hesitatingly*). Then was he—I don't know how to express it—was he—regular enough in his habits to be fit for the post? Eh?

MRS. ELVSTED. For the last two years his conduct has been irreproachable.

TESMAN. Has it indeed? Fancy that, Hedda!

HEDDA. I hear it.

MRS. ELVSTED. Perfectly irreproachable, I assure you! In every respect. But all the same—now that I know he is here—in this great town—and with a large sum of money in his hands—I can't help being in mortal fear for him.

TESMAN. Why did he not remain where he was? With you and your husband? Eh?

MRS. ELVSTED. After his book was published he was too restless and unsettled to remain with us.

TESMAN. Yes, by-the-bye, Aunt Julia told me he had published a new book.

MRS. ELVSTED. Yes, a big book, dealing with the march of civilization—in broad outline, as it were. It came out about a fortnight ago. And since it has sold so well, and been so much read—and made such a sensation——

TESMAN. Has it indeed? It must be something he has had lying by since his better days.

MRS. ELVSTED. Long ago, you mean?

TESMAN. Yes.

MRS. ELVSTED. No, he has written it all since he has been with us—within the last year.

TESMAN. Isn't that good news. Hedda? Think of that.

MRS. ELVSTED. Ah, yes, if only it would last!

HEDDA. Have you seen him here in town?

MRS. ELVSTED. No, not yet. I have had the greatest difficulty in finding out his address. But this morning I discovered it at last.

HEDDA (*looks searchingly at her*). Do you know, it seems to me a little odd of your husband—h'm——

MRS. ELVSTED (*starting nervously*). Of my husband! What?

HEDDA. That he should send you to town on such an errand—that he does not come himself and look after his friend.

MRS. ELVSTED. Oh no, no—my husband has no time. And besides, I—I had some shopping to do.

HEDDA (*with a slight smile*). Ah, that is a different matter.

MRS. ELVSTED (*rising quickly and uneasily*). And now I beg and implore you, Mr. Tesman—receive Eilert Lövborg kindly if he comes to you! And that he is sure to do. You see you were such great friends in the old days. And then you are interested in the same studies—the same branch of science—so far as I can understand.

TESMAN. We used to be, at any rate.

MRS. ELVSTED. That is why I beg so earnestly that you—you too—will keep a sharp eye upon him. Oh, you will promise me that, Mr. Tesman—won't you?

TESMAN. With the greatest of pleasure, Mrs. Rysing——

HEDDA. Elvsted.

TESMAN. I assure you I shall do all I possibly can for Eilert. You may rely upon me.

MRS. ELVSTED. Oh, how very, very kind of you! (*Presses his hands.*) Thanks, thanks, thanks! (*Frightened.*) You see, my husband is very fond of him!

HEDDA (*rising*). You ought to write to him, Tesman. Perhaps he may not care to come to you of his own accord.

TESMAN. Well, perhaps it would be the right thing to do, Hedda? Eh?

HEDDA. And the sooner the better. Why not at once?

MRS. ELVSTED (*imploringly*). Oh, if you only would!

TESMAN. I'll write this moment. Have you his address. Mrs.—Mrs. Elvsted.

MRS. ELVSTED. Yes. (*Takes a slip of paper from her pocket, and hands it to him.*) Here it is.

TESMAN. Good, good. Then I'll go in—— (*Looks about him.*) By-the-bye,—my slippers? Oh, here. (*Takes the packet, and is about to go.*)

HEDDA. Be sure you write him a cordial, friendly letter. And a good long one too.

TESMAN. Yes, I will.

MRS. ELVSTED. But please, please don't say a word to show that I have suggested it.

TESMAN. No, how could you think I would? Eh? (*He goes out to the right, through the inner room.*)

HEDDA (*goes up to* MRS. ELVSTED, *smiles, and says in a low voice*). There. We have killed two birds with one stone.

MRS. ELVSTED. What do you mean?

HEDDA. Could you not see that I wanted him to go?

MRS. ELVSTED. Yes, to write the letter——

HEDDA. And that I might speak to you alone.

MRS. ELVSTED (*confused*). About the same thing?

HEDDA. Precisely.

MRS. ELVSTED (*apprehensively*). But there is nothing more, Mrs. Tesman! Absolutely nothing!

HEDDA. Oh, yes, but there is. There is a great deal more—I can see that. Sit here—and we'll have a cosy, confidential chat. (*She forces* MRS. ELVSTED *to sit in the easy-chair beside the stove, and seats herself on one of the footstools.*)

MRS. ELVSTED (*anxiously, looking at her watch*). But, my dear Mrs. Tesman— I was really on the point of going.

HEDDA. Oh, you can't be in such a hurry.—Well? Now tell me something about your life at home.

MRS. ELVSTED. Oh, that is just what I care least to speak about.

HEDDA. But to me, dear——? Why, weren't we school-fellows?

MRS. ELVSTED. Yes, but you were in the class above me. Oh, how dreadfully afraid of you I was then!

HEDDA. Afraid of me?

MRS. ELVSTED. *Yes*, dreadfully. For when we met on the stairs you used always to pull my hair.

HEDDA. Did I, really?

MRS. ELVSTED. Yes, and once you said you would burn it off my head.

HEDDA. Oh, that was all nonsense, of course.

MRS. ELVSTED. Yes, but I was so silly in those days.—And since then, too— we have drifted so far—far apart from each other. Our circles have been so entirely different.

HEDDA. Well then, we must try to drift together again. Now listen! At school we said *du* to each other; and we called each other by our Christian names——

MRS. ELVSTED. No, I am sure you must be mistaken.

HEDDA. No, not at all! I can remember quite distinctly. So now we are going to renew our old friendship. (*Draws the footstool closer to* MRS. ELVSTED.) There now! (*Kisses her cheek.*) You must say *du* to me and call me Hedda.

MRS. ELVSTED (*presses and pats her hands*). Oh, how good and kind you are! I am not used to such kindness.

HEDDA. There, there, there! And I shall say *du* to you, as in the old days, and call you my dear Thora.

MRS. ELVSTED. My name is Thea.

HEDDA. Why, of course! I meant Thea. (*Looks at her compassionately.*) So you are not accustomed to goodness and kindness, Thea? Not in your own home?

MRS. ELVSTED. Oh, if I only had a home! But I haven't any; I have never had a home.

HEDDA (*looks at her for a moment*). I almost suspected as much.

MRS. ELVSTED (*gazing helplessly before her*). Yes—yes—yes.

HEDDA. I don't quite remember—was it not as housekeeper that you first went to Mr. Elvsted's?

MRS. ELVSTED. I really went as governess, But his wife—his late wife—was an invalid,—and rarely left her room. So I had to look after the housekeeping as well.

HEDDA. And then—at last—you became mistress of the house.

MRS. ELVSTED (*sadly*). Yes, I did.

HEDDA. Let me see—about how long ago was that?

MRS. ELVSTED. My marriage?

HEDDA. Yes.

MRS. ELVSTED. Five years ago.

HEDDA. To be sure; it must be that.

MRS. ELVSTED. Oh, those five years——! Or at all events the last two or three

of them! Oh, if you [1] could only imagine——

HEDDA (*giving her a little slap on the hand*). De? Fie, Thea!

MRS. ELVSTED. Yes, yes, I will try—— Well if—you could only imagine and understand——

HEDDA (*lightly*). Eilert Lövborg has been in your neighborhood about three years, hasn't he?

MRS. ELVSTED (*looks at her doubtfully*). Eilert Lövborg? Yes—he has.

HEDDA. Had you known him before, in town here?

MRS. ELVSTED. Scarcely at all. I mean— I knew him by name of course.

HEDDA. But you saw a good deal of him in the country?

MRS. ELVSTED. Yes, he came to us every day. You see, he gave the children lessons; for in the long run I couldn't manage it all myself.

HEDDA. No, that's clear.—And your husband——? I suppose he is often away from home?

MRS. ELVSTED. Yes. Being Sheriff, you know, he has to travel about a good deal in his district.

HEDDA (*leaning against the arm of the chair*). Thea—my poor, sweet Thea—now you must tell me everything—exactly as it stands.

MRS. ELVSTED. Well then, you must question me.

HEDDA. What sort of a man is your husband, Thea? I mean—you know— in everyday life. Is he kind to you?

MRS. ELVSTED (*evasively*). I am sure he means well in everything.

HEDDA. I should think he must be altogether too old for you. There is at least twenty years' difference between you, is there not?

[1] Mrs. Elvsted here uses the formal pronoun *De*, whereupon Hedda rebukes her. In her next speech Mrs. Elvsted says *du*.

MRS. ELVSTED (*irritably*). Yes, that is true, too. Everything about him is repellent to me! We have not a thought in common. We have no single point of sympathy—he and I.

HEDDA. But is he not fond of you all the same? In his own way?

MRS. ELVSTED. Oh, I really don't know. I think he regards me simply as a useful property. And then it doesn't cost much to keep me. I am not expensive.

HEDDA. That is stupid of you.

MRS. ELVSTED (*shakes her head*). It cannot be otherwise—not with him. I don't think he really cares for any one but himself—and perhaps a little for the children.

HEDDA. And for Eilert Lövborg, Thea.

MRS. ELVSTED (*looking at her*). For Eilert Lövborg? What puts that into your head?

HEDDA. Well, my dear—I should say, when he sends you after him all the way to town—— (*Smiling almost imperceptibly.*) And besides, you said so yourself, to Tesman.

MRS. ELVSTED (*with a little nervous twitch*). Did I? Yes, I suppose I did. (*Vehemently, but not loudly.*) No—I may just as well make a clean breast of it at once! For it must all come out in any case.

HEDDA. Why, my dear Thea——?

MRS. ELVSTED. Well, to make a long story short: My husband did not know that I was coming.

HEDDA. What! Your husband didn't know it!

MRS. ELVSTED. No, of course not. For that matter, he was away from home himself—he was traveling. Oh, I could bear it no longer, Hedda! I couldn't indeed—so utterly alone as I should have been in future.

HEDDA. Well? And then?

MRS. ELVSTED. So I put together some of my things—what I needed most—as quietly as possible. And then I left the house.

HEDDA. Without a word?

MRS. ELVSTED. Yes—and took the train straight to town.

HEDDA. Why, my dear, good Thea—to think of you daring to do it!

MRS. ELVSTED (*rises and moves about the room*). What else could I possibly do?

HEDDA. But what do you think your husband will say when you go home again?

MRS. ELVSTED (*at the table, looks at her*). Back to him.

HEDDA. Of course.

MRS. ELVSTED. I shall never go back to him again.

HEDDA (*rising and going towards her*). Then you have left your home—for good and all?

MRS. ELVSTED. Yes. There was nothing else to be done.

HEDDA. But then—to take flight so openly.

MRS. ELVSTED. Oh, it's impossible to keep things of that sort secret.

HEDDA. But what do you think people will say of you, Thea?

MRS. ELVSTED. They may say what they like for aught *I* care. (*Seats herself wearily and sadly on the sofa.*) I have done nothing but what I had to do.

HEDDA (*after a short silence*). And what are your plans now? What do you think of doing?

MRS. ELVSTED. I don't know yet. I only know this, that I must live here, where Eilert Lövborg is—if I am to live at all.

HEDDA (*takes a chair from the table, seats herself beside her, and strokes her hands*). My dear Thea—how did this—this friendship—between you and Eilert Lövborg come about?

MRS. ELVSTED. Oh, it grew up gradually. I gained a sort of influence over him.

HEDDA. Indeed?

MRS. ELVSTED. He gave up his old habits. Not because I asked him to, for I never dared do that. But of course he saw how repulsive they were to me; and so he dropped them.

HEDDA (*concealing an involuntary smile of scorn*). Then you have reclaimed him —as the saying goes—my little Thea.

MRS. ELVSTED. So he says himself, at any rate. And he, on his side, has made a real human being of me—taught me to think, and to understand so many things.

HEDDA. Did he give you lessons too, then?

MRS. ELVSTED. No, not exactly lessons. But he talked to me—talked about such an infinity of things. And then came the lovely, happy time when I began to share in his work—when he allowed me to help him!

HEDDA. Oh, he did, did he?

MRS. ELVSTED. Yes! He never wrote anything without my assistance.

HEDDA. You were two good comrades, in fact?

MRS. ELVSTED (*eagerly*). Comrades! Yes, fancy, Hedda—that is the very word he used!—Oh, I ought to feel perfectly happy; and yet I cannot; for I don't know how long it will last.

HEDDA. Are you no surer of him than that?

MRS. ELVSTED (*gloomily*). A woman's shadow stands between Eilert Lövborg and me.

HEDDA (*looks at her anxiously*). Who can that be?

MRS. ELVSTED. I don't know. Some one he knew in his—in his past. Some one he has never been able wholly to forget.

HEDDA. What has he told you—about this?

MRS. ELVSTED. He has only once—quite vaguely—alluded to it.

HEDDA. Well! And what did he say?

MRS. ELVSTED. He said that when they parted, she threatened to shoot him with a pistol.

HEDDA (*with cold composure*). Oh, nonsense! No one does that sort of thing here.

MRS. ELVSTED. No. And that is why I think it must have been that redhaired singing woman whom he once——

HEDDA. Yes, very likely.

MRS. ELVSTED. For I remember they used to say of her that she carried loaded firearms.

HEDDA. Oh—then of course it must have been she.

MRS. ELVSTED (*wringing her hands*). And now just fancy, Hedda—I hear that this singing-woman—that she is in town again! Oh, I don't know what to do——

HEDDA (*glancing towards the inner room*). Hush! Here comes Tesman. (*Rises and whispers.*) Thea—all this must remain between you and me.

MRS. ELVSTED (*springing up*). Oh, yes, yes! for heaven's sake——!

[GEORGE TESMAN, *with a letter in his hand, comes from the right through the inner room.*]

TESMAN. There now—the epistle is finished.

HEDDA. That's right. And now Mrs. Elvsted is just going. Wait a moment—I'll go with you to the garden gate.

TESMAN. Do you think Berta could post the letter, Hedda dear?

HEDDA (*takes it*). I will tell her to.

[BERTA *enters from the hall.*]

BERTA. Judge Brack wishes to know if Mrs. Tesman will receive him.

HEDDA. Yes, ask Judge Brack to come in. And look here—put this letter in the post.

BERTA (*taking the letter*). Yes, ma'am. [*She*

opens the door for JUDGE BRACK *and goes out herself.* BRACK *is a man of forty-five; thick-set, but well-built and elastic in his movements. His face is roundish with an aristocratic profile. His hair is short, still almost black, and carefully dressed. His eyes are lively and sparkling. His eyebrows thick. His moustaches are also thick, with short-cut ends. He wears a well-cut walking-suit, a little too youthful for his age.* 10 *He uses an eye-glass, which he now and then lets drop.*]

JUDGE BRACK (*with his hat in his hand, bowing*). May one venture to call so early in the day?

HEDDA. Of course one may.

TESMAN (*presses his hand*). You are welcome at any time. (*Introducing him.*) Judge Brack—Miss Rysing——

HEDDA. Oh——!   20

BRACK (*bowing*). Ah—delighted——

HEDDA (*looks at him and laughs*). It's nice to have a look at you by daylight, Judge!

BRACK. Do you find me—altered?

HEDDA. A little younger, I think.

BRACK. Thank you so much.

TESMAN. But what do you think of Hedda—eh? Doesn't she look flourishing? She has actually——   30

HEDDA. Oh, do leave me alone. You haven't thanked Judge Brack for all the trouble he has taken——

BRACK. Oh, nonsense—it was a pleasure to me——

HEDDA. Yes, you are a friend indeed. But here stands Thea all impatience to be off—so *au revoir* Judge. I shall be back again presently. (*Mutual salutations.* MRS. ELVSTED *and* HEDDA *go out by* 40 *the hall door.*)

BRACK. Well,—is your wife tolerably satisfied——

TESMAN. Yes, we can't thank you sufficiently. Of course she talks of a little re-arrangement here and there; and

one or two things are still wanting. We shall have to buy some additional trifles.

BRACK. Indeed!

TESMAN. But we won't trouble you about these things. Hedda says she herself will look after what is wanting.—— Shan't we sit down? Eh?

BRACK. Thanks, for a moment. (*Seats himself beside the table.*) There is something I wanted to speak to you about, my dear Tesman.

TESMAN. Indeed? Ah, I understand! (*Seating himself.*) I suppose it's the serious part of the frolic that is coming now. Eh?

BRACK. Oh, the money question is not so very pressing; though, for that matter, I wish we had gone a little more economically to work.

TESMAN. But that would never have done, you know! Think of Hedda, my dear fellow! You, who know her so well——. I couldn't possibly ask her to put up with a shabby style of living!

BRACK. No, no—that is just the difficulty.

TESMAN. And then—fortunately—it can't be long before I receive my appointment.

BRACK. Well, you see—such things are often apt to hang fire for a time.

TESMAN. Have you heard anything definite? Eh?

BRACK. Nothing exactly definite—— (*Interrupting himself.*) But, by-the-bye —I have one piece of news for you.

TESMAN. Well?

BRACK. Your old friend, Eilert Lövborg, has returned to town.

TESMAN. I know that already.

BRACK. Indeed! How did you learn it?

TESMAN. From that lady who went out with Hedda.

BRACK. Really? What was her name? I didn't quite catch it.

TESMAN. Mrs. Elvsted.

BRACK. Aha—Sheriff Elvsted's wife? Of course—he has been living up in their regions.

TESMAN. And fancy—I'm delighted to hear that he is quite a reformed character!

BRACK. So they say.

TESMAN. And then he has published a new book—eh?

BRACK. Yes, indeed he has.

TESMAN. And I hear it has made some sensation!

BRACK. Quite an unusual sensation.

TESMAN. Fancy—isn't that good news! A man of such extraordinary talents—— I felt so grieved to think that he had gone irretrievably to ruin.

BRACK. That was what everybody thought.

TESMAN. But I cannot imagine what he will take to now! How in the world will he be able to make his living? Eh?

[*During the last words,* HEDDA *has entered by the hall door.*]

HEDDA (*to* BRACK, *laughing with a touch of scorn*). Tesman is forever worrying about how people are to make their living.

TESMAN. Well, you see, dear—we were talking about poor Eilert Lövborg.

HEDDA (*glancing at him rapidly*). Oh, indeed? (*Seats herself in the arm-chair beside the stove and asks indifferently.*) What is the matter with him?

TESMAN. Well—no doubt he has run through all his property long ago; and he can scarcely write a new book every year—eh? So I really can't see what is to become of him.

BRACK. Perhaps I can give you some information on that point.

TESMAN. Indeed!

BRACK. You must remember that his relations have a good deal of influence.

TESMAN. Oh, his relations, unfortunately,

have entirely washed their hands of him.

BRACK. At one time they called him the hope of the family.

TESMAN. At one time, yes! But he has put an end to all that.

HEDDA. Who knows? (*With a slight smile.*) I hear they have reclaimed him up at Sheriff Elvsted's——

BRACK. And then this book that he has published——

TESMAN. Well, well, I hope to goodness they may find something for him to do. I have just written to him. I asked him to come and see us this evening, Hedda dear.

BRACK. But, my dear fellow, you are booked for my bachelors' party this evening. You promised on the pier last night.

HEDDA. Had you forgotten, Tesman?

TESMAN. Yes, I had utterly forgotten.

BRACK. But it doesn't matter, for you may be sure he won't come.

TESMAN. What makes you think that? Eh?

BRACK (*with a little hesitation, rising and resting his hands on the back of his chair*). My dear Tesman—and you too, Mrs. Tesman—I think I ought not to keep you in the dark about something that—that——

TESMAN. That concerns Eilert——?

BRACK. Both you and him.

TESMAN. Well, my dear Judge, out with it.

BRACK. You must be prepared to find your appointment deferred longer than you desired or expected.

TESMAN (*jumping up uneasily*). Is there some hitch about it? Eh?

BRACK. The nomination may perhaps be made conditional on the result of a competition——

TESMAN. Competition! Think of that, Hedda!

HEDDA (*leans farther back in the chair*). Aha—aha!

TESMAN. But who can my competitor be? Surely not——?

BRACK. Yes, precisely—Eilert Lövborg.

TESMAN (*clasping his hands*). No, no—it's quite inconceivable! Quite impossible! Eh?

BRACK. H'm—that is what it may come too, all the same.

TESMAN. Well but, Judge Brack—it would show the most incredible lack of consideration for me. (*Gesticulates with his arms.*) For—just think—I'm a married man. We have been married on the strength of these prospects, Hedda and I; and run deep into debt; and borrowed money from Aunt Julia too. Good heavens, they had as good as promised me the appointment. Eh?

BRACK. Well, well, well—no doubt you will get it in the end; only after a contest.

HEDDA (*immovable ιn her arm-chair*). Fancy, Tesman, there will be a sort of sporting interest in that.

TESMAN. Why, my dearest Hedda, how can you be so indifferent about it.

HEDDA (*as before*). I am not at all indifferent. I am most eager to see who wins.

BRACK. In any case, Mrs. Tesman, it is best that you should know how matters stand. I mean—before you set about the little purchases I hear you are threatening.

HEDDA. This can make no difference.

BRACK. Indeed! Then I have no more to say. Good-bye! (*To* TESMAN.) I shall look in on my way back from my afternoon walk, and take you home with me.

TESMAN. Oh yes, yes—your news has quite upset me.

HEDDA (*reclining, holds out her hand*). Good-bye, Judge; and be sure you call in the afternoon.

BRACK. Many thanks. Good-bye, good-bye!

TESMAN (*accompanying him to the door*). Good-bye, my dear Judge! You must really excuse me—— (JUDGE BRACK *goes out by the hall door.*)

TESMAN (*crosses the room*). Oh, Hedda—one should never rush into adventures. Eh?

HEDDA (*looks at him, smiling*). Do you do that?

TESMAN. Yes, dear—there is no denying —it was adventurous to go and marry and set up house upon mere expectations.

HEDDA. Perhaps you are right there.

TESMAN. Well—at all events, we have our delightful home, Hedda! Fancy, the home we both dreamed of—the home we were in love with, I may almost say. Eh?

HEDDA (*rising slowly and wearily*). It was part of our compact that we were to go into society—to keep open house.

TESMAN. Yes, if you only knew how I had been looking forward to it! Fancy—to see you as hostess—in a select circle? Eh? Well, well, well—for the present we shall have to get on without society, Hedda—only to invite Aunt Julia now and then.—Oh, I intended you to lead such an utterly different life, dear——!

HEDDA. Of course I cannot have my man in livery just yet.

TESMAN. Oh no, unfortunately. It would be out of the question for us to keep a footman, you know.

HEDDA. And the saddle-horse I was to have had——

TESMAN (*aghast*). The saddle-horse!

HEDDA. ——I suppose I must not think of that now.

TESMAN. Good heavens, no!—that's as clear as daylight.

HEDDA (*goes up the room*). Well, I shall

have one thing at least to kill time with in the meanwhile.

TESMAN (*beaming*). Oh, thank heaven for that! What is it, Hedda? Eh?

HEDDA (*in the middle doorway, looks at him with covert scorn*). My pistols, George.

TESMAN (*in alarm*). Your pistols!

HEDDA (*with cold eyes*). General Gabler's pistols. (*She goes out through the inner room, to the left.*)

TESMAN (*rushes up to the middle doorway and calls after her*). No, for heaven's sake, Hedda darling—don't touch those dangerous things! For my sake, Hedda! Eh?

ACT II

The room at the TESMANS' as in the first Act, except that the piano has been removed, and an elegant little writing-table with bookshelves put in its place. A smaller table stands near the sofa at the left. Most of the bouquets have been taken away. MRS. ELVSTED'S bouquet is upon the large table in front.—It is afternoon.

HEDDA, dressed to receive callers, is alone in the room. She stands by the open glass door, loading a revolver. The fellow to it lies in an open pistol-case on the writing-table.

HEDDA (*looks down the garden, and calls*). So you are here again, Judge!

BRACK (*is heard calling from a distance*). As you see, Mrs. Tesman!

HEDDA (*raises the pistol and points*). Now I'll shoot you, Judge Brack!

BRACK (*calling unseen*). No, no, no! Don't stand aiming at me!

HEDDA. This is what comes of sneaking in by the back way.[1] (*She fires.*)

BRACK (*nearer*). Are you out of your senses——!

HEDDA. Dear me—did I happen to hit you?

BRACK (*still outside*). I wish you would let these pranks alone!

HEDDA. Come in then, Judge.

[JUDGE BRACK, *dressed as though for a men's party, enters by the glass door. He carries a light overcoat over his arm.*]

[1] "Bagveje" means both "back ways" and "underhand courses."

BRACK. What the deuce—haven't you tired of that sport, yet? What are you shooting at?

HEDDA. Oh, I am only firing in the air.

BRACK (*gently takes the pistol out of her hand*). Allow me, madam! (*Looks at it.*) Ah—I know this pistol well! (*Looks around.*) Where is the case? Ah, here it is. (*Lays the pistol in it, and shuts it.*) Now we won't play at that game any more to-day.

HEDDA. Then what in heaven's name would you have me do with myself?

BRACK. Have you had no visitors?

HEDDA (*closing the glass door*). Not one. I suppose all our set are still out of town.

BRACK. And is Tesman not at home either?

HEDDA (*at the writing-table, putting the pistol-case in a drawer which she shuts*). No. He rushed off to his aunt's directly after lunch; he didn't expect you so early.

BRACK. H'm—how stupid of me not to have thought of that!

HEDDA (*turning her head to look at him*). Why stupid?

BRACK. Because if I had thought of it I should have come a little—earlier.

HEDDA (*crossing the room*). Then you would have found no one to receive you; for I have been in my room changing my dress ever since lunch.

BRACK. And is there no sort of little

chink that we could hold a parley through?

HEDDA. You have forgotten to arrange one.

BRACK. That was another piece of stupidity.

HEDDA. Well, we must just settle down here—and wait. Tesman is not likely to be back for some time yet.

BRACK. Never mind; I shall not be impatient.

[HEDDA *seats herself in the corner of the sofa.* BRACK *lays his overcoat over the back of the nearest chair, and sits down, but keeps his hat in his hand. A short silence. They look at each other.*]

HEDDA. Well?

BRACK (*in the same tone*). Well?

HEDDA. I spoke first.

BRACK (*bending a little forward*). Come, let us have a cosy little chat, Mrs. Hedda.

HEDDA (*leaning further back in the sofa*). Does it not seem like a whole eternity since our last talk? Of course I don't count those few words yesterday evening and this morning.

BRACK. You mean since our last confidential talk? Our last tête-à-tête?

HEDDA. Well, yes—since you put it so.

BRACK. Not a day has passed but I have wished that you were home again.

HEDDA. And I have done nothing but wish the same thing.

BRACK. You? Really, Mrs. Hedda? And I thought you had been enjoying your tour so much!

HEDDA. Oh, yes, you may be sure of that!

BRACK. But Tesman's letters spoke of nothing but happiness.

HEDDA. Oh, Tesman! You see, he thinks nothing so delightful as grubbing in libraries and making copies of old parchments, or whatever you call them.

BRACK (*with a spice of malice*). Well, that is his vocation in life—or part of it at any rate.

HEDDA. Yes, of course; and no doubt when it's your vocation—— But *I!* Oh, my dear Mr. Brack, how mortally bored I have been.

BRACK (*sympathetically*). Do you really say so? In downright earnest?

HEDDA. Yes, you can surely understand it——! To go for six whole months without meeting a soul that knew anything of our circle, or could talk about the things we are interested in.

BRACK. Yes, yes—I too should feel that a deprivation.

HEDDA. And then, what I found most intolerable of all——

BRACK. Well?

HEDDA. ——was being everlastingly in the company of—one and the same person——

BRACK (*with a nod of assent*). Morning, noon, and night, yes—at all possible times and seasons.

HEDDA. I said "everlastingly."

BRACK. Just so. But I should have thought, with our excellent Tesman, one could——

HEDDA. Tesman is—a specialist, my dear Judge.

BRACK. Undeniably.

HEDDA. And specialists are not at all amusing to travel with. Not in the long run at any rate.

BRACK. Not even—the specialist one happens to love?

HEDDA. Faugh—don't use that sickening word!

BRACK (*taken aback*). What do you say, Mrs. Hedda?

HEDDA (*half laughing, half irritated*). You should just try it! To hear of nothing but the history of civilization, morning, noon, and night——

BRACK. Everlastingly.

HEDDA. Yes, yes, yes! And then all this

about the domestic industry of the middle ages——! That's the most disgusting part of it!

BRACK (*looks searchingly at her*). But tell me—in that case, how am I to understand your——? H'm——

HEDDA. My accepting George Tesman, you mean?

BRACK. Well, let us put it so.

HEDDA. Good heavens, do you see any-thing so wonderful in that?

BRACK. Yes and no—Mrs. Hedda.

HEDDA. I had positively danced myself tired, my dear Judge. My day was done—— (*With a slight shudder.*) Oh no—I won't say that; nor think it either!

BRACK. You have assuredly no reason to.

HEDDA. Oh, reasons—— (*Watching him closely.*) And George Tesman—after all, you must admit that he is correctness itself.

BRACK. His correctness and respectability are beyond all question.

HEDDA. And I don't see anything absolutely ridiculous about him.—Do you?

BRACK. Ridiculous? N—no—I shouldn't exactly say so——

HEDDA. Well—and his powers of research, at all events, are untiring.—I see no reason why he should not one day come to the front, after all.

BRACK (*looks at her hesitatingly*). I thought that you, like every one else, expected him to attain the highest distinction.

HEDDA (*with an expression of fatigue*). Yes, so I did.—And then, since he was bent, at all hazards, on being allowed to provide for me—I really don't know why I should not have accepted his offer?

BRACK. No—if you look at it in that light——

HEDDA. It was more than my other adorers were prepared to do for me, my dear Judge.

BRACK (*laughing*). Well, I can't answer for all the rest; but as for myself, you know quite well that I have always entertained a—a certain respect for the marriage tie—for marriage as an institution, Mrs. Hedda.

HEDDA (*jestingly*). Oh, I assure you I have never cherished any hopes with respect to you.

BRACK. All I require is a pleasant and intimate interior, where I can make myself useful in every way, and am free to come and go as—as a trusted friend——

HEDDA. Of the master of the house, do you mean?

BRACK (*bowing*). Frankly—of the mistress first of all; but of course of the master, too, in the second place. Such a triangular friendship—if I may call it so—is really a great convenience for all parties, let me tell you.

HEDDA. Yes, I have many a time longed for some one to make a third on our travels. Oh—those railway-carriage tête-à-têtes——!

BRACK. Fortunately your wedding journey is over now.

HEDDA (*shaking her head*). Not by a long —long way. I have only arrived at a station on the line.

BRACK. Well, then the passengers jump out and move about a little, Mrs. Hedda.

HEDDA. I never jump out.

BRACK. Really?

HEDDA. No—because there is always some one standing by to——

BRACK (*laughing*). To look at your ankles, do you mean?

HEDDA. Precisely.

BRACK. Well but, dear me——

HEDDA (*with a gesture of repulsion*). I won't have it. I would rather keep my seat where I happen to be—and continue the tête-à-tête.

BRACK. But suppose a third person were to jump in and join the couple.

HEDDA. Ah—that is quite another matter!

BRACK. A trusted, sympathetic friend ——

HEDDA. ——with a fund of conversation on all sorts of lively topics——

BRACK. ——and not the least bit of a specialist!

HEDDA (*with an audible sigh*). Yes, that would be a relief indeed.

BRACK (*hears the front door open, and glances in that direction*). The triangle is completed.

HEDDA (*half aloud*). And on goes the train.

[GEORGE TESMAN, *in a gray walking-suit, with a soft felt hat, enters from the hall. He has a number of unbound books under his arm and in his pockets.*]

TESMAN (*goes up to the table beside the corner settee*). Ouf—what a load for a warm day—all these books. (*Lays them on the table.*) I'm positively perspiring, Hedda. Hallo—are you there already, my dear Judge? Eh? Berta didn't tell me.

BRACK (*rising*). I came in through the garden.

HEDDA. What books have you got there?

TESMAN (*stands looking them through*). Some new books on my special subjects—quite indispensable to me.

HEDDA. Your special subjects?

BRACK. Yes, books on his special subjects, Mrs. Tesman. (BRACK *and* HEDDA *exchange a confidential smile.*)

HEDDA. Do you need still more books on your special subjects?

TESMAN. Yes, my dear Hedda, one can never have too many of them. Of course one must keep up with all that is written and published.

HEDDA. Yes, I suppose one must.

TESMAN (*searching among his books*). And look here—I have got hold of Eilert Lövborg's new book too. (*Offering it to her.*) Perhaps you would like to glance through it, Hedda? Eh?

HEDDA. No, thank you. Or rather—afterwards perhaps.

TESMAN. I looked into it a little on the way home.

BRACK. Well, what do you think of it—as a specialist?

TESMAN. I think it shows quite remarkable soundness of judgment. He never wrote like that before. (*Putting the books together.*) Now I shall take all these into my study. I'm longing to cut the leaves——! And then I must change my clothes. (*To* BRACK.) I suppose we needn't start just yet? Eh?

BRACK. Oh, dear no—there is not the slightest hurry.

TESMAN. Well then, I will take my time. (*Is going with his books, but stops in the doorway and turns.*) By-the-bye, Hedda—Aunt Julia is not coming this evening.

HEDDA. Not coming? Is it that affair of the bonnet that keeps her away?

TESMAN. Oh, not at all. How could you think such a thing of Aunt Julia? Just fancy——! The fact is, Aunt Rina is very ill.

HEDDA. She always is.

TESMAN. Yes, but to-day she is much worse than usual, poor dear.

HEDDA. Oh, then it's only natural that her sister should remain with her. I must bear my disappointment.

TESMAN. And you can't imagine, dear, how delighted Aunt Julia seemed to be—because you had come home looking so flourishing!

HEDDA (*half aloud, rising*). Oh, those everlasting aunts!

TESMAN. What?

HEDDA (*going to the glass door*). Nothing.

TESMAN. Oh, all right. (*He goes through the inner room, out to the right.*)

BRACK. What bonnet were you talking about?

HEDDA. Oh, it was a little episode with Miss Tesman this morning. She had laid down her bonnet on the chair there—(*Looks at him and smiles.*)—And I pretended to think it was the ser-10 vant's.

BRACK (*shaking his head*). Now my dear Mrs. Hedda, how could you do such a thing? To that excellent old lady, too!

HEDDA (*nervously crossing the room*). Well, you see—these impulses come over me all of a sudden; and I cannot resist them. (*Throws herself down in the easy-chair by the stove.*) Oh, I don't know how to explain it. 20

BRACK (*behind the easy-chair*). You are not really happy—that is at the bottom of it.

HEDDA (*looking straight before her*). I know of no reason why I should be—happy. Perhaps you can give me one?

BRACK. Well—amongst other things, because you have got exactly the home you had set your heart on.

HEDDA (*looks up at him and laughs*). Do 30 you too believe in that legend?

BRACK. Is there nothing in it, then?

HEDDA. Oh, yes, there is something in it.

BRACK. Well?

HEDDA. There is this in it, that I made use of Tesman to see me home from evening parties last summer——

BRACK. I, unfortunately, had to go quite a different way.

HEDDA. That's true. I know you were 40 going a different way last summer.

BRACK (*laughing*). Oh fie, Mrs. Hedda! Well, then—you and Tesman——?

HEDDA. Well, we happened to pass here one evening; Tesman, poor fellow, was writhing in the agony of having

to find conversation; so I took pity on the learned man——

BRACK (*smiles doubtfully*). You took pity? H'm——

HEDDA. Yes, I really did. And so—to help him out of his torment—I happened to say, in pure thoughtlessness, that I should like to live in this villa.

BRACK. No more than that?

HEDDA. Not that evening.

BRACK. But afterwards?

HEDDA. Yes, my thoughtlessness had consequences, my dear Judge.

BRACK. Unfortunately that too often happens, Mrs. Hedda.

HEDDA. Thanks! So you see it was this enthusiasm for Secretary Falk's villa that first constituted a bond of sympathy between George Tesman and me. From that came our engagement and our marriage, and our wedding journey, and all the rest of it. Well, well, my dear Judge—as you make your bed so you must lie, I could almost say.

BRACK. This is exquisite! And you really cared not a rap about it all the time.

HEDDA. No, heaven knows I didn't.

BRACK. But now? Now that we have made it so homelike for you?

HEDDA. Uh—the rooms all seem to smell of lavender and dried rose-leaves.— But perhaps it's Aunt Julia that has brought that scent with her.

BRACK (*laughing*). No, I think it must be a legacy from the late Mrs. Secretary Falk.

HEDDA. Yes, there is an odor of mortality about it. It reminds me of a bouquet—the day after the ball. (*Clasps her hands behind her head, leans back in her chair and looks at him.*) Oh, my dear Judge—you cannot imagine how horribly I shall bore myself here.

BRACK. Why should not you, too, find some sort of vocation in life, Mrs Hedda?

HEDDA. A vocation—that should attract me?

BRACK. If possible, of course.

HEDDA. Heaven knows what sort of a vocation that could be. I often wonder whether—— (*Breaking off.*) But that would never do either.

BRACK. Who can tell? Let me hear what it is.

HEDDA. Whether I might not get Tesman to go into politics, I mean.

BRACK (*laughing*). Tesman? No, really now, political life is not the thing for him—not at all in his line.

HEDDA. No, I daresay not.—But if I could get him into it all the same?

BRACK. Why—what satisfaction could you find in that? If he is not fitted for that sort of thing, why should you want to drive him into it?

HEDDA. Because I am bored, I tell you! (*After a pause.*) So you think it quite out of the question that Tesman should ever get into the ministry?

BRACK. H'm—you see, my dear Mrs. Hedda—to get into the ministry, he would have to be a tolerably rich man.

HEDDA (*rising impatiently*). Yes, there we have it! It is this genteel poverty I have managed to drop into——! (*Crosses the room.*) That is what makes life so pitiable! So utterly ludicrous! —For that's what it is.

BRACK. Now *I* should say the fault lay elsewhere.

HEDDA. Where, then?

BRACK. You have never gone through any really stimulating experience.

HEDDA. Anything serious, you mean?

BRACK. Yes, you may call it so. But now you may perhaps have one in store.

HEDDA (*tossing her head*). Oh, you're thinking of the annoyances about this wretched professorship! But that must be Tesman's own affair. I assure you I shall not waste a thought upon it.

BRACK. No, no, I daresay not. But suppose now that what people call—in elegant language—a solemn responsibility were to come upon you? (*Smiling.*) A new responsibility, Mrs. Hedda?

HEDDA (*angrily*). Be quiet! Nothing of that sort will ever happen!

BRACK (*warily*). We will speak of this again a year hence—at the very outside.

HEDDA (*curtly*). I have no turn for anything of the sort, Judge Brack. No responsibilities for me!

BRACK. Are you so unlike the generality of women as to have no turn for duties which——?

HEDDA (*beside the glass door*). Oh, be quiet, I tell you!—I often think there is only one thing in the world I have any turn for.

BRACK (*drawing near to her*). And what is that, if I may ask?

HEDDA (*stands looking out*). Boring myself to death. Now you know it. (*Turns, looks towards the inner room, and laughs.*) Yes, as I thought! Here comes the Professor.

BRACK (*softly, in a tone of warning*). Come, come, come, Mrs. Hedda!

[GEORGE TESMAN, *dressed for the party, with his gloves and hat in his hand, enters from the right through the inner room.*]

TESMAN. Hedda, has no message come from Eilert Lövborg? Eh?

HEDDA. No.

TESMAN. Then you'll see he'll be here presently.

BRACK. Do you really think he will come?

TESMAN. Yes, I am almost sure of it. For what you were telling us this morning must have been a mere floating rumor.

BRACK. You think so?

TESMAN. At any rate, Aunt Julia said she

did not believe for a moment that he would ever stand in my way again. Fancy that!

BRACK. Well then, that's all right.

TESMAN (*placing his hat and gloves on a chair on the right*). Yes, but you must really let me wait for him as long as possible.

BRACK. We have plenty of time yet. None of my guests will arrive before seven or half-past.

TESMAN. Then meanwhile we can keep Hedda company, and see what happens. Eh?

HEDDA (*placing* BRACK'S *hat and overcoat upon the corner settee*). And at the worst Mr. Lövborg can remain here with me.

BRACK (*offering to take his things*). Oh, allow me, Mrs. Tesman!—What do you mean by "At the worst"?

HEDDA. If he won't go with you and Tesman.

TESMAN (*looks dubiously at her*). But, Hedda dear—do you think it would quite do for him to remain with you? Eh? Remember, Aunt Julia can't come.

HEDDA. No, but Mrs. Elvsted is coming. We three can have a cup of tea together.

TESMAN. Oh, yes, that will be all right.

BRACK (*smiling*). And that would perhaps be the safest plan for him.

HEDDA. Why so?

BRACK. Well, you know, Mrs. Tesman, how you used to gird at my little bachelor parties. You declared they were adapted only for men of the strictest principles.

HEDDA. But no doubt Mr. Lövborg's principles are strict enough now. A converted sinner—— (BERTA *appears at the hall door*.)

BERTA. There's a gentleman asking if you are at home, ma'am——

HEDDA. Well, show him in.

TESMAN (*softly*). I'm sure it is he! Fancy that!

[EILERT LÖVBORG *enters from the hall. He is slim and lean; of the same age as* TESMAN, *but looks older and somewhat worn-out. His hair and beard are of a blackish brown, his face long and pale, but with patches of color on the cheek-bones. He is dressed in a well-cut black visiting suit, quite new. He has dark gloves and a silk hat. He stops near the door, and makes a rapid bow, seeming somewhat embarrassed.*]

TESMAN (*goes up to him and shakes him warmly by the hand*). Well, my dear Eilert—so at last we meet again!

EILERT LÖVBORG (*speaks in a subdued voice*). Thanks for your letter, Tesman. (*Approaching* HEDDA.) Will you too shake hands with me, Mrs. Tesman?

HEDDA (*taking his hand*). I am glad to see you, Mr. Lövborg. (*With a motion of her hand.*) I don't know whether you two gentlemen——?

LÖVBORG (*bowing slightly*). Judge Brack, I think.

BRACK (*doing likewise*). Oh, yes,—in the old days——

TESMAN (*to* LÖVBORG, *with his hands on his shoulders*). And now you must make yourself entirely at home, Eilert! Mustn't he, Hedda?—For I hear you are going to settle in town again? Eh?

LÖVBORG. Yes, I am.

TESMAN. Quite right, quite right. Let me tell you, I have got hold of your new book; but I haven't had time to read it yet.

LÖVBORG. You may spare yourself the trouble.

TESMAN. Why so?

LÖVBORG. Because there is very little in it.

TESMAN. Just fancy—how can you say so?

BRACK. But it has been very much praised, I hear.

LÖVBORG. That was what I wanted; so I put nothing into the book but what every one would agree with.

BRACK. Very wise of you.

TESMAN. Well but, my dear Eilert——!

LÖVBORG. For now I mean to win myself a position again—to make a fresh start.

TESMAN (*a little embarrassed*). Ah, that is what you wish to do? Eh?

LÖVBORG (*smiling, lays down his hat, and draws a packet, wrapped in paper, from his coat pocket*). But when this one appears, George Tesman, you will have to read it. For this is the real book—the book I have put my true self into.

TESMAN. Indeed? And what is it?

LÖVBORG. It is the continuation.

TESMAN. The continuation? Of what?

LÖVBORG. Of the book.

TESMAN. Of the new book?

LÖVBORG. Of course.

TESMAN. Why, my dear Eilert—does it not come down to our own days?

LÖVBORG. Yes, it does; and this one deals with the future.

TESMAN. With the future! But, good heavens, we know nothing of the future!

LÖVBORG. No; but there is a thing or two to be said about it all the same. (*Opens the packet.*) Look here——

TESMAN. Why, that's not your handwriting.

LÖVBORG. I dictated it. (*Turning over the pages.*) It falls into two sections. The first deals with the civilizing forces of the future. And here is the second— (*running through the pages towards the end*) —forecasting the probable line of development.

TESMAN. How odd now! I should never have thought of writing anything of that sort.

HEDDA (*at the glass door, drumming on the pane*). H'm—I daresay not.

LÖVBORG (*replacing the manuscript in its paper and laying the packet on the table*). I brought it, thinking I might read you a little of it this evening.

TESMAN. That was very good of you, Eilert. But this evening——? (*Looking at* BRACK.) I don't quite see how we can manage it——

LÖVBORG. Well then, some other time. There is no hurry.

BRACK. I must tell you, Mr. Lövborg—there is a little gathering at my house this evening—mainly in honor of Tesman, you know——

LÖVBORG (*looking for his hat*). Oh—then I won't detain you——

BRACK. No, but listen—will you not do me the favor of joining us?

LÖVBORG (*curtly and decidedly*). No, I can't—thank you very much.

BRACK. Oh, nonsense—do! We shall be quite a select little circle. And I assure you we shall have a "lively time," as Mrs. Hed—as Mrs. Tesman says.

LÖVBORG. I have no doubt of it. But nevertheless——

BRACK. And then you might bring your manuscript with you, and read it to Tesman at my house. I could give you a room to yourselves.

TESMAN. Yes, think of that, Eilert,—why shouldn't you? Eh?

HEDDA (*interposing*). But, Tesman, if Mr. Lövborg would really rather not! I am sure Mr. Lövborg is much more inclined to remain here and have supper with me.

LÖVBORG (*looking at her*). With you, Mrs. Tesman?

HEDDA. And with Mrs. Elvsted.

LÖVBORG. Ah—— (*Lightly.*) I saw her for a moment this morning.

HEDDA. Did you? Well, she is coming this evening. So you see you are almost bound to remain, Mr. Lövborg, or she will have no one to see her home.

LÖVBORG. That's true. Many thanks, Mrs. Tesman—in that case I will remain.

HEDDA. Then I have one or two orders to give the servant——

[*She goes to the hall door and rings.* BERTA *enters.* HEDDA *talks to her in a whisper, and points toward the inner room.* BERTA *nods and goes out again.*]

TESMAN (*at the same time, to* LÖVBORG). Tell me, Eilert—is it this new subject—the future—that you are going to lecture about?

LÖVBORG. Yes.

TESMAN. They told me at the bookseller's, that you are going to deliver a course of lectures this autumn.

LÖVBORG. That is my intention. I hope you won't take it ill, Tesman.

TESMAN. Oh no, not in the least! But——?

LÖVBORG. I can quite understand that it must be disagreeable to you.

TESMAN (*cast down*). Oh, I can't expect you, out of consideration for me, to——

LÖVBORG. But I shall wait till you have received your appointment.

TESMAN. Will you wait? Yes, but—yes, but—are you not going to compete with me? Eh?

LÖVBORG. No; it is only the moral victory I care for.

TESMAN. Why, bless me—then Aunt Julia was right after all! Oh yes—I knew it! Hedda! Just fancy—Eilert Lövborg is not going to stand in our way!

HEDDA (*curtly*). Our way? Pray leave me out of the question. 40

[*She goes up towards the inner room, where* BERTA *is placing a tray with decanters and glasses on the table.* HEDDA *nods approval, and comes forward again.* BERTA *goes out.*]

TESMAN (*at the same time*). And you, Judge Brack—what do you say to this? Eh?

BRACK. Well, I say that a moral victory—h'm—may be all very fine——

TESMAN. Yes, certainly. But all the same——

HEDDA (*looking at* TESMAN *with a cold smile*). You stand there looking as if you were thunderstruck——

TESMAN. Yes—so I am—I almost think——

BRACK. Don't you see, Mrs. Tesman, a thunderstorm has just passed over?

HEDDA (*pointing towards the inner room*). Will you not take a glass of cold punch, gentlemen?

BRACK (*looking at his watch*). A stirrup-cup? Yes, it wouldn't come amiss.

TESMAN. A capital idea, Hedda! Just the thing! Now that the weight has been taken off my mind——

HEDDA. Will you not join them, Mr. Lövborg?

LÖVBORG (*with a gesture of refusal*). No, thank you. Nothing for me.

BRACK. Why, bless me—cold punch is surely not poison.

LÖVBORG. Perhaps not for every one.

HEDDA. I will keep Mr. Lövborg company in the meantime.

TESMAN. Yes, yes, Hedda dear, do.

[*He and* BRACK *go into the inner room, seat themselves, drink punch, smoke cigarettes, and carry on a lively conversation during what follows.* EILERT LÖVBORG *remains beside the stove.* HEDDA *goes to the writing-table.*]

HEDDA (*raising her voice a little*). Do you care to look at some photographs, Mr. Lövborg? You know Tesman and I made a tour in the Tyrol on our way home?

[*She takes up an album, and places it on the table beside the sofa, in the further corner of which she seats herself.* EILERT LÖVBORG *approaches, stops, and looks at her.*

Then he takes a chair and seats himself at her left, with his back towards the inner room.]

HEDDA (*opening the album*). Do you see this range of mountains, Mr. Lövborg? It's the Ortler group. Tesman has written the name underneath. Here it is: "The Ortler group near Meran."

LÖVBORG (*who has never taken his eyes off her, says softly and slowly*). Hedda— Gabler!

HEDDA (*glancing hastily at him*). Ah! Hush!

LÖVBORG (*repeats softly*). Hedda Gabler!

HEDDA (*looking at the album*). That was my name in the old days—when we two knew each other.

LÖVBORG. And I must teach myself never to say Hedda Gabler again— never, as long as I live.

HEDDA (*still turning over the pages*). Yes, you must. And I think you ought to practice in time. The sooner the better, I should say.

LÖVBORG (*in a tone of indignation*). Hedda Gabler married? And married to— George Tesman!

HEDDA. Yes—so the world goes.

LÖVBORG. Oh, Hedda, Hedda—how could you [1] throw yourself away!

HEDDA (*looks sharply at him*). What? I can't allow this!

LÖVBORG. What do you mean? (TESMAN *comes into the room and goes toward the sofa.*)

HEDDA (*hears him coming and says in an indifferent tone*). And this is a view from the Val d'Ampezzo, Mr. Lövborg. Just look at these peaks! (*Looks affectionately up at* TESMAN.) What's the name of these curious peaks, dear?

TESMAN. Let me see? Oh, those are the Dolomites.

HEDDA. Yes, that's it!—Those are the Dolomites, Mr. Lövborg.

TESMAN. Hedda dear,—I only wanted to ask whether I shouldn't bring you a little punch after all? For yourself at any rate—eh?

HEDDA. Yes, do, please; and perhaps a few biscuits.

TESMAN. No cigarettes?

HEDDA. No.

TESMAN. Very well.

[*He goes into the inner room and out to the right.* BRACK *sits in the inner room, and keeps an eye from time to time on* HEDDA *and* LÖVBORG.]

LÖVBORG (*softly, as before*). Answer me, Hedda—how could you go and do this?

HEDDA (*apparently absorbed in the album*). If you continue to say *du* to me I won't talk to you.

LÖVBORG. May I not say *du* when we are alone?

HEDDA. No. You may think it; but you mustn't say it.

LÖVBORG. Ah, I understand. It is an offense against George Tesman, whom you [2]—love.

HEDDA (*glances at him and smiles*). Love? What an idea!

LÖVBORG. You don't love him then!

HEDDA. But I won't hear of any sort of unfaithfulness! Remember that.

LÖVBORG. Hedda—answer me one thing ——

HEDDA. Hush! (TESMAN *enters with a small tray from the inner room.*)

TESMAN. Here you are! Isn't this tempting? (*He puts the tray on the table.*)

HEDDA. Why do you bring it yourself?

TESMAN (*filling the glasses*). Because I think it's such fun to wait upon you, Hedda.

HEDDA. But you have poured out two

[1] He uses the familiar *du*.

[2] From this point onward Lövborg uses the formal *De*.

glasses. Mr. Lövborg said he wouldn't have any——

TESMAN. No, but Mrs. Elvsted will soon be here, won't she?

HEDDA. Yes, by-the-bye—Mrs. Elvsted——

TESMAN. Had you forgotten her? Eh?

HEDDA. We were so absorbed in these photographs. (*Shows him a picture.*) Do you remember this little village?

TESMAN. Oh, it's that one just below the Brenner Pass. It was there we passed the night——

HEDDA. ——and met that lively party of tourists.

TESMAN. Yes, that was the place. Fancy —if we could only have had you with us, Eilert! Eh? (*He returns to the inner room and sits beside* BRACK.)

LÖVBORG. Answer me this one thing, Hedda——

HEDDA. Well?

LÖVBORG. Was there no love in your friendship for me either? Not a spark —not a tinge of love in it?

HEDDA. I wonder if there was? To me it seems as though we were two good comrades—two thoroughly intimate friends. (*Smilingly.*) You especially were frankness itself.

LÖVBORG. It was you that made me so.

HEDDA. As I look back upon it all, I think there was really something beautiful, something fascinating— something daring—in—in that secret intimacy—that comradeship which no living creature so much as dreamed of.

LÖVBORG. Yes, yes, Hedda! Was there not?—When I used to come to your father's in the afternoon—and the General sat over at the window reading his papers—with his back towards us——

HEDDA. And we two on the corner sofa——

LÖVBORG. Always with the same illustrated paper before us——

HEDDA. For want of an album, yes.

LÖVBORG. Yes, Hedda, and when I made my confessions to you—told you about myself, things that at that time no one else knew! There I would sit and tell you of my escapades— my days and nights of devilment. Oh, Hedda—what was the power in you that forced me to confess these things?

HEDDA. Do you think it was any power in me?

LÖVBORG. How else can I explain it? And all those—those roundabout questions you used to put to me——

HEDDA. Which you understood so particularly well——

LÖVBORG. How could you sit and question me like that? Question me quite frankly——

HEDDA. In roundabout terms, please observe.

LÖVBORG. Yes, but frankly nevertheless. Cross-question me about—all that sort of thing?

HEDDA. And how could you answer, Mr. Lövborg?

LÖVBORG. Yes, that is just what I can't understand—in looking back upon it. But tell me now, Hedda—was there not love at the bottom of our friendship? On your side, did you not feel as though you might purge my stains away if I made you my confessor? Was it not so?

HEDDA. No, not quite.

LÖVBORG. What was your motive, then?

HEDDA. Do you think it quite incomprehensible that a young girl—when it can be done—without any one knowing——

LÖVBORG. Well?

HEDDA. ——should be glad to have a peep, now and then, into a world which——

LÖVBORG. Which——?

HEDDA. ——which she is forbidden to know anything about?

LÖVBORG. So that was it?

HEDDA. Partly. Partly—I almost think.

LÖVBORG. Comradeship in the thirst for life. But why should not that, at any rate, have continued?

HEDDA. The fault was yours.

LÖVBORG. It was you that broke with me.

HEDDA. Yes, when our friendship threatened to develop into something more serious. Shame upon you, Eilert Lövborg! How could you think of wronging your—your frank comrade?

LÖVBORG (clenching his hands). Oh, why did you not carry out your threat? Why did you not shoot me down?

HEDDA. Because I have such a dread of scandal.

LÖVBORG. Yes, Hedda, you are a coward at heart.

HEDDA. A terrible coward. (Changing her tone.) But it was a lucky thing for you. And now you have found ample consolation at the Elvsteds'.

LÖVBORG. I know what Thea has confided to you.

HEDDA. And perhaps you have confided to her something about us?

LÖVBORG. Not a word. She is too stupid to understand anything of that sort.

HEDDA. Stupid?

LÖVBORG. She is stupid about matters of that sort.

HEDDA. And I am cowardly. (Bends over towards him, without looking him in the face, and says more softly.) But now I will confide something to you.

LÖVBORG (eagerly). Well?

HEDDA. The fact that I dared not shoot you down——

LÖVBORG. Yes!

HEDDA. ——that was not my most arrant cowardice—that evening.

LÖVBORG (looks at her a moment, understands, and whispers passionately). Oh, Hedda! Hedda Gabler! Now I begin to see a hidden reason beneath our comradeship! You [1] and I——! After all, then, it was your craving for life——

HEDDA (softly, with a sharp glance). Take care! Believe nothing of the sort!

[Twilight has begun to fall. The hall door is opened from without by BERTA.]

HEDDA (closes the album with a bang and calls smilingly). Ah, at last! My darling Thea,—come along!

[MRS. ELVSTED enters from the hall. She is in evening dress. The door is closed behind her.]

HEDDA (on the sofa, stretches out her arms towards her). My sweet Thea—you can't think how I have been longing for you!

[MRS. ELVSTED, in passing, exchanges slight salutations with the gentlemen in the inner room, then goes up to the table and gives HEDDA her hands. EILERT LÖVBORG has risen. He and MRS. ELVSTED greet each other with a silent nod.]

MRS. ELVSTED. Ought I to go in and talk to your husband for a moment?

HEDDA. Oh, not at all. Leave those two alone. They will soon be going.

MRS. ELVSTED. Are they going out?

HEDDA. Yes, to a supper-party.

MRS. ELVSTED (quickly, to LÖVBORG). Not you?

LÖVBORG. No.

HEDDA. Mr. Lövborg remains with us.

MRS. ELVSTED (takes a chair and is about to seat herself at his side). Oh, how nice it is here!

HEDDA. No, thank you, my little Thea! Not there! You'll be good enough to come over here to me. I will sit between you.

[1] In this speech he once more says du. Hedda addresses him throughout as De.

MRS. ELVSTED. Yes, just as you please.

[*She goes round the table and seats herself on the sofa on* HEDDA'S *right.* LÖVBORG *re-seats himself on his chair.*]

LÖVBORG (*after a short pause, to* HEDDA). Is not she lovely to look at?

HEDDA (*lightly stroking her hair*). Only to look at?

LÖVBORG. Yes. For we two—she and I—we are two real comrades. We have absolute faith in each other; so we can sit and talk with perfect frankness——

HEDDA. Not round about, Mr. Lövborg?

LÖVBORG. Well——

MRS. ELVSTED (*softly clinging close to* HEDDA). Oh, how happy I am, Hedda; for, only think, he says I have inspired him too.

HEDDA (*looks at her with a smile*). Ah! Does he say that, dear?

LÖVBORG. And then she is so brave, Mrs. Tesman!

MRS. ELVSTED. Good heavens—am I brave?

LÖVBORG. Exceedingly—where your comrade is concerned.

HEDDA. Ah, yes—courage! If one only had that!

LÖVBORG. What then? What do you mean?

HEDDA. Then life would perhaps be live-able, after all. (*With a sudden change of tone.*) But now, my dearest Thea, you really must have a glass of cold punch.

MRS. ELVSTED. No, thanks—I never take anything of that kind.

HEDDA. Well then, you, Mr. Lövborg.

LÖVBORG. Nor I, thank you.

MRS. ELVSTED. No, he doesn't either.

HEDDA (*looks fixedly at him*). But if I say you shall?

LÖVBORG. It would be no use.

HEDDA (*laughing*). Then I, poor creature, have no sort of power over you?

LÖVBORG. Not in that respect.

HEDDA. But seriously, I think you ought to—for your own sake.

MRS. ELVSTED. Why, Hedda——!

LÖVBORG. How so?

HEDDA. Or rather on account of other people.

LÖVBORG. Indeed?

HEDDA. Otherwise people might be apt to suspect that—in your heart of hearts—you did not feel quite secure —quite confident of yourself.

MRS. ELVSTED (*softly*). Oh please, Hedda——

LÖVBORG. People may suspect what they like—for the present.

MRS. ELVSTED (*joyfully*). Yes, let them!

HEDDA. I saw it plainly in Judge Brack's face a moment ago.

LÖVBORG. What did you see?

HEDDA. His contemptuous smile, when you dared not go with them into the inner room.

LÖVBORG. Dared not? Of course I pre-ferred to stop here and talk to you.

MRS. ELVSTED. What could be more natural, Hedda?

HEDDA. But the Judge could not guess that. And I saw, too, the way he smiled and glanced at Tesman when you dared not accept his invitation to this wretched little supper-party of his.

LÖVBORG. Dared not! Do you say I dared not?

HEDDA. *I* don't say so. But that was how Judge Brack understood it.

LÖVBORG. Well, let him.

HEDDA. Then you are not going with them?

LÖVBORG. I will stay here with you and Thea.

MRS. ELVSTED. Yes, Hedda—how can you doubt that?

HEDDA (*smiles and nods approvingly to* LÖVBORG). Firm as a rock! Faithful to your principles, now and forever!

Ah, that is how a man should be! (*Turns to* MRS. ELVSTED *and caresses her.*) Well now, what did I tell you, when you came to us this morning in such a state of distraction——

LÖVBORG (*surprised*). Distraction!

MRS. ELVSTED (*terrified*). Hedda—oh Hedda——!

HEDDA. You can see for yourself; you haven't the slightest reason to be in such mortal terror—— (*Interrupting herself.*) There! Now we can all three enjoy ourselves!

LÖVBORG (*who has given a start*). Ah—what is all this, Mrs. Tesman?

MRS. ELVSTED. Oh my God, Hedda! What are you saying? What are you doing?

HEDDA. Don't get excited! That horrid Judge Brack is sitting watching you.

LÖVBORG. So she was in mortal terror! On my account!

MRS. ELVSTED (*softly and piteously*). Oh, Hedda—now you have ruined everything!

LÖVBORG (*looks fixedly at her for a moment. His face is distorted*). So that was my comrade's frank confidence in me?

MRS. ELVSTED (*imploringly*). Oh, my dearest friend—only let me tell you——

LÖVBORG (*takes one of the glasses of punch, raises it to his lips, and says in a low, husky voice*). Your health, Thea! [*He empties the glass, puts it down, and takes the second.*]

MRS. ELVSTED (*softly*). Oh, Hedda, Hedda—how could you do this?

HEDDA. *I* do it? *I*? Are you crazy?

LÖVBORG. Here's to your health too, Mrs. Tesman. Thanks for the truth. Hurrah for the truth! [*He empties the glass and is about to re-fill it.*]

HEDDA (*lays her hand on his arm*). Come, come—no more for the present. Re-member you are going out to supper.

MRS. ELVSTED. No, no, no!

HEDDA. Hush! They are sitting watching you.

LÖVBORG (*putting down the glass*). Now, Thea—tell me the truth——

MRS. ELVSTED. Yes.

LÖVBORG. Did your husband know that you had come after me?

MRS. ELVSTED (*wringing her hands*). Oh, Hedda—do you hear what he is asking?

LÖVBORG. Was it arranged between you and him that you were to come to town and look after me? Perhaps it was the Sheriff himself that urged you to come? Aha, my dear—no doubt he wanted my help in his office! Or was it at the card-table that he missed me?

MRS. ELVSTED (*softly, in agony*). Oh, Lövborg, Lövborg——!

LÖVBORG (*seizes a glass and is on the point of filling it*). Here's a glass for the old Sheriff too!

HEDDA (*preventing him*). No more just now. Remember you have to read your manuscript to Tesman.

LÖVBORG (*calmly, putting down the glass*). It was stupid of me all this, Thea—to take it in this way, I mean. Don't be angry with me, my dear, dear comrade. You shall see—both you and the others—that if I was fallen once—now I have risen again! Thanks to you, Thea.

MRS. ELVSTED (*radiant with joy*). Oh, heaven be praised——!

[BRACK *has in the meantime looked at his watch. He and* TESMAN *rise and come into the drawing-room*].

BRACK (*takes his hat and overcoat*). Well, Mrs. Tesman, our time has come.

HEDDA. I suppose it has.

LÖVBORG (*rising*). Mine too, Judge Brack.

MRS. ELVSTED (*softly and imploringly*). Oh, Lövborg, don't do it!

HEDDA (*pinching her arm*). They can hear you!

MRS. ELVSTED (*with a suppressed shriek*). Ow!

LÖVBORG (*to* BRACK). You were good enough to invite me.

BRACK. Well, are you coming after all?

LÖVBORG. Yes, many thanks.

BRACK. I'm delighted——

LÖVBORG (*to* TESMAN, *putting the parcel of MS. in his pocket*). I should like to show you one or two things before I send it to the printer's.

TESMAN. Fancy—that will be delightful. But, Hedda dear, how is Mrs. Elvsted to get home? Eh?

HEDDA. Oh, that can be managed somehow.

LÖVBORG (*looking towards the ladies.*) Mrs. Elvsted? Of course, I'll come again and fetch her. (*Approaching.*) At ten or thereabouts, Mrs. Tesman? Will that do?

HEDDA. Certainly. That will do capitally.

TESMAN. Well, then, that's all right. But you must not expect me so early, Hedda.

HEDDA. Oh, you may stop as long—as long as ever you please.

MRS. ELVSTED (*trying to conceal her anxiety*). Well then, Mr. Lövborg—I shall remain here until you come.

LÖVBORG (*with his hat in his hand*). Pray do, Mrs. Elvsted.

BRACK. And now off goes the excursion train, gentlemen! I hope we shall have a lively time, as a certain fair lady puts it.

HEDDA. Ah, if only the fair lady could be present unseen——!

BRACK. Why unseen?

HEDDA. In order to hear a little of your liveliness at first hand, Judge Brack.

BRACK (*laughing*). I should not advise the fair lady to try it.

TESMAN (*also laughing*). Come, you're a nice one Hedda! Fancy that!

BRACK. Well, good-bye, good-bye, ladies.

LÖVBORG (*bowing*). About ten o'clock, then.

[BRACK, LÖVBORG, *and* TESMAN *go out by the hall door. At the same time* BERTA *enters from the inner room with a lighted lamp, which she places on the dining-room table; she goes out by the way she came.*]

MRS. ELVSTED (*who has risen and is wandering restlessly about the room*). Hedda—Hedda—what will come of all this?

HEDDA. At ten o'clock—he will be here. I can see him already—with vine-leaves in his hair—flushed and fearless——

MRS. ELVSTED. Oh, I hope he may.

HEDDA. And then, you see—then he will have regained control over himself. Then he will be a free man for all his days.

MRS. ELVSTED. Oh God!—if he would only come as you see him now!

HEDDA. He will come as I see him—so, and not otherwise! (*Rises and approaches* THEA). You may doubt him as long as you please; I believe in him. And now we will try——

MRS. ELVSTED. You have some hidden motive in this, Hedda!

HEDDA. Yes, I have. I want for once in my life to have power to mold a human destiny.

MRS. ELVSTED. Have you not the power?

HEDDA. I have not—and have never had it.

MRS. ELVSTED. Not your husband's?

HEDDA. Do you think that is worth the trouble? Oh, if you could only understand how poor I am. And fate has made you so rich! (*Clasps her passionately in her arms.*) I think I must burn your hair off, after all.

MRS. ELVSTED. Let me go! Let me go! I am afraid of you, Hedda!

BERTA (*in the middle doorway*). Tea is laid in the dining room, ma'am.

HEDDA. Very well. We are coming.

MRS. ELVSTED. No, no, no! I would rather go home alone! At once!

HEDDA. Nonsense! First you shall have a cup of tea, you little stupid. And then—at ten o'clock—Eilert Lövborg will be here—with vine-leaves in his hair. (*She drags* MRS. ELVSTED *almost by force towards the middle doorway.*)

ACT III

The room at the TESMANS'. *The curtains are drawn over the middle doorway, and also over the glass door. The lamp, half turned down, and with a shade over it, is burning on the table. In the stove, the door of which stands open, there has been a fire, which is now nearly burnt out.*

MRS. ELVSTED, *wrapped in a large shawl, and with her feet upon a foot-rest, sits close to the stove, sunk back in the arm-chair.* HEDDA, *fully dressed, lies sleeping upon the sofa, with a sofa-blanket over her.*

MRS. ELVSTED (*after a pause, suddenly sits up in her chair, and listens eagerly. Then she sinks back again wearily, moaning to herself*). Not yet!—Oh God—oh God —not yet!

[BERTA *slips in by the hall door. She has a letter in her hand.*]

MRS. ELVSTED (*turns and whispers eagerly*). Well—has any one come?

BERTA (*softly*). Yes, a girl has brought this letter.

MRS. ELVSTED (*quickly, holding out her hand*). A letter! Give it to me!

BERTA. No, it's for Dr. Tesman, ma'am.

MRS. ELVSTED. Oh, indeed.

BERTA. It was Miss Tesman's servant that brought it. I'll lay it here on the table.

MRS. ELVSTED. Yes, do.

BERTA (*laying down the letter*). I think I had better put out the lamp. It's smoking.

MRS. ELVSTED. Yes, put it out. It must soon be daylight now.

BERTA (*putting out the lamp*). It is daylight already, ma'am.

MRS. ELVSTED. Yes, broad day! And no one come back yet——!

BERTA. Lord bless you, ma'am! I guessed how it would be.

MRS. ELVSTED. You guessed?

BERTA. Yes, when I saw that a certain person had come back to town—and that he went off with them. For we've heard enough about that gentleman before now.

MRS. ELVSTED. Don't speak so loud. You will waken Mrs. Tesman.

BERTA (*looks towards the sofa and sighs*). No, no—let her sleep, poor thing. Shan't I put some wood on the fire?

MRS. ELVSTED. Thanks, not for me.

BERTA. Oh, very well. (*She goes softly out by the hall door.*)

HEDDA (*is awakened by the shutting of the door, and looks up*). What's that——?

MRS. ELVSTED. It was only the servant——

HEDDA (*looking about her*). Oh, we're here——! Yes now I remember. (*Sits erect upon the sofa, stretches herself, and rubs her eyes.*) What o'clock is it, Thea?

MRS. ELVSTED (*looks at her watch*). It's past seven.

HEDDA. When did Tesman come home?

MRS. ELVSTED. He has not come.

HEDDA. Not come home yet?

MRS. ELVSTED (*rising*). No one has come.

HEDDA. Think of our watching and waiting here till four in the morning——

MRS. ELVSTED (*wringing her hands*). And how I watched and waited for him!

HEDDA (*yawns, and says with her hand before her mouth*). Well, well—we might have spared ourselves the trouble.

MRS. ELVSTED. Did you get a little sleep?

HEDDA. Oh yes; I believe I have slept pretty well. Have you not?

MRS. ELVSTED. Not for a moment. I couldn't, Hedda!—not to save my life.

HEDDA (*rises and goes towards her*). There, there, there! There's nothing to be so alarmed about. I understand quite well what has happened.

MRS. ELVSTED. Well, what do you think? Won't you tell me?

HEDDA. Why, of course it has been a very late affair at Judge Brack's——

MRS. ELVSTED. Yes, yes, that is clear enough. But all the same——

HEDDA. And then, you see, Tesman hasn't cared to come home and ring us up in the middle of the night. (*Laughing.*) Perhaps he wasn't inclined to show himself either—immediately after a jollification.

MRS. ELVSTED. But in that case—where can he have gone?

HEDDA. Of course he has gone to his aunts' and slept there. They have his old room ready for him.

MRS. ELVSTED. No, he can't be with them; for a letter has just come for him from Miss Tesman. There it lies.

HEDDA. Indeed? (*Looks at the address.*) Why yes, it's addressed in Aunt Julia's own hand. Well then, he has remained at Judge Brack's. And as for Eilert Lövborg—he is sitting, with vine-leaves in his hair, reading his manuscript.

MRS. ELVSTED. Oh Hedda, you are just saying things you don't believe a bit.

HEDDA. You really are a little blockhead, Thea.

MRS. ELVSTED. Oh yes, I suppose I am.

HEDDA. And how mortally tired you look.

MRS. ELVSTED. Yes, I am mortally tired.

HEDDA. Well then, you must do as I tell you. You must go into my room and lie down for a little while.

MRS. ELVSTED. Oh no, no—I shouldn't be able to sleep.

HEDDA. I am sure you would.

MRS. ELVSTED. Well, but your husband is certain to come soon now; and then I want to know at once——

HEDDA. I shall take care to let you know when he comes.

MRS. ELVSTED. Do you promise me, Hedda?

HEDDA. Yes, rely upon me. Just you go in and have a sleep in the meantime.

MRS. ELVSTED. Thanks; then I'll try to. (*She goes off through the inner room.*)

[*Hedda goes up to the glass door and draws back the curtains. The broad daylight streams into the room. Then she takes a little hand-glass from the writing-table, looks at herself in it, and arranges her hair. Next she goes to the hall door and presses the bell-button.*]

[BERTA *presently appears at the hall door.*]

BERTA. Did you want anything, ma'am?

HEDDA. Yes; you must put some more wood in the stove. I am shivering.

BERTA. Bless me—I'll make up the fire at once. (*She rakes the embers together and lays a piece of wood upon them; then stops and listens.*) That was a ring at the front door, ma'am.

HEDDA. Then go to the door. I will look after the fire.

BERTA. It'll soon burn up. (*She goes out by the hall door.*)

[HEDDA *kneels on the foot-rest and lays some more pieces of wood in the stove.*]

[*After a short pause,* GEORGE TESMAN *enters from the hall. He looks tired and rather serious. He steals on tiptoe towards the middle doorway and is about to slip through the curtains.*]

HEDDA (*at the stove, without looking up*). Good morning.

TESMAN (*turns*). Hedda! (*Approaching her.*) Good heavens—are you up so early? Eh?

HEDDA. Yes, I am up very early this morning.

TESMAN. And I never doubted you were still sound asleep! Fancy that, Hedda!

HEDDA. Don't speak so loud. Mrs. Elvsted is resting in my room.

TESMAN. Has Mrs. Elvsted been here all night?

HEDDA. Yes, since no one came to fetch her.

TESMAN. Ah, to be sure.

HEDDA (*closes the door of the stove and rises*). Well, did you enjoy yourself at Judge Brack's?

TESMAN. Have you been anxious about me? Eh?

HEDDA. No, I should never think of being anxious. But I asked if you had enjoyed yourself.

TESMAN. Oh yes,—for once in a way. Especially the beginning of the evening; for then Eilert read me part of his book. We arrived more than an hour too early—fancy that! And Brack had all sorts of arrangements to make—so Eilert read to me.

HEDDA (*seating herself by the table on the right*). Well? Tell me, then——

TESMAN (*sitting on a footstool near the stove*). Oh Hedda, you can't conceive what a book that is going to be! I believe it is one of the most remarkable things that have ever been written. Fancy that!

HEDDA. Yes, yes; I don't care about that——

TESMAN. I must make a confession to you, Hedda. When he had finished reading—a horrid feeling came over me.

HEDDA. A horrid feeling?

TESMAN. I felt jealous of Eilert for having had it in him to write such a book. Only think, Hedda!

HEDDA. Yes, yes, I am thinking!

TESMAN. And then how pitiful to think that he—with all his gifts—should be irreclaimable after all.

HEDDA. I suppose you mean that he has more courage than the rest?

TESMAN. No, not at all—I mean that he is incapable of taking his pleasures in moderation.

HEDDA. And what came of it all—in the end?

TESMAN. Well, to tell the truth, I think it might best be described as an orgy, Hedda.

HEDDA. Had he vine-leaves in his hair?

TESMAN. Vine-leaves? No, I saw nothing of the sort. But he made a long, rambling speech in honor of the woman who had inspired him in his work—that was the phrase he used.

HEDDA. Did he name her?

TESMAN. No, he didn't; but I can't help thinking he meant Mrs. Elvsted. You may be sure he did.

HEDDA. Well—where did you part from him?

TESMAN. On the way to town. We broke up—the last of us at any rate—all together; and Brack came with us to get a breath of fresh air. And then, you see, we agreed to take Eilert home; for he had had far more than was good for him.

HEDDA. I daresay.

TESMAN. But now comes the strange part of it, Hedda; or, I should rather say, the melancholy part of it. I declare I am almost ashamed—on Eilert's account—to tell you——

HEDDA. Oh, go on——

TESMAN. Well, as we were getting near town, you see, I happened to drop a little behind the others. Only for a minute or two—fancy that!

HEDDA. Yes, yes, yes, but——?

TESMAN. And then, as I hurried after them—what do you think I found by the wayside? Eh? 10

HEDDA. Oh, how should I know!

TESMAN. You mustn't speak of it to a soul, Hedda! Do you hear! Promise me, for Eilert's sake. (*Draws a parcel, wrapped in paper, from his coat pocket*). Fancy, dear—I found this.

HEDDA. Is not that the parcel he had with him yesterday?

TESMAN. Yes, it is the whole of his pre- 20 cious, irreplaceable manuscript! And he had gone and lost it, and knew nothing about it. Only fancy, Hedda! So deplorably——

HEDDA. But why did you not give him back the parcel at once?

TESMAN. I didn't dare to—in the state he was then in——

HEDDA. Did you not tell any of the others that you had found it? 30

TESMAN. Oh, far from it! You can surely understand that, for Eilert's sake, I wouldn't do that.

HEDDA. So no one knows that Eilert Lövborg's manuscript is in your possession?

TESMAN. No. And no one must know it.

HEDDA. Then what did you say to him afterwards?

TESMAN. I didn't talk to him again at all; 40 for when we got in among the streets, he and two or three of the others gave us the slip and disappeared. Fancy that!

HEDDA. Indeed! They must have taken him home then.

TESMAN. Yes, so it would appear. And Brack, too, left us.

HEDDA. And what have you been doing with yourself since?

TESMAN. Well, I and some of the others went home with one of the party, a jolly fellow, and took our morning coffee with him; or perhaps I should rather call it our night coffee—eh? But now, when I have rested a little, and given Eilert, poor fellow, time to have his sleep out, I must take this back to him.

HEDDA (*holds out her hand for the packet*). No—don't give it to him! Not in such a hurry, I mean. Let me read it first.

TESMAN. No, my dearest Hedda, I mustn't, I really mustn't.

HEDDA. You must not?

TESMAN. No—for you can imagine what a state of despair he will be in when he awakens and misses the manuscript. He has no copy of it, you must know! He told me so.

HEDDA (*looking searchingly at him*). Can such a thing not be reproduced? Written over again?

TESMAN. No, I don't think that would be possible. For the inspiration, you see——

HEDDA. Yes, yes—I suppose it depends on that. (*Lightly.*) But, by-the-bye—here is a letter for you.

TESMAN. Fancy——!

HEDDA (*handing it to him.*) It came early this morning.

TESMAN. It's from Aunt Julia! What can it be? (*He lays the packet on the other footstool, opens the letter, runs his eye through it, and jumps up.*) Oh, Hedda —she says that poor Aunt Rina is dying!

HEDDA. Well, we were prepared for that.

TESMAN. And that if I want to see her

again, I must make haste. I'll run in to them at once.

HEDDA (*suppressing a smile*). Will you run?

TESMAN. Oh, dearest Hedda—if you could only make up your mind to come with me! Just think!

HEDDA (*rises and says wearily, repelling the idea*). No, no, don't ask me. I will not look upon sickness and death. I loathe all sorts of ugliness.

TESMAN. Well, well, then——! (*Bustling around.*) My hat—My overcoat——? Oh, in the hall—I do hope I mayn't come too late, Hedda! Eh?

HEDDA. Oh, if you run——

[BERTA *appears at the hall door.*]

BERTA. Judge Brack is at the door, and wishes to know if he may come in.

TESMAN. At this time! No, I can't possibly see him.

HEDDA. But I can. (*To* BERTA.) Ask Judge Brack to come in. (BERTA *goes out.*)

HEDDA (*quickly whispering*). The parcel, Tesman! (*She snatches it up from the stool.*)

TESMAN. Yes, give it to me!

HEDDA. No, no, I will keep it till you come back.

[*She goes to the writing-table and places it in the book-case.* TESMAN *stands in a flurry of haste, and cannot get his gloves on.*]

[JUDGE BRACK *enters from the hall.*]

HEDDA (*nodding to him*). You are an early bird, I must say.

BRACK. Yes, don't you think so? (*To* TESMAN.) Are you on the move, too?

TESMAN. Yes, I must rush off to my aunts'. Fancy—the invalid one is lying at death's door, poor creature.

BRACK. Dear me, is she indeed? Then on no account let me detain you. At such a critical moment——

TESMAN. Yes, I must really rush—Good-bye! Good-bye! (*He hastens out by the hall door.*)

HEDDA (*approaching*). You seem to have made a particularly lively night of it at your rooms, Judge Brack.

BRACK. I assure you I have not had my clothes off, Mrs. Hedda.

HEDDA. Not you, either?

BRACK. No, as you may see. But what has Tesman been telling you of the night's adventures?

HEDDA. Oh, some tiresome story. Only that they went and had coffee somewhere or other.

BRACK. I have heard about that coffee-party already. Eilert Lövborg was not with them, I fancy?

HEDDA. No, they had taken him home before that.

BRACK. Tesman, too?

HEDDA. No, but some of the others, he said.

BRACK (*smiling*). George Tesman is really an ingenuous creature, Mrs. Hedda.

HEDDA. Yes, heaven knows he is. Then is there something behind all this?

BRACK. Yes, perhaps there may be.

HEDDA. Well then, sit down, my dear Judge, and tell your story in comfort.

[*She seats herself to the left of the table.* BRACK *sits near her, at the long side of the table.*]

HEDDA. Now then?

BRACK. I had special reasons for keeping track of my guests—or rather of some of my guests—last night.

HEDDA. Of Eilert Lövborg among the rest, perhaps?

BRACK. Frankly, yes.

HEDDA. Now you make me really curious——

BRACK. Do you know where he and one or two of the others finished the night, Mrs. Hedda?

HEDDA. If it is not quite unmentionable, tell me.

BRACK. Oh no, it's not at all unmentionable. Well, they put in an appearance at a particularly animated soirée.

HEDDA. Of the lively kind?

BRACK. Of the very liveliest——

HEDDA. Tell me more of this, Judge Brack—— 10

BRACK. Lövborg, as well as the others, had been invited in advance. I knew all about it. But he had declined the invitation; for now, as you know, he has become a new man.

HEDDA. Up at the Elvsteds', yes. But he went after all, then?

BRACK. Well, you see, Mrs. Hedda—unhappily the spirit moved him at my rooms last evening——

HEDDA. Yes, I hear he found inspiration.

BRACK. Pretty violent inspiration. Well, I fancy that altered his purpose; for we men folk are unfortunately not always so firm in our principles as we ought to be.

HEDDA. Oh, I am sure you are an exception, Judge Brack. But as to Lövborg——?

BRACK. To make a long story short—he 30 landed at last in Mademoiselle Diana's rooms.

HEDDA. Mademoiselle Diana's?

BRACK. It was Mademoiselle Diana that was giving the soirée, to a select circle of her admirers and her lady friends.

HEDDA. Is she a red-haired woman?

BRACK. Precisely.

HEDDA. A sort of a—singer?

BRACK. Oh yes—in her leisure moments. 40 And moreover a mighty huntress —of men—Mrs. Hedda. You have no doubt heard of her. Eilert Lövborg was one of her most enthusiastic protectors—in the days of his glory.

HEDDA. And how did all this end?

BRACK. Far from amicably, it appears. After a most tender meeting, they seem to have come to blows——

HEDDA. Lövborg and she?

BRACK. Yes. He accused her or her friends of having robbed him. He declared that his pocket-book had disappeared—and other things as well. In short, he seems to have made a furious disturbance.

HEDDA. And what came of it all?

BRACK. It came to a general scrimmage, in which the ladies as well as the gentlemen took part. Fortunately the police at last appeared on the scene.

HEDDA. The police too?

BRACK. Yes. I fancy it will prove a costly frolic for Eilert Lövborg, crazy being that he is.

HEDDA. How so? 20

BRACK. He seems to have made a violent resistance—to have hit one of the constables on the head and torn the coat off his back. So they had to march him off to the police-station with the rest.

HEDDA. How have you learnt all this?

BRACK. From the police themselves.

HEDDA (gazing straight before her). So that is what happened. Then he had no vine-leaves in his hair.

BRACK. Vine-leaves, Mrs. Hedda?

HEDDA (changing her tone). But tell me now, Judge—what is your real reason for tracking out Eilert Lövborg's movements so carefully?

BRACK. In the first place, it could not be entirely indifferent to me if it should appear in the police-court that he came straight from my house.

HEDDA. Will the matter come into court, then?

BRACK. Of course. However, I should scarcely have troubled so much about that. But I thought that, as a friend of the family, it was my duty to supply you and Tesman with a full account of his nocturnal exploits.

HEDDA. Why so, Judge Brack?

BRACK. Why, because I have a shrewd suspicion that he intends to use you as a sort of blind.

HEDDA. Oh, how can you think such a thing!

BRACK. Good heavens, Mrs. Hedda—we have eyes in our head. Mark my 10 words! This Mrs. Elvsted will be in no hurry to leave town again.

HEDDA. Well, even if there should be anything between them, I suppose there are plenty of other places where they could meet.

BRACK. Not a single home. Henceforth, as before, every respectable house will be closed against Eilert Lövborg.

HEDDA. And so ought mine to be, you 20 mean?

BRACK. Yes. I confess it would be more than painful to me if this personage were to be made free of your house. How superfluous, how intrusive, he would be, if he were to force his way into——

HEDDA. ——into the triangle?

BRACK. Precisely. It would simply mean that I should find myself homeless. 30

HEDDA (*looks at him with a smile*). So you want to be the one cock in the basket —that is your aim.

BRACK (*nods slowly and lowers his voice*). Yes, that is my aim. And for that I will fight—with every weapon I can command.

HEDDA (*her smile vanishing*). I see you are a dangerous person—when it comes to the point.   40

BRACK. Do you think so?

HEDDA. I am beginning to think so. And I am exceedingly glad to think— that you have no sort of hold over me.

BRACK (*laughing equivocally*). Well, well, Mrs. Hedda—perhaps you are right

there. If I had, who knows what I might be capable of?

HEDDA. Come, come now, Judge Brack. That sounds almost like a threat.

BRACK (*rising*). Oh, not at all! The triangle, you know, ought, if possible, to be spontaneously constructed.

HEDDA. There I agree with you.

BRACK. Well, now I have said all I had to say; and I had better be getting back to town. Good-bye, Mrs. Hedda. (*He goes towards the glass door.*)

HEDDA (*rising*). Are you going through the garden?

BRACK. Yes, it's a short cut for me.

HEDDA. And then it is the back way, too.

BRACK. Quite so. I have no objection to back ways. They may be piquant enough at times.

HEDDA. When there is ball practice going on, you mean?

BRACK (*in the doorway, laughing to her*). Oh, people don't shoot their tame poultry, I fancy.

HEDDA (*also laughing*). Oh no, when there is only one cock in the basket——

[*They exchange laughing nods of farewell. He goes. She closes the door behind him.*

[HEDDA, *who has become quite serious, stands for a moment looking out. Presently she goes and peeps through the curtain over the middle doorway. Then she goes to the writing-table, takes* LÖVBORG'S *packet out of the bookcase, and is on the point of looking through its contents.* BERTA *is heard speaking loudly in the hall.* HEDDA *turns and listens. Then she hastily locks up the packet in the drawer, and lays the key on the inkstand.*

[EILERT LÖVBORG, *with his great coat on and his hat in his hand, tears open the hall door. He looks somewhat confused and irritated.*]

LÖVBORG (*looking towards the hall*). And I tell you I must and will come in! There!

[*He closes the door, turns and sees* HEDDA, *at once regains his self-control, and bows.*]

HEDDA (*at the writing-table*). Well, Mr. Lövborg, this is rather a late hour to call for Thea.

LÖVBORG. You mean rather an early 10 hour to call on you. Pray pardon me.

HEDDA. How do you know that she is still here?

LÖVBORG. They told me at her lodgings that she had been out all night.

HEDDA (*going to the oval table*). Did you notice anything about the people of the house when they said that?

LÖVBORG (*looks inquiringly at her*). Notice anything about them?

HEDDA. I mean, did they seem to think it odd?

LÖVBORG (*suddenly understanding*). Oh yes, of course! I am dragging her down with me! However, I didn't notice anything.—I suppose Tesman is not up yet?

HEDDA. No—I think not——

LÖVBORG. When did he come home?

HEDDA. Very late.

LÖVBORG. Did he tell you anything?

HEDDA. Yes, I gathered that you had had an exceedingly jolly evening at Judge Brack's.

LÖVBORG. Nothing more?

HEDDA. I don't think so. However, I was so dreadfully sleepy——

[MRS. ELVSTED *enters through the curtains of the middle doorway.*]

MRS. ELVSTED (*going towards him*). Ah, 40 Lövborg! At last——!

LÖVBORG. Yes, at last. And too late!

MRS. ELVSTED (*looks anxiously at him*). What is too late?

LÖVBORG. Everything is too late now. It is all over with me.

MRS. ELVSTED. Oh no, no—don't say that!

LÖVBORG. You will say the same when you hear——

MRS. ELVSTED. I won't hear anything!

HEDDA. Perhaps you would prefer to talk to her alone! If so, I will leave you.

LÖVBORG. No, stay—you too. I beg you to stay.

MRS. ELVSTED. Yes, but I won't hear anything, I tell you.

LÖVBORG. It is not last night's adventures that I want to talk about.

MRS. ELVSTED. What is it then——?

LÖVBORG. I want to say that now our ways must part.

MRS. ELVSTED. Part!

HEDDA (*involuntarily*). I knew it!

LÖVBORG. You can be of no more service 20 to me, Thea.

MRS. ELVSTED. How can you stand there and say that! No more service to you! Am I not to help you now, as before? Are we not to go on working together?

LÖVBORG. Henceforward I shall do no work.

MRS. ELVSTED (*despairingly*). Then what am I to do with my life?

LÖVBORG. You must try to live your life 30 as if you had never known me.

MRS. ELVSTED. But you know I cannot do that!

LÖVBORG. Try if you cannot, Thea. You must go home again——

MRS. ELVSTED (*in vehement protest*). Never in this world! Where you are, there will I be also! I will not let myself be driven away like this! I will remain here! I will be with you when the book appears.

HEDDA (*half aloud, in suspense*). Ah yes— the book!

LÖVBORG (*looks at her*). My book and Thea's; for that is what it is.

MRS. ELVSTED. Yes, I feel that it is. And

that is why I have a right to be with you when it appears! I will see with my own eyes how respect and honor pour in upon you afresh. And the happiness—the happiness—oh, I must share it with you!

LÖVBORG. Thea—our book will never appear.

HEDDA. Ah!

MRS. ELVSTED. Never appear!

LÖVBORG. Can never appear.

MRS. ELVSTED (in agonized foreboding). Lövborg—what have you done with the manuscript?

HEDDA (looks anxiously at him). Yes, the manuscript——?

MRS. ELVSTED. Where is it?

LÖVBORG. Oh Thea—don't ask me about it!

MRS. ELVSTED. Yes, yes, I will know. I demand to be told at once.

LÖVBORG. The manuscript—Well then —I have torn the manuscript into a thousand pieces.

MRS. ELVSTED (shrieks). Oh no, no——!

HEDDA (involuntarily). But that's not——

LÖVBORG (looks at her). Not true, you think?

HEDDA (collecting herself). Oh well, of course—since you say so. But it sounded so improbable——

LÖVBORG. It is true, all the same.

MRS. ELVSTED (wringing her hands). Oh God—oh God, Hedda—torn his own work to pieces!

LÖVBORG. I have torn my own life to pieces. So why should I not tear my life-work too——?

MRS. ELVSTED. And you did this last night?

LÖVBORG. Yes, I tell you! Tore it into a thousand pieces and scattered them on the fiord—far out. There there is cool sea-water at any rate—let them drift upon it—drift with the current and the wind. And then presently they will sink—deeper and deeper— as I shall, Thea.

MRS. ELVSTED. Do you know, Lövborg, that what you have done with the book—I shall think of it to my dying day as though you had killed a little child.

LÖVBORG. Yes, you are right. It is a sort of child-murder.

MRS. ELVSTED. How could you, then——! Did not the child belong to me too?

HEDDA (almost inaudibly). Ah, the child ——

MRS. ELVSTED (breathing heavily). It is all over then. Well, well, now I will go, Hedda.

HEDDA. But you are not going away from town?

MRS. ELVSTED. Oh, I don't know what I shall do. I see nothing but darkness before me. (She goes out by the hall door.)

HEDDA (stands waiting for a moment). So you are not going to see her home, Mr. Lövborg?

LÖVBORG. I? Through the streets? Would you have people see her walking with me?

HEDDA. Of course I don't know what else may have happened last night. But is it so utterly irretrievable?

LÖVBORG. It will not end with last night—I know that perfectly well. And the thing is that now I have no taste for that sort of life either. I won't begin it anew. She has broken my courage and my power of braving life out.

HEDDA (looking straight before her). So that pretty little fool has had her fingers in a man's destiny. (Looks at him.) But all the same, how could you treat her so heartlessly?

LÖVBORG. Oh, don't say that it was heartless!

HEDDA. To go and destroy what has filled her whole soul for months and years! You do not call that heartless!

LÖVORG. To you I can tell the truth, Hedda.

HEDDA. The truth?

LÖVBORG. First promise me—give me your word—that what I now confide to you Thea shall never know.

HEDDA. I give you my word.

LÖVBORG. Good. Then let me tell you that what I said just now was untrue. 10

HEDDA. About the manuscript?

LÖVBORG. Yes. I have not torn it to pieces—nor thrown it into the fiord.

HEDDA. No, n— But—where is it then!

LÖVBORG. I have destroyed it none the less—utterly destroyed it, Hedda!

HEDDA. I don't understand.

LÖVBORG. Thea said that what I had done seemed to her like a child-murder.

HEDDA. Yes, so she said.

LÖVBORG. But to kill his child—that is not the worst thing a father can do to it.

HEDDA. Not the worst?

LÖVBORG. No. I wanted to spare Thea from hearing the worst.

HEDDA. Then what is the worst?

LÖVBORG. Suppose now, Hedda, that a man—in the small hours of the morning—came home to his child's mother 30 after a night of riot and debauchery, and said: "Listen—I have been here and there—in this place and in that. And I have taken our child with me— to this place and to that. And I have lost the child—utterly lost it. The devil knows into what hands it may have fallen—who may have had their clutches on it."

HEDDA. Well—but when all is said and 40 done, you know—that was only a book——

LÖVBORG. Thea's pure soul was in that book.

HEDDA. Yes, so I understand.

LÖVBORG. And you can understand, too, that for her and me together no future is possible.

HEDDA. What path do you mean to take then?

LÖVBORG. None. I will only try to make an end of it all—the sooner the better.

HEDDA (a step nearer to him). Eilert Lövborg—listen to me. Will you not try to—to do it beautifully?

LÖVBORG. Beautifully? (Smiling.) With vine-leaves in my hair, as you used to dream in the old days——?

HEDDA. No, no. I have lost my faith in the vine-leaves. But beautifully, nevertheless! For once in a way!— Good-bye! You must go now—and do not come here any more.

LÖVBORG. Good-bye, Mrs. Tesman. And give George Tesman my love. (He is on the point of going.)

HEDDA. No, wait! I must give you a memento to take with you.

[She goes to the writing-table and opens the drawer and the pistol-case; then returns to LÖVBORG with one of the pistols.]

LÖVBORG (looks at her). This? Is this the memento?

HEDDA (nodding slowly). Do you recognize it? It was aimed at you once.

LÖVBORG. You should have used it then.

HEDDA. Take it—and do you use it now.

LÖVBORG (puts the pistol in his breast pocket). Thanks!

HEDDA. And beautifully, Eilert Lövborg. Promise me that!

LÖVBORG. Good-bye, Hedda Gabler. (He goes out by the hall door.)

[HEDDA listens for a moment at the door. Then she goes up to the writing-table, takes out the packet of manuscript, peeps under the cover, draws a few of the sheets half out, and looks at them. Next she goes over and seats herself in the arm-chair beside the stove, with the packet in her lap. Presently she opens the stove door, and then the packet.]

HEDDA (*throws one of the quires into the fire and whispers to herself*). Now I am burning your child, Thea!—Burning it, curly-locks! (*Throwing one or two more* quires into the stove.) Your child and Eilert Lövborg's. (*Throws the rest in.*) I am burning—I am burning your child.

ACT IV

The same rooms at the TESMANS'. *It is evening. The drawing-room is in darkness. The back room is lighted by the hanging lamp over the table. The curtains over the glass door are drawn close.*

HEDDA, *dressed in black, walks to and fro in the dark room. Then she goes into the back room and disappears for a moment to the left. She is heard to strike a few chords on the piano. Presently she comes in sight again, and returns to the drawing-room.*

BERTA *enters from the right, through the inner room, with a lighted lamp, which she places on the table in front of the corner settee in the drawing-room. Her eyes are red with weeping, and she has black ribbons in her cap. She goes quietly and circumspectly out to the right.*

HEDDA, *goes up to the glass door, lifts the curtain a little aside, and looks out into the darkness.*

Shortly afterwards, MISS TESMAN, *in mourning, with a bonnet and veil on, comes in from the hall.* HEDDA *goes towards her and holds out her hand.*

MISS TESMAN. Yes, Hedda, here I am, in mourning and forlorn; for now my poor sister has at last found peace.

HEDDA. I have heard the news already, as you see. Tesman sent me a card.

MISS TESMAN. Yes, he promised me he would. But nevertheless I thought that to Hedda—here in the house of life—I ought myself to bring the tidings of death.

HEDDA. That was very kind of you.

MISS TESMAN. Ah, Rina ought not to have left us just now. This is not the time for Hedda's house to be a house of mourning.

HEDDA (*changing the subject*). She died quite peacefully, did she not, Miss Tesman?

MISS TESMAN. Oh, her end was so calm, so beautiful. And then she had the unspeakable happiness of seeing George once more—and bidding him good-bye.—Has he come home yet?

HEDDA. No. He wrote that he might be detained. But won't you sit down?

MISS TESMAN. No thank you, my dear, dear Hedda. I should like to, but I have so much to do. I must prepare my dear one for her rest as well as I can. She shall go to her grave looking her best.

HEDDA. Can I not help you in any way?

MISS TESMAN. Oh, you must not think of it! Hedda Tesman must have no hand in such mournful work. Nor let her thoughts dwell on it either—not at this time.

HEDDA. One is not always mistress of one's thoughts——

MISS TESMAN (*continuing*). Ah yes, it is the way of the world. At home we shall be sewing a shroud; and here there will soon be sewing too, I suppose—but of another sort, thank God!

[GEORGE TESMAN *enters by the hall door.*]

HEDDA. Ah, you have come at last!

TESMAN. You here, Aunt Julia? With Hedda? Fancy that!

MISS TESMAN. I was just going, my dear boy. Well, have you done all you promised?

TESMAN. No; I'm really afraid I have

forgotten half of it. I must come to you again to-morrow. To-day my brain is all in a whirl. I can't keep my thoughts together.

MISS TESMAN. Why, my dear George, you mustn't take it in this way.

TESMAN. Mustn't——? How do you mean?

MISS TESMAN. Even in your sorrow you must rejoice, as I do—rejoice that she is at rest.

TESMAN. Oh yes, yes—you are thinking of Aunt Rina.

HEDDA. You will feel lonely now, Miss Tesman.

MISS TESMAN. Just at first, yes. But that will not last very long, I hope. I daresay I shall soon find an occupant for poor Rina's little room.

TESMAN. Indeed? Who do you think will take it? Eh?

MISS TESMAN. Oh, there's always some poor invalid or other in want of nursing, unfortunately.

HEDDA. Would you really take such a burden upon you again?

MISS TESMAN. A burden! Heaven forgive you, child—it has been no burden to me.

HEDDA. But suppose you had a total stranger on your hands——

MISS TESMAN. Oh, one soon makes friends with sick folk; and it's such an absolute necessity for me to have some one to live for. Well, heaven be praised, there may soon be something in this house, too, to keep an old aunt busy.

HEDDA. Oh, don't trouble about anything here.

TESMAN. Yes, just fancy what a nice time we three might have together, if——?

HEDDA. If——?

TESMAN (uneasily). Oh, nothing. It will all come right. Let us hope so—eh?

MISS TESMAN. Well, well, I daresay you two want to talk to each other.

(Smiling.) And perhaps Hedda may have something to tell you too, George. Good-bye! I must go home to Rina. (Turning at the door.) How strange it is to think that now Rina is with me and with my poor brother as well!

TESMAN. Yes, fancy that, Aunt Julia! Eh?

[MISS TESMAN goes out by the hall door.]

HEDDA (follows TESMAN coldly and searchingly with her eyes). I almost believe your Aunt Rina's death affects you more than it does your Aunt Julia.

TESMAN. Oh, it's not that alone. It's Eilert I am so terribly uneasy about.

HEDDA (quickly). Is there anything new about him?

TESMAN. I looked in at his rooms this afternoon, intending to tell him the manuscript was in safe keeping.

HEDDA. Well, did you not find him?

TESMAN. No. He wasn't at home. But afterwards I met Mrs. Elvsted, and she told me that he had been here early this morning.

HEDDA. Yes, directly after you had gone.

TESMAN. And he said that he had torn his manuscript to pieces—eh?

HEDDA. Yes, so he declared.

TESMAN. Why, good heavens, he must have been completely out of his mind! And I suppose you thought it best not to give it back to him, Hedda?

HEDDA. No, he did not get it.

TESMAN. But of course you told him that we had it?

HEDDA. No. (Quickly.) Did you tell Mrs. Elvsted?

TESMAN. No; I thought I had better not. But you ought to have told him. Fancy, if, in desperation, he should go and do himself some injury! Let me have the manuscript, Hedda! I will take it to him at once. Where is it?

HEDDA (*cold and immovable, leaning on the arm-chair*). I have not got it.

TESMAN. Have not got it? What in the world do you mean?

HEDDA. I have burnt it—every line of it.

TESMAN (*with a violent movement of terror*). Burnt! Burnt Eilert's manuscript!

HEDDA. Don't scream so. The servant might hear you.

TESMAN. Burnt! Why, good God——! No, no, no! It's impossible!

HEDDA. It is so, nevertheless.

TESMAN. Do you know what you have done, Hedda? It's unlawful appropriation of lost property. Fancy that! Just ask Judge Brack, and he'll tell you what it is.

HEDDA. I advise you not to speak of it—either to Judge Brack, or to any one else.

TESMAN. But how could you do anything so unheard-of? What put it into your head? What possessed you? Answer me that—eh?

HEDDA (*suppressing an almost imperceptible smile*). I did it for your sake, George.

TESMAN. For my sake!

HEDDA. This morning, when you told me about what he had read to you——

TESMAN. Yes, yes—what then?

HEDDA. You acknowledged that you envied him his work.

TESMAN. Oh, of course I didn't mean that literally.

HEDDA. No matter—I could not bear the idea that any one should throw you into the shade.

TESMAN (*in an outburst of mingled doubt and joy*). Hedda! Oh, is this true? But—but—I never knew you to show your love like that before. Fancy that!

HEDDA. Well, I may as well tell you that—just at this time—— (*Impatiently, breaking off.*) No, no; you can ask Aunt Julia. She will tell you, fast enough.

TESMAN. Oh, I almost think I understand you, Hedda! (*Clasps his hands together.*) Great heavens! do you really mean it! Eh?

HEDDA. Don't shout so. The servant might hear.

TESMAN (*laughing in irrepressible glee*). The servant! Why, how absurd you are, Hedda. It's only my old Berta! Why, I'll tell Berta myself.

HEDDA (*clenching her hands together in desperation*). Oh, it is killing me,—it is killing me, all this!

TESMAN. What is, Hedda? Eh?

HEDDA (*coldly, controlling herself*). All this—absurdity— George.

TESMAN. Absurdity! Do you see anything absurd in my being overjoyed at the news! But after all perhaps I had better not say anything to Berta.

HEDDA. Oh—why not that too?

TESMAN. No, no, not yet! But I must certainly tell Aunt Julia. And then that you have begun to call me George too! Fancy that! Oh, Aunt Julia will be so happy—so happy.

HEDDA. When she hears that I have burnt Eilert Lövborg's manuscript—for your sake?

TESMAN. No, by-the-bye—that affair of the manuscript—of course nobody must know about that. But that you love me so much, Hedda—Aunt Julia must really share my joy in that! I wonder, now, whether this sort of thing is usual in young wives? Eh?

HEDDA. I think you had better ask Aunt Julia that question too.

TESMAN. I will indeed, some time or other. (*Looks uneasy and downcast again.*) And yet the manuscript—the manuscript! Good God! it is terrible to think what will become of poor Eilert now.

[MRS. ELVSTED, *dressed as in the first Act, with hat and cloak, enters by the hall door.*]

MRS. ELVSTED (*greets them hurriedly, and says in evident agitation*). Oh, dear Hedda, forgive my coming again.

HEDDA. What is the matter with you, Thea?

TESMAN. Something about Eilert Lövborg again—eh?

MRS. ELVSTED. Yes! I am dreadfully afraid some misfortune has happened to him.

HEDDA (*seizes her arm*). Ah,—do you think so?

TESMAN. Why, good Lord—what makes you think that, Mrs. Elvsted?

MRS. ELVSTED. I heard them talking of him at my boarding-house—just as I came in. Oh, the most incredible rumors are afloat about him today.

TESMAN. Yes, fancy, so I heard too! And I can bear witness that he went straight home to bed last night. Fancy that!

HEDDA. Well, what did they say at the boarding-house?

MRS. ELVSTED. Oh, I couldn't make out anything clearly. Either they knew nothing definite, or else——They stopped talking when they saw me; and I did not dare to ask.

TESMAN (*moving about uneasily*). We must hope—we must hope that you misunderstood them, Mrs. Elvsted.

MRS. ELVSTED. No, no; I am sure it was of him they were talking. And I heard something about the hospital or——

TESMAN. The hospital?

HEDDA. No—surely that cannot be!

MRS. ELVSTED. Oh, I was in such mortal terror! I went to his lodgings and asked for him there.

HEDDA. You could make up your mind to that, Thea!

MRS. ELVSTED. What else could I do? I really could bear the suspense no longer.

TESMAN. But you didn't find him either—eh?

MRS. ELVSTED. No. And the people knew nothing about him. He hadn't been home since yesterday afternoon, they said.

TESMAN. Yesterday! Fancy, how could they say that?

MRS. ELVSTED. Oh, I am sure something terrible must have happened to him.

TESMAN. Hedda dear—how would it be if I were to go and make inquiries——?

HEDDA. No, no—don't you mix yourself up in this affair.

[JUDGE BRACK, *with his hat in his hand, enters by the hall door, which* BERTA *opens, and closes behind him. He looks grave and bows in silence.*]

TESMAN. Oh, is that you, my dear Judge? Eh?

BRACK. Yes. It was imperative I should see you this evening.

TESMAN. I can see you have heard the news about Aunt Rina.

BRACK. Yes, that among other things.

TESMAN. Isn't it sad—eh?

BRACK. Well, my dear Tesman, that depends on how you look at it.

TESMAN (*looks doubtfully at him*). Has anything else happened?

BRACK. Yes.

HEDDA (*in suspense*). Anything sad, Judge Brack?

BRACK. That, too, depends on how you look at it, Mrs. Tesman.

MRS. ELVSTED (*unable to restrain her anxiety*). Oh! it is something about Eilert Lövborg!

BRACK (*with a glance at her*). What makes you think that, Madam? Perhaps you have already heard something——?

MRS. ELVSTED (*in confusion*). No, nothing at all, but——

TESMAN. Oh, for heaven's sake, tell us!

BRACK (*shrugging his shoulders*). Well, I

regret to say Eilert Lövborg has been taken to the hospital. He is lying at the point of death.

MRS. ELVSTED (*shrieks*). Oh God! Oh God——

TESMAN. To the hospital! And at the point of death.

HEDDA (*involuntarily*). So soon then——

MRS. ELVSTED (*wailing*). And we parted in anger, Hedda!

HEDDA (*whispers*). Thea—Thea—be careful!

MRS. ELVSTED (*not heeding her*). I must go to him! I must see him alive!

BRACK. It is useless, Madam. No one will be admitted.

MRS. ELVSTED. Oh, at least tell me what has happened to him? What is it?

TESMAN. You don't mean to say that he has himself—— Eh?

HEDDA. Yes, I am sure he has.

TESMAN. Hedda, how can you——?

BRACK (*keeping his eyes fixed upon her*). Unfortunately you have guessed quite correctly, Mrs. Tesman.

MRS. ELVSTED. Oh, how horrible!

TESMAN. Himself, then! Fancy that!

HEDDA. Shot himself!

BRACK. Rightly guessed again, Mrs. Tesman.

MRS. ELVSTED (*with an effort at self-control*). When did it happen, Mr. Brack?

BRACK. This afternoon—between three and four.

TESMAN. But, good Lord, where did he do it? Eh?

BRACK (*with some hesitation*). Where? Well—I suppose at his lodgings.

MRS. ELVSTED. No, that cannot be; for I was there between six and seven.

BRACK. Well, then, somewhere else. I don't know exactly. I only know that he was found——. He had shot himself—in the breast.

MRS. ELVSTED. Oh, how terrible! That he should die like that!

HEDDA (*to* BRACK). Was it in the breast?

BRACK. Yes—as I told you.

HEDDA. Not in the temple?

BRACK. In the breast, Mrs. Tesman.

HEDDA. Well, well—the breast is a good place, too.

BRACK. How do you mean, Mrs. Tesman?

HEDDA (*evasively*). Oh, nothing—nothing.

TESMAN. And the wound is dangerous, you say—eh?

BRACK. Absolutely mortal. The end has probably come by this time.

MRS. ELVSTED. Yes, yes, I feel it. The end! The end! Oh, Hedda——!

TESMAN. But tell me, how have you learnt all this?

BRACK (*curtly*). Through one of the police. A man I had some business with.

HEDDA (*in a clear voice*). At last a deed worth doing!

TESMAN (*terrified*). Good heavens, Hedda! what are you saying?

HEDDA. I say there is beauty in this.

BRACK. H'm, Mrs. Tesman——

TESMAN. Beauty! Fancy that!

MRS. ELVSTED. Oh, Hedda, how can you talk of beauty in such an act!

HEDDA. Eilert Lövborg has himself made up his account with life. He has had the courage to do—the one right thing.

MRS. ELVSTED. No, you must never think that was how it happened! It must have been in delirium that he did it.

TESMAN. In despair!

HEDDA. That he did not. I am certain of that.

MRS. ELVSTED. Yes, yes! In delirium! Just as when he tore up our manuscript.

BRACK (*starting*). The manuscript? Has he torn that up?

MRS. ELVSTED. Yes, last night.

TESMAN (*whispers softly*). Oh, Hedda, we shall never get over this.

BRACK. H'm, very extraordinary.

TESMAN (*moving about the room*). To think of Eilert going out of the world in this way! And not leaving behind him the book that would have immortalized his name——

MRS. ELVSTED. Oh, if only it could be put together again! 10

TESMAN. Yes, if it only could! I don't know what I would not give——

MRS. ELVSTED. Perhaps it can, Mr. Tesman.

TESMAN. What do you mean?

MRS. ELVSTED (*searches in the pocket of her dress*). Look here. I have kept all the loose notes he used to dictate from.

HEDDA (*a step forward*). Ah——!

TESMAN. You have kept them, Mrs. 20 Elvsted! Eh?

MRS. ELVSTED. Yes, I have them here. I put them in my pocket when I left home. Here they still are——

TESMAN. Oh, do let me see them!

MRS. ELVSTED (*hands him a bundle of papers*). But they are in such disorder— all mixed up.

TESMAN. Fancy, if we could make something out of them, after all! Perhaps 30 if we two put our heads together——

MRS. ELVSTED. Oh, yes, at least let us try——

TESMAN. We will manage it! We must! I will dedicate my life to this task.

HEDDA. You, George? Your life?

TESMAN. Yes, or rather all the time I can spare. My own collections must wait in the meantime. Hedda—you understand, eh? I owe this to Eilert's 40 memory.

HEDDA. Perhaps.

TESMAN. And so, my dear Mrs. Elvsted, we will give our whole minds to it. There is no use in brooding over what can't be undone—eh? We must

try to control our grief as much as possible, and——

MRS. ELVSTED. Yes, yes, Mr. Tesman, I will do the best I can.

TESMAN. Well then, come here. I can't rest until we have looked through the notes. Where shall we sit? Here? No, in there, in the back room. Excuse me, my dear Judge. Come with me, Mrs. Elvsted.

MRS. ELVSTED. Oh, if only it were possible!

[TESMAN *and* MRS. ELVSTED *go into the back room. She takes off her hat and cloak. They both sit at the table under the hanging lamp, and are soon deep in an eager examination of the papers.* HEDDA *crosses to the stove and sits in the arm-chair. Presently* BRACK *goes up to her.*]

HEDDA (*in a low voice*). Oh, what a sense of freedom it gives one, this act of Eilert Lövborg's.

BRACK. Freedom, Mrs. Hedda? Well, of course, it is a release for him——

HEDDA. I mean for me. It gives me a sense of freedom to know that a deed of deliberate courage is still possible in this world,—a deed of spontaneous beauty.

BRACK (*smiling*). H'm—my dear Mrs. Hedda——

HEDDA. Oh, I know what you are going to say. For you are a kind of a specialist too, like—you know!

BRACK (*looking hard at her*). Eilert Lövborg was more to you than perhaps you are willing to admit to yourself. Am I wrong?

HEDDA. I don't answer such questions. I only know Eilert Lövborg has had the courage to live his life after his own fashion. And then—the last great act, with its beauty! Ah! that he should have the will and the strength to turn away from the banquet of life—so early.

BRACK. I am sorry, Mrs. Hedda,—but I fear I must dispel an amiable illusion.

HEDDA. Illusion?

BRACK. Which could not have lasted long in any case.

HEDDA. What do you mean?

BRACK. Eilert Lövborg did not shoot himself voluntarily.

HEDDA. Not voluntarily?

BRACK. No. The thing did not happen exactly as I told it.

HEDDA (in suspense). Have you concealed something? What is it?

BRACK. For poor Mrs. Elvsted's sake I idealized the facts a little.

HEDDA. What are the facts?

BRACK. First, that he is already dead.

HEDDA. At the hospital?

BRACK. Yes—without regaining consciousness.

HEDDA. What more have you concealed?

BRACK. This—the event did not happen at his lodgings.

HEDDA. Oh, that can make no difference.

BRACK. Perhaps it may. For I must tell you—Eilert Lövborg was found shot in—in Mademoiselle Diana's boudoir.

HEDDA (makes a motion as if to rise, but sinks back again). That is impossible, Judge Brack! He cannot have been there again to-day.

BRACK. He was there this afternoon. He went there, he said, to demand the return of something which they had taken from him. Talked wildly about a lost child——

HEDDA. Ah—so that was why——

BRACK. I thought probably he meant his manuscript; but now I hear he destroyed that himself. So I suppose it must have been his pocketbook.

HEDDA. Yes, no doubt. And there—there he was found?

BRACK. Yes, there. With a pistol in his breast-pocket, discharged. The ball had lodged in a vital part.

HEDDA. In the breast—yes.

BRACK. No—in the bowels.

HEDDA (looks up at him with an expression of loathing). That too! Oh, what curse is it that makes everything I touch turn ludicrous and mean?

BRACK. There is one point more, Mrs. Hedda—another disagreeable feature in the affair.

HEDDA. And what is that?

BRACK. The pistol he carried——

HEDDA (breathless). Well? What of it?

BRACK. He must have stolen it.

HEDDA (leaps up). Stolen it! That is not true! He did not steal it!

BRACK. No other explanation is possible. He must have stolen it—— Hush!

[TESMAN and MRS. ELVSTED have risen from the table in the back room, and come into the drawing room.]

TESMAN (with the papers in both his hands). Hedda dear, it is almost impossible to see under that lamp. Think of that!

HEDDA. Yes, I am thinking.

TESMAN. Would you mind our sitting at your writing-table—eh?

HEDDA. If you like. (Quickly.) No, wait! Let me clear it first!

TESMAN. Oh, you needn't trouble, Hedda. There is plenty of room.

HEDDA. No, no; let me clear it, I say! I will take these things in and put them on the piano. There! (She has drawn out an object, covered with sheet music, from under the book-case, places several other pieces of music upon it, and carries the whole into the inner room, to the left. TESMAN lays the scraps of paper on the writing-table, and moves the lamp there from the corner table. HEDDA returns.)

HEDDA (behind MRS. ELVSTED's chair, gently ruffling her hair). Well, my sweet Thea,—how goes it with Eilert Lövborg's monument?

MRS. ELVSTED (*looks dispiritedly up at her*). Oh, it will be terribly hard to put in order.

TESMAN. We must manage it. I am determined. And arranging other people's papers is just the work for me.

[HEDDA *goes over to the stove, and seats herself on one of the foot-stools.* BRACK *stands over her, leaning on the arm-chair.*]

HEDDA (*whispers*). What did you say 10 about the pistol?

BRACK (*softly*). That he must have stolen it.

HEDDA. Why stolen it?

BRACK. Because every other explanation ought to be impossible, Mrs. Hedda.

HEDDA. Indeed?

BRACK (*glances at her*). Of course Eilert Lövborg was here this morning. Was 20 he not?

HEDDA. Yes.

BRACK. Were you alone with him?

HEDDA. Part of the time.

BRACK. Did you not leave the room whilst he was here?

HEDDA. No.

BRACK. Try to recollect. Were you not out of the room a moment?

HEDDA. Yes, perhaps just a moment— 30 out in the hall.

BRACK. And where was your pistol-case during that time?

HEDDA. I had it locked up in——

BRACK. Well, Mrs. Hedda?

HEDDA. The case stood there on the writing-table.

BRACK. Have you looked since, to see whether both the pistols are there?

HEDDA. No. 40

BRACK. Well, you need not. I saw the pistol found in Lövborg's pocket, and I knew it at once as the one I had seen yesterday—and before, too.

HEDDA. Have you it with you?

BRACK. No; the police have it.

HEDDA. What will the police do with it?

BRACK. Search till they find the owner.

HEDDA. Do you think they will succeed?

BRACK (*bends over her and whispers*). No, Hedda Gabler—not so long as I say nothing.

HEDDA (*looks frightened at him*). And if you do not say nothing,—what then?

BRACK (*shrugs his shoulders*). There is always the possibility that the pistol was stolen.

HEDDA (*firmly*). Death rather than that.

BRACK (*smiling*). People say such things —but they don't do them.

HEDDA (*without replying*). And supposing the pistol was stolen, and the owner is discovered? What then?

BRACK. Well, Hedda—then comes the scandal.

HEDDA. The scandal!

BRACK. Yes, the scandal—of which you are mortally afraid. You will, of course be brought before the court— both you and Mademoiselle Diana. She will have to explain how the thing happened—whether it was an accidental shot or murder. Did the pistol go off as he was trying to take it out of his pocket, to threaten her with? Or did she tear the pistol out of his hand, shoot him, and push it back into his pocket? That would be quite like her; for she is an able-bodied young person, this same Mademoiselle Diana.

HEDDA. But *I* have nothing to do with all this repulsive business.

BRACK. No. But you will have to answer the question: Why did you give Eilert Lövborg the pistol? And what conclusions will people draw from the fact that you did give it to him?

HEDDA (*lets her head sink*). That is true. I did not think of that.

BRACK. Well, fortunately, there is no danger, so long as I say nothing.

HEDDA (*looks up at him*). So I am in your power, Judge Brack. You have me at your beck and call, from this time forward.

BRACK (*whispers softly*). Dearest Hedda —believe me— I shall not abuse my advantage.

HEDDA. I am in your power none the less. Subject to your will and your demands. A slave, a slave then! (*Rises impetuously.*) No, I cannot endure the thought of that! Never!

BRACK (*looks half-mockingly at her*). People generally get used to the inevitable.

HEDDA (*returns his look*). Yes, perhaps. (*She crosses to the writing-table. Suppressing an involuntary smile, she imitates* TESMAN'S *intonations.*) Well? Are you getting on, George? Eh?

TESMAN. Heaven knows, dear. In any case it will be the work of months.

HEDDA (*as before*). Fancy that! (*Passes her hands softly through* MRS. ELVSTED'S *hair.*) Doesn't it seem strange to you, Thea? Here are you sitting with Tesman—just as you used to sit with Eilert Lövborg?

MRS. ELVSTED. Ah, if I could only inspire your husband in the same way.

HEDDA. Oh, that will come too—in time.

TESMAN. Yes, do you know, Hedda—I really think I begin to feel something of the sort. But won't you go and sit with Brack again?

HEDDA. Is there nothing I can do to help you two?

TESMAN. No, nothing in the world. (*Turning his head.*) I trust to you to keep Hedda company, my dear Brack.

BRACK (*with a glance at* HEDDA). With the very greatest of pleasure.

HEDDA. Thanks. But I am tired this evening. I will go in and lie down a little on the sofa.

TESMAN. Yes, do dear—eh?

[HEDDA *goes into the back room and draws the curtains. A short pause. Suddenly she is heard playing a wild dance on the piano.*]

MRS. ELVSTED (*starts from her chair*). Oh— what is that?

TESMAN (*runs to the doorway*). Why, my dearest Hedda—don't play dance music to-night! Just think of Aunt Rina! And of Eilert too!

HEDDA (*puts her head out between the curtains*). And of Aunt Julia. And of all the rest of them.—After this, I will be quiet. (*Closes the curtains again.*)

TESMAN (*at the writing-table*). It's not good for her to see us at this distressing work. I'll tell you what, Mrs. Elvsted,—you shall take the empty room at Aunt Julia's, and then I will come over in the evenings, and we can sit and work there—eh?

HEDDA (*in the inner room*). I hear what you are saying, Tesman. But how am *I* to get through the evenings out here?

TESMAN (*turning over the papers*). Oh, I daresay Judge Brack will be so kind as to look in now and then, even though I am out.

BRACK (*in the arm-chair, calls out gaily*). Every blessed evening, with all the pleasure in life, Mrs. Tesman! We shall get on capitally together, we two!

HEDDA (*speaking loud and clear*). Yes, don't you flatter yourself we will, Judge Brack? Now that you are the one cock in the basket——

[*A shot is heard within.* TESMAN, MRS. ELVSTED, *and* BRACK *leap to their feet.*]

TESMAN. Oh, now she is playing with those pistols again.

[*He throws back the curtains and runs in, followed by* MRS. ELVSTED. HEDDA *lies stretched on the sofa, lifeless. Confusion and cries.* BERTA *enters in alarm from the right.*]

TESMAN (*shrieks to* BRACK). Shot herself! Shot herself in the temple! Fancy that!

BRACK (*half-fainting in the arm-chair*). Good God!—people don't do such things.

AUGUST STRINDBERG

O N JANUARY 3, 1924, the Province-
town presented Strindberg's *The
Spook Sonata*. The playbill carried a brief
program article by a rapidly rising
young playwright, Eugene O'Neill,
entitled "Strindberg and Our Theatre."
This important statement opened with
these words: "In creating a modern
theater which we hope will liberate for
significant expression a fresh elation and
joy in experimental production, it is the
most apt symbol of our good intentions
that we start with a play by August
Strindberg; for Strindberg was the
precursor of all modernity in our present theater. . . . Strindberg still remains among the most modern of
moderns, the greatest interpreter in the
theater of the characteristic spiritual
conflicts which constitute the drama—
the blood—of our lives today." That
pronouncement by the leading American dramatist (who has been reticent
with words of tribute) for the most original and influential group in American
drama would be significant, even if
exaggerated by young enthusiasm, as
an indication of the powerful impact
this Swedish giant had upon his own
and the generation that followed him.

The man who called forth this handsome praise first lived those "characteristic spiritual conflicts" before he
made them into dramas of world
interest. For August Strindberg was an
intense, fiery, and tortured genius. All
his portraits show a turbulent energy
flashing from his haunted eyes, his
sensitive mouth, and his bristling mustache. The voluminous and intimate
autobiographical confessions that came
from his pen give us an embarrassingly
complete picture of his life and bare his
innermost soul. He was born at Stockholm in 1849 under circumstances that
left his spirit scarred. His father was a
merchant of some standing; his mother
was a servant who had already borne
two children to the merchant before
she was married to him shortly before
the birth of August. Strindberg in a
frenzy of self torment, feeling that he
was unwanted, referred to himself as
"the bondwoman's son." This attitude
of humiliation was no doubt forced
upon him by the wretched circumstances of his early life. The father lost
his business, many children were born,
and poverty closed in upon them.
Strindberg was one of eleven people
crowded into three rooms; he remembered this melancholy brooding period
as a miserable succession of scoldings,
cuffings, and commands to sit on a
chair and keep still. Analysts have
remarked a close causal connection
between his hatred for women and their
war upon him, and these early years of
hostility from his mother and domination by an older sister.

From the outset life was for Strindberg a great weight to be borne. His
mother died when he was thirteen. His
father soon married again, this time his
former housekeeper. She had little
affection for August Strindberg who
failed to win her sympathy or her
friendship. His experiences at school
brought him little satisfaction. He
spoke of this period as "a preparation

61

for hell and not for life." His unhappiness lay within himself or his stars, for his exceptional, though erratic, abilities were early observed by his teachers. He did not submit willingly to discipline or direction, but followed the wayward drive that pushed him into his singular channel. He picked up an astonishing miscellany of learning in his wide and feverish reading and experiments.

The unhappy Strindberg, poor and frustrated but energetic, entered the University of Upsala when he was eighteen. After one semester, during which he went without a fire in his barren attic room, he was forced out by his poverty. He tried teaching in his home school, and worked at various jobs during the next five years while intermittently attending the university. He was critical of the entire institution, and once in a cynical moment said that the one solid remains of his years there was a smart tailored coat. In the midst of this wretched and unpromising mental turmoil he felt the urge to write. He began to turn out poetry and plays that won mild recognition. He worked at journalism, but failed to support himself by writing alone. He was given a post in the Royal Library at Stockholm. During the eight years there (1874–1882) he studied hard, wrote, and began to publish stories and historical essays about Stockholm and the people of Sweden—an interest that bore rich fruit in his early historical plays.

At the age of twenty-six Strindberg married a woman who divorced her husband for him—the first of three marriages, each of which began well but ended in separation and recriminations. During this first marriage he wrote with tremendous determination. He turned out a novel that was heatedly discussed, his plays attracted attention, and in 1883 he decided he could now leave Stockholm and enter upon a full-time career as a writer. He went to Switzerland where he wrote the stories called *Marriage* which caused an uproar among the conservatives in Sweden. The book was first confiscated and then released when Strindberg himself went back to contest the action. This book, followed by a second on the same subject in 1886, gave clear indication of the bent of Strindberg's realism in that period of feminism and the naturalistic movement, and defined the basic views dramatized during the next two years in the famous plays dealing with marriage and the sex war: *The Father, Comrades*, and *Miss Julia*.

From this period to the close of his life, Strindberg was a self-torturing, half-maddened soul seeking escape from things as they were, in the illusion that in the next experiment in living he would find peace. He went from place to place: Bavaria, Denmark, Berlin, Paris, only to be followed by the same fears, to be disturbed by the same disharmonies. He was irresistibly drawn to women in this search for completion, only to be repelled by his disappointment and driven into a confirmed state of bitterness against the entire sex. He was convinced that the "new woman" betrayed herself and the man to whom she should be united in peace and mutual support by denying her privileges and obligations as woman in the campaign for "equality madness." It was Strindberg's personal tragedy to seek desperately for the serenity and poise of an Emerson while looking with starting eyes into the black mystery of his own throbbing libido.

Driven by the inferno within, he wrote at high pitch about the things that persecuted him. The dramas reflect this soul tension, but the record itself may be read in the torrential outpourings of his autobiographies from 1893 to 1903: *The Son of a Bondswoman, Fermentation Time, The Author, The Confessions of a Fool, Inferno, Legends,* and *Alone.* The last four of these volumes are especially interesting because they trace his bitter experiences through the adult years: the breakup of his first marriage, the attack on his wife as a vampire, his succeeding marriages, the onslaught of his persecution mania and his months in a private hospital, and finally the period of comparative calm under the influence of his daughter and the religious power of Swedenborg. Here the expressionistic plays take up the record, as we shall note below.

He lived on at this feverish pace until 1912, when he died of cancer at his native Stockholm where he had been living chiefly since the foundation of his own Intimate Theatre there in 1897. Of the one hundred fifteen published works which he left behind him, fifty-six were in dramatic form.

This brief biographical sketch will at least suggest "the characteristic spiritual conflicts" (as O'Neill labeled them) of Strindberg which "constitute the drama—the blood—of our lives today." The permanent expression of these conflicts is revealed at white heat in the best of the fifty-six plays. Since Strindberg was a man of the times as well as an eccentric genius, it is natural to find that his plays fall conveniently into certain rough groupings that enable us to see his work as a whole. He began, like Ibsen who was twenty-one years older, with historical romance represented by *Master Olof* (1872) and folklore fantasy represented by *The Wanderings of Lucky-Per* (1883). These plays are mentioned now only because their author wrote greater ones later on. They show few symptoms of the stark, acrid realism that was soon to startle Europe.

Following these apprentice pieces, Strindberg wrote essays, stories, and novels, some of them sensational, and then presented the four great naturalistic dramas that placed him among the giants of the contemporary theatre. The first of these was *The Father* (1887). For cold, bitter, unrelieved intensity and for remorseless exposure of the black, selfish heart of a female at war with a man, *The Father* has never been surpassed. Representing this conflict are Laura and her husband, a captain of cavalry, at the climax of some twenty years of marriage. They have reached the peak of the repulsion following the attraction of sex. Laura is weary of the captain and jealous of him and his growing reputation. Through the years she has practised a petty, womanish tyranny over him, wearing him down with a canny ruthlessness foreign to the nature of the captain.

The immediate struggle centers around their seventeen year old daughter Bertha. The father sees that she too is being ruined by the selfish, domineering possessiveness of Laura, and determines to send the child to boarding school and freedom. He reckons without the embattled Laura who menaces him and makes war upon him by getting rid of the captain's friendly doctor, taunting him, driving him to distraction with diabolical insinuations that Bertha is not his child, that the father is not wanted and no longer needed, and torturing him until he throws a lighted lamp at her. Then she has him pronounced insane, the nurse slips a straightjacket on him, and the captain falls with a stroke as the triumphant Laura clasps her daughter to her breast with the pointed cry, "My child, my own child!"

That is naturalism with a vengeance, crisp, firm and tight in structure, and uncompromising in its grim picture of the results of the marital struggle in which victor and vanquished alike are defeated and lost. *The Father* was performed at the Théâtre Libre in Paris in 1887. It has been revived again and again, and has been frequently reprinted as an example of Strindberg's naturalistic dramas.

Comrades, which followed the next year, was a sombre comedy on the same general theme. It shows woman at her worst—childish, petty, ungenerous, jealous, taking mean advantage of the "comradeship" arrangement with her husband. Bertha and Axel are both artists. She tries to subdue him as Laura had subdued the Captain. She almost succeeds because Axel, who prefers to appease her, is reluctant to assert himself even though, as he says, "It's as if you were drawing a net about me while I sit absorbed in my work." When Bertha's mean and covetous soul is revealed after she wins a prize for a picture that Axel had painted, Axel rouses himself and drives her away. He determines to meet his comrades at the cafe; "at home I want a wife." The tone of the piece is well sounded by Carl: "They only need real men—and human beings can be made even out of women."

Creditors (1890), a long one act play, is made of the same stuff, and tells the story of a vampirish literary woman who had written a scurrilous novel about her first husband, and is now destroying her second by usurping his strength. Both men are her creditors; without them, and even with them, she is nothing. The theme is stated by Gustav, the first husband, who returns to open the eyes of his successor: "For look you, the woman is the man's child. If she doesn't become his, he becomes hers and then we have a topsy-turvy world." These plays on the misery of men and women at war and in competition in marriage reached their most despairing climax in *The Dance of Death* in 1901.

We have chosen *Miss Julia* (1888) to represent Strindberg's powerful contribution to naturalistic drama. The play was designated by the author as "A Naturalistic Tragedy." In his introduction Edwin Björkman, who made the translation reprinted here, wrote: "Among more than half a hundred plays produced by Strindberg during his lifetime, none has won such widespread attention as *Miss Julia*, both on account of its masterful construction and its gripping theme. . . . It represents, first of all, its author's most determined and most daring endeavor to win the modern stage for Naturalism."

In his own famous preface to the play, Strindberg analysed in great detail the origin, theory, structure, and method of presentation of *Miss Julia*. It was based on an actual incident that impressed Strindberg deeply when he heard it. He found well-suited to his idea of tragedy the sad situation of a fortunately placed individual falling from station and perishing. He said he discovered the "joy of life in its violent and cruel struggles." He explained Miss Julia's fate as a complex of many factors: "her mother's fundamental instincts; her father's mistaken upbringing of the girl; her own nature, and the suggestive influence of her fiancé on a weak and degenerate brain"; and the whole combination of the circumstances of this particular Midsummer Eve, with her father away, herself in an excited physical state, and other factors that led up to the fatal moment with the lackey in the secluded room. This "remnant of the old military nobility" went down before "the new nobility of nerves and brain."

The valet, Strindberg says, "is the kind that builds new stock. . . . He has already risen in the world, and is strong enough not to be sensitive about using other people's services." But he is emotionally callous, "having at once the slave's brutality and the master's lack of squeamishness." And he shows us how the servant classes "look at life from beneath." The character, Christine the cook, Strindberg described as "a female slave, full of servility and sluggishness acquired in front of the kitchen fire, and stuffed full of morality and religion that are meant to serve her at once as cloak and scapegoat."

The grim tragedy which these three act out is cast into an unbroken unit of an hour and a half playing time relieved by expertly arranged pantomime. Strindberg said he had not done anything new, since that could not be done, but that he had tried to modernize the form for "the new men of a new time." Though it was immediately produced by the Students' Association of the Copenhagen University, by the Freie Bühne in Berlin, by Antoine in Paris, and by Strindberg at his own Intimate Theatre in Stockholm in 1906, *Miss Julia* has been in English a play of the library rather than of the theatre. No public performance was given in England until January, 1939. The movement of which it was a part is now passed, but the play retained enough of its original power to arouse controversy for over three decades, and it still represents most characteristically Strindberg's unique contribution to the naturalistic theatre.

The other important and influential contribution of Strindberg to the drama was in the imaginative plays out of which the modern movement of expressionism arose, as O'Neill's program note documents. Following the harrowing experiences of his breakdown and mental anguish in the 1890s, though he again took up the historical drama to good effect, Strindberg concentrated his creative energy and his extraordinarily powerful imagination on a series of symbolic plays that have the reality appropriate only to a dream. To the awake eye of the man making his living under the morning sun, they are distorted in setting and action to the point of incommunicability. Actually they are soul-searching explorations into the illusive regions of the spirit where precision is impossible. Strindberg, who had voyaged much and often in these treacherous zones, devised a new mode of communication to suggest, if not to specify exactly, what he saw there. He drew upon a set of symbols, he invented parables, he created a dream or a ghost world to provoke the imagination into understanding. Of these once baffling and still somewhat strange plays, the greatest are *To Damascus* (Parts I & II, 1898; III, 1904); *The Dream Play* (1902); and *The Spook Sonata* (1907).

The long symbolic play *To Damascus* seems to have sprung from Strindberg's soul crisis as described and analysed in the autobiography *Inferno* (1898). By eschewing objective reality and congruity and assuming the world of a dream, Strindberg was able to concentrate upon the abstract essence of the struggle rather than upon the details of its physical manifestation. For in a dream, anything can happen; there are no improbabilities, no limitations of space, no logical sequence of time, no restraint on the forms assumed by the characters. Strindberg uses all the liberties in *To Damascus* to allegorize his struggle for peace through religious faith and acceptance. The title links the journey to that of Saul on his way to conversion, and gives the necessary clue to the theme of the drama.

The Dream Play is less involved than *To Damascus*. As the title implies, and the insubstantial settings and figures of the drama illustrate, the play is a poet's dream. The daughter of the gods comes to earth to see for herself the extent and the necessity of the misery which we mortals bear and yet must bear. All is timeless, spaceless, and in defiance of natural logic. The play becomes a sequence of parabolic scenes, each centering about a symbol, such as the flowers growing out of the dirt, the billposter and his green dipnet, the porteress and her shawl, the door with the four leaf clover window, the daughter pasting up the cracks in the room, the four faculties of knowledge, the hairpin, Fairhaven vs. Foulstrand, the coalheavers and the oppressers (used by O'Neill in *The Hairy Ape*), and many others. *The Dream Play* is full of the tragedy of life, but touched with pity and pathos. Suffering, the daughter of the gods discovers, is inherent in the state of being. Even she is driven to a domestic quarrel against her wish. The world is made that way.

The Spook Sonata, here presented in the Palmstierna, Fagan translation as *The Ghost Sonata*, is fully representative of this pregnant form of the modern drama. Behind the imaginative treat-ment that gives the play its peculiar effect may be discovered the realities from which it takes its rise. The Colonel's wife is seen as a mummy in a closet. The white marble statue featured in the set, "surrounded by palms, and strongly illumined by the sunlight," represents her as the girl she was long ago before she was unfaithful to her husband. The Death Screen, emphatic in the third scene, is kept in readiness to be placed before her death bed. It is drawn instead before the closet where The Old Man hangs himself under the hypnotic suggestion of the Mummy after he had disclosed that he, not her husband, was the father of her daughter, The Young Lady of the play. So the evil goes on perpetuating itself.

The Young Lady and the Student enact the sub-plot of the drama. They are engaged, but the bitter ironies and doubts of the Student about the nature of life wound her soul, and symbolically the golden harp that was to strike "fire and purple" among the hyacinths by the Buddha with the shallot bulb in his lap, is struck dumb and deaf, "the strings give no sound," "a curse lies on the whole creation and on life," and The Young Lady sinks into death. Then the Student utters a prayer to the Buddha, and the harp begins to hum softly the spook sonata: "Blest is he who doeth good."

This play, stimulating alike in content and in form, gave impetus to the expressionistic drama which has attracted so many of the world's most talented playwrights in recent years. And perhaps the best conclusion to be drawn from the passionate labors of this goaded genius is expressed at the close of O'Neill's program note with which we began. "Strindberg knew and suffered with our struggles years before many of us were born. He expressed it by intensifying the method of his time and by foreshadowing both in content and form the methods to come. All that is enduring in what we loosely call 'Expressionism'—all that is artistically valid and sound theater—can be traced back through Wedekind to Strindberg's *The Dream Play, There Are Crimes and Crimes, The Spook Sonata*, etc.

"Hence, *The Spook Sonata* at our Playhouse. One of the most difficult of Strindberg's 'behind-life' (if I may coin the term) plays to interpret with insight and distinction—but the difficult is properly our special task, or we have no good reason for existing. Truth, in the theater as in life, is eternally difficult, just as the easy is the everlasting lie.

"So pray with us—and (although we don't need it, of course, but it may do some good) for us."

MISS JULIA

A Naturalistic Tragedy

CHARACTERS

MISS JULIA, *aged twenty-five*
JEAN, *a valet, aged thirty*
CHRISTINE, *a cook, aged thirty-five*

The action takes place on Midsummer Eve, in the kitchen of the count's country house.

A large kitchen: the ceiling and the side walls are hidden by draperies and hangings. The rear wall runs diagonally across the stage, from the left side and away from the spectators. On this wall, to the left, there are two shelves full of utensils made of copper, iron, and tin. The shelves are trimmed with scalloped paper.

A little to the right may be seen three-fourths of the big arched doorway leading to the outside. It has double glass doors, through which are seen a fountain with a cupid, lilac shrubs in bloom, and the tops of some Lombardy poplars.

On the left side of the stage is seen the corner of a big cookstove built of glazed bricks; also a part of the smoke-hood above it.

From the right protrudes one end of the servants' dining-table of white pine, with a few chairs about it.

The stove is dressed with bundled branches of birch. Twigs of juniper are scattered on the floor.

On the table end stands a big Japanese spice pot full of lilac blossoms.

An icebox, a kitchen-table, and a wash-stand.

Above the door hangs a big old-fashioned bell on a steel spring, and the mouthpiece of a speaking-tube appears at the left of the door.

CHRISTINE *is standing by the stove, frying something in a pan. She has on a dress of light-coloured cotton, which she has covered up with a big kitchen apron.*

JEAN *enters, dressed in livery and carrying a pair of big, spurred riding-boots, which he places on the floor in such manner that they remain visible to the spectators.*

JEAN. To-night Miss Julia is crazy again; absolutely crazy.

CHRISTINE. So you're back again?

JEAN. I took the count to the station, and when I came back by the barn, I went in and had a dance, and there I saw the young lady leading the dance with the gamekeeper. But when she caught sight of me, she rushed right up to me and asked me to dance the ladies' waltz with her. And ever since she's been waltzing like—well, I never saw the like of it. She's crazy!

CHRISTINE. And has always been, but never the way it's been this last fortnight, since her engagement was broken.

JEAN. Well, what kind of a story was that anyhow? He's a fine fellow, isn't he, although he isn't rich? Ugh, but

MISS JULIA: Translated by Edwin Björkman. Reprinted by permission of Charles Scribner's Sons.

they're so full of notions. (*Sits down at the end of the table.*) It's peculiar anyhow, that a young lady—hm!—would rather stay at home with the servants—don't you think?—than go with her father to their relatives!

CHRISTINE. Oh, I guess she feels sort of embarrassed by that rumpus with her fellow.

JEAN. Quite likely. But there was some 10 backbone to that man just the same. Do you know how it happened, Christine? I saw it, although I didn't care to let on.

CHRISTINE. No, did you?

JEAN. Sure, I did. They were in the stable-yard one evening, and the young lady was training him, as she called it. Do you know what that meant? She made him leap over her 20 horse-whip the way you teach a dog to jump. Twice he jumped and got a cut each time. The third time he took the whip out of her hand and broke it into a thousand bits. And then he got out.

CHRISTINE. So that's the way it happened! You don't say!

JEAN. Yes, that's how that thing happened. Well, Christine, what have 30 you got that's tasty?

CHRISTINE (*serves from the pan and puts the plate before* JEAN). Oh, just some kidney which I cut out of the veal roast.

JEAN (*smelling the food*). Fine! That's my great *délice*. (*Feeling the plate.*) But you might have warmed the plate.

CHRISTINE. Well, if you ain't harder to please than the count himself! (*Pulls his hair playfully.*)   40

JEAN (*irritated*). Don't pull my hair! You know how senstive I am.

CHRISTINE. Well, well, it was nothing but a love pull, you know.

[JEAN *eats.* CHRISTINE *opens a bottle of beer.*]

JEAN. Beer—on Midsummer Eve? No, thank you! Then I have something better myself. (*Opens a table-drawer and takes out a bottle of claret with yellow cap.*) Yellow seal, mind you! Give me a glass—and you use those with stems when you drink it *pure*.

CHRISTINE (*returns to the stove and puts a small pan on the fire*). Heaven preserve her that gets you for a husband, Mr. Finicky!

JEAN. Oh, rot! You'd be glad enough to get a smart fellow like me. And I guess it hasn't hurt you that they call me your beau. (*Tasting the wine.*) Good! Pretty good! Just a tiny bit too cold. (*He warms the glass with his hands.*) We got this at Dijon. It cost us four francs per litre, not counting the bottle. And there was the duty besides. What is it you're cooking—with that infernal smell?

CHRISTINE. Oh, it's some deviltry the young lady is going to give Diana.

JEAN. You should choose your words with more care, Christine. But why should you be cooking for a bitch on a holiday eve like this? Is she sick?

CHRISTINE. Ye-es, she is sick. She's been running around with the gatekeeper's pug—and now's there's trouble—and the young lady just won't hear of it.

JEAN. The young lady is too stuck up in some ways and not proud enough in others—just as was the countess while she lived. She was most at home in the kitchen and among the cows, but she would never drive with only one horse. She wore her cuffs till they were dirty, but she had to have cuff buttons with a coronet on them. And speaking of the young lady, she doesn't take proper care of herself and her person. I might say even that she's lacking in refinement. Just now, when she was dancing in the barn, she pulled the gamekeeper away from Anna and asked him herself to come and dance with her. We wouldn't act in that way. But that's just how it is: when upper-class people want to demean themselves, then they grow —mean! But she's splendid! Magnificent! Oh, such shoulders! And— and so on!

CHRISTINE. Oh, well, don't brag too much! I've heard Clara talking, who tends to her dressing.

JEAN. Pooh, Clara! You're always jealous of each other. I, who have been out riding with her— And then the way she dances!

CHRISTINE. Say, Jean, won't you dance with me when I'm done?

JEAN. Of course I will.

CHRISTINE. Do you promise?

JEAN. Promise? When I say so, I'll do it. Well, here's thanks for the good food. It tasted fine! (*Puts the cork back into the bottle.*)

JULIA (*appears in the doorway, speaking to somebody on the outside*). I'll be back in a minute. You go right on in the meantime.

[JEAN *slips the bottle into the table-drawer and rises respectfully.*]

JULIA (*enters and goes over to* CHRISTINE *by the wash-stand*). Well, is it done yet?

[CHRISTINE *signs to her that* JEAN *is present.*]

JEAN (*gallantly*). The ladies are having secrets, I believe.

JULIA (*strikes him in the face with her handkerchief*). That's for you, Mr. Pry!

JEAN. Oh, what a delicious odor that violet has!

JULIA (*with coquetry*). Impudent! So you know something about perfumes also? And know pretty well how to dance— Now don't peep! Go away!

JEAN (*with polite impudence*). Is it some kind of witches' broth the ladies are cooking on Midsummer Eve—something to tell fortunes by and bring out the lucky star in which one's future love is seen?

JULIA (*sharply*). If you can see that, you'll have good eyes, indeed! (*To* CHRISTINE.) Put it in a pint bottle and cork it well. Come and dance a *schottische* with me now, Jean.

JEAN (*hesitatingly*). I don't want to be impolite, but I had promised to dance with Christine this time——

JULIA. Well, she can get somebody else —can't you, Christine? Won't you let me borrow Jean from you?

CHRISTINE. That isn't for me to say. When Miss Julia is so gracious, it isn't for him to say no. You just go along, and be thankful for the honour, too!

JEAN. Frankly speaking, but not wishing to offend in any way, I cannot help wondering if it's wise for Miss Julia to dance twice in succession with the same partner, especially as the people here are not slow in throwing out hints——

JULIA (*flaring up*). What is that? What kind of hints? What do you mean?

JEAN (*submissively*). As you don't want to understand, I have to speak more plainly. It don't look well to prefer one servant to all the rest who are expecting to be honoured in the same unusual way——

JULIA. Prefer! What ideas! I'm surprised! I, the mistress of the house, deign to honour this dance with my presence, and when it so happens that I actually want to dance, I want to dance with one who knows how to lead, so that I am not made ridiculous.

JEAN. As you command, Miss Julia! I am at your service!

JULIA (*softened*). Don't take it as a

command. To-night we should enjoy
ourselves as a lot of happy people,
and all rank should be forgotten. Now
give me your arm. Don't be afraid,

Christine! I'll return your beau to
you!

[JEAN *offers his arm to* MISS JULIA *and leads
her out.*]

PANTOMIME

*Must be acted as if the actress were really
alone in the place. When necessary she turns
her back to the public. She should not look in
the direction of the spectators, and she
should not hurry as if fearful that they might
become impatient.*   10

CHRISTINE *is alone. A schottische tune
played on a violin is heard faintly in the
distance.*

While humming the tune, CHRISTINE
clears off the table after JEAN, *washes the
plate at the kitchen-table, wipes it, and puts
it away in a cupboard.*

*Then she takes off her apron, pulls out a
small mirror from one of the table-drawers
and leans it against the flower jar on the* 20
*table; lights a tallow candle and heats a
hairpin, which she uses to curl her front hair.*

*Then she goes to the door and stands there
listening. Returns to the table. Discovers
the handkerchief which* MISS JULIA *has left
behind, picks it up, and smells it, spreads it
out absent-mindedly and begins to stretch it,
smooth it, fold it up, and so forth.*

JEAN (*enters alone*). Crazy, that's what 30
she is! The way she dances! And the
people stand behind the doors and
grin at her. What do you think of it,
Christine?

CHRISTINE. Oh, she has her time now,
and then she is always a little queer
like that. But are you going to dance
with me now?

JEAN. You are not mad at me because I
disappointed you?   40

CHRISTINE. No!—Not for a little thing
like that, you know! And also, I
know my place——

JEAN (*putting his arm around her waist*).
You are a sensible girl, Christine, and
I think you'll make a good wife——

JULIA (*enters and is unpleasantly surprised;
speaks with forced gayety*). Yes, you are
a fine partner—running away from
your lady!

JEAN. On the contrary, Miss Julia. I
have, as you see, looked up the one I
deserted.

JULIA (*changing tone*). Do you know,
there is nobody that dances like you!
—But why do you wear your livery
on an evening like this? Take it off
at once!

JEAN. Then I must ask you to step outside for a moment, as my black coat
is hanging right here.

[*Points toward the right and goes in that
direction.*]

JULIA. Are you bashful on my account?
Just to change a coat? Why don't you
go into your own room and come
back again? Or, you can stay right
here, and I'll turn my back on you.

JEAN. With your permission, Miss Julia.

[*Goes further over to the right; one of his arms
can be seen as he changes his coat.*]

JULIA (*to* CHRISTINE). Are you and Jean
engaged, that he's so familiar with
you?

CHRISTINE. Engaged? Well, in a way.
We call it that.

JULIA. Call it?

CHRISTINE. Well, Miss Julia, you have
had a fellow of your own, and——

JULIA. We were really engaged——

CHRISTINE. But it didn't come to anything just the same——

[JEAN *enters, dressed in black frock coat and black derby.*]

JULIA. *Très gentil, Monsieur Jean! Très gentil!*

JEAN. *Vous voulez plaisanter, Madame!*

JULIA. *Et vous voulez parler français!* Where did you learn it?

JEAN. In Switzerland, while I worked as *sommelier* in one of the big hotels at Lucerne.

JULIA. But you look like a real gentleman in your frock coat! Charming! (*Sits down at the table.*)

JEAN. Oh, you flatter me.

JULIA (*offended*). Flatter—you!

JEAN. My natural modesty does not allow me to believe that you could be paying genuine compliments to one like me, and so I dare to assume that you are exaggerating, or, as we call it, flattering.

JULIA. Where did you learn to use your words like that? You must have been to the theatre a great deal?

JEAN. That, too. I have been to a lot of places.

JULIA. But you were born in this neighbourhood?

JEAN. My father was a cotter on the county attorney's property right by here, and I can recall seeing you as a child, although you, of course, didn't notice me.

JULIA. No, really!

JEAN. Yes, and I remember one time in particular—but of that I can't speak.

JULIA. Oh, yes, do! Why—just for once.

JEAN. No, really, I cannot do it now. Another time, perhaps.

JULIA. Another time is no time. Is it as bad as that?

JEAN. It isn't bad, but it comes a little hard. Look at that one! (*Points to* CHRISTINE, *who has fallen asleep on a chair by the stove.*)

JULIA. She'll make a pleasant wife. And perhaps she snores, too.

JEAN. No, she doesn't, but she talks in her sleep.

JULIA (*cynically*). How do you know?

JEAN (*insolently*). I have heard it.

[*Pause during which they study each other.*]

JULIA. Why don't you sit down?

JEAN. It wouldn't be proper in your presence.

JULIA. But if I order you to do it?

JEAN. Then I obey.

JULIA. Sit down, then!—But wait a moment! Can you give me something to drink first?

JEAN. I don't know what we have got in the icebox. I fear it is nothing but beer.

JULIA. And you call that nothing? My taste is so simple that I prefer it to wine.

JEAN (*takes a bottle of beer from the icebox and opens it; gets a glass and a plate from the cupboard, and serves the beer*). Allow me!

JULIA. Thank you. Don't you want some yourself?

JEAN. I don't care very much for beer, but if it is a command, of course——

JULIA. Command?—I should think a polite gentleman might keep his lady company.

JEAN. Yes, that's the way it should be. (*Opens another bottle and takes out a glass.*)

JULIA. Drink my health now!

[JEAN *hesitates.*]

JULIA. Are you bashful—a big, grown-up man?

JEAN (*kneels with mock solemnity and raises his glass*). To the health of my liege lady!

JULIA. Bravo!—And now you must also kiss my shoe in order to get it just right.

[JEAN *hesitates a moment; then he takes hold*

of her foot and touches it lightly with his lips.]

JULIA. Excellent! You should have been on the stage.

JEAN (*rising to his feet*). This won't do any longer, Miss Julia. Somebody might see us.

JULIA. What would that matter?

JEAN. Oh, it would set the people talking—that's all! And if you only knew how their tongues were wagging up there a while ago——

JULIA. What did they have to say? Tell me— Sit down now!

JEAN (*sits down*). I don't want to hurt you, but they were using expressions —which cast reflections of a kind that —oh, you know it yourself! You are not a child, and when a lady is seen alone with a man, drinking—no matter if he's only a servant—and at night—then——

JULIA. Then what? And besides, we are not alone. Isn't Christine with us?

JEAN. Yes—asleep!

JULIA. Then I'll wake her. (*Rising.*) Christine, are you asleep?

CHRISTINE (*in her sleep*). Blub-blub-blub-blub!

JULIA. Christine!—Did you ever see such a sleeper.

CHRISTINE (*in her sleep*). The count's boots are polished—put on the coffee —yes, yes, yes—my—my—pooh!

JULIA (*pinches her nose*). Can't you wake up?

JEAN (*sternly*). You shouldn't bother those that sleep.

JULIA (*sharply*). What's that?

JEAN. One who has stood by the stove all day has a right to be tired at night. And sleep should be respected.

JULIA (*changing tone*). It is fine to think like that, and it does you honour— I thank you for it. (*Gives* JEAN *her hand.*) Come now and pick some lilacs for me.

[*During the following scene* CHRISTINE *wakes up. She moves as if still asleep and goes out to the right in order to go to bed.*]

JEAN. With you, Miss Julia?

JULIA. With me!

JEAN. But it won't do! Absolutely not!

JULIA. I can't understand what you are thinking of. You couldn't possibly imagine——

JEAN. No, not I, but the people.

JULIA. What? That I am fond of the valet?

JEAN. I am not at all conceited, but such things have happened—and to the people nothing is sacred.

JULIA. You are an aristocrat, I think.

JEAN. Yes, I am.

JULIA. And I am stepping down——

JEAN. Take my advice, Miss Julia, don't step down. Nobody will believe you did it on purpose. The people will always say that you fell down.

JULIA. I think better of the people than you do. Come and see if I am not right. Come along! (*She ogles him.*)

JEAN. You're mighty queer, do you know!

JULIA. Perhaps. But so are you. And for that matter, everything is queer. Life, men, everything—just a mush that floats on top of the water until it sinks, sinks down! I have a dream that comes back to me ever so often. And just now I am reminded of it. I have climbed to the top of a column and sit there without being able to tell how to get down again. I get dizzy when I look down, and I must get down, but I haven't the courage to jump off. I cannot hold on, and I am longing to fall, and yet I don't fall. But there will be no rest for me until I get down, no rest until I get down, down on the ground. And if I did reach the ground, I should want to get still further down, into the ground itself— Have you ever felt like that?

JEAN. No, my dream is that I am lying under a tall tree in a dark wood. I want to get up, up to the top, so that I can look out over the smiling landscape, where the sun is shining, and so that I can rob the nest in which lie the golden eggs. And I climb and climb, but the trunk is so thick and smooth, and it is so far to the first branch. But I know that if I could only reach that first branch, then I should go right on to the top as on a ladder. I have not reached it yet, but I am going to, if it only be in my dreams.

JULIA. Here I am chattering to you about dreams! Come along! Only into the park!

[*She offers her arm to him, and they go toward the door.*]

JEAN. We must sleep on nine midsummer flowers to-night, Miss Julia— then our dreams will come true.

[*They turn around in the doorway, and* JEAN *puts one hand up to his eyes.*]

JULIA. Let me see what you have got in your eye.

JEAN. Oh, nothing—just some dirt—it will soon be gone.

JULIA. It was my sleeve that rubbed against it. Sit down and let me help you. (*Takes him by the arm and makes him sit down; takes hold of his head and bends it backwards; tries to get out the dirt with a corner of her handkerchief.*) Sit still now, absolutely still! (*Slaps him on the hand.*) Well, can't you do as I say? I think you are shaking—a big, strong fellow like you! (*Feels his biceps.*) And with such arms!

JEAN (*ominously*). Miss Julia!

JULIA. Yes, Monsieur Jean.

JEAN. *Attention! Je ne suis qu' un homme.*

JULIA. Can't you sit still!— There now!

Now it's gone. Kiss my hand now, and thank me.

JEAN (*rising*). Miss Julia, listen to me. Christine has gone to bed now— Won't you listen to me?

JULIA. Kiss my hand first.

JEAN. Listen to me!

JULIA. Kiss my hand first!

JEAN. All right, but blame nobody but yourself!

JULIA. For what?

JEAN. For what? Are you still a mere child at twenty-five? Don't you know that it is dangerous to play with fire?

JULIA. Not for me. I am insured.

JEAN (*boldly*). No, you are not. And even if you were, there are inflammable surroundings to be counted with.

JULIA. That's you, I suppose?

JEAN. Yes. Not because I am I, but because I am a young man——

JULIA. Of handsome appearance—what an incredible conceit! A Don Juan, perhaps. Or a Joseph? On my soul, I think you are a Joseph!

JEAN. Do you?

JULIA. I fear it almost.

[JEAN *goes boldly up to her and takes her around the waist in order to kiss her.*]

JULIA (*gives him a cuff on the ear*). Shame!

JEAN. Was that in play or in earnest?

JULIA. In earnest.

JEAN. Then you were in earnest a moment ago also. Your playing is too serious, and that's the dangerous thing about it. Now I am tired of playing, and I ask to be excused in order to resume my work. The count wants his boots to be ready for him, and it is after midnight already.

JULIA. Put away the boots.

JEAN. No, it's my work, which I am bound to do. But I have not undertaken to be your playmate. It's something I can never become— I hold myself too good for it.

JULIA. You're proud!

JEAN. In some ways, and not in others.

JULIA. Have you ever been in love?

JEAN. We don't use that word. But I have been fond of a lot of girls, and once I was taken sick because I couldn't have the one I wanted: sick, you know, like those princes in the Arabian Nights who cannot eat or drink for sheer love. 10

JULIA. Who was it?

[JEAN *remains silent.*]

JULIA. Who was it?

JEAN. You cannot make me tell you.

JULIA. If I ask you as an equal, ask you as—a friend: who was it?

JEAN. It was you.

JULIA (*sits down*). How funny!

JEAN. Yes, as you say—it was ludicrous. That was the story, you see, which I 20 didn't want to tell you a while ago. But now I am going to tell it. Do you know how the world looks from below—no, you don't. No more than do hawks and falcons, of whom we never see the back because they are always floating about high up in the sky. I lived in the cotter's hovel, together with seven other children, and a pig—out there on the grey 30 plain, where there isn't a single tree. But from our windows I could see the wall around the count's park, and apple-trees above it. That was the Garden of Eden; and many fierce angels were guarding it with flaming swords. Nevertheless I and some other boys found our way to the Tree of Life—now you despise me?

JULIA. Oh, stealing apples is something 40 all boys do.

JEAN. You may say so now, but you despise me nevertheless. However— once I got into the Garden of Eden with my mother to weed the onion beds. Near by stood a Turkish pavil-

lion, shaded by trees and covered with honeysuckle. I didn't know what it was used for, but I had never seen a more beautiful building. People went in and came out again, and one day the door was left wide open. I stole up and saw the walls covered with pictures of kings and emperors, and the windows were hung with red, fringed curtains— now you know what I mean. I— (*Breaks off a lilac sprig and holds it under* MISS JULIA'S *nose*.)—I had never been inside the manor, and I had never seen anything but the church—and this was much finer. No matter where my thoughts ran, they returned always—to that place. And gradually a longing arose within me to taste the full pleasure of—*enfin!* I sneaked in, looked and admired. Then I heard somebody coming. There was only one way out for fine people, but for me there was another, and I could do nothing else but choose it.

[JULIA, *who has taken the lilac sprig, lets it drop on the table.*]

JEAN. Then I started to run, plunged through a hedge of raspberry bushes, chased right across a strawberry plantation, and came out on the terrace where the roses grow. There I caught sight of a pink dress and pair of white stockings—that was you! I crawled under a pile of weeds —right into it, you know—into stinging thistles and wet, ill-smelling dirt. And I saw you walking among the roses, and I thought: if it be possible for a robber to get into heaven and dwell with the angels, then it is strange that a cotter's child, here on God's own earth, cannot get into the park and play with the count's daughter.

JULIA (*sentimentally*). Do you think all

poor children have the same thoughts as you had in this case?

JEAN (*hesitatingly at first; then with conviction*). If *all* poor—yes—of course. Of course!

JULIA. It must be a dreadful misfortune to be poor.

JEAN (*in a tone of deep distress and with rather exaggerated emphasis*). Oh, Miss Julia! Oh!— A dog may lie on her ladyship's sofa; a horse may have his nose patted by the young lady's hand, but a servant—(*Changing his tone.*)— oh well, here and there you meet one made of different stuff, and he makes a way for himself in the world, but how often does it happen?— However, do you know what I did? I jumped into the mill brook with my clothes on, and was pulled out, and got a licking. But the next Sunday, when my father and the rest of the people were going over to my grandmother's, I fixed it so that I could stay at home. And then I washed myself with soap and hot water, and put on my best clothes, and went to church, where I could see you. I did see you, and went home determined to die. But I wanted to die beautifully and pleasantly, without any pain. And then I recalled that it was dangerous to sleep under an elder bush. We had a big one that was in full bloom. I robbed it of all its flowers, and then I put them in the big box where the oats were kept and lay down in them. Did you ever notice the smoothness of oats? Soft to the touch as the skin of the human body! However, I pulled down the lid and closed my eyes—fell asleep and was waked up a very sick boy. But I didn't die, as you can see. What I wanted—that's more than I can tell. Of course, there was not the least

hope of winning you—but you symbolised the hopelessness of trying to get out of the class into which I was born.

JULIA. You narrate splendidly, do you know! Did you ever go to school?

JEAN. A little. But I have read a lot of novels and gone to the theatre a good deal. And besides, I have listened to the talk of better-class people, and from that I have learned most of all.

JULIA. Do you stand around and listen to what we are saying?

JEAN. Of course! And I have heard a lot, too, when I was on the box of the carriage, or rowing the boat. Once I heard you, Miss Julia, and one of your girl friends——

JULIA. Oh!— What was it you heard then?

JEAN. Well, it wouldn't be easy to repeat. But I was rather surprised, and I couldn't understand where you had learned all those words. Perhaps, at bottom, there isn't quite so much difference as they think between one kind of people and another.

JULIA. You ought to be ashamed of yourself! We don't live as you do when we are engaged.

JEAN (*looking hard at her*). Is it so certain?— Well, Miss Julia, it won't pay to make yourself out so very innocent to me——

JULIA. The man on whom I bestowed my love was a scoundrel.

JEAN. That's what you always say— afterwards.

JULIA. Always?

JEAN. Always, I believe, for I have heard the same words used several times before, on similar occasions.

JULIA. What occasions?

JEAN. Like the one of which we were speaking. The last time——

JULIA (*rising*). Stop! I don't want to hear any more!

JEAN. Nor did *she*—curiously enough! Well, then I ask permission to go to bed.

JULIA (*gently*). Go to bed on Midsummer Eve?

JEAN. Yes, for dancing with that mob out there has really no attraction for me.

JULIA. Get the key to the boat and take me out on the lake— I want to watch the sunrise.

JEAN. Would that be wise?

JULIA. It sounds as if you were afraid of your reputation.

JEAN. Why not? I don't care to be made ridiculous, and I don't care to be discharged without a recommendation, for I am trying to get on in the world. And then I feel myself under a certain obligation to Christine.

JULIA. So it's Christine now——

JEAN. Yes, but it's you also— Take my advice and go to bed!

JULIA. Am I to obey you?

JEAN. For once—and for your own sake! The night is far gone. Sleepiness makes us drunk, and the head grows hot. Go to bed! And besides—if I am not mistaken—I can hear the crowd coming this way to look for me. And if we are found together here, you are lost!

CHORUS (*is heard approaching*).
Through the fields come two ladies a-walking,
Treederee-derallah, treederee-derah.
And one has her shoes full of water,
Treederee-derallah-lah.

They're talking of hundreds of dollars,
Treederee-derallah, treederee-derah.

But have not between them a dollar
Treederee-derallah-lah.

This wreath I give you gladly,
Treederee-derallah, treederee-derah.
But love another madly,
Treederee-derallah-lah.

JULIA. I know the people, and I love them, just as they love me. Let them come, and you'll see.

JEAN. No, Miss Julia, they don't love you. They take your food and spit at your back. Believe me. Listen to me— can't you hear what they are singing?— No, don't pay any attention to it!

JULIA (*listening*). What is it they are singing?

JEAN. Oh, something scurrilous. About you and me.

JULIA. How infamous! They ought to be ashamed! And the treachery of it!

JEAN. The mob is always cowardly. And in such a fight as this there is nothing to do but to run away.

JULIA. Run away? Where to? We cannot get out. And we cannot go into Christine's room.

JEAN. Oh, we cannot? Well, into my room, then! Necessity knows no law. And you can trust me, for I am your true and frank and respectful friend.

JULIA. But think only—think if they should look for you in there!

JEAN. I shall bolt the door. And if they try to break it open, I'll shoot!— Come! (*Kneeling before her.*) Come!

JULIA (*meaningly*). And you promise me ——?

JEAN. I swear!

[MISS JULIA *goes quickly out to the right* JEAN *follows her eagerly.*]

BALLET

The peasants enter. They are decked out in their best and carry flowers in their hats. A fiddler leads them. On the table they place a barrel of small-beer and a keg of "brännvin," or white Swedish whiskey, both of them decorated with wreathes woven out of leaves. First they drink. Then they form in ring and sing and dance to the melody heard before:
"Through the fields come two ladies a-walking."
The dance finished, they leave singing.

JULIA (*Enters alone. On seeing the disorder in the kitchen, she claps her hands together. Then she takes out a powder-puff and begins to powder her face*).

JEAN (*enters in a state of exaltation*). There you see! And you heard, didn't you? Do you think it possible to stay here?

JULIA. No, I don't think so. But what are we to do?

JEAN. Run away, travel, far away from here.

JULIA. Travel? Yes—but where?

JEAN. To Switzerland, the Italian lakes —you have never been there?

JULIA. No. Is the country beautiful?

JEAN. Oh! Eternal summer! Orange trees! Laurels! Oh!

JULIA. But then—what are we to do down there?

JEAN. I'll start a hotel, everything first class, including the customers.

JULIA. Hotel?

JEAN. That's the life, I tell you! Constantly new faces and new languages. Never a minute free for nerves or brooding. No trouble about what to do—for the work is calling to be done: night and day, bells that ring, trains that whistle, 'busses that come and go; and gold pieces raining on the counter all the time. That's the life for you!

JULIA. Yes, that is life. And I?

JEAN. The mistress of everything, the chief ornament of the house. With your looks—and your manners—oh, success will be assured! Enormous! You'll sit like a queen in the office and keep the slaves going by the touch of an electric button. The guests will pass in review before your throne and timidly deposit their treasures on your table. You cannot imagine how people tremble when a bill is presented to them—I'll salt the items, and you'll sugar them with your sweetest smiles. Oh, let us get away from here— (*Pulling a time-table from his pocket.*)—at once, with the next train! We'll be in Malmö at 6.30; in Hamburg at 8.40 to-morrow morning; in Frankfort and Basel a day later. And to reach Como by way of the St. Gotthard it will take us—let me see—three days. Three days!

JULIA. All that is all right. But you must give me some courage—Jean. Tell me that you love me. Come and take me in your arms.

JEAN (*reluctantly*). I should like to—but I don't dare. Not in this house again. I love you—beyond doubt—or, can you doubt it, Miss Julia?

JULIA (*with modesty and true womanly feeling*). Miss?—Call me Julia. Between us there can be no barriers hereafter. Call me Julia!

JEAN (*disturbed*). I cannot! There will be barriers between us as long as we stay in this house—there is the past, and there is the count—and I have never met another person for whom I felt such respect. If I only catch sight of his gloves on a chair I feel small. If I only hear that bell up there, I jump like a shy horse. And even now, when I see his boots standing there so stiff and perky, it is as if something made my back bend. (*Kicking at the boots.*) It's nothing but superstition and tradition hammered into us from childhood—but it can be as easily forgotten again. Let us only get to another country, where they have a republic, and you'll see them bend their backs double before my liveried porter. You see, backs have to be bent, but not mine. I wasn't born to that kind of thing. There's better stuff in me—character—and if I only get hold of the first branch, you'll see me do some climbing. To-day I am a valet, but next year I'll be a hotel owner. In ten years I can live on the money I have made, and then I'll go to Roumania and get myself an order. And I may—note that I say *may*—end my days as a count.

JULIA. Splendid, splendid!

JEAN. Yes, in Roumania the title of count can be had for cash, and so you'll be a countess after all. My countess!

JULIA. What do I care about all I now cast behind me! Tell me that you love me: otherwise—yes, what am I otherwise?

JEAN. I will tell you so a thousand times—later. But not here. And above all, no sentimentality, or everything will be lost. We must look at the matter in cold blood, like sensible people. (*Takes out a cigar, cuts off the point, and lights it.*) Sit down there now, and I'll sit here, and then we'll talk as if nothing had happened.

JULIA (*in despair*). Good Lord! Have you then no feelings at all?

JEAN. I? No one is more full of feeling than I am. But I know how to control myself.

JULIA. A while ago you kissed my shoe—and now!

JEAN (*severely*). Yes, that was then. Now we have other things to think of.

JULIA. Don't speak harshly to me!

JEAN. No, but sensibly. One folly has been committed—don't let us commit any more! The count may be here at any moment, and before he comes our fate must be settled. What do you think of my plans for the future? Do you approve of them?

JULIA. They seem acceptable, on the whole. But there is one question: a big undertaking of that kind will require a big capital—have you got it?

JEAN (*chewing his cigar*). I? Of course! I have my expert knowledge, my vast experience, my familiarity with several languages. That's the very best kind of capital, I should say.

JULIA. But it won't buy you a railroad ticket even.

JEAN. That's true enough. And that is just why I am looking for a backer to advance the needful cash.

JULIA. Where could you get one all of a sudden?

JEAN. It's for you to find him if you want to become my partner.

JULIA. I cannot do it, and I have nothing myself. (*Pause.*)

JEAN. Well, then that's off——

JULIA. And——

JEAN. Everything remains as before.

JULIA. Do you think I am going to stay under this roof as your concubine? Do you think I'll let the people point their fingers at me? Do you think I can look my father in the face after this? No, take me away from here, from all this humiliation and disgrace!— Oh, what have I done? My God, my God! (*Breaks into tears.*)

JEAN. So we have got around to that tune now!— What you have done? Nothing but what many others have done before you.

JULIA (*crying hysterically*). And now you're despising me!— I'm falling, I'm falling!

JEAN. Fall down to me, and I'll lift you up again afterwards.

JULIA. What horrible power drew me to you? Was it the attraction which the strong exercises on the weak—the one who is rising on one who is falling? Or was it love? This—love! Do you know what love is?

JEAN. I? Well, I should say so! Don't you think I have been there before?

JULIA. Oh, the language you use, and the thoughts you think!

JEAN. Well, that's the way I was brought up, and that's the way I am. Don't get nerves now and play the exquisite, for now one of us is just as good as the other. Look here, my girl, let me treat you to a glass of something superfine.

[*He opens the table-drawer, takes out the wine bottle and fills up two glasses that have already been used.*]

JULIA. Where did you get that wine?

JEAN. In the cellar.

JULIA. My father's Burgundy!

JEAN. Well, isn't it good enough for the son-in-law?

JULIA. And I am drinking beer—I!

JEAN. It shows merely that I have better taste than you.

JULIA. Thief!

JEAN. Do you mean to tell on me?

JULIA. Oh, oh! The accomplice of a house thief! Have I been drunk, or have I been dreaming all this night? Midsummer Eve! The feast of innocent games——

JEAN. Innocent—hm!

JULIA (*walking back and forth*). Can there be another human being on earth so unhappy as I am at this moment?

JEAN. But why should you be? After such a conquest? Think of Christine in there. Don't you think she has feelings also?

JULIA. I thought so a while ago, but I don't think so any longer. No, a menial is a menial——

JEAN. And a whore a whore!

JULIA (*on her knees, with folded hands*). O God in heaven, make an end of this wretched life! Take me out of the filth into which I am sinking! Save me! Save me!

JEAN. I cannot deny that I feel sorry for you. When I was lying among the onions and saw you up there among the roses—I'll tell you now—I had the same nasty thoughts that all boys have.

JULIA. And you who wanted to die for my sake!

JEAN. Among the oats. That was nothing but talk.

JULIA. Lies in other words!

JEAN (*beginning to feel sleepy*). Just about. I think I read the story in a paper, and it was about a chimney-sweep who crawled into a wood-box full of lilacs because a girl had brought suit against him for not supporting her kid——

JULIA. So that's the sort you are——

JEAN. Well, I had to think of something —for it's the high-faluting stuff that the women bite on.

JULIA. Scoundrel!

JEAN. Rot!

JULIA. And now you have seen the back of the hawk——

JEAN. Well, I don't know——

JULIA. And I was to be the first branch ——

JEAN. But the branch was rotten——

JULIA. I was to be the sign in front of the hotel——

JEAN. And I the hotel.——

JULIA. Sit at your counter, and lure your customers, and doctor your bills——

JEAN. No, that I should have done myself——

JULIA. That a human soul can be so steeped in dirt!

JEAN. Well, wash it off!

JULIA. You lackey, you menial, stand up when I talk to you!

JEAN. You lackey-love, you mistress of a menial—shut up and get out of here! You're the right one to come and tell me that I am vulgar. People of my kind would never in their lives act as vulgarly as you have acted to-night. Do you think any servant girl would go for a man as you did? Did you ever see a girl of my class throw herself at anybody in that way? I have never seen the like of it except among beasts and prostitutes.

JULIA (crushed). That's right: strike me, step on me—I haven't deserved any better! I am a wretched creature. But help me! Help me out of this, if there be any way to do so!

JEAN (in a milder tone). I don't want to lower myself by a denial of my share in the honour of seducing. But do you think a person in my place would have dared to raise his eyes to you, if the invitation to do so had not come from yourself? I am still sitting here in a state of utter surprise——

JULIA. And pride——

JEAN. Yes, why not? Although I must confess that the victory was too easy to bring with it any real intoxication.

JULIA. Strike me some more!

JEAN (rising). No! Forgive me instead what I have been saying. I don't want to strike one who is disarmed, and least of all a lady. On one hand I cannot deny that it has given me pleasure to discover that what has dazzled us below is nothing but cat-gold; that the hawk is simply grey on the back also; that there is powder on the tender cheek; that there may be black borders on the polished nails; and that the handkerchief may be dirty, although it smells of perfume. But on the other hand it hurts me to have discovered that what I was striving to reach is neither better nor more genuine. It hurts me to see you sinking so low that you are far beneath your own cook—it hurts me as it hurts to see the Fall flowers beaten down by the rain and turned into mud.

JULIA. You speak as if you were already above me?

JEAN. Well, so I am. Don't you see: I could have made a countess of you, but you could never make me a count.

JULIA. But I am born of a count, and that's more than you can ever achieve.

JEAN. That's true. But I might be the father of counts—if——

JULIA. But you are a thief—and I am not.

JEAN. Thief is not the worst. There are other kinds still farther down. And then, when I serve in a house, I regard myself in a sense as a member of the family, as a child of the house, and you don't call it theft when children pick a few of the berries that load down the vines. (His passion is aroused once more.) Miss Julia, you are a magnificent woman, and far too good for one like me. You were swept along by a spell of intoxication, and now you want to cover up your mistake by making yourself believe that you are in love with me. Well, you are not, unless possibly my looks might tempt you—in which case your love is no better than mine. I could never rest satisfied with having you care for nothing in me but the mere animal, and your love I can never win.

JULIA. Are you so sure of that?

JEAN. You mean to say that it might be possible? That I might love you: yes, without doubt—for you are beautiful, refined (*Goes up to her and takes hold of her hand.*), educated, charming when you want to be so, and it is not likely that the flame will ever burn out in a man who has once been set on fire by you. (*Puts his arm around her waist.*) You are like burnt wine with strong spices in it, and one of your kisses——

[*He tries to lead her away, but she frees herself gently from his hold.*]

JULIA. Leave me alone! In that way you cannot win me.

JEAN. How then?— Not in that way! Not by caresses and sweet words! Not by thought for the future, by escape from disgrace! How then?

JULIA. How? How? I don't know— Not at all! I hate you as I hate rats, but I cannot escape from you!

JEAN. Escape *with* me!

JULIA (*straightening up*). Escape? Yes, we must escape!— But I am so tired. Give me a glass of wine.

[JEAN *pours out wine.*]

JULIA (*looks at her watch*). But we must have a talk first. We have still some time left. (*Empties her glass and holds it out for more.*)

JEAN. Don't drink so much. It will go to your head.

JULIA. What difference would that make?

JEAN. What difference would it make? It's vulgar to get drunk— What was it you wanted to tell me?

JULIA. We must get away. But first we must have a talk—that is, I must talk, for so far you have done all the talking. You have told me about your life. Now I must tell you about mine, so that we know each other right to the bottom before we begin the journey together.

JEAN. One moment, pardon me! Think first, so that you don't regret it afterwards, when you have already given up the secrets of your life.

JULIA. Are you not my friend?

JEAN. Yes, at times—but don't rely on me.

JULIA. You only talk like that—and besides, my secrets are known to everybody. You see, my mother was not of noble birth, but came of quite plain people. She was brought up in the ideas of her time about equality, and woman's independence, and that kind of thing. And she had a decided aversion to marriage. Therefore, when my father proposed to her, she said she wouldn't marry him—and then she did it just the same. I came into the world—against my mother's wish, I have come to think. Then my mother wanted to bring me up in a perfectly natural state, and at the same time I was to learn everything that a boy is taught, so that I might prove that a woman is just as good as a man. I was dressed as a boy, and was taught how to handle a horse, but could have nothing to do with the cows. I had to groom and harness and go hunting on horseback. I was even forced to learn something about agriculture. And all over the estate men were set to do women's work, and women to do men's—with the result that everything went to pieces and we became the laughing-stock of the whole neighbourhood. At last my father must have recovered from the spell cast over him, for he rebelled, and everything was changed to suit his own ideas. My mother was taken sick—what kind of sickness it was I don't know, but she fell often into convulsions, and she used to hide herself in the garret or in the garden, and sometimes she stayed out all night. Then came the big fire, of which you have heard. The house, the stable, and the barn were burned down, and this under circumstances which made it look as if the fire had been set on purpose. For the disaster occurred the day after our insurance expired, and the money sent for renewal of the policy had been delayed by the messenger's carelessness, so that it came too late. (*She fills her glass again and drinks.*)

JEAN. Don't drink any more.

JULIA. Oh, what does it matter!— We were without a roof over our heads and had to sleep in the carriages. My father didn't know where to get money for the rebuilding of the house. Then my mother suggested that he try to borrow from a childhood friend of hers, a brick manufacturer living not far from here. My father got the loan, but was not permitted to pay any interest, which astonished him. And so the house was built up again. (*Drinks again.*) Do you know who set fire to the house?

JEAN. Her ladyship, your mother!

JULIA. Do you know who the brick manufacturer was?

JEAN. Your mother's lover?

JULIA. Do you know to whom the money belonged?

JEAN. Wait a minute—no, that I don't know.

JULIA. To my mother.

JEAN. In other words, to the count, if there was no settlement.

JULIA. There was no settlement. My mother possessed a small fortune of her own which she did not want to leave in my father's control, so she invested it with—her friend.

JEAN. Who copped it.

JULIA. Exactly! He kept it. All this came to my father's knowledge. He couldn't bring suit; he couldn't pay his wife's lover; he couldn't prove that it was his wife's money. That was my mother's revenge because he had made himself master in his own house. At that time he came near shooting himself—it was even rumoured that he had tried and failed. But he took a new lease of life, and my mother had to pay for what she had done. I can tell you that those were five years I'll never forget! My sympathies were with my father, but I took my mother's side because I was not aware of the true circumstances. From her I learned to suspect and hate men—for she hated the whole sex, as you have probably heard—and I promised her on my oath that I would never become a man's slave.

JEAN. And so you became engaged to the County Attorney.

JULIA. Yes, in order that he should be my slave.

JEAN. And he didn't want to?

JULIA. Oh, he wanted, but I wouldn't let him. I got tired of him.

JEAN. Yes, I saw it—in the stable-yard.

JULIA. What did you see?

JEAN. Just that—how he broke the engagement.

JULIA. That's a lie! It was I who broke it. Did he say he did it, the scoundrel?

JEAN. Oh, he was no scoundrel, I guess. So you hate men, Miss Julia?

JULIA. Yes! Most of the time. But now and then—when the weakness comes over me—oh, what shame!

JEAN. And you hate me too?

JULIA. Beyond measure! I should like to kill you like a wild beast——

JEAN. As you make haste to shoot a mad dog. Is that right? 10

JULIA. That's right!

JEAN. But now there is nothing to shoot with—and there is no dog. What are we to do then?

JULIA. Go abroad.

JEAN. In order to plague each other to death?

JULIA. No—in order to enjoy ourselves: a couple of days, a week, as long as enjoyment is possible. And then— 20 die!

JEAN. Die? How silly! Then I think it's much better to start a hotel.

JULIA (without listening to JEAN).—At Lake Como, where the sun is always shining, and the laurels stand green at Christmas, and the oranges are glowing.

JEAN. Lake Como is a rainy hole, and I could see no oranges except in the 30 groceries. But it is a good place for tourists, as it has a lot of villas that can be rented to loving couples, and that's a profitable business—do you know why? Because they take a lease for six months—and then they leave after three weeks.

JULIA (naïvely). Why after three weeks?

JEAN. Because they quarrel, of course. But the rent has to be paid just the 40 same. And then you can rent the house again. And that way it goes on all the time, for there is plenty of love—even if it doesn't last long.

JULIA. You don't want to die with me?

JEAN. I don't want to die at all. Both because I am fond of living, and because I regard suicide as a crime against the Providence which has bestowed life on us.

JULIA. Do you mean to say that *you* believe in God?

JEAN. Of course, I do. And I go to church every other Sunday. Frankly speaking, now I am tired of all this, and now I am going to bed.

JULIA. So! And you think that will be enough for me? Do you know what you owe a woman that you have spoiled?

JEAN (takes out his purse and throws a silver coin on the table). You're welcome! I don't want to be in anybody's debt.

JULIA (pretending not to notice the insult). Do you know what the law provides ——

JEAN. Unfortunately the law provides no punishment for a woman who seduces a man.

JULIA (as before). Can you think of any escape except by our going abroad and getting married, and then getting a divorce?

JEAN. Suppose I refuse to enter into this mésaillance?

JULIA. Mésaillance——

JEAN. Yes, for me. You see, I have better ancestry than you, for nobody in my family was ever guilty of arson.

JULIA. How do you know?

JEAN. Well, nothing is known to the contrary, for we keep no pedigrees—except in the police bureau. But I have read about your pedigree in a book that was lying on the drawing-room table. Do you know who was your first ancestor? A miller who let his wife sleep with the king one night during the war with Denmark. I have no such ancestry. I have none at all, but i can become an ancestor myself.

JULIA. That's what I get for unburdening my heart to one not worthy of it; for sacrificing my family's honour——

JEAN. Dishonour! Well, what was it I told you? You shouldn't drink, for then you talk. And you *must* not talk!

JULIA. Oh, how I regret what I have done! How I regret it! If at least you loved me! 10

JEAN. For the last time: what do you mean? Am I to weep? Am I to jump over your whip? Am I to kiss you, and lure you down to Lake Como for three weeks, and so on? What am I to do? What do you expect? This is getting to be rather painful! But that's what comes from getting mixed up with women. Miss Julia! I see that you are un-20 happy; I know that you are suffering; but I cannot understand you. We never carry on like that. There is never any hatred between us. Love is to us a play, and we play at it when our work leaves us time to do so. But we have not the time to do so all day and all night, as you have. I believe you are sick—I am sure you are sick.

JULIA. You should be good to me—and 30 now you speak like a human being.

JEAN. All right, but be human yourself. You spit on me, and then you won't let me wipe myself—on you!

JULIA. Help me, help me! Tell me only what I am to do—where I am to turn?

JEAN. O Lord, if I only knew that myself!

JULIA. I have been exasperated, I have 40 been mad, but there ought to be some way of saving myself.

JEAN. Stay right here and keep quiet. Nobody knows anything.

JULIA. Impossible! The people know, and Christine knows.

JEAN. They don't know, and they would never believe it possible.

JULIA (*hesitating*). But—it might happen again.

JEAN. That's true.

JULIA. And the results?

JEAN (*frightened*). The results! Where was my head when I didn't think of that! Well, then there is only one thing to do—you must leave. At once! I can't go with you, for then everything would be lost, so you must go alone—abroad—anywhere!

JULIA. Alone? Where?— I can't do it.

JEAN. You must! And before the count gets back. If you stay, then you know what will happen. Once on the wrong path, one wants to keep on, as the harm is done anyhow. Then one grows more and more reckless—and at last it all comes out. So you must get away! Then you can write to the count and tell him everything, except that it was me. And he would never guess it. Nor do I think he would be very anxious to find out.

JULIA. I'll go if you come with me.

JEAN. Are you stark mad, woman? Miss Julia to run away with her valet! It would be in the papers in another day, and the count could never survive it.

JULIA. I can't leave! I can't stay! Help me! I am so tired, so fearfully tired. Give me orders! Set me going, for I can no longer think, no longer act——

JEAN. Do you see now what good-for-nothings you are! Why do you strut and turn up your noses as if you were the lords of creation? Well, I am going to give you orders. Go up and dress. Get some travelling money, and then come back again.

JULIA (*in an undertone*). Come up with me!

JEAN. To your room? Now you're crazy again! (*Hesitates a moment.*) No, you must go at once! (*Takes her by the hand and leads her out.*)

JULIA (*on her way out*). Can't you speak kindly to me, Jean?

JEAN. An order must always sound unkind. Now you can find out how it feels!

[JULIA *goes out.* JEAN, *alone, draws a sigh of relief; sits down at the table; takes out a note-book and a pencil; figures aloud from time to time; dumb play until* CHRISTINE *enters dressed for church; she has a false shirt front and a white tie in one of her hands.*]

CHRISTINE. Goodness gracious, how the place looks! What have you been up to anyhow?

JEAN. Oh, it was Miss Julia who dragged in the people. Have you been sleeping so hard that you didn't hear anything at all?

CHRISTINE. I have been sleeping like a log.

JEAN. And dressed for church already?

CHRISTINE. Yes, didn't you promise to come with me to communion to-day?

JEAN. Oh, yes, I remember now. And there you've got the finery. Well, come on with it. (*Sits down;* CHRISTINE *helps him to put on the shirt front and the white tie. Pause.*)

JEAN (*sleepily*). What's the text to-day?

CHRISTINE. Oh, about John the Baptist beheaded, I guess.

JEAN. That's going to be a long story, I'm sure. My, but you choke me! Oh, I'm so sleepy, so sleepy!

CHRISTINE. Well, what has been keeping you up all night? Why, man, you're just green in the face!

JEAN. I have been sitting here talking with Miss Julia.

CHRISTINE. She hasn't an idea of what's proper, that creature! (*Pause.*)

JEAN. Say, Christine.

CHRISTINE. Well?

JEAN. Isn't it funny anyhow, when you come to think of it? Her!

CHRISTINE. What is it that's funny?

JEAN. Everything! (*Pause.*)

CHRISTINE (*seeing the glasses on the table that are only half emptied*). So you've been drinking together also?

JEAN. Yes.

CHRISTINE. Shame on you! Look me in the eye!

JEAN. Yes.

CHRISTINE. Is it possible? Is it possible?

JEAN (*after a moment's thought*). Yes, it is!

CHRISTINE. Ugh! That's worse than I could ever have believed. It's awful!

JEAN. You are not jealous of her, are you?

CHRISTINE. No, not of her. Had it been Clara or Sophie, then I'd have scratched your eyes out. Yes, that's the way I feel about it, and I can't tell why. Oh my, but that was nasty!

JEAN. Are you mad at her then?

CHRISTINE. No, but at you! It was wrong of you, very wrong! Poor girl! No, I tell you, I don't want to stay in this house any longer, with people for whom it is impossible to have any respect.

JEAN. Why should you have any respect for them?

CHRISTINE. And you who are such a smarty can't tell that! You wouldn't serve people who don't act decently, would you? It's to lower oneself, I think.

JEAN. Yes, but it ought to be a consolation to us that they are not a bit better than we.

CHRISTINE. No, I don't think so. For if they're no better, then it's no use trying to get up to them. And just think of the count! Think of him who has had so much sorrow in his day!

No, I don't want to stay any longer in this house— And with a fellow like you, too. If it had been the county Attorney—if it had only been some one of her own sort——

JEAN. Now look here!

CHRISTINE. Yes, yes! You're all right in your way, but there's after all some difference between one kind of people and another— No, but this is something I'll never get over!— And the young lady who was so proud, and so tart to the men, that you couldn't believe she would ever let one come near her—and such a one at that! And she who wanted to have poor Diana shot because she had been running around with the gate-keeper's pug!— Well, I declare!— But I won't stay here any longer, and next October I get out of here.

JEAN. And then?

CHRISTINE. Well, as we've come to talk of that now, perhaps it would be just as well if you looked for something, seeing that we're going to get married after all.

JEAN. Well, what could I look for? As a married man I couldn't get a place like this.

CHRISTINE. No, I understand that. But you could get a job as a janitor, or maybe as a messenger in some government bureau. Of course, the public loaf is always short in weight, but it comes steady, and then there is a pension for the widow and the children——

JEAN (making a face). That's good and well, but it isn't my style to think of dying all at once for the sake of wife and children. I must say that my plans have been looking toward something better than that kind of thing.

CHRISTINE. Your plans, yes—but you've got obligations also, and those you had better keep in mind!

JEAN. Now don't you get my dander up by talking of obligations! I know what I've got to do anyhow. (Listening for some sound on the outside.) However, we've plenty of time to think of all this. Go in now and get ready, and then we'll go to church.

CHRISTINE. Who is walking around up there?

JEAN. I don't know, unless it be Clara.

CHRISTINE (going out). It can't be the count, do you think, who's come home without anybody hearing him?

JEAN (scared). The count? No, that isn't possible, for then he would have rung for me.

CHRISTINE (as she goes out). Well, God help us all! Never have I seen the like of it!

[The sun has risen and is shining on the tree tops in the park. The light changes gradually until it comes slantingly in through the windows. JEAN goes to the door and gives a signal.]

JULIA (enters in travelling dress and carrying a small bird-cage covered up with a towel; this she places on a chair). Now I am ready.

JEAN. Hush! Christine is awake.

JULIA (showing extreme nervousness during the following scene). Did she suspect anything?

JEAN. She knows nothing at all. But, my heavens, how you look!

JULIA. How do I look?

JEAN. You're as pale as a corpse, and —pardon me, but your face is dirty.

JULIA. Let me wash it then— Now! (She goes over to the washstand and washes her face and hands.) Give me a towel— Oh!— That's the sun rising!

JEAN. And then the ogre bursts.

JULIA. Yes, ogres and trolls were abroad last night!— But listen, Jean. Come with me, for now I have the money.

JEAN (*doubtfully*). Enough?

JULIA. Enough to start with. Come with me, for I cannot travel alone to-day. Think of it—Midsummer Day, on a stuffy train, jammed with people who stare at you—and standing still at stations when you want to fly. No, I cannot! I cannot! And then the memories will come: childhood memories of Midsummer Days, when the inside of the church was turned into a green forest—birches and lilacs; the dinner at the festive table with relatives and friends; the afternoon in the park, with dancing and music, flowers and games! Oh, you may run and run, but your memories are in the baggage-car, and with them remorse and repentance!

JEAN. I'll go with you—but at once, before it's too late. This very moment!

JULIA. Well, get dressed then. (*Picks up the cage.*)

JEAN. But no baggage! That would only give us away.

JULIA. No, nothing at all! Only what we can take with us in the car.

JEAN (*has taken down his hat*). What have you got there? What is it?

JULIA. It's only my finch. I can't leave it behind.

JEAN. Did you ever! Dragging a bird-cage along with us! You must be raving mad! Drop the cage!

JULIA. The only thing I take with me from my home! The only living creature that loves me since Diana deserted me! Don't be cruel! Let me take it along!

JEAN. Drop the cage, I tell you! And don't talk so loud—Christine can hear us.

JULIA. No, I won't let it fall into strange hands. I'd rather have you kill it!

JEAN. Well, give it to me, and I'll wring its neck.

JULIA. Yes, but don't hurt it. Don't—no, I cannot!

JEAN. Let me—I can!

JULIA (*takes the bird out of the cage and kisses it*). Oh, my little birdie, must it die and go away from its mistress!

JEAN. Don't make a scene, please. Don't you know it's a question of your life, of your future? Come, quick! (*Snatches the bird away from her, carries it to the chopping-block and picks up an axe.* MISS JULIA *turns away.*)

JEAN. You should have learned how to kill chickens instead of shooting with a revolver—(*Brings down the axe.*)—then you wouldn't have fainted for a drop of blood.

JULIA (*screaming*). Kill me too! Kill me! You who can take the life of an innocent creature without turning a hair! Oh, I hate and despise you! There is blood between us! Cursed be the hour when I first met you! Cursed be the hour when I came to life in my mother's womb!

JEAN. Well, what's the use of all that cursing? Come on!

JULIA (*approaching the chopping-block as if drawn to it against her will*). No, I don't want to go yet. I cannot—I must see—Hush! There's a carriage coming up the road. (*Listening without taking her eyes off the block and the axe.*) You think I cannot stand the sight of blood. You think I am as weak as that—oh, I should like to see your blood, your brains, on that block there. I should like to see your whole sex swimming in blood like that thing there. I think I could drink out of your skull, and bathe my feet in your open breast, and eat your heart from the spit!— You think I am weak; you think I love you because the fruit of my womb was yearning for your seed; you think I want to carry your offspring under my heart and nourish it with my blood—bear your children and take your name! Tell me, you, what are you called anyhow? I have never heard your family name—and maybe you haven't any. I should become Mrs. "Hovel," or Mrs. "Backyard"—you dog there, 10 that's wearing my collar; you lackey with my coat of arms on your buttons—and I should share with my cook, and be the rival of my own servant. Oh! Oh! Oh!— You think I am a coward and want to run away! No, now I'll stay—and let the lightning strike! My father will come home—will find his chiffonier opened—the money gone! Then he'll 20 ring—twice for the valet—and then he'll send for the sheriff—and then I shall tell everything! Everything! Oh, but it will be good to get an end to it—if it only be the end! And then his heart will break, and he dies!— So there will be an end to all of us— and all will be quiet—peace—eternal rest!— And then the coat of arms will be shattered on the coffin—and 30 the count's line will be wiped out— but the lackey's line goes on in the orphan asylum—wins laurels in the gutter, and ends in jail.

JEAN. There spoke the royal blood! Bravo, Miss Julia! Now you put the miller back in his sack!

[CHRISTINE *enters dressed for church and carrying a hymn-book in her hand*.]

JULIA (*hurries up to her and throws herself* 40 *into her arms as if seeking protection*). Help me, Christine! Help me against this man!

CHRISTINE (*unmoved and cold*). What kind of performance is this on the Sabbath morning? (*Catches sight of the chopping-block*.) My, what a mess you have made!— What's the meaning of all this? And the way you shout and carry on!

JULIA. You are a woman, Christine, and you are my friend. Beware of that scoundrel!

JEAN (*a little shy and embarrassed*). While the ladies are discussing I'll get myself a shave. (*Slinks out to the right*.)

JULIA. You must understand me, and you must listen to me.

CHRISTINE. No, really, I don't understand this kind of trolloping. Where are you going in your travelling-dress—and he with his hat on— what?— What?

JULIA. Listen, Christine, listen, and I'll tell you everything——

CHRISTINE. I don't want to know anything——

JULIA. You must listen to me——

CHRISTINE. What is it about? Is it about this nonsense with Jean? Well, I don't care about it at all, for it's none of my business. But if you're planning to get him away with you, we'll put a stop to that!

JULIA (*extremely nervous*). Please try to be quiet, Christine, and listen to me. I cannot stay here, and Jean cannot stay here—and so we must leave——

CHRISTINE. Hm, hm!

JULIA (*brightening up*). But now I have got an idea, you know. Suppose all three of us should leave—go abroad —go to Switzerland and start a hotel together—I have money, you know— and Jean and I could run the whole thing—and you, I thought, could take charge of the kitchen— Wouldn't that be fine!— Say yes, now! And come along with us! Then everything is fixed!— Oh, say yes! (*She puts her arms around* CHRISTINE *and pats her*.)

CHRISTINE (*coldly and thoughtfully*). Hm, hm!

JULIA (*presto tempo*). You have never travelled, Christine—you must get out and have a look at the world. You cannot imagine what fun it is to travel on a train—constantly new people—new countries—and then we get to Hamburg and take in the Zoological Gardens in passing—that's what you like—and then we go to the theatres and to the opera—and when we get to Munich, there, you know, we have a lot of museums, where they keep Rubens and Raphael and all those big painters, you know — Haven't you heard of Munich, where King Louis used to live—the king, you know, that went mad— And then we'll have a look at his castle—he has still some castles that are furnished just as in a fairy tale— and from there it isn't very far to Switzerland—and the Alps, you know —just think of the Alps, with snow on top of them in the middle of the summer—and there you have orange trees and laurels that are green all the year around——

[JEAN *is seen in the right wing, sharpening his razor on a strop which he holds between his teeth and his left hand; he listens to the talk with a pleased mien and nods approval now and then.*]

JULIA (*tempo prestissimo*). And then we get a hotel—and I sit in the office, while Jean is outside receiving tourists—and goes out marketing—and writes letters— That's a life for you— Then the train whistles, and the 'bus drives up, and it rings upstairs, and it rings in the restaurant—and then I make out the bills—and I am going to salt them, too— You can never imagine how timid tourists are when they come to pay their bills! And you—you will sit like a queen in the kitchen. Of course, you are not going to stand at the stove yourself. And you'll have to dress neatly and nicely in order to show yourself to people— and with your looks—yes, I am not flattering you—you'll catch a husband some fine day—some rich Englishman, you know—for those fellows are so easy (*Slowing down.*) to catch—and then we grow rich—and we build us a villa at Lake Como—of course, it is raining a little in that place now and then—but (*Limply.*) the sun must be shining sometimes— although it looks dark—and—then— or else we can go home again—and come back—here—or some other place——

CHRISTINE. Tell me, Miss Julia, do you believe in all that yourself?

JULIA (*crushed*). Do I believe in it myself?

CHRISTINE. Yes.

JULIA (*exhausted*). I don't know: I believe no longer in anything. (*She sinks down on the bench and drops her head between her arms on the table.*) Nothing! Nothing at all!

CHRISTINE (*turns to the right, where* JEAN *is standing*). So you were going to run away!

JEAN (*abashed, puts the razor on the table*). Run away? Well, that's putting it rather strong. You have heard what the young lady proposes, and though she is tired out now by being up all night, it's a proposition that can be put through all right.

CHRISTINE. Now you tell me: did you mean me to act as cook for that one there——?

JEAN (*sharply*). Will you please use decent language in speaking to your mistress! Do you understand?

CHRISTINE. Mistress!

JEAN. Yes!

CHRISTINE. Well, well! Listen to him!

JEAN. Yes, it would be better for you to listen a little more and talk a little less. Miss Julia is your mistress, and what makes you disrespectful to her now should make you feel the same way about yourself.

CHRISTINE. Oh, I have always had enough respect for myself——

JEAN. To have none for others!

CHRISTINE. —not to go below my own station. You can't say that the count's cook has had anything to do with the groom or the swineherd. You can't say anything of the kind!

JEAN. Yes, it's your luck that you have had to do with a gentleman.

CHRISTINE. Yes, a gentleman who sells the oats out of the count's stable!

JEAN. What's that to you who get a commission on the groceries and bribes from the butcher?

CHRISTINE. What's that?

JEAN. And so you can't respect your master and mistress any longer! You—you!

CHRISTINE. Are you coming with me to church? I think you need a good sermon on top of such a deed.

JEAN. No, I am not going to church to-day. You can go by yourself and confess your own deeds.

CHRISTINE. Yes, I'll do that, and I'll bring back enough forgiveness to cover you also. The Saviour suffered and died on the cross for all our sins, and if we go to him with a believing heart and a repentant mind, he'll take all our guilt on himself.

JULIA. Do you believe that, Christine?

CHRISTINE. It is my living belief, as sure as I stand here, and the faith of my childhood which I have kept since I was young, Miss Julia. And where sin abounds, grace abounds too.

JULIA. Oh, if I had your faith! Oh, if——

CHRISTINE. Yes, but you don't get it without the special grace of God, and that is not bestowed on every-body——

JULIA. On whom is it bestowed then?

CHRISTINE. That's just the great secret of the work of grace, Miss Julia, and the Lord has no regard for persons, but there those that are last shall be the foremost——

JULIA. Yes, but that means he has regard for those that are last.

CHRISTINE (*going right on*). —and it is easier for a camel to go through a needle's eye than for a rich man to get into heaven. That's the way it is, Miss Julia. Now I am going, however —alone—and as I pass by, I'll tell the stableman not to let out the horses if anybody should like to get away before the count comes home. Good-bye! (*Goes out.*)

JEAN. Well, ain't she a devil!— And all this for the sake of a finch!

JULIA (*apathetically*). Never mind the finch!— Can you see any way out of this, any way to end it?

JEAN (*ponders*). No!

JULIA. What would you do in my place?

JEAN. In your place? Let me see. As one of gentle birth, as a woman, as one who has—fallen. I don't know—yes, I do know!

JULIA (*picking up the razor with a significant gesture*). Like this?

JEAN. Yes!— But please observe that I myself wouldn't do it, for there is a difference between us.

JULIA. Because you are a man and I a woman? What is the difference?

JEAN. It is the same—as—that between man and woman.

JULIA (*with the razor in her hand*). I want to, but I cannot!— My father

couldn't either, that time he should
have done it.

JEAN. No, he should not have done it,
for he had to get his revenge first.

JULIA. And now it is my mother's turn
to revenge herself again, through me.

JEAN. Have you not loved your father,
Miss Julia?

JULIA. Yes, immensely, but I must have
hated him, too. I think I must have
been doing so without being aware
of it. But he was the one who reared
me in contempt for my own sex—
half woman and half man! Whose
fault is it, this that has happened?
My father's—my mother's—my own?
My own? Why, I have nothing that
is my own. I haven't a thought that
didn't come from my father; not a
passion that didn't come from my
mother; and now this last—this
about all human creatures being
equal—I got that from him, my
fiancé—whom I call a scoundrel for
that reason! How can it be my own
fault? To put the blame on Jesus, as
Christine does—no, I am too proud
for that, and know too much—
thanks to my father's teachings—
And that about a rich person not
getting into heaven, it's just a lie, and
Christine, who has money in the
savings-bank, wouldn't get in anyhow. Whose is the fault?— What does
it matter whose it is? For just the
same I am the one who must bear the
guilt and the results——

JEAN. Yes, but——

[*Two sharp strokes are rung on the bell.*
MISS JULIA *leaps to her feet.* JEAN
changes his coat.]

JEAN. The count is back. Think if
Christine—— (*Goes to the speaking-
tube, knocks on it, and listens.*)

JULIA. Now he has been to the chiffonier!

JEAN. It is Jean, your lordship! (*Listening again, the spectators being unable to
hear what the count says.*) Yes, your
lordship! (*Listening.*) Yes, your lordship! At once! (*Listening.*) In a minute, your lordship! (*Listening.*) Yes,
yes! In half an hour!

JULIA (*with intense concern*). What did he
say? Lord Jesus, what did he say?

JEAN. He called for his boots and
wanted his coffee in half an hour.

JULIA. In half an hour then! Oh, I am
so tired. I can't do anything; can't
repent, can't run away, can't stay,
can't live—can't die! Help me now!
Command me, and I'll obey you
like a dog! Do me this last favour—
save my honour, and save his name!
You know what my will ought to do,
and what it cannot do—now give
me your will, and make me do it!

JEAN. I don't know why—but now I
can't either—I don't understand—
It is just as if this coat here made a—
I cannot command you—and now,
since I've heard the count's voice—
now—I can't quite explain it—but—
Oh, that damned menial is back in
my spine again. I believe if the count
should come down here, and if he
should tell me to cut my own throat
—I'd do it on the spot!

JULIA. Make believe that you are he,
and that I am you!— You did some
fine acting when you were on your
knees before me—then you were the
nobleman—or—have you ever been
to a show and seen one who could
hypnotize people?

[JEAN *makes a sign of assent.*]

JULIA. He says to his subject: get the
broom. And the man gets it. He
says: sweep. And the man sweeps.

JEAN. But then the other person must
be asleep.

JULIA (*ecstatically*). I am asleep already—
there is nothing in the whole room

but a lot of smoke—and you look like a stove—that looks like a man in black clothes and a high hat—and your eyes glow like coals when the fire is going out—and your face is a lump of white ashes. (*The sunlight has reached the floor and is now falling on JEAN.*) How warm and nice it is! (*She rubs her hands as if warming them before a fire.*) And so light—and so peaceful!

JEAN (*takes the razor and puts it in her hand*). There's the broom! Go now, while it is light—to the barn—and —— (*Whispers something in her ear.*)

JULIA (*awake*). Thank you! Now I shall have rest! But tell me first—that the foremost also receive the gift of grace. Say it, even if you don't believe it.

JEAN. The foremost? No, I can't do that!— But wait—Miss Julia—I know! You are no longer among the foremost—now when you are among the—last!

JULIA. That's right. I am among the last of all: I am the very last. Oh!—

But now I cannot go— Tell me once more that I must go!

JEAN. No, now I can't do it either. I cannot!

JULIA. And those that are foremost shall be the last.

JEAN. Don't think, don't think! Why, you are taking away my strength, too, so that I become a coward— What? I thought I saw the bell moving!— To be that scared of a bell! Yes, but it isn't only the bell— there is somebody behind it—a hand that makes it move—and something else that makes the hand move—but if you cover up your ears—just cover up your ears! Then it rings worse than ever! Rings and rings, until you answer it—and then it's too late— then comes the sheriff—and then—

[*Two quick rings from the bell.*]

JEAN (*shrinks together; then he straightens himself up*). It's horrid! But there's no other end to it!— Go!

[JULIA *goes firmly out through the door.*]

CURTAIN.

THE GHOST SONATA

CHARACTERS

THE OLD MAN, *Mr. Hummel, a Merchant*
ARKENHOLTZ, *a Student*
THE MILKMAID, *a Vision*
THE JANITRESS
THE JANITOR
THE DEAD MAN, *a Consul*
THE LADY IN BLACK, *the daughter of the Janitress and the Dead Man*
THE COLONEL

THE MUMMY, *the Colonel's wife*
HIS DAUGHTER, *the daughter of the Old Man*
THE NOBLEMAN, *called Baron Skanskorg.*
    Engaged to the daughter of the Janitress
JOHANSSON, *a Servant of Mr. Hummel*
BENGTSSON, *the Colonel's valet*
THE FIANCÉE, *Mr. Hummel's former fiancée, a white-haired old woman*

SCENE I

The ground floor and first floor of the façade of a modern house, but only the corner of the house which on the ground floor terminates in a round drawing-room, above which, on the first floor, is a balcony with a flagstaff.

Through the open windows of the drawing-room is visible, when the blinds are up, a white marble statue of a young woman, surrounded by palms, and strongly illumined by the sunlight. In the window to the left are to be seen pots of hyacinths (blue, white and pink).

On the balcony rail on the first floor in the corner, a blue silk bed quilt and two white pillows. The windows to the left are hung with white sheets. It is a bright Sunday morning.

In the foreground in front of the house is a green bench.

To the right in the foreground a street fountain, to the left an advertisement column.

In the background to the left the front door, showing the staircase with steps of white marble and banister of brass with a

mahogany rail; on both sides of the door on the pavement stand tubs with laurels.

The round drawing-room at the corner looks out also on a side street which is supposed to lead in towards the background.

To the left of the front door is a window, on the ground floor, with a window mirror.

As the curtain rises, several distant church bells ring.

The doors in the façade are open: a woman dressed in dark clothes stands motionless on the steps.

The JANITRESS sweeps the entrance hall, then she rubs the brass on the door, and waters the laurels.

By the advertisement column sits the OLD MAN in a wheeled chair, reading a newspaper: he has white hair and beard and spectacles.

The MILKMAID enters from the corner with bottles in a wire basket, she wears summer clothes, with brown shoes, black stockings and a white cap; she takes off her cap and hangs it on the fountain; wipes the

THE GHOST SONATA: Translated by Erik Palmstierna and James Bernard Fagan. Reprinted by permission of the Strindberg estate representative.

perspiration from her forehead; takes a drink from the cup, washes her hands and arranges her hair, mirroring herself in the water.

The bell of a steamer is heard to ring, and the bass notes of an organ in a neighbouring church pierce the silence now and then.

After a couple of minutes' silence, when the girl has finished her toilet, the STUDENT *enters from the left; he has had a sleepless night and is unshaven. He goes straight to the fountain.*

[*Pause.*]

STUDENT. May I have the cup?

[*The* MILKMAID *draws the cup towards her.*]
Haven't you nearly finished?

[*The* MILKMAID *looks at him with horror.*]

OLD MAN (*to himself*). Who is he talking to?—I don't see anybody!—Is he crazy? (*He continues to look at them with great surprise.*)

STUDENT. Why do you stare at me? Do I look so awful?—Well, I've had no sleep. I suppose you think I have been making a night of it. . . .

[*The* MILKMAID *as before.*]
You think I've been drinking?—Do I smell of it?

[*The* MILKMAID *as before.*]
I know I haven't shaved . . . give me a drink of water, girl, I have earned it! (*Pause.*) Well! Then I suppose I've got to tell you that I spent the whole night dressing wounds and nursing the injured. You see, I was present when that house collapsed last night . . . that's all.

[*The* MILKMAID *rinses the cup, and gives him a drink.*]
Thanks!

[*The* MILKMAID *motionless.*]
(*Slowly.*) Would you do me a great favour? (*Pause.*) My eyes are inflamed, as you can see, and my hands have been touching wounds and corpses. To touch my eyes with them would be dangerous. . . . Will you take my handkerchief which is clean, dip it in the fresh water, and bathe my poor eyes with it.—Will you do that?—Won't you act the good Samaritan?

[*The* MILKMAID *hesitates, but does as he has asked.*]
Thank you, my dear! (*He takes out his purse.*)

[*The* MILKMAID *makes a deprecatory gesture.*]
Pardon my absent-mindedness, I am only half awake. . . .

OLD MAN (*to the* STUDENT). Excuse a stranger, but I heard you mention last night's accident . . . I was just reading about it in the paper. . . .

STUDENT. Is it already in the papers?

OLD MAN. All about it. Even your portrait. They greatly regret though that they have not been able to learn the name of the brave young student who did such splendid work. . . .

STUDENT (*glancing at the paper*). That's me! Ha!

OLD MAN. Whom were you talking to just now?

STUDENT. Didn't you see? (*Pause.*)

OLD MAN. What's your name?—Would it be impertinent—to ask—your name?

STUDENT. What does it matter? I don't care for publicity.—Blame is always mixed up with any praise you may get.—To belittle has become an art. —Besides I ask no reward. . . .

OLD MAN. Wealthy are you?

STUDENT. Not at all . . . on the contrary! Poor as a durmouse.

OLD MAN. That's queer. . . . It seems to me as if I had heard that voice. When I was young, I had a friend who always said durmouse instead of dormouse.—Until now he was the one person I had ever heard using that pronunciation. You are the other one.—Is it possible you are a relative of Mr. Arkenholtz, the merchant?

STUDENT. He was my father.

OLD MAN. Strange are the ways of fate. . . . I saw you once when you were an infant, under very trying circumstances. . . .

STUDENT. Yes. They say I came into the world in the middle of a bankruptcy. . . .

OLD MAN. Exactly!

STUDENT. May I ask your name?

OLD MAN. I am Mr. Hummel. . . .

STUDENT. You . . . ? Then I remember. . . .

OLD MAN. You have often heard my name mentioned at home? Have you?

STUDENT. Yes!

OLD MAN. And not in a pleasant way, I suppose?

[STUDENT *remains silent.*]

Yes, I should think so!—You were told, I suppose, that I had ruined your father?—All who are ruined by foolish speculations think themselves ruined by the man they tried to fool. (*Pause.*) Now the fact is your father robbed me of seventeen thousand crowns. All my savings at that time.

STUDENT. It is queer how the same story can be told in two quite different ways.

OLD MAN. You don't think I am lying?

STUDENT. How can I tell what to think? My father never lied!

OLD MAN. No, that's right, a father never lies . . . but I, too, am a father, and that is why. . . .

STUDENT. What are you driving at?

OLD MAN. I saved your father from misery, and he repaid me with the ruthless hatred that is born of the obligation to be grateful . . . he taught his family to speak ill of me.

STUDENT. Perhaps you made him ungrateful by poisoning the assistance you gave him with needless humiliation.

OLD MAN. All assistance is humiliating, sir.

STUDENT (*pause*). What do you want from me?

OLD MAN. Not the money back. But if you will render me a small service now and then, I shall consider myself well paid. I am a cripple as you see. Some people say it is my own fault. Others blame my parents. I prefer to blame life itself, with its pitfalls. To escape one of these pitfalls is to walk headlong into another. As it is, I cannot climb stairs or ring door-bells, therefore I beg you: help me!

STUDENT. What can I do?

OLD MAN. Give my chair a push, to begin with, so that I can read the play-bills on that column. I want to see what they are playing to-night. . . .

STUDENT (*wheels the chair*). Have you no attendant?

OLD MAN. Yes, but he has gone on an errand . . . He'll be back soon . . . Are you a medical student?

STUDENT. No, I am studying languages. What profession to choose, I don't know. . . .

OLD MAN. I see!—Are you good at mathematics?

STUDENT. Not too bad.

OLD MAN. That's good!—Perhaps you would like a job?

STUDENT. Yes, why not?

OLD MAN (*studying the play-bills*). Splendid! They are playing "The Valkyrie" at the *matinée*. . . . The Colonel will be there and his daughter, and as he always has the end seat in the sixth row, I'll put you next. . . . Will you please go over to that telephone kiosk and order a ticket for seat 82 in the sixth row?

STUDENT. Must I go to the Opera in the afternoon?

OLD MAN. Yes! you do as I tell you, and you'll get on! I wish to see you happy, rich and honoured. Your debut last night as the brave rescuer will make you famous by to-morrow, and then your name will be worth a great deal.

STUDENT (goes to the telephone box). What a funny adventure. . . .

OLD MAN. Are you a sportsman?

STUDENT. Yes, worse luck. . . .

OLD MAN. Then we'll turn it into better luck! 'Phone up now! (Reads his paper.)

[The DARK LADY has come out on to the pavement and talks with the JANITRESS. The OLD MAN listens, but the audience hears nothing. The STUDENT re-enters.] It is all right?

STUDENT. All right.

OLD MAN. Do you see that house?

STUDENT. Well, yes, I have seen it before . . . I passed it yesterday when the sun was shining on the window-panes—and imagining all the beauty and luxury within—I said to my companion: "Just think of having a flat up there on the fourth floor, a beautiful young wife, two pretty little children, and twenty thousand crowns a year. . . ."

OLD MAN. So that's what you said? That's what you said? Well! well! I also am very fond of this house. . . .

STUDENT. Do you speculate in houses?

OLD MAN. Mm-yah! But not in the way you mean. . . .

STUDENT. Do you know the people who live there?

OLD MAN. All of them. A man of my age knows everybody, including their parents, and grandparents, and one is always related in some way to people. —I am just eighty—but nobody knows me—not quite.—Human destinies interest me. . . .

[The blinds of the round drawing-room are drawn up; the COLONEL is seen inside in mufti. After having looked at the thermometer he goes into the room and stands in front of the marble statue.] Look, that's the Colonel; you will sit next him this afternoon. . . .

STUDENT. Is that—the Colonel? I understand nothing of all this, it's just like a story. . . .

OLD MAN. My whole life has been like a collection of stories, sir. But though the stories are different, they hang together on a common thread, and the dominant theme recurs regularly.

STUDENT. Whom does that statue in there represent?

OLD MAN. His wife, of course. . . .

STUDENT. Was she so lovable then?

OLD MAN. Mm-yah! Yes!

STUDENT. Speak out!

OLD MAN. Oh, we can't judge people, young man!—If I told you that she'd left him, that he beat her, that she returned to him, that she married him a second time, and that she is sitting there now like a mummy, worshipping her own statue, then you would think me crazy.

STUDENT. I don't understand!

OLD MAN. I thought not!—And there is the window with the hyacinths. His daughter lives there. . . . She is out riding now; she will be home soon. . . .

STUDENT. And who is the Dark Lady, talking to the Janitress?

OLD MAN. Well, that's a bit complicated, but it is connected with the dead man up there, where you see the white sheets. . . .

STUDENT. Who was he then?

OLD MAN. A human being like you or me, but the most conspicuous thing about him was his vanity. . . . If you were a Sunday child you would presently see him come out of that door to look at the flag of the Consulate flying at half-mast.—You see, he was a Consul, and he revelled in coronets and lions and plumed hats and coloured ribbons. 10

STUDENT. You said Sunday child.— They say I was born on a Sunday. . . .

OLD MAN. No! Were you . . . ? Oh, I should have known . . . the colour of your eyes shows it . . . then you can see what other people can't. Have you noticed anything of that kind?

STUDENT. Of course I don't know what other people see, but at times . . . Oh! One doesn't talk of such things! 20

OLD MAN. I was almost sure of it, but you can tell me because I—I understand—such things. . . .

STUDENT. Yesterday, for instance . . . I was drawn to that little side street, where the house fell down afterwards. . . . I got there, I stopped in front of that house, which I had never seen before . . . then I noticed a crack in the wall. . . . I could hear floor beams snapping. . . . I rushed forward and picked up a child close to the wall . . . a second later the house came tumbling down . . . I was saved, but in my arms which I thought held the child, there was nothing at all. . . . 30

OLD MAN. Well! . . . I must say of all the things . . . tell me one thing. Why did you make those gestures by the fountain just now? Why were you talking to yourself? 40

STUDENT. Didn't you see the Milkmaid I was talking to?

OLD MAN (horrified). A milkmaid?

STUDENT. Yes, the girl who handed me the cup.

OLD MAN. Oh! That's how it is? . . . Well, I cannot see things, but there are things I can do.

[A white-haired old lady is now seen to sit down at the window with the window mirror.]

Look at the old woman in the window! Do you see her?—Good! She was my fiancée once upon a time, sixty years ago . . . I was twenty— Never mind, she does not recognize me! We meet every day, and it makes no impression on me, although in those days we had vowed to love each other eternally . . . eternally!

STUDENT. How foolish you were in those old days! We never talk to our girls like that.

OLD MAN. Forgive us, young man! We didn't know any better!—but can't you see that that old woman was once young and pretty?

STUDENT. It doesn't show. Oh! yes, I feel she has beautiful eyes, although I cannot see them.

[The JANITRESS comes out with a basket and strews chopped fir branches, as is usual in Sweden when a funeral is to be held.]

OLD MAN. Ah! The Janitress—Hm! That Dark Lady is her daughter by the man who is dead, and that's why her husband was made Janitor . . . but the Dark Lady has a lover; he is a nobleman with great expectations. He is now getting a divorce from his present wife, who is giving him a big house to get rid of him. This elegant lover is the son-in-law of the dead man, and you can see his bed-clothes being aired on the balcony upstairs . . . that's a bit complicated, I should say!

STUDENT. Yes, it's awfully complicated!

OLD MAN. It certainly is, inside and out, however simple it looks.

STUDENT. But then who was the dead man?

OLD MAN. You've asked me that already, and I answered. If you could look round the corner, where the servants' entrance is, you would see a lot of poor people whom he used to help . . . when he was in the mood. . . . 10

STUDENT. He was a charitable man, then?

OLD MAN. Yes . . . at times.

STUDENT. Not always?

OLD MAN. No-o! . . . people are like that! Come, sir, turn my chair towards the sun, I feel so cold. You see, the blood congeals, when you can't move about.—Death isn't very far away from me, I know, but I have 20 a few things to do before it comes— hold my hand and feel how cold I am.

STUDENT. Yes, yes, terribly. (*He shrinks back.*)

OLD MAN. Don't leave me, I am tired now, and lonely, but I haven't always been like this, you know. I have an enormously long life behind me— enormously long—I have made people unhappy, and people have 30 made me unhappy, and one thing balances the other, but before I die, I want to see you happy . . . our destinies are intertwined through your father—and other things. . . .

STUDENT. But let go my hand, you know you are taking my strength. You are freezing me. What do you want with me?

OLD MAN. Patience, and you'll see and 40 understand. . . . There comes the young lady.

STUDENT. The Colonel's daughter?

OLD MAN. His daughter—yes! Look at her!—did you ever see such a masterpiece?

STUDENT. She resembles the marble statue there. . . .

OLD MAN. It is her mother, you know!

STUDENT. You are right—never did I see such a woman of woman born.— Lucky the man who wins her for a wife and for his home!

OLD MAN. *You* see it then!—Her beauty is not discovered by everybody . . . so it is written!

[*The* YOUNG LADY *comes in from the left; she is dressed in modern English riding costume, walks slowly, without noticing anyone, to the door, where she stops to say a few words to the* JANITRESS, *and enters the house.*]

[*The* STUDENT *covers his eyes with the hands.*]

OLD MAN. Are you crying?

STUDENT. In the face of what is hopeless, is there anything *but* despair?

OLD MAN. I can open doors and hearts, if I only find an arm to do my will . . . serve me, and you shall have power. . . .

STUDENT. Is it then a bargain? Must I sell my soul?

OLD MAN. Don't sell anything!—You see, all my life I have been accustomed to *take*. Now I have a craving to give,—to give! But no one will accept . . . I am rich, very rich, but I have no heirs, except a scamp who is tormenting the life out of me. . . . Become my son; inherit me while I am still alive, enjoy life, and let me look on from a distance, at least.

STUDENT. What am I to do?

OLD MAN. First go and hear "The Valkyrie"!

STUDENT. That's settled—but what else?

OLD MAN. To-night you shall be in there, in the Round Room!

STUDENT. How shall I get there?

OLD MAN. By means of "The Valkyrie"!

STUDENT. Why have you chosen me to be your instrument? Did you know me before?

OLD MAN. Of course I did! I have had my eye on you for a long time . . . but now look there at the balcony, the maid is raising the flag to half-mast for the dead Consul . . . and now she turns the mattresses. . . . Do you notice that blue quilt?—It was made to cover two, now it will only cover one. . . .

[*The* YOUNG LADY *appears at her window, having changed her dress in the meantime; she waters the hyacinths.*]

There is my little girl. Look at her—look!—She is talking to her flowers; isn't she like that blue hyacinth herself? . . . She gives them drink, pure water only—and they transform the water into colour and fragrance. . . . There comes the Colonel with the paper!—He shows her about the house that fell down . . . now he points to your portrait! She is not indifferent . . . she is reading about your brave deed . . . it is clouding over, I think. . . . I wonder if it is going to rain? I shall be in a nice fix then, unless Johansson comes back soon. . . .

[*The sun has disappeared, and it is growing darker, the white-haired old woman at the window mirror closes her window.*]

Now my fiancée is closing the window . . . seventy-nine years . . . the only mirror she uses is the window mirror, for there she sees not herself, but the world outside—from two angles, but the world can see her, and she hasn't thought of that . . . handsome old lady after all. . . .

[*Now the* DEAD MAN, *wrapped in a winding sheet, comes out of the door.*]

STUDENT. Good God, what do I see?

OLD MAN. What *do* you see?

STUDENT. Don't *you* see? In the doorway, the Dead Man?

OLD MAN. I see nothing, but I expected this! Tell me . .

STUDENT. He comes out into the street. . . . (*Pause.*) Now, he turns his head and looks at the flag.

OLD MAN. What did I say? He will probably count the wreaths; also look at the visiting cards . . . woe to him who is missing!

STUDENT. Now he turns the corner. . . .

OLD MAN. He's going to count the poor at the back door . . . the poor are so decorative, you know: "Followed by the blessings of many." Yes, but my blessing he won't get!—Between ourselves—he was a great scoundrel. . . .

STUDENT. But charitable. . . .

OLD MAN. Charitable scoundrel, always thinking of his grand funeral. . . . When he knew his end was near he cheated the State out of fifty thousand crowns. . . . Now his daughter goes about with another woman's husband, and wonders what is in his will. . . . The scoundrel, he can hear every word we say, and he is welcome to it! —There comes Johansson. . . .

[JOHANSSON *enters from the left.*]

OLD MAN. Report!

[JOHANSSON *speaking inaudibly.*]

Not at home you say? You are an ass!—Any telegram? Nothing! . . . Go on! Six o'clock to-night? That's good!—The special edition?—with his name in full!—Arkenholtz, student, born . . . parents . . . splendid! I think it's beginning to rain. . . . What did he really say? So—so! He wouldn't? Well, then he must!— Here comes the nobleman!—Push me round the corner, Johansson, so that I can hear what the poor people say. . . . And, Arkenholtz, wait for me here . . . understand!—Hurry up, hurry up!

[JOHANSSON *wheels the chair round the corner. The* STUDENT *remains looking at the* YOUNG LADY, *who is now loosening the earth in the flower pot. The* NOBLEMAN *in mourning enters and speaks to the* DARK LADY, *who has been walking to and fro on the pavement.*]

NOBLEMAN. Well! What's to be done?— We've got to wait.

DARK LADY. But I can't wait!

NOBLEMAN. Is that so? Oh, go to the country then!

DARK LADY. I don't want to.

NOBLEMAN. Come this way, or they'll hear what we are saying.

[*They move towards the advertising column and continue their talk inaudibly.*]

[*Enter* JOHANSSON *from the right, to the* STUDENT.]

JOHANSSON. The master asks you, sir, not to forget that other matter!

STUDENT (*slowly*). Look here—tell me first: who is your master?

JOHANSSON. Well! He is so many things, and has been everything.

STUDENT. Is he in his right mind?

JOHANSSON. Yes, what is *that?*—All his life he has been looking for a Sunday child he says, but that may be a lie.

STUDENT. What does he want? Is he avaricious?

JOHANSSON. He wants power . . . The whole day long he travels about in his chariot like the Thunder God himself . . . He looks at houses, tears them down, opens up new streets, builds new squares . . . but he also breaks into houses, sneaks through windows, plays havoc with human destinies, kills his enemies, and never forgives.—Can you imagine, sir, that this crippled thing was once a Don Juan, but one who never kept his women?

STUDENT. How can that be?

JOHANSSON. He is so full of guile that he makes the women leave him when he is tired of them . . . meanwhile, he is like a horse thief on the human market, he steals human beings in all kinds of ways . . . Why, he has literally stolen me out of the hands of the law . . . You see, I had been guilty of a slip which he alone knew of. Instead of putting me in jail, he made me a slave. I slave and get only my food, not a bit too good either . . .

STUDENT. What does he want to do in this house then?

JOHANSSON. Well, that I won't say! It is so complicated.

STUDENT. I think I'd better get away from this. . . .

JOHANSSON. Look! The young lady has dropped her bracelet out of the window. . . .

[*The* YOUNG LADY *drops a bracelet out of the open window. The* STUDENT *advances slowly, picks up the bracelet and hands it to the* YOUNG LADY, *who thanks him stiffly. The* STUDENT *goes back to* JOHANSSON.]

So you mean to get away? . . . That is not so easy as one might think, when *he* has got his net over one's head . . . And he fears nothing between heaven and earth . . . Yes, one thing . . . or rather one person.

STUDENT. Wait now, perhaps I know!

JOHANSSON. How can you know?

STUDENT. I'm guessing! Is it . . . a little milkmaid he fears?

JOHANSSON. He always turns away whenever he meets a milk-cart . . . And he also talks in his sleep . . . He must have been in Hamburg at one time, I think. . . .

STUDENT. Is the man to be trusted?

JOHANSSON. You may trust him—to do anything!

STUDENT. What is he doing there round the corner now?

JOHANSSON. Listening to the poor . . . sowing a little word, picking out a stone at a time, until the house tumbles down . . . metaphorically speaking . . . You see, I am an educated man, I used to be in a book-shop . . . Are you going now?

STUDENT. I find it hard to be ungrateful 10 . . . Once he saved my father, and now he asks a small service in return . . .

JOHANSSON. What is that?

STUDENT. To go and see "The Valkyrie" . . .

JOHANSSON. That's beyond me . . . But he is always up to new tricks . . . Look at him now, talking to the policeman . . . He is always thick 20 with the police. He uses them; he snares them in their own interests. He ties their hands with false promises and expectations, while all the time he is pumping them.—You'll see that he is received in the Round Room before the day is over!

STUDENT. What does he want there? What has he to do with the Colonel? 30

JOHANSSON. I think I can guess, . . . but I'm not sure. But you'll see for yourself, when you get there! . . .

STUDENT. I shall never get there. . . .

JOHANSSON. That depends on yourself! —Go to "The Valkyrie." . . .

STUDENT. Is that the way?

JOHANSSON. Yes, if *he* has said so.—Look

at him there.—Look at him in his war chariot, drawn in triumph by the beggars, who get nothing for their pains, only a hint of a treat at his funeral.

[*The* OLD MAN *appears standing in his wheeled chair drawn by one of the* BEGGARS, *and followed by the rest.*]

OLD MAN. Honour to the noble youth who, at the risk of his own, saved many lives in yesterday's accident! Three cheers for Arkenholtz!

[*The* BEGGARS *bare their heads, but do not cheer. The* YOUNG LADY *at the window waves her handkerchief. The* COLONEL *stares out from the window. The* FIANCÉE *rises at her window. The* MAID *on the balcony hoists the flag to the top.*]

And one cheer more, citizens! It is Sunday, to be sure, but the ass in the pit and the corn in the field will absolve us, and although I am not a Sunday child, I have the gift of prophecy as well as healing, for once I restored a drowned person to life . . . that was in Hamburg on a Sunday morning like this. . . .

[*The* MILKMAID *enters, seen only by the* STUDENT *and the* OLD MAN. *She raises her arms like a drowning person, while gazing fixedly at the* OLD MAN.]

OLD MAN (*sits down, then collapses, stricken with horror*). Get me out of this, Johansson!   Quick!—Arkenholtz, don't forget "The Valkyrie" !

STUDENT. What is all this?

JOHANSSON. We'll see! we'll see!

CURTAIN

SCENE II

In the Round Drawing-Room. A stove of white glazed bricks decorated with a mirror and with pendulum clock and candelabras in the background. To the right the entrance lobby, behind which may be seen a green room with mahogany furniture. To the left stands the statue, which is shaded by palms, and can be concealed by curtains. A door to the left in the background leads to the Hyacinth Room where the YOUNG LADY *sits*

reading. One observes the back of the COLO-
NEL *in the Green Room, where he sits writing.*

[BENGTSSON, *the valet, enters from the lobby
dressed in livery. He is followed by* JO-
HANSSON *in evening dress with white tie.*]
BENGTSSON. Johansson, *you* must wait at
table, while I take the coats. Ever
done it?
JOHANSSON. I'd have you know, Mr. 10
Bengtsson, that though I push a war
chariot in the daytime, I wait in
private houses at night, and I have
always dreamt of getting into this
place . . . queer sort of people?
Hm?
BENGTSSON. Oh, yes, a little out of the
ordinary, one might say.
JOHANSSON. Is it a musical party or
what?   20
BENGTSSON. The usual Ghost supper, as
we call it. They drink tea, don't say a
single word, or else the Colonel does
all the talking. And then they crunch
their biscuits, all at the same time,
so that it sounds like rats in an attic.
JOHANSSON. Why do you say Ghost
supper?
BENGTSSON. They look like ghosts . . .
and they have kept this up for twenty 30
years, always the same people saying
the same things, or saying nothing at
all for fear of being found out.
JOHANSSON. Is there not a lady in the
house too?
BENGTSSON. Oh yes, but she's a little
cracked; she sits in a cupboard,
because her eyes cannot bear the
light . . . She sits in there . . . (*He
points at a papered door in the wall.*)   40
JOHANSSON. In there?
BENGTSSON. Well, didn't I say they were
a little out of the ordinary . . .
JOHANSSON. What does she look like
then?
BENGTSSON. Like a mummy . . . care

to look at her, Mr. Johansson? (*He
opens the papered door.*) There she sits!
JOHANSSON. Good Lord!
MUMMY (*babbling*). Why does he open
the door, haven't I told him to keep
it closed . . .
BENGTSSON (*in a namby-pamby tone*). Ta,
ta, ta, ta. Polly very nice now. Then
she'll get something good!—Pretty
Polly.
MUMMY (*parrot-like*). Pretty Polly! Are
you there, Jacob? Currrrr!
BENGTSSON. She thinks herself a parrot,
and maybe she's right. . . . (*To the
MUMMY.*) Whistle for us, Polly!
[*The* MUMMY *whistles.*]
JOHANSSON. Well, I've seen a few things
in my day, but this beats everything!
BENGTSSON. Don't you see, a house gets
old, it becomes mouldy, so when
people sit a long time together tormenting each other, they become
crazy. This lady here.—Shut up,
Polly! That mummy has been sitting
here for forty years—same husband,
same furniture, same relatives, same
friends. . . . (*He closes the paper door.*)
And the goings on in this house—
well, it's beyond me . . . look at
that statue . . . that's the lady as a
girl!
JOHANSSON. Good Lord!—is that the
mummy?
BENGTSSON. Yes!—it's enough to make
you weep!—But this woman by the
power of imagination or somehow
has acquired some of the qualities of
the talkative bird.—She can't stand
cripples or sick people, for instance
. . . she can't stand the sight of her
own daughter because she is sick. . . .
JOHANSSON. Is the young lady sick?
BENGTSSON. Didn't you know that, Mr.
Johansson?
JOHANSSON. No! . . . And the Colonel,
who is he?

BENGTSSON. Hm, you'll see!

JOHANSSON (*looking at the statue*). It's horrible to think that . . . how old is the lady?

BENGTSSON. Nobody knows . . . But at thirty-five she is said to have looked like nineteen, and that is what she made the Colonel believe . . . in this house . . . Do you know what that black Japanese screen beside the couch is for?—They call it the death screen, and it is brought out when anyone is going to die, same as in a hospital. . . .

JOHANSSON. What a horrible house . . . And the Student was longing to get in as if it had been paradise . . .

BENGTSSON. *What* Student? Oh, him! The one who is coming here to-night . . . the Colonel and the young lady happened to meet him at the Opera and both took a fancy to him. . . . Hm! . . . but now it's my turn to ask questions: Who is your master? The Director in the Bath chair . . . ?

JOHANSSON. Well! Well!—Is he coming here too?

BENGTSSON. He's not invited.

JOHANSSON. He comes uninvited! if need be!

[*The* OLD MAN *appears in the lobby in frock-coat and top hat and crutches. He steals forward and listens.*]

BENGTSSON. He is a regular old devil, isn't he?

JOHANSSON. Full fledged!

BENGTSSON. He *looks* like Old Harry!

JOHANSSON. And he's a wizard too! I think—because he passes through locked doors. . . .

OLD MAN (*comes forward and pinches* JOHANSSON'S *ear*). Scoundrel!—take care! (*To* BENGTSSON.) Tell the Colonel I am here!

BENGTSSON. Yes, but we are expecting some guests . . .

OLD MAN. I know! But my visit is as good as expected, though not exactly looked forward to. . . .

BENGTSSON. I see! What's the name? Director Hummel!

OLD MAN. Exactly. Yes!

[BENGTSSON *crosses the lobby to the Green Room, the door of which he closes behind him.*]

(*To* JOHANSSON.) Vanish!

[JOHANSSON *hesitates.*]

Vanish!

[JOHANSSON *disappears into the lobby.*]

[*The* OLD MAN *inspects the room and stops in front of the statue in great astonishment.*]

Amelia! . . . It is she! . . . She! (*He strolls about the room fingering objects, arranges his wig in front of the mirror, returns to the statue.*)

MUMMY (*from the cupboard*). Prretty Polly!

OLD MAN (*startled*). What was that? Is there a parrot in the room? But I don't see it!

MUMMY. Are you there, Jacob?

OLD MAN. The house is haunted!

MUMMY. Jacob!

OLD MAN. I'm frightened . . . So that's the kind of secret they have been hiding in this house! (*Looks at a picture with his back turned to the cupboard.*) And that's he . . . he!

[*The* MUMMY *opens the door, approaches behind the* OLD MAN, *and snatches his wig.*]

MUMMY. Currrr! Is that Jacob! Currrr!

OLD MAN (*jumps up*). God in Heaven! Who is it?

MUMMY (*speaking in a natural voice*). Is that you, Jacob?

OLD MAN. My name is Jacob . . .

MUMMY (*moved*). And my name is Amelia!

OLD MAN. No, no, no . . . Oh, my God!

MUMMY. Yes, it is! And once looked like that! (*Pointing to the statue.*) Life's an edifying thing, isn't it?—I live mostly in the cupboard to avoid seeing and being seen. . . . But you, Jacob, what do you seek here?

OLD MAN. My child! Our child . . .

MUMMY. There she sits.

OLD MAN. Where?

MUMMY. There, in the Hyacinth Room!

OLD MAN (*looking at the* YOUNG LADY). Yes, that is she! (*Pause.*) And what does her father say, I mean the Colonel? . . . Your husband?

MUMMY. Once when I was angry with him, I told him everything.

OLD MAN. Well?

MUMMY. He didn't believe me, but answered: "That's what all wives say when they wish to kill their husbands."—It was a dreadful crime none the less. His whole life then became a fake, his family tree as well; sometimes I take a look in the peerage, and I say to myself: There she is with her false birth certificate like any servant girl, and the punishment for that is hard labour.

OLD MAN. Well, it's quite common; you gave a false date for your birth I remember. . . .

MUMMY. It was my mother who made me do it . . . I was not to blame! . . . But after all, Jacob, the greater share in our crime was yours. . . .

OLD MAN. No, your husband was the cause of that crime when he took my fiancée from me!—I was born a man who cannot forgive till he has punished.—It was to me an imperative duty . . . and is still!

MUMMY. What do you seek in this house? What do you want? How did you get in?—Does it concern my daughter? If you touch her you shall die!

OLD MAN. I mean well by her!

MUMMY. But you must spare her father!

OLD MAN. No!

MUMMY. Then you shall die; in this room, behind that screen. . . .

OLD MAN. Maybe . . . but I can't let go when I have got my teeth in. . . .

MUMMY. You want to marry her to the student? Why? He is nothing and has nothing.

OLD MAN. He will be rich, thanks to me!

MUMMY. Are you invited here to-night?

OLD MAN. No, but I mean to get an invitation for this Ghost supper!

MUMMY. Do you know who are coming?

OLD MAN. Not exactly.

MUMMY. The Baron . . . who lives above here and whose father-in-law was buried this afternoon. . . .

OLD MAN. The man who is getting a divorce to marry the daughter of the Janitress . . . the man who once was your—lover!

MUMMY. Another guest will be your former fiancée who was seduced by my husband. . . .

OLD MAN. A pretty collection. . . .

MUMMY. Oh God, if we might die! *If* we might die.

OLD MAN. But why do you keep together then?

MUMMY. Crime and guilt bind us together!—We have broken our bonds and gone apart innumerable times, but we are always drawn together again. . . .

OLD MAN. And now I think the Colonel is coming.

MUMMY. Then I will go in to Adèle. . . . (*Pause.*) Consider what you do, Jacob! Spare him. . . .

[*Pause, she goes out.*]

[*The* COLONEL *enters, cold and reserved.*]

COLONEL. Be seated, please!

[*The* OLD MAN *sits down deliberately. Pause.*]

(*Staring fixedly at him.*) You wrote this letter, sir?

OLD MAN. Yes!

COLONEL. Your name is Hummel? Eh?

OLD MAN. Yes!

[*Pause.*]

COLONEL. As I learn that you have bought up all my debts, overdue notes, I conclude that I am in your hands. Now what do you want?

OLD MAN. I want payment, in one way or another.

COLONEL. In what way?

OLD MAN. A very simple one—let us not talk of the money—just put up with me in your house as a guest!

COLONEL. If so little will satisfy you . . .

OLD MAN. Thanks!

COLONEL. Anything more?

OLD MAN. Discharge Bengtsson!

COLONEL. Why should I? My devoted servant, who has been with me a lifetime—and who has the medal for long and faithful service—why should I?

OLD MAN. He does possess these excellent qualities, but only in your imagination.—He is not the man he appears to be.

COLONEL. Who *is?*

OLD MAN (*taken aback*). True! But Bengtsson must go!

COLONEL. Do you mean to rule my household?

OLD MAN. Yes!—As everything I see here belongs to me—furniture, curtains, dinner ware, linen . . . and so on!

COLONEL. Anything else?

OLD MAN. Everything! All that is to be seen is mine! I own it!

COLONEL. Granted. It *is* yours! But my unsullied family honour and my good name belong to myself!

OLD MAN. No, not even that! (*Pause.*) You are not a nobleman!

COLONEL. How dare you!

OLD MAN (*takes out a paper*). If you'll read this extract from *The Armorial Gazette*, you will see that the family whose name you are using has been extinct for a century!

COLONEL (*reading*). I have heard rumours to that effect, but the name was my father's before it was mine. . . . (*Reading.*) That is true. You are right, you are right. . . . I am not a nobleman!—not even that!—Then I take off my signet ring.—Oh, I remember now . . . it belongs to you! . . . Please!

OLD MAN (*putting the ring into his pocket*). Now let us continue!—You're no Colonel either!

COLONEL. Am I not?

OLD MAN. No, you once held a temporary rank of Colonel for a short time, in the American Volunteer Force, but after the war in Cuba and the reorganization of the Army, all such titles were abolished. . . .

COLONEL. Is that true?

OLD MAN (*with a gesture toward his pocket*). Would you like to read?

COLONEL. No, it's unnecessary! . . . Who are you? What right have you to sit there stripping me naked in this fashion?

OLD MAN. You'll see by and by! But as to stripping you naked . . . do you know who you are?

COLONEL. How dare you?

OLD MAN. Take off that wig, and have a look at yourself in the mirror, but take out that set of false teeth at the same time and shave off your moustache, let Bengtsson remove your metal stays, and perhaps a certain X.Y.Z., a lackey, will recognize himself; once a cupboard lover in a certain kitchen . . .

[*The* COLONEL *makes a movement toward*

a bell on the table; the OLD MAN *forestalls him.*]
Don't touch that bell, and don't call Bengtsson, if you do I'll have him arrested . . . and—now the guests are coming, keep quiet, and we will go on playing our old parts!

COLONEL. Who are you? I recognize the voice and the eyes. . . .

OLD MAN. Don't try to find out, only be 10 silent and obey!

[*The* STUDENT *enters, and bows to the* COLONEL.]

STUDENT. How do you do, sir?

COLONEL. Welcome to my house, young man! Your splendid behaviour in connection with that great disaster has brought your name to everybody's lips, and I count it an honour to receive you in my home. . . .   20

STUDENT. My humble descent, sir . . . your illustrious name and noble birth . . .

COLONEL. May I introduce Mr. Arkenholtz—Mr. Hummel. . . . The ladies are in there, Mr. Arkenholtz—if you please—I must conclude my conversation with Mr. Hummel. . . .

[*The* STUDENT *is shown into the Hyacinth Room, where he remains visible, standing* 30 *beside the* YOUNG LADY *and talking timidly to her.*]
A splendid young man, musical, sings, writes poetry . . . if he were only a nobleman, if he belonged to our class I don't think I should object. . . . Well . . .

OLD MAN. To what?

COLONEL. Oh, my daughter . . .

OLD MAN. *Your* daughter?—But apropos 40 of that why is she always sitting in there?

COLONEL. She has to spend all her time in the Hyacinth Room when she is not out! That is a peculiarity of hers . . . Ah . . . here comes Miss Betty von Holsteinkrona, a charming creature . . . a secular Canoness, with a pension just enough to suit her birth and position. . . .

OLD MAN (*to himself*). My fiancée!

[*The* FIANCÉE *enters, white-haired and odd-looking.*]

COLONEL. Miss von Holsteinkrona— Mr. Hummel.

[*The* FIANCÉE *curtsies and takes a seat.*]

[*The* NOBLEMAN *in mourning enters and seats himself. He looks mysterious.*]
Baron Skanskorg. . . .

OLD MAN (*aside without rising*). That's the jewellery thief, I think. . . . (*To the* COLONEL.) Bring in the Mummy, and our gathering will be complete. . . .

COLONEL (*in the door of the Hyacinth Room*). Polly!

[MUMMY *enters.*]

MUMMY. Currrrr!

COLONEL. Should the young people come in too?

OLD MAN. No, not the young people! They must be spared. . . .

[*All are seated in a circle, silent.*]

COLONEL. Shall we order the tea now?

OLD MAN. What's the use! No one cares for tea, why should we sit here and be hypocrites.

[*Pause.*]

COLONEL. Shall we sit and talk then?

OLD MAN (*speaking slowly and with pauses*). Talk of the weather which we know all about; ask one another's state of health, which we know just as well; I prefer silence, then thoughts become audible and we can see the past; silence can hide nothing . . . but words can. I read the other day that the difference of languages had its origin in the desire amongst savage peoples to keep their tribal secrets hidden from outsiders. Thus every language is a code, and he who finds the key can understand every language in the world, which does not prevent secrets from leaking out without a key, and especially when paternity has to be proved, but, of course, legal proof is another matter. Two false witnesses suffice to prove anything on which they agree, but you don't bring witnesses in the adventure which I have in mind. Nature herself has planted in man a sense of modesty, which tends to hide what should be hidden. But we slip into situations unawares, and sometimes by a chance the greatest secret is unveiled, the mask is torn from the impostor, the villain is exposed. . . .

[*Pause, all look at each other in silence.*] How silent you have become!

[*Long silence.*]

Here, for instance, in this respectable house, in this attractive home, where beauty and culture and wealth join hands . . .

[*Long silence.*]

All of us who sit here, we know who we are . . . don't we? I need not say that. . . . And you know me, although you pretend ignorance. . . . There again sits my daughter, *mine*, that you know too. . . . She has lost the desire to live without knowing why . . . is withering away in this air charged with crime and deceit and falsehood of every kind . . . that is why I brought her a friend in whose company she may enjoy the light and heat that is given out by noble deeds. . . .

[*Long silence.*]

That was my mission in this house, to pull out the weeds, to expose the crimes, to settle all accounts, so that these young people can start afresh in this home which I give to them!

[*Long silence.*]

Now I grant you all a safe-conduct.

Everybody may leave in his proper turn: Whoever stays will be arrested!

[*Long silence.*]

Do you hear the ticking of the clock like a deathwatch in the wall! Can you hear what it says? "It's time! It's time! It's time!"—When it strikes shortly, your time will be up, and then you can go, but not before. You may notice, that the clock shakes its fist at you before it strikes.—Listen! There it is! "Better beware," it says. —And I can strike, too . . . (*He strikes the table with one of his crutches.*) Do you hear?

[*Silence.*]

MUMMY (*goes up to the clock and stops it, then in a clear and serious voice*). But I can stop the course of time.—I can wipe out the past and undo what is done. Not with bribes, nor with threats—but with suffering and repentance. (*Turns to the* OLD MAN.) We are miserable human beings, that we know. We have failed and we have sinned, we like the rest. We are not what we seem, but in our souls we are better than we seem, because we hate our sins. But when you, Jacob Hummel, with a false name, sit there in judgment on us, you prove yourself worse than us, miserable sinners though we be. Even you are not what you seem—you are a thief of human souls. For you stole me once upon a time by false promises. You killed the Consul, whom they buried this afternoon, strangling him with debts. You have now stolen the Student, binding him with an imaginary claim against his father, whonever owed you a halfpenny. . . .

[*The* OLD MAN, *after trying to rise and say something, sinks back into his chair. He is seen to shrink more and more during the following.*]

But there is one dark spot in your life which I do not quite know and yet suspect . . . I believe Bengtsson knows about it! (*She rings the bell on the table.*)

OLD MAN. No! not Bengtsson, not him!

MUMMY. So he does know! (*She rings again.*)

[*The little* MILKMAID *now appears in the door of the lobby, unseen by all except the* OLD MAN, *who shrinks back in horror. The* MILKMAID *vanishes when* BENGTSSON *enters.*]

Do you know this man, Bengtsson?

BENGTSSON. Oh, yes, I know him, and he me. Life has its ups and downs, as you know. I have been in his service, another time he has been in mine. He was a cupboard lover in my kitchen, fed by my cook for two whole years— because he had to be away at three o'clock the dinner was made ready at two, and the house had to eat the leavings of that brute—and he also drank the soup stock, and we had to fill it up with water—he sat out there like a vampire, and sucked the juice out of the house, so that we became like skeletons—and he nearly got us into jail when we called the cook a thief.

Later I met this man in Hamburg under another name, he was a money-lender then, a bloodsucker. But while there, he was accused of having lured a young girl out on to the ice, to drown her, because she had seen him commit a crime, and he was afraid of being exposed. . . .

MUMMY (*making a pass with her hand over the face of the* OLD MAN). That is you! And now, give up the notes and the will!

[JOHANSSON *appears in the lobby door and watches the scene with great interest, as*

his slavery has now come to an end. The OLD MAN *produces a bundle of papers and throws it on the table.*]

(*Stroking the* OLD MAN's *back*), Eh, Jacob. Is Jacob there?

OLD MAN (*like a parrot*). Jacob is there! Pretty Polly! Currrr!

MUMMY. May the clock strike?

OLD MAN (*clucks*). The clock may strike! (*Imitating a cuckoo clock.*) Cuckoo, cuckoo, cuckoo . . . cuckoo . . .

MUMMY (*opening the cupboard door*). Now the clock has struck!—Rise, and enter the cupboard, where I have spent twenty years repenting our crime.—There hangs a rope which may stand for the one with which you strangled the Consul up there, and with which you meant to strangle your benefactor . . . Go!

[*The* OLD MAN *enters the cupboard.*]

(*She closes the door.*) Bengtsson! put up the screen! the Death Screen!

[BENGTSSON *places the screen in front of the door.*]

It is finished!—God have mercy on his soul!

ALL. Amen!

[*Long silence.*]

[*The* YOUNG LADY *appears in the Hyacinth Room with a harp on which she accompanies the* STUDENT's *recitation.*]

Song with prelude.

I saw the Sun; then lo! methought
Mine eyes beheld the Hidden Power.
All men's actions have their guerdon,
Blest is he who doeth good.
No deed that we have wrought in anger
Can find in evil its atonement.
Comfort him whom thou hast grieved,
With goodness: this alone availeth.
He feareth not who doeth no evil:
Good is to be innocent.

CURTAIN

SCENE III

A room in rather bizarre style with Orien-
tal motives. Hyacinths of all colours every-
where. On the tiled stove a huge, seated
Buddha, in whose lap rests a bulb from
which the stalk of a shallot (Allium asca-
lonicum) rises, spreading its almost globular
cluster of white, starlike flowers.

An open door in the right background
leads into the Round Drawing-Room where
the COLONEL *and the* MUMMY *are seated idle* 10
and silent. A part of the Death Screen is also
visible. Another door to the left leads to the
pantry and the kitchen. The STUDENT, *the*
YOUNG LADY *(Adèle) at the table. She at*
her harp, he standing.

YOUNG LADY. Now sing to my flowers!
STUDENT. Is this the flower of your soul?
YOUNG LADY. The one and only! Do
you love the hyacinth?   20
STUDENT. I love it above all other
flowers. Its virginal shape rises slender
and straight out of the bulb which
rests on the water and sends its pure
white rootlets down into the colour-
less fluid. I love the colours of it, the
snow-white innocent pure one, the
honey-yellow sweet one, the youthful pink, the ripe red, but above all
the blue, the blue of the dewdrop, 30
deep-eyed, full of faith . . . I love
them all, more than gold and pearls,
have loved them since I was a child,
have admired them, because they
possess every fine quality that I lack
. . . yet! . . .
YOUNG LADY. What?
STUDENT. My love is not returned, for
these beautiful blossoms hate me. . . .
YOUNG LADY. How?   40
STUDENT. Their fragrance, pure and
powerful as the early winds of spring
which have passed over melting
snows, confuses my senses, deafens me,

blinds me, crowds me out of the
room, bombards me with poisoned
arrows that put woe in my heart and
fever in my head! Do you not know
the legend of that flower?
YOUNG LADY. Tell me!
STUDENT. But first to solve its riddle.
The bulb is the earth, resting on the
water or buried in the soil. Now the
stalk rises, straight as the axis of the
world and at its top are the six-
pointed star flowers.
YOUNG LADY. Above the earth—the
stars! Oh! that is a great thought,
where did you get it? How did you
discover it?
STUDENT. Let me see!—In your eyes!
—Why it is an image of the Cosmos
. . . And that is why Buddha sits
holding the earth-bulb, with brooding eyes watching to see it grow out-
wards and upwards, transforming
itself into a heaven—the poor earth
will be a heaven! That is what the
Buddha waits for!
YOUNG LADY. I see now—is not the
snowflake six-pointed too, like the
hyacinth lily?
STUDENT. You are right!—Thus the
snowflakes are falling stars . . .
YOUNG LADY. And the snowdrop is a
snow star . . . grown out of the
snow.
STUDENT. But Sirius, the largest and
most beautiful of all the red and
yellow stars in the firmament, is the
Narcissus, with its yellow and red
chalice and its six white rays. . . .
YOUNG LADY. Have you seen the shallot
blossom?
STUDENT. Indeed, I have!—It carries
its flowers within a ball, a globe
resembling the celestial one, and
strewn with white stars. . . .

YOUNG LADY. How glorious! Whose thought was that?

STUDENT. Yours!

YOUNG LADY. Yours!

STUDENT. Ours!—We two have given birth to something; we are wedded. . . .

YOUNG LADY. Not yet. . .

STUDENT. What remains?

YOUNG LADY. Waiting, trials, patience! 10

STUDENT. Well, try me! (*Pause.*) Tell me! Why do your parents sit in there so quietly, not saying a single word?

YOUNG LADY. Because they have nothing to say to each other, and because neither believes what the other says. My father puts it like this: What is the use of talking, when you can't impose upon each other?

STUDENT. That's horrible. . . .

YOUNG LADY. Here comes the Cook! . . . look at her, how big and fat she is. . . .

STUDENT. What does she want?

YOUNG LADY. She will ask me about the dinner; you see, I am looking after the house during my mother's illness. . . .

STUDENT. Have we to bother about the kitchen?

YOUNG LADY. We must eat . . . look at the Cook, I can't bear the sight of her. . . .

STUDENT. What kind of a monster is she?

YOUNG LADY. She belongs to the Hummel family of vampires. She is eating us. . . .

STUDENT. Why not discharge her?

YOUNG LADY. She won't go! We can do 40 nothing with her, and we've got her because of our sins . . . don't you see that we are pining and wasting away? . . .

STUDENT. Don't you get food then?

YOUNG LADY. Yes, many dishes, but all the nourishment is gone. . . . She boils the life out of the beef, gives us the fibre and water, while she drinks the stock herself. And when there's a roast, she first boils out the sap, eats the gravy and drinks the juice. Everything she touches loses its savour. It is as if she sucked with her eyes. We get the grounds when she has had the coffee. She drinks the wine and fills the bottle up with water. . . .

STUDENT. Kick her out!

YOUNG LADY. We can't!

STUDENT. Why?

YOUNG LADY. We don't know! She won't leave! And no one can make her—she has taken all our strength from us.

STUDENT. Will you let me dispose of her?

YOUNG LADY. No! It has to be as it is, I suppose!—Here she is! She will ask me what there is to be for dinner; I say so-and-so, she objects and gets her own way.

STUDENT. Let her decide for herself then!

YOUNG LADY. She won't decide.

STUDENT. What a strange house; it is bewitched!

YOUNG LADY. Yes!—but now she turns back, seeing you here!

COOK (*in the doorway*). No, that's not the reason! (*She grins so that her teeth show.*)

STUDENT. Out you get!

COOK. When it pleases me! (*Pause.*) Now it does please me! (*She disappears.*)

YOUNG LADY. Don't lose your temper!— Practise patience; she is part of the ordeal we face in this house! But we have a housemaid too, and we have to do the rooms again after her!

STUDENT. Now I am done! Cor in aethere! Music!

YOUNG LADY. Wait!

STUDENT. Music!

YOUNG LADY. Patience!—This room is named the Room of Ordeal.—It is beautiful to look at, but is only full of imperfections. . . .

STUDENT. Incredible! Yet such things have to be borne! It is very beautiful, although a little cold. Why don't you have a fire?

YOUNG LADY. Because the chimney smokes.

STUDENT. Can't you sweep the chimney?

YOUNG LADY. It doesn't help! . . . Do you see that writing-desk?

STUDENT. Remarkably handsome!

YOUNG LADY. But one leg is too short; every day I put a piece of cork under that leg; every day the housemaid takes it away when she sweeps the room; every day I have to cut a new piece. The penholder and writing materials too are spotted with ink every morning, and I have to clean them after that woman, as sure as the sun rises. (*Pause.*) What is the worst thing you can think of?

STUDENT. To count the washing! Ugh!

YOUNG LADY. That's what I have to do! Ugh!

STUDENT. Anything else?

YOUNG LADY. To be waked out of your sleep and have to get up and rehook the window . . . which the house-maid has left unlatched.

STUDENT. Anything else!

YOUNG LADY. To get up on a ladder and tie on the cord which the housemaid has torn from the window blind.

STUDENT. Anything else!

YOUNG LADY. To sweep after her; to dust after her; to start the fire again, after she has merely thrown some wood into the stove! To watch the damper in the stove; to wipe every glass; to lay the table over again; to open the wine bottles; to see that the rooms are aired; to remake my bed; to rinse the water-bottle that is green with sediment; to buy matches and soap, which are always lacking; to wipe the chimneys and cut the wicks to keep the lamps from smoking . . . and to keep them from going out when we have company, I have to fill them myself. . . .

STUDENT. Music!

YOUNG LADY. Wait!—The labour comes first, the labour of keeping the dirt of life at a distance!

STUDENT. But aren't you wealthy? Why not have two servants!

YOUNG LADY. That wouldn't help! Even if there were three! It is troublesome to live, and at times I get tired . . . think then if there were a nursery as well!

STUDENT. The greatest of joys . . .

YOUNG LADY. And the most expensive. . . . Is life worth so much trouble?

STUDENT. I suppose it depends on the reward you expect for your labours . . . to win your hand I would shrink from nothing.

YOUNG LADY. Don't say that!—You can never get me!

STUDENT. Why?

YOUNG LADY. You mustn't ask. (*Pause.*)

STUDENT. You dropped your bracelet out of the window . . .

YOUNG LADY. Because my hand had grown so small. . . .

[*Pause. The* COOK *appears with a Japanese bottle in her hand.*]

There is the one who eats me and all of us alive.

STUDENT. What has she in her hand?

COOK. This is the colouring bottle with letters like scorpions on it. It's the soy that turns water into bouillon, and that takes the place of gravy. You can make cabbage soup out of it, you can make mock turtle soup out of it.

STUDENT. Get out!

COOK. You take the sap out of us, and

we out of you; we keep the blood and give you back the water—with the colouring. It is colour that counts! —Now I am going, but I'll stay just the same, as long as I please!

[*She goes out.*]

STUDENT. Why has Bengtsson got a medal?

YOUNG LADY. For his great merits.

STUDENT. Has he no faults?

YOUNG LADY. Yes, great ones, but faults bring you no medals.

[*Both smile.*]

STUDENT. You have many secrets in this house. . . .

YOUNG LADY. As in all houses . . . permit us to keep ours! (*Pause.*)

STUDENT. Do you care for frankness?

YOUNG LADY. Within reason!

STUDENT. At times I am overwhelmed with a craving to say all I think; yet I know the world would go to pieces if one were perfectly frank. (*Pause.*) I attended a funeral the other day . . . in the church—it was very solemn and beautiful

YOUNG LADY. That of Mr. Hummel?

STUDENT. Yes, that of my pretended benefactor!—An elderly friend of the deceased acted as mace bearer and stood at the head of the coffin. I was particularly impressed by the dignified manner and moving words of the clergyman—I cried and we all cried.—Afterwards we went to a restaurant and there I learned that the man with the mace had been too friendly with the dead man's son . . .

[*The* YOUNG LADY *stares at him, trying to make out his meaning.*]

I learned too, that the dead man had borrowed money from his son's devoted friend . . . (*Pause.*) Next day the clergyman was arrested for embezzling the church funds!—Nice, isn't it!

YOUNG LADY. Oh! (*Pause.*)

STUDENT. Do you know what I am thinking about you now?

YOUNG LADY. Don't tell me, or I'll die!

STUDENT. I must, otherwise I shall die!
. . .

YOUNG LADY. It is only in a madhouse you say all that you think. . . .

STUDENT. Exactly! My father finished up in a madhouse. . . .

YOUNG LADY. Was he sick?

STUDENT. No, he was well, but he was mad! You see, it broke out once, and these are the circumstances . . . Like all of us, he had his circle of acquaintances, he called them friends for short. They were a lot of scoundrels, of course, as people mostly are; he had to have some society, however, as he couldn't be all alone. As you know, no one tells people what he thinks of them, in everyday life, and he didn't either. Of course he knew how false they were, he sounded the depths of their perfidy, but he was a wise man and well brought up, and so he always remained polite. One day, however, he gave a big party— it was in the evening and he was tired out by a hard day's work and the double strain of keeping silent and talking rot to his guests . . .

[*The* YOUNG LADY *is horrified.*]

Well, at the dinner table he rapped for silence, raised his glass to begin to speak . . . then something loosened the trigger, and in a long speech he stripped the whole company naked, one by one, told them all their treacheries and tired out sat down in the middle of the table and shouted at them "Go to Hell!"

YOUNG LADY. Oh!

STUDENT. I was present, and I shall never forget what happened after that! . . . Father and mother came to blows, the guests rushed to the doors . . . and my father was taken to a madhouse, where he died! (*Pause*.) By keeping still too long water stagnates and rots, and so it is in this house too, for there is something very rotten here. And yet I thought it paradise itself when I saw you enter the first time . . . it was a Sunday morning, and I stood gazing into these rooms. I saw a Colonel who was no Colonel. I had a generous benefactor who was a thief and had to hang himself. I saw a mummy who was not a mummy, and a virgin— how about the virginity by the by? . . . Where is beauty to be found? In nature, and in my mind when it is in its Sunday clothes. Where, honour and faith! In fairy tales and children's plays. Where can I find anything that fulfils its promise? . . . In my imagination!—Now your flowers have poisoned me, and I have given the poison back to you—I asked you to become my wife in a home full of poetry, and song and music; and then the Cook appeared . . . Sursum corda! Try once more to strike fire and purple out of the golden harp . . . try, I ask you, I implore you on my knees. . . . Well, then I'll do it myself! (*He picks up the harp, but the strings give no sound*.) It is dumb and deaf! To think that the most beautiful flowers are so poisonous, are the most poisonous. A curse lies on the whole creation and on life. . . . Why would you not be my bride? Because the well-spring of life in you is sick . . . now I feel the vampire in the kitchen begins to suck my life. She must be a Lamia, one of those that suck the blood of children. It is always in the servants' quarters that the seed-leaves of the children are

nipped, if that has not already happened in the bedroom . . . there are poisons that destroy the sight, and poisons that open the eyes.—I seem to have been born with the last, for I cannot see the ugly as the beautiful, or call evil good—I cannot! Jesus Christ descended into hell. That meant His pilgrimage on earth, to this madhouse, this jail, this morgue —this earth. And the madmen killed him when he wished to liberate them, but the robber was set free. The robber always gets sympathy! Woe, woe! to all of us! Saviour of the world, save us, we perish!

[*The* YOUNG LADY *has collapsed. She seems to be dying. She manages to ring a bell.* BENGTSSON *enters.*]

YOUNG LADY. Bring the screen! Quick! —I am dying!

[BENGTSSON *comes back with the screen, opens it and places it in front of the* YOUNG LADY.]

STUDENT. The liberator is coming! Welcome, thou pale and gentle one!— Sleep beauteous, unhappy innocent creature, whose sufferings are undeserved. Sleep without dreaming, and when you wake again . . . may you be greeted by a sun that does not burn, in a home with no dust, by friends without stain, by a love without flaw! . . . Thou wise and gentle Buddha, who sittest waiting there to see a Heaven sprout from the earth, endow us with patience in the hour of trial, and with purity of will, so that our hope be not cherished in vain!

[*The strings of the harp hum softly, and a white light floods the room.*]

I saw the Sun; then lo! methought
Mine eyes beheld the Hidden Power.
All men's actions have their guerdon,
Blest is he who doeth good.

No deed that we have wrought in anger
Can find in evil its atonement.
Comfort him whom thou hast grieved,
With goodness: this alone availeth.
He feareth not who doeth no evil:
Good is to be innocent.

[*A faint moaning sound is heard from behind the screen.*]

STUDENT. You poor little child, you child of this world of illusion, guilt, suffering, and death; this world of eternal change, disappointment and pain! May the Lord of Heaven have mercy on you in your journey.

[*The whole room disappears, and in its place appears "The Island of the Dead" by Böecklin as background. Soft music, very quiet and pleasantly sad, is heard from the distant island.*]

CURTAIN

GERHART HAUPTMANN

THE NAME OF Gerhart Hauptmann is naturally bracketed with that of Ibsen, Strindberg, and Chekhov as one of the founders of modern drama. Since the evening of October 20, 1889, when the Freie Bühne, the new German theatrical organization modeled on the Théâtre Libre in Paris, produced his first play with tumultuous effect, he has been steadily before the public of the world as the greatest playwright of Germany. That play was called *Before Dawn*. It was a bloody slice of life in the best naturalistic form. The scene is Silesia; the people are, most of them, degenerate beyond redemption; and their lives are a mess. A corrupt heredity and a hostile environment have made tragic ruin of the Krause family. They suddenly got hold of money through the discovery of coal on their farm. Old man Krause has become a drunken and vicious sot. One of his daughters is also a confirmed drunkard whose offspring are either stillborn or die of alcoholism in early childhood. Her husband is a lecher who is now lusting after the one gentle creature in the play, Krause's younger daughter Helene. Krause's second wife is also carrying on with a corrupt neighbor boy whom she wants to marry to Helene. Helene returns to this degradation from a Moravian convent. She falls in love with a visiting social worker, Alfred Loth, and it looks as if she at least might be rescued from disaster. But Loth makes inquiries into her family background and hustles promptly away from danger. Helene lays hold of

the big hunting knife that has been conspicuously hanging on the wall and stabs herself. And as the curtain falls, old Krause, roaring drunk again, staggers in singing a licentious tavern song.

The relation of this play to *Ghosts*, *The Power of Darkness*, the novels of Zola, and such works is obvious. Like them it was lauded or attacked by the critics according to their position on the new naturalistic movement in letters. Those who denied the existence of such people, or believed that this kind of subject matter was unavailable to dramatists, called Hauptmann "the painter of the putrid" and the "glorifier of the unclean," though just in what respects *Before Dawn* "glorified" the Krauses is mystifying. The enthusiastic and able group who were encouraging naturalism and making stage production of its plays possible, hailed young Hauptmann as "a budding Goethe, the coming glory of the New Movement." Hauptmann, with the help of his friends and sponsors, soon won the day. Before the 1890's were well under way, Hauptmann was a dramatist famed throughout the world for his exact and objective portrayal of lowly types from his native province.

The Silesian background of *Before Dawn* and many of the more celebrated plays was not accidental. Hauptmann, christened Gerhart Johanne Robert, was born in the village of Obersalzbrunn in that district on November 15, 1862. His family was peasant stock, but at the time of his birth Gerhart's father

117

was the proprietor of a well-known and prosperous hotel, "Zur Preussischen Krone," just outside the village. Hauptmann's grandfather, like his own father before him, had been a weaver, but had given up that trade to become a waiter. He worked hard and intelligently to better himself, and within a few years he had risen to a position as independent keeper of an inn at Obersalzbrunn. Gerhart's father inherited this establishment. This public house furnished the future dramatist an admirable vantage point from which to view the life about him; his own family tradition was rich in human experience; and the combination was useful to him in his dramas. His mother was a member of a pious Moravian family. Her zeal and emotional intensity had a profound effect upon Hauptmann. This may be observed in *Rose Bernd*, *The Fool in Christ*, and especially in *Hannele*, wherein he showed how deeply he understood the emotional nature of the Christian religion and the faith of the little child which it exalts.

Hauptmann was a poor student at the village school. He failed to improve measurably during the four years he spent at the Realschule at Breslau, whither he went in 1874 with his two older brothers, Carl and Georg. He was distinguished only for indifference and inattention to the curriculum. When his father experienced difficulties because of competitors and changing conditions in the village, Hauptmann was withdrawn from the school and placed under the supervision of a maternal uncle near Striegan to study agriculture. But Hauptmann was certainly not cut out for a farmer. He learned more about people and lonely lives than he did about agriculture. The experience of these years provided him

with more invaluable dramatic materials for the future. *Before Dawn* drew upon the peasants and the countryside, and many individual characters throughout his plays were created from the people he knew in and about Striegan.

As Hauptmann's boredom with agriculture intensified, a strong desire to be an artist formed within him, and on the advice of his brother Carl he returned to Breslau in 1880 to enter the Royal College of Art. He stayed there, with some interruptions, until the spring of 1882, when he went on to the University of Jena where his brother Carl was a student. He remained there less than a year, but he was finally beginning to find himself and settle down to work. As his biographer Ludwig Lewishon remarks, "the value of this restless shifting in his early years is apparent. For the discontent that marked his unquiet youth made for a firm retention of impressions. Observation, in the saying of Balzac, springs from suffering, and Hauptmann saw the Silesian country folk and the artists of Breslau with an almost morbid exactness of vision."

At this point, although he had tried his hand at two dramas (*Germans and Romans* and *Ingeborg*, glorifying Germanic history and myth), instead of following the prescribed course of study at Breslau, Hauptmann decided to go to Rome in the warm south and become a sculptor. He sailed from Hamburg in 1883 on a cargo steamer owned by his prosperous merchant brother Georg, making calls at all the important Spanish and Mediterranean ports. He was so inspired by all that he saw and felt that he wrote a Childe Haroldish poem about it ponderously titled *Promethidenlos*. This was published in 1885, and was Hauptmann's first book.

Its only value to us is its autobiographical nature and the forecast of the poet of *Hannele* and *The Sunken Bell*. On this journey which seems to have lasted some six months, he spent more of his time writing than in the practice of sculpture; but he went again to Rome in the spring of 1884 and ambitiously set up an atelier. There he caught typhoid fever and had to return to Hamburg where his future wife nursed him back to health. He married Marie Thienemann early in 1885; she was very well-to-do and they had no need to worry about making a living. They established themselves at Erkner, a suburb of Berlin, and Hauptmann after a short period of continued uncertainty plunged unreservedly into literature.

Hauptmann had selected a propitious moment. Germany attained national greatness with her victories over Austria and France. She looked toward parallel glories in literature. These glories however did not immediately appear; they had to await a new generation who could interpret the new spirit of the nation. Premonitory voices were soon heard. The brothers Heinrich and Julius Hart lamented the way German drama imitated the French and avoided fresh and original approaches to human experience. Michael Conrad began to edit the magazine *Die Gesellschaft* in 1885 to support the faithful naturalism of Zola with its passion for science and objective observation. The following year the society *Durch* was established to canalize the enthusiasm of the young artistic group around Berlin. Arno Holz and Johannes Schlaf were formulating theories and experimenting with methods for creating the illusion of life through the medium of exact speech—"consistent naturalism." Otto Brahm and Paul Schlenther founded the Freie Bühne to produce plays that could not pass the official censor or survive the economic pressures of the commercial theatre.

These men and many others were creating the intellectual atmosphere of the young Germany and encouraging production. Their creed was summed up by Michael Conrad when he said that literature and criticism must be "liberated from the tyranny of the conventional young lady." Hauptmann himself has left in his *The Rats* (1911) a comprehensive picture of the conflict between the old and the new concept of what a play should be and how it should be produced and acted. The body of the play is stark naturalism, and there is a close parallel between the title and the people whose lives are depicted in this dark and musty tenement and storage house. Bruno, the brutal moron who toys with a rat trap and casually commits the murder, is simply a rat. All the characters are caught in various traps provided by the mysterious purposes of life itself. But as a sub-plot Hauptmann presents an old-style romantic director, Hassenreuter, who tries to teach to his rebellious pupil Spitta all the out-moded elocutionary tricks of voice and gesture. And in protest the pupil states the theory of this young school of writers:

"Spitta: Yes, all this stilted, rhetorical stuff is quite foreign to my nature. . . . I don't care for the whole sonorous bombast of the 'Bride of Messina.'

"Hassenreuter: . . . You asserted the other day that, in certain circumstances, a barber or a scrubwoman might as fittingly be the protagonist of a tragedy as Lady Macbeth or King Lear!

"Spitta: Before art as before the law all men are equal, sir."

Hauptmann's career was begun in this high-pitched and crusading period at the close of the 1880's. His house at Erkner, "the last in the village, half buried in woods and with far prospects over the heaths and deep green, melancholy waters of Brandenburg," was a frequent meeting place for these young literary leaders. His own bent was toward sympathetic brooding over the lowly and oppressed people who needed a champion. His talent was for reproducing the stresses of his time rather than for original invention or interpretation. His abilities fitted in perfectly with the naturalistic movement and its dedication to exact and plotless reproduction of the lives of little creatures beaten by the world and forgotten by literature.

Following his first successes Hauptmann retired to his native Silesia in 1891. A stream of plays came from his pen, most of them dealing with the poor and the oppressed, some in the astringent vein of "consistent naturalism," others relieved by the beauty of poetic form and feeling. His reputation continuously ascended until about 1912, and then began to level off before the period of actual decline following the World War. He visited America in 1892. Vienna unexpectedly honored him with the coveted Grillparzer prize for *Hannele* (1893). Oxford University conferred upon him an honorary degree in 1905. He was awarded the Nobel Prize for Literature in 1912, presumably in recognition of *The Weavers*. The award coincided with his successful novel *Atlantis*, which attracted especial attention in America, not so much for the merits of its story of the obsessed German physician who was wrecked with his paramour in the Atlantic Ocean, as for its apparent description of Ameri-

cans whom Hauptmann had met on his journey to this country, and the extraordinary coincidence of the sinking of the *Titanic* paralleling the vivid description of the wreck in *Atlantis*.

Hauptmann was elaborately honored by his country on the occasion of his sixtieth birthday in 1922. By decree of President Ebert a great celebration and dramatic festival was held at Breslau as a tribute to him, and the presidential proclamation called him "the bearer of the Republic's banner . . . the spiritual president of the state." Hauptmann came down from his villa above Agentendorf in the Silesian Mountains and spoke on the new spirit of Germany. In the same year Hauptmann was decorated with the Vienna Cross. He made a speech of acceptance at the University of Vienna that sounded ominous to his liberal admirers. He condemned the Versailles treaty as "grotesque," described the state of his people as a "purgatory," and called for a new religion that would substitute for the old Christian philosophies a worship of the state. He took an active political interest in post-war Germany that seemed to be more and more in keeping with the views of the rising Nazis. Adolf Hitler, who drove most of Germany's literary men into exile or concentration camps, burnt their books, and confiscated their property, canonized Hauptmann in 1933 with the compliment, "*Sein Titel ist die 'Goldene Harfe.'*"

Little has been heard of the dramatist since the rise of Hitler. Bits of news appear from time to time to the effect that he who was once rebellious and secular is now "complacent and religious," that he lives "in an air tight chamber, apart from world events" in his native Silesia, and that he is a mouthpiece of the Nazis. Bernard Sobel confirms the report that Hauptmann was "the model of the renegade playwright who, in the face of German National Socialism, deserts the cause of humanity in S. N. Berhman's *Rain from Heaven.*" Whatever the truth about his life in the terrible decade of the 1930's, the fact remains that much of his prestige as a man has gone down in ruins outside of Germany. Fortunately we have to do with the young dramatist in the eager years of the 1890's and the first decade of the present century. The man and the dramas of that golden period have retained their lustre.

Hauptmann's first plays are very good models of the naturalistic drama. They keep faithfully to the free plotless movement of life itself, eschewing all theatrical tricks and stage devices. The natural flow of life itself is transferred to the stage, and the common speech, dialect, and colloquialisms are reproduced. They usually treat the sordid side of life that had been neglected in the preceding romantic period. *The Festival of Peace* (1890) is a heavily ironic title for a drama of father-son quarrels in a mal-adjusted family. *Lonely Lives* (1891) is a grim portrait of Johannes Vockerat, who, with his difficult domestic and artistic problems, is much like Hauptmann himself; for the play is based on the breakdown of Hauptmann's own marriage, and presents the problems and the heartaches which he himself was facing in those critical years. It also pictures one of the new women in Anna Mahr, and it ends with the conventional suicide of the hero. It sounds like *Rosmersholm,* to which it was indebted.

Colleague Crampton (1892), his fourth play, was the first of the comedies of which *The Beaver Coat* (1893) is probably the best example. Crampton was drawn with some malice and a little sympathy from Hauptmann's own indifferent academic experiences. *The Weavers* also came in 1892 and is rightly regarded as one of Hauptmann's best plays. To modern readers accustomed to plays about the ill-fed third of the nation written with a bristling ideology, *The Weavers* seems passive and without hope. For Hauptmann was content merely to exhibit with faithful accuracy the serious dislocation in the economic life of this group of weavers to which his own grandfather and great grandfather belonged. It is nobody's fault; it is the system. Much of the telling effect of the play is achieved by the irony of the last scene, and the extreme pathos of the ending. The play is one of the best examples of German Naturalism, and it is important as the first great play on the proletariat and its mob conflict with the owners of the means of production. The presentation of the play aroused heated controversy.

At this point in Hauptmann's career he introduced a new dimension into his dramas and wrote the tender *Hannele* (1893). The basic incident and the physical setting are as sombre and desolate as those in *Before Dawn,* but the bare room of the almshouse and the wretched pallet on which Hannele lies are softened by the appearance of the angels and the poetic rendering of Hannele's vision. The play unites successfully the naturalism of *The Weavers* and the poetic symbolism of *The Sunken Bell.* It was presented at the Royal Theatre in Berlin, November 13, 1893. Antoine came up from Paris to the première; he was so enchanted with its realistic beginning and its mystic-symbolical ending that he presented it

at the Théâtre Libre. Some critics
thought it might excite too much sympathy for the poor; others abused
Hauptmann for deserting naturalism;
but most people were impressed by the
poetic charm of the performance. The
results were the same when it was
produced in New York in 1894. It was
presented there again in 1910 by
Harrison Grey Fiske with Mrs. Fiske
in the title role, and has had other
performances since that time.

Hannele is static in the style of Maeterlinck, whose popular success was contemporary with the shift in Hauptmann's manner. But it is saved from
imitativeness by its firm handling of the
realistic setting and dialogue, as it
avoids sentimentality by its authentic
poetry. Though Hauptmann is better
known for The Weavers, Rose Bernd, and
Michael Kramer in one style, and The
Sunken Bell in another, his Hannele must
be counted among the finest of his
works. As Edward E. Hale, Jr., wrote
in 1900, "If one could read but one
play of Hauptmann's, the one to read
would be Hannele Himmelfahrt. . . . It
is in fact, although the shortest, yet the
greatest of its author's plays." And he
adds that it is the only one of the plays
not equalled by somebody else. Hannele
in its simplicity reflects all human aspi-
ration and pathos, and in apparent
defeat affirms the unconquerable
courage and hope of life itself.

HANNELE

A Dream Poem

CHARACTERS

HANNELE

GOTTWALD (afterwards The Stranger),
    a Schoolmaster

SISTER MARTHA, *a Deaconess*

TULPE

HETE (Hedwig)   ⎫ *Inmates of an Alms-*

PLESCHKE   ⎬ *house*

HANKE   ⎭

SEIDEL, *a Woodcutter*

BERGER, *a Magistrate*

SCHMIDT, *a Police Official*

DR. WACHLER

APPARITIONS INTRODUCED DURING HANNELE'S DELIRIUM

MATTERN (a Mason), *supposed to be*
    Hannele's Father

THE FORM OF HANNELE'S DEAD MOTHER

A GREAT DARK ANGEL

THREE ANGELS OF LIGHT

THE DEACONESS

GOTTWALD

GOTTWALD'S PUPILS

PLESCHKE

HANKE AND OTHER PAUPERS

SEIDEL

A VILLAGE DOCTOR

FOUR YOUTHS, CLAD IN WHITE

NUMEROUS BRIGHT ANGELS, GREAT AND
    SMALL

MOURNERS

WOMEN, ETC.

"Suffer little Children to come unto Me, and forbid them not. For of such is the Kingdom of Heaven."

ACT I

Scene—A room in the Almshouse of a village in the mountains. Bare walls. A door at centre, back. To the left of this door is a small window. Before the window are a rickety table and a bench. Near the table and to the left of it is a stove.

To the right of the door is a pallet with a straw mattress and a few ragged cover= lets.

It is a stormy December evening.

At the table, seated and singing a hymn which she reads from a hymn book, by the light of a tallow candle, sits TULPE, an old, ragged pauper.

HANNELE: Rendered into English verse by Charles Henry Meltzer. This play is published by arrangement with Harrison Grey Fiske, sole owner of the publishing and acting rights by contract with Gerhart Hauptmann and Carl and Theodor Rosenfeld. In its present form it is dedicated to the reading public only and no performance of it can be given without Mr. Fiske's permission.

TULPE (*sings in a cracked, quavering voice*).
Jesus, lover of my soul,
Let me to Thy bosom fly,
While the waves of tr-ouble. . . .
[*Enter* HEDWIG, *familiarly known as* HETE,
*a disreputable woman of about thirty, with
curly hair. Round her head is wrapped a
thick cloth. She carries a bundle under her
arm. Her dress is light and shabby.*]
HETE (*blowing on her fingers*). Mercy on 10
us, nice weather we're havin'. (*Drops
her bundle on the table and goes on blowing her fingers, standing alternately on
each of her feet, which are shod in worn-
out old boots.*) We ain't had such
weather for an age.
TULPE. What have yer got in there?
HETE (*grinning and whining with pain, sits
on the bench by the stove and tries to take
off her boots*). Oh, Lord! My blessed 20
toes are just burnin'!
TULPE (*unties Hete's bundle, in which are
seen a loaf, a packet of chicory, a bag of
coffee, a few pairs of stockings, etc.*). Ain't
there nothin' for me in your bundle?
HETE (*at first too busy with her boots to
mind* TULPE. *Suddenly snatches at the
bundle and collects its contents*).
Tulpe! (*One of* HETE's *feet is bare. She
piles her belongings together and carries* 30
them off to the pallet.) Now you'd best
leave my things alone—D'you think
I've been trampin' about and freezin'
all the bones in my body for *you*, eh?
TULPE. Ah, yer needn't make such a
fuss about it, you fool! (*Rises, closes
her hymn book, and wipes it carefully with
her skirt.*) I don't want none of the
rubbish you've been beggin' for.
HETE (*hiding her property under the mattress*). 40
Beggin'? I'd like to know who's done
most beggin'—you or me! You've
done nothin' else all your life. And
you're no chicken, neither.
TULPE. Don't you fly out about it. We
know the sort er life *you've* led. Pastor

told you what he thought of *you*, he
did. I didn't tramp about the streets
when *I* was a girl. *I* was respect'ble.
HETE. I s'pose that's why you were sent
to jail!
TULPE. You'll get there fast enough,
don't you fear, my beauty. Just you
let me get a sight of a gendarme,
that's all. I could tell him a thing or
two about you, 's sure 's yer live!
HETE. Oh, shut up! I don't care for
your gendarmes. Let 'em come and
see if I don't tell 'em somethin' as'll
make you feel uncomfort'ble.
TULPE. Yer can't say nothin' against
me!
HETE. Oh, I can't, can't I? Who stole
the overcoat from the innkeeper's
little boy, eh?
[TULPE *makes as though to spit at* HETE.]
That's what you call manners, I
s'pose? Yer shan't have nothin' now,
just to spite yer.
TULPE. Ah, go on! I wouldn't take
anythin' from the likes er you, anyhow.
HETE. No, and you won't get nothin'.
[PLESCHKE *and* HANKE *appear outside the
open door, against which they have been
literally blown by the howling wind.*
PLESCHKE, *a scrofulous, childish old man,
in rags, bursts out laughing.* HANKE, *a
good-for-nothing blackguard, blasphemes.
They are seen to shake the snow off their
hats and cloaks. Each carries a bundle.*]
PLESCHKE. Lord, how it do blow! One
er these 'ere nights, you see if the
old shanty ain't smashed to bits!
[*At sight of the newcomers,* HETE *hurriedly drags her bundle from beneath the
mattress, picks it up and runs past the men
into the courtyard and up a flight of stairs.*]
PLESCHKE (*calling after* HETE). Hey!
Hulloa! Yer in a hurry! Wot are yer
runnin' away fur? We won't hurt yer,
will we, Hanke?

TULPE (*busy at the stove with a saucepan*). Oh, she ain't right in her head. She thinks you'll steal her bundle.

PLESCHKE (*enters*). Lord save us! That's rough on us, that is! Evenin'! G'd evenin'! Good Lord, what weather! Hang me if I wasn't a'most blown off my feet! (*Limps to the table, lays his bundle down, and wags his white-haired, feeble head at* TULPE. *Pants from fatigue, coughs and tries to warm himself. Meanwhile,* HANKE *enters, lays his beggar's bag against the door and shivers with cold as he puts fuel into the stove.*)

TULPE. Where er you been?

PLESCHKE (*stuttering*). Where—where have I been? Quite a way, quite a way. Up in the hills.

TULPE. Brought anythin' back?

PLESCHKE. Lots—lots of things. Th' priest giv' me this 'ere five-pfenniger, and down at th' inn they give me—er—give me—er—a bowl er soup——

TULPE. Hand it over, and I'll warm it up. (*Takes a pot out of the bundle, sets it on the table and stirs the contents of the saucepan.*)

PLESCHKE. I—I've got somethin' else in here—sausage. The butcher give it to me. Ay, the butcher.

TULPE. Where's the money?

PLESCHKE. Oh, the money's all right. Here's the money.

TULPE. Give it t'me. I'll take care of it for yer.

HETE (*re-enters*). Yer blamed old fool, why d' yer let her have it? (*She goes to the stove.*)

TULPE. You mind yer own business.

HANKE. Don't worry. He's her sweet-heart.

HETE. Saints alive!

HANKE. It's only right he should bring her home a trifle now and then, ain't it?

PLESCHKE (*stammering*). You—you ought —oughter know—better, you ought. Can't yer leave a poor old man alone an'—n—not make game of him?

HETE (*mimicking* PLESCHKE). W—why d—don't yer l—let the poor old man alone? Pleschke, yer gettin' shaky. You won't last much longer.

PLESCHKE (*threatening her with a stick*). Y—you'd best c—clear outer this!

HETE. I'd like to see you make me clear out.

PLESCHKE. Clear out! D'ye hear?

TULPE. Catch her one on the head. It'll do her good.

PLESCHKE. Clear out!

HANKE. Oh, drop it! Leave her alone. [HETE, *taking advantage of* HANKE's *having turned his back to defend her from* PLESCHKE, *makes a grab at his bag and tries to steal something from it.* TULPE *sees her and shakes with laughter.*]

HANKE. I don't see much to laugh about.

TULPE (*still laughing*). He don't see nothin' to laugh at!

PLESCHKE. Oh, Lord, just look at her!

TULPE. Yer'd best look arter yer bag, or maybe you'll miss somethin'.

HANKE (*turns and sees that he has been tricked*). You would, would you, you devil! (*Rushes after* HETE.) Just you let me get at you!

[*Tramping of feet, as* HANKE *runs up the staircase after* HETE. *Smothered cries.*]

PLESCHKE. Well, well, well! She's a smart 'un. (*He laughs.*)

[TULPE *joins in his laughter, which is interrupted by the sound of the sudden opening and shutting of a door.*]

W—what was that?

[*Howling wind heard outside. Snow dashes against the window-panes. Then all is quiet for a moment. The schoolmaster,* GOTTWALD, *a man of two and thirty, with a dark beard, enters, carrying* HANNELE MATTERN, *a girl of about fourteen. The child whimpers. Her long red hair streams over the schoolmaster's shoulders. Her face is pressed against his throat, her arms hang straight and limp. The rags in which she is clothed barely cover her.* GOTTWALD *takes no notice of* PLESCHKE *and* TULPE, *carries the child in tenderly, and lays her on the bed, which stands on the right near the wall. He is followed by* SEIDEL, *a wood-cutter, who carries a lantern in one hand. He also carries a saw, an axe, and a bundle of rags. On his grey head he wears a shabby old hat.*]

PLESCHKE (*staring stupidly at the newcomers*). Hulloa, hulloa, hulloa! W— what's the matter?

GOTTWALD (*laying his overcoat and some blankets over* HANNELE). Hot bricks, Seidel! Quick!

SEIDEL (*to* TULPE). Don't stand there doin' nothin'. Heat some bricks. Look sharp!

TULPE. What's the matter with the girl?

SEIDEL. I've no time for talkin'. (*Exit with* TULPE.)

GOTTWALD (*trying to soothe* HANNELE). There, there, don't you fear. We'll soon put you right.

HANNELE (*her teeth chattering*). I'm afraid! I'm afraid!

GOTTWALD. Fear nothing. We won't let any harm come to you.

HANNELE. It's father! It's father!

GOTTWALD. Why, he's not here, my dear.

HANNELE. I'm afraid of father. Oh, if he should come!

GOTTWALD. Ssh! Ssh! He won't come.

[*Hurried steps are heard on the staircase.* HETE *bustles in, with an iron grater in her hand.*]

HETE (*holding up the grater*). Just look what Hanke's got!

[HANKE *rushes in after* HETE *and tries to take the grater from her. She flings it into the middle of the room.*]

HANNELE (*screams with terror*). He's coming! He's coming! (*She half rises, leans forward, with anguish on her pale, sick, pinched little face, and stares at the place from which the noise comes.* HETE *dodges away from* HANKE *and runs into the back room.* HANKE *goes to pick up the grater.*)

HANKE (*astonished*). I'll give you a taste of it presently, you slut, you!

GOTTWALD (*to* HANNELE). It's all right, my child. (*to* HANKE). What are you doing here?

HANKE. What am *I* doin' here?

HETE (*putting her head in at the back door*). 'Tain't his! He stole it!

HANKE (*threatening*). You wait a bit! I'll get even with you.

GOTTWALD. I beg you to be quiet. The child's ill.

HANKE (*picks up the grater and draws back abashed*). Why, what's the matter?

SEIDEL (*enters with two bricks*). These ought to do.

GOTTWALD (*examining the bricks*). Are they warm enough?

SEIDEL. Oh, they'll warm her. (*He puts one of the bricks under Hannele's feet.*)

GOTTWALD. Put the other one there. (*Points to another place.*)

SEIDEL. She don't seem much warmer yet.

GOTTWALD. The child's shivering with cold.

[TULPE *has entered, following* SEIDEL. *Behind her enter* HETE *and* PLESCHKE *and several other paupers, who stand in the doorway whispering and fussing about inquisitively.* TULPE *moves to the bedside and stands there with her arms a-kimbo.*]

TULPE. Brandy and hot water 'ud do her good.

SEIDEL (*pulls out a flask. So do* PLESCHKE *and* HANKE). There's just a drop left.

TULPE (*at the stove*). Bring it here.

SEIDEL. Is the water hot?

TULPE. Scaldin' !

GOTTWALD. You'd better put in a lump of sugar.

HETE. Where d' yer s'pose we'd get sugar from?

TULPE. Ah, shut up! Yer know yer 've got some stowed away.

HETE. Yer lie, I ain't got no sugar. (*Laughs nervously.*)

TULPE. It's *you* that's lyin'. I saw yer bring it in. 10

SEIDEL (*to* HETE). Run and get it, can't you?

HANKE (*to* HETE). What are yer waitin' for?

HETE (*doggedly*). Fetch it yerself.

PLESCHKE. Get the sugar!

HETE. Yer can get all yer want at the grocer's. (*Exit.*)

SEIDEL. And if you don't get some at the grocer's, double quick time—— Well, 20 you'll see! That's all I've got to say. You won't want more nor I'll give you, my lass.

PLESCHKE (*who has been out, returns*). Ah, she's a bad lot, she is.

SEIDEL. I'd like to have the handlin' of her. I'd take her down a bit, I would, if I was the Burgomaster. She's got no business to be in an almshouse— a great, big, healthy slut like her. 30 Why don't she work?

PLESCHKE. H—here's a—b—b—bit of sugar.

HANKE (*sniffing the aroma of the grog*). I'd like to be ill myself, I would!

[SCHMIDT *enters with a lantern. His manner is important and impressive.*]

SCHMIDT. Now then, make room there. The Judge 'll be here in a moment.

[BERGER, *the magistrate, enters. His manner* 40 *stamps him as a retired officer. He wears a short beard. Although his hair is grizzled, he seems still youthful and good-looking. He wears a well-cut, long overcoat. His cocked hat is set jauntily on his head. One of his characteristics is a boyish swagger.*]

THE PAUPERS. Evenin', Judge. Evenin', Captain!

BERGER. Evenin'. (*Takes off his hat and cloak and puts them down with his stick. With a commanding gesture.*) Out with you, the whole lot of you!

[SCHMIDT *hustles* THE PAUPERS *into the back room.*]

BERGER. Evenin', Schoolmaster. (*Holds out his hand.*) How are you getting on?

GOTTWALD. We've just pulled the child out of the water!

SEIDEL (*stepping forward*). Excuse me, Judge. (*Makes a military salute.*) I was working later than usual down at t' smithy. You see, I was puttin' a new clamp round my axe—and just as I was comin' out er—t' smithy—down yonder by the pond, Judge—you know the big pond—it's pretty nigh as big as a lake—— (BERGER *makes an impatient gesture.*) Yes, Judge. Well, there's a corner in that pond as never freezes over—I can call to mind when I was a boy——

BERGER. Never mind that. Go on with your story.

SEIDEL (*saluting again*). Yes, Cap'n. Well —as I was sayin', I'd just come out o' t' smithy and was standin', in th' moonlight, when I heard some one cryin'. At first I thought it was only some one makin' believe, as you might say. But happenin' to look toward the pond, I saw somethin' in the water! Yes, Judge. Where it never freezes over. I called out to say I was a-comin', but she'd fainted! Well, I just ran back and fetched a plank from t' smithy and laid it over the hole—and in a moment I had brought her safe to land again.

BERGER. Bravo, Seidel. We don't hear that sort of tale every day. We hear more about quarrelling and fighting, and head-breaking, down in the village . . . And then, I suppose, you brought her straight up here?

SEIDEL. Excuse me, Judge. It was the teacher——

GOTTWALD. I happened to be passing by on my way home from a lecture. So I took her to my house first and got my wife to find some warm clothes for her.

BERGER. What do you make of the affair?

SEIDEL (*hesitating*). Well, you see—h'm. She's Mattern's step-daughter.

BERGER (*seems shocked*). That ragged little thing Mattern's step-daughter?

SEIDEL. Ay. Her mother died six weeks ago. . . . There ain't much more to tell. She kicked and scratched because she thought I was her stepfather.

BERGER (*thinking of* MATTERN, *mutters*). The scoundrel!

SEIDEL. He's bin sittin' at the inn, drinkin' hard, ever since yesterday. It takes a cask to fill *him* up, it does.

BERGER. He'll have a score to settle with me, for this job. (*Bends over* HANNELE.) Now, my child. Listen. You needn't cry about it. What's the girl looking at me like that for? . . . I won't hurt you. What's your name? . . . A little louder, please. I can't hear you—— (*He rises.*) The child seems very stubborn.

GOTTWALD. She's only frightened . . . Hannele!

HANNELE (*gasping*). Yes, sir!

GOTTWALD. Do as the Judge bids you, child.

HANNELE (*shivering*). Dear Lord, I'm freezing!

SEIDEL (*bringing in the grog*). There. Take a drop o' this, my lass.

HANNELE (*as before*). Dear Lord, I'm hungry!

GOTTWALD (*to the Magistrate*). It's no use. We can't make her drink.

HANNELE. It hurts!

GOTTWALD. Where does it hurt you, little one?

HANNELE. Oh, I'm afraid! I'm afraid!

BERGER. Who's frightening you, my dear? Come, come, now. Tell us all about it. Don't be afraid. What was that?—I can't understand a word you're saying. Try and remember how it happened. Did your stepfather ill-treat you?—Did he beat you or lock you up or—turn you out into the street?—It's hard to get anything out of her——

SEIDEL. Ay! She ain't fond er chatterin'! Choppin' trees is easier nur makin' *her* talk. She's as still as a mouse, *she* is.

BERGER. If we only had facts to go on— we might have the fellow locked up.

GOTTWALD. She's terribly afraid of him.

SEIDEL. 'Tain't the first time, neither, as he's been caught at this sort of game. Jest you ask the folks about him. They'll tell you what sort of man he is. It's a wonder she wasn't killed years ago.

BERGER. What has he done to her?

SEIDEL. Done?—Druv her out o' doors o' nights. That's what he's done to her. Sent her out a-beggin' in the snow. That's what he's done. And if she didn't bring him back enough to get him roarin' drunk, out she'd have to go agen. That's what he's done. Many's the night she's froze and cried her eyes out, she has.

GOTTWALD. It wasn't quite so bad while her mother lived.

BERGER. Well, anyhow, we'll have the man arrested. He's a notorious drunkard. Now, my little maid, just look me straight in the face.

HANNELE (*imploringly*). Oh please, please, please!

SEIDEL. 'Tain't no use you're asking questions. You won't get nothin' out o' her.

GOTTWALD (*gently*). Hannele!

HANNELE. Yes, sir.

GOTTWALD. Do you know me?

HANNELE. Yes, sir.

GOTTWALD. Who am I?

HANNELE. Teacher, sir—Teacher Gottwald.

GOTTWALD. That's right. We're getting along famously. Now, my dear child, tell us all about it. Don't be afraid. How is it you did not stay at home instead of going down to the pond by the blacksmith's? Eh?

HANNELE. I'm afraid! I'm afraid!

BERGER. We'll go away, and you can say all you have to say to the schoolmaster.

HANNELE. (*shyly and mysteriously*). He called me!

GOTTWALD. Who called you, my dear?

HANNELE. The Lord Jesus.

GOTTWALD. Where did the Lord Jesus call you?

HANNELE. From the water.

GOTTWALD. Where?

HANNELE. Why, from the bottom of the water.

BERGER (*changing his mind and putting on his overcoat*). We'd better have the doctor fetched. I daresay he's not left the inn yet.

GOTTWALD. I have sent for one of the Sisters. The child needs very careful nursing.

BERGER. I'll go for the doctor at once. (*to* SCHMIDT). Bring the policeman to me at the inn, Schmidt. We'll have the fellow locked up. Good-night, Schoolmaster. (BERGER *and* SCHMIDT *exeunt.* HANNELE *falls asleep.*)

SEIDEL (*after a pause*). He won't lock him up. Not much.

GOTTWALD. Why not?

SEIDEL. He knows why, *he* does. *Who's the girl's father*, eh?

GOTTWALD. Stuff, Seidel. That's all gossip.

SEIDEL. All right. I knows what I knows.

GOTTWALD. You mustn't mind what people say. Half are lies.—I only wish the doctor would make haste.

SEIDEL (*softly*). She won't get over it. You'll see.

[*Enter* DR. WACHLER, *a grave-looking man of four-and-thirty.*]

DR. WACHLER. Good evening!

GOTTWALD. Good evening, Doctor.

SEIDEL (*helping the* DOCTOR *to take off his fur overcoat*). Good evening, Herr Doctor.

DR. WACHLER (*warming his hands at the stove*). I should like another candle. [*The sound of a barrel-organ comes from the adjoining room.*] They must have lost their wits!

SEIDEL (*at the half-closed door of the back room*). Can't you keep quiet in there? (*Noise ceases.* SEIDEL *goes into the back room.*)

DR. WACHLER. Herr Gottwald, I believe?

GOTTWALD. That is my name.

DR. WACHLER. I hear she tried to drown herself?

GOTTWALD. She saw no other way out of her troubles, poor child.

[*Short pause.*]

DR. WACHLER (*watching* HANNELE *beside her bed*). Has she been talking in her sleep?

HANNELE. Millions and millions of stars!

[DR. WACHLER *and* GOTTWALD *watch the child. Through the window the moonlight streams on the group.*] Why are you pulling at my bones? Don't! Don't! It hurts, oh it *does* hurt so!

DR. WACHLER (*carefully loosening the collar of* HANNELE'S *chemise*). Her body is a mass of bruises!

SEIDEL. Ah, and that's how her mother looked when she was put in her coffin!

DR. WACHLER. Shocking! Shocking!

HANNELE (*in a changed, peevish voice*). I won't go home. I won't! I want to go to Dame Holle.—Let me go to the pond.—Let me go!—Oh, that dreadful, dreadful smell!—Father, you've been drinking brandy again!—Hark! 10 how the wind blows in the wood!—There was a storm in the hills this morning.—Oh, I do hope there won't be a fire.—Do you hear? Oh, what a storm!—It'll blow the tailor away, if he hasn't put his goose in his pocket!

[*Enter* SISTER MARTHA.]

GOTTWALD. Good evening, Sister. (SISTER MARTHA *bends her head in response.* 20 GOTTWALD *joins her at the back of the stage, where she is getting everything ready for nursing.*)

HANNELE. Where's mother? In heaven? How far away it is! (*She opens her eyes, stares about her in a dazed way, rubs her eyes slowly and says in an almost inaudible voice.*) Where am I?

DR. WACHLER (*bending over her*). You're with friends, Hannele.

HANNELE. I'm thirsty.

DR. WACHLER. Water!

[SEIDEL, *who has brought in another candle, goes out to get some water.*]

DR. WACHLER. Does it pain you anywhere? (HANNELE *shakes her head.*) No. That's first-rate. We'll soon put you right.

HANNELE. Please, sir, are you the doctor?

DR. WACHLER. Yes, my dear.

HANNELE. Am I very, very ill?

DR. WACHLER. No, no! Not *very* ill.

HANNELE. Are you going to make me well again?

DR. WACHLER (*examining her quickly*). Does that hurt? No! Does that? Ah, this is the place!—Don't be frightened! I won't hurt you. Is this where the pain is?

GOTTWALD (*returning to the bedside*). Answer the doctor, Hannele.

HANNELE (*earnestly, imploringly, tearfully*). Oh, *dear* Teacher Gottwald!

GOTTWALD. Come, come! Attend to what the Doctor says and answer his questions. (HANNELE *shakes her head.*) No? Why not?

HANNELE. Oh, do, *do* let me go to mother!

GOTTWALD (*deeply moved—strokes her hair gently*). Don't, don't say that, my child!

[*Short pause. The* DOCTOR *lifts his head, draws a long breath and reflects for a moment.* SISTER MARTHA *has brought the lighted candle from the table and stands nearby, holding it.*]

DR. WACHLER (*beckons to* SISTER MARTHA). One moment, Sister.

[*The* DOCTOR *and* SISTER MARTHA *retire to the table. The* DOCTOR *gives the* SISTER *some instructions in an undertone.* GOTTWALD *glances at* HANNELE, *the* SISTER, *and the* DOCTOR *alternately. He stands waiting, hat in hand.*]

30 [DR. WACHLER *ends his quiet talk with* SISTER MARTHA.]

I'll look in again later on. I'll have the medicine sent round. (*To* GOTTWALD.) It seems they have arrested the man at the inn.

SISTER MARTHA. Yes. So they say.

DR. WACHLER (*putting on his overcoat. To* SEIDEL). You'd better come to the apothecary's with me.

40 [*The* DOCTOR, GOTTWALD *and* SEIDEL *take leave of* SISTER MARTHA *quietly as they move toward the door.*]

GOTTWALD (*in a casual way*). What do you think of the case, doctor?

[DOCTOR, GOTTWALD *and* SEIDEL *exeunt.* SISTER MARTHA, *who is now alone with*

HANNELE, *pours some milk into a bowl. Meanwhile,* HANNELE *opens her eyes and watches her.*]

HANNELE. Have you come from Jesus?

SISTER MARTHA. What did you say, dear?

HANNELE. Have you come from the Lord Jesus?

SISTER MARTHA. Why, Hannele, have you forgotten me? I'm Sister Martha. Don't you remember coming to see 10 us one day and praying and singing those beautiful hymns?

HANNELE (*nodding joyfully*). Oh yes, yes. Such beautiful, beautiful hymns!

SISTER MARTHA. I've come to nurse you, in God's name, till you get well.

HANNELE. I don't want to get well.

SISTER MARTHA (*bringing her the milk*). The doctor says you must take a little of this milk, to make you strong again. 20

HANNELE (*turns away*). I don't *want* to get well.

SISTER MARTHA. Don't want to get well? That's not sensible, my dear. There, let me tie your hair up. (*She ties her hair.*)

HANNELE (*crying quietly*). I don't want to get well.

SISTER MARTHA. Well, I declare! Why not?

HANNELE. Oh, how I *long* to go to 30 heaven, Sister.

SISTER MARTHA. We all long for that, darling. But we must be patient and wait until God calls us, and then, if we repent of our sins——

HANNELE (*eagerly*). I *do* repent, Sister! Indeed, indeed I do!

SISTER MARTHA.—and if we believe in the Lord Jesus——

HANNELE. I *do* believe in Him! 40

SISTER MARTHA. Then you may wait in peace, my child.—Let me smooth your pillow for you.—There. Now go to sleep.

HANNELE. I can't sleep.

SISTER MARTHA. Oh yes, you can, if you try.

HANNELE. Sister Martha!

SISTER MARTHA. Well, dear?

HANNELE. Sister! Are there any—any unpardonable sins?

SISTER MARTHA. We won't talk about that now. You must not excite yourself.

HANNELE. Please, please, please! Won't you tell me?

SISTER MARTHA. Yes, yes. There *are* sins that God won't pardon—sins against the Holy Ghost!

HANNELE. Oh, do you think I've committed one?

SISTER MARTHA. Nonsense. Why, only very, *very* wicked people, like Judas, who betrayed our Lord, could commit those sins.

HANNELE. You don't know—you don't know.

SISTER MARTHA. Hush. You must go to sleep.

HANNELE. I'm so afraid.

SISTER MARTHA. You need not be.

HANNELE. But if I have committed one?

SISTER MARTHA. Oh, but you haven't.

HANNELE (*clings to the* SISTER *and stares into the darkness*). Sister! Sister!

SISTER MARTHA. Hush, dear, hush!

HANNELE. Sister!

SISTER MARTHA. What is it?

HANNELE. He's coming. Can't you hear him?

SISTER MARTHA. I hear nothing.

HANNELE. That's his voice—outside! Hark!

SISTER MARTHA. Whose voice?

HANNELE. Father's! Father's! There he is!

SISTER MARTHA. Where? I don't see him.

HANNELE. Look!

SISTER MARTHA. Where?

HANNELE. At the foot of the bed!

SISTER MARTHA. It's only this coat and hat, darling. We'll take the nasty things away and give them to Daddy Pleschke. And then I'll bring some water and we'll make a compress for you. You won't be afraid if I leave you alone for a few moments, will you? Lie quite still till I come back.

HANNELE. Was it really only the coat and hat, Sister? How silly of me. 10

SISTER MARTHA. Keep quite still. I'll be back directly. (*She goes out, but returns, as the courtyard is pitch dark.*) I'll put the candle outside in the courtyard for a minute. (*Shaking her finger tenderly at* HANNELE.) Now mind! Keep still! (*She goes out.*)

[*It is almost dark in the room. As soon as the* SISTER *has gone, the figure of* MATTERN, *the mason, appears at the foot of the bed.* 20 *He has a drunken and unkempt look, tangled red hair, and a shabby old soldier's cap. In his left hand he holds his tools. Round his right wrist is a cord. He stares threateningly at* HANNELE *as if about to strike. A pale light envelopes the apparition and streams on to the bed.* HANNELE *covers her face with her hands in terror. She writhes and moans piteously.*]

THE APPARITION (*in a hoarse and exas-* 30 *perated voice*). Where are you? Loafin' agen, as usual, eh? I'll teach yer to skulk, you little devil, you. So you've been tellin' tales, have you? Tellin' the folks I ill-uses you, eh? I beats you, eh? Aren't you ashamed to tell such lies? You ain't no child of mine. Get up, you lazy baggage. I don't want to have nothin' more to do with you. I've half a mind to turn you out 40 into the gutter. Get up and light the fire. D'ye hear? If I keeps you it's out o' charity. Now then, up with you? You won't, won't you? Well then, look out——

[HANNELE, *with an effort, rises. Her eyes*

remain closed. She drags herself to the stove, opens the stove-door, and falls senseless as SISTER MARTHA *returns with a lighted candle and a jug of water. The apparition vanishes.* SISTER MARTHA *staggers, stares at* HANNELE *as she lies among the ashes, and exclaims.*]

SISTER MARTHA. Saints alive! (*She puts down the candle and the jug, hastens to* HANNELE, *and lifts her from the floor. Hearing her cry, the inmates of the Almshouse rush in.*) I just left her for a moment to fetch some water and she got out of bed. Here, Hedwig, give me a hand!

HANKE. You'd best be careful, or you'll hurt her.

PLESCHKE. It d——don't seem nat'ral to me, Sister. Someone must a-be-witched the girl.

TULPE. That's what's wrong wi' her.

HANKE (*loudly*). She won't last long, she won't.

SISTER MARTHA (*when with* HEDWIG'S *assistance she has put* HANNELE *to bed again*). That may be all very true, my good man, but you really must not excite the child.

HANKE. You're makin' quite a fuss about her, ain't you?

PLESCHKE (*to* HANKE). You're a bad lot you are—a reg'lar out an' out bad lot. Ain't you got sense enough to know—as—as—sick folk mustn't be excited?

HETE (*mimicking him*). S—sick folk mustn't be excited——

SISTER MARTHA. I really must request you——

TULPE. Quite right, Sister.—You get out o' here!

HANKE. When we wants to go, we'll go, and not before.

HETE. The stable's good enough for the likes of *us*.

PLESCHKE. Don't you make no fuss—

you'll find a place to sleep in, you will.

[*The inmates of the Almshouse go out.*]

HANNELE (*opens her eyes. She seems terrified*). Has he gone?

SISTER MARTHA. They've all gone, Hannele. Did they frighten you?

HANNELE (*still terrified*). Has father gone?

SISTER MARTHA. He hasn't been here.

HANNELE. Oh, yes, he has, Sister!

SISTER MARTHA. You dreamt it, my dear.

HANNELE (*sighing deeply*). Oh, dear Lord Jesus! Dear, dear Lord Jesus! Won't you please, please, take me away from here! (*Her tone changes.*)
"Oh, would He but come
And guide my way home!
I'm worn and I'm weary
No more can I roam!"
Yes, yes. I'm sure He will, Sister.

SISTER MARTHA. What, dear?

HANNELE. He's promised to take me to Him, Sister.

SISTER MARTHA. H'm. (*Coughs.*)

HANNELE. He's promised.

SISTER MARTHA. Who has promised?

HANNELE (*whispering mysteriously into the Sister's ear*). The dear Lord—Gottwald!

SISTER MARTHA. Get off to sleep again, Hannele, that's a good girl.

HANNELE. Isn't he handsome, Sister? Don't you think teacher's handsome? His name is Heinrich!—Did you know that? What a beautiful name! (*Fervently.*) Dear, good, kind Heinrich! Sister, when I grow up, we're going to be married!
"And when the priest had made them one,
The bride grew pink as heather;
The bridegroom kissed her trembling lips,
And off they rode together."
He has such a lovely beard. (*Entranced.*) And, oh, his head's covered with such sweet white clover!—Hark! He's calling me! Don't you hear?

SISTER MARTHA. Do go to sleep, my pet. No one is calling.

HANNELE. It was the voice of—Jesus. Iark! He's calling me again. Oh, I hear Him quite plainly. "Hannele!" "Hannele!"—Let us go to Him!

SISTER MARTHA. When God calls He will find me ready!

HANNELE (*her head is now bathed in moonlight. She makes a gesture as though she were inhaling some sweet perfume*). Don't you smell them, Sister?

SISTER MARTHA. No, Hannele.

HANNELE. Lilacs! (*Her ecstasy increases.*) Listen! Listen! (*A sweet voice is faintly heard in the far distance.*) Is that the angels singing? Don't you hear?

SISTER MARTHA. Yes, dear, I hear. But now you must turn round and have a good long sleep.

HANNELE. Can you sing that, too?

SISTER MARTHA. Sing what, my child?

HANNELE. "Sleep, darling, sleep!"

SISTER MARTHA. Would you like me to?

HANNELE (*lies back and strokes the* SISTER's *hand*). Mother, mother! Sing to me!

SISTER MARTHA (*extinguishes the light, bends over the bed, and softly intones the following verses to the accompaniment of distant music*).
"Sleep, darling, sleep!
In the garden goes a sheep.
(*She sings the rest in darkness.*)
A little lamb with thee shall play,
From dawn to sunset, all the day.
Sleep, darling, sleep!"

[*Twilight fills the room.* SISTER MARTHA *has gone. The pale and ghostly form of a woman appears and seats itself on the side of the bed. She is slightly bent and seems to rest on her thin bare arms. Her feet are bare. Her long white locks stream over her shoulders and onto the bed. Her face seems worn and wasted. Her sunken eyes, though closed, seem fixed on* HANNELE. *Her voice sounds as the voice of one speaking in her sleep. Before she speaks, her lips are seen to move, as though it cost her a great effort to get the words out. She is prematurely aged. Her cheeks are hollow, and she is clad in miserable clothes.*]

THE FEMALE APPARITION. Hannele!

HANNELE (*her eyes, also, are closed*). Mother, dearest mother! Is it you?

THE FEMALE APPARITION. It is I.—I have washed the feet of my Saviour with my tears, and I have dried them with my hair.

HANNELE. Do you bring me good tidings?

THE FEMALE APPARITION. Yes!

HANNELE. Have you come far?

THE FEMALE APPARITION. Hundreds of thousands of miles, through the night!

HANNELE. How strange you look, mother!

THE FEMALE APPARITION. As the children of earth look, so I look!

HANNELE. There are buttercups and daisies on your lips. Your voice rings out like music.

THE FEMALE APPARITION. It is no true ring, my child.

HANNELE. Mother, dear mother, your beauty dazzles me!

THE FEMALE APPARITION. The angels in heaven are a thousandfold more radiant!

HANNELE. Why are you not like them?

THE FEMALE APPARITION. I suffered for your sake.

HANNELE. Mother mine, won't you stay with me?

THE FEMALE APPARITION (*rising*). I cannot stay!

HANNELE. Is it beautiful where you have come from?

THE FEMALE APPARITION. There the wide meadows are sheltered from the wind and storm and hail. God shields them.

HANNELE. Can you rest there when you are tired?

THE FEMALE APPARITION. Yes!

HANNELE. Can you get food to eat there, when you are hungry?

THE FEMALE APPARITION. There is meat and fruit for all who hunger, and golden wine for those who thirst. (*She shrinks away.*)

HANNELE. Are you going, mother?

THE FEMALE APPARITION. God calls me!

HANNELE. Does He call loudly?

THE FEMALE APPARITION. He calls *me* loudly!

HANNELE. My heart is parched within me, mother!

THE FEMALE APPARITION. God will cool it with roses and with lilies.

HANNELE. Mother, will God redeem me?

THE FEMALE APPARITION. Do you know this flower I hold here in my hand?

HANNELE. It's golden sesame![1] The key of heaven!

THE FEMALE APPARITION. (*puts it into* HANNELE's *hand*). Take it and keep it as God's pledge. Farewell!

HANNELE. Mother! Mother, don't leave me!

THE FEMALE APPARITION (*shrinks away*). A little while and ye shall not see me, and again a little while and ye shall see me.

HANNELE. I'm afraid!

THE FEMALE APPARITION (*shrinking still farther away*). Even as the snowdrifts on the hills are swept away by the winds, so shall thy troubles be lifted from thee.

HANNELE. Don't go!

---

[1] In the German the flower is *Himmelschlussel,* that is "Key of heaven," but in English, cowslip. "Sesame" seems more appropriate and suggestive.—C. H. M.

THE FEMALE APPARITION. The Children
of Heaven are as lightnings in the
Night. Sleep!
[*The room gradually grows dark. Pretty
voices of young children are heard singing
the second verse of "Sleep, darling,
sleep."*]
"Sleep, darling, sleep!
Bright guests their vigils keep——
[*A gold-green light suddenly floods the room.* 10
Three radiant ANGELS, *crowned with
roses, and having the forms of beautiful
winged youths, appear and take up the
song. In their hands they hold music.* THE
FEMALE APPARITION *has vanished.*]
The guests who guard thee thro' the
    night
Are angels from the realms of Light.
Sleep, darling, sleep!"
HANNELE (*opens her eyes and gazes rap-* 20
turously at the Angels). Angels! (*Her
joy and her amazement grow, but she
seems still in doubt.*) Angels!! (*Triumphantly.*) Angels!!!
[*Short pause. Then the* ANGELS *sing the
following strophes from the music in their
hands.*]
        FIRST ANGEL
The sunlight that glints on the moun-
    tain   30

No gladness, or gold, had for thee.
For thee there was sorrow and sadness
In valley and forest and lea.
        SECOND ANGEL
Thy hunger cried out to the reaper
In vain, as he garnered the grain.
For milk thy poor lips went a-thirst-
    ing—
They thirsted again and again.
        THIRD ANGEL
The buds and the blossoms of springtide.
In scarlet and purple arrayed,
For others had savour and sweetness.
And faded—as thou, too, must fade.
        [*Brief pause.*]
        FIRST ANGEL
From out of the darkness of space
    A greeting we bring.
A message of love and of grace
    We bear on our wing.
        SECOND ANGEL
In the hem of our raiment we bring thee
    The fragrance of May.
The rose of the morn, newly born,
    Illumines our way.
        THIRD ANGEL
A glory of green and of glamour
    We leave in the skies.
The splendour of God is reflected
    And shines in our eyes!

ACT II

*The scene is as it was before the appear-
ance of the* ANGELS.
THE DEACONESS (SISTER MARTHA) *sits
beside* HANNELE'S *bed. She lights the
candle again and* HANNELE *awakes. Her
inward rapture is still shown in the expression of her face. As soon as she recog-
nises* SISTER MARTHA *she breaks into joyous
talk.*

HANNELE. Sister! Sister Martha! Do   40
you know who has been here? Angels!
Angels, Sister!

SISTER MARTHA. Aha! You're wide
    awake again.
HANNELE. Yes, yes. Only think of it.
    (*Impulsively.*) Angels! Angels! Real
    angels, from heaven, Sister Martha,
    with great, big wings!
SISTER MARTHA. What sweet dreams you
    must have had, dear.
HANNELE. Why do you speak of dreams?
    Look, look! See what I have in my
    hand! (*She holds out an imaginary
    flower to her.*)
SISTER MARTHA. What is it, dearest?

HANNELE. Can't you see?

SISTER MARTHA. H'm.

HANNELE. Look at it, Sister. Only look!

SISTER MARTHA. I see, dear.

HANNELE. Smell how sweet it is!

SISTER MARTHA (*pretending to smell*). Beautiful!

HANNELE. Take care, take care. You'll crush it.

SISTER MARTHA. Oh no, I mustn't do that, my dear. What do you call this wonderful flower? 10

HANNELE. Why, golden sesame, of course!

SISTER MARTHA. Oh!

HANNELE. Of course it is. Can't you see? Bring the light here. Quick! Quick!

SISTER MARTHA. Ah! Now I see.

HANNELE. Isn't it beautiful? 20

SISTER MARTHA. Yes, yes. But you mustn't talk so much, my child. You must keep quite, quite still, or else the doctor will be angry. Now you must take the medicine he sent for you.

HANNELE. Oh, Sister, why will you worry so much about me? You don't know what has happened—do you, now? Who do you think it was gave me this lovely golden sesame? Guess, guess.—What's sesame for? Don't you know, Sister? 30

SISTER MARTHA. Ssh! You can tell me all about it in the morning, when you are strong, and bright, and well again.

HANNELE. I *am* well. (*She tries to rise and puts her feet out of bed.*)

SISTER MARTHA. You mustn't do that, Hannele, dear.

HANNELE (*waving her away, gets out of bed and walks a few steps*). Please—please do leave me alone. I must go away—away. (*She starts and stares fixedly at something.*) Oh, dear Lord Jesus! 40

[*The figure of an* ANGEL, *clad in black and with black wings, appears. The* ANGEL *is tall, majestic and beautiful. In his hands he holds a long, wavy sword, the hilt of which is wrapped in crape. The* ANGEL *is seated near the stove. He is silent and serious. He gazes steadily and calmly at* HANNELE. *A supernatural white light fills the room.*] Who are you? (*Pause.*) Are you an angel? (*No answer.*) Is it me you want? (*No answer.*) I am Hannele Mattern. Have you come for *me*? (*Again no answer.*)

[*During this incident,* SISTER MARTHA *has stood looking on, perplexed and thoughtful, with folded hands. She slowly passes out of the room.*] Has God made you dumb? Are you an angel? (*No answer.*) Are you one of God's good angels? (*No answer.*) Will you be kind to me? (*No answer.*) Are you an enemy? (*No answer.*) Why have you hidden that sword in the folds of your dress? (*Silence.*) I'm so cold, so cold. Your look chills me. You're icy cold. (*Still silence.*) Who are you? (*No answer. Terror suddenly overmasters her. She screams and turns as if appealing for help to someone behind her.*) Mother! Mother!

[*A figure, dressed like the* DEACONESS, *but younger and more beautiful, and with great white wings, enters the room.* HANNELE *hurries toward the figure, and clutches at her hand.*] Mother, mother! There's someone in the room!

DEACONESS. Where?

HANNELE. There—there!

DEACONESS. Why do you tremble so?

HANNELE. I'm afraid.

DEACONESS. Fear nothing. I am with you.

HANNELE. My teeth are chattering. I can't *help* it, mother! He terrifies me!

DEACONESS. Fear not, my child. He is your friend.

HANNELE. Who is it, mother?

DEACONESS. Do you not know him?

HANNELE. Who is he?

DEACONESS. He is Death!

HANNELE. Death! (*She stares fixedly and fearfully at the Angel for a moment.*) Must it—must it be?

DEACONESS. Death is the gate, Hannele!

HANNELE. Is there no other, mother dear?

DEACONESS. There is no other.

HANNELE. Will you be cruel to me, Death?—He won't answer! Why won't he answer any of my questions, mother?

DEACONESS. The voice of God has answered you already.

HANNELE. Oh, dear Lord God, I have so often longed for this. But now— now I am afraid!

DEACONESS. Get ready, Hannele.

HANNELE. For death, mother?

DEACONESS. For death.

HANNELE (*timidly, after a pause*). Shall I have to wear these ragged clothes, when they put me into the coffin?

DEACONESS. God will clothe you. (*She produces a small silver bell and rings it. In response there enters—silently, like all the following apparitions—a little hump-backed* VILLAGE TAILOR, *carrying on his arm a bridal dress, a veil and a wreath. In one hand he has a pair of crystal slippers. He has a comical, see-saw gait, bows silently to the* ANGEL *and the* DEACONESS, *and lastly, and obsequiously, to* HANNELE.)

THE VILLAGE TAILOR (*bobbing and bowing*). Johanna Katherina Mattern, your most obedient. (*Clears his throat.*) Your father, his Excellency the Count, has done me the honour of ordering this bridal robe for you.

DEACONESS (*takes the dress from the* TAILOR *and attires* HANNELE). I will help you to put it on, Hannele.

HANNELE (*joyfully*). Oh, how it rustles.

DEACONESS. It's white silk, Hannele.

HANNELE. Won't the people be astonished to see me so beautifully dressed in my coffin!

THE VILLAGE TAILOR. Johanna Katherina Mattern——(*He clears his throat.*) The village is full of it. (*He clears his throat.*) It's full of the good luck your death is bringing you. (*Clears his throat.*) Your father, his Excellency the Count—(*Coughs.*) has just been talking to the Burgomaster about it.

DEACONESS (*puts wreath on* HANNELE'S *head*). Lift up your head, you heavenly bride!

HANNELE (*trembling with childish pleasure*). Oh, Sister Martha, I'm so glad I am to die. (*Breaking off suddenly and doubtfully.*) You *are* Sister Martha, are you not?

DEACONESS. Yes, my child.

HANNELE. No, no. You're not Sister Martha. You are my mother!

DEACONESS. Yes.

HANNELE. Are you both of them?

DEACONESS. The children of heaven are all one in God.

THE VILLAGE TAILOR. If I may say so, Princess Hannele——(*He kneels to put on the slippers.*) these slippers are the smallest in the land. Hedwig, and Agnes, and Liese, and Martha, and Minna, and Anna, and Käthe, and Gretchen, and the rest of them all have such very large feet. (*He puts on the slippers.*) But they fit you— they fit you! We've found the bride! Princess Hannele's feet are the smallest!—Is there anything else I can do for you? (*Bows and scrapes.*) Your servant, Princess. Your servant. (*He goes.*)

HANNELE. Who would have dreamt it, mother?

DEACONESS. Now you need not take any more of that nasty physic.

HANNELE. No.

DEACONESS. Soon you will be as bright and blithe as a lark, now, darling.

HANNELE. Oh, yes!

DEACONESS. Come, dear, and lie down on your death-bed. (*She takes* HAN-NELE *by the hand, leads her gently to the bed and waits while* HANNELE *lies down.*)

HANNELE. Now I'll soon know what death is, won't I?

DEACONESS. You will, Hannele.

HANNELE (*lying on her back and playing with an imaginary flower*). I have a pledge here!

DEACONESS. Press it closely to your breast.

HANNELE (*growing frightened again and glancing at the* ANGEL). Must it—must it be?

DEACONESS. It must.

[*Sounds of a funeral march heard in the remote distance.*]

HANNELE (*listening*). That's Master Seyfried and the musicians announcing the funeral.

[*The* ANGEL *rises.*]
Oh, he's getting up!

[*The storm outside gains strength. The* ANGEL *draws nearer to* HANNELE.]
Sister! Mother! He's coming to me! Where are you? I can't see you! (*Appealing to the* ANGEL.) Make haste, thou dark and silent spirit! (*Speaking as though a heavy weight oppressed her.*) He's pressing me down! (*The* ANGEL *solemnly lifts up his sword.*) He'll crush me to pieces! (*With anguish.*) Help, Sister, help!

[*The* DEACONESS *steps majestically between the* ANGEL *and* HANNELE, *and lays her hands protectingly on the child's heart. She speaks loftily, impressively and with authority.*]

DEACONESS. He dare not. I lay my consecrated hands upon thy heart.

[*The dark* ANGEL *vanishes. Silence.*]

[*The* DEACONESS *lapses into meditation and her lips move as if in prayer. The sound of the funeral march has continued through this scene. A noise as of many tramping feet is heard. The form of the schoolmaster,* GOTTWALD, *appears in the central doorway. The funeral march ceases.*

GOTTWALD *is dressed in mourning and bears a bunch of lovely bluebells in his hand. He takes off his hat reverently, and on entering makes a gesture as though he would have silence. Behind him are ranged his pupils—boys and girls, in Sunday clothes. At the gesture of the* SCHOOLMASTER, *they stop chattering, and seem afraid to cross the threshold.* GOTTWALD *approaches the* DEACONESS *with a radiant look upon his face.*]

GOTTWALD. Good day, Sister Martha.

DEACONESS. Good day, Teacher Gottwald.

GOTTWALD (*shakes his head sadly as he looks at* HANNELE). Poor little maid.

DEACONESS. Why are you so sad, Teacher Gottwald?

GOTTWALD. Is she not dead?

DEACONESS. Is that a thing to grieve over? She has found peace at last. I envy her.

GOTTWALD (*sighing*). Ay, she is free from care and sorrow now. It is all for the best.

DEACONESS (*looking steadfastly at* HANNELE). How fair she seems.

GOTTWALD. Yes, very fair. Death seems to have clothed her with beauty.

DEACONESS. God has made her beautiful, because she loved Him.

GOTTWALD. Yes, she was always good and pious. (*Sighs heavily, opens his hymn book, and peers into it sadly.*)

DEACONESS (*peering into the same hymn book*). We should not repine. We must be patient.

GOTTWALD. And yet my heart is heavy.

DEACONESS. You do not mourn to know that she is saved?

GOTTWALD. I mourn to think that two fair flowers have withered.

DEACONESS. I do not understand you.

GOTTWALD. I have two faded violets in this book. How like they are to the dead eyes of my poor little Hannele.

DEACONESS. They will grow bright and blue again in Heaven.

GOTTWALD. Oh, Lord, how long must we still wander in this vale of tears! (*His tone changes abruptly. He becomes bustling and business-like. Produces a hymn book.*) I thought it would be a good idea to sing the first hymn here—in the house—"Jesus, my Guide——"

DEACONESS. It is a beautiful hymn and Hannele Mattern was a pious child.

GOTTWALD. And then, you know, when we get to the churchyard, we can sing, "Now lettest Thou thy servant." (*He turns to the school children and addresses them.*) Hymn No. 62! (*Intones hymn, slowly beating time.*) "Now let-test-Thou-thy-servant, De-pa-ar-art-in-peace——" (*The children chime in.*) Children, have you all warm clothes on? It will be cold out yonder in the churchyard. Come in and take one last look at our poor Hannele. (*The children enter and range themselves about the bed.*) See how beautiful death has made the child. Once she was clad in rags. Now she wears silken raiment. She went bare-footed once. Now she has crystal slippers on her feet. Ere very long she will be taken to a house all built of gold, where she will never more know thirst or hunger.

Do you remember how you used to mock at her and call her Princess Rag-Tag?—Now she is going away from us to be a real princess in heaven. If any of you have offended her, now is the time to beg for her forgiveness. If you do not, she will tell her Heavenly Father how unkind you were to her, and it will go hard with you.

A CHILD (*stepping forward*). Dear Princess Hannele, please, please forgive me and don't tell God that I used to call you Princess Rag-Tag.

ALL THE CHILDREN (*together*). We are all very, very sorry.

GOTTWALD. That's right, children. Hannele will forgive you. Now, boys and girls, go inside and wait till I join you.

DEACONESS. Come into the back room with me and I will tell you what you must all do if you want to join the bright angels some day, like Hannele. (*She goes out.* THE CHILDREN *follow. The door closes.*)

GOTTWALD (*alone with Hannele. He lays his flowers at her feet*). My dear, dear Hannele, here are the violets I have brought you. (*Kneels by the bedside. His voice trembles.*) Do not forget me in your new felicity. (*He sobs and lays his head against the folds of her dress.*) My heart is breaking at the thought of parting from you.

[*Voices are heard without.* GOTTWALD *rises and lays a covering over* HANNELE. *Two aging women, dressed as if for a funeral, and with handkerchiefs and yellow-edged hymn books in their hands, push their way into the room.*]

FIRST WOMAN (*glancing round*). We're ahead of them all.

SECOND WOMAN. No, we ain't. There's the Teacher. Good day, Teacher.

GOTTWALD. Good day.

FIRST WOMAN. You're takin' it to heart, Teacher. Well, well, I allow she was a sweet child. My, what a busy little thing she was, to be sure.

SECOND WOMAN. Say, Teacher, we've heard as how she killed herself. It ain't true, is it?

THIRD WOMAN (*appears*). T'ud be a mortal sin!

SECOND WOMAN. Ay, that it would.

THIRD WOMAN. The minister, *he* says, there ain't no pardon for it.

GOTTWALD. The Saviour said, "Suffer little children to come unto me, and forbid them not."

FOURTH WOMAN (*enters*). Dear, dear, what weather we're havin'. We'll all be froze, I guess, before we've done. I hope the parson won't keep us long in the churchyard. The snow's a foot deep in the churchyard.

FIFTH WOMAN (*enters*). Th' parson won't have no prayers read over her. He says as how consecrated ground ain't no place for the likes er her.

PLESCHKE (*enters*). Ha' yer heard the news? A grand stranger's bin to see the parson. He says that Mattern's Hannele's a saint.

HANKE (*hurrying in*). They bringin' her a crystal coffin.

SEVERAL VOICES (*together*). A crystal coffin!

HANKE. Reckon it'll cost a pretty sum.

SEVERAL VOICES (*together*). A crystal coffin!

SEIDEL (*enters*). Thur's strange goin's on down in the village. An angel's bin thur—an angel as big 's a poplar, they do say. An' thur's more of 'em down at th' blacksmith's—little uns, they be, no bigger nor babies. (*Looking at* HANNELE.) She don't look like a beggar, she don't.

SEVERAL VOICES (*scattered*). No, she don't look like a beggar—
A crystal coffin!—Did you ever hear the like!—And angels in the village!

[FOUR YOUTHS CLAD IN WHITE *enter, bearing a crystal coffin, which they put down close to* HANNELE'S *bed. They whisper to each other excitedly and curiously.*]

GOTTWALD (*slightly raising the cloth*). Would you like to have a look at the dead child?

FIRST WOMAN (*peeping at* HANNELE). Just look at her hair. Why, if it ain't shinin' just like gold.

GOTTWALD (*drawing the cloth completely from the body which is flooded with a pale light*). Have you seen her silk dress and crystal slippers?

[*All utter exclamations of surprise, and draw back.*]

SEVERAL VOICES (*confusedly*). Lord, how beautiful!—
Why, that ain't our Hannele!—
That can't be Mattern's Hannele!—
Well, if it ain't wonderful!

PLESCHKE. She's a saint, sure enough.

[*The* FOUR YOUTHS *lay* HANNELE *reverently in the crystal coffin.*]

HANKE. I told you there wouldn't be no buryin' for *her*.

FIRST WOMAN. I reckon they'll put her into the church.

SECOND WOMAN. I don't believe the girl's dead at all. She looks too lifelike for that.

PLESCHKE. G— gi' me— gi' me— a feather.—We'll soon see if she's dead.
—Just gi' me a feather—— (*They give him a feather. He holds it before her lips.*) It don't stir! The girl's dead, sure enough, she is. There ain't no life left in her.

THIRD WOMAN. I'd kinder like to give her this bit o' rosemary. (*She puts a sprig into the coffin.*)

FOURTH WOMAN. She can have my lavender, too.

FIFTH WOMAN. Why, where's Mattern?

FIRST WOMAN. Ay, where's Mattern?

SECOND WOMAN. Where he allus is, drinkin' down at th' inn.

FIRST WOMAN. May be he don't know what's happened?

SECOND WOMAN. He don't know nothin' when he's full o' drink.

PLESCHKE. Wot? Ain't no one told him there's a dead body in the house?

THIRD WOMAN. He might er found that out for hisself. 10

FOURTH WOMAN. I'm not accusin' anyone, I ain't. But it *do* seem odd the man who killed the child, as you might say, shouldn't know nothin' about it.

SEIDEL. That's what I say, and every one in th' village ud say the same. Why, she's got a bruise on her as big as my fist.

FIFTH WOMAN. He's the devil's own 20 child, is Mattern.

SEIDEL. I saw that there bruise when I was helpin' to put her to bed. I tell yer, it was as big as my fist. That's what settled her business.

FIRST WOMAN. He's the man as done it.

ALL (*whispering angrily to one another*). That's what he is.

SECOND WOMAN. I call him a murderer.

ALL. He's a murderer, a murderer! 30 [*The drunken voice of* MATTERN, *the mason, is heard without.*]

MATTERN (*without*). Lemme in, d'ye hear. Lemme in! I ain't done no harm to nobody. (*He appears in the doorway and bawls.*) Where are you hidin', you good-for-nothin' hussy? (*He staggers.*) I'll give you till I count five. Then look out. Now then. One— two—three— and one makes—Come 40 out, damn you, you hussy. What d'ye mean by makin' me lose my temper? Lemme get a sight of you, that's all, and I'll break every bone in your body. (*He stumbles, recovers and stares stupidly at the silent by-standers.*) What are you starin' at me for? (*No answer.*) What d' ye want? Devil take you all. I ain't done nothin' to the girl. Come out, d' ye hear? And mighty quick about it, too. (*He chuckles to himself.*) I know what I'm about, if I *have* had a drop too much. What, you ain't gone yet—— (*Savagely.*) Don't stand there glarin' at me or I'll——

[*A man wearing a long, shabby, brown robe enters. He is about thirty years old. His hair is long and dark. His face is the face of the schoolmaster,* GOTTWALD. *In his left hand he holds a soft hat. He has sandals on his feet. He seems weary and travel-stained. He interrupts the mason by laying his hand gently on his arm.* MATTERN *turns round roughly. The stranger looks him steadily and calmly in the face.*]

THE STRANGER (*gently*). Mattern, the mason, God's peace be with thee.

MATTERN. Where do *you* come from? What do you want?

THE STRANGER (*appealing*). My feet are weary and blood-stained. Give me water wherewith to wash them. The burning sun has parched my tongue. Give me wine, wherewith to cool it. No food has passed my lips since early morn. Give me bread, wherewith to still my hunger.

MATTERN. It's none of my business. If you'd been working, like an honest man, instead o' trampin' up and down the country roads, you'd be all right. *I* have to work for my livin'.

THE STRANGER. I am a workman.

MATTERN. You're a vagabond, you are. Honest workmen don't starve.

THE STRANGER. For *my* work no man pays me.

MATTERN. You're a vagabond.

THE STRANGER (*faintly, submissively, but pressingly*). I am a physician. Hast thou not need of me?

MATTERN. Not I. I'm not sick. No doctors for me.

THE STRANGER (*his voice trembling with emotion*). Mattern, the mason, bethink thee! Though thou hast denied me water, I will heal thee. Though thou hast refused me bread, yet I can make thee well. God is my witness.

MATTERN. Be off with you, d'ye hear? 10 Be off. My bones are sound. I don't want nothin' to do with doctors. Will you clear out?

THE STRANGER. Mattern, the mason, bethink thee well. I will wash thy feet. I will give thee wine. Thou shalt have sweet, white bread to eat. Set thy foot upon my head, and I will still heal thee, as God liveth.

MATTERN. You won't go, won't you, 20 eh? I'll have to throw you out?

THE STRANGER (*impressively*). Mattern, the mason, dost thou not know what lies within this house?

MATTERN. There ain't nothin' lyin' here but what belongs to the place, 'ceptin' you. Off you go, damn you!

THE STRANGER (*simply*). Thy daughter lies here, sick.

MATTERN. She don't want no doctors 30 to cure her complaint. She's lazy. That's wot's the matter with her. I'll cure her, and mighty quick, too, if she don't stop skulkin'.

THE STRANGER (*loftily*). Mattern, the mason, I come to thee as a messenger.

MATTERN. A messenger? Who sent you, eh?

THE STRANGER. I come from the Father, and I go unto the Father. What hast 40 thou done with His child?

MATTERN. P'raps you know where she's hidin' herself better than I do. What are His children to me? He don't seem to trouble himself much about them.

THE STRANGER (*directly*). There is one dead within these walls.

MATTERN (*sees* HANNELE, *approaches the coffin silently, and looks in, muttering*). Where the devil did she get all them fine clothes and that ere crystal coffin?

[*The coffin-bearers whisper together angrily,* "*Murderer!*" "*Murderer!*" MATTERN, *softly and stammering.*]

I—n-never did ye n-no harm. I was kind to you, I was. I didn't deny you nothin'—— (*Brutally, to the* STRANGER.) Wot d'yer want? Come, speak out and ha' done with it? 'Tain't no business of mine.

THE STRANGER. Mattern the mason, hast thou nothing to say to me?

[*The coffin-bearers grow more and more excited, and frequent exclamations of* "*Murderer!*" "*Murderer!*" *are heard.*] Hast thou not sinned? Hast thou never dragged her from sleep at night and beaten her till she grew faint with pain and anguish?

MATTERN (*frenzied with excitement*). May Heaven strike me dead if I have!

[*Faint blue lightning and distant thunder.*]

ALL (*scattered voices*). It's thundering!— Thunder in mid-winter!— He's perjured himself!— The murderer's perjured himself!

THE STRANGER (*gently and persuasively*). Hast thou still nothing to confess, Mattern?

MATTERN (*panic-struck*). Those whom the Lord loveth, He chasteneth. That's what I did to the girl. I treated her as though she was my own child, I did.

THE WOMEN (*rushing at him*). Murderer! Murderer!

MATTERN. She lied to me and cheated me.

THE STRANGER. Is this the truth?

MATTERN. So help me God!

[*The golden sesame appears in* HANNELE'S *clapsed hands. A mystic greenish-yellow light streams from it. The sight dismays* MATTERN, *who recoils in terror.*]

THE STRANGER. Mattern the mason, thou hast lied to me.

ALL (*scattered voices*). A miracle! A miracle!

PLESCHKE. The girl's a saint, sure. He's perjured hisself, he has.   10

MATTERN (*shouting*). I'll go hang myself! (*He presses his hands to his temples and goes.*)

THE STRANGER (*advances to the coffin and turns to the bystanders, who draw back in awe of his now noble and imposing form*). Be not afraid! (*He stops and presses* HANNELE'S *hand. Then in a gentle tone*). The maiden is not dead. She sleepeth. (*Earnestly.*) Johanna Mat- 20 tern!

[*A golden-green light steals into the room.* HANNELE *opens her eyes and, with the help of* THE STRANGER'S *hand, rises, not yet daring to fix her eyes on him. She leaves the coffin and sinks upon her knees before* THE STRANGER. *The bystanders flee in consternation.* THE STRANGER *and* HANNELE *remain alone.* THE STRANGER'S *shabby gown falls from his shoulders.* 30 *Beneath it is a robe of white and gold.*]

THE STRANGER (*tenderly*). Hannele!

HANNELE (*with rapture, bending her head low*). 'Tis he!

THE STRANGER. Dost thou know me?

HANNELE. I have waited for thee.

THE STRANGER. Canst thou name my name?

HANNELE (*trembling with awe*). Holy! Holy! Holy!   40

THE STRANGER. I know thy sorrow and thy pain.

HANNELE. I have longed for thy coming.

THE STRANGER. Arise!

HANNELE. Thy dress is spotless. I am ashamed.

THE STRANGER (*laying his right hand on* HANNELE'S *head*). Thy shame I take from thee. (*He lifts her face gently and touches her eyelids.*) I fill thine eyes with everlasting light. Thy soul shall be all sunshine. Eternal brightness shall be thine, from dawn till eve and then till dawn again. Receive all radiant things, and feast thine eyes on all the glories of the deep blue sea and azure sky and fair green trees, forever and forever. (*He touches her ears.*) Let thine ears be opened to the music of the millions upon millions of God's angels. (*He touches her lips.*) Thus do I loose thy stammering tongue and quicken it with the life of thine own soul and my soul, and the soul of God Almighty.

[HANNELE *trembling convulsively with rapture, tries to rise, but cannot. She sobs and buries her head in* THE STRANGER'S *robe*].

With these thy tears I cleanse thee from the dust and stain of earth. I will raise thee high above the stars of God.

[THE STRANGER *lays his hand on the child's head and speaks the lines following to the accompanying strains of soft music. As he speaks, the forms of many angels appear, crowding through the doorway. Some are tall, some short. Some are radiant winged boys and girls. They swing incense-censers and strew flowers, and spread rich stuffs on the floor.*]

THE STRANGER

The Realm of Righteousness is filled with light and joy.

God's everlasting peace reigns there without alloy.

[*Harps are heard, at first played softly, then gradually swelling louder and louder.*]

Its mansions are marble, its roofs are of gold,

Through its rivulets ripple wines ruddy
and old.
In its silver-white streets blow the lily
and rose,
In its steeples the chiming of joy-bells
grows.
The beautiful butterflies frolic and
play
On its ramparts, rich-robed in the
mosses of May.
Swans, twelve, soft as snow, ring them
round in the sky,
And their wings thrill the air with sweet
sounds as they fly.
And louder and louder the symphonies
swell
Till their resonance reaches from heav'n
to hell.
Forever and ever, through aeons un-
ending,
With music majestic their progress
attending,
They soar above Zion and meadow and
sea,
And their path is made lambent with
mystery.
The blessèd below, in the regions of
Light,
Wander on, hand in hand, and rejoice
in their flight.
In the depths of the radiant, the ruby-
red waves,
Swan dives down after swan, as its
plumage it laves.
So they wash themselves clean in the
clear, deep red
Of the blood that the Lord, their dear
Saviour, had shed,
And they pass from the glory of flood
and of foam,
To the rest and the bliss of their
heavenly home.

[THE STRANGER *turns to the* ANGELS, *who
have ended their work. With timid joy
they draw near and form a semi-circle
round* HANNELE *and* THE STRANGER.]

Bring hither finest linen, children
mine—
My fair, my pretty turtle-doves, come
hither.
Surround her weak and wasted little
frame
With comfort and with warmth, to
keep her free
From frost and fever, pain and weary
10 woe.
Be tender with her. Shield her from
rude touch,
And bear her swiftly up, on pinions
light.
Above the waving grasses of the lea,
Beyond the shimmering wastes of
moonlit space
Beyond the meads and groves of Paradise,
20 Into the cool and shade of boundless
peace.
Then, while she rests upon her silken
bed,
Prepare for her, in alabaster bath,
Water from mountain brook, and purple wine, and milk of antelope,
To wash away the stain of earthly ill!
From off the bushes break the budding
sprays,
30 Lilac and jessamine, with dew bent low,
And let their moisture from the petals
flow
Softly upon her, as the showers in May.
Take linen rare and fine, to dry her
limbs
With loving hands, as ye would lily-
leaves.
From jewell'd chalices pour the re-
viving wine,
40 Pressed from the patient heart of
fragrant fruit.

.   .   .   .   .   .

Delight her lips with sweets, her heart
delight
With all the dazzling splendours of the
morn.

Enchant her eyes with stately palaces.
Let humming-birds, in iris hues ar-
rayed,
From walls of malachite flash gold and
green.
Beneath her feet spread velvets, richly
wrought,
And strew her path with daffodils and
tulips.
To fan her cheek let palms in cadence 10
sway
And make her life unceasing holiday.
Where the red poppies rear their
beauteous heads
And happy children dance to meet the
day,
Bid her repose, free now from tear and
sigh,
And witch her soul with gentle har-
mony.

THE ANGELS (*sing in chorus*).
We bear thee away to the Heavenly
Rest,
Lullaby, into the Land of the Blest,
Lullaby, into the Land of the Blest!
[*The stage grows gradually dark, as the*
ANGELS *sing. Out of the darkness the*
sound of their song is heard more and
more faintly. Then the stage grows light.
The interior of the Almshouse is seen,
exactly as before the first apparition.
HANNELE—*a poor, sick child, once more*
lies on the bed. DOCTOR WACHLER *bends*
over her, with a stethoscope. The DEA-
CONESS (SISTER MARTHA) *stands by,*
watching anxiously, and holding a candle
in her hand. The ANGELS' *song ceases.*]
DR. WACHLER (*rising*). You are right!
DEACONESS. Is she dead?
20 DR. WACHLER (*sadly*). She is dead.

ANTON CHEKHOV

ANTON CHEKHOV became "the most beloved of all authors" among the Russians. The phrase is from Nemirovitch-Dantchenko, co-founder with Stanislavsky of the Moscow Art Theatre. Chekhov's name is inseparably linked with that organization which first succeeded in producing his plays to bring out their full value on the stage. Nemirovitch-Dantchenko, who has every right to speak, called the Moscow Art Theatre "the Theatre of Chekhov," and devoted much of *My Life in the Russian Theatre* to an affectionate memoir of the dramatist. Chekhov's name also stands for a masterpiece of modern drama, *The Cherry Orchard*. Though his other plays are esteemed and are occasionally revived, it is this last and finest of them that gives him his high rank in the company of Ibsen. It was the culminating creation of a gentle and versatile man. He was only forty-three when he died, but he had labored successfully in three different careers: as a physician, winning the affection of the poor among whom he would occasionally practise when their need was compelling, although he had given up medicine for letters; as a short-story writer; and finally as a dramatist. The alert personality of Chekhov synthesized these apparently divergent activities and levied tribute on an interesting total experience to produce his dramas.

We have extensive knowledge of the dramatist through the memoirs of his friends and from his own notebooks and letters. They give us an illuminating picture of Chekhov as a man and as an artist. He was born January 17, 1860, in the Ukraine city of Taganrog on the northwest corner of the Sea of Azov. The people of this sun-warmed province are said to be less sombre and melancholy than the standard Russian. Chekhov's father was not softened by the locale, for he was harsh, exacting, and ritualistic in his demands. If Anton failed to sing well during the incessant religious ceremonies, he was beaten. He remembered his childhood with sorrow. In a characteristic sentence, he wrote at the age of thirty-four: "I began to believe in progress in my early childhood, because of the tremendous difference between the time when I was still whipped and the time I was not." Many of the sad and despairing outcries wrung from the characters in the plays arose without doubt from the memory of his own unhappy lot as a "little convict."

Chekhov's family had formerly been serfs on the Cherry-Orchard lands of the decaying aristocracy. By hard work and determination his grandfather accumulated enough to buy his freedom for 3,500 rubles in 1841. In Anton's day this kindly grandfather was supervisor of Count Platov's estate on the steppes back of Taganrog. Anton lived with him during the summers, and remembered him with affection though he made him work "from dawn to dusk." There he learned much for future use about this phase of Russian life. His father was a grocer in Taganrog. Anton hated the melancholy hours he was forced to spend behind the counter learning the trade,

147

but out of the experience and the observation of the types that came daily to the store, he later made some of his best stories. His mother was genial and full of understanding; she softened the bitterness of Anton's early years with her affection and her stories of life in the vast Russia to the North.

Chekhov's school life was no escape from unpleasantness. He was placed in "The School of the Emperor Constantine," presided over by an eccentric Greek master, where he formed a profound distaste for all things Greek. Two years later, through the foresight of his mother, he was transferred to the Classical Gymnasium where his naturally sunny personality and love of life began to expand. By ingenious disguises he managed to witness many performances at the theatre though attendance was forbidden him and the penalties for discovery were severe. He was far from brilliant as a student, but his observation of people and their traits of character developed at school as well as at the grocery store, and his masters and fellow students were all later embedded in his writings. When Chekhov was sixteen his father failed in business, his effects were sold, and the family moved to Moscow. Chekhov stayed behind at the Gymnasium and as tutor to the nephew of the man who bought out his father. He rode horseback in the country with his pupil, and, except for the first of the attacks of illness that were to cut short his life, his last days in Taganrog were not unpleasant. He began reading more widely, and became more interested in the theatre and in the idea of writing. More than ever he was ambitious to rise to freedom and independence.

In 1879 Chekhov went to Moscow where his father worked in a store and the family endured poverty. Chekhov entered the medical school at the University of Moscow and took his degree in 1884. The necessity for self support and the need of his family had, in the meantime, compelled Chekhov to earn money, and he found that he could do this by writing. He won some success in the magazines with short humorous pieces, and in the year of his graduation he published a collection of them that excited interest. He was happy to be a doctor, but the prospect of a literary career was even more attractive to him. He did not seriously practice medicine, partially because of his failing health; but he gave his services generously in time of need, notably during the cholera epidemic of 1892 when he served as a district physician. Like Maugham, Schintzler, and some other celebrated dramatists, Chekhov made more of his knowledge and skill as a physician to write with penetrating understanding about the sick lives of men than to attempt to cure them. The nervous, sensitive, shrewd Chekhov, with his singular mixture of humor, sentiment, and tears, seemed to be fashioned especially for studying humanity and interpreting sick and dying Russia at the close of the last century.

The reputation of Chekhov as a writer was first established with his short stories. A second collection of them was issued in 1886. They were generally well received, and more of them flowed easily from his pen. At the time of his death he was more famous as the author of over four hundred sketches and stories than as a dramatist. This was due, in no small part at least, to the moribund condition of the Russian theatre in the eighties and early nineties. Chekhov loved the theatre enough to speak his scorn for the low estate to which it had fallen and the kind of plays it presented. In *The Sea Gull*, a strongly autobiographical play in which he introduced himself as Trigorin, and expressed his own views on the theatre, he caused the young Treplieff to say: "I despise the modern stage . . . to me the theatre is merely the vehicle of convention and prejudice." In anger he cried out at his actress mother, "Go back to your beloved stage and act the miserable ditch-water plays you so much admire!" Yet Chekhov aspired to write plays as eagerly as Treplieff. He had made up plays as a schoolboy and enjoyed seeing them acted by amateurs. He had been writing and producing them without much success for at least ten years before the Moscow Art Theatre was formed.

The first of these of any importance, *Ivanov*, was presented on November 17, 1887, at Korsh's private theatre in Moscow. Korsh knew Chekhov's humorous pieces, and Chekhov had twice visited Korsh's Theatre, one of the best among the many small theatres of Russia. Korsh invited Chekhov to write a play for the company, and the result was *Ivanov*. He had written it in just two weeks. Despite its many faults, it suggested the qualities that, fully developed, distinguished *Uncle Vanya* and *The Cherry Orchard*. Ivanov, the central figure, is afflicted with the heavy sadness of so many of Chekhov's characters. He neglects his frail and sickly wife, hastens her death by his conduct, and then is tormented by his remorse. "I am a broken man," he laments, "I am old at thirty. . . . I wander like a shadow among other men, not knowing whether I am alive or what it is that I want. . . . So I carry my sadness with me wherever I go. . . . Yes, I am lost forever." Weary, discouraged, hopeless, and without faith, he commits suicide.

Ivanov was a minor success which made news. A riot broke out in the audience, Chekhov's sister fainted, and students were taken out of the gallery by the police. Critics representing the taste of that day, which had condemned Ibsen's *A Doll's House* and *Ghosts* as repulsive and degrading, called *Ivanov* "bold, cynical, immoral, disgusting." The author himself said, "This play may be bad, yet I have created a type of literary significance." And that was right. Its basic structure and tone are clear indications of the style that reached perfection sixteen years later in *The Cherry Orchard*.

The reception of *Ivanov* encouraged Chekhov to write more plays. In the next few years he produced several one act pieces in a variety of moods. The most popular of these were *The Bear*, really a vaudeville skit; an amusing farce called *The Proposal* that was a favorite in the provincial theatre; and the more ambitious dramatic study, *The Swan Song*, that was produced at Korsh's Theatre. He also attempted a serious play on a significant theme entitled *The Wood Spirit*, sometimes translated as *The Wood Demon*. It was refused by the Imperial theatres, but was given a production, with little success, at Abramova's Theatre in December, 1889. Chekhov was disappointed, but he took the failure resignedly. He professed surprise "that such strange things should come from my pen." And he explained his maturing conviction that plays should be "just as complex and as simple as life is. People dine and at the same time their happiness is made or their lives are broken."

After these failures, Chekhov, in accordance with the advice of a friend, gave up the attempt to write plays, and went traveling. In a typically jocular paragraph of autobiography in a letter to his friend V. A. Tikhonov, he summarized his activities: "In 1890 I made a journey to Saghalien across Siberia, returning by sea. In 1891 I made a tour of Europe, where I drank splendid wine and ate oysters. In 1892 I was at a birthday party where I had a spree with V. A. Tikhonov." It was seven years before he returned to the stage and presented *The Sea Gull*, a drama of lyrical moods, of emotional distress, and of extensive symbolism. The central idea of this play and some of its basic episodes were drawn directly from actual occurrences in the life of an artist who at one time stayed with Chekhov. Chekhov made these episodes into a parable on the ineffectiveness of the moody artists of the 1880's and 1890's, and the tragedy of their frustrations. It was produced at the Alexandriski Theatre, St. Petersburg, in October, 1896, and it was a failure. In the same year he reworked *The Wood Demon*, turning it into another study of the deep melancholy of the age. It was printed as *Uncle Vanya* in 1897, and was played throughout the province.

All these efforts preceded the now celebrated alliance of Chekhov with the Moscow Art Theatre. That association was fortunate for both. Chekhov's decade of playwriting had defined his view of life and his extremely individual approach to dramaturgy. But the poetic atmosphere of the plays, the delicate nuances upon which his effects depend, and the relative subordination of plot action to tenuous and illusive soul states, asked entirely too much of the actors and directors even among the small, experimental theatres that flourished in Russia in the 1890's. Chekhov was discontented, and thought his plays were failures. After the unsuccessful staging of *The Sea Gull*, Chekhov exclaimed bitterly, "Never will I write these plays or try to produce them, not if I live to be 700 years old."

Chekhov could not foresee that two young Russians of genius, Nemirovitch-Dantchenko and Stanislavsky, at their famous eighteen-hour conference, June 21, 1897, would plan to organize and train a company to produce effectively the very kind of play that Chekhov had just renounced, and we accept with indulgent understanding these outbursts of inconsistency. The details of their dramatic principles, and the manner in which the Moscow Art Theatre under Stanislavsky transformed the theory into a system, are set down in his *My Life in Art* (1938) and *An Actor Prepares* (1936), and in Dantchenko's *My Life in the Russian Theatre* (1936). The central point was their determination, at whatever cost in time and training, to create "a theatre of inner feeling," and to go beyond surface realism to the surrender of the personality of the actor to that of the character in the play. They might have had in mind the crucial obstacle in the way of a Chekhov success on the stage; for his plays must be acted perfectly or admit defeat. Their interest is in the group as a whole, not on a central character or two; and each individual in the entire group is meticulously but not obtrusively studied in relation to each of the others and to their environment. The natural impulse of the reader or watcher is always to give his attention to one or two people. But Chekhov deliberately decentralizes the interest and attention, and makes the action seem casual. In *The Cherry Orchard* Charlotte says, with life-like incongruity, "My little dog eats nuts." And Lopakhin thrusts his head in at the door where Barbara and Anya are sighing over the doomed property and, "mooing like a cow," cries "Moooo!" and goes away again. These irrelevancies might easily ruin some plays, but in Chekhov's dramas they may be as pertinent and eloquent as the big scene itself.

The Chekhov plays now passed into the hands of a company that could make an artistic and living unit of all their silences, extraneous talk and behavior, and their central tragedy; and could capture an audience with them. Chekhov was filled with new enthusiasm when he saw the company at work in September, 1898; and he wrote, "The *mise-en-scène* is remarkable, never before seen in Russia. Among other things they are putting on my ill-fated *The Sea Gull.*" To this day a sea gull decorates the programs of the Moscow Art Theatre, in recognition of their first staging of Chekhov. This play was followed by successful productions of *Uncle Vanya* in 1899, and *The Three Sisters* in 1901.

The Cherry Orchard was produced at the Moscow Art Theatre on January 17, 1904. It reached a higher level than any of the earlier plays. The theme is universal; every generation sees it reenacted in some form as the pattern of life of individuals, families, towns, and even nations is broken up by economic and cultural changes to which they are no longer resilient enough or imaginative enough to respond with vigor and dispatch. There is dramatic pathos in the dispossession of the charming and cultivated Madame Ranevsky, who scatters money about, and sighs over her lost world, of which she and her orchard are the symbols; of Gayef, her impractical brother, who practises billiards with an imaginary cue and balls; and all the rest of them, who are held by tradition and sentiment to the decaying order that produced them. They have no skill or competence in a world that is changing before their averted eyes and carries their destruction with it. They dreamily and passively hope in the face of inevitable disaster that something will turn up to save them. Their habit of life has robbed them of action; they cannot even answer yes or no to the crude but aggressive Lopakhin, son of ex-slaves of this very land, who buys the estate and supplants them as master.

The thesis is not obtrusive. Chekhov, like Maugham, insisted that the solution of problems was the business of the specialist in the field, not of the dramatist. He presented realistically the spectacle of life as an end in itself. His characters are abundantly rich in personality, their own sorrows and despairs, their personal problems and defeats, forming an undersong to the rhythmic flow of the larger drama in whose meshes they are caught and carried along. Their suppressed, melancholy cries answer like an echo of the symbolic sound of the ax at the roots of the Cherry Orchard. By choosing superior people, cultivated, complex, subtle, and distressed, Chekhov gave to realism a beauty and a delicacy that would have been inappropriate to the outcasts and the degenerates in plays like Gorky's *The Lower Depths* and Hauptmann's *Before Dawn.* The finesse of the acting of the Moscow Art company and the studied realism of the setting, with open doors in the rear and people in the rooms beyond the scene of the action to give depth and naturalness, allowed these qualities to come through with superb artistry. The company has played *The Cherry Orchard* in most of the theatrical capitals of the world. Their first production in America was at Jolson's Fifty-ninth Street Theatre on January 22, 1923. The play has been translated several times into English since

1908, when M. S. Mandell made a version for the Dramatic Department of the Yale Courant under the title, *The Cherry Garden*. George Claderon's excellent translation was made in 1912.

Chekhov's health had long been precarious, compelling him to live in the warmer south. The ravages of tuberculosis began to undermine him. He was seriously ill when *The Cherry Orchard* was produced, with his wife as the incomparable Madame Ranevsky. Nevertheless he journeyed to Moscow to see the performance. Later in the year he went to the Black Forest in the hope of finding relief, and with plans for another play. He died at Badenweiler on July 2, 1904, less than six months after the opening of *The Cherry Orchard*. His body was brought back to Moscow and buried within the walls of Novodevichii Convent whose cupolas he had loved to watch at sunset and whose quiet cemetery among the poplar trees he had loved to visit.

THE CHERRY ORCHARD

CHARACTERS

MADAME RANÉVSKY, *a landowner*
ÁNYA, *her daughter, aged seventeen*
BARBARA, *her adopted daughter, aged twenty-seven*
LEONÍD GÁYEF, *brother of Madame Ranévsky*
LOPÁKHIN, *a merchant*
PETER TROPHÍMOF, *a student*
SIMEÓNOF-PÍSHTCHIK, *a landowner*

CHARLOTTE, *a governess*
EPHIKHÓDOF, *a clerk*
DUNYÁSHA, *a housemaid*
FIRS, *man-servant, aged eighty-seven*
YÁSHA, *a young man-servant*
TRAMP
Stationmaster, Post-Office Official, Guests, Servants, etc.

The action takes place on Madame Ranévsky's property.

ACT I

A room which is still called the nursery. One door leads to ÁNYA's *room. Dawn; the sun will soon rise. It is already May; the cherry trees are in blossom, but it is cold in the garden and there is a morning frost. The windows are closed.*

Enter DUNYÁSHA *with a candle, and* LOPÁKHIN *with a book in his hand.]*

LOPÁKHIN. So the train has come in, 10 thank Heaven. What is the time?

DUNYÁSHA. Nearly two. (*Putting the candle out.*) It is light already.

LOPÁKHIN. How late is the train? A couple of hours at least. (*Yawning and stretching.*) What do you think of me? A fine fool I have made of myself. I came on purpose to meet them at the station and then I went and fell asleep, fell asleep as I sat in my 20 chair. What a nuisance it is! You might have woke me up anyway.

DUNYÁSHA. I thought that you had gone. (*She listens.*) That sounds like them driving up.

LOPÁKHIN (*listening*). No; they have got to get the luggage out and all that. (*A pause.*) Madame Ranévsky has been five years abroad. I wonder what she has become like. What a splendid creature she is! So easy and simple in her ways. I remember when I was a youngster of fifteen my old father (he used to keep the shop here in the village then) struck me in the face with his fist and set my nose bleeding. We had come, for some reason or other, I forget what, into the courtyard, and he had been drinking. Madame Ranévsky—I remember it like yesterday, still a young girl, and oh, so slender—brought me to the wash-hand stand, here, in this very room, in the nursery. "Don't cry, little peasant," she said, "it'll mend by your wed-

THE CHERRY ORCHARD: Translated, with text notes, by George Calderon. Reprinted by permission of and special arrangement with Mr. Mitchell Kennerley.

ding." [1] (*A pause.*) "Little peasant"!
... My father, it is true, was a
peasant, and here am I in a white
waistcoat and brown boots; a silk
purse out of a sow's ear, as you might
say; just turned rich, with heaps of
money, but when you come to look
at it, still a peasant of the peasants.
(*Turning over the pages of the book.*)
Here's this book that I was reading 10
and didn't understand a word of it;
I just sat reading and fell asleep.

DUNYÁSHA. The dogs never slept all
night; they knew that their master
and mistress were coming.

LOPÁKHIN. What's the matter with you,
Dunyásha? You're all . . .

DUNYÁSHA. My hands are trembling;
I feel quite faint.

LOPÁKHIN. You are too refined, Dun- 20
yásha; that's what it is. You dress
yourself like a young lady; and look
at your hair! You ought not to do it;
you ought to remember your place.

[*Enter* EPHIKHÓDOF *with a nosegay. He is
dressed in a short jacket and brightly
polished boots which squeak noisily. As
he comes in he drops the nosegay.*]

EPHIKHÓDOF (*picking it up*). The gardener has sent this; he says it is to go 30
in the dining-room. (*Handing it to*
DUNYÁSHA.)

LOPÁKHIN. And bring me some quass.

DUNYÁSHA. Yes, sir. (*Exit* DUNYÁSHA.)

EPHIKHÓDOF. There's a frost this morning, three degrees, and the cherry
trees all in blossom. I can't say I
think much of our climate; (*Sighing.*)
that is impossible. Our climate is not
adapted to contribute; and I should 40
like to add, with your permission,
that only two days ago I bought myself a new pair of boots, and I venture to assure you they do squeak

[1] *It'll mend by your wedding:* a proverbial
phrase.

beyond all bearing. What am I t
grease them with?

LOPÁKHIN. Get out; I'm tired of you.

EPHIKHÓDOF. Every day some misfor
tune happens to me; but do
grumble? No; I am used to it; I ca
afford to smile.

[*Enter* DUNYÁSHA, *and hands a glass o
quass to* LOPÁKHIN.]

EPHIKHÓDOF. I must be going. (*H
knocks against a chair, which falls to th
ground.*) There you are! (*In a voice o
triumph.*) You see, if I may venture
on the expression, the sort of inci
dents *inter alia*. It really is astonish
ing! (*Exit* EPHIKHÓDOF.)

DUNYÁSHA. To tell you the truth, Yer
molái Alexéyitch, Ephikhódof ha
made me a proposal.

LOPÁKHIN. Hmph!

DUNYÁSHA. I hardly know what to do
He is such a well-behaved youn
man, only so often when he talks on
doesn't know what he means. It i
all so nice and full of good feeling
but you can't make out what i
means. I fancy I am rather fond o
him. He adores me passionately. H
is a most unfortunate man; ever
day something seems to happen to
him. They call him "Twenty-tw
misfortunes," that's his nickname.

LOPÁKHIN (*listening*). There, surely tha
is them coming!

DUNYÁSHA. They're coming! Oh, wha
is the matter with me? I am all
turning cold.

LOPÁKHIN. Yes, there they are, and n
mistake. Let's go and meet them
Will she know me again, I wonder
It is five years since we met.

DUNYÁSHA. I am going to faint! . . . I
am going to faint!

[*Two carriages are heard driving up to th
house.* LOPÁKHIN *and* DUNYÁSHA *exeun
quickly. The stage remains empty. A*

hubbub begins in the neighboring rooms. FIRS *walks hastily across the stage, leaning on a walking-stick. He has been to meet them at the station. He is wearing an old-fashioned livery and a tall hat; he mumbles something to himself, but not a word is audible. The noise behind the scenes grows louder and louder. A voice says: "Let's go this way." Enter* MADAME RANÉVSKY, ÁNYA, CHARLOTTE, 10 *leading a little dog on a chain, all dressed in traveling-dresses;* BARBARA *in greatcoat, with a kerchief over her head,* GÁYEF, SIMEÓNOF-PÍSHTCHIK, LOPÁKHIN, DUNYÁSHA, *carrying parcel and umbrella, servants with luggage, all cross the stage.*]

ÁNYA. Come through this way. Do you remember what room this is, mamma?

MADAME RANÉVSKY (*joyfully, through her* 20 *tears*). The nursery.

BARBARA. How cold it is. My hands are simply frozen. (*To* MADAME RANÉVSKY.) Your two rooms, the white room and the violet room, are just the same as they were, mamma.

MADAME RANÉVSKY. My nursery, my dear, beautiful nursery! This is where I used to sleep when I was a little girl. (*Crying.*) I am like a little 30 girl still. (*Kissing* GÁYEF *and* BARBARA *and then* GÁYEF *again.*) Barbara has not altered a bit; she is just like a nun; and I knew Dunyásha at once. (*Kissing* DUNYÁSHA.)

GÁYEF. Your train was two hours late. What do you think of that? There's punctuality for you!

CHARLOTTE (*to* SIMEÓNOF-PÍSHTCHIK). My little dog eats nuts. 40

PÍSHTCHIK (*astonished*). You don't say so! Well, I never!

[*Exeunt all but* ÁNYA *and* DUNYÁSHA.]

DUNYÁSHA. At last you've come! (*She takes off* ÁNYA'*s overcoat and hat.*)

ÁNYA. I have not slept for four nights on the journey. I am frozen to death.

DUNYÁSHA. It was Lent when you went away. There was snow on the ground; it was freezing; but now! Oh, my dear! (*Laughing and kissing her.*) How I have waited for you, my joy, my light! Oh, I must tell you something at once, I cannot wait another minute.

ÁNYA (*without interest*). What, again?

DUNYÁSHA. Ephikhódof, the clerk, proposed to me in Easter Week.

ÁNYA. Same old story. . . . (*Putting her hair straight.*) All my hairpins have dropped out. (*She is very tired, staggering with fatigue.*)

DUNYÁSHA. I hardly know what to think of it. He loves me! Oh, how he loves me!

ÁNYA (*looking into her bedroom, affectionately*). My room, my windows, just as if I had never gone away! I am at home again! When I wake up in the morning I shall run out into the garden. . . . Oh, if only I could get to sleep! I have not slept the whole journey from Paris, I was so nervous and anxious.

DUNYÁSHA. Monsieur Trophímof arrived the day before yesterday.

ÁNYA (*joyfully*). Peter?

DUNYÁSHA. He is sleeping outside in the bath-house; he is living there. He was afraid he might be in the way. (*Looking at her watch.*) I'd like to go and wake him, only Mamzelle Barbara told me not to. "Mind you don't wake him," she said.

[*Enter* BARBARA *with bunch of keys hanging from her girdle.*]

BARBARA. Dunyásha, go and get some coffee, quick. Mamma wants some coffee.

DUNYÁSHA. In a minute! (*Exit* DUNYÁSHA.)

BARBARA. Well, thank Heaven, you

have come. Here you are at home again. (*Caressing her.*) My little darling is back! My pretty one is back!

ÁNYA. What I've had to go through!

BARBARA. I can believe you.

ÁNYA. I left here in Holy Week. How cold it was! Charlotte would talk the whole way and keep doing conjuring tricks. What on earth made you tie Charlotte round my neck? 10

BARBARA. Well, you couldn't travel alone, my pet. At seventeen!

ÁNYA. When we got to Paris, it was so cold! There was snow on the ground. I can't talk French a bit. Mamma was on the fifth floor of a big house. When I arrived there were a lot of Frenchmen with her, and ladies, and an old Catholic priest with a book, and it was very uncomfortable and full of 20 tobacco smoke. I suddenly felt so sorry for mamma, oh so sorry! I took her head in my arms and squeezed it and could not let it go, and then mamma kept kissing me and crying.

BARBARA (*crying*). Don't go on; don't go on!

ÁNYA. She's sold her villa near Mentone already. She's nothing left, absolutely nothing; and I hadn't a 30 farthing either. We only just managed to get home. And mamma won't understand! We get out at a station to have some dinner, and she asks for all the most expensive things and gives the waiters a florin each for a tip; and Charlotte does the same. And Yásha wanted his portion, too. It was too awful! Yásha is mamma's new manservant. We 40 have brought him back with us.

BARBARA. I've seen the rascal.

ÁNYA. Come, tell me all about everything! Has the interest on the mortgage been paid?

BARBARA. How could it be?

ÁNYA. Oh, dear! Oh, dear!

BARBARA. The property will be sold in August.

ÁNYA. Oh, dear! Oh, dear!

LOPÁKHIN (*looking in at the door and mooing like a cow*). Moo-oo! (*He goes away again.*)

BARBARA (*laughing through her tears, and shaking her fist at the door*). Oh, I should like to give him one!

ÁNYA (*embracing* BARBARA *softly*). Barbara, has he proposed to you? (BARBARA *shakes her head.*)

ÁNYA. And yet I am sure he loves you. Why don't you come to an understanding? What are you waiting for?

BARBARA. I don't think anything will come of it. He has so much to do; he can't be bothered with me; he hardly takes any notice. Confound the man! I can't bear to see him! Every one talks about our marriage; every one congratulates me; but, as a matter of fact, there is nothing in it; it's all a dream. (*Changing her tone.*) You've got on a brooch like a bee.

ÁNYA (*sadly*). Mamma bought it me. (*Going into her room, talking gayly, like a child.*) When I was in Paris, I went up in a balloon!

BARBARA. How glad I am you are back, my little pet! my pretty one!

[DUNYÁSHA *has already returned with a coffee-pot and begins to prepare the coffee.*

BARBARA (*standing by the door*). I trudge about all day looking after things and I think and think. What are we to do? If only we could marry you to some rich man it would be a load off my mind. I would go into a retreat, and then to Kief, to Moscow I would tramp about from one holy place to another, always tramping and tramping. What bliss!

ÁNYA. The birds are singing in the garden. What time is it now?

BARBARA. It must be past two. It is time to go to bed, my darling. (*Following* ÁNYA *into her room.*) What bliss!

[*Enter* YÁSHA *with a shawl and a traveling-bag.*]

YÁSHA (*crossing the stage, delicately*). May I pass this way, mademoiselle?

DUNYÁSHA. One would hardly know you, Yásha. How you've changed abroad! 10

YÁSHA. Ahem! And who may you be?

DUNYÁSHA. When you left here I was a little thing like that. (*Indicating with her hand.*) My name is Dunyásha, Theodore Kozoyédof's daughter. Don't you remember me?

YÁSHA. Ahem! You little cucumber! (*He looks round cautiously, then embraces her. She screams and drops a saucer. Exit* 20 YÁSHA *hastily.*)

BARBARA (*in the doorway, crossly*). What's all this?

DUNYÁSHA (*crying*). I've broken a saucer.

BARBARA. Well, it brings luck.

[*Enter* ÁNYA *from her room.*]

ÁNYA. We must tell mamma that Peter's here.

BARBARA. I've told them not to wake him.

ÁNYA (*thoughtfully*). It's just six years 30 since papa died. And only a month afterwards poor little Grisha was drowned in the river; my pretty little brother, only seven years old! It was too much for mamma; she ran away, ran away without looking back. (*Shuddering.*) How well I can understand her, if only she knew! (*A pause.*) Peter Trophímof was Grisha's tutor; 40 he might remind her.

[*Enter* FIRS *in long coat and white waistcoat.*]

FIRS (*going over to the coffee-pot, anxiously*). My mistress is going to take coffee here. (*Putting on white gloves.*) Is the coffee ready? (*Sternly, to* DUNYÁSHA.) Here, girl, where's the cream?

DUNYÁSHA. Oh, dear! Oh, dear! (*Exit* DUNYÁSHA *hastily.*)

FIRS (*bustling about the coffee-pot*). Ah, you . . . job-lot! [1] (*Mumbling to himself.*) She's come back from Paris. The master went to Paris once in a post-chaise. (*Laughing.*)

BARBARA. What is it, Firs?

FIRS. I beg your pardon? (*Joyfully.*) My mistress has come home; at last I've seen her. Now I'm ready to die. [*He cries with joy. Enter* MADAME RANÉVSKY, LOPÁKHIN, GÁYEF, *and* PÍSHTCHIK; PÍSHTCHIK *in Russian breeches and coat of fine cloth.* GÁYEF *as he enters makes gestures as if playing billiards.*]

MADAME RANÉVSKY. What was the expression? Let me see. "I'll put the red in the corner pocket; double into the middle—"

GÁYEF. I'll chip the red in the right-hand top. Once upon a time, Lyuba, when we were children, we used to sleep here side by side in two little cots, and now I'm fifty-one, and can't bring myself to believe it.

LOPÁKHIN. Yes, time flies.

GÁYEF. Who's that?

LOPÁKHIN. Time flies, I say.

GÁYEF. There's a smell of patchouli!

ÁNYA. I am going to bed. Good-night, mamma. (*Kissing her mother.*)

MADAME RANÉVSKY. My beloved little girl! (*Kissing her hands.*) Are you glad you're home again? I can't come to my right senses.

ÁNYA. Good-night, uncle.

GÁYEF (*kissing her face and hands*). God bless you, little Ánya. How like your mother you are! (*To* MADAME

---

[1] *Job-lot.* In the original, *nedotëpa*, a word invented by Tchekhov, and now established as classical. Derived from *ne*, not, and *dotyápat*, to finish chopping.

RANÉVSKY.) You were just such another girl at her age, Lyuba.

[ÁNYA *shakes hands with* LOPÁKHIN *and* SIMEÓNOF-PÍSHTCHIK, *and exit, shutting her bedroom door behind her.*]

MADAME RANÉVSKY. She's very, very tired.

PÍSHTCHIK. It must have been a long journey.

BARBARA (*to* LOPÁKHIN *and* PÍSHTCHIK). Well, gentlemen, it's past two; time you were off.

MADAME RANÉVSKY (*laughing*). You haven't changed a bit, Barbara! (*Drawing her to herself and kissing her.*) I'll just finish my coffee, then we'll all go. (FIRS *puts a footstool under her feet.*) Thank you, friend. I'm used to my coffee. I drink it day and night. Thank you, you dear old man. (*Kissing* FIRS.)

BARBARA. I'll go and see if they've got all the luggage. (*Exit* BARBARA.)

MADAME RANÉVSKY. Can it be me that's sitting here? (*Laughing.*) I want to jump and wave my arms about. (*Pausing and covering her face.*) Surely I must be dreaming! God knows I love my country. I love it tenderly. I couldn't see out of the window from the train, I was crying so. (*Crying.*) However, I must drink my coffee. Thank you, Firs; thank you, you dear old man. I'm so glad to find you still alive.

FIRS. The day before yesterday.

GÁYEF. He's hard of hearing.

LOPÁKHIN. I've got to be off for Kharkof by the five-o'clock train. Such a nuisance! I wanted to stay and look at you and talk to you. You're as splendid as you always were.

PÍSHTCHIK (*sighing heavily*). Handsomer than ever and dressed like a Parisian . . . Perish my wagon and all its wheels!

LOPÁKHIN. Your brother, Leoníd Andréyitch, says I'm a snob, a moneygrubber. He can say what he likes. I don't care a hang. Only I want you to believe in me as you used to; I want your wonderful, touching eyes to look at me as they used to. Merciful God in heaven! My father was your father's serf, and your grandfather's serf before him; but you, you did so much for me in the old days that I've forgotten everything, and I love you like a sister—more than a sister.

MADAME RANÉVSKY. I can't sit still! I can't do it! (*Jumping up and walking about in great agitation.*) This happiness is more than I can bear. Laugh at me! I am a fool! (*Kissing a cupboard.*) My darling old cupboard! (*Caressing a table.*) My dear little table!

GÁYEF. Nurse is dead since you went away.

MADAME RANÉVSKY (*sitting down and drinking coffee*). Yes, Heaven rest her soul. They wrote and told me.

GÁYEF. And Anastási is dead. Squinteyed Peter has left us and works in the town at the Police Inspector's now. (GÁYEF *takes out a box of sugar candy from his pocket, and begins to eat it.*)

PÍSHTCHIK. My daughter Dáshenka sent her compliments.

LOPÁKHIN. I long to say something charming and delightful to you. (*Looking at his watch.*) I'm just off; there's no time to talk. Well, yes, I'll put it in two or three words. You know that your cherry orchard is going to be sold to pay the mortgage: the sale is fixed for the 22d of August; but don't you be uneasy, my dear lady; sleep peacefully; there's a way out of it. This is my plan. Listen to me carefully. Your property is only fifteen miles from the town; the railway runs close beside it; and if only you will cut up the cherry orchard and the land along the river into building lots and let it off on lease for villas, you will get at least two thousand five hundred pounds a year out of it.

GÁYEF. Come, come! What rubbish you're talking!

MADAME RANÉVSKY. I don't quite understand what you mean, Yermolái Alexéyitch.

LOPÁKHIN. You will get a pound a year at least for every acre from the tenants, and if you advertise the thing at once, I am ready to bet whatever you like, by the autumn you won't have a clod of that earth left on your hands. It'll all be snapped up. In two words, I congratulate you; you are saved. It's a first-class site, with a good deep river. Only, of course you will have to put it in order and clear the ground; you will have to pull down all the old buildings—this house, for instance, which is no longer fit for anything; you'll have to cut down the cherry orchard. . . .

MADAME RANÉVSKY. Cut down the cherry orchard! Excuse me, but you don't know what you are talking about. If there is one thing that's interesting, remarkable in fact, in the whole province, it's our cherry orchard.

LOPÁKHIN. There's nothing remarkable about the orchard except that it's a very big one. It only bears once every two years, and then you don't know what to do with the fruit. Nobody wants to buy it.

GÁYEF. Our cherry orchard is mentioned in Andréyevsky's Encyclopaedia.

LOPÁKHIN (looking at his watch). If we don't make up our minds or think of any way, on the 22d of August the cherry orchard and the whole property will be sold by auction. Come, make up your mind! There's no other way out of it, I swear—absolutely none.

FIRS. In the old days, forty or fifty years ago, they used to dry the cherries and soak 'em and pickle 'em, and make jam of 'em; and the dried cherries . . .

GÁYEF. Shut up, Firs.

FIRS. The dried cherries used to be sent in wagons to Moscow and Kharkof. A heap of money! The dried cherries were soft and juicy and sweet and sweet-smelling then. They knew some way in those days.

MADAME RANÉVSKY. And why don't they do it now?

FIRS. They've forgotten. Nobody remembers how to do it.

PÍSHTCHIK (to MADAME RANÉVSKY). What about Paris? How did you get on? Did you eat frogs?

MADAME RANÉVSKY. Crocodiles.

PÍSHTCHIK. You don't say so! Well, I never!

LOPÁKHIN. Until a little while ago there was nothing but gentry and peasants in the villages; but now villa residents have made their appearance. All the towns, even the little ones, are surrounded by villas now. In another twenty years the villa resident will have multiplied like anything. At present he only sits and drinks tea on his veranda, but it is quite likely that he will soon take to cultivating his three acres of land, and then your old cherry orchard will become fruitful, rich and happy. . . .

GÁYEF (angry). What gibberish!

[*Enter* BARBARA *and* YÁSHA.]

BARBARA (*taking out a key and noisily unlocking an old-fashioned cupboard*). There are two telegrams for you, mamma. Here they are.

MADAME RANÉVSKY (*tearing them up without reading them*). They're from Paris. I've done with Paris.

GÁYEF. Do you know how old this cupboard is, Lyuba? A week ago I pulled out the bottom drawer and saw a date burnt in it. That cupboard was made exactly a hundred years ago. What do you think of that, eh? We might celebrate its jubilee. It's only an inanimate thing, but for all that it's a historic cupboard.

PÍSHTCHIK (*astonished*). A hundred years? Well, I never!

GÁYEF (*touching the cupboard*). Yes, it's a wonderful thing. . . . Beloved and venerable cupboard; honor and glory to your existence, which for more than a hundred years has been directed to the noble ideals of justice and virtue. Your silent summons to profitable labor has never weakened in all these hundred years. (*Crying.*) You have upheld the courage of succeeding generations of our mankind; you have upheld faith in a better future and cherished in us ideals of goodness and social consciousness. (*A pause.*)

LOPÁKHIN. Yes. . . .

MADAME RANÉVSKY. You haven't changed, Leoníd.

GÁYEF (*embarrassed*). Off the white in the corner, chip the red in the middle pocket!

LOPÁKHIN (*looking at his watch*). Well, I must be off.

YÁSHA (*handing a box to* MADAME RANÉVSKY). Perhaps you'll take your pills now.

PÍSHTCHIK. You oughtn't to take medicine, dear lady. It does you neither good nor harm. Give them here, my friend. (*He empties all the pills into the palm of his hand, blows on them, puts them in his mouth, and swallows them down with a draught of quass.*) There!

MADAME RANÉVSKY (*alarmed*). Have you gone off your head?

PÍSHTCHIK. I've taken all the pills.

LOPÁKHIN. Greedy feller!

[*Every one laughs.*]

FIRS (*mumbling*). They were here in Easter Week and finished off a gallon of pickled gherkins.

MADAME RANÉVSKY. What's he talking about?

BARBARA. He's been mumbling like that these three years. We've got used to it.

YÁSHA. Advancing age.

[CHARLOTTE *crosses in a white frock, very thin, tightly laced, with a lorgnette at her waist.*]

LOPÁKHIN. Excuse me, Charlotte Ivánovna, I've not paid my respects to you yet. (*He prepares to kiss her hand.*)

CHARLOTTE (*drawing her hand away*). If one allows you to kiss one's hand, you will want to kiss one's elbow next, and then one's shoulder.

LOPÁKHIN. I'm having no luck to-day. (*All laugh.*) Charlotte Ivánovna, do us a conjuring trick.

MADAME RANÉVSKY. Charlotte, do do us a conjuring trick.

CHARLOTTE. No, thank you. I'm going to bed. (*Exit* CHARLOTTE.)

LOPÁKHIN. We shall meet again in three weeks. (*Kissing* MADAME RANÉVSKY'S *hand.*) Meanwhile, good-bye. I must be off. (*To* GÁYEF.) So-long. (*Kissing* PÍSHTCHIK.) Ta-ta. (*Shaking hands with* BARBARA, *then with* FIRS *and* YÁSHA.) I hate having to go. (*To* MADAME RANÉVSKY.) If you make up your mind about the villas, let me know, and I'll raise you five thousand pounds at once. Think it over seriously.

BARBARA (*angrily*). For Heaven's sake, do go!

LOPÁKHIN. I'm going, I'm going. (*Exit LOPÁKHIN.*)

GÁYEF. Snob! . . . However, *pardon!* Barbara's going to marry him; he's Barbara's young man.

BARBARA. You talk too much, uncle.

MADAME RANÉVSKY. Why, Barbara, I shall be very glad. He's a nice man.

PÍSHTCHIK. Not a doubt of it. . . . A most worthy individual. My Dáshenka, she says . . . oh, she says . . . lots of things. (*Snoring and waking up again at once.*) By the by, dear lady, can you lend me twenty-five pounds? I've got to pay the interest on my mortgage to-morrow.

BARBARA (*alarmed*). We can't! We can't!

MADAME RANÉVSKY. It really is a fact that I haven't any money.

PÍSHTCHIK. I'll find it somewhere. (*Laughing.*) I never lose hope. Last time I thought, "Now I really am done for, I'm a ruined man," when behold, they ran a railway over my land and paid me compensation. And so it'll be again; something will happen, if not to-day, then to-morrow. Dáshenka may win the twenty-thousand-pound prize; she's got a ticket in the lottery.

MADAME RANÉVSKY. The coffee's finished. Let's go to bed.

FIRS (*brushing GÁYEF's clothes, admonishingly*). You've put on the wrong trousers again. Whatever am I to do with you?

BARBARA (*softly*). Ánya is asleep. (*She opens the window quietly.*) The sun's up already; it isn't cold now. Look, mamma, how lovely the trees are.

Heavens! what a sweet air! The starlings are singing!

GÁYEF (*opening the other window*). The orchard is all white. You've not forgotten it, Lyuba? This long avenue going straight on, straight on, like a ribbon between the trees? It shines like silver on moonlight nights. Do you remember? You've not forgotten?

MADAME RANÉVSKY (*looking out into the garden*). Oh, my childhood, my pure and happy childhood! I used to sleep in this nursery. I used to look out from here into the garden. Happiness awoke with me every morning; and the orchard was just the same then as it is now; nothing is altered. (*Laughing with joy.*) It is all white, all white! Oh, my cherry orchard! After the dark and stormy autumn and the frosts of winter you are young again and full of happiness; the angels of heaven have not abandoned you. Oh! if only I could free my neck and shoulders from the stone that weighs them down! If only I could forget my past!

GÁYEF. Yes; and this orchard will be sold to pay our debts, however impossible it may seem. . . .

MADAME RANÉVSKY. Look! There's mamma walking in the orchard . . . in a white frock! (*Laughing with joy.*) There she is!

GÁYEF. Where?

BARBARA. Heaven help you!

MADAME RANÉVSKY. There's no one there really. It only looked like it; there on the right where the path turns down to the summer-house; there's a white tree that leans over and looks like a woman.

[*Enter* TROPHÍMOF *in a shabby student uniform and spectacles.*]

MADAME RANÉVSKY. What a wonderful

orchard, with its white masses of blossom and the blue sky above!

TROPHÍMOF. Lyubóf Andréyevna! (*She looks round at him.*) I only want to say, "How do you do," and go away at once. (*Kissing her hand eagerly.*) I was told to wait till the morning, but I hadn't the patience.

[MADAME RANÉVSKY *looks at him in astonishment.*]

BARBARA (*crying*). This is Peter Trophímof.

TROPHÍMOF. Peter Trophímof; I was Grisha's tutor, you know. Have I really altered so much?

[MADAME RANÉVSKY *embraces him and cries softly.*]

GÁYEF. Come, come, that's enough, Lyuba!

BARBARA (*crying*). I told you to wait till to-morrow, you know, Peter.

MADAME RANÉVSKY. My little Grisha! My little boy! Grisha . . . my son. . . .

BARBARA. It can't be helped, mamma. It was the will of God.

TROPHÍMOF (*gently, crying*). There, there!

MADAME RANÉVSKY (*crying*). He was drowned. My little boy was drowned. Why? What was the use of that, my dear? (*In a softer voice.*) Ánya's asleep in there, and I am speaking so loud, and making a noise. . . . But tell me, Peter, why have you grown so ugly? Why have you grown so old?

TROPHÍMOF. An old woman in the train called me a "mouldy gentleman."

MADAME RANÉVSKY. You were quite a boy then, a dear little student, and now your hair's going and you wear spectacles. Are you really still a student? (*Going toward the door.*)

TROPHÍMOF. Yes, I expect I shall be a perpetual student.

MADAME RANÉVSKY (*kissing her brother*

and then BARBARA). Well, go to bed. You've grown old too, Leoníd.

PÍSHTCHIK (*following her*). Yes, yes; time for bed. Oh, oh, my gout! I'll stay the night here. Don't forget, Lyubóf Andréyevna, my angel, to-morrow morning . . . twenty-five.

GÁYEF. He's still on the same string.

PÍSHTCHIK. Twenty-five . . . to pay the interest on my mortgage.

MADAME RANÉVSKY. I haven't any money, my friend.

PÍSHTCHIK. I'll pay you back, dear lady. It's a trifling sum.

MADAME RANÉVSKY. Well, well, Leoníd will give it you. Let him have it, Leoníd.

GÁYEF (*ironical*). I'll give it him right enough! Hold your pocket wide! [1]

MADAME RANÉVSKY. It can't be helped. . . . He needs it. He'll pay it back.

[*Exeunt* MADAME RANÉVSKY, TROPHÍMOF, PÍSHTCHIK, *and* FIRS. GÁYEF, BARBARA, *and* YÁSHA *remain.*]

GÁYEF. My sister hasn't lost her old habit of scattering the money. (*To* YÁSHA.) Go away, my lad! You smell of chicken.

YÁSHA (*laughing*). You're just the same as you always were, Leoníd Andréyevitch!

GÁYEF. Who's that? (*to* BARBARA.) What does he say?

BARBARA (*to* YÁSHA). Your mother's come up from the village. She's been waiting for you since yesterday in the servants' hall. She wants to see you.

YÁSHA. What a nuisance she is!

BARBARA. You wicked, unnatural son!

YÁSHA. Well, what do I want with her? She might just as well have waited till to-morrow. (*Exit* YÁSHA.)

BARBARA. Mamma is just like she used to be; she hasn't changed a bit. If

[1] *Hold your pocket wide:* a proverbial piece of irony.

she had her way, she'd give away everything she has.

GÁYEF. Yes. (*A pause.*) If people recommend very many cures for an illness, that means that the illness is incurable. I think and think, I batter my brains; I know of many remedies, very many, and that means really that there is none. How nice it would be to get a fortune left one by some- 10 body! How nice it would be if Ánya could marry a very rich man! How nice it would be to go to Yaroslav and try my luck with my aunt the Countess. My aunt is very, very rich, you know.

BARBARA (*crying softly*). If only God would help us!

GÁYEF. Don't howl! My aunt is very rich, but she does not like us. In the 20 first place, my sister married a solicitor, not a nobleman. (ÁNYA *appears in the doorway.*) She married a man who was not a nobleman, and it's no good pretending that she has led a virtuous life. She's a dear, kind, charming creature, and I love her very much, but whatever mitigating circumstances one may find for her, there's no getting round it that she's 30 a sinful woman. You can see it in her every gesture.

BARBARA (*whispering*). Ánya is standing in the door!

GÁYEF. Who's that? (*A pause.*) It's very odd, something's got into my right eye. I can't see properly out of it. Last Thursday when I was down at the District Court . . .

[ÁNYA *comes down.*] 40

BARBARA. Why aren't you asleep, Ánya?

ÁNYA. I can't sleep. It's no good trying.

GÁYEF. My little pet! (*Kissing* ÁNYA'S *hands and face.*) My little girl! (*Crying.*) You're not my niece; you're

my angel; you're my everything. Trust me, trust me. . . .

ÁNYA. I do trust you, uncle. Every one loves you, every one respects you; but dear, dear uncle, you ought to hold your tongue, only to hold your tongue. What were you saying just now about mamma?—about your own sister? What was the good of saying that?

GÁYEF. Yes, yes. (*Covering his face with her hand.*) You're quite right; it was awful of me! Lord, Lord! Save me from myself! And a little while ago I made a speech over a cupboard. What a stupid thing to do! As soon as I had done it, I knew it was stupid.

BARBARA. Yes, really, uncle. You ought to hold your tongue. Say nothing; that's all that's wanted.

ÁNYA. If only you would hold your tongue, you'd be so much happier!

GÁYEF. I will! I will! (*Kissing* ÁNYA'S *and* BARBARA'S *hands.*) I'll hold my tongue. But there's one thing I must say; it's business. Last Thursday, when I was down at the District Court, a lot of us were there together, we began to talk about this and that, one thing and another, and it seems I could arrange a loan on note of hand to pay the interest into the bank.

BARBARA. If only Heaven would help us!

GÁYEF. I'll go in on Tuesday and talk it over again. (*To* BARBARA.) Don't howl! (*To* ÁNYA.) Your mamma shall have a talk with Lopákhin. Of course he won't refuse her. And as soon as you are rested you must go to see your grandmother, the Countess, at Yaroslav. We'll operate from three points, and the trick is done. We'll pay the interest, I'm certain of it.

(*Taking sugar candy.*) I swear on my honor, or whatever you will, the property shall not be sold. (*Excitedly.*) I swear by my hope of eternal happiness! There's my hand on it. Call me a base, dishonorable man if I let it go to auction. I swear by my whole being!

ÁNYA (*calm again and happy*). What a dear you are, uncle, and how clever! 10 (*Embraces him.*) Now I'm easy again. I'm easy again! I'm happy!

[*Enter* FIRS.]

FIRS (*reproachfully*). Leoníd Andréyevitch, have you no fear of God? When are you going to bed?

GÁYEF. I'm just off—just off. You get along, Firs. I'll undress myself all right. Come, children, by-bye! Details to-morrow, but now let's go to 20 bed. (*Kissing* ÁNYA *and* BARBARA.) I'm a good Liberal, a man of the eighties. People abuse the eighties, but I think that I may say I've suffered something for my convictions in my time. It's not for nothing that the peasants love me. We ought to know the peasants; we ought to know with what . . .

ÁNYA. You're at it again, uncle!   30

BARBARA. Why don't you hold your tongue, uncle?

FIRS (*angrily*). Leoníd Andréyevitch!

GÁYEF. I'm coming; I'm coming. Now go to bed. Off two cushions in the middle pocket! I start another life! . . . (*Exit, with* FIRS *hobbling after him.*)

ÁNYA. Now my mind is at rest. I don't want to go to Yaroslav; I don't like 40

grandmamma; but my mind is at rest, thanks to Uncle Leoníd. (*She sits down.*)

BARBARA. Time for bed. I'm off. Whilst you were away there's been a scandal. You know that nobody lives in the old servants' quarters except the old people, Ephim, Pauline, Evstignéy, and old Karp. Well, they took to having in all sorts of queer fish to sleep there with them. I didn't say a word. But at last I heard they had spread a report that I had given orders that they were to have nothing but peas to eat; out of stinginess, you understand? It was all Evstignéy's doing. "Very well," I said to myself, "you wait a bit." So I sent for Evstignéy. (*Yawning.*) He comes. "Now then, Evstignéy," I said, "you old imbecile, how do you dare . . ." (*Looking at* ÁNYA.) Ánya, Ánya! (*A pause.*) She's asleep. (*Taking* ÁNYA's *arm.*) Let's go to bed. Come along. (*Leading her away.*) Sleep on, my little one! Come along; come along! (*They go towards* ÁNYA's *room. In the distance beyond the orchard a shepherd plays his pipe.* TROPHÍMOF *crosses the stage and, seeing* BARBARA *and* ÁNYA, *stops.*) 'Sh! She's asleep, she's asleep! Come along, my love.

ÁNYA (*drowsily*). I'm so tired! Listen to the bells! Uncle, dear uncle! Mamma! Uncle!

BARBARA. Come along, my love! Come along. (*Exeunt* BARBARA *and* ÁNYA *to the bedroom.*)

TROPHÍMOF (*with emotion*). My sunshine! My spring!

ACT II

In the open fields; an old crooked half-ruined shrine. Near it a well; big stones, apparently old tombstones; an old bench.

Road to the estate beyond. On one side rise dark poplar trees. Beyond them begins the cherry orchard. In the distance a row of

telegraph poles, and, far away on the horizon, the dim outlines of a big town, visible only in fine, clear weather. It is near sunset.
CHARLOTTE, YÁSHA, *and* DUNYÁSHA *sit on the bench.* EPHIKHÓDOF *stands by them and plays on a guitar; they meditate.* CHARLOTTE *wears an old peaked cap.*[1] *She has taken a gun from off her shoulders and is mending the buckle of the strap.*

CHARLOTTE (*thoughtfully*). I have no proper passport. I don't know how old I am; I always feel I am still young. When I was a little girl my father and mother used to go about from one country fair to another, giving performances, and very good ones, too. I used to do the *salto mortale* and all sorts of tricks. When papa and mamma died, an old German lady adopted me and educated me. Good! When I grew up I became a governess. But where I come from and who I am, I haven't a notion. Who my parents were—very likely they weren't married—I don't know. (*Taking a cucumber from her pocket and beginning to eat.*) I don't know anything about it. (*A pause.*) I long to talk so, and I have no one to talk to, I have no friends or relations.

EPHIKHÓDOF (*playing on the guitar and singing*).
"What is the noisy world to me?
Oh, what are friends and foes?"
How sweet it is to play upon a mandolin!

DUNYÁSHA. That's a guitar, not a mandolin. (*She looks at herself in a handglass and powders her face.*)

EPHIKHÓDOF. For the madman who loves, it is a mandolin. (*Singing.*)

"Oh, that my heart were cheered
By the warmth of requited love."
[YÁSHA *joins in.*]

CHARLOTTE. How badly these people do sing! Foo! Like jackals howling!

DUNYÁSHA (*to* YÁSHA). What happiness it must be to live abroad!

YÁSHA. Of course it is; I quite agree with you. (*He yawns and lights a cigar.*)

EPHIKHÓDOF. It stands to reason. Everything abroad has attained a certain culmination.[2]

YÁSHA. That's right.

EPHIKHÓDOF. I am a man of cultivation; I have studied various remarkable books, but I cannot fathom the direction of my preferences; do I want to live or do I want to shoot myself, so to speak? But in order to be ready for all contingencies I always carry a revolver in my pocket. Here it is. (*Showing revolver.*)

CHARLOTTE. That's done. I'm off. (*Slinging the rifle over her shoulder.*) You're a clever fellow, Ephikhódof, and very alarming. Women must fall madly in love with you. Brrr! (*Going.*) These clever people are all so stupid; I have no one to talk to. I am always alone, always alone; I have no friends or relations, and who I am, or why I exist, is a mystery. (*Exit slowly.*)

EPHIKHÓDOF. Strictly speaking, without touching upon other matters, I must protest *inter alia* that destiny treats me with the utmost rigor, as a tempest might treat a small ship. If I labor under a misapprehension, how is it that when I woke up this morning, behold, so to speak, I perceived sitting on my chest a spider of preternatural dimensions, like that? (*Indicating with both hands.*) And if I

---

[1] *Furázhka*, the commonest men's headgear in Russia, shaped like a yachting cap.

[2] *Culmination.* This represents a similar blunder of Ephikhódof's in the original.

go to take a draught of quass, I am sure to find something of the most indelicate character, in the nature of a cockroach. (*A pause.*) Have you read Buckle? (*A pause.—to* DUNYÁSHA.) I should like to trouble you, Avdotya Fëdorovna,[1] for a momentary interview.

DUNYÁSHA. Talk away.

EPHIKHÓDOF. I should prefer to conduct it *tête-à-tête.* (*Sighing.*)

DUNYÁSHA (*confused*). Very well, only first please fetch me my cloak.[2] It's by the cupboard. It's rather damp here.

EPHIKHÓDOF. Very well, mademoiselle. I will go and fetch it, mademoiselle. Now I know what to do with my revolver. (*Takes his guitar and exit, playing.*)

YÁSHA. Twenty-two misfortunes! Between you and me, he's a stupid fellow. (*Yawning.*)

DUNYÁSHA. Heaven help him, he'll shoot himself! (*A pause.*) I have grown so nervous, I am always in a twitter. I was quite a little girl when they took me into the household, and now I have got quite disused to common life, and my hands are as white as white, like a lady's. I have grown so refined, so delicate and genteel, I am afraid of everything. I'm always frightened. And if you deceive me, Yásha, I don't know what will happen to my nerves.

YÁSHA (*kissing her*). You little cucumber! Of course every girl ought to behave herself properly; there's nothing I dislike as much as when girls aren't proper in their behavior.

[1] *Avdotya Fëdorovna* (the ë is to be pronounced like the *yach* in *yacht*.) Dunya (diminutive Dunyásha), stands for Avdotya, formally Evdokiya, representing the Greek Eudoxia.
[2] *Cloak. Talmotchka,* a diminutive of *talma,* a sort of big cape, named after the tragedian.

DUNYÁSHA. I've fallen dreadfully in love with you. You're so educated; you can talk about anything! (*A pause.*)

YÁSHA (*yawning*). Yes. . . . The way I look at it is this; if a girl falls in love with anybody, then I call her immoral. (*A pause.*) How pleasant it is to smoke one's cigar in the open air. (*Listening.*) There's some one coming. It's the missis and the rest of 'em. . . . (DUNYÁSHA *embraces him hastily.*) Go towards the house as if you'd just been for a bathe. Go by this path or else they'll meet you and think that I've been walking out with you. I can't stand that sort of thing.

DUNYÁSHA (*coughing softly*). Your cigar has given me a headache.

[*Exit* DUNYÁSHA. YÁSHA *remains sitting by the shrine.*]

[*Enter* MADAME RANÉVSKY, GÁYEF, *and* LOPÁKHIN.]

LOPÁKHIN. You must make up your minds once and for all. Time waits for no man. The question is perfectly simple. Are you going to let off the land for villas or not? Answer in one way; yes or no? Only one word!

MADAME RANÉVSKY. Who's smoking horrible cigars here? (*She sits down.*)

GÁYEF. How handy it is now they've built that railway. (*Sitting.*) We've been into town for lunch and back again. . . . Red in the middle! I must just go up to the house and have a game.

MADAME RANÉVSKY. There's no hurry.

LOPÁKHIN. Only one word—yes or no! (*Entreatingly.*) Come, answer the question!

GÁYEF (*yawning*). Who's that?

MADAME RANÉVSKY (*looking into her purse*). I had a lot of money yesterday, but there's hardly any left now. Poor Barbara tries to save money by feeding us all on milk soup; the old people in the kitchen get nothing but peas, and yet I go squandering aimlessly. . . . (*Dropping her purse and scattering gold coins; vexed.*) There, I've dropped it all!

YÁSHA. Allow me, I'll pick it up. (*Collecting the coins.*)

MADAME RANÉVSKY. Yes, please do, Yásha! Whatever made me go into town for lunch? I hate your horrid restaurant with the organ, and the tablecloths all smelling of soap. Why do you drink so much, Leoníd? Why do you eat so much? Why do you talk so much? You talked too much at the restaurant again, and most unsuitably, about the seventies, and the decadents. And to whom? Fancy talking about decadents to the waiters!

LOPÁKHIN. Quite true.

GÁYEF (*with a gesture*). I'm incorrigible, that's plain. (*Irritably to* YÁSHA.) What do you keep dodging about in front of me for?

YÁSHA (*laughing*). I can't hear your voice without laughing.

GÁYEF (*to* MADAME RANÉVSKY). Either he or I . . .

MADAME RANÉVSKY. Go away, Yásha; run along.

YÁSHA (*handing* MADAME RANÉVSKY *her purse*). I'll go at once. (*Restraining his laughter with difficulty.*) This very minute. (*Exit* YÁSHA.)

LOPÁKHIN. Derigánof, the millionaire, wants to buy your property. They say he'll come to the auction himself.

MADAME RANÉVSKY. How did you hear?

LOPÁKHIN. I was told so in town.

GÁYEF. Our aunt at Yaroslav has promised to send something; but I don't know when, or how much.

LOPÁKHIN. How much will she send?

Ten thousand pounds? Twenty thousand pounds?

MADAME RANÉVSKY. Oh, come. . . . A thousand or fifteen hundred at the most.

LOPÁKHIN. Excuse me, but in all my life I never met anybody so frivolous as you two, so crazy and unbusinesslike! I tell you in plain Russian your property is going to be sold, and you don't seem to understand what I say.

MADAME RANÉVSKY. Well, what are we to do? Tell us what you want us to do.

LOPÁKHIN. Don't I tell you every day? Every day I say the same thing over and over again. You must lease off the cherry orchard and the rest of the estate for villas; you must do it at once, this very moment; the auction will be on you in two twos! Try and understand. Once you make up your mind there are to be villas, you can get all the money you want, and you're saved.

MADAME RANÉVSKY. Villas and villa residents, oh, please, . . . it's so vulgar!

GÁYEF. I quite agree with you.

LOPÁKHIN. I shall either cry, or scream, or faint. I can't stand it! You'll be the death of me. (*To* GÁYEF.) You're an old woman!

GÁYEF. Who's that?

LOPÁKHIN. You're an old woman! (*Going.*)

MADAME RANÉVSKY (*frightened*). No; don't go. Stay here, there's a dear! Perhaps we shall think of some way.

LOPÁKHIN. What's the good of thinking!

MADAME RANÉVSKY. Please don't go; I want you. At any rate, it's gayer when you're here. (*A pause.*) I keep expecting something to happen, as if the house were going to tumble down about our ears.

GÁYEF (*in deep abstraction*). Off the

cushion on the corner; double into the middle pocket . . .

MADAME RANÉVSKY. We have been very, very sinful!

LOPÁKHIN. You! What sins have you committed?

GÁYEF (*eating candy*). They say I've devoured all my substance in sugar candy. (*Laughing.*)

MADAME RANÉSVKY. Oh, the sins that I have committed . . . I've always squandered money at random like a mad-woman; I married a man who made nothing but debts. My husband drank himself to death on champagne; he was a fearful drinker. Then for my sins I fell in love and went off with another man; and immediately—that was my first punishment—a blow full on the head . . . here, in this very river . . . my little boy was drowned; and I went abroad, right, right away, never to come back any more, never to see this river again. . . . I shut my eyes and ran, like a mad thing, and *he* came after me, pitiless and cruel. I bought a villa at Mentone, because he fell ill there, and for three years I knew no rest day or night; the sick man tormented and wore down my soul. Then, last year, when my villa was sold to pay my debts, I went off to Paris, and he came and robbed me of everything, left me and took up with another woman, and I tried to poison myself. . . . It was all so stupid, so humiliating. . . . Then suddenly I longed to be back in Russia, in my own country, with my little girl. . . . (*Wiping away her tears.*) Lord, Lord, be merciful to me; forgive my sins! Do not punish me any more! (*Taking a telegram from her pocket.*) I got this to-day from Paris. . . . He asks to be forgiven, begs me to go back. . . . (*Tearing up the telegram.*) Isn't that music that I hear? (*Listening.*)

GÁYEF. That's our famous Jewish band. You remember? Four fiddles, a flute, and a double bass.

MADAME RANÉVSKY. Does it still exist? We must make them come up sometime; we'll have a dance.

LOPÁKHIN (*listening*). I don't hear anything. (*Singing softly.*)
"The Germans for a fee will turn
A Russ into a Frenchman."
(*Laughing.*) I saw a very funny piece at the theater last night; awfully funny!

MADAME RANÉVSKY. It probably wasn't a bit funny. You people oughtn't to go and see plays; you ought to try to see yourselves; to see what a dull life you lead, and how much too much you talk.

LOPÁKHIN. Quite right. To tell the honest truth, our life's an imbecile affair. (*A pause.*) My papa was a peasant, an idiot; he understood nothing; he taught me nothing; all he did was to beat me, when he was drunk, with a walking-stick. As a matter of fact I'm just as big a blockhead and idiot as he was. I never did any lessons; my handwriting's abominable; I write so badly I'm ashamed before people; like a pig.

MADAME RANÉVSKY. You ought to get married.

LOPÁKHIN. Yes, that's true.

MADAME RANÉVSKY. Why not marry Barbara? She's a nice girl.

LOPÁKHIN. Yes.

MADAME RANÉVSKY. She's a nice straightforward creature; works all day; and what's most important, she loves you. You've been fond of her for a long time.

LOPÁKHIN. Well, why not? I'm quite willing. She's a very nice girl. (*A pause.*)

GÁYEF. I've been offered a place in a bank. Six hundred pounds a year. Do you hear?

MADAME RANÉVSKY. You in a bank! Stay where you are.

[*Enter* FIRS, *carrying an overcoat.*]

FIRS (*to* GÁYEF). Put this on, please, 10 master; it's getting damp.

GÁYEF (*putting on the coat*). What a plague you are, Firs!

FIRS. What's the use. . . . You went off and never told me. (*Examining his clothes.*)

MADAME RANÉVSKY. How old you've got, Firs!

FIRS. I beg your pardon?

LOPÁKHIN. She says how old you've got! 20

FIRS. I've been alive a long time. When they found me a wife, your father wasn't even born yet. (*Laughing.*) And when the Liberation came I was already chief valet. But I wouldn't have any Liberation then; I stayed with the master. (*A pause.*) I remember how happy everybody was, but why they were happy they didn't know themselves.   30

LOPÁKHIN. It was fine before then. Anyway they used to flog 'em.

FIRS (*mishearing him*). I should think so! The peasants minded the masters, and the masters minded the peasants, but now it's all higgledy-piggledy; you can't make head or tail of it.

GÁYEF. Shut up, Firs. I must go into town again to-morrow. I've been 40 promised an introduction to a general who'll lend money on a bill.

LOPÁKHIN. You'll do no good. You won't even pay the interest; set your mind at ease about that.

MADAME RANÉVSKY (*to* LOPÁKHIN).

He's only talking nonsense. There's no such general at all.

[*Enter* TROPHÍMOF, ÁNYA, *and* BARBARA.]

GÁYEF. Here come the others.

ÁNYA. Here's mamma.

MADAME RANÉVSKY (*tenderly*). Come along, come along . . . my little ones. . . . (*Embracing* ÁNYA *and* BARBARA.) If only you knew how much I love you both! Sit beside me . . . there, like that.

[*Every one sits.*]

LOPÁKHIN. The Perpetual Student's always among the girls.

TROPHÍMOF. It's no affair of yours.

LOPÁKHIN. He's nearly fifty and still a student.

TROPHÍMOF. Stop your idiotic jokes!

LOPÁKHIN. What are you losing your temper for, silly?

TROPHÍMOF. Why can't you leave me alone?

LOPÁKHIN (*laughing*). I should like to know what your opinion is of me.

TROPHÍMOF. My opinion of you, Yermolái Alexéyitch, is this. You're a rich man; you'll soon be a millionaire. Just as a beast of prey which devours everything that comes in its way is necessary for the conversion of matter, so you are necessary, too.

[*All laugh.*]

BARBARA. Tell us something about the planets, Peter, instead.

MADAME RANÉVSKY. No. Let's go on with the conversation we were having yesterday.

TROPHÍMOF. What about?

GÁYEF. About the proud man.

TROPHÍMOF. We had a long talk yesterday, but we didn't come to any conclusion. There is something mystical in the proud man in the sense in which you use the words. You may be right from your point of view, but, if we look at it simple-mindedly, what room is there for pride? Is there any sense in it, when man is so poorly constructed from the physiological point of view, when the vast majority of us are so gross and stupid and profoundly unhappy? We must give up admiring ourselves. The only thing to do is to work.

GÁYEF. We shall die all the same.

TROPHÍMOF. Who knows? And what does it mean, to die? Perhaps man has a hundred senses, and when he dies only the five senses that we know perish with him, and the other ninety-five remain alive.

MADAME RANÉVSKY. How clever you are, Peter!

LOPÁKHIN (ironically). Oh, extraordinary!

TROPHÍMOF. Mankind marches forward, perfecting its strength. Everything that is unattainable for us now will one day be near and clear; but we must work; we must help with all our force those who seek for truth. At present only a few men work in Russia. The vast majority of the educated people that I know seek after nothing, do nothing, and are as yet incapable of work. They call themselves the "Intelligentsia," they say "thou" and "thee" to the servants, they treat the peasants like animals, learn nothing, read nothing serious, do absolutely nothing, only talk about science, and understand little or nothing about art. They are all serious; they all have solemn faces; they only discuss important subjects; they philosophize; but meanwhile the vast majority of us, ninety-nine per cent, live like savages; at the least thing they curse and punch people's heads; they eat like beasts and sleep in dirt and bad air; there are bugs everywhere, evil smells, damp and moral degradation. . . . It's plain that all our clever conversations are only meant to distract our own attention and other people's. Show me where those crèches are, that they're always talking so much about; or those reading-rooms. They are only things people write about in novels; they don't really exist at all. Nothing exists but dirt, vulgarity, and Asiatic ways. I am afraid of solemn faces; I dislike them; I am afraid of solemn conversations. Let us rather hold our tongues.

LOPÁKHIN. Do you know, I get up at five every morning; I work from morning till night; I am always handling my own money or other people's, and I see the sort of men there are about me. One only has to begin to do anything to see how few honest and decent people there are. Sometimes, as I lie awake in bed, I think: "O Lord, you have given us mighty forests, boundless fields and immeasurable horizons, and, we living in their midst, ought really to be giants."

MADAME RANÉVSKY. Oh, dear, you want giants! They are all very well in fairy stories; but in real life they are rather alarming.

[EPHIKHÓDOF passes at the back of the scene, playing on his guitar.]

MADAME RANÉVSKY (pensively). There goes Ephikhódof.

ÁNYA (pensively). There goes Ephikhódof.

GÁYEF. The sun has set.

TROPHÍMOF. Yes.

GÁYEF (as if declaiming, but not loud). O Nature, wonderful Nature, you glow with eternal light; beautiful and indifferent, you whom we call our mother, uniting in yourself both life and death, you animate and you destroy . . .

BARBARA (*entreatingly*). Uncle!

ÁNYA. You're at it again, uncle.

TROPHÍMOF. You'd far better double the red into the middle pocket.

GÁYEF. I'll hold my tongue! I'll hold my tongue!

[*They all sit pensively. Silence reigns, broken only by the mumbling of old* FIRS. *Suddenly a distant sound is heard as if from the sky, the sound of a string breaking, dying away, melancholy.*]

MADAME RANÉVSKY. What's that?

LOPÁKHIN. I don't know. It's a lifting-tub given way somewhere away in the mines. It must be a long way off.

GÁYEF. Perhaps it's some sort of bird . . . a heron, or something.

TROPHÍMOF. Or an owl. . . .

MADAME RANÉVSKY (*shuddering*). There is something uncanny about it!

FIRS. The same thing happened before the great misfortune: the owl screeched and the samovar kept humming.

GÁYEF. What great misfortune?

FIRS. The Liberation. (*A pause.*)

MADAME RANÉVSKY. Come, every one, let's go in; it's getting late. (*To* ÁNYA.) You've tears in your eyes. What is it, little one? (*Embracing her.*).

ÁNYA. Nothing, mamma. I'm all right.

TROPHÍMOF. There's some one coming.

[*A* TRAMP *appears in a torn white peaked cap and overcoat. He is slightly drunk.*]

TRAMP. Excuse me, but can I go through this way straight to the station?

GÁYEF. Certainly. Follow this path.

TRAMP. I am uncommonly obliged to you, sir. (*Coughing.*) We're having lovely weather. (*Declaiming.*) "Brother, my suffering brother". . . "Come forth to the Volga. Who moans?" . . . (*To* BARBARA.) Mademoiselle, please spare a sixpence for a hungry fellow-countryman.

[BARBARA, *frightened, screams.*]

LOPÁKHIN (*angrily*). There's a decency for every indecency to observe!

MADAME RANÉVSKY. Take this; here you are. (*Fumbling in her purse.*) I haven't any silver. . . . Never mind, take this sovereign.

TRAMP. I am uncommonly obliged to you, madam. (*Exit* TRAMP. *Laughter.*)

BARBARA (*frightened*). I'm going! I'm going! Oh, mamma, there's nothing for the servants to eat at home, and you've gone and given this man a sovereign.

MADAME RANÉVSKY. What's to be done with your stupid old mother? I'll give you up everything I have when I get back. Yermolái Alexéyitch, lend me some more money.

LOPÁKHIN. Very good.

MADAME RANÉVSKY. Come along, every one; it's time to go in. We've settled all about your marriage between us, Barbara. I wish you joy.

BARBARA (*through her tears*). You mustn't joke about such things, mamma.

LOPÁKHIN. Amelia, get thee to a nunnery, go!

GÁYEF. My hands are all trembling; it's ages since I had a game of billiards.

LOPÁKHIN. Amelia, nymphlet, in thine orisons remember me.[1]

MADAME RANÉVSKY. Come along. It's nearly supper-time.

BARBARA. How he frightened me! My heart is simply throbbing.

LOPÁKHIN. Allow me to remind you, the cherry orchard is to be sold on the 22d of August. Bear that in mind; bear that in mind!

[*Exeunt* OMNES *except* TROPHÍMOF *and* ÁNYA.]

ÁNYA (*laughing*). Many thanks to the

---

[1] There is a wretched pun in the original: Ophelia is called Okhmelia (from *okhmelét,* to get drunk).

Tramp for frightening Barbara; at last we are alone.

TROPHÍMOF. Barbara's afraid we shall go and fall in love with each other. Day after day she never leaves us alone. With her narrow mind she cannot understand that we are above love. To avoid everything petty, everything illusory, everything that prevents one from being free and happy, that is the whole meaning and purpose of our life. Forward! We march on irresistibly towards that bright star which burns far, far before us! Forward! Don't tarry, comrades!

ÁNYA (*clasping her hands*). What beautiful things you say! (*A pause.*) Isn't it enchanting here to-day!

TROPHÍMOF. Yes, it's wonderful weather.

ÁNYA. What have you done to me, Peter? Why is it that I no longer love the cherry orchard as I did? I used to love it so tenderly; I thought there was no better place on earth than our garden.

TROPHÍMOF. All Russia is our garden. The earth is great and beautiful; it is full of wonderful places. (*A pause.*) Think, Ánya, your grandfather, your great-grandfather and all your ancestors were serf owners, owners of living souls. Do not human spirits look out at you from every tree in the orchard, from every leaf and every stem? Do you not hear human voices? . . . Oh! it is terrible. Your orchard frightens me. When I walk through it in the evening or at night, the rugged bark on the trees glows with a dim light, and the cherry trees seem to see all that happened a hundred and two hundred years ago in painful and oppressive dreams. Well, well, we have fallen at least two hundred years behind the times.

We have achieved nothing at all as yet; we have not made up our minds how we stand with the past; we only philosophize, complain of boredom, or drink vodka. It is so plain that, before we can live in the present, we must first redeem the past, and have done with it; and it is only by suffering that we can redeem it, only by strenuous, unremitting toil. Understand that, Ánya.

ÁNYA. The house we live in has long since ceased to be our house; and I shall go away, I give you my word.

TROPHÍMOF. If you have the household keys, throw them in the well and go away. Be free, be free as the wind.

ÁNYA (*enthusiastically*). How beautifully you put it!

TROPHÍMOF. Believe what I say, Ánya; believe what I say. I'm not thirty yet; I am still young, still a student; but what I have been through! I am hungry as the winter; I am sick, anxious, poor as a beggar. Fate has tossed me hither and thither; I have been everywhere, everywhere. But wherever I have been, every minute, day and night, my soul has been full of mysterious anticipations. I feel the approach of happiness, Ánya; I see it coming. . . .

ÁNYA (*pensively*). The moon is rising.

[EPHIKHÓDOF *is heard still playing the same sad tune on his guitar. The moon rises. Somewhere beyond the poplar trees,* BARBARA *is heard calling for* ÁNYA: "*Ánya, where are you?*"]

TROPHÍMOF. Yes, the moon is rising. (*A pause.*) There it is, there is happiness; it is coming towards us, nearer and nearer; I can hear the sound of its footsteps. . . . And if we do not see it, if we do not know it, what does it matter? Others will see it.

BARBARA (*without*). Ánya? Where are you?

TROPHÍMOF. There's Barbara again! (*Angrily.*) It really is too bad!

ÁNYA. Never mind. Let us go down to the river. It's lovely there.

TROPHÍMOF. Come on!

[*Exeunt* ÁNYA *and* TROPHÍMOF.]

BARBARA (*without*). Ánya! Ánya!

ACT III

A sitting-room separated by an arch from a big drawing-room behind. Chandelier lighted. The Jewish band mentioned in Act II is heard playing on the landing. Evening. In the drawing-room they are 10 *dancing the grand rond.* SIMEÓNOF-PÍSHTCHIK *is heard crying, "Promenade à une paire!"*

The dancers come down into the sitting-room. The first pair consists of PÍSHT-CHIK *and* CHARLOTTE; *the second of* TROPHÍMOF *and* MADAME RANÉVSKY; *the third of* ÁNYA *and the* POST-OFFICE OFFICIAL; *the fourth of* BARBARA *and the* STATIONMASTER, *etc., etc.* BARBARA 20 *is crying softly and wipes away the tears as she dances. In the last pair comes* DUNYÁSHA. *They cross the sitting-room.*

PÍSHTCHIK. "Grand rond, balancez . . . Les cavaliers à genou et remerciez vos dames."

[FIRS *in evening dress carries seltzer water across on a tray.* PÍSHTCHIK *and* TROPH-ÍMOF *come down into the sitting-room.*] 30

PÍSHTCHIK. I am a full-blooded man; I've had two strokes already; it's hard work dancing, but, as the saying goes, "If you run with the pack, bark or no, but anyway wag your tail." I'm as strong as a horse. My old father, who was fond of his joke, rest his soul, used to say, talking of our pedigree, that the ancient stock of the Simeónof-Píshtchiks was de- 40 scended from that very horse that Caligula made a senator. . . . (*Sitting.*) But the worst of it is, I've got

no money. A hungry dog believes in nothing but meat. (*Snoring and waking up again at once.*) I'm just the same . . . It's nothing but money, money, with me.

TROPHÍMOF. Yes, it's quite true, there is something horse-like about your build.

PÍSHTCHIK. Well, well . . . a horse is a jolly creature . . . you can sell a horse.

[*A sound of billiards being played in the next room.* BARBARA *appears in the drawing-room beyond the arch.*]

TROPHÍMOF (*teasing her*). Madame Lopákhin! Madame Lopákhin.

BARBARA (*angrily*). Mouldy gentleman!

TROPHÍMOF. Yes, I'm a mouldy gentleman, and I'm proud of it.

BARBARA (*bitterly*). We've hired the band, but where's the money to pay for it? (*Exit* BARBARA.)

TROPHÍMOF (*to* PÍSHTCHIK). If the energy which you have spent in the course of your whole life in looking for money to pay the interest on your loans had been diverted to some other purpose, you would have had enough of it, I dare say, to turn the world upside down.

PÍSHTCHIK. Nietzsche the philosopher, a very remarkable man, very famous, a man of gigantic intellect, says in his works that it's quite right to forge bank notes.

TROPHÍMOF. What, have you read Nietzsche?

PÍSHTCHIK. Well . . . Dáshenka told me. . . . But I'm in such a hole, I'd forge 'em for twopence. I've got to pay thirty-one pounds the day after to-morrow. . . . I've got thirteen pounds already. (*Feeling his pockets; alarmed.*) My money's gone! I've lost my money! (*Crying.*) Where's my money got to? (*Joyfully.*) Here it is, inside the lining. . . . It's thrown 10 me all in a perspiration.

[*Enter* MADAME RANÉVSKY *and* CHARLOTTE.]

MADAME RANÉVSKY (*humming a lezginka[1]*). Why is Leoníd so long? What can he be doing in the town? (*To* DUNYÁSHA.) Dunyásha, ask the musicians if they'll have some tea.

TROPHÍMOF. The sale did not come off, in all probability. 20

MADAME RANÉVSKY. It was a stupid day for the musicians to come; it was a stupid day to have this dance. . . . Well, well, it doesn't matter. . . . (*She sits down and sings softly to herself.*)

CHARLOTTE (*giving* PÍSHTCHIK *a pack of cards*). Here is a pack of cards. Think of any card you like.

PÍSHTCHIK. I've thought of one.

CHARLOTTE. Now shuffle the pack. 30 That's all right. Give them here, oh, most worthy Mr. Píshtchik. Ein, zwei, drei! Now look and you'll find it in your side pocket.

PÍSHTCHIK (*taking a card from his side pocket*). The Eight of Spades! You're perfectly right. (*Astonished.*) Well, I never!

CHARLOTTE (*holding the pack on the palm of her hand, to* TROPHÍMOF). Say 40 quickly, what's the top card?

TROPHÍMOF. Well, say the Queen of Spades.

[1] *Lezginka.* A lively Caucasian dance in two-four time, popularized by Glinka, and by Rubinstein in his opera, *Demon.*

CHARLOTTE. Right! (*To* PÍSHTCHIK.) Now, then, what's the top card?

PÍSHTCHIK. Ace of Hearts.

CHARLOTTE. Right! (*She claps her hands; the pack of cards disappears.*) What a beautiful day we've been having.

[*A mysterious female* VOICE *answers her as if from under the floor:* "*Yes, indeed, a charming day, mademoiselle.*"]

CHARLOTTE. You are my beautiful ideal.

THE VOICE. "*I think you also ferry peautiful, mademoiselle.*"

STATIONMASTER (*applauding*). Bravo, Miss Ventriloquist!

PÍSHTCHIK (*astonished*). Well, I never! Bewitching Charlotte Ivánovna, I'm head over ears in love with you.

CHARLOTTE. In love! (*Shrugging her shoulders.*) Are you capable of love? Guter Mensch, aber schlechter Musikant!

TROPHÍMOF (*slapping* PÍSHTCHIK *on the shoulder*). You old horse!

CHARLOTTE. Now, attention, please; one more trick. (*Taking a shawl from a chair.*) Now here's a shawl, and a very pretty shawl; I'm going to sell this very pretty shawl. (*Shaking it.*) Who'll buy? who'll buy?

PÍSHTCHIK (*astonished*). Well, I never!

CHARLOTTE. Ein, zwei, drei! (*She lifts the shawl quickly; behind it stands ÁNYA, who drops a curtsy, runs to her mother, kisses her, then runs up into the drawing-room amid general applause.*)

MADAME RANÉVSKY (*applauding*). Bravo! bravo!

CHARLOTTE. Once more. Ein, zwei, drei! (*She lifts up the shawl; behind it stands BARBARA, bowing.*)

PÍSHTCHIK (*astonished*). Well, I never!

CHARLOTTE. That's all. (*She throws the shawl over* PÍSHTCHIK, *makes a curtsy and runs up into the drawing-room.*)

PÍSHTCHIK (*hurrying after her*). You little

rascal . . . there's a girl for you, there's a girl. . . . (*Exit.*)

MADAME RANÉVSKY. And still no sign of Leoníd. What he's doing in the town so long, I can't understand. It must be all over by now; the property's sold; or the auction never came off; why does he keep me in suspense so long?

BARBARA (*trying to soothe her*). Uncle has bought it, I am sure of that.

TROPHÍMOF (*mockingly*). Of course he has.

BARBARA. Grannie sent him a power of attorney to buy it in her name and transfer the mortgage. She's done it for Ánya's sake. I'm perfectly sure that Heaven will help us and uncle will buy it.

MADAME RANÉVSKY. Your Yaroslav grannie sent fifteen hundred pounds to buy the property in her name— she doesn't trust us—but it wouldn't be enough even to pay the interest. (*Covering her face with her hands.*) My fate is being decided to-day, my fate. . . .

TROPHÍMOF (*teasing* BARBARA). Madame Lopákhin!

BARBARA (*angrily*). Perpetual Student! He's been sent down twice from the University.

MADAME RANÉVSKY. Why do you get angry, Barbara? He calls you Madame Lopákhin for fun. Why not? You can marry Lopákhin if you like; he's a nice, interesting man; you needn't if you don't; nobody wants to force you, my pet.

BARBARA. I take it very seriously, mamma, I must confess. He's a nice man and I like him.

MADAME RANÉVSKY. Then marry him. There's no good putting it off that I can see.

BARBARA. But, mamma, I can't pro-pose to him myself. For two whole years everybody's been talking about him to me, every one; but he either says nothing or makes a joke of it. I quite understand. He's making money; he's always busy; he can't be bothered with me. If I only had some money, even a little, even ten pounds, I would give everything up and go right away. I would go into a nunnery.

TROPHÍMOF (*mocking*). What bliss!

BARBARA (*to* TROPHÍMOF). A student ought to be intelligent. (*In a gentler voice, crying.*) How ugly you've grown, Peter; how old you've grown! (*She stops crying; to* MADAME RANÉVSKY.) But I can't live without work, mamma. I must have something to do every minute of the day.

[*Enter* YÁSHA.]

YÁSHA (*trying not to laugh*). Ephikhó-dof has broken a billiard cue. (*Exit* YÁSHA.)

BARBARA. What's Ephikhódof doing here? Who gave him leave to play billiards? I don't understand these people. (*Exit* BARBARA.)

MADAME RANÉVSKY. Don't tease her, Peter. Don't you see that she's unhappy enough already.

TROPHÍMOF. I wish she wouldn't be so fussy, always meddling in other people's affairs. The whole summer she's given me and Ánya no peace; she is afraid we'll work up a romance between us. What business is it of hers? I'm sure I never gave her any grounds; I'm not likely to be so commonplace. We are above love!

MADAME RANÉVSKY. Then I suppose I must be beneath love. (*Deeply agitated.*) Why doesn't Leoníd come? Oh, if only I knew whether the property's sold or not! It seems such an impossible disaster, that I don't know what to think. . . . I'm bewildered . . . I shall burst out screaming, I shall do something idiotic. Save me, Peter; say something to me, say something. . . .

TROPHÍMOF. Whether the property is sold to-day or whether it's not sold, surely it's all one? It's all over with it long ago; there's no turning back; the path is overgrown. Be calm, dear Lyubóf Andréyevna. You mustn't deceive yourself any longer; for once you must look the truth straight in the face.

MADAME RANÉVSKY. What truth? You can see what's truth, and what's untruth, but I seem to have lost the power of vision; I see nothing. You settle every important question so boldly; but tell me, Peter, isn't that because you're young, because you have never solved any question of your own as yet by suffering? You look boldly ahead; isn't it only that you don't see or divine anything terrible in the future; because life is still hidden from your young eyes? You are bolder, honester, deeper than we are, but reflect, show me just a finger's breadth of consideration, take pity on me. Don't you see? I was born here, my father and mother lived here, and my grandfather; I love this house; without the cherry orchard my life has no meaning for me, and if it *must* be sold, then for Heaven's sake, sell me too! (*Embracing* TROPHÍMOF *and kissing him on the forehead.*) My little boy was drowned here. (*Crying.*) Be gentle with me, dear, kind Peter.

TROPHÍMOF. You know I sympathize with all my heart.

MADAME RANÉVSKY. Yes, yes, but you ought to say it somehow differently. (*Taking out her handkerchief and drop-ping a telegram.*) I am so wretched to-day, you can't imagine! All this noise jars on me, my heart jumps at every sound. I tremble all over; but I can't shut myself up; I am afraid of the silence when I'm alone. Don't be hard on me, Peter; I love you like a son. I would gladly let Ánya marry you, I swear it; but you must work, Peter; you must get your degree. You do nothing; Fate tosses you about from place to place; and that's not right. It's true what I say, isn't it? And you must do something to your beard to make it grow better. (*Laughing.*) I can't help laughing at you.

TROPHÍMOF (*picking up the telegram*). I don't wish to be an Adonis.

MADAME RANÉVSKY. It's a telegram from Paris. I get them every day. One came yesterday, another to-day. That savage is ill again; he's in a bad way. . . . He asks me to forgive him, he begs me to come; and I really ought to go to Paris and be with him. You look at me sternly; but what am I to do, Peter? What am I to do? He's ill, he's lonely, he's unhappy. Who is to look after him? Who is to keep him from doing stupid things? Who is to give him his medicine when it's time? After all, why should I be ashamed to say it? I love him, that's plain. I love him, I love him. . . . My love is like a stone tied round my neck; it's dragging me down to the bottom; but I love my stone. I can't live without it. (*Squeezing* TROPHÍMOF's *hand.*) Don't think ill of me, Peter; don't say anything! Don't say anything!

TROPHÍMOF (*crying*). Forgive my bluntness, for Heaven's sake; but the man has simply robbed you.

MADAME RANÉVSKY. No, no, no! (*Stopping her ears.*) You mustn't say that!

TROPHÍMOF. He's a rascal; everybody sees it but yourself; he's a petty rascal, a ne'er-do-well . . .

MADAME RANÉVSKY (*angry but restrained*). You're twenty-six or twenty-seven, and you're still a Lower School boy![1]

TROPHÍMOF. Who cares?

MADAME RANÉVSKY. You ought to be a 10 man by now; at your age you ought to understand people who love. You ought to love some one yourself, you ought to be in love! (*Angrily.*) Yes, yes! It's not purity with you; it's simply you're a smug, a figure of fun, a freak. . . .

TROPHÍMOF (*horrified*). What does she say?

MADAME RANÉVSKY. "I am above love!" 20 You're not above love; you're simply what Firs calls a "job-lot." At your age you ought to be ashamed not to have a mistress!

TROPHÍMOF (*aghast*). This is awful! What does she say? (*Going quickly up into the drawing-room, clasping his head with his hands.*) This is something awful! I can't stand it; I'm off . . . (*Exit, but returns at once.*) All is over between 30 us! (*Exit to landing.*)

MADAME RANÉVSKY (*calling after him*). Stop, Peter! Don't be ridiculous; I was only joking! Peter!

[TROPHÍMOF *is heard on the landing going quickly down the stairs, and suddenly falling down them with a crash.* ÁNYA *and* BARBARA *scream. A moment later the sound of laughter.*]

MADAME RANÉVSKY. What has hap- 40 pened?

[ÁNYA *runs in.*]

ÁNYA (*laughing*). Peter's tumbled downstairs. (*She runs out again.*)

[1] Literally, a gymnasist of the second form (from the bottom).

MADAME RANÉVSKY. What a ridiculous fellow he is!

[*The* STATIONMASTER *stands in the middle of the drawing-room beyond the arch and recites Alexey Tolstoy's poem, "The Sinner." Everybody stops to listen, but after a few lines the sound of a waltz is heard from the landing and he breaks off. All dance.* TROPHÍMOF, ÁNYA, BARBARA, *and* MADAME RANÉVSKY *enter from the landing.*]

MADAME RANÉVSKY. Come, Peter, come, you pure spirit. . . . I beg your pardon. Let's have a dance. (*She dances with* TROPHÍMOF. ÁNYA *and* BARBARA *dance.*)

[*Enter* FIRS, *and stands his walking-stick by the side door. Enter* YÁSHA *by the drawing-room; he stands looking at the dancers.*]

YÁSHA. Well, grandfather?

FIRS. I'm not feeling well. In the old days it was generals and barons and admirals that danced at our dances, but now we send for the Postmaster and the Stationmaster, and even they make a favor of coming. I'm sort of weak all over. The old master, their grandfather, used to give us all sealing wax, when we had anything the matter. I've taken sealing wax every day for twenty years and more. Perhaps that's why I'm still alive.

YÁSHA. I'm sick of you, grandfather. (*Yawning.*) I wish you'd die and have done with it.

FIRS. Ah! you . . . job-lot. (*He mumbles to himself.*)

[TROPHÍMOF *and* MADAME RANÉVSKY *dance beyond the arch and down into the sitting-room.*]

MADAME RANÉVSKY. *Merci.* I'll sit down. (*Sitting.*) I'm tired.

[*Enter* ÁNYA.]

ÁNYA (*agitated*). There was somebody in the kitchen just now saying that the cherry orchard was sold to-day.

MADAME RANÉVSKY. Sold? Who to?

ÁNYA. He didn't say who to. He's gone. (*She dances with* TROPHÍMOF. *Both dance up into the drawing-room.*)

YÁSHA. It was some old fellow chattering; a stranger.

FIRS. And still Leoníd Andréyitch doesn't come. He's wearing his light overcoat, *demi-saison;* he'll catch cold as like as not. Ah, young wood, green wood!

MADAME RANÉVSKY. This is killing me. Yásha, go and find out who it was sold to.

YÁSHA. Why, he's gone long ago, the old man. (*Laughs.*)

MADAME RANÉVSKY (*vexed*). What are you laughing at? What are you glad about?

YÁSHA. He's a ridiculous fellow is Ephikhódof. Nothing in him. Twenty-two misfortunes!

MADAME RANÉVSKY. Firs, if the property is sold, where will you go to?

FIRS. Wherever you tell me, there I'll go.

MADAME RANÉVSKY. Why do you look like that? Are you ill? You ought to be in bed.

FIRS (*ironically*). Oh, yes, I'll go to bed, and who'll hand the things round, who'll give orders? I've the whole house on my hands.

YÁSHA. Lyubóf Andréyevna! Let me ask a favor of you; be so kind; if you go to Paris again, take me with you, I beseech you. It's absolutely impossible for me to stay here. (*Looking about; sotto voce.*) What's the use of talking? You can see for yourself this is a barbarous country; the people have no morals; and the boredom! The food in the kitchen is something shocking, and on the top of it old Firs going about mumbling irrelevant nonsense. Take me back with you; be so kind!

[*Enter* PÍSHTCHIK.]

PÍSHTCHIK. May I have the pleasure . . . a bit of a waltz, charming lady? (MADAME RANÉVSKY *takes his arm.*) All the same, enchanting lady, you must let me have eighteen pounds. (*Dancing.*) Let me have . . . eighteen pounds. (*Exeunt dancing through the arch.*)

YÁSHA (*singing to himself*).
"Oh, wilt thou understand
The turmoil of my soul?"

[*Beyond the arch appears a figure in gray tall hat and check trousers, jumping and waving its arms. Cries of "Bravo, Charlotte Ivánovna."*]

DUNYÁSHA (*stopping to powder her face*). Mamselle Ánya tells me I'm to dance; there are so many gentlemen and so few ladies. But dancing makes me giddy and makes my heart beat, Firs Nikoláyevitch; and just now the gentleman from the postoffice said something so nice to me, oh so nice! It quite took my breath away. [*The music stops.*]

FIRS. What did he say to you?

DUNYÁSHA. He said, "You are like a flower."

YÁSHA (*yawning*). Cad! (*Exit* YÁSHA.)

DUNYÁSHA. Like a flower! I am so ladylike and refined, I dote on compliments.

FIRS. You'll come to a bad end.

[*Enter* EPHIKHÓDOF.]

EPHIKHÓDOF. You are not pleased to see me, Avdótya Fyódorovna, no more than if I were some sort of insect. (*Sighing.*) Ah! Life! Life!

DUNYÁSHA. What do you want?

EPHIKHÓDOF. Undoubtedly perhaps you are right. (*Sighing.*) But of course, if one regards it, so to speak, from the point of view, if I may allow myself the expression, and with apologies for my frankness, you have finally reduced me to a state of mind. I quite appreciate my destiny; every day some misfortune happens to me, and I have long since grown accustomed to it, and face my fortune with a smile. You have passed your word to me, and although I . . .

DUNYÁSHA. Let us talk of this another time, if you please; but now leave me in peace. I am busy meditating. (*Playing with her fan.*)

EPHIKHÓDOF. Every day some misfortune befalls me, and yet if I may venture to say so, I meet them with smiles and even laughter.

[*Enter* BARBARA *from the drawing-room.*]

BARBARA (*to* EPHIKHÓDOF). Haven't you gone yet, Simeon? You seem to pay no attention to what you're told. (*To* DUNYÁSHA.) You get out of here, Dunyásha. (*To* EPHIKHÓDOF.) First you play billiards and break a cue, and then you march about the drawing-room as if you were a guest!

EPHIKHÓDOF. Allow me to inform you that it's not your place to call me to account.

BARBARA. I'm not calling you to account; I'm merely talking to you. All you can do is to walk about from one place to another, without ever doing a stroke of work; and why on earth we keep a clerk at all Heaven only knows.

EPHIKHÓDOF (*offended*). Whether I work, or whether I walk, or whether I eat, or whether I play billiards is a question to be decided only by my elders and people who understand.

BARBARA (*furious*). How dare you talk to me like that! How dare you! I don't understand things, don't I? You clear out of here this minute! Do you hear me? This minute!

EPHIKHÓDOF (*flinching*). I must beg you to express yourself in genteeler language.

BARBARA (*beside herself*). You clear out this instant second! Out you go! (*Following him as he retreats towards the door.*) Twenty-two misfortunes! Make yourself scarce! Get out of my sight!

[*Exit* EPHIKHÓDOF.]

EPHIKHÓDOF (*without*). I shall lodge a complaint against you.

BARBARA. What! You're coming back, are you? (*Seizing the walking-stick left at the door by* FIRS.) Come on! Come on! Come on! I'll teach you! Are you coming? Are you coming? Then take that. (*She slashes with the stick.*)

[*Enter* LOPÁKHIN.]

LOPÁKHIN. Many thanks; much obliged.

BARBARA (*still angry, but ironical*). Sorry!

LOPÁKHIN. Don't mention it. I'm very grateful for your warm reception.

BARBARA. It's not worth thanking me for. (*She walks away, then looks round and asks in a gentle voice:*) I didn't hurt you?

LOPÁKHIN. Oh, no, nothing to matter. I shall have a bump like a goose's egg, that's all.

[*Voices from the drawing-room: "Lopàkhin has arrived! Yermolái Alexéyitch!"*]

PÍSHTCHIK. Let my eyes see him, let my ears hear him! (*He and* LOPÁKHIN *kiss.*) You smell of brandy, old man. We're having a high time, too.

[*Enter* MADAME RANÉVSKY.]

MADAME RANÉVSKY. Is it you, Yermolái Alexéyitch? Why have you been so long? Where is Leoníd?

LOPÁKHIN. Leoníd Andréyitch came back with me. He's just coming.

MADAME RANÉVSKY (*agitated*). What happened? Did the sale come off? Tell me, tell me!

LOPÁKHIN (*embarrassed, afraid of showing his pleasure*). The sale was all over by four o'clock. We missed the train and had to wait till half-past eight. (*Sighing heavily.*) Ouf! I'm rather giddy. . . .

[*Enter* GÁYEF. *In one hand he carries parcels; with the other he wipes away his tears.*]

MADAME RANÉVSKY. What happened, Lénya? Come, Lénya? (*Impatiently, crying.*) Be quick, be quick, for Heaven's sake!

GÁYEF (*answering her only with an up-and-down gesture of the hand; to* FIRS, *crying*). Here, take these. . . . Here are some anchovies and Black Sea herrings. I've had nothing to eat all day. Lord, what I've been through! (*Through the open door of the billiard-room comes the click of the billiard balls and* YÁSHA'S *voice: "Seven, eighteen!"* GÁYEF'S *expression changes; he stops crying.*) I'm frightfully tired. Come and help me change, Firs. (*He goes up through the drawing-room,* FIRS *following.*)

PÍSHTCHIK. What about the sale? Come on, tell us all about it.

MADAME RANÉVSKY. Was the cherry orchard sold?

LOPÁKHIN. Yes.

MADAME RANÉVSKY. Who bought it?

LOPÁKHIN. I did. (*A pause.* MADAME RANÉVSKY *is overwhelmed at the news. She would fall to the ground but for the chair and table by her.* BARBARA *takes the keys from her belt, throws them on the floor in the middle of the sitting-room, and exit.*) I bought it. Wait a bit; don't hurry me; my head's in a whirl; I can't speak. . . . (*Laughing.*) When we got to the sale, Derigánof was there already. Leoníd Andréyitch had only fifteen hundred pounds, and Derigánof bid three

thousand more than the mortgage right away. When I saw how things stood, I went for him and bid four thousand. He said four thousand five hundred. I said five thousand five hundred. He went up by five hundreds, you see, and I went up by thousands. . . . Well, it was soon over. I bid nine thousand more than the mortgage, and got it; and now the cherry orchard is mine! Mine! (*Laughing.*) Heavens alive! Just think of it! The cherry orchard is mine! Tell me that I'm drunk; tell me that I'm off my head; tell me that it's all a dream! . . . (*Stamping his feet.*) Don't laugh at me! If only my father and my grandfather could rise from their graves and see the whole affair, how their Yermolái, their flogged and ignorant Yermolái, who used to run about barefooted in the winter, how this same Yermolái had bought a property that hasn't its equal for beauty anywhere in the whole world! I have bought the property where my father and grandfather were slaves, where they weren't even allowed into the kitchen. I'm asleep, it's only a vision, it isn't real. . . . 'Tis the fruit of imagination, wrapped in the mists of ignorance. (*Picking up the keys and smiling affectionately.*) She's thrown down her keys; she wants to show that she's no longer mistress here. . . . (*Jingling them together.*) Well, well, what's the odds? (*The musicians are heard tuning up.*) Hey, musicians, play! I want to hear you. Come, every one, and see Yermolái Lopákhin lay his axe to the cherry orchard, come and see the trees fall down! We'll fill the place with villas; our grandsons and great-grandsons shall see a new life here. . . . Strike up, music!

[*The band plays.* MADAME RANÉVSKY *sinks into a chair and weeps bitterly.*] LOPÁKHIN (*reproachfully.*) Oh, why, why, didn't you listen to me? You can't put the clock back now, poor dear. (*Crying.*) Oh, that all this were past and over! Oh, that our unhappy topsy-turvy life were changed! PÍSHTCHIK (*taking him by the arm, sotto voce*). She's crying. Let's go into the drawing-room and leave her alone to . . . Come on. (*Taking him by the arm, and going up toward the drawing-room.*) LOPÁKHIN. What's up? Play your best, musicians! Let everything be as I want. (*Ironically.*) Here comes the new squire, the owner of the cherry orchard! (*Knocking up by accident against a table and nearly throwing down the candelabra.*) Never mind, I can pay for everything! [*Exit with* PÍSHTCHIK. *Nobody remains in the drawing-room or sitting-room*

except MADAME RANÉVSKY, *who sits huddled together, weeping bitterly. The band plays softly.*] [*Enter* ÁNYA *and* TROPHÍMOF *quickly.* ÁNYA *goes to her mother and kneels before her.* TROPHÍMOF *stands in the entry to the drawing-room.*] ÁNYA. Mamma! Are you crying, mamma? My dear, good, sweet mamma! Darling, I love you! I bless you! The cherry orchard is sold; it's gone; it's quite true, it's quite true. But don't cry, mamma, you've still got life before you, you've still got your pure and lovely soul. Come with me, darling; come away from here. We'll plant a new garden, still lovelier than this. You will see it and understand, and happiness, deep, tranquil happiness will sink down on your soul, like the sun at eventide, and you'll smile, mamma. Come, darling, come with me!

ACT IV

Same scene as Act I. There are no window curtains, no pictures. The little furniture left is stacked in a corner, as if for sale. A feeling of emptiness. By the door to the hall and at the back of the scene are piled portmanteaux, bundles, etc. The door is open and the voices of BARBARA *and* ÁNYA *are audible.*

LOPÁKHIN *stands waiting.* YÁSHA *holds a tray with small tumblers full of champagne.* EPHIKHÓDOF *is tying up a box in the hall. A distant murmur of voices behind the scene; the* PEASANTS *have come to say good-bye.*

GÁYEF (*without*). Thank you, my lads, thank you.
YÁSHA. The common people have come to say good-bye. I'll tell you what I think, Yermolái Alexéyitch;

they're good fellows but rather stupid.
[*The murmur of voices dies away.*]

[*Enter* MADAME RANÉVSKY *and* GÁYEF *from the hall. She is not crying, but she is pale, her face twitches, she cannot speak.*]
GÁYEF. You gave them your purse, Lyuba. That was wrong, very wrong! MADAME RANÉVSKY. I couldn't help it. I couldn't help it! (*Exeunt both.*) LOPÁKHIN (*calling after them through the doorway*). Please come here! Won't you come here? Just a glass to say good-bye. I forgot to bring any from the town, and could only raise one bottle at the station. Come along. (*A pause.*) What, won't you have any? (*Returning from the door.*) If I'd known, I wouldn't have bought it. I shan't

have any either. (YÁSHA *sets the tray down carefully on a chair*.) Drink it yourself, Yásha.

YÁSHA. Here's to our departure! Good luck to them that stay! (*Drinking*.) This isn't real champagne, you take my word for it.

LOPÁKHIN. Sixteen shillings a bottle. (*A pause*.) It's devilish cold in here.

YÁSHA. The fires weren't lighted to-day; we're all going away. (*He laughs*.)

LOPÁKHIN. What are you laughing for?

YÁSHA. Just pleasure.

LOPÁKHIN. Here we are in October, but it's as calm and sunny as summer. Good building weather. (*Looking at his watch and speaking off*.) Don't forget that there's only forty-seven minutes before the train goes. You must start for the station in twenty minutes. Make haste.

[*Enter* TROPHÍMOF *in an overcoat, from out of doors*.]

TROPHÍMOF. I think it's time we were off. The carriages are round. What the deuce has become of my goloshes? I've lost 'em. (*Calling off*.) Ánya, my goloshes have disappeared. I can't find them anywhere!

LOPÁKHIN. I've got to go to Kharkof. I'll start in the same train with you. I'm going to spend the winter at Kharkof. I've been loafing about all this time with you people, eating my head off for want of work. I can't live without work, I don't know what to do with my hands; they dangle about as if they didn't belong to me.

TROPHÍMOF. Well, we're going now, and you'll be able to get back to your beneficent labors.

LOPÁKHIN. Have a glass.

TROPHÍMOF. Not for me.

LOPÁKHIN. Well, so you're off to Moscow?

TROPHÍMOF. Yes, I'll see them into the town, and go on to Moscow to-morrow.

LOPÁKHIN. Well, well, . . . I suppose the professors haven't started their lectures yet; they're waiting till you arrive.

TROPHÍMOF. It's no affair of yours.

LOPÁKHIN. How many years have you been up at the University?

TROPHÍMOF. Try and think of some new joke; this one's getting a bit flat. (*Looking for his goloshes*.) Look here, I dare say we shan't meet again, so let me give you a bit of advice as a keepsake: Don't flap your hands about! Get out of the habit of flapping. Building villas, prophesying that villa residents will turn into small freeholders, all that sort of thing is flapping, too. Well, when all's said and done, I like you. You have thin, delicate, artist fingers; you have a delicate artist soul.

LOPÁKHIN (*embracing him*). Good-bye, old chap. Thank you for everything. Take some money off me for the journey if you want it.

TROPHÍMOF. What for? I don't want it.

LOPÁKHIN. But you haven't got any.

TROPHÍMOF. Yes, I have. Many thanks. I got some for a translation. Here it is, in my pocket. (*Anxiously*.) I can't find my goloshes anywhere!

BARBARA (*from the next room*). Here, take your garbage away! (*She throws a pair of goloshes on the stage*.)

TROPHÍMOF. What are you so cross about, Barbara? Humph! . . . But those aren't *my* goloshes!

LOPÁKHIN. In the spring I sowed three thousand acres of poppy and I have cleared four thousand pounds net profit. When my poppies were in flower, what a picture they made!

So you see, I cleared four thousand pounds; and I wanted to lend you a bit because I've got it to spare. What's the good of being stuck up? I'm a peasant. . . . As man to man . . .

TROPHÍMOF. Your father was a peasant; mine was a chemist; it doesn't prove anything. (LOPÁKHIN *takes out his pocket-book with paper money.*) Shut up, shut up. . . . If you offered me twenty thousand pounds I would not take it. I am a free man; nothing that you value so highly, all of you, rich and poor, has the smallest power over me; it's like thistledown floating on the wind. I can do without you; I can go past you; I'm strong and proud. Mankind marches forward to the highest truth, to the highest happiness possible on earth, and I march in the foremost ranks.

LOPÁKHIN. Will you get there?

TROPHÍMOF. Yes. (*A pause.*) I will get there myself, or I will show others the way.

[*The sound of axes hewing is heard in the distance.*]

LOPÁKHIN. Well, good-bye, old chap; it is time to start. Here we stand swaggering to each other, and life goes by all the time without heeding us. When I work for hours without getting tired, I get easy in my mind and I seem to know why I exist. But God alone knows what most of the people in Russia were born for. . . . Well, who cares? It doesn't affect the circulation of work. They say Leoníd Andréyitch has got a place; he's going to be in a bank and get six hundred pounds a year. . . . He won't sit it out, he's too lazy.

ÁNYA (*in the doorway*). Mamma says, will you stop them cutting down the orchard till she has gone?

TROPHÍMOF. Really, haven't you got tact enough for that? (*Exit* TROPHÍMOF *by the hall.*)

LOPÁKHIN. Of course, I'll stop them at once.—What fools they are! (*Exit after* TROPHÍMOF.)

ÁNYA. Has Firs been sent to the hospital?

YÁSHA. I told 'em this morning. They're sure to have sent him.

ÁNYA (*To* EPHIKHÓDOF, *who crosses.*) Simeon Pantaléyitch, please find out if Firs has been sent to the hospital.

YÁSHA (*offended*). I told George this morning. What's the good of asking a dozen times?

EPHIKHÓDOF. Our centenarian friend, in my conclusive opinion, is hardly worth tinkering; it's time he was despatched to his forefathers. I can only say I envy him. (*Putting down a portmanteau on a bandbox and crushing it flat.*) There you are! I knew how it would be! (*Exit.*)

YÁSHA (*jeering*). Twenty-two misfortunes!

BARBARA (*without*). Has Firs been sent to the hospital?

ÁNYA. Yes.

BARBARA. Why didn't they take the note to the doctor?

ÁNYA. We must send it after them. (*Exit* ÁNYA.)

BARBARA (*from the next room*). Where's Yásha? Tell him his mother is here. She wants to say good-bye to him.

YÁSHA (*with a gesture of impatience*). It's enough to try the patience of a saint!

[DUNYÁSHA *has been busying herself with the luggage. Seeing* YÁSHA *alone, she approaches him.*]

DUNYÁSHA. You might just look once at me, Yásha. You are going away, you are leaving me. (*Crying and throwing her arms round his neck.*)

YÁSHA. What's the good of crying? (*Drinking champagne.*) In six days I shall be back in Paris. To-morrow we take the express, off we go, and that's the last of us! I can hardly believe it's true. *Vive la France!* This place don't suit me. I can't bear it . . . it can't be helped. I have had enough barbarism; I'm fed up. (*Drinking champagne.*) What's the good of crying? You be a good girl, and you'll have no call to cry. 10

DUNYÁSHA (*powdering her face and looking into a glass*). Write me a letter from Paris. I've been so fond of you, Yásha, ever so fond! I am a delicate creature, Yásha.

YÁSHA. Here's somebody coming. (*He busies himself with the luggage, singing under his breath.*)

[*Enter* MADAME RANÉVSKY, GÁYEF, ÁNYA, *and* CHARLOTTE.] 20

GÁYEF. We'll have to be off; it's nearly time. (*Looking at* YÁSHA.) Who is it smells of red herring?

MADAME RANÉVSKY. We must take our seats in ten minutes. (*Looking round the room.*) Good-bye dear old house; good-bye, grandpapa! When winter is past and spring comes again, you will be here no more; they will have pulled you down. Oh, think of all 30 these walls have seen! (*Kissing* ÁNYA *passionately.*) My treasure, you look radiant, your eyes flash like two diamonds. Are you happy?—very happy?

ÁNYA. Very, very happy. We're beginning a new life, mamma.

GÁYEF (*gayly*). She's quite right; everything's all right now. Till the cherry orchard was sold we were all agitated 40 and miserable; but once the thing was settled finally and irrevocably, we all calmed down and got jolly again. I'm a bank clerk now; I'm a financier . . . red in the middle! And you, Lyuba, whatever you may

say, you're looking ever so much better, not a doubt about it.

MADAME RANÉVSKY. Yes, my nerves are better; it's quite true. (*She is helped on with her hat and coat.*) I sleep well now. Take my things out, Yásha. We must be off. (*To* ÁNYA.) We shall soon meet again, darling. . . . I'm off to Paris; I shall live on the money your grandmother sent from Yaroslav to buy the property. God bless your grandmother! I'm afraid it won't last long.

ÁNYA. You'll come back very, very soon, won't you, mamma? I'm going to work and pass the examination at the Gymnase and get a place and help you. We'll read all sorts of books together, won't we, mamma? (*Kissing her mother's hands.*) We'll read in the long autumn evenings, we'll read heaps of books, and a new, wonderful world will open up before us. (*Meditating.*) . . . Come back, mamma!

MADAME RANÉVSKY. I'll come back, my angel. (*Embracing her.*)

[*Enter* LOPÁKHIN. CHARLOTTE *sings softly.*]

GÁYEF. Happy Charlotte, she's singing.

CHARLOTTE (*taking a bundle of rags, like a swaddled baby*). Hush-a-bye, baby, on the tree-top . . . (*The baby answers,* "*Wah, wah.*") Hush, my little one, hush, my pretty one! ("*Wah, wah.*") You'll break your mother's heart. (*She throws the bundle down on the floor again.*) Don't forget to find me a new place, please. I can't do without it.

LOPÁKHIN. We'll find you a place, Charlotte Ivánovna, don't be afraid.

GÁYEF. Everybody's deserting us. Barbara's going. Nobody seems to want us.

CHARLOTTE. There's nowhere for me to live in the town. I'm obliged to go. (*Hums a tune.*) What's the odds?

[*Enter* PÍSHTCHIK.]

LOPÁKHIN. Nature's masterpiece!

PÍSHTCHIK (*panting*). Oy, oy, let me get my breath again! . . . I'm done up! . . . My noble friends! . . . Give me some water.

GÁYEF. Wants some money, I suppose. No, thank you; I'll keep out of harm's way. (*Exit.*)

PÍSHTCHIK. It's ages since I have been here, fairest lady. (*To* LOPÁKHIN.) You here? Glad to see you, you man of gigantic intellect. Take this; it's for you. (*Giving* LOPÁKHIN *money.*) Forty pounds! I still owe you eighty-four.

LOPÁKHIN (*amazed, shrugging his shoulders*). It's like a thing in a dream! Where did you get it from?

PÍSHTCHIK. Wait a bit. . . . I'm hot. . . . A most remarkable thing! Some Englishmen came and found some sort of white clay on my land. (*To* MADAME RANÉVSKY.) And here's forty pounds for you, lovely, wonderful lady. (*Giving her money.*) The rest another time. (*Drinking water.*) Only just now a young man in the train was saying that some . . . some great philosopher advises us all to jump off roofs. . . . Jump, he says, and there's an end of it. (*With an astonished air.*) Just think of that! More water!

LOPÁKHIN. Who were the Englishmen?

PÍSHTCHIK. I leased them the plot with the clay on it for twenty-four years. But I haven't any time now . . . I must be getting on. I must go to Znoikof's, to Kardamónof's. . . . I owe everybody money. (*Drinking.*) Good-bye to every one; I'll look in on Thursday.

MADAME RANÉVSKY. We're just moving into town, and to-morrow I go abroad.

PÍSHTCHIK. What! (*Alarmed.*) What are you going into town for? Why, what's happened to the furniture? . . . Trunks? . . . Oh, it's all right. (*Crying.*) It's all right. People of powerful intellect . . . those Englishmen. It's all right. Be happy . . . God be with you . . . it's all right. Everything in this world has to come to an end. (*Kissing* MADAME RANÉVSKY's *hand.*) If ever the news reaches you that *I* have come to an end, give a thought to the old . . . horse, and say, "Once there lived a certain Simeónof-Píshtchik, Heaven rest his soul." . . . Remarkable weather we're having. . . . Yes. . . . (*Goes out deeply moved. Returns at once and says from the doorway:*) Dáshenka sent her compliments. (*Exit.*)

MADAME RANÉVSKY. Now we can go. I have only two things on my mind. One is poor old Firs. (*Looking at her watch.*) We can still stay five minutes.

ÁNYA. Firs has been sent to the hospital already, mamma. Yásha sent him off this morning.

MADAME RANÉVSKY. My second anxiety is Barbara. She's used to getting up early and working, and now that she has no work to do she's like a fish out of water. She has grown thin and pale and taken to crying, poor dear. . . . (*A pause.*) You know very well, Yermolái Alexéyitch, I always hoped . . . to see her married to you, and as far as I can see, you're looking out for a wife. (*She whispers to* ÁNYA, *who nods to* CHARLOTTE, *and both exeunt.*) She loves you; you like her; and I can't make out why you seem to fight shy of each other. I don't understand it.

LOPÁKHIN. I don't understand it either, to tell you the truth. It all seems so odd. If there's still time I'll do it this moment. Let's get it over and have done with it; without you there, I feel as if I should never propose to her.

MADAME RANÉVSKY. A capital idea! After all, it doesn't take more than a minute. I'll call her at once.

LOPÁKHIN. And here's the champagne all ready. (*Looking at the glasses.*) Empty; some one's drunk it. (YÁSHA *coughs.*) That's what they call lapping it up and no mistake!

MADAME RANÉVSKY (*animated*). Capital! We'll all go away. . . . *Allez*, Yásha. I'll call her. (*At the door.*) Barbara, leave all that and come here. Come along! (*Exeunt* MADAME RANÉVSKY *and* YÁSHA.)

LOPÁKHIN (*looking at his watch*). Yes. [*A pause. A stifled laugh behind the door; whispering; at last enter* BARBARA.]

BARBARA (*examining the luggage*). Very odd; I can't find it anywhere . . .

LOPÁKHIN. What are you looking for?

BARBARA. I packed it myself, and can't remember. (*A pause.*)

LOPÁKHIN. Where are you going to-day, Varvára Mikháilovna?

BARBARA. Me? I'm going to the Ragulins. I'm engaged to go and keep house for them, to be housekeeper or whatever it is.

LOPÁKHIN. Oh, at Yáshnevo? That's about fifty miles from here. (*A pause.*) Well, so life in this house is over now.

BARBARA (*looking at the luggage*). Wherever can it be? Perhaps I put it in the trunk. . . . Yes, life here is over now; there won't be any more . . .

LOPÁKHIN. And I'm off to Kharkof at once . . . by the same train. A lot of business to do. I'm leaving Ephikhódof to look after this place. I've taken him on.

BARBARA. Have you?

LOPÁKHIN. At this time last year snow was falling already, if you remember; but now it's fine and sunny. Still, it's cold for all that. Three degrees of frost.

BARBARA. Were there? I didn't look. (*A pause.*) Besides, the thermometer's broken. (*A pause.*)

A VOICE (*at the outer door*). Yermolái Alexéyitch!

LOPÁKHIN (*as if he had only been waiting to be called*). I'm just coming! (*Exit* LOPÁKHIN *quickly.*)

[BARBARA *sits on the floor, puts her head on a bundle and sobs softly. The door opens and* MADAME RANÉVSKY *comes in cautiously.*]

MADAME RANÉVSKY. Well? (*A pause.*) We must be off.

BARBARA (*no longer crying, wiping her eyes*). Yes, it's time, mamma. I shall get to the Ragulins all right to-day, so long as I don't miss the train.

MADAME RANÉVSKY (*calling off*). Put on your things, Ánya.

[*Enter* ÁNYA, *then* GÁYEF *and* CHARLOTTE. GÁYEF *wears a warm overcoat with a hood. The servants and drivers come in.* EPHIKHÓDOF *busies himself about the luggage.*]

MADAME RANÉVSKY. Now we can start on our journey.

ÁNYA (*delighted*). We can start on our journey!

GÁYEF. My friends, my dear, beloved friends! Now that I am leaving this house forever, can I keep silence? Can I refrain from expressing those emotions which fill my whole being at such a moment?

ÁNYA (*pleadingly*). Uncle!

BARBARA. Uncle, what's the good?

GÁYEF (*sadly*). Double the red in the middle pocket. I'll hold my tongue.

[*Enter* TROPHÍMOF, *then* LOPÁKHIN.]

TROPHÍMOF. Come along, it's time to start.

LOPÁKHIN. Ephikhódof, my coat.

MADAME RANÉVSKY. I must sit here another minute. It's just as if I had never noticed before what the walls and ceilings of the house were like. I look at them hungrily, with such tender love . . .

GÁYEF. I remember, when I was six years old, how I sat in this window on Trinity Sunday, and watched father starting out for church.

MADAME RANÉVSKY. Has everything been cleared out?

LOPÁKHIN. Apparently everything. (*To* EPHIKHÓDOF, *putting on his overcoat.*) See that everything 's in order, Ephikhódof.

EPHIKHÓDOF (*in a hoarse voice*). You trust me, Yermolái Alexéyitch.

LOPÁKHIN. What's up with your voice?

EPHIKHÓDOF. I was just having a drink of water. I swallowed something.

YÁSHA (*contemptuously*). Cad!

MADAME RANÉVSKY. We're going, and not a soul will be left here.

LOPÁKHIN. Until the spring.

[BARBARA *pulls an umbrella out of a bundle of rugs, as if she were brandishing it to strike.* LOPÁKHIN *pretends to be frightened.*]

BARBARA. Don't be so silly! I never thought of such a thing.

TROPHÍMOF. Come, we'd better go and get in. It's time to start. The train will be in immediately.

BARBARA. There are your goloshes, Peter, by that portmanteau. (*Crying.*) What dirty old things they are!

TROPHÍMOF (*putting on his goloshes*). Come along.

GÁYEF (*much moved, afraid of crying*). The train . . . the station . . . double the red in the middle; doublette to pot the white in the corner.[1] . . .

[1] If you make your ball hit the cushion and run across into a pocket, it is a double; if I hit the cushion myself and pot you on the rebound, it is a doublette.

MADAME RANÉVSKY. Come on!

LOPÁKHIN. Is every one here? No one left in there? (*Locking the door.*) There are things stacked in there; I must lock them up. Come on!

ÁNYA. Good-bye, house! Good-bye, old life!

TROPHÍMOF. Welcome, new life!

[*Exit with* ÁNYA. BARBARA *looks round the room, and exit slowly. Exeunt* YÁSHA, *and* CHARLOTTE *with her dog.*]

LOPÁKHIN. Till the spring, then. Go on, everybody. So-long! (*Exit.*)

[MADAME RANÉVSKY *and* GÁYEF *remain alone. They seem to have been waiting for this, throw their arms round each other's necks and sob restrainedly and gently, afraid of being overheard.*]

GÁYEF (*in despair*). My sister! my sister!

MADAME RANÉVSKY. Oh, my dear, sweet, lovely orchard! My life, my youth, my happiness, farewell! Farewell!

ÁNYA (*calling gayly, without*). Mamma!

TROPHÍMOF (*gay and excited*). Aoo!

MADAME RANÉVSKY. One last look at the walls and the windows. . . . Our dear mother used to love to walk up and down this room.

GÁYEF. My sister! my sister!

ÁNYA (*without*). Mamma!

TROPHÍMOF (*without*). Aoo!

MADAME RANÉVSKY. We're coming.

[*Exeunt. The stage is empty. One hears all the doors being locked, and the carriages driving away. All is quiet. Amid the silence the thud of the axes on the trees echoes sad and lonely. The sound of footsteps.* FIRS *appears in the doorway, right. He is dressed, as always, in his long coat and white waistcoat; he wears slippers. He is ill.*]

FIRS (*going to the door, left, and trying the handle*). Locked. They've gone. (*Sitting on the sofa.*) They've forgotten me. Never mind! I'll sit here. Leoníd

Andréyitch is sure to put on his cloth coat instead of his fur. (*He sighs anxiously.*) He hadn't me to see. Young wood, green wood! (*He mumbles something incomprehensible.*) Life has gone by as if I'd never lived. (*Lying down.*) I'll lie down. There's no strength left in you; there's

nothing, nothing. Ah, you . . . joblot!

[*He lies motionless. A distant sound is heard, as if from the sky, the sound of a string breaking, dying away, melancholy. Silence ensues, broken only by the stroke of the axe on the trees far away in the cherry orchard.*]

MAXIM GORKY

ON NEW YEAR'S EVE, 1902, the Moscow Art Theatre performed for the first time *The Lower Depths* by Maxim Gorky. It was the most thunderous triumph in the history of that organization. The audience, the actors, and the play achieved the rare perfection of complete fusion in their tripartite roles. The author was given a tremendous ovation that brought him twenty times before the audience, and the company took endless curtain calls. Gorky's masterpiece had had its première. Despite the passing years and the stupendous changes in the twentieth century world, *The Lower Depths* has retained its full flavor. It is one of the great plays to come out of Russia, and it is now an established classic in modern European drama.

The Lower Depths, variously known as *At the Bottom*, *The Submerged*, *In the Depths*, *A Night's Shelter*, *A Night's Lodging*, from the Russian title *Na Dnye* meaning "on the bottom," was Gorky's second play. The *Smug Citizen*, his first play, written more or less simultaneously during the first several months of the new century, had been presented with moderate success at St. Petersburg in the preceding April by the Moscow Art Theatre. But Gorky already enjoyed a vast reputation as a character and a writer before he began to write for the stage. Both *The Smug Citizen* and *The Lower Depths* were the natural artistic flowering and condensation in terms of drama of the diverse and melancholy struggle for life to which Gorky had been condemned. By force of genius he made his way up from the lowest depths of a wretched and beaten outcast in the world to the proud position, in his later years, of first artist in the Soviet state. His career is a drama in itself, and it contributes largely to an understanding of his play.

Maxim Gorky, meaning "Maxim the bitter one," was the pen name of Alexei Maximovich Pyeshkov, born March 14, 1868, at Nizhni Novgorod, an important commercial city on the Volga, just below the mouth of the Oka. His father, a dyer and upholsterer, died early, and his mother soon married a cruel and penniless member of Russia's decaying nobility. The boy Maxim—or Alexei, as he was then called—went to live with the tempestuous, lower middle class family of his maternal grandfather, the Kashirins. The grandfather was a tyrant. He taught Maxim to read the characters of Church Slavic and frequently gave him severe beatings and religious lectures. Gorky took sanctuary from this brutality and coarseness in the warm, sympathetic affection of Grandmother Kashirin whose God, unlike her husband's, was kind and eternally good. Gorky could be almost happy while listening to her relate fairy tales and stories of her own life. He had no friends among the other boys in the neighborhood; they regarded him as an enemy and referred to him as the "Kashirin brat." Despite his unusual size and strength Maxim often came in torn and bleeding from the streets, to face the interminable moral sermons of his grandfather. He intensely disliked the few months he spent in a local school, and considered them a waste of time. He preferred the rough humor of the sweating stevedores who toiled on the barges along the Volga, or the mystery of the forest near the home of the Kashirins where he might catch songbirds to sell on market-days. "The forest," he wrote later in his autobiography, "called up a feeling of peace and solace in my heart, and in that time also my senses acquired a peculiar keenness, my hearing and sight became more acute, my memory more retentive, my storehouse of impressions widened."

The generally drab period of his childhood came to an end in 1878 when his mother died. Maxim, not quite ten years old, was told by his grandfather to get out and earn his own way. He began as a "boy" in a bootshop. He already knew about hardship and cruelty, but the brutality and hypocrisy of Russian business methods filled him with revulsion, and he soon ran off. He became a servant in the home of a draughtsman, but this too was unendurable, and he found a job as dishwasher on a Volga steamer. Oddly enough this new venture first revealed to him the world of literature. Smouri, the steamer's cook and Gorky's immediate superior, owned an *Ivanhoe*, a *Tom Jones*, and books by Gogol and Dumas-père, which he encouraged the boy to read. Maxim read greedily with wonder and delight. After another short stay at the draughtsman's and a second venture as galley-helper on a steamer, Gorky was apprenticed at an icon workshop where he was taught how to lure customers from rival shops, how to cheat and lie about the value and age of images. It shocked him to

know that the employees were thieves and that the master knew and accepted the fact. He left the icon workshop to serve two more years with the draughtsman, this time as an overseer. He continued to borrow books and read steadily.

Gorky's desire for learning became so strong that in 1884, at the age of fifteen, he set out for Kazan on the Volga with the hope that he might study at the University there. The hope was short lived, for Gorky was one of the despised people, and formal education was denied him. He remained at Kazan, nevertheless, fascinated by the medieval charm of its cathedral, its storied Kremlin, and its ancient relics of Mohammedan culture. He earned a bare sustenance as a stevedore on the river docks, and later worked as a gardener, janitor, choir singer and baker's apprentice. This period in Gorky's life is vividly described in his stories *Konovalov*, *Twenty-six men and a Girl*, and *The Master*. His work at the bakery entailed long hours and sometimes, while waiting for the bread to rise, Gorky eased his boredom by writing verses. But his existence was intolerably dull, despite occasional meetings with the young university radicals and continued efforts at self-education. In despair he shot himself in the winter of 1887. The bullet penetrated his lung and lodged in his back. He recovered, and in humiliation returned a month later to the grind in the bakery. The experience preyed on his mind until he purged it somewhat in his story *An Incident in the Life of Makar*. Gorky summarized the effects of these first years in *Reminiscences of My Youth:* "From direct observation I saw that the whole structure of society was almost completely devoid of human sympathy. Life was unfolding itself before me as an endless chain of hostility and cruelty, as an unceasing and sordid struggle for the possession of worthless objects. To me, personally, books were the only necessity, everything else possessed no importance in my eyes. . . . As I sucked the stimulating honey out of books, I was conscious of growing mentally and of speaking with greater assurance."

In the summer of 1888 Gorky continued his migration down the Volga, stopping at Krasnovidovo to enjoy the companionship of Romas, a Ukrainian shopkeeper with a flair for literature and a fine collection of books; then moving on southward to the mouth of the river where he led the life of a vagabond, consorting with all types of people and adding richly to his store of experiences. He joined a band of Kalmuck fishermen on the Caspian Sea; he served as night-watchman at a railroad station in Dobrinka, walking about from six in the evening until six in the morning and occasionally encountering Cossacks intent on stealing food supplies from the warehouses. Sometimes the station master released him to sing at entertainments and parties which often degenerated into wild, drunken orgies. He wandered on from place to place, and finally returned in the autumn of 1889 to his native village, where he was almost immediately sent to jail for associating with political suspects. After his release, he was given a physical examination at an army recruiting station, but was declared unfit for active service because of his punctured lung and a leg injury which he had suffered during his labors as a longshoreman on the Volga.

For nearly two years Gorky remained in Nizhni Novgorod working in a brewery, peddling *kvas*—a Russian variety of fermented cider—clerking in a distillery office, and finally, as a copyist, in the law office of A. I. Lanin. In his autobiographical works Gorky speaks highly of Lanin's friendship and later dedicated to him his first volume of collected stories. These were important years for Gorky; he began to find himself and to make literary friendships, particularly with Korolenko, then the most popular writer in Russia. To him Gorky submitted a poem called *The Song of an Old Oak.* Korolenko's criticism was both honest and severe, and when the manuscript was returned, Gorky thrust it into the burning stove. He was not yet ripe for literature, and he resumed his restless wanderings.

In the spring of 1890 he went down the Volga again, crossed the Ukraine, visited Bessarabia, and the Crimea, and finally, in the autumn of 1891, arrived at Tiflis, the capital of Georgia, in the very heart of the Caucasus, where he worked in the paymaster's office of a railroad company. He lived for a time with Kalyuzhny, a revolutionary figure who had once spent several years at enforced labor in the mines of Siberia. With Kalyuzhny's encouragement, Gorky wrote his first prose story, *Makar Chudra,* which appeared in a Tiflis newspaper in September 1892. When the editors requested him to sign his story, he casually and for the first time wrote his name "Maxim Gorky." The literary career of Alexey Pyeshkov had begun.

Elated with this success, Gorky returned to Nizhni Novgorod, resumed his work for Lanin, and once more submitted his literary pieces for the helpful criticism of Korolenko. Gorky later wrote in *Reminiscences:* "Korolenko was the first to tell me in impressive human language of the meaning of form and the beauty of idiom. I was astonished at the clear and simple truth of his words, and as I listened I had an uncanny feeling that writing was not an easy matter." Among the stories that now poured forth was the famous *Chelkash*, which appeared in the paper edited by Korolenko.

Gorky spent most of the next eight years as a journalist and fiction writer in or near his native city. He developed tuberculosis of the lungs, however, and in 1897 went to the Crimea and the Ukraine for treatment. The next year he was arrested and sent to Tiflis, where he was imprisoned in the Metekh Fortress. His revolutionary sympathies, which were often boldly promulgated in his journalistic writings, kept him under constant police surveillance. Back in Nizhni Novgorod, Gorky published two volumes of his *Sketches and Stories* in March 1898. A third volume soon followed. These were enthusiastically received by public and critics alike. Gorky's fame spread rapidly and, at the age of thirty, he took his place among the most popular writers in Russia.

Gorky's connection with the Moscow Art Theatre came through his friendship with Anton Chekhov, who superseded Korolenko as the young writer's critical mentor. He wrote a letter to Chekhov and sent him his books in November 1898. Chekhov wrote at once; he was struck with Gorky's talent and potential greatness, but he sternly criticised his lack of grace and self-restraint. In March 1899 Gorky went to the Crimea and met Chekhov in person. They became warm friends.

Chekhov urgently advised Gorky to get out of backwoods Nizhni Novgorod and go to Moscow or St. Petersburg. He tried to polish off some of Gorky's hobo crudities. He introduced him to the Moscow Art group that, touring southward, had stopped to see Chekhov. Gorky needed their encouragement, and they needed new playwrights for their theatre. Their union with Gorky was almost as inspired as that with Chekhov. Russia was living in disturbed days in an atmosphere of expectancy. Gorky knew these undercurrents at first hand, having experienced the misery of the submerged millions as had no other writer in Russia. His vivid, even horrifying stories had already made his name potent as the revealer and champion of the brutalized and the oppressed. He was watched by the Czar's Ogpu. He was the one man in all Russia to do the play that the young and ambitious Nemirovich-Danchenko and Stanislavsky wanted for their new theatre. They urged him, and Chekhov urged him to the refrain of "Write a play! Write! Write! Write!" So Gorky, forced by the authorities to live at his native village, wrote his first plays—while his own residence and personal movements were spied upon and checked by the secret agents.

Gorky's dramas were invariably treated as symbols of the emergence of oppressed Russia, and their performance was consequently restricted and under tight government control and censorship. The Moscow Art Theatre continued to produce them whenever possible at home and abroad. The performance of his *Children of the Sun*, a grim and fatalistic domestic drama in the naturalistic style, provoked a near riot in Moscow in the tempestuous days following the Revolution of 1905, although there is little besides the title passage to offer hope: "Fear of death is all that keeps men from being bold, beautiful, and free; but we—we are the

Children of the Sun, radiant source of life; born to the sun, we shall conquer the dark fear of death." Gorky had written the play while imprisoned in the Peter and Paul fortress in St. Petersburg following his arrest in Riga after the bloody Red Sunday outbreak in January 1905.

Released on bail, Gorky went to the Crimea for his health, then to Finland where he wrote his play *Barbarians*. He became virtually a political exile. In 1906 he made a goodwill visit to America, hoping to obtain financial support for the revolutionary movement. But he blundered into an offence against American public opinion by bringing with him Maria Andreyeva, a Russian actress who was not his wife, and by openly supporting the cause of American labor and advocating strikes. The nation raised its eyebrows; the Russian embassy, which had been steadily defaming him, was victorious. While in America Gorky wrote his novel, *Mother*, which was later dramatized.

Gorky then settled on the island of Capri, where he began his intimate friendship with Lenin. He did not return to Russia until 1914, when he was granted amnesty. For a time he lived in Finland under the watchful eye of the police. After the War, which Gorky actively opposed, he devoted his efforts to the preservation and development of culture and education in Russia at a time when the hysterical masses, who had come to power in 1917, wanted to destroy everything associated with the deposed intelligentsia. He aided the hard hit Russian scholars, and undertook to edit a collection of *World Literature*, a gathering of masterpieces from all countries to be published by the state.

In 1921 Gorky became seriously ill with tuberculosis; at the insistence of his friend Lenin, he went to a German sanatorium for treatment. When his health improved sufficiently he journeyed to Italy and settled at Capo di Sorrento. The Mussolini regime searched his villa once but otherwise left him unmolested. In this pleasant environment Gorky wrote many of his novels, short stories, and essays. He carried on an enormous correspondence with young, aspiring Soviet writers, whom he was ever eager to help.

In March 1928, Gorky's sixtieth birthday was the occasion for a national celebration in Russia. The government of the Soviet Union, the literary, educational, and scientific bodies in the country joined to pay tribute to the "proletarian writer" who had attained international renown. In the same year Gorky returned to Russia and became an official spokesman of the Stalin regime, toward which he was friendly and sympathetic. He wielded enormous influence in Russia's world of letters. He renewed his interest in drama and wrote two new plays in a projected trilogy on the decay of the Russian bourgeoise: *Yegor Bulychov and Others* (1932), and *Dostigaev and Others* (1933). In 1932 he was actively involved in the abolition of the Association of Russian Proletarian Authors, an organization which for several years had had a deadening effect on Russian literature.

In September 1932 the entire Soviet Union celebrated a national holiday to commemorate the fortieth anniversary of Gorky's literary career. At the Moscow Opera House Stalin headed a distinguished company which gathered to praise the achievements of the man who was then Russia's most distinguished living writer. During the proceedings the author's birthplace was renamed Gorky.

After establishing his permanent residence in Moscow, Gorky continued his allegiance to the Soviet Union and remained a benevolent leader of Russia's world of letters until his death on June 18, 1936.

Gorky's great fame in the contemporary theatre rests, but rests firmly, on *The Lower Depths*. In that play he succeeded in bringing to a convincing life in art that outcast band of thieves, fences, and prostitutes, the cap-maker, the meat-pie vendor, the locksmith, the shoemaker, the alcoholic actor, the consumptive and dying young wife, and the fallen baron, "creatures that once were men" now heaped upon each other in this lodging for the night at the bottom of a grimy cave-like cellar. They are summoned up from the intolerable wretchedness seen and personally endured by Gorky. His motive and his theme were summed up after an account of a horrifying episode in front of a brothel in his autobiography: "Why do I relate these abominations? So that you may know, kind sirs, that it is not all past and done with! . . . I know of genuine horrors, everyday terrors, and I have an undeniable right to excite you unpleasantly by telling you about them, in order that you may remember how we live, and under what circumstances. A low and unclean life it is, ours, and that is the truth. . . . I am a lover of humanity, and I have no desire to make anyone miserable; but one must not be sentimental, nor hide the grim truth with the mothy words of beautiful lies. Let us face life as it is."

Gorky builds his play on the belief that human beings drawn from the life with pity and understanding carry their own power and need no clever stage tricks to intensify their appeal; the author, as Gorky once put it, is merely their host at the party. The desperate, brutalized, degraded people in the play must make whatever impact such a spectacle in life itself makes upon us personally. The action is even more static than in Chekhov's plays. It is devoid of form in action; it is a series of tenuously related tableaux, without the usual stitching of an unfolding plot. Luka, alone, with his gentle humanity and his subtle alteration of the lives in this cellar, gives a rhythmic continuity to its decentralized structure. The group itself—not any individual member of it—is the hero. It has the unstudied casualness of life itself surprised and spied upon without its knowledge. In fact, when the Moscow Art company was rehearsing the play, Gorky took the actors to the cave-lodgings around the Khitrov Market to give them fuller understanding of the submerged creatures they were to recreate on the stage, and he taught Olga Knipper (Chekhov's wife) how to give verisimilitude to the part of Nastya, "a street-walker." Its tone is resigned before the spectacle of these broken spirits who have abandoned hope. For this reason the Russia since the revolution of 1917 has pointed to the play as a prize exhibit in the horrors of the past before the awakening of the social conscience, and contrasts its despair with the enthusiasm of later Russian plays that exude optimism and propaganda for the new order and the five year plans. But the communists, it is reported, disapproved of the character of Luka and his pale cast of thought.

The Lower Depths was promptly translated into other languages. Max Reinhardt produced it with great sucess at the Kleine Theatre in Berlin, January 23, 1903. The Stage Society in London produced it at the Court Theatre on November 29, 1903. The German version was presented in New York at the Old Irving Place Theatre in the winter of 1903. The English version did not reach America until Arthur Hopkins presented it at the Plymouth Theatre in 1919, and then most of the critics, except Ludwig Lewisohn, described it as an "apotheosis of gloom" or "a triumph of the dismal and the dirty." It has had many successful performances here and abroad since then, it is a favored drama in the Moscow Art Theatre, and it has been translated time and again into English. The version that follows is the very fine one by Jenny Covan.

THE LOWER DEPTHS

MIKHAIL IVANOFF KOSTILYOFF, *keeper of a night lodging*
VASSILISA KARPOVNA, *his wife*
NATASHA, *her sister*
MIEDVIEDIEFF, *her uncle, a policeman*
VASKA PEPEL, *a young thief*
ANDREI MITRITCH KLESHTCH, *a locksmith*
ANNA, *his wife*
NASTYA, *a street-walker*
KVASHNYA, *a vendor of meat-pies*

BUBNOFF, *a cap-maker*
THE BARON
SATINE
THE ACTOR
LUKA, *a pilgrim*
ALYOSHKA, *a shoemaker*
KRIVOY ZOB ⎫
THE TARTAR ⎭ *Porters*
NIGHT LODGERS, TRAMPS AND OTHERS

The action takes place in a Night Lodging and in "The Waste," an area in its rear.

ACT I

A cellar resembling a cave. The ceiling, which merges into stone walls, is low and grimy, and the plaster and paint are peeling off. There is a window, high up on the right wall, from which comes the light. The right corner, which constitutes PEPEL'S *room, is partitioned off by thin boards. Close to the corner of this room is* BUBNOFF'S *wooden bunk. In the left corner stands a large Russian stove. In the stone wall, left, is a door leading to the kitchen where live* KVASHNYA, *the* BARON, *and* NASTYA. *Against the wall, between the stove and the door, is a large bed covered with dirty chintz. Bunks line the walls. In the foreground, by the left wall, is a block of wood with a vise and a small anvil fastened to it, and another smaller block of wood somewhat further towards the back.* KLESHTCH *is seated on the smaller block, trying keys into old locks. At his feet are two large bundles of various keys, wired together, also a battered tin samo-*var, *a hammer, and pincers. In the center are a large table, two benches, and a stool, all of which are of dirty, unpainted wood. Behind the table* KVASHNYA *is busying herself with the samovar. The* BARON *sits chewing a piece of black bread, and* NASTYA *occupies the stool, leans her elbows on the table, and reads a tattered book. In the bed, behind curtains,* ANNA *lies coughing.* BUBNOFF *is seated on his bunk, attempting to shape a pair of old trousers with the help of an ancient hat shape which he holds between his knees. Scattered about him are pieces of buckram, oilcloth, and rags.* SATINE, *just awakened, lies in his bunk, grunting. On top of the stove, the* ACTOR, *invisible to the audience, tosses about and coughs.*

It is an early spring morning.

THE BARON. And then?

KVASHNYA. No, my dear, said I, keep away from me with such proposals.

THE LOWER DEPTHS: Translated from the Russian by Jenny Covan. Reprinted by permission of Coward-McCann, Inc.

I've been through it all, you see—and not for a hundred baked lobsters would I marry again!

BUBNOFF (*to* SATINE). What are you grunting about? (SATINE *keeps on grunting.*)

KVASHNYA. Why should I, said I, a free woman, my own mistress, enter my name into somebody else's passport and sell myself into slavery—no! Why —I wouldn't marry a man even if he were an American prince!

KLESHTCH. You lie!

KVASHNYA. Wha-at?

KLESHTCH. You lie! You're going to marry Abramka. . . .

THE BARON (*snatching the book out of* NASTYA'S *hand and reading the title*). "Fatal Love" . . . (*laughs.*)

NASTYA (*stretching out her hand*). Give it back—give it back! Stop fooling!

[*The* BARON *looks at her and waves the book in the air.*]

KVASHNYA (*to* KLESHTCH). You crimson goat, you—calling me a liar! How dare you be so rude to me?

THE BARON (*hitting* NASTYA *on the head with the book*). Nastya, you little fool!

NASTYA (*reaching for the book*). Give it back!

KLESHTCH. Oh—what a great lady . . . but you'll marry Abramka just the same—that's all you're waiting for . . .

KVASHNYA. Sure! Anything else? You nearly beat your wife to death!

KLESHTCH. Shut up, you old bitch! It's none of your business!

KVASHNYA. Ho-ho! can't stand the truth, can you?

THE BARON. They're off again! Nastya, where are you?

NASTYA (*without lifting her head*). Hey— go away!

ANNA (*putting her head through the curtains*). The day has started. For God's sake, don't row!

KLESHTCH. Whining again!

ANNA. Every blessed day . . . let me die in peace, can't you?

BUBNOFF. Noise won't keep you from dying.

KVASHNYA (*walking up to* ANNA). Little mother, how did you ever manage to live with this wretch?

ANNA. Leave me alone—get away from me. . . .

KVASHNYA. Well, well! You poor soul . . . how's the pain in the chest— any better?

THE BARON. Kvashnya! Time to go to market. . . .

KVASHNYA. We'll go presently. (*To* ANNA.) Like some hot dumplings?

ANNA. No, thanks. Why should I eat?

KVASHNYA. You must eat. Hot food— good for you! I'll leave you some in a cup. Eat them when you feel like it. Come on, sir! (*To* KLESHTCH.) You evil spirit! (*Goes into kitchen.*)

ANNA (*coughing*). Lord, Lord . . .

THE BARON (*painfully pushing forward* NASTYA'S *head*). Throw it away—little fool!

NASTYA (*muttering*). Leave me alone—I don't bother you . . .

[*The* BARON *follows* KVASHNYA, *whistling.*]

SATINE (*sitting up in his bunk*). Who beat me up yesterday?

BUBNOFF. Does it make any difference who?

SATINE. Suppose they did—but why did they?

BUBNOFF. Were you playing cards?

SATINE. Yes!

BUBNOFF. That's why they beat you.

SATINE. Scoundrels!

THE ACTOR (*raising his head from the top of the stove*). One of these days they'll beat you to death!

SATINE. You're a jackass!

THE ACTOR. Why?

SATINE. Because a man can die only once!

THE ACTOR (*after a silence*). I don't understand—

KLESHTCH. Say! You crawl from that stove—and start cleaning house! Don't play the delicate primrose!

THE ACTOR. None of your business!

KLESHTCH. Wait till Vassilisa comes— she'll show you whose business it is!

THE ACTOR. To hell with Vassilisa! Today is the Baron's turn to clean. . . . Baron!

[*The* BARON *comes from the kitchen.*]

THE BARON. I've no time to clean . . . I'm going to market with Kvashnya.

THE ACTOR. That doesn't concern me. Go to the gallows if you like. It's your turn to sweep the floor just the same— I'm not going to do other people's work . . .

THE BARON. Go to blazes! Nastya will do it. Hey there—fatal love! Wake up! (*Takes the book away from* NASTYA.)

NASTYA (*getting up*). What do you want? Give it back to me! You scoundrel! And that's a nobleman for you!

THE BARON (*Returning the book to her*). Nastya! Sweep the floor for me—will you?

NASTYA (*goes to kitchen*). Not so's you'll notice it!

KVASHNYA (*to the* BARON *through kitchen door*). Come on—you! They don't need you! Actor! You were asked to do it, and now you go ahead and attend to it—it won't kill you . . .

THE ACTOR. It's always I . . . I don't understand why. . . .

[*The* BARON *comes from the kitchen, across his shoulders a wooden beam from which hang earthen pots covered with rags.*]

THE BARON. Heavier than ever!

SATINE. It paid you to be born a Baron, eh?

KVASHNYA (*to* ACTOR). See to it that you sweep up! (*Crosses to outer door, letting the* BARON *pass ahead.*)

THE ACTOR (*climbing down from the stove*). It's bad for me to inhale dust. (*With pride.*) My organism is poisoned with alcohol. (*Sits down on a bunk, meditating.*)

SATINE. Organism—organon. . . .

ANNA. Andrei Mitritch. . . .

KLESHTCH. What now?

ANNA. Kvashnya left me some dumplings over there—you eat them!

KLESHTCH (*coming over to her*). And you— don't you want any?

ANNA. No. Why should I eat? You're a workman—you need it.

KLESHTCH. Frightened, are you? Don't be! You'll get all right!

ANNA. Go and eat! It's hard on me. . . . I suppose very soon . . .

KLESHTCH (*walking away*). Never mind— maybe you'll get well—you can never tell! (*Goes into kitchen.*)

THE ACTOR (*loud, as if he had suddenly awakened*). Yesterday the doctor in the hospital said to me: "Your organism," he said, "is entirely poisoned with alcohol . . ."

SATINE (*smiling*). Organon . . .

THE ACTOR (*stubbornly*). Not organon— organism!

SATINE. Sibylline. . . .

THE ACTOR (*shaking his fist at him*). Nonsense! I'm telling you seriously . . . if the organism is poisoned . . . that means it's bad for me to sweep the floor—to inhale the dust . . .

SATINE. Macrobistic . . . hah!

BUBNOFF. What are you muttering?

SATINE. Words—and here's another one for you—transcendentalistic . . .

BUBNOFF. What does it mean?

SATINE. Don't know—I forgot . . .

BUBNOFF. Then why did you say it?

SATINE. Just so! I'm bored, brother, with human words—all our words. Bored!

I've heard each one of them a thousand times surely.

THE ACTOR. In Hamlet they say: "Words, words, words!" It's a good play. I played the grave-digger in it once. . . .

[KLESHTCH *comes from the kitchen.*]

KLESHTCH. Will you start playing with the broom?

THE ACTOR. None of your business. (*Striking his chest.*) Ophelia! O—remember me in thy prayers!

[*Back stage is heard a dull murmur, cries, and a police whistle.* KLESHTCH *sits down to work, filing screechily.*]

SATINE. I love unintelligible, obsolete words. When I was a youngster—and worked as a telegraph operator—I read heaps of books. . . .

BUBNOFF. Were you really a telegrapher?

SATINE. I was. There are some excellent books—and lots of curious words . . . Once I was an educated man, do you know?

BUBNOFF. I've heard it a hundred times. Well, so you were! That isn't very important! Me—well—once I was a furrier. I had my own shop—what with dyeing the fur all day long, my arms were yellow up to the elbows, brother. I thought I'd never be able ever to get clean again—that I'd go to my grave, all yellow! But look at my hands now—they're plain dirty—that's what!

SATINE. Well, and what then?

BUBNOFF. That's all!

SATINE. What are you trying to prove?

BUBNOFF. Oh, well—just matching thoughts—no matter how much dye you get on yourself, it all comes off in the end—yes, yes—

SATINE. Oh—my bones ache!

THE ACTOR (*sits, nursing his knees*). Education is all rot. Talent is the thing. I knew an actor—who read his parts by heart, syllable by syllable—but he played heroes in a way that . . . why—the whole theater would rock with ecstasy!

SATINE. Bubnoff, give me five kopecks.

BUBNOFF. I only have two—

THE ACTOR. I say—talent, that's what you need to play heroes. And talent is nothing but faith in yourself, in your own powers—

SATINE. Give me five kopecks and I'll have faith that you're a hero, a crocodile, or a police inspector—Kleshtch, give me five kopecks.

KLESHTCH. Go to hell! All of you!

SATINE. What are you cursing for? I know you haven't a kopeck in the world!

ANNA. Andrei Mitritch—I'm suffocating—I can't breathe—

KLESHTCH. What shall I do?

BUBNOFF. Open the door into the hall.

KLESHTCH. All right. You're sitting on the bunk, I on the floor. You change places with me, and I'll let you open the door. I have a cold as it is.

BUBNOFF (*unconcernedly*). I don't care if you open the door—it's your wife who's asking—

KLESHTCH (*morosely*). I don't care who's asking—

SATINE. My head buzzes—ah—why do people have to hit each other over the heads?

BUBNOFF. They don't only hit you over the head, but over the rest of the body as well. (*Rises.*) I must go and buy some thread—our bosses are late to-day—seems as if they've croaked. (*Exit.*)

[ANNA *coughs;* SATINE *is lying down motionless, his hands folded behind his head.*]

THE ACTOR (*looks about him morosely, then goes to* ANNA). Feeling bad, eh?

ANNA. I'm choking—

THE ACTOR. If you wish, I'll take you into the hallway. Get up, then, come! (*He helps her to rise, wraps some sort of a rag about her shoulders, and supports her toward the hall.*) It isn't easy. I'm sick myself—poisoned with alcohol . . . (KOSTILYOFF *appears in the doorway.*)

KOSTILYOFF. Going for a stroll? What a nice couple—the gallant cavalier and the lady fair!

THE ACTOR. Step aside, you—don't you see that we're invalids?

KOSTILYOFF. Pass on, please! (*Hums a religious tune, glances about him suspiciously, and bends his head to the left as if listening to what is happening in* PEPEL'S *room.* KLESHTCH *is jangling his keys and scraping away with his file, and looks askance at the other.*) Filing?

KLESHTCH. What?

KOSTILYOFF. I say, are you filing? (*Pause.*) What did I want to ask? (*Quick and low.*) Hasn't my wife been here?

KLESHTCH. I didn't see her.

KOSTILYOFF (*carefully moving toward* PEPEL'S *room*). You take up a whole lot of room for your two rubles a month. The bed—and your bench—yes—you take up five rubles' worth of space, so help me God! I'll have to put another half ruble to your rent—

KLESHTCH. You'll put a noose around my neck and choke me . . . you'll croak soon enough, and still all you think of is half rubles—

KOSTILYOFF. Why should I choke you? What would be the use? God be with you—live and prosper! But I'll have to raise you half a ruble—I'll buy oil for the ikon lamp, and my offering will atone for my sins, and for yours as well. You don't think much of your sins—not much! Oh, Andrushka, you're a wicked man! Your wife is dying because of your wickedness—no one loves you, no one respects you—your work is squeaky, jarring on every one.

KLESHTCH (*shouts*). What do you come here for—just to annoy me? [SATINE *grunts loudly.*]

KOSTILYOFF (*with a start*). God, what a noise! [*The* ACTOR *enters.*]

THE ACTOR. I've put her down in the hall and wrapped her up.

KOSTILYOFF. You're a kindly fellow. That's good. Some day you'll be rewarded for it.

THE ACTOR. When?

KOSTILYOFF. In the Beyond, little brother —there all our deeds will be reckoned up.

THE ACTOR. Suppose you reward me right now?

KOSTILYOFF. How can I do that?

THE ACTOR. Wipe out half my debt.

KOSTILYOFF. He-ho! You're always jesting, darling—always poking fun . . . can kindliness of heart be repaid with gold? Kindliness—it's above all other qualities. But your debt to me —remains a debt. And so you'll have to pay me back. You ought to be kind to me, an old man, without seeking for reward!

THE ACTOR. You're a swindler, old man! (*Goes into kitchen.*)

[KLESHTCH *rises and goes into the hall.*]

KOSTILYOFF (*to* SATINE). See that squeaker—? He ran away—he doesn't like me!

SATINE. Does anybody like you besides the Devil.

KOSTILYOFF (*laughing*). Oh—you're so quarrelsome! But I like you all—I understand you all, my unfortunate downtrodden, useless brethren . . . (*Suddenly, rapidly.*) Is Vaska home?

SATINE. See for yourself—

KOSTILYOFF (*goes to the door and knocks*). Vaska!

[*The* ACTOR *appears at the kitchen door, chewing something.*]

PEPEL. Who is it?

KOSTILYOFF. It's I—I, Vaska!

PEPEL. What do you want?

KOSTILYOFF (*stepping aside*). Open!

SATINE (*without looking at* KOSTILYOFF).
He'll open—and she's there—
[*The* ACTOR *makes a grimace.*]

KOSTILYOFF (*in a low, anxious tone*). Eh?
Who's there? What?

SATINE. Speaking to me?

KOSTILYOFF. What did you say?

SATINE. Oh—nothing—I was just talking to myself—

KOSTILYOFF. Take care, brother. Don't
carry your joking too far! (*Knocks
loudly at door.*) Vassily!

PEPEL (*opening door*). Well? What are
you disturbing me for?

KOSTILYOFF (*peering into room*). I—you
see—

PEPEL. Did you bring the money?

KOSTILYOFF. I've something to tell you—

PEPEL. Did you bring the money?

KOSTILYOFF. What money? Wait—

PEPEL. Why—the seven rubles for the
watch—well?

KOSTILYOFF. What watch, Vaska? Oh,
you—

PEPEL. Look here. Yesterday, before witnesses, I sold you a watch for ten
rubles, you gave me three—now let
me have the other seven. What are
you blinking for? You hang around
here—you disturb people—and don't
seem to know yourself what you're
after.

KOSTILYOFF. Sh-sh! Don't be angry,
Vaska. The watch—it is—

SATINE. Stolen!

KOSTILYOFF (*sternly*). I do not accept
stolen goods—how can you imagine—

PEPEL (*taking him by the shoulder*). What
did you disturb me for? What do you
want?

KOSTILYOFF. I don't want—anything.
I'll go—if you're in such a state—

PEPEL. Be off, and bring the money!

KOSTILYOFF. What ruffians! I—I—
(*Exit.*)

THE ACTOR. What a farce!

SATINE. That's fine—I like it.

PEPEL. What did he come here for?

SATINE (*laughing*). Don't you understand? He's looking for his wife. Why
don't you beat him up once and for
all, Vaska?

PEPEL. Why should I let such trash interfere with my life?

SATINE. Show some brains! And then
you can marry Vassilisa—and become our boss—

PEPEL. Heavenly bliss! And you'd smash
up my household and, because I'm a
soft-hearted fool, you'll drink up everything I possess. (*Sits on a bunk.*)
Old devil—woke me up—I was having such a pleasant dream. I dreamed
I was fishing—and I caught an enormous trout—such a trout as you only
see in dreams! I was playing him—
and I was so afraid the line would
snap. I had just got out the gaff—
and I thought to myself—in a moment—

SATINE. It wasn't a trout, it was Vassilisa—

THE ACTOR. He caught Vassilisa a long
time ago.

PEPEL (*angrily*). You can all go to the
devil—and Vassilisa with you—
[KLESHTCH *comes from the hall.*]

KLESHTCH. Devilishly cold!

THE ACTOR. Why didn't you bring Anna
back? She'll freeze, out there—

KLESHTCH. Natasha took her into the
kitchen—

THE ACTOR. The old man will kick her
out—

KLESHTCH (*sitting down to his work*). Well
—Natasha will bring her in here—

SATINE. Vassily—give me five kopecks!

THE ACTOR (*to* SATINE). Oh, you—always five kopecks—Vassya—give us twenty kopecks—

PEPEL. I'd better give it to them now before they ask for a ruble. Here you are!

SATINE. Gibraltar! There are no kindlier people in the world than thieves!

KLESHTCH (*morosely*). They earn their money easily—they don't work—

SATINE. Many earn it easily, but not many part with it so easily. Work? Make work pleasant—and maybe I'll work too. Yes—maybe. When work's a pleasure, life's, too. When it's toil, then life is a drudge. (*To the* ACTOR.) You, Sardanapalus! Come on!

THE ACTOR. Let's go, Nebuchadnezzar! I'll get as drunk as forty thousand topers!

[*They leave.*]

PEPEL (*yawning*). Well, how's your wife?

KLESHTCH. It seems as if soon—(*Pause.*)

PEPEL. Now I look at you—seems to me all that filing and scraping of yours is useless.

KLESHTCH. Well—what else can I do?

PEPEL. Nothing.

KLESHTCH. How can I live?

PEPEL. People manage, somehow.

KLESHTCH. Them? Call them people? Muck and dregs—that's what they are! I'm a workman—I'm ashamed even to look at them. I've slaved since I was a child. . . . D'you think I shan't be able to tear myself away from here? I'll crawl out of here, even if I have to leave my skin behind —but crawl out I will! Just wait . . . my wife'll die . . . I've lived here six months, and it seems like six years.

PEPEL. Nobody here's any worse off than you . . . say what you like . . .

KLESHTCH. No worse is right. They've neither honor nor conscience.

PEPEL (*indifferently*). What good does it do—honor or conscience? Can you get them on their feet instead of on their uppers—through honor and conscience? Honor and conscience are needed only by those who have power and energy . . .

BUBNOFF (*coming back*). Oh—I'm frozen.

PEPEL. Bubnoff! Got a conscience?

BUBNOFF. What? A conscience?

PEPEL. Exactly!

BUBNOFF. What do I need a conscience for? I'm not rich.

PEPEL. Just what I said: honor and conscience are for the rich—right! And Kleshtch is upbraiding us because we haven't any!

BUBNOFF. Why—did he want to borrow some of it?

PEPEL. No—he has plenty of his own. . .

BUBNOFF. Oh—are you selling it? You won't sell much around here. But if you had some old boxes, I'd buy them—on credit . . .

PEPEL (*didactically*). You're a jackass, Andrushka! On the subject of conscience you ought to hear Satine—or the Baron . . .

KLESHTCH. I've nothing to talk to them about!

PEPEL. They have more brains than you —even if they're drunkards . . .

BUBNOFF. He who can be drunk and wise at the same time is doubly blessed . . .

PEPEL. Satine says every man expects his neighbor to have a conscience, but— you see—it isn't to any one's advantage to have one—that's a fact.

[NATASHA *enters, followed by* LUKA *who carries a stick in his hand, a bundle on his back, a kettle and a teapot slung from his belt.*]

LUKA. How are you, honest folks?

PEPEL (*twisting his mustache*). Aha— Natasha!

BUBNOFF (*to* LUKA). I was honest—up to spring before last.

NATASHA. Here's a new lodger . . .

LUKA. Oh, it's all the same to me. Crooks—I don't mind them, either. For my part there's no bad flea—they're all black—and they all jump— . . . Well, dearie, show me where I can stow myself.

NATASHA (*pointing to kitchen door*). Go in there, grand-dad.

LUKA. Thanks, girlie! One place is like another—as long as an old fellow keeps warm, he keeps happy . . .

PEPEL. What an amusing old codger you brought in, Natasha!

NATASHA. A hanged sight more interesting than you! . . . Andrei, your wife's in the kitchen with us—come and fetch her after a while . . .

KLESHTCH. All right—I will . . .

NATASHA. And be a little more kind to her—you know she won't last much longer.

KLESHTCH. I know . . .

NATASHA. Knowing won't do any good—it's terrible—dying—don't you understand?

PEPEL. Well—look at me—I'm not afraid . . .

NATASHA. Oh—you're a wonder, aren't you?

BUBNOFF (*whistling*). Oh—this thread's rotten . . .

PEPEL. Honestly, I'm not afraid! I'm ready to die right now. Knife me to the heart—and I'll die without making a sound . . . even gladly—from such a pure hand . . .

NATASHA (*going out*). Spin that yarn for some one else!

BUBNOFF. Oh—that thread is rotten—rotten—

NATASHA (*at hallway door*). Don't forget your wife, Andrei!

KLESHTCH. All right.

PEPEL. She's a wonderful girl!

BUBNOFF. She's all right.

PEPEL. What makes her so curt with me? Anyway—she'll come to no good here . . .

BUBNOFF. Through you—sure!

PEPEL. Why through me? I feel sorry for her . . .

BUBNOFF. As the wolf for the lamb!

PEPEL. You lie! I feel very sorry for her . . . very . . . very sorry! She has a tough life here—I can see that . . .

KLESHTCH. Just wait till Vassilisa catches you talking to her!

BUBNOFF. Vassilisa? She won't give up so easily what belongs to her—she's a cruel woman!

PEPEL (*stretching himself on the bunk*). You two prophets can go to hell!

KLESHTCH. Just wait—you'll see!

LUKA (*singing in the kitchen*). "In the dark of the night the way is black . . ."

KLESHTCH. Another one who yelps!

PEPEL. It's dreary! Why do I feel so dreary? You live—and everything seems all right. But suddenly a cold chill goes through you—and then everything gets dreary . . .

BUBNOFF. Dreary? Hm-hm—

PEPEL. Yes—yes—

LUKA (*sings*). "The way is black . . ."

PEPEL. Old fellow! Hey there!

LUKA (*looking from kitchen door*). You call me?

PEPEL. Yes. Don't sing!

LUKA (*coming in*). You don't like it?

PEPEL. When people sing well I like it—

LUKA. In other words—I don't sing well?

PEPEL. Evidently!

LUKA. Well, well—and I thought I sang well. That's always the way: a man imagines there's one thing he can do well, and suddenly he finds out that other people don't think so . . .

PEPEL (*laughs*). That's right . . .

BUBNOFF. First you say you feel dreary—and then you laugh!

PEPEL. None of your business, raven!

LUKA. Who do they say feels dreary?

PEPEL. I do.

[*The* BARON *enters.*]

LUKA. Well, well—out there in the kitchen there's a girl reading and crying! That's so! Her eyes are wet with tears . . . I say to her: "What's the matter, darling?" And she says: "It's so sad!" "What's so sad?" say I. "The book!" says she.—And that's how 10 people spend their time. Just because they're bored . . .

THE BARON. She's a fool!

PEPEL. Have you had tea, Baron?

THE BARON. Yes. Go on!

PEPEL. Well—want me to open a bottle?

THE BARON. Of course. Go on!

PEPEL. Drop on all fours, and bark like a dog!

THE BARON. Fool! What's the matter 20 with you? Are you drunk?

PEPEL. Go on—bark a little! It'll amuse me. You're an aristocrat. You didn't even consider us human formerly, did you?

THE BARON. Go on!

PEPEL. Well—and now I am making you bark like a dog—and you will bark, won't you?

THE BARON. All right. I will. You jack- 30 ass! What pleasure can you derive from it, since I myself know that I have sunk almost lower than you. You should have made me drop on all fours in the days when I was still above you.

BUBNOFF. That's right . . .

LUKA. I say so, too!

BUBNOFF. What's over, is over. Remain only trivialities. We know no class dis- 40 tinctions here. We've shed all pride and self-respect. Blood and bone—man —just plain man—that's what we are!

LUKA. In other words, we're all equal . . . and you, friend, were you really a Baron?

THE BARON. Who are you? A ghost?

LUKA (*laughing*). I've seen counts and princes in my day—this is the first time I meet a baron—and one who's decaying—at that!

PEPEL (*laughing*). Baron, I blush for you!

THE BARON. It's time you knew better, Vassily . . .

LUKA. Hey-hey—I look at you, brothers —the life you're leading . . .

BUBNOFF. Such a life! As soon as the sun rises, our voices rise, too—in quarrels!

THE BARON. We've all seen better days— yes! I used to wake up in the morning and drink my coffee in bed—coffee— with cream! Yes—

LUKA. And yet we're all human beings. Pretend all you want to, put on all the airs you wish, but man you were born, and man you must die. And as I watch I see that the wiser people get, the busier they get—and though from bad to worse, they still strive to improve—stubbornly—

THE BARON. Who are you, old fellow? Where do you come from?

LUKA. I?

THE BARON. Are you a tramp?

LUKA. We're all of us tramps—why— I've heard said that the very earth we walk on is nothing but a tramp in the universe.

THE BARON (*severely*). Perhaps. But have you a passport?

LUKA (*after a short pause*). And what are you—a police inspector?

PEPEL (*delighted*). You scored, old fellow! Well, Barosha, you got it this time!

BUBNOFF. Yes—our little aristocrat got his!

THE BARON (*embarrassed*). What's the matter? I was only joking, old man. Why, brother, I haven't a passport, either.

BUBNOFF. You lie!

THE BARON. Oh—well—I have some

sort of papers—but they have no value—

LUKA. They're papers just the same—and no papers are any good—

PEPEL. Baron—come on to the saloon with me—

THE BARON. I'm ready. Good-bye, old man—you old scamp—

LUKA. Maybe I am one, brother—

PEPEL (*near doorway*). Come on—come on! 10

[*Leaves,* BARON *following him quickly.*]

LUKA. Was he really once a Baron?

BUBNOFF. Who knows? A gentleman—? Yes. That much he's even now. Occasionally it sticks out. He never got rid of the habit.

LUKA. Nobility is like small-pox. A man may get over it—but it leaves marks . . .

BUBNOFF. He's all right all the same—occasionally he kicks—as he did about your passport . . . 20

[ALYOSHKA *comes in, slightly drunk, with a concertina in his hand, whistling.*]

ALYOSHKA. Hey there, lodgers!

BUBNOFF. What are you yelling for?

ALYOSHKA. Excuse me—I beg your pardon! I'm a well-bred man—

BUBNOFF. On a spree again?   30

ALYOSHKA. Right you are! A moment ago Medyakin, the precinct captain, threw me out of the police station and said: "Look here—I don't want as much as a smell of you to stay in the streets—d'you hear?" I'm a man of principles, and the boss croaks at me —and what's a boss anyway—pah!— it's all bosh—the boss is a drunkard. I don't make any demands on life. I 40 want nothing—that's all. Offer me one ruble, offer me twenty—it doesn't affect me. [NASTYA *comes from the kitchen*). Offer me a million—I won't take it! And to think that I, a respectable man, should be ordered

about by a pal of mine—and he a drunkard! I won't have it—I won't!

[NASTYA *stands in the doorway, shaking her head at* ALYOSHKA.]

LUKA (*good-naturedly*).   Well,   boy, you're a bit confused—

BUBNOFF. Aren't men fools!

ALYOSHKA (*stretches out on the floor*). Here, eat me up alive—and I don't want anything. I'm a desperate man. Show me one better! Why am I worse than others? There! Medyakin said: "If you show yourself on the streets I smash your face!" And yet I shall go out—I'll go—and stretch out in the middle of the street—let them choke me—I don't want a thing!

NASTYA. Poor fellow—only a boy—and he's already putting on such airs—

ALYOSHKA (*kneeling before her*). Lady! Mademoiselle! *Parlez français—? Prix courrant?* I'm on a spree—

NASTYA (*in a loud whisper*). Vassilisa!

VASSILISA (*opens door quickly; to* ALYOSHKA). You here again?

ALYOSHKA. How do you do—? Come in —you're welcome—

VASSILISA. I told you, young puppy, that not a shadow of you should stick around here—and you're back—eh?

ALYOSHKA. Vassilisa Karpovna . . . shall I tune up a funeral march for you?

VASSILISA [*seizing him by the shoulders*). Get out!

ALYOSHKA (*moving towards the door*). Wait —you can't put me out this way! I learned this funeral march a little while ago! It's refreshing music . . . wait—you can't put me out like that!

VASSILISA. I'll show whether I can or not. I'll rouse the whole street against you—you foul-mouthed creature— you're too young to bark about me—

ALYOSHKA (*running out*). All right—I'll go—

VASSILISA. Look out—I'll get you yet!

ALYOSHKA (*opens the door and shouts*). Vassilisa Karpovna—I'm not afraid of you—(*Hides.*)

[LUKA *laughs.*]

VASSILISA. Who are you?

LUKA. A passer-by—a traveler . . .

VASSILISA. Stopping for the night or going to stay here?

LUKA. I'll see.

VASSILISA. Have you a passport?

LUKA. Yes.

VASSILISA. Give it to me.

LUKA. I'll bring it over to your house—

VASSILISA. Call yourself a traveler? If you'd say a tramp—that would be nearer the truth—

LUKA (*sighing*). You're not very kindly, mother!

[VASSILISA *goes to door that leads to* PEPEL'S *room.* ALYOSHKA *pokes his head through the kitchen door.*]

ALYOSHKA. Has she left?

VASSILISA (*turning around*). Are you still here?

[ALYOSHKA *disappears, whistling.* NASTYA *and* LUKA *laugh.*]

BUBNOFF (*to* VASSILISA). He isn't here—

VASSILISA. Who?

BUBNOFF. Vaska.

VASSILISA. Did I ask you about him?

BUBNOFF. I noticed you were looking around—

VASSILISA. I am looking to see if things are in order, you see? Why aren't the floors swept yet? How often did I give orders to keep the house clean?

BUBNOFF. It's the actor's turn to sweep—

VASSILISA. Never mind whose turn it is! If the health inspector comes and fines me, I'll throw out the lot of you—

BUBNOFF (*calmly*). Then how are you going to earn your living?

VASSILISA. I don't want a speck of dirt! (*Goes to kitchen; to* NASTYA.) What are you hanging round here for? Why's

your face all swollen up? Why are you standing there like a dummy? Go on—sweep the floor! Did you see Natalia? Was she here?

NASTYA. I don't know—I haven't seen her . . .

VASSILISA. Bubnoff! Was my sister here?

BUBNOFF. She brought him along.

VASSILISA. That one—was he home?

BUBNOFF. Vassily? Yes—Natalia was here talking to Kleshtch—

VASSILISA. I'm not asking you whom she talked to. Dirt everywhere—filth—oh, you swine! Mop it all up—do you hear? (*Exit rapidly.*)

BUBNOFF. What a savage beast she is!

LUKA. She's a lady that means business!

NASTYA. You grow to be an animal, leading such a life—any human being tied to such a husband as hers . . .

BUBNOFF. Well—that tie isn't worrying her any—

LUKA. Does she always have these fits?

BUBNOFF. Always. You see, she came to find her lover—but he isn't home—

LUKA. I guess she was hurt. Oh-ho! Everybody is trying to be boss—and is threatening everybody else with all kinds of punishment—and still there's no order in life . . . and no cleanliness—

BUBNOFF. All the world likes order—but some people's brains aren't fit for it. All the same—the room should be swept—Nastya—you ought to get busy!

NASTYA. Oh, certainly? Anything else? Think I'm your servant? (*Silence.*) I'm going to get drunk to-night—dead-drunk!

BUBNOFF. Fine business!

LUKA. Why do you want to get drunk, girlie? A while ago you were crying—and now you say you'll get drunk—

NASTYA (*defiantly*). I'll drink—then I cry again—that's all there's to it!

BUBNOFF. That's nothing!

LUKA. But for what reason—tell me! Every pimple has a cause! (NASTYA *remains silent, shaking her head.*) Oh— you men—what's to become of you? All right—I'll sweep the place. Where's your broom?

BUBNOFF. Behind the door—in the hall—
[LUKA *goes into the hall.*]
Nastinka!

NASTYA. Yes?

BUBNOFF. Why did Vassilisa jump on Alyoshka?

NASTYA. He told her that Vaska was tired of her and was going to get rid of her—and that he's going to make up to Natasha—I'll go away from here—I'll find another lodging-house—

BUBNOFF. Why? Where?

NASTYA. I'm sick of this—I'm not wanted here!

BUBNOFF (*calmly*). You're not wanted anywhere—and, anyway, all people on earth are superfluous—
[NASTYA *shakes her head. Rises and slowly, quietly, leaves the cellar.* MIEDVIEDIEFF *comes in.* LUKA, *with the broom, follows him.*]

MIEDVIEDIEFF. I don't think I know you—

LUKA. How about the others—d'you know them all?

MIEDVIEDIEFF. I must know everybody in my precinct. But I don't know you.

LUKA. That's because, uncle, the whole world can't stow itself away in your precinct—some of it was bound to remain outside . . . (*Goes into kitchen.*)

MIEDVIEDIEFF (*crosses to* BUBNOFF). It's true—my precinct is rather small— yet it's worse than any of the very largest. Just now, before getting off duty, I had to bring Alyoshka, the shoemaker, to the station house. Just

imagine—there he was, stretched right in the middle of the street, playing his concertina and yelping: "I want nothing, nothing!" Horses going past all the time—and with all the traffic going on, he could easily have been run over—and so on! He's a wild youngster—so I just collared him—he likes to make mischief—

BUBNOFF. Coming to play checkers tonight?

MIEDVIEDIEFF. Yes—I'll come—how's Vaska?

BUBNOFF. Same as ever—

MIEDVIEDIEFF. Meaning—he's getting along—?

BUBNOFF. Why shouldn't he? He's able to get along all right.

MIEDVIEDIEFF (*doubtfully*). Why shouldn't he? (LUKA *goes into hallway, carrying a pail.*) M-yes—there's a lot of talk about Vaska. Haven't you heard?

BUBNOFF. I hear all sorts of gossip . . .

MIEDVIEDIEFF. There seems to have been some sort of talk concerning Vassilisa. Haven't you heard about it?

BUBNOFF. What?

MIEDVIEDIEFF. Oh—why—generally speaking. Perhaps you know—and lie. Everybody knows—(*Severely.*) You mustn't lie, brother!

BUBNOFF. Why should I lie?

MIEDVIEDIEFF. That's right. Dogs! They say that Vaska and Vassilisa . . . but what's that to me? I'm not her father. I'm her uncle. Why should they ridicule me? (KVASHNYA *comes in.*) What are people coming to? They laugh at everything. Aha—you here?

KVASHNYA. Well—my love-sick garrison —? Bubnoff! He came up to me again on the marketplace and started pestering me about marrying him . . .

BUBNOFF. Go to it! Why not? He has money and he's still a husky fellow.

MIEDVIEDIEFF. Me—? I should say so!

KVASHNYA. You ruffian! Don't you dare touch my sore spot! I've gone through it once already, darling. Marriage to a woman is just like jumping through a hole in the ice in winter. You do it once, and you remember it the rest of your life . . .

MIEDVIEDIEFF. Wait! There are different breeds of husbands . . .

KVASHNYA. But there's only one of me! When my beloved husband kicked the bucket, I spent the whole day all by my lonely—just bursting with joy. I sat and simply couldn't believe it was true. . . .

MIEDVIEDIEFF. If your husband beat you without cause, you should have complained to the police.

KVASHNYA. I complained to God for eight years—and he didn't help.

MIEDVIEDIEFF. Nowadays the law forbids to beat your wife . . . all is very strict these days—there's law and order everywhere. You can't beat up people without due cause. If you beat them to maintain discipline—all right . . .

LUKA (comes in with ANNA). Well—we finally managed to get here after all. Oh, you! Why do you, weak as you are, walk about alone? Where's your bunk?

ANNA (pointing). Thank you, grand-dad.

KVASHNYA. There—she's married—look at her!

LUKA. The little woman is in very bad shape . . . she was creeping along the hallway, clinging to the wall and moaning—why do you leave her by herself?

KVASHNYA. Oh, pure carelessness on our part, little father—forgive us! Her maid, it appears, went out for a walk . . .

LUKA. Go on—poke fun at me . . . but, all the same, how can you neglect a human being like that? No matter who or what, every human life has its worth . . .

MIEDVIEDIEFF. There should be supervision! Suppose she died suddenly—? That would cause a lot of bother . . . we must look after her!

LUKA. True, sergeant!

MIEDVIEDIEFF. Well—yes—though I'm not a sergeant—ah—yet!

LUKA. No! But you carry yourself most martially!

[Noise of shuffling feet is heard in the hallway. Muffled cries.]

MIEDVIEDIEFF. What now—a row?

BUBNOFF. Sounds like it?

KVASHNYA. I'll go and see . . .

MIEDVIEDIEFF. I'll go, too. It is my duty! Why separate people when they fight? They'll stop sooner or later of their own accord. One gets tired of fighting. Why not let them fight all they want to—freely? They wouldn't fight half as often—if they'd remember former beatings . . .

BUBNOFF (climbing down from his bunk). Why don't you speak to your superiors about it?

KOSTILYOFF (throws open the door and shouts). Abram! Come quick—Vassilisa is killing Natasha—come quick.

[KVASHNYA, MIEDVIEDIEFF, and BUBNOFF rush into hallway; LUKA looks after them, shaking his head.]

ANNA. Oh God—poor little Natasha . . .

LUKA. Who's fighting out there?

ANNA. Our landladies—they're sisters . . .

LUKA (crossing to ANNA). Why?

ANNA. Oh—for no reason—except that they're both fat and healthy . . .

LUKA. What's your name?

ANNA. Anna . . . I look at you . . .

you're like my father—my dear
father . . . you're as gentle as he
was—and as soft. . . .

LUKA. Soft! Yes! They pounded me till
I got soft! (*Laughs tremulously.*)

CURTAIN

ACT II

Same as Act I—Night.
On the bunks near the stove SATINE, *the*
BARON, KRIVOY ZOB, *and the* TARTAR *play*
cards. KLESHTCH *and the* ACTOR *watch*
them. BUBNOFF, *on his bunk, is playing*
checkers with MIEDVIEDIEFF. LUKA *sits on*
a stool by ANNA'S *bedside. The place is lit*
by two lamps, one on the wall near the card
players, the other is on BUBNOFF'S *bunk.*

THE TARTAR. I'll play one more game—
then I'll stop . . .
BUBNOFF. Zob! Sing! (*He sings.*)
"The sun rises and sets . . ."
ZOB (*joining in*).
"But my prison is dark, dark . . ."
THE TARTAR (*to* SATINE). Shuffle the
cards—and shuffle them well. We
know your kind—
ZOB AND BUBNOFF (*together*).
"Day and night the wardens
Watch beneath my window . . ."
ANNA. Blows—insults—I've had nothing
but that all my life long . . .
LUKA. Don't worry, little mother!
MIEDVIEDIEFF. Look where you're mov-
ing!
BUBNOFF. Oh, yes—that's right . . .
THE TARTAR (*threatening* SATINE *with his*
fist). You're trying to palm a card?
I've seen you—you scoundrel . . .
ZOB. Stop it, Hassan! They'll skin us
anyway . . . come on, Bubnoff!
ANNA. I can't remember a single day
when I didn't go hungry . . . I've
been afraid, waking, eating, and
sleeping . . . all my life I've trembled—afraid I wouldn't get another
bite . . . all my life I've been in

rags—all through my wretched life—
and why . . . ?
LUKA. Yes, yes, child—you're tired—
never you mind!
THE ACTOR (*to* ZOB). Play the Jack—the
Jack, devil take you!
THE BARON. And we play the King!
KLESHTCH. They always win.
SATINE. Such is our habit.
MIEDVIEDIEFF. I have the Queen!
BUBNOFF. And so have I!
ANNA. I'm dying . . .
KLESHTCH. Look, look! Prince, throw up
the game—throw it up, I tell you!
THE ACTOR. Can't he play without your
assistance?
THE BARON. Look out, Andrushka, or
I'll beat the life out of you!
THE TARTAR. Deal once more—the
pitcher went after water—and got
broke—and so did I!
[KLESHTCH *shakes his head and crosses to*
BUBNOFF.]
ANNA. I keep on thinking—is it possible
that I'll suffer in the other world as I
did in this—is it possible? There,
too?
LUKA. Nothing of the sort! Don't you
disturb yourself! You'll rest there
. . . be patient. We all suffer, dear,
each in our own way. . . . (*Rises and*
goes quickly into kitchen.)
BUBNOFF (*sings*).
"Watch as long as you please . . ."
ZOB. "I shan't run away . . ."
BOTH (*together*).
"I long to be free, free—
Alas! I cannot break my chains. . . ."
THE TARTAR (*yells*). That card was up
his sleeve!

THE BARON (*embarrassed*). Do you want me to shove it up your nose?

THE ACTOR (*emphatically*). Prince! You're mistaken—nobody—ever . . .

THE TARTAR. I saw it! You cheat! I won't play!

SATINE (*gathering up the cards*). Leave us alone, Hassan . . . you knew right along that we're cheats—why did you play with us?

THE BARON. He lost forty kopecks and he yelps as if he had lost a fortune! And a Prince at that!

THE TARTAR (*excitedly*). Then play honest!

SATINE. What for?

THE TARTAR. What do you mean "what for"?

SATINE. Exactly. What for?

THE TARTAR. Don't you know?

SATINE. I don't. Do you?

[*The* TARTAR *spits out, furiously; the others laugh at him.*]

ZOB (*good-naturedly*). You're a funny fellow, Hassan! Try to understand this! If they should begin to live honestly, they'd die of starvation inside of three days.

THE TARTAR. That's none of my business. You must live honestly!

ZOB. They did you brown! Come and let's have tea. . . . (*Sings.*)
"O my chains, my heavy chains . . ."

BUBNOFF (*sings*).
"You're my steely, clanking wardens . . ."

ZOB. Come on, Hassanka! (*Leaves the room, singing.*)
"I cannot tear you, cannot break you . . ."

[*The* TARTAR *shakes his fist threateningly at the* BARON, *and follows the other out of the room.*]

SATINE (*to* BARON, *laughing*). Well, Your Imperial Highness, you've again sat down magnificently in a mud puddle!

You've learned a lot—but you're an ignoramus when it comes to palming a card.

THE BARON (*spreading his hands*). The Devil knows how it happened. . . .

THE ACTOR. You're not gifted—you've no faith in yourself—and without that you can never accomplish anything . . .

MIEDVIEDIEFF. I've one Queen—and you've two—oh, well . . .

BUBNOFF. One's enough if she has brains—play!

KLESHTCH. You lost, Abram Ivanovitch?

MIEDVIEDIEFF. None of your business—see? Shut up!

SATINE. I've won fifty-three kopecks.

THE ACTOR. Give me three of them . . . though, what'll I do with them?

LUKA (*coming from kitchen*). Well—the Tartar was fleeced all right, eh? Going to have some vodka?

THE BARON. Come with us.

SATINE. I wonder what you'll be like when you're drunk.

LUKA. Same as when I'm sober.

THE ACTOR. Come on, old man—I'll recite verses for you . . .

LUKA. What?

THE ACTOR. Verses. Don't you understand?

LUKA. Verses? And what do I want with verses?

THE ACTOR. Sometimes they're funny—sometimes sad.

SATINE. Well, poet, are you coming? (*Exit with the* BARON.)

THE ACTOR. I'm coming. I'll join you. For instance, old man, here's a bit of verse—I forget how it begins—I forget . . . (*Brushes his hand across his forehead.*)

BUBNOFF. There! Your Queen is lost—go on, play!

MIEDVIEDIEFF. I made the wrong move.

THE ACTOR. Formerly, before my organism was poisoned with alcohol, old man, I had a good memory. But now it's all over with me, brother. I used to declaim these verses with tremendous success—thunders of applause . . . you have no idea what applause means . . . it goes to your head like vodka! I'd step out on the stage—stand this way—(*Strikes a pose.*)—I'd stand there and . . . (*Pause.*) I can't remember a word—I can't remember! My favorite verses—isn't it ghastly, old man?

LUKA. Yes—is there anything worse than forgetting what you loved? Your very soul is in the thing you love!

THE ACTOR. I've drunk my soul away, old man—brother, I'm lost . . . and why? Because I had no faith . . . I'm done with . . .

LUKA. Well—then—cure yourself! Nowadays they have a cure for drunkards. They treat you free of charge, brother. There's a hospital for drunkards—where they're treated for nothing. They've owned up, you see, that even a drunkard is a human being, and they're only too glad to help him get well. Well—then—go to it!

THE ACTOR (*thoughtfully*). Where? Where is it?

LUKA. Oh—in some town or other . . . what do they call it—? I'll tell you the name presently—only, in the meanwhile, get ready. Don't drink so much! Take yourself in hand—and bear up! And then, when you're cured, you'll begin life all over again. Sounds good, brother, doesn't it, to begin all over again? Well—make up your mind!

THE ACTOR (*smiling*). All over again—from the very beginning—that's fine . . . yes . . . all over again . . . (*Laughs.*) Well—then—I can, can't I?

LUKA. Why not? A human being can do anything—if he only makes up his mind.

THE ACTOR (*suddenly, as if coming out of a trance*). You're a queer bird! See you anon! (*Whistles.*) Old man—*au revoir!* (*Exit.*)

ANNA. Grand-dad!

LUKA. Yes, little mother?

ANNA. Talk to me.

LUKA (*close to her*). Come on—let's chat . . .

[KLESHTCH, *glancing around, silently walks over to his wife, looks at her, and makes queer gestures with his hands, as though he wanted to say something.*]

LUKA. What is it, brother?

KLESHTCH (*quietly*). Nothing . . .

[*Crosses slowly to hallway door, stands on the threshold for a few seconds, and exit.*]

LUKA (*looking after him*). Hard on your man, isn't it?

ANNA. He doesn't concern me much . . .

LUKA. Did he beat you?

ANNA. Worse than that—it's he who's killed me—

BUBNOFF. My wife used to have a lover—the scoundrel—how clever he was at checkers!

MIEDVIEDIEFF. Hm-hm—

ANNA. Grand-dad! Talk to me, darling —I feel so sick . . .

LUKA. Never mind—it's always like this before you die, little dove—never mind, dear! Just have faith! Once you're dead, you'll have peace—always. There's nothing to be afraid of —nothing. Quiet! Peace! Lie quietly! Death wipes out everything. Death is kindly. You die—and you rest—that's what they say. It is true, dear! Because—where can we find rest on this earth?

[PEPEL *enters. He is slightly drunk, disheveled, and sullen. Sits down on bunk near door, and remains silent and motionless.*]

ANNA. And how is it—there? More suffering?

LUKA. Nothing of the kind! No suffering! Trust me! Rest—nothing else! They'll lead you into God's presence, and they'll say: "Dear God! Behold! Here is Anna, Thy servant!"

MIEDVIEDIEFF (*sternly*). How do you know what they'll say up there? Oh, you . . . 10

[PEPEL, *on hearing* MIEDVIEDIEFF'S *voice, raises his head and listens.*]

LUKA. Apparently I do know, Mr. Sergeant!

MIEDVIEDIEFF (*conciliatory*). Yes—it's your own affair—though I'm not exactly a sergeant—yet—

BUBNOFF. I jump two!

MIEDVIEDIEFF. Damn—play!

LUKA. And the Lord will look at you 20 gently and tenderly and He'll say: "I know this Anna!" Then He'll say: "Take Anna into Paradise. Let her have peace. I know. Her life on earth was hard. She is very weary. Let Anna rest in peace!"

ANNA (*choking*). Grandfather—if it were only so—if there were only rest and peace . . .

LUKA. There won't be anything else! 30 Trust me! Die in joy and not in grief. Death is to us like a mother to small children . . .

ANNA. But—perhaps—perhaps I get well . . . ?

LUKA (*laughing*). Why—? Just to suffer more?

ANNA. But—just to live a little longer . . . just a little longer! Since there'll be no suffering hereafter, I could bear 40 it a little longer down here . . .

LUKA. There'll be nothing in the hereafter . . . but only . . .

PEPEL (*rising*). Maybe yes—maybe no!

ANNA (*frightened*). Oh—God!

LUKA. Hey—Adonis!

MIEDVIEDIEFF. Who's that yelping?

PEPEL (*crossing over to him*). I! What of it?

MIEDVIEDIEFF. You yelp needlessly—that's what! People ought to have some dignity!

PEPEL. Block-head! And that's an uncle for you—ho-ho!

LUKA (*to* PEPEL, *in an undertone*). Look here—don't shout—this woman's dying—her lips are already grey—don't disturb her!

PEPEL. I've respect for you, grand-dad. You're all right, you are! You lie well, and you spin pleasant yarns. Go on lying, brother—there's little fun in this world . . .

BUBNOFF. Is the woman really dying?

LUKA. You think I'm joking?

BUBNOFF. That means she'll stop coughing. Her cough was very disturbing. I jump two!

MIEDVIEDIEFF. I'd like to murder you!

PEPEL. Abramka!

MIEDVIEDIEFF. I'm not Abramka to you!

PEPEL. Abrashka! Is Natasha ill?

MIEDVIEDIEFF. None of your business!

PEPEL. Come—tell me! Did Vassilisa beat her up very badly?

MIEDVIEDIEFF. That's none of your business, either! It's a family affair! Who are you anyway?

PEPEL. Whoever I am, you'll never see Natasha again if I choose!

MIEDVIEDIEFF (*throwing up the game*). What's that? Who are you alluding to? My niece by any chance? You thief!

PEPEL. A thief whom you were never able to catch!

MIEDVIEDIEFF. Wait—I'll catch you yet—you'll see—sooner than you think!

PEPEL. If you catch me, God help your whole nest! Do you think I'll keep quiet before the examining magistrate? Every wolf howls! They'll ask me: "Who made you steal and showed you where?" "Mishka Kostilyoff and his wife!" "Who was your fence?" "Mishka Kostilyoff and his wife!"

MIEDVIEDIEFF. You lie! No one will believe you!

PEPEL. They'll believe me all right—because it's the truth! And I'll drag you into it, too. Ha! I'll ruin the lot of you—devils—just watch!

MIEDVIEDIEFF (confused). You lie! You lie! And what harm did I do to you, you mad dog?

PEPEL. And what good did you ever do me?

LUKA. That's right!

MIEDVIEDIEFF (to LUKA). Well—what are you croaking about? Is it any of your business? This is a family matter!

BUBNOFF (to LUKA). Leave them alone! What do we care if they twist each other's tails?

LUKA (peacefully). I meant no harm. All I said was that if a man isn't good to you, then he's acting wrong. . . .

MIEDVIEDIEFF (uncomprehending). Now then—we all of us here know each other—but you—who are you? (Frowns and exit.)

LUKA. The cavalier is peeved! Oh-ho, brothers, I see your affairs are a bit tangled up!

PEPEL. He'll run to complain about us to Vassilisa . . .

BUBNOFF. You're a fool, Vassily. You're very bold these days, aren't you? Watch out! It's all right to be bold when you go gathering mushrooms, but what good is it here? They'll break your neck before you know it!

PEPEL. Well—not as fast as all that! You don't catch us Yaroslavl boys napping! If it's going to be war, we'll fight . . .

LUKA. Look here, boy, you really ought to go away from here—

PEPEL. Where? Please tell me!

LUKA. Go to Siberia!

PEPEL. If I go to Siberia, it'll be at the Tsar's expense!

LUKA. Listen! You go just the same! You can make your own way there. They need your kind out there . . .

PEPEL. My way is clear. My father spent all his life in prison, and I inherited the trait. Even when I was a small child, they called me thief—thief's son.

LUKA. But Siberia is a fine country—a land of gold. Any one who has health and strength and brains can live there like a cucumber in a hothouse.

PEPEL. Old man, why do you always tell lies?

LUKA. What?

PEPEL. Are you deaf? I ask—why do you always lie?

LUKA. What do I lie about?

PEPEL. About everything. According to you, life's wonderful everywhere—but you lie . . . why?

LUKA. Try to believe me. Go and see for yourself. And some day you'll thank me for it. What are you hanging round here for? And, besides, why is truth so important to you? Just think! Truth may spell death to you!

PEPEL. It's all one to me! If that—let it be that!

LUKA. Oh—what a madman! Why should you kill yourself?

BUBNOFF. What are you two jawing about, anyway? I don't understand. What kind of truth do you want, Vaska? And what for? You know the truth about yourself—and so does everybody else . . .

PEPEL. Just a moment! Don't crow!

Let him tell me! Listen, old man! Is there a God?

[LUKA *smiles silently.*]

BUBNOFF. People just drift along—like shavings on a stream. When a house is built—the shavings are thrown away!

PEPEL. Well? Is there a God? Tell me.

LUKA (*in a low voice*). If you have faith, there is; if you haven't, there isn't . . . whatever you believe in, exists . . .

[PEPEL *looks at* LUKA *in staring surprise.*]

BUBNOFF. I'm going to have tea—come on over to the restaurant!

LUKA (*to* PEPEL). What are you staring at?

PEPEL. Oh—just because! Wait now—you mean to say . . .

BUBNOFF. Well—I'm off.

[*Goes to door and runs into* VASSILISA.]

PEPEL. So—you . . .

VASSILISA (*to* BUBNOFF). Is Nastasya home?

BUBNOFF. No. (*Exit.*)

PEPEL. Oh—you've come—?

VASSILISA (*crossing to* ANNA). Is she alive yet?

LUKA. Don't disturb her!

VASSILISA. What are you loafing around here for?

LUKA. I'll go—if you want me to . . .

VASSILISA (*turning towards* PEPEL'S *room*). Vassily! I've some business with you . . .

[LUKA *goes to hallway door, opens it, and shuts it loudly, then warily climbs into a bunk, and from there to the top of the stove.*]

VASSILISA (*calling from* PEPEL'S *room*). Vaska—come here!

PEPEL. I won't come—I don't want to . . .

VASSILISA. Why? What are you angry about?

PEPEL. I'm sick of the whole thing . . .

VASSILISA. Sick of me, too?

PEPEL. Yes! Of you, too!

[VASSILISA *draws her shawl about her, pressing her hands over her breast. Crosses to* ANNA, *looks carefully through the bed curtains, and returns to* PEPEL.] Well—out with it!

VASSILISA. What do you want me to say? I can't force you to be loving, and I'm not the sort to beg for kindness. Thank you for telling me the truth.

PEPEL. What truth?

VASSILISA. That you're sick of me—or isn't it the truth? (PEPEL *looks at her silently. She turns to him.*) What are you staring at? Don't you recognize me?

PEPEL (*sighing*). You're beautiful, Vassilisa! (*She puts her arm about his neck, but he shakes it off.*) But I never gave my heart to you. . . . I've lived with you and all that—But I never really liked you . . .

VASSILISA (*quietly*). That so? Well—?

PEPEL. What is there to talk about? Nothing. Go away from me!

VASSILISA. Taken a fancy to some one else?

PEPEL. None of your business! Suppose I have—I wouldn't ask you to be my match-maker!

VASSILISA (*significantly*). That's too bad . . . perhaps I might arrange a match . . .

PEPEL (*suspiciously*). Who with?

VASSILISA. You know—why do you pretend? Vassily—let me be frank. (*With lower voice.*) I won't deny it—you've offended me . . . it was like a bolt from the blue . . . you said you loved me—and then all of a sudden . . .

PEPEL. It wasn't sudden at all. It's been a long time since I . . . woman, you've no soul! A woman must have a soul . . . we men are beasts—we must be taught—and you, what have you taught me—?

VASSILISA. Never mind the past! I know—no man owns his own heart—you don't love me any longer . . . well and good, it can't be helped!

PEPEL. So that's over. We part peaceably, without a row—as it should be!

VASSILISA. Just a moment! All the same, when I lived with you, I hoped you'd help me out of this swamp—I thought you'd free me from my husband and my uncle—from all this life—and perhaps, Vassya, it wasn't you whom I loved—but my hope—do you understand I waited for you to drag me out of this mire . . .

PEPEL. You aren't a nail—and I'm not a pair of pincers! I thought you had brains—you are so clever—so crafty . . .

VASSILISA (leaning closely towards him). Vassa—Let's help each other!

PEPEL. How?

VASSILISA (low and forcibly). My sister—I know you've fallen for her . . .

PEPEL. And that's why you beat her up, like the beast you are! Look out, Vassilisa! Don't you touch her!

VASSILISA. Wait. Don't get excited. We can do everything quietly and pleasantly. You want to marry her. I'll give you money . . . three hundred rubles—even more than . . .

PEPEL (moving away from her). Stop! What do you mean?

VASSILISA. Rid me of my husband! Take that noose from around my neck . . .

PEPEL (whistling softly). So that's the way the land lies! You certainly planned it cleverly . . . in other words, the grave for the husband, the gallows for the lover, and as for yourself . . .

VASSILISA. Vassya! Why the gallows? It doesn't have to be yourself—but one of your pals! And supposing it were yourself—who'd know? Natalia

—just think—and you'll have money—you go away somewhere . . . you free me forever—and it'll be very good for my sister to be away from me—the sight of her enrages me. . . . I get furious with her on account of you, and I can't control myself. I tortured the girl—I beat her up—beat her up so that I myself cried with pity for her—but I'll beat her—and I'll go on beating her!

PEPEL. Beast! Bragging about your beastliness?

VASSILISA. I'm not bragging—I speak the truth. Think now, Vassa. You've been to prison twice because of my husband—through his greed. He clings to me like a bed-bug—he's been sucking the life out of me for the last four years—and what sort of a husband is he to me? He's forever abusing Natasha—calls her a beggar—he's just poison, plain poison, to every one . . .

PEPEL. You spin your yarn cleverly . . .

VASSILISA. Everything I say is true. Only a fool could be as blind as you. . . .

[KOSTILYOFF enters stealthily and comes forward noisily.]

PEPEL (to VASSILISA). Oh—go away!

VASSILISA. Think it over! (Sees her husband.) What? You? Following me?

[PEPEL leaps up and stares at KOSTILYOFF savagely.]

KOSTILYOFF. It's I, I! So the two of you were here alone—you were—ah—conversing? (Suddenly stamps his feet and screams.) Vassilisa—you bitch! You beggar! You damned hag! (Frightened by his own screams which are met by silence and indifference on the part of the others.) Forgive me, O Lord . . . Vassilisa—again you've led me into the path of sin. . . . I've been looking for you everywhere

It's time to go to bed. You forgot to fill the lamps—oh, you . . . beggar! Swine! (*Shakes his trembling fist at her, while* VASSILISA *slowly goes to door, glancing at* PEPEL *over her shoulder.*)

PEPEL (*to* KOSTILYOFF). Go away— clear out of here—

KOSTILYOFF (*yelling*). What? I? The Boss? I get out? You thief!

PEPEL (*sullenly*). Go away, Mishka!

KOSTILYOFF. Don't you dare—I—I'll show you.

[PEPEL *seizes him by the collar and shakes him. From the stove come loud noises and yawns.* PEPEL *releases* KOSTILYOFF *who runs into the hallway, screaming.*]

PEPEL (*jumping on a bunk*). Who is it? Who's on the stove?

LUKA (*raising his head*). Eh?

PEPEL. You?

LUKA (*undisturbed*). I—I myself—oh, dear Jesus!

PEPEL (*shuts hallway door, looks for the wooden closing bar, but can't find it*). The devil! Come down, old man!

LUKA. I'm climbing down—all right . . .

PEPEL (*roughly*). What did you climb on that stove for?

LUKA. Where was I to go?

PEPEL. Why—didn't you go out into the hall?

LUKA. The hall's too cold for an old fellow like myself, brother.

PEPEL. You overheard?

LUKA. Yes—I did. How could I help it? Am I deaf? Well, my boy, happiness is coming your way. Real, good fortune I call it!

PEPEL (*suspiciously*). What good fortune—?

LUKA. In so far as I was lying on the stove . . .

PEPEL. Why did you make all that noise?

LUKA. Because I was getting warm . . .

it was your good luck . . . I though if only the boy wouldn't make a mistake and choke the old man . .

PEPEL. Yes—I might have done it . . how terrible . . .

LUKA. Small wonder! It isn't difficult to make a mistake of that sort.

PEPEL (*smiling*). What's the matter? Did you make the same sort of mistake once upon a time?

LUKA. Boy, listen to me. Send that woman out of your life! Don't let her near you! Her husband—she'll get rid of him herself—and in a shrewder way than you could—yes! Don't you listen to that devil! Look at me: I am bald-headed—know why? Because of all these women. . . . Perhaps I knew more women than I had hair on the top of my head— but this Vassilisa—she's worse than the plague. . . .

PEPEL. I don't understand . . . I don't know whether to thank you—or— well . . .

LUKA. Don't say a word! You won't improve on what I said. Listen: take the one you like by the arm, and march out of here—get out of here— clean out . . .

PEPEL (*sadly*). I can't understand people. Who is kind and who isn't? It's all a mystery to me . . .

LUKA. What's there to understand? There's all breeds of men . . . they all live as their hearts tell them . . . good to-day, bad to-morrow! But if you really care for that girl . . . take her away from here and that's all there is to it. Otherwise go away alone . . . you're young—you're in no hurry for a wife . . .

PEPEL (*taking him by the shoulder*). Tell me! Why do you say all this?

LUKA. Wait. Let me go. I want a look at Anna . . . she was coughing so terribly . . . (*Goes to* ANNA'S *bed, pulls the curtains, looks, touches her.* PEPEL, *thoughtfully and distraught, follows him with his eyes.*) Merciful Jesus Christ! Take into Thy keeping the soul of this woman Anna, newcomer amongst the blessed!

PEPEL (*softly*). Is she dead?

Without approaching, he stretches himself and looks at the bed.]　　　10

LUKA (*gently*). Her sufferings are over! Where's her husband?

PEPEL. In the saloon, most likely . . .

LUKA. Well—he'll have to be told . . .

PEPEL (*shuddering*). I don't like corpses!

LUKA (*going to door*). Why should you like them? It's the living who demand our love—the living . . .

PEPEL. I'm coming with you . . .

LUKA. Are you afraid?　　　20

PEPEL. I don't like it . . .

They go out quickly. The stage is empty and silent for a few moments. Behind the door is heard a dull, staccato, incomprehensible noise. Then the ACTOR *enters.*]

THE ACTOR (*stands at the open door, supporting himself against the jamb, and shouts*). Hey, old man—where are you—? I just remembered—listen . . . (*Takes two staggering steps for-*　30 *ward and, striking a pose, recites.*) "Good people! If the world cannot find

A path to holy truth,

Glory be to the madman who will enfold all humanity

In a golden dream . . ."

NATASHA *appears in the doorway behind the* ACTOR.]

Old man! (*Recites.*)　　　40

"If to-morrow the sun were to forget

To light our earth,

To-morrow then some madman's thought

Would bathe the world in sunshine. . . ."

NATASHA (*laughing*). Scarecrow! You're drunk!

THE ACTOR (*turns to her*). Oh—it's you? Where's the old man, the dear old man? Not a soul here, seems to me . . . Natasha, farewell—right—farewell!

NATASHA (*entering*). Don't wish me farewell, before you've wished me how-d'you-do!

THE ACTOR (*barring her way*). I am going. Spring will come—and I'll be here no longer—

NATASHA. Wait a moment! Where do you propose going?

THE ACTOR. In search of a town—to be cured—And you, Ophelia, must go away! Take the veil! Just imagine —there's a hospital to cure—ah— organisms for drunkards—a wonderful hospital—built of marble—with marble floors . . . light—clean— food—and all gratis! And a marble floor—yes! I'll find it—I'll get cured —and then I shall start life anew. . . . I'm on my way to regeneration, as King Lear said. Natasha, my stage name is . . . Svertchkoff— Zavoloushski . . . do you realize how painful it is to lose one's name? Even dogs have their names . . .

[NATASHA *carefully passes the* ACTOR, *stops at* ANNA'S *bed and looks.*]

To be nameless—is not to exist!

NATASHA. Look, my dear—why—she's dead. . . .

THE ACTOR (*shakes his head*). Impossible . . .

NATASHA (*stepping back*). So help me God—look . . .

BUBNOFF (*appearing in doorway*). What is there to look at?

NATASHA. Anna—she's dead!

BUBNOFF. That means—she's stopped coughing! (*Goes to* ANNA'S *bed, looks, and returns to his bunk.*) We must tell

Kleshtch—it's his business to know . . .

THE ACTOR. I'll go—I'll say to him—she lost her name—(*Exit.*)

NATASHA (*in centre of room*). I, too—some day—I'll be found in the cellar—dead. . . .

BUBNOFF (*spreading out some rags on his bunk*). What's that? What are you muttering?

NATASHA. Nothing much . . .

BUBNOFF. Waiting for Vaska, eh? Take care—Vassilisa'll break your head!

NATASHA. Isn't it the same who breaks it? I'd much rather he'd do it!

BUBNOFF (*lying down*). Well—that's your own affair . . .

NATASHA. It's best for her to be dead—yet it's a pity . . . oh, Lord—why do we live?

BUBNOFF. It's so with all . . . we're born, live, and die—and I'll die, too—and so'll you—what's there to be gloomy about?

[*Enter* LUKA, *the* TARTAR, ZOB, *and* KLESHTCH. *The latter comes after the others, slowly, shrunk up.*)

NATASHA. Sh-sh! Anna!

ZOB. We've heard—God rest her soul . . .

THE TARTAR (*to* KLESHTCH). We must take her out of here. Out into the hall! This is no place for corpses—but for the living . . .

KLESHTCH (*quietly*). We'll take her out—

[*Everybody goes to the bed,* KLESHTCH *looks at his wife over the others' shoulders.*]

ZOB (*to the* TARTAR). You think she'll smell? I don't think she will—she dried up while she was still alive . . .

NATASHA. God! If they'd only a little pity . . . if only some one would say a kindly word—oh, you . . .

LUKA. Don't be hurt, girl—never mind! Why and how should we pity the dead? Come, dear! We don't pity the living—we can't even pity ou own selves—how can we?

BUBNOFF (*yawning*). And, besides, whei you're dead, no word will help you—when you're still alive, even sick, i may. . . .

THE TARTAR (*stepping aside*). The polic must be notified . . .

ZOB. The police—must be done! Kleshtch! Did you notify the po lice?

KLESHTCH. No—she's got to be buried—and all I have is forty kopecks—

ZOB. Well—you'll have to borrow then—otherwise we'll take up a col lection . . . one'll give five kopecks, others as much as they can. But the police must be notified at once—oi they'll think you killed her or God knows what not . . .

[*Crosses to the* TARTAR's *bunk and prepares to lie down by his side.*]

NATASHA (*going to* BUBNOFF's *bunk*). Now—I'll dream of her . . . I always dream of the dead . . . I'm afraid to go out into the hall by myself—it's dark there . . .

LUKA (*following her*). You better fear the living—I'm telling you . . .

NATASHA. Take me across the hall, grandfather.

LUKA. Come on—come on—I'll take you across—

[*They go away. Pause.*]

ZOB (*to the* TARTAR). Oh-ho! Spring will soon be here, little brother, and it'll be quite warm. In the villages the peasants are already making ready their ploughs and harrows, preparing to till . . . and we . . . Hassan? Snoring already? Damned Mohammedan!

BUBNOFF. Tartars love sleep!

KLESHTCH (*in centre of room, staring in front of him*). What am I to do now?

ZOB. Lie down and sleep—that's all . . .

KLESHTCH (*softly*). But—she . . . how about . . .

[*No one answers him.* SATINE *and the* ACTOR *enter.*]

THE ACTOR (*yelling*). Old man! Come here, my trusted Duke of Kent!

SATINE. Miklookha-Maklai is coming—ho-ho!

THE ACTOR. It has been decided upon! Old man, where's the town—where are you?

SATINE. Fata Morgana, the old man bilked you from top to bottom! There's nothing—no towns—no people—nothing at all!

THE ACTOR. You lie!

THE TARTAR (*jumping up*). Where's the boss? I'm going to the boss. If I can't sleep, I won't pay! Corpses—drunkards . . . (*Exit quickly.*)

[SATINE *looks after him and whistles.*]

BUBNOFF (*in a sleepy voice*). Go to bed, boys—be quiet . . . night is for sleep . . .

THE ACTOR. Yes—so—there's a corpse here. . . . "Our net fished up a corpse. . . ." Verses—by Béranger. . . .

SATINE (*screams*). The dead can't hear . . . the dead do not feel—Scream!—Roar! . . . the dead don't hear!

[*In the doorway appears* LUKA.]

CURTAIN

ACT III

"*The Waste,*" *a yard strewn with rubbish and overgrown with weeds. Back, a high brick wall which shuts out the sight of the sky. Near it are elder-bushes. Right, the dark, wooden wall of some sort of house, barn or stable. Left, the grey tumbledown wall of* KOSTILYOFF'S *night asylum. It is built at an angle so that the further corner reaches almost to the center of the yard. Between it and the wall runs a narrow passage. In the grey, plastered wall are two windows, one on a level with the ground, the other about six feet higher up and closer to the brick wall. Near the latter wall is a big sledge turned upside down and a beam about twelve feet long. Right of the wall is a heap of old planks. Evening. The sun is setting, throwing a crimson light on the brick wall. Early spring, the snow having only recently melted. The elder-bushes are not yet in bud.*

NATASHA *and* NASTYA *are sitting side by side on the beam.* LUKA *and the* BARON *are on the sledge.* KLESHTCH *is stretched on the pile of planks to the right.* BUBNOFF'S *face is at the ground floor window.*

NASTYA (*with closed eyes, nodding her head in rhythm to the tale she is telling in a sing-song voice*). So then at night he came into the garden. I had been waiting for him quite a while. I trembled with fear and grief—he trembled, too . . . he was as white as chalk—and he had the pistol in his hand . . .

NATASHA (*chewing sun-flower seeds*). Oh—are these students really such desperate fellows? . . .

NASTYA. And he says to me in a dreadful voice: "My precious darling . . ."

BUBNOFF. Ho-ho! Precious—?

THE BARON. Shut up! If you don't like it, you can lump it! But don't interrupt her. . . . Go on . . .

NASTYA. "My one and only love," he says, "my parents," he says, "refuse to give their consent to our wedding—and threaten to disown me because of my love for you. Therefore," he says, "I must take my life." And his pistol was huge—and loaded with ten bullets . . . "Farewell," he says, "beloved comrade! I have made up my mind for good and all . . . I can't live without you . . ." and I replied: "My unforgettable friend—my Raoul. . . ."

BUBNOFF (*surprised*). What? What? Krawl—did you call him—?

THE BARON. Nastya! But last time his name was Gaston. . . .

NASTYA (*jumping up*). Shut up, you bastards! Ah—you lousy mongrels! You think for a moment that you can understand love—true love? My love was real honest-to-God love! (*To the* BARON.) You good-for-nothing! . . . educated, you call yourself—drinking coffee in bed, did you?

LUKA. Now, now! Wait, people! Don't interfere! Show a little respect to your neighbors . . . it isn't the word that matters, but what's in back of the word. That's what matters! Go on, girl! it's all right!

BUBNOFF. Go on, crow! See if you can make your feathers white!

THE BARON. Well—continue!

NATASHA. Pay no attention to them . . . what are they? They're just jealous . . . they've nothing to tell about themselves . . .

NASTYA (*sits down again*). I'm going to say no more! If they don't believe me they'll laugh. (*Stops suddenly, is silent for a few seconds, then, shutting her eyes, continues in a loud and intense voice, swaying her hands as if to the rhythm of far music.*) And then I replied to him: "Joy of my life! My bright moon! And I, too, I can't live without you— because I love you madly, so madly —and I shall keep on loving you as long as my heart beats in my bosom. But—" I say—"don't take your young life! Think how necessary it is to your dear parents whose only happiness you are. Leave me! Better that

I should perish from longing for you, my life! I alone! I—ah—as such, such! Better that I should die—it doesn't matter . . . I am of no use to the world—and I have nothing, nothing at all—"

[*Covers her face with her hand and weeps gently.*]

NATASHA (*in a low voice*). Don't cry— don't!

[LUKA, *smiling, strokes* NASTYA'S *head.*]

BUBNOFF (*laughs*). Ah—you limb of Satan!

THE BARON (*also laughs*). Hey, old man? Do you think it's true? It's all from that book, *Fatal Love* . . . it's all nonsense! Let her alone!

NATASHA. And what's it to you? Shut up —or God'll punish you!

NASTYA (*bitterly*). God damn your soul! You worthless pig! Soul—bah!—you haven't got one!

LUKA (*takes* NASTYA'S *hand*). Come, dear! it's nothing! Don't be angry—I know —I believe you! You're right, not they! If you believe you had a real love affair, then you did—yes! And as for him—don't be angry with a fellow-lodger . . . maybe he's really jealous, and that's why he's laughing. Maybe he never had any real love— maybe not—come on—let's go!

NASTYA (*pressing her hand against her breast*). Grandfather! So help me God —it happened! It happened! He was a student, a Frenchman—Gastotcha was his name—he had a little black beard—and patent leathers—may God strike me dead if I'm lying! And he loved me so—my God, how he loved me!

LUKA. Yes, yes, it's all right. I believe you! Patent leathers, you said? Well, well, well—and you loved him, did you? (*Disappears with her around the corner.*)

THE BARON. God—isn't she a fool, though? She's good-hearted—but such a fool—it's past belief!

BUBNOFF. And why are people so fond of lying—just as if they were up before the judge—really!

NATASHA. I guess lying is more fun than speaking the truth—I, too . . .

THE BARON. What—you, too? Go on!

NATASHA. Oh—I imagine things—in-vent them—and I wait—

THE BARON. For what?

NATASHA (smiling confusedly). Oh—I think that perhaps—well—to-morrow somebody will really appear—some one—oh—out of the ordinary—or something'll happen—also out of the ordinary. . . . I've been waiting for it—oh—always. . . . But, really, what is there to wait for? (Pause.)

THE BARON (with a slight smile). Nothing—I expect nothing! What is past, is past! Through! Over with! And then what?

NATASHA. And then—well—to-morrow I imagine suddenly that I'll die—and I get frightened . . . in summer it's all right to dream of death—then there are thunder storms—one might get struck by lightning . . .

THE BARON. You've a hard life . . . your sister's a wicked-tempered devil!

NATASHA. Tell me—does anybody live happily? It's hard for all of us—I can see that . . .

KLESHTCH (who until this moment has sat motionless and indifferent, jumps up suddenly). For all? You lie! Not for all! If it were so—all right! Then it wouldn't hurt—yes!

BUBNOFF. What in hell's bit you? Just listen to him yelping!

[KLESHTCH lies down again and grunts.]

THE BARON. Well—I'd better go and make my peace with Nastinka—if I don't, she won't treat me to vodka . . .

BUBNOFF. Hm—people love to lie . . . with Nastya—I can see the reason why. She's used to painting that mutt of hers—and now she wants to paint her soul as well . . . put rouge on her soul, eh? But the others—why do they? Take Luka for instance—he lies a lot . . . and what does he get out of it? He's an old fellow, too—why does he do it?

THE BARON (smiling and walking away). All people have drab-colored souls—and they like to brighten them up a bit . . .

LUKA (appearing from round the corner). You, sir, why do you tease the girl? Leave her alone—let her cry if it amuses her . . . she weeps for her own pleasure—what harm is it to you?

THE BARON. Nonsense, old man! She's a nuisance. Raoul to-day, Gaston to-morrow—always the same old yarn, though! Still—I'll go and make up with her. (Leaves.)

LUKA. That's right—go—and be nice to her. Being nice to people never does them any harm . . .

NATASHA. You're so good, little father—why are you so good?

LUKA. Good, did you say? Well—call it that! (Behind the brick wall is heard soft singing and the sounds of a concertina.) Some one has to be kind, girl—some one must pity people! Christ pitied everybody—and he said to us: "Go and do likewise!" I tell you—if you pity a man when he most needs it, good comes of it. Why—I used to be a watchman on the estate of an engineer near Tomsk—all right—the house was right in the middle of a forest—lonely place—winter came—and I remained all by myself. Well—one night I heard a noise—

NATASHA. Thieves?

LUKA. Exactly! Thieves creeping in! I took my gun—I went out. I looked and saw two of them opening a window—and so busy that they didn't even see me. I yell: "Hey there—get out of here!" And they turn on me with their axes—I warn them to stand back, or I'd shoot—and as I speak, I keep on covering them with my gun, first the one, then the other —they go down on their knees, as if to implore me for mercy. And by that time I was furious—because of those axes, you see—and so I say to them: "I was chasing you, you scoundrels— and you didn't go. Now you go and break off some stout branches!"—and they did so—and I say: "Now—one of you lie down and let the other one flog him!" So they obey me and flog each other—and then they begin to implore me again. "Grandfather," they say, "for God's sake give us some bread! We're hungry!" There's thieves for you, my dear! (*Laughs.*) And with an ax, too! Yes—honest peasants, both of them! And I say to them, "You should have asked for bread straight away!" And they say: "We got tired of asking—you beg and beg—and nobody gives you a crumb —it hurts!" So they stayed with me all that winter—one of them, Stepan, would take my gun and go shooting in the forest—and the other, Yakoff, was ill most of the time—he coughed a lot . . . and so the three of us together looked after the house . . . then spring came . . . "Good-bye, grandfather," they said—and they went away—back home to Russia . . .

NATASHA. Were they escaped convicts?

LUKA. That's just what they were—escaped convicts—from a Siberian prison camp . . . honest peasants. If I hadn't felt sorry for them—they might have killed me—or maybe worse—and then there would have been trial and prison and afterwards Siberia—what's the sense of it? Prison teaches no good—and Siberia doesn't either—but another human being can . . . yes, a human being can teach another one kindness—very simply! (*Pause.*)

BUBNOFF. Hm—yes—I, for instance, don't know how to lie . . . why—as far as I'm concerned, I believe in coming out with the whole truth and putting it on thick . . . why fuss about it?

KLESHTCH (*again jumps up as if his clothes were on fire, and screams*). What truth? Where is there truth? (*Tearing at his ragged clothes.*) Here's truth for you! No work! No strength! That's the only truth! Shelter—there's no shelter! You die—that's the truth! Hell! What do I want with the truth? Let me breathe! Why should I be blamed? What do I want with truth? To live—Christ Almighty!—they won't let you live—and that's another truth!

BUBNOFF. He's mad!

LUKA. Dear Lord . . . listen to me, brother—

KLESHTCH (*trembling with excitement*). They say: there's truth! You, old man, try to console every one . . . I tell you—I hate every one! And there's your truth—God curse it— understand? I tell you—God curse it!

[*Rushes away round the corner, turning as he goes.*]

LUKA. Ah—how excited he got! Where did he run off to?

NATASHA. He's off his head . . .

BUBNOFF. God—didn't he say a whole

lot, though? As if he was playing drama—he gets those fits often . . . he isn't used to life yet . . .

PEPEL (*comes slowly round the corner*). Peace on all this honest gathering! Well, Luka, you wily old fellow—still telling them stories?

LUKA. You should have heard how that fellow carried on!

PEPEL. Kleshtch—wasn't it? What's wrong with him? He was running like one possessed!

LUKA. You'd do the same if your own heart were breaking!

PEPEL (*sitting down*). I don't like him . . . he's got such a nasty, bad temper— and so proud! (*Imitating* KLESHTCH.) "I'm a workman!" And he thinks everyone's beneath him. Go on working if you feel like it—nothing to be so damned haughty about! If work is the standard—a horse can give us points—pulls like hell and says nothing! Natasha—are your folks at home?

NATASHA. They went to the cemetery— then to night service . . .

PEPEL. So that's why you're free for once —quite a novelty.

LUKA (*to* BUBNOFF, *thoughtfully*). There— you say—truth! Truth doesn't always heal a wounded soul. For instance, I knew of a man who believed in a land of righteousness . . .

BUBNOFF. In what?

LUKA. In a land of righteousness. He said: "Somewhere on this earth there must be a righteous land—and wonderful people live there—good people! They respect each other, help each other, and everything is peaceful and good!" And so that man—who was always searching for this land of righteousness—he was poor and lived miserably—and when things got to be so bad with him that it seemed there was nothing else for him to do except lie down and die— even then he never lost heart—but he'd just smile and say: "Never mind! I can stand it! A little while longer— and I'll have done with this life—and I'll go in search of the righteous land!"—it was his one happiness— the thought of that land . . .

PEPEL. Well? Did he go there?

BUBNOFF. Where? Ho-ho!

LUKA. And then to this place—in Siberia, by the way—there came a convict—a learned man with books and maps—yes, a learned man who knew all sorts of things—and the other man said to him: "Do me a favor—show me where is the land of righteousness and how I can get there." At once the learned man opened his books, spread out his maps, and looked and looked and he said—no—he couldn't find this land anywhere . . . everything was correct—all the lands on earth were marked—but not this land of righteousness . . .

PEPEL (*in a low voice*). Well? Wasn't there a trace of it?

[BUBNOFF *roars with laughter.*]

NATASHA. Wait . . . well, little father?

LUKA. The man wouldn't believe it. . . . "It must exist," he said, "look carefully. Otherwise," he says, "your books and maps are of no use if there's no land of righteousness." The learned man was offended. "My plans," he said, "are correct. But there exists no land of righteousness anywhere." Well, then the other man got angry. He'd lived and lived and suffered and suffered, and had believed all the time in the existence of this land—and now, according to the plans, it didn't exist at all. He felt robbed! And he said to the learned man: "Ah—you scum of the earth!

You're not a learned man at all—but just a damned cheat!"—and he gave him a good wallop in the eye—then another one . . . (*After a moment's silence.*) And then he went home and hanged himself!

[*All are silent.* LUKA, *smiling, looks at* PEPEL *and* NATASHA.]

PEPEL (*low-voiced*). To hell with this story—it isn't very cheerful . . .

NATASHA. He couldn't stand the disappointment . . .

BUBNOFF (*sullen*). Ah—it's nothing but a fairy-tale . . .

PEPEL. Well—there is the righteous land for you—doesn't exist, it seems . . .

NATASHA. I'm sorry for that man . . .

BUBNOFF. All a story—ho-ho!—land of righteousness—what an idea! (*Exit through window.*)

LUKA (*pointing to window*). He's laughing! (*Pause.*) Well, children, God be with you! I'll leave you soon . . .

PEPEL. Where are you going to?

LUKA. To the Ukraine—I heard they discovered a new religion there—I want to see—yes! People are always seeking—they always want something better—God grant them patience!

PEPEL. You think they'll find it?

LUKA. The people? They will find it! He who seeks, will find! He who desires strongly, will find!

NATASHA. If only they could find something better—invent something better . . .

LUKA. They're trying to! But we must help them, girl—we must respect them . . .

NATASHA. How can I help them? I am helpless myself!

PEPEL (*determined*). Again—listen—I'll speak to you again, Natasha—here—before him—he knows everything . . . run away with me?

NATASHA. Where? From one prison to another?

PEPEL. I told you—I'm through with being a thief, so help me God! I'll quit! If I say so, I'll do it! I can read and write—I'll work—He's been telling me to go to Siberia on my own hook—let's go there together, what do you say? Do you think I'm not disgusted with my life? Oh—Natasha—I know . . . I see . . . I console myself with the thought that there are lots of people who are honored and respected—and who are bigger thieves than I! But what good is that to me? It isn't that I repent . . . I've no conscience . . . but I do feel one thing: One must live differently. One must live a better life . . . one must be able to respect one's own self . . .

LUKA. That's right, friend! May God help you! It's true! A man must respect himself!

PEPEL. I've been a thief from childhood on. Everybody always called me "Vaska—the thief—the son of a thief!" Oh—very well then—I am a thief— . . . just imagine—now, perhaps, I'm a thief out of spite—perhaps I'm a thief because no one ever called me anything different. . . . Well, Natasha—?

NATASHA (*sadly*). Somehow I don't believe in words—and I'm restless to-day—my heart is heavy . . . as if I were expecting something . . . it's a pity, Vassily, that you talked to me to-day . . .

PEPEL. When should I? It isn't the first time I speak to you . . .

NATASHA. And why should I go with you? I don't love you so very much—sometimes I like you—and other times the mere sight of you makes me sick . . . it seems—no—I don't really love you . . . when one really loves, one sees no fault. . . . But I do see . . .

PEPEL. Never mind—you'll love me after a while! I'll make you care for me . . . if you'll just say yes! For over a year I've watched you . . . you're a decent girl . . . you're kind—you're reliable—I'm very much in love with you . . .

VASSILISA, *in her best dress, appears at window and listens.*]

NATASHA. Yes—you love me—but how about my sister? . . .

PEPEL (*confused*). Well, what of her? There are plenty like her . . .

LUKA. You'll be all right, girl! If there's no bread, you have to eat weeds . . .

PEPEL (*gloomily*). Please—feel a little sorry for me! My life isn't all roses— it's a hell of a life . . . little happiness in it . . . I feel as if a swamp were sucking me under . . . and whatever I try to catch and hold on to, is rotten . . . it breaks . . . Your sister—oh—I thought she was different . . . if she weren't so greedy after money . . . I'd have done anything for her sake, if she were only all mine . . . but she must have someone else . . . and she has to have money—and freedom . . . because she doesn't like the straight and narrow . . . she can't help me. But you're like a young fir-tree . . . you bend, but you don't break . . .

LUKA. Yes—go with him, girl, go! He's a good lad—he's all right! Only tell him every now and then that he's a good lad so that he won't forget it— and he'll believe you. Just you keep on telling him "Vasya, you're a good man—don't you forget it!" Just think, dear, where else could you go except with him? Your sister is a savage beast . . . and as for her husband, there's little to say of him?

He's rotten beyond words . . . and all this life here, where will it get you? But this lad is strong . . .

NATASHA. Nowhere to go—I know—I thought of it. The only thing is—I've no faith in anybody—and there's no place for me to turn to . . .

PEPEL. Yes, there is! But I won't let you go that way—I'd rather cut your throat!

NATASHA (*smiling*). There—I'm not his wife yet—and he talks already of killing me!

PEPEL (*puts his arms around her*). Come, Natasha! Say yes!

NATASHA (*holding him close*). But I'll tell you one thing, Vassily—I swear it before God . . . the first time you strike me or hurt me any other way, I'll have no pity on myself . . . I'll either hang myself . . . or . . .

PEPEL. May my hand wither if ever I touch you!

LUKA. Don't doubt him, dear! He needs you more than you need him!

VASSILISA (*from the window*). So now they're engaged! Love and advice!

NATASHA. They've come back—oh, God —they saw—oh, Vassily . . .

PEPEL. Why are you frightened? Nobody'll dare touch you now!

VASSILISA. Don't be afraid, Natalia! He won't beat you . . . he don't know how to love or how to beat . . . I know!

LUKA (*in a low voice*). Rotten old hag— like a snake in the grass . . .

VASSILISA. He dares only with the word!

KOSTILYOFF (*enters*). Natashka! What are you doing here, you parasite? Gossiping? Kicking about your family? And the samovar not ready? And the table not cleared?

NATASHA (*going out*). I thought you were going to church . . .?

KOSTILYOFF. None of your business **what**

we intended doing! Mind your own affairs—and do what you're told!

PEPEL. Shut up, you! She's no longer your servant! Don't go, Natalia—don't do a thing!

NATASHA. Stop ordering me about—you're commencing too soon! (*Leaves.*)

PEPEL (*to* KOSTILYOFF). That's enough. You've used her long enough—now she's mine!

KOSTILYOFF. Yours? When did you buy her—and for how much?

[VASSILISA *roars with laughter.*]

LUKA. Go away, Vasya!

PEPEL. Don't laugh, you fools—or first thing you know I'll make you cry!

VASSILISA. Oh, how terrible! Oh—how you frighten me!

LUKA. Vassily—go away! Don't you see —she's goading you on . . . ridicul-ing you, don't you understand? . . .

PEPEL. Yes . . . You lie, lie! You won't get what you want!

VASSILISA. Nor will I get what I don't want, Vasya!

PEPEL (*shaking his fist at her*). We'll see . . . (*Exit.*)

VASSILISA (*disappearing through window*). I'll arrange some wedding for you . . .

KOSTILYOFF (*crossing to* LUKA). Well, old man, how's everything?

LUKA. All right!

KOSTILYOFF. You're going away, they say—?

LUKA. Soon.

KOSTILYOFF. Where to?

LUKA. I'll follow my nose . . .

KOSTILYOFF. Tramping, eh? Don't like stopping in one place all the time, do you?

LUKA. Even water won't pass beneath a stone that's sunk too firmly in the ground, they say . . .

KOSTILYOFF. That's true for a stone. But man must settle in one place. Men can't live like cockroaches, crawling about wherever they want. . . . A man must stick to one place—and not wander about aimlessly . . .

LUKA. But suppose his home is wherever he hangs his hat?

KOSTILYOFF. Why, then—he's a vagabond—useless . . . a human being must be of some sort of use—he must work . . .

LUKA. That's what you think, eh?

KOSTILYOFF. Yes—sure . . . just look! What's a vagabond? A strange fellow . . . unlike all others. If he's a real pilgrim then he's some good in the world . . . perhaps he discovered a new truth. Well—but not every truth is worth while. Let him keep it to himself and shut up about it! Or else—let him speak in a way which no one can understand . . . don't let him interfere . . . don't let him stir up people without cause! It's none of his business how other people live! Let him follow his own righteous path . . . in the woods—or in a monastery—away from everybody! He mustn't interfere—nor condemn other people—but pray—pray for all of us—for all the world's sins—for mine—for yours—for everybody's. To pray—that's why he forsakes the world's turmoil! That's so! (*Pause.*) But you—what sort of a pilgrim are you—? An honest person must have a passport . . . all honest people have passports . . . yes! . . .

LUKA. In this world there are people—and also just plain men . . .

KOSTILYOFF. Don't coin wise sayings! Don't give me riddles! I'm as clever as you . . . what's the difference—people and men?

LUKA. What riddle is there? I say—there's sterile and there's fertile ground . . . whatever you sow in it, grows . . . that's all . . .

KOSTILYOFF. What do you mean?

LUKA. Take yourself for instance . . . if the Lord God himself said to you: "Mikhailo, be a man!"—it would be useless—nothing would come of it— you're doomed to remain just as you are . . .

KOSTILYOFF. Oh—but do you realize that my wife's uncle is a policeman, and that if I . . .   10

VASSILISA (coming in). Mikhail Ivanitch— come and have your tea . . .

KOSTILYOFF (to LUKA). You listen! Get out! You leave this place—hear?

VASSILISA. Yes—get out, old man! Your tongue's too long! And—who knows —you may be an escaped convict . . .

KOSTILYOFF. If I ever see sign of you again after to-day—well—I've warned you!   20

LUKA. You'll call your uncle, eh? Go on —call him! Tell him you've caught an escaped convict—and maybe uncle'll get a reward—perhaps all of three kopecks . . .

BUBNOFF (in the window). What are you bargaining about? Three kopecks— for what?

LUKA. They're threatening to sell me . . .

VASSILISA (to her husband). Come . . .   30

BUBNOFF. For three kopecks? Well— look out, old man—they may even do it for one!

KOSTILYOFF (to BUBNOFF). You have a habit of jumping up like a jack-in-the-box!

VASSILISA. The world is full of shady people and crooks—

LUKA. Hope you'll enjoy your tea!

VASSILISA (turning). Shut up! You rotten 40 toadstool! (Leaves with her husband.)

LUKA. I'm off to-night.

BUBNOFF. That's right. Don't outstay your welcome!

LUKA. True enough.

BUBNOFF. I know. Perhaps I've escaped the gallows by getting away in time . . .

LUKA. Well?

BUBNOFF. That's true. It was this way. My wife took up with my boss. He was great at his trade—could dye a dog's skin so that it looked like a rac-coon's—could change cat's skin into kangaroo—muskrats, all sorts of things. Well—my wife took up with him—and they were so mad about each other that I got afraid they might poison me or something like that—so I commenced beating up my wife—and the boss beat me . . . we fought savagely! Once he tore off half my whiskers—and broke one of my ribs . . . well, then I, too, got en-raged. . . . I cracked my wife over the head with an iron yard-measure —well—and altogether it was like an honest-to-God war! And then I saw that nothing really could come of it . . . they were planning to get the best of me! So I started planning— how to kill my wife—I thought of it a whole lot . . . but I thought better of it just in time . . . and got away . . .

LUKA. That was best! Let them go on changing dogs into raccoons!

BUBNOFF. Only—the shop was in my wife's name . . . and so I did my-self out of it, you see? Although, to tell the truth, I would have drunk it away . . . I'm a hard drinker, you know . . .

LUKA. A hard drinker—oh . . .

BUBNOFF. The worst you ever met! Once I start drinking, I drink every-thing in sight, I'll spend every bit of money I have—everything except my bones and my skin . . . what's more, I'm lazy . . . it's terrible how I hate work!

[Enter SATINE and the ACTOR, quarreling.]

SATINE. Nonsense! You'll go nowhere—it's all a damned lie! Old man, what did you stuff him with all those fairy-tales for?

THE ACTOR. You lie! Grandfather! Tell him that he lies!—I am going away. I worked to-day—I swept the streets . . . and I didn't have a drop of vodka. What do you think of that? Here they are—two fifteen-kopeck pieces—and I'm sober!

SATINE. Why—that's absurd! Give it to me—I'll either drink it up—or lose it at cards . . .

THE ACTOR. Get out—this is for my journey . . .

LUKA (to SATINE). And you—why are you trying to lead him astray?

SATINE. Tell me, soothsayer, beloved by the gods, what's my future going to be? I've gone to pieces, brother—but everything isn't lost yet, grandfather . . . there are sharks in this world who got more brains than I!

LUKA. You're cheerful, Constantine—and very agreeable!

BUBNOFF. Actor, come over here! (*The* ACTOR *crosses to window, sits down on the sill before* BUBNOFF, *and speaks in a low voice with him.*)

SATINE. You know, brother, I used to be a clever youngster. It's nice to think of it. I was a devil of a fellow . . . danced splendidly, played on the stage, loved to amuse people . . . it was awfully gay . . .

LUKA. How did you get to be what you are?

SATINE. You're inquisitive, old man! You want to know everything? What for?

LUKA. I want to understand the ways of men—I look at you, and I don't understand. You're a bold lad, Constantine, and you're no fool . . . yet, all of a sudden . . .

SATINE. It's prison, grandfather—I spent four years and seven months in prison . . . afterwards—where could I go?

LUKA. Aha! What were you there for?

SATINE. On account of a scoundrel—whom I killed in a fit of rage . . . and despair . . . and in prison I learned to play cards. . . .

LUKA. You killed—because of a woman?

SATINE. Because of my own sister. . . . But look here—leave me alone! I don't care for these cross-examinations—and all this happened a long time ago. It's already nine years since my sister's death. . . . Brother, she was a wonderful girl . . .

LUKA. You take life easily! And only a while ago that locksmith was here—and how he did yell!

SATINE. Kleshtch?

LUKA. Yes—"There's no work," he shouted; "there isn't anything . . ."

SATINE. He'll get used to it. What could I do?

LUKA (softly). Look—here he comes!

[KLESHTCH *walks in slowly, his head bowed low.*]

SATINE. Hey, widower! Why are you so down in the mouth? What are you thinking?

KLESHTCH. I'm thinking—what'll I do? I've no food—nothing—the funeral ate up all . . .

SATINE. I'll give you a bit of advice . . . do nothing! Just be a burden to the world at large!

KLESHTCH. Go on—talk—I'd be ashamed of myself . . .

SATINE. Why—people aren't ashamed to let you live worse than a dog. Just think . . . you stop work—so do I—so do hundreds, thousands of others—everybody—understand?—everybody'll quit working . . . nobody'll do a damned thing—and then what'll happen?

KLESHTCH. They'll all starve to death . . .

LUKA (*to* SATINE). If those are your notions, you ought to join the order of Béguines—you know—there's some such organization . . .

SATINE. I know—grandfather—and they're no fools . . .

[NATASHA *is heard screaming behind* KOS-TILYOFF'S *window: "What for? Stop!* 10 *What have I done?"*]

LUKA (*worried*). Natasha! That was she crying—oh, God . . .

[*From* KOSTILYOFF'S *room is heard noise, shuffling, breaking of crockery, and* KOS-TILYOFF'S *shrill cry: "Ah! Heretic! Bitch!"*]

VASSILISA. Wait, wait—I'll teach her—there, there!

NATASHA. They're beating me—killing 20 me . . .

SATINE (*shouts through the window*). Hey—you there— . . .

LUKA (*trembling*). Where's Vassily—? Call Vaska—oh, God—listen, brothers . . .

THE ACTOR (*running out*). I'll find him at once!

BUBNOFF. They beat her a lot these days . . .

SATINE. Come on, old man—we'll be witnesses . . .

LUKA (*following* SATINE). Oh—witnesses —what for? Vassily—he should be called at once!

NATASHA. Sister—sister dear! Va-a-a . . .

BUBNOFF. They've gagged her—I'll go and see . . .

[*The noise in* KOSTILYOFF'S *room dies down* 40 *gradually as if they had gone into the hallway. The old man's cry: "Stop!" is heard. A door is slammed noisily, and the latter sound cuts off all the other noises sharply. Quiet on the stage. Twilight.*]

KLESHTCH (*seated on the sledge, indiffer-*

ently, rubbing his hands; mutters at first indistinguishably, then). What then? One must live. (*Louder.*) Must have shelter—well? There's no shelter, no roof—nothing . . . there's only man —man alone—no hope . . . no help . . .

[*Exit slowly, his head bent. A few moments of ominous silence, then somewhere in the hallway a mass of sounds, which grows in volume and comes nearer. Individual voices are heard.*]

VASSILISA. I'm her sister—let go . . .

KOSTILYOFF. What right have you . . .?

VASSILISA. Jail-bird!

SATINE. Call Vaska—quickly! Zob—hit him!

[*A police whistle. The* TARTAR *runs in, his right hand in a sling.*]

THE TARTAR. There's a new law for you —kill only in daytime!

[*Enter* ZOB, *followed by* MIEDVIEDIEFF.]

ZOB. I handed him a good one!

MIEDVIEDIEFF. You—how dare you fight?

THE TARTAR. What about yourself? What's your duty?

MIEDVIEDIEFF (*running after*). Stop—give back my whistle!

KOSTILYOFF (*runs in*). Abram! Stop him! Hold him! He's a murderer—he . . .

[*Enter* KVASHNYA *and* NASTYA *supporting* NATASHA *who is disheveled.* SATINE *backs away, pushing away* VASSILISA *who is trying to attack her sister, while, near her,* ALYOSHKA *jumps up and down like a madman, whistles into her ear, shrieking, roaring. Also other ragged men and women.*]

SATINE (*to* VASSILISA). Well—you damned bitch!

VASSILISA. Let go, you jail-bird! I'll tear you to pieces—if I have to pay for it with my own life!

KVASHNYA (*leading* NATASHA *aside*). You Karpovna—that's enough—stand back—aren't you ashamed? Or are you crazy?

MIEDVIEDIEFF (*seizes* SATINE). Aha— caught at last!

SATINE. Zob—beat them up! Vaska— Vaska . . .

[*They all, in a chaotic mass, struggle near the brick wall. They lead* NATASHA *to the right, and set her on a pile of wood.* PEPEL *rushes in from the hallway and, silently, with powerful movements, pushes the crowd aside.*]

PEPEL. Natalia, where are you . . . you . . .

KOSTILYOFF (*disappearing behind a corner*). Abram! Seize Vaska! Comrades— help us get him! The thief! The rob- ber!

PEPEL. You—you old bastard! (*Aiming a terrific blow at* KOSTILYOFF. KOSTILYOFF *falls so that only the upper part of his body is seen.* PEPEL *rushes to* NA- TASHA.)

VASSILISA. Beat Vaska! Brothers! Beat the thief!

MIEDVIEDIEFF (*yells to* SATINE). Keep out of this—it's a family affair . . . they're relatives—and who are you? . . .

PEPEL (*to* NATASHA). What did she do to you? She used a knife?

KVASHNYA. God—what beasts! They've scalded the child's feet with boiling water!

NASTYA. They overturned the samo- var . . .

THE TARTAR. Maybe an accident—you must make sure—you can't exactly tell . . .

NATASHA (*half fainting*). Vassily—take me away—

VASSILISA. Good people! Come! Look! He's dead! Murdered!

[*All crowd into the hallway near* KOSTILYOFF. BUBNOFF *leaves the crowd and crosses to* PEPEL.]

BUBNOFF (*in a low voice, to* PEPEL). Vaska —the old man is done for!

PEPEL (*looks at him, as though he does not understand*). Go—for help—she must be taken to the hospital . . . I'll set- tle with them . . .

BUBNOFF. I say—the old man—some- body's killed him . . .

[*The noise on the stage dies out like a fire under water. Distinct, whispered exclama- tions: "Not really?" "Well—let's go away, brothers!" "The devil!" "Hold on now!" "Let's get away before the police come!" The crowd disappears.* BUBNOFF, *the* TARTAR, NASTYA, *and* KVASHNYA, *rush up to* KOSTILYOFF'S *body.*]

VASSILISA (*rises and cries out triumphantly*). Killed—my husband's killed! Vaska killed him! I saw him! Brothers, I saw him! Well—Vasya—the po- lice!

PEPEL (*moves away from* NATASHA). Let me alone. (*Looks at* KOSTILYOFF; *to* VASSILISA.) Well—are you glad? (*Touches the corpse with his foot.*) The old bastard is dead! Your wish has been granted! Why not do the same to you? (*Throws himself at her.*)

[SATINE *and* ZOB *quickly overpower him, and* VASSILISA *disappears in the passage.*]

SATINE. Come to your senses!

ZOB. Hold on! Not so fast!

VASSILISA (*appearing*). Well, Vaska, dear friend? You can't escape your fate. . . . police—Abram—whistle!

MIEDVIEDIEFF. Those devils tore my whistle off!

ALYOSHKA. Here it is! (*Whistles,* MIEDVIE- DIEFF *runs after him.*)

SATINE (*leading* PEPEL *to* NATASHA). Don't be afraid, Vaska! Killed in a row! That's nonsense—only manslaughter —you won't have to serve a long term . . .

VASSILISA. Hold Vaska—he killed him— I saw it!

SATINE. I, too, gave the old man a couple of blows—he was easily fixed . . . you call me as witness, Vaska!

PEPEL. I don't need to defend myself . . . I want to drag Vassilisa into this mess—and I'll do it—she was the one who wanted it . . . she was the one who urged me to kill him—she goaded me on . . .

NATASHA (*sudden and loud*). Oh—I understand—so that's it, Vassily? Good people! They're both guilty—my sister and he—they're both guilty! They had it all planned! So, Vassily, that's why you spoke to me a while ago—so that she should overhear everything—? Good people! She's his mistress—you know it—everybody knows it—they're both guilty! She—she urged him to kill her husband—he was in their way—and so was I! And now they've maimed me . . .

PEPEL. Natalia! What's the matter with you? What are you saying?

SATINE. Oh—hell!

VASSILISA. You lie. She lies. He—Vaska killed him . . .

NATASHA. They're both guilty! God damn you both!

SATINE. What a mix-up! Hold on, Vassily—or they'll ruin you between them!

ZOB. I can't understand it—oh—what a mess!

PEPEL. Natalia! It can't be true! Surely you don't believe that I—with her—

SATINE. So help me God, Natasha! Just think . . .

VASSILISA (*in the passage*). They've killed my husband—Your Excellency! Vaska Pepel, the thief, killed him, Captain! I saw it—everybody saw it . . .

NATASHA (*tossing about in agony; her mind wandering*). Good people—my sister and Vaska killed him! The police—listen—this sister of mine—here—she urged, coaxed her lover—there he stands—the scoundrel! They both killed him! Put them in jail! Bring them before the judge! Take me along, too! To prison! Christ Almighty—take me to prison, too!

CURTAIN

ACT IV

Same as Act I. But PEPEL'S *room is no longer there, and the partition has been removed. Furthermore, there is no anvil at the place where* KLESHTCH *used to sit and work. In the corner, where* PEPEL'S *room used to be, the* TARTAR *lies stretched out, rather restless, and groaning from time to time.* KLESHTCH *sits at one end of the table, repairing a concertina and now and then testing the stops. At the other end of the table sit* SATINE, *the* BARON, *and* NASTYA. *In front of them stand a bottle of vodka, three bottles of beer, and a large loaf of black bread. The* ACTOR *lies on top of the stove, shifting about and coughing. It is night. The stage is lit by a lamp in the middle of the table. Outside the wind howls.*

KLESHTCH. Yes . . . he disappeared during the confusion and noise . . .

THE BARON. He vanished under the very eyes of the police—just like a puff of smoke . . .

SATINE. That's how sinners flee from the company of the righteous!

NASTYA. He was a dear old soul! But you—you aren't men—you're just—oh—like rust on iron!

THE BARON (*drinks*). Here's to you, my lady!

SATINE. He was an inquisitive old fellow—yes! Nastenka here fell in love with him . . .

NASTYA. Yes! I did! Madly! It's true! He saw everything—understood everything . . .

SATINE (*laughing*). Yes, generally speaking, I would say that he was—oh—like mush to those who can't chew. . . .

THE BARON (*laughing*). Right! Like plaster on a boil!

KLESHTCH. He was merciful—you people don't know what pity means . . .

SATINE. What good can I do you by pitying you?

KLESHTCH. You needn't have pity—but you needn't harm or offend your fellow-beings, either!

THE TARTAR (*sits up on his bunk, nursing his wounded hand carefully*). He was a fine old man. The law of life was the law of his heart. . . . and he who obeys this law, is good, while he who disregards it, perishes . . .

THE BARON. What law, Prince?

THE TARTAR. There are a number—different ones—you know . . .

THE BARON. Proceed!

THE TARTAR. Do not do harm unto others—such is the law!

SATINE. Oh—you mean the Penal Code, criminal and correctional, eh?

THE BARON. And also the Code of Penalties inflicted by Justices of the Peace!

THE TARTAR. No. I mean the Koran. It is the supreme law—and your own soul ought to be the Koran—yes!

KLESHTCH (*testing his concertina*). It wheezes like all hell! But the Prince speaks the truth—one must live abiding by the law—by the teachings of the Gospels . . .

SATINE. Well—go ahead and do it!

THE BARON. Just try it!

THE TARTAR. The Prophet Mohammed gave to us the law. He said: "Here is the law! Do as it is written therein!" Later on a time will arrive when the Koran will have outlived its purpose—and time will bring forth its own laws—every generation will create its own . . .

SATINE. To be sure! Time passed on—and gave us—the Criminal Code . . . It's a strong law, brother—it won't wear off so very soon!

NASTYA (*banging her glass on the table*). Why—why do I stay here—with you? I'll go away somewhere—to the ends of the world!

THE BARON. Without any shoes, my lady?

NASTYA. I'll go—naked, if must be—creeping on all fours!

THE BARON. That'll be rather picturesque, my lady—on all fours!

NASTYA. Yes—and I'll crawl if I have to—anything at all—as long as I don't have to see your faces any longer—oh, I'm so sick of it all—the life—the people—everything!

SATINE. When you go, please take the actor along—he's preparing to go to the very same place—he has learned that within a half mile's distance of the end of the world there's a hospital for diseased organons . . .

THE ACTOR (*raising his head over the top of the stove*). A hospital for organisms—you fool!

SATINE. For organons—poisoned with vodka!

THE ACTOR. Yes! He will go! He will indeed! You'll see!

THE BARON. Who is he, sir?

THE ACTOR. I!

THE BARON. Thanks, servant of the goddess—what's her name—? The goddess of drama—tragedy—whatever is her name—?

THE ACTOR. The muse, idiot! Not the goddess—the muse!

ATINE. Lachesis—Hera—Aphrodite—Atropos—oh! To hell with them all! You see—Baron—it was the old man who stuffed the actor's head full with this rot . . .

THE BARON. Tht old maan's a fool . . .

THE ACTOR. Ignoramuses! Beasts! Melpomene—that's her name! Heartless brutes! Bastards! You'll see! He'll go! "On with the orgy, dismal spirits!"—10 poem—ah—by Béranger! Yes—he'll find some spot where there's no—no . . .

THE BARON. Where there's nothing, sir?

THE ACTOR. Right! Nothing! "This hole shall be my grave—I am dying—ill and exhausted . . ." Why do you exist? Why?

THE BARON. You! God or genius or orgy—or whatever you are—don't roar so 20 loud!

THE ACTOR. You lie! I'll roar all I want to!

NASTYA (lifting her head from the table and throwing up her hands). Go on! Yell! Let them listen to you!

THE BARON. Where is the sense, my lady?

SATINE. Leave them alone, Baron! To hell with the lot! Let them yell—let them knock their damned heads off if 30 they feel like it! There's a method in their madness! Don't you go and interfere with people as that old fellow did! Yes—it's he—the damned old fool—he bewitched the whole gang of us!

KLESHTCH. He persuaded them to go away—but failed to show them the road . . .

THE BARON. That old man was a hum- 40 bug!

NASTYA. Liar! You're a humbug yourself!

THE BARON. Shut up, my lady!

KLESHTCH. The old man didn't like truth very much—as a matter of fact he strongly resented it—and wasn't he right, though? Just look—where is there any truth? And yet, without it, you can't breathe! For instance, our Tartar Prince over there, crushed his hand at his work—and now he'll have to have his arm amputated—and there's the truth for you!

SATINE (striking the table with his clenched fist). Shut up! You sons of bitches! Fools! Not another word about that old fellow! (To the BARON.) You, Baron, are the worst of the lot! You don't understand a thing, and you lie like the devil! The old man's no humbug! What's the truth? Man! Man—that's the truth! He understood man—you don't! You're all as dumb as stones! I understand the old man—yes! He lied—but lied out of sheer pity for you . . . God damn you! Lots of people lie out of pity for their fellow-beings! I know! I've read about it! They lie—oh—beautifully, inspiringly, stirringly! Some lies bring comfort, and others bring peace—a lie alone can justify the burden which crushed a workman's hand and condemns those who are starving! I know what lying means! The weakling and the one who is a parasite through his very weakness—they both need lies—lies are their support, their shield, their armor! But the man who is strong, who is his own master, who is free and does not have to suck his neighbors' blood—he needs no lies! To lie—it's the creed of slaves and masters of slaves! Truth is the religion of the free man!

THE BARON. Bravo! Well spoken! Hear, hear! I agree! You speak like an honest man!

SATINE. And why can't a crook at times speak the truth—since honest people at times speak like crooks? Yes—I've forgotten a lot—but I still know a thing or two! The old man? Oh—he's wise! He affected me as acid affects a dirty old silver coin! Let's drink to his health! Fill the glasses . . . (NASTYA *fills a glass with beer and hands it to* SATINE, *who laughs.*) The old man lives within himself . . . he looks upon all the world from his own angle. Once I asked him: "Grand-dad, why do people live?" (*Tries to imitate* LUKA'S *voice and gestures.*) And he replied: "Why, my dear fellow, people live in the hope of something better! For example—let's say there are carpenters in this world, and all sorts of trash . . . people . . . and they give birth to a carpenter the like of which has never been seen upon the face of the earth . . . he's way above everybody else, and has no equal among carpenters! The brilliancy of his personality was reflected on all his trade, on all the other carpenters, so that they advanced twenty years in one day! This applies to all other trades—blacksmiths and shoemakers and other workmen—and all the peasants —and even the aristocrats live in the hopes of a higher life! Each individual thinks that he's living for his own self, but in reality he lives in the hope of something better. A hundred years—sometimes longer—do we expect, live for the finer, higher life . . ." (NASTYA *stares intently into* SATINE'S *face.* KLESHTCH *stops working and listens. The* BARON *bows his head very low, drumming softly on the table with his fingers. The* ACTOR, *peering down from the stove, tries to climb noiselessly into the bunk.*) "Every one, brothers, every one lives in the hope of something better. That's why we must respect each and every human being! How do we know who he

is, why he was born, and what he is capable of accomplishing? Perhaps his coming into the world will prove to be our good fortune . . . Especially must we respect little children! Children—need freedom! Don't interfere with their lives! Respect children!" (*Pause.*)

THE BARON (*thoughtfully*). Hm—yes—something better?—That reminds me of my family . . . an old family dating back to the time of Catherine . . . all noblemen, soldiers, originally French—they served their country and gradually rose higher and higher. In the days of Nicholas the First my grandfather, Gustave DeBille, held a high post—riches—hundreds of serfs . . . horses—cooks—

NASTYA. You liar! It isn't true!

THE BARON (*jumping up*). What? Well—go on—

NASTYA. It isn't true.

THE BARON (*screams*). A house in Moscow! A house in Petersburg! Carriages! Carriages with coats of arms!

[KLESHTCH *takes his concertina and goes to one side, watching the scene with interest.*]

NASTYA. You lie!

THE BARON. Shut up!—I say—dozens of footmen . . .

NASTYA (*delighted*). You lie!

THE BARON. I'll kill you!

NASTYA (*ready to run away*). There were no carriages!

SATINE. Stop, Nastenka! Don't infuriate him!

THE BARON. Wait—you bitch! My grandfather . . .

NASTYA. There was no grandfather! There was nothing!

[SATINE *roars with laughter.*]

THE BARON (*worn out with rage, sits down on bench*). Satine! Tell that slut—what—? You, too, are laughing? You

—don't believe me either? (*Cries out in despair, pounding the table with his fists.*) It's true—damn the whole lot of you!

NASTYA (*triumphantly*). So—you're crying? Understand now what a human being feels like when nobody believes him?

KLESHTCH (*returning to the table*). I thought there'd be a fight . . .

THE TARTAR. Oh—people are fools! It's too bad . . .

THE BARON. I shall not permit any one to ridicule me! I have proofs—documents—damn you!

SATINE. Forget it! Forget about your grandfather's carriages! You can't drive anywhere in a carriage of the past!

THE BARON. How dare she—just the same—?

NASTYA. Just imagine! How dare I—?

SATINE. You see—she does dare! How is she any worse than you are? Although, surely, in her past there wasn't even a father and mother, let alone carriages and a grandfather . . .

THE BARON (*quieting down*). Devil take you—you do know how to argue dispassionately—and I, it seems—I've no will-power . . .

SATINE. Acquire some—it's useful . . . (*Pause.*) Nastya! Are you going to the hospital?

NASTYA. What for?

SATINE. To see Natasha.

NASTYA. Oh—just woke up, did you? She's been out of the hospital for some time—and they can't find a trace of her . . .

SATINE. Oh—that woman's a goner!

KLESHTCH. It's interesting to see whether Vaska will get the best of Vassilisa, or the other way around—?

NASTYA. Vassilisa will win out! She's shrewd! And Vaska will go to the gallows!

SATINE. For manslaughter? No—only to jail . . .

NASTYA. Too bad—the gallows would have been better . . . that's where all of you should be sent . . . swept off into a hole—like filth . . .

SATINE (*astonished*). What's the matter? Are you crazy?

THE BARON. Oh—give her a wallop—that'll teach her to be less impertinent . . .

NASTYA. Just you try to touch me!

THE BARON. I shall!

SATINE. Stop! Don't insult her! I can't get the thought of the old man out of my head! (*Roars with laugher.*) Don't offend your fellow-beings! Suppose I were offended once in such a way that I'd remember it for the rest of my life? What then? Should I forgive? No, no!

THE BARON (*to* NASTYA). You must understand that I'm not your sort . . . you—ah—you piece of dirt!

NASTYA. You bastard! Why—you live off me like a worm off an apple!

[*The men laugh amusedly.*]

KLESHTCH. Fool! An apple—?

THE BARON. You can't be angry with her—she's just an ass—

NASTYA. You laugh! Liars? Don't strike you as funny, eh?

THE ACTOR (*morosely*). Give them a good beating!

NASTYA. If I only could! (*Takes a cup from the table and throws it on the floor.*) That's what I'd like to do to you all!

THE TARTAR. Why break dishes—eh—silly girl?

THE BARON (*rising*). That'll do! I'll teach her manners in half a second!

NASTYA (*running toward door*). Go to hell!

SATINE (*calling after her*). Hey! That's enough! Whom are you trying to frighten? What's all the row about, anyway?

NASTYA. Dogs! I hope you'll croak! Dogs! (*Runs out.*)

THE ACTOR (*morosely*). Amen!

THE TARTAR. Allah! Mad women, these Russians! They're bold, wilful; Tartar women aren't like that! They know the law and abide by it. . . .

KLESHTCH. She ought to be given a sound hiding!

THE BARON. The slut!

KLESHTCH (*testing the concertina*). It's ready! But its owner isn't here yet— that young fellow is burning his life away . . .

SATINE. Care for a drink—now?

KLESHTCH. Thanks . . . it's time to go to bed . . .

SATINE. Getting used to us?

KLESHTCH (*drinks, then goes to his bunk*). It's all right . . . there are people everywhere—at first you don't notice it . . . but after a while you don't mind. . . .

[*The* TARTAR *spreads some rags over his bunk, then kneels on them and prays.*]

THE BARON (*to* SATINE, *pointing at the* TARTAR). Look!

SATINE. Stop! He's a good fellow! Leave him alone! (*Roars with laughter.*) I feel kindly to-day—the devil alone knows the reason why . . .

THE BARON. You always feel kindly when you're drunk—you're even wiser at such times . . .

SATINE. When I'm drunk? Yes—then I like everything—right—He prays? That's fine! A man may believe or not—that's his own affair—a man is free—he pays for everything himself —belief or unbelief—love—wisdom . . . a man pays for everything —and that's just why he's free! Man is—truth! And what is man? It's neither you nor I nor they—oh, no—it's you and they and I and the old man —and Napoleon—Mohammed—all in one! (*Outlines vaguely in the air the contour of a human being.*) Do you understand? It's tremendous! It contains the beginning and the end of everything—everything is in man— and everything exists for him! Man alone exists—everything else is the creation of his hands and his brain! Man! It is glorious! It sounds—oh— so big! Man must be respected—not degraded with pity—but respected, respected! Let us drink to man, Baron! (*Rises.*) It is good to feel that you are a man! I'm a convict, a murderer, a crook—granted!—When I'm out on the street people stare at me as if I were a scoundrel—they draw away from me—they look after me and often they say: "You dog! You humbug! Work!" Work? And what for? to fill my belly? (*Roars with laughter.*) I've always despised people who worry too much about their bellies. It isn't right, Baron! It isn't! Man is loftier than that! Man stands above hunger!

THE BARON. You—reason things out. . . . Well and good—it brings you a certain amount of consolation. . . . Personally I'm incapable of it . . . I don't know how. (*Glances around him and then, softly, guardedly.*) Brother—I am afraid—at times. Do you understand? Afraid!—Because— what next?

SATINE. Rot! What's a man to be afraid of?

THE BARON (*pacing up and down*). You know—as far back as I can remember, there's been a sort of fog in my brain. I was never able to understand anything. Somehow I feel embarrassed—it seems to me that all my life I've done nothing but change clothes

—and why? I don't understand! I studied—I wore the uniform of the Institute for the Sons of the Nobility . . . but what have I learned? I don't remember! I married—I wore a frock-coat—then a dressing-gown . . . but I chose a disagreeable wife . . . and why? I don't understand. I squandered everything that I possessed—I wore some sort of a grey jacket and brick-colored trousers—but how did I happen to ruin myself? I haven't the slightest idea. . . . I had a position in the Department of State. . . . I wore a uniform and a cap with insignia of rank. . . . I embezzled government funds . . . so they dressed me in a convict's garb—and later on I got into these clothes here—and it all happened as in a dream—it's funny . . .

SATINE. Not very! It's rather—silly!

THE BARON. Yes—silly! I think so, too. Still—wasn't I born for some sort of purpose?

SATINE (*laughing*). Probably—a man is born to conceive a better man. (*Shaking his head.*)—It's all right!

THE BARON. That she-devil Nastya! Where did she run to? I'll go and see —after all, she . . . (*Exit; pause.*)

THE ACTOR. Tartar! (*Pause.*) Prince! (*The* TARTAR *looks round.*) Say a prayer for me . . .

THE TARTAR. What?

THE ACTOR (*softly*). Pray—for me!

THE TARTAR (*after a silence*). Pray for your own self!

THE ACTOR (*quickly crawls off the stove and goes to the table, pours out a drink with shaking hands, drinks, then almost runs to passage*). All over!

SATINE. Hey, proud Sicambrian! Where are you going?

[SATINE *whistles.* MIEDVIEDIEFF *enters, dressed in a woman's flannel shirtwaist; followed by* BUBNOFF. *Both are slightly drunk.* BUBNOFF *carries a bunch of pretzels in one hand, a couple of smoked fish in the other, a bottle of vodka under one arm, another bottle in his coat pocket.*]

MIEDVIEDIEFF. A camel is something like a donkey—only it has no ears. . . .

BUBNOFF. Shut up! You're a variety of donkey yourself!

MIEDVIEDIEFF. A camel has no ears at all, at all—it hears through its nostrils . . .

BUBNOFF (*to* SATINE). Friend! I've looked for you in all the saloons and all the cabarets! Take this bottle—my hands are full . . .

SATINE. Put the pretzels on the table—then you'll have one hand free—

BUBNOFF. Right! Hey—you donkey—look! Isn't he a clever fellow?

MIEDVIEDIEFF. All crooks are clever—I know! They couldn't do a thing without brains. An honest man is all right even if he's an idiot . . . but a crook must have brains. But, speaking about camels, you're wrong . . . you can ride them—they have no horns . . . and no teeth either . . .

BUBNOFF. Where's everybody? Why is there no one here? Come on out . . . I treat! Who's in the corner?

SATINE. How soon will you drink up everything you have? Scarecrow!

BUBNOFF. Very soon! I've very little this time. Zob—where's Zob?

KLESHTCH (*crossing to table*). He isn't here . . .

BUBNOFF. Waughrr! Bull-dog! Brr-zz-zz! —Turkey-cock! Don't bark and don't growl! Drink—make merry—and don't be sullen!—I treat everybody—Brother, I love to treat—if I were rich, I'd run a free saloon! So help me God, I would! With an orchestra and a lot of singers! Come, every one! Drink and eat—listen to the music—

and rest in peace! Beggars—come, all
you beggars—and enter my saloon
free of charge! Satine—you can have
half my capital—just like that!

SATINE. You better give me all you have
straight away!

BUBNOFF. All my capital? Right now?
Well—here's a ruble—here's twenty
kopecks—five kopecks—sun-flower
seeds—and that's all!

SATINE. That's splendid! It'll be safer
with me—I'll gamble with it . . .

MIEDVIEDIEFF. I'm a witness—the money
was given you for safe-keeping. How
much is it?

BUBNOFF. You? You're a camel—we
don't need witnesses . . .

ALYOSHKA (comes in barefoot). Brothers,
I got my feet wet!

BUBNOFF. Go on and get your throat wet
—and nothing'll happen—you're a
fine fellow—you sing and you play—
that's all right! But it's too bad you
drink—drink, little brother, is harmful, very harmful . . .

ALYOSHKA. I judge by you! Only when
you're drunk do you resemble a human being . . . Kleshtch! Is my
concertina fixed? (Sings and dances.)
"If my mug were not so attractive,
My sweetheart wouldn't love me at
all . . ."
Boys, I'm frozen—it's cold . . .

MIEDVIEDIEFF. Hm—and may I ask
who's this sweetheart?

BUBNOFF. Shut up! From now on,
brother, you are neither a policeman
nor an uncle!

ALYOSHKA. Just auntie's husband!

BUBNOFF. One of your nieces is in jail—
the other one's dying . . .

MIEDVIEDIEFF (proudly). You lie! She's
not dying—she disappeared—without trace . . . (SATINE roars.)

BUBNOFF. All the same, brothers—a man
without nieces isn't an uncle!

ALYOSHKA. Your Excellency! Listen to
the drummer of the retired billy-
goats' brigade! (Sings.)
"My sweetheart has money,
I haven't a cent.
But I'm a cheerful,
Merry lad!"
Oh—isn't it cold!

[Enter ZOB. From now until the final curtain
men and women drift in, undress, and
stretch out on the bunks, grumbling.]

ZOB. Bubnoff! Why did you run off?

BUBNOFF. Come here—sit down—
brother, let's sing my favorite ditty,
eh?

THE TARTAR. Night was made for sleep!
Sing your songs in the daytime!

SATINE. Well—never mind, Prince—
come here!

THE TARTAR. What do you mean—
never mind? There's going to be a
noise—there always is when people
sing!

BUBNOFF (crossing to the TARTAR). Count
—ah—I mean Prince—how's your
hand? Did they cut it off?

THE TARTAR. What for? We'll wait and
see—perhaps it won't be necessary . . . a hand isn't made of iron—
it won't take long to cut it off . . .

ZOB. It's your own affair, Hassanka!
You'll be good for nothing without
your hand. We're judged by our
hands and backs—without the pride
of your hand, you're no longer a human being. Tobacco-carting—that's
your business! Come on—have a
drink of vodka—and stop worrying!

KVASHNYA (comes in). Ah, my beloved
fellow-lodgers! It's horrible outside—
snow and slush . . . is my policeman
here?

MIEDVIEDIEFF. Right here!

KVASHNYA. Wearing my blouse again?
And drunk, eh? What's the idea?

MIEDVIEDIEFF. In celebration of Bubnoff's birthday . . . besides, it's cold . . .

KVASHNYA. Better look out—stop fooling about and go to sleep!

MIEDVIEDIEFF (*goes to kitchen*). Sleep? I can—I want to—it's time—(*Exit.*)

SATINE. What's the matter? Why are you so strict with him?

KVASHNYA. You can't be otherwise, friend. You have to be strict with his sort. I took him as a partner. I thought he'd be of some benefit to me—because he's a military man—and you're a rough lot . . . and I am a woman—and now he's turned drunkard—that won't do at all!

SATINE. You picked a good one for partner!

KVASHNYA. Couldn't get a better one. You wouldn't want to live with me . . . you think you're too fine! And even if you did it wouldn't last more than a week . . . you'd gamble me and all I own away at cards!

SATINE (*roars with laughter*). That's true, landlady—I'd gamble . . .

KVASHNYA. Yes, yes. Alyoshka!

ALYOSHKA. Here he is—I, myself!

KVASHNYA. What do you mean by gossiping about me?

ALYOSHKA. I? I speak out everything—whatever my conscience tells me. There, I say, is a wonderful woman! Splendid meat, fat, bones—over four hundred pounds! But brains—? Not an ounce!

KVASHNYA. You're a liar! I've a lot of brains! What do you mean by saying I beat my policeman?

ALYOSHKA. I thought you did—when you pulled him by the hair!

KVASHNYA (*laughs*). You fool! You aren't blind, are you? Why wash dirty linen in public? And—it hurts his feelings—that's why he took to drink . . .

ALYOSHKA. It's true, evidently, that even a chicken likes vodka . . . (SATINE *and* KLESHTCH *roar with laughter.*)

KVASHNYA. Go on—show your teeth! What sort of a man are you anyway, Alyoshka?

ALYOSHKA. Oh—I am first-rate! Master of all trades! I follow my nose!

BUBNOFF (*near the* TARTAR'S *bunk*). Come on! At all events—we won't let you sleep! We'll sing all night. Zob!

ZOB. Sing—? All right . . .

ALYOSHKA. And I'll play . . .

SATINE. We'll listen!

THE TARTAR (*smiling*). Well—Bubnoff—you devil—bring the vodka—we'll drink—we'll have a hell of a good time! The end will come soon enough —and then we'll be dead!

BUBNOFF. Fill his glass, Satine! Zob—sit down! Ah—brothers—what does a man need after all? There, for instance, I've had a drink—and I'm happy! Zob! Start my favorite song! I'll sing—and then I'll cry. . . .

ZOB (*begins to sing*).
"The sun rises and sets . . ."

BUBNOFF (*joining in*).
"But my prison is all dark . . . ."
[*Door opens quickly.*]

THE BARON (*on the threshold; yells*). Hey—you—come—come here! Out in the waste—in the yard . . . over there . . . The actor—he's hanged himself. . . .

[*Silence. All stare at the* BARON. *Behind him appears* NASTYA, *and slowly, her eyes wide with horror, she walks to the table.*]

SATINE (*in a matter-of-fact voice*). Damned fool—he ruined the song . . . !

CURTAIN

EDMOND ROSTAND

EDMOND ROSTAND died of influenza on December 2, 1918, just three weeks after the frenzied celebration of the Armistice which he had prayed he might live to see. Ill though he was, he had summoned his failing strength to join the hysterical throngs shouting in the streets of Paris. As that gay and victorious city honored him with an imposing funeral, even the lowliest Parisian on the boulevard knew that the French capital was paying homage to the author of the most popular and best loved play in France, the incomparable *Cyrano de Bergerac*. A score of cataclysmic years had passed since it was first presented, but its popularity continued; another two decades and more have gone by, and its vitality is undiminished, its plume erect. *Cyrano* is *de rigueur* in the history and the library of modern drama.

Cyrano de Bergerac stormed and captured Paris when it was first presented at the Théâtre de la Porte Saint-Martin on the night of December 28, 1897. The ecstatic audience rose to its feet at the close of each of the five acts and cheered for minutes on end. Its triumph was even greater than the two other supreme moments in the French theatre: the presentation of Corneille's *The Cid* at the Hôtel de Bourgogne in 1636 (when the real Cyrano, by the way, was a great boy of seventeen years), and Hugo's *Hernani* which, in 1830, caused a pitched battle in the pit between the conservative and the romantic literary factions. The play, shrewdly advertized well in advance, was acted by the reigning idol of the Paris stage, Benoit Constant

Coquelin of the romantic gestures and the orchestral voice trained for the poetic flights of a Cyrano. Its presentation was also admirably timed. The naturalistic plays, like *The Power of Darkness, Before Sunrise, Ghosts*, etc., had monopolized critical discussion and their champions had announced the demise of moribund romanticism. André Antoine at his Théâtre Libre had for ten years kept these plays of human miseries, degeneracies, crimes, and social problems before the public while the enemies raged against their picture of life and their degradation of the stage. The romantic tradition, however, always manages to elude the grave prepared for it from time to time by the realists. The rich imagination that produced *Faust* in one age, and *Peer Gynt* in another, only abided its time to reappear. The coming together of Rostand, Coquelin, and a hospitable public provided the right combination at the right moment, but the agent of the coalescence, the romantic drama *Cyrano de Bergerac*, proved to be not only for the moment but for the years.

It was written especially for Coquelin by a frail young man nearing thirty who was known only to a very limited art circle in the cliquish Paris of the 1890's. Rostand had been born at Marseilles, April 1, 1868, in a family of repute in journalism, finance, and economics. He had gone to the Lycée de Marseilles, had studied law at the Collège Stanislas in Paris, and had been admitted to the bar, but had immediately given up law for letters. At the age of twenty he had written and had produced his first play, *The Red Glove*. At twenty-two he had published a little volume of poems in the mode of the time, *Les Musardises;* and at twenty-three he had produced another amateurish play, *The Two Pierrots*. His extravagant drama on romantic love, *The Romancers*, had won some success at the Comédie Française, and the Toirac prize in 1894. His *The Princess Faraway* had told in an engaging manner the old legend of the twelfth century Provencal poet, Jaufré Rudel, who, at the mere report of her beauty, fell in love with the Countess of Tripoli whom he had never seen, and sailed promptly away to Syria where he died in her arms. It was written for Sarah Bernhardt and was produced on April 5, 1895. He had followed this success with another play for Bernhardt, *La Samaritaine*, an unfortunate excursion into the story of Jesus and the woman of Samaria, presented in April, 1897.

This was Rostand's modest background of accomplishment when *Cyrano* made its sensational hit. Coquelin, in an account of his first association with the dramatist, tells how he reluctantly took a moment out of his busy life to go to Sarah Bernhardt's hotel on her insistence to hear Rostand read *The Princess Faraway*. He was even more impressed by Rostand and his reading than with the play itself. He walked home afterwards with Rostand, talking with him about his work and his ambitions. At Rostand's door, Coquelin impulsively exclaimed: "In my opinion, you are destined to become the greatest dramatic poet of the age; I bind myself here and now to take any play you write (in which there is a part for me) without reading it, to cancel any engagements I may have on hand, and produce your piece with the least possible delay." After that flattering, and no doubt breathtaking, offer and invitation nothing remained to the still obscure young dramatist except to do a play worthy of the great actor who had so confidently committed himself.

Rostand happily hit upon the intriguing life and character of that noble Gascon poet and dramatist of the Seventeenth Century, Savinien Cyrano de Bergerac (1619–1655). Cyrano in his turbulent youth had fought hundreds of duels over insults to his prodigious nose. He was wounded at the siege of Arras when he was twenty-one, and spent most of the rest of his short life in writing and in the study of philosophy and physics. He was meanly cut down at the age of thirty-six by a knock on the head with a piece of wood that somehow or other (Rostand selects murder by a lackey) fell from a window under which he was passing one night on his way home. The man himself, virile, gay, quick to a quarrel and dexterous with his sword, physically ugly to the ludicrous, but at heart gentle, unselfish, and honorable in the extreme, was ready-made for Rostand's purpose; he needed but a slight exaggeration and idealization of his natural traits to make him into a captivating romantic hero. Rostand had only to reproduce accurately the picturesque times of the first half of the Seventeenth Century to provide his play with its irresistible atmosphere and to create for his hero a worthy stage.

That Rostand succeeded has never been a subject for debate. The only question seems to have been what superlatives would best apply. Clayton Hamilton, who as a youth could hardly wait for the boat to bring over a copy of the text after Coquelin's triumph, who read the play in French to a crowd of homesick and cheering Frenchmen in a café on Sixth Avenue, who attended every performance by Coquelin and Bernhardt during their first week in New York in 1900, and who persuaded Walter Hampden to revive it for post-War audiences, won the crown. After nearly a quarter of a century of devotion to *Cyrano*, he still called it "the most intoxicating play of modern times, . . . the most entrancing and contagious play that had ever yet been shown at any time on any stage." These extravagant responses help readers and spectators of a later generation better to understand the spirit of the fin-de-siècle world that went wild over this play.

Cyrano de Bergerac is a remarkable achievement, and easily maintains its high place in modern drama. It is tingling with life and action, with wit, pathos, and humor, in the large and expansive idiom of romance in the grand manner. Its verse is by turns gay and sparkling, richly sentimental and theatrical, sincere and moving. Splendorous is perhaps the best single word for this human and poetic outburst in an age of restricted naturalism. The action, concocted expressly for the theatre, but firmly rooted in its original sources, is continuously dominated by Cyrano. He wins everybody by the revelation of the heart of gold that beats behind the frame with its preposterous nasality. His speech is interwoven with words and phrases from the real Cyrano, and he is surrounded by the world of Molière. His brave, honest, generous spirit achieves greatness through the gesture of renunciation exalted in romantic fiction and cherished by the great Victorians. Unlike the passive victims in naturalistic tragedies, Cyrano, who had dreamed of a heroic death "with an honest sword in his heart," only to be killed "in a trap, from behind, by a lackey, with a log," rises to nobility in dying, carrying forth "unblemished and unbent" his white plume.

Rostand ever afterwards fed on the tremendous popularity of *Cyrano*. He wrote four more plays: *L'Aiglon* (1900), *Chantecler* (1910), *The Sacred Wood* (1910), and *Don Juan's Last Night* (1921). The first two have become a part of dramatic literature. *L'Aiglon* showed how the Duke of Reichstadt, son of Napoleon, was destroyed by the incompatible combination of the Napoleonic heart in the weak Hapsburg frame and spirit. As in naturalistic drama of the period, the hereditary and environmental elements are supreme, and when badly mixed in a poor Eaglet, the retort bursts. The devices of the play, however, the scene between the Duke and his Royal Austrian Grandfather, the melodrama of Flambeau and his decoration, the mirror scene with Metternich, the Wagram scene that so nearly approached expressionism, and the elaborate ending, are all in the extravagant manner of Rostand's romanticism. Actresses from Sarah Bernhardt and Maude Adams to Eva LaGallienne have taken satisfaction in playing the role of the effeminate young duke. *Chantecler* is a beast fable in the long tradition by which man's qualities are isolated and simplified by reproducing them in their nearest correspondent in the barn-lot. It is more deeply thought through than the more famous *Cyrano de Bergerac*. Rostand himself declared that *Chantecler* was "a poem rather than a play," and that Chantecler was a character "used to express my own dreams, and to make live, before my eyes, a little of myself."

Shortly after Bernhardt's production

of *L'Aiglon* in 1900, Rostand at the age of thirty-three was elected to the French Academy; he was the youngest man ever to be so honored. Ill health forced him to leave Paris; he lived the rest of his life for the most part in retirement at "Arnaga," his estate at Cambo-les-Bains, in the Basque country. Here under the shadow of the Pyrenees, he nursed his health, wrote very slowly, and amused himself by planning his garden and its walks, and looking at the mountains behind his pergolas hung with grapevines.

CYRANO DE BERGERAC

CHARACTERS

CYRANO DE BERGERAC	A SPECTATOR
CHRISTIAN DE NEUVILLETTE	A WATCHMAN
COMTE DE GUICHE	BERTRANDOU THE FIFER
RAGUENEAU	A CAPUCHIN
LE BRET	TWO MUSICIANS
CAPTAIN CARBON DE CASTEL-JALOUX	SEVEN CADETS
LIGNIÈRE	THREE MARQUISES
DE VALVERT	POETS
MONTFLEURY	PASTRYCOOKS
BELLEROSE	
JODELET	ROXANE
CUIGY	SISTER MARTHA
BRISSAILLE	LISE
A BORE	THE SWEETMEAT VENDER
A MOUSQUETAIRE	MOTHER MARGARET
OTHER MOUSQUETAIRE	THE DUENNA
A SPANISH OFFICER	SISTER CLAIRE
A LIGHT-CAVALRY MAN	AN ACTRESS
A DOORKEEPER	A SOUBRETTE
A BURGHER	A FLOWER-GIRL
HIS SON	PAGES
A PICKPOCKET	

The crowd, bourgeois, marquises, mousquetaires, pickpockets, pastrycooks, poets, Gascony Cadets, players, fiddlers, pages, children, Spanish soldiers, spectators, précieuses, actresses, bourgeoises, nuns, etc.

ACT I

A PLAY AT THE HOTEL DE BOURGOGNE

The great hall of the Hotel de Bourgogne, in 1640. A sort of tennis-court arranged and decorated for theatrical performances.

The hall is a long rectangle, seen obliquely, so that one side of it constitutes the background, which runs from the position of the front wing at the right, to the line of the furthest wing at the left, and forms an angle with the stage, which is equally seen obliquely.

This stage is furnished, on both sides, along the wings, with benches. The drop-curtain is composed of two tapestry hangings,

CYRANO DE BEGERAC: Translated from the French by Gertrude Hall. Copyright, 1898, 1926, by Doubleday, Doran & Company, Inc. Reprinted by permission of and special arrangement with Doubleday, Doran & Company, Inc.

which can be drawn apart. Above a harlequin cloak, the royal escutcheon. Broad steps lead from the raised platform of the stage into the house. On either side of these steps, the musicians' seats. A row of candles fills the office of footlights.

   Two galleries run along the side; the lower one is divided into boxes. No seats in the pit, which is the stage proper. At the back of the pit, that is to say, at the right, in the front, a few seats raised like steps, one above the other; and, under a stairway which leads to the upper seats, and of which the lower end only is visible, a stand decked with small candelabra, jars full of flowers, flagons and glasses, dishes heaped with sweetmeats, etc. 10

   In the center of the background, under the box-tier, the entrance to the theater, large door which half opens to let in the spectators. On the panels of this door, and in several corners, and above the sweetmeat stand, red playbills announcing LA CLORISE. 20

   At the rise of the curtain, the house is nearly dark, and still empty. The chandeliers are let down in the middle of the pit, until time to light them.

   The audience, arriving gradually. Cavaliers, burghers, lackeys, pages, fiddlers, etc.

   A tumult of voices is heard beyond the door; enter brusquely a CAVALIER. 30

DOORKEEPER (*running in after him*). Not so fast! Your fifteen pence!

CAVALIER. I come in admission free!

DOORKEEPER. And why?

CAVALIER. I belong to the king's light cavalry!

DOORKEEPER (*to another* CAVALIER *who has entered*). You?

SECOND CAVALIER. I do not pay! 40

DOORKEEPER. But . . .

SECOND CAVALIER. I belong to the mousquetaires!

FIRST CAVALIER (*to the* SECOND). It does not begin before two. The floor is empty. Let us have a bout with foils.

(*They fence with foils they have brought.*)

A LACKEY (*entering*). Pst! . . . Flanquin!

OTHER LACKEY (*arrived a moment before*). Champagne? . . .

FIRST LACKEY (*taking a pack of cards from his doublet and showing it to* SECOND LACKEY). Cards. Dice. (*Sits down on the floor.*) Let us have a game.

SECOND LACKEY (*sitting down likewise*). You rascal, willingly!

FIRST LACKEY (*taking from his pocket a bit of candle which he lights and sticks on the floor*). I prigged an eyeful of my master's light!

ONE OF THE WATCH (*to a* FLOWER-GIRL, *who comes forward*). It is pleasant getting here before the lights. (*Puts his arm around her waist.*)

ONE OF THE FENCERS (*taking a thrust*). Hit!

ONE OF THE GAMBLERS. Clubs!

THE WATCHMAN (*pursuing the girl*). A kiss!

THE FLOWER-GIRL (*repulsing him*). We shall be seen!

THE WATCHMAN (*drawing her into a dark corner*). No, we shall not!

A MAN (*sitting down on the floor with others who have brought provisions*). By coming early, you get a comfortable chance to eat.

A BURGHER (*leading his son*). This should be a good place, my boy. Let us stay here.

ONE OF THE GAMBLERS. Ace wins!

A MAN (*taking a bottle from under his cloak and sitting down*). A proper toper, toping Burgundy (*drinks*), I say should tope it in Burgundy House!

THE BURGHER (*to his son*). Might one not suppose we had stumbled into some house of evil fame? (*Points with his cane at the drunkard.*) Guzzlers! . . . (*In breaking guard one of the fencers jostles him.*) Brawlers! . . . (*He falls between the gamblers.*) Gamesters! . . .

THE WATCHMAN (*behind him, still teasing the flower-girl*). A kiss!

THE BURGHER (*dragging his son precipitately away*). Bless my soul! . . . And to reflect that in this very house, my son, were given the plays of the great Rotrou!

THE YOUTH. And those of the great Corneille!

[*A band of* PAGES *holding hands rush in performing a farandole and singing.*]

PAGES. Tra la la la la la la la! . . . 10

DOORKEEPER (*severely to the* PAGES). Look, now! . . . you pages, you! none of your tricks!

FIRST PAGE (*with wounded dignity*). Sir! . . . this want of confidence . . . (*As soon as the doorkeeper has turned away, briskly to the* SECOND PAGE.) Have you a string about you?

SECOND PAGE. With a fish-hook at the end!

FIRST PAGE. We will sit up there and angle for wigs!

A PICKPOCKET (*surrounded by a number of individuals of dubious appearance*). Come, now, my little hopefuls, and learn your A B C's of trade. Being as you're not used to hooking . . .

SECOND PAGE (*shouting to other* PAGES *who have already taken seats in the upper gallery*). Ho! . . . Did you bring any 30 pea-shooters?

THIRD PAGE (*from above*). Yes! . . . And pease! . . . (*Shoots down a volley of pease.*)

THE YOUTH (*to his father*). What are we going to see?

THE BURGHER. Clorise.

THE YOUTH. By whom?

THE BURGHER. By Balthazar Baro. Ah, what a play it is! . . . (*Goes toward* 40 *the back on his son's arm.*)

PICKPOCKET (*to his disciples*). Particularly the lace-ruffles at the knees, . . . you're to snip off carefully!

A SPECTATOR (*to another, pointing toward an upper seat*). Look! On the first night of the Cid, I was perched up there!

PICKPOCKET (*with pantomimic suggestion of spiriting away*). Watches . . .

THE BURGHER (*coming forward again with his son*). The actors you are about to see, my son, are among the most illustrious . . .

PICKPOCKET (*with show of subtracting with furtive little tugs*). Pocket-handkerchiefs . . .

THE BURGHER. Montfleury . . .

SOMEBODY (*shouting from the upper gallery*). Make haste, and light the chandeliers!

THE BURGHER. Bellerose, l'Épy, the Beaupré, Jodelet . . .

A PAGE (*in the pit*). Ah! . . . Here comes the goody-seller!

THE SWEETMEAT VENDER (*appearing behind the stand*). Oranges . . . Milk . . . Raspberry cordial . . . citron-wine . . . (*Hubbub at the door.*)

FALSETTO VOICE (*outside*). Make room, ruffians!

ONE OF THE LACKEYS (*astonished*). The marquises . . . in the pit!

OTHER LACKEY. Oh, for an instant only!

[*Enter a band of foppish* YOUNG MARQUISES.]

ONE OF THE MARQUISES (*looking around the half-empty house*). What? . . . We happen in like so many linen-drapers? Without disturbing anybody? treading on any feet? . . . Too bad! too bad! too bad! (*He finds himself near several other gentlemen, come in a moment before.*) Cuigy, Brissaille! (*Effusive embraces.*)

CUIGY. We are of the faithful indeed. We are here before the lights.

THE MARQUIS. Ah, do not speak of it! . . . It has put me in such a humor!

OTHER MARQUIS. Be comforted, marquis . . . here comes the candle-lighter!

THE AUDIENCE (*greeting the arrival of the candle-lighter*). Ah! . . . (*Many gather around the chandeliers while they are being*

lighted. A few have taken seats in the galleries.)
[LIGNIÈRE *enters, arm in arm with* CHRISTIAN DE NEUVILLETTE. LIGNIÈRE, *in somewhat disordered apparel, appearance of gentlemanly drunkard.* CHRISTIAN, *becomingly dressed, but in clothes of a slightly obsolete elegance.*]
CUIGY. Lignière!
BRISSAILLE (*laughing*). Not tipsy yet?
LIGNIÈRE (*low to* CHRISTIAN). Shall I present you? (CHRISTIAN *nods assent.*) Baron de Neuvillette . . . (*Exchange of bows.*)
THE AUDIENCE (*cheering the ascent of the first lighted chandelier*). Ah! . . .
CUIGY (*to* BRISSAILLE, *looking at* CHRISTIAN). A charming head . . . charming!
FIRST MARQUIS (*who has overheard*). Pooh! . . .
LIGNIÈRE (*presenting* CHRISTIAN). Messieurs de Cuigy . . . de Brissaille . . .
CHRISTIAN (*bowing*). Delighted! . . .
FIRST MARQUIS (*to* SECOND). He is a pretty fellow enough, but is dressed in the fashion of some other year!
LIGNIÈRE (*to* CUIGY). Monsieur is lately arrived from Touraine.
CHRISTIAN. Yes, I have been in Paris not over twenty days. I enter the Guards tomorrow, the Cadets.
FIRST MARQUIS (*looking at those who appear in the boxes*). There comes the président Aubry!
SWEETMEAT VENDER. Oranges! Milk!
THE FIDDLERS (*tuning*). La . . . la . . .
CUIGY (*to* CHRISTIAN, *indicating the house which is filling*). A good house! . . .
CHRISTIAN. Yes, crowded.
FIRST MARQUIS. The whole of fashion!
(*They give the names of the women, as, very brilliantly attired, these enter the boxes. Exchange of bows and smiles.*)
SECOND MARQUIS. Mesdames de Guéménée . . .

CUIGY. De Bois-Dauphin . . .
FIRST MARQUIS. Whom . . . time was . . . we loved! . . .
BRISSAILLE. . . . de Chavigny . . .
SECOND MARQUIS. Who still plays havoc with our hearts!
LIGNIÈRE. *Tiens!* Monsieur de Corneille has come back from Rouen!
THE YOUTH (*to his father*). The Academy is present?
THE BURGHER. Yes . . . I perceive more than one member of it. Yonder are Boudu, Boissat and Cureau . . . Porchères, Colomby, Bourzeys, Bourdon, Arbaut . . . All names of which not one will be forgotten. What a beautiful thought it is!
FIRST MARQUIS. Attention! Our précieuses are coming into their seats . . . Barthénoide, Urimédonte, Cassandace, Félixérie . . .
SECOND MARQUIS. Ah, how exquisite are their surnames! . . . Marquis, can you tell them off, all of them?
FIRST MARQUIS. I can tell them off, all of them, marquis!
LIGNIÈRE (*drawing* CHRISTIAN *aside*). Dear fellow, I came in here to be of use to you. The lady does not come. I revert to my vice!
CHRISTIAN (*imploringly*). No! No! . . . You who turn into ditties Town and Court, stay by me; you will be able to tell me for whom it is I am dying of love!
THE LEADER OF THE VIOLINS (*rapping on his desk with his bow*). Gentlemen! . . . (*He raises his bow.*)
SWEETMEAT VENDER. Macaroons . . . Citronade . . . (*The fiddles begin playing.*)
CHRISTIAN. I fear . . . oh, I fear to find that she is fanciful and intricate! I dare not speak to her, for I am of a simple wit. The language written and spoken in these days bewilders and

baffles me. I am a plain soldier . . . shy, to boot.—She is always at the right, there, the end: the empty box.

LIGNIÈRE (*with show of leaving*). I am going.

CHRISTIAN (*still attempting to detain him*). Oh, no! . . . Stay, I beseech you!

LIGNIÈRE. I cannot. D'Assoucy is expecting me at the pot-house. Here is a mortal drought!

SWEETMEAT VENDER (*passing before him with a tray*). Orangeade? . . .

LIGNIÈRE. Ugh!

SWEETMEAT VENDER. Milk? . . .

LIGNIÈRE. Pah! . . .

SWEETMEAT VENDER. Lacrima? . . .

LIGNIÈRE. Stop! (*To* CHRISTIAN.) I will tarry a bit. . . . Let us see this lacrima? (*Sits down at the sweetmeat stand. The* VENDER *pours him a glass of lacrima.*)

[*Shouts among the audience at the entrance of a little, merry-faced, roly-poly man.*]

AUDIENCE. Ah, Ragueneau! . . .

LIGNIÈRE (*to* CHRISTIAN). Ragueneau, who keeps the great cookshop.

RAGUENEAU (*attired like a pastrycook in his Sunday best, coming quickly toward* LIGNIÈRE). Monsieur, have you seen Monsieur de Cyrano?

LIGNIÈRE (*presenting* RAGUENEAU *to* CHRISTIAN). The pastrycook of poets and of players!

RAGUENEAU (*abashed*). Too much honor. . . .

LIGNIÈRE. No modesty! . . . Mecaenas! . . .

RAGUENEAU. It is true, those gentlemen are among my customers. . . .

LIGNIÈRE. Debitors! . . . A considerable poet himself. . . .

RAGUENEAU. It has been said! . . .

LIGNIÈRE. Daft on poetry!

RAGUENEAU. It is true that for an ode . . .

LIGNIÈRE. You are willing to give at any time a tart!

RAGUENEAU. . . . let. A tart-let.

LIGNIÈRE. Kind soul, he tries to cheapen his charitable acts! And for a triolet were you not known to give . . . ?

RAGUENEAU. Rolls. Just rolls.

LIGNIÈRE (*severely*). Buttered! . . . And the play, you are fond of the play?

RAGUENEAU. It is with me a passion!

LIGNIÈRE. And you settle for your entrance fee with a pastry currency. Come now, among ourselves, what did you have to give today for admittance here?

RAGUENEAU. Four custards . . . eighteen lady-fingers. (*He looks all around.*) Monsieur de Cyrano is not here. I wonder at it.

LIGNIÈRE. And why?

RAGUENEAU. Montfleury is billed to play.

LIGNIÈRE. So it is, indeed. That ton of man will today entrance us in the part of Phoedo . . . Phoedo! . . . But what is that to Cyrano?

RAGUENEAU. Have you not heard? He interdicted Montfleury, whom he has taken in aversion, from appearing for one month upon the stage.

LIGNIÈRE (*who is at his fourth glass.*) Well?

RAGUENEAU. Montfleury is billed to play.

CUIGY (*who has drawn near with his companions*). He cannot be prevented.

RAGUENEAU. He cannot? . . . Well, I am here to see!

FIRST MARQUIS. What is this Cyrano?

CUIGY. A crack-brain!

SECOND MARQUIS. Of quality?

CUIGY. Enough for daily uses. He is a cadet in the Guards. (*Pointing out a gentleman who is coming and going about the pit, as if in search of somebody.*) But his friend Le Bret can tell you. (*Calling.*) Le Bret! . . . (LE BRET comes toward them.) You are looking for Bergerac?

LE BRET. Yes. I am uneasy.

CUIGY. Is it not a fact that he is a most uncommon fellow?

LE BRET (affectionately). The most exquisite being he is that walks beneath the moon!

RAGUENEAU. Poet!

CUIGY. Swordsman!

BRISSAILLE. Physicist!

LE BRET. Musician!

LIGNIÈRE. And what an extraordinary aspect he presents!

RAGUENEAU. I will not go so far as to say that I believe our grave Philippe de Champaigne will leave us a portrait of him; but, the bizarre, excessive, whimsical fellow that he is would certainly have furnished the late Jacques Callot with a type of madcap fighter for one of his masques. Hat with triple feather, doublet with twice-triple skirt, cloak which his interminable rapier lifts up behind, with pomp, like the insolent tail of a cock; prouder than all the Artabans that Gascony ever bred, he goes about in his stiff Punchinello ruff, airing a nose. . . . Ah, gentlemen, what a nose is that! One cannot look upon such a specimen of the nasigera without exclaiming, "No! truly, the man exaggerates." . . . After that, one smiles, one says: "He will take it off." . . . But Monsieur de Bergerac never takes it off at all.

LE BRET (shaking his head). He wears it always . . . and cuts down whoever breathes a syllable in comment.

RAGUENEAU (proudly). His blade is half the shears of Fate!

FIRST MARQUIS (shrugging his shoulders). He will not come!

RAGUENEAU. He will. I wager you a chicken à la Ragueneau.

FIRST MARQUIS (laughing). Very well!

[Murmur of admiration in the house. ROXANE has appeared in her box. She takes a seat in the front, her duenna at the back. CHRISTIAN, engaged in paying the SWEETMEAT VENDER, does not look.)

SECOND MARQUIS (uttering a series of small squeals). Ah, gentlemen, she is horrifically enticing!

FIRST MARQUIS. A strawberry set in a peach, and smiling!

SECOND MARQUIS. So fresh, that being near her, one might catch cold in his heart!

CHRISTIAN (looks up, sees ROXANE, and, agitated, seizes LIGNIÈRE by the arm). That is she!

LIGNIÈRE (looking). Ah, that is she! . . .

CHRISTIAN. Yes. Tell me at once. . . . Oh, I am afraid! . . .

LIGNIÈRE (sipping his wine slowly). Magdeleine Robin, surnamed Roxane. Subtle. Euphuistic.

CHRISTIAN. Alack-a-day!

LIGNIÈRE. Unmarried. An orphan. A cousin of Cyrano's . . . the one of whom they were talking.

[While he is speaking, a richly dressed nobleman, wearing the order of the Holy Ghost on a blue ribbon across his breast, enters ROXANE's box, and, without taking a seat, talks with her a moment.]

CHRISTIAN (starting). That man? . . .

LIGNIÈRE (who is beginning to be tipsy, winking). Hé! Hé! Comte de Guiche. Enamored of her. But married to the niece of Armand de Richelieu. Wishes to manage a match between Roxane and certain sorry lord, one Monsieur de Valvert, vicomte and . . . easy. She does not subscribe to his views, but De Guiche is powerful: he can persecute to some purpose a simple commoner. But I have duly set forth his shady machinations in a song which . . . Ho! he must bear me a grudge! The end was wicked . . . Listen! . . . (*He rises, staggering, and lifting his glass, is about to sing.*)

CHRISTIAN. No. Good evening.

LIGNIÈRE. You are going? . . .

CHRISTIAN. To find Monsieur de Valvert.

LIGNIÈRE. Have a care. You are the one who will get killed. (*Indicating* ROXANE *by a glance.*) Stay. Someone is looking . . .

CHRISTIAN. It is true . . . (*He remains absorbed in the contemplation of* ROXANE. *The pickpockets, seeing his abstracted air, draw nearer to him.*)

LIGNIÈRE. Ah, you are going to stay. Well, I am going. I am thirsty! And I am looked for . . . at all the public houses! (*Exit unsteadily.*)

LE BRET (*who has made the circuit of the house, returning toward* RAGUENEAU, *in a tone of relief*). Cyrano is not here.

RAGUENEAU. And yet . . .

LE BRET. I will trust to Fortune he has not seen the announcement.

THE AUDIENCE. Begin! Begin!

ONE OF THE MARQUISES (*watching* DE GUICHE, *who comes from* ROXANE'S *box, and crosses the pit, surrounded by obsequious satellites, among whom the* VICOMTE DE VALVERT). Always a court about him, De Guiche!

OTHER MARQUIS. Pf! . . . Another Gascon!

FIRST MARQUIS. A Gascon, of the cold and supple sort. That sort succeeds. Believe me, it will be best to offer him our duty. (*They approach* DE GUICHE.)

SECOND MARQUIS. These admirable ribbons! What color, Comte de Guiche? Should you call it Kiss-me-Sweet or . . . Expiring Fawn?

DE GUICHE. This shade is called Sick Spaniard.

FIRST MARQUIS. Appropriately called, for shortly, thanks to your valor, the Spaniard will be sick indeed, in Flanders!

DE GUICHE. I am going upon the stage. Are you coming? (*He walks toward the stage, followed by all the* MARQUISES *and men of quality. He turns and calls.*) Valvert, come!

CHRISTIAN (*who has been listening and watching them, starts on hearing that name*). The vicomte! . . . Ah, in his face . . . in his face I will fling my . . . (*He puts his hand to his pocket and finds the pickpocket's hand. He turns.*) Hein?

PICKPOCKET. Aï!

CHRISTIAN (*without letting him go*). I was looking for a glove.

PICKPOCKET (*with an abject smile*). And you found a hand. (*In a different tone, low and rapid.*) Let me go . . . I will tell you a secret.

CHRISTIAN (*without releasing him*). Well?

PICKPOCKET. Lignière who has just left you . . .

CHRISTIAN (*as above*). Yes? . . .

PICKPOCKET. Has not an hour to live. A song he made annoyed one of the great, and a hundred men—I am one of them—will be posted to-night . . .

CHRISTIAN. A hundred? . . . By whom?

PICKPOCKET. Honor . . .

CHRISTIAN (*shrugging his shoulders*). Oh! . . .

PICKPOCKET (*with great dignity*). Among rogues!

CHRISTIAN. Where will they be posted?

PICKPOCKET. At the Porte de Nesle, on his way home. Inform him.

CHRISTIAN (*letting him go*). But where can I find him?

PICKPOCKET. Go to all the taverns: the Golden Vat, the Pine-Apple, the Belt and Bosom, the Twin

CHRISTIAN. Yes. I will run! . . . Ah, the blackguards! A hundred against one! . . . (*Looks lovingly toward* ROX- ANE.) Leave her! . . . (*Furiously, looking toward* VALVERT.) And him! . . . But Lignière must be prevented. (*Exit running.*)

[DE GUICHE, *the* MARQUISES, *all the gentry have disappeared behind the curtain, to place themselves on the stage-seats. The pit is crowded. There is not an empty seat in the boxes or the gallery.*]

THE AUDIENCE. Begin!

A BURGHER (*whose wig goes sailing off at the end of a string held by one of the* PAGES *in the upper gallery*). My wig!

SCREAMS OF DELIGHT. He is bald! . . . The pages! . . . Well done! . . . Ha, ha, ha! . . .

THE BURGHER (*furious, shaking his fist*). Imp of Satan! . . .

[*Laughter and screams, beginning very loud and decreasing suddenly. Dead silence.*]

LE BRET (*astonished*). This sudden hush? . . . (*One of the spectators whispers in his ear.*) Ah? . . .

THE SPECTATOR. I have it from a reliable quarter.

RUNNING MURMURS. Hush! . . . Has he come? No! . . . Yes, he has! In the box with the grating. . . . The cardinal! . . . the cardinal! . . . the cardinal! . . .

ONE OF THE PAGES. What a shame! . . . Now we shall have to behave!

[*Knocking on the stage. Complete stillness. Pause.*]

VOICE OF ONE OF THE MARQUISES (*breaking the deep silence, behind the curtain*). Snuff that candle!

OTHER MARQUIS (*thrusting his head out between the curtains*). A chair! (*A chair is passed from hand to hand, above the* heads. *The* MARQUIS *takes it and disappears, after kissing his hand repeatedly toward the boxes.*)

A SPECTATOR. Silence!

[*Once more, the three knocks. The curtain opens. Tableau. The* MARQUISES *seated at the sides, in attitudes of languid haughtiness. The stage-setting is the faint-colored bluish sort usual in a pastoral. Four small crystal candelabra light the stage. The violins play softly.*]

LE BRET (*to* RAGUENEAU, *under breath*). Is Montfleury the first to appear?

RAGUENEAU (*likewise under breath*). Yes. The opening lines are his.

LE BRET. Cyrano is not here.

RAGUENEAU. I have lost my wager.

LE BRET. Let us be thankful. Let us be thankful.

[*A bagpipe is heard.* MONTFLEURY *appears upon the stage, enormous, in a conventional shepherd's costume, with a rose-wreathed hat set jauntily on the side of his head, breathing into a be-ribboned bagpipe.*]

THE PIT (*applauding*). Bravo, Montfleury! Montfleury!

MONTFLEURY (*after bowing, proceeds to play the part of* PHOEDO).
Happy the man who, freed from Fashion's fickle sway,
In exile self-prescribed whiles peaceful hours away;
Who when Zephyrus sighs amid the answering trees . . .

A VOICE (*from the middle of the pit*). Rogue! Did I not forbid you for one month? (*Consternation. Everyone looks around. Murmurs.*)

VARIOUS VOICES. Hein? What? What is the matter? (*Many in the boxes rise to see.*)

CUIGY. It is he!

LE BRET (*alarmed*). Cyrano!

THE VOICE. King of the Obese! Incontinently vanish! . . .

THE WHOLE AUDIENCE (*indignant*). Oh!
. . .

MONTFLEURY. But . . .

THE VOICE. You stop to muse upon the matter?

SEVERAL VOICES (*from the pit and the boxes*). Hush! . . . Enough! . . . Proceed, Montfleury. . . . Fear nothing!

MONTFLEURY (*in an unsteady voice*). Happy 10 the man who, freed from Fashion's f—— . . .

THE VOICE (*more threatening than before*). How is this? Shall I be constrained, Man of the Monster Belly, to enforce my regulation . . . regularly? (*An arm holding a cane leaps above the level of the heads.*)

MONTFLEURY (*in a voice growing fainter and fainter*). Happy the man . . . 20 (*The cane is wildly flourished.*)

THE VOICE. Leave the stage!

THE PIT. Oh! . . .

MONTFLEURY (*choking*). Happy the man who freed . . .

CYRANO (*appears above the audience, standing upon a chair, his arms folded on his chest, his hat at a combative angle, his moustache on end, his nose terrifying*). Ah! I shall lose my temper! (*Sensa-* 30 *tion at sight of him.*)

MONTFLEURY (*to the* MARQUISES). Messieurs, I appeal to you!

ONE OF THE MARQUISES (*languidly*). But go ahead! . . . Play!

CYRANO. Fat man, if you attempt it, I will dust the paint off you with this!

THE MARQUIS. Enough!

CYRANO. Let every little lordling keep silence in his seat, or I will ruffle his 40 ribbons with my cane!

ALL THE MARQUISES (*rising*). This is too much! . . . Montfleury. . . .

CYRANO. Let Montfleury go home, or stay, and, having cut his ears off, I will disembowel him!

A VOICE. But . . .

CYRANO. Let him go home, I said!

OTHER VOICE. But after all . . .

CYRANO. It is not yet done? (*With show of turning up his sleeves.*) Very well, upon that stage, as on a platter trimmed with green, you shall see me carve that mount of brawn . . .

MONTFLEURY (*calling up his whole dignity*). Monsieur, you cast indignity, in my person, upon the Muse!

CYRANO (*very civilly*). Monsieur, if that lady, with whom you have naught to do, had the pleasure of beholding you . . . just as you stand, there, like a decorated pot! . . . she could not live, I do protest, but she hurled her buskin at you!

THE PIT. Montfleury! . . . Montfleury! . . . Give us Baro's piece!

CYRANO (*to those shouting around him*). I beg you will show some regard for my scabbard: it is ready to give up the sword! (*The space around him widens.*)

THE CROWD (*backing away*). Hey . . . softly, there!

CYRANO (*to* MONTFLEURY). Go off!

THE CROWD (*closing again, and grumbling*). Oh! . . . Oh!

CYRANO (*turning suddenly*). Has somebody objections? (*The crowd again pushes away from him.*)

A VOICE (*at the back, singing*).
Monsieur de Cyrano, one sees,
Inclines to be tyrannical;
In spite of that tyrannicle
We shall see La Clorise!

THE WHOLE AUDIENCE (*catching up the tune*). La Clorise! La Clorise!

CYRANO. Let me hear that song again, and I will do you all to death with my stick!

A BURGHER. Samson come back! . . .

CYRANO. Lend me your jaw, good man!

A LADY (*in one of the boxes*). This is unheard of!

A MAN. It is scandalous!

A BURGHER. It is irritating, to say no more.

A PAGE. What fun it is!

THE PIT. Ksss! . . . Montfleury! . . . Cyrano! . . .

CYRANO. Be still! . . .

THE PIT (*in uproar*). Hee-haw! . . . Baaaaah! . . . Bow-wow! . . . Cockadoodledoooooo!

CYRANO. I will . . .

A PAGE. Meeeow!

CYRANO. I order you to hold your tongues! . . . I dare the floor collectively to utter another sound! . . . I challenge you, one and all! . . . I will take down your names . . . Step forward, budding heroes! Each in his turn. You shall be given numbers. Come, which one of you will open the joust with me? You, monsieur? No! You? No! The first that offers is promised all the mortuary honors due the brave. Let all who wish to die hold up their hands! (*Silence.*) It is modesty that makes you shrink from the sight of my naked sword? Not a name? Not a hand?—Very good. Then I proceed. (*Turning toward the stage where* MONT-FLEURY *is waiting in terror.*) As I was saying, it is my wish to see the stage cured of this tumor. Otherwise . . . (*Claps hand to his sword.*) the lancet!

MONTFLEURY. I . . .

CYRANO (*gets down from his chair, and sits in the space that has become vacant around him, with the ease of one at home*). Thrice will I clap my hands, O plenilune! At the third clap . . . eclipse!

THE PIT (*diverted*). Ah! . . .

CYRANO (*clapping his hands*). One! . . .

MONTFLEURY. I . . .

A VOICE (*from one of the boxes*). Do not go! . . .

THE PIT. He will stay! . . . He will go! . . .

MONTFLEURY. Messieurs, I feel . . .

CYRANO. Two! . . .

MONTFLEURY. I feel it will perhaps be wiser . . .

CYRANO. Three! . . .

[MONTFLEURY *disappears, as if through a trap-door. Storm of laughter, hissing, catcalls.*]

THE HOUSE. Hoo! . . . Hoo! . . .Milksop! . . . Come back! . . .

CYRANO (*beaming, leans back in his chair and crosses his legs*). Let him come back, if he dare!

A BURGHER. The spokesman of the company!

[BELLEROSE *comes forward on the stage and bows.*]

THE BOXES. Ah, there comes Bellerose!

BELLEROSE (*with elegant bearing and diction*). Noble ladies and gentlemen . . .

THE PIT. No! No! Jodelet . . . We want Jodelet! . . .

JODELET (*comes forward, speaks through his nose*). Pack of swine!

THE PIT. That is right! . . . Well said! . . . Bravo!

JODELET. Don't bravo me! . . . The portly tragedian, whose paunch is your delight, felt sick! . . .

THE PIT. He is a poltroon! . . .

JODELET. He was obliged to leave . . .

THE PIT. Let him come back!

SOME. No!

OTHERS. Yes! . . .

A YOUTH (*to* CYRANO). But, when all is said, monsieur, what good grounds have you for hating Montfleury?

CYRANO (*amiably, sitting as before*). Young gosling, I have two, whereof each, singly, would be ample. Primo: He is an execrable actor, who bellows, and with grunts that would disgrace a water-carrier launches the verse

that should go forth as if on pinions!
. . . Secundo: is my secret.

THE OLD BURGHER (*behind* CYRANO).
But without compunction you deprive
us of hearing La Clorise. I am determined . . .

CYRANO (*turning his chair around so as to
face the old gentleman; respectfully*).
Venerable mule, old Baro's verses
being what they are, I do it without 10
compunction, as you say.

THE PRÉCIEUSES (*in the boxes*). Ha! . . .
Ho! . . . Our own Baro! . . . My
dear, did you hear that? How can
such a thing be said? . . . Ha! . . .
Ho! . . .

CYRANO (*turning his chair so as to face the
boxes; gallantly*). Beautiful creatures,
do you bloom and shine, be ministers
of dreams, your smiles our anodyne. 20
Inspire poets, but poems . . . spare to
judge!

BELLEROSE. But the money which must
be given back at the door!

CYRANO (*turning his chair to face the
stage*). Bellerose, you have said the
only intelligent thing that has, as
yet, been said! Far from me to
wrong by so much as a fringe the
worshipful mantle of Thespis. . . . 30
(*He rises and flings a bag upon the
stage.*) Catch! . . . and keep quiet!

THE HOUSE (*dazzled*). Ah! . . .
Oh! . . .

JODELET (*nimbly picking up the bag,
weighing it with his hand*). For such a
price, you are authorized, monsieur,
to come and stop the performance
every day!

THE HOUSE. Hoo! . . . Hoo! . . .   40

JODELET. Should we be hooted in a
body! . . .

BELLEROSE. The house must be evac-
uated!

JODELET. Evacuate it!

[*The audience begins to leave;* CYRANO
*looking on with a satisfied air. The crowd,
however, becoming interested in the following scene, the exodus is suspended. The
women in the boxes who were already
standing and had put on their wraps,
stop to listen and end by resuming their
seats.*]

LE BRET (*to* CYRANO). What you have
done . . . is mad!

A BORE. Montfleury! . . . the eminent
actor! . . . What a scandal! . . .
But the Duc de Candale is his patron!
. . . Have you a patron, you?

CYRANO. No!

THE BORE. You have not?

CYRANO. No!

THE BORE. What? You are not pro-
tected by some great nobleman under
the cover of whose name . . .

CYRANO (*exasperated*). No, I have told
you twice. Must I say the same thing
thrice? No, I have no protector . . .
(*Hand on sword.*) but this will do.

THE BORE. Then, of course, you will
leave town.

CYRANO. That will depend.

THE BORE. But the Duc de Candale has
a long arm . . .

CYRANO. Not so long as mine . . .
(*Pointing to his sword.*) pieced out with
this!

THE BORE. But you cannot have the
presumption . . .

CYRANO. I can, yes.

THE BORE. But . . .

CYRANO. And now, . . . face about!

THE BORE. But . . .

CYRANO. Face about, I say . . . or
else, tell me why you are looking at
my nose.

THE BORE (*bewildered*). I . . .

CYRANO (*advancing upon him*). In what
is it unusual?

THE BORE (*backing*). Your worship is
mistaken.

CYRANO (*same business as above*). It is

flabby and pendulous, like a proboscis?

THE BORE. I never said . . .

CYRANO. Or hooked like a hawk's beak?

THE BORE. I . . .

CYRANO. Do you discern a mole upon the tip?

THE BORE. But . . .

CYRANO. Or is a fly disporting himself thereon? What is there wonderful about it?

THE BORE. Oh . . .

CYRANO. Is it a freak of nature?

THE BORE. But I had refrained from casting so much as a glance at it!

CYRANO. And why, I pray, should you not look at it?

THE BORE. I had . . .

CYRANO. So it disgusts you?

THE BORE. Sir . . .

CYRANO. Its color strikes you as unwholesome?

THE BORE. Sir . . .

CYRANO. Its shape, unfortunate?

THE BORE. But far from it!

CYRANO. Then wherefore that depreciating air? . . . Perhaps monsieur thinks it a shade too large?

THE BORE. Indeed not. No, indeed. I think it small . . . small—I should have said, minute!

CYRANO. What? How? Charge me with such a ridiculous defect? Small, my nose? Ho! . . .

THE BORE. Heavens!

CYRANO. Enormous, my nose! . . . Contemptible stutterer, snub-nosed and flat-headed, be it known to you that I am proud, proud of such an appendage! inasmuch as a great nose is properly the index of an affable, kindly, courteous man, witty, liberal, brave, such as I am! and such as you are for evermore precluded from supposing yourself, deplorable rogue! For the inglorious surface my hand encounters above your ruff, is no less devoid—— (*Strikes him.*)

THE BORE. Aï, aï! . . .

CYRANO. Of pride, alacrity and sweep, of perception and of gift, of heavenly spark, of sumptuousness, to sum up all, of NOSE, than that (*Turns him around by the shoulders and suits the action to the word.*), which stops my boot below your spine!

THE BORE (*running off*). Help! The watch! . . .

CYRANO. Warning to the idle who might find entertainment in my organ of smell. . . . And if the facetious fellow be of birth, my custom is, before I let him go to chasten him, in front, and higher up, with steel, and not with hide!

DE GUICHE (*who has stepped down from the stage with the* MARQUISES). He is becoming tiresome!

VALVERT (*shrugging his shoulders*). It is empty bluster!

DE GUICHE. Will no one take him up?

VALVERT. No one? . . . Wait! I will have one of those shots at him! (*He approaches* CYRANO *who is watching him, and stops in front of him, in an attitude of silly swagger.*) Your . . . your nose is . . . errr . . . Your nose . . . is very large!

CYRANO (*gravely*). Very.

VALVERT (*laughs*). Ha! . . .

CYRANO (*imperturbable*). Is that all?

VALVERT. But . . .

CYRANO. Ah, no, young man, that is not enough! You might have said, dear me, there are a thousand things . . . varying the tone . . . For instance . . . here you are:—Aggressive: "I, monsieur, if I had such a nose, nothing would serve but I must cut it off!" Amicable: "It must be in your way while drinking; you ought to have a special beaker made!" Descriptive: "It is a crag! . . . a peak! . . . a promontory! . . . A promontory, did I say? . . . It is a peninsula!" Inquisitive: "What may the office be of that oblong receptacle? Is it an inkhorn or a scissor-case?" Mincing: "Do you so dote on birds, you have, fond as a father, been at pains to fit the little darlings with a roost?" Blunt: "Tell me, monsieur, you, when you smoke, is it possible you blow the vapor through your nose without a neighbor crying 'The chimney is afire'?" Anxious: "Go with caution. I beseech, lest your head, dragged over by that weight, should drag you over!" Tender: "Have a little sunshade made for it! It might get freckled!" Learned: "None but the beast, monsieur, mentioned by Aristophanes, the hippocampelephantocamelos, can have borne beneath his forehead so much cartilage and bone!" Offhand: "What, comrade, is that sort of peg in style? Capital to hang one's hat upon!" Emphatic: "No wind can hope, O lordly nose, to give the whole of you a cold, but the Nor-Wester!" Dramatic: "It is the Red Sea when it bleeds!" Admiring: "What a sign for a perfumer's shop!" Lyrical: "Art thou a Triton, and is that thy conch?" Simple: "A monument! When is admission free?" Deferent: "Suffer, monsieur, that I should pay you my respects: that is what I call possessing a house of your own!" Rustic: "Hi, boys! Call that a nose? Ye don't gull me! It's either a prize carrot or else a stunted gourd!" Military: "Level against the cavalry!" Practical: "Will you put it up for raffle? Indubitably, sir, it

will be the feature of the game!" And finally in parody of weeping Pyramus: "Behold, behold the nose that traitorously destroyed the beauty of its master! and is blushing for the same!"—That, my dear sir, or something not unlike, is what you would have said to me, had you the smallest leaven of letters or of wit; but of wit, O most pitiable of objects made by God, you never had a rudiment, and of letters, you have just those that are needed to spell "fool!"—But, had it been otherwise, and had you been possessed of the fertile fancy requisite to shower upon me, here, in this noble company, that volley of sprightly pleasantries, still should you not have delivered yourself of so much as a quarter of the tenth part of the beginning of the first. . . . For I let off these good things at myself, and with sufficient zest, but do not suffer another to let them off at me!

DE GUICHE (*attempting to lead away the amazed vicomte*). Let be, vicomte!

VALVERT. That insufferable haughty bearing! . . . A clodhopper without . . . without so much as gloves . . . who goes abroad without points . . . or bowknots! . . .

CYRANO. My foppery is of the inner man. I do not trick myself out like a popinjay, but I am more fastidious, if I am not so showy. I would not sally forth, by any chance, not washed quite clean of an affront; my conscience foggy about the eye, my honor crumpled, my nicety black-rimmed. I walk with all upon me furbished bright. I plume myself with independence and straightforwardness. It is not a handsome figure, it is my soul, I hold erect as in a brace. I go decked with exploits in place of

ribbon bows. I taper to a point my
wit like a moustache. And at my
passage through the crowd true
sayings ring like spurs!

VALVERT. But, sir . . .

CYRANO. I am without gloves? . . . a
mighty matter! I only had one left,
of a very ancient pair, and even that
became a burden to me . . . I left
it in somebody's face.   10

VALVERT. Villain, clod-poll, flat-foot,
refuse of the earth!

CYRANO (*taking off his hat and bowing as if
the* VICOMTE *had been introducing himself*). Ah? . . . And mine, Cyrano-
Savinien-Hercule of Bergerac!

VALVERT (*exasperated*). Buffoon!

CYRANO (*giving a sudden cry, as if seized
with a cramp*). Aï! . . .

VALVERT (*who had started toward the* 20
back, turning). What is he saying now?

CYRANO (*screwing his face as if in pain*). It
must have leave to stir . . . it has a
cramp! It is bad for it to be kept still
so long!

VALVERT. What is the matter?

CYRANO. My rapier prickles like a foot
asleep!

VALVERT (*drawing*). So be it!

CYRANO. I shall give you a charming 30
little hurt!

VALVERT (*contemptuous*). A poet!

CYRANO. Yes, a poet, . . . and to such
an extent, that while we fence, I will,
hop! extempore, compose you a
ballade!

VALVERT. A ballade?

CYRANO. I fear you do not know what
that is.

VALVERT. But . . .   40

CYRANO (*as if saying a lesson*). The ballade is composed of three stanzas of
eight lines each . . .

VALVERT (*stamps with his feet*). Oh! . . .

CYRANO (*continuing*). And an envoi of
four.

VAVLERT. You . . .

CYRANO. I will with the same breath
fight you and compose one. And at
the last line, I will hit you.

VALVERT. Indeed you will not!

CYRANO. No? . . . (*Declaiming.*)
Ballade of the duel which in Burgundy House
Monsieur de Bergerac fought with a
jackanapes.

VALVERT. And what is that, if you
please?

CYRANO. That is the title.

THE AUDIENCE (*at the highest pitch of
excitement*). Make room! . . .Good
sport! . . . Stand aside! . . . Keep
still! . . .

[*Tableau. A ring, in the pit, of the interested; the* MARQUISES *and* OFFICERS
scattered among the BURGHERS *and*
COMMON PEOPLE. *The* PAGES *have
climbed on the shoulders of various ones,
the better to see. All the women are
standing in the boxes. At the right,*
DE GUICHE *and his attendant gentlemen. At
left,* LE BRET, RAGUENEAU, CUIGY, *etc.*]

CYRANO (*closing his eyes a second*). Wait.
I am settling upon the rhymes. There.
I have them. (*In declaiming, he suits
the action to the word.*)
Of my broad felt made lighter,
I cast my mantle broad,
And stand, poet and fighter,
To do and to record.
I bow, I draw my sword . . .
En garde! with steel and wit
I play you at first abord . . .
At the last line, I hit! (*They begin
fencing.*)

You should have been politer;
Where had you best be gored?
The left side or the right—ah?
Or next your azure cord?
Or where the spleen is stored?
Or in the stomach pit?

Come we to quick accord . . .
At the last line, I hit!

You falter, you turn whiter?
You do so to afford
Your foe a rhyme in "iter"? . . .
You thrust at me—I ward—
And balance is restored.
Laridon! Look to your spit! . . .
No, you shall not be floored
Before my cue to hit! (*He announces solemnly.*)

ENVOI

Prince, call upon the Lord! . . .
I skirmish . . . feint a bit . . .
I lunge! . . . I keep my word!
(*The* VICOMTE *staggers;* CYRANO *bows.*)
At the last line, I hit!
[*Acclamations. Applause from the boxes.
Flowers and handkerchiefs are thrown.
The* OFFICERS *surround and congratulate*
CYRANO. RAGUENEAU *dances with delight.* LE BRET *is tearfully joyous and at
the same time highly troubled. The friends
of the* VICOMTE *support him off the stage.*]
THE CROWD (*in a long shout*). Ah! . . .
A LIGHT-CAVALRY MAN. Superb!
A WOMAN. Sweet!
RAGUENEAU. Astounding!
A MARQUIS. Novel!
LE BRET. Insensate!
THE CROWD (*pressing around* CYRANO).
Congratulations! . . . Well done!
. . . Bravo! . . .
A WOMAN'S VOICE. He is a hero!
A MOUSQUETAIRE (*striding swiftly toward*
CYRANO, *with outstretched hand*). Monsieur, will you allow me? It was quite,
quite excellently done, and I think I
know whereof I speak. But, as a fact,
I expressed my mind before, by
making a huge noise. . . . (*He retires.*)
CYRANO (*to* CUIGY). Who may the
gentleman be?

CUIGY. D'Artagnan.
LE BRET (*to* CYRANO, *taking his arm*).
Come, I wish to talk with you.
CYRANO. Wait till the crowd has
thinned. (*To* BELLEROSE.) I may
remain?
BELLEROSE (*deferentially*). Why, certainly! . . . (*Shouts are heard outside.*)
JODELET (*after looking*). They are hooting Montfleury.
BELLEROSE (*solemnly*). Sic transit! . . .
(*In a different tone, to the doorkeeper and
the candle snuffer.*) Sweep and close.
Leave the lights. We shall come
back, after eating, to rehearse a new
farce for tomorrow. (*Exeunt* JODELET
and BELLEROSE, *after bowing very low
to* CYRANO.)
THE DOORKEEPER (*to* CYRANO). Monsieur
will not be going to dinner?
CYRANO. I? . . . No. (*The doorkeeper
withdraws.*)
LE BRET (*to* CYRANO). And this, because? . . .
CYRANO (*proudly*). Because . . . (*In a
different tone, having seen that the doorkeeper is too far to overhear.*) I have not
a penny!
LE BRET (*making the motion of flinging a
bag*). How is this? The bag of crowns
. . .
CYRANO. Monthly remittance, thou
lastedst but a day!
LE BRET. And to keep you the remainder of the month? . . .
CYRANO. Nothing is left!
LE BRET. But then, flinging that bag,
what a child's prank!
CYRANO. But what a gesture! . . .
THE SWEETMEAT VENDER (*coughing behind her little counter*). Hm! . . .
(CYRANO *and* LE BRET *turn toward her.
She comes timidly forward.*) Monsieur,
to know you have not eaten . . .
makes my heart ache. (*Pointing to the
sweetmeat-stand.*) I have there all that

is needed . . . (*Impulsively.*) Help yourself!

CYRANO (*taking off his hat*). Dear child, despite my Gascon pride, which forbids that I should profit at your hand by the most inconsiderable of dainties, I fear too much lest a denial should grieve you: I will accept therefore . . . (*He goes to the stand and selects.*) Oh, a trifle! . . . A grape off this . . . (*She proffers the bunch, he takes a single grape.*) No . . . one! This glass of water . . . (*She starts to pour wine into it, he stops her.*) No . . . clear! And half a macaroon. (*He breaks in two the macaroon, and returns half.*)

LE BRET. This comes near being silly!

SWEETMEAT VENDER. Oh, you will take something more! . . .

CYRANO. Yes. Your hand to kiss. (*He kisses the hand she holds out to him, as if it were that of a princess.*)

SWEETMEAT VENDER. Monsieur, I thank you. (*Curtseys.*) Good-evening! (*Exit.*)

CYRANO (*to* LE BRET). I am listening. (*He establishes himself before the stand, sets the macaroon before him.*) Dinner! (*Does the same with the glass of water.*) Drink! (*And with the grape.*) Dessert! (*He sits down.*) La! let me begin! I was as hungry as a wolf! (*Eating.*) You were saying?

LE BRET. That if you listen to none but those great boobies and swashbucklers your judgment will become wholly perverted. Inquire, will you, of the sensible, concerning the effect produced today by your prowesses.

CYRANO. (*finishing his macaroon*). Enormous!

LE BRET. The cardinal . . .

CYRANO (*beaming*). He was there, the cardinal?

LE BRET. Must have found what you did . . .

CYRANO. To a degree, original.

LE BRET. Still . . .

CYRANO. He is a poet. It cannot be distasteful to him wholly that one should deal confusion to a fellow-poet's play.

LE BRET. But, seriously, you make too many enemies!

CYRANO (*biting into the grape*). How many, thereabouts, should you think I made tonight?

LE BRET. Eight and forty. Not mentioning the women.

CYRANO. Come, tell them over!

LE BRET. Montfleury, the old merchant, De Guiche, the Vicomte, Baro, the whole Academy . . .

CYRANO. Enough! You steep me in bliss!

LE BRET. But whither will the road you follow lead you? What can your object be?

CYRANO. I was wandering aimlessly; too many roads were open . . . too many resolves, too complex, allowed of being taken. I took . . .

LE BRET. Which?

CYRANO. By far the simplest of them all. I decided to be, in every matter, always, admirable!

LE BRET (*shrugging his shoulders*). That will do.—But tell me, will you not, the motive—look, the true one!— of your dislike to Montfleury.

CYRANO (*rising*). That old Silenus, who has not seen his knees this many a year, still believes himself a delicate desperate danger to the fair. And as he struts and burrs upon the stage, makes sheep's-eyes at them with his moist frog's-eyes. And I have hated him . . . oh, properly! . . . since the night he was so daring as to cast his glance on her . . . her, who— Oh, I thought I saw a slug crawl over a flower!

LE BRET (*amazed*). Hey? What? Is it possible? . . .

CYRANO (*with a bitter laugh*). That I should love? (*In a different tone, seriously.*) I love.

LE BRET. And may one know? . . . You never told me . . .

CYRANO. Whom I love? . . . Come, think a little. The dream of being beloved, even by the beautiless, is made, to me, an empty dream indeed by this good nose, my forerunner ever by a quarter of an hour. Hence, whom should I love? . . . It seems superfluous to tell you! . . . I love . . . it was inevitable! . . . the most beautiful that breathes!

LE BRET. The most beautiful? . . .

CYRANO. No less, in the whole world! And the most resplendent, and the most delicate of wit, and among the golden-haired . . . (*With overwhelming despair.*) Still the superlative!

LE BRET. Dear me, what is this fair one?

CYRANO. All unawares, a deadly snare, exquisite without concern to be so. A snare of nature's own, a musk-rose, in which ambush Love lies low. Who has seen her smile remembers the ineffable! There is not a thing so common but she turns it into prettiness; and in the merest nod or beck she can make manifest all the attributes of a goddess. No, Venus! you cannot step into your iridescent shell, nor, Dian, you, walk through the blossoming groves, as she steps into her chair and walks in Paris!

LE BRET. Sapristi! I understand! It is clear!

CYRANO. It is pellucid.

LE BRET. Magdeleine Robin, your cousin?

CYRANO. Yes, Roxane.

LE BRET. But, what could be better? You love her? Tell her so! You covered yourself with glory in her sight a moment since.

CYRANO. Look well at me, dear friend, and tell me how much hope you think can be justly entertained with this protuberance. Oh, I foster no illusions! . . . Sometimes, indeed, yes, in the violet dusk, I yield, even I! to a dreamy mood. I penetrate some garden that lies sweetening the hour. With my poor great devil of a nose I sniff the April. . . . And as I follow with my eyes some woman passing with some cavalier, I think how dear would I hold having to walk beside me, linked like that, slowly, in the soft moonlight, such a one! I kindle—I forget—and then . . . then suddenly I see the shadow of my profile upon the garden-wall!

LE BRET (*touched*). My friend . . .

CYRANO. Friend, I experience a bad half hour sometimes, in feeling so unsightly . . . and alone.

LE BRET (*in quick sympathy, taking his hand*). You weep?

CYRANO. Ah, God forbid! That? Never! No, that would be unsightly to excess! That a tear should course the whole length of this nose! Never, so long as I am accountable, shall the divine loveliness of tears be implicated with so much gross ugliness! Mark me well, nothing is so holy as are tears, nothing! and never shall it be that, rousing mirth through me, a single one of them shall seem ridiculous!

LE BRET. Come, do not despond! Love is a lottery.

CYRANO (*shaking his head*). No! I love Cleopatra: do I resemble Caesar? I worship Berenice: do I put you in mind of Titus?

LE BRET. But your courage . . . and your wit!—The little girl who but a moment ago bestowed on you that very modest meal, her eyes, you must have seen as much, did not exactly hate you!

CYRANO (*impressed*). That is true!

LE BRET. You see? So, then!—But Roxane herself, in following your duel, went lily-pale.

CYRANO. Lily-pale? . . .

LE BRET. Her mind, her heart as well, are struck with wonder! Be bold, speak to her, in order that she may . . .

CYRANO. Laugh in my face! . . . No, there is but one thing upon earth I fear. . . . It is that.

THE DOORKEEPER (*admitting the* DUENNA *to* CYRANO). Monsieur, you are inquired for.

CYRANO (*seeing the* DUENNA). Ah, my God! . . . her duenna!

THE DUENNA (*with a great curtsey*). Somebody wishes to know of her valorous cousin where one may, in private, see him.

CYRANO (*upset*). See me?

THE DUENNA (*with curtsey*). See you. There are things for your ear.

CYRANO. There are . . . ?

THE DUENNA (*other curtsey*). Things.

CYRANO (*staggering*). Ah, my God! . . .

THE DUENNA. Somebody intends, tomorrow, at the earliest roses of the dawn, to hear Mass at Saint Roch.

CYRANO (*upholds himself by leaning on* LE BRET). Ah, my God!

THE DUENNA. That over, where might one step in a moment, have a little talk?

CYRANO (*losing his senses*). Where? . . . I . . . But . . . Ah, my God!

THE DUENNA. Expedition, if you please.

CYRANO. I am casting about . . .

THE DUENNA. Where?

CYRANO. At . . . at . . . at Ragueneau's . . . the pastrycook's.

THE DUENNA. He lodges?

CYRANO. In . . . In Rue . . . Ah, my God! my God! . . . St. Honoré.

THE DUENNA (*retiring*). We will be there. Do not fail. At seven.

CYRANO. I will not fail. (*Exit* DUENNA.)

CYRANO (*falling on* LE BRET'S *neck*). To me . . . from her . . . a meeting!

LE BRET. Well, your gloom is dispelled?

CYRANO. Ah, to whatever end it may be, she is aware of my existence!

LE BRET. And now you will be calm?

CYRANO (*beside himself*). Now, I shall be fulminating and frenetical! I want an army all complete to put to rout! I have ten hearts and twenty arms . . . I cannot now be suited with felling dwarfs to earth. . . . (*At the top of his lungs.*) Giants are what I want!

[*During the last lines, on the stage at the back, shadowy shapes of players have been moving about. The rehearsal has begun; the fiddlers have resumed their places.*]

A VOICE (*from the stage*). Hey! Psst! Over there! A little lower. We are trying to rehearse!

CYRANO (*laughing*). We are going! (*He goes toward the back.*)

[*Through the street door, enter* CUIGY, BRISSAILLE, *several* OFFICERS *supporting* LIGNIÈRE *in a state of complete intoxication.*]

CUIGY. Cyrano!

CYRANO. What is this?

CUIGY. A *turdus vinaticus* we are bringing you.

CYRANO (*recognizing him*). Lignière! Hey, what has happened to you?

CUIGY. He is looking for you.

BRISSAILLE. He cannot go home.

CYRANO. Why?

LIGNIÈRE (*in a thick voice, showing him a bit of crumpled paper*). This note bids me beware . . . A hundred men against me . . . on account of lampoon . . . Grave danger threatening me . . . Porte de Nesle . . . must pass it to get home. Let me come and sleep under your roof.

CYRANO. A hundred, did you say?—You shall sleep at home!

LIGNIÈRE (*frightened*). But . . .

CYRANO (*in a terrible voice, pointing to the lighted lantern which the* DOORKEEPER *stands swinging as he listens to this scene*). Take that lantern (LIGNIÈRE *hurriedly takes it.*) and walk! . . . I swear to 10 tuck you in your bed tonight myself. (*To the* OFFICERS.) You, follow at a distance. You may look on!

CUIGY. But a hundred men . . .

CYRANO. Are not one man too many for my mood tonight! (*The players, in their several costumes, have stepped down from the stage and come nearer.*)

LE BRET. But why take under your especial care . . .   20

CYRANO. Still Le Bret is not satisfied!

LE BRET. That most commonplace of sots?

CYRANO (*slapping* LIGNIÈRE *on the shoulder*). Because this sot, this cask of muscatel, this hogshead of rosolio, did once upon a time a wholly pretty thing. On leaving Mass, having seen her whom he loved take holy-water, as the rite prescribes, he, whom the sight of water puts to flight, ran to the 30 holy-water bowl, and stooping over, drank it dry. . . .

AN ACTRESS (*in the costume of soubrette*). *Tiens*, that was nice!

CYRANO. Was it not, soubrette?

THE SOUBRETTE (*to the others*). But why are they, a hundred, all against one poor poet?

CYRANO. Let us start! (*To the* OFFICERS.) And you, gentlemen, when you see 40 me attack, whatever you may suppose to be my danger, do not stir to second me!

ANOTHER OF THE ACTRESSES (*jumping from the stage*). Oh, I will not miss seeing this!

CYRANO. Come!

ANOTHER ACTRESS (*likewise jumping from the stage, to an elderly actor*). Cassandre, will you not come?

CYRANO. Come, all of you! the Doctor, Isabel, Leander, all! and you shall lend, charming fantastic swarm, an air of Italian farce to the Spanish drama in view. Yes, you shall be a tinkling heard above a roar, like bells about a tambourine!

ALL THE WOMEN (*in great glee*). Bravo! . . . Hurry! . . . A mantle! . . . A hood!

JODELET. Let us go!

CYRANO (*to the fiddlers*). You will favor us with a tune, messieurs the violinists!

[*The fiddlers fall into the train. The lighted candles which furnished the footlights are seized and distributed. The procession becomes a torchlight procession.*]

CYRANO. Bravo! Officers, beauty in fancy dress, and, twenty steps ahead . . . (*he takes the position he describes*). I, by myself, under the feather stuck, with her own hand, by Glory, in my hat! Proud as a Scipio trebly Nasica!—It is understood? Formal interdiction to interfere with me!— We are ready? One! Two! Three! Doorkeeper, open the door! (*The* DOORKEEPER *opens wide the folding door. A picturesque corner of Old Paris appears, bathed in moonlight.*)

CYRANO. Ah! . . . Paris floats in dim nocturnal mist. . . . The sloping bluish roofs are washed with moonlight . . . A setting, exquisite indeed, offers itself for the scene about to be enacted. . . . Yonder, under silvery vapor wreathes, like a mysterious magic mirror, glimmers the Seine. . . . And you shall see what you shall see!

ALL. To the Porte de Nesle!

CYRANO (*standing on the threshold*). To the Porte de Nesle! (*Before crossing it, he turns to the* SOUBRETTE.) Were you not asking, mademoiselle, why upon that solitary rhymster a hundred men were set? (*He draws his sword, and tranquilly.*) Because it was well known he is a friend of mine! (*Exit.*)

[*To the sound of the violins, by the flickering light of the candles, the procession*—LIGNIÈRE *staggering at the head, the* ACTRESSES *arm in arm with the* OFFICERS, *the players capering behind—follows out into the night.*]

CURTAIN

ACT II

THE COOKSHOP OF POETS

RAGUENEAU'S *shop, vast kitchen at the corner of Rue St. Honoré and Rue de l'Arbre-Sec, which can be seen at the back, through the glass door, gray in the early dawn.*

At the left, in front, a counter overhung by a wrought-iron canopy from which geese, ducks, white peacocks are hanging. In large china jars, tall nosegays composed of the simpler flowers mainly sunflowers. On the same side, in the middle distance, an enormous fire- 10 *place, in front of which, between huge andirons, each of which supports a small iron pot, roasting meats drip into appropriate pans.*

At the right, door in the front wing. In the middle distance, a staircase leading to a loft, the interior of which is seen through open shutters; a spread table lighted by a small Flemish candelabrum, shows it to be an eating room. A wooden gallery continuing the stairway, suggests other similar rooms to 20 *which it may lead.*

In the center of the shop, an iron hoop— which can be lowered by means of a rope— to which large roasts are hooked.

In the shadow, under the stairway, ovens are glowing. Copper molds and saucepans are shining; spits turning, hams swinging, pastry pyramids showing fair. It is the early beginning of the workday. Bustling of hurried scul- 30 *lions, portly cooks and young cook's-assistants; swarming of caps decorated with hen feathers and guinea-fowl wings. Wicker crates and broad sheets of tin are brought in loaded with brioches and tarts.*

There are tables covered with meats and cakes; others, surrounded by chairs, await customers. In a corner, a smaller table, littered with papers. At the rise of the curtain, RAGUENEAU *is discovered seated at this table, writing with an inspired air, and counting upon his fingers.*

FIRST PASTRYCOOK (*bringing in a tall molded pudding*). Nougat of fruit!

SECOND PASTRYCOOK (*bringing in the dish he names*). Custard!

THIRD PASTRYCOOK (*bringing in a fowl roasted in its feathers*). Peacock!

FOURTH PASTRYCOOK (*bringing in a tray of cakes*). Mince-pies!

FIFTH PASTRYCOOK (*bringing in a deep earthen dish*). Beef stew!

RAGUENEAU (*laying down his pen, and looking up*). Daybreak already plates with silver the copper pans! Time, Ragueneau, to smother within thee the singing divinity! The hour of the lute will come anon—now is that of the ladle! (*He rises; speaking to one of the cooks.*) You, sir, be so good as to lengthen this gravy—it is too thick!

THE COOK. How much?

RAGUENEAU. Three feet. (*Goes farther.*)

THE COOK. What does he mean?

FIRST PASTRYCOOK. Let me have the tart!

SECOND PASTRYCOOK. The dumpling!

RAGUENEAU (*standing before the fireplace*). Spread thy wings, Muse, and fly further, that thy lovely eyes may not be reddened at the sordid kitchen fire! (*To one of the cooks, pointing at some small loaves of bread.*) You have improperly placed the cleft in those loaves; the caesura belongs in the middle—between the hemistichs! (*To another of the* COOKS, *pointing at an unfinished pastry.*) This pastry palace requires a roof! (*To a young cook's appren-* tice, *who, seated upon the floor, is putting fowls on a spit.*) And you, on that long spit, arrange, my son, in pleasing alternation, the modest pullet and the splendid turkey-cock—even as our wise Malherbe alternated of old the greater with the lesser lines, and so with roasted fowls compose a poem!

ANOTHER APPRENTICE (*coming forward with a platter covered by a napkin*). Master, in your honor, see what I have baked. . . . I hope you are pleased with it!

RAGUENEAU (*ecstatic*). A lyre!

THE APPRENTICE. Of pie-crust!

RAGUENEAU (*touched*). With candied fruits!

THE APPRENTICE. And the strings, see— of spun sugar!

RAGUENEAU (*giving him money*). Go, drink my health! (*Catching sight of* LISE *who is entering.*) Hush! My wife! . . . Move on, and hide that money. (*To* LISE, *showing her the lyre, with a constrained air.*) Fine, is it not?

LISE. Ridiculous! (*She sets a pile of wrapping-paper on the counter.*)

RAGUENEAU. Paper bags? Good. Thanks. (*He examines them.*) Heavens! My beloved books! The masterpieces of my friends—dismembered—torn!—to fashion paper bags for penny pies!— Ah, the abominable case is re-enacted of Orpheus and the Maenads!

LISE (*drily*). And have I not an unquestionable right to make what use I can

of the sole payment ever got from your paltry scribblers of uneven lines?

RAGUENEAU. Pismire! Forbear to insult those divine, melodious crickets!

LISE. Before frequenting that low crew, my friend, you did not use to call me a Maenad—no, nor yet a pismire!

RAGUENEAU. Put poems to such a use!

LISE. To that use and no other!

RAGUENEAU. If with poems you do this, I should like to know, Madame, what you do with prose!

[*Two children have come into the shop.*]

RAGUENEAU. What can I do for you, little ones?

FIRST CHILD. Three patties.

RAGUENEAU (*waiting on them*). There you are! Beautifully browned, and piping hot.

SECOND CHILD. Please, will you wrap them for us?

RAGUENEAU (*starting, aside*). There goes one of my bags! (*To the children.*) You want them wrapped, do you? (*He takes one of the paper bags, and as he is about to put in the patties, reads.*) "No otherwise, Ulysses, from Penelope departing. . . ." Not this one! (*He lays it aside and takes another. At the moment of putting in the patties, he reads.*) "Phoebus of the aureate locks . . ." Not that one! (*Same business.*)

LISE (*out of patience*). Well, what are you waiting for?

RAGUENEAU. Here we are. Here we are. Here we are. (*He takes a third bag and resigns himself.*) The sonnet to Phyllis! . . . It is hard, all the same.

LISE. It is lucky you made up your mind. (*Shrugging her shoulders.*) Nicodemus! (*She climbs on a chair and arranges dishes on a sideboard.*)

RAGUENEAU (*taking advantage of her back being turned, calls back the children who had already reached the door*). Psst! . . . Children! Give me back the sonnet to

Phyllis, and you shall have six patties instead of three! (*The children give back the paper-bag, joyfully take the patties and exeunt.* RAGUENEAU *smooths out the crumpled paper and reads declaiming.*) "*Phyllis!*" . . . Upon that charming name, a grease-spot! . . . "*Phyllis!*" . . . [*Enter brusquely* CYRANO.]

CYRANO. What time is it?

RAGUENEAU (*bowing with eager deference*). Six o'clock.

CYRANO (*with emotion*). In an hour! (*He comes and goes in the shop.*)

RAGUENEAU (*following him*). Bravo! I too was witness . . .

CYRANO. Of what?

RAGUENEAU. Your fight.

CYRANO. Which?

RAGUENEAU. At the Hotel de Bourgogne.

CYRANO (*with disdain*). Ah, the duel!

RAGUENEAU (*admiringly*). Yes—the duel in rhyme.

LISE. He can talk of nothing else.

CYRANO. Let him! . . . It does no harm.

RAGUENEAU (*thrusting with a spit he has seized*). "*At the last line, I hit!*" "*At the last line, I hit!*"—How fine that is! (*With growing enthusiasm.*) "*At the last line, I*"——

CYRANO. What time, Ragueneau?

RAGUENEAU (*remaining fixed in the attitude of thrusting, while he looks at the clock*). Five minutes past six.—"*I hit!*" (*He recovers from his duelling posture.*) Oh, to be able to make a ballade!

LISE (*to* CYRANO, *who in passing her counter has absentmindedly shaken hands with her*). What ails your hand?

CYRANO. Nothing. A scratch.

RAGUENEAU. You have been exposed to some danger?

CYRANO. None whatever.

LISE (*shaking her finger at him*). I fear that is a fib!

CYRANO. From the swelling of my nose? The fib in that case must have been

good-sized. . . . (*In a different tone.*) I am expecting someone. You will leave us alone in here.

RAGUENEAU. But how can I contrive it? My poets shortly will be coming . . .

LISE (*ironically*). For breakfast!

CYRANO. When I sign to you, you will clear the place of them.—What time is it?

RAGUENEAU. It is ten minutes past six.

CYRANO (*seating himself nervously at* RAGUENEAU'S *table and helping himself to paper*). A pen?

RAGUENEAU (*taking one from behind his ear, and offering it*). A swan's quill.

A MOUSQUETAIRE (*with enormous moustachios, enters; in a stentorian voice*). Good-morning! (LISE *goes hurriedly to him, toward the back.*)

CYRANO (*turning*). What is it?

RAGUENEAU. A friend of my wife's—a warrior—terrible, from his own report.

CYRANO (*taking up the pen again, and waving* RAGUENEAU *away*). Hush! . . . (*To himself.*) Write to her, . . . fold the letter, . . . hand it to her, . . . and make my escape. . . . (*Throwing down the pen.*) Coward! . . . But may I perish if I have the courage to speak to her, . . . to say a single word. . . . (*To* RAGUENEAU.) What time is it?

RAGUENEAU. A quarter past six.

CYRANO (*beating his breast*). A single word of all I carry here! . . . Whereas in writing . . . (*He takes up the pen again.*) Come, let us write it then, in very deed, the love-letter I have written in thought so many times, I have but to lay my soul beside my paper, and copy! (*He writes.*)

[*Beyond the glass door, shadowy lank hesitating shabby forms are seen moving.*]

[*Enter the* POETS, *clad in black, with hanging hose, sadly mudsplashed.*]

LISE (*coming forward, to* RAGUENEAU). Here they come, your scarecrows!

FIRST POET (*entering, to* RAGUENEAU). Brother in art! . . .

SECOND POET (*shaking both* RAGUENEAU'S *hands*). Dear fellow-bard. . . .

THIRD POET. Eagle of pastrycooks (*sniffs the air*), your eyrie smells divine!

FOURTH POET. Phoebus turned baker!

FIFTH POET. Apollo master-cook!

RAGUENEAU (*surrounded, embraced, shaken by the hand*). How at his ease a man feels at once with them!

FIRST POET. The reason we are late, is the crowd at the Porte de Nesle!

SECOND POET. Eight ugly ruffians, ripped open with the sword, lie weltering on the pavement.

CYRANO (*raising his head a second*). Eight? I thought there were only seven. (*Goes on with his letter.*)

RAGUENEAU (*to* CYRANO). Do you happen to know who is the hero of this event?

CYRANO (*negligently*). I? . . . No.

LISE (*to the* MOUSQUETAIRE). Do you?

THE MOUSQUETAIRE (*turning up the ends of his moustache*). Possibly!

CYRANO (*writing; from time to time he is heard murmuring a word or two*). . . . "*I love you . . .*"

FIRST POET. A single man, we were told, put a whole gang to flight!

SECOND POET. Oh, it was a rare sight! The ground was littered with pikes, and cudgels . . .

CYRANO (*writing*). . . . "*Your eyes . . .*"

THIRD POET. Hats were strewn as far as the Goldsmiths' square!

FIRST POET. Sapristi! He must have been a madman of mettle. . . .

CYRANO (*as above*). "*. . . your lips . . .*"

FIRST POET. An infuriate giant, the doer of that deed!

CYRANO (*same business*). "*. . . but when I see you, I come near to swooning with a tender dread . . .*"

SECOND POET (*snapping up a tart*). What have you lately written, Ragueneau?

CYRANO (*same business*). "*. . . who loves you devotedly . . .*" (*In the act of signing the letter, he stops, rises, and tucks it inside his doublet.*) No need to sign it. I deliver it myself.

RAGUENEAU (*to* SECOND POET). I have rhymed a recipe.

THIRD POET (*establishing himself beside a tray of cream puffs*). Let us hear this recipe!

FOURTH POET (*examining a brioche of which he has possessed himself*). It should not wear its cap so saucily on one side . . . it scarcely looks well! . . . (*Bites off the top.*)

FIRST POET. See, the spice-cake there, ogling a susceptible poet with eyes of almond under citron brows! . . . (*He takes the spice cake.*)

SECOND POET. We are listening!

THIRD POET (*slightly squeezing a cream puff between his fingers*). This puff creams at the mouth. . . . I water!

SECOND POET (*taking a bite out of the large pastry lyre*). For once the Lyre will have filled my stomach!

RAGUENEAU (*who has made ready to recite, has coughed, adjusted his cap, struck an attitude*). A recipe in rhyme!

SECOND POET (*to* FIRST POET, *nudging him*). Is it breakfast, with you?

FIRST POET (*to* SECOND POET). And with you, is it dinner?

RAGUENEAU. *How Almond Cheese-Cakes should be made.*

Briskly beat to lightness due,
    Eggs, a few;
With the eggs so beaten, beat—
Nicely strained for this same use—
    Lemon-juice,
Adding milk of almonds, sweet.

With fine pastry dough, rolled flat,
    After that,

Line each little scalloped mold;
Round the sides, light-fingered, spread
  Marmalade;
Pour the liquid eggy gold,

Into each delicious pit;
  Prison it
In the oven—and, bye and bye,
Almond cheese-cakes will in gay
  Blond array   10
Bless your nostril and your eye!

THE POETS (*their mouths full*). Exquisite! . . . Delicious!

ONE OF THE POETS (*choking*). Humph! (*They go toward the back, eating.* CYRANO, *who has been watching them, approaches* RAGUENEAU.)

CYRANO. While you recite your works to them, have you a notion how they stuff?

RAGUENEAU (*low, with a smile*). Yes, I see them . . . without looking, lest they should be abashed. I get a double pleasure thus from saying my verses over: I satisfy a harmless weakness of which I stand convicted, at the same time as giving those who have not fed a needed chance to feed!

CYRANO (*slapping him on the shoulder*). You, . . . I like you! (RAGUENEAU 30 *joins his friends.* CYRANO *looks after him; then, somewhat sharply.*) Hey, Lise! (LISE, *absorbed in tender conversation with the* MOUSQUETAIRE, *starts and comes forward toward* CYRANO.) Is that captain . . . laying siege to you?

LISE (*offended*). My eyes, sir, have ever held in respect those who meant hurt to my character. . . .

CYRANO. For eyes so resolute . . . I 40 thought yours looked a little languishing!

LISE (*choking with anger*). But . . .

CYRANO (*bluntly*). I like your husband. Wherefore, Madame Lise, I say he shall not be sc . . . horned!

LISE. But . . .

CYRANO (*raising his voice so as to be heard by the* MOUSQUETAIRE). A word to the wise! (*He bows to the* MOUSQUETAIRE, *and after looking at the clock, goes to the door at the back and stands in watch.*)

LISE (*to the* MOUSQUETAIRE, *who has simply returned* CYRANO's *bow*). Really . . . I am astonished at you. . . . Defy him . . . to his face!

THE MOUSQUETAIRE. To his face, indeed! . . . to his face! . . . (*He quickly moves off.* LISE *follows him.*)

CYRANO (*from the door at the back, signalling to* RAGUENEAU *that he should clear the room*). Pst! . . .

RAGUENEAU (*urging the* POETS *toward the door at the right*). We shall be much more comfortable in there. . . .

CYRANO (*impatiently*). Pst! . . . Pst! . . .

RAGUENEAU (*driving along the* POETS). I want to read you a little thing of mine. . . .

FIRST POET (*despairingly, his mouth full*). But the provisions. . . .

SECOND POET. Shall not be parted from us! (*They follow* RAGUENEAU *in procession, after making a raid on the eatables.*)

CYRANO. If I feel that there is so much as a glimmer of hope . . . I will out with my letter! . . .

[ROXANE, *masked, appears behind the glass door, followed by the* DUENNA.]

CYRANO (*instantly opening the door*). Welcome! (*Approaching the* DUENNA.) Madame, a word with you!

THE DUENNA. A dozen.

CYRANO. Are you fond of sweets?

THE DUENNA. To the point of indigestion!

CYRANO (*snatching some paper bags off the counter*). Good. Here are two sonnets of Benserade's . . .

THE DUENNA. Pooh!

CYRANO. Which I fill for you with grated almond drops.

THE DUENNA (*with a different expression*). Ha!

CYRANO. Do you look with favor upon the cate they call a trifle?

THE DUENNA. I affect it out of measure, when it has whipped cream inside.

CYRANO. Six shall be yours, thrown in with a poem by Saint-Amant. And in these verses of Chapelain I place this wedge of fruit-cake, light by the side of them. . . . Oh! And do you like tarts . . . little jam ones . . . fresh?

THE DUENNA. I dream of them at night!

CYRANO (*loading her arms with crammed paper bags*). Do me the favor to go and eat these in the street.

THE DUENNA. But . . .

CYRANO (*pushing her out*). And do not come back till you have finished it! (*He closes the door upon her, comes forward toward* ROXANE, *and stands, bareheaded, at a respectful distance.*) Blessed forevermore among all hours the hour in which, remembering that so lowly a being still draws breath, you were so gracious as to come to tell me . . . to tell me? . . .

ROXANE (*who has removed her mask*). First of all, that I thank you. For that churl, that coxcomb yesterday, whom you taught manners with your sword, is the one whom a great nobleman, who fancies himself in love with me . . .

CYRANO. De Guiche?

ROXANE (*dropping her eyes*). Has tried to force upon me as a husband.

CYRANO. Honorary? (*Bowing.*) It appears, then, that I fought, and I am glad of it, not for my graceless nose, but your thrice-beautiful eyes.

ROXANE. Further than that . . . I wished . . . But, before I can make the confession I have in mind to make, I must find in you once more the . . . almost brother, with whom as a child I used to play, in the park—do you remember?—by the lake!

CYRANO. I have not forgotten. Yes . . . you came every summer to Bergerac.

ROXANE. You used to fashion lances out of reeds . . .

CYRANO. The silk of the tasselled corn furnished hair for your doll . . .

ROXANE. It was the time of long delightful games . . .

CYRANO. And somewhat sour berries . . .

ROXANE. The time when you did everything I bade you!

CYRANO. Roxane, wearing short frocks, was known as Magdeleine.

ROXANE. Was I pretty in those days?

CYRANO. You were not ill-looking.

ROXANE. Sometimes, in your venturesome climbings you used to hurt yourself. You would come running to me, your hand bleeding. And, playing at being your mamma, I would harden my voice and say . . . (*She takes his hand.*) "Will you never keep out of mischief?" (*She stops short, amazed.*) Oh, it is too much! Here you have done it again! (CYRANO *tries to draw back his hand.*) No! Let me look at it! . . . Aren't you ashamed? A great boy like you! . . . How did this happen, and where?

CYRANO. Oh, fun . . . near the Porte de Nesle.

ROXANE (*sitting down at a table and dipping her handkerchief into a glass of water*). Let me have it.

CYRANO (*sitting down too*). So prettily, so cheeringly maternal!

ROXANE. And tell me, while I wash this naughty blood away . . . with how many were you fighting?

CYRANO. Oh, not quite a hundred.

ROXANE. Tell me about it.

CYRANO. No. What does it matter? You tell me, you . . . what you were going to tell me before, and did not dare . . .

ROXANE (*without releasing his hand*). I do dare, now. I have breathed in courage with the perfume of the past. Oh, yes, now I dare. Here it is. There is someone whom I love.

CYRANO. Ah! . . .

ROXANE. Oh, he does not know it.

CYRANO. Ah! . . .

ROXANE. As yet. . . .

CYRANO. Ah! . . .

ROXANE. But if he does not know it, he soon will.

CYRANO. Ah! . . .

ROXANE. A poor boy who until now has loved me timidly, from a distance, without daring to speak. . . .

CYRANO. Ah! . . .

ROXANE. No, leave me your hand. It is hot, this will cool it. . . . But I have read his heart in his face.

CYRANO. Ah! . . .

ROXANE (*completing the bandaging of his hand with her small pocket-handkerchief*). And, cousin, is it not a strange coincidence—that he should serve exactly in your regiment!

CYRANO. Ah! . . .

ROXANE (*laughing*). Yes. He is a cadet, in the same company!

CYRANO. Ah! . . .

ROXANE. He bears plain on his forehead the stamp of wit, of genius! He is proud, noble, young, brave, handsome. . . .

CYRANO (*rising, pale*). Handsome! . . .

ROXANE. What . . . what is the matter?

CYRANO. With me? . . . Nothing! . . . It is . . . it is . . . (*Showing his hand, smiling.*) You know! . . . It smarts a little . . .

ROXANE. In short, I love him. I must tell you, however, that I have never seen him save at the play.

CYRANO. Then you have never spoken to each other?

ROXANE. Only with our eyes.

CYRANO. But, then . . . how can you know? . . .

ROXANE. Oh, under the lindens of Place Royale, people will talk. A trustworthy gossip told me many things!

CYRANO. A cadet, did you say?

ROXANE. A cadet, in your company.

CYRANO. His name?

ROXANE. Baron Christian de Neuvillette.

CYRANO. What? He is not in the cadets.

ROXANE. He is! He certainly is, since morning. Captain Carbon de Castel-Jaloux.

CYRANO. And quickly, quickly, she throws away her heart! . . . But my poor little girl . . .

THE DUENNA (*opening the door at the back*). Monsieur de Bergerac, I have eaten them, every one!

CYRANO. Now read the poetry printed upon the bags! (*The* DUENNA *disappears.*) My poor child, you who can endure none but the choicest language, who savor eloquence and wit, . . . if he should be a barbarian!

ROXANE. No! No! . . . He has hair like one of D'Urfé's heroes!

CYRANO. If he had on proof as homely a wit as he has pretty hair!

ROXANE. No! No! . . . I can see at a single glance, his utterances are fine, pointed . . .

CYRANO. Ah, yes! A man's utterances are invariably like his moustache! . . . Still, if he *were* a ninny? . . .

ROXANE (*stamping with her foot*). I should die, there!

CYRANO (*after a time*). You bade me come here that you might tell me this? I scarcely see the appropriateness, madame.

ROXANE. Ah, it was because someone yesterday let death into my soul by telling me that in your company you are all Gascons, . . . all!

CYRANO. And that we pick a quarrel with every impudent fledgling, not Gascon, admitted by favor to our thoroughbred Gascon ranks? That is what you heard?

ROXANE. Yes, and you can imagine how distracted I am for him!

CYRANO (in his teeth). You well may be!

ROXANE. But I thought, yesterday, when you towered up, great and invincible, giving his due to that miscreant, standing your ground against those caitiffs, I thought "Were he but willing, he of whom all are in awe . . ."

CYRANO. Very well, I will protect your little baron.

ROXANE. Ah, you will . . . you will protect him for me? . . . I have always felt for you the tenderest regard!

CYRANO. Yes, yes.

ROXANE. You will be his friend?

CYRANO. I will!

ROXANE. And never shall he have to fight a duel?

CYRANO. I swear it.

ROXANE. Oh, I quite love you! . . . Now I must go. (*She hurriedly resumes her mask, throws a veil over her head; says absentmindedly.*) But you have not yet told me about last night's encounter. It must have been amazing! . . . Tell him to write to me. (*She kisses her hand to him.*) I love you dearly!

CYRANO. Yes, yes.

ROXANE. A hundred men against you? . . . Well, adieu. We are fast friends.

CYRANO. Yes, yes.

ROXANE. Tell him to write me! . . . A hundred men! You shall tell me another time. I must not linger now . . . A hundred men! What a heroic thing to do!

CYRANO (*bowing*). Oh, I have done better since!

[*Exit* ROXANE. CYRANO *stands motionless, staring at the ground. Silence. The door at the right opens.* RAGUENEAU *thrusts in his head.*]

RAGUENEAU. May we come back?

CYRANO (*without moving*). Yes . . .

[RAGUENEAU *beckons, his friends come in again. At the same time, in the doorway at the back, appears* CARBON DE CASTEL-JALOUX, *costume of a Captain of the Guards. On seeing* CYRANO, *he gesticulates exaggeratedly by way of signal to someone out of sight.*]

CARBON DE CASTEL-JALOUX. He is here!

CYRANO (*looking up*). Captain!

CARBON DE CASTEL-JALOUX (*exultant*). Hero! We know all! . . . About thirty of my cadets are out there! . . .

CYRANO (*drawing back*). But . . .

CARBON DE CASTEL-JALOUX (*trying to lead him off*). Come! . . . You are in request!

CYRANO. No!

CARBON DE CASTEL-JALOUX. They are drinking across the way, at the Cross of the Hilt.

CYRANO. I . . .

CARBON DE CASTEL-JALOUX (*going to the door and shouting toward the street corner, in a voice of thunder*). The hero refuses. He is not in the humor!

A VOICE (*outside*). Ah, *sandious!* . . . (*Tumult outside, noise of clanking swords and of boots drawing nearer.*)

CARBON DE CASTEL-JALOUX (*rubbing his hands*). Here they come, across the street. . . .

THE CADETS (*entering the cookshop*). *Mille dious!* . . . *Capdedious!* . . . *Mordious!* . . . *Pocapdedious!* . . .

RAGUENEAU (*backing in alarm*). Messieurs, are you all natives of Gascony?

THE CADETS. All!

ONE OF THE CADETS (to CYRANO). Bravo!

CYRANO. Baron!

OTHER CADET (shaking both CYRANO's hands). Vivat!

CYRANO. Baron!

THIRD CADET. Let me hug you to my heart!

CYRANO. Baron!

SEVERAL GASCONS. Let us hug him!

CYRANO (not knowing which one to answer). Baron! . . . baron! . . . your pardon!

RAGUENEAU. Messieurs, are you all barons?

THE CADETS. All!

RAGUENEAU. Are they truly?

FIRST CADET. Our coats of arms piled up would dwindle in the clouds!

LE BRET (entering, running to CYRANO). They are looking for you! A crowd, gone mad as March, led by those who were with you last night.

CYRANO (alarmed). You never told them where to find me? . . .

LE BRET (rubbing his hands). I did.

A BURGHER (entering, followed by a number of others). Monsieur, the Marais is coming in a body!

[The street outside has filled with people. Sedan-chairs, coaches stop before the door.]

LE BRET (smiling, low to CYRANO). And Roxane?

CYRANO (quickly). Be quiet!

THE CROWD (outside). Cyrano! (A rabble bursts into the cookshop. Confusion. Shouting.)

RAGUENEAU (standing upon a table). My shop is invaded! They are breaking everything! It is glorious!

PEOPLE (pressing round CYRANO). My friend . . . my friend. . . .

CYRANO. I had not so many friends . . . yesterday!

LE BRET. This is success!

A YOUNG MARQUIS (running toward CY-RANO, with outstretched hands). If you knew, my dear fellow . . .

CYRANO. Dear? . . . Fellow? . . . Where was it we stood sentinel together?

OTHER MARQUIS. I wish to present you, sir, to several ladies, who are outside in my coach. . . .

CYRANO (coldly). But you, to me, by whom will you first be presented?

LE BRET (astonished). But what is the matter with you?

CYRANO. Be still!

A MAN OF LETTERS (with an inkhorn). Will you kindly favor me with the details of . . .

CYRANO. No.

LE BRET (nudging him). That is Theophrastus Renaudot, the inventor of the gazette.

CYRANO. Enough!

LE BRET. A sheet close packed with various information! It is an idea, they say, likely to take firm root and flourish!

A POET (coming forward). Monsieur . . .

CYRANO. Another!

THE POET. I am anxious to make a pentacrostic on your name.

SOMEBODY ELSE (likewise approaching CYRANO). Monsieur . . .

CYRANO. Enough, I say! (At the gesture of impatience which CYRANO cannot repress, the crowd draws away.)

[DE GUICHE appears, escorted by officers; among them CUIGY, BRISSAILLE, those who followed CYRANO at the end of the first act. CUIGY hurries toward CYRANO.]

CUIGY (to CYRANO). Monsieur de Guiche! (Murmurs. Everyone draws back.) He comes at the request of the Marshal de Gaussion.

DE GUICHE (bowing to CYRANO). Who wishes to express his admiration for your latest exploit, the fame of which has reached him.

THE CROWD. Bravo!

CYRANO (*bowing*). The Marshal is qualified to judge of courage.

DE GUICHE. He would scarcely have believed the report, had these gentlemen not been able to swear they had seen the deed performed.

CUIGY. With our own eyes!

LE BRET (*low to* CYRANO, *who wears an abstracted air*). But . . .

CYRANO. Be silent!

LE BRET. You appear to be suffering . . .

CYRANO (*starting, and straightening himself*). Before these people . . . (*His moustache bristles; he expands his chest.*) I . . . suffering? . . . You shall see!

DE GUICHE (*in whose ear* CUIGY *has been whispering*). But this is by no means the first gallant achievement marking your career. You serve in the madcap Gascon company, do you not?

CYRANO. In the cadets, yes.

ONE OF THE CADETS (*in a great voice*). Among his countrymen!

DE GUICHE (*considering the* GASCONS, *in line behind* CYRANO). Ah, ha!—All these gentlemen then of the formidable aspect, are the famous . . .

CARBON DE CASTEL-JALOUX. Cyrano!

CYRANO. Captain? . . .

CARBON DE CASTEL-JALOUX. My company, I believe, is here in total. Be so obliging as to present it to the Count.

CYRANO (*taking a step toward* DE GUICHE, *and pointing at the* CADETS).
They are the Gascony Cadets
Of Carbon de Castel-Jaloux;
Famed fighters, liars, desperates,
They are the Gascony Cadets!
All, better-born than pickpockets,
Talk couchant, rampant, . . . pendent, too!
They are the Gascony Cadets
Of Carbon de Castel-Jaloux!

Cat-whiskered, eyed like falconets,
Wolf-toothed and heron-legged, they hew
The rabble down that snarls and threats . . .
Cat-whiskered, eyed like falconets!
Great pomp of plume hides and offsets
Holes in those hats they wear askew . . .
Cat-whiskered, eyed like falconets,
They drive the snarling mob, and hew!

The mildest of their sobriquets
Are Crack-my-crown and Run-me-through,
Mad drunk on glory Gascon gets!
These boasters of soft sobriquets
Whenever rapier rapier whets
Are met in punctual rendezvous. . . .
The mildest of their sobriquets
Are Crack-my-crown and Run-me-through!

They are the Gascony Cadets
That give the jealous spouse his due!
Lean forth, adorable coquettes
They are the Gascony Cadets,
With plumes and scarfs and aigulets!
The husband gray may well look blue. . . .
They are the Gascony Cadets
That give the jealous spouse his due!

DE GUICHE (*nonchalantly seated in an armchair which* RAGUENEAU *has hurriedly brought for him*). A gentleman provides himself today, by way of luxury, with a poet. May I look upon you as mine?

CYRANO. No, your lordship, as nobody's.

DE GUICHE. My uncle Richelieu yesterday found your spontaneity diverting. I shall be pleased to be of use to you with him.

LE BRET (*dazzled*). Great God!

DE GUICHE. I cannot think I am wrong in supposing that you have rhymed a tragedy?

LE BRET (*whispering to* CYRANO). My boy, your Agrippina will be played!

DE GUICHE. Take it to him. . . .

CYRANO (*tempted and pleased*). Really . .

DE GUICHE. He has taste in such matters. He will no more than, here and there, alter a word, recast a passage. . . .

CYRANO (*whose face has instantly darkened*). Not to be considered, monsieur! My blood runs cold at the thought of a single comma added or suppressed.

DE GUICHE. On the other hand, my dear sir, when a verse finds favor with him, he pays for it handsomely.

CYRANO. He scarcely can pay me as I pay myself, when I have achieved a verse to my liking, by singing it over to myself!

DE GUICHE. You are proud.

CYRANO. You have observed it?

ONE OF THE CADETS (*coming in with a number of disreputable, draggled tattered hats threaded on his sword*). Look, Cyrano! at the remarkable feathered game we secured this morning near the Porte de Nesle! The hats of the fugitives!

CARBON DE CASTEL-JALOUX. *Spolioe opimoe!*

ALL (*laughing*). Ha! Ha! Ha! . . .

CUIGY. The one who planned that military action, my word! must be proud of it today!

BRISSAILLE. Is it known who did it?

DE GUICHE. I!—(*The laughter stops short.*) They had instructions to chastise—a matter one does not attend to in person—a drunken scribbler. (*Constrained silence.*)

THE CADET (*under breath, to* CYRANO, *indicating the hats*). What can we do with them? They are oily. . . . Make them into a hotch pot?

CYRANO (*taking the sword with the hats, and bowing, as he shakes them off at* DE GUICHE'S *feet*). Monsieur, if you should care to return them to your friends? . . .

DE GUICHE (*rises, and in a curt tone*). My chair and bearers, at once. (To CYRANO, *violently.*) As for you, sir . . .

A VOICE (*in the street, shouting*). The chairmen of Monseigneur the Comte de Guiche!

DE GUICHE (*who has recovered control over himself, with a smile*). Have you read Don Quixote?

CYRANO. I have. And at the name of that divine madman, I uncover . . .

DE GUICHE. My advice to you is to ponder . . .

A CHAIRMAN (*appearing at the back*). The chair is at the door!

DE GUICHE. The chapter of the wind mills.

CYRANO (*bowing*). Chapter thirteen.

DE GUICHE. For when a man attacks them, it often happens . . .

CYRANO. I have attacked, am I to infer, a thing that veers with every wind?

DE GUICHE. That one of their far-reaching canvas arms pitches him down into the mud!

CYRANO. Or up among the stars!

[*Exit* DE GUICHE. *He is seen getting into his chair. The gentlemen withdraw whispering.* LE BRET *goes to the door with them. The crowd leaves. The* CADETS *remain seated at the right and left at tables where food and drink is brought to them.*]

CYRANO (*bowing with a derisive air to those who leave without daring to take leave of him*). Gentlemen . . . gentlemen . . . gentlemen. . . .

LE BRET (*coming forward, greatly distressed, lifting his hands to Heaven*). Oh, in what a pretty pair of shoes . . .

CYRANO. Oh, you! . . . I expect you to grumble!

LE BRET. But yourself, you will agree with me that invariably to cut the throat of opportunity becomes an exaggeration! . . .

CYRANO. Yes. I agree. I do exaggerate.

LE BRET (*triumphant*). You see, you admit it! . . .

CYRANO. But for the sake of principle, and of example, as well, I think it a good thing to exaggerate as I do!

LE BRET. Could you but leave apart, once in a while, your mousquetaire of a soul, fortune, undoubtedly, fame . . . 10

CYRANO. And what should a man do? Seek some grandee, take him for patron, and like the obscure creeper clasping a tree-trunk, and licking the bark of that which props it up, attain to height by craft instead of strength? No, I thank you. Dedicate, as they all do, poems to financiers? Wear motley in the humble hope of seeing the lips of a minister distend for once in a 20 smile not ominous of ill? No, I thank you. Eat every day a toad? Be threadbare at the belly with grovelling? Have his skin dirty soonest at the knees? Practice feats of dorsal elasticity? No, I thank you. With one hand stroke the goat while with the other he waters the cabbage? Make gifts of senna that counter-gifts of rhubarb may accrue, and indefatigably 30 swing his censer in some beard? No, I thank you. Push himself from lap to lap, become a little great man in a great little circle, propel his ship with madrigals for oars and in his sails the sighs of the elderly ladies? No, I thank you. Get the good editor Sercy to print his verses at proper expense? No, I thank you. Contrive to be nominated Pope in conclaves held by im- 40 beciles in wineshops? No, I thank you. Work to construct a name upon the basis of a sonnet, instead of constructing other sonnets? No, I thank you. Discover talent in tyros, and in them alone? Stand in terror of what ga-

zettes may please to say, and say to himself, "At whatever cost, may I figure in the Paris Mercury!" No, I thank you. Calculate, cringe, peak, prefer making a call to a poem—petition, solicit, apply? No, I thank you! No, I thank you! No, I thank you! But . . . sing, dream, laugh, loaf, be single, be free, have eyes that look squarely, a voice with a ring; wear, if he chooses, his hat hindside afore; for a yes, for a no, fight a duel or turn a ditty! . . . Work, without concern of fortune or of glory, to accomplish the heart's-desired journey to the moon! Put forth nothing that has not its spring in the very heart, yet, modest, say to himself, "Old man, be satisfied with blossoms, fruits, yea, leaves alone, so they be gathered in your garden and not another man's!" Then, if it happen that to some small extent he triumph, be obliged to render of the glory, to Caesar, not one jot, but honestly appropriate it all. In short, scorning to be the parasite, the creeper, if even failing to be the oak, rise, not perchance to a great height, . . . but rise alone!

LE BRET. Alone? Good! but not one against all! How the devil did you contract the mania that possesses you for making enemies, always, everywhere?

CYRANO. By seeing you make friends, and smile to those same flocks of friends with a mouth that takes for model an old purse! I wish not to be troubled to return bows in the street, and I exclaim with glee, "An enemy the more!"

LE BRET. This is mental aberration!

CYRANO. I do not dispute it. I am so framed. To displease is my pleasure. I love that one should hate me. Dear friend, if you but know how much better a man walks under the exciting fire of hostile eyes, and how amused he may become over the spots on his doublet, spattered by Envy and Cowardice! . . . You, the facile friendship wherewith you surround yourself, resembles those wide Italian collars, loose and easy, with a perforated pattern, in which the neck looks like a woman's. They are more com- 10 fortable, but of less high effect; for the brow not held in proud position by any constraint from them, falls to nodding this way and that. . . . But for me every day Hatred starches and flutes the ruff whose stiffness holds the head well in place. Every new enemy is another plait in it, adding compulsion, but adding, as well, a ray: for, similar in every point to the Spanish 20 ruff, Hatred is a bondage, . . . but is a halo, too!

LE BRET (*after a pause, slipping his arm through* CYRANO's). To the hearing of all be proud and bitter, . . . but to me, below breath, say simply that she does not love you!

CYRANO (*sharply*). Not a word!

[CHRISTIAN *has come in and mingled with the* CADETS; *they ignore him; he has finally* 30 *gone to a little table by himself, where* LISE *waits on him.*]

ONE OF THE CADETS (*seated at a table at the back, glass in hand*). Hey, Cyrano! (CYRANO *turns toward him.*) Your story!

CYRANO. Presently! (*He goes toward the back on* LE BRET's *arm. They talk low.*)

THE CADET (*rising and coming toward the front*). The account of your fight! It will be the best lesson (*Stopping in front* 40 *of the table at which* CHRISTIAN *is sitting.*) for this timorous novice!

CHRISTIAN (*looking up*). . . . Novice?

OTHER CADET. Yes, sickly product of the North!

CHRISTIAN. Sickly?

FIRST CADET (*impressively*). Monsieur de Neuvillette, it is a good deed to warn you that there is a thing no more to be mentioned in our company than rope in the house of the hanged!

CHRISTIAN. And what is it?

OTHER CADET (*in a terrifying voice*). Look at me! (*Three times, darkly, he places his finger upon his nose.*) You have understood?

CHRISTIAN. Ah, it is the . . .

OTHER CADET. Silence! . . . Never must you so much as breathe that word, or . . . (*He points toward* CYRANO *at the back talking with* LE BRET.) You will have him, over there, to deal with!

OTHER CADET (*who while* CHRISTIAN *was turned toward the first, has noiselessly seated himself on the table behind him.*) Two persons were lately cut off in their pride by him for talking through their noses. He thought it personal.

OTHER CADET (*in a cavernous voice, as he rises from under the table where he had slipped on all fours*). Not the remotest allusion, ever, to the fatal cartilage, . . . unless you fancy an early grave!

OTHER CADET. A word will do the business! What did I say? . . . A word? . . . A simple gesture! Make use of your pocket-handkerchief, you will shortly have use for your shroud!

[*Silence. All around* CHRISTIAN *watch him, with folded arms. He rises and goes to* CARBON DE CASTEL-JALOUX, *who in conversation with an officer, affects to notice nothing.*]

CHRISTIAN. Captain!

CARBON DE CASTEL-JALOUX (*turning and looking him rather contemptuously up and down*). Monsieur?

CHRISTIAN. What is the proper course for a man when he finds gentlemen of the South too boastful?

CARBON DE CASTEL-JALOUX. He must

prove to them that one can be of the North, yet brave. (*He turns his back upon him.*)

CHRISTIAN. I am much obliged.

FIRST CADET (*to* CYRANO). And now, the tale of your adventure!

ALL. Yes, yes, now let us hear!

CYRANO (*coming forward among them*). My adventure? (*All draw their stools nearer, and sit around him, with craned necks.* CHRISTIAN *sits astride a chair.*) Well, then, I was marching to meet them. The moon up in the skies was shining like a silver watch, when suddenly I know not what careful watch-maker having wrapped it in a cottony cloud, there occurred the blackest imaginable night; and, the streets being no-wise lighted—*mordious!*—you could see no further than . . .

CHRISTIAN. Your nose. (*Silence. Every one slowly gets up; all look with terror at* CYRANO. *He has stopped short, amazed. Pause.*)

CYRANO. Who is that man?

ONE OF THE CADETS (*low*). He joined this morning.

CYRANO (*taking a step toward* CHRISTIAN). This morning?

CARBON DE CASTEL-JALOUX (*low*). His name is Baron de Neuvill . . .

CYRANO (*stopping short*). Ah, very well. . . . (*He turns pale, then red, gives evidence of another impulse to throw himself upon* CHRISTIAN.) I . . . (*He conquers it, and says in a stifled voice.*) Very well. (*He takes up his tale.*) As I was saying . . . (*With a burst of rage.*) Mordious! . . . (*He continues in a natural tone.*) one could not see in the very least. (*Consternation. All resume their seats, staring at one another.*) And I was walking along, reflecting that for a very insignificant rogue I was probably about to offend some great prince who would bear me a lasting grudge, that, in brief, I was about to thrust my . . .

CHRISTIAN. Nose . . . (*All get up.* CHRISTIAN *has tilted his chair and is rocking on the hind legs.*)

CYRANO (*choking*). Finger . . . between the tree and the bark; for the aforesaid prince might be of sufficient power to trip me and throw me . . .

CHRISTIAN. On my nose . . .

CYRANO (*wipes the sweat from his brow*). But, said I, "Gascony forward! Never falter when duty prompts! Forward, Cyrano!" and, saying this, I advance —when suddenly, in the darkness, I barely avoid a blow . . .

CHRISTIAN. Upon the nose . . .

CYRANO. I ward it . . . and thereupon find myself . . .

CHRISTIAN. Nose to nose . . .

CYRANO (*springing toward him*). Ventre-Saint-Gris! . . . (*All the* GASCONS *rush forward, to see;* CYRANO, *on reaching* CHRISTIAN, *controls himself and proceeds.*) . . . with a hundred drunken brawlers, smelling . . .

CHRISTIAN. To the nose's limit . . .

CYRANO (*deathly pale, and smiling*). . . . . of garlic and of grease. I leap forward, head lowered . . .

CHRISTIAN. Nose to the wind! . . .

CYRANO. And I charge them. I knock two breathless and run a third through the body. One lets off at me: Paf! and I retort . . .

CHRISTIAN. Pif!

CYRANO (*exploding*). Death and damnation! Go—all of you! (*All the* CADETS *make for the door.*)

FIRST CADET. The tiger is roused at last!

CYRANO. All! and leave me with this man.

SECOND CADET. Bigre! When we see him again, it will be in the shape of mince-meat!

RAGUENEAU. Mince-meat? . . .

OTHER CADET. In one of your pies.

RAGUENEAU. I feel myself grow white and flabby as a table-napkin!

CARBON DE CASTEL-JALOUX. Let us go!

OTHER CADET. Not a smudge of him will be left!

OTHER CADET. What these walls are about to behold gives me gooseflesh to think upon!

OTHER CADET (*closing the door at the right*). 10 Ghastly! . . . Ghastly!

[*All have left, by the back or the sides, a few up the stairway.* CYRANO *and* CHRISTIAN *remain face to face, and look at each other a moment.*]

CYRANO. Embrace me!

CHRISTIAN. Monsieur . . .

CYRANO. Brave fellow.

CHRISTIAN. But what does this . . .

CYRANO. Very brave fellow. I wish you 20 to.

CHRISTIAN. Will you tell me? . . .

CYRANO. Embrace me, I am her brother.

CHRISTIAN. Whose?

CYRANO. Hers!

CHRISTIAN. What do you mean?

CYRANO. Roxane's!

CHRISTIAN (*running to him*). Heavens! You, her brother?

CYRANO. Or the same thing: her first 30 cousin.

CHRISTIAN. And she has . . .

CYRANO. Told me everything!

CHRISTIAN. Does she love me?

CYRANO. Perhaps!

CHRISTIAN (*seizing his hands*). How happy I am, monsieur, to make your acquaintance! . . .

CYRANO. That is what I call a sudden sentiment!

CHRISTIAN. Forgive me! . . .

CYRANO (*looking at him, laying his hand upon his shoulder*). It is true that he is handsome, the rascal!

CHRISTIAN. If you but knew, monsieur, how greatly I admire you! . . .

CYRANO. But all those noses which you . . .

CHRISTIAN. I take them back!

CYRANO. Roxane expects a letter tonight . . .

CHRISTIAN. Alas!

CYRANO. What is the matter?

CHRISTIAN. I am lost if I cease to be dumb!

CYRANO. How is that?

CHRISTIAN. Alas! I am such a dunce that I could kill myself for shame!

CYRANO. But, no . . . no. . . . You are surely not a dunce, if you believe you are! Besides, you scarcely attacked me like a dunce.

CHRISTIAN. Oh, it is easy to find words in mounting to the assault! Indeed, I own to a certain cheap military readiness, but when I am before women, I have not a word to say. . . . Yet their eyes, when I pass by, express a kindness toward me . . .

CYRANO. And do their hearts not express the same when you stop beside them?

CHRISTIAN. No! . . . for I am of those— I recognize it, and am dismayed!— who do not know how to talk of love.

CYRANO. *Tiens!* . . . It seems to me that if Nature had taken more pains with my shape, I should have been of those who do know how to talk of it.

CHRISTIAN. Oh, to be able to express things gracefully!

CYRANO. Oh, to be a graceful little figure of a passing mousquetaire!

CHRISTIAN. Roxane is a précieuse, . . . there is no chance but that I shall be a disillusion to Roxane!

CYRANO (*looking at* CHRISTIAN). If I had, to express my soul, such an interpreter! . . .

CHRISTIAN (*desperately*). I ought to have eloquence! . . .

CYRANO (*abruptly*). Eloquence I will lend you! . . . And you, to me, shall lend all-conquering physical charm . . . and between us we will compose a hero of romance!

CHRISTIAN. What?

CYRANO. Should you be able to say, as your own, things which I day by day would teach you?

CHRISTIAN. You are suggesting? . . .

CYRANO. Roxane shall not have disillusions! Tell me, shall we win her heart, we two as one? Will you submit to feel, transmitted from my leather doublet into your doublet stitched with silk, the soul I wish to share?

CHRISTIAN. But Cyrano! . . .

CYRANO. Christian, will you?

CHRISTIAN. You frighten me!

CYRANO. Since you fear, left to yourself, to chill her heart, will you consent— and soon it will take fire, I vouch for it!—to contribute your lips to my phrases?

CHRISTIAN. Your eyes shine! . . .

CYRANO. Will you?

CHRISTIAN. What, would it please you so much?

CYRANO (*with rapture*). It would . . . (*Remembering, and confining himself to expressing an artistic pleasure.*) . . . amuse me! It is an experiment fit surely to tempt a poet. Will you complete me, and let me in exchange complete you? We will walk side by side: you in full light, I in your shadow. . . . I will be wit to you . . . you, to me, shall be good looks!

CHRISTIAN. But the letter, which should be sent to her without delay? . . . Never shall I be able . . .

CYRANO (*taking from his doublet the letter written in the first part of the act*). The letter? Here it is!

CHRISTIAN. How? . . .

CYRANO. It only wants the address.

CHRISTIAN. I . . .

CYRANO. You can send it without uneasiness. It is a good letter.

CHRISTIAN. You had? . . .

CYRANO. You shall never find us—poets! —without epistles in our pockets to the Chlorises . . . of our imagining! For we are those same that have for mistress a dream blown into the bubble of a name! Take—you shall convert this feigning into earnest; I was sending forth at random these confessions and laments: you shall make the wandering birds to settle . . . Take it! You shall see . . . I was as eloquent as if I had been sincere! Take, and have done!

CHRISTIAN. But will it not need to be altered in any part? . . . Written without object, will it fit Roxane?

CYRANO. Like a glove!

CHRISTIAN. But . . .

CYRANO. Trust to the blindness of love . . . and vanity! Roxane will never question that it was written for her.

CHRISTIAN. Ah, my friend! (*He throws himself into* CYRANO'S *arms. They stand embraced.*)

ONE OF THE CADETS (*opening the door a very little*). Nothing more . . . The stillness of death . . . I dare not look . . . (*He thrusts in his head.*) What is this?

ALL THE CADETS (*entering and seeing* CYRANO *and* CHRISTIAN *locked in each other's arms*). Ah! . . . Oh! . . .

ONE OF THE CADETS. This passes bounds! (*Consternation.*)

THE MOUSQUETAIRE (*impudent*). Ouais?

CARBON DE CASTEL-JALOUX. Our demon is waxen mild as an apostle; smitten upon one nostril, he turns the other also!

THE MOUSQUETAIRE. It is in order now to speak of his nose, is it? (*Calling* LISE, *with a swaggering air.*) Hey, Lise! now listen and look. (*Pointedly sniffing the air.*) Oh, . . . oh, . . . it is surprising! . . . what an odor! (*Going to* CYRANO.) But monsieur must have smelled it, too? Can you tell me what it is, so plain in the air?

CYRANO (*beating him*). Why, sundry blows! (*Joyful antics of the* CADETS *in beholding* CYRANO *himself again.*)

CURTAIN

ACT III

ROXANE'S KISS

A small square in the old Marais. Old-fashioned houses. Narrow streets seen in perspective. At the right, ROXANE'S *house and the wall of her garden, above which spreading* 10 *tree-tops. Over the house-door, a balcony and window. A bench beside the doorstep.*

The wall is overclambered by ivy, the balcony wreathed with jasmine.

By means of the bench and projecting stones in the wall, the balcony can easily be scaled.

On the opposite side, old house in the same style of architecture, brick and stone, with entrance-door. The door-knocker is swaddled 20 *in linen.*

At the rise of the curtain, the DUENNA *is seated on the bench. The window on* ROXANE'S *balcony is wide open.*

RAGUENEAU, *in a sort of livery, stands near the* DUENNA; *he is finishing the tale of his misfortunes, drying his eyes.*

RAGUENEAU. And then, she eloped with a mousquetaire! Ruined, forsaken, I 30 was hanging myself. I had already taken leave of earth, when Monsieur de Bergerac, happening along, unhanged me, and proposed me to his cousin as her steward. . . .

THE DUENNA. But how did you fall into such disaster?

RAGUENEAU. Lise was fond of soldiers, I, of poets! Mars ate up all left over by Apollo. Under those circumstances, 40 you conceive, the pantry soon was bare.

THE DUENNA (*rising and calling toward the open window*). Roxane, are you ready? . . . They are waiting for us! . . .

ROXANE'S VOICE (*through the window*). I am putting on my mantle!

THE DUENNA (*to* RAGUENEAU, *pointing at the door opposite*). It is over there, opposite, we are expected. At Clomire's. She holds a meeting in her little place. A disquisition upon the Softer Sentiments is to be read.

RAGUENEAU. Upon the Softer Sentiments?

THE DUENNA (*coyly*). Yes! . . . (*Calling toward the window.*) Roxane, you must make haste, or we shall miss the disquisition upon the Softer Sentiments!

ROXANE'S VOICE. I am coming! (*A sound of string-instruments is heard, drawing nearer.*)

CYRANO'S VOICE (*singing in the wings*). La! la! la! la! la! . . .

THE DUENNA (*surprised*). We are to have music?

CYRANO (*enters followed by two* PAGES *with theorbos*). I tell you it is a demi-semi-quaver! . . . you demi-semi-noddle!

FIRST PAGE (*ironically*). Monsieur knows then about quavers, semi and demi?

CYRANO. I know music, as do all Gassendi's disciples!

THE PAGE (*playing and singing*). La! la!

CYRANO (*snatching the theorbo from him and continuing the musical phrase*). I can carry on the melody. . . . La, la, la, la, . . .

OXANE (*appearing on the balcony*). It is you?

YRANO (*singing upon the tune he is continuing*). I, indeed, who salute your lilies and present my respects to your ro-o-oses! . . .

OXANE. I am coming down! (*She leaves the balcony.*) 10

HE DUENNA (*pointing at the* PAGES). What is the meaning of these two virtuosi?

YRANO. A wager I won from D'Assoucy. We were disputing upon a question of grammar. Yes! No! Yes! No! Suddenly pointing at these two tall knaves, expert at clawing strings, by whom he constantly goes attended, he said, "I wager a day long of music!" He lost. Until therefore 20 the next rise of the sun, I shall have dangling after me these archlute players, harmonious witnesses of all I do! . . . At first I liked it very well, but now it palls a little. (*To the musicians.*) Hey! . . . Go, from me, to Montfleury, and play him a pavane! . . . (*The* PAGES *go toward the back. To the* DUENNA.) I have come to inquire of Roxane, as I do every eve- 30 ning . . . (*To the* PAGES *who are leaving.*) Play a long time . . . and out of tune! (*To the* DUENNA.) . . . whether in the friend of her soul she can still detect no fault?

OXANE (*coming out of the house*). Ah, how beautiful he is, what wit he has, how deeply I love him!

YRANO (*smiling*). Christian has so much wit? . . .

OXANE. Cousin, more than yourself! 40

YRANO. I grant you.

OXANE. There is not one alive, I truly believe, more apt at turning those pretty nothings which yet are everything. . . . Sometimes he is of an

absent mood, his muse is woolgathering, then, suddenly, he will say the most enchanting things!

CYRANO. (*incredulous*). Come! . . .

ROXANE. Oh, it is too bad! Men are all alike, narrow, narrow: because he is handsome, he cannot possibly be witty!

CYRANO. So he talks of the heart in acceptable fashion?

ROXANE. Talks, cousin, is feeble. . . . He dissertates!

CYRANO. And writes? . . .

ROXANE. Still better! Listen now to this . . . (*Declaiming.*) "*The more of my heart you steal from me, the more heart I have!*" (*Triumphantly to* CYRANO.) Well? . . .

CYRANO. Pooh!

ROXANE. And to this: "*Since you have stolen my heart, and since I must suffer, to suffer with send me your own!*"

CYRANO. Now he has too much heart, now he has not enough, . . . just what does he want, in the matter of quantity?

ROXANE. You vex me! You are eaten up with jealousy . . .

CYRANO (*starting*). *Hein?*

ROXANE. Author's jealousy! And this, could anything be more exquisitely tender? "*Unanimously, believe it, my heart cries out to you, and if kisses could be sent in writing, Love, you should read my letter with your lips . . .*"

CYRANO (*in spite of himself smiling with satisfaction*). Ha! Ha! Those particular lines seem to me . . . ho! . . . ho! . . . (*remembering himself, disdainfully*) . . . puny, pretty . . .

ROXANE. This, then . . .

CYRANO (*delighted*). You know his letters by heart?

ROXANE. All!

CYRANO. It is flattering, one cannot deny.

ROXANE. In this art of expressing love he is a master!

CYRANO (*modest*). Oh, . . . a master!

ROXANE (*peremptory*). A master!

CYRANO. As you please, then . . . a master!

THE DUENNA (*who had gone toward the back, coming quickly forward*). Monsieur de Guiche! (*To* CYRANO, *pushing him toward the house.*) Go in! It is perhaps better that he should not see you here! it might put him on the scent . . .

ROXANE (*to* CYRANO). Yes, of my dear secret! He loves me, he is powerful, . . . he must not find out! He might cut in sunder our loves . . . with an axe!

CYRANO (*going into the house*). Very well, very well.

[DE GUICHE *appears.*]

ROXANE (*to* DE GUICHE, *with a curtsey*). I was leaving the house.

DE GUICHE. I have come to bid you farewell.

ROXANE. You are going away?

DE GUICHE. To war.

ROXANE. Ah!

DE GUICHE. I have my orders. Arras is besieged.

ROXANE. Ah! . . . it is besieged?

DE GUICHE. Yes. . . . I see that my departure does not greatly affect you.

ROXANE. Oh! . . .

DE GUICHE. As for me, I own it wrings my heart. Shall I see you again? . . . When? . . . You know that I am made commander-in-general?

ROXANE (*uninterested*). I congratulate you.

DE GUICHE. Of the Guards.

ROXANE (*starting*). Ah, . . . of the Guards?

DE GUICHE. Among whom your cousin serves, . . . the man of the boasts and tirades. I shall have opportunity in plenty to retaliate upon him down there.

ROXANE (*suffocating*). What? The Guards are going down there?

DE GUICHE. Surely. It is my regiment.

ROXANE (*falls sitting upon the bench aside*). Christian!

DE GUICHE. What is it troubles you?

ROXANE (*greatly moved*). This departure . . . grieves me mortally. When one cares for a person . . . to know him away at the war!

DE GUICHE (*surprised and charmed*). For the first time you utter a kind and feeling word, when I am leaving!

ROXANE (*in a different tone, fanning herself*). So . . . you are thinking of revenge upon my cousin?

DE GUICHE (*smiling*). You side with him?

ROXANE. No . . . against him.

DE GUICHE. Do you see much of him?

ROXANE. Very little.

DE GUICHE. He is everywhere to be met with one of the cadets . . . (*Trying to remember*) that Neu . . . ville . . . . . . viller . . .

ROXANE. A tall man?

DE GUICHE. Light-haired.

ROXANE. Red-haired.

DE GUICHE. Good-looking.

ROXANE. Pooh!

DE GUICHE. But a fool!

ROXANE. He looks like one. (*In a different tone.*) Your vengeance upon Cyrano is then to place him within reach of shot, which is the thing of all he loves! . . . A miserable vengeance! . . . I know, I do, what would more seriously concern him.

DE GUICHE. And that is?

ROXANE. Why . . . that the regiment should march, and leave him behind with his beloved cadets, arms folded the whole war through, in Paris! That is the only way to cast down a man like him. You wish to punish him? Deprive him of danger.

DE GUICHE. A woman! A woman! None but a woman could devise a vengeance of the sort!

ROXANE. His friends will gnaw their fists, and he his very soul, with chagrin at not being under fire; and you will be abundantly avenged!

DE GUICHE (coming nearer). Then you do love me a little? (Roxane smiles.) I wish to see in this fact of your espousing my grudge a proof of affection, Roxane . . .

ROXANE. . . . You may!

DE GUICHE (showing several folded papers). I have here upon me the orders to be transmitted at once to each of the companies . . . except . . . (He takes one from among the others.) This one! . . . the company of the cadets . . . (He puts it in his pocket.) This, I will keep. (Laughing.) Ah, ah, ah! Cyrano! his belligerent humor! . . . So you sometimes play tricks upon people, you? . . .

ROXANE. Sometimes.

DE GUICHE (very near her). I love you to distraction! This evening . . . listen, . . . it is true that I must be gone. But to go when I feel that it is a matter for your caring! Listen! . . . There is, not far from here, in Rue Orléans, a convent founded by the Capuchins. Father Athanasius. A layman may not enter. But the good fathers . . . I fear no difficulty with them! They will hide me up their sleeve . . . their sleeve is wide. They are the Capuchins that serve Richelieu at home. Fearing the uncle, they proportionately fear the nephew. I shall be thought to have left. I will come to you masked. Let me delay by a single day, wayward enchantress!

ROXANE. But if it should transpire . . . your fame . . .

DE GUICHE. Bah!

ROXANE. But . . . the siege . . . Arras!

DE GUICHE. Must wait! Allow me, I beg . . .

ROXANE. No!

DE GUICHE. I beseech!

ROXANE (tenderly). No! Love itself bids me forbid you!

DE GUICHE. Ah!

ROXANE. You must go! (Aside.) Christian will stay! (Aloud.) For my sake be heroic . . . Antony!

DE GUICHE. Ah heavenly word upon your lips! . . . Then you love the one who . . .

ROXANE. Who shall have made me tremble for his sake . . .

DE GUICHE (in a transport of joy). Ah, I will go! (He kisses her hand.) Are you satisfied with me?

ROXANE. My friend, I am. (Exit DE GUICHE.)

THE DUENNA (dropping a mocking curtsey toward his back). My friend, we are!

ROXANE (to the DUENNA). Not a word of what I have done: Cyrano would never forgive me for defrauding him of his war! (She calls toward the house.) Cousin! (CYRANO comes out.) We are going to Clomire's. (She indicates the house opposite.) Alcandre has engaged to speak, and so has Lysimon.

THE DUENNA (putting her little finger to her ear). Yes, but my little finger tells me that we shall be too late to hear them!

CYRANO (to ROXANE). Of all things do not miss the trained monkeys! (They have reached COLMIRE'S door.)

THE DUENNA. See! . . . See! they have muffled the door-knocker! (To the door-knocker.) You have been gagged, that your voice should not disturb the beautiful lecture, . . . little brutal disturber! (*She lifts it with infinite care and knocks softly.*)

ROXANE (*seeing the door open*). Come! (*From the threshold to* CYRANO.) If Christian should come, as probably he will, say he must wait!

CYRANO (*hurriedly, as she is about to disappear*). Ah! (*She turns.*) Upon what shall you, according to your custom, question him today? 10

ROXANE. Upon . . .

CYRANO (*eagerly*). Upon? . . .

ROXANE. But you will be silent . . .

CYRANO. As that wall!

ROXANE. Upon nothing! I will say: Forward! Free rein! No curb! Improvise! Talk of love! Be magnificent!

CYRANO (*smiling*). Good.

ROXANE. Hush!

CYRANO. Hush!

ROXANE. Not a word! (*She goes in and closes the door.*)

CYRANO (*bowing, when the door is closed*). A thousand thanks! (*The door opens again and* ROXANE *looks out.*)

ROXANE. He might prepare his speeches . . .

CYRANO. Ah, no! . . . the devil, no!

BOTH (*together*). Hush! . . . (*The door closes.*) 30

CYRANO (*calling*). Christian! (*Enter* CHRISTIAN.) I know all that we need to. Now make ready your memory. This is your chance to cover yourself with glory. Let us lose no time. Do not look sullen, like that. Quick! Let us go to your lodgings and I will rehearse you . . .

CHRISTIAN. No!

CYRANO. What? 40

CHRISTIAN. No, I will await Roxane here.

CYRANO. What insanity possesses you? Come quickly and learn . . .

CHRISTIAN. No, I tell you! I am weary of borrowing my letters, my words

. . . of playing a part, and living in constant fear. . . . It was very well at first, but now I feel that she loves me. I thank you heartily. I am no longer afraid. I will speak for myself . . .

CYRANO. *Ouais?* . . .

CHRISTIAN. And what tells you that I shall not know how? I am not such an utter blockhead, after all! You shall see! Your lessons have not been altogether wasted. I can shift to speak without your aid! And, that failing, by Heaven! I shall still know enough to take her in my arms! (*Catching sight of* ROXANE *who is coming out from* CLOMIRE'S.) She is coming! Cyrano, no, do not leave me! . . .

CYRANO (*bowing to him*). I will not meddle, monsieur. (*He disappears behind the garden wall.*)

ROXANE (*coming from Clomire's house with a number of people from whom she is taking leave. Curtseys and farewells.*) Barthénoide! . . . Alcandre! . . . Crémoine! . . .

THE DUENNA (*comically desperate*). We missed the disquisition upon the Softer Sentiments! (*She goes into* ROXANE'S *house.*)

ROXANE (*still taking leave of this one and that*). Urimédonte! . . . Good-bye! (*All bow to* ROXANE, *to one another, separate and go off by the various streets.* ROXANE *sees* CHRISTIAN.)

ROXANE. You are here! (*She goes to him.*) Evening is closing round. . . . Wait! . . . They have all gone. . . . The air is so mild. . . . Not a passer in sight. . . . Let us sit here. . . . Talk! . . . I will listen.

CHRISTIAN (*sits beside her, on the bench. Silence*). I love you.

ROXANE (*closing her eyes*). Yes. Talk to me of love.

CHRISTIAN. I love you.

ROXANE. Yes. That is the theme. Play variations upon it.

CHRISTIAN. I love . . .

ROXANE. Variations!

CHRISTIAN. I love you so much . . .

ROXANE. I do not doubt it. What further? . . .

CHRISTIAN. And further . . . I should be so happy if you loved me! Tell me, Roxane, that you love me . . .

ROXANE (*pouting*). You proffer cider to me when I was hoping for champagne! . . . Now tell me a little *how* you love me?

CHRISTIAN. Why . . . very, very much.

ROXANE. Oh! . . . unravel, disentangle your sentiments!

CHRISTIAN. Your throat! . . . I want to kiss it! . . .

ROXANE. Christian!

CHRISTIAN. I love you! . . .

ROXANE (*attempting to rise*). Again! . . .

CHRISTIAN (*hastily, holding her back*). No, I do not love you! . . .

ROXANE (*sitting down again*). That is fortunate!

CHRISTIAN. I adore you!

ROXANE (*rising and moving away*). Oh! . . .

CHRISTIAN. Yes, . . . love makes me into a fool!

ROXANE (*drily*). And I am displeased at it! as I should be displeased at your no longer being handsome.

CHRISTIAN. But . . .

ROXANE. Go, and rally your routed eloquence!

CHRISTIAN. I . . .

ROXANE. You love me. I have heard it. Good-evening. (*She goes toward the house.*)

CHRISTIAN. No, no, not yet! . . . I wish to tell you . . .

ROXANE (*pushing open the door to go in*). That you adore me. Yes, I know. No! No! Go away! . . . Go! . . . Go! . . .

CHRISTIAN. But I . . . (*She closes the door in his face.*)

CYRANO (*who has been on the scene a moment, unnoticed*). Unmistakably a success.

CHRISTIAN. Help me!

CYRANO. No, sir, no.

CHRISTIAN. I will go kill myself if I am not taken back into favor at once . . . at once!

CYRANO. And how can I . . . how, the devil? . . . make you learn on the spot . . .

CHRISTIAN (*seizing him by the arm*). Oh, there! . . . Look! . . . See! (*Light has appeared in the balcony window.*)

CYRANO (*with emotion*). Her window!

CHRISTIAN. Oh, I shall die!

CYRANO. Not so loud!

CHRISTIAN (*in a whisper*). I shall die!

CYRANO. It is a dark night. . . .

CHRISTIAN. Well?

CYRANO. All may be mended. But you do not deserve . . . There! stand there, miserable boy! . . . in front of the balcony! I will stand under it and prompt you.

CHRISTIAN. But . . .

CYRANO. Do as I bid you!

THE PAGES (*reappearing at the back, to* CYRANO). Hey!

CYRANO. Hush! (*He signs to them to lower their voices.*)

FIRST PAGE (*in a lower voice*). We have finished serenading Montfleury!

CYRANO (*low, quickly*). Go and stand out of sight. One at this street corner, the other at that; and if anyone comes near, play! . . .

SECOND PAGE. What sort of tune, Monsieur the Gassendist?

CYRANO. Merry if it be a woman, mournful if it be a man. (*The* PAGES

disappear, one at each street corner. To
CHRISTIAN.) Call her!

CHRISTIAN. Roxane!

CYRANO (*picking up pebbles and throwing
them at the window-pane*). Wait! A few
pebbles . . .

ROXANE (*opening the window*). Who is
calling me?

CHRISTIAN. It is I . . .

ROXANE. Who is . . . I?

CHRISTIAN. Christian!

ROXANE (*disdainfully*). Oh, you!

CHRISTIAN. I wish to speak with you.

CYRANO (*under the balcony, to* CHRISTIAN).
Speak low! . . .

ROXANE. No, your conversation is too
common. You may go home!

CHRISTIAN. In mercy! . . .

ROXANE. No . . . you do not love me
any more!

CHRISTIAN (*whom* CYRANO *is prompting*).
You accuse me . . . just Heaven!
of loving you no more . . . when I
can love you no more!

ROXANE (*who was about to close her window, stopping*). Ah, that is a little
better! . . .

CHRISTIAN (*same business*). To what a
. . . size has Love grown in my . . .
sigh-rocked soul which the . . . cruel
cherub has chosen for his cradle!

ROXANE (*stepping nearer to the edge of the
balcony*). That is distinctly better!
. . . But, since he is so cruel, this
Cupid, you were unwise not to
smother him in his cradle!

CHRISTIAN (*same business*). I tried to, but,
madame, the . . . attempt was futile. This . . . new-born Love is
. . . a little Hercules . . .

ROXANE. Much, much better!

CHRISTIAN (*same business*). . . . Who
found it merest baby-play to . . .
strangle the serpents . . . twain,
Pride and . . . Mistrust.

ROXANE (*leaning her elbows on the bal-*

cony-rail). Ah, that is very good
indeed! . . . But why do you speak
so slowly and stintedly? Has your
imagination gout in its wings?

CYRANO (*drawing* CHRISTIAN *under the
balcony, and taking his place*). Hush!
It is becoming too difficult!

ROXANE. Tonight your words come
falteringly. . . . Why is it?

CYRANO (*talking low like* CHRISTIAN).
Because of the dark. They have to
grope to find your ear.

ROXANE. My words do not find the
same difficulty.

CYRANO. They reach their point at
once? Of course they do! That is
because I catch them with my heart.
My heart, you see, is very large,
your ear particularly small. . . .
Besides, your words drop . . . that
goes quickly; mine have to climb
. . . and that takes longer!

ROXANE. They have been climbing
more nimbly, however, in the last
few minutes.

CYRANO. They are becoming used to
this gymnastic feat!

ROXANE. It is true that I am talking
with you from a very mountain top!

CYRANO. It is sure that a hard word
dropped from such a height upon
my heart would shatter it!

ROXANE (*with the motion of leaving*). I will
come down.

CYRANO (*quickly*). Do not!

ROXANE (*pointing at the bench at the foot
of the balcony*). Then do you get up on
the seat! . . .

CYRANO (*drawing away in terror*). No!

ROXANE. How do you mean . . . No?

CYRANO (*with ever-increasing emotion*).
Let us profit a little by this chance of
talking softly together without seeing
each other . . .

ROXANE. Without seeing each other?
. . .

CYRANO. Yes, to my mind, delectable! Each guesses at the other, and no more. You discern but the trailing blackness of a mantle, and I a dawn-gray glimmer which is a summer gown. I am a shadow merely, a pearly phantom are you! You can never know what these moments are to me! If ever I was eloquent . . .

ROXANE. You were!   10

CYRANO. My words never till now surged from my very heart . . .

ROXANE. And why?

CYRANO. Because, till now, they must strain to reach you through . . .

ROXANE. What?

CYRANO. Why, the bewildering emotion a man feels who sees you, and whom you look upon! . . . But this eve-ning, it seems to me that I am speak-20 ing to you for the first time!

ROXANE. It is true that your voice is altogether different.

CYRANO (coming nearer, feverishly). Yes, altogether different, because, pro-tected by the dark, I dare at last to be myself. I dare . . . (He stops, and distractedly.) What was I saying? . . . I do not know. . . . All this . . . forgive my incoherence! . . . is so 30 delicious . . . is so new to me!

ROXANE. So new? . . .

CYRANO (in extreme confusion, still trying to mend his expressions). So new . . . yes, new, to be sincere; the fear of being mocked always constrains my heart . . .

ROXANE. Mocked . . . for what?

CYRANO. Why . . . for its impulses, its flights! . . . Yes, my heart always 40 cowers behind the defence of my wit. I set forth to capture a star . . . and then, for dread of laughter, I stop and pick a flower . . . of rhetoric.

ROXANE. That sort of flower has its pleasing points . . .

CYRANO. But yet, tonight, let us scorn it!

ROXANE. Never before had you spoken as you are speaking! . . .

CYRANO. Ah, if far from Cupid-darts and quivers, we might seek a place of somewhat fresher things! If in-stead of drinking, flat sip by sip, from a chiselled golden thimble, drops distilled and dulcified, we might try the sensation of quenching the thirst of our souls by stooping to the level of the great river, and set-ting our lips to the stream!

ROXANE. But yet, wit . . . fancy . . . delicate conceits . . .

CYRANO. I gave my fancy leave to frame conceits, before, to make you linger, . . . but now it would be an affront to this balm-breathing night, to Nature and the hour, to talk like characters in a pastoral performed at Court! . . . Let us give Heaven leave, looking at us with all its earnest stars, to strip us of disguise and artifice: I fear, . . . oh, fear! . . . lest in our mistaken alchemy sentiment should be sub-tilized to evaporation; lest the life of the heart should waste in these empty pastimes, and the final re-finement of the fine be the undoing of the refined!

ROXANE. But yet, wit, . . . aptness, . . . ingenuity . . .

CYRANO. I hate them in love! Criminal, when one loves, to prolong over-much that paltry thrust and parry! The moment, however, comes inevi-tably—and I pity those for whom it never comes!—in which, we ap-prehending the noble depth of the love we harbor, a shallow word hurts us to utter!

ROXANE. If . . . if, then, that moment has come for us two, what words will you say to me?

CYRANO. All those, all those, all those that come to me! Not in formal nosegay order, . . . I will throw them you in a wild sheaf! I love you, choke with love, I love you, dear. . . . My brain feels, I can bear no more, it is too much. . . . Your name is in my heart the golden clapper in a bell; and as I know no rest, Roxane, always the heart is shaken, and ever rings your name! . . . Of you, I remember all, all have I loved! Last year, one day, the twelfth of May, in going out at morning you changed the fashion of your hair. . . . I have taken the light of your hair for my light, and as having stared too long at the sun, on everything one sees a scarlet wheel, on everything when I come from my chosen light, my dazzled eye sets swimming golden blots! . . .

ROXANE (*in a voice unsteady with emotion*). Yes . . . this is love . . .

CYRANO. Ah, verily! The feeling which invades me, terrible and jealous, is love . . . with all its mournful frenzy! It is love, yet self-forgetting more than the wont of love! Ah, for your happiness now readily would I give mine, though you should never know it, might I but, from a distance, sometimes, hear the happy laughter bought by my sacrifice! Every glance of yours breeds in me new strength, new valor! Are you beginning to understand? Tell me, do you grasp my love's measure? Does some little part of my soul make itself felt of you there in the darkness? . . . Oh, what is happening to me this evening is too sweet, too deeply dear! I tell you all these things, and you listen to me, you! Not in my least modest hoping did I ever hope so much! I have now only to die! It is because

of words of mine that she is trembling among the dusky branches! For you are trembling, like a flower among leaves! Yes, you tremble, . . . for whether you will or no, I have felt the worshipped trembling of your hand all along this thrilled and blissful jasmine-bough! (*He madly kisses the end of a pendent bough.*)

ROXANE. Yes, I tremble . . . and weep . . . and love you . . . and am yours! . . . For you have carried me away . . . away! . . .

CYRANO. Then, let death come! I have moved you, I! . . . There is but one thing more I ask . . .

CHRISTIAN (*under the balcony*). A kiss!

ROXANE (*drawing hastily back*). What?

CYRANO. Oh!

ROXANE. You ask? . . .

CYRANO. Yes . . . I . . . (*To* CHRISTIAN.) You are in too great haste!

CHRISTIAN. Since she is so moved, I must take advantage of it!

CYRANO (*to* ROXANE). I . . . Yes, it is true I asked . . . but, merciful heavens! . . . I knew at once that I had been too bold.

ROXANE (*a shade disappointed*). You insist no more than so?

CYRANO. Indeed, I insist . . . without insisting! Yes! yes! but your modesty shrinks! . . . I insist, but yet . . . the kiss I begged . . . refuse it me!

CHRISTIAN (*to* CYRANO, *pulling at his mantle*). Why?

CYRANO. Hush, Christian!

ROXANE (*bending over the balcony-rail*). What are you whispering?

CYRANO. Reproaches to myself for having gone too far; I was saying "Hush, Christian!" (*The theorbos are heard playing.*) Your pardon! . . . a second! . . . Someone is coming! (ROXANE *closes the window.* CYRANO *listens to the theorbos, one of which plays*

a lively and the other a lugubrious tune.)
CYRANO. A dance? . . . A dirge? . . .
What do they mean? Is it a man or a
woman? . . . Ah, it is a monk!
[*Enter a* CAPUCHIN MONK, *who goes from
house to house, with a lantern, examining
the doors.*]
CYRANO (*to the* CAPUCHIN). What are
you looking for, Diogenes?
THE CAPUCHIN. I am looking for the 10
house of Madame . . .
CHRISTIAN. He is in the way!
THE CAPUCHIN. Magdeleine Robin . . .
CYRANO (*pointing up one of the streets*).
This way! . . . Straight ahead . . .
go straight ahead . . .
THE CAPUCHIN. I thank you. I will say
ten Aves for your peace. (*Exit.*)
CYRANO. My good wishes speed your
cowl! (*He comes forward toward* CHRIS- 20
TIAN.)
CHRISTIAN. Insist upon the kiss! . . .
CYRANO. No, I will not!
CHRISTIAN. Sooner or later . . .
CYRANO. It is true! It must come, the
moment of inebriation when your
lips shall imperiously be impelled
toward each other, because the one
is fledged with youthful gold and the
other is so soft a pink! . . . (*To* 30
himself.) I had rather it should be
because . . . (*Sound of the window
reopening;* CHRISTIAN *hides under the
balcony.*)
ROXANE (*stepping forward on the balcony*).
Are you there? We were speaking
of . . . of . . . of a . . .
CYRANO. Kiss. The word is sweet. Why
does your fair lip stop at it? If the
mere word burns it, what will be of 40
the thing itself? Do not make it into a
fearful matter, and then fear! Did
you not a moment ago insensibly
leave playfulness behind and slip
without trepidation from a smile to a
sigh, from a sigh to a tear? Slip but

a little further in the same blessed
direction: from a tear to a kiss there
is scarcely a dividing shiver!
ROXANE. Say no more!
CYRANO. A kiss! When all is said, what
is a kiss? An oath of allegiance taken
in closer proximity, a promise more
precise, a seal on a confession, a rose-
red dot upon the letter i in loving;
a secret which elects the mouth for
ear; an instant of eternity murmuring like a bee; balmy communion
with a flavor of flowers; a fashion of
inhaling each other's heart, and of
tasting, on the brink of the lips, each
other's soul!
ROXANE. Say no more . . . no more!
CYRANO. A kiss, madame, is a thing so
noble that the Queen of France, on
the most fortunate of lords, bestowed
one, did the queen herself!
ROXANE. If that be so . . .
CYRANO (*with increasing fervor*). Like
Buckingham I have suffered in
long silence, like him I worship a
queen, like him I am sorrowful and
unchanging . . .
ROXANE. Like him you enthrall through
the eyes the heart that follows you!
CYRANO (*to himself, sobered*). True, I am
handsome . . . I had forgotten!
ROXANE. Come then and gather it, the
supreme flower . . .
CYRANO (*pushing* CHRISTIAN *toward the
balcony*). Go!
ROXANE. . . . tasting of the heart.
CYRANO. Go! . . .
ROXANE. . . . murmuring   like   a
bee . . .
CYRANO. Go!
CHRISTIAN (*hesitating*). But now I feel as
if I ought not!
ROXANE. . . . making Eternity an in-
stant . . .
CYRANO (*pushing* CHRISTIAN). Scale the
balcony, you donkey! (CHRISTIAN

springs toward the balcony, and climbs by means of bench, the vine, the posts and balusters.)

CHRISTIAN. Ah, Roxane! (*He clasps her to him, and bends over her lips.*)

CYRANO. Ha! . . . What a turn of the screw to my heart! . . . Kiss, banquet of Love at which I am Lazarus, a crumb drops from your table even to me, here in the shade. . . . Yes, 10 in my outstretched heart a little falls, as I feel that upon the lip pressing her lip Roxane kisses the words spoken by me! . . . (*The theorbos are heard.*) A merry tune . . . a mournful one . . . The monk! (*He goes through the pretence of arriving on the spot at a run, as if from a distance; calling.*) Ho, there!

ROXANE. What is it? 20

CYRANO. It is I. I was passing this way. Is Christian there?

CHRISTIAN (*astonished*). Cyrano!

ROXANE. Good-evening, cousin!

CYRANO. Cousin, good-evening!

ROXANE. I will come down. (ROXANE *disappears in the house.*)

[CAPUCHIN *re-enters at the back.*]

CHRISTIAN (*seeing him*). Oh, again! (*He follows* ROXANE.) 30

THE CAPUCHIN. It is here she lives, I am certain . . . Magdeleine Robin.

CYRANO. You said Ro-lin.

THE CAPUCHIN. No, bin, . . . b,i,n, bin!

ROXANE (*appearing upon the threshold, followed by* RAGUENEAU *carrying a lantern, and* CHRISTIAN). What is it?

THE CAPUCHIN. A letter.

CHRISTIAN. What? 40

THE CAPUCHIN (*to* ROXANE). Oh, the contents can be only of a sacred character! It is from a worthy nobleman who . . .

ROXANE (*to* CHRISTIAN). It is from De Guiche!

CHRISTIAN. He dares to . . . ?

ROXANE. Oh, he will not trouble me much longer! (*Opening the letter.*) I love you, and if . . . (*By the light of* RAGUENEAU's *lantern she reads, aside, low.*) Mademoiselle: The drums are beating. My regiment is buckling on its corselet. It is about to leave. I am thought to have left already, but lag behind. I am disobeying you. I am in the convent here. I am coming to you, and send you word by a friar, silly as a sheep, who has no suspicion of the import of this letter. You smiled too sweetly upon me an hour ago: I must see you smile again. Provide to be alone, and deign graciously to receive the audacious worshipper, forgiven already, I can but hope, who signs himself your—etc. . . . (*To the* CAPUCHIN.) Father, this is what the letter tells me . . . Listen: (*All draw nearer; she reads aloud.*) Mademoiselle: The wishes of the cardinal may not be disregarded, however hard compliance with them prove. I have therefore chosen as bearer of this letter a most reverend, holy, and sagacious Capuchin; it is our wish that he should at once, in your own dwelling, pronounce the nuptial blessing over you. Christian must secretly become your husband. I send him to you. You dislike him. Bow to Heaven's will in resignation, and be sure that it will bless your zeal, and sure, likewise, mademoiselle, of the respect of him who is and will be ever your most humble and . . . etc.

THE CAPUCHIN (*beaming*). The worthy gentleman! . . . I knew it! You remember that I said so: The contents of that letter can be only of a sacred character!

ROXANE (*low, to* CHRISTIAN). I am a fluent reader, am I not?

CHRISTIAN. Hm!

ROXANE (*with feigned despair*). Ah . . . it is horrible!

THE CAPUCHIN (*who has turned the light of his lantern upon* CYRANO). You are the one?

CHRISTIAN. No, I am.

THE CAPUCHIN (*turning the light upon him, and as if his good looks aroused suspicion*). But . . . 10

ROXANE (*quickly*). Postscript: You will bestow upon the convent two hundred and fifty crowns.

THE CAPUCHIN. The worthy, worthy gentleman! (*To* ROXANE.) Be reconciled!

ROXANE (*with the expression of a martyr*). I will endeavor! (*While* RAGUENEAU *opens the door for the* CAPUCHIN, *whom* CHRISTIAN *is showing into the house*, 20 ROXANE *says low to* CYRANO.) De Guiche is coming! . . . Keep him here! Do not let him enter until . . .

CYRANO. I understand! (*To the* CAPUCHIN.) How long will it take to marry them?

THE CAPUCHIN. A quarter of an hour.

CYRANO (*pushing all toward the house*). Go in! I shall be here!

ROXANE (*to* CHRISTIAN). Come! (*They* 30 *go in.*)

CYRANO. How can I detain De Guiche for a quarter of an hour? (*He jumps upon the bench, climbs the wall toward the balcony-rail.*) So! . . . I climb up here! . . . I know what I will do! . . . (*The theorbos play a melancholy tune.*) Ho, it is a man! (*The tune quavers lugubriously.*) Ho, ho, this time there is no mistake! (*He is on the balcony; he* 40 *pulls the brim of his hat over his eyes, takes off his sword, wraps his cloak about him, and bends over the balcony-rail.*) No, it is not too far! (*He climbs over the balcony-rail, and reaching for a long bough that projects beyond the garden wall, holds on to*

it with both hands, ready to let himself drop.) I shall make a slight commotion in the atmosphere!

DE GUICHE (*enters masked, groping in the dark*). What can that thrice-damned Capuchin be about?

CYRANO. The devil! if he should recognize my voice? (*Letting go with one hand, he makes show of turning a key*). Cric! crac! (*Solemnly.*) Cyrano, resume the accent of Bergerac!

DE GUICHE (*looking at* ROXANE'S *house*). Yes, that is it. I can scarcely see. This mask bothers my eyes! (*He is about to enter* ROXANE'S *house;* CYRANO *swings from the balcony, holding on to the bough, which bends and lets him down between the door and* DE GUICHE. *He intentionally drops very heavily, to give the effect of dropping from a great height, and lies flattened upon the ground, motionless, as if stunned.*)

DE GUICHE. What is it? (*When he looks up, the bough has swung into place; he sees nothing but the sky.*) Where did this man drop from?

CYRANO (*rising to a sitting posture*). From the moon!

DE GUICHE. From the . . . ?

CYRANO (*in a dreamy voice*). What time is it?

DE GUICHE. Is he mad?

CYRANO. What time? What country? What day? What season?

DE GUICHE. But . . .

CYRANO. I am dazed!

DE GUICHE. Monsieur . . .

CYRANO. I have dropped from the moon like a bomb!

DE GUICHE (*impatiently*). What are you babbling about?

CYRANO (*rising, in a terrible voice*). I tell you I have dropped from the moon!

DE GUICHE (*backing a step*). Very well. You have dropped from the moon! . . . He is perhaps a lunatic!

CYRANO (*walking up close to him*). Not metaphorically, mind that!

DE GUICHE. But . . .

CYRANO. A hundred years ago, or else a minute—for I have no conception how long I have been falling—I was up there, in that saffron-colored ball!

DE GUICHE (*shrugging his shoulders*). You were. Now, let me pass!

CYRANO (*standing in his way*). Where am I? Be frank with me! Keep nothing from me! In what region, among what people, have I been shot like an aerolite?

DE GUICHE. I wish to pass!

CYRANO. While falling I could not choose my way, and have no notion where I have fallen! Is it upon a moon, or is it upon an earth, I have 20 been dragged by my posterior weight?

DE GUICHE. I tell you, sir . . .

CYRANO (*with a scream of terror at which* DE GUICHE *starts backward a step*). Great God! . . . In this country men's faces are soot-black!

DE GUICHE (*lifting his hand to his face*). What does he mean?

CYRANO (*still terrified*). Am I in Algeria? Are you a native? . . .

DE GUICHE (*who has felt his mask*). Ah, my 30 mask!

CYRANO (*pretending to be easier*). So I am in Venice! . . . Or am I in Genoa?

DE GUICHE (*attempting to pass*). A lady is expecting me!

CYRANO (*completely reassured*). Ah, then I am in Paris.

DE GUICHE (*smiling in spite of himself*). The rogue is not far from amusing! 40

CYRANO. Ah, you are laughing!

DE GUICHE. I laugh . . . but intend to pass!

CYRANO (*beaming*). To think I should strike Paris! (*Quite at his ease, laughing, brushing himself, bowing.*) I arrived—

pray, pardon my appearance!—by the last whirlwind. I am rather unpresentable—Travel, you know! My eyes are still full of star-dust. My spurs are clogged with bristles off a planet. (*Appearing to pick something off his sleeve.*) See, on my sleeve, a comet's hair! (*He makes a feint of blowing it away.*)

DE GUICHE (*beside himself*). Sir . . .

CYRANO (*as* DE GUICHE *is about to pass, stretching out his leg as if to show something on it, thereby stopping him*). Embedded in my calf, I have brought back one of the Great Bear's teeth . . . and as, falling too near to Trident, I strained aside to clear one of its prongs, I landed sitting in Libra, . . . yes, one of the scales! . . . and now my weight is registered up there! (*Quickly preventing* DE GUICHE *from passing, and taking hold of a button on his doublet.*) And if, monsieur, you should take my nose between your fingers and compress it . . . milk would result!

DE GUICHE. What are you saying? Milk? . . .

CYRANO. Of the Milky Way.

DE GUICHE. Go to the devil!

CYRANO. No! I am sent from Heaven literally. (*Folding his arms.*) Will you believe—I discovered it in passing—that Sirius at night puts on a nightcap? (*Confidentially.*) The lesser Bear is too little yet to bite. . . . (*Laughing.*) I tumbled plump through Lyra, and snapped a string! . . . (*Magnificent.*) But I intend setting all this down in a book, and the golden stars I have brought back caught in my shaggy mantle, when the book is printed, will be seen serving as asterisks!

DE GUICHE. I have stood this long enough! I want . . .

CYRANO. I know perfectly what you want!

DE GUICHE. Man . . .

CYRANO. You want to know, from me, at first hand, what the moon is made of, and whether that monumental pumpkin is inhabited?

DE GUICHE (*shouting*). Not in the very least! I want . . .

CYRANO. To know how I got there? I got there by a method of my own invention.

DE GUICHE (*discouraged*). He is mad! . . . stark!

CYRANO (*disdainfully*). Do not imagine that I resorted to anything so absurd as Regiomontanus's eagle, or anything so lacking in enterprise as Archytas's pigeon! . . .

DE GUICHE. The madman is erudite . . .

CYRANO. I drew up nothing that had ever been thought of before! (DE GUICHE *has succeeded in getting past* CYRANO, *and is nearing* ROXANE'S *door;* CYRANO *follows him, ready to buttonhole him.*) I invented no less than six ways of storming the blue fort of Heaven!

DE GUICHE (*turning around*). Six, did you say?

CYRANO (*volubly*). One way was to stand naked in the sunshine, in a harness thickly studded with glass phials, each filled with morning dew. The sun in drawing up the dew, you see, could not have helped drawing me up too!

DE GUICHE (*surprised, taking a step toward* CYRANO). True. That is one!

CYRANO (*taking a step backward, with a view to drawing* DE GUICHE *away from the door*). Or else, I could have let the wind into a cedar coffer, then rarefied the imprisoned element by means of cunningly adjusted burning-glasses, and soared up with it!

DE GUICHE (*taking another step toward* CYRANO). Two!

CYRANO (*backing*). Or else, mechanic as well as artificer, I could have fashioned a giant grasshopper, with steel joints, which, impelled by successive explosions of salt peter, would have hopped with me to the azure meadows where graze the starry flocks!

DE GUICHE (*unconsciously following* CYRANO, *and counting on his fingers*). That makes three!

CYRANO. Since smoke by its nature ascends, I could have blown into an appropriate globe a sufficient quantity to ascend with me!

DE GUICHE (*as above, more and more astonished*). Four!

CYRANO. Since Phoebe, the moon-goddess, when she is at wane, is greedy, O beeves! of your marrow, . . . with that marrow have besmeared myself!

DE GUICHE (*amazed*). Five!

CYRANO (*who while talking has backed, followed by* DE GUICHE, *to the further side of the square, near a bench*). Or else, I could have placed myself upon an iron plate, have taken a magnet of suitable size, and thrown it in the air! That way is a very good one! The magnet flies upward, the iron instantly after; the magnet no sooner overtaken than you fling it up again. . . . The rest is clear! You can go upward indefinitely.

DE GUICHE. Six! . . . But here are six excellent methods! Which of the six, my dear sir, did you select?

CYRANO. A seventh!

DE GUICHE. Did you, indeed? And what was that?

CYRANO. I give you a hundred guesses!

DE GUICHE. I must confess that I should like to know!

CYRANO (*imitating the noise of the surf, and making great mysterious gestures*). Hoo-ish! hoo-ish!

DE GUICHE. Well! What is that?

CYRANO. Cannot you guess?

DE GUICHE. No!

CYRANO. The tide! . . . At the hour in which the moon attracts the deep, I lay down upon the sands, after a sea-bath . . . and, my head being drawn up first—the reason of this, you see, that the hair will hold a quantity of water in its mop!—I rose in the air, straight, beautifully straight, like an angel. I rose . . . I rose softly . . . without an effort . . . when, suddenly, I felt a shock. Then . . .

DE GUICHE (lured on by curiosity, taking a seat on the bench). Well, . . . then?

CYRANO. Then . . . (Resuming his natural voice.) The time is up, monsieur, and I release you. They are married.

DE GUICHE (getting to his feet with a leap). I am dreaming or drunk! That voice? (The door of ROXANE's house opens; lackeys appear carrying lighted candelabra. CYRANO removes his hat.) And that nose! . . . Cyrano!

CYRANO (bowing). Cyrano. They have exchanged rings within the quarter of the hour.

DE GUICHE. Who have? (He turns round. Tableau. Behind the lackey stand ROXANE and CHRISTIAN holding hands. THE CAPUCHIN follows them smiling. RAGUENEAU holds high a flambeau. The DUENNA closes the procession, bewildered, in her bedgown.) Heavens! (To ROXANE.) You! (Recognizing CHRISTIAN with amazement.) He? (Bowing to ROXANE.) Your astuteness compels my admiration! (To CYRANO.) My compliments to you, ingenious inventor of flying machines. Your experiences would have beguiled a saint on the threshold of Paradise! Make a note of them. . . . They can be used again, with profit, in a book!

CYRANO (bowing). I will confidently follow your advice.

THE CAPUCHIN (to DE GUICHE, pointing at the lovers, and wagging his great white beard with satisfaction). A beautiful couple, my son, brought together by you!

DE GUICHE (eyeing him frigidly). As you say! (To ROXANE.) And now proceed, Madame, to take leave of your husband.

ROXANE. What?

DE GUICHE (to CHRISTIAN). The regiment is on the point of starting. You are to join it!

ROXANE. To go to war?

DE GUICHE. Of course!

ROXANE. But the cadets are not going!

DE GUICHE. They are! (Taking out the paper which he had put in his pocket.) Here is the order. (To CHRISTIAN.) I beg you will take it to the Captain, baron, yourself.

ROXANE (throwing herself in CHRISTIAN's arms). Christian!

DE GUICHE (to CYRANO, with a malignant laugh). The wedding night is somewhat far as yet!

CYRANO (aside). He thinks that he is giving me great pain!

CHRISTIAN (to ROXANE). Oh, once more, dear! . . . Once more!

CYRANO. Be reasonable . . . Come! . . . Enough!

CHRISTIAN (still clasping ROXANE). Oh, it is hard to leave her. . . . You cannot know . . .

CYRANO (trying to draw him away). I know. (Drums are heard in the distance sounding a march.)

DE GUICHE (at the back). The regiment is on its way!

ROXANE (to CYRANO, while she clings to CHRISTIAN whom he is trying to draw away). Oh! . . . I entrust him to your care! Promise that under no circumstance shall his life be placed in danger!

CYRANO. I will endeavor . . . but obviously cannot promise . . .

ROXANE (*same business*). Promise that he will be careful of himself!

CYRANO. I will do my best, but . . .

ROXANE (*as above*). That during this terrible siege he shall not take harm from the cold! 10

CYRANO. I will try, but . . .

ROXANE (*as above*). That he will be true to me!

CYRANO. Of course, but yet, you see . . .

ROXANE (*as above*). That he will write to me often!

CYRANO (*stopping*). Ah, that . . . I promise freely!

CURTAIN

ACT IV

THE GASCONY CADETS

The post occupied at the siege of Arras by the company of CARBON DE CASTEL-JALOUX. *At the back, across the whole stage, sloping earthwork. Beyond this is seen a plain stretching to the horizon; the country is covered with constructions relating to the siege. In the distance, against the sky, the outlines of the walls and roofs of Arras. Tents; scattered arms; drums, etc. It is shortly before sunrise. The East is yellow.* 20 *Sentinels at even intervals. Camp-fires. The* GASCONY CADETS *lie asleep, rolled in their cloaks.* CARBON DE CASTEL-JALOUX *and* LE BRET *are watching. All are very pale and gaunt.* CHRISTIAN *lies sleeping among the others, in his military cape, in the foreground, his face lighted by one of the camp-fires. Silence.*

LE BRET. It is dreadful!

CARBON. Yes. Nothing left.

LE BRET. *Mordious!*

CARBON (*warning him by a gesture to speak lower*). Curse in a whisper! You will wake them! . . . (*To the* CADETS.) Hush! Go to sleep! (*To* LE BRET.) Who sleeps dines.

LE BRET. Who lies awake misses two good things . . . What a situation! (*A few shots are heard in the distance.*) 40

CARBON. The devil take their popping! They will wake my young ones! . . .

(*To the* CADETS *who lift their heads.*) Go to sleep! (*The* CADETS *lie down again. Other shots are heard, nearer.*)

ONE OF THE CADETS (*stirring*). The devil! Again?

CARBON. It is nothing. It is Cyrano getting home. (*The heads which had started up, go down again.*)

A SENTINEL (*outside*). *Ventrebleu!* Who goes there?

CYRANO'S VOICE. Bergerac!

THE SENTINEL (*upon the embankment*). *Ventrebleu!* Who goes there?

CYRANO (*appearing at the top of the embankment*). Bergerac, blockhead! (*He comes down.* LE BRET *goes to him, uneasy.*)

LE BRET. Ah, thank God!

CYRANO (*warning him by a sign to wake no one*). Hush!

LE BRET. Wounded?

CYRANO. Do you not know that it has become a habit with them to miss me?

LE BRET. To me, it seems a little excessive that you should, every morning, for the sake of taking a letter, risk . . .

CYRANO (*stopping in front of* CHRISTIAN). I promised that he would write often. (*He looks at* CHRISTIAN.) He sleeps. He has grown pale. If the poor little girl could know that he is starving. . . . But handsome as ever!

LE BRET. Go at once and sleep.

CYRANO. Le Bret, do not grumble! Learn this: I nightly cross the Spanish lines at a point where I know beforehand everyone will be drunk.

LE BRET. You ought sometime to bring us back some victuals!

CYRANO. I must be lightly burdened to flit through! . . . But I know that there will be events before the evening. The French, unless I am much mistaken, will eat or die. 10

LE BRET. Oh, tell us!

CYRANO. No, I am not certain . . . You will see!

CARBON. What a shameful reversal of the order of things, that the besieger should be starved!

LE BRET. Alas! never was more complicated siege than this of Arras: We besiege Arras, and, caught in a 20 trap, are ourselves besieged by the Cardinal-prince of Spain. . . .

CYRANO. Someone now ought to come and besiege him.

LE BRET. I am not joking!

CYRANO. Oh, oh!

LE BRET. To think, ungrateful boy, that every day you risk a life precious as yours, solely to carry . . . (CYRANO 30 goes toward one of the tents.) Where are you going?

CYRANO. I am going to write another.

[He lifts the canvas flap, and disappears in the tent. Daybreak has brightened. Rosy flush. The city of Arras at the horizon catches a golden light. The report of a cannon is heard, followed at once by a drum-call, very far away, at the left. Other drums beat, nearer. The drum-calls 40 answer one another, come nearer, come very near, and go off, decreasing, dying in the distance, toward the right, having made the circuit of the camp. Noise of general awakening. Voices of officers in the distance.]

CARBON (with a sigh). The réveillé . . . Ah, me! . . . (The CADETS stir in their cloaks, stretch.) An end to the succulent slumbers! I know but too well what their first word will be!

ONE OF THE CADETS (sitting up). I am famished!

OTHER CADET. I believe I am dying!

ALL. Oh! . . .

CARBON. Get up!

THIRD CADET. I cannot go a step!

FOURTH CADET. I have not strength to stir!

FIRST CADET (looking at himself in a bit of armor). My tongue is coated: it must be the weather that is indigestible!

OTHER CADET. Anyone who wants them, can have all my titles of nobility for a Chester cheese . . . or part of one!

OTHER CADET. If my stomach does not have something put into it to take up the attention of my gastric juice, I shall retire into my tent before long . . . like Achilles!

OTHER CADET. Yes, they ought to provide us with bread!

CARBON (going to the tent into which CYRANO has retired; low). Cyrano!

OTHER CADETS. We cannot stand this much longer!

CARBON (as above, at the door of the tent). To the rescue, Cyrano! You who succeed so well always in cheering them, come and make them pluck up spirits!

SECOND CADET (falling upon FIRST CADET who is chewing something). What are you chewing, man?

FIRST CADET. A bit of gun-tow fried in axle-grease . . . using a burganet as frying pan. The suburbs of Arras are not precisely rich in game. . . .

OTHER CADET (entering). I have been hunting!

OTHER CADET (the same). I have been fishing!

ALL (*rising and falling upon the newcomers*).
What?—what did you catch?—A
pheasant?—A carp?—Quick, quick!
. . . Let us see!

THE HUNTSMAN. A sparrow!

THE ANGLER. A gudgeon!

ALL (*exasperated*). Enough of this! Let us
revolt!

CARBON. To the rescue, Cyrano! (*It is
now broad daylight.*)   10

CYRANO (*coming out of the tent, tranquil,
a pen behind his ear, a book in his hand*).
What is the matter? (*Silence. To
FIRST CADET.*) Why do you go off like
that, with that slouching gait?

THE CADET. I have something away
down in my heels which incon-
veniences me.

CYRANO. And what is that?

THE CADET. My stomach.   20

CYRANO. That is where mine is, too.

THE CADET. Then you too must be in-
convenienced.

CYRANO. No. The size of the hollow
within me merely increases my sense
of my size.

SECOND CADET. I happen to have teeth,
long ones!

CYRANO. The better will you bite . . .
in good time!

THIRD CADET. I reverberate like a drum!

CYRANO. You will be of use . . . to
sound the charge!

OTHER CADET. I have a buzzing in my
ears!

CYRANO. A mistake. Empty belly, no
ears. You hear no buzzing.

OTHER CADET. Ah, a trifling article to
eat . . . and a little oil upon it!

CYRANO (*taking off the CADET's morion   40
and placing it in his hand*). That is
seasoned.

OTHER CADET. What is there we could
devour?

CYRANO (*tossing him the book he has been
holding*). Try the Iliad!

OTHER CADET. The minister, in Paris,
makes his four meals a day!

CYRANO. You feel it remiss in him not
to send you a bit of partridge?

THE SAME. Why should he not? And
some wine!

CYRANO. Richelieu, some Burgundy, if
you please?

THE SAME. He might, by one of his
Capuchins!

CYRANO. By his Eminence, perhaps, in
sober gray?

OTHER CADET. No ogre was ever so
hungry!

CYRANO. You may have your fill yet of
humble-pie!

FIRST CADET (*shrugging his shoulders*).
Forever jests! . . . puns! . . . *mots!*

CYRANO. *Le mot* forever, indeed! And I
would wish to die, on a fine evening,
under a rose-flushed sky, delivering
myself of a good *mot* in a good cause!
. . . Ah, yes, the best were indeed,
far from fever-bed and potion, pierced
with the only noble weapon, by an
adversary worthy of oneself, to fall
upon a glorious field, the point of a
sword through his heart, the point of
a jest on his lips! . . .

ALL (*in a wail*). I am hungry!   30

CYRANO (*folding his arms*). God ha'
mercy! can you think of nothing but
eating? . . . Come here, Bertrandou
the fifer, once the shepherd! Take
from the double case one of your fifes:
breathe into it, play to this pack of
guzzlers and of gluttons our homely
melodies, of haunting rhythm, every
note of which appeals like a little
sister, through whose every strain
are heard strains of beloved voices
. . . mild melodies whose slowness
brings to mind the slowness of the
smoke upcurling from our native
hamlet hearths . . . melodies that
seem to speak to a man in his native

dialect! . . . (*The old fifer sits down and makes ready his fife.*) Today let the fife, martial unwillingly, be reminded, while your fingers upon its slender stem flutter like birds in a delicate minuet, that before being ebony it was reed; surprise itself by what you make it sing, . . . let it feel restored to it the soul of its youth, rustic and peaceable! (*The old man begins playing Languedoc tunes.*) Listen, Gascons! It is no more, beneath his fingers, the shrill fife of the camp, but the soft flute of the woodland! It is no more, between his lips, the whistling note of battle, but the lowly lay of goatherds leading their flocks to feed! . . . Hark! . . . It sings of the valley, the heath, the forest! . . . of the little shepherd, sunburned under his crimson cap! . . . the green delight of evening on the river! . . . Hark, Gascons all! It sings of Gascony! (*Every head has drooped; all eyes have grown dreamy; tears are furtively brushed away with a sleeve, the hem of a cloak.*)

CARBON (*to* CYRANO, *low*). You are making them weep!

CYRANO. With homesickness! . . . a nobler pain than hunger . . . not physical: mental! I am glad the seat of their suffering should have removed . . . that the gripe should now afflict their hearts!

CARBON. But you weaken them, making them weep!

CYRANO (*beckoning to a drummer*). Never fear! The hero in their veins is quickly roused. It is enough to . . . (*He signs to the drummer who begins drumming.*)

ALL (*starting to their feet and snatching up their arms*). Hein? . . . What? . . . What is it?

CYRANO (*smiling*). You see? . . . The sound of the drum was enough!

Farewell dreams, regrets, old homestead, love . . . What comes with the fife with the drum may go . . .

ONE OF THE CADETS (*looking off at the back*). Ah! ah . . . Here comes Monsieur de Guiche!

ALL THE CADETS (*grumbling*). Hoo . . .

CYRANO (*smiling*). Flattering murmur . . .

ONE OF THE CADETS. He bores us! . . .

OTHER CADET. Showing himself off, with his broad point collar on top of his armor! . . .

OTHER CADET. As if lace were worn with steel!

FIRST CADET. Convenient, if you have a boil on your neck to cover . . .

SECOND CADET. There is another courtier for you!

OTHER CADET. His uncle's own nephew!

CARBON. He is a Gascon, nevertheless!

FIRST CADET. Not genuine! . . . Never trust him. For a Gascon, look you, must be something of a madman: nothing is so deadly to deal with as a Gascon who is completely rational!

LE BRET. He is pale!

OTHER CADET. He is hungry, as hungry as any poor devil of us! But his corselet being freely embellished with gilt studs, his stomach-ache is radiant in the sun!

CYRANO (*eagerly*). Let us not appear to suffer, either! You, your cards, your pipes, your dice . . . (*All briskly set themselves to playing with cards and dice, on the heads of drums, on stools, on cloaks spread over the ground. They light long tobacco pipes.*) And I will be reading Descartes. . . . (*He walks to and fro, forward and backward, reading a small book which he has taken from his pocket. Tableau.*)

[*Enter* DE GUICHE. *Everyone appears absorbed and satisfied.* DE GUICHE *is very pale. He goes toward* CARBON.]

DE GUICHE (*to* CARBON). Ah, good-morning. (*They look at each other attentively. Aside, with satisfaction.*) He is pale as plaster.

CARBON (*same business*). His eyes are all that is left of him.

DE GUICHE (*looking at the* CADETS). So here are the wrongheaded rascals? . . . Yes, gentlemen, it is reported to me on every side that I am your 10 scoff and derision; that the cadets, highland nobility, Béarn clod-hoppers, Périgord baronets, cannot express sufficient contempt for their colonel; call me intriguer, courtier, find it irksome to their taste that I should wear, with my cuirass, a collar of Genoese point, and never cease to air their wondering indignation that a man should be a Gascon 20 without being a vagabond! (*Silence. The* CADETS *continue smoking and playing.*) Shall I have you punished by your captain? . . . I do not like to.

CARBON. Did you otherwise, however, . . . I am free, and punish only . . .

DE GUICHE. Ah? . . .

CARBON. My company is paid by myself, belongs to me. I obey no orders but such as relate to war.   30

DE GUICHE. Ah, is it so? Enough, then. I will treat your taunts with simple scorn. My fashion of deporting myself under fire is well known. You are not unaware of the manner in which yesterday, at Bapaume, I forced back the columns of the Comte de Bucquoi; gathering my men together to plunge forward like an avalanche, three times I charged him. . . .   40

CYRANO (*without lifting his nose from his book*). And your white scarf?

DE GUICHE (*surprised and self-satisfied*). You heard of that circumstance? . . . In fact, it happened that as I was wheeling about to collect my men for the third charge, I was caught in a stream of fugitives which bore me onward to the edge of the enemy. I was in danger of being captured and cut off with an arquebuse, when I had the presence of mind to untie and let slip to the ground the white scarf which proclaimed my military grade. Thus was I enabled, undistinguished, to withdraw from among the Spaniards, and thereupon returning with my reinspirited men, to defeat them. Well? . . . What do you say to the incident?

[*The* CADETS *have appeared not to be listening; at this point, however, hands with cards and dice-boxes remain suspended in the air; no pipe-smoke is ejected; all express expectation.*]

CYRANO. That never would Henry the Fourth, however great the number of his opponents, have consented to diminish his presence by the size of his white plume.

[*Silent joy. Cards fall, dice rattle, smoke upwreathes.*]

DE GUICHE. The trick was successful, however!

[*As before, expectation suspends gambling and smoking.*]

CYRANO. Very likely. But one should not resign the honor of being a target. (*Cards, dice, smoke, fall, rattle, and upwreathe, as before, in expression of increasing glee.*) Had I been at hand when you allowed your scarf to drop —the quality of our courage, monsieur, shows different in this—I would have picked it up and worn it. . . .

DE GUICHE. Ah, yes—more of your Gascon bragging! . . .

CYRANO. Bragging? . . . Lend me the scarf. I engage to mount, ahead of all, to the assault, wearing it crosswise upon my breast!

DE GUICHE. A Gascon's offer, that too! You know that the scarf was left in the enemy's camp, by the banks of the Scarpe, where bullets since then have hailed . . . whence no one can bring it back!

CYRANO (*taking a white scarf from his pocket and handing it to* DE GUICHE). Here it is.

[*Silence. The* CADETS *smother their laughter behind cards and in dice-boxes.* DE GUICHE *turns around, looks at them; instantly they become grave; one of them, with an air of unconcern, whistles the tune played earlier by the fifer.*]

DE GUICHE (*taking the scarf*). I thank you. I shall be able with this shred of white to make a signal . . . which I was hesitating to make. . . . (*He goes to the top of the bank and waves the scarf.*)

ALL. What now? . . . What is this?

THE SENTINEL (*at the top of the bank*). A man . . . over there . . . running off . . .

DE GUICHE (*coming forward again*). It is a supposed Spanish spy. He is very useful to us. The information he carries to the enemy is that which I give him—so that their decisions are influenced by us.

CYRANO. He is a scoundrel!

DE GUICHE (*coolly tying on his scarf*). He is a convenience. We were saying? . . . Ah, I was about to tell you. Last night, having resolved upon a desperate stroke to obtain supplies, the Marshal secretly set out for Dourlens. The royal sutlers are encamped there. He expects to join them by way of the tilled fields; but, to provide against interference, he took with him troops in such number that, certainly, if we were now attacked, the enemy would find easy

work. Half of the army is absent from the camp.

CARBON. If the Spaniards knew that, it might be serious. But they do not know.

DE GUICHE. They do. And are going to attack us.

CARBON. Ah!

DE GUICHE. My pretended spy came to warn me of their intention. He said, moreover: I can direct the attack. At what point shall it be? I will lead them to suppose it the least strong, and they will center their efforts against it. I answered: Very well. Go from the camp. Look down the line. Let them attack at the point I signal from.

CARBON (*to the* CADETS). Gentlemen, get ready! (*All get up. Noise of swords and belts being buckled on.*)

DE GUICHE. They will be here in an hour.

FIRST CADET. Oh! . . . if there is a whole hour! . . . (*All sit down again, and go on with their games.*)

DE GUICHE (*to* CARBON). The main object is to gain time. The Marshal is on his way back.

CARBON. And to gain time?

DE GUICHE. You will be so obliging as to keep them busy killing you.

CYRANO. Ah, this is your revenge!

DE GUICHE. I will not pretend that if I had been fond of you, I would have thus singled out you and yours; but, as your bravery is unquestionably beyond that of others, I am serving my King at the same time as my inclination.

CYRANO. Suffer me, monsieur, to express my gratitude.

DE GUICHE. I know that you affect fighting one against a hundred. You will not complain of lacking opportunity. (*He goes toward the back with* CARBON.)

CYRANO (*to the* CADETS). We shall now be able, gentlemen, to add to the Gascon escutcheon, which bears, as it is, six chevrons, or and azure, the chevron that was wanting to complete it—blood-red! (DE GUICHE *at the back speaks low with* CARBON. *Orders are given. All is made ready to repel an attack.* CYRANO *goes toward* CHRISTIAN, *who stands motionless, with folded arms.*) 10

CYRANO (*laying his hand on* CHRISTIAN'S *shoulder*). Christian?

CHRISTIAN(*shaking his head*). Roxane!

CYRANO. Ah me!

CHRISTIAN. I wish I might at least put my whole heart's last blessing in a beautiful letter!

CYRANO. I mistrusted that it would come today . . . (*He takes a letter from his doublet.*) and I have written 20 your farewells.

CHRISTIAN. Let me see!

CYRANO. You wish to see it? . . .

CHRISTIAN (*taking the letter*). Yes! (*He opens the letter, begins to read, stops short.*) Ah? . . .

CYRANO. What?

CHRISTIAN. That little round blister?

CYRANO (*hurriedly taking back the letter, and looking at it with an artless air*). A 30 blister?

CHRISTIAN. It is a tear!

CYRANO. It looks like one, does it not? . . . A poet, you see, is sometimes caught in his own snare—that is what constitutes the interest, the charm! . . . This letter, you must know, is very touching. In writing it I apparently made myself shed tears.

CHRISTIAN. Shed tears? . . . 40

CYRANO. Yes, because . . . well, to die is not terrible at all . . . but never to see her again . . . never! . . . that, you know, is horrible beyond all thinking. . . . And, things

having taken the turn they have, I shall not see her . . . (CHRISTIAN *looks at him.*) we shall not see her . . . (*Hastily.*) you will not see her. . . .

CHRISTIAN (*snatching the letter from him*). Give me the letter! (*Noise in the distance.*)

VOICE OF A SENTINEL. *Ventrebleu*, who goes there? (*Shots. Noise of voices, tinkling of bells.*)

CARBON. What is it?

THE SENTINEL (*on the top of the bank*). A coach! (*All run to see.*) (*Noisy exclamations.*) What?—In the camp?—It is driving into the camp!—It comes from the direction of the enemy! The devil! Fire upon it!—No! the coachman is shouting something!—What does he say?—He shouts: Service of the King!

DE GUICHE. What? Service of the King?

[*All come down from the bank and fall into order.*]

CARBON. Hats off, all!

DE GUICHE (*at the corner*). Service of the King! Stand back, low rabble, and give it room to turn around with a handsome sweep!

[*The coach comes in at a trot. It is covered with mud and dust. The curtains are drawn. Two lackeys behind. It comes to a standstill.*]

CARBON (*shouting*). Salute!

[*Drums roll. All the* CADETS *uncover.*]

DE GUICHE. Let down the steps!

[*Two men hurry forward. The coach door opens.*]

ROXANE (*stepping from the carriage*). Good-morning!

[*At the sound of a feminine voice, all the men, in the act of bowing low, straighten themselves. Consternation.*]

DE GUICHE. Service of the King! You?

ROXANE. Of the only King! . . . of Love!

CYRANO. Ah, great God!

CHRISTIAN (*rushing to her*). You! Why are you here?

ROXANE. This siege lasted too long!

CHRISTIAN. Why have you come?

ROXANE. I will tell you!

CYRANO (*who at the sound of her voice has started, then stood motionless without venturing to look her way*). God! . . . can I trust myself to look at her?

DE GUICHE. You cannot remain here. 10

ROXANE. But I can—I can, indeed! Will you favor me with a drum? (*She seats herself upon a drum brought forward for her.*) There! I thank you! (*She laughs.*) They fired upon my carriage. (*Proudly.*) A patrol!—It does look rather as if it were made out of a pumpkin, does it not? like Cinderella's coach! and the footmen made out of rats! (*Blowing a kiss to* 20 CHRISTIAN.) How do you do? (*Looking at them all.*) You do not look over-joyed! . . . Arras is a long way from Paris, do you know it? (*Catching sight of* CYRANO.) Cousin, delighted!

CYRANO (*coming toward her*). But how did you . . . ?

ROXANE. How did I find the army? Dear me, cousin, that was simple: I followed straight along the line of 30 devastation. . . . Ah, I should never have believed in such horrors had I not seen them! Gentlemen, if that is the service of your King, I like mine better!

CYRANO. But this is mad! . . . By what way did you come?

ROXANE. Way? . . . I drove through the Spaniards' camp.

FIRST CADET. Ah, what will keep lovely 40 woman from her way!

DE GUICHE. But how did you contrive to get through their lines?

LE BRET. That must have been difficult . . .

ROXANE. No, not very. I simply drove through them, in my coach, at a trot. If a hidalgo, with arrogant front, showed likely to stop us, I put my face at the window, wearing my sweetest smile, and, those gentlemen being—let the French not grudge my saying so!—the most gallant in the world, . . . I passed!

CARBON. Such a smile is a passport, certainly! . . . But you must have been not unfrequently bidden to stand and deliver where you were going?

ROXANE. Not unfrequently, you are right. Whereupon I would say, "I am going to see my lover!" At once, the fiercest looking Spaniard of them all would gravely close my carriage door; and, with a gesture the King might emulate, motion aside the musket-barrels levelled at me; and, superb at once for grace and haughti-ness, bringing his spurs together, and lifting his plumed hat, bow low and say, "Pass, señorita, pass!"

CHRISTIAN. But, Roxane. . .

ROXANE. I said, "My lover!" yes, for-give me!—You see, if I had said, "My husband!" they would never have let me by!

CHRISTIAN. But . . .

ROXANE. What troubles you?

DE GUICHE. You must leave at once.

ROXANE. I?

CYRANO. At once!

LE BRET. As fast as you can.

CHRISTIAN. Yes, you must.

ROXANE. But why?

CHRISTIAN (*embarrassed*). Because . . .

CYRANO (*embarrassed too*). In three quarters of an hour . . .

DE GUICHE (*the same*). Or an hour . . .

CARBON (*the same*). You had much better . . .

LE BRET (*the same*). You might . . .

ROXANE. I shall remain. You are going to fight.

ALL. Oh, no! . . . No!

ROXANE. He is my husband! (*She throws herself in* CHRISTIAN'*s arms.*) Let me be killed with you!

CHRISTIAN. How your eyes shine!

ROXANE. I will tell you why they shine!

DE GUICHE (*desperately*). It is a post of horrible probabilities!

ROXANE (*turning toward him*). What—of horrible? . . .   10

CYRANO. In proof of which he appointed us to it! . . .

ROXANE. Ah, you wish me made a widow?

DE GUICHE. I swear to you . . .

ROXANE. No! Now I have lost all regard. . . . Now I will surely not go. . . . Besides, I think it fun!

CYRANO. What? The précieuse contained a heroine?   20

ROXANE. Monsieur de Bergerac, I am a cousin of yours!

ONE OF THE CADETS. Never think but that we will take good care of you!

ROXANE (*more and more excited*). I am sure you will, my friends!

OTHER CADET. The whole camp smells of iris!

ROXANE. By good fortune I put on a hat that will look well in battle! (*Glancing* 30 *toward* DE GUICHE.) But perhaps it is time the Count should go.—The battle might begin.

DE GUICHE. Ah, it is intolerable!—I am going to inspect my guns, and coming back.—You still have time: think better of it!

ROXANE. Never!

        [*Exit* DE GUICHE.]

CHRISTIAN (*imploring*). Roxane!   40

ROXANE. No!

FIRST CADET. She is going to stay!

ALL (*hurrying about, pushing one another, snatching things from one another*). A comb!—Soap!—My jacket is torn, a needle!—A ribbon!—Lend me your pocket-mirror!—My cuffs!—Curling-irons!—A razor!

ROXANE (*to* CYRANO, *who is still pleading with her*). No! Nothing shall prevail upon me to stir from this spot!

CARBON (*after having, like the others, tightened his belt, dusted himself, brushed his hat, straightened his feather, pulled down his cuffs, approaches* ROXANE, *and ceremoniously*). It is, perhaps, proper, since you are going to stay, that I should present to you a few of the gentlemen about to have the honor of dying in your presence . . . (ROXANE *bows, and stands waiting, with her arm through* CHRISTIAN'*s.*) Baron Peyrescous de Colignac!

THE CADET (*bowing*). Madame!

CARBON (*continuing to present the* CADETS). Baron de Casterac de Cahuzac—Vidame de Malgouyre Estressac Lesbas d'Escarabiot—Chevalier d'Antignac-Juzet—Baron Hillot de Blagnac-Saléchan de Castel Crabioules . . .

ROXANE. But how many names have you apiece?

BARON HILLOT. Innumerable!

CARBON (*to* ROXANE). Open your hand with the handkerchief!

ROXANE (*opens her hand; the handkerchief drops*). Why? (*The whole company starts forward to pick it up.*)

CARBON (*instantly catching it*). My company had no flag! Now, my word, it will have the prettiest one in the army!

ROXANE (*smiling*). It is rather small!

CARBON (*fastening the handkerchief on the staff of his captain's spear*). But it is lace!

ONE OF THE CADETS (*to the others*). I could die without a murmur, having looked upon that beautiful face, if I had so much as a walnut inside me! . . .

CARBON (*who has overheard, indignant*).

Shame! . . . to talk of food when an exquisite woman . . .

ROXANE. But the air of the camp is searching, and I myself am hungry: Patties, jellied meat, light wine . . . are what I should like best! Will you kindly bring me some? (*Consternation.*)

ONE OF THE CADETS. Bring you some?

OTHER CADET. And where, great God, shall we get them? 10

ROXANE (*quietly*). In my coach.

ALL. What?

ROXANE. But there is much to be done, carving and boning and serving. Look more closely at my coachman, gentlemen, and you will recognize a precious individual: the sauces, if we wish, can be warmed over . . .

THE CADETS (*springing toward the coach*). It is Ragueneau! (*Cheers.*) Oh! Oh! 20

ROXANE (*watching them*). Poor fellows!

CYRANO (*kissing her hand.*) Kind fairy!

RAGUENEAU (*standing upon the box-seat like a vender at a public fair*). Gentlemen! (*Enthusiasm.*)

THE CADETS. Bravo! Bravo!

RAGUENEAU. How should the Spaniards, when so much beauty passed, suspect the repast? (*Applause.*)

CYRANO (*low to* CHRISTIAN). Hm! Hm! 30 Christian!

RAGUENEAU. Absorbed in gallantry, no heed took they . . . (*He takes a dish from the box-seat.*) . . . of galantine! (*Applause. The galantine is passed from hand to hand.*)

CYRANO (*low to* CHRISTIAN). A word with you. . . .

RAGUENEAU. Venus kept their eyes fixed upon herself, while Diana slipped past 40 with the . . . (*He brandishes a joint.*) game! (*Enthusiasm. The joint is seized by twenty hands at once.*)

CYRANO (*low to* CHRISTIAN). I must speak with you.

ROXANE (*to the* CADETS *who come forward, their arms full of provisions*). Spread it all upon the ground! (*Assisted by the two imperturbable footmen who were on the back of the coach, she arranges everything on the grass.*)

ROXANE (*to* CHRISTIAN *whom* CYRANO *is trying to draw aside*). Make yourself useful, sir!

[CHRISTIAN *comes and helps her.* CYRANO *gives evidence of uneasiness.*]

RAGUENEAU. A truffled peacock!

FIRST CADET (*radiant, comes forward cutting a large slice of ham*). Praise the pigs, we shall not go to our last fight with nothing in our b . . . (*Correcting himself at sight of* ROXANE.) hm . . . stomachs!

RAGUENEAU (*flinging the carriage cushions*). The cushions are stuffed with snipe! (*Tumult. The cushions are ripped open. Laughter. Joy.*)

RAGUENEAU (*flinging bottles of red wine*). Molten ruby! (*Bottles of white wine.*) Fluid topaz!

ROXANE (*throwing a folded tablecloth to* CYRANO). Unfold the cloth: Hey! . . . be nimble!

RAGUENEAU (*waving one of the coach lanterns*). Each lantern is a little larder!

CYRANO (*low to* CHRISTIAN, *while together they spread the cloth*). I must speak with you before you speak with her . . .

RAGUENEAU. The handle of my whip, behold, is a sausage!

ROXANE (*pouring wine, dispensing it*). Since we are the ones to be killed, *morbleu,* we will not fret ourselves about the rest of the army! Everything for the Gascons! . . . And if De Guiche comes, nobody must invite him! (*Going from one to the other.*) Gently! You have time . . . You must not eat so fast! There, drink. What are you crying about?

FIRST CADET. It is too good!

ROXANE. Hush! White wine or red?—Bread for Monsieur de Carbon!—A knife!—Pass your plate!—You prefer crust?—A little more?—Let me help you.—Champagne?—A wing?—

CYRANO (*following* ROXANE, *his hands full of dishes, helping her*). I adore her!

ROXANE (*going to* CHRISTIAN). What will you take?

CHRISTIAN. Nothing! 10

ROXANE. Oh, but you must take something! This biscuit—in a little Muscatel—just a little?

CHRISTIAN (*trying to keep her from going*). Tell me what made you come?

ROXANE. I owe myself to those poor fellows . . . Be patient . . . By and by . . .

LE BRET (*who had gone toward the back to pass a loaf of bread on the end of a pike to* 20 *the* SENTINEL *upon the earthwork*). De Guiche!

CYRANO. Presto! Vanish basket, flagon, platter and pan! Hurry! Let us look as if nothing were! (*To* RAGUENEAU.) Take a flying leap onto your box!—Is everything hidden? (*In a wink, all the eatables have been pushed into the tents, or hidden under clothes, cloaks, hats.*)

[*Enter* DE GUICHE, *hurriedly; he stops short,* 30 *sniffing the air. Silence.*]

DE GUICHE. What a good smell!

ONE OF THE CADETS (*singing, with effect of mental abstraction*). To lo lo lo. . . .

DE GUICHE (*stopping and looking at him closely*). What is the matter with you—you, there? You are red as a crab.

THE CADET. I? Nothing . . . It is just my blood. . . . We are going to fight: it tells . . . 40

OTHER CADET. Poom . . . poom . . . poom . . .

DE GUICHE (*turning*). What is this?

THE CADET (*slightly intoxicated*). Nothing . . . A song . . . just a little song.

DE GUICHE. You look in good spirits, my boy!

THE CADET. Danger affects me that way!

DE GUICHE (*calling* CARBON DE CASTEL-JALOUX *to give an order*). Captain, I . . . (*He stops at sight of his face.*) Peste! You look in good spirits, too.

CARBON (*flushed, holding a bottle behind him; with an evasive gesture*). Oh! . . .

DE GUICHE. I had a cannon left over, which I have ordered them to place (*He points in the wing.*) there, in that corner, and which your men can use, if necessary . . .

ONE OF THE CADETS (*swaying from one foot to the other*). Charming attention!

OTHER CADET (*smiling sugarily*). Our thanks for your gracious thoughtfulness!

DE GUICHE. Have they gone mad? . . . (*Drily.*) As you are not accustomed to handling a cannon, look out for its kicking . . .

FIRST CADET. Ah, pfft! . . .

DE GUICHE (*going toward him, furious*). But . . .

THE CADET. A cannon knows better than to kick a Gascon!

DE GUICHE (*seizing him by the arm and shaking him*). You are all tipsy: on what?

THE CADET (*magnificently*). The smell of powder!

DE GUICHE (*shrugs his shoulders, pushes aside the* CADET, *and goes rapidly toward* ROXANE). Quick, Madame! what have you condescended to decide?

ROXANE. I remain.

DE GUICHE. Retire, I beseech you.

ROXANE. No.

DE GUICHE. If you are determined, then . . . Let me have a musket!

CARBON. What do you mean?

DE GUICHE. I, too, will remain.

CYRANO. At last, monsieur, an instance of pure and simple bravery!

FIRST CADET. Might you be a Gascon, lace collar notwithstanding?

DE GUICHE. I do not leave a woman in danger.

SECOND CADET (*to* FIRST CADET). Look here! I think he might be given something to eat! (*All the food reappears, as if by magic.*)

DE GUICHE (*his eyes brightening*). Provisions?

THIRD CADET. Under every waistcoat!

DE GUICHE (*mastering himself, haughtily*). Do you imagine that I will eat your leavings?

CYRANO (*bowing*). You are improving!

DE GUICHE (*proudly, falling at the last of the sentence into a slightly* GASCON *accent*). I will fight before I eat!

FIRST CADET (*exultant*). Fight! Eat! . . . He spoke with an accent!

DE GUICHE (*laughing*). I did?

(THE CADET. He is one of us! (*All fall to dancing.*)

CARBON (*who a moment before disappeared behind the earthworks, reappearing at the top*). I have placed my pikemen. They are a determined troop . . . (*He points at a line of pikes projecting above the bank.*)

DE GUICHE (*to* ROXANE, *bowing*). Will you accept my hand and pass them in review? (*She takes his hand; they go toward the bank. Everyone uncovers and follows.*)

CHRISTIAN (*going to* CYRANO, *quickly*). Speak! Be quick!

[*As* ROXANE *appears at the top of the bank, the pikes disappear, lowered in a salute, and a cheer goes up;* ROXANE *bows.*]

PIKEMEN (*outside*). Vivat!

CHRISTIAN. What did you want to tell me?

CYRANO. In case Roxane . . .

CHRISTIAN. Well?

CYRANO. Should speak to you of the letters . . .

CHRISTIAN. Yes, the letters. I know!

CYRANO. Do not commit the blunder of appearing surprised . . .

CHRISTIAN. At what?

CYRANO. I must tell you! . . . It is quite simple, and merely comes into my mind today because I see her. You have . . .

CHRISTIAN. Hurry!

10 CYRANO. You . . . you have written to her oftener than you suppose . . .

CHRISTIAN. Oh, have I?

CYRANO. Yes. It was my business, you see. I had undertaken to interpret your passion, and sometimes I wrote without having told you I should write.

CHRISTIAN. Ah?

CYRANO. It is very simple.

20 CHRISTIAN. But how did you succeed since we have been so closely surrounded, in . . . ?

CYRANO. Oh, before daybreak I could cross the lines . . .

CHRISTIAN (*folding his arms*). Ah, that is very simple, too? . . . And how many times a week have I been writing? Twice? Three times? Four? . . .

CYRANO. More.

30 CHRISTIAN. Every day?

CYRANO. Yes, every day . . . twice.

CHRISTIAN (*violently*). And you cared so much about it that you were willing to brave death. . . .

CYRANO (*seeing* ROXANE *who returns*). Be still . . . Not before her! (*He goes quickly into his tent.* CADETS *come and go at the back.* CARBON *and* DE GUICHE *give orders.*)

40 ROXANE (*running to* CHRISTIAN). And now, Christian . . .

CHRISTIAN (*taking her hands*). And now, you shall tell me why, over these fearful roads, through these ranks of rough soldiery, you risked your dear self to join me?

ROXANE. Because of the letters!

CHRISTIAN. The . . . ? What did you say?

ROXANE. It is through your fault that I have been exposed to such and so many dangers. It is your letters that have gone to my head! Ah, think how many you have written me in a month, each one more beautiful . . .

CHRISTIAN. What? . . . Because of a few 10 little love letters . . .

ROXANE. Say nothing! You cannot understand! Listen: The truth is that I took to idolizing you one evening, when, below my window, in a voice I did not know before, your soul began to reveal itself. . . . Think then what the effect should be of your letters, which have been like your voice heard constantly for one month, your voice 20 of that evening, so tender, caressing . . . You must bear it as you can, I have come to you! Prudent Penelope would not have stayed at home with her eternal tapestry, if Ulysses, her lord, had written as you write . . . but, impulsive as Helen, have tossed aside her yarns, and flown to join him!

CHRISTIAN. But . . . 30

ROXANE. I read them, I re-read them, in reading I grew faint . . . I became your own indeed! Each fluttering leaf was like a petal of your soul wafted to me . . . In every word of those letters, love is felt as a flame would be felt—love, compelling, sincere, profound . . .

CHRISTIAN. Ah, sincere, profound? . . . You say that it can be felt, Roxane? 40

ROXANE. He asks me!

CHRISTIAN. And so you came? . . .

ROXANE. I came—oh Christian, my own, my master! If I were to kneel at your feet you would lift me, I know. It is my soul therefore which kneels, and never can you lift it from that posture!—I came to implore your pardon—as it is fitting, for we are both perhaps about to die!—your pardon for having done you the wrong, at first, in my shallowness, of loving you . . . for mere looking!

CHRISTIAN (in alarm). Ah, Roxane! . . .

ROXANE. Later, dear one, grown less shallow—similar to a bird which flutters before it can fly—your gallant exterior appealing to me still, but your soul appealing equally, I loved you for both! . . .

CHRISTIAN. And now?

ROXANE. Now at last yourself are vanquished by yourself. I love you for your soul alone . . .

CHRISTIAN (drawing away). Ah, Roxane!

ROXANE. Rejoice! For to be loved for that wherewith we are clothed so fleetingly must put a noble heart to torture. . . . Your dear thought at last casts your dear face in shadow: the harmonious lineaments whereby at first you pleased me, I do not see them, now my eyes are open!

CHRISTIAN. Oh!

ROXANE. You question your own triumph?

CHRISTIAN (sorrowfully). Roxane!

ROXANE. I understand, you cannot conceive of such a love in me?

CHRISTIAN. I do not wish to be loved like that! I wish to be loved quite simply . . .

ROXANE. For that which other women till now have loved in you? Ah, let yourself be loved in a better way.

CHRISTIAN. No . . . I was happier before! . . .

ROXANE. Ah, you do not understand! It is now that I love you most, that I truly love you. It is that which makes you, you—can you not grasp it?—that I worship . . . And did you no longer walk our earth like a young martial Apollo . . .

CHRISTIAN. Say no more!

ROXANE. Still would I love you! . . . Yes, though a blight should have fallen upon your face and form . . .

CHRISTIAN. Do not say it!

ROXANE. But I do say it . . . I do!

CHRISTIAN. What? If I were ugly, distinctly, offensively?

ROXANE. If you were ugly, dear, I swear it!

CHRISTIAN. God!

ROXANE. And you are glad, profoundly glad?

CHRISTIAN (*in a smothered voice*). Yes . . .

ROXANE. What is it?

CHRISTIAN (*pushing her gently away*). Nothing. I have a word or two to say to someone: your leave, for a second . . .

ROXANE. But . . .

CHRISTIAN (*pointing at a group of* CADETS *at the back*). In my selfish love, I have kept you from those poor brothers. . . . Go, smile on them a little, before they die, dear . . . go!

ROXANE (*moved*). Dear Christian! (*She goes toward the* GASCONS *at the back; they respectfully gather around her.*)

CHRISTIAN (*calling toward* CYRANO'S *tent*). Cyrano!

CYRANO (*appears, armed for battle*). What is it? . . . How pale you are!

CHRISTIAN. She does not love me any more!

CYRANO. What do you mean?

CHRISTIAN. She loves you.

CYRANO. No!

CHRISTIAN. She only loves my soul!

CYRANO. No!

CHRISTIAN. Yes! Therefore it is you she loves . . . and you love her . . .

CYRANO. I . . .

CHRISTIAN. I know it!

CYRANO. It is true.

CHRISTIAN. To madness!

CYRANO. More.

CHRISTIAN. Tell her then.

CYRANO. No!

CHRISTIAN. Why not?

CYRANO. Look at me!

CHRISTIAN. She would love me grown ugly.

CYRANO. She told you so?

CHRISTIAN. With the utmost frankness!

CYRANO. Ah! I am glad she should have told you that! But, believe me, believe me, place no faith in such a mad asseveration! Dear God, I am glad such a thought should have come to her, and that she should have spoken it—but believe me, do not take her at her word: Never cease to be the handsome fellow you are. . . . She would not forgive me!

CHRISTIAN. That is what I wish to discover.

CYRANO. No! no!

CHRISTIAN. Let her choose between us! You shall tell her everything.

CYRANO. No . . . No . . . I refuse the ordeal!

CHRISTIAN. Shall I stand in the way of your happiness because my outside is not so much amiss?

CYRANO. And I? shall I destroy yours, because, thanks to the hazard that sets us upon earth, I have the gift of expressing . . . what you perhaps feel?

CHRISTIAN. You shall tell her everything!

CYRANO. He persists in tempting me . . . It is a mistake . . . and cruel!

CHRISTIAN. I am weary of carrying about, in my own self, a rival!

CYRANO. Christian!

CHRISTIAN. Our marriage . . . contracted without witnesses . . . can be annulled . . . if we survive!

CYRANO. He persists! . . .

CHRISTIAN. Yes. I will be loved for my sole self, or not at all!—I am going to see what they are about. Look! I will walk to the end of the line and back . . . Tell her, and let her pronounce between us.

CYRANO. She will pronounce for you.

CHRISTIAN. I can but hope she will! (*Calling.*) Roxane!

CYRANO. No! No!

ROXANE (*coming forward*). What is it?

CHRISTIAN. Cyrano has something to tell you . . . something important! (ROXANE *goes hurriedly to* CYRANO. *Exit* CHRISTIAN.)

ROXANE. Something important?

CYRANO (*distractedly*). He is gone! . . . (*To* ROXANE.) Nothing whatever! He attaches—but you must know him of old!—he attaches importance to trifles . . .

ROXANE (*quickly*). He did not believe what I told him a moment ago? . . . I saw that he did not believe . . .

CYRANO (*taking her hand*). But did you in very truth tell him the truth?

ROXANE. Yes. Yes. I should love him even . . . (*She hesitates a second.*)

CYRANO (*smiling sadly*). You do not like to say it before me?

ROXANE. But . . .

CYRANO. I shall not mind! . . . Even if he were ugly?

ROXANE. Yes . . . Ugly. (*Musket shots outside.*) They are firing!

CYRANO (*ardently*). Dreadfully ugly?

ROXANE. Dreadfully.

CYRANO. Disfigured?

ROXANE. Disfigured!

CYRANO. Grotesque?

ROXANE. Nothing could make him grotesque . . . to me.

CYRANO. You would love him still?

ROXANE. I believe that I should love him more . . . if that were possible!

CYRANO (*losing his head, aside*). My God,

perhaps she means it . . . perhaps it is true . . . and that way is happiness! (*To* ROXANE.) I . . . Roxane . . . listen!

LE BRET (*comes in hurriedly; calls softly*). Cyrano!

CYRANO (*turning*). Hein?

LE BRET. Hush! (*He whispers a few words to* CYRANO.)

CYRANO (*letting* ROXANE's *hand drop, with a cry*). Ah! . . .

ROXANE. What ails you?

CYRANO (*to himself, in consternation*). It is finished! (*Musket reports.*)

ROXANE. What is it? What is happening? Who is firing? (*She goes to the back to look off.*)

CYRANO. It is finished. . . . My lips are sealed forevermore!

[CADETS *come in, attempting to conceal something they carry among them; they surround it, preventing* ROXANE's *seeing it.*]

ROXANE. What has happened?

CYRANO (*quickly stopping her as she starts towards them*). Nothing!

ROXANE. These men? . . .

CYRANO (*drawing her away*). Pay no attention to them!

ROXANE. But what were you about to say to me before?

CYRANO. What was I about to say? . . . Oh, nothing! . . . Nothing whatever, I assure you. (*Solemnly.*) I swear that Christian's spirit, that his soul, were . . . (*In terror, correcting himself.*) are the greatest that . . .

ROXANE. Were? . . . (*With a great cry.*) Ah! . . . (*Runs to the group of* CADETS, *and thrusts them aside.*)

CYRANO. It is finished!

ROXANE (*seeing* CHRISTIAN *stretched out in his cloak*). Christian!

LE BRET (*to* CYRANO). At the enemy's first shot!

[ROXANE *throws herself on* CHRISTIAN's

body. *Musket reports. Clashing of swords. Tramping. Drums.*]

CARBON (*sword in hand*). The attack! To your muskets! (*Followed by the* CADETS *he goes to the further side of the earthworks.*)

ROXANE. Christian!

CARBON'S VOICE (*beyond the earthworks*). Make haste!

ROXANE. Christian!

CARBON. Fall into line!

ROXANE. Christian!

CARBON. Measure . . . match!

[RAGUENEAU *has come running in with water in a steel cap.*]

CHRISTIAN (*in a dying voice*). Roxane!

CYRANO (*quick, low in* CHRISTIAN'S *ear, while* ROXANE, *distracted, dips into the water a fragment of linen torn from her breast to bind his wound*). I have told her everything! . . . You are still the one she loves! (CHRISTIAN *closes his eyes.*)

ROXANE. What, dear love?

CARBON. Muzzle . . . high!

ROXANE (*to* CYRANO). He is not dead? . . .

CARBON. Open charge . . . with teeth!

ROXANE. I feel his cheek grow cold against my own!

CARBON. Take aim!

ROXANE. A letter on his breast. . . . (*She opens it.*) To me!

CYRANO (*aside*). My letter!

CARBON. Fire! (*Musket shots. Cries. Roar of battle.*)

CYRANO (*trying to free his hand which* ROX-ANE *clasps kneeling*). But, Roxane, they are fighting.

ROXANE (*clinging*). No! . . . Stay with me a little! . . . He is dead. You are the only one that truly knew him. . . . (*She cries subduedly.*) Was he not an exquisite being . . . an exceptional, marvellous being? . . .

CYRANO (*standing bareheaded*). Yes, Roxane.

ROXANE. A poet without his peer, . . . one verily to reverence?

CYRANO. Yes, Roxane.

ROXANE. A sublime spirit?

CYRANO. Yes, Roxane.

ROXANE. A profound heart, such as the profane could never have understood . . . a soul as noble as it was charming? . . .

CYRANO (*firmly*). Yes, Roxane.

ROXANE (*throwing herself on* CHRISTIAN'S *body*). And he is dead!

CYRANO (*aside, drawing his sword*). And I have now only to die, since, without knowing it, she mourns my death in his!

[*Trumpets in the distance.*]

DE GUICHE (*reappears on the top of the bank, bareheaded, his forehead bloody; in a thundering voice*). The signal they promised! The flourish of trumpets! . . . The French are entering the camp with supplies! . . . Stand fast a little longer!

ROXANE. Upon his letter . . . blood, . . . tears!

A VOICE (*outside, shouting*). Surrender!

VOICES OF THE CADETS. No!

RAGUENEAU (*who from the top of the coach is watching the battle beyond the bank*). The conflict rages hotter! . . .

CYRANO (*to* DE GUICHE *pointing at* ROXANE). Take her away! . . . I am going to charge.

ROXANE (*kissing the letter, in a dying voice*). His blood! . . . his tears!

RAGUENEAU (*leaping from the coach and running to* ROXANE). She is fainting!

DE GUICHE (*at the top of the bank, to the* CADETS, *madly*). Stand fast!

VOICE (*outside*). Surrender!

VOICES OF THE CADETS. No!

CYRANO (*to* DE GUICHE). Your courage none will question . . . (*Pointing at* ROXANE.) Fly for the sake of saving her!

DE GUICHE (*runs to* ROXANE *and lifts her in his arms*). So be it! But we shall win the day if you can hold out a little longer . . .

CYRANO. We can. (*To* ROXANE, *whom* DE GUICHE, *helped by* RAGUENEAU, *is carrying off insensible.*) Good-bye, Roxane!

Tumult. Cries. CADETS *reappear, wounded, and fall upon the stage.* CYRANO *dashing* 10 *forward to join the combatants is stopped on the crest of the bank by* CARBON *covered with blood.*]

CARBON. We are losing ground . . . I have got two halberd wounds . . .

CYRANO (*yelling to the* GASCONS). Steadfast! . . . Never give them an inch! . . . Brave boys! (*To* CARBON.) Fear nothing! I have various deaths to avenge: Christian's and all my 20 hopes'! (*They come down.* CYRANO *brandishes the spear at the head of which* ROXANE'S *handkerchief is fastened.*) Float free, little cobweb flag, embroidered with her initials! (*He drives the spear-staff into the earth; shouts to the* CADETS.) Fall on them, boys! . . . Crush them! (*To the fifer.*) Fifer, play! (*The fifer plays. Some of the wounded get* to *their feet again. Some of the* CADETS, *coming down the bank, group themselves around* CYRANO *and the little flag. The coach, filled and covered with men, bristles with muskets and becomes a redoubt.*)

ONE OF THE CADETS (*appears upon the top of the bank backing while he fights; he cries*). They are coming up the slope! (*Falls dead.*)

CYRANO. We will welcome them!
[*Above the bank suddenly rises a formidable array of enemies. The great banners of the Imperial Army appear.*]

CYRANO. Fire! (*General discharge.*)

CRY (*among the hostile ranks*). Fire! (*Shots returned.* CADETS *drop on every side.*)

A SPANISH OFFICER (*taking off his hat*). What are these men, so determined all to be killed?

CYRANO (*declaiming, as he stands in the midst of flying bullets*).
They are the Gascony Cadets
Of Carbon de Castel-Jaloux;
Famed fighters, liars, desperates . . .
(*He leaps forward, followed by a handful of survivors.*)
They are the Gascony Cadets! . . .
(*The rest is lost in the confusion of battle.*)
CURTAIN

ACT V

CYRANO'S GAZETTE

Fifteen years later, 1655. The park belonging to the convent of the Sisters of the Cross, in Paris.

Superb shade-trees. At the left, the house; several doors opening on to broad terrace with steps. In the center of the stage, huge trees standing alone in a clear oval space. At the right, first wing, a semicircular stone seat, surrounded by large box-trees.

All along the back of the stage, an avenue of chestnut-trees, which leads, at the right, fourth wing, to the door of a chapel seen through trees. Through the double row of trees overarching the avenue are seen lawns, other avenues, clumps of trees, the further recesses of the park, the sky.

The chapel opens by a small side-door into a colonnade, overrun by a scarlet creeper; the colonnade comes forward and is lost to sight behind the box-tree at the right.

It is Autumn. The leaves are turning, above the still fresh grass. Dark patches of evergreens, box and yew. Under each tree a mat of yellow leaves. Fallen leaves litter the whole stage, crackle underfoot, lie thick on the terrace and the seats.

Between the seat at the right and the tree in the center, a large embroidery frame, in front of which a small chair. Baskets full of wools, in skeins and balls. On the frame, a piece of tapestry, partly done.

At the rise of the curtain, nuns come and go in the park; a few are seated on the stone seat around an older nun; leaves are falling.

SISTER MARTHA (*to* MOTHER MARGARET). 10 Sister Claire, after putting on her cap went back to the mirror, to see herself again.

MOTHER MARGARET (*to* SISTER CLAIRE). It was unbecoming, my child.

SISTER CLAIRE. But Sister Martha, today, after finishing her portion, went back to the tart for a plum. I saw her!

MOTHER MARGARET (*to* SISTER MARTHA). My child, it was ill done.

SISTER CLAIRE. I merely glanced! . . .

SISTER MARTHA. The plum was about so big! . . .

MOTHER MARGARET. This evening, when Monsieur Cyrano comes, I will tell him.

SISTER CLAIRE (*alarmed*). No! He will laugh at us!

SISTER MARTHA. He will say that nuns are very vain!

SISTER CLAIRE. And very greedy!

MOTHER MARGARET. And really very good.

SISTER CLAIRE. Mother Margaret, is it not true that he has come here every Saturday in the last ten years?

MOTHER MARGARET. Longer! Ever since his cousin brought among our linen coifs her coif of crape, the worldly symbol of her mourning, which set- 40 tled like a sable bird amidst our flock of white some fourteen years ago.

SISTER MARTHA. He alone, since she took her abode in our cloister, has art to dispel her never-lessening sorrow.

ALL THE NUNS. He is so droll!—It is merry when he comes!—He teases us —He is delightful!—We are greatl attached to him!—We are makin Angelica paste to offer him!

SISTER MARTHA. He is not, however, very good Catholic!

SISTER CLAIRE. We will convert him.

THE NUNS. We will! We will!

MOTHER MARGARET. I forbid your re newing that attempt, my children Do not trouble him: he might no come so often!

SISTER MARTHA. But . . . God!

MOTHER MARGARET. Set your hearts a rest: God must know him of old!

SISTER MARTHA. But every Saturday when he comes, he says to me as soor as he sees me, "Sister, I ate meat, yes terday!"

20 MOTHER MARGARET. Ah, that is what he says? . . . Well, when he last said it he had eaten nothing for two days.

SISTER MARTHA. Mother!

MOTHER MARGARET. He is poor.

SISTER MARTHA. Who told you?

MOTHER MARGARET. Monsieur Le Bret.

SISTER MARTHA. Does no one offer him assistance?

30 MOTHER MARGARET. No, he would take offence.

[*In one of the avenues at the back, appear* ROXANE, *in black, wearing a widow' coif and long mourning veil;* DE GUICHE, *markedly older, magnificently dressed, walks beside her. They go very slowly.* MOTHER MARGARET *gets up.*]

MOTHER MARGARET. Come, we must go within. Madame Magdeleine is walk ing in the park with a visitor.

SISTER MARTHA (*low to* SISTER CLAIRE). Is not that the Marshal-duke de Grammont?

SISTER CLAIRE (*looking*). I think it is!

SISTER MARTHA. He has not been to see her in many months!

THE NUNS. He is much engaged!—The Court!—The Camp!——

SISTER CLAIRE. Cares of this world! (*Exeunt.* DE GUICHE *and* ROXANE *come forward silently, and stop near the embroidery frame. A pause.*)

DE GUICHE. And so you live here, uselessly fair, always in mourning?

ROXANE. Always.

DE GUICHE. As faithful as of old?   10

ROXANE. As faithful.

DE GUICHE (*after a time*). Have you forgiven me?

ROXANE. Since I am here. (*Other silence.*)

DE GUICHE. And he was really such a rare being?

ROXANE. To understand, one must have known him!

DE GUICHE. Ah, one must have known him! . . . Perhaps I did not know 20 him well enough. And his last letter, still and always, against your heart?

ROXANE. I wear it on this velvet, as a more holy scapular.

DE GUICHE. Even dead, you love him?

ROXANE. It seems to me sometimes he is but half dead, that our hearts have not been severed, that his love still wraps me round, no less than ever 30 living!

DE GUICHE (*after another silence*). Does Cyrano come here to see you?

ROXANE. Yes, often. That faithful friend fulfils by me the office of gazette. His visits are regular. He comes: when the weather is fine, his armchair is brought out under the trees. I wait for him here with my work; the hour strikes; on the last stroke, I hear—I 40 do not even turn to see who comes!— his cane upon the steps; he takes his seat; he rallies me upon my neverending tapestry; he tells off the events of the week, and . . . (LE BRET *appears on the steps.*) Ah, Le Bret! (LE

BRET *comes down the steps.*) How does your friend?

LE BRET. Ill.

THE DUKE. Oh!

ROXANE. He exaggerates! . . .

LE BRET. All is come to pass as I foretold: neglect! poverty! his writings ever breeding him new enemies! Fraud he attacks in every embodiment: usurpers, pious pretenders, plagiarists, asses in lions' skins . . . all! He attacks all!

ROXANE. No one, however, but stands in profound respect of his sword. They will never succeed in silencing him.

DE GUICHE (*shaking his head*). Who knows?

LE BRET. What I fear is not the aggression of man; what I fear is loneliness and want and winter creeping upon him like stealthy wolves in his miserable attic; they are the insidious foes that will have him by the throat at last! . . . Every day he tightens his belt by an eyelet; his poor great nose is pinched, and turned the sallow of old ivory; the worn black serge you see him in is the only coat he has!

DE GUICHE. Ah, there is one who did not succeed! . . . Nevertheless, do not pity him too much.

LE BRET (*with a bitter smile*). Marshal! . . .

DE GUICHE. Do not pity him too much: he signed no bonds with the world; he has lived free in his thought as in his actions.

LE BRET (*as above*). Duke . . .

DE GUICHE (*haughtily*). I know, yes: I have everything, he has nothing. . . . But I should like to shake hands with him. (*Bowing to* ROXANE.) Good-bye.

ROXANE. I will go with you to the door. (DE GUICHE *bows to* LE BRET *and goes with* ROXANE *toward the terrace steps.*)

DE GUICHE (*stopping, while she goes up the steps*). Yes, sometimes I envy him. You see, when a man has succeeded too well in life, he is not unlikely to feel—dear me! without having committed any very serious wrong!—a multitudinous disgust of himself, the sum of which does not constitute a real remorse, but an obscure uneasiness; and a ducal mantle, while it 10 sweeps up the stairs of greatness, may trail in its furry lining a rustling of sere illusions and regrets, as, when you slowly climb toward those doors, your black gown trails the withered leaves.

ROXANE (*ironical*). Are you not unusually pensive? . . .

DE GUICHE. Ah, yes! (*As he is about to leave, abruptly.*) Monsieur Le Bret! 20 (*To* ROXANE.) Will you allow me? A word. (*He goes to* LE BRET, *and lowering his voice.*) It is true that no one will dare overtly to attack your friend, but many have him in particular disrelish; and someone was saying to me yesterday, at the Queen's, "It seems not unlikely that this Cyrano will meet with an accident."

LE BRET. Ah? . . .   30

DE GUICHE. Yes. Let him keep indoors. Let him be cautious.

LE BRET (*lifting his arms toward Heaven*). Cautious! . . . He is coming here. I will warn him. Warn him! . . . Yes, but . . .

ROXANE (*who has been standing at the head of the steps, to a nun who comes toward her*). What is it?

THE NUN. Ragueneau begs to see you, 40 Madame.

ROXANE. Let him come in. (*To* DE GUICHE *and* LE BRET.) He comes to plead distress. Having determined one day to be an author, he became in turn precentor . . .

LE BRET. Bath-house keeper . . .

ROXANE. Actor . . .

LE BRET. Beadle . . .

ROXANE. Barber . . .

LE BRET. Arch-lute teacher . . .

ROXANE. I wonder what he is now!

RAGUENEAU (*entering precipitately*). Ah, madame! (*He sees* LE BRET.) Monsieur!

ROXANE (*smiling*). Begin telling your misfortunes to Le Bret. I am coming back.

RAGUENEAU. But, madame . . .

[ROXANE *leaves without listening, with the* DUKE. RAGUENEAU *goes to* LE BRET.]

RAGUENEAU. It is better so. Since you are here, I had liefer not tell her! Less than half an hour ago, I was going to see your friend. I was not thirty feet from his door, when I saw him come out. I hurried to catch up with him. He was about to turn the corner. I started to run, when from a window below which he was passing—was it pure mischance? It may have been!— a lackey drops a block of wood . . .

LE BRET. Ah, the cowards! . . . Cyrano!

RAGUENEAU. I reach the spot, and find him . . .

LE BRET. Horrible!

RAGUENEAU. Our friend, monsieur, our poet, stretched upon the ground, with a great hole in his head!

LE BRET. He is dead?

RAGUENEAU. No, but . . . God have mercy! I carried him to his lodging . . . Ah, his lodging! You should see that lodging of his!

LE BRET. Is he in pain?

RAGUENEAU. No, monsieur, he is unconscious.

LE BRET. Has a doctor seen him?

RAGUENEAU. One came . . . out of good nature.

LE BRET. My poor, poor Cyrano! . . .

We must not tell Roxane outright.
And the doctor? . . .

RAGUENEAU. He talked . . . I hardly
grasped . . . of fever . . . cerebral
inflammation! Ah, if you should see
him, with his head done up in
cloths! . . . Let us hurry . . . No
one is there to tend him . . . And he
might die if he attempted to get up!

LE BRET (*dragging* RAGUENEAU *off at the*
right). This way. Come, it is shorter
through the chapel.

ROXANE (*appearing at the head of the steps,*
catching sight of LE BRET *hurrying off*
through the colonnade which leads to the
chapel side-door). Monsieur Le Bret!
(LE BRET *and* RAGUENEAU *make their*
escape without answering.) Le Bret not
turning back when he is called? . . .
Poor Ragueneau must be in some new
trouble! (*She comes down the steps.*) How
beautiful . . . how beautiful, this
golden-hazy waning day of September at its wane! My sorrowful mood,
which the exuberant gladness of April
offends, Autumn, the dreamy and
subdued, lures on to smile . . . (*She*
sits down at her embroidery frame. Two
NUNS *come from the house bringing a large*
armchair which they place under the tree.)
Ah, here comes the classic armchair
in which my old friend always sits!

SISTER MARTHA. The best in the convent
parlor!

ROXANE. I thank you, sister. (*The nuns*
withdraw.) He will be here in a moment. (*She adjusts the embroidery frame*
before her.) There! The clock is striking . . . My   wools! . . . . The
clock has struck? . . . I wonder at
this! . . . Is it possible that for the
first time he is late? . . . It must be
that the sister who keeps the door . . .
my thimble? ah, here it is! . . . is de-
taining him to exhort him to repentance . . . (*A pause.*) She exhorts him

at some length! . . . He cannot be
much longer . . . A withered leaf!
(*She brushes away the dead leaf which has*
dropped on the embroidery.) Surely nothing could keep . . . My scissors? . . .
in my workbag! . . . could keep him
from coming!

A NUN (*appearing at the head of the steps*).
Monsieur de Bergerac!

ROXANE (*without turning round*). What was
I saying? . . . (*She begins to embroider.*
CYRANO *appears, exceedingly pale, his hat*
drawn down over his eyes. The NUN *has*
shown him into the garden, withdraws. He
comes down the steps very slowly, with evi-
dent difficulty to keep on his feet, leaning
heavily on his cane. ROXANE *proceeds with*
her sewing.) Ah, these dull soft
shades! . . . How shall I match
them? (*To* CYRANO, *in a tone of friendly*
chiding.) After fourteen years, for the
first time you are late!

CYRANO (*who has reached the armchair and*
seated himself, in a jolly voice which con-
trasts with his face). Yes, it seems incredible! I am savage at it. I was detained, spite of all I could do! . . .

ROXANE. By? . . .

CYRANO. A somewhat inopportune call.

ROXANE (*absent-minded, sewing*). Ah,
yes . . . some troublesome fellow!

CYRANO. Cousin, it was a troublesome
Madam.

ROXANE. You excused yourself?

CYRANO. Yes. I said, "Your pardon, but
this is Saturday, on which day I am
due in a certain dwelling. On no account do I ever fail. Come back in an
hour!"

ROXANE (*lightly*). Well, she will have to
wait some time to see you. I shall not
let you go before evening.

CYRANO. Perhaps . . . I shall have to
go a little earlier. (*He closes his eyes and*
is silent a moment. SISTER MARTHA *is seen*
crossing the park from the chapel to the ter-

race. ROXANE *sees her and beckons to her by a slight motion of her head.*)

ROXANE (*to* CYRANO). Are you not going to tease Sister Martha today?

CYRANO (*quickly, opening his eyes*). I am indeed! (*In a comically gruff voice.*) Sister Martha, come nearer! (*The* NUN *demurely comes toward him.*) Ha! ha! ha! Beautiful eyes, ever studying the ground! 10

SISTER MARTHA (*lifting her eyes and smiling*). But . . . (*She sees his face and makes a gesture of surprise.*) Oh!

CYRANO (*low, pointing at* ROXANE). Hush! . . . It is nothing! (*In swaggering voice, aloud.*) Yesterday, I ate meat!

SISTER MARTHA. I am sure you did! (*Aside.*) That is why he is so pale! (*Quickly, low.*) Come to the refectory presently. I shall have ready for you 20 there a good bowl of broth . . . You will come!

CYRANO. Yes, yes, yes.

SISTER MARTHA. Ah, you are more reasonable today?

ROXANE (*hearing them whisper*). She is trying to convert you?

SISTER MARTHA. Indeed I am not!

CYRANO. It is true, you, usually almost discursive in the holy cause, are read- 30 ing me no sermon! You amaze me! (*With comical fury.*) I will amaze you, too! Listen, you are authorized . . . (*With the air of casting about in his mind, and finding the jest he wants.*) Ah, now I shall amaze you! to . . . pray for me, this evening . . . in the chapel.

ROXANE. Oh! oh!

CYRANO (*laughing*). Sister Martha . . . lost in amazement! 40

SISTER MARTHA (*gently*). I did not wait for your authorization. (*She goes in.*)

CYRANO (*turning to* ROXANE, *who is bending over her embroidery*). The devil, tapestry . . . the devil, if I hope to live to see the end of you!

ROXANE. I was waiting for that jest.

[*A slight gust of wind makes the leaves fall.*]

CYRANO. The leaves!

ROXANE (*looking up from her work and gazing off toward the avenues*). They are the russet gold of a Venetian beauty's hair . . . Watch them fall!

CYRANO. How consummately they do it! In that brief fluttering from bough to ground, how they contrive still to put beauty! And though foredoomed to moulder upon the earth that draws them, they wish their fall invested with the grace of a free bird's flight!

ROXANE. Serious, you?

CYRANO (*remembering himself*). Not at all, Roxane!

ROXANE. Come, never mind the falling leaves! Tell me the news, instead . . . Where is my budget?

CYRANO. Here it is!

ROXANE. Ah!

CYRANO (*growing paler and paler, and struggling with pain*). Saturday, the nineteenth: The king having filled his dish eight times with Cette preserves, and emptied it, was taken with a fever; his distemper, for high treason, was condemned to be let blood, and now the royal pulse is rid of febriculosity! On Sunday: at the Queen's great ball, were burned seven hundred and sixty-three wax candles; our troops, it is said, defeated Austrian John; four sorcerers were hanged; Madame Athis's little dog had a distressing turn, the case called for a . . .

ROXANE. Monsieur de Bergerac, leave out the little dog!

CYRANO. Monday, . . . nothing, or next to it: Lygdamire took a fresh lover.

ROXANE. Oh!

CYRANO (*over whose face is coming a change more and more marked*). Tuesday: the

whole Court assembled at Fontaine-
bleau. Wednesday, the fair Monglat
said to Count Fiesco "No!" Thursday, Mancini, Queen of France, . . .
or little less. Twenty-fifth, the fair
Monglat said to Count Fiesco "Yes!"
And Saturday, the twenty-sixth . . .
(*He closes his eyes. His head drops on his
breast. Silence.*)

ROXANE (*surprised at hearing nothing further,* 10
*turns, looks at him and starts to her feet in
alarm*). Has he fainted? (*She runs to
him, calling.*) Cyrano!

CYRANO (*opening his eyes, in a faint voice*).
What is it? . . . What is the matter!
(*He sees* ROXANE *bending over him, hurriedly readjusts his hat, pulling it more
closely over his head, and shrinks back in
his armchair in terror.*) No! no! I assure
you, it is nothing! . . . Do not mind 20
me!

ROXANE. But surely . . .

CYRANO. It is merely the wound I received at Arras . . . Sometimes . . .
you know . . . even now . . .

ROXANE. Poor friend!

CYRANO. But it is nothing . . . It will
pass . . . (*He smiles with effort.*) It has
passed.

ROXANE. Each one of us has his wound: 30
I too have mine. It is here, never to
heal, that ancient wound . . . (*She
places her hand on her breast.*) It is here,
beneath the yellowing letter on which
are still faintly visible tear-drops and
drops of blood!
[*The light is beginning to grow less.*]

CYRANO. His letter? . . . Did you not
once say that some day . . . you
might show it to me?

ROXANE. Ah! . . . Do you wish? . . .
His letter?

CYRANO. Yes . . . today . . . I wish
to . . .

ROXANE (*handing him the little bag from her
neck*). Here!

CYRANO. I may open it?

ROXANE. Open it . . . read! (*She goes
back to her embroidery frame, folds it up,
orders her wools.*)

CYRANO. "Good-bye, Roxane! I am going to die!"

ROXANE (*stopping in astonishment*). You are
reading it aloud?

CYRANO (*reading*). "It is fated to come
this evening, beloved, I believe! My
soul is heavy, oppressed with love it
had not time to utter . . . and now
Time is at end! Never again, never
again shall my worshipping
eyes . . ."

ROXANE. How strangely you read his
letter!

CYRANO (*continuing*). ". . . whose passionate revel it was, kiss in its fleeting
grace your every gesture. One, usual
to you, of tucking back a little curl,
comes to my mind . . . and I cannot refrain from crying out . . ."

ROXANE. How strangely you read his
letter! . . .
[*The darkness gradually increases.*]

CYRANO. "and I cry out: Good-bye!"

ROXANE. You read it . . .

CYRANO. "my dearest, my darling, . . .
my treasure . . ."

ROXANE. . . . in a voice . . .

CYRANO. ". . . my love! . . ."

ROXANE. . . . in a voice . . . a voice
which I am not hearing for the first
time! (ROXANE *comes quietly nearer to
him, without his seeing it; she steps behind
his armchair, bends noiselessly over his
shoulder, looks at the letter. The darkness
deepens.*)

CYRANO. ". . . My heart never desisted
for a second from your side . . . and
I am and shall be in the world that
has no end, the one who loved you
without measure, the one . . ."

ROXANE (*laying her hand on his shoulder*).
How can you go on reading? It is

dark. (CYRANO *starts, and turns round; sees her close to him, makes a gesture of dismay and hangs his head. Then, in the darkness which has completely closed round them, she says slowly, clasping her hands.*) And he, for fourteen years, has played the part of the comical old friend who came to cheer me!

CYRANO. Roxane!

ROXANE. So it was you.

CYRANO. No, no, Roxane!

ROXANE. I ought to have divined it, if only by the way in which he speaks my name!

CYRANO. No, it was not I!

ROXANE. So it was you!

CYRANO. I swear to you . . .

ROXANE. Ah, I detect at last the whole generous imposture: The letters . . . were yours!

CYRANO. No!

ROXANE. The tender fancy, the dear folly . . . yours!

CYRANO. No!

ROXANE. The voice in the night, was yours!

CYRANO. I swear to you that it was not!

ROXANE. The soul . . . was yours!

CYRANO. I did not love you, no!

ROXANE. And you loved me!

CYRANO. Not I . . . it was the other!

ROXANE. You loved me!

CYRANO. No!

ROXANE. Already your denial comes more faintly!

CYRANO. No, no, my darling love, I did not love you!

ROXANE. Ah, how many things within the hour have died . . . how many have been born! Why, why have . . . been silent these long years, when on this letter, in which he had no part, the tears were yours?

CYRANO (*handing her the letter*). Because . . . the blood was his.

ROXANE. Then why let the sublime bond of this silence be loosed today?

CYRANO. Why?

[LE BRET *and* RAGUENEAU *enter running.*

LE BRET. Madness! Monstrous madness! . . . Ah, I was sure of it! There he is!

CYRANO (*smiling and straightening himself*). Tiens! Where else?

LE BRET. Madame, he is likely to have got his death by getting out of bed!

ROXANE. Merciful God! A moment ago, then . . . that faintness . . . that . . . ?

CYRANO. It is true. I had not finished telling you the news. And on Saturday, the twenty-sixth, an hour after sundown, Monsieur de Bergerac died of murder done upon him. (*He takes off his hat; his head is seen wrapped in bandages.*)

ROXANE. What is he saying? . . . Cyrano? . . . Those bandages about his head? . . . Ah, what have they done to you? . . . Why? . . .

CYRANO. "Happy who falls, cut off by a hero, with an honest sword through his heart!" I am quoting from myself! . . . Fate will have his laugh at us! . . . Here am I killed, in a trap, from behind, by a lackey, with a log! Nothing could be completer! In my whole life I shall have not had anything I wanted . . . not even a decent death!

RAGUENEAU. Ah, monsieur! . . .

CYRANO. Ragueneau, do not sob like that! (*Holding out his hand to him.*) And what is the news with you, these latter days, fellow-poet?

RAGUENEAU (*through his tears*). I am candle-snuffer at Molière's theater.

CYRANO. Molière!

RAGUENEAU. But I intend to leave no later than tomorrow. Yes, I am indignant! Yesterday, they were giving

Scapin, and I saw that he has appropriated a scene of yours.

LE BRET. A whole scene?

RAGUENEAU. Yes, monsieur. The one in which occurs the famous "What the devil was he doing in . . ."

LE BRET. Molière has taken that from you!

CYRANO. Hush! hush! He did well to take it! (*To* RAGUENEAU.) The scene was very effective, was it not?

RAGUENEAU. Ah, monsieur, the public laughed . . . laughed!

CYRANO. Yes, to the end, I shall have been the one who prompted . . . and was forgotten! (*To* ROXANE.) Do you remember that evening on which Christian spoke to you from below the balcony? There was the epitome of my life: while I have stood below in darkness, others have climbed to gather the kiss and glory! It is well done, and on the brink of my grave I approve it: Molière has genius . . . Christian was a fine fellow! (*At this moment, the chapel bell having rung, the* NUNS *are seen passing at the back, along the avenue, on their way to service.*) Let them hasten to their prayers . . . the bell is summoning them . . .

ROXANE (*rising and calling*). Sister! Sister!

CYRANO (*holding her back*). No! No! do not leave me to fetch anybody! When you came back I might not be here to rejoice . . . (*The* NUNS *have gone into the chapel; the organ is heard.*) I longed for a little music . . . it comes in time!

ROXANE. I love you . . . you shall live!

CYRANO. No! for it is only in the fairy-tale that the shy and awkward prince when he hears the beloved say "I love you!" feels his ungainliness melt and drop from him in the sunshine of those words! . . . But you would always know full well, dear Heart, that there had taken place in your poor slave no beautifying change!

ROXANE. I have hurt you . . . I have wrecked your life, I! . . . I!

CYRANO. You? . . . The reverse! Woman's sweetness I had never known. My mother . . . thought me unflattering. I had no sister. Later, I shunned Love's crossroad in fear of mocking eyes. To you I owe having had, at least, among the gentle and fair, a friend. Thanks to you there has passed across my life the rustle of a woman's gown.

LE BRET (*calling his attention to the moonlight peering through the branches*). Your other friend, among the gentle and fair, is there . . . she comes to see you!

CYRANO (*smiling to the moon*). I see her!

ROXANE. I never loved but one . . . and twice I lose him!

CYRANO. Le Bret, I shall ascend into the opalescent moon, without need this time of a flying-machine!

ROXANE. What are you saying?

CYRANO. Yes, it is there, you may be sure, I shall be sent for my Paradise. More than one soul of those I have loved must be apportioned there . . . There I shall find Socrates and Galileo!

LE BRET (*in revolt*). No! No! It is too senseless, too cruel, too unfair! So true a poet! So great a heart! To die . . . like this! To die! . . .

CYRANO. As ever . . . Le Bret is grumbling!

LE BRET (*bursting into tears*). My friend! My friend!

CYRANO (*lifting himself, his eyes wild*). They are the Gascony Cadets! . . . Man in the gross . . . Eh, yes! . . . the weakness of the weakest point . . .

LE BRET. Learned . . . even in his delirium! . . .

CYRANO. Copernicus said . . .

ROXANE. Oh!

CYRANO. But what the devil was he doing . . . and what the devil was he
doing in that galley?

Philosopher and physicist,
Musician, rhymester, duellist,
Explorer of the upper blue,
Retorter apt with point and point,
Lover as well—not for his peace!   10
Here lies Hercule Savinien
De Cyrano de Bergerac,
Who was everything . . . but of account!
But your pardons, I must go . . . I
wish to keep no one waiting . . . See,
a moonbeam, come to take me home!
(*He has dropped in his chair;* ROXANE'S
*weeping calls him back to reality; he looks
at her and gently stroking her mourning* 20
veil.) I do not wish . . . indeed, I do
not wish . . . that you should sorrow
less for Christian, the comely and the
kind! Only I wish that when the everlasting cold shall have seized upon my
fibres, this funereal veil should have a
twofold meaning, and the mourning
you wear for him be worn for me
too . . . a little!

ROXANE. I promise . . .   30

CYRANO (*seized with a great shivering,
starts to his feet*). Not there! No! Not
in an elbow-chair! (*All draw nearer to
help him.*) Let no one stay me! No one!
(*He goes and stands against the tree.*)
Nothing but this tree! (*Silence.*) She
comes, Mors, the indiscriminate
Madam! . . . Already I am booted
with marble . . . gauntleted with
lead! (*He stiffens himself.*) Ah, since 40
she is on her way, I will await her
standing . . . (*He draws his sword.*)
Sword in hand!

LE BRET. Cyrano!

ROXANE (*swooning*). Cyrano! (*All start
back, terrified.*)

CYRANO. I believe she is looking at
me . . . that she dares to look at my
nose, the bony baggage who has
none! (*He raises his sword.*) What are
you saying? That it is no use? . . .
I know it! But one does not fight because there is hope of winning!
No! . . . no! . . . it is much finer
to fight when it is no use! . . . What
are all those? You are a thousand
strong? . . . Ah, I know you
now . . . all my ancient enemies!
. . . Hypocrisy? . . . (*He   beats
with his sword, in the vacancy.*) Take
this! and this! Ha! Ha! Compro-
mises? . . . and Prejudices? and das-
tardly Expedients? (*He strikes.*) That
I should come to terms, I? . . .
Never! Never! . . . Ah, you are there
too, you, bloated and pompous Silli-
ness! I know full well that you will
lay me low at last . . . No matter:
whilst I have breath, I will fight you,
I will fight you, I will fight you! (*He
waves his sword in great sweeping circles,
and stops, panting.*) Yes, you have
wrested from me everything, laurel
as well as rose . . . Work your
wills! . . . Spite of your worst, something will still be left me to take
whither I go . . . and tonight when
I enter God's house, in saluting,
broadly will I sweep the azure threshold with what despite of all I carry
forth unblemished and unbent . . .
(*He starts forward, with lifted sword.*) and
that is . . . (*The sword falls from his
hands, he staggers, drops in the arms of*
LE BRET *and* RAGUENEAU.)

ROXANE (*bending over him and kissing his
forehead*). That is? . . .

CYRANO (*opens his eyes again, recognizes her
and says with a smile*). . . . My plume!

CURTAIN

MAURICE MAETERLINCK

MAURICE MAETERLINCK

THE MOST POWERFUL current in modern drama has been that of naturalism. The plays that roused the theatre from its mid-nineteenth century torpor and gave it its sensational place of influence in the contemporary world were bold slices of life, usually cut from sick or diseased areas of the body social. There is no room for argument about the fact of the potency of these plays. They startled the age; they dramatized serious problems; they created the "useful theatre" or public forum type of drama; and they cultivated a more adult concept of the nature of "entertainment" in the theatre. For a time in the eighties and nineties naturalistic drama threatened to monopolize the serious stage. But the opposition to its one-sided obsession was not silent. Antoine's theatre was not without rivals in Le Théâtre des Poètes, Le Théâtre des Artes, and other organizations.

The naturalists' doctrinaire assumption of a limited view of man's spiritual capacity, their willing acceptance of the narrow and rather arrogant positivistic philosophy that accompanied the advance of science in the late nineteenth century, aroused vigorous antagonism. It is true that man is a low, unclean, depraved, and often vicious creature, and that his abominations are legitimate clinical data for representation on the stage. It is an even more engrossing phenomenon that his brutish skull is capable of idealism, mysticism, and poetry. Drama was invented to display these ennobling qualities as well as the cruder struggles. It may

content itself with a realistic reproduction on the stage of the visible and audible aspects of life. It may also draw upon the allied arts of music, rhythmic movements, and poetry to stimulate the imagination, and to suggest or shadow forth nuances untapped by cold, objective realism.

Maurice Maeterlinck is preeminent among the modern playwrights who have cultivated this form of the poetic or symbolistic drama. Because he wrote in French, because Paris was the center of his success, and perhaps also because he has lived most of his life in France, Maeterlinck is quite naturally thought of as belonging to French literature. He was born a Belgian of an old and honored Flemish family at Ghent. The date was August 29, 1862. His natural predilection for mysticism was fostered at the Jesuit College of Sainte-Barbe in his native city. He was entranced by the somber melancholy of medieval tales and legends of fated lovers. His interest in religion and his curiosity about the occult and the supernatural also began in this period; in later years he was to reach a wide audience throughout the world with books like *The Intelligence of the Flowers, Our Eternity,* and numerous essays about subjects on the outposts of reason like theosophy, spiritism, and clairvoyance. He was graduated from this school in 1885; he then turned dutifully to the study of law at the University of Ghent. Like so many other young men of his generation, he found the law tiresome, and practiced it only long enough to "lose a case or two." He longed for freedom in the life of a man of letters. In that day literature and Paris were synonymous, and Maeterlinck, in 1886, followed the familiar pattern that led straight to the cafes of Montmarte.

Maeterlinck at twenty-four, round faced and misty eyed, with a mind in revolt against the severe discipline of legal training and stirred with literary ambitions, was a hospitable spirit for the exciting movement in French poetry newly christened Symbolism. Paul Verlaine was then the master of the school, following the publication of his collected poems, mystical and "decadent," under the titles *Sagesse* (1881) and *Jadis et Naguère* (1885). As an eager young disciple, Maeterlinck got to know the leaders in French poetry, Verlaine, Mallarme, Mirabeau, and others who were making a cult of Rimbaud. He particularly came under the spell of Villiers de L'Isle Adam, to whom his kindred-spirited contemporary, William Butler Yeats, also looked up as master. He heard these impassioned young men of the eighties read their verses and theorize about the art of poetry over a bottle of wine and a stack of plates at the cafe shrines. Rimbaud had scornfully dismissed "all the old fools" who had "stuck to the false conception of the *ego.*" The poet, he announced, goes through the barrier of reality into the infinity beyond our view; he is the instrument through which speaks "the voice of the Eternal." "I am present at the birth of my thought, I look at it and I listen." Hugo Von Hofmannsthal stated the theory more concretely: "A certain gesture with which you leaped from a tall wagon; a sultry, starless summer night; the odour of moist stones in a hallway; the sensation of icy water

which a fountain made to sparkle over your hands—all your inner life is bound to a few thousand of such earthly things, all your exaltations, all your yearning, all your ecstasies." If we substitute for these examples a ring, sunlight, moonglow, forests, gardens, fountains, a castle tower, a vault, a flock of sheep, a maid lost in the woods, and a few dozen such earthly and romantic objects from the land of faery, we shall be well into the realm of the King of Allemonde where Pelléas and Mélisande love and die.

Maeterlinck's infatuated sojourn in Paris was cut off at the end of a year by the death of his father, and he returned to Ghent to live for the next seven years. But his head was drunk with glimpses of this fragile sphere of the soul's ecstasy and the power of poetry to arrest those fleeting moments and make them reproducible experiences through the magic of word symbols, music, and poetic form. He and his young Belgian friends tried to confer literary distinction on their native land by bringing out a few issues of a little magazine in the Paris manner, imitatively called La Pléiade. Still under the spell of his French models, he began to publish his own compositions. The first was *The Massacre of the Innocents*, a sketch in prose; it was followed in 1889 by the inevitable volume of slender verse, somber and vague, called *Serres Chaudes;* and by his first play, a five act tragedy, *The Princess Maleine.*

From 1889 on, Maeterlinck's production was steady and voluminous. By 1901 he had written a dozen plays in dolesome mood, of mystery, legend, and parable, and had become the founder of symbolistic drama and its most celebrated figure. *Monna Vanna,* which appeared in 1902, surprised the

Maeterlinck public because it avoided the pensive world of Tintagiles, Francesca da Rimini, and The Seven Princesses for the stern realism of a problem play set in besieged Pisa at the end of the fifteenth century. Since 1902 his plays have alternated between conventional drama and his early symbolistic subjects and methods, and he has given much of his time to essays and expository writing on flowers, bees, and the mysteries of life, death, and immortality.

Maeterlinck's life has been a favored one, and in a public way rather uneventful though interesting. After his first successes he again left Ghent, in 1896, for Paris. When he had had enough of the admiring and often contentious theatrical and literary circles in Paris, he changed his residence to his restored Benedictine abbey at Saint Wandrille in Normandy, a romantic estate ideally appropriate to the author of Pelléas and Mélisande; or he retired to his villa (Les Abeilles) set in a magnificent garden in the mountains of southern France between Grasse and Nice. He was awarded the Nobel prize for literature in 1911 following the international success of The Blue Bird. The title of count was conferred on him in 1932.

Maeterlinck was one of the vast flock of famous Europeans who invaded America right after the World War to travel the lecture circuits at war-debt prices. His English was too feeble to support a performance, and both lecturer and audience were quite unhappy over it. Maeterlinck went away not liking Americans very well. But twenty years later, in July, 1940, following the obliteration of Belgium and the fall of France, he returned to find sanctuary on these shores. Like so many among "the world's dwindling community of civilized minds" he had been overtaken by a Fate not unlike that which in his own plays strangled Maleine, poisoned Tintagile, and shut up Alladine and Palomides in the dark subterranean grottoes and pushed them at last over the rock into the water "all enwrapped in gloom." Yet the doom in the plays is eery, pensive, and romantic, whereas the destructiveness of the Nazis was harsh, savage, and terrible. Maeterlinck had expected to live out the rest of his days peacefully in good living. On landing in New York he explained to interviewers: "I had my money in a bank in Brussels. The Germans occupied Belgium. I had my house and belongings in Nice. The Germans have occupied France. All is gone." He had nothing left, he said, but royalties from The Blue Bird. And like Rostand with his Cyrano de Bergerac, Maeterlinck was known to the American public as the author of that one play about little Tyltyl and Mytyl and their quest for happiness.

As we have already intimated, Maeterlinck's work in general falls into two periods divided by the year 1902 and the play Monna Vanna. Despite the popular fame of The Blue Bird (1908), Maeterlinck holds his tenuous place in modern drama because of his early symbolistic plays, chiefly on subjects long familiar to literature through frequent retellings. His own contribution is the peculiar magic of the atmosphere in which he bathes the ancient legends until they take on the appearance of something new. This is, of course, the investiture of Symbolism. For Maeterlinck attempted by means of images and sounds to thrust beyond the bounds of the senses into the "world beyond the world." Neither the process nor the product may be defined with exactitude; if this could be done, the whole structure of symbolism would fall, for then it would be back in the realm of reason, the very world it tried to dethrone and from which it tried to escape.

Maeterlinck's plays are all intensely personal, like lyric poetry. They have been aptly labeled "still-life" dramas. They are plays for puppets, simple, repetitive, and weighted with homily or with the mood of forlorn maidens "sole-sitting by the shores of old romance." *The Princess Maleine* (1889) is a series of vague vignettes, accompanied by romantic terrors as it works up to the strangulation of Maleine. *The Intruder* (1890), an artistic one-act play, deals simply with the quiet visitation of Death. The blind grandfather, the father, the uncle, and the three daughters sit in "a dimly lighted room in an old country-house" talking about rain, the stars, and homely family matters in tense and pregnant simplicity, while in the next room a child is born and its mother dies. The Sister of Mercy in black garments announces the Intruder by bowing to the family and making the sign of the cross. The play ends with the grandfather feeling his way round the table in the darkness, deeply agitated, crying "Where are you going?—Where are you going?— The girls have left me all alone!" *The Blind*, also of 1890, is one of Maeterlinck's strongest allegorical plays. The six blind men and the six blind women are seen groping about in a symbolic forest whither they have been led by a priest who is dead. There they are, lost, blind, and without guidance. They try to find their way but fail, for the woman to whom they listen is not prophetic but mad, the dog leads them only to the dead priest, and the sound of footsteps among them is but an illusion. We have eyes but do not see in the faithless, error-filled world; and the priests are dead.

The Seven Princesses (1891) is a Maeterlinckian parallel on the old fairy tale of the sleeping beauties who have grown weary to death of their seven years of waiting for their prince. *Pelléas and Mélisande* of which we shall treat later, came in 1892, followed by *Alladine and Palomide* in 1894. This tragedy in five short acts closely resembles the greater and better known *Pelléas and Mélisande*. Alladine is a sad, fairy-like child, "a little Greek slave, who has come from the depths of Arcady," attended by her lamb, and loved by the aging King Ablamore. Palomides is betrothed to King Ablamore's daughter, but is thrown by fate, like Pelléas, into the arms of Alladine. The maddened king takes his terrible revenge upon them. It was their starcrossed destiny to love and to die.

Interior or *Home* (*L'Intérieur*), a one-act play of the same year, has somewhat of the mood and technical mastery of Synge's *Riders to the Sea* which it suggests. The kindly, wise grandfather knows of the death of his granddaughter who has just been drowned in the river. It is his sorrow to break the news to the family. They are gathered about the lamp and may be seen from the garden where the grandfather stands, reflecting: "They are so secure of their little life, and do not dream that so many others know more of it than they, and that I, poor old man, at two steps from their door, hold all their little happiness, like a wounded bird, in the hollow of my old hands, and dare not open them." But the crowd is gathering, and he must enter and speak. His mission and its pitiful effects are witnessed by Martha, Mary, and The Stranger, and reported in hushed, broken phrases.

And so the plays kept coming from Maeterlinck's pen: *The Death of Tintagiles* (1894), a sad little piece about the innocent child brought to a castle where the sea roars, the trees moan, and "they seem to watch lest the smallest happiness come near"; *Aglavaine and Sélysette* (1896), the title being the names of the two sentimental women in love with Sélysette's husband; *Sister Beatrice* (1900) retelling the oft-told tale of the nun whose vows were broken for love; and *Ariadne and Bluebeard* (1901) an ingenious turn of that famous legend. These last two pieces, though much like their predecessors, were librettos, indicating the close alliance between Maeterlinck's kind of drama and the kindred art of music. And with those compositions we arrive at *Monna Vanna*.

Monna Vanna appeared in 1902, the year of Brieux's sensational problem play *Damaged Goods*, the year between Shaw's *Three Plays for Puritans* (1901) and *Man and Superman* (1903). By 1902 the excitement over the revival of poetic drama that had raised hope throughout the nineties had grown passive. The social problem play was the fashion and even Maeterlinck yielded to it. He had apparently carried his allegories and his insubstantial atmospheric plays of the preceding decade as far as they would go. He now withdrew his sponsorship of "static" marionette drama and turned to a subject that might have been chosen by any number of realistic dramatists of the time—and as a matter of fact it was. For the people of *Monna Vanna* are no longer the pale,

forlorn, fate-driven lovers of the symbolistic plays; they are more nearly sensual creatures of bone and blood who face the stern facts of war. The action revolves around the problem of a woman's honor, whether it is a jewel more to be valued than the sack and rape of a beleaguered city.

Pisa is invested, her powder is gone, her walls breached, and her people starving. Prinzivalle, the enemy captain, offers to lift the siege and revenge himself upon his double-crossing Florentine masters by sending into Pisa hundreds of wagons of Tuscany grain and forage, Sienna fruit and wine, German powder, lead, six hundred Apulian cattle, and twice as many sheep. The one condition is that Monna Vanna, wife of the Commander of the Garrison of Pisa, shall come for one night to his tent, alone, clad only in her cloak. Vanna goes, is honorably treated with high chivalry by Prinzivalle who has long worshipped her from afar, and returns unmolested with the enemy captain himself to Pisa. The third act shows Vanna, confronted by the accusations of her jealous husband, putting the two men to the test. She finds her suspicious lord wanting in character, and as the curtain falls she is clearly planning in her heart to rescue the noble captain from his dungeon and to escape with him from Pisa.

Obviously the basic situation is not very different from that in *Alladine and Palomides* and such plays, but the mood, method and treatment are more conventional theatre, despite the long, rhetorical dialogue and the relatively little action for a play with so dramatic a setting as a war in Renaissance Italy. The characters act resolutely from comprehensible motives; Alladine, Mélisande, and such heroines are passive and unexplained, but Vanna makes her own choice and bravely passes through the enemy's lines, sacrificing herself to save her city. Yet the Maeterlinckian touch is unmistakable; especially in the scenes where the elderly Marco reveals to his son the condition under which Pisa may be spared (it suggests the comparable scene in *L'Intérieur*); and in the scene between Vanna and Prinzivalle in his tent.

Of the dozen plays since *Monna Vanna* only one need detain us further. That is *The Blue Bird* (1908). The others like *Joyzelle* (1903), a weak and imitative piece; *Mary Magdalene* (1910), in which the heroine's virtue is tested and found inviolable; *The Burgomaster of Stilemonde* (1918), Maeterlinck's contribution to the plays of the World War, etc., neither enriched the contemporary drama nor added to the fame of the author. But *The Blue Bird* captivated the world and endeared Maeterlinck to the childish of heart. If the play is examined by the cool and rational mind, it vanishes like a morning cloud. Ludwig Lewisohn tried to reduce it to absurdity by summing up in a few propositions what he called its "cheap and shallow optimism." The series of little allegories say in substance "that the dead live in our memories of them (Act II, Scene I), that simple pleasures are best and most harmless (III, II), that man is conquering disease (III, I), and that he will more and more subdue the forces of nature (V, III), and finally, that happiness need not be sought afar but waits for us at home." But such an approach man-handles this charming little idyll of Mytyl, Tyltyl, the Dog and the Cat; of Daddy Tyl, Mummy Tyl, the Fairy Berylune and Neighbour Berlingot, and all the allegorical figures in this search for the bluebird of happiness. It is designed for children and appeals not to the intellect of an adult but to the imagination of childhood. It had an overwhelming success in London, in New York, and at the Moscow Art Theatre.

This brief survey of the life of the author and the nature of the plays may perhaps provide a setting for Maeterlinck's masterpiece of symbolistic drama, the delicately planned and executed *Pelléas and Mélisande* (1892). This, the young dramatist's fifth play, was composed while his enthusiasm for the form and the mood was at its height. It shows in one delicately wrought drama most if not all the qualities peculiar to its type. Its source is, of course, the famous passage at the end of the fifth canto of Dante's *Inferno* in which the fatal love of Francesca for Paolo, the younger brother of her husband Gianciotto of Rimini, is immortalized. In the hands of a determined naturalist, this story would have been just another sordid triangle in which the guilty couple were stabbed to death by the deformed husband to whom Francesca had been married for political reasons. Dante permits the beauty and dignity of their love to lend grace to their sin. Francesca weeps and tells how she came to love Paolo: "'One day, for pastime, we read of Lancelot, how love constrained him; we were alone, and without all suspicion. Several times that reading urged our eyes to meet, and changed the colour of our faces; but one moment alone it was that overcame us. When we read how the fond smile was kissed by such a lover, he, who shall never be divided from me, kissed my mouth all trembling: the book, and he who wrote it, was a Galeotto; that day we read in it no farther.'"

Gabriele D'Annunzio, Stephen Phillips, George Boker, and other playwrights have attempted to dramatize this story with varying degrees of verisimilitude but with unmistakable humanity. Maeterlinck deliberately casts over it the misty veil of unreality. He detaches the characters from the natural world, but permits their actions vaguely to parallel the original tragic course in this nebulous kingdom of unhappy dreams which his fancy has created. Here Fate rules over its passive victims with an absolutism equalled only by the stern grip of heredity and environment on the poor wretches of naturalism. All these tragic lovers were destined for their affinities before they ever met: his kiss was on her lips ere she was born. Palomides felt a power so mighty moving him toward Alladine that he "must perforce give way to it. . . ." In his confession to Astolaine he says, "I feel that I never shall be what I had hoped that I might become. . . . Fate has stepped but towards me: or I, it may be, have beckoned to Fate; for we never know whether we ourselves have gone forth or Fate have come seeking us." We do what was ordained, said Ablamore. And just so does Fate take possession of Pelléas and Mélisande, and Arkel repeats the wisdom of Ablamore. As Pelléas stands kissing Mélisande in the park by the fountain just before his brother Golaud stabs him, he laments, "We do not what we will."

This element of fatalism helps to create the forlorn loveliness of the atmosphere of *Pelléas and Mélisande*. Neither of the pensive children seeks the torment of the forbidden love, but they are unable to stay the current of destruction. Neither of them is accounted for or motivated beyond their fatality to love. They are haunted by the ineffable sadness of old romance where the sea is always perilous and the magic casements open upon dungeons and death. They are like bewildered children clinging tearfully to each other while they await their doom. The somber beauty is created and intensified by the power of the symbolic series of tableaux to stimulate our creative imagination. They draw upon our own banked-up associations from childhood reading about magic fountains in gloomy forests, of phantom ships, castle corridors, and Guendolen from her tower showering her golden hair around her knight with the woe of the scarlet coated witch and Rapunzel upon it. Little Yniold makes the magic kingdom still more misty and unreal by his tearful simplicity and otherworldness as he reports to Golaud the nature of Mélisande's love for Pelléas, and muses over the flock of sheep going to the slaughter. In the first scene, the opening of the gate that can never be cleaned foreshadows the corresponding scene in the last act where the old servant again opens the gate; "the little princess was nearly dead, and the great Golaud had still his sword in his side . . . there was blood on the sill. . . ." The moment that overcame Pelléas and Mélisande was not the reading of Galeotto but the tossing of her wedding ring into the sun and its falling into the fountain.

A score or so of these suggestive touches and the fragile drama is evoked. It has the quality of romantic opera. Claude Debussy paralleled it in music, working ten years on the labor of love. Its apparent naivete, monotony, and répetitiveness suggest a libretto rather than a spoken dialogue. It loses some of its magic in the violence of translation, for it is artistically wrought in its illusive French cadences; but much abides, also, to preserve its character as the best of the symbolistic dramas of the nineties. Its key of fatalistic sadness is never far removed from the mood of the human heart. And even Maeterlinck's own lament on landing as a fugitive in New York was only a paraphrase of Golaud's exclamation; "It is not my fault! . . . It is not my fault!" and of Arkel's reply, "The human soul is very silent. . . . It suffers so timorously. . . . But the sadness, Golaud. . . . The sadness of all we see! . . . My God! . . . My God! . . . I shall never understand it all. . . ."

PELLÉAS AND MÉLISANDE

CHARACTERS

ARKËL, *King of Allemonde*
PELLÉAS } *grandsons of Arkël*
GOLAUD }
MÉLISANDE, *wife of Golaud*
Servants, Beggars, etc.

GENEVIÈVE, *mother of Pelléas and Golaud*
YNIOLD, *son of Golaud*
   (*by a former marriage*)
A PHYSICIAN
THE PORTER

ACT I

SCENE I. *The gate of the castle*

MAIDSERVANTS (*within*). Open the gate! Open the gate!
PORTER (*within*). Who is there? Why do you come and wake me up? Go out by the little gates; there are enough of them! . . .
A MAIDSERVANT (*within*). We have come to wash the threshold, the gate, and the steps; open, then! open!
ANOTHER MAIDSERVANT (*within*). There are going to be great happenings!
THIRD MAIDSERVANT (*within*). There are going to be great fêtes! Open quickly!
THE MAIDSERVANTS. Open! open!
PORTER. Wait! wait! I do not know whether I shall be able to open it; . . . it is never opened. . . . Wait till it is light. . . .
FIRST MAIDSERVANT. It is light enough without; I see the sunlight through the chinks. . . .
PORTER. Here are the great keys. . . . Oh! oh! how the bolts and the locks grate! . . . Help me! help me! . . .

MAIDSERVANTS. We are pulling; we are pulling. . . .
SECOND MAIDSERVANT. It will not open. . . .
FIRST MAIDSERVANT. Ah! ah! It is opening! it is opening slowly!
PORTER. How it shrieks! how it shrieks! It will wake up everybody. . . .
SECOND MAIDSERVANT (*appearing on the threshold*). Oh, how light it is already out-of-doors!
FIRST MAIDSERVANT. The sun is rising on the sea!
PORTER. It is open. . . . It is wide open! [*All the maidservants appear on the threshold and pass over it.*]
FIRST MAIDSERVANT. I am going to wash the sill first. . . .
SECOND MAIDSERVANT. We shall never be able to clean all this.
OTHER MAIDSERVANTS. Fetch the water! fetch the water!
PORTER. Yes, yes; pour on water; pour on water; pour on all the water of the Flood! You will never come to the end of it. . . .

329

SCENE II. *A forest*

MÉLISANDE *discovered at the brink of a spring.*

[*Enter* GOLAUD.]

GOLAUD. I shall never be able to get out of this forest again.—God knows where that beast has led me. And yet I thought I had wounded him to death; and here are traces of blood. 10 But now I have lost sight of him; I believe I am lost myself—my dogs can no longer find me—I shall retrace my steps. . . . I hear weeping . . . Oh! oh! what is there yonder by the water's edge? . . . A little girl weeping by the water's edge? (*He coughs.*) She does not hear me. I cannot see her face. (*He approaches and touches* MÉLISANDE *on the shoulder.*) Why 20 weepest thou? (MÉLISANDE *trembles, starts up, and would flee.*) Do not be afraid. You have nothing to fear. Why are you weeping here all alone?

MÉLISANDE. Do not touch me! do not touch me!

GOLAUD. Do not be afraid. . . . I will not do you any . . . Oh, you are beautiful!

MÉLISANDE. Do not touch me! do not 30 touch me! or I throw myself in the water! . . .

GOLAUD. I will not touch you. . . . See, I will stay here, against the tree. Do not be afraid. Has any one hurt you?

MÉLISANDE. Oh! yes! yes! yes! . . . (*She sobs profoundly.*)

GOLAUD. Who has hurt you?

MÉLISANDE. Every one! every one!

GOLAUD. What hurt have they done you? 40

MÉLISANDE. I will not tell! I cannot tell! . . .

GOLAUD. Come; do not weep so. Whence come you?

MÉLISANDE. I have fled! . . . fled . . . fled. . . .

GOLAUD. Yes; but whence have you fled?

MÉLISANDE. I am lost! . . . lost! . . . Oh! oh! lost here. . . . I am not of this place. . . . I was not born there. . . .

GOLAUD. Whence are you? Where were you born?

MÉLISANDE. Oh! oh! far away from here! . . . far away . . . far away. . . .

GOLAUD. What is it shining so at the bottom of the water?

MÉLISANDE. Where?—Ah! it is the crown he gave me. It fell as I was weeping. . . .

GOLAUD. A crown?—Who was it gave you a crown?—I will try to get it. . . .

MÉLISANDE. No, no; I will have no more of it! I will have no more of it! . . . I had rather die . . . die at once. . . .

GOLAUD. I could easily pull it out. The water is not very deep.

MÉLISANDE. I will have no more of it! If you take it out, I throw myself in its place! . . .

GOLAUD. No, no; I will leave it there. It could be reached without difficulty, nevertheless. It seems very beautiful. —Is it long since you fled?

MÉLISANDE. Yes, yes! . . . Who are you?

GOLAUD. I am Prince Golaud—grandson of Arkël, the old King of Allemonde.

MÉLISANDE. Oh, you have gray hairs already. . . .

GOLAUD. Yes; some, here, by the temples . . .

MÉLISANDE. And in your beard, too. . . . Why do you look at me so?

GOLAUD. I am looking at your eyes.— Do you never shut your eyes?

MÉLISANDE. Oh, yes; I shut them at night. . . .

GOLAUD. Why do you look astonished?

MÉLISANDE. You are a giant.

GOLAUD. I am a man like the rest. . . .

MÉLISANDE. Why have you come here?

GOLAUD. I do not know, myself. I was hunting in the forest. I was chasing a wild boar. I mistook the road.— You look very young. How old are you?

MÉLISANDE. I am beginning to be cold.

GOLAUD. Will you come with me! 10

MÉLISANDE. No, no; I will stay here.

GOLAUD. You cannot stay here all alone. You cannot stay here all night long. . . . What is your name?

MÉLISANDE. Mélisande.

GOLAUD. You cannot stay here, Mélisande. Come with me. . . .

MÉLISANDE. I will stay here. . . .

GOLAUD. You will be afraid, all alone. We do not know what there may be 20 here . . . all night long . . . all alone . . . it is impossible. Mélisande, come, give me your hand. . .

MÉLISANDE. Oh, do not touch me! . . .

GOLAUD. Do not scream. . . . I will not touch you again. But come with me. The night will be very dark and very cold. Come with me. . . .

MÉLISANDE. Where are you going? . . .

GOLAUD. I do not know. . . . I am 30 lost too. . . . (*Exeunt.*)

SCENE III. *A hall in the castle*

ARKËL *and* GENEVIÈVE *discovered.*

GENEVIÈVE. Here is what he writes to his brother Pelléas: "I found her all in tears one evening, beside a spring in the forest where I had lost myself. I do not know her age, nor who she is, nor whence she comes, and I dare 40 not question her, for she must have had a sore fright; and when you ask her what has happened to her, she falls at once a-weeping like a child, and sobs so heavily you are afraid. Just as I found her by the springs, a crown of gold had slipped from her hair and fallen to the bottom of the water. She was clad, besides, like a princess, though her garments had been torn by the briers. It is now six months since I married her and I know no more about it than on the day of our meeting. Meanwhile, dear Pelléas, thou whom I love more than a brother, although we were not born of the same father; meanwhile make ready for my return. . . . I know my mother will willingly forgive me. But I am afraid of the King, our venerable grandsire, I am afraid of Arkël, in spite of all his kindness, for I have undone by this strange marriage all his plans of state, and I fear the beauty of Mélisande will not excuse my folly to eyes so wise as his. If he consents nevertheless to receive her as he would receive his own daughter, the third night following this letter, light a lamp at the top of the tower that overlooks the sea. I shall perceive it from the bridge of our ship; otherwise I shall go far away again and come back no more. . . ." What say you of it?

ARKËL. Nothing. He has done what he probably must have done. I am very old, and nevertheless I have not yet seen clearly for one moment into myself; how would you that I judge what others have done? I am not far from the tomb and do not succeed in judging myself. . . . One always mistakes when one does not close his eyes. That may seem strange to us; but that is all. He is past the age to marry and he weds, like a child, a little girl he finds by a spring. . . . That may seem strange to us, because we never see but the reverse of destinies . . . the reverse even of our own. . . . He has always followed my counsels hitherto; I had thought to make him happy in sending him to ask the hand of Princess Ursula. . . . He could not remain alone; since the death of his wife he has been sad to be alone; and that marriage would have put an end to long wars and old hatreds. . . . He would not have it so. Let it be as he would have it; I have never put myself athwart a destiny; and he knows better than I his future. There happen perhaps no useless events. . . .

GENEVIÈVE. He has always been so prudent, so grave and so firm. . . . If it were Pelléas, I should understand. . . . But he . . . at his age. . . . Who is it he is going to introduce here?—An unknown found along the roads. . . . Since his wife's death, he has no longer lived for aught but his son, the little Yniold, and if he were about to marry again, it was because you had wished it. . . . And now . . . a little girl in the forest. . . . He has forgotten everything. . . . —What shall we do? . . .

[Enter PELLÉAS.]

ARKËL. Who is coming in there?

GENEVIÈVE. It is Pelléas. He has been weeping.

ARKËL. Is it thou, Pelléas?—Come a little nearer, that I may see thee in the light. . . .

PELLÉAS. Grandfather, I received another letter at the same time as my brother's; a letter from my friend Marcellus. . . . He is about to die and calls for me. He would see me before dying. . . .

ARKËL. Thou wouldst leave before thy brother's return?—Perhaps thy friend is less ill than he thinks. . . .

PELLÉAS. His letter is so sad you can see death between the lines. . . . He says he knows the very day when death must come. . . . He tells me I can arrive before it if I will, but that there is no more time to lose. The journey is very long, and if I await Golaud's return, it will be perhaps too late. . . .

ARKËL. Thou must wait a little while, nevertheless. . . . We do not know what this return has in store for us. And, besides, is not thy father here, above us, more sick perhaps than thy friend. . . . Couldst thou choose between the father and the friend? . . . (Exit.)

GENEVIÈVE. Have a care to keep the lamp lit from this evening, Pelléas. . . . (Exeunt severally.)

SCENE IV. *Before the castle*

[Enter GENEVIÈVE and MÉLISANDE.]

MÉLISANDE. It is gloomy in the gardens. And what forests, what forests all about the palaces. . . .

GENEVIÈVE. Yes; that astonished me too when I came hither; it astonishes everybody. There are places where you never see the sun. But one gets used to it so quickly. . . . It is long ago, it is long ago. . . . It is nearly forty years that I have lived here. . . . Look toward the other side, you will have the light of the sea. . . .

MÉLISANDE. I hear a noise below us. . . .

GENEVIÈVE. Yes; it is some one coming up toward us. . . . Ah! it is Pelléas. He seems still tired from having waited so long for you. . . .

MÉLISANDE. He has not seen us.

GENEVIÈVE. I think he has seen us but does not know what he should do. . . . Pelléas, Pelléas, is it thou? . . .

[Enter PELLÉAS.]

PELLÉAS. Yes! . . . I was coming toward the sea. . . .

GENEVIÈVE. So were we; we were seeking the light. It is a little lighter here than elsewhere; and yet the sea is gloomy.

PELLÉAS. We shall have a storm tonight. There has been one every night for some time, and yet it is so calm now. . . . One might embark unwittingly and come back no more.

MÉLISANDE. Something is leaving the port. . . .

PELLÉAS. It must be a big ship. . . . The lights are very high, we shall see it in a moment, when it enters the band of light. . . .

GENEVIÈVE. I do not know whether we shall be able to see it . . . there is still a fog on the sea. . . .

PELLÉAS. The fog seems to be rising slowly. . . .

MÉLISANDE. Yes; I see a little light down there, which I had not seen. . . .

PELLÉAS. It is a lighthouse; there are others we cannot see yet.

MÉLISANDE. The ship is in the light. . . . It is already very far away. . . .

PELLÉAS. It is a foreign ship. It looks larger than ours. . . .

MÉLISANDE. It is the ship that brought me here! . . .

PELLÉAS. It flies away under full sail. . . .

MÉLISANDE. It is the ship that brought me here. It has great sails. . . . I recognized it by its sails.

PELLÉAS. There will be a rough sea tonight.

MÉLISANDE. Why does it go away tonight? . . . You can hardly see it any longer. . . . Perhaps it will be wrecked. . . .

PELLÉAS. The night falls very quickly. . . . (A silence.)

GENEVIÈVE. No one speaks any more? . . . You have nothing more to say to each other? . . . It is time to go in. Pelléas, show Mélisande the way. I must go see little Yniold a moment. (Exit.)

PELLÉAS. Nothing can be seen any longer on the sea. . . .

MÉLISANDE. I see more lights.

PELLÉAS. It is the other lighthouses. . . . Do you hear the sea? . . . It is the wind rising. . . . Let us go down this way. Will you give me your hand?

MÉLISANDE. See, see, my hands are full. . . .

PELLÉAS. I will hold you by the arm, the road is steep and it is very gloomy there. . . . I am going away perhaps tomorrow. . . .

MÉLISANDE. Oh! . . . why do you go away? (Exeunt.)

ACT II

SCENE I. *A fountain in the park*

[*Enter* PELLÉAS *and* MÉLISANDE.]

PELLÉAS. You do not know where I have brought you?—I often come to sit here, toward noon, when it is too hot in the gardens. It is stifling today, even in the shade of the trees.

MÉLISANDE. Oh, how clear the water is! . . .

PELLÉAS. It is as cool as winter. It is an old abandoned spring. It seems to have been a miraculous spring—it opened the eyes of the blind—they still call it "Blind Man's Spring."

MÉLISANDE. It no longer opens the eyes of the blind?

PELLÉAS. Since the King has been nearly blind himself, no one comes any more. . . .

MÉLISANDE. How alone one is here! . . . There is no sound.

PELLÉAS. There is always a wonderful silence here. . . . One could hear the water sleep. . . . Will you sit down on the edge of the marble basin? There is one linden where the sun never comes. . . .

MÉLISANDE. I am going to lie down on the marble.—I should like to see the bottom of the water. . . .

PELLÉAS. No one has ever seen it. It is as deep, perhaps, as the sea. It is not known whence it comes. Perhaps it comes from the bottom of the earth. . . .

MÉLISANDE. If there were anything shining at the bottom, perhaps one could see it. . . .

PELLÉAS. Do not lean over so. . . .

MÉLISANDE. I would like to touch the water. . . .

PELLÉAS. Have a care of slipping. . . . I will hold your hand. . . .

MÉLISANDE. No, no, I would plunge both hands in it. . . . You would say my hands were sick today. . . .

PELLÉAS. Oh! oh! take care! take care! Mélisande! . . . Mélisande! . . . Oh! your hair! . . .

MÉLISANDE (*starting upright*). I cannot . . . I cannot reach it. . . .

PELLÉAS. Your hair dipped in the water. . . .

MÉLISANDE. Yes, it is longer than my arms. . . . It is longer than I. . . .

[*A silence.*]

PELLÉAS. It was at the brink of a spring, too, that he found you?

MÉLISANDE. Yes. . . .

PELLÉAS. What did he say to you?

MÉLISANDE. Nothing;—I no longer remember. . . .

PELLÉAS. Was he quite near you?

MÉLISANDE. Yes; he would have kissed me.

PELLÉAS. And you would not?

MÉLISANDE. No.

PELLÉAS. Why would you not?

MÉLISANDE. Oh! oh! I saw something pass at the bottom of the water. . . .

PELLÉAS. Take care! take care!—You will fall! What are you playing with?

MÉLISANDE. With the ring he gave me.

PELLÉAS. Take care; you will lose it. . .

MÉLISANDE. No, no; I am sure of my hands. . . .

PELLÉAS. Do not play so, over so deep a water. . . .

MÉLISANDE. My hands do not tremble.

PELLÉAS. How it shines in the sunlight! Do not throw it so high in the air. . . .

MÉLISANDE. Oh! . . .

PELLÉAS. It has fallen?

MÉLISANDE. It has fallen into the water!

PELLÉAS. Where is it? where is it? . . .

MÉLISANDE. I do not see it sink! . . .

PELLÉAS. I think I see it shine. . . .

MÉLISANDE. My ring?

PELLÉAS. Yes, yes; down yonder. . . .

MÉLISANDE. Oh! oh! It is so far away from us! . . . no, no, that is not it . . . that is not it . . . It is lost . . . lost. . . . There is nothing any more but a great circle on the water. . . . What shall we do? What shall we do now? . . .

PELLÉAS. You need not be so troubled for a ring. It is nothing. . . . We shall find it again, perhaps. Or else we shall find another. . . .

MÉLISANDE. No, no; we shall never find it again; we shall never find any others either. . . . And yet I thought I had it in my hands. . . . I had already shut my hands, and it is fallen in spite of all. . . . I threw it too high, toward the sun. . . .

PELLÉAS. Come, come, we will come back another day; . . . come, it is time. They will come to meet us. It was striking noon at the moment the ring fell.

MÉLISANDE. What shall we say to Golaud if he asks where it is?

PELLÉAS. The truth, the truth, the truth. . . . (*Exeunt.*)

SCENE II. *An apartment in the castle*

GOLAUD *discovered, stretched upon his bed;* MÉLISANDE, *by his bedside.*

GOLAUD. Ah! ha! all goes well; it will amount to nothing. But I cannot understand how it came to pass. I was hunting quietly in the forest. All at once my horse ran away, without cause. Did he see anything unusual? . . . I had just heard the twelve strokes of noon. At the twelfth stroke he suddenly took fright and ran like a blind madman against a tree. I heard no more. I do not yet know what happened. I fell, and he must have fallen on me. I thought I had the whole forest on my breast; I thought my heart was crushed. But my heart is sound. It is nothing, apparently. . . .

MÉLISANDE. Would you like a little water?

GOLAUD. Thanks, thanks; I am not thirsty.

MÉLISANDE. Would you like another pillow? . . . There is a little spot of blood on this.

GOLAUD. No, no; it is not worth while. I bled at the mouth just now. I shall bleed again, perhaps. . . .

MÉLISANDE. Are you quite sure? . . . You are not suffering too much?

GOLAUD. No, no; I have seen a good many more like this. I was made of iron and blood. . . . These are not the little bones of a child; do not alarm yourself. . . .

MÉLISANDE. Close your eyes and try to sleep. I shall stay here all night. . . .

GOLAUD. No, no; I do not wish you to tire yourself so. I do not need any-thing; I shall sleep like a child. . . . What is the matter, Mélisande? Why do you weep all at once? . . .

MÉLISANDE (*bursting into tears*). I am . . . I am ill too. . . .

GOLAUD. Thou art ill? . . . What ails thee, then; what ails thee, Mélisande? . . .

MÉLISANDE. I do not know. . . . I am ill here. . . . I had rather tell you today; my lord, my lord, I am not happy here. . . .

GOLAUD. Why, what has happened, Mélisande? What is it? . . . And I suspected nothing. . . . What has happened? . . . Someone has done thee harm? . . . Someone has given thee offense?

MÉLISANDE. No, no; no one has done me the least harm. . . . It is not that. . . . It is not that. . . . But I can live here no longer. I do not know why. . . . I would go away, go away! . . . I shall die if I am left here. . . .

GOLAUD. But something has happened? You must be hiding something from me? . . . Tell me the whole truth, Mélisande. . . . Is it the King? . . . Is it my mother? . . . Is it Pelléas? . . .

MÉLISANDE. No, no; it is not Pelléas. It is not anybody. . . . You could not understand me. . . .

GOLAUD. Why should I not understand? . . . If you tell me nothing, what will you have me do? . . . Tell me everything and I shall understand everything.

MÉLISANDE. I do not know myself what it is. . . . I do not know just what it is. . . . If I could tell you, I would tell you. . . . It is something stronger than I. . . .

GOLAUD. Come; be reasonable, Mélisande.—What would you have me

do?—You are no longer a child.—
Is it I whom you would leave?

MÉLISANDE. Oh! no, no; it is not that.
. . . I would go away with you.
. . . It is here that I can live no
longer. . . . I feel that I shall not
live a long while. . . .

GOLAUD. But there must be a reason,
nevertheless. You will be thought
mad. It will be thought child's
dreams.—Come, is it Pelléas, perhaps?—I think he does not often
speak to you.

MÉLISANDE. Yes, yes; he speaks to me
sometimes. I think he does not like
me; I have seen it in his eyes. . . .
But he speaks to me when he meets
me. . . .

GOLAUD. You must not take it ill of him.
He has always been so. He is a little
strange. And just now he is sad; he
thinks of his friend Marcellus, who is
at the point of death, and whom he
cannot go to see. . . . He will
change, he will change, you will see;
he is young. . . .

MÉLISANDE. But it is not that . . . it is
not that. . . .

GOLAUD. What is it, then?—Can you
not get used to the life one leads here?
Is it too gloomy here?—It is true the
castle is very old and very somber.
. . . It is very cold, and very deep.
And all those who dwell in it, are
already old. And the country may
seem gloomy too, with all its forests,
all its old forests without light. But
that may all be enlivened if we will.
And then, joy, joy, one does not have
it every day; we must take things as
they come. But tell me something;
no matter what; I will do everything
you could wish. . . .

MÉLISANDE. Yes, yes; it is true. . . .
You never see the sky here. I saw it
for the first time this morning. . . .

GOLAUD. It is that, then, that makes you
weep, my poor Mélisande?—It is
only that, then?—You weep, not to
see the sky?—Come, come, you are
no longer at the age when one may
weep for such things. . . . And then,
is not the summer yonder? You will
see the sky every day.—And then,
next year. . . . Come, give me your
hand; give me both your little hands.
(*He takes her hands.*) Oh! oh! these
little hands that I could crush like
flowers. . . .—Hold! where is the
ring I gave you?

MÉLISANDE. The ring?

GOLAUD. Yes; our wedding-ring, where
is it?

MÉLISANDE. I think . . . I think it has
fallen. . . .

GOLAUD. Fallen?—Where has it fallen?
—You have not lost it?

MÉLISANDE. No, no; it fell . . . it must
have fallen . . . but I know where
it is. . . .

GOLAUD. Where is it?

MÉLISANDE. You know . . . you know
well . . . the grotto by the sea-
shore? . . .

GOLAUD. Yes.

MÉLISANDE. Well then, it is there. . . .
It must be it is there. . . . Yes, yes;
I remember. . . . I went there this
morning to pick up shells for little
Yniold. . . . There were some very
fine ones. . . . It slipped from my
finger . . . then the sea came in;
and I had to go out before I had
found it.

GOLAUD. Are you sure it is there?

MÉLISANDE. Yes, yes; quite sure. . . . I
felt it slip . . . then, all at once, the
noise of the waves. . . .

GOLAUD. You must go look for it at
once.

MÉLISANDE. I must go look for it at once?

GOLAUD. Yes.

MÉLISANDE. Now?—at once?—in the dark?

GOLAUD. Now, at once, in the dark. You must go look for it at once. I had rather have lost all I have than have lost that ring. You do not know what it is. You do not know whence it came. The sea will be very high tonight. The sea will come to take it before you. . . . Make haste. You 10 must go look for it at once. . . .

MÉLISANDE. I dare not. . . . I dare not go alone. . . .

GOLAUD. Go, go with no matter whom. But you must go at once, do you understand?—Make haste; ask Pelléas to go with you.

MÉLISANDE. Pelléas?—With Pelléas?—But Pelléas would not. . . .

GOLAUD. Pelléas will do all you ask of 20 him. I know Pelléas better than you do. Go, go; hurry! I shall not sleep until I have the ring.

MÉLISANDE. Oh! oh! I am not happy! . . . I am not happy! . . . (*Exit, weeping.*)

SCENE III. *Before a grotto*

[*Enter* PELLÉAS *and* MÉLISANDE.]

PELLÉAS (*speaking with great agitation*). 30 Yes; it is here; we are there. It is so dark you cannot tell the entrance of the grotto from the rest of the night. . . . There are no stars on this side. Let us wait till the moon has torn through that great cloud; it will light up the whole grotto, and then we can enter without danger. There are dangerous places, and the path is very narrow between two lakes whose 40 bottom has not yet been found. I did not think to bring a torch or a lantern, but I think the light of the sky will be enough for us.—You have never gone into this grotto?

MÉLISANDE. No. . . .

PELLÉAS. Let us go in; let us go in. . . . You must be able to describe the place where you lost the ring, if he questions you. . . . It is very big and very beautiful. There are stalactites that look like plants and men. It is full of blue darks. It has not been explored to the end. There are great treasures hidden there, it seems. You will see the remains of ancient shipwrecks there. But you must not go far in it without a guide. There have been some who never have come back. I myself dare not go forward too far. We will stop the moment we no longer see the light of the sea or the sky. When you strike a little light there, you would say the vault was covered with stars like the sky. It is bits of crystal or salt, they say, that shine so in the rock.—Look, look, I think the sky is going to clear. . . . Give me your hand; do not tremble, do not tremble so. There is no danger; we will stop the moment we no longer see the light of the sea. . . . Is it the noise of the grotto that frightens you? It is the noise of night or the noise of silence. . . . Do you hear the sea behind us?—It does not seem happy tonight. . . . Ah! look, the light! . . . [*The moon lights up abundantly the entrance and part of the darkness of the grotto; and at a certain depth are seen three old beggars with white hair, seated side by side, leaning upon each other and asleep against a boulder.*]

MÉLISANDE. Ah!

PELLÉAS. What is it?

MÉLISANDE. There are . . . there are. . . . (*She points out the three beggars.*)

PELLÉAS. Yes, yes; I have seen them too. . . .

MÉLISANDE. Let us go! . . . Let us go! . . .

PELLÉAS. Yes . . . it is three old poor

men fallen asleep. . . . There is a famine in the country. . . . Why have they come to sleep here? . . .

MÉLISANDE. Let us go! . . . Come, come. . . . Let us go! . . .

PELLÉAS. Take care; do not speak so loud. . . . Let us not wake them. . . . They are still sleeping heavily. . . . Come.

MÉLISANDE. Leave me, leave me; I prefer 10 to walk alone. . . .

PELLÉAS. We will come back another day. . . . (*Exeunt.*)

SCENE IV. *An apartment in the castle*

ARKËL *and* PELLÉAS *discovered.*

ARKËL. You see that everything retains you here just now and forbids you this useless journey. We have concealed your father's condition from 20 you until now; but it is perhaps hopeless; and that alone should suffice to stop you on the threshold. But there are so many other reasons. . . . And it is not in the day when our enemies awake, and when the people are dying of hunger and mur-

mur about us, that you have the right to desert us. And why this journey? Marcellus is dead; and life has graver duties than the visit to a tomb. You are weary, you say, of your inactive life; but activity and duty are not found on the highways. They must be waited for upon the threshold, and let in as they go by; and they go by every day. You have never seen them? I hardly see them any more myself; but I will teach you to see them, and I will point them out to you the day when you would make them a sign. Nevertheless, listen to me; if you believe it is from the depths of your life this journey is exacted, I do not forbid your undertaking it, for you must know better than I the events you must offer to your being or your fate. I shall ask you only to wait until we know what must take place ere long. . . .

PELLÉAS. How long must I wait?

ARKËL. A few weeks; perhaps a few days. . . .

PELLÉAS. I will wait. . . .

ACT III

SCENE I. *An apartment in the castle*

PELLÉAS *and* MÉLISANDE *discovered.* 30 MÉLISANDE *plies her distaff at the back of the room.*

PELLÉAS. Yniold does not come back; where has he gone?

MÉLISANDE. He had heard something in the corridor; he has gone to see what it is.

PELLÉAS. Mélisande. . . .

MÉLISANDE. What is it?

PELLÉAS . . . Can you see still to work 40 there? . . .

MÉLISANDE. I work as well in the dark. . . .

PELLÉAS. I think everybody is already

asleep in the castle. Golaud does not come back from the chase. It is late, nevertheless. . . . He no longer suffers from his fall? . . .

MÉLISANDE. He said he no longer suffered from it.

PELLÉAS. He must be more prudent; his body is no longer as supple as at twenty years. . . . I see the stars through the window and the light of the moon on the trees. It is late; he will not come back now. (*Knocking at the door.*) Who is there? . . . Come in! . . .

[*Little* YNIOLD *opens the door and enters the room.*]

It was you knocking so? . . . That

is not the way to knock at doors. It is as if a misfortune had arrived; look, you have frightened little mother.

YNIOLD. I only knocked a tiny little bit.

PELLÉAS. It is late; little father will not come back tonight; it is time for you to go to bed.

YNIOLD. I shall not go to bed before you do.

PELLÉAS. What? . . . What is that you are saying?

YNIOLD. I say . . . not before you . . . not before you . . . (*Bursts into sobs and takes refuge by* MÉLISANDE.)

MÉLISANDE. What is it, Yniold? . . . What is it? why do you weep all at once?

YNIOLD (*sobbing*). Because . . . oh! oh! because . . .

MÉLISANDE. Because what? . . . Because what? . . . Tell me . . .

YNIOLD. Little mother . . . little mother . . . you are going away. . . .

MÉLISANDE. But what has taken hold of you, Yniold? . . . I have never dreamed of going away. . . .

YNIOLD. Yes, you have; yes, you have; little father has gone away. . . . Little father does not come back, and you are going to go away too. . . . I have seen it . . . I have seen it. . . .

MÉLISANDE. But there has never been any idea of that, Yniold. . . . Why, what makes you think that I would go away? . . .

YNIOLD. I have seen it . . . I have seen it. . . . You have said things to uncle that I could not hear . . .

PELLÉAS. He is sleepy. . . . He has been dreaming. . . . Come here, Yniold; asleep already? . . . Come and look out at the window; the swans are fighting with the dogs. . . .

YNIOLD (*at the window*). Oh! oh! they are chasing the dogs! . . . They are chasing them! . . . Oh! oh! the

water! . . . the wings! . . . the wings! . . . they are afraid. . . .

PELLÉAS (*coming back by* MÉLISANDE). He is sleepy; he is struggling against sleep; his eyes were closing. . . .

MÉLISANDE (*singing softly as she spins*). Saint Daniel and Saint Michaël. . . Saint Michaël and Saint Raphaël. . . .

YNIOLD (*at the window*). Oh! oh! little mother! . . .

MÉLISANDE (*rising abruptly*). What is it, Yniold? . . . What is it? . . .

YNIOLD. I saw something at the window!

[PELLÉAS *and* MÉLISANDE *run to the window.*]

PELLÉAS. What is there at the window? . . . What have you seen? . . .

YNIOLD. Oh! oh! I saw something! . . .

PELLÉAS. But there is nothing. I see nothing. . . .

MÉLISANDE. Nor I. . . .

PELLÉAS. Where did you see something? Which way? . . .

YNIOLD. Down there, down there! . . . It is no longer there. . . .

PELLÉAS. He does not know what he is saying. He must have seen the light of the moon on the forest. There are often strange reflections . . . or else something must have passed on the highway . . . or in his sleep. For see, see, I believe he is quite asleep. . . .

YNIOLD (*at the window*). Little father is there! little father is there!

PELLÉAS (*going to the window*). He is right; Golaud is coming into the courtyard.

YNIOLD. Little father! . . . little father! . . . I am going to meet him! . . . (*Exit, running.—A silence.*)

PELLÉAS. They are coming up the stair.

[*Enter* GOLAUD *and little* YNIOLD *with a lamp.*]

GOLAUD. You are still waiting in the dark?

YNIOLD. I have brought a light, little mother, a big light! . . . (*He lifts the lamp and looks at* MÉLISANDE.) You have been weeping, little mother? . . . You have been weeping? . . . (*He lifts the lamp toward* PELLÉAS *and looks in turn at him.*) You too, you too, you have been weeping? . . . Little father, look, little father; they have both been weeping. . . .

GOLAUD. Do not hold the light under their eyes so. . . .

SCENE II. *One of the towers of the castle. A watchman's round passes under a window in the tower.*

MÉLISANDE (*at the window, combing her unbound hair*).

My long locks fall foaming
To the threshold of the tower—
My locks await your coming
All along the tower,
And all the long, long hour,
And all the long, long hour.

Saint Daniel and Saint Michaël,
Saint Michaël and Saint Raphaël.

I was born on a Sunday,
A Sunday at high noon. . . .

[*Enter* PELLÉAS *by the watchman's round.*]

PELLÉAS. Holà! Holà! ho! . . .

MÉLISANDE. Who is there?

PELLÉAS. I, I, and I! . . . What art thou doing there at the window, singing like a bird that is not native here?

MÉLISANDE. I am doing my hair for the night. . . .

PELLÉAS. Is it that I see upon the wall? . . . I thought you had some light. . . .

MÉLISANDE. I have opened the window; it is too hot in the tower. . . . It is beautiful tonight. . . .

PELLÉAS. There are innumerable stars; I have never seen so many as tonight; . . . but the moon is still upon the sea. . . . Do not stay in the shadow, Mélisande; lean forward a little till I see your unbound hair. . . .

MÉLISANDE. I am frightful so. . . . (*She leans out at the window.*)

PELLÉAS. Oh! oh! Mélisande! . . . oh, thou art beautiful! . . . thou art beautiful so! . . . Lean out! . . . lean out! . . . Let me come nearer thee . . .

MÉLISANDE. I cannot come nearer thee. . . . I am leaning out as far as I can. . . .

PELLÉAS. I cannot come up higher; . . . give me at least thy hand tonight . . . before I go away. . . . I leave tomorrow. . . .

MÉLISANDE. No, no, no! . . .

PELLÉAS. Yes, yes, yes; I leave, I shall leave tomorrow. . . . Give me thy hand, thy hand, thy little hand upon my lips. . . .

MÉLISANDE. I give thee not my hand if thou wilt leave. . . .

PELLÉAS. Give, give, give! . . .

MÉLISANDE. Thou wilt not leave?

PELLÉAS. I will wait; I will wait. . . .

MÉLISANDE. I see a rose in the shadows. . . .

PELLÉAS. Where? . . . I see only the boughs of the willow hanging over the wall. . . .

MÉLISANDE. Farther down, farther down, in the garden; farther down, in the somber green. . . .

PELLÉAS. It is not a rose. . . . I will go see by and by, but give me thy hand first; first thy hand. . . .

MÉLISANDE. There, there; . . . I cannot lean out farther. . . .

PELLÉAS. I cannot reach thy hand with my lips. . . .

MÉLISANDE. I cannot lean out farther.

. . . I am on the point of falling. . . . —Oh! oh! my hair is falling down the tower! (*Her tresses fall suddenly over her head, as she is leaning out so, and stream over* PELLÉAS.)

PELLÉAS. Oh! oh! what is it? . . . Thy hair, thy hair is falling down to me! . . . All thy locks, Mélisande, all thy locks have fallen down the tower! . . . I hold them in my hands; I hold them in my mouth. . . . I hold them in my arms; I put them about my neck. . . . I will not open my hands again tonight. . . .

MÉLISANDE. Let me go! let me go! . . . Thou wilt make me fall! . . .

PELLÉAS. No, no, no; . . . I have never seen such hair as thine, Mélisande! . . . See, see, see; it comes from so high and yet it floods me to the heart! . . . And yet it floods me to the knees! . . . And it is sweet, sweet as if it fell from heaven! . . . I see the sky no longer through thy locks. Thou seest, thou seest? . . . I can no longer hold them with both hands; there are some on the boughs of the willow. . . . They are alive like birds in my hands, . . . and they love me, they love me more than thou! . . .

MÉLISANDE. Let me go; let me go! . . . Someone might come. . . .

PELLÉAS. No, no, no; I shall not set thee free tonight. . . . Thou art my prisoner tonight; all night, all night! . . .

MÉLISANDE. Pelléas! Pelléas! . . .

PELLÉAS. I tie them, I tie them to the willow boughs. . . . Thou shalt not go away now; . . . thou shalt not go away now. . . . Look, look, I am kissing thy hair. . . . I suffer no more in the midst of thy hair. . . . Hearest thou my kisses along thy hair? . . . They mount along thy hair. . . . Each hair must bring thee some. . . . Thou seest, thou seest, I can open my hands. . . . My hands are free, and thou canst not leave me now. . . .

MÉLISANDE. Oh! oh! thou hurtest me. . . . (*Doves come out of the tower and fly about them in the night.*)—What is that, Pelléas?—What is it flying about me?

PELLÉAS. It is the doves coming out of the tower. . . . I have frightened them; they are flying away. . . .

MÉLISANDE. It is my doves, Pelléas.— Let us go away, let me go; they will not come back again. . . .

PELLÉAS. Why will they not come back again?

MÉLISANDE. They will be lost in the dark. . . . Let me go; let me lift my head. . . . I hear a noise of footsteps. . . . Let me go!—It is Golaud! . . . I believe it is Golaud! . . . He has heard us. . . .

PELLÉAS. Wait. Wait! . . . Thy hair is about the boughs. . . . It is caught there in the darkness. . . . Wait, wait! . . . It is dark. . . .

[*Enter* GOLAUD, *by the watchman's round.*]

GOLAUD. What do you here?

PELLÉAS. What do I here? . . . I . . .

GOLAUD. You are children. . . . Mélisande, do not lean out so at the window; you will fall. . . . Do you not know it is late? It is nearly midnight.—Do not play so in the darkness.—You are children . . . (*Laughing nervously.*) What children! . . . What children! . . . (*Exit, with* PELLÉAS.)

SCENE III. *The vaults of the castle*

[*Enter* GOLAUD *and* PELLÉAS.]

GOLAUD. Take care; this way, this way. —You have never penetrated into these vaults?

PELLÉAS. Yes; once, of old; but it was long ago. . . .

GOLAUD. They are prodigious great; it is a succession of enormous crypts that end, God knows where. The whole castle is builded on these crypts. Do you smell the deathly odor that reigns here?—That is what I wished to show you. In my opinion, it comes from the little underground 10 lake I am going to have you see. Take care; walk before me, in the light of my lantern. I will warn you when we are there. (*They continue to walk in silence.*) Hey! hey! Pelléas! stop! stop! (*He seizes him by the arm.*) For God's sake! . . . Do you not see?—One step more, and you had been in the gulf! . . .

PELLÉAS. But I did not see it! . . . 20 The lantern no longer lighted me. . . .

GOLAUD. I made a misstep . . . but if I had not held you by the arm . . . Well, this is the stagnant water that I spoke of to you. . . . Do you perceive the smell of death that rises?— Let us go to the end of this overhanging rock, and do you lean over a little. It will strike you in the 30 face.

PELLÉAS. I smell it already; . . . you would say a smell of the tomb.

GOLAUD. Farther, farther. . . . It is this that on certain days has poisoned the castle. The King will not believe it comes from here.—The crypt should be walled up in which this standing water is found. It is time, besides, to examine these vaults a 40 little. Have you noticed those lizards on the walls and pillars of the vaults? —There is a labor hidden here you would not suspect; and the whole castle will be swallowed up one of these nights, if it is not looked out

for. But what will you have? Nobody likes to come down this far. . . . There are strange lizards in many of the walls. . . . Oh! here . . . do you perceive the smell of death that rises?

PELLÉAS. Yes; there is a smell of death rising about us. . . .

GOLAUD. Lean over; have no fear. . . . I will hold you . . . give me . . . no, no, not your hand . . . it might slip . . . your arm, your arm! . . . Do you see the gulf? (*Moved.*)— Pelléas? Pelléas? . . .

PELLÉAS. Yes; I think I see the bottom of the gulf. . . . Is it the light that trembles so? . . . You . . . (*He straightens up, turns, and looks at* GOLAUD.)

GOLAUD (*with a trembling voice*). Yes; it is the lantern. . . . See, I shook it to lighten the walls. . . .

PELLÉAS. I stifle here; . . . let us go out. . . .

GOLAUD. Yes; let us go out. . . . (*Exeunt in silence.*)

SCENE IV. *A terrace at the exit of the vaults*

[*Enter* GOLAUD *and* PELLÉAS.]

PELLÉAS. Ah! I breathe at last! . . . I thought, one moment, I was going to be ill in those enormous crypts; I was on the point of falling. . . . There is a damp air there, heavy as a laden dew, and darkness thick as a poisoned paste. . . . And now, all the air of all the sea! . . . There is a fresh wind, see; fresh as a leaf that has just opened, over the little green waves. . . . Hold! the flowers have just been watered at the foot of the terrace, and the smell of the verdure and the wet roses comes up to us. . . . It must be nearly noon; they are already in the shadow of the tower. . . . It is noon; I hear the bells ringing, and the children are going down to the beach to bathe. . . . I did not know that we had stayed so long in the caverns. . . .

ƍOLAUD. We went down toward eleven o'clock. . . .

ᴘELLÉAS. Earlier; it must have been earlier; I heard it strike half past ten.

ɢOLAUD. Half past ten or a quarter to eleven. . . .

PELLÉAS. They have opened all the windows of the castle. It will be unusually hot this afternoon. . . . Look, there is mother with Mélisande at a window of the tower. . . .

ɜOLAUD. Yes; they have taken refuge on the shady side.—Speaking of Mélisande, I heard what passed and what was said last night. I am quite aware all that is but child's play; but it need not be repeated. Mélisande is very young and very impressionable; and she must be treated the more circumspectly that she is perhaps with child at this moment. . . . She is very delicate, hardly woman; and the least emotion might bring on a mishap. It is not the first time I have noticed there might be something between you. . . . You are older than she; it will suffice to have told you. . . . Avoid her as much as possible; without affectation, moreover; without affectation. . . . — What is it I see yonder on the highway toward the forest? . . .

ᴘELLÉAS. Some herds they are leading to the city. . . .

ɢOLAUD. They cry like lost children; you would say they smelt the butcher already.—It will be time for dinner. —What a fine day! What a capital day for the harvest! . . . (*Exeunt.*)

SCENE V. *Before the castle*

[*Enter* GOLAUD *and little* YNIOLD.]

GOLAUD. Come, we are going to sit down here, Yniold; sit on my knee; we shall see from here what passes in the forest. I do not see you any more at all now. You abandon me too; you are always at little mother's. . . . Why, we are sitting just under little mother's windows.—Perhaps she is saying her evening prayer at this moment. . . . But tell me, Yniold, she is often with your Uncle Pelléas, isn't she?

YNIOLD. Yes, yes; always, little father; when you are not there, little father. . . .

GOLAUD. Ah!—Look; someone is going by with a lantern in the garden.— But I have been told they did not like each other. . . . It seems they often quarrel; . . . no? Is it true?

YNIOLD. Yes, yes; it is true.

GOLAUD. Yes?—Ah! ah!—But what do they quarrel about?

YNIOLD. About the door.

GOLAUD. What?—about the door?— What are you talking about?—No, come, explain yourself; why do they quarrel about the door?

YNIOLD. Because it won't stay open.

GOLAUD. Who wants it to stay open?— Come, why do they quarrel?

YNIOLD. I don't know, little father, about the light.

GOLAUD. I am not talking to you about the light; we will talk of that by and by. I am talking to you about the door. Answer what I ask you; you must learn to talk; it is time. . . . Do not put your hand in your mouth so; . . . come. . . .

YNIOLD. Little father! little father! . . . I won't do it any more. . . . (*He cries.*)

GOLAUD. Come; what are you crying for now? What has happened?

YNIOLD. Oh! oh! little father, you hurt me. . . .

GOLAUD. I hurt you?—Where did I hurt you? I did not mean to. . . .

YNIOLD. Here, here; on my little arm. . . .

GOLAUD. I did not mean to; come, don't cry any more, and I will give you something tomorrow.

YNIOLD. What, little father?

GOLAUD. A quiver and some arrows; but tell me what you know about the door.

YNIOLD. Big arrows?

GOLAUD. Yes, yes; very big arrows.— But why don't they want the door to be open?—Come, answer me sometime!—No, no; do not open your mouth to cry. I am not angry. We are going to have a quiet talk, like Pelléas and little mother when they are together. What do they talk about when they are together?

YNIOLD. Pelléas and little mother?

GOLAUD. Yes; what do they talk about?

YNIOLD. About me; always about me.

GOLAUD. And what do they say about you?

YNIOLD. They say I am going to be very big.

GOLAUD. Oh, plague of my life! . . . I am here like a blind man searching for his treasure at the bottom of the ocean! . . . I am here like a new-born child lost in the forest, and you . . . Come, come, Yniold, I was wandering; we are going to talk seriously. Do Pelléas and little mother never speak of me when I am not there? . . .

YNIOLD. Yes, yes, little father; they are always speaking of you.

GOLAUD. Ah! . . . And what do they say of me?

YNIOLD. They say I shall grow as big as you are.

GOLAUD. You are always by them?

YNIOLD. Yes, yes, always, always, little father.

GOLAUD. They never tell you to go play somewhere else?

YNIOLD. No, little father; they are afraid when I am not there.

GOLAUD. They are afraid? . . . What makes you think they are afraid?

YNIOLD. Little mother always says, "Don't go away; don't go away!" . . . They are unhappy, but they laugh. . . .

GOLAUD. But that does not prove they are afraid.

YNIOLD. Yes, yes, little father; she is afraid. . . .

GOLAUD. Why do you say she is afraid?

YNIOLD. They always weep in the dark.

GOLAUD. Ah! ah! . . .

YNIOLD. That makes one weep too.

GOLAUD. Yes, yes! . . .

YNIOLD. She is pale, little father.

GOLAUD. Ah! ah! . . . patience, my God, patience! . . .

YNIOLD. What, little father?

GOLAUD. Nothing, nothing, my child.— I saw a wolf go by in the forest.— Then they get on well together?— I am glad to learn they are on good terms.—They kiss each other sometimes?—No? . . .

YNIOLD. Kiss each other, little father? —No, no—ah! yes, little father, yes, yes; once . . . once when it rained. . . .

GOLAUD. They kissed?—But how, how did they kiss?

YNIOLD. So, little father, so! . . . (*He gives him a kiss on the mouth, laughing.*) Ah! ah! your beard, little father! . . . It pricks! it pricks! it pricks! It is getting all gray, little father, and your hair, too; all gray, all gray, all gray. . . . (*The window under which they are sitting is lighted up at this moment, and the light falls upon them.*)

Ah! ah! little mother has lit her lamp. It is light, little father; it is light. . . .

GOLAUD. Yes; it is beginning to be light. . . .

YNIOLD. Let us go there, too, little father; let us go there, too. . . .

GOLAUD. Where do you want to go?

YNIOLD. Where it is light, little father.

GOLAUD. No, no, my child; let us stay in the dark a little longer. . . . One cannot tell, one cannot tell yet. . . . Do you see those poor people down there trying to kindle a little fire in the forest?—It has rained. And over there, do you see the old gardener trying to lift that tree the wind has blown down across the road?—He cannot; the tree is too big; the tree is too heavy, and it will lie where it fell. All that cannot be helped. . . . I think Pelléas is mad. . . .

YNIOLD. No, little father, he is not mad; he is very good.

GOLAUD. Do you want to see little mother?

YNIOLD. Yes, yes; I want to see her!

GOLAUD. Don't make any noise; I am going to hoist you up to the window. It is too high for me, for all I am so big. . . . (*He lifts the child.*) Do not make the least noise; little mother would be terribly afraid. . . . Do you see her?—Is she in the room?

YNIOLD. Yes. . . . Oh, how light it is!

GOLAUD. She is alone?

YNIOLD. Yes; . . . no, no; Uncle Pelléas is there, too.

GOLAUD. He— . . .!

YNIOLD. Ah! ah! little father! you have hurt me! . . .

GOLAUD. It is nothing; be still; I will not do it any more; look, look, Yniold! . . . I stumbled; speak lower. What are they doing?—

YNIOLD. They are not doing anything, little father; they are waiting for something.

GOLAUD. Are they near each other?

YNIOLD. No, little father.

GOLAUD. And . . . and the bed? Are they near the bed?

YNIOLD. The bed, little father?—I can't see the bed.

GOLAUD. Lower, lower; they will hear you. Are they speaking?

YNIOLD. No, little father; they do not speak.

GOLAUD. But what are they doing?— They must be doing something. . . .

YNIOLD. They are looking at the light.

GOLAUD. Both?

YNIOLD. Yes, little father.

GOLAUD. They do not say anything?

YNIOLD. No, little father; they do not close their eyes.

GOLAUD. They do not come near each other?

YNIOLD. No, little father; they do not stir.

GOLAUD. They are sitting down?

YNIOLD. No, little father; they are standing upright against the wall.

GOLAUD. They make no gestures?— They do not look at each other?— They make no signs? . . .

YNIOLD. No, little father.—Oh! oh! little father; they never close their eyes. . . . I am terribly afraid. . . .

GOLAUD. Be still. They do not stir yet?

YNIOLD. No, little father.—I am afraid, little father; let me come down! . . .

GOLAUD. Why, what are you afraid of? —Look! look! . . .

YNIOLD. I dare not look any more, little father! . . . Let me come down! . . .

GOLAUD. Look! look! . . .

YNIOLD. Oh! oh! I am going to cry, little father!—Let me come down! let me come down! . . .

GOLAUD. Come; we will go see what has happened. (*Exeunt.*)

ACT IV

SCENE I. *A corridor in the castle*

[*Enter* PELLÉAS *and* MÉLISANDE, *meeting.*]

PELLÉAS. Where goest thou? I must speak to thee tonight. Shall I see thee?

MÉLISANDE. Yes.

PELLÉAS. I have just left my father's room. He is getting better. The physician has told us he is saved. . . . And yet this morning I had a presenti- 10 ment this day would end ill. I have had a rumor of misfortune in my ears for some time. . . . Then, all at once there was a great change; today it is no longer anything but a question of time. All the windows in his room have been thrown open. He speaks; he seems happy. He does not speak yet like an ordinary man, but already his ideas no longer all come from the 20 other world. . . . He recognized me. He took my hand and said with that strange air he has had since he fell sick: "Is it thou, Pelléas? Why, why, I had not noticed it before, but thou hast the grave and friendly look of those who will not live long. . . . You must travel; you must travel. . . ." It is strange; I shall obey him. . . . My mother listened to 30 him and wept for joy.—Hast thou not been aware of it?—The whole house seems already to revive; you hear breathing, you hear speaking, you hear walking. . . . Listen; I hear some one speaking behind that door. Quick, quick! answer quickly! where shall I see thee?

MÉLISANDE. Where wouldst thou?

PELLÉAS. In the park; near "Blind 40 Man's Spring."—Wilt thou?—Wilt thou come?

MÉLISANDE. Yes.

PELLÉAS. It will be the last night;—I am going to travel, as my father said. Thou wilt not see me more. . . .

MÉLISANDE. Do not say that, Pelléas. . . . I shall see thee always; I shall look upon thee always. . . .

PELLÉAS. Thou wilt look in vain. . . . I shall be so far away thou couldst no longer see me. . . . I shall try to go very far away. . . . I am full of joy, and you would say I had all the weight of heaven and earth on my body today. . . .

MÉLISANDE. What has happened, Pelléas?—I no longer understand what you say. . . .

PELLÉAS. Go, go; let us separate. I hear someone speaking behind that door. . . . It is the strangers who came to the castle this morning. . . . They are going out. . . . Let us go; it is the strangers. . . . (*Exeunt severally.*)

SCENE II. *An apartment in the castle*

ARKËL *and* MÉLISANDE *discovered.*

ARKËL. Now that Pelléas's father is saved, and sickness, the old hand-maid of Death, has left the castle, a little joy and a little sunlight will at last come into the house again. . . . It was time!—For, since thy coming, we have only lived here whispering about a closed room. . . . And truly I have pitied thee, Mélisande. . . . Thou camest here all joyous, like a child seeking a gala-day, and at the moment thou enteredst in the vestibule I saw thy face change, and probably thy soul, as the face changes in spite of us when we enter at noon into a grotto too gloomy and too cold. . . . And since—since, on account of all that, I have often no longer understood thee. . . . I observed thee, thou wert there, listless, perhaps, but with the strange, astray look of one awaiting ever a great trouble, in the sunlight, in a beautiful garden. . . . I cannot explain. . . . But I was sad to see thee so; for thou art too young and too beautiful to live already day and night under the breath of Death. . . . But now all that will change. At my age—and there, perhaps, is the surest fruit of 10 my life—at my age I have gained I know not what faith in the fidelity of events, and I have always seen that every young and beautiful being creates about itself young, beautiful, and happy events. . . . And it is thou who wilt now open the door for the new era I have glimpses of. . . . Come here; why dost thou stay there without answering and without lift- 20 ing thine eyes?—I have kissed thee but once only hitherto—the day of thy coming; and yet old men need sometimes to touch with their lips a woman's forehead or a child's cheek, to believe still in the freshness of life and avert awhile the menaces. . . . Art thou afraid of my old lips? How I have pitied thee these months! . . .

MÉLISANDE. Grandfather, I have not 30 been unhappy. . . .

ARKËL. Perhaps you were of those who are unhappy without knowing it, . . . and they are the most unhappy. . . . Let me look at thee, so, quite near, a moment: . . . we have such need of beauty beside Death. . . .

[*Enter* GOLAUD.]

GOLAUD. Pelléas leaves tonight.

ARKËL. Thou hast blood on thy fore- 40 head.—What hast thou done?

GOLAUD. Nothing, nothing. . . . I have passed through a hedge of thorns.

MÉLISANDE. Bend down your head a little, my lord. . . . I will wipe your forehead. . . .

GOLAUD (*repulsing her*). I will not that you touch me, do you understand? Go, go!—I am not speaking to you.— Where is my sword?—I come to seek my sword. . . .

MÉLISANDE. Here; on the praying-stool.

GOLAUD. Bring it. (*To* ARKËL.) They have just found another peasant dead of hunger, along by the sea. You would say they all meant to die under our eyes. (*To* MÉLISANDE.) Well, my sword?—Why do you tremble so? —I am not going to kill you. I would simply examine the blade. I do not employ the sword for these uses. Why do you examine me like a beggar?— I do not come to ask alms of you. You hope to see something in my eyes without my seeing anything in yours?—Do you think I may know something? (*To* ARKËL.)—Do you see those great eyes?—It is as if they were proud of their richness. . . .

ARKËL. I see there only a great inno-cence. . . .

GOLAUD. A great innocence! . . . They are greater than innocence. . . . They are purer than the eyes of a lamb. . . . They would give God lessons in innocence! A great inno-cence! Listen: I am so near them I feel the freshness of their lashes when they wink; and yet I am less far away from the great secrets of the other world than from the smallest secret of those eyes! . . . A great inno-cence! . . . More than innocence! You would say the angels of heaven celebrated there an eternal baptism! . . . I know those eyes! I have seen them at their work! Close them! close them! or I shall close them for a long while! . . . Do not put your right hand to your throat so; I am saying a very simple thing. . . . I have no under-thought. . . . If I had an under-thought, why should I not say it? Ah! ah!—Do not attempt to flee!—Here!—Give me that hand! —Ah! your hands are too hot. . . . Go away! Your flesh disgusts me! . . . Here!—There is no more question of fleeing now! (*He seizes her by the hair.*) You shall follow me on your knees!—On your knees!—On your knees before me!—Ah! ah! your long hair serves some purpose at last! . . . Right, . . . left!—Left, . . . right! —Absalom! Absalom.—Forward! back! To the ground! to the ground! . . . You see, you see; I laugh already like an old man. . . .

ARKËL (*running up*). Golaud! . . .

GOLAUD (*affecting a sudden calm*). You will do as you may please, look you. —I attach no importance to that.— I am too old; and, besides, I am not a spy. I shall await chance; and then . . . Oh! then! . . . simply because it is the custom; simply because it is the custom. . . . (*Exit.*)

ARKËL. What ails him?—He is drunk?

MÉLISANDE (*in tears*). No, no; he does not love me any more. . . . I am not happy! . . . I am not happy! . . .

ARKËL. If I were God, I would have pity on men's hearts. . . .

SCENE III. *A terrace of the castle*

Little YNIOLD *discovered, trying to lift a boulder.*

YNIOLD. Oh, this stone is heavy! . . . It is heavier than I am. . . . It is heavier than everybody. . . . It is heavier than everything that ever happened. . . . I can see my golden ball between the rock and this naughty stone, and I cannot reach it. . . . My little arm is not long enough, . . . and this stone won't be lifted. . . . I can't lift it, . . . and nobody could lift it. . . . It is heavier than the whole house; . . . you would think it had roots in the earth. . . . (*The bleatings of a flock heard far away.*) —Oh! oh! I hear the sheep crying. . . . (*He goes to look, at the edge of the terrace.*) Why! there is no more sun. . . . They are coming . . . the little sheep . . . they are coming. . . . There is a lot of them! . . . There is a lot of them! . . . They are afraid of the dark. . . . They crowd together! They crowd together! . . . They can hardly walk any more. . . . They are crying! They are crying! And they go quick! . . . They go quick! . . . They are already at the great crossroads. Ah! ah! They don't know where they ought to go any more. . . . They don't cry any more. . . . They wait. . . . Some of them want to go to the right. . . . They all want to go to the right. . . . They cannot! . . . The shepherd is throwing earth at them. . . . Ah! ah! They are going to pass by here. . . . They obey! They obey! They are going to pass under the terrace. . . . They are going to pass under the rocks. I am going to see them near by. . . . Oh! oh! what a lot of them! . . . What a lot of them! The whole road is full of them! . . . They all keep still now. . . . Shepherd! shepherd! why don't they speak any more?

THE SHEPHERD (*who is out of sight*). Because it is no longer the road to the stable . . .

YNIOLD. Where are they going?— Shepherd! shepherd!—Where are they going?—He doesn't hear me any more. They are too far away already. . . . They go quick. . . . They are not making a noise any more. . . . It is no longer the road to the stable. . . . Where are they going to sleep tonight?—Oh! oh!—It is too dark. . . . I am going to tell something to somebody. . . . (*Exit.*)

SCENE IV. *A fountain in the park*

[*Enter* PELLÉAS.]

PELLÉAS. It is the last evening . . . the last evening. It must all end. I have played like a child about a thing I did not guess. . . . I have played a-dream about the snares of fate. . . . Who has awakened me all at once? I shall flee, crying out for joy and woe like a blind man fleeing from his burning house. . . . I am going to tell her I shall flee. . . . My father is out of danger; and I have no more reason to lie to myself. . . . It is late; she does not come. . . . I should do better to go away without seeing her again. . . . I must look well at her this time. . . . There are some things that I no longer recall. . . . It seems at times as if I had not seen her for a hundred years. . . . And I have not yet looked upon her look. . . . There remains nought to me if I go away thus. And all those memories . . . it is as if I were to take away a little water in a muslin bag. . . . I must see her one last time, to the bottom of her heart. . . . I must tell her all that I have never told her.

[*Enter* MÉLISANDE.]

MÉLISANDE. Pelléas!

PELLÉAS. Mélisande!—Is it thou, Mélisande?

MÉLISANDE. Yes.

PELLÉAS. Come hither; do not stay at the edge of the moonlight.—Come hither. We have so many things to tell each other. . . . Come hither in the shadow of the linden.

MÉLISANDE. Let me stay in the light. . . .

PELLÉAS. We might be seen from the windows of the tower. Come hither; here, we have nothing to fear.—Take care; we might be seen . . .

MÉLISANDE. I wish to be seen. . . .

PELLÉAS. Why, what doth ail thee?— Thou wert able to come out without being seen?

MÉLISANDE. Yes; your brother slept. . . .

PELLÉAS. It is late.—In an hour they will close the gates. We must be careful. Why art thou come so late?

MÉLISANDE. Your brother had a bad dream. And then my gown was caught on the nails of the gate. See, it is torn. I lost all this time, and ran. . . .

PELLÉAS. My poor Mélisande! . . . I should almost be afraid to touch thee. . . . Thou art still out of breath, like a hunted bird. . . . It is for me, for me, thou doest all that? . . . I hear thy heart beat as if it were mine. . . . Come hither . . . nearer, nearer me. . . .

MÉLISANDE. Why do you laugh?

PELLÉAS. I do not laugh;—or else I laugh for joy, unwittingly. . . . It were a weeping matter, rather. . . .

MÉLISANDE. We have come here before. . . . I recollect. . . .

PELLÉAS. Yes . . . yes . . . Long months ago.—I knew not then. . . . Knowest thou why I asked thee to come here tonight?

MÉLISANDE. No.

PELLÉAS. It is perhaps the last time I shall see thee. . . . I must go away forever. . . .

MÉLISANDE. Why sayest thou always thou wilt go away? . . .

PELLÉAS. I must tell thee what thou knowest already?—Thou knowest not what I am going to tell thee?

MÉLISANDE. Why, no; why, no, I know nothing—. . .

PELLÉAS. Thou knowest not why I must go afar. . . . Thou knowest not it is because . . . (*He kisses her abruptly.*) I love thee. . . .

MÉLISANDE (*in a low voice*). I love thee, too. . . .

PELLÉAS. Oh! oh! What saidst thou, Mélisande? . . . I hardly heard it! . . . Thou sayest that in a voice coming from the end of the world! . . . I hardly heard thee. . . . Thou lovest me?—Thou lovest me, too? . . . Since when lovest thou me? . . . [10]

MÉLISANDE. Since always. . . . Since I saw thee. . . .

PELLÉAS. Oh, how thou sayest that! . . . Thy voice seems to have blown across the sea in spring! . . . I have never heard it until now; . . . one would say it had rained on my heart! . . . [20] Thou sayest that so frankly! . . . Like an angel questioned! . . . I cannot believe it, Mélisande! . . . Why shouldst thou love me?—Nay, why dost thou love me?—Is what thou sayest true?—Thou dost not mock me?—Thou dost not lie a little, to make me smile? . . .

MÉLISANDE. No; I never lie; I lie but to thy brother. . . .

PELLÉAS. Oh, how thou sayest that! . . . Thy voice! thy voice! . . . It is cooler and more frank than the water is! . . . It is like pure water on my lips! . . . It is like pure water on my hands. . . . Give me, give me thy hands! . . . Oh, how small thy hands are! . . . I did not know thou wert so beautiful! . . . I have never seen anything so beautiful before thee. [40] . . . I was full of unrest; I sought throughout the country. . . . And I found not beauty. . . . And now I have found thee! . . . I have found thee! . . . I do not think there could be on the earth a fairer woman!

. . . Where art thou?—I no longer hear thee breathe. . . .

MÉLISANDE. Because I look on thee. . . .

PELLÉAS. Why dost thou look so gravely on me?—We are already in the shadow.—It is too dark under this tree.—Come into the light. We cannot see how happy we are. Come, come; so little time remains to us. . . .

MÉLISANDE. No, no; let us stay here. . . . I am nearer thee in the dark. . . .

PELLÉAS. Where are thine eyes?—Thou art not going to fly me?—Thou dost not think of me just now.

MÉLISANDE. Oh, yes; oh, yes; I only think of thee. . . .

PELLÉAS. Thou wert looking elsewhere. . . .

MÉLISANDE. I saw thee elsewhere. . . .

PELLÉAS. Thy soul is far away. . . . What ails thee, then?—Meseems thou art not happy. . . .

MÉLISANDE. Yes, yes; I am happy, but I am sad. . . .

PELLÉAS. One is sad often when one loves. . . .

MÉLISANDE. I weep always when I think of thee. . . .

[30] PELLÉAS. I, too. . . . I, too, Mélisande. . . . I am quite near thee; I weep for joy and yet . . . (*He kisses her again.*) —Thou art strange when I kiss thee so. . . . Thou art so beautiful that one would think thou wert about to die. . . .

MÉLISANDE. Thou, too. . . .

PELLÉAS. There, there. . . . We do not what we will. . . . I did not love thee the first time I saw thee. . . .

MÉLISANDE. Nor I . . . nor I. . . . I was afraid. . . .

PELLÉAS. I could not admit thine eyes. . . . I would have gone away at once . . . and then . . .

MÉLISANDE. And I—I would not have

come. . . . I do not yet know why—
I was afraid to come. . . .

PELLÉAS. There are so many things one
never knows. We are ever waiting;
and then. . . . What is that noise?—
They are closing the gates! . . .

MÉLISANDE. Yes, they have closed the
gates. . . .

PELLÉAS. We cannot go back now?—
Hearest thou the bolts?—Listen! listen! . . . The great chains! . . .
The great chains! . . . It is too late;
it is too late! . . .

MÉLISANDE. All the better! all the better!
all the better! . . .

PELLÉAS. Thou—. . . ? Behold, behold! . . . It is no longer we who
will it so! . . . All's lost, all's saved!
All is saved tonight!—Come, come.
. . . My heart beats like a madman
—up to my very throat. . . . (*They
embrace.*) Listen! Listen! My heart is
almost strangling me. . . . Come!
come! . . . Ah, how beautiful it is
in the shadows! . . .

MÉLISANDE. There is someone behind us!

PELLÉAS. I see no one. . . .

MÉLISANDE. I heard a noise. . . .

PELLÉAS. I hear only thy heart in the
dark. . . .

MÉLISANDE. I heard the crackling of dead
leaves. . . .

PELLÉAS. Because the wind is silent all at
once. . . . It fell as we were kissing.
. . .

MÉLISANDE. How long our shadows are
tonight! . . .

PELLÉAS. They embrace to the very end
of the garden. Oh, how they kiss far
away from us! . . . Look! look! . . .

MÉLISANDE (*in a stifled voice*). A-a-h!—
He is behind a tree!

PELLÉAS. Who?

MÉLISANDE. Golaud!

PELLÉAS.   Golaud!—Where?—I   see
nothing. . . .

MÉLISANDE. There . . . at the end of
our shadows. . . .

PELLÉAS. Yes, yes; I saw him. . . . Let
us not turn abruptly. . . .

MÉLISANDE. He has his sword. . . .

PELLÉAS. I have not mine. . . .

MÉLISANDE. He saw us kiss. . . .

PELLÉAS. He does not know we have
seen him. . . . Do not stir; do not
turn your head. . . . He would rush
headlong on us. . . . He will remain
there while he thinks we do not
know. He watches us. . . . He is still
motionless. . . . Go, go at once this
way. . . . I will wait for him. . . .
I will stop him. . . .

MÉLISANDE. No, no, no! . . .

PELLÉAS. Go! Go! He has seen all! . . .
He will kill us! . . .

MÉLISANDE. All the better! all the better!
all the better! . . .

PELLÉAS. He comes! He comes! . . .
Thy mouth! . . . Thy mouth! . . .

MÉLISANDE. Yes! . . . yes! yes! . . .
(*They kiss desperately.*)

PELLÉAS. Oh! oh! All the stars are falling! . . .

MÉLISANDE. Upon me, too! upon me, too!

PELLÉAS. Again! Again! . . . Give!
Give!

MÉLISANDE. All! all! all! . . .

[GOLAUD *rushes upon them, sword in hand,
and strikes* PELLÉAS, *who falls at the
brink of the fountain.* MÉLISANDE *flees
terrified.*]

MÉLISANDE (*fleeing*). Oh! Oh! I have no
courage! . . . I have no courage!
. . .

[GOLAUD *pursues her through the wood in
silence.*]

ACT V

SCENE I. *A lower hall in the castle*

The women servants discovered, gathered together, while without children are playing before one of the ventilators of the hall.

AN OLD SERVANT. You will see, you will see, my daughters; it will be tonight. —Someone will come to tell us by and by. . . .

ANOTHER SERVANT. They will not come to tell us. . . . They don't know what they are doing any longer. . . .

THIRD SERVANT. Let us wait here. . . .

FOURTH SERVANT. We shall know well enough when we must go up. . . .

FIFTH SERVANT. When the time is come, we shall go up of ourselves. . . .

SIXTH SERVANT. There is no longer a sound heard in the house. . . .

SEVENTH SERVANT. We ought to make the children keep still, who are playing before the ventilator.

EIGHTH SERVANT. They will be still of themselves by and by.

NINTH SERVANT. The time has not yet come. . . .

[*Enter an old Servant.*]

THE OLD SERVANT. No one can go in the room any longer. I have listened more than an hour. . . . You could hear the flies walk on the doors. . . . I heard nothing. . . .

FIRST SERVANT. Has she been left alone in the room?

THE OLD SERVANT. No, no; I think the room is full of people.

FIRST SERVANT. They will come, they will come, by and by. . . .

THE OLD SERVANT. Lord! Lord! It is not happiness that has come into the house. . . . One may not speak, but if I could say what I know. . . .

SECOND SERVANT. It was you who found them before the gate?

THE OLD SERVANT. Why, yes! why, yes! It was I who found them. The porter says it was he who saw them first; but it was I who waked them. He was sleeping on his face and would not get up.—And now he comes saying, "It was I who saw them first." Is that just?—See, I burned myself lighting a lamp to go down cellar. Now what was I going to do down cellar?—I can't remember any more what I was going to do down cellar.—At any rate, I got up very early; it was not yet very light; I said to myself, I will go across the courtyard, and then I will open the gate. Good; I go down the stairs on tiptoe, and I open the gate as if it were an ordinary gate. . . . My God! My God! What do I see? Divine a little what I see! . . .

FIRST SERVANT. They were before the gate?

THE OLD SERVANT. They were both stretched out before the gate! . . . Exactly like poor folk that are too hungry. . . . They were huddled together like little children who are afraid. . . . The little princess was nearly dead, and the great Golaud had still his sword in his side. . . . There was blood on the sill. . . .

SECOND SERVANT. We ought to make the children keep still. . . . They are screaming with all their might before the ventilator. . . .

THIRD SERVANT. You can't hear yourself speak. . . .

FOURTH SERVANT. There is nothing to be done: I have tried already; they won't keep still. . . .

FIRST SERVANT. It seems he is nearly cured?

THE OLD SERVANT. Who?

FIRST SERVANT. The great Golaud.

THIRD SERVANT. Yes, yes; they have taken him to his wife's room. I met them just now, in the corridor. They were holding him up as if he were drunk. He cannot yet walk alone.

THE OLD SERVANT. He could not kill himself; he is too big. But she is hardly wounded, and it is she who is going to die. . . . Can you understand that?

FIRST SERVANT. You have seen the wound?

THE OLD SERVANT. As I see you, my daughter.—I saw everything, you understand. . . . I saw it before all the others. . . . A tiny little wound under her little left breast—a little wound that wouldn't kill a pigeon. Is it natural?

FIRST SERVANT. Yes, yes; there is some-20 thing underneath. . . .

SECOND SERVANT. Yes; but she was delivered of her babe three days ago. . . .

THE OLD SERVANT. Exactly! . . . She was delivered on her deathbed; is that a little sign?—And what a child! Have you seen it?—A wee little girl a beggar would not bring into the world. . . . A little wax figure that 30 came much too soon; . . . a little wax figure that must live in lambs' wool. . . . Yes, yes; it is not happiness that has come into the house. . . .

FIRST SERVANT. Yes, yes; it is the hand of God that has been stirring. . . .

SECOND SERVANT. Yes, yes; all that did not happen without reason. . . .

THIRD SERVANT. It is as good Lord 40 Pelléas . . . where is he?—No one knows. . . .

THE OLD SERVANT. Yes, yes; everybody knows. . . . But nobody dare speak of it. . . . One does not speak of this; . . . one does not speak of that;

. . . one speaks no more of anything; . . . one no longer speaks truth. . . . But *I* know he was found at the bottom of Blind Man's Spring; . . . but no one, no one could see him. . . . Well, well, we shall only know all that at the last day. . . .

FIRST SERVANT. I dare not sleep here any longer. . . .

10 THE OLD SERVANT. Yes, yes; once illfortune is in the house, one keeps silence in vain. . . .

THIRD SERVANT. Yes; it finds you all the same. . . .

THE OLD SERVANT. Yes, yes; but we do not go where we would. . . .

FOURTH SERVANT. Yes, yes; we do not do what we would. . . .

FIRST SERVANT. They are afraid of us 20 now. . . .

SECOND SERVANT. They all keep silence. . . .

THIRD SERVANT. They cast down their eyes in the corridors.

FOURTH SERVANT. They do not speak any more except in a low voice.

FIFTH SERVANT. You would think they had all done it together.

SIXTH SERVANT. One doesn't know what 30 they have done. . . .

SEVENTH SERVANT. What is to be done when the masters are afraid? . . .
[*A silence.*]

FIRST SERVANT. I no longer hear the children screaming.

SECOND SERVANT. They are sitting down before the ventilator.

THIRD SERVANT. They are huddled against each other.

40 THE OLD SERVANT. I no longer hear anything in the house. . . .

FIRST SERVANT. You no longer even hear the children breathe. . . .

THE OLD SERVANT. Come, come; it is time to go up. . . . (*Exeunt, in silence.*)

SCENE II. *An apartment in the castle*

ARKËL, GOLAUD, *and the* PHYSICIAN *discovered in one corner of the room.* MÉLISANDE *is stretched upon her bed.*

THE PHYSICIAN. It cannot be of that little wound she is dying; a bird would not have died of it. . . . It is not you, then, who have killed her, good my lord; do not be so disconsolate. . . . 10 She could not have lived. . . . She was born without reason . . . to die; and she dies without reason. . . . And then, it is not sure we shall not save her. . . .

ARKËL. No, no; it seems to me we keep too silent, in spite of ourselves, in her room. . . . It is not a good sign. . . . Look how she sleeps . . . slowly, slowly; . . . it is as if her soul 20 was cold forever. . . .

GOLAUD. I have killed her without cause! I have killed her without cause! . . . Is it not enough to make the stones weep? . . . They had kissed like little children. . . .They had simply kissed. . . . They were brother and sister. . . . And I, and I at once! . . . I did it in spite of myself, look you. . . . I did it in spite of myself. 30 . . .

THE PHYSICIAN. Stop; I think she is waking. . . .

MÉLISANDE. Open the window; . . . open the window. . . .

ARKËL. Shall I open this one, Mélisande?

MÉLISANDE. No, no; the great window . . . the great window. . . . It is to see . . . 40

ARKËL. Is not the sea air too cold to-night?

THE PHYSICIAN. Do it; do it. . . .

MÉLISANDE. Thanks. . . . Is it sunset?

ARKËL. Yes; it is sunset on the sea; it is late.—How are you, Mélisande?

MÉLISANDE. Well, well.—Why do you ask that? I have never been better.—And yet it seems to me I know something. . . .

ARKËL. What sayest thou?—I do not understand thee. . . .

MÉLISANDE. Neither do I understand all I say, you see. . . . I do not know what I am saying. . . . I do not know what I know. . . . I no longer say what I would. . . .

ARKËL. Why, yes! why, yes! . . . I am quite happy to hear thee speak so; thou hast raved a little these last days, and one no longer understood thee. . . . But now all that is far away. . . .

MÉLISANDE. I do not know. . . .—Are you all alone in the room, grandfather?

ARKËL. No; there is the physician, besides, who cured thee. . . .

MÉLISANDE. Ah! . . .

ARKËL. And then there is still someone else. . . .

MÉLISANDE. Who is it?

ARKËL. It is . . . thou must not be frightened. . . . He does not wish thee the least harm, be sure. . . . If thou'rt afraid, he will go away. . . . He is very unhappy. . . .

MÉLISANDE. Who is it?

ARKËL. It is thy . . . thy husband. . . . It is Golaud. . . .

MÉLISANDE. Golaud is here? Why does he not come by me?

GOLAUD (*dragging himself toward the bed*). Mélisande . . . Mélisande. . . .

MÉLISANDE. Is it you, Golaud? I should hardly recognize you any more. . . . It is the evening sunlight in my eyes. . . . Why look you on the walls? You have grown thin and old. . . . Is it a long while since we saw each other?

GOLAUD. (*To* ARKËL *and the* PHYSICIAN.) Will you withdraw a moment, if you please, if you please? . . . I will leave the door wide open. . . . One moment only. . . . I would say something to her; else I could not die. . . . Will you?—Go clear to the end of the corridor; you can come back at once, at once. . . . Do not refuse me this. . . , I am a wretch. . . . (*Exit* ARKËL *and the* PHYSICIAN.) —Mélisande, hast thou pity on me, as I have pity on thee? . . . Mélisande? . . . Dost thou forgive me, Mélisande? . . .

MÉLISANDE. Yes, yes, I do forgive thee. . . . What must I forgive? . . .

GOLAUD. I have wrought thee so much ill, Mélisande. . . . I cannot tell thee the ill I have wrought thee. . . . But I see it, I see it so clearly today . . . since the first day. . . . And all I did not know till now leaps in my eyes tonight. . . . And it is all my fault, all that has happened, all that will happen. . . . If I could tell it, thou wouldst see as I do! . . . I see all! I see all! . . . But I loved thee so! . . . I loved thee so! . . . But now there is someone dying. . . It is I who am dying. . . . And I would know . . . I would ask thee. . . . Thou'lt bear me no ill-will . . . I would . . . The truth must be told to a dying man. . . . He must know the truth, or else he could not sleep. . . . Swearest thou to tell me the truth?

MÉLISANDE. Yes.

GOLAUD. Didst thou love Pelléas?

MÉLISANDE. Why yes; I loved him.— Where is he?

GOLAUD. Thou dost not understand me? —Thou wilt not understand me?—It seems to me . . . it seems to me . . . Well, then, here: I ask thee if thou lovedst him with a forbidden love? . . . Wert thou . . . were you guilty? Say, say, yes, yes, yes! . . .

MÉLISANDE. No, no; we were not guilty. —Why do you ask that?

GOLAUD. Mélisande! . . . tell me the truth, for the love of God!

MÉLISANDE. Why have I not told the truth?

GOLAUD. Do not lie so any more, at the moment of death!

MÉLISANDE. Who is dying?—Is it I?

GOLAUD. Thou, thou! And I, I too, after thee! . . . And we must have the truth. . . . We must have the truth at last, dost thou understand? . . . Tell me all! Tell me all! I forgive thee all! . . .

MÉLISANDE. Why am I going to die?—I did not know it. . . .

GOLAUD. Thou knowest it now! . . . It is time! It is time! . . . Quick! quick! . . . The truth! the truth! . . .

MÉLISANDE. The truth . . . the truth . . .

GOLAUD. Where art thou?—Mélisande! —Where art thou?—It is not natural! Mélisande! Where art thou!—Where goest thou? (*Perceiving* ARKËL *and the* PHYSICIAN *at the door of the room.*)— Yes, yes; you may come in. . . . I know nothing; it is useless. . . . It is too late; she is already too far away from us. . . . I shall never know! . . . I shall die here like a blind man! . . .

ARKËL. What have you done? You will kill her. . . .

GOLAUD. I have already killed her. . . .

ARKËL. Mélisande. . . .

MÉLISANDE. Is it you, grandfather?

ARKËL. Yes, my daughter. . . . What would you have me do?

MÉLISANDE. Is it true that the winter is beginning? . . .

ARKËL. Why dost thou ask?

MÉLISANDE. Because it is cold, and there are no more leaves. . . .

ARKËL. Thou art cold?—Wilt thou have the windows closed?

MÉLISANDE. No, no, . . . not till the sun be at the bottom of the sea.—It sinks slowly; then it is the winter beginning?

ARKËL. Yes.—Thou dost not like the winter?

MÉLISANDE. Oh! no. I am afraid of the cold.—I am so afraid of the great cold. . . .

ARKËL. Dost thou feel better?

MÉLISANDE. Yes, yes; I have no longer all those qualms. . . .

ARKËL. Wouldst thou see thy child?

MÉLISANDE. What child?

ARKËL. Thy child.—Thou art a mother. . . . Thou hast brought a little daughter into the world. . . .

MÉLISANDE. Where is she?

ARKËL. Here. . . .

MÉLISANDE. It is strange. I cannot lift my arms to take her. . . .

ARKËL. Because you are still very weak. . . . I will hold her myself; look. . . .

MÉLISANDE. She does not laugh. . . . She is little. . . . She is going to weep too. . . . I pity her. . . .

[*The room has been invaded, little by little, by the women servants of the castle, who range themselves in silence along the walls and wait.*]

GOLAUD (*rising abruptly*). What is the matter?—What are all these women coming here for? . . .

THE PHYSICIAN. It is the servants. . . .

ARKËL. Who was it called them?

THE PHYSICIAN. It was not I. . . .

GOLAUD. Why do you come here?—No one has asked for you. . . . What come you here to do?—But what is it, then?—Answer me! . . .

[*The servants make no answer.*]

ARKËL. Do not speak too loud. . . . She is going to sleep; she has closed her eyes. . . .

GOLAUD. It is not . . . ?

THE PHYSICIAN. No, no; see, she breathes. . . .

ARKËL. Her eyes are full of tears.—It is her soul weeping now. . . . Why does she stretch her arms out so?—What would she?

THE PHYSICIAN. It is toward the child, without doubt. . . . It is the struggle of motherhood against . . .

GOLAUD. At this moment?—At this moment?—You must say. Say! Say! . . .

THE PHYSICIAN. Perhaps.

GOLAUD. At once? . . . Oh! oh! I must tell her. . . .—Mélisande! . . . Mélisande! . . . Leave me alone! leave me alone with her! . . .

ARKËL. No, no; do not come near. . . . Trouble her not. . . . Speak no more to her. . . . You know not what the soul is. . . .

GOLAUD. It is not my fault! . . . It is not my fault!

ARKËL. Hush! . . . Hush! . . . We must speak softly now.—She must not be disturbed. . . . The human soul is very silent. . . . The human soul likes to depart alone. . . . It suffers so timorously. . . . But the sadness, Golaud . . . the sadness of all we see! . . . Oh! oh! oh! . . .

[*At this moment, all the servants fall suddenly on their knees at the back of the chamber.*]

ARKËL (*turning*). What is the matter!

THE PHYSICIAN (*approaching the bed and feeling the body*). They are right. . . .

[*A long silence.*]

ARKËL. I saw nothing.—Are you sure?

THE PHYSICIAN. Yes, yes.

ARKËL. I heard nothing. . . . So quick, so quick! . . . All at once! . . . She goes without a word. . . .

GOLAUD (*sobbing*). Oh! oh! oh!

ARKËL. Do not stay here, Golaud. . . . She must have silence now. . . . Come, come. . . . It is terrible, but it is not your fault. . . . 'Twas a little being, so quiet, so fearful, and so silent. . . . 'Twas a poor little mysterious being, like everybody. . . . She lies there as if she were the big sister of her child. . . . Come, come. . . . My God! My God! . . . I shall never understand it at all. . . . Let us not stay here.—Come; the child must not stay here in this room. . . . She must live now in her place. . . . It is the poor little one's turn. . . . (*They go out in silence.*)

PAUL CLAUDEL

THE TIDINGS BROUGHT TO MARY is a liturgical drama of a species rare in our time. Its ceremonial nature was affirmed by Lugné-Poë and the Théâtre de l'Ouevre when they chose Christmas Eve for its first performance in Paris in 1912; and again by the Theatre Guild when they introduced it to New York on Christmas Day, 1922. The mood of veneration and piety is rapturous and seraphic, in startling contrast to the prevailing atmosphere of cold objectivity and controlled observation that laves modern drama and fiction. The play is equally significant as a self-contained work of art, and as the product of an unusual dramatist. Claudel's intuitive and emotional experience with life has been quite different from that of most contemporary writers. It has convinced him of the truth of mystical visions unknown to most of us except partially and then through the intellect rather than as an act of faith.

The author of this play might have been describing his own consecration when he caused Pièrre de Craon to exclaim in wonder to the saintly Violaine, "Who are you, young girl, and what part in you has God reserved to Himself?" For some part of Paul Claudel was reserved when the successful consul, ambassador, and diplomat was fashioned, and that part was uppermost when he wrote *The Tidings Brought to Mary*. It was rooted in the pious traditions of his fathers' lands and in the faith of the generations of peasants that tilled them. It was brought to life by his own sudden conversion to the church.

Claudel's transformation began with the discovery of Rimbaud's poetry. He was eighteen years old, and he had been living for about five years in Paris, where his family had moved after the death of his grandfather. He was now a student at the Lycée Louis-le-Grand where the great skeptic, Ernest Renan, had patted him on the head when he received a prize. In June, 1886, he bought a copy of *Vogue* which contained Rimbaud's *Illuminations*. The effect was startling. He emerged at last, he said, "from that hideous world of Taine, of Renan, and of the other Molocks of the 19th century, from that prison, from that frightful mechanism entirely governed by perfect and inflexible laws, which, to make it worse, were knowable and teachable . . . I had a revelation of the supernatural."

Rimbaud's supernaturalism, empty of meaning though it was, led Claudel to the still greater and more revolutionary experience of conversion at Notre Dame on Christmas Day, 1886. We may read it in his own words: "I was beginning then to write, and it seemed to me that in the Catholic ceremonies, considered as a higher form of dilettantism, I was finding a means of excitation which happened to be possessed by some decadent services and rites. It was in such a mood that, elbowed and pushed about by the crowd, I attended with only a moderate amount of pleasure the High Mass. Then, not having anything better to do I returned to Vespers. The choir boys in white robes, and the young men of the junior seminary of St. Nich-

359

olas du Chardonnet, who accompanied them, were just about to sing that which I learned later to be the *Magnificat.* I was myself not sitting, but erect, standing by the second pillar at the entrance to the choir, at the right, on the sacristy side.—And it is then that was produced the event which dominates all my life. In an instant my heart was touched and I believed. I believed with such a clinging force, such a lifting up of my being, with so powerful a conviction, with such a certitude void of any kind of doubt, that since that time, not all the books, nor all the reasonings, nor all the vicissitudes of an agitated life, have been able to shake my faith, nor indeed to touch it. I had had all of a sudden a heart-rending sense of Innocence, of the eternal infancy of God, an unspeakable revelation."

The young man who had met God and experienced this mystical joy while the incense, the music, and the high ceremony had pressed upon him in the candlelight of Notre Dame, had come down from the fertile province in the Oisne-Aisne-Marne valley to the northeast of Paris. It is a mellow region steeped in the middle ages. Its cornfields and vineyards have been trampled century upon century by the feet of armies (and lately by the steel treads of tanks), marching against the storied cathedral towns of Laon, Soissons, and Rheims; but its peasants have survived each passing invasion to perpetuate their religious lore, not as a treasured legend, but as a living faith. Its legends are of a piece with that of Santa Maria Maggiore in Rome, where, in August, 352, the Virgin caused a patch of snow to appear covering the exact area set apart for the church; and of San Paolo alle Tre Fontane outside the city, where three fountains sprang up on the spots where St.

Paul's severed head rebounded from the ground. The peasants believe that the stones for the cathedral on the hill at Laon were dragged up there by the oxen of their own accord. Indeed Claudel's conversion at Notre Dame would seem an ideal and conclusive religious experience for a susceptible and poetic young man whose roots had been sunk in such uncommon rich soil. And under the effect of that tremendous experience he became the spokesman in poetry and drama for this vision of the meaning of life.

Claudel was born in the heart of chivalric France at Villeneuve-sur-Fère-en-Tardenois on August 6, 1868. His father was a reasonably well-to-do broker in mortgages and securities. The ancestral family-house, where they lived surrounded by the fields of Champagne, belonged to his mother's family. He attended a lycée in Paris, trained for the law with a view to the consular service, and at the age of twenty-four became vice-consul at New York in 1893. That was the beginning of a long and distinguished career that took him slowly round the world during the next forty years. He became vice-consul at Boston, consul at Foochow and other Chinese ports, and First Secretary at Pekin in 1906. After thirteen crucial years of study, meditation, and self-discipline in far away China, he was transferred to the hectic scene of pre-war Europe; to Prague in 1909, to Frankfort as Consul-General in 1911, to Hamburg in 1913. In the midst of the World War he became Minister at Rio de Janeiro, and at its close, Minister at Copenhagen. From 1921 to 1926 he was the French Ambassador at Tokyo, from 1926 to 1933 the Ambassador to the United States, and from 1933 to 1935 Ambassador to Belgium.

In 1935 he retired and took up residence again in Paris.

The poet and dramatist, it will be noted, survived the worldly demands made upon the statesman and the diplomat. The combination is not rare in France, nor does it seem unusual or surprising in French culture as it does in American—where it is all but nonexistent. The variety of experience with different nations in troubled times enlarged his catholic understanding and reaffirmed the universality of the human spirit and the will of God. It did not diffuse his energy or his central vision, but sharpened and deepened them. Particularly his long acquaintance with China and the Far East impressed him profoundly, as may be seen in his understanding studies of those civilizations in *Religion of the Signe, The Inner Wall of Tokyo, The Black Bird in the Rising Sun, La Connaissance de l'Est, Le Repos du Septième Jour*, a Chinese tragedy, and other writings.

Claudel has gone his own way in poetry and the drama, but his work is not unrelated to the movements of his country. As a youth in Paris he had been impressed by Baudelaire and the symbolists who gathered around Mallarmé. Like other young men of the time, he felt, as we have noted, the hypnosis of Rimbaud's *Illuminations*. His artistic maturity was concomitant with the mood of dissatisfaction with a naturalism that exalted scientific materialism and was preoccupied with our animality instead of with our souls and imagination. He also quickly saw the deadend of sterility down which the symbolists and the art-for-art's-sake aesthetes of the eighties and nineties were plunging for lack of a large and noble purpose. For both movements left out the illusive but no less real experience of

which Coleridge sang in "The Aeolian Harp," and which Wordsworth felt above Tintern Abbey when, his body almost asleep, he became a living soul and saw into the heart of things. This belief in the "something more" that once gave support to existence, this intuitive assurance of the heart that reason and the physical senses are not enough to apprehend the tormenting mystery of life, rescued Claudel's work from a decaying movement and gave it strength and purpose. The great Christian writers of the ages of faith were, he was sure, the only true mystics and symbolists; they were not lost in mere aesthetic sensations that were certain to pall, but they were aflame with zeal to reveal the nature of God and unite man to Him in the harmony of the universe.

Claudel's poetic creed, upon which the poems, the hymns and prayers, and even the religious dramas are formed, is painstakingly set down in his *Art Poétique*. Readers have found this work abstruse, and Claudel observed regretfully that it "has not been understood by anybody, so to say." No doubt many facets of his meaning in this tightly-phrased work escape us. But his central point is that the poet is like the original Adam in a new world—the namer of things. As a poet, Claudel attempts to reveal his perception of God, with whom he talks easily and informally, and his understanding of the universe which he has inspected, recognized, meditated upon, and named in sounds and symbols. This concept may be difficult to state abstractly, but the concrete poetic product is reasonably clear. Enough comes through in this treatise, or may be deduced from a sympathetic reading of his plays, to give us a comfortable illusion of understanding somewhat of the nature of his incommunicable world.

And a diplomat who has translated Aeschylus's *Agamemnon* and *Eumenides*, and written ritualistic dramas after a troubled day at the French Embassy, seems, somehow, to have retained a reassuring earthiness that we gladly welcome.

Claudel has written some fourteen plays since 1890 when *Tête d'Or*, which he called "the drama of earth possession," was published. They have included *The City* (1893) in which the conflicts of our time between science and poetry, world and spirit are dramatized, the title referring to the City of God; the loosely connected trilogy on retribution and sacrifice comprised in *L'Otage* (The Hostage) 1911, *Le Pain Dur* (Hard Bread) 1918, and *Le Père Humilie* (The Humiliated Father) 1920; *The Satin Slipper; or The Worst is Not the Surest*, 1924, and *The Book of Christopher Columbus*, 1929. All these plays contribute in one way or another to Claudel's Hound-of-Heaven theme, and all of them present difficulties in production that are usually overcome only by imaginative reading in the library.

The Tidings Brought to Mary is easily Claudel's masterpiece. It is one with the mystery plays. We are carried back into the living middle ages where the miracle that climaxes the drama offers no stumbling block to simple faith. Violaine's resurrection to life of Mara's dead child, the change in the color of its eyes, the drop of milk on its mouth, are as natural to this world as the sound of the feet of the Maid of Orleans and the clatter of armour on the crusaders marching to the tomb of Jesus that are heard in the background. The pilgrimage of Anne Vercours, who feels constrained to leave his well-loved acres and his wife to go to Jerusalem, "to that great hole in the earth—that the Cross made when it was set there," is as natural to this world as the fat barn at Cambernon and the bells of Monsanvierge being answered by faraway Rheims through the stillness of Michaelmas. The farm life of Picardy, the faith of the people, the strains caused by human weakness, the courage of human strength, the history of the time and the age of miracles are all woven into a play that aims at the permanent truths behind the changing aspects of thought and life.

The structure is simple, but the play is vibrant with the controlled excitement of Violaine and Pièrre, of Jacque and Mara, of Anne and Elizabeth his wife, and the forces of spirit that have caught them up. The tension mounts to the celebration of the miracle, the tidings that bind Mara to Mary, and to the rhapsody on life and death after Anne's return from his eight years of pilgrimage. Some of Claudel's own love of the earth and all creation that "seems to rest with God in a profound mystery" is tensely spoken by Anne as he ecstatically greets his farm:

Hail, Monsanvierge, lofty dwelling! . . .
All the aromatic odours of exile are little
  to me
Compared with this walnut leaf I crush
  between my fingers.
Hail, Earth, powerful and subdued!

The verse is written in rhythmic units based on breathing, akin to passages in Isaiah and in Walt Whitman, and adaptable to English translation.

This drama has been extraordinarily successful in Germany as well as in France. It profoundly affected the London audience which saw the first English performance in June, 1917, and listened to it "with that grave attention which is better than applause." At the splendid Theatre Guild performance, staged by T. Komisarjevsky and Lee

Simonson, the New York audiences were lukewarm, and found the Catholic mysticism "tormented, obscure, and sickly." The play is, of course, startlingly out of the mode of modern drama. For full appreciation of its beauty and power one must surrender his disbelief to the atmosphere of the legend, miracle, credulity, and faith of a by-gone age. Under those happy circumstances it achieves the high purpose of poetry, as Stephen Spender once so aptly stated it: "Poetry does not state truth, it states the conditions within which something felt is true."

THE TIDINGS BROUGHT TO MARY

CHARACTERS

ANNE VERCORS
ELISABETH, *his wife*
VIOLAINE, *his elder daughter*
MARA, *his younger daughter*
PIERRE DE CRAON
JACQUES HURY

THE MAYOR OF CHEVOCHE
WORKMEN
AN APPRENTICE
COUNTRYWOMEN
A NUN

The action takes place in France some time in the Middle Ages

PROLOGUE

The barn at Combernon. It is a lofty edifice, with square pillars that support a vaulted roof. It is empty except for the right wing, which is still filled with straw; and straws are scattered about on the floor, which is of well-trampled earth. At the back is a large double door in the thick wall, with complicated bars and bolts. On the valves of the door are painted rude images of St. Peter and St. Paul, one holding the keys, the other the sword. The scene is lighted by a large yellow wax candle in an iron socket fastened to one of the pillars.

The scenes of the drama take place at the close of the Middle Ages, seen conventionally, as mediaeval poets might have imagined classic antiquity.

The time is night, merging into the hours of dawn.

Enter, on a heavy horse, a man wearing a black cloak, and with a leathern bag on the horse's croup behind him, PIERRE DE CRAON. *His gigantic shadow moves across the wall, the floor, the pillars.*

Suddenly, from behind a pillar, VIOLAINE 20

steps out to meet him. She is tall and slender, and her feet are bare. Her gown is of coarse woollen stuff, and upon her head is a linen coif at once peasant-like and monastic.

VIOLAINE (*laughingly raising her hands toward him, with the forefingers crossed*). Halt, my lord cavalier! Dismount!

PIERRE DE CRAON. Violaine! (*He gets off the horse.*)

VIOLAINE. Softly, Master Pierre! Is that the way one leaves the house, like a thief without an honest greeting to the ladies?

10 PIERRE DE CRAON. Violaine, take yourself off. It is the dead of night, and we are here alone, the two of us.

And you know that I am not such a very safe man.

VIOLAINE. I am not afraid of you, mason! A man is not wicked merely because he wants to be!

And a man doesn't do with me just as he wills!

Poor Pierre! You did not even succeed in killing me
With your wretched knife! Nothing
but a little snick on my arm which
nobody has seen.

PIERRE DE CRAON. Violaine, you must
forgive me.

VIOLAINE. It is for that I came.

PIERRE DE CRAON. You are the first
woman I ever laid hands on. The 10
devil, who always seizes his chance,
took possession of me.

VIOLAINE. But you found me stronger
than him.

PIERRE DE CRAON. Violaine, I am even
more dangerous now than I was
then.

VIOLAINE. Must we then fight once
more?

PIERRE DE CRAON. Even my very pres- 20
ence here is baleful. (*Silence.*)

VIOLAINE. I don't know what you mean.

PIERRE DE CRAON. Had I not my work?
Stones enough to choose and
gather, wood enough to join, and
metals to melt and mould.
My own work, that suddenly I should
lay an impious and lustful hand on
the work of another, a living being?

VIOLAINE. In my father's house, the 30
house of your host! Lord! what
would they have said if they had
known? But I concealed it well.
And they all take you for a sincere
and blameless man, just as they did
before.

PIERRE DE CRAON. Under appearances,
God judges the heart.

VIOLANE. We three then will guard the
secret.   40

PIERRE DE CRAON. Violaine!

VIOLAINE. Master Pierre?

PIERRE DE CRAON. Stand there near the
candle that I may see you well.
(*She stands, smiling, under the candle.
He looks a long while at her.*)

VIOLAINE. Have you looked at me long
enough?

PIERRE DE CRAON. Who are you, young
girl, and what part in you has God
reserved to himself?
That the hand which touches you
with fleshly desire should in that
same instant be thus
Withered, as if it had approached too
near the mystery of his dwelling-
place?

VIOLAINE. What has happened to you,
then, since last year?

PIERRE DE CRAON. The very next day
after that one you remember . . .

VIOLAINE. Well——?

PIERRE DE CRAON. I discovered in my
side the horrible scourge.

VIOLAINE. The scourge, you say? What
scourge?

PIERRE DE CRAON. Leprosy, the same we
read of in the book of Moses.

VIOLAINE. What is leprosy?

PIERRE DE CRAON. Have you never heard
of the woman who lived alone
among the rocks of the Gèyn?
Veiled from head to foot, and with a
rattle in her hand?

VIOLAINE. That malady, Master Pierre?

PIERRE DE CRAON. Such a scourge it
is
That he who has it in its most mali-
cious form
Must be set apart at once,
For there is no living man so healthy
that leprosy cannot taint him.

VIOLAINE. Why, then, are you still at
liberty among us?

PIERRE DE CRAON. The Bishop gave me a
dispensation, and you must know
how few people I see,
Except my workmen to give them orders, and my malady is as yet secret
and concealed.
And, were I not there, who would
give away those newborn churches

whom God has confided to my care, on their wedding day?

VIOLAINE. Is that why nobody has seen you this time at Combernon?

PIERRE DE CRAON. I could not avoid returning here,

Because it is my duty to open the side of Monsanvierge

And to unseal the wall for each new flight of doves that seek entrance into the high Ark whose gates may only open toward heaven!

And this time we led to the altar an illustrious victim, a solemn censer,

The Queen herself, mother of the King, ascending in her own person,

For her son deprived of his kingdom.

And now I return to Rheims.

VIOLAINE. Maker of doors, let me open this one for you.   20

PIERRE DE CRAON. Was there no one else at the farm to do me this service?

VIOLAINE. The servant likes to sleep, and willingly gave me the keys.

PIERRE DE CRAON. Have you no fear or horror of the leper?

VIOLAINE. There is God, He knows how to protect me.

PIERRE DE CRAON. Give me the key, then.

VIOLAINE. No. Let me. You do not understand the working of these old doors.

Indeed! Do you take me for a dainty damsel

Whose taper fingers are used to nothing rougher than the spur, light as the bone of a bird, that arms the heel of her new knight?

You shall see! (*She turns the keys in the* 40 *two grinding locks and draws the bolts.*)

PIERRE DE CRAON. This iron is very rusty.

VIOLAINE. The door is no longer used. But the road is shorter this way. (*She strains at the bar.*)

I have opened the door!

PIERRE DE CRAON. What could resist such an assailant?

What a dust! the old valve from top to bottom creaks and moves,

The black spiders run away, the old nests crumble, and the door at last opens from the centre.

[*The door opens; through the darkness can be seen the meadows and the harvest. A feeble glimmer in the east.*]

VIOLAINE. This little rain has done everybody good.

PIERRE DE CRAON. The dust in the road will be well laid.

VIOLAINE (*in a low voice, affectionately*). Peace to you, Pierre!

[*Silence. And, suddenly, sonorous and clear and very high in the heaven, the first tolling of the Angelus.* PIERRE *takes off his hat, and both make the sign of the cross.*]

VIOLAINE (*her hands clasped and her face raised to heaven, in a voice beautifully clear and touching*). Regina Caeli, Laetare, alleluia!

[*Second tolling.*]

PIERRE DE CRAON (*in a hollow voice*). Quia quem meruisti portare, alleluia!

[*Third tolling.*]

VIOLAINE. Resurrexit sicut dixit, alleluia!

PIERRE DE CRAON. Ora pro nobis Deum. (*Pause.*)

VIOLAINE. Gaude et laetare, Virgo Maria, alleluia!

PIERRE DE CRAON. Quia resurrexit dominus vere, alleluia!

[*Peal of the Angelus.*]

PIERRE DE CRAON (*very low*). Oremus.

Deus qui per resurrectionem Filii tui Domini Nostri Jesu Christi mundum laetificare dignatus es, praesta, quaesumus, ut per ejus Genitricem Virginem Mariam perpetuae capiamus gaudia vitae. Per eundem Dominum Nostrum Jesum

Christum qui tecum vivit et regnat in unitate Spiritus Sancti Deus per omnia saecula saeculorum.

VIOLAINE. Amen. (*Both cross themselves.*)

PIERRE DE CRAON. How early the Angelus rings!

VIOLAINE. They say matins up there at midnight like the Carthusians.

PIERRE DE CRAON. I shall be at Rheims this evening. 10

VIOLAINE. Know you well the road?

First along this hedge,

And then by that low house in the grove of elder bushes, under which you will see five or six beehives.

And a hundred paces further on you reach the King's Highway. (*A pause.*)

PIERRE DE CRAON. Pax tibi.

How all creation seems to rest with 20 God in a profound mystery!

That which was hidden grows visible again with Him, and I feel on my face a breath as fresh as roses.

Praise thy God, blessed earth, in tears and darkness!

The fruit is for man, but the flower is for God and the sweet fragrance of all things born.

Thus the virtue of the holy soul that 30 is hidden is subtly revealed, as the mint leaf by its odour.

Violaine, who have opened the door for me, farewell!

I shall never return again to you.

O young tree of the knowledge of Good and Evil, behold how my dissolution begins because I have laid my hands upon you,

And already my soul and body are 40 being divided, as the wine in the vat from the crushed grape! What matters it? I had no need of woman.

I have never possessed a corruptible woman.

The man who in his heart has preferred God, sees when he dies his guardian Angel.

The time will soon come when another door opens,

When he who in this life has pleased but few, having finished his work, falls asleep in the arms of the eternal Bird:

When through translucent walls looms on all sides the sombre Paradise,

And the censers of the night mingle their scent with the odour of the noisome wick as it sputters out.

VIOLAINE. Pierre de Craon, I know that you do not expect to hear from me any false sighs, "Poor fellows!" or "Poor Pierres."

Because to him who suffers the consolation of a joyous comforter is not of much worth, for his anguish is not to us what it is to him.

Suffer with our Lord.

But know that your evil act is forgotten

So far as it concerns me, and that I am at peace with you,

And that I do not scorn or abhor you because you are stricken with the pest and malady,

But I shall treat you like a healthy man, and like Pierre de Craon, our old friend, whom I respect and love and fear.

What I say to you is true.

PIERRE DE CRAON. Thank you, Violaine.

VIOLAINE. And now I have something to ask you.

PIERRE DE CRAON. Speak.

VIOLAINE. What is this beautiful story that my father has told us? What is this "Justice" that you are building at Rheims, and that will be more beautiful than Saint-Rémy and Notre-Dame?

PIERRE DE CRAON. It is the church which the guilds of Rheims gave me to build on the site of the old Parcaux-Ouilles,[1]

There where the old Marc-de-l'Evêque [2] was burned down yesteryear.

Firstly, as a thank-offering to God for seven fat summers while distress reigned everywhere else in the king- 10 dom,

For abundant grain and fruit, for cheap and beautiful wool,

For cloth and parchment profitably sold to the merchants of Paris and Germany.

Secondly, for the liberties acquired, the privileges conferred by our Lord the King,

The old order issued against us by 20 Bishops Felix II and Abondant de Cramail

Rescinded by the Pope,

And all that by the aid of the bright sword and Champenois coins.

For such is the Christian commonwealth, without servile fear,

But that each should have his right, according to justice, in marvellous diversity,

That charity may be fulfilled.

VIOLAINE. But of which King and of which Pope do you speak? For there are two, and one does not know which is the good one.

PIERRE DE CRAON. The good one is he who is good to us.

VIOLAINE. You do not speak rightly.

PIERRE DE CRAON. Forgive me. I am only an ignorant man.

VIOLAINE. And whence comes this name given to the new parish?

PIERRE DE CRAON. Have you never heard of Saint Justice who was

martyred in an anise field in the time of the Emperor Julian?

(The anise seeds which they put in our gingerbread at the Easter fair.)

As we were trying to divert the waters of a subterranean spring, to make way for our foundations,

We discovered her tomb, with this inscription on a slab of stone, broken in two: Justitia Ancilla Domini in Pace.

The fragile little skull was broken like a nut—she was a child of eight years—

And a few milk teeth still adhere to the jaw.

For which all Rheims is filled with admiration, and many signs and miracles follow the body

Which we have laid in a chapel, to await the completion of our work.

But under the great foundation stone we have left, like seed, the little teeth.

VIOLAINE. What a beautiful story! And father also told us that all the ladies of Rheims give their jewels for the building of the Justice.

30 PIERRE DE CRAON. We have a great heap of them, and many Jews around them like flies.

[VIOLAINE *has been looking down and turning hesitatingly a massive gold ring which she wears on her fourth finger.*]

PIERRE DE CRAON. What ring is that, Violaine?

VIOLAINE. A ring that Jacques gave me. (*Silence.*)

40 PIERRE DE CRAON. I congratulate you.
    [*She holds out the ring to him.*]

VIOLAINE. It is not yet settled. My father has said nothing.

Well! That is what I wanted to tell you.

Take my beautiful ring, which is all I

---

[1] Sheep-fold.
[2] The bishop's still.

have, and Jacques gave it to me secretly.

PIERRE DE CRAON. But I do not want it!

VIOLAINE. Take it quickly, or I shall no longer have the strength to part with it. (*He takes the ring.*)

PIERRE DE CRAON. What will your betrothed say?

VIOLAINE. He is not really my betrothed yet. 10

The loss of a ring does not change the heart. He knows me. He will give me another of silver. This one was too fine for me.

PIERRE DE CRAON (*examining it*). It is of vegetable gold which, in former times, they knew how to make with an alloy of honey.

It is as supple as wax, and nothing can break it. 20

VIOLAINE. Jacques turned it up in the ground when he was ploughing, in a place where they sometimes find old swords turned quite green, and pretty bits of glass.

I was afraid to wear such a pagan thing, which belongs to the dead.

PIERRE DE CRAON. I accept this pure gold.

VIOLAINE. And kiss my sister Justice for 30 me.

PIERRE DE CRAON (*looking suddenly at her, as if struck with an idea*). Is that all you have to give me for her? a bit of gold taken off your finger?

VIOLAINE. Will that not be enough to pay for one little stone?

PIERRE DE CRAON. But Justice is a large stone herself.

VIOLAINE (*laughing*). I am not from the 40 same quarry.

PIERRE DE CRAON. The stone needed for the base is not the stone needed for the pinnacle.

VIOLAINE. Then, if I am a stone, may it be that useful one that grinds the corn, coupled to the twin millstone.

PIERRE DE CRAON. And Justitia also was only a humble little girl at her mother's side,

Until the moment God called her to the confession of faith.

VIOLAINE. But nobody wishes me ill! Is it necessary that I should go preach the Gospel to the Saracens?

PIERRE DE CRAON. It is not for the stone to choose its own place, but for the Master of the Work who chose the stone.

VIOLAINE. Then praised be God who has given me mine now, and I have no longer to seek it. And I ask him for no other.

I am Violaine, I am eighteen years old, my father's name is Anne Vercors, my mother's name is Elisabeth,

My sister's name is Mara, my betrothed is named Jacques. There, that is all, there is nothing more to know.

Everything is perfectly clear, all is arranged beforehand, and I am very glad.

I am free, I have nothing to trouble me; another will lead me, the poor man, and he knows everything that there is to do.

Sower of steeples, come to Combernon! we will give you stone and wood, but you shall not have the daughter of the house!

And, besides, is this not already the house of God, the land of God, the service of God?

Have we not charge over lonely Monsanvierge, which we must feed and guard, providing it with bread, wine, and wax,

Being a dependency of this lonely eyrie of angels with half-spread wings?

Thus, as the great lords have their dovecot, we too have ours, which is known from a great distance away.

PIERRE DE CRAON. One day as I went through the forest of Fisme, I heard two beautiful oak trees talking together,

Praising God for making them immovable on the spot where they were born. 10

Now one of them, in the prow of an ocean raft, makes war upon the Turks,

The other, felled under my care, supports Jehanne, the good bell in the tower of Laon, whose voice is heard ten leagues away.

Young girl, in my craft one does not keep one's eyes in one's pocket.

I know the good stone under the juni- 20 per trees, and the good wood like a master woodpecker;

In the same way, men and women.

VIOLAINE. But not girls, Master Pierre! That is too subtle for you.

And in the first place, there is nothing at all to know.

PIERRE DE CRAON (*in a low voice*). You love him dearly, Violaine?

VIOLAINE (*lowering her eyes*). That is a 30 great mystery between us two.

PIERRE DE CRAON. Blessed be thou in thy pure heart!

Holiness is not to get oneself stoned by the Turks, or to kiss a leper on the mouth,

But to obey promptly God's commands.

Whether it be

To stay where we are, or to ascend 40 higher.

VIOLAINE. Ah, how beautiful the world is, and how happy I am!

PIERRE DE CRAON (*speaking low*). Ah, how beautiful the world is, and how unhappy I am!

VIOLAINE (*pointing to the sky*). Man of the city, listen! (*Pause.*)

Do you hear high up there that little soul singing?

PIERRE DE CRAON. It is the lark!

VIOLAINE. It is the lark, alleluia! The lark of the Christian earth, alleluia, alleluia!

Do you hear it cry four times, he! he! he! he! higher, higher!

Do you see it, the eager little cross, with its wings spread, like the seraphim who have only wings and no feet, singing shrilly before the throne of God?

PIERRE DE CRAON. I hear it.

And it is thus I heard it once at dawn, on the day we dedicated my daughter Notre-Dame de la Couture,

And a golden point gleamed at the topmost pinnacle of this great thing I had made, like a star new-born!

VIOLAINE. Pierre de Craon, if you had done with me as you would,

Would you be more happy now because of that, or I more beautiful?

PIERRE DE CRAON. No, Violaine.

VIOLAINE. And would I still be the same Violaine whom you loved?

PIERRE DE CRAON. No, not she, but another.

VIOLAINE. And which is better, Pierre, That I share my joy with you, or that I share your pain?

PIERRE DE CRAON. Sing far up in the highest heaven, lark of France!

VIOLAINE. Forgive me, for I am too happy, because he whom I love Loves me, and I am sure of him, and I know he loves me, and all is equal between us.

And because God made me to be happy and not for evil nor any sorrow.

PIERRE DE CRAON. Mount to heaven in a single flight!

As for me, to ascend a little I must have the whole of a cathedral, with its deep foundations.

VIOLAINE. And tell me that you forgive Jacques for marrying me.

PIERRE DE CRAON. No, I do not forgive him.

VIOLAINE. Hatred does you no good, Pierre, and makes me grieve.

PIERRE DE CRAON. It is you who make 10 me speak.

Why do you force me to show the ugly wound that no one sees?

Let me go, and ask me nothing more. We shall not see each other any more.

All the same, I carry away his ring!

VIOLAINE. Leave your hatred in its place, and I will give it back to you when you have need of it. 20

PIERRE DE CRAON. But besides, Violaine, I am very wretched.

It is hard to be a leper, to bear this shameful wound, knowing that there is no cure and that there is no help for it,

But that each day it spreads and bites deeper; and to be alone and to suffer one's own poison, to feel oneself alive in corruption,

Not only to taste death once, aye, ten 30 times, but to miss nothing, even to the end, of the horrible alchemy of the tomb!

It is you who have brought this evil upon me by your beauty, for before I saw you I was pure and happy,

My heart lost in my work and ideas, under another's command. 40

And now that I command in my turn, and draw the plans,

Behold, you turn your face toward me with that poisonous smile.

VIOLAINE. The poison was not in me, Pierre!

PIERRE DE CRAON. I know it, it was in me, and it is still there, and this sick flesh has not cured the tainted soul!

O little soul, was it possible that I should see you and not love you?

VIOLANE. And certainly you have shown that you love me.

PIERRE DE CRAON. It is my fault if the fruit hangs on the branch?

And who is he who loves and does not desire all?

VIOLAINE. And that is why you tried to destroy me?

PIERRE DE CRAON. Man, cruelly injured, has his infernal shades, too, like woman.

VIOLAINE. In what have I failed you?

PIERRE DE CRAON. O image of eternal Beauty, thou art not for me!

VIOLAINE. I am not an image!

That is not the way to speak!

PIERRE DE CRAON. Another takes from you that which was for me.

VIOLAINE. The image remains.

PIERRE DE CRAON. Another takes Violaine from me, and leaves me this tainted flesh and this consumed mind.

VIOLAINE. Be a man, Pierre! Be worthy of the flame which consumes you!

And if one must be consumed, let it be like the Paschal-candle, flaming on its golden candelabrum in the midst of the choir for the glory of all the Church!

PIERRE DE CRAON. So many sublime pinnacles! But shall I never see the roof of my own little house under the trees?

So many belfries whose circling shadows write the hour for all the city! But shall I never design an oven, and the room for the children?

VIOLAINE. It was not for me to take for myself alone what belongs to all.

PIERRE DE CRAON. When will the wedding be, Violaine?

VIOLAINE. At Michaelmas, I suppose, when the harvest is done.

PIERRE DE CRAON. On that day, when the bells of Monsanvierge have spoken and are silent, listen well and you will hear me answer them far away at Rheims.

VIOLAINE. Who takes care of you there? 10

PIERRE DE CRAON. I have always lived like a workman; it is enough for me if I have a bunch of straw between two stones, a leathern coat, and a little bacon on my bread.

VIOLAINE. Poor Pierre!

PIERRE DE CRAON. I am not to be pitied for that; we are set apart.

I do not live as other men, as I am always under the ground with the 20 foundations, or in the sky with the belfry.

VIOLAINE. Well! We could never have lived together! My head swims if I only go up to the hayloft.

PIERRE DE CRAON. This church alone will be my wife, drawn from my side like an Eve of stone, in the slumber of pain.

May I soon feel my great structure 30 rising under me, and lay my hand on this indestructible thing I have made, whose parts hold firmly together, this solid work which I have constructed of strong stone that the Holy Sacrament may be placed there, my work that God inhabits!

I shall never come down again! It is I at whom they point, that group of 40 young girls with arms interlaced, on the chequered pavement a hundred feet below!

VIOLAINE. You must come down. Who knows but I shall have need of you some day?

PIERRE DE CRAON. Farewell, Violaine, my soul, I shall never see you again!

VIOLAINE. Who knows that you will never see me again?

PIERRE DE CRAON. Farewell, Violaine!

How many things I have already done! How many things remain for me to do, how much building up of habitations!

Darkness, with God.

Not the hours of the office in a breviary, but the real hours of a cathedral, where the sun brings light and shade successfully to every part.

I take away your ring,

And of its little circle I will make golden seed!

"God caused the deluge to cease," as says the baptismal psalm,

And I, between the walls of the Justice, shall imprison the gold of the dawn!

The light of day changes, but not that which I shall distil under those arches,

Like the light of the human soul, that the Host may dwell in the midst of it.

The soul of Violaine, my child, in whom my heart delights.

There are churches like pits, and others which are like furnaces,

And others so delicately put together, adjusted with such art, that they seem as if they would ring like a bell under a finger-tap.

But that which I am going to build will lie under its own shadow like condensed gold, and like a pyx full of manna!

VIOLAINE. O Master Pierre, what a beautiful stained-glass window you gave to the monks of Clinchy!

PIERRE DE CRAON. The staining of glass is not my art, though I know something of it.

But, before the glass is made, the architect, by his knowledge of arrangement, makes the stone framework like a filter in the waves of God's Light,

And gives to the whole edifice its individual lustre, as to a pearl.

[MARA VERCORS *enters and watches them without being seen.*]

And now farewell! The sun is risen, 10 and I ought already to be far on my road.

VIOLAINE. Farewell, Pierre!

PIERRE DE CRAON. Farewell, Violaine!

VIOLAINE. Poor Pierre! (*She looks at him with eyes full of tears, hesitates, and offers him her hand. He seizes it, and while he holds it between his own she leans towards him and kisses him on the face.*)

[MARA *makes a gesture of surprise and goes out.*]

[PIERRE DE CRAON *and* VIOLAINE *go out by the different doors.*]

ACT I

SCENE ONE

The kitchen of Combernon, a spacious room having a great fireplace with an emblazoned mantel; in the middle of the room a long table and all the domestic utensils, as in a picture by Breughel. THE MOTHER, *stooping before the hearth, tries to revive the fire.* 20 ANNE VERCORS, *standing, looks at her. He is a tall and strong man of sixty years, with a full blond beard streaked with much white.*

THE MOTHER (*without turning around*). Why do you look at me like that?

ANNE VERCORS (*thinking*). The end, already! It is like coming to the last page in a picture book.   30 "When the night had passed, the woman having revived the household fire . . .," and the humble and touching story is finished.

It is as if I were no longer here. There she is, before my eyes, yet seeming already like something only remembered. (*Aloud.*)

O wife, it is a month since we were married   40

With a ring which is shaped like *Oui*,

A month of which each day is a year.

And for a long time you were fruitless

Like a tree which gives nothing but shade.

And one day we looked at each other

And it was the middle of our life,

Elisabeth! and I saw the first wrinkles on thy forehead and around thine eyes.

And, as on our wedding day,

We clasped and embraced each other, no longer with lightness of heart,

But with the tenderness and compassion and piety of our mutual trust.

And between us was our child and the modesty

Of this sweet narcissus, Violaine.

And then the second was born to us,

Mara the black. Another daughter, and not a son. (*Pause.*)

Well now, say what you have to say, for I know

When you begin speaking without looking at you, saying something and nothing. Come now!

THE MOTHER. You know well that one can tell you nothing. You are never there, and I must even catch you to sew on a button.

And you do not listen to one, but like a watchdog you watch,

Only attentive to the noises of the door.

But men never understand anything.

ANNE VERCORS. Now the little girls are grown up.

THE MOTHER. They? No.

ANNE VERCORS. To whom are we going to marry them all?

THE MOTHER. Marry them, Anne, say you? We have plenty of time to think of that.

ANNE VERCORS. Oh, deceit of woman! Tell me! When think you anything But first you do not say just the contrary; maliciousness! I know thee.

THE MOTHER. I won't say anything more.

ANNE VERCORS. Jacques Hury.

THE MOTHER. Well?

ANNE VERCORS. There. I will give him Violaine . . .

And he will take the place of the son I have not had. He is an upright and industrious man.

I have known him since he was a little lad, and his mother gave him to us.

It is I who have taught him everything,

Grain, cattle, servants, arms, tools, our neighbours, our betters, custom —God—

The weather, the nature of this ancient soil,

How to reflect before speaking.

I have seen him develop into a man while he was looking at me and the beard grow around his kind face,

As he is now, straight-backed and tight like the ears of the barley.

And he was never one of those who contradict, but who reflect, like the earth which receives all kinds of grain.

And that which is false, not taking root, dies;

And so, one may not say that he believes in truth, but rather that it grows within him, having found nourishment.

THE MOTHER. How do you know, if they love each other or not?

ANNE VERCORS. Violaine Will do what I tell her.

As for him, I know that he loves her, and you too know it.

Yet the blockhead dares not speak to me. But I will give her to him if he wants her. So shall it be.

THE MOTHER. Yes. No doubt that is as it should be.

ANNE VERCORS. Have you nothing more to say?

THE MOTHER. What, then?

ANNE VERCORS. Very well, I will go seek him.

THE MOTHER. What, seek him? Anne!

ANNE VERCORS. I want everything to be settled at once. I will tell you why presently.

THE MOTHER. What have you to tell me? —Anne, listen a moment. . . . I fear. . . .

ANNE VERCORS. Well?

THE MOTHER. Mara Slept in my room this winter, while you were ill, and we talked at night in our beds.

Surely he is an honest lad, and I love him like my own child, almost.

He has no property, that is true, but he is a good ploughman, and comes of a good family.

We could give them Our Demi-muids farm with the lower fields which are too far away for us.

—I, too, wanted to speak to you of him.

ANNE VERCORS. Well?

THE MOTHER. Well, nothing. No doubt Violaine is the eldest.

ANNE VERCORS. Come, come, what then?

THE MOTHER. What then? How do you know surely that he loves her?— Our old friend, Master Pierre

THE TIDINGS BROUGHT TO MARY

(Why did he keep away from us
this time without seeing anybody?),
You saw him last year when he came,
And how he looked at her while she
served us.—
Certainly he has no land, but he earns
much money.
—And she, while he spoke,
How she listened to him, with her
eyes wide open like a child's,   10
Forgetting to pour the drink for us,
so that I had to scold her!
—And Mara, you know her. You
know how hard-headed she is!
If she has a notion then
That she will marry Jacques—heigh-
ho! She is hard as iron.
I don't know! Perhaps it would be
better . . .

ANNE VERCORS. What is all this non-   20
sense?

THE MOTHER. Very well! Very well! we
can talk like that. You must not
get angry.

ANNE VERCORS. It is my will.
Jacques shall marry Violaine.

THE MOTHER. Well! he shall marry her,
then.

ANNE VERCORS. And now, mother, I
have something else to tell you,   30
poor old woman! I am going away.

THE MOTHER. You are going away? You
are going away, old man? What is
that you say?

ANNE VERCORS. That is why Jacques
must marry Violaine without delay, and take my place here.

THE MOTHER. Lord! You are going
away! You mean it? And where are
you going?   40

ANNE VERCORS (pointing vaguely toward the
south). Down there.

THE MOTHER. To Château?

ANNE VERCORS. Farther than Château.

THE MOTHER (lowering her voice). To
Bourges, to the other King?

ANNE VERCORS. To the King of Kings,
to Jerusalem.

THE MOTHER. Lord! (She sits down.)
Is it because France is not good
enough for you?

ANNE VERCORS. There is too much sorrow in France.

THE MOTHER. But we are very comfortable here and nobody troubles
Rheims.

ANNE VERCORS. That is it.

THE MOTHER. That is what?

ANNE VERCORS. The very thing; we are
too happy,
And the others not happy enough.

THE MOTHER. Anne, that is not our
fault.

ANNE VERCORS. It is not theirs, either.

THE MOTHER. I don't know. I know that
you are there and that I have two
children.

ANNE VERCORS. But you see, surely, that
everything is upset and put out of
its right place, and everybody seeks
distractedly to find where that
place is.
And the smoke we see sometimes in
the distance is not merely the smoke
of burning straw.
And these crowds of poor people who
come to us from every side.
There is no longer a King reigning
over France, according to the pre-
diction of the prophet.[1]

THE MOTHER. That is what you read to
us the other day?

[1] "For, behold the Lord, the Lord of hosts,
doth take away from Jerusalem and from
Judah, the stay and the staff, the whole stay of
bread, and the whole stay of water.
"The mighty man, and the man of war, the
judge, and the prophet, and the prudent, and
the ancient.
"The captain of fifty, and the honourable
man, and the counsellor, and the cunning
artificer, and the eloquent orator.
"And I will give children to be their princes,
and babes shall rule over them."—Isaiah iii.
1-5

ANNE VERCORS. In the place of the King
we have two children.

The English one, in his island,

And the other one, so little that
among the reeds of the Loire he
cannot be seen.

In place of the Pope we have three
Popes, and instead of Rome, I
don't know what council or other
in Switzerland.

All is struggling and moving,

Having no longer any counterweight
to steady it.

THE MOTHER. And you, also, where do
you want to go?

ANNE VERCORS. I can no longer stay
here.

THE MOTHER. Anne, have I done anything to grieve you?

ANNE VERCORS. No, my Elisabeth.   20

THE MOTHER. Here you abandon me in
my old age.

ANNE VERCORS. Give me leave to go,
yourself.

THE MOTHER. You do not love me any
more and you are no longer happy
with me.

ANNE VERCORS. I am weary of being
happy.

THE MOTHER. Scorn not the gift which 30
God has given you.

ANNE VERCORS. God be praised who has
overwhelmed me with his goodness!

For these thirty years now I have held
this sacred fief from my father, and
God has sent rain on my furrows.

For ten years there has not been one
hour of my work

That he has not repaid four times
over and more,   40

As if it were not his will to keep open
his account with me, or leave anything owing.

All else perished, yet I was spared;

So that I shall appear before him
empty and without a claim, among

those who have received their re
ward.

THE MOTHER. It is enough to have
grateful heart.

ANNE VERCORS. But I am not satisfie
with his benefits,

And because I have received them
shall I leave the greater good t
others?

10 THE MOTHER. I do not understand you

ANNE VERCORS. Which receives more
the full or the empty vessel?

And which has need of the mos
water, the cistern or the spring?

THE MOTHER. Ours is nearly dried u
by this long hot summer.

ANNE VERCORS. Such has been the evil o
this world, that each has wanted t
enjoy his own as if it had been
created for him,

And not at all as if he had received it
by the will of God,

The lord his estate, the father his
children,

The King his Kingdom and the
scholar his rank.

That is why God has taken away from
them all these things which can be
taken away,

And has sent to each man deliverance
and fasting.

And why is the portion of others not
mine also?

THE MOTHER. You have your duty here
with us.

ANNE VERCORS. Not if you will absolve
me from it.

THE MOTHER. I will not absolve you.

ANNE VERCORS. You see that what I had
to do is done.

The two children are reared, and
Jacques is there to take my place.

THE MOTHER. Who calls you far away
from us?

ANNE VERCORS (smiling). An angel blowing a trumpet.

HE MOTHER. What trumpet?

NNE VERCORS. The soundless trumpet that is heard by all.

The trumpet that calls all men from time to time that the portions may be distributed afresh.

The trumpet in the valley of Jehosaphat before it has made a sound,

That of Bethlehem when Augustus numbered the people. 10

The trumpet of the Assumption, when the apostles were assembled.

The voice which takes the place of the Word when the Chief no longer speaks

To the body that seeks union with him.

HE MOTHER. Jerusalem is so far away!

NNE VERCORS. Paradise is still farther.

HE MOTHER. God in the tabernacle is 20 with us even here.

NNE VERCORS. But not that great hole in the earth.

HE MOTHER. What hole?

NNE VERCORS. That the Cross made when it was set there.

Behold how it draws everything to itself.

There is the stitch which cannot be undone, the knot which cannot be 30 untied,

The heritage of all, the interior boundary stone that can never be uprooted,

The centre and the navel of the world, the element by which all humanity is held together.

THE MOTHER. What can one pilgrim alone do?

ANNE VERCORS. I am not alone! A great 40 multitude rejoice and depart with me!

The multitude of all my dead,

Those souls, one above the other, of whom nothing is left now but the tombstones, all those stones bap-

tized with me who claim their rightful place in the structure!

And as it is true that the Christian is never alone, but is in communion with all his brothers,

The whole kingdom is with me, invoking, and drawing near to the Seat of God, taking anew its course toward him,

And I am its deputy and I carry it with me

To lay it once again upon the eternal Pattern.

THE MOTHER. Who knows but that we shall need you here?

ANNE VERCORS. Who knows but that I am needed elsewhere?

Everything is shaking; who knows but that I obstruct God's plan by remaining here

Where the need there was of me is past?

THE MOTHER. I know you are an inflexible man.

ANNE VERCORS (tenderly, changing his voice). To me you are always young and beautiful, and very great is the love I feel for my black-haired sweet Elisabeth.

THE MOTHER. My hair is grey!—

ANNE VERCORS. Say yes, Elisabeth. . . .

THE MOTHER. Anne, you have not left me in all these thirty years. What will become of me without my chief and my companion?

ANNE VERCORS. . . . The yes which will separate us now, very low,

As round as the oui that formerly made us one. (Silence.)

THE MOTHER (speaking very low). Yes, Anne.

ANNE VERCORS. Have patience, Zabillet! I shall soon return.

Can you not have faith in me a little while, though I am not here!

Soon will come another separation.

Come, put food for two days in a bag.
It is time I was off.

THE MOTHER. What? Today, even today?

ANNE VERCORS. Even today. (*Her head
droops and she does not move. He takes
her in his arms but she does not respond.*)
Farewell, Elisabeth.

THE MOTHER. Alas, old man, I shall
never see you again.

ANNE VERCORS. And now I must seek 10
Jacques.

SCENE TWO

[*Enter* MARA.]

MARA (*to* THE MOTHER). Go, and tell him
she is not to marry him.

THE MOTHER. Mara! How is this? You
were there?

MARA. Go, I tell you, and tell him she is
not to marry him.   20

THE MOTHER. What she? What he? What
do you know of her marrying
him?

MARA. I was there. I heard it all.

THE MOTHER. Very well, my child! Your
father wishes it.
You have seen I did what I could, and
his mind is not changed.

MARA. Go and tell him that she is not to
marry him, or I will kill myself!   30

THE MOTHER. Mara!

MARA. I will hang myself in the wood-
house, there where we found the cat
hung.

THE MOTHER. Mara! Wicked girl!

MARA. There again she has taken him
away from me! Now she has taken
him away!
It was always I who was to be his
wife, and not she.
She knows very well it is I.   40

THE MOTHER. She is the eldest.

MARA. What does that matter?

THE MOTHER. It is your father who
wishes it.

MARA. I don't care.

THE MOTHER. Jacques Hury
Loves her.

MARA. That is not true! I know we
enough that you do not love me!
You have always loved her best! Ol
when you talk of your Violaine it i
like talking of sugar,
It is like sucking a cherry just whei
you are about to spit out th
stone!
But Mara the magpie! She is as hard
as iron, she is as sour as the wil
cherry!
Added to that, there's always the tall
of your Violaine being so beautiful
And behold, she is now to have Com
bernon!
What does she know how to do, the
ferret? which of us two can drive
the cart?
She thinks herself like Saint Onze
millevierges!
But, as for me, I am Mara Vercors
who hates injustice and deceit,
Mara who speaks the truth, and it is
that which makes the servant:
angry!
Let them be angry! I scorn them. No
one of the women dares stir in my
presence, the hypocrites! Everything goes as smoothly as at the
mill.
—And yet everything is for her and
nothing for me.

THE MOTHER. You will have your share.

MARA. Aye, truly! The sandy ground up
yonder! ooze and mud that it needs
five oxen to plough! the bad ground
of Chinchy.

THE MOTHER. It brings in good profit all
the same.

MARA. Surely.
Long-rooted reeds and cow-wheat,
senna, and mullein!
I shall have enough to make my
herb-tea.

HE MOTHER. Bad girl; you know well
enough that is not true!
You know well no wrong is done you!
But you have always been wicked!
When you were little
You would not cry when you were
beaten.
Tell me, you black-skinned child, you
ugly one!
Is she not the eldest?
What have you against her?
Jealous girl! Yet she has always done
what you wish.
Very well! She will be married first,
and you will be married, you also,
afterwards!
And it is too late to do differently,
anyhow, because your father is go-
ing away—oh, how sad I am!
He has gone to speak to Violaine and 20
he will look for Jacques.

MARA. That's true! Go at once! Go, go at
once!

THE MOTHER. Go where?

MARA. Mother, come now! You know
well I am the one. Tell him she is
not to marry him, *maman!*

THE MOTHER. Surely I shall do no such
thing.

MARA. Only tell him what I have said. 30
Tell him that I will kill myself. Do
you understand? (*She looks fixedly at
her.*)

THE MOTHER. Ha!

MARA. Do you believe I will not do it?

THE MOTHER. Alack, I know you would!

MARA. Go then!

THE MOTHER. O
Obstinate!

MARA. You have nothing to do with it. 40
Only to repeat to him just what I have
said.

THE MOTHER. And he—how do you
know he will be willing to marry
you?

MARA. Certainly he will not.

THE MOTHER. Well. . . .

MARA. Well?

THE MOTHER. Don't think that I shall advise him to do your will!— on the
contrary!
I will only tell him what you have
said. It is very sure
That she will not be so silly as to give
in to you, if she will listen to me.

10 MARA. Perhaps.—Go.—Do as I say.
(*She goes out.*)

SCENE THREE

[*Enter* ANNE VERCORS *and* JACQUES HURY,
afterwards VIOLAINE, *and then the farm
labourers and servants.*]

ANNE VERCORS (*stopping*). Heh! what is
that thou tell'st me?

JACQUES HURY. Just as I say! This time I
took him in the act, with the prun-
ing-hook in his hand!
I came up softly behind him and all
of a sudden
Flac! I threw myself full length on
him,
As you throw yourself on a hare in her
hole at harvest
And there beside him was a bunch of
twenty young poplars, the ones you
set such store by!

ANNE VERCORS. Why did he not come to
me? I should have given him the
wood he needed.

JACQUES HURY. The wood he needs is the
handle of my whip!
It is not need but wickedness, the idea
of doing wrong!
These ne'er-do-wells from Chevoche
are always ready to do anything
Out of bravado, and to defy people!
But as to that man, I will cut off his
ears with my little knife!

ANNE VERCORS. No.

JACQUES HURY. At least let me tie him by
his wrists to the harrow, before the
big gate,

With his face turned against the teeth;
with Faraud the dog to watch him.

ANNE VERCORS. Not that either.

JACQUES HURY. What is to be done then?

ANNE VERCORS. Send him home.

JACQUES HURY. With his bundle of wood?

ANNE VERCORS. And with another that
thou wilt give him.

JACQUES HURY. Father, that is not right.

ANNE VERCORS. Thou canst tie his faggot 10
around, that he may not lose any
of it.

That will help him in crossing the
ford at Saponay.

JACQUES HURY. It is not well to be lax
about one's rights.

ANNE VERCORS. I know it, it is not well!
Jacques, behold how lazy and old I
am, weary of fighting and defending. 20
Once I was harsh like thee.

There is a time to take and a time to
let take.

The budding tree must be protected,
but the tree where the fruit hangs
do not trouble thyself about.

Let us be unjust in very little, lest
God be unjust to me in much.

—And besides, thou wilt do now as
thou wilt, for thou art placed over 30
Combernon in my stead.

JACQUES HURY. What do you say?

THE MOTHER. He is going a pilgrim to
Jerusalem.

JACQUES HURY. Jerusalem?

ANNE VERCORS. It is true. I start this very
moment.

JACQUES HURY. What? What does that
mean?

ANNE VERCORS. Thou hast heard very 40
well.

JACQUES HURY. Thou wilt leave us like
that, when the work is at its heavi-
est?

ANNE VERCORS. It is not necessary to
have two masters at Combernon.

JACQUES HURY. My father, I am only
your son!

ANNE VERCORS. Thou wilt be the father
here, in my stead.

JACQUES HURY. I do not understand you

ANNE VERCORS. I am going away. Take
Combernon from me

As I took it from my father, and he
from his,

And Radulphe the Frank, first of our
line, from Saint Rémy de Rheims,

Who from Genevieve of Paris received
this land, pagan and bristling with
seedlings and wild thorns.

Radulphe and his children made it
Christian by iron and by fire

And laid it naked and broken under
the waters of baptism.

Hill and plain scored they with equal
furrows,

As an industrious scholar copies line
after line the word of God.

And they began to build Monsanvierge on the mountain, in that
place where Evil was worshipped,

(And at first there was naught but a
cabin made of logs and reeds,
whose door the Bishop came to
seal,

And two holy recluses were left to
guard it),

And at the mountain's base, Combernon, a dwelling armed and provisioned.

Thus this land is free that we hold
from Saint Rémy in heaven, paying
tithes up there to this flight, one
moment stayed, of murmuring
doves.

For everything is of God, and those
who live in Him reap without ceasing the fruits of their works,

Which pass and come back to us
again in their time in magnificent
succession:

As over the various harvests every day

in summer float those great clouds that drift toward Germany.

The cattle here are never sick, the udders and the wells are never dry; the grain is as solid as gold, the straw as firm as iron.

And for defence against pillagers we have arms, and the walls of Combernon, and the King, our neighbour.

Gather this harvest that I have sown, 10 as in the past I myself have filled again the furrows my father ploughed.

O joyful work of the farmer, for which the sun is as bright as our glistening ox, and the rain is our banker, and God works with us every day, making of everything the best!

Others look to men for their rewards, but we receive ours straight from 20 heaven itself,

A hundred for one, the full ear for a seed, and the tree for a nut.

For such is the justice of God to us, and the measure with which He repays us.

The earth cleaves to the sky, the body to the spirit, all things that He has created are in communion, all have need of one another.   30

Take the handles of the plough in my stead, that the earth may bring forth bread as God Himself has wished.

Give food to all creatures, men and animals, to spirits and bodies, and to immortal souls.

You, women, labourers, look! Behold the son

I have chosen, Jacques! I am going away and he stays in my place. 40 Obey him.

JACQUES HURY. May it be done according to your will.

ANNE VERCORS. Violaine! My child, first born instead of the son I have not had!

Heir of my name in whom I too shall be given to another!

Violaine, when thou shalt have a husband, do not scorn the love of thy father.

For thou canst not give back to a father what he has given thee, when thou wouldst.

Between husband and wife everything is equal; what they do not know they accept, one from the other, with faith.

This is the mutual religion, this is the servitude through which the wife's breast grows large with milk!

But the father, seeing his children separate from him, recognizes what was once within himself. My daughter, know thy father!

A Father's love

Asks no return, and the child has no need either to win or merit it:

As it was his before the beginning, so it remains

His blessing and his inheritance, his help, his honour, his right, his justification!

My soul is never divided from the soul I have transmitted.

What I have given can never be given back. Only know, O my child, that I am thy father!

And of my issue there is no male. Only women have I brought into the world.

Nothing but that thing in us which gives and which is given.

—And now the hour of parting is come.

VIOLAINE. Father! Do not say such a cruel thing!

ANNE VERCORS. Jacques, you are the man whom I love. Take her! I give you my daughter, Violaine. Take my name from her.

Love her, for she is as pure as gold.

All the days of thy life, like bread, of which one never tires.

She is simple and obedient, sensitive and reserved.

Do not cause her any sorrow, and give her only kindness.

Everything here is thine, except what will be given to Mara, in accordance with my plan.

JACQUES HURY. What, my father, your daughter, your property . . .

ANNE VERCORS. I give you all at once, as all is mine.

JACQUES HURY. But who knows if she still cares for me?

ANNE VERCORS. Who knows?

[VIOLAINE *looks at* JACQUES *and forms "Yes" with her lips, without speaking.*]

JACQUES HURY. You care for me, Violaine?

VIOLAINE. My father wishes it.

JACQUES HURY. You wish it too?

VIOLAINE. I wish it too.

JACQUES HURY. Violaine!

How shall we get on together?

VIOLAINE. Consider well while there is yet time!

JACQUES HURY. Then I take you by God's command, and I will nevermore let you go. (*He takes her by both hands.*)

I have you and hold you, your hand and the arm with it, and all that comes with the arm.

Parents, your daughter is no longer yours! She is mine only!

ANNE VERCORS. Well, they are married; it is done!

What say you, mother?

THE MOTHER. I am very glad! (*She weeps.*)

ANNE VERCORS. She weeps, my wife!

There! that is how they take our children from us and we shall be left alone,

The old woman who lives on a little milk and a small bit of cake,

And the old man with his ears full of white hairs like the heart of an artichoke.

—Let them make ready the wedding-dress!

—Children, I shall not be at your wedding.

VIOLAINE. What, father!

THE MOTHER. Anne!

ANNE VERCORS. I am going. Now.

VIOLAINE. O father! before we are married.

ANNE VERCORS. It must be. Your mother will explain all to you.

[*Enter* MARA.]

THE MOTHER. How long shall you stay over there?

ANNE VERCORS. I do not know. It may be but a short time.

I shall soon be coming back. (*Silence.*)

VOICE OF A CHILD (*in the distance*). Oriole, oriole! all alone!

Who eats the wild cherry and throws out the stone!

ANNE VERCORS. The oriole, rosy and golden, whistles in the heart of the tree.

What does he say? that after these long days of heat

The rain last night was like a shower of gold falling upon the earth.

What does he say? he says it is good weather for ploughing.

What more does he say? that the weather is fine, that God is great, and that it is still two hours of noon.

What more does the little bird say?

That it is time for the old man to go Elsewhere, and leave the world to itself.

—Jacques, I leave to you all my property—protect these women.

JACQUES HURY. What, are you really going?

ANNE VERCORS. I believe he has heard nothing.

JACQUES HURY. Like that, right away?

ANNE VERCORS. The hour is come.

THE MOTHER. You will not go without first eating?

[*During this time the women servants have prepared the table for the farm meal.*]

ANNE VERCORS (*to a woman servant*). Ho! my bag, my hat!

Bring my shoes! bring my cloak!

I have not time enough to share this meal with you.

THE MOTHER. Anne! How long wilt thou stay over there? One year, two years? More than two years?

ANNE VERCORS. One year. Two years. Yes, that is it.

Put on my shoes.

[THE MOTHER *kneels before him and puts on his shoes.*]

For the first time I leave thee, O house!

Combernon, lofty dwelling!

Watch faithfully over it all! Jacques will be here in my stead.

There is the hearth where there is always fire, there is the long table where I give food to my people.

All take your places! Just once more I will cut the bread. . . . (*He seats himself at the head of the long table, with* THE MOTHER *at his right. All the men and women servants stand, each at his place. He takes the bread, making the sign of the cross above it with the knife, and cuts it; and gives it to* VIOLAINE *and* MARA *to pass. The last piece he keeps himself. Then he turns solemnly toward* THE MOTHER *and opens his arms.*)

Farewell, Elisabeth!

THE MOTHER (*weeping in his arms*). Thou wilt never see me more.

ANNE VERCORS (*in a lower tone*). Farewell, Elisabeth. (*He turns toward* MARA, *looks gravely at her for a long time, and then holds out his hand to her.*)

Farewell, Mara! be virtuous.

MARA (*kissing his hand*). Farewell, father!

[*Silence.* ANNE VERCORS *stands, looking before him as if he did not see* VIOLAINE, *who stands full of agitation at his side. At last he turns slightly toward her, and she puts her arms around his neck, sobbing, with her face against his breast.*]

ANNE VERCORS (*to the men servants, as if he noticed nothing*). Farewell, all!

I have always dealt justly by you. If anyone denies this, he lies.

I am not like other masters. But I praise when praise is due, and I reprove when reproof is due.

Now that I am going away, do your duty as if I were there.

For I shall return. I shall return some time when you do not expect me. (*He shakes hands with them all.*)

Let my horse be brought! (*Silence. He leans toward* VIOLAINE, *who continues to embrace him.*)

What is it, little child?

You have exchanged a husband for thy father.

VIOLAINE. Alas! Father! Alas! (*He removes her hands gently from around his neck.*)

THE MOTHER. Tell me when will you return.

ANNE VERCORS. I cannot tell.

Perhaps it will be in the morning, perhaps at mid-day, when you are eating.

And perhaps, awaking some night, you will hear my step on the road.

Farewell! (*He goes.*)

ACT II

SCENE ONE

A fortnight later. The beginning of July. Noon.

A large orchard planted with regular rows of round trees. Higher, and a little withdrawn, the wall and towers and long buildings with tiled roofs of Combernon. Then, the side of the hill, which rises abruptly, and on its summit the massive stone arch of Monsanvierge, 10 *without door or window, with its five towers like those of the Cathedral of Laon, and in its side the great white scar made for the recent entrance of the Queen Mother of France.*

Everything vibrates under an ardent sun.

[*A woman's voice on high, from the height of the highest tower of Monsanvierge.*]

Salve regina mater misericordiae
Vita dulcedo et spes nostra salve
Ad te clamamus exules filii hevae   20
Ad te suspiramus gementes et flentes
  in hac lacrymarum valle eia ergo
  advocata nostra illos tuos miseri-
  cordes oculos ad nos converte
Et jesum benedictum fructum ventris
  tui nobis post hoc exilium ostende
O clemens
O pia
O dulcis virgo maria
[*Long pause during which the stage remains* 30
  empty.]
        [*Enter* THE MOTHER *and* MARA.]
MARA. What did she say?
THE MOTHER. I drew her out as we
  talked, without seeming to.
  You see how she has lost her gay
  spirits these last few days.
MARA. She never talks much.
THE MOTHER. But she does not laugh any 40
  more.
  That troubles me.
  Perhaps it is because Jacquin is away,
  but he returns today.
  —And her father too is gone.

MARA. That is all thou saidst to her?
THE MOTHER. That is what I said to her,
  and the rest of it without changing
  a word, just as you said it to me:
  Jacquin and you: that you love him
  and all.
  And I added, and I said it over two or
  three times, that this time she must
  not be foolish, and not resist at all,
  Or break off the marriage, which is
  as good as made, against the
  father's will.
  What would people think of it?
MARA. And what did she answer?
THE MOTHER. She began to laugh, and I,
  I began to cry.
MARA. I will make her laugh!
THE MOTHER. It was not the laughter I
  love of my little girl, and I began
  to cry.
  And I said, "No, no, Violaine, my
  child!" not knowing any longer
  what I said.
  But she, without speaking, made a
  sign with her hand that she wanted
  to be alone.
  Ah! what misery we have with our
  children!
MARA. Hush!
THE MOTHER. What is it?   30
  I am sorry for what I have done.
MARA. Well! Do you see her down there
  in the paddock? She is walking behind the trees.
  Now she is out of sight.
[*Silence. From behind the scene is heard the
  blast of a horn.*]
THE MOTHER. There is Jacquin come
  back. I know the sound of his horn.
40 MARA. Let us go further off. (*They move off.*)

SCENE TWO
        [*Enter* JACQUES HURY.]
JACQUES HURY (*looking all around*). I don't
  see her.

And yet she sent word
That she wanted to see me this morn-
ing,
Here.

[*Enter* MARA. *She advances to* JACQUES, *and
at six paces before him drops a ceremo-
nious courtesy.*]

JACQUES HURY. Good morning, Mara.

MARA. My lord, your servant!

JACQUES HURY. What is this foolery? 10

MARA. Do I not owe you respect? Are
you not the master here, dependent
only upon God, like the King of
France himself and the Emperor
Charlemagne?

JACQUES HURY. Jest if you like, but it is
true all the same! Yes, Mara, it is
glorious! Dear sister, I am too
happy!

MARA. I am not your *dear* sister! I am 20
your servant because I must be.
Man of Braine! son of a serf! I am
not your sister; you are not of our
blood!

JACQUES HURY. I am the husband of
Violaine.

MARA. You are not that yet.

JACQUES HURY. I shall be tomorrow.

MARA. Who knows?

JACQUES HURY. Mara, I have thought 30
deeply about it,
And I believe you have only dreamed
that story you told me the other day.

MARA. What story?

JACQUES HURY. Don't pretend not to
know.
That story about the mason, that secret kiss at dawn.

MARA. It is possible. I did not see well.
Yet I have good eyes. 40

JACQUES HURY. And it has been whispered to me that the man is a leper!

MARA. I do not love you, Jacques.
But you have the right to know all.
All must be pure and clear at
Monsanvierge, which is held up

like a monstrance before all the
kingdom.

JACQUES HURY. All that will be explained
in a moment.

MARA. You are clever and nothing can
escape you.

JACQUES HURY. I see at any rate that you
don't love me.

MARA. There! there! What did I say?
what did I say?

JACQUES HURY. Everybody here is not of
your mind.

MARA. You speak of Violaine? I blush for
that little girl.
It is shameful to give oneself like that,
Soul, body, heart, skin, the outside,
the inside, and the root.

JACQUES HURY. I know that she belongs
entirely to me.

MARA. Yes.
How grandly he speaks! how sure he
is of the things that belong to him!
Brainard of Braine!
Only those things belong to one that
one has made, or taken, or earned.

JACQUES HURY. But, Mara, I like you,
and I have nothing against you.

MARA. Without doubt—like all the rest
of the things here?

JACQUES HURY. It is no fault of mine that
you are not a man, and that I take
your property from you!

MARA. How proud and satisfied he is!
Look at him, he can hardly keep
from laughing!
There now! don't do yourself harm!
Laugh! (*He laughs.*)
I know your face well, Jacques.

JACQUES HURY. You are angry because
you cannot make me unhappy.

MARA. Like the other day while the
father was talking,
When one of your eyes smiled and the
other wept—without tears.

JACQUES HURY. Am I not master of a fine
estate?

MARA. And the father was old, wasn't he? You know a thing or two more than he does?

JACQUES HURY. To each man his day.

MARA. That is true, Jacques, you are a tall and handsome young man.

See him, how he blushes.

JACQUES HURY. Don't torment me.

MARA. All the same, it is a pity!

JACQUES HURY. What is a pity?

MARA. Farewell, husband of Violaine! Farewell, master of Monsanvierge —ah—ah!

JACQUES HURY. I will show you that so I am.

MARA. Then understand the spirit of this place, Brainard of Braine!

He thinks that everything is his, like a peasant; you will be shown the contrary!

Like a peasant who sees nothing higher than himself as he stands in the midst of his flat little field!

But Monsanvierge belongs to God, and the master of Monsanvierge is God's man, who has nothing

For himself, having received everything for another.

That is the lesson passed on here from father to son. There is no higher position than ours.

Take on the spirit of your masters, peasant! (*She makes as if to go and turns back.*)

Ah!

Violaine, when I met her,

Gave me a message for you.

JACQUES HURY. Why did you not say so sooner?

MARA. She is waiting for you near the fountain.

SCENE THREE

The fountain of the Adoue. It is a large square orifice cut in a vertical wall, built of blocks of limestone. A thin stream of water drips from it with a melancholy sound. Thank-offerings of crosses made of straw and bouquets of faded flowers are hung on the wall.

The fountain is surrounded with luxurious trees, and with a bower of rosebushes whose abundant blossoms thickly star the green foliage.

JACQUES HURY (*he looks at* VIOLAINE *who comes along the winding path. She is all golden, and glows brilliantly at moments when the sun falls upon her between the leaves*). O my betrothed among the flowery branches, hail!

[VIOLAINE *enters and stands before him. She is clothed in a linen gown with a kind of dalmatic of cloth-of-gold decorated with large red and blue flowers. Her head is crowned with a diadem of enamel and gold.*]

Violaine, how beautiful you are!

VIOLAINE. Jacques! Good morning, Jacques! Ah, how long you stayed down there!

JACQUES HURY. I had to get rid of everything, and sell, in order to be perfectly free.

To be the man of Monsanvierge only and yours.

—What is this wonderful dress?

VIOLAINE. I wore it for you. I had spoken to you about it. Do you not recognize it?

It is the habit of the nuns of Monsanvierge, except only the maniple, the habit they wear in the choir,

The deacon's dalmatic which they have the privilege of wearing, something priestly, as they themselves are holy sacrifices,

And the women of Combernon have the right to wear it twice:

First, on the day of their betrothal, Secondly, on the day of their death.

JACQUES HURY. It is really true, then,

that this is the day of our betrothal, Violaine?

VIOLAINE. Jacques, there is yet time, we are not married yet!

If you have only wanted to please my father there is still time to withdraw; it concerns no one but us. Say but a word, and I would not want you any more, Jacques.

For nothing has yet been put in writing, and I do not know if I still please you.

JACQUES HURY. How beautiful you are, Violaine!

And how beautiful is the world of which you are the portion reserved for me.

VIOLAINE. It is you, Jacques, who are all that is best in the world.

JACQUES HURY. Is it true that you are willing to belong to me?

VIOLAINE. Yes, it is true! good morning, my beloved! I am yours.

JACQUES HURY. Good morning, my wife! Good morning, sweet Violaine!

VIOLAINE. These are good things to hear, Jacques!

JACQUES HURY. You must always be there! Tell me that you will always be the same, the angel who is sent to me!

VIOLAINE. For evermore all that is mine shall always be yours.

JACQUES HURY. And as for me, Violaine.
. . .

VIOLAINE. Say nothing. I ask you nothing. You are there, and that is enough for me. Good morning, Jacques!

Ah, how beautiful this hour is, and I ask for nothing more.

JACQUES HURY. Tomorrow will be still more beautiful!

VIOLAINE. Tomorrow I shall have taken off my gorgeous robe.

JACQUES HURY. But you will be so near to me that I shall no longer be able to see you.

VIOLAINE. Very near to you indeed!

JACQUES HURY. Your place is ready.

Violaine, what a solitary spot this is, and how secretly I am here with you!

VIOLAINE (*in a low tone*). Your heart is enough.

Go to, I am with you, and say not a word more.

JACQUES HURY. But tomorrow, before everybody,

I will take this Queen in my arms.

VIOLAINE. Take her, and do not let her go.

Ah, take your little one with you so that they can never find her, and never do her any harm!

JACQUES HURY. And you will not regret then the linen and the gold?

VIOLAINE. Was I wrong to make myself beautiful for one poor little hour?

JACQUES HURY. No, my beautiful lily, I can never tire of looking at you in your glory!

VIOLAINE. O Jacques! tell me again that you think me beautiful!

JACQUES HURY. Yes, Violaine!

VIOLAINE. The most beautiful of all, and the other women are nothing to you?

JACQUES HURY. Yes, Violaine.

VIOLAINE. And that you love me only, as the tenderest husband loves the poor creature who has given herself to him?

JACQUES HURY. Yes, Violaine.

VIOLAINE. Who gives herself to him with all her heart, Jacques, believe me, and holds nothing back.

JACQUES HURY. And you, Violaine, do you not believe me then?

VIOLAINE. I believe you, I believe you, Jacques!

I believe in you! I have confidence in you, my darling!

JACQUES HURY. Why, then, do you seem troubled and frightened?
Show me your left hand. (*She shows it.*)
My ring is gone.

VIOLAINE. I will explain that to you presently, you will be satisfied.

JACQUES HURY. I am satisfied, Violaine. I have faith in you.

VIOLAINE. I am more than a ring, Jacques. I am a great treasure.

JACQUES HURY. Yes, Violaine.

VIOLAINE. Ah, if I give myself to you,
Will you not know how to save your little one who loves you?

JACQUES HURY. There you are doubting me again.

VIOLAINE. Jacques! After all I do no harm in loving you. It is God's will, and my father's.
It is you who have charge of me! And who knows if you will not know perfectly how to defend and save me?
It is enough that I give myself entirely to you.
The rest is your affair, and no longer mine.

JACQUES HURY. And is it like this you give yourself to me, my flower-o'-the-sun?

VIOLAINE. Yes, Jacques.

JACQUES HURY. Who then can take you out of my arms?

VIOLAINE. Ah, how big the world is, and how alone we are!

JACQUES HURY. Poor child! I know that your father is gone.
And I too no longer have anyone with me to tell me what should be done, and what is good or ill.
You must help me, Violaine, as I love you.

VIOLAINE. My father has abandoned me.

JACQUES HURY. But I remain to you, Violaine.

VIOLAINE. Neither my mother nor my sister love me, though I have done them no wrong.
And nothing is left to me but this tall, terrible man whom I do not know.
[*He tries to take her in his arms. She pushes him away quickly.*]
Do not touch me, Jacques!

JACQUES HURY. Am I then a leper?

VIOLAINE. Jacques, I want to speak to you—ah, but it is hard!
Do not fail me, who now have only you!

JACQUES HURY. Who would do you harm?

VIOLAINE. Know what you do in taking me for your wife!
Let me speak to you very humbly, my lord Jacques,
Who are about to receive my soul and my body from the hands of God according to his command, and my father's who made them.
And know the dowry I bring to you which is not like those of other women,
But this holy mountain wrapped in prayer day and night before God, like an altar smoking always,
And this lamp whose light is never suffered to go out, and whose oil it is our duty to replenish.
And no man is witness to our marriage, but that Lord whose fief we alone hold,
Who is the Omnipotent, the God of the Armies.
And it is not the sun of July that lights us, but the light of his countenance.
To the holy be the holy things! Who knows if our heart be pure?
Never until now has a male been lacking to our race, and always the sacred place has been handed down from father to son,
And behold, for the first time it falls

into the hands of a woman, and becomes with her the object of desire.

JACQUES HURY. Violaine—no: I am not a scholar nor a monk nor a saint.

I am not the lay-servant of Monsanvierge, nor the keeper of its turning-box.

I have a duty and I will perform it,

Which is to feed these murmuring birds, 10

And to fill each morning the basket they lower from the sky.

That is written down. That is right.

I have understood that, and I have fixed it in my head, and you must not ask any more of me.

You must not ask me to understand what is above me, and why these holy women have imprisoned themselves up there in that pigeon-house. 20

To the heavenly be heaven, and the earth to the earthly.

For the wheat will not grow by itself, and a good ploughman is necessary.

And I can say without boasting that such I am, and no one can teach me that, not even your father himself perhaps,

For he was old and set in his ways. 30

To each one his own place, and that is justice.

And your father, in giving you to me, Together with Monsanvierge, knew what he was doing, and that was just.

VIOLAINE. But Jacques, I do not love you because it is just.

And even if it were not just, I would love you the same, and more.

JACQUES HURY. I do not understand you, 40 Violaine.

VIOLAINE. Jacques, do not make me speak! You love me so much, and I can only do you harm.

Let me alone! there cannot be justice between us two! but only faith and

charity. Go away from me while there is yet time.

JACQUES HURY. I do not understand, Violaine.

VIOLAINE. My beloved, do not force me to tell you my great secret.

JACQUES HURY. A great secret, Violaine?

VIOLAINE. So great that all is over, and you will not ask to marry me any more.

JACQUES HURY. I do not understand you.

VIOLAINE. Am I not beautiful enough just now, Jacques? What more do you ask of me?

What does one ask of a flower

Except to be beautiful and fragrant for a moment, poor flower, and then—the end.

The flower's life is short, but the joy it has given for a minute

Is not of those things which have a beginning and an end.

Am I not beautiful enough? Is something lacking? Ah! I see thine eyes, my beloved! Is there anything in thee at this moment that does not love me, and that doubts me?

Is my soul not enough? Take it, and I am still here, and absorb to its depths that which is all thine!

To die requires but a moment, and to die in each other would not annihilate us more than love, and does one need to live when one is dead?

What more wouldst thou do with me? Fly, take thyself away! Why dost thou wish to marry me? Why dost thou wish

To take for thyself what belongs only to God?

The hand of God is upon us, and thou canst not defend me!

O Jacques, we shall never be husband and wife in this world!

JACQUES HURY. Violaine, what are these strange words, so tender, so bitter?

By what threatening and gloomy paths are you leading me?

I believe you wish to put me to the proof, and to triumph over me, who am but a simple and rough man.

Ah! Violaine, how beautiful you are like this! and yet I am afraid, and I see you in clothing that terrifies me!

For this is not a woman's dress, but the robe of one who offers the sacri- [10] fice at the altar,

Of him who waits upon the priest, leaving the side uncovered and the arms free!

Ah, I see, it is the spirit of Monsanvierge which lives in you, the supreme flower outside of this sealed garden!

Ah, do not turn to me that face which is no longer of this world! that is no [20] longer my dear Violaine.

There are enough angels to serve the mass in heaven!

Have pity on me, who am only a man without wings, who rejoiced in this companion God had given me, and that I should hear her sigh with her head resting on my shoulder!

Sweet bird! the sky is beautiful, but it is beautiful too to be taken captive! [30]

And the sky is beautiful! but this is a beautiful thing too, and even worthy of God, the heart of a man that can be filled, leaving no part empty.

Do not torment me by depriving me of your face!

And no doubt I am a dull and ugly man,

But I love you, my angel, my queen, [40] my darling!

VIOLAINE. So I have warned you in vain, and you want to take me for your wife, and you will not give up your plan?

JACQUES HURY. Yes, Violaine.

VIOLAINE. When a man takes a woman for his wife they are then one soul in one body, and nothing will ever separate them.

JACQUES HURY. Yes, Violaine.

VIOLAINE. You wish it!

Then it is not right that I should reserve anything, or keep to myself any longer

This great, this unspeakable secret.

JACQUES HURY. Again this secret, Violaine?

VIOLAINE. So great, truly, Jacques,

That your heart will be saturated with it,

And you will ask nothing more of me,

And that we shall never be torn apart from each other.

A secret so deep

That neither life, Jacques, nor hell, nor Heaven itself

Will ever end it, or will ever end this

Moment in which I have revealed it, here in the burning

Heat of this terrible sun which almost prevents us from seeing each other!

JACQUES HURY. Speak, then!

VIOLAINE. But tell me first once more that you love me.

JACQUES HURY. I love you!

VIOLAINE. And that I am your wife and your only love?

JACQUES HURY. My wife, my only love.

VIOLAINE. Tell me, Jacques: neither my face nor my soul has sufficed thee, and that is not enough?

And have you been misled by my proud words? Then learn of the fire which consumes me!

Know this flesh which you have loved so much!

Come nearer to me. (*He comes nearer.*)

Nearer! nearer still! close against my side. Sit down on that bench. (*Silence.*)

And give me your knife.

[*He gives her his knife. She cuts the linen of her gown, at her side upon the heart, under the left breast, and leaning towards him she opens the slit with her hands and shows him the flesh where the first spot of leprosy has appeared. Silence.*]

JACQUES HURY (*slightly turning away his face*). Give me the knife. (*She gives it to him. Silence. Then Jacques moves a few steps away from her, half turning his back, and he does not look at her again until the end of the Act.*)

JACQUES HURY. Violaine, I am not mistaken? What is this silver flower emblazoned on your flesh?

VIOLAINE. You are not mistaken.

JACQUES HURY. It is the malady? it is the malady, Violaine?

VIOLAINE. Yes, Jacques.

JACQUES HURY. Leprosy!

VIOLAINE. Surely you are hard to convince. And you had to see it to believe.

JACQUES HURY. And which leprosy is the most hideous,
That of the soul or that of the body?

VIOLAINE. I cannot say as to the other. I only know that of the body, which is bad enough.

JACQUES HURY. No, you know not the other, reprobate?

VIOLAINE. I am not a reprobate.

JACQUES HURY. Infamous woman, reprobate,
Infamous in your soul and in your flesh!

VIOLAINE. So you do not ask any more to marry me, Jacques?

JACQUES HURY. Scoff no more, child of the devil!

VIOLAINE. Such is that great love you had for me.

JACQUES HURY. Such is this lily that I had chosen.

VIOLAINE. Such is the man who takes the place of my father.

JACQUES HURY. Such is the angel that God had sent me.

VIOLAINE. Ah, who will tear us apart from each other? I love you, Jacques, and you will defend me, and I know that in thy arms I have nothing to fear.

JACQUES HURY. Do not mock thyself with these horrible words!

VIOLAINE. Tell me,
Have I broken my word? My soul was not enough for thee? Have you enough now of my flesh?
Will you forget henceforth your Violaine, and the heart she revealed to thee?

JACQUES HURY. Go farther away from me!

VIOLAINE. Go to, I am far enough away, Jacques; you have nothing to fear.

JACQUES HURY. Yes, yes.
Further than you were from that measled pig of yours!
That maker of bones whereon the flesh rots!

VIOLAINE. Is it of Pierre de Craon that you speak?

JACQUES HURY. It is of him I speak, him you kissed on the mouth.

VIOLAINE. And who has told you that?

JACQUES HURY. Mara saw you with her own eyes.
And she has told me all, as it was her duty to do,
And I, fool that I was, did not believe it!
Come, confess it! confess it then! It is true! Say that it is true!

VIOLAINE. It is true, Jacques.
Mara always speaks the truth.

JACQUES HURY. And it is true that you kissed him on the face?

VIOLAINE. It is true.

JACQUES HURY. O damned one! are the flames of hell so savory that you have thus lusted after them while you were still alive?

VIOLAINE (*speaking very low*). No, not damned.

But sweet, sweet Violaine! sweet, sweet Violaine!

JACQUES HURY. And you do not deny that this man had you and possessed you?

VIOLAINE. I deny nothing, Jacques.

JACQUES HURY. But I love you still, Violaine! 10

Ah, this is too cruel!

Tell me something, even if you have nothing to say, and I will believe it! Speak, I beg you! tell me it is not true!

VIOLAINE. I cannot turn all black in a minute, Jacques; but in a few months, a few months more,

You will not recognize me any longer.

JACQUES HURY. Tell me that all this is 20 not true.

VIOLAINE. Mara always speaks the truth, and then there is that flower upon my body that you have seen.

JACQUES HURY. Farewell, Violaine.

VIOLAINE. Farewell, Jacques.

JACQUES HURY. Tell me, what shall you do, wretched woman?

VIOLAINE. Take off this robe. Leave this house. 30

Fulfill the law. Show myself to the priest.

Go to . . .

JACQUES HURY. Well?

VIOLAINE. . . . the place set apart for people like me.

The lazar-house of the Géyn, over there.

JACQUES HURY. When?

VIOLAINE. Today—this very evening. 40 (*Long silence.*)

There is nothing else to be done.

JACQUES HURY. We must avoid any scandal.

Go, take off your robe and put on a travelling dress, and I will tell you

what it is right to do. (*They go out.*)

SCENE FOUR

The kitchen at Combernon, as in Act I.

THE MOTHER. Every day the weather is fine. It has not rained for eight days. (*She listens.*)

Now and then I hear the bells of Arcy.

Dong! Dong!

How warm it is, and how large everything looks!

What is Violaine doing? and Jacques? What have they to talk about so long?

I am sorry for what I said to her. (*She sighs.*)

And what is the crazy old man doing? Where is he now?

Ah! (*She bows her head.*)

MARA (*entering quickly*). They are coming here. I think the marriage is broken off. Do you hear me?

Be silent,

And say nothing.

THE MOTHER. What?

O wicked girl! wretch! You have got what you wished for!

MARA. Let it alone. It is only for a moment.

There was no other way

It could be done. So, now it is I

He must marry and not she. It will be better for her like that. It must be thus. Do you hear?

Be silent!

THE MOTHER. Who told you that?

MARA. Was there need for me to be told? I saw it all in their faces. I came upon them all warm. I understood everything in no time at all.

And Jacques, poor fellow, I pity him.

THE MOTHER. I am sorry for what I said!

MARA. You have said nothing; you know nothing—be silent!

And if they say anything to you, no matter what they tell you,

Agree with them, do everything they wish. There is nothing more to do.

THE MOTHER. I hope all is for the best.

SCENE FIVE

[*Enter* JACQUES HURY, *then* VIOLAINE *all in black, dressed as for a journey.*]

THE MOTHER. What is the matter, Jacques? What is the matter, Violaine? 10

Why have you put on this dress, as if you were going away?

VIOLAINE. I, too, am going away.

THE MOTHER. Going away? You going away, too? Jacques! what has happened between you?

JACQUES HURY. Nothing has happened.

But you know that I went to see my mother at Braine, and have only 20 just returned.

THE MOTHER. Well?

JACQUES HURY. You know, she is old and feeble.

She says she wishes to see and bless Her daughter-in-law before she dies.

THE MOTHER. Can she not come to the wedding?

JACQUES HURY. She is ill, she cannot 30 wait.

And this harvest time, too, when there is so much to be done

Is not the time to be married.

We have just been talking about it, Violaine and I, just now, very pleasantly,

And we have decided that it is best to wait till

The autumn. 40

Until then she will stay at Braine with my mother.

THE MOTHER. Is this your wish, Violaine?

VIOLAINE. Yes, mother.

THE MOTHER. But what! Do you wish to go away this very day?

VIOLAINE. This very evening.

JACQUES HURY. I shall go with her.

Time is short and work pressing in this month of hay and harvest. I have already stayed away too long.

THE MOTHER. Stay, Violaine! Do not go away from us, thou too!

VIOLAINE. It is only for a short time, mother!

THE MOTHER. A short time, you promise?

JACQUES HURY. A short time, and when autumn comes

Here she will be with us again, never to go away any more.

THE MOTHER. Ah, Jacques! Why do you let her go away?

JACQUES HURY. Do you think it is not hard for me?

MARA. Mother, what they both say is reasonable.

THE MOTHER. It is hard to see my child leave me.

VIOLAINE. Do not be sad mother!

What does it matter that we should wait a few days?

It is only a little time to pass.

Am I not sure of your affection? and of Mara's? and of Jacques', my betrothed?

Is it not so, Jacques? He is mine as I am his, and nothing can separate us? Look at me, dear Jacques. See how he weeps to see me go away!

This is not the time for weeping, mother! am I not young and beautiful and loved by everybody?

My father has gone away, it is true, but he has left me the tenderest of husbands, the friend who will never forsake me.

So it is not the time to weep, but to rejoice.

Ah, dear mother, how beautiful life is, and how happy I am!

MARA. And you, Jacques, what do you say? You do not look very happy.

JACQUES HURY. Is it not natural that I should be sad?

MARA. Come! it is only a separation for a few months!

JACQUES HURY. Too long for my heart.

MARA. Listen, Violaine, how well he said that!

And how is this, my sister, you so sad too? Smile at me with that charming mouth! Raise those blue eyes that our father loved so much. See Jacques! Look at your wife and see how beautiful she is when she smiles!

She will not be taken away from you! who would be sad who has a little sun like this to shine in his home?

Love her well for us, cruel man! Tell her to be brave!

JACQUES HURY. Courage, Violaine!

You have not lost me; we are not lost to each other!

You see that I do not doubt your love; but do you doubt mine?

Do I doubt you, Violaine? Do I not love you, Violaine? Am I not sure of you, Violaine?

I have talked about you to my mother, and you may imagine how happy she will be to see you.

It is hard to leave the house of your parents.

But where you are going you will have a safe shelter where no one can break in.

Neither your love nor your innocence, dear Violaine, has anything to fear.

THE MOTHER. These are very loving words,

And yet there is something in them, and in what you said to me, my child,

I don't know what—something strange which does not please me.

MARA. I see nothing strange, mother.

THE MOTHER. Violaine! If I hurt you just now, my child,

Forget what I said.

VIOLAINE. You have not hurt me.

THE MOTHER. Then let me embrace you. (*She opens her arms to her.*)

VIOLAINE. No, mother.

THE MOTHER. What?

VIOLAINE. No.

MARA. Violaine, that is wrong! Do you fear to have us touch thee? Why do you treat us thus, like lepers?

VIOLAINE. I have made a vow.

MARA. What vow?

VIOLAINE. That nobody shall touch me.

MARA. Until you return here? (*Silence. She lowers her head.*)

JACQUES HURY. Let her alone. You see she is troubled.

THE MOTHER. Go away for a moment. (*They move away.*)

Farewell, Violaine!

You will not deceive me, my child; you will not deceive the mother who bore thee.

What I have said to you is hard; but look at me, I am full of trouble, and I am old.

You—you are young, and you will forget.

My man is gone, and now here is my child turning away from me.

One's own sorrow is nothing, but the sorrow one has caused to others

Makes bitter the bread in the mouth.

Think of that, my sacrificed lamb, and say to yourself: Thus I have caused sorrow to no one.

I counselled thee as I thought for the best. Don't bear malice, Violaine! Save your sister. Must she be left to be ruined?

And God will be with you, who is your recompense.

That is all. You will never see my old face again. May God be with thee!

And you do not wish to kiss me, but I can at least give you my blessing, sweet, sweet Violaine!

VIOLAINE. Yes, mother! yes, mother! (*She kneels, and* THE MOTHER *makes the sign of the cross above her.*)

JACQUES HURY (*returning*). Come, Violaine, it is time to go.

MARA. Go and pray for us.

10

VIOLAINE (*calling*). I give you my dresses, Mara, and all my things! Have no fear of them; you know that I have not touched them.

I did not go into that room.

—Ah, ah! my poor wedding-dress that was so pretty! (*She stretches out her arms as if to find support. All remain at a distance from her. She goes out tottering, followed by* JACQUES.)

ACT III

SCENE ONE

Eight years later. Chevoche. A large forest sparsely grown with lofty oaks and birches, with an undergrowth of pines, firs, and a few holly trees. A wide straight road has just been cut through the woods to the horizon. Workmen are removing the last stumps of trees and preparing the roadway. There is a camp at one side, with huts made of faggots, a pot 20 over a camp-fire, etc. The camp lies in a sandpit, where a few workmen are engaged in loading a cart with a fine white sand. An apprentice of PIERRE DE CRAON, *squatting among the dry gorse bushes, oversees the work. On either side of the new road stand two colossi made of faggots, with collars and smocks of white cloth, each with a red cross on its breast. A barrel forms the head of each colossus, with its edge cut into saw-teeth to simulate a crown, 30 and a sort of face roughly painted on it in red. A long trumpet is fitted to the bunghole, and held in place by a board as if by an arm.*

It is the end of the day. There is snow on the ground and in the sky.

It is Christmas Eve.

THE MAYOR OF CHEVOCHE. There. Now the King can come. 40

A WORKMAN. 'A can coom an' a' likes. We've done our part well.

THE MAYOR (*looking around with satisfac-* tion). It's mighty beautiful! Fact is, it can hold everybody, as many as there are, men, women, and tiny children.

And to think 'twas the worst part, with all these bad weeds and these briars, and the marsh.

It ain't the wise ones of Bruyères can teach us anything.

A WORKMAN. Their road has a beard, and teeth too, wi' all those stumps they's left us! (*They laugh.*)

THE APPRENTICE (*pedantically, in a voice frightfully sharp and shrill*). Vox clamantis in deserto: Parate vias Domini et erunt prava in directa et aspera in vias planas.

It is true you have done your work well. I congratulate you, good people. It is like the road at Corpus Christi. (*Pointing to the Giants.*)

And who, gentlemen, are these two beautiful and reverend persons?

A WORKMAN. Beant they handsome? It was fathe' Vincent, the old drunkard, thet made 'em.

'A said it's th' great King of Abyssinia an' his wife Bellotte.

THE APPRENTICE. For my part I thought they were Gog and Magog.

THE MAYOR. 'Tis the two Angels of Chevoche who come to salute the King their lord.

They'll be set a-fire when 'a passes.
Listen! (*All listen.*)

A WORKMAN. Oh, no, that beant him yet.
We'd hear the bells o' Bruyères a-
ringin'.

ANOTHER. 'A won't be here afore midnight. 'A supped at Fisme.

ANOTHER. 'Tis a good place to see from,
here.
I shallna budge.   10

ANOTHER. Hast 'a eat, Perrot? I've on'y
a mossel o' bread, all froze.

THE MAYOR. Don't be afraid. The's a
quarter o' pork in the pot and some
big sausages, and the roebuck we
killed,
And three ells o' blood-sausages, and
apples, and a good little keg of
Marne wine.

THE APPRENTICE. I stay with you.   20

A WOMAN. And there's a good little
Christmas for you.

THE APPRENTICE. It was on Christmas
Day that King Clovis was baptized
at Rheims.

ANOTHER WOMAN. 'Tis Christmas Day
that oor King Charles comes back
to get hi'self crowned.

ANOTHER. 'Tis a village girl, sent by
God, Who brings him back to his 30
own.

ANOTHER. Jeanne, they call her!

ANOTHER. The Maid!

ANOTHER. Who was born on Twelfth
Night!

ANOTHER. Who drove the English away
from Orleans when they besieged
it!

ANOTHER WORKMAN. And who's goin' to
drive 'em out of France too, all of 40
'em! Amen.

ANOTHER WORKMAN (*humming*). Noel!
Cock-a-doodle-do! Noel! Noel
come again! Rrr! how cauld it be!
(*He wraps himself closer in his cloak.*)

A WOMAN. Mus' look well t' see if the's a

little man all in red clothes by th'
King. That's her.

ANOTHER WOMAN. On a tall black horse.

THE FIRST WOMAN. On'y six months
agone her was keepin' her father's
cows.

ANOTHER WOMAN. And now her carries a
banner where Jesus is in writin'.

A WORKMAN. An' that the English run
away before like mice.

ANOTHER WORKMAN. Let the wicked
Bourguignons o' Saponay beware!

ANOTHER WORKMAN. They'll be at
Rheims at the break o' day.

ANOTHER WORKMAN. What be they doin',
those down there?

THE APPRENTICE. The two bells of the Cathedral, Baudon and Baude, will be
rung at the Gloria at midnight, and
they will never stop swinging and
clanging until the French come.
Everybody will keep a lighted candle
in his house until morning.
They expect the King to be there for
the Mass at dawn, which is "Lux
fulgebit."
All the clergy will go out to meet him,
three hundred priests and the Archbishop in copes of gold, and the
monks, the Mayor and the vestry.
All that will be very beautiful on the
snow, in the bright merry sunshine,
with all the people singing "Noel"!
And they say that the King intends to
get down from his horse, and enter
his good city riding upon an ass,
like our Lord.

THE MAYOR. How comes it that you did
not stay down there?

THE APPRENTICE. Master Pierre de
Craon sent me here to get sand.

THE MAYOR. What! He busies himself
about sand at such a time?

THE APPRENTICE. He says there is not
much time.

THE MAYOR. But how could he employ

himself better than in making this road, as we do?

THE APPRENTICE. He says that his work is not to make roads for the King, but a dwelling for God.

THE MAYOR. Of what use would Rheims be if the King could not reach it?

THE APPRENTICE. But what use would the road be if there is no church at the end of it? 10

THE MAYOR. He is not a good Frenchman.

THE APPRENTICE. He says that he knows nothing but his work. If anybody talks politics to us, we blacken his nose with the bottom of the frying-pan.

THE MAYOR. He has not even been able to finish his Justice, though 'tis ten years they've been working on 20 it.

THE APPRENTICE. On the contrary! All the stone is polished and the wood-work is in place; it's only the spire that has not yet done growing.

THE MAYOR. They never work on it.

THE APPRENTICE. The master is preparing the glass for his windows now, and that is why he sends us here for sand; 30
Though that is not his craft.
All winter he has worked among his furnaces.
To make light, my poor people, is more difficult than to make gold,
To breathe on this heavy matter and make it transparent, "according as our bodies of mud shall be changed into bodies of glory,"
As Saint Paul said. 40
And he says that he must find for each colour
The mother-colour itself, just as God himself made it.
That is why, into his great clean vessels, full of shining water, he pours

jacinth, ultra-marine, rich gold, vermilion.
And he watches these beautiful rose-coloured liquids to see what happens to them in the sunshine, and by virtue of the grace of God, and how they mingle and bloom in the matrass.
And he says there is not one colour which he cannot make out of his own knowledge alone,
As his body makes red and blue.
Because he wishes the Justice of Rheims to shine like the morning on the day of her nuptials.

THE MAYOR. They say he has leprosy.

THE APPRENTICE. That is not true! I saw him naked last summer.
While he bathed in the Aisne at Soissons. I know what I say!
His flesh is as healthy as a child's.

THE MAYOR. It is queer, all the same. Why did he keep himself hidden so long?

THE APPRENTICE. That is a lie.

THE MAYOR. I know, I am older than you. You mustn't get angry, little man. It doesn't matter if he be sick in the body.
It isn't with his body he works.

THE APPRENTICE. Better not let him hear you say that! I remember how he punished one of us because he stayed all the time in his corner, drawing:
He sent him up on the scaffolding to serve the masons all day and pass them their hods and their stones,
Saying that by the end of the day he would know two things better than he could learn them by rule and design: the weight a man can carry and the height of his body.
And as the grace of God multiplies each of our good deeds,
So he taught us about what he calls

"the shekel of the Temple," and this dwelling of God of which each man who does all that his body is capable of doing is like a secret foundation;

What means the thumb, and the hand, and the arm's length, and the spread of both our arms, and the arm extended, and the circle it makes,

And the foot and the step;

And how all these things are never the same.

Do you think Father Noah was indifferent to the body when he built the ark? and are these things of no account:

The number of paces from the door to the altar, and the height the eye may be lifted to, and the number of souls the two sides of the Church may hold all at the same time?

For the heathen artist made everything from the outside, but we make all from within, like the bees,

And as the soul does for the body: nothing is lifeless, everything lives, Everything gives thanks in action.

THE MAYOR. The little man talks well.

A WORKMAN. Hear him, like a magpie, all full of his master's words.

THE APPRENTICE. Speak with respect of Pierre de Craon!

THE MAYOR. 'Tis true he's a burgher of Rheims, and they call him Master of the Compass.

As they used to call Messire Loys The Master of the Rule.

ANOTHER. Throw some wood on the fire, Perrot. Look, it's beginning to snow.

[It snows. Night has come. Enter MARA dressed in black, carrying a bundle under her cloak.]

MARA. Are these the people of Chevoche?

THE MAYOR. 'Tis ourselves.

MARA. Praised be Jesus Christ.

THE MAYOR. Amen!

MARA. Is it around here I'll find the little cell of the Géyn?

THE MAYOR. Where the leper woman lives?

MARA. Yes.

THE MAYOR. Not exactly here, but close by.

ANOTHER. You want to see the leper woman?

MARA. Yes.

A MAN. She can't be seen; she always wears a veil over her face, as it's ordered.

ANOTHER. And well ordered! it isn't myself as wants to see her.

MARA. It's a long time you've had her?

A MAN. A'most eight years, and we'd like it well not to have her at all.

MARA. Is that because she has done harm?

A MAN. No, but all t'same it's unlucky to have these varmint kind of folk near by.

THE MAYOR. And then, 'tis the parish that feeds her.

A MAN. By the way, I bet they've forgot to take her her bite to eat for three days, with all these doings about the road!

A WOMAN. And what do you want o' this woman?

[MARA makes no reply, but stands, looking at the fire.]

A WOMAN. A person would say it's a child you're a-holdin' in your arms?

ANOTHER WOMAN. It's a fearsome cold to take out little children at such an hour.

MARA. It is not cold.

[Silence. There is heard from the darkness under the trees, the sound of a wooden rattle.]

AN OLD WOMAN. Wait! there's her!

there's her click-click! Holy Virgin! what a pity her ain't dead!

A WOMAN. 'A comes to ask for her food. No fear her'll forget that!

A MAN. What a plague 'tis to feed such varmint.

ANOTHER. Toss her somethin'. She mustn't come anigh to us. First thing you know she'd give us the poison. 10

ANOTHER. No meat, Perrot. It's fast day, it's Christmas Eve! (*They laugh.*) Throw her this mossel o' bread that's froze. Good enough for the like o' her!

A MAN (*calling*). Heigh, No-face! Heigh, Jeanne, I say, hallo, rotting one!

[*The black form of the leper woman is seen on the snow.* MARA *looks at her.*]

Catch it! (*He throws her swiftly a piece of 20 bread. She stoops and picks it up and goes away.* MARA *follows her.*)

A MAN. Where is it she's going?

ANOTHER. Here, woman! hallo! where be you going, what be you doing?

[MARA *and* THE WOMAN *go farther away.*]

SCENE TWO

They disappear within the forest, leaving their tracks upon the snow. The night 30 brightens. The brilliant moon, surrounded by an immense halo, lights up a hillock covered with heather and white sand. Enormous sandstone rocks, fantastically formed, rise here and there like beasts belonging to the fossil ages, like inexplicable monuments or idols with deformed heads and limbs. And the leper woman conducts MARA *to the cave where she lives, a kind of low cavern in which it is impossible to stand upright. The back of the cave is closed, 40 leaving only an opening for the smoke.*

SCENE THREE

VIOLAINE. Who is this
That does not fear to walk with the leper woman?

You must know that it is dangerous to be near her, and her breath is deadly.

MARA. It is I, Violaine.

VIOLAINE. O voice, so long unheard! Is it you, mother?

MARA. It is I, Violaine.

VIOLAINE. It is your voice and another. Let me light this fire, for it is very cold. And this torch, too. (*She lights a fire of turf and heather by means of live embers which she takes from a pot, and then the torch.*)

MARA. It is I, Violaine; Mara, your sister.

VIOLAINE. Dear sister, hail! How good of you to come! But do you not fear me?

MARA. I fear nothing in this world.

VIOLAINE. How much your voice has become like *Maman's! (Silence.)*

MARA. Violaine, our dear mother is no more.

VIOLAINE. When did she die?

MARA. In that same month after your departure.

VIOLAINE. Knowing nothing?

MARA. I do not know.

VIOLAINE. Poor *Maman!*
May God have thy soul in his keeping!

MARA. And our father has not yet come back.

VIOLAINE. And you two?

MARA. It is well with us.

VIOLAINE. Everything at home is as you wish it?

MARA. Everything is well.

VIOLAINE. I know it could not be otherwise
With Jacques and you.

MARA. You should see what we have done! We have three more ploughs. You would not recognize Combernon And we are going to pull down those old walls,
Now that the King has come back.

VIOLAINE. And are you happy together, Mara?

MARA. Yes. We are happy. He loves me As I love him.

VIOLAINE. God be praised.

MARA. Violaine!
You do not see what I hold in my arms?

VIOLAINE. I cannot see.

MARA. Lift your veil, then.

VIOLAINE. Under that I have another.

MARA. You cannot see any more?

VIOLAINE. I have no longer any eyes.
The soul lives alone in the ruined body.

MARA. Blind!
How then are you able to walk so straight?

VIOLAINE. I hear.

MARA. What do you hear?

VIOLAINE. I hear all things exist with me.

MARA (significantly). And I, Violaine, do you hear me?

VIOLAINE. God has given me the same intelligence
Which He has given to us all.

MARA. Do you hear me, Violaine?

VIOLAINE. Ah, poor Mara!

MARA. Do you hear me, Violaine?

VIOLAINE. What would you have of me, dear sister?

MARA. To join you in praise of this God who has struck you with the pestilence.

VIOLAINE. Then let us praise Him, on this Eve of His Nativity.

MARA. It is easy to be a saint when leprosy helps us.

VIOLAINE. I do not know, not being one.

MARA. We must turn to God when everything else is gone.

VIOLAINE. He at least will not fail us.

MARA (softly). Perhaps, who knows? Violaine, tell me!

VIOLAINE. Life fails, but not the death where I now live.

MARA. Heretic! are you sure, then, of your salvation?

VIOLAINE. I am sure of the goodness of Him who has provided for everything.

MARA. We see His first instalment.

VIOLAINE. I have faith in God who has ordained my destiny.

MARA. What do you know of Him who is invisible, who is never manifest?

VIOLAINE. He is not more invisible to me now than all the rest.

MARA (ironically). He is with you, little dove, and He loves you!

VIOLAINE. As with all who are wretched, Himself with me.

MARA. Surely how very great is His love!

VIOLAINE. As the love of the fire for the wood it flames above.

MARA. He has cruelly punished you.

VIOLAINE. Not more than it was due to me.

MARA. And already, he to whom you had submitted your body has forgotten you?

VIOLAINE. I have not submitted my body!

MARA. Sweet Violaine! lying Violaine!
Did I not see you tenderly kiss Pierre de Craon the morning of that beautiful day in June?

VIOLAINE. You saw all, and there was nothing else.

MARA. Why, then, did you kiss him so feelingly?

VIOLAINE. The poor man was a leper, and I, I was so happy that day!

MARA. In all innocence, wasn't it?

VIOLAINE. Like a little girl who kisses a poor little boy.

MARA. Ought I to believe that, Violaine?

VIOLAINE. It is true.

MARA. Don't say, too, that it was of your own will you abandoned Jacques to me?

VIOLAINE. No, not of my own will. I

loved him! I am not so good as that.

MARA. Ought he to have loved you the same, though you were a leper?

VIOLAINE. I did not expect it.

MARA. Who would love a leper woman?

VIOLAINE. My heart is pure!

MARA. But what did Jacques know of that? He believes you guilty.

VIOLAINE. Our mother had told me that you loved him.

MARA. Don't say it was she who made you a leper.

VIOLAINE. God in His goodness warned me.

MARA. So that when our mother spoke to you . . .

VIOLAINE. It was His voice that I heard.

MARA. But why allow yourself to seem guilty?

VIOLAINE. Should I have done nothing, then, on my part?
Poor Jacquin! Was it necessary to leave him still regretting me?

MARA. Say that you did not love him at all.

VIOLAINE. I did not love him, Mara.

MARA. But I would never have let him go like that.

VIOLAINE. Was it I who let him go?

MARA. It would have killed me.

VIOLAINE. And am I living?

MARA. Now I am happy with him.

VIOLAINE. Peace be unto you!

MARA. And I have given him a child, Violaine! a dear little girl. A sweet little girl.

VIOLAINE. Peace be unto you!

MARA. Our happiness is great. But yours is greater, with God.

VIOLAINE. And I too knew what happiness was eight years ago, and my heart was ravished with it.
So much, that I madly asked God— ah!—that it might last for ever!

And God heard me in a strange manner! Will my leprosy ever be cured? No, no, as long as there remains a particle of my flesh to be devoured. Will the love in my heart be cured? Never, as long as my immortal soul lives to nourish it.
Does your husband understand you, Mara?

MARA. What man understands a woman?

VIOLAINE. Happy is she who can be known, heart and soul, who can give herself utterly.
Jacques—what would he have done with all that I could have given him?

MARA. You have transferred your faith to Another?

VIOLAINE. Love has ended in pain, and pain has ended in love.
The wood we set on fire gives not only ashes, but a flame as well.

MARA. But of what use is this blind fire that gives to others
Neither light nor heat?

VIOLAINE. Is it not something that it does me service?
Do not begrudge to a creature consumed,
Afflicted to the uttermost depths, this light that illumines her within!
And if you could pass but one night only in my skin, you would not say that this fire gives no heat.
Man is the priest, but it is not forbidden to woman to be victim.
God is miserly, and does not permit any creature to be set on fire
Unless some impurity be burned with him,
His own, or that which surrounds him, as when the living embers in the censer are stirred.
And truly these are unhappy times.
The people have no father. They look

around, and they know no longer where the King is, or the Pope.

That is why my body agonizes here for all Christendom which is perishing.

Powerful is suffering when it is as voluntary as sin!

You saw me kiss that leper, Mara?

Ah, the chalice of sorrow is deep,

And who once sets his lip to it can never withdraw it again of his own free will.

MARA. Take my sorrow upon thee, too!

VIOLAINE. I have already taken it.

MARA. Violaine! if there is still something living, that was once my sister, under that veil and in that ruined body,

Remember that we were children together! Have pity upon me!

VIOLAINE. Speak, dear sister. Have faith! Tell me all!

MARA. Violaine, I am a wretched woman, and my pain is greater than yours!

VIOLAINE. Greater, sister?

MARA (with a loud cry, opens her cloak and lifts up the corpse of a baby). Look! take it!

VIOLAINE. What is this?

MARA. Look, I tell you! take it! Take it, I give it to you. (She lays the corpse in her arms.)

VIOLAINE. Ah! I feel a rigid little body! a poor little cold face!

MARA. Ha! ha! Violaine! My child! my little girl!

That is her sweet little face! that is her poor little body!

VIOLAINE (speaking low). Dead, Mara?

MARA. Take her, I give her to you!

VIOLAINE. Peace, Mara!

MARA. They wanted to take her away from me, but I would not let them! and I ran away with her.

But you, take her, Violaine. Here,

take her; you see, I give her to you.

VIOLAINE. What do you wish me to do, Mara?

MARA. What do I wish you to do? do you not understand?

I tell you she is dead! I tell you she is dead!

VIOLAINE. Her soul lives with God. She follows the Lamb. She is with all the blessed little girls.

MARA. But for me she is dead!

VIOLAINE. You readily give me her body! give the rest to God.

MARA. No! no! no! You shall never trick me with your nunnish rigmaroles! No, I shall never be silenced.

This milk that burns my breast cries out to God like the blood of Abel!

Have I got fifty children to tear out of my body? have I got fifty souls to tear out of my soul?

Do you know what it is to be rent in two in order to bring into the world this little wailing creature?

And the midwife told me I should have no more children.

But if I had a hundred children it would not be my little Aubaine.

VIOLAINE. Accept, submit.

MARA. Violaine, you know well I have a hard head. I am one who never gives up, and who accepts nothing.

VIOLAINE. Poor sister!

MARA. Violaine, they are so sweet, these little ones, and it hurts you so when this cruel little mouth bites your breast!

VIOLAINE (caressing the face). How cold her little face is!

MARA (speaking low). He knows nothing yet.

VIOLAINE (also speaking low). He was not home?

MARA. He has gone to Rheims to sell his grain.

She died suddenly, in two hours.

VIOLAINE. Whom was she like?

MARA. Like him, Violaine. She is not only mine, she is his, too. Only her eyes are like mine.

VIOLAINE. Poor Jacquin!

MARA. It was not to hear you say poor Jacquin! that I came here.

VIOLAINE. What do you wish of me, then?

MARA. Violaine, do you want to know? 10 Tell me, do you know what a soul is that damns itself,

Of its own will, to all eternity?

Do you know what it is in the heart that really blasphemes?

There is a devil who, while I was running, sang me a little song,

Do you wish to hear the things he taught me?

VIOLAINE. Do not say these horrible 20 things!

MARA. Then give me back my child that I gave you.

VIOLAINE. You gave me only a corpse.

MARA. And you, give it back to me alive!

VIOLAINE. Mara, what do you dare to say?

MARA. I will not have it that my child is dead.

VIOLAINE. Is it in my power to bring the 30 dead to life?

MARA. I don't know, I have only you to help me.

VIOLAINE. Is it in my power to bring the dead to life, like God?

MARA. Of what use are you, then?

VIOLAINE. To suffer and to supplicate!

MARA. But of what use is it to suffer and supplicate if you give me not back my child? 40

VIOLAINE. God knows. It is enough for Him that I serve Him.

MARA. But I—I am deaf, and I do not hear! and I cry to you from the depths where I am fallen!
Violaine! Violaine!

Give me back that child I gave you! See! I give in, I humiliate myself! have pity on me!

Have pity on me, Violaine, and give me back that child you took from me.

VIOLAINE. Only He who took it can give it back!

MARA. Give it back to me then! Ah, I know it is all your fault.

VIOLAINE. My fault!

MARA. Then let it not be yours.
It is mine, forgive me!
But give her back to me, my sister!

VIOLAINE. But you see it is dead.

MARA. You lie! it is not dead! Ah! figure-of-two, ah, heart-of-a-sheep! Ah, if I had access to your God as you have,

He would not take my little ones away from me so easily!

VIOLAINE. Ask me to re-create heaven and earth!

MARA. But it is written that you may blow on that mountain and cast it into the sea.

VIOLAINE. I can, if I am a saint.

MARA. You must be a saint when a wretched being prays to you.

VIOLAINE. Ah, supreme temptation!
I swear, and I declare, and I protest before God that I am not a saint!

MARA. Then give me back my child.

VIOLAINE. O my God, you see into my heart.
I swear, and I declare, and I protest before God that I am not a saint!

MARA. Violaine, give me back my child!

VIOLAINE. Why will you not leave me in peace?
Why do you come thus to torment me in my tomb?
Am I of any worth? do I influence God? am I like God?
It is God himself you are asking me to judge.

MARA. I ask you only for my child.
(*Pause.*)

VIOLAINE (*raising her finger*). Listen.

[*Silence. A distant, almost imperceptible, sound of bells.*]

MARA. I hear nothing.

VIOLAINE. The Christmas bells, the bells announcing the midnight Mass!
O Mara, a little child is born to us!

MARA. Then give me back mine.   10

[*Trumpets in the distance.*]

VIOLAINE. What is that?

MARA. It is the King going to Rheims.
Have you not heard of the road the peasants have cut through the forest?
And they can keep all the wood they cut.
It is a little shepherdess who guides the King through the middle of France 20
To Rheims, to be crowned there.

VIOLAINE. Praised be God, who does all these wonderful things!

[*Again the sound of bells, very distinct.*]

MARA. How loud the bells ring for the *Gloria!*
The wind blows this way.
They are ringing in three villages all at once.

VIOLAINE. Let us pray, with all the uni- 30 verse!
Thou art not cold, Mara?

MARA. I am cold only in my heart.

VIOLAINE. Let us pray. It is long since we celebrated Christmas together.
Fear nothing. I have taken your grief upon myself. Look! and that which you have given me lies close against my heart.
Do not weep! This is not the time to 40 weep, when the salvation of all mankind is already born.

[*Bells in the distance, less clear.*]

MARA. The snow has stopped, and the stars are shining.

VIOLAINE. Look! Do you see this Book?

The priest who visits me now and then left it with me.

MARA. I see it.

VIOLAINE. Take it, will you? and read me the Christmas Service, the First Lesson of each of the three Nocturnes.

[MARA *takes the Book and reads.*]

PROPHECY OF ISAIAH[1]

1 Nevertheless, the dimness shall not be such as was in her vexation, when at the first he lightly afflicted the land of Zebulun and the land of Naphtali, and afterward did more grievously afflict her by the way of the sea, beyond Jordan, in Galilee of the nations.

2 The people that walked in darkness have seen a great light: they that dwell in the land of the shadow of death, upon them hath the light shined.

3 Thou hast multiplied the nation, and not increased the joy: they joy before thee according to the joy in harvest, and as men rejoice when they divide the spoil.

4 For thou hast broken the yoke of his burden; and the staff of his shoulder, the rod of his oppressor, as in the day of Midian.

5 For every battle of the warrior is with confused noise, and garments rolled in blood; but this shall be with burning and fuel of fire.

6 For unto us a child is born, unto us a son is given, and the government shall be upon his shoulder; and his name shall be called Wonderful, Counsellor, The mighty God, The everlasting Father, the Prince of Peace.

VIOLAINE (*raising her face*). Listen! (*Silence.*)

[1] Isaiah ix, 1–6.

VOICES OF ANGELS IN HEAVEN, *heard only by* VIOLAINE:

CHOIR.[1] Hodie nobis de caelo pax vera descendit, hodie per totum mundum melliflui facti sunt caeli.

A VOICE.[2] Hodie illuxit nobis dies redemptionis novae, reparationis antiquae, felicitatis aeternae.

CHOIR. Hodie per totum mundum melliflui facti sunt caeli. 10

[VIOLAINE *lifts her finger in warning. Silence.* MARA *listens and looks uneasily.*]

MARA. I hear nothing.

VIOLAINE. Read on, Mara.

MARA (*continuing to read*).

SERMON OF SAINT LEO, POPE

Our Saviour, dearly beloved, was today born: let us rejoice. For there should be no loop-hole open to sor- 20 row on the birthday of Life, which, the fear of Death being at last consumed, filleth us with the joy of eternity promised. No one from this gladness is excluded, as one and the same cause for happiness exists for us all: for Our Lord, the destroyer of sin and Death, having found no one exempt from sin, came to deliver everyone. Let the 30 sinless exult insomuch as his palm is at hand; let the sinful rejoice . . .

[*Suddenly a brilliant and prolonged sound of trumpets very near. Shouts resound through the forest.*]

MARA. The King! The King of France!

[*Again and again the blare of the trumpets, unutterably piercing, solemn, and triumphant.*]

MARA (*in a low voice*). The King of France 40 who goes to Rheims! (*Silence.*) Violaine! (*Silence.*)

[1] The voices are like those of heroic young men singing solemnly in unison, with retarded movement and very simple cadence at the end of phrases.
[2] Like the voice of a child.

Do you hear me, Violaine? (*Silence. She goes on with the reading.*)

. . . Let the sinful rejoice insomuch as forgiveness is offered to him. Let the Gentile be of good cheer, because he is bidden to share life. For the Son of God, according to the fulness of this time which the inscrutable depth of the Divine counsel hath disposed, took on Himself the nature of mankind so that He might reconcile it to its maker, and that this deviser of Death, Satan, by that which he had vanquished might be in his turn conquered.

VOICES OF ANGELS (*heard only by* VIOLAINE, *as before*).

CHOIR. O magnum mysterium et admirabile sacramentum ut animalia viderint dominum natum jacentem in praesepio! Beata virgo cujus viscera meruerunt portare dominum christum.

A VOICE. Ave, Maria, gratia plena, dominus tecum.

CHOIR. Beata virgo cujus viscera meruerunt portare dominum christum. (*Pause.*)

MARA. Violaine, I am not worthy to read this Book! Violaine, I know that my heart is too hard, and I am sorry for it: I wish I could be different.

VIOLAINE. Read on, Mara. You do not know who chants the responses. (*Silence.*)

MARA (*with an effort takes up the Book, and reads in a trembling voice*).

The Holy Gospel according to Saint Luke.[3] (*They both stand up.*)

1 And it came to pass in those days, that there went out a decree from Caesar Augustus, that all the world should be taxed. (*And the rest.*)

[*They sit down.*]

[3] Luke ii, 1.

HOMILY OF SAINT GREGORY, POPE

[*She stops, overcome by emotion.—The trumpets sound a last time in the distance.*]

Forasmuch as, by the grace of God, we are this day thrice to celebrate the solemnities of Mass, we may not speak at length on the gospel that hath just been read. However, the birth of our Redeemer bids us ad-10 dress you at least in a few words. Wherefore, at the time of this birth, should there have been a census of all the people except clearly to manifest that He who was appearing in the flesh just then was numbering his Elect for eternity? On the contrary, the Prophet saith of the wicked: they shall be deleted from the Book of the Living and 20 they shall not be written down among the Righteous. It is meet also that He should be born in Bethlehem. For Bethlehem means the House of Bread, and Jesus Christ saith of Himself: I am the Living Bread descended from Heaven. Therefore had the place in which our Lord was born been called the House of Bread in order 30 that He who was to feed our hearts with internal satiety should there appear in the substance of flesh. He was born, not in the house of his parents, but by the roadside, no doubt to show that by taking on humanity He was being born in a place strange to Him.

VOICES OF ANGELS.

CHOIR. Beata viscera mariae virginis 40 quae portaverunt aeterni patris filium; et beata ubera quae lactaverunt christum dominum.

Qui hodie pro salute mundi de virgine nasci dignatus est.

A VOICE. Dies sanctificatus illuxit nobis; venite, gentes, et adorate dominum.

CHOIR. Qui hodie pro salute mundi de virgine nasci dignatus est. (*Long silence.*)

VOICES OF ANGELS (*again, almost imperceptible*).

CHOIR. Verbum caro factum est et habitavit in nobis: et vidimus gloriam ejus, gloriam quasi unigeniti a patre, plenum gratiae et veritatis.

A VOICE. Omnia per ipsum facta sunt et sine ipso factum est nihil.

CHOIR. Et vidimus gloriam ejus, gloriam quasi unigeniti a patre, plenum gratiae et veritatis.

A VOICE. Gloria patri et filio et spiritui sancto.

CHOIR. Et vidimus gloriam ejus, gloriam quasi unigeniti a patre, plenum gratiae et veritatis. (*Long silence.*)

VIOLAINE (*suddenly cries out in a stifled voice*). Ah!

MARA. What is it?

[*With her hand* VIOLAINE *makes a sign to be silent.—Silence.—The first flush of dawn appears.*]

[VIOLAINE *puts her hand under her cloak as if to fasten her dress again.*]

MARA. Violaine, I see something moving under your cloak!

VIOLAINE (*as if she were awakening little by little*). Is it you, Mara? good morning, sister. I feel the breath of the new-born day on my face.

MARA. Violaine! Violaine! is it your arm that stirs? Again I see something moving.

VIOLAINE. Peace, Mara, it is Christmas Day, when all joy is born!

MARA. What joy is there for me unless my child lives?

VIOLAINE. And for us, too—a little child is born to us!

MARA. In the name of the living God, what say you?

VIOLAINE. "Behold, I bring thee glad tidings . . ."

MARA. Your cloak—it moves again!

[*The little bare foot of a baby, moving lazily, appears in the opening of the cloak.*]

VIOLAINE. ". . . Because a man has appeared in the world!"

[MARA *falls upon her knees, with a deep sigh, her forehead on the knees of her sister.* VIOLAINE *caresses her.*]

VIOLAINE. Poor sister! she weeps. She, too, has had too much sorrow. (*Silence.* VIOLAINE *kisses her head.*)

Take it, Mara! Would you leave the child always with me?

MARA (*she takes the child from under the cloak and looks at it wildly*). It lives!

VIOLAINE (*she walks out of the cave a few steps upon the heather. By the first light of the bitter cold morning can be seen, first, the pine and birch trees hoary with frost, then, at the end of an immense snow-covered plain, seeming very small on the top of its hill, but clearly etched in the pure air, the five-towered silhouette of Monsanvierge*). Glory to God!

MARA. It lives!

VIOLAINE. Peace on earth to men!

MARA. It lives! it lives!

VIOLAINE. It lives and we live.

And the face of the Father appeared on the earth born again and comforted.

MARA. My child lives!

VIOLAINE (*raising her finger*). Listen! (*Silence.*)

I hear the Angelus ringing at Monsanvierge. (*She crosses herself and prays. The child awakes.*)

MARA (*whispering*). It is I, Aubaine; dost know me? (*The child moves about and whines.*)

What is it, my joy? What is it, my treasure? (*The child opens its eyes, looks at its mother and begins to cry.* MARA *looks closely at it.*)

Violaine!

What does this mean? Its eyes were black,

And now they are blue like yours. (*Silence.*)

Ah!

And what is this drop of milk I see on its lips?

ACT IV

SCENE ONE

Night. The large kitchen, as in Act I, empty. A lamp is on the table. The outer door is half open.

MARA *enters from without, and carefully closes the door. She stands still for a moment in the centre of the room, looking toward the door, and listening.*

Then she takes the lamp and goes out by another door without making any sound.

The stage remains dark. Nothing can be seen but the fire of some live coals on the hearth.

SCENE TWO

Two or three blasts of a horn are heard in the distance. Sounds of calling. Movement in the farm. Then the noise of opening doors, and the grinding of approaching cart-wheels. Loud knocks at the door.

VOICE FROM WITHOUT (*calling*). Hallo!

[*Noise in the upper story of a window opening.*]

VOICE OF JACQUES HURY. Who is there?

VOICE FROM WITHOUT. Open the door!

VOICE OF JACQUES HURY. What do you want?

VOICE FROM WITHOUT. Open the door!

VOICE OF JACQUES HURY. Who are you?

VOICE FROM WITHOUT. Open the door so that I can tell you! (*Pause.*)

[JACQUES HURY, *with a candle in his hand, enters the room; he opens the door. After a slight pause, enter* PIERRE DE CRAON, *carrying the body of a woman wrapped up in his arms. He lays his burden very carefully upon the table. Then he lifts his head. The two men stare at each other in the candlelight.*]

PIERRE DE CRAON. Jacques Hury, do you not recognize me?

JACQUES HURY. Pierre de Craon?

PIERRE DE CRAON. It is I. (*They continue to look at each other.*)

JACQUES HURY. And what is this you bring me?

PIERRE DE CRAON. I found her half-buried in my sand-pit, there where I seek what I need

For my glass ovens, and for the mortar—

Half-hidden under a great cart-load of sand, under a cart standing on end from which they had taken off the backboard. She is still alive. It is I who took it upon myself to bring her to you

Here.

JACQUES HURY. Why here?

PIERRE DE CRAON. That at least she might die under her father's roof!

JACQUES HURY. There is no roof here but mine.

PIERRE DE CRAON. Jacques, here is Violaine.

JACQUES HURY. I know no Violaine.

PIERRE DE CRAON. Have you never heard of the Leper Woman of Chevoche?

JACQUES HURY. What does that matter to me?

You lepers, it is for you to scrape each other's sores.

PIERRE DE CRAON. I am not a leper any more;

I was cured long ago.

JACQUES HURY. Cured?

PIERRE DE CRAON. Year after year the disease grew less, and I am now healthy.

JACQUES HURY. And this one, she too will be cured presently.

PIERRE DE CRAON. You are more leprous than she and I.

JACQUES HURY. But I don't ask to be taken out of my hole in the sand.

PIERRE DE CRAON. And even if she had been guilty, you ought to remember.

JACQUES HURY. Is it true that she kissed you on the mouth?

PIERRE DE CRAON (*looking at him*). It is true, poor child!

JACQUES HURY. She moves, she is coming to herself.

PIERRE DE CRAON. I leave you with her. (*He goes out.*)

SCENE THREE

[JACQUES HURY *sits down near the table and looks silently at* VIOLAINE.]

VIOLAINE (*coming to herself and stretching forth her hand*). Where am I, and who is there?

JACQUES HURY. At Monsanvierge, and it is I who am near you. (*Pause.*)

VIOLAINE (*speaking as she used to do*). Good morning, Jacques. (*Silence.*)

Jacques, you still care for me, then?

JACQUES HURY. The wound is not healed.

VIOLAINE. Poor boy!

And I, too, have I not suffered a little too?

JACQUES HURY. What possessed you to kiss that leper on the mouth!

VIOLAINE. Jacques! you must reproach me quickly with all you have in your heart against me, that we may finish with all that.

For we have other things still to say.

And I want to hear you say just once

again those words I loved so much: *Dear Violaine! Sweet Violaine!* For the time that remains to us is short.

JACQUES HURY. I have nothing more to say to you.

VIOLAINE. Come here, cruel man! (*He approaches her, where she lies.*) Come nearer to me. (*She takes his hand and draws him to her. He kneels awkwardly at her side.*)

Jacques, you must believe me. I swear it before God, who is looking upon us! I was never guilty with Pierre de Craon.

JACQUES HURY. Why, then, did you kiss him?

VIOLAINE. Ah, he was so sad and I was so happy.

JACQUES HURY. I don't believe you. (*She lays her hand a moment on his head.*)

VIOLAINE. Do you believe me now? (*He hides his face in her dress and sobs heavily.*)

JACQUES HURY. Ah, Violaine! cruel Violaine!

VIOLAINE. Not cruel, but sweet, sweet Violaine!

JACQUES HURY. It is true, then? yes, it was only I you loved? (*Silence. She gives him her other hand.*)

VIOLAINE. Jacques, no doubt it was all too beautiful, and we should have been too happy.

JACQUES HURY. You have cruelly deceived me.

VIOLAINE. Deceived? this silver flower on my side did not lie.

JACQUES HURY. What was I to believe, Violaine?

VIOLAINE. If you had believed in me, Who knows but what you might have cured me?

JACQUES HURY. Was I not to believe my own eyes?

VIOLAINE. That is true. You ought to have believed your own eyes, that is right.

One does not marry a leper. One does not marry an unfaithful woman.

Do not regret anything, Jacques. There, it is better as it is.

JACQUES HURY. Did you know that Mara loved me?

VIOLAINE. I knew it. My mother herself had told me.

JACQUES HURY. Thus everything was in league with her against me!

VIOLAINE. Jacques, there is already enough sorrow in the world. It is best not to be willingly the cause of a great sorrow to others.

JACQUES HURY. But what of my sorrow?

VIOLAINE. That is another thing, Jacques. Are you not happy to be with me?

JACQUES. Yes, Violaine.

VIOLAINE. Where I am, there is patience, not sorrow. (*Silence.*) The world's grief is great.

It is too hard to suffer, and not to know why.

But that which others do not know, I have learned, and thou must share my knowledge.

Jacques, have we not been separated long enough now? should we let any barrier remain between us? Must it still be that death shall separate us?

Only that which is ill should perish, and that which should not perish is that which suffers.

Happy is he who suffers, and who knows why.

Now my task is finished.

JACQUES HURY. And mine begins.

VIOLAINE. What! do you find the cup where I have drunk so bitter?

JACQUES HURY. And now I have lost you for ever!

VIOLAINE. Tell me, why lost?

JACQUES HURY. You are dying.

VIOLAINE. Jacques, you must understand me!

Of what use is the finest perfume in a sealed vase? it serves for nothing.

JACQUES HURY. No, Violaine.

VIOLAINE. Of what use has my body been to me, having hidden away my heart so that you could not see it, but you saw only the scar on the outside of the worthless shell.

JACQUES HURY. I was hard and blind!

VIOLAINE. Now I am broken utterly, and the perfume is set free.

And behold, you believe everything, simply because I laid my hand on your head.

JACQUES HURY. I believe. I do not doubt any more.

VIOLAINE. And tell me, where is the Justice in all that, this justice you spoke of so proudly?

JACQUES HURY. I am no longer proud.

VIOLAINE. Come, leave Justice alone. It is not for us to call her and to make her come.

JACQUES HURY. Violaine, how you have suffered in these eight long years!

VIOLAINE. But not in vain. Many things are consumed in the flame of a heart that burns.

JACQUES HURY. Deliverance is near.

VIOLAINE. Blessed be the hand that led me that night!

JACQUES HURY. What hand?

VIOLAINE. That silent hand that clasped mine, and led me, when I was coming back with my food.

JACQUES HURY. Led you where?

VIOLAINE. Where Pierre de Craon found me.

Under a great mound of sand, a whole cart-load heaped upon me. Did I place myself there, all alone?

JACQUES HURY (rising). Who has done that?

God's Blood! who has done that?

VIOLAINE. I don't know. It matters little. Do not curse.

JACQUES HURY. I shall find out the truth about that.

VIOLAINE. No, you shall find out the truth about nothing.

JACQUES HURY. Tell me all!

VIOLAINE. I have told you all. What would you learn of a blind woman?

JACQUES HURY. You shall not put me off the track.

VIOLAINE. Do not waste words. I have only a little more time to be with you.

JACQUES HURY. I shall always have Mara.

VIOLAINE. She is your wife, and she is my sister, born of the same father and the same mother, and of the same flesh,

Both of us, here beside Monsanvierge. (Silence.)

[JACQUES stands a moment motionless as if trying to control himself. Then he sits down again.]

JACQUES HURY. There are no more recluses at Monsanvierge.

VIOLAINE. What did you say?

JACQUES HURY. The last one died last Christmas. No mouth comes any more to the wicket of the nourishing church of this holy monastery, so the priest tells us who used to give them communion.

VIOLAINE. The mountain of God

Is dead, and we share the heritage, Mara and I.

JACQUES HURY. And Violaine was the secret offshoot of the Holy Tree, growing from some subterranean root.

God would not have taken her from me, if she had been entirely filled by me, leaving no part of her empty,

"God's part," as good women call it.

VIOLAINE. What's to be done? so much the worse!

JACQUES HURY. Stay! do not go!

VIOLAINE. I stay, I am not going.

Tell me, Jacques, do you remember that hour at noon, and that great scorching sun, and that spot on the flesh under my breast that I showed to you?

JACQUES HURY. Ah!

VIOLAINE. You remember? did I not tell you truly that you could never more tear me out of your soul?

This of myself is in you for ever. I do not wish you any more to be happy, it is not proper that you should laugh,

In this time when you are still far away from me.

JACQUES HURY. Ah! Ah! Violaine!

VIOLAINE. Have this from me, my well-beloved!

The communion on the cross, the bitterness like the bitterness of myrrh,

Of the sick man who sees the shadow upon the dial, and of the soul that receives its call!

And for you age is already come. But how hard it is to renounce when the heart is young!

JACQUES HURY. And from me you have not wanted to accept anything!

VIOLAINE. Think you that I know nothing about you, Jacques?

JACQUES HURY. My mother knew me.

VIOLAINE. To me also, O Jacques, you have caused much pain!

JACQUES HURY. You are a virgin and I have no part in you.

VIOLAINE. What! must I tell you everything?

JACQUES HURY. What do you still conceal?

VIOLAINE. It is necessary. This is not the time to keep anything back.

JACQUES HURY. Speak louder.

VIOLAINE. Have they not told you, then, that your child was dead?

Last year, while you were at Rheims?

JACQUES HURY. Several people told me. But Mara swears that it only slept And I have never been able to draw from her the whole story.

They say she went to find you.

I should have known everything in time. I wanted to learn the whole truth.

VIOLAINE. That is true. You have the right to know all.

JACQUES HURY. What did she go to ask of you?

VIOLAINE. Have you never noticed that the eyes of your little girl are changed?

JACQUES HURY. They are blue now, like yours.

VIOLAINE. It was Christmas night. Yes, Jacques, it is true, she was dead. Her little body was stiff and icy.

I know it; all night I held her in my arms.

JACQUES HURY. Who then restored her to life?

VIOLAINE. God only, and with God the faith and the despair of her mother.

JACQUES HURY. But you had nothing to do with it?

VIOLAINE. O Jacques, to you only I will tell a great mystery.

It is true, when I felt this dead body upon my own, the child of your flesh, Jacques. . . .

JACQUES HURY. Ah, my little Aubaine!

VIOLAINE. You love her very much?

JACQUES HURY. Go on.

VIOLAINE. . . . My heart contracted, and the iron entered into me.

Behold what I held in my arms for my Christmas night, and all that remained of our race, a dead child!

All of yours that I should ever possess in this life!

And I listened to Mara, who read me the Service for this Holy night: the babe who has been given to us, the gospel of Joy.

Ah, do not say that I know nothing of you!

Do not say that I do not know what it is to suffer for you!

Nor that I do not know the effort and the partition of the woman who gives life!

JACQUES HURY. You do not mean that the child was really brought back to life?

VIOLAINE. What I know is that it was dead, and that all of a sudden I felt its head move!

And life burst from me in a flash, at one bound, and my mortified flesh bloomed again!

Ah, I know what it is, that little blind mouth that seeks, and those pitiless teeth!

JACQUES HURY. O Violaine! (*Silence. He makes as if to rise.* VIOLAINE *feebly forces him to remain seated.*)

VIOLAINE. Do you forgive me now?

JACQUES HURY. Oh, the duplicity of women!

Ah, you are the daughter of your mother!

Tell me! it is not you that you would have me forgive!

VIOLAINE. Whom, then?

JACQUES HURY. What hand was that which took yours the other night, and so kindly led you?

VIOLAINE. I do not know.

JACQUES HURY. But I think that I know.

VIOLAINE. You do not know.

Leave that to us, it is an affair between women.

JACQUES HURY. My affair is to have justice done.

VIOLAINE. Ah, leave thy Justice alone!

JACQUES HURY. I know what remains for me to do.

VIOLAINE. You know nothing at all, poor fellow.

You have no understanding of women,

And what poor creatures they are, stupid and hard-headed and knowing only one thing.

Do not confuse everything between you and her, as with you and me.

Was it really her hand alone? I do not know. And you do not know either. And of what good would it be to know?

Keep what you have. Forgive.

And you, have you never needed to be forgiven?

JACQUES HURY. I am alone.

VIOLAINE. Not alone, with this beautiful little child I have given back to you,

And Mara, my sister, your wife, of the same flesh as myself. Who, with me, knows you better?

It is necessary for you to have the strength and the deed, it is necessary for you to have a duty plainly laid down and final.

That is why I have this sand in my hair.

JACQUES HURY. Happiness is ended for me.

VIOLAINE. It is ended, what does that matter?

Happiness was never promised to you. Work, that is all that is asked of you.—*And Monsanvierge belongs only to you now.*—

Question the old earth and she will

always answer you with bread
and wine.
As for me I have finished with her,
and I go beyond.
Tell me, what is the day you will
pass far from me? It will soon pass.
And when your turn shall come, and
when you see the great door creak
and move,
I shall be on the other side and you
will find me waiting. (*Silence.*)

JACQUES HURY. O my betrothed, through
the blossoming branches, hail!

VIOLAINE. You remember?
Jacques! Good morning, Jacques!
[*The first rays of dawn appear.*]
And now I must be carried away
from here.

JACQUES HURY. Carried away?

VIOLAINE. This is not the place for a
leper to die in.
Let me be carried to that shelter my
father built for the poor at the door
of Monsanvierge. (*He makes as if to
take her. She waves him away with her
hand.*)
No, Jacques, no, not you.

JACQUES HURY. What, not even this last
duty to you?

VIOLAINE. No it is not right that you
should touch me.
Call Pierre de Craon.
He has been a leper, though God has
cured him. He has no horror of me.
And I know that to him I am like a
brother, and woman has no more
power over his soul. (*JACQUES HURY
goes out and returns several minutes later
with* PIERRE DE CRAON. *She does not
speak. The two men look at her in silence.*)

VIOLAINE. Jacques!

JACQUES HURY. Violaine!

VIOLAINE. Has the year been good and
the grain fine and abundant?

JACQUES HURY. So abundant that we do
not know where to put it all.

VIOLAINE. Ah!
How beautiful a great harvest is!
Yes, even now I remember it, and I
think it beautiful.

JACQUES HURY. Yes, Violaine.

VIOLAINE. How beautiful it is
To live! (*Speaking low and with deep
fervour.*) and how great is the glory
of God!

JACQUES HURY. Live, then, and stay
with us.

VIOLAINE. But how good it is to die too!
When all is really ended, and over
us spreads little by little
The darkness, as of a deep shade.
(*Silence.*)

PIERRE DE CRAON. She does not speak
any more.

JACQUES HURY. Take her. Carry her
where I have told you.
For, as to me, she does not wish me
to touch her.
Very gently! Gently, gently, I tell
you. Do not hurt her.
[*They go out,* PIERRE *carrying the body. The
door stands open. Long pause.*]

SCENE FOUR

On the threshold of the door appears ANNE
VERCORS *in the habit of a traveller, a staff
in his hand and a sack slung on his back.*

ANNE VERCORS. Open?
Is the house empty, that all the doors
should be open?
Who has come in so early before me?
or who is it that has gone out? (*He
looks around a long time.*)
I recognize the old room, nothing
is changed.
Here is the fireplace, here is the table.
Here is the ceiling with its strong
beams.
I am like an animal that smells all
around him, and who knows his
resting-place and his home.

Hail, house! It is I. Here is the master come back.

Hail, Monsanvierge, lofty dwelling!

From far away, since yesterday morning and the day before, on the top of the hill I recognized the Arch with the five towers.

But why is it that the bells ring no more? neither yesterday nor this morning 10 Have I heard in the sky, with the Angel ninefold sonorous, tidings of Jesus brought three times, three times to the heart of Mary.

Monsanvierge! how often I have thought of thy walls,

While, under my captive feet, I made the water rise into the garden of the old man of Damascus.

(Oh, the morning, and the im-20 placable afternoon!

Oh, the eternal noria and the eyes we lift toward Lebanon!)

And all the aromatic odours of exile are little to me

Compared with this walnut-leaf I crush between my fingers.

Hail, Earth, powerful and subdued! Here it is not sand that we plough, and soft alluvium, 30

But the deep earth itself that we work with the whole strength of our body and of the six oxen who pull and form slowly under the ploughshare of the great trench,

And, as far as my eyes can see, everything has responded to the upheaval man has caused.

Already I have seen all my fields, and perceived that everything is 40 well cared for. God be praised! Jacques does his work well. (*He lays his sack on the table.*)

Earth, I have been to seek for thee a little earth,

A little earth for my burial, that which God himself chose for his own at Jerusalem. (*Pause.*)

I would not come back last night. I waited for daylight.

And I passed the night under a stack of new straw, thinking, sleeping, praying, looking around, remembering, giving thanks,

Listening to hear, if I could, the voice of my wife, or of my daughter Violaine, or of a crying child.

When I awoke I saw that the night was brighter.

And up there, above the dark crest of Monsanvierge, resplendent, from Arabia,

The morning star rose over France, like a herald rising in the solitude!

And then I came to the house.

Hallo! Is there anybody here? (*He raps on the table with his staff. . . . Curtain, which remains down a few minutes.*)

SCENE FIVE

The farther end of the garden. Afternoon of the same day. End of the summer.

The trees are heavy with fruit. The branches of some of them, bending to the ground, are held up by props. The dried and tarnished leaves, mingled with the red and yellow of apples, seem like tapestry.

Below, flooded with light, lies the immense plain as it would be after the harvest; with stubble, and already some ploughed earth. The white roads and the villages can be seen. There are rows of haystacks, looking very small, and here and there a poplar. Far away, in another direction, are flocks of sheep. The shadows of large clouds pass over the plain.

In the middle, where the scene descends toward the background, from which the tops of the trees in a little wood are seen to emerge, there is a semi-circular stone bench, reached by three steps, and with lions' heads at each

end of its back. ANNE VERCORS *is sitting there, with* JACQUES HURY *at his right side.*

ANNE VERCORS. The golden end of Autumn
Will soon
Despoil the fruit tree and the vine.
And in the morning the white sun,
A single flash of a fireless diamond,
will blend with the white vesture of 10
the earth:
And the evening is near when he who
walks beneath the aspen
Shall hear the last leaf on its summit.
Now, behold, making equal the days
and nights,
Counterpoising the long hours of
labour with its projecting sign,
athwart the celestial Door
Interposes the royal Balance. 20
JACQUES HURY. Father, since thou hast
been gone,
Everything, the painful story, and the
plot of these women, and the pitfall made to take us in,
Thou know'st, and I have told thee
Still another thing, with my mouth
against thine ear,
Where is thy wife? where is thy
daughter Violaine? 30
And lo, thou talkest of the straw we
twist, and of the great black grape
Which fills the hand of the vinedresser, the hand he thrusts under
the vine-branch!
Already
The crooked Scorpion and the retreating Sagittarius
Have appeared on the dial of night.
ANNE VERCORS. Let the old man exult in 40
the warm season! O truly blessed
place! O bosom of the Fatherland!
O grateful, fecund earth!
The carts passing along the road
Leave straw among the fruited
branches!

JACQUES HURY. O Violaine! O cruel
Violaine! desire of my soul, you
have betrayed me!
O hateful garden! O love useless and
denied! O garden planted in an
evil hour!
Sweet Violaine! perfidious Violaine!
Oh, the silence and the depth of
woman!
Art thou then really gone, my soul?
Having deceived me, she goes away;
and having undeceived me, with
fatal sweet words,
She goes again, and I, bearing this
poisoned arrow, it will be necessary
That I live on and on! like the beast
we take by the horn, drawing his
head out of the manger,
Like the horse we loose from the
single-tree in the evening with a
lash of the whip on his back!
O ox, it is thou that walkest ahead,
but we two make but one team.
Only that the furrow be made, that is
all they ask of us.
That is why everything that was not
necessary to my task, everything
has been taken away from me.
ANNE VERCORS. Monsanvierge is dead,
and the fruit of your labour is for
you alone.
JACQUES HURY. It is true. (*Silence.*)
ANNE VERCORS. Have they looked well
to provisioning the chapel for tomorrow?
Is there enough to eat and drink for
all those we shall have to entertain?
JACQUES HURY. Old man! It is your
daughter we are going to lay in the
earth, and behold what you find to
say!
Surely you have never loved her!
But the old man, like the miser who
after warming his hands at his pot
of embers hoards their heat in his
bosom,

He suffices for himself alone.

ANNE VERCORS. Everything must be done.

Things must be done honourably
. . . Elisabeth, my wife, hidden heart!

[*Enter* PIERRE DE CRAON.]

ANNE VERCORS. Is everything ready?

PIERRE DE CRAON. They are working at the coffin. 10

They are digging the grave where you ordered,

Close up by the church there, near that of the last chaplain, your brother.

Within it they have put the earth you brought back.

A great black ivy-vine

Comes out of the priestly tomb, and, crossing the wall,

Enters almost into the sealed arch.

. . . Tomorrow, in the early morning. Everything is ready.

[JACQUES HURY *weeps, his face in his cloak. In the path is seen a nun, like a woman who hunts for flowers.*]

ANNE VERCORS. What are you looking for, Sister?

VOICE OF THE NUN (*hollow and smothered*). Some flowers, to lay on her heart, 30 between her hands.

ANNE VERCORS. There are no more flowers, there is nothing but fruit.

JACQUES HURY. Push aside the leaves and you will find the last violet!

And the Immortelle is still in the bud, and nothing is left to us but the dahlia and the poppy. (*The nun is no longer there.*)

PIERRE DE CRAON. The two Sisters, who 40 care for the sick, one quite young the other very old,

Have dressed her, and Mara has sent her wedding-dress for her.

Truly, she was only a leper, but she was honourable in the sight of God.

She reposes in a deep sleep
As one who knows in whose care she is.

I saw her before they had laid her in the coffin.

Her body is still supple.

Oh, while the Sister finished dressing her, with her arm around her waist,

Holding her in a sitting posture, how her head fell backward

Like that of the still warm partridge the hunter picks in his hand!

ANNE VERCORS. My child! my little daughter I carried in my arms before she knew how to walk!

The fat little girl who awoke with bursts of laughter in her little sabot of a bed.

All that is over. Ah! ah! O God! Alas!

20 PIERRE DE CRAON. Don't you want to see her before they nail down the coffin-lid?

ANNE VERCORS. No. The child disowned
Goes away secretly.

JACQUES HURY. Never again in this life shall I see her face.

[PIERRE DE CRAON *sits down at the left of* ANNE VERCORS. *Long pause. The sound of a hammer on planks. They remain silent, listening.* MARA *is seen to pass at the side of the stage holding a child in her arms wrapped in a black shawl. Then she re-enters slowly at the back, and comes and stands in front of the bench where the three men are sitting. They stare at her, except* JACQUES HURY, *who looks at the ground.*]

MARA (*her head lowered*). Hail, father! Hail to you all.

You stare at me and I know what you think: "Violaine is dead.

The beautiful ripe fruit, the good golden fruit

Has fallen from the branch, and, bitter without, hard as a stone within,

Only the wintry nut remains to us."
Who loves me? Who has ever loved
me? (*She lifts her head with a savage
gesture.*)
Well! here I am! what have you to
say to me? Say everything! What
have you against me?
What makes you look at me like that,
with your eyes saying: It is thou!
It is true, it is I!   10
It is true, it was I who killed her,
It was I the other night who took her
by the hand, having gone to seek
her,
While Jacques was not there,
And I who made her fall into the
sandpit, and who turned over upon
her
That loaded cart. Everything was
ready, there was only a bolt to   20
pull out,
I did that,
Jacques! and it is I, too, who said to
my mother,
Violaine—to talk to her that day
when you came back from Braine.
For I longed ardently to marry you,
and if I could not I had decided to
hang myself the day of your wed-
ding.   30
Now God, who sees into hearts, had
already let her take the leprosy.
—But Jacques never stopped thinking
of her.
That is why I killed her.
What then? What else was there to do?
What more could be done
So that the one I love and who is
mine
Should be mine entirely, as I am his   40
entirely,
And that Violaine should be shut
out?
I did what I could.
And you in your turn, answer! Your
Violaine that you loved,

How then did you love her, and which
was worth the most,
Your love, do you think, or my
hatred?
You all loved her! and here is her
father who abandons her, and her
mother who advises her!
And her betrothed, how he has
believed in her!
Certainly you loved her,
As we say we love a gentle animal, a
pretty flower, and that was all the
feeling there was in your love!
Mine was of another kind;
Blind, never letting go anything once
taken, like a deaf thing that does
not hear!
For him to have me entirely, it was
necessary to me to have him entirely!
What have I done after all that I
must defend myself? who has been
the most faithful to him, I or Violaine?
Violaine who betrayed him for I
know not what leper, giving in,
said she, to God's council in a kiss?
I honour God. Let him stay where
he is! Our miserable life is so short!
Let him leave us in peace!
Is it my fault if I loved Jacques? was
it for my happiness, or for the
burning away of my soul?
What could I do to defend myself, I
who am not beautiful, nor agreeable, a poor woman who can only
give pain?
That is why I killed her in my despair!
O poor, unskilful crime!
O disgrace to her that no one loves
and with whom nothing succeeds!
What ought to have been done,
since I loved him and he did not
love me? (*She turns toward* JACQUES.)
And you, O Jacques, why do you not
speak?

Why turn you your face to the ground,
without a word to say,
Like Violaine, the day when you accused her unjustly?
Do you not know me? I am your wife.
Truly I know that I do not seem to
you either beautiful or agreeable,
but look, I have dressed myself for
you, I have added to that pain
that I can give you. And I am the 10
sister of Violaine.
It is born of pain! This love is not
born of joy, it is born of pain! the
pain which suffices for those who
have no joy!
No one is glad to see it, ah, it is not
the flower in its season,
But that which is under the flowers
that wither, the earth itself, the
miserly earth under the grass, the 20
earth that never fails!
Know me then!
I am your wife and you can do nothing to change that!
One inseparable flesh, the contact
by the centre and by the soul, and
for confirmation this mysterious
parentage between us two.
Which is, that I have had a child of
yours.   30
I have committed a great crime. I
have killed my sister; but I have
not sinned against you. And I tell
you that you have nothing to reproach me with. And what do the
others matter to me?
That is what I had to say, and now do
what you will. (*Silence.*)
ANNE VERCORS. What she says is true.
Go, Jacques, forgive her!   40
JACQUES HURY. Come then, Mara.
[*She comes nearer and stands before them,
forming with her child a single object
upon which the two men extend together
their right hands. Their arms cross,
and* JACQUES' *hand is laid on the head*

of the child, that of ANNE *on the head
of* MARA.]
JACQUES HURY. It is Violaine who forgives you.
It is through her, Mara, that I forgive
you.
Guilty woman, it is she who reunites us.
MARA. Alas! alas! dead words and without a ray of light!
O Jacques, I am no longer the same!
There is something in me that is
ended. Have no fear. All that is
nothing to me.
Something in me is broken, and I am
left without strength, like a woman
widowed and without children.
[*The child laughs vaguely and looks all
around, with little cries of delight.*]
ANNE VERCORS (*caressing it*). Poor Violaine!
And you, little child! How blue its
eyes are!
MARA (*melting into tears*). Father! father!
ah!
It was dead, and it was she who
brought it back to life! (*She goes
away, and sits down alone. The sun
goes down. It rains here and there on
the plain, and the lines of the rain can
be seen crossing the rays of the sun. An
immense rainbow unfurls.*)
VOICE OF A CHILD. Hi! Hi! look at the
beautiful rainbow!
[*Other voices cease in the distance. Great
flocks of pigeons fly about, turning,
scattering, and alighting here and there
in the stubble.*]
ANNE VERCORS. The earth is set free.
The place is empty.
The harvest is all gathered, and the
birds of heaven
Pick up the lost grain.
PIERRE DE CRAON. Summer is over, the
season sleeps in a time of quiet,
everywhere the foliage rustles in
the breeze of September.

The sky has turned blue again, and while the partridges call from their covert,

The buzzard soars in the liquid air.

JACQUES HURY. Everything is yours. Father! take back again all this property you vested in me.

ANNE VERCORS. No, Jacques, I no longer possess anything, and this is no more mine. He who went away will not return, and that which is once given cannot be

Taken back. Here is a new Combernon, a new Monsanvierge.

PIERRE DE CRAON. The other is dead. The virgin mountain is dead, and the scar in her side will never open again.

ANNE VERCORS. It is dead. My wife, too, is dead, my daughter is dead, the holy Maid

Has been burned and thrown to the winds, not one of her bones remains on the earth.

But the King and the Pope have been given back again to France and to the whole world.

The schism comes to an end, and once more the Throne rises above all men. 30

I returned by Rome, I kissed the foot of Saint Peter, I ate the consecrated bread standing with people from the Four Divisions of the Earth,

While the bells of the Quirinal and of the Lateran, and the voice of Santa Maria Maggiore,

Saluted the ambassadors of these new nations who come from the Orient 40 and the Occident all together into the City,

Asia found again, and this Atlantic world beyond the Pillars of Hercules!

And this very evening when the Angelus shall ring, at the same hour when the star Al-Zohar glows in the unfurled heaven,

Begins the year of Jubilee which the new Pope grants,

The annulment of debts, the liberation of prisoners, the suspension of war, the closing of the courts, the restitution of all property.

PIERRE DE CRAON. Truce for one year and peace for one day only.

ANNE VERCORS. What does it matter? peace is good, but war will find us armed.

O Pierre! this is a time when women and newborn infants teach sages and old men!

Here am I shocked like a Jew because the face of the Church is darkened, and because she totters on her road forsaken by all men.

And I wanted once more to clasp the empty tomb, to put my hand in the hole left by the cross.

But my little daughter Violaine has been wiser.

Is the object of life only to live? will the feet of God's children be fastened to this wretched earth?

It is not to live, but to die, and not to hew the cross, but to mount upon it, and to give all that we have, laughing!

There is joy, there is freedom, there is grace, there is eternal youth! and as God lives, the blood of the old man on the sacrificial cloth, near that of the young man,

Makes a stain as red and fresh as that of the yearling lamb!

O Violaine! child of grace! flesh of my flesh! As far as the smoky fire of my farm is distant from the morning star,

When on the sun's breast that beautiful virgin lays her illumined head,

May thy father see thee on high
through all eternity in the place
which has been kept for thee!
As God lives, where the little child
goes the father should go also!
What is the worth of the world compared to life? and what is the worth
of life if not to be given?
And why torment ourselves when it
is so simple to obey?   10
It is thus that Violaine follows at
once without hesitation the hand
that takes hers.
PIERRE DE CRAON. O father! I was the
last who held her in my arms,
because she entrusted herself to
Pierre de Craon, knowing that
there is no longer in his heart the
desire of the flesh.
And the young body of this divine 20
brother lay in my arms like a tree
that has been cut down and droops
Already, as the glowing colour of the
pomegranate blossoms everywhere
flames from the bud that can no
longer sheathe it,
So the splendour of the angel that
knows not death embraces our
little sister.
The odour of Paradise exhaled in 30
my arms from this broken tabernacle.
Do not weep, Jacques, my friend.
ANNE VERCORS. Do not weep, my son.
JACQUES HURY. Pierre, give me back
that ring she gave thee.
PIERRE DE CRAON. I cannot!
Any more than the ripened spike of
corn can give back the seed in the
earth from which sprang its stem. 40
Of that bit of gold I have made a
fiery gem.
And the vessel of everlasting Day
where the seed of the ultimate
goodness of saintly souls is treasured.

Justitia is finished and lacks only the
woman that I shall set there at the
blossoming of my supreme lily.
ANNE VERCORS. You are powerful in
works, Pierre, and I have seen on
my way the churches you have
brought to birth.
PIERRE DE CRAON. Blessed be God who
has made me a father of churches,
And who has endowed my soul with
understanding and the sense of the
three dimensions!
And who has debarred me as a leper
and freed me from all temporal
care,
To the end that I should raise up
from the soil of France Ten Wise
Virgins whose oil is never exhausted, and who compose a vessel
of prayers!
What is this *soul*, or bolt of wood, that
the lutemaker inserts between the
front and the back of his instrument,
Compared to this great enclosed lyre,
and of these columnar Powers in
the night, whose number and distance I have calculated?
Never from the outside do I carve
an image.
But, like father Noah, from the
middle of my enormous Arch,
I work from within, and see everything rise simultaneously around
me!
And what is matter which the hand
can chisel compared to the spirit
we strive to enshrine,
Or to the hallowed space left empty
by a reverent soul shrinking back
in the presence of its God?
Nothing is too deep for me: my wells
descend as far as the waters of the
Mother-spring.
Nothing is too high for the spire that
mounts to heaven and steals God's
lightning from him!

Pierre de Craon will die, but the Ten Virgins, his daughters,
Will remain like the Widow's cruse
In which the flour and the sacred measures of the oil and wine are renewed for ever.

ANNE VERCORS. Yes, Pierre. Whoever trusts himself to stone will not be deceived.

PIERRE DE CRAON. Oh, how beautiful is 10 stone, and how soft it is in the hands of the architect! and how right and beautiful a thing is his whole completed work!
How faithful is stone, and how well it preserves the idea, and what shadows it makes!
And if a vine grows well on the least bit of wall, and the rosebush above it blooms, 20
How beautiful it is, and how true it is altogether!
Have you seen my little church of l'Epine, which is like a glowing brasier and a rosebush in full bloom?
And Saint Jean de Vertus like a handsome young man in the midst of the Craie Champenoise? And Mont-Saint Martin which will be 30 mellow in fifty years?
And Saint-Thomas of Fond-d'Ardenne that you can hear in the evening bellowing like a bull in the midst of its marshes?
But Justitia that I have made last, Justitia my daughter is more beautiful!

ANNE VERCORS. I shall go there and leave my staff for a thank-offering. 40

PIERRE DE CRAON. She is dedicated in my heart, nothing is lacking, she is whole.
And for the roof,
I have found the stone I sought, not quarried by iron,

Softer than alabaster and closer-grained than a grindstone.
As the fragile teeth of the little Justitia serve as a foundation for my great structure,
So also at the summit, in the wide sky, I shall set this other Justice,
Violaine the leper in glory, Violaine the blind in the sight of everybody.
And I shall make her with her hands crossed on her breast, like the spike of grain still half-prisoned in its tegmen,
And her eyes blindfolded.

ANNE VERCORS. Why blindfolded?

PIERRE DE CRAON. That, seeing not, she may the better hear
The sound of the city and the fields, and man's voice at the same time with the voice of God.
For she is Justice herself, who listens and conceives in her heart the perfect harmony.
This is she who is a refuge from storms, and a shade from the heat at the rising of the dog-star.

JACQUES HURY. But Violaine is not a stone for me, and stone does not suffice me!
And I do not wish the light of her beautiful eyes to be veiled!

ANNE VERCORS. The light of her soul is with us. I have not lost thee, Violaine! How beautiful thou art, my child!
And how beautiful is the bride when on her wedding-day she shows herself to her father in her splendid wedding-gown, sweetly embarrassed.
Walk before me, Violaine, my child, and I will follow thee. But sometimes turn thy face toward me, that I may see thine eyes!
Violaine! Elisabeth! soon again I shall be with you.

As for you, Jacques, perform your task in your turn, as I have done mine! The end is near.

It is here, the end of all that is given me of the day, of the year, and of my own life!

It is six o'clock. The shadow of the Grès-qui-va-boire reaches the brook.

Winter comes, night comes; yet a little more night, [10]

A short watch!

All my life I have worked with the Sun and aided him in his task.

But now, by the fireside, in the light of the lamp,

All alone I must begin the night.

PIERRE DE CRAON. O husbandman, your work is finished. See the empty land, see the harvested earth, and [20] already the plough attacks the stubble!

And now, what you have begun it is my part to complete.

As you have opened the furrow, I dig the pit wherein to preserve the grain, I prepare the tabernacle.

And as it is not you who cause the harvest to ripen, but the sun, so it is also with grace. [30]

And nothing, unless it issue from the seed, can develop into the ear.

And certainly, Justice is beautiful. But how much more beautiful

Is this fruitful tree of mankind, which the seed of the Eucharist engenders and makes grow.

This too makes one complete whole, unified.

Ah, if all men understood architec- [40] ture as I do,

Who would willingly fail to follow his vocation and renounce the sacred place assigned to him in the Temple?

ANNE VERCORS. Pierre de Craon, you have many thoughts, but for me this setting sun suffices.

All my life I have done the same thing that he does, cultivating the earth, rising and returning home with him.

And now I go into the night, and I am not afraid, and I know that there too all is clear and in order, in the season of this great heavenly winter which sets all things in motion.

The night sky where everything is at work, and which is like a great ploughing, and a room with only one person in it.

And there the eternal Ploughman drives the seven oxen, with his gaze set upon a fixed star,

As ours is set upon the green branch that marks the end of the furrow.

The sun and I, side by side

Have worked, and the product of our work does not concern us. Mine is done.

I bow to what must be, and now I am willing to be dissolved.

And herein lies peace for him who knows it, and joy and grief in equal parts.

My wife is dead. Violaine is dead. That is right.

I do not desire to hold any more that weak and wrinkled old hand. And as for Violaine, when she was eight years old, when she came and threw herself against my legs,

How I loved that strong little body! And little by little the impetuous, frolicsome roughness of the laughing child

Melted into the tenderness of the maiden, into the pain and heaviness of love, and when I went away

I saw already in her eyes one un-

known blossom among the flowers
of her springtime.

PIERRE DE CRAON. The call of death,
like a solemn lily.

ANNE VERCORS. Blessed be death in
which all the petitions in the Pater-
noster are satisfied.

PIERRE DE CRAON. For my part, it was
by herself and from her innocent
lips 10
That I received freedom and dismissal from this life.

[*The sun is in the western sky, as high as a
tall tree.*]

ANNE VERCORS. Behold the sun in the sky,
As he is in the pictures where the
Master awakes the workman at the
Eleventh Hour.

[*The door of the barn is heard to creak.*]

JACQUES HURY. What is that? 20

ANNE VERCORS. They have come to the
barn for straw
To lay in the bottom of the grave.

[*Silence:—Sound in the distance of a washer-
woman beating linen.*]

VOICE OF A CHILD (*without*).
Marguerite of Paris, pray!
Lend to me thy shoes of gray!
To walk in Paradise a way!
How fair it is! 30
How warm it is!
I hear the little bird say it is!
He goes pa—a—a—a!

JACQUES HURY. That is not the door of
the barn, it is the sound of the
tomb opening!
And, having looked at me with her
blind eyes, she that I loved passes
to the other side.
And I too, I have looked at her like 40
one who is blind, and I did not
doubt without proofs.
I never doubted her who accused her.
I have made my choice, and she that
I chose has been given to me. What
shall I say? It is right.

It is right.
Happiness is not for me, but desire!
it will never be torn from me.
And not Violaine, radiant and unblemished,
But the leper bending over me with a
bitter smile and the devouring
wound in her side! (*Silence.*)

[*The sun is behind the trees. It shines through
the branches. The shadows of the leaves
cover the ground and the seated people.
Here and there a golden bee shines in
the sunny interstices.*]

ANNE VERCORS. Here am I seated, and
from the top of the mountain I see
all the country at my feet.
And I recognized the roads, and I
count the farms and villages, and I
know them by name, and all the
people who live in them.
The plain is lost to view toward the
north.
And elsewhere, rising again, the hill
surrounds this village like a theatre.
And everywhere, all the while,
Green and pink in the spring, blue
and flaxen in the summer, brown
in winter or all white with snow,
Before me, at my side, around me,
I see always the Earth, like an unchanging sky all painted with
changing colours.
Having a form as much its own as a
person's, it is always there present
with me.
Now that is finished.
How many times have I risen from
my bed and gone to my work!
And now here is evening, and the
sun brings home the men and the
animals as if he led them by his
hand. (*He raises himself slowly and
painfully, and slowly stretches out his
arms to their full length, while the sun,
grown yellow, covers him.*)

Ah! ah!

Here am I stretching out my arms in the rays of the sun.

Evening is come! Have pity upon every man, Lord, in that hour when he has finished his task and stands before Thee like a child whose hands are being examined.

Mine are free. My day is finished. I have planted the grain and I have harvested it, and with this bread 10 that I have mac̄ all my children have made their communion.

Now I have finished.

A moment ago there was someone with me.

And now, wife and child having gone away,

I remain alone to say grace at the empty table.

Both of them are dead, but I, live, on the threshold of death, and I am filled with inexplicable joy!

[*The Angelus is rung from the church down below. First toll of three strokes.*]

JACQUES HURY (*hollowly*). The Angel of God proclaims peace to us, and the child thrills in the bosom of its mother.

[*Second toll.*]

PIERRE DE CRAON. "Men of little faith, 30 why do you weep?"

[*Third toll.*]

ANNE VERCORS. "Because I go to my father and to your father."

[*Profound silence. Then peal.*]

PIERRE DE CRAON. Thus the Angelus speaks as if with three voices, in May When the unmarried man comes home, having buried his mother,

"Voice-of-the-Rose" speaks in the 40 silvery evening.

O Violaine! O woman through whom comes temptation!

For, not yet knowing what I would do, I turned my eyes where you then did turn thine.

Truly I have always thought that joy was a good thing.

But now I have everything!

I possess everything, under my hands, and I am like a person who, seeing a tree laden with fruit,

And having mounted a ladder, feels the thick branches yield under his body.

I must talk under the tree, like a flute which is neither low nor shrill! How the water

Raises me! Thanksgiving unseals the stone of my heart!

How I live, thus! How I grow greater, thus mingled with my God, like the vine and the olive-tree.

[*The sun goes down.* MARA *turns her head toward her husband and looks at him.*]

20 JACQUES HURY. See her, looking at me.

See her returning to me with the night! (*Sound of a cracked bell near by. First toll.*)

ANNE VERCORS. It is the little bell of the sisters that rings the Angelus in its turn.

[*Silence. Then another bell is heard, very high up, at Monsanvierge, sounding in its turn the triple toll, admirably sonorous and solemn.*]

JACQUES HURY. Listen!

PIERRE DE CRAON. A miracle!

ANNE VERCORS. It is Monsanvierge come to life again! The Angelus, ringing once more, brings to the listening heavens and earth the wonted tidings.

PIERRE DE CRAON. Yes, Voice-of-the-Rose, God is born!

40 [*Second toll of the bell of the sisters. It strikes the third note just as Monsanvierge strikes the first.*]

ANNE VERCORS. God makes himself man.

JACQUES HURY. He is dead!

PIERRE DE CRAON. He is risen!

[*Third toll of the bell of the sisters. Then the*

peal. Pause. Then, nearly lost in the distance, are heard the three strokes of the third toll up on the heights.]

ANNE VERCORS. This is not the toll of the Angelus, it is the communion bells!

PIERRE DE CRAON. The three strokes are gathered like an ineffable sacrifice into the bosom of the Virgin without sin.

[*Their faces are turned toward the heights; they listen as if awaiting the peal, which does not come.*]

GREGORIO MARTÍNEZ SIERRA

G. MARTÍNEZ SIERRA, the most popular modern Spanish dramatist in America, is an excellent representative of his country's contribution to the contemporary theatre. Spanish drama has not been in the forefront of modern world currents: it has not been particularly conscious of or concerned with the stirring movements whose contagion touched almost all other European states. It has sometimes paralleled the techniques and subject interests of other countries, but that seems a coincidence among a group of dramatists who have in general gone their own self-contained way. One does not go to the Iberian peninsula in search of things that are new or forward-looking.

This does not mean, however, that Spain has not had her giants in the contemporary theatre. José Echegaray (1832–1916), celebrated for *The Great Galeoto* (1881), the masterpiece among his eighty-odd plays, received the Nobel Prize in Literature in 1905—the second dramatist to be so honored. Jacinto Benavente (1866), almost as prolific as Echegaray, was Spain's leading dramatist among the young men who were known as the Generation of '98, and who tried to free their theatre from its older tradition. They were issuing manifestoes at the time Echegaray was being honored in 1905. Benavente himself received the Nobel prize in 1922. His popular and much reprinted *The Passion Flower* was a big success in America with Nance O'Neill as Raimunda. The Theatre Guild chose to launch its career in 1919 with Benavente's *The Bonds of Interest*, and Eva Le Gallienne opened her Civic Repertory Theatre in 1926 with his *Saturday Night*. Such signal distinction was due to the humanity of Benavente rather than to any novelty or departure in his plays; for the plays gave no hint of the forthcoming *Liliom*'s, *R.U.R.*'s, *The Great God Brown*'s and such advanced achievements which were to give the Guild its prestige. Besides Echegaray and Benavente a few other Spanish dramatists have been represented in English by a play or two, notably the socially conscious Benito Pérez Galdós with his anti-clerical *Electra*, and other plays; and the brothers Álverez Quintero with their engaging comedies of Andalusia: *The Lady from Alfaqueque* presented at the Civic Repertory Theatre, *A Hundred Years Old* in which Otis Skinner starred, *Malvaloca*, and others.

Martínez Sierra belongs with those few who have chosen to dramatize the gentler passions and the tenderer sentiments. He was born in Madrid on March 6, 1881. He attended the University of Madrid with only indifferent success as a scholar. In 1899 he married Maria de la O Lejárrago, a woman of talent and distinction from the wine region of Rioja which served as the setting of some of the later plays of her husband. Throughout the years they have written in intimate collaboration under Martínez Sierra's name without revealing the nature or the extent of their individual contribution.

Martínez Sierra did not begin to write for the theatre until 1907, a decade after the appearance of his first book, *The Song of Labor*, for which Benavente himself wrote an introduction and arranged publication. During the next ten years he wrote poems, essays, short stories and novels, and four dialogues called *Theatre of Dreams* that were strongly touched with the mystical influence of Maeterlinck. It was the great and versatile Benavente who drew him into the theatre. During the period of ferment following the Spanish-American War, Benavente had founded an Art Theatre at Madrid, and had been especially hospitable to the young men of talent. Martínez Sierra joined this company as an actor in the opening performance of Benavente's *A Long Farewell*, and continued to appear with the organization for nearly ten years. This first-hand, practical discipline in the working theatre was of first importance to him as a playwright. The continued tutelage of Benavente made a profound impression upon him, which Martínez Sierra handsomely acknowledged: "As I listened to him talk, the fundamental laws of the modern theatre were revealed to me, and I have profited by his instruction unceasingly."

Martínez Sierra's first play was a collaboration with his old friend Santiago Rusiñol—a comedy called *Life and Sweetness*, presented in Madrid in 1907. They did two other plays together; then Martínez Sierra came forward independently with a success of his own, a two-act comedy, *The Shadow of the Father* (1909). This was followed in 1910 by *The Mistress of the House*. These two plays were bare forerunners of the triumphant drama of the next year, *The Cradle Song*, dedicated to Benavente, which carried Martínez Sierra's name to the four corners of the world. Martínez Sierra built rapidly and solidly

upon the reputation thus established. He has written more than fifty plays of all varieties, many of them works of genius or of great distinction. At the same time he was managing his own theatre in Madrid, established in 1916 as the Teatro Eslava, directing his own stock company there, and taking it on several international tours, including one to New York in 1927. In addition to his own plays, he presented his translations of fifty or more of the plays of Ibsen, Björnson, Brieux, Barrie, Shakespeare, and others. As though this were not enough activity for one man, or in this case for the combined energies of Martínez Sierra and his versatile wife, he established and directed his own highly successful publishing house in Madrid, edited a literary periodical, edited a library of World Classics in translation, translated Maeterlinck, wrote voluminously about social questions and in support of the feminist movement for the liberation and exaltation of women for the advancement of modern Spain, and served in Hollywood with the Fox Studios as translator, adapter, and director of plays for Spanish speaking countries—including some of his own.

Out of all this activity it is fairly easy to sift the plays that belong permanently to the modern theatre. Thanks especially to the efforts of John Garrett Underhill and of Helen and Harley Granville-Barker, most of these plays are available in excellent English translations. Many of them, as might be expected, are light comedies aimed at nothing more, though it is enough, than an evening's entertainment in the theatre. Some of the best of these are short plays, a form in which the delicate art and slender plot structure congenial to Martínez Sierra are particularly at home. *The Lover* (1913) is an amusing comedy about a harmless lunatic who fell in love with his queen, followed her about, hid in her garden, slept in the house with her orang-outang, gathered up souvenirs of the queen, including a pair of her slippers, and had the good fortune to serve her when her carriage overturned. The queen, musing upon Shakespeare's sonnet "When forty winters shall besiege thy brow," grants this lover his boon—a pass over the railways of the Kingdom—and reflects in the tag line, "The poet was right:—We have been born too late into a world which has grown too old!"

Poor John (1912) is equally harmless and gentle. John, aged 22, is a hapless boy for whom things always go wrong. He is desperately in love with Mariana, just turned twenty. She loves him like a needy child, recognizing the truth of the village saying about poor John: "He is as modest as a mallow and as good as God's bread." Poor John, tenderly rejected by Mariana, even fails to commit suicide because he falls into a boat. His final words in the play are a rejection of the role of godfather to the first of Mariana's proposed ten children because the child might inherit John's poor luck; "besides, when things go wrong with him, I don't want to hear you saying forever: 'Poor John!' " This fragile one act play depends for its effect on "the humble truth" of the character drawing of good little people. *Madame Pepita* (1912), of conventional three act length, is an intricately plotted comedy centering in the intrigues around Madame Pepita, aged thirty-eight, her daughter, and nine other characters. For Madame Pepita, a dressmaker, inherits the fortune of a titled Russian who had deceived her, is besieged by a penniless count, and

saved by a good man; her daughter escapes the count's son, marries the young artist, and all is well in the best of all possible comic worlds. These plays are adequate samples in the lighter manner of the output from the fecund mine of the Martínez Sierras.

In the more serious vein and in a higher region of dramatic art are the four plays which really distinguish the name of Martínez Sierra. They see life through the poetic temperament and with the vibrancy of religious faith. *A Lily Among Thorns* (1911) is a study of the miraculous effect which the mere presence of Sister Teresa has upon the worldlings foregathered in a house of ill repute on a night when revolution breaks into violence in the streets of a big Spanish town. Fleeing from the wreckage of her convent, Sister Teresa comes unwittingly to this house. In one of the fine scenes she confronts the men and girls in their revelry, as one of the girls, wounded in the street fighting, is borne into the house. The Sister completely dominates the scene as she takes charge of the ministrations to the girl; the room is transformed, the men slink away, the girls grow serious, the revelry gives way to rosaries, and the Madame closes the play with the words: "Good God . . . if they're not all telling their beads there with that nun! Poor girls! But that's what I always say! No matter what you do . . . or what you come to . . . there's religion!"

The Kingdom of God (1915), one of Martínez Sierra's best plays, was made famous in America through the splendid acting of Ethel Barrymore. It is a full-flavored and well-rounded study of three periods in the life of Sister Gracia who has dedicated her life without reserve to ministering to the needy of the world. Her treasures are not laid up on earth. In the first act Sister Gracia at nineteen is giving her youth, against the protests of her mother and the scorn of her sister, to the varied inmates of an asylum for poor old men. In the second, now a woman of twenty-nine, she is attending the wretched creatures in a maternity home for unfortunates, and a pathetic, disconsolate illegitimate lot they are. In these surroundings it is not surprising to find Sister Gracia, whose order takes vows year by year, rejecting the physician's offer of marriage. In the final act she is seventy, Mother of an orphanage, governing the disputatious children who break into quarrels without warning. In Martínez Sierra's best manner, and in the best Spanish style is the scene where Juan de Dios, one of her former charges, fetches her the ear of his first bull: "Oh, Reverend Mother, I have dreamed of this day . . . and I've kept myself for it . . . yes, I have . . . like one of God's blessed angels." And the aged Mother charges the boys, and receives their solemn promise "that you will help to build on earth the Kingdom of God." Men suffer "but they work and hope."

The Two Shepherds (1913) is one of Martínez Sierra's most successful character studies in the two-act form of which he is fond. Here are the sentimental tragedies of a forceful old priest and his worthy colleague, a doctor, who fail to meet the new technical requirements laid upon their callings by their superiors, though both are excellent men and do more for the community than their successors ever will despite their skill at passing examinations Their flavor may be taken from one exchange between the priest and the doctor:

"Don Antonio: . . . to get these folk to heaven I've to drag them by the scruffs of their necks. . . .

"Don Francisco: Well I have to vaccinate 'em by main force to keep them on earth a little longer."

This pair and the Spanish village in which they work, are vividly evoked in the play, simple and unpretentious though it is.

This brief view of some of Martínez Sierra's typical and most widely known plays may perhaps serve to place *The Cradle Song* in the larger perspective of this dramatist's voluminous work. This play has been a favorite among audiences throughout the world since its triumphant première at the Teatro Lara, Madrid, in 1911. Translated into many languages, it has had many notable productions, including one at the Times Square Theatre, New York, in 1921, Eva Le Gallienne's successful presentation at the Civic Repertory Theatre in 1927, the production by Mary Shaw's company that toured the United States, the popular cinema version starring Dorothea Vieck, and numerous performances at the Abbey Theatre, the Playhouses of Oxford, Liverpool, and numerous university and little theatres everywhere. Its unfailing tenderness, its simplicity, and its beauty of character and spirit have made an irresistible appeal to the sentiments of the human heart in an age that has taken pride in its affectation of being hard-boiled.

The Cradle Song seems to owe much of its authority and verisimilitude to the hand of Maria Martínez Sierra. According to the English translator, John Garrett Underhill, it is "a reminiscence of Maria's youth in Carabanchel, a town in which her father was convent doctor and where her sister took the veil, the Sister Joanna of the Cross of the play." Its theme is great in its simplicity and timeless in its appeal, for it sets forth in living form the sacrifices in normal life exacted of these Nuns by their vows. They have stifled but not effaced their natural maternal instincts that long for expression and satisfaction. These are especially strong in Sister Joanna, who dreams of her little brothers and sisters ("I was always carrying one about in my arms"), who thinks of the Blessed Jesus as a child in the Madonna's arms, and whose pent-up love rushes out to enfold the foundling child Teresa. Teresa drove away her melancholy, gave her something warm and alive to love. "For earthly love," she says, bidding her Teresa goodbye, ". . . I mean . . . it seems to me it is like a flower, that we find by the side of the road—a little brightness that God grants us to help us pass through life, for we are weak and frail; a drop of honey spread upon our bread each day, which we should receive gladly, but with trembling, and keeping our hearts whole, daughter, for it will surely pass away." And when, for Sister Joanna, this happiness has passed, we see her, as the curtain falls, remaining unnoticed and alone after the Nuns have filed out; "with a cry, she falls upon her knees beside an empty chair."

On this slender thread of tremulous sentiment is woven the pattern of the play, made up of the daily gestures of grace and goodness, the harmless, guarded, and well-intentioned gossip of the convent, and the little acts of kindness and of love. There are no heroics, no villains, no great tragic dénouement. Its pictorial quality is clear and convincing. It is radiant with humanity, poetic in conception, treatment, and diction, and warm with heart-felt emotion—and these rare qualities are united to produce a harmonious work of artistic simplicity and permanence.

THE CRADLE SONG

Comedy in Two Acts with an Interlude in Verse

CHARACTERS

SISTER JOANNA OF THE CROSS, *18 years of age*

TERESA, *aged 18*

THE PRIORESS, *aged 40*

THE VICARESS, *aged 40*

THE MISTRESS OF NOVICES, *aged 36*

SISTER MARCELLA, *aged 19*

SISTER MARÍA JESÚS, *aged 19*

SISTER SAGRARIO, *aged 18*

SISTER INEZ, *aged 50*

SISTER TORNERA, *aged 30*

THE DOCTOR, *aged 60*

ANTONIO, *aged 25*

THE POET

A COUNTRYMAN

Also a Lay Sister, Two Monitors, and several other Nuns, as desired.

ACT I

A room opening upon the cloister of a Convent of Enclosed Dominican Nuns. The walls are tinted soberly; the floor is tiled. Three arches at the rear. In the right wall a large door with a wicket in it, leading to a passage communicating with the exterior. A grilled peephole for looking out. Above the door a bell which may be rung from the street. Beside the door an opening containing a revolving box, or wheel, on which objects may be placed and passed in from the outside without the recipient's being seen, or a view of the interior disclosed. Not far from this wheel, a pine table stands against one of the piers of the cloister. Ancient paintings relieve the walls. Through the arches the cloister garden may be seen, with a well in the middle; also a number of fruit trees, some greenery and a few rose bushes. Beneath the arches, potted flowers—roses, carnations, sweet basil, herb Louisa and balsam apple—together with a number of wooden benches and rush-seated chairs, and three arm chairs.

As the curtain rises THE PRIORESS *is discovered seated in the largest of the arm chairs, and* THE MISTRESS OF NOVICES *and* THE VICARESS *in the smaller ones, the former on the right, the latter on the left, well to the front. The other* NUNS *are grouped about them, seated also. The novices,* SISTER MARCELLA, SISTER JOANNA OF THE CROSS, SISTER MARÍA JESÚS *and* SISTER SAGRARIO *stand somewhat to the right,* SISTER JOANNA OF THE CROSS *occupying the centre of the stage. The* LAY SISTER *and* SISTER TORNERA *remain standing by the table at the rear.*

It is broad day light. The scene is one of cheerfulness and animation.

SISTER SAGRARIO. Yes, do! Do! Do let her read them!

SISTER MARCELLA. Yes, do Mother! Do say yes!

PRIORESS. Very well. You may read them since you have written them.

SISTER JOANNA OF THE CROSS. I am very much ashamed.

MISTRESS OF NOVICES. These are the temptations of self-love, my child.

VICARESS. And the first sin in the world was pride.

SISTER JOANNA OF THE CROSS. They are very bad. I know you will all laugh at me.

VICARESS. In that way we shall mortify 10 your vanity.

MISTRESS OF NOVICES. Besides, since we are not at school here, all that our Mother will consider in them will be the intention.

PRIORESS. Begin. And do not be afraid.

SISTER JOANNA OF THE CROSS (reciting). To our Beloved Mother on the day of her Blessed Saint—her birthday:

Most reverend Mother,   20
On this happy day
Your daughters unite
For your welfare to pray.
We are the sheep
Who under your care
Are seeking out Heaven—
The path that leads there.
On one side the roses,
On the other the thorn,
On the top of the mountain
Jesus of Mary born.
To Jesus we pray
Long years for your life,
And of the Virgin María
Freedom from strife;
And may the years vie
In good with each other,
In holiness and joy,
Our dearly-loved Mother!

[*The nuns applaud and all speak at once.*]
SOME. Good! Very good!
OTHERS. Oh, how pretty!
SISTER TORNERA. They are like the Jewels of the Virgin!
SISTER INEZ (*depreciatively*). She has copied them out of a book.

SISTER JOANNA OF THE CROSS (*carried away by her triumph*). Long live our Mother!

ALL (*enthusiastically*). Long live our Mother!

PRIORESS. Come, you must not flatter me, my children. The verses are very pretty. Many thanks, my daughter. I did not know that we had a poet in the house. You must copy them out for me on a piece of paper, so that I may have them to read.

SISTER JOANNA OF THE CROSS. They are copied already, reverend Mother. If your Reverence will be pleased to accept them . . . (*She offers her a roll of parchment, tied elaborately with blue ribbons. The verses are written on the parchment and embellished with a border of flowers, doves and hearts, all of which have been painted by hand.*)

PRIORESS (*taking and unrolling the parchment*). Bless me! What clear writing and what a beautiful border! Can you paint too?

SISTER JOANNA OF THE CROSS. No, reverend Mother. Sister María Jesús copied out the verses, and Sister Sagrario painted the border. Sister Marcella tied the bows.

SISTER MARCELLA. So it is a remembrance from all the novices.

PRIORESS. And all the while I knew nothing about it! The children have learned how to dissimulate very skilfully.

SISTER JOANNA OF THE CROSS. We had permission from Mother Anna St. Francis. She gave us the ribbon and the parchment.

PRIORESS. No wonder, then. So the Mother Mistress of Novices knows also how to keep secrets?

MISTRESS OF NOVICES. Once . . . Only for today . . .

SISTER JOANNA OF THE CROSS. Today you must forgive everything.

PRIORESS (*smiling*). The fault is not a grave one.

VICARESS (*acridly*). Not unless it leads them to pride themselves upon their accomplishments. The blessed mother Santa Teresa de Jesús never permitted her daughters to do fancy work. Evil combats us where we least expect it, and ostentation is not becoming in a heart which has vowed itself to poverty and humility.

MISTRESS OF NOVICES. Glory be to God, Mother Vicaress, but why must your Reverence always be looking for five feet on the cat? (SISTER MARCELLA *laughs flagrantly*.)

VICARESS. That laugh was most inopportune.

SISTER MARCELLA (*pretending repentance, but still continuing to laugh in spite of herself*). I beg your pardon, your Reverence, I didn't mean it. This sister has such temptations to laugh, and she can't help it.

VICARESS. Biting your tongue would help it.

SISTER MARCELLA. Don't you believe it, your Reverence. No indeed it wouldn't!

PRIORESS (*thinking it best to intervene*). Come, you must not answer back, my daughter. Today I wish to punish nobody.

VICARESS (*muttering*). Nor today, nor never!

PRIORESS (*aroused*). What does your Reverence mean by that, Mother Vicaress?

VICARESS (*very meekly*). What we all know, reverend Mother—that the patience of your Reverence is inexhaustible.

PRIORESS. Surely your Reverence is not sorry that it is so?

VICARESS (*belligerently*). Not upon my account, no. For by the grace of God I am able to fulfil my obligation and accommodate myself to the letter and spirit of our holy rule. But there are those who are otherwise, who, encouraged by leniency, may stumble and even fall . . .

PRIORESS. Has your Reverence anything definite in mind to say? If so, say it.

VICARESS. I have noticed for some time —and the Lord will absolve me of malice—that these "temptations to laugh" of which Sister Marcella speaks, have been abounding in this community; and these, taken with other manifestations of self-indulgence, not any less effervescent, are signs of a certain relaxation of virtue and deportment.

PRIORESS. I hardly think we need trouble ourselves upon that account. Providence has been pleased of late to bring into our fold some tender lambs, and perhaps they do frisk a little sometimes in the pastures of the Lord. But the poor children mean no harm. Am I right in your opinion, Mother Mistress of Novices?

MISTRESS OF NOVICES. You are always right in my opinion, reverend Mother. *Gaudeamus autem in Domino!*

VICARESS. Your Reverences of course know what you are doing. I have complied with my obligation.

[*The bell rings at the entrance.* SISTER TORNERA, *who is an active little old woman, goes up to the grille and looks through it, after first having made a reverence to the* PRIORESS.]

SISTER TORNERA. *Ave Maria Purissima!*

A VOICE (*outside, hoarse and rough*). Conceived without sin. Is it permitted to speak with the Mother Abbess?

SISTER TORNERA. Say what you have need of, brother.

VOICE. Then here's a present for her from my lady, the mayor's wife, who wishes her happiness, and sends her this present, and she's sorry she can't come herself to tell her; but she can't, and you know the reason . . . (*The* PRIORESS *sighs, lifting up her eyes to heaven, and the others do the same, all sighing in unison.*) And even if she could on that account, she couldn't do it, because she's sick in bed, and you know the reason . . . 10

SISTER TORNERA. God's will be done! Can the poor woman get no rest? Tell her that we will send her a jar of ointment in the name of the blessed Saint Clara, and say that these poor sisters never forget her in their prayers. They pray every day that the Lord will send her comfort. (*She turns the wheel by the grille, and a basket appears, neatly covered with a* 20 *white cloth.*) Ah!—and the reverend Mother thanks her for this remembrance. And may God be with you, brother. (*Approaching the others with the basket, which she has taken from the wheel.*) Poor lady! What tribulations our Lord sends into this world upon the cross of matrimony!

PRIORESS. And to her more than anybody. Such a submissive creature, 30 and married to a perfect prodigal!

MISTRESS OF NOVICES. Now that we are on the subject, your Reverences, and have the pot by the handle, so to speak, do your Reverences know that the blasphemies of that man have completely turned his head? You heard the bells of the parish church ringing at noon yesterday? Well, that was because the mayor ordered them 40 to be rung, because in the election at Madrid yesterday the republicans had the majority.

ALL. God bless us! God bless us!

VICARESS. Did the priest give his consent to that?

SISTER INEZ. The priest is another sheep of the same color—he belongs to the same flock, may the Lord forgive me if I lack charity! Didn't your Reverences hear the sacrilege he committed upon our poor chaplain, who is holier than God's bread? Well, he told him that he was more liberal than the mayor, and that the next thing he knew, when he least expected it, he was going to sing the introitus to the mass to the music of the Hymn of Riego!

PRIORESS. Stop! Enough! It is not right to repeat such blasphemies.

MISTRESS OF NOVICES. Yes, calumnies invented by unbelievers, the evil-minded . . .

SISTER INEZ. No such thing! Didn't Father Calixtus tell me himself while he was dressing for mass this morning? We'll have to put a new strip pretty soon down the middle of his chasuble.

PRIORESS. What? Again?

SISTER INEZ. Yes. It's all worn out; it looks terribly. Poor Father Calixtus is so eloquent! Pounding on his chest all the time, he simply tears the silk to pieces.

VICARESS. God's will be done, the man is a saint!

PRIORESS. And all this while we have been forgetting the present from the mayor's wife. Bring it nearer, Sister.

SISTER SAGRARIO. Mercy! What a big basket!

SISTER TORNERA. It's very light, though.

SISTER INEZ. Ha! It's easy to see what sister has a sweet tooth!

SISTER MARÍA JESÚS. As if she didn't like sweets! (*Aside.*)

SISTER MARCELLA. Now, Sister Inez, what did we see you doing this morning? You know we caught you licking the cake pan yourself.

SISTER INEZ. I? Licking the pan? Your Sister licking the pan? Oh, what a slander! *Jesús!*

PRIORESS. Come, you must not be displeased, Sister Inez; for it was said only in pleasantry. Ah, Sister Marcella! Sister Marcella! Do have a little more circumspection and beg your Sister's pardon.

SISTER MARCELLA (*kneeling before* SISTER INEZ). Pardon me, Sister, as may God pardon you, and give me your hand to kiss as a penance for having offended you.

PRIORESS. That is the way my children should behave, humbly and with contrition. Sister Inez, give Sister Marcella your hand to kiss, since she begs it of you so humbly.

SISTER MARCELLA (*spitefully, after kissing her hand*). *Ay!* But what a smell of vanilla you have on your fingers, Sister! Goody! We're going to have cookies for lunch. (*The others laugh.*)

SISTER INEZ (*irritated, almost in tears*). Vanilla? God-a-mercy! Vanilla! Look at me! Do my fingers smell of vanilla?

PRIORESS (*imposing silence*). Surely the devil must be in you, Sister Marcella, and may God forgive you for it! Go and kneel in the corner there with your face to the wall, and make the cross with your arms while you repeat a greater station. May the Lord forgive you for it!

SISTER MARCELLA. Willingly, reverend Mother.

SISTER INEZ (*rubbing her hands under her scapular*). Too bad! Too bad! *Ay! Ay! Ay!*

SISTER MARCELLA (*aside*). Old box of bones! (*She goes and kneels in the corner, right, but keeps smiling and turning her head while she lets herself sink back on her heels, as if not taking the penance too seriously.*)

PRIORESS. You may uncover the basket now, Sister. Let us see what is in it.

SISTER TORNERA. With your permission, reverend Mother. Why! It's a cage!

SISTER SAGRARIO. With a canary in it!

ALL. A canary! A canary! Why, so it is! Let me see! How lovely!

MISTRESS OF NOVICES. Isn't it pretty?

SISTER MARÍA JESÚS. The dear! Isn't it cunning, though?

SISTER JOANNA OF THE CROSS. It looks as if it were made of silk.

SISTER INEZ. I wonder if it can sing?

PRIORESS. Of course it can sing. The mayor's wife would never send us a canary that couldn't sing.

SISTER SAGRARIO. What a beautiful cage! Why, there's a scroll on the front!

MISTRESS OF NOVICES. That isn't a scroll. It has letters on it.

SISTER MARÍA JESÚS. Why, so it has! Look and see what they say.

MISTRESS OF NOVICES. "The Convent of Dominican Nuns!"

SISTER INEZ (*laughing*). I'd call that a pretty airy convent!

VICARESS. The good woman is holier than God's bread.

PRIORESS. She could not have sent me anything that would have pleased me better. I have always been anxious to have a canary.

SISTER INEZ. The Carmelite Sisters have two lovely canaries, and they say last year on Holy Thursday they hung them in the door of the tomb they have in the church for Easter, and it was like a miracle to hear them sing.

MISTRESS OF NOVICES. Then if ours sings, we can hang him in the church this year, and take the music box away.

PRIORESS. No, for the music box is a present from the chaplain, and he would rightly be offended. We will have the box and the canary there together, and when we wind up the box, it will encourage the bird to sing.

SISTER JOANNA OF THE CROSS. Oh, look at him now—he's taking his bath!

SISTER SAGRARIO. See how he jumps.

PRIORESS. What wonders God performs!

VICARESS. And yet there are misguided creatures who pretend that the world made itself!

SISTER INEZ. Sister Marcella stuck her tongue out at me.

SISTER MARCELLA. Oh, reverend Mother! I did nothing of the kind!

VICARESS. How nothing of the kind? Didn't I see it with my own eyes? And I was struck dumb!

SISTER MARCELLA. I said nothing of the kind . . . as . . . as that I had stuck my tongue out at Sister Inez. I stuck it out because there was a fly on the end of my nose, and since I had my arms out making the cross, I had to frighten him away with something.

SISTER JOANNA OF THE CROSS. Reverend Mother, since this is your Saint's day, won't you please excuse Sister Marcella this time?

SISTER MARÍA JESÚS. Yes, reverend Mother! I am sure she won't do anything that's wrong again.

PRIORESS. Sister Inez is the one who has been offended, and she is the only one who has the right to request her pardon.

NOVICES. She does! She does! You do, don't you, Sister Inez?

SISTER INEZ (*with a wry face*). Your Reverence will pardon her when your Reverence thinks best.

PRIORESS. Then come here, my erring daughter.—She knows that I pardon her because of the day, and so as not to spoil the pleasure of her sisters.

SISTER MARCELLA. May God reward you, reverend Mother!

PRIORESS. And set your veil straight, for this is the Lord's house, and it looks as if you were going on an excursion. —And now to your cells, every one. (*To the* NOVICES.) What are you whispering about?

SISTER SAGRARIO. We were not whispering, Mother . . . We wanted to ask you something.

SISTER MARÍA JESÚS. And we are afraid to do it.

PRIORESS. Is it as bad as that?

SISTER MARÍA JESÚS. No, it isn't bad. But ——

SISTER JOANNA OF THE CROSS. Your Reverence might think so.

PRIORESS. I might? I am not so evil-minded.

SISTER SAGRARIO. I . . . I . . . Our Mother Mistress will tell you.

MISTRESS OF NOVICES. They mean me.— Do you want me to?

NOVICES. Yes! Yes! Do!

MISTRESS OF NOVICES. With God's help I will try. Though I don't know for certain, I think what they want is for your Reverence to give them permission to talk a little, while they are waiting for the beginning of the *fiesta*. Am I right?

NOVICES. Yes! Yes! You are! Do, Mother, do!

SISTER MARCELLA. Long live our Mother!

PRIORESS. Silence! Silence! What? Haven't they had talking enough to-day after the dispensation I allowed them this morning?

VICARESS. The appetite always grows by what it feeds on. It is an unruly monster, and woe to her who gives it rein. If they came under my authority, I would not give them opportunity to make a single slip, for the holy Apostle Saint James has said and well said: "He who saith that he hath not offended by his tongue, lies."

SISTER MARCELLA. Ah, Sister Crucifixion! Don't spoil this holiday for our Mother.

VICARESS. Spoil it, eh? Who pays any attention to what I say in this house?

PRIORESS. Will you promise not to whisper nor offend the Lord with foolish talk?

NOVICES. We promise.

PRIORESS. Then you may talk as much as you like until the hour for prayers.

NOVICES. Thanks, thanks! (*The bell rings at the entrance twice.*)

SISTER TORNERA. Two rings! The doctor!

PRIORESS. Cover your faces. (*The NUNS lower their veils over their faces.*) And pass out through the cloister.

[*The NUNS begin to file out slowly and disappear through the cloister.*]

SISTER SAGRARIO (*approaching the PRIORESS*). This Sister has a felon, reverend Mother.

PRIORESS. Remain then—and you too, Sister María Jesús. (*To SISTER TORNERA.*) Open, Sister. (*The PRIORESS, SISTER TORNERA, SISTER SAGRARIO and SISTER MARÍA JESÚS remain. SISTER TORNERA unchains, unbolts and opens the door. The DOCTOR enters. He is about sixty years of age.*)

SISTER TORNERA. *Ave Maria Purissima!*

DOCTOR. Conceived without sin. (*He comes in.*) Good morning, Sister.

SISTER TORNERA. Good morning, Doctor.

DOCTOR. Well, what progress are we making in holiness today?

SISTER TORNERA (*laughing*). Ho, ho, Doctor!

DOCTOR. Enough! Enough! No doubt, no doubt! (*Discovering the PRIORESS.*) Congratulations, Mother.

PRIORESS. What? A heretic, and yet you remember the days of the saints?

DOCTOR. You are the saint, Mother; you are the saint.

PRIORESS. Ah! You must not scandalize me before my novices.

DOCTOR. Novices? Where, where? I said so when I came in. I smell fresh meat.

PRIORESS. Don José! Don José!

DOCTOR. But I say no more. Come! To work! To work! . . . What is the trouble with these white lambs?

SISTER SAGRARIO. Your handmaid has a felon, Doctor.

DOCTOR. Eh? On the hand? And such a lovely hand! Well, we shall have to lance it, Sister.

SISTER SAGRARIO (*alarmed*). What? Not now?

DOCTOR. No, tomorrow, Sister. Tomorrow, unless it yields first to a poultice and five *Pater nosters*. Remember, not one less!

SISTER SAGRARIO (*in perfect earnest*). No, Doctor.

DOCTOR. And this other one, eh?

PRIORESS. Ah, Doctor! She has been giving me a great deal of worry. She falls asleep in the choir; she sighs continually without being able to assign any reason; she cries over nothing whatever; she has no appetite for anything but salads . . .

DOCTOR. How old are you?

SISTER MARÍA JESÚS. Eighteen.

DOCTOR. How long have you been in this holy house?

SISTER MARÍA JESÚS. Two years and a half.

DOCTOR. And how many more do you remain before you come to profession?

SISTER MARÍA JESÚS. Two and a half more, if the Lord should be pleased to grant this unworthy novice grace to become his bride.

DOCTOR. Let me see the face.

PRIORESS. Lift your veil. (SISTER MARÍA JESÚS *lifts her veil.*)

DOCTOR. Hm! The Lord has not bad

taste. A little pale, but well rounded, well rounded.

ISTER TORNERA. Don José! But who ever heard of such a doctor?

DOCTOR. So, we have melancholy then, a constant disposition to sigh, combined with loss of appetite—well, there is nothing else for it, Sister: a cold bath every morning and afterwards a few minutes' exercise in the garden. 10

ISTER TORNERA (*somewhat scandalized*). Exercise? Don José!

DOCTOR. Unless we write at once home to her mother to hurry and fetch her and find us a good husband for her.

SISTER MARÍA JESÚS. Oh, Don José! But this Sister has taken her vows to the Church!

DOCTOR. Well, in that case cold water. There is nothing else for it. For mel- 20 ancholy at eighteen, matrimony or cold water.

SISTER SAGRARIO (*summoning her courage*). You always talk so much about it, Doctor, why don't you get married yourself?

DOCTOR. Because I am sixty, daughter; and it is fifteen years since I have felt melancholy. Besides, whom do you expect me to marry when all the 30 pretty girls go into convents?

PRIORESS. Doctor, doctor! This conversation will become displeasing to me.

DOCTOR. Is this all the walking infirmary?

SISTER TORNERA. Yes, Doctor.

DOCTOR. And the invalid? How is she?

SISTER TORNERA. She is the same to-day, Doctor. Poor Sister Maria of Con- 40 solation hasn't closed her eyes all night! Don't you remember? Yesterday she said she felt as if she had a viper gnawing at her vitals? Well, to-day she has a frog in her throat.

DOCTOR. Goodness gracious! Come, let me see, let me see. What a continual war the devil does wage against these poor sisters!—Long life, Mother, and happy days!

PRIORESS. Long life to you, Doctor. (*To* SISTER TORNERA.) Go with him, Sister, and meanwhile these children will take care of the gate. (SISTER TORNERA *takes a bell from the table and, her veil covering her face, precedes the* DOCTOR *through the cloister, ringing solemnly in warning. They disappear.*) I must repair to the choir; I fear that today I have fallen behind in devotion and prayer.

SISTER MARÍA JESÚS. Will your Reverence give us permission to call the others?

PRIORESS. Yes, call them; but be careful that you commit no frivolity. (*The* PRIORESS *goes out.*)

SISTER MARÍA JESÚS (*approaching one of the arches of the cloister*). Sister Marcella! Sister Joanna of the Cross! Pst! Come out! We are watching the grille and we have permission to talk.

[SISTER MARCELLA *and* SISTER JOANNA OF THE CROSS *re-enter.*]

SISTER SAGRARIO. What shall we talk about?

SISTER JOANNA OF THE CROSS. Let Sister Marcella tell us a story.

SISTER MARCELLA. Yes, so that you'll all be shocked.

SISTER MARÍA JESÚS. *Ay!* We are not such hypocrites as that, Sister.

SISTER MARCELLA. Or so that Sister Sagrario can run and tell on us to the Mother Mistress.

SISTER SAGRARIO. Oh, thank you, Sister!

SISTER MARCELLA. It wouldn't be the first time either.

SISTER SAGRARIO. You needn't mind me, Sisters. I am going to sit here in the corner and work, and you can talk about whatever you please. I shan't hear you. (*She takes a pair of pincers, some beads and a piece of wire out of her pocket, and sitting down in a corner, begins to string a rosary.*)

SISTER JOANNA OF THE CROSS. Oh, come on, Sister! Don't be foolish. (*They all surround her, and finally she allows herself to be persuaded, after many expressions of protest, like a small child who says "I won't play."*)

SISTER SAGRARIO. Why! If they haven't forgotten the canary!

SISTER MARCELLA. Poor thing! How do you like to be left in this nest of silly women, little fellow? Let's open the cage.

SISTER MARÍA JESÚS. What for?

SISTER MARCELLA. So that he can fly away, silly, if he wants to.

SISTER SAGRARIO. No, no!

SISTER MARÍA JESÚS. Our Mother wouldn't like that.

SISTER MARCELLA. He would like it, though. Come on! (*She opens the door of the cage.*) Fly out, sweetheart! Fly away, the world is yours. You are free!

SISTER JOANNA OF THE CROSS. He doesn't fly out.

SISTER MARÍA JESÚS. He doesn't budge.

SISTER MARCELLA. Stupid, don't you see what a bright, sunny day it is?

SISTER JOANNA OF THE CROSS. They say canaries are born in cages and, see, now he doesn't care to fly away.

SISTER MARÍA JESÚS. He'd rather stay shut up all his life like us nuns.

SISTER MARCELLA. Then you're a great fool, birdie. (*She shuts the door of the cage.*) God made the air for wings and He made wings to fly with. While he might be soaring away above the clouds, he is satisfied to stay here all day shut up in his cage, hopping between two sticks and a leaf of lettuce! What sense is there in a bird? *Ay*, Mother! And what wouldn't I give to be a bird!

SISTER JOANNA OF THE CROSS. Yes! Wha wouldn't you give to be a bird?

SISTER MARÍA JESÚS. They say that the swallows fly away every year over the ocean, and nobody knows where they go.

SISTER SAGRARIO. I often dream that I am flying in the night time—that i, not flying, but floating—just floating in the air without wings.

SISTER MARCELLA. I often dream that I am running fast—oh so fast!—and that I am skipping down stairs, without ever touching my feet to the ground, or to the stairs.

SISTER SAGRARIO. Isn't it nice, though? And how disappointed you are when you wake up and find out after all that it isn't so, that it was only a dream!

SISTER MARCELLA. I have dreamed that dream so many times, that now when I wake up, I hardly know whether it is the truth or a dream.

SISTER JOANNA OF THE CROSS. What do you suppose it is that makes you dream the same dream so many times?

SISTER MARCELLA. I don't know, unless it is because it is the things you want to do, and you can't, and so you do them in dreams.

SISTER MARÍA JESÚS. What nice things you want to do!

SISTER SAGRARIO. But then what good would it be if you could do them? For instance, if we had wings like birds, where would we fly?

SISTER MARCELLA. I? I would fly to the end of the world!

SISTER MARÍA JESÚS. I? To the Holy Land, to Mount Calvary!

SISTER JOANNA OF THE CROSS. I would fly to Bethlehem and to the garden of Nazareth, where the Virgin lived with the child.

SISTER SAGRARIO. How do you know that there is a garden at Nazareth?

SISTER JOANNA OF THE CROSS. Of course there's a garden there, with a brook running by it. The song says so:
"The Virgin washed his garments
And hung them on the rose.
The little angels sing
And the water onward flows" . . .
(*Simply.*) There was a garden, too, by our house in the village, with a big rosebush on the border of a brook that ran by it; and I used to kneel beside the brook, and sing that song while I washed my baby brother's clothes, for there were seven of us children, and I was the oldest. (*Feelingly.*) And that's what I miss most! (*Drying her eyes with her hands.*) Ay, Mother! And I always cry when I think of that baby boy! But it isn't right, I know . . . He loved me more than he did mother, and the day that they took me away to the Convent, and I left home, he cried—he cried so that he nearly broke his little baby heart!

SISTER MARCELLA. I have a brother and a sister, but they are both older than I am. My sister married two years ago, and now she has a baby. (*With an air of importance.*) She brought him here once to show me.

SISTER JOANNA OF THE CROSS (*interrupting her, greatly interested*). I remember. He stuck his little hand in through the grille and your sister kissed it. Did you ever think how soft babies' hands are? Whenever I take communion I try to think I am receiving our Lord as a little child, and I take and press him like this to my heart, and then it seems to me that he is so little and so helpless that he can't refuse me anything. And then I think that he is crying, and I pray to the Virgin to

come and help me quiet him. And if I wasn't ashamed, because I know you would all laugh at me, I'd croon to him then, and rock him to sleep, and sing him baby songs.

[*The bell rings by the grille.*]

SISTER SAGRARIO. The bell! I wonder who it is?

SISTER JOANNA OF THE CROSS. Better ask. That's why they left us here.

SISTER MARÍA JESÚS. Who'll do it? I won't. I'm afraid.

SISTER SAGRARIO. So am I.

SISTER MARCELLA. You're not usually so bashful, I must say. I'll ask, though I was the last to enter the house. (*Going up to the grille, she says in a timid voice:*) Ave Maria Purissima! (*A moment's silence.*) No one answers.

SISTER JOANNA OF THE CROSS. Try again. Say it louder.

SISTER MARCELLA (*raising her voice*). Ave Maria Purissima!

SISTER SAGRARIO. Nothing this time, either.

SISTER MARÍA JESÚS (*summoning her courage, in a high-pitched voice*). Ave Maria Purissima!

[*Another silence. The Novices look at each other in surprise.*]

SISTER MARCELLA. It is very strange.

SISTER MARÍA JESÚS. It must be spirits.

SISTER SAGRARIO. Oh, I'm afraid!

SISTER JOANNA OF THE CROSS. Nonsense! It's some little boy who has rung the bell on his way home from school, so as to be funny.

SISTER MARÍA JESÚS. Peep through the hole and see if anybody is there.

SISTER MARCELLA (*stooping down to look*). No, nobody. But it looks as if there was something on the wheel. Yes . . .

SISTER JOANNA OF THE CROSS. Let me see! Yes . . . Can't you turn it? (*She turns the wheel, and a second basket appears, carefully covered with a white cloth like the first.*) A basket!

SISTER SAGRARIO. Another present for our Mother.

SISTER MARÍA JESÚS. Of course it is! And here's a paper tied fast to it.

SISTER JOANNA OF THE CROSS (*reading, but without unfolding the paper*). "For the Mother Prioress."

SISTER SAGRARIO. Didn't I tell you?

SISTER MARCELLA. Somebody wants to give her a surprise.

SISTER JOANNA OF THE CROSS. I wonder if it's Don Calixtus, the chaplain?

SISTER MARCELLA. Of course it is, child!

SISTER MARÍA JESÚS. Or maybe it's the Doctor.

SISTER JOANNA OF THE CROSS. No. He was just here and he didn't say anything about it.

SISTER SAGRARIO. All the same it might be from him. Maybe he wants to keep it a secret.

SISTER MARÍA JESÚS. Let's take it off the wheel.

SISTER MARCELLA (*lifting and carrying it to the table*). We'd better put it here by the canary. My! But it's heavy!

SISTER SAGRARIO. I wonder what it is?

SISTER MARCELLA. Let's lift the corner and see.

SISTER MARÍA JESÚS. No, for curiosity is a sin.

SISTER MARCELLA. What of it? Come on! Let's do it. Who will ever know? (*She lifts the corner of the cloth a little and starts back quickly with a sharp cry.*) Ay!!

SISTER JOANNA OF THE CROSS (*hurrying to look*). Jesús!

SISTER MARÍA JESÚS. Ave Maria! (*Looking too.*)

SISTER SAGRARIO (*following*). God bless us!

[*The Convent is aroused at the cry of* SISTER MARCELLA. *Presently the* PRIORESS, *the* VICARESS, *the* MISTRESS OF NOVICES *and*

the other NUNS *enter from different directions.*]

PRIORESS. What is the matter? Who called out?

VICARESS. Who gave that shout?

MISTRESS OF NOVICES. Is anything wrong? (*The four Novices, trembling, stand with their backs to the basket, their bodies hiding it completely.*)

VICARESS. It is easy to see it was Sister Marcella.

PRIORESS. What has happened? Speak! Why are you all standing in a row like statues?

MISTRESS OF NOVICES. Has any thing happened to you?

SISTER JOANNA OF THE CROSS. No, reverend Mother, not to us; but——

SISTER MARÍA JESÚS. No, reverend Mother; it's . . .

SISTER MARCELLA. Someone rang the bell by the wheel . . . and we looked . . . and there was nobody there . . . and they left a basket . . . this basket . . . and . . . and your Sister had the curiosity to undo it . . .

VICARESS. Naturally, you couldn't do otherwise.

SISTER MARCELLA. And it's . . .

PRIORESS. Well? What is it?

SISTER MARCELLA. It's . . . I . . . I think it would be better for your Reverence to look yourself.

PRIORESS. By all means! Let me see. (*She goes up to the basket and uncovers it.*) Ave Maria! (*In a hoarse whisper.*) A baby!

ALL (*variously affected*). A baby? (*The* VICARESS, *horrified, crosses herself.*)

PRIORESS (*falling back*). Your Reverences may see for yourselves. (*The* NUNS *hurry up to the basket and surround it.*)

VICARESS. Ave Maria! How can such an insignificant object be so pink?

MISTRESS OF NOVICES. It's asleep.

SISTER JOANNA OF THE CROSS. See it open its little hands!

ISTER MARÍA JESÚS. Why! It has hair under the edge of its cap!

ISTER SAGRARIO. It is like an angel!

VICARESS. A pretty angel for the Lord to send us.

ISTER JOANNA OF THE CROSS (*as if she had been personally offended*). *Ay*, Mother Vicaress! You mustn't say that.

PRIORESS (*tenderly*). Where do you come from, little one? 10

VICARESS. From some nice place, you may be sure.

PRIORESS. Who can tell, Mother? There is so much poverty in the world, so much distress.

VICARESS. There is so much vice, reverend Mother.

MISTRESS OF NOVICES. You say that there was nobody at the grille?

SISTER MARCELLA. Nobody; no, Mother. 20 The bell rang; we answered . . . but there was nobody there.

SISTER SAGRARIO (*picking up the paper which has fallen on the floor*). Here is a paper which came with it.

PRIORESS (*taking the paper*). "For the Mother Prioress."

VICARESS. An appropriate present for your Reverence.

PRIORESS. Yes, it is a letter. 30

[*She unfolds the paper and begins to read.*]

"Reverend Mother:

Forgive the liberty which a poor woman takes, trusting in your Grace's charity, of leaving at the grille this newborn babe. I, my lady, am one of those they call women of the street, and I assure you I am sorry for it; but this is the world, and you can't turn your back on it, and it costs as much 40 to go down as it does to go up, and that is what I am writing to tell you, my lady. The truth is this little girl hasn't any father, that is to say it is the same as if she didn't have any, and I —who am her mother—I leave her

here, although it costs me something to leave her; for although one is what one is, one isn't all bad, and I love her as much as any mother loves her baby, though she is the best lady in the land. But all the same, though she came into this world without being wanted by anyone, she doesn't deserve to be the daughter of the woman she is, above all, my lady, of her father, and I don't want her to have to blush for having been born the way she was, nor for having the mother she has, and to tell it to me to my face, and I pray you by everything you hold dear, my lady, that you will protect her and keep her with you in this holy house, and you won't send her to some orphanage or asylum, for I was brought up there myself, and I know what happens in them, although the sisters are kind—yes, they are—and have pity. And some day, when she grows up and she asks for her mother, you must tell her that the devil has carried her away, and I ask your pardon, for I must never show myself to her, nor see her again, nor give you any care nor trouble, so you can do this good work in peace, if you will do it, for I implore you again, my lady, that you will do it for the memory of your own dear mother, and God will reward you, and she will live in peace, and grow up as God wills, for what the eyes have not seen the heart cannot understand, my lady."

VICARESS. Bless us! *Ave Maria!*

MISTRESS OF NOVICES. Poor woman!

SISTER JOANNA OF THE CROSS. Baby dear! Darling baby!

VICARESS. What pretty mothers the Lord selects for his children!

PRIORESS. God moves in his own ways, Sister. God moves in his own ways.

SISTER INEZ. Is that all the letter says?

PRIORESS. What more could it say?

[*The* DOCTOR *and* SISTER TORNERA *have reentered during the reading.*]

DOCTOR. Exactly. What more could it say?

PRIORESS. What do you think, Don José?

DOCTOR. I think that somebody has made you a very handsome present.

PRIORESS. But what are we going to do with it? Because I . . . this poor woman . . . she has put this poor creature into our hands, and I would protect her willingly, as she asks, and keep her here with us . . .

NOVICES. Yes, yes, Mother! Do! Do!

MISTRESS OF NOVICES. Silence!

PRIORESS. But I don't know if we can . . . that is, if it is right, if it is according to law . . . for, when we enter this holy rule, we renounce all our rights . . . and to adopt a child legally . . . I don't know whether it can be done. How does it seem to you?

DOCTOR. I agree with you. Legally, you have no right to maternity.

VICARESS. And even if we had, would it be proper for our children to be the offspring of ignominy and sin?

PRIORESS. I would not raise that question, reverend Mother, for the child is not responsible for the sin in which she was born, and her mother, in renouncing her motherhood, has bitterly paid the penalty.

VICARESS. Yes, it didn't cost her much to renounce it.

PRIORESS. Do we know, Mother? Do we know?

VICARESS. We can guess. It is easy enough to go scattering children about the world if all you have to do is leave them to be picked up afterwards by the first person who happens along.

DOCTOR. How easy it is might be a matter for discussion. There are aspects of it which are not so easy.

SISTER SAGRARIO. Oh! She's opened her mouth!

SISTER JOANNA OF THE CROSS. The little angel is hungry.

SISTER MARÍA JESÚS. She's sucking her thumb!

SISTER JOANNA OF THE CROSS. Make her take her thumb out of her mouth She'll swallow too much and then she'll have a pain.

SISTER SAGRARIO. Don't suck your fingers baby.

SISTER JOANNA OF THE CROSS. Isn't she good, though? You stop her playing and she doesn't cry.

PRIORESS. There is another thing we must consider. What are we to do for a nurse?

SISTER JOANNA OF THE CROSS. The gardener's wife has a little boy she is nursing now.

PRIORESS. In that case I hardly think she would care to be responsible for two.

SISTER JOANNA OF THE CROSS. But it won't be any trouble—she's so tiny! Besides, we can help her out with cow's milk and a little pap. The milk will keep on the ice and we can clear it with a dash of tea.

DOCTOR. It is easy to see Sister Joanna of the Cross has had experience with children.

SISTER JOANNA OF THE CROSS. Your handmaid has six little brothers and sisters. Ah, reverend Mother! Give her to me to take care of and then you will see how strong she'll grow up.

VICARESS. Nothing else was needed to complete the demoralization of the Novices. You can see for yourselves how naturally they take to this dissipation.

PRIORESS. I want you to tell me frankly

what you think—all of you. (*All speak at once.*)

MISTRESS OF NOVICES. Your Sister thinks, reverend Mother . . .

SISTER TORNERA. Your handmaid . . .

SISTER INEZ. It seems to me . . .

PRIORESS (*smiling*). But one at a time.

SISTER TORNERA. It is an angel which the Lord has sent us, and your Sister thinks that we ought to receive her 10 like an angel, with open arms.

MISTRESS OF NOVICES. Of course we ought. Suppose, your Reverences, it hadn't been a little girl, but . . . I don't know—some poor animal, a dog, a cat, or a dove, like the one which flew in here two years ago and fell wounded in the garden trying to get away from those butchers at the pigeon-traps. Wouldn't we have taken it in? 20 Wouldn't we have cared for it? And wouldn't it have lived happy forever afterward in its cage? And how can we do less for a creature with a soul than for a bird?

SISTER TORNERA. We must have charity.

VICARESS. I am glad the Mother Mistress of Novices has brought up the incident of that bird, for it will absolve me from bringing it up, as it might 30 seem, with some malice. It was against my advice that that creature was received into this house, and afterward we had good reason to regret it, with this one saying "Yes, I caught him!" and that one, "No, I took care of him!" and another "He opens his beak whenever I pass by!" and another, "See him flap his wings! He does it at me!"—vanities, sophis- 40 tries, deceits all of them, snares of the devil continually! And if all this fuss was about a bird, what will happen to us with a child in the house? This one will have to dress it, that one will have to wash it, another will be boasting,

"It is looking at me!" another that it's at her that it googles most . . . There is Sister Joanna of the Cross making faces at it already!

SISTER JOANNA OF THE CROSS. What did your Reverence say?

VICARESS. Dissipation and more dissipation! Your Reverences should remember that when we passed behind these bars, we renounced forever all personal, all selfish affection.

MISTRESS OF NOVICES. Is it selfish to give a poor foundling a little love?

VICARESS. It is for us. Our God is a jealous God. The Scriptures tell us so.

MISTRESS OF NOVICES. Bless us! Mercy me!

VICARESS. And this quite apart from other infractions of our order which such indulgence must involve. For example, your Reverences—and I among the first—take no account of the fact that at this very moment we are transgressing our rule. We are conversing with our faces unveiled in the presence of a man.

PRIORESS. That is true.

DOCTOR. Ladies, as far as I am concerned—Take no account of me. . . .

PRIORESS. No, Doctor, you are of no account. I beg your pardon, Don José; I hardly know what I am saying.— Your Reverence is right. Cover yourselves—that is, it makes no difference . . . The harm has been done . . . only once. . . . But comply with your consciences . . . (*The* VICARESS *covers her face. The others, hesitating, wait for the* PRIORESS, *who makes a movement to do so, but then desists. The* VICARESS, *when she is covered, cannot see that she has become the victim of the rest.*) But where were we? I confess that my heart prompts me to keep the child.

VICARESS. The Doctor already has told us that we have no right to maternity.

MISTRESS OF NOVICES. But the child is God's child, and she is returning to her father's mansion.

VICARESS. God has other mansions for his abandoned children.

SISTER JOANNA OF THE CROSS. Don't send her to the asylum!

SISTER SAGRARIO. No!

PRIORESS. Her mother entreats us.

VICARESS. Her mother is not her mother. She has abandoned her.

PRIORESS. She has not abandoned her. She has entrusted her to others who seemed worthier to undertake her keeping.

VICARESS. Unholy egotism!

MISTRESS OF NOVICES. Christian heroism!

VICARESS. So? We are coining phrases, are we? Is this a convent, or an illustrated weekly?

MISTRESS OF NOVICES. Life is hard to some people, and thorny.

VICARESS. Yes, and into the details of it, it is not becoming for us to go, since by the grace of God we have been relieved from the temptations and the frailties of the world.

MISTRESS OF NOVICES. All the more, then, we ought to have compassion on those who have fallen and are down.

VICARESS. Compassion? Mush and sentiment!

MISTRESS OF NOVICES. The veil of charity!

PRIORESS. Silence! And let us not begin by rending it, irritating ourselves and aggravating each other.—Don José, I suppose this birth will have to be reported?

DOCTOR. It will, madam. To the Register.

SISTER JOANNA OF THE CROSS. But then they will take her away?

DOCTOR. If nobody wants her. But if you have made up your minds you would like to keep her, I think I can propose a solution.

PRIORESS. A solution that is legal?

DOCTOR. Perfectly. Thanks be to God I am a single man. But, although I am not a saint, yet I cannot take to myself the credit of having augmented the population of this country by so much as a single soul. I have not a penny, that is true, but like everybody else, I have a couple of family names. They are at the service of this little stranger, if they will be of use to her. She will have no father and no mother—I cannot help that—but she will have an honorable name.

PRIORESS. Do you mean to say?——

DOCTOR. That I am willing to adopt her; exactly—and to entrust her to your care, because my own house . . . The fact is the hands of Doña Cecilia are a little rough for handling these tiny Dresden dolls, and perhaps I might prove a bit testy myself. The neighbors all say that the air grows blue if my coat rubs against me as I walk down the street.

[All laugh.]

DOCTOR. Besides I am sure Sister Crucifixion is better equipped for the robing of saints.

VICARESS. Doctor, God help us both!

DOCTOR. Is it agreed?

PRIORESS. God reward you for it! Yes, in spite of everything. We shall notify the Superior immediately. It is not necessary that the child should live in the cloister. She can remain with the gardener's wife until she has grown older, and enter here later when she has the discretion to do so. She has been entrusted to our hands, and it is our duty to take care of her—a duty of conscience.

DOCTOR. If I cannot be of further service, I will go. And I will speak to the Register.

PRIORESS. As you go, be so kind as to ask

the gardener's wife to come in. We must see if she will take charge of the child and nurse her. And tell her also to bring with her some of her little boy's clothes.

SISTER JOANNA OF THE CROSS. Yes, for we shall have to make a change immediately.

SISTER SAGRARIO. We shall?

VICARESS. Not a change, but a beginning.

DOCTOR. Good afternoon, ladies.

ALL. Good afternoon, Don José. (*The* DOCTOR *goes out.*)

[*A pause.*]

PRIORESS. Sisters, may God pardon us if we have acted in this with aught but the greatest purity of motive. I hope and pray that His grace will absolve us of offense, nor find us guilty of having loved too much one of His poor children. The child shall be brought up in the shadow of this house, for we may say that her guardian angel has delivered her at the door. From this hour forth we are all charged with the salvation of her soul. The Lord has entrusted to us an angel and we must return to Him a saint. Watch and pray.

ALL. Watch and pray. We will, reverend Mother.

PRIORESS. And now bring her to me, Sister Joanna of the Cross, for as yet it can scarcely be said that I have seen her. (*Looking at the child.*) Lamb of God! Sleeping as quietly in her basket as if it were a cradle of pure gold! What is it that children see when they are asleep that brings to their faces an expression of such peace?

SISTER JOANNA OF THE CROSS. They see God and the Virgin Mary.

SISTER MARÍA JESÚS. Maybe the angel who watches over them whispers in their ears and tells them about heaven.

PRIORESS. Who can say? But it is a comfort to the soul to see a child asleep.

SISTER MARÍA JESÚS. It makes you want to be a saint, reverend Mother.

SISTER SAGRARIO. Will your Reverence grant me permission to give her a kiss?

SISTER MARÍA JESÚS. Oh, no! For it hasn't been baptized yet, and it is a sin to kiss a heathen!

PRIORESS. She is right. We must send for the Chaplain and have her baptized immediately.

MISTRESS OF NOVICES. What shall we call her?

SISTER INEZ. Teresa, after our beloved Mother.

SISTER TORNERA. María of the Miracles.

SISTER SAGRARIO. Bienvenida. (*A large bell rings outside.*)

PRIORESS. The summons to the choir! We can decide later. Let us go. (*The* NUNS *file out slowly, looking at the child as they go.*) Remain with her, Sister Joanna of the Cross—you understand children; and wait for the coming of the gardener's wife. Follow the devotions from where you are, and do not let your attention falter.

[*All the* NUNS *go out, except* SISTER JOANNA OF THE CROSS, *who bends over the basket; then sinks on her knees beside it. The choir is heard within, led by a single* NUN *in solo, the responses being made in chorus, in which* SISTER JOANNA OF THE CROSS *joins. While the* NUN *is leading,* SISTER JOANNA OF THE CROSS *talks and plays with the child; then she makes her responses with the others.*]

VOICE WITHIN. *In nomine Patri et Filio et Spiritui Sancto.* (SISTER JOANNA OF THE CROSS *crosses herself and says with the other* NUNS:)

VOICES WITHIN AND SISTER JOANNA OF THE CROSS. *Amen!*

SISTER JOANNA OF THE CROSS (*to the child*). **Pretty one! Pretty one!**

VOICE WITHIN. *Deus in adjutorium meum intende.*

VOICES WITHIN AND SISTER JOANNA OF THE CROSS. *Domine ad adjuvandum me festina.*

SISTER JOANNA OF THE CROSS (*to the child*). Do you love me, sweetheart? Do you love me?

VOICE WITHIN. *Gloria Patri et Filio et Spiritui Sancto.* 10

VOICES WITHIN IN CHORUS. *Sicut erat in principio et nunc et semper et insecula seculorum. Amen! Allelulia!*

[*But this time* SISTER JOANNA OF THE CROSS *makes no response. Instead she bends over the basket, embracing the child passionately, oblivious of all else, and says:*]

SISTER JOANNA OF THE CROSS. Little one! Little one! Whom do you love?

CURTAIN

INTERLUDE

SPOKEN BY THE POET

You came tonight to listen to a play;
Instead into a convent you made way.
Singular hardihood! Almost profanation!
What will a poet not do to create sensation?
Pardon, good nuns, him who disturbs the rest
And troubles the serene quietude of your nest,
Kindling amid the shades of this chaste bower
The flame of love you have renounced and flower.
Nay! Do not frown because I have said love,
For you must know, chaste brides of God above,   20
That which you have deemed charity and pity,
The act of mercy, clemency for the pretty,
Unfriended foundling fate has brought along,
Yearning of adoption and the cradle song,
No other is than love's fire, divine and human
Passion ever brooding in the heart of woman.

Ah, love of woman, by whose power we live,
Offend so often—but to see forgive!
Whence do you draw your grace but from above?
Whence simply! Simply from maternal love!   30
Yes, we are children, woman, in your arms;
Your heart is bread, you soothe our wild alarms,
Like children give us the honey of your breast,
In a cradle always your lover sinks to rest
Although he prostitutes our grovelling flesh.
Mother if lover, mother if sister too,
Mother by pure essence, day long and night through,
Mother if you laugh, or if with us you cry,
In the core of being, in fibre and in mesh,
Every woman carries, so God has willed on high,   40
A baby in her bosom, sleeping eternally!

So being women, you are lovers, nuns;
Despite the ceintured diamond which runs
Across your virgin shields, showing in your lives
How to be mothers without being wives.
And in this child of all, you have poured all
The honey of your souls, and blended all
The fire of the sun, all fragrance and all light,
The first sweet morning kiss, the last good-night,
Till all her being tenderness exhales,
Her heart the home of love and nightingales.   **10**
A hundred times a woman but no saint.
The nuns pray in the choir; outside her plaint
A song; her prayer, gay rippling laughter.
Mass and the May morning slip by, she running after
Or dreaming in the garden. The roses smell
So sweetly! No child this for the hermits' cell.
She loves Heaven, but in good company;
And before the altar of the Virgin see
Her with a boy, ruddier than the candle's flame,
Who calls her "Sister," the nuns "Aunt" for name.   **20**
A smiling, bashful boy, who soon will grow
To be a strong man, learn to give a blow
And take one, conquer worlds and redress wrong,
Justice in his heart, and on his lips a song!
Sometimes she takes the cat up, calls it "Dear!"
The nuns cross themselves, religiously severe.
"The child is mad," they say. Ah! No such thing!
With her into the convent entered Spring.

This then the simple story. The poet would
Have told it day by day, if well he could,   **30**
In shining glory. But the task were vain.
The glory of our daily lives is plain.
For life builds up itself in such a way,
The water runs so clear, so bright the day,
That time is lulled to sleep within these walls.
An age or moment? Which passes? Who recalls?
The wheel turns round, but no one notes the turn.
What matter if the sisters' locks that burn
With gold, in time to silvery gray have paled?
Their hoods conceal it. And the pinks have failed   **40**
In the cheeks, and the lilies on the brow.
There are no mirrors. The sisters then as now
May walk in the garden, believe it still is May.

Among these hours which softly slip away,
This timeless time, we shyly pause at that

In which there is most warmth, the concordat
Of youth and incense, breaking of the spring.
The years have passed, the child is ripening.
The curtain rises on a soul in flower,
And a love chapter claims us for an hour.
It is quiet afternoon, quiet breeding;
The nuns are sewing and their sister reading:

ACT II

Parlor of a Convent.

At the rear, a grille with a double row of bars. A curtain of dark woolen cloth hangs over the grill and intercepts the view of the outer parlor, to which visitors are admitted. This is without decoration, and may be brightly illuminated at the proper moment 10 *from the garden. A number of oil paintings of saints hang upon the walls—all of them very old and showing black stains. With them a carved crucifix or large black wooden cross. A small window furnished with heavy curtains, which, when drawn, shut off the light completely, is cut in the wall of the inner parlor on either side of the grille, high up toward the ceiling. A pine table, a carved arm chair, two other arm chairs, smaller chairs* 20 *and benches, together with all the materials necessary for sewing.*

THE PRIORESS, *the* MISTRESS OF NOVICES, SISTERS INEZ *and* TORNERA, SISTER SAGRARIO, SISTER JOANNA OF THE CROSS, SISTER MARCELLA, SISTER MARÍA JESÚS *and the other* NUNS *are discovered upon the rise of the curtain. Only the* VICARESS *is absent. All are seated, sewing, with the exception of* SISTER MARÍA JESÚS, *who stands in the cen-* 30 *tre, to the left of the* PRIORESS'S *chair, reading. A bride's trousseau is spread out upon the table and chairs. It is embroidered elaborately, trimmed with lace and tied with blue silk ribbons. A new trunk stands against the wall on the right, the trays being distributed about the benches and upon the floor.*

Eighteen years have passed. It must be remembered that the NUNS *have changed in ap-*

pearance, and those who were novices have now professed and have exchanged the white for the black veil.

SISTER MARÍA JESÚS (*reading and intoning*). "The Treasury of Patience, the Meditations of an Afflicted Soul in the presence of its God."

SISTER MARCELLA (*sighing*). *Ay!*

SISTER MARÍA JESÚS (*reading*). "First Meditation: The Sorrows of an Unhappy Spirit, Submerged in a Sea of Woe."

[*Outside,* TERESA'S *voice is heard, singing gaily.*]

TERESA. "Come singing and bringing
Flowers from the field,
Flowers from the field,
Sweet gardens, to Mary.
Flowers you must yield
For Love's sanctuary!"

[*The reader stops, and, smiling, glances in the direction of the window through which the voice is heard. The other* NUNS *smile also, complacently.*]

PRIORESS (*with affected severity*). The child interrupts us continually.

SISTER INEZ. And a day like to-day!

SISTER JOANNA OF THE CROSS (*sympathetically*). She sings like a lark.

MISTRESS OF NOVICES (*indulgently*). She is so young!

SISTER MARCELLA. *Ay*, Mother!

PRIORESS. Continue reading, Sister María Jesús.

SISTER MARÍA JESÚS (*reading*). "The Sorrows of an Unhappy Spirit, Submerged in a Sea of Woe. My God, O my God, save me, for every moment I die! Overwhelmed, I sink in the midst of this terrible storm. Every moment I am buffeted and borne down. I am sucked into the uttermost depths, and there is no health in me!"

TERESA (*singing*).

"From the glory of your brightness,
   Radiantly sweet,   10
O, let me stoop and bend me
   To kiss your feet!
Let me stoop and bend me
   To kiss your feet!"

[*Again the reader stops. The* NUNS *smile again.*]

PRIORESS. Sister Sagrario, will you step out into the garden and ask the child not to sing? We are reading.

[SISTER SAGRARIO *goes out, right, after mak-* 20 *ing the customary reverence.*] Continue, Sister, continue.

SISTER MARÍA JESÚS (*reading*). "There is no health in me. I cannot support myself; I cannot resist the shock of the horrible onrushing waves."

TERESA (*singing*).

"You too were happy, Mary,
   Happy in his love,
Flowers of love and springtime   30
   That bloom above!"

[*The song is broken off suddenly, as if the* NUN *had arrived and commanded* TERESA *to stop. A moment later, there is a sound of light laughter.*]

PRIORESS. It cannot be helped. (*Smiling.*) The child was born happy and she will die so. (*To the reader.*) Continue.

SISTER MARCELLA. Ay, Lady of Sorrows!

PRIORESS. But Sister Marcella, my   40 daughter, why do you sigh like this? Are you unwell?

SISTER MARCELLA. No, reverend Mother. But your daughter has temptations to melancholy.

PRIORESS. The Lord protect and keep you. You know how it displeases me to see the shadow of melancholy enter this house.

SISTER MARCELLA (*making a reverence*). Ay, reverend Mother, pardon me and assign me some penance if I sin, but your daughter cannot help it.

PRIORESS. Who was thinking of sin? Go out into the garden and take a little sunshine, daughter; that is what you need.

SISTER MARCELLA. Ay, reverend Mother, you don't know what you say! For when your daughter sees the flowers in the garden, and the blue sky so bright above them, and the sun so beautiful overhead, the temptation comes upon her then to sigh more than ever. Ay!

PRIORESS. If that is the case, return to your seat and let us pray that it may cease. But do not let me hear you sigh again, for I do not wish to send you to the prison to brighten your spirit with solitude and confinement.

SISTER MARCELLA. As your Reverence desires. (*Returning to her seat.*) Ay, my soul! (*The* PRIORESS *raises her eyes to heaven in resignation.*)

A NUN. Ay, Blessed Virgin!

ANOTHER. Ay, Jesús!

PRIORESS (*somewhat ruffled*). What? Is this an epidemic? Nothing is wanting now but that we should begin to sigh in chorus. Remember, it is with gladness and thanksgiving that the Lord is to be served "*in hymnis et canticis,*" for the second of the fruits of the Spirit is joy and there is none higher but love, from which it springs. (*A Pause.* SISTER MARÍA JESÚS *reopens the book, and without waiting for the signal from the* PRIORESS, *resumes reading.*)

SISTER MARÍA JESÚS (*reading*). "I cannot resist the shock of the horrible onrushing waves. They break over me unceasingly; irresistibly they bear me down."

PRIORESS. Close the book, Sister María Jesús, for the blessed father who wrote it, alas, he too was of a melancholy turn of mind!

[SISTER MARÍA JESÚS *closes the book, makes a reverence and sits down to sew. The* MOTHER VICARESS *appears in the door on the left, accompanied solemnly by two other* NUNS.]

VICARESS (*greatly agitated*). *Ave Maria Purissima!*

PRIORESS. Conceived without sin.

VICARESS. Have I permission, reverend Mother?

PRIORESS. Enter and speak. (*Looking at her.*) If I am not mistaken, your Reverence is greatly disturbed.

VICARESS. You are not mistaken, reverend Mother. No, and I dare affirm it is not for a slight reason. Your Reverence will be judge if this is the time and place to confront with a charge of *ipso facto* a member of this community.

PRIORESS. Speak, if the knowledge of the fault in public will not in itself constitute a scandal and a cause of offense.

VICARESS. In the opinion of your handmaid all cause of scandal will be avoided by looking the offense straight in the face.

PRIORESS. Speak then.

VICARESS (*making a profound inclination*). I obey. Reverend Mother, while making the round of my inspection of the cells with these two monitors, as your Reverence has been pleased to command . . . (*The two* MONITORS *each make a reverence.*) And coming to the cell of Sister Marcella . . . (*All the* NUNS *look at* SISTER MARCELLA, *who lowers her eyes.*) I found under the mattress of the bed—in itself a suspicious

circumstance and sufficient to constitute a sin—an object which should never be found in the hands of a religious, an object which, to say nothing of the sin against the rule of holy poverty which the private possession and concealment of any property whatever must presuppose, is by its very nature a root of perdition and an origin and source of evil.

PRIORESS. Conclude, Mother, in God's name! For you keep us in suspense. What is this object?

VICARESS. Disclose it, sister. (*To one of the* MONITORS.)

[*The* MONITOR *makes a reverence, and draws from her sleeve a piece of glass, covered on one side with quick-silver.*]

PRIORESS. A piece of looking-glass.

VICARESS. Exactly, a piece of looking-glass! (*Horrified silence on the part of the community.*)

PRIORESS. What has Sister Marcella to say to this?

SISTER MARCELLA (*leaving her place and kneeling before the* PRIORESS). Mother, I confess my guilt and I beseech your pardon.

PRIORESS. Rise. (SISTER MARCELLA *rises.*) Unhappy woman! What was the use of this piece of glass?

VICARESS. To look at herself in it, and amuse herself with the sight of her beauty, thus offending her Maker with pride and vain glory, and the exhibition of her taste.

SISTER MARCELLA (*humbly*). No, reverend Mother; no!

VICARESS. Or else to dress herself up and fix herself by it, and makes faces and grimaces such as they do on the streets in these days. (*The* VICARESS, *who has taken the mirror, looks at herself in it for a moment, then turns it hurriedly away.*)

SISTER MARCELLA. No, reverend Mother.

PRIORESS. For what then?

SISTER MARCELLA. For nothing, reverend Mother.

PRIORESS. What? For nothing?

SISTER MARCELLA. Your daughter means for nothing evil. On the contrary . . .

VICARESS. Ha! Now I suppose we are going to hear that it is a virtue in a religious to have a glass!

SISTER MARCELLA. No, reverend Mother, 10 it is not a virtue. But your Reverences know already that your Sister suffers from temptations to melancholy.

VICARESS. Yes, yes . . .

SISTER MARCELLA. And when they seize upon her too strongly, they put it into her head to climb trees and run along the tops of walls, and jump over the fences in the garden, and to throw herself into the water of the fountain, 20 and since your Sister knows that, in a religious, these . . . these . . .

VICARESS. These extravagances.

SISTER MARCELLA. Are unbecoming, your Sister catches a sunbeam in the mirror and makes it dance among the leaves and across the ceiling of her cell, and over the walls opposite, and so she consoles herself and imagines that it is a butterfly or a bird, and can go 30 wherever it pleaseth.

VICARESS. It can, and stay there.

PRIORESS. For this fault, Sister Marcella . . . (SISTER MARCELLA *kneels.*) which, without being a grave one, yet is more than a little, considered according to the constitution of our rule, I assign you this penance. Tonight, before you retire, you are to repeat four times in your cell the psalm "*Quam* 40 *dilecta.*" Rise, and return to your seat. (SISTER MARCELLA *obeys, but before seating herself she makes a reverence before each of the* NUNS.) (*To the* VICARESS.) You may be seated. (*The* VICARESS *and the two* MONITORS *seat themselves.*)

(*Three light knocks on the door. It is* TERESA *who says:*)

TERESA. *Ave Maria Purissima!*

PRIORESS. Conceived without sin.

TERESA. May I come in?

PRIORESS. Come in. (TERESA *enters. She is eighteen, very pretty, very sunny and very gay, with nothing about her to suggest the mystic or the religious. She is dressed simply in gray and wears a white apron. She has a flower in her hair, which is arranged modestly, and without an excess of curls or ornament.*) Where are you coming from in such a hurry? You are all out of breath.

TERESA (*speaks always with the greatest simplicity, without affectation or pretense of any sort*). From dressing the altar of the Virgin.

PRIORESS. Did that put you out of breath?

TERESA. No, Mother. It's because I wanted it to be all in white today, and there weren't white flowers enough in the garden, so I had to climb up and cut some branches off the acacia.

MISTRESS OF NOVICES. Did you climb a tree?

TERESA. Yes, I climbed two; there weren't enough blossoms on one.

MISTRESS OF NOVICES. *Jesús!*

VICARESS. *Ave María!*

TERESA. I wish you could see the view from the top of the big acacia! (SISTER MARCELLA'S *eyes open wide with envy.*)

VICARESS. Child, you have put yourself beyond the pale of God's mercy!

SISTER JOANNA OF THE CROSS. You might have fallen! It's too terrible to think of!

TERESA. Fallen? No, Mother. Why, I've climbed it a hundred times!

PRIORESS. Then you must not do it again.

MISTRESS OF NOVICES (*regretfully*). It is too late to forbid her now.

PRIORESS (*sorrowfully*). That is true.

SISTER INEZ. It is the last day she will dress the altar.

SISTER JOANNA OF THE CROSS. The very last!

TERESA. Ah, Mothers! You mustn't talk like this. Don't be sad.

VICARESS. No, we had better behave like you do, though it doesn't seem possible when you consider the day that it is, and you laughing and carrying on like one possessed!

PRIORESS. The Mother is right. A little more feeling today, daughter, a manner more subdued, would not have been out of place.

TERESA. You are right, reverend Mothers—you always are, in the holiness, which like a halo surrounds your reverend heads; but when a girl wants to laugh she wants to laugh, although, as Mother Anna St. Francis says, it may be the solemnest day of her life.

MISTRESS OF NOVICES. It is a solemn day, a very solemn day. You are leaving this house in which you have passed eighteen years, without scarcely so much as taking thought how it was you came to be here. Tomorrow, you will be your own mistress, and you will have upon your conscience the responsibilities of a wife.

VICARESS. Which believe me, are not light. Men are selfish, fickle . . .

TERESA (*timidly*). Antonio is very good.

VICARESS. However good he may be, he is a man, and men are accustomed to command. They have been from the beginning of the world, and it has affected their character. And since you are very independent yourself, and like to have your own way . . .

TERESA. Yes, I have been spoiled I know; but you will see now how good I will be. It will come out all right.

SISTER JOANNA OF THE CROSS. Do you want to spoil the day for her?

TERESA. No, Mother—no; you won't spoil it, for I am very, very happy. You have all been so good to me!

VICARESS. Nonsense! No such thing.

TERESA. But it isn't nonsense. I know this is God's house, but you might have closed the doors to me, and you have flung them wide open, freely. I have lived here eighteen years and in all this time, to the very moment that I am leaving it, you have never once reminded me that I have lived here on your charity.

SISTER JOANNA OF THE CROSS. Don't say such things!

TERESA. Yes, I must say them. On your charity, on your alms—like a poor beggar and an outcast. I don't mind saying it nor thinking it, for I have been so happy here—yes, I am happy now—happier than the daughter of a king: for I love you all so much that I want to kiss even the walls and hug the trees, for even the walls and the trees have been kind to me. This has been the Convent of my Heart!

SISTER MARCELLA. It has been your home. If you had only been content always to remain in it!

PRIORESS. We must not talk like this. God moves in His own ways.

MISTRESS OF NOVICES. And in all of them His children may do His service.

VICARESS. The child was not born to be a religious. The things of the world appeal to her too strongly.

TERESA. It is true. The world appeals to me—poor me! It seems to me sometimes as if everybody loved me, as if everything was calling to me everywhere to come. I have been so happy in this house, and yet, all the time, I have been thinking how great the world was, how wonderful! Whenever

I have gone out into the street, how my heart leaped! I felt as if I were going to fly, it was so light! My brain was in a whirl. Then I was so glad to come back again into this house, it felt so good, as if you were all taking me up once more into your arms, as if I had fallen to sleep in them again and was warm, folded beneath the shelter of the everlasting wings. 10

VICARESS. The wings of your good angel, who stood waiting at the door—stood waiting till you came.

PRIORESS. Why should he have to wait? Her good angel always has gone with her, and surely there never has been a time when he has had to turn away his face. Am I right, daughter?

TERESA. You are, Mother. (*Sincerely.*)

SISTER JOANNA OF THE CROSS. They 20 needn't have asked her that!

SISTER MARÍA JESÚS (*rising*). Here are the bows for the corset covers. Do you want them pinned or sewed?

SISTER INEZ. Sewed, I say.

SISTER MARÍA JESÚS. Down the middle?

MISTRESS OF NOVICES. Of course, down the middle.

SISTER MARÍA JESÚS. The reason I asked was because in the pattern they are 30 all fastened down the side.

MISTRESS OF NOVICES (*bending over to examine the fashion plates with* SISTER INEZ *and* SISTER MARÍA JESÚS.) Yes. Don't you see? She is right.

SISTER INEZ. That's funny! But they are pretty that way.

MISTRESS OF NOVICES. I say it's absurd.

SISTER MARÍA JESÚS. What do you think, Mother Crucifixion? 40

VICARESS. Don't ask me; I don't think. I neither understand nor wish to understand these things—pomp and vanity, artifices of the devil, who, they tell me, is very well acquainted with the dressmakers of Paris, and takes part in their designs and encourages their abbreviations. Take it away, take that paper out of my sight, for it never should have entered this holy house!

SISTER MARCELLA. *Ay*, but we have to know the fashions, Mother!

VICARESS. The fashions! The fashions! Go to hell and you will find the fashions! Any other place would be too far behind.

SISTER MARÍA JESÚS. But you don't want the child to be married, do you, in the dress of the year of the ark?

VICARESS. A pure heart and an upright spirit are what she should be married in, and if that is the case, no one is going to notice whether she has one bow more or less.

SISTER MARCELLA. They say men pay a great deal of attention to such things, Mother Crucifixion.

SISTER MARÍA JESÚS. And we must render unto Caesar the things which are Caesar's, and unto God the things which are God's.

VICARESS. So! We have philosophers, have we, in the house?

SISTER INEZ. Hand me the scissors, if you will. I want to cut off these ends.

SISTER JOANNA OF THE CROSS. I think now everything is ready to put in the trunk.

PRIORESS. Yes, for the carriage will be waiting.

[TERESA *kneels on the floor beside the trunk. The* NUNS *hand her the various articles of the trousseau, which they remove from the benches and the table.*]

SISTER INEZ. Here are the chemises.

SISTER MARCELLA. And the lace petticoats.

SISTER JOANNA OF THE CROSS. Put them in the other tray, so they won't get wrinkled.

SISTER INEZ. Lord of Mercy! What a tuck!—What bungler ran this tuck?

MISTRESS OF NOVICES. You must not say anything against the sister who ran it, Sister; say it would look better if it were redampened and ironed.

TERESA. But it looks splendidly; really it does! Give it to me! Here—let me have them. This is too much trouble for you to take.   10

PRIORESS. Have you everything?

SISTER MARCELLA. The handkerchiefs?

SISTER JOANNA OF THE CROSS. The dressing-jackets?

VICARESS. Here is some edging that was left over, embroidered by hand. You had better put it in the trunk in case of accident.

MISTRESS OF NOVICES. And the patterns—you might need them.   20

SISTER INEZ. Here is a sachet, my child. It is filled with thyme and lavender and has lime peel in it. It will give a fresh scent to your clothes.

SISTER MARCELLA. She'll have real perfumes soon enough.

SISTER MARÍA JESÚS. Yes, expensive ones.

SISTER INEZ. They may be more expensive, but they won't be any better—I can tell you that; for these are plants 30 that God has made, and they smell sweetly, and of a good conscience. I have them in all the presses in the sacristy, and it is a joy to smell them when you go up the steps to the altar.

TERESA. I think we have everything.

PRIORESS. Yes, everything. Now turn the key. Does it lock securely? (TERESA gets up.) And hang the key around 40 your neck with the rosaries, for we have fastened it on a ribbon for you. Take care you don't lose it. The lock is an English one, and not every key will open it.

TERESA. Yes, Mother.

VICARESS. It will be a miracle if she has it tomorrow.

SISTER JOANNA OF THE CROSS. She will settle down soon under the responsibilities of a wife.

MISTRESS OF NOVICES. Well? Are you satisfied?

TERESA. Satisfied is too little, Mother. It does not express it. I don't deserve what you have done for me.

VICARESS. Yes, you do; you deserve it. And you might as well tell the truth as a falsehood. You have a good heart; you are a sensible girl. When you said what you did, you were thinking of your clothes; but you need have no scruples. Everything that you take away with you from this house, and more too, you have earned by your labor. That is the truth and you know it. Maybe we have taught you here how to sew and embroider, but you have worked for us in the convent, and outside of it. You owe us nothing. Besides, you had two hundred and fifty pesetas from the doctor to buy the material. Here . . . (*Producing a paper from under her scapular.*) is the account of the way they have been spent, so you can see for yourself and answer for it, since delicacy will not permit that we should be asked how it was used.

TERESA (*embarrassed and confused*). What do you mean? Why, Mother Crucifixion!

VICARESS. That is all there is to it. You will find the account is correct. (TERESA *takes the paper and having folded it, puts it in her dress.*)

PRIORESS (*to the* NUNS *who have been working*). You may remove the table and gather up these things.

TERESA. No, Mother—let me do it. I will pick up everything. (*The* PRIORESS *makes a sign and all the* NUNS *rise and leave the room, except only herself, the* VICARESS, *the* MISTRESS OF NOVICES, *and* SISTER JOANNA OF THE CROSS.)

PRIORESS (*to* TERESA). What time do you go?

TERESA. My father is coming for me at five, but . . . Antonio has asked me . . . before I go . . . to say that he would like to see you all and thank you, and tell you how happy and grateful he is to you for the little girl you have brought up.

PRIORESS. We shall be very glad to see him.

VICARESS. Glad or not glad, no matter; it is our obligation. He cannot expect to carry her off like a thief in the night, and have no woman ask a question.

TERESA. I will call you when he comes.

[*The* PRIORESS, *the* VICARESS *and the* MISTRESS OF NOVICES *go out.* TERESA *and* SISTER JOANNA OF THE CROSS *remain behind picking up and arranging the papers, patterns and scraps that have been left on the seats or about the floor. They say nothing but presently* TERESA *throws herself on her knees before the* NUN.]

TERESA. Sister Joanna of the Cross!

SISTER JOANNA OF THE CROSS. What do you want, my child?

TERESA. Now that we are alone, bless me while there is no one here to see—no, not one—for you are my mother, more than all the rest!

SISTER JOANNA OF THE CROSS. Get up. (TERESA *gets up.*) Don't talk like that! We are all equal in God's house.

TERESA. But in my heart you are the first. You mustn't be angry at what I say. How can I help it? Is it my fault, though I have struggled against it all my life, that I have come to love you so?

SISTER JOANNA OF THE CROSS. Yes, you have struggled. You have been wilful

. . . (*Then seeking at once to excuse her.*) But it was because you were strong and well. When a child is silent and keeps to herself in a corner, it is a sign that she is sick or thinking of some evil. But you . . .

TERESA. Ay, Mother! Where do you suppose that I came from?

SISTER JOANNA OF THE CROSS. From Heaven, my daughter, as all of us have come.

TERESA. Do you really think that we have all come from Heaven?

SISTER JOANNA OF THE CROSS. At least you have come from Heaven to me. You say that I am your mother more than the rest; I don't know—it may be. But I know that for years you have been all my happiness and joy.

TERESA. Mother!

SISTER JOANNA OF THE CROSS. I was so glad to hear you laugh and see you run about the cloisters! It was absurd, but I always felt—not now, for you are grown-up now—but for years I always felt as if you must be I, myself, scampering and playing. For I was just your age now, a little more or less, when you came into the Convent. And it seemed to me as if I was a child again and had just begun to live. You were so little, so busy—yes, you were —but I was busy too, if you only knew, before I entered here, at home in our house in the village. I was always singing and dancing, although we were very poor. My mother went out every day to wash in the river or to do housework—she had so many children!—and I was always carrying one about in my arms. And when I entered here, as I could do, thanks to some good ladies, who collected the money for my dowry—God reward them for it—although I had a real vocation, I was sorrowful and homesick thinking of my little brothers and sisters! How I used to cry in the dark corners, and I never dared to say a word! Then the Mother told me that if my melancholy didn't leave me she would be obliged to send me home. And then you came and I forgot everything! That is why I say you came to me from Heaven. And I don't want you to think I am angry, or ashamed—or that it has ever given me a moment's pain to have loved you.

TERESA. Is that the reason that you scold me so?

SISTER JOANNA OF THE CROSS. When have I ever scolded you?

TERESA. Oh, so many times! But no matter. I always tell Antonio, Sister Joanna of the Cross is my mother. She is my mother, my real mother! So now he always calls you mother whenever he speaks of you.

SISTER JOANNA OF THE CROSS. My daughter, will you be happy with him?

TERESA. Of course! I am sure I will. He is so good, he is so happy! He says he doesn't know where it is all his happiness comes from, because his father, who is dead now, was more mournful than a willow, and his mother, poor lady, whenever anything happened to her that was good, burst right out crying. How do you suppose it was she ever managed to have such a boy? It must be that sad mothers have happy children. How does it seem to you?

SISTER JOANNA OF THE CROSS. How do I know?

TERESA. It must be that way. The first boy I have is going to be—what is the solemnest thing in the world? No, the first is going to be an architect, like his father; but the second can be a missionary, and go to China if he wants to, and convert the heathen. Just think what it would be to have a son who was a saint! I shouldn't have to be so humble in heaven, then, should I? I should have influence. And here you are all the time, Sister Joanna of the Cross, praying for me and preparing miracles. So you see I have a good start already.

SISTER JOANNA OF THE CROSS. How you do love to talk!

TERESA. Isn't it foolish, Mother? Don't I? Listen! When you were little didn't you ever want to be a boy? I did. I used to cry because I thought then that I could have been anything I wanted to be—this, that, I didn't care what it was—Captain-General, Archbishop, yes, Pope, even! Or something else. It used to make me mad to think that because I was a girl I couldn't even be an acolyte. But now, since—well, since I love Antonio, and he loves me, I don't care; it doesn't make any difference any more, because if I am poor and know nothing, he is wise and strong; and if I am foolish and of no account, he is, oh, of so much worth! And if I have to stay behind at home and hide myself in the corner, he can go out into the world and mount, oh, so high —wherever a man can go—and instead of making me envious, it makes me so happy! Ah, Sister Joanna of the Cross, when she truly loves a man, how humble it makes a girl!

SISTER JOANNA OF THE CROSS. Do you really love him so?

TERESA. More than life itself! And that is all too little. Maybe it's a sin, but I can tell you. Do you believe that we will meet in Heaven the persons we have loved on earth? Because if I don't meet him there and I can't go on loving him always just the same as

I do now, no, more than I do now
. . .

SISTER JOANNA OF THE CROSS (*interrupting*).
Hush! Peace! You mustn't say such
things. It is a sin.

TERESA. *Ay*, sister Joanna of the Cross!
How sweet it is to be in love!

SISTER JOANNA OF THE CROSS. But he . . .
he . . . Does he love you too, so
much?   10

TERESA. Yes, he loves me. How much, I
don't know; but it doesn't make any
matter. What makes me happy is that
I love him. You needn't think that
sometimes—very seldom though—I
haven't been afraid that perhaps some
day he might stop loving me. It used
to make me sad. But if I had ever
thought that some day I could stop
loving him . . . No, it would be bet- 20
ter to die first; for then, what would
be the good of life?

SISTER JOANNA OF THE CROSS. Ah, my
child! To continue in God's love!

TERESA. Do you know how I would like
to spend my life? All of it? Sitting on
the ground at his feet, looking up into
his eyes, just listening to him talk.
You don't know how he can talk. He
knows everything—everything that   30
there is to know in the world, and he
tells you such things! The things that
you always have known yourself, in
your heart, and you couldn't find out
how to say them. Even when he
doesn't say anything, if he should be
speaking some language which you
didn't understand, it is wonderful
. . . his voice . . . I don't know
how to explain it, but it is his voice— 40
a voice that seems as if it had been
talking to you ever since the day you
were born! You don't hear it only
with your ears, but with your whole
body. It's like the air which you see
and breathe and taste, and which

smells so sweetly in the garden beneath the tree of paradise. Ah,
Mother! The first day that he said to
me "Teresa"—you see what a simple
thing it was, my name, Teresa—why,
it seemed to me as if nobody ever had
called me by my name before, as if I
never had heard it, and when he went
away, I ran up and down the street
saying to myself "Teresa, Teresa,
Teresa!" under my breath, without
knowing what I was doing, as if I
walked on air!

SISTER JOANNA OF THE CROSS. You
frighten me, my child.

TERESA. Do I? Why?

SISTER JOANNA OF THE CROSS. Because
you love him so. For earthly love . . .
I mean . . . it seems to me it is like a
flower, that we find by the side of the
road—a little brightness that God
grants us to help us pass through life,
for we are weak and frail; a drop of
honey spread upon our bread each
day, which we should receive gladly,
but with trembling, and keeping our
hearts whole, daughter, for it will
surely pass away.

TERESA. It cannot pass away!

SISTER JOANNA OF THE CROSS. It may; and
then what will be left to your soul, if
you have set your all on this delight,
and it has passed away?

TERESA (*humbly*). You mustn't be angry
with me, Mother. No! Look at me! It
isn't wrong, I know. Loving him, I
. . . he is so good, he is so good . . .
and good, it cannot pass away!

SISTER JOANNA OF THE CROSS. Is he a good
Christian?

TERESA. He is good, Sister.

SISTER JOANNA OF THE CROSS. But does he
fear God?

TERESA. One day he said to me: "I love
you because you know how to pray."
Don't you see? And another time: "I

feel a devotion toward you as toward some holy thing." He! Devotion! To me! And whenever I think of that, it seems to me as if I was just growing better, as if all at once I was capable of everything there was to do or suffer in the world—so as to have him always feel that way!

SISTER JOANNA OF THE CROSS. I hear some one in the parlor. Draw the curtains.

[TERESA, *pulling the cord, draws the curtains over the windows, shutting off the light. The fore part of the stage remains in shadow, but the outer parlor is brightly illuminated.* ANTONIO *has entered and may be seen through the crack where the curtains join. He is twenty-five years of age, well-built, manly and sensitive of feature. He remains alone and his footsteps may be heard on the boards as he paces nervously up and down.*]

TERESA (*in a low voice, going up to the* NUN). Yes. It is he.

SISTER JOANNA OF THE CROSS (*seizing her hand*). Ah! How tall he is!

TERESA. Yes, he is tall. Doesn't he look splendidly though?

SISTER JOANNA OF THE CROSS. Yes, he does. Has he golden hair?

TERESA. No, it's the light; his hair is dark brown, and his eyes are between violet and blue. It's too bad you can't see them. They are so beautiful! When he talks, they sparkle.

SISTER JOANNA OF THE CROSS. How old is he?

TERESA. Just twenty-five.

[ANTONIO *crosses from one side to the other, and continues to pace back and forth.*]

SISTER JOANNA OF THE CROSS. He seems to be of a very active disposition.

TERESA. That is because he is impatient. Shall I speak to him and tell him you are here?

SISTER JOANNA OF THE CROSS (*falling back*). No!

TERESA. Why not? He loves you dearly. (*In a low voice, going up to the grille.*) Good afternoon, Antonio.

ANTONIO (*looking about from one side to the other*). Teresa? Where are you?

TERESA (*laughing*). Here, boy, here; behind the grille. It is easy to see you are not accustomed to calling on nuns.

ANTONIO. Can't you run back the curtain?

TERESA. No, because I am not alone. Can't you guess who is with me? My mother.

ANTONIO. Sister Joanna of the Cross?

TERESA (*to the* NUN, *delighted because he has guessed it*). There! Do you see? (*To* ANTONIO.) Sister Joanna of the Cross —exactly. We have been watching you through the grille, and she says that she thinks you are a very handsome young man.

SISTER JOANNA OF THE CROSS. Goodness gracious! You mustn't pay any attention to what she says.

TERESA. Don't be angry, Mother. I think so myself.

ANTONIO. You never told me that before.

TERESA. That is because in here, where you can't see me, I'm not so embarrassed to tell you. Listen! We have to send in word now that you are here; but I want you to tell my mother something first, for if you stand there like a blockhead without opening your mouth, I am going to be very much ashamed, after all the time I have spent in singing your praises.

ANTONIO. What do you want me to tell her?

TERESA. What you have in your heart.

ANTONIO. But I don't know whether it is proper to tell it to a religious, although it is in my heart, for I love her dearly.

TERESA. Ah! I tell her that a million times a day.

ANTONIO. Then let us tell her together two million; because I must say to you, Madam, that it is impossible to know Teresa and not to love you.

TERESA. What a treasure is this mother of mine!

SISTER JOANNA OF THE CROSS. For shame, my child! (*Blushing, to* ANTONIO.) I 10 also have a great affection for you, sir, for this child has been teaching me to love you. She is a little blind perhaps, and trusting, for that is natural. She knows nothing of the world, and we—how were we to teach her? And now you are going to take her far away; but don't take her heart away from us, sir, and break ours, when we let her hand go.   20

ANTONIO. Madam, I swear to you now that I shall always kneel in reverence before the tenderness and virtue which you have planted in her soul.

TERESA. I told you that he was very good, Mother.

SISTER JOANNA OF THE CROSS. May God make you both very happy. And may God remain with you, for his hand-maid must go now and seek the 30 Mother.

ANTONIO. But you are coming back?

SISTER JOANNA OF THE CROSS. With the Sisters . . . Yes, I think so. Good-bye. I have been so happy to know you.

[SISTER JOANNA OF THE CROSS *goes out, greatly moved.* TERESA *remains standing by the grille until the* NUN *has disappeared, without speaking a word.*]   40

ANTONIO. Now you can draw back the curtain.

TERESA. Yes, a little. (*She runs back the curtain a little way.*) But it won't do you any good, because you won't be able to see me. Do you really like my mother? Do you really? Why are you so silent? What are you thinking about?

ANTONIO. I don't know; it is very strange. Since I have come into this room, since I have heard your mother speak, and have heard you, behind this grille, without knowing for certain where you were in the dark, I have been almost afraid to love you. But ah—how I do love you!

TERESA. I like that better.

ANTONIO. Teresa!

TERESA. What is it?

ANTONIO. Will you never forget, will you carry with you always wherever you go, this peace and this calm?

TERESA. With you, Antonio?

ANTONIO. Yes, into the world, beyond these walls; for in the world we make so much useless noise. And you—I see it now—you are the mistress of peace and of calm.

TERESA (*laughing*). I the mistress of calm? As if I hadn't been a little flyaway all my life, without an idea in my head! Mother Crucifixion says that since I was passed in on the wheel there hasn't been one moment in this house of what the rules call "profound calm." I know I don't talk much when I am with you—we have been together such a little while, and it has been all too short to listen to you; but you will see when I grow bolder and am not afraid. You will have to put cotton in your ears then. Ah, Antonio! Only think, we are going to have all our lives to be together and listen to each other talk and tell each other things—that is, all our lives for you to tell me things, because I . . . you will find out soon enough. Tell me really, truly, Antonio: aren't you going to be awfully ashamed to have such an ignorant wife?

ANTONIO. Ignorant or learned?

TERESA. I? Learned? In what?

ANTONIO. In a science which I did not know, and which you have taught to me.

TERESA. You are joking.

ANTONIO. I am in earnest. Until I met you, I knew nothing; I did not even know myself.

TERESA. Pshaw! 10

ANTONIO. You mustn't laugh. Did it ever seem to you, Teresa, that our soul was like a palace?

TERESA. Of course it is! It is like a castle. Santa Teresa says so: The soul is like a castle—the interior of a castle, all made of one diamond above and below. And it has seven courts, and in the last is stored a great treasure . . .

ANTONIO. Then in the innermost cham-20 ber of my soul was stored the love I have for you, and if you had not come and opened the door yourself, and helped me to find it, I should have passed all my life in ignorance, without knowing anything was there.

TERESA. Don't repeat such heresies!

ANTONIO. Is it a heresy—the love I bear for you? No, it is a religion—the only one for me! My girl! Seven courts, 30 you say? Then with a great effort I had passed into the first and I was running here and there aimlessly, and you don't know what horrible things I found—everywhere I stumbled on. They were my own traits. I was cold, selfish, proud, without trust or faith, without other ambitions than material desires—to pass through life easily and well, to be the first in my own 40 petty world, incapable of sacrifice, of abnegation, of compassion, of disinterested love.

TERESA. No! No! You were no such thing.

ANTONIO. But I lived as if I were! What difference did it make? But then one day I heard your voice, and summoned by you, I again searched through the castle, and in the other courts I began to find—ah! under how many cobwebs, all covered-up with dust—humility and devotion, warmth of heart, pity and faith in so many holy things. And then I found my honor, self-respect and sympathy with my fellow man, in which we live, Teresa, for without it nothing else is life, and I began to be a man when I first loved you. For in these things you are the master, and I have learned them all from you!

TERESA. Hush! They are coming.

[TERESA *falls back from the grille, after first drawing the curtains again. The* NUNS *in single file enter silently, the youngest first, followed at last by the* MISTRESS OF NOVICES, *the* VICARESS *and the* PRIORESS. *The* PRIORESS *seats herself in the armchair at the left of the grille; the* VICARESS *and the* MISTRESS OF NOVICES *in two other chairs at the right. The remaining* NUNS *stand or are seated round about.* TERESA *supports herself with her hand on the back of the* PRIORESS'S *chair.* SISTER JOANNA OF THE CROSS *approaches her and takes her by the other hand. There is absolute silence as the* NUNS *enter and find their places. They look at each other with expectant attention, and some nod and smile among themselves. When they are seated, there follows an interval of further silence.*]

PRIORESS. *Ave Maria Purissima!* (AN-TONIO, *somewhat embarrassed, and endeavoring vainly to penetrate the darkness behind the grille, does not answer. The* PRIORESS, *after waiting a moment, turns her head and smiles indulgently at the community.*) Good afternoon, young man.

ANTONIO. Good afternoon, Madam—or Madams—for behind the mystery of this screen, it is impossible for me to see whether I am speaking with one or with many. (*The* NUNS *smile quietly and discreetly.*)

PRIORESS (*in a low voice*). Run back the curtain, Sister Inez. (*The Sister runs back the curtain.*) You are speaking with the entire community, which takes great pleasure in knowing you.

ANTONIO. Ladies, the pleasure and the honor are mine, and they are much greater than you will be ready to imagine.

SISTER INEZ. Bless us! But isn't he a polite and polished talker?

SISTER TORNERA. Keep still! I want to hear what he has to say.

ANTONIO. For a long time I have desired greatly to visit you. Teresa knows it, and she must have told it to you.

PRIORESS. That is true. She has indeed. And we have greatly appreciated your desire.

ANTONIO. But the first time I was in this place it was Advent and the second it was Lent; and both times Teresa informed me that it was impossible for me to see you.

VICARESS. Clearly. In seasons of penitence we receive no visitors.

ANTONIO. But now it is May and past Easter time.

MISTRESS OF NOVICES. How well acquainted he is with the calendar! Surely you must be very devout, sir.

ANTONIO. I am, Madam—very; but chiefly in the worship of certain saints who as yet are not on the altars.

SISTER INEZ. What a nice compliment! Saints, did he say? (*Laughing.*) He *is* a polished talker.

ANTONIO. Ladies, after a hundred years they will be lighting candles to you, and invoking you in prayers, and in gratitude they will be bringing you thank offerings of crutches and wooden legs.

SISTER TORNERA (*laughing*). Does he think we are going to be the patrons of rheumatism?

MISTRESS OF NOVICES. After a hundred years? You are giving us a century of Purgatory.

ANTONIO. No, Madam, by all that is holy! I am giving you a century of life, and entrance thereafter directly into the choir of seraphim.

PRIORESS. I fear you speak frivolously, Señor Don Antonio.

ANTONIO. Madam, I was never more earnest in my life. Whenever I think of death, you have no idea of the peace which enters my soul. I remember how many saintly white hands will be stretched down to me to help me into Paradise—for I suppose that you will be able to exercise a little influence on behalf of one of the family.

SISTER SAGRARIO (*laughing*). One of the family?

VICARESS. Certainly. We are all God's children.

ANTONIO. But I shall be so in a double sense; first, in my own birthright, and then as your son-in-law, who are his brides.

VICARESS. Ah! It is not meet to jest about holy things.

ANTONIO. Madam, you are right. And you will pardon me all the inconsequences which I have said, for I swear to you that they have been nothing but nervousness and fear.

MISTRESS OF NOVICES. You are not afraid of us?

ANTONIO. I am, Madam, very—because of the respect and admiration in which I hold you all. I came here more disturbed than I ever have been before in my whole life. I do not know whether I should thank you, or whether I should beg your pardon.

PRIORESS. Beg our pardon?

ANTONIO. Yes, because I fear that I am not worthy of the treasure which you are entrusting to me.

PRIORESS. We know already through the doctor that you are an honorable young man.

MISTRESS OF NOVICES. And the love which our daughter bears you is our guarantee. Surely the Lord would not permit His child, brought up in His fear, to throw herself away upon an evil man.

ANTONIO. I am not evil, no; but I am a man, and you, ladies, with all the great piety of your souls, have been nurturing a flower for the skies. When I first knew her, my heart whispered to me that I had met a saint. She was a miracle. When I first dared to speak to her, there came over me a fear and a trembling that were out of the course of nature; and when I told her that I loved her, my heart stopped, and bade me to fall on my knees, and now that I have come here to beg my happiness of you, I don't know what I can promise you in token of my gratitude, nor how I can give you thanks enough for the great honor which you do me.

VICARESS. It may be you are speaking more truly than you think, Señor Don Antonio.

MISTRESS OF NOVICES. Why, Mother!

VICARESS. No, let me speak. For he has said well. The girl is not one of those worldly creatures who take to their husbands a great store of physical beauty. That is certain. You cannot call her ugly, but it is the most that can be said. Nor does she bring with her any dower. She is poorer than the poor. But she carries in her heart a treasure, the only one which we have been able to give her, which is more priceless than silver or gold, and that is the fear of God. For this, sir, you must be answerable to us, and we ask you your word now, that you will always respect it in her and in her children, if you should have any, if it should be God's holy will.

ANTONIO. Teresa shall always be the absolute mistress of her conscience and of my house, and my children shall ever be that which she desires. I pledge my word.

PRIORESS. You will never have reason to regret it, for she is a good and prudent girl.

VICARESS. And not hypocritical, for, although, as you have said, we have nurtured her for the skies, we have never permitted ourselves to believe that she was to reach them through the cloister.

SISTER MARÍA JESÚS. Do you mean to take her very far away?

ANTONIO. Yes, Madam. That is to say, there is no longer in the world either far or near. We sail next week. I am going to America as the resident director of a firm of architects.

PRIORESS. Yes, we know already.

ANTONIO. That is the reason for this haste. I do not wish to go alone.

SISTER TORNERA. Aren't you afraid the child will be seasick? They say you do get a terrible shaking-up upon the sea.

SISTER MARÍA JESÚS. You must promise us to take good care of her.

SISTER INEZ. If she gets overheated never let her drink cold water. She is very pig-headed about that.

SISTER MARCELLA. But you mustn't forget that she is accustomed to cold baths.

SISTER INEZ. If she takes cold or gets a

cough, make her drink a glass of hot milk with a teaspoonful of hot rum in it, with plenty of sugar, for that's the only thing that will make her sweat.

TERESA. I think perhaps I had better attend to these matters myself, Sister.

SISTER INEZ. Yes, you'd be a pretty one to attend to them! Don't you mind what she says, Señor Don Antonio, for she is spoiled utterly. If you don't give her medicines and force the spoon down her throat, she might be dying for all you'd know, but she'd never ask for them herself.

PRIORESS. We had better not confuse him with too many recommendations. Surely he knows the more important precautions already.

ANTONIO (*smiling*). Perhaps it would be better if you wrote them out for me on a piece of paper.

SISTER TORNERA. A good idea! (*Laughing.*) If we began where does he think we'd leave off?

SISTER SAGRARIO. How many days will you be on the ship?

ANTONIO. Two weeks.

SISTER MARCELLA. Mercy! What an age! Suppose there should be a storm?

MISTRESS OF NOVICES. It will be at least two weeks more before we can get letters back.

ANTONIO. We will telegraph when we arrive and we will send you a message from the middle of the ocean, so that you will hear from us the same day.

SISTER INEZ. Mother of God! Can they send messages now from the middle of the ocean? How do the words come?

TERESA. Flying through the air, like birds.

SISTER INEZ. What will men invent next? When your handmaid was in the world, they came by a wire, and yet it seemed the work of the devil.

ANTONIO. I should not advise you, Madam, to believe that the devil is ever very far away from these inventions.

SISTER INEZ. Whether he is or not, when the telegram comes it will be safest to sprinkle it with holy water.

PRIORESS. Ah, Sister Inez, you are so simple! Don't you see that the young man is only joking?

VICARESS. It is five o'clock—the hour we were to expect your father.

ANTONIO. I do not wish to molest you further.

PRIORESS. You do not molest us, but we must close the parlor at five.

ANTONIO. You will pardon me if I commit a terrible breach of etiquette, but I should like to ask you one favor before I go.

PRIORESS. If it is in our power to grant . . .

ANTONIO. Although, as it seems, you have run back a curtain, yet the mystery of this screen still remains a mystery to me, a poor sinner, inscrutable as before; and I should be sorry to go away without having seen you face to face. Is it too much to ask?

PRIORESS. For us this is a day of giving. Draw back the curtains, Teresa.

[TERESA *draws back the curtain from one window, a* NUN *that from the other, lighting up the room.*]

ANTONIO (*bowing*). Ladies! . . .

VICARESS. Well? How does the vision appear to you?

ANTONIO. I shall never forget it as long as I live.

PRIORESS. Then may God go with you, and may you live a thousand years. (*Taking* TERESA *by the hand.*) Here is her hand. See, we give her to you with a great love, and may you make her happy.

ANTONIO. I answer for her happiness with my life.

PRIORESS. And may God go with you.

MISTRESS OF NOVICES. Teresa will give you from us two scapularies, the remembrances of a nun. They are not worth anything, but they have lain beside the reliquary of our father, the blessed Saint Dominic. Keep them in memory of this day. 10

ANTONIO. I shall treasure them, ladies, from this hour. And I pray you, remember me always in your prayers.

VICARESS. And upon your part do not forget to pray with them from time to time, for although it lies within the province of everyone to help our souls along the way to heaven, yet we must take the first steps ourselves. And may God go with you. 20

ALL. God go with you.

ANTONIO. Ladies! . . . (*He retires and disappears.*)

[*A* NUN *draws the curtain over the grille. Then a moment's silence. Some of the* NUNS *sigh and say:*]

NUNS. Ah, Lord! Good Lord! May it be God's holy will! (*The bell by the door rings twice.*)

VICARESS. I thought so—your father. 30

[TERESA *stands in the midst of the group of* NUNS, *bewildered, looking from one to the other, greatly moved.* SISTER TORNERA *goes to open the door.*]

PRIORESS. Ask him to come in.

[*The* DOCTOR *enters on the arm of* SISTER TORNERA. *He is now very old, but neither decrepit nor cast down.*]

DOCTOR. Good afternoon, ladies; good afternoon, daughter. 40

TERESA (*kissing his hand*). Good afternoon, father.

DOCTOR. The whole assembly—the parting, eh? Well, did you see the young man? (*The* NUNS *do not answer.*) A fine fellow, isn't he? He is waiting outside. We have an hour in the coach before we arrive at the station, so you had better get ready now, daughter. (TERESA *goes out with* SISTER JOANNA OF THE CROSS.) Ah! The trunk? Good! Carry it to the door. The boys outside will take care of it. (*Two* NUNS *lift the trunk and carry it out by the door on the right.*) There, that is done. (*He seats himself in the* PRIORESS'S *chair.*) Well, how are we today?

PRIORESS. You see, Doctor.

MISTRESS OF NOVICES. Who would ever have believed it eighteen years ago?

DOCTOR. Eighteen years? We are growing old, Mother. We are growing old.

PRIORESS. That is not the worst of it.

SISTER INEZ. How old are you now, Doctor?

DOCTOR. Seventy-eight, Sister. 20

SISTER INEZ. No one would ever think it.

DOCTOR (*attempting a witticism so as to cheer up the* NUNS). That is because I am preserved in sanctity, like a fly in thick syrup. (*But none of the* NUNS *laugh.*) A little mournful to-day, eh?

SISTER MARCELLA. What else did you expect?

SISTER SAGRARIO. She is not even going to be married in our chapel.

DOCTOR. No, his mother is old and sick, and naturally she wants him to be with her, so they must be married in her house.

PRIORESS. Naturally. Poor woman! (*A pause.*)

MISTRESS OF NOVICES. She is going so far away!

DOCTOR. But she will come back, 40 Mother. She will come back.

PRIORESS. She knows nothing of the world.

DOCTOR. There is no cause to be alarmed. He is an honorable man.

VICARESS. Yes, he seems to be one.

[TERESA *and* SISTER JOANNA OF THE CROSS

re-enter. It is plain that they have both been crying. TERESA, *wearing a mantilla, and with her coat on, carries a shawl over her arm for use as a wrap on the voyage. She stops in the middle of the room and stands still, not daring to say good-bye.*]

DOCTOR. Well? Are we ready now?

TERESA. Yes . . . Now . . .

DOCTOR. Then say good-bye. It is late. We must be going, daughter.

PRIORESS. Yes, you must not delay.

TERESA (*throwing herself on her knees before the* PRIORESS *and kissing her scapular*). Mother!

PRIORESS. Rise, my daughter, rise.

TERESA. Bless me, Mother! Bless me!

PRIORESS. May God bless you; so. Rise.

(*As* TERESA *rises, the* NUN *embraces her.*)

TERESA. Mother! I don't know what to say to you . . . I don't know how to leave you . . . but you must forgive me all the wrong I have ever done in all these years. I have been foolish, wilful. I have made so much trouble for you all. You must forgive me. I would like to do something great, something splendid for you all. But—but may God reward you! May God reward you! God reward you! (*She bursts into tears.*)

PRIORESS. My daughter, come! You must not cry. You must not allow yourself to be afflicted so.

TERESA. I am not afflicted, Mother; but . . . it's . . . Mother, I can never forget you! You must pray for me, pray for me! And you must never forget me!

PRIORESS. Ah, no, my child! Never! We will pray God to help you, and to be with you, and you must pray to Him for guidance and for counsel always, whenever you are troubled or perplexed in anything. For the liberty which they enjoy in the world is like a sword in the hands of a child, and life

at best is hard, and bitter oftentimes.

MISTRESS OF NOVICES. Be thankful that your heart is well steeled to resist all the temptations that may come. Is it not, my daughter?

TERESA. It is, Mother.

PRIORESS. Will you promise always to be reverent and good?

TERESA. Yes! Yes, Mother!

VICARESS. Remember that your obligation is greater than that of others, because you have come forth from God's own house.

TERESA. Yes! Yes, Mother!

PRIORESS. Remember all the blessings He has showered upon you from the cradle; remember that your whole life has been as a miracle, that you have lived here as few have ever lived, that you have been brought up as few have ever been brought up, like the Holy Virgin herself, in the very temple of the Lord.

MISTRESS OF NOVICES. As He was to the Evangelist, so God has been to you a father and a mother, more than to any other living thing.

PRIORESS. Remember that you are the rose of His garden and the grain of incense upon His altar.

TERESA. Yes! Mother, yes! I will! . . . I will remember all . . . all . . . all . . .

MISTRESS OF NOVICES. And do not forget each day to make an examination of your soul.

TERESA. No, Mother.

SISTER JOANNA OF THE CROSS. And write often.

TERESA. Yes, Mother.

DOCTOR. It is time to go, Teresa.

TERESA (*throwing herself suddenly into his arms*). Oh, father! Promise me never to leave them! Never abandon them!

DOCTOR. Child of my heart! Ah, may they never abandon me!—for this is my house. For more than forty years I have been coming here day by day, hour by hour, and now there is nobody within these walls who is older than I. I have no children. I have had my loves—yes, a moment's flame—but it was so long ago! I have forgotten them. And these Sisters, who have been mothers to you, have been daughters to me; and now, when I come, they no longer even cover their faces before me. Why should they? It seems to me as if I had seen them born. And in this house (*Greatly moved.*) I should like to die, so that they might close my eyes, and say a prayer for me when life itself has closed!

MISTRESS OF NOVICES. Who is thinking of dying, Doctor?

PRIORESS. It is time to go.

TERESA (*looking from one to the other*). Aren't you going to embrace me?

[*The* NUNS, *after hesitating and glancing a moment doubtfully at the* MOTHER PRIORESS, *embrace* TERESA *in turn, in perfect silence. Only* SISTER JOANNA OF THE CROSS, *taking her into her arms, says:*]

SISTER JOANNA OF THE CROSS. My child!

PRIORESS. May you find what you seek in the world, daughter, for so we hope and so we pray to God. But if it should not be so, remember, this is your Convent.

TERESA. Thanks . . . thanks . . . (*Sobbing.*)

DOCTOR. Come, daughter, come . . .

[*The* DOCTOR *and* TERESA *go to the door, but* TERESA *turns when she reaches the* threshold *and embraces* SISTER JOANNA OF THE CROSS, *passionately. Then she disappears.* SISTER JOANNA OF THE CROSS *rests her head against the grille, her back to the others, and weeps silently. A pause. The bells of the coach are heard outside as it drives away.*]

MISTRESS OF NOVICES. They are going now.

[*The chapel bell rings summoning the* NUNS *to choir.*]

PRIORESS. The summons to the choir.

MISTRESS OF NOVICES. Come, Sisters! Let us go there.

[*All make ready to go out sadly. The* VICARESS, *sensing the situation, to her mind demoralizing, feels it to be her duty to provide a remedy. She, too, is greatly moved, but making a supreme effort to control herself, says in a voice which she in vain endeavors to make appear calm, but which is choked in utterance by tears:*]

VICARESS. One moment. I have observed of late . . . that some . . . in the prayer . . . have not been marking sufficiently the pauses in the middle of the lines, while on the other hand, they drag out the last words interminably. Be careful of this, for your Reverences know that the beauty of the office lies in rightly marking the pauses, and in avoiding undue emphasis on the end of the phrase. Let us go there.

[*The* NUNS *file out slowly.* SISTER JOANNA OF THE CROSS, *unnoticed, remains alone. With a cry, she falls upon her knees beside an empty chair.*]

CURTAIN

FERENC MOLNAR

THE Hungarian, Ferenc Molnar, has been one of the most continuously popular European dramatists in America. In the decade beginning on the night of April 20, 1921, when the Theatre Guild first presented *Liliom*, hardly a season went by without one or more Molnar plays to brighten Broadway. His work coincided with the international mood of romantic fantasy, boulevard sophistication, and light-hearted cynicism that laid hold of the world after the Armistice. Twenty of his plays, most of which had been produced in New York, were published in English translation in 1929.

The Molnar plays were, for the most part, good, light theatrical entertainment that stopped well outside the bounds of critical study. They were expertly put together, enlivened by wit and shrewd observations of the surface of life, and were pleasantly diverting. Many were in the irresponsible man-of-the-world (or of many worlds, as Molnar said) vein so brilliantly cultivated by Arthur Schnitzler in the gay man-and-mistress, or Max-Anatole-Ilona situations. Such situations came to signify Budapest as well as old Vienna, where no serious problems intruded upon the privileged, and God was not censorious when his children had their fling. In fact it was Molnar, the man-about-town and café celebrity, who made Budapest an important center of the international theatre; and it was his popularity in America that led a wit to suggest to the Theatre Guild, when that organization wanted a name for its new theatre, that they call it Budapesthouse.

Molnar was born on January 12, 1878, of a wealthy Jewish family. His early years were spent at a parochial school, his later ones at the Royal College of Science, and the University of Geneva. He much preferred the gayety of the Central Café to the discipline of college, and his own spirited writing to the study of law and the preparation of briefs. He turned to journalism as a profession at the age of eighteen. Throughout his adult life he has contributed an extraordinary variety of sketches, stories, human interest articles, humorous skits, and other occasional pieces for newspapers at home and abroad. He was once famous for his articles from the Austrian front during the World War; they were even published in London and New York. He married his Budapest editor's daughter, Margaret Vaszi; then Sari Fedak, the opera-singer and actress, who once toured America; and then her actress rival, Lily Darvas, who had appeared in several of his plays.

Molnar began in his youth to play at theatricals. In an autobiographical sketch he said that he staged his first play in a neighbor's basement "with the aid of all sorts of blue bottles filched from the surgery of my father, a physician," and that it "ended in a riot." That was somewhere in the early nineties. He entered seriously into play-making in 1902 with *The Doctor;* followed with *Jozsi*, based upon some of his sketches, in 1904; and became famous with the international success of *The Devil* in 1907. This was an intrigue play wherein the Devil is the Galeotto who prepares and directs the adultery of Olga and Karl, in the usual husband-wife-artist triangle, and patters amusing cynicisms about woman and her ways as he carries out his little plot. *The Devil* was the precursor of a series of plays in the same vein. For Molnar was quite at home in this world of dilettantism, with its romantic flitting from infatuation to infatuation, and its playful, unconcerned instability. In fact his own private but well-publicized experiences and escapades furnished the occasion and not a little of the material for several of his most popular plays.

The Guardsman (1911) was fashioned from the same tinsel as *The Devil*, and it proved to be his best play in this sophisticated genre. It was first played in New York in 1913 under the title *Where Ignorance Is Bliss*, but it had only sixteen performances. The Theatre Guild opened its season of 1924 with a revival of the play under its present title. With Alfred Lunt and Lynn Fontanne it was performed two hundred forty-eight times, then was taken on tour, and finally was made into a successful motion picture. It is a triangle play, but the hackneyed situation is ingeniously varied by having the suspicious husband, himself an actor, pretend to go on a journey. He then disguises himself as a Russian guardsman, and returns to try the faithfulness of his actress wife who is restless and dreamy after a few months of marriage. Both the Guardsman and his wife carry out the experiment in the grand style. The play turns back upon itself and rounds out an evening by having the actress quietly announce next day that she knew who he was from the minute when he first appeared in her ante-room at the opera, and she had merely played up to his part; behind

that front the actor-husband cannot go. Molnar, of course, makes the most of the situation to comment brightly upon pride, jealousy, and the frivolities of life.

Among the many other successes were several plays that rose above the level of the general average. *The Wolf*, or *The Phantom Rival* (1912), restated the oft-handled theme (Ibsen's *The Lady from the Sea*, Barry's *In a Garden*, Sherwood's *Reunion in Vienna*, etc.), wherein the memory of an earlier, romantic love interferes with a later marriage until the woman is cured of her phantasm by meeting her now quite unromantic and middle-aged first lover face-to-face across the intervening years. *Carnival* (1917) was written especially for Sari Fedak, an opera-singer who had engaged Molnar's fancy. It tells of a lovely lady who is married to an old and watchful husband. He keeps her isolated in the country, where she releases her suppressed longings by exploits of daring horsemanship. But she does go to Budapest for her annual carnival. She meets her young lover, puts him to the test of valor, and finds him uncourageous and selfish. She then goes back to her husband and her horses in the country.

The Swan (1914) achieved wide success, particularly in France where it won for Molnar the French Cross of the Legion of Honor. American audiences in the early twenties were pleased with its dramatic but untroubled romance and flocked to see it. It poked fun at royalty and all the elaborate ceremony surrounding a rather seedy court. The visiting Prince Albert, bashful without his mother, sleeps fifteen hours a day, and every single movement he makes is noted by a flunkey at the key hole who hastens to relay the news to the Queen his hostess. It makes amusing comedy of all the resources, including a poor professor, employed by the widow-queen to make Prince Albert aware of the Princess Alexandra, her daughter, The Swan. The intrigue is elaborately wound up, and then lightly resolved as Prince Albert's resistance is broken down and the royal couple marry and prepare to live unhappily ever afterwards. The play is sparkling, sometimes hilarious, at the expense of the useless classes, represented by professors and kings. And the title, which recurs several times, is given its final interpretation in Dominica's lines near the end: "Natural history teaches that the swan is nothing but an aristocratic duck. That is why she must stay on the mirror of the water. She is a bird, but she may never fly. She knows a song, but she may never sing until she is about to die. Yes, dear, glide on the water . . . head high . . . stately silence . . . and the song— never!"

The Swan, produced by Charles Frohman in October, 1923, had a long and profitable run in New York with Eva LeGallienne, Basil Rathbone, and Philip Merivale. At the same time and almost next door to it Arthur Hopkins was presenting Edna St. Vincent Millay's adaptation of Molnar's *Launzi* (1922), a romantic fantasy about the hopeless passion of an eighteen year old girl. She became deranged and lived in the illusion of death with a pair of angel's wings fastened on her shoulders. Thinking that she would be borne up by these magic wings, she attempted to soar upward from her tower window, but went down.

There were other fantasies even more extreme. *The Red Mill* (1923), adapted as *Mima* and presented in New York by David Belasco in 1928, ran through one hundred eighty performances. The Red Mill is a soul-corrupter, a special invention of the Devil and his staff, guaranteed to debase the most righteous of men within an hour. It must be tested out, however, and that is difficult in hell, where no good man is. A traffic accident furnishes a good victim for the experiment in the person of a young forester who had got into hell by mistake. He is put into the Red Mill where Mima reduces him to sin in record time. But the forces of goodness in man triumph in spite of the Devil's technique, and they bring about an explosion that wrecks the mill.

Yet another of Molnar's dramas, *The Play's the Thing* (1924), adapted in English by P. G. Wodehouse, was included by Burns Mantle in *Best Plays of 1926–1927*. The English title, borrowed from Hamlet, fits the theme of the play. A composer is writing an opera for his fiancée. He overhears a young baritone declaring his love for her in the next room. The composer and his collaborator decide to test the honesty of the couple in a scientific psychological manner. A little play is devised that reproduces the overheard words in a fitting situation, and the young couple are compelled to enact it before the suspicious composer. Everything is resolved when he learns that they had only been rehearsing their roles.

These are samples of the best of the prolific compositions that came from Molnar's pen. They are still coming. Like so many other distinguished European writers, he was caught in the Nazi upheavals, and fled to the United States. His new play, *Delicate Story*, produced in New York on December 4, 1940, was withdrawn after two weeks. It was in Molnar's traditional style of the eternal triangle, this time a Swiss delicatessen-keeper, his wife, and a young man who must soon go back home to enter the army. As in *The Play's the Thing*, *The Guardsman*, and others, everything has really been quite all right. It is now plain that Molnar was first a precursor and then a symbol of the post-War mood. He was content to prepare the brittle fantasies, and the worldly sentimentalisms with which the theatres of Budapest pleased their entertainment-seeking audiences, and which the America of the twenties found new, sophisticated, and amusing.

Had Molnar not written *Liliom* he would not appear in this anthology in competition with so many other important men in modern European drama. He would be admired for his skill in contriving, for occasional bursts of imagination, and for a few surpassing scenes of power and insight. He would be remembered in a bright corner of the encyclopedia of contemporary drama as the clever Hungarian who wore a monocle under an arched brow in a round face, slept through the day, wrote, talked, and tasted life at night, and kept the theatres honorably in their business of amusing the public.

In his masterpiece, Molnar seemed to gather up his diverse qualities and concentrate them in a single work of art. His talents for stagecraft, for building up character by seizing upon a few essential human traits that flash light into the hidden recesses of the heart; for giving resonance to the surface appearance by revealing unsuspected depths of controlled emotion beneath it; his compassion and his humor; his astringent realism and his grotesque fantasy; his gifts of style and sense of movement; his originality and inventiveness; all the qualities that were partial or dispersed in his other works coalesced in *Liliom*. The mute love-tragedy of Liliom and Julie

took deep hold upon the fashionable author of the smart comedies. The froth boiled away and left a genuine and moving play about a cocky amusement park barker, an inarticulate maid, and the way the elemental mystery of life stirred them for its own unfathomable ends.

Molnar got to know the people and the milieu of *Liliom* in his eager young days as a reporter on the prowl through the slums and odd corners of Budapest spying out human interest stories for his paper. He was only thirty-one when his play was first presented to a puzzled audience at Budapest in December, 1909. He mingled the squalor and violence of the lower depths with the immortal spirit of love and compassion, and joined the simple flow of realistic action with the extravaganza of expressionism without destroying both. The contrasts in the play are violent and bold: the tough world of the opening scene, and the tremulous dialogue between Julie and Liliom on the park bench under the acacia tree as night gathers, the lamps come on, and the noise of the calliope drifts in upon them; the opening of the scene at the railroad embankment where the hard-boiled Liliom breaks into a moment of poetic dreaming as he hears the rails singing under the train all the way to Vienna, the telegraph wires humming, and the sparrow listening, followed by the pathetic robbery scene and suicide; Liliom bleeding to death while the cops complain of their pay and working conditions; and a dozen such effective dramatic alterations.

Primarily it is Liliom's play, the seemingly empty braggart who can find no way to express his twisted soul except in violence, and is afraid when he feels the softening tenderness of Julie's love for him. He bullies women, gambles, drinks, attempts robbery and murder, beats Julie, and commits suicide; and yet the revelation of his sympathetic qualities, his exaltation over Julie's expected child, his exuberant humanity, redeem him in our eyes. His dying words to Julie were: "It's all the same to me who was right.—It's so dumb. Nobody's right—but they all think they are right.—A lot they know!" He carries his earthly perversities into his own concept of another world, properly represented as a heavenly police court and city jail purgatory, where fifteen years of flames fail to alter his impulsive violence; he slaps Louise, for whom he stole a star, and returns to the Liliom hell between the two Heavenly Policemen. But in at least three scenes it is also Julie's play:

as she sits by Liliom under the acacia tree, as she declares to the dead Liliom her unspoken love for him, and in the final moment before the curtain when she explains to Louise that "It is possible, dear—that someone may beat you and beat you and beat you—and not hurt you at all." Her unbent strength and beauty of spirit give to the play much of its charm and pathos.

Liliom has kept its popularity on the stage through frequent revivals (Burgess Meredith and Ingrid Bergman played it again for seven weeks in the spring of 1940), and it is an established part of contemporary drama. Benjamin F. Glazer's translation makes it as good in English as in the original.

LILIOM

A Legend in Seven Scenes and a Prologue

CHARACTERS

LILIOM	LINZMAN
JULIE	THE DOCTOR
MARIE	THE MAGISTRATE
MRS. MUSKAT	TWO MOUNTED POLICEMEN
LOUISE	TWO PLAINCLOTHES POLICEMEN
MRS. HOLLUNDER	TWO HEAVENLY POLICEMEN
FICSUR	THE RICHLY DRESSED MAN
YOUNG HOLLUNDER	THE POORLY DRESSED MAN
WOLF BEIFELD	THE GUARD
THE CARPENTER	A SUBURBAN POLICEMAN

THE PROLOGUE

An amusement park on the outskirts of Budapest on a late afternoon in Spring. Barkers stand before the booths of the sideshows haranguing the passing crowd. The strident music of a calliope is heard; laughter, shouts, the scuffle of feet, the signal bells of merry-go-round.

The merry-go-round is at center. LILIOM *stands at the entrance, a cigarette in his mouth, coaxing the people in. The girls regard him with idolizing glances and screech with pleasure as he playfully pushes them through entrance. Now and then some girl's escort resents the familiarity, whereupon* LILIOM'S *demeanor becomes ugly and menacing, and the cowed escort slinks through the entrance behind his girl or contents himself with a muttered resentful comment.*

One girl hands LILIOM *a red carnation; he rewards her with a bow and a smile. When the soldier who accompanies her pro-*

tests, LILIOM *cows him with a fierce glance and a threatening gesture.* MARIE *and* JULIE *come out of the crowd and* LILIOM *favors them with particular notice as they pass into the merry-go-round.*

MRS. MUSKAT *comes out of the merry-go-round, bringing* LILIOM *coffee and rolls.* LILIOM *mounts the barker's stand at the entrance, where he is elevated over every one on the stage. Here he begins his harangue. Everybody turns toward him. The other booths are gradually deserted. The tumult makes it impossible for the audience to hear what he is saying, but every now and then some witticism of his provokes a storm of laughter which is audible above the din. Many people enter the merry-go-round. Here and there one catches a phrase "Room for one more on the zebra's back," "Which of you ladies?" "Ten heller for adults, five for children," "Step right up——"*

It is growing darker. A lamplighter

LILIOM: Translated from the Hungarian by Benjamin Glazer. Published by Liveright Publishing Corporation.

crosses the stage, and begins unperturbedly lighting the colored gas-lamps. The whistle of a distant locomotive is heard. Suddenly the tumult ceases, the lights go out, and the curtain falls in darkness.

END OF PROLOGUE

SCENE I

A lonely place in the park, half hidden by trees and shrubbery. Under a flowering acacia 10 *tree stands a painted wooden bench. From the distance, faintly, comes the tumult of the amusement park. It is the sunset of the same day.*
When the curtain rises the stage is empty.

[MARIE *enters quickly, pauses at center, and looks back.*]

MARIE. Julie, Julie! (*There is no answer.*) Do you hear me, Julie? Let her be! 20 Come on. Let her be. (*Starts to go back.*)
   [JULIE *enters, looks back angrily.*]

JULIE. Did you ever hear of such a thing? What's the matter with the woman anyway?

MARIE (*looking back again*). Here she comes again.

JULIE. Let her come. I didn't do anything to her. All of a sudden she comes up to me and begins to raise a 30 row.

MARIE. Here she is. Come on, let's run. (*Tries to urge her off.*)

JULIE. Run? I should say not. What would I want to run for? I'm not afraid of her.

MARIE. Oh, come on. She'll only start a fight.

JULIE. I'm going to stay right here. Let her *start* a fight.   40

MRS. MUSKAT (*entering*). What do you want to run away for? (*To* JULIE.) Don't worry. I won't eat you. But there's one thing I want to tell you, my dear. Don't let me catch you in my carousel again. I stand for a whole lot, I have to in my business. It makes no difference to me whether my customers are ladies or the likes of you—as long as they pay their money. But when a girl misbehaves herself on my carousel—out she goes. Do you understand?

JULIE. Are you talking to me?

MRS. MUSKAT. Yes, you! You—chambermaid, you! In my carousel——

JULIE. Who did anything in your old carousel? I paid my fare and took my seat and never said a word, except to my friend here.

MARIE. No, she never opened her mouth. Liliom came over to her of his own accord.

MRS. MUSKAT. It's all the same. I'm not going to get in trouble with the police, and lose my license on account of you—you shabby kitchen maid!

JULIE. Shabby yourself.

MRS. MUSKAT. You stay out of my carousel! Letting my barker fool with you! Aren't you ashamed of yourself?

JULIE. What did you say?

MRS. MUSKAT. I suppose you think I have no eyes in my head. I see everything that goes on in my carousel. During the whole ride she let Liliom fool with her—the shameless hussy!

JULIE. He did not fool with me! I don't let any man fool with me!

MRS. MUSKAT. He leaned against you all through the ride!

JULIE. He leaned against the panther. He always leans against something, doesn't he? Everybody leans where he wants. I couldn't tell him not to lean, if he always leans, could I? But he didn't lay a hand on me.

MRS. MUSKAT. Oh, didn't he? And I suppose he didn't put his hand around your waist, either?

MARIE. And if he did? What of it?

MRS. MUSKAT. You hold your tongue!

No one's asking you—just you keep out of it.

JULIE. He put his arm around my waist —just the same as he does to all the girls. He always does that.

MRS. MUSKAT. I'll teach him not to do it any more, my dear. No carryings on in my carousel! If you are looking for that sort of thing, you'd better go to the circus! You'll find lots of soldiers there to carry on with!

JULIE. You keep your soldiers for yourself!

MARIE. Soldiers! As if we wanted soldiers!

MRS. MUSKAT. Well, I only want to tell you this, my dear, so that we understand each other perfectly. If you ever stick your nose in my carousel again, you'll wish you hadn't! I'm not going to lose my license on account of the likes of you! People who don't know how to behave, have got to stay out!

JULIE. You're wasting your breath. If I feel like riding on your carousel I'll pay my ten heller and I'll ride. I'd like to see any one try to stop me!

MRS. MUSKAT. Just come and try it, my dear—just come and try it.

MARIE. We'll see what'll happen.

MRS. MUSKAT. Yes, you will see something happen that never happened before in this park.

JULIE. Perhaps you think you could throw me out!

MRS. MUSKAT. I'm sure of it, my dear.

JULIE. And suppose I'm stronger than you?

MRS. MUSKAT. I'd think twice before I'd dirty my hands on a common servant girl. I'll have Liliom throw you out. He knows how to handle your kind.

JULIE. You think Liliom would throw me out.

MRS. MUSKAT. Yes, my dear, so fast that you won't know what happened to you!

JULIE. He'd throw me——

[*Stops suddenly, for* MRS. MUSKAT *has turned away. Both look off stage until* LILIOM *enters, surrounded by four giggling servant girls.*]

LILIOM. Go away! Stop following me, or I'll smack your face!

A LITTLE SERVANT GIRL. Well, give me back my handkerchief.

LILIOM. Go on now——

THE FOUR SERVANT GIRLS (*simultaneously*). What do you think of him?— My handkerchief!—Give it back to her!—That's a nice thing to do!

THE LITTLE SERVANT GIRL (*to* MRS. MUSKAT). Please, lady, make him——

MRS. MUSKAT. Oh, shut up!

LILIOM. Will you get out of here? (*Makes a threatening gesture—the* FOUR SERVANT GIRLS *exit in voluble but fearful haste.*)

MRS. MUSKAT. What have you been doing now?

LILIOM. None of your business. (*Glances at* JULIE.) Have you been starting with her again?

JULIE. Mister Liliom, please——

LILIOM (*steps threateningly toward her*). Don't yell!

JULIE (*timidly*). I didn't yell.

LILIOM. Well, don't. (*To* MRS. MUSKAT.) What's the matter? What has she done to you?

MRS. MUSKAT. What has she done? She's been impudent to me. Just as impudent as she could be! I put her out of the carousel. Take a good look at this innocent thing, Liliom. She's never to be allowed in my carousel again!

LILIOM (*to* JULIE). You heard that. Run home, now.

MARIE. Come on. Don't waste your time with such people. (*Tries to lead* JULIE *away.*)

JULIE. No, I won't——

MRS. MUSKAT. If she ever comes again, you're not to let her in. And if she gets in before you see her, throw her out. Understand?

LILIOM. What has she done, anyhow?

JULIE (*agitated and very earnest*). Mister Liliom—tell me please—honest and truly—if I come into the carousel, will you throw me out?

MRS. MUSKAT. Of course he'll throw you out.

MARIE. She wasn't talking to you.

JULIE. Tell me straight to my face, Mister Liliom, would you throw me out?

[*They face each other. There is a brief pause.*]

LILIOM. Yes, little girl, if there was a reason—but if there was no reason, why should I throw you out?

MARIE (*to* MRS. MUSKAT). There, you see!

JULIE. Thank you, Mister Liliom.

MRS. MUSKAT. And I tell you again, if this little slut dares to set her foot in my carousel, she's to be thrown out! I'll stand for no indecency in my establishment.

LILIOM. What do you mean—indecency?

MRS. MUSKAT. I saw it all. There's no use denying it.

JULIE. She says you put your arm around my waist.

LILIOM. Me?

MRS. MUSKAT. Yes, I saw you. Don't play the innocent.

LILIOM. Here's something new! I'm not to put my arm around a girl's waist any more! I suppose I'm to ask your permission before I touch another girl!

MRS. MUSKAT. You can touch as many girls as you want and as often as you want—for my part you can go as far as you like with any of them—but not this one—I permit no indecency in my carousel.

[*There is a long pause.*]

LILIOM (*to* MRS. MUSKAT). And now I'll ask you please to shut your mouth.

MRS. MUSKAT. What?

LILIOM. Shut your mouth quick, and go back to your carousel.

MRS. MUSKAT. What?

LILIOM. What did she do to you, anyhow? Tryin' to start a fight with a little pigeon like that . . . just because I touched her?—You come to the carousel as often as you want to, little girl. Come every afternoon, and sit on the panther's back, and if you haven't got the price, Liliom will pay for you. And if any one dares to bother you, you come and tell *me*.

MRS. MUSKAT. You reprobate!

LILIOM. Old witch!

JULIE. Thank you, Mister Liliom.

MRS. MUSKAT. You seem to think that I can't throw you out, too. What's the reason I can't? Because you are the best barker in the park? Well, you are very much mistaken. In fact, you can consider yourself thrown out already. You're discharged!

LILIOM. Very good.

MRS. MUSKAT (*weakening a little*). I can discharge you any time I feel like it.

LILIOM. Very good, you feel like discharging me. I'm discharged. That settles it.

MRS. MUSKAT. Playing the high and mighty, are you? Conceited pig! Good-for-nothing!

LILIOM. You said you'd throw me out, didn't you? Well, that suits me; I'm thrown out.

MRS. MUSKAT (*softening*). Do you have to take up every word I say?

LILIOM. It's all right; it's all settled. I'm a good-for-nothing. And a conceited pig. And I'm discharged.

MRS. MUSKAT. Do you want to ruin my business?

LILIOM. A good-for-nothing? Now I

know! And I'm discharged! Very good.

MRS. MUSKAT. You're a devil, you are . . . and that woman——

LILIOM. Keep away from her!

MRS. MUSKAT. I'll get Hollinger to give you such a beating that you'll hear all the angels sing . . . and it won't be the first time, either.

LILIOM. Get out of here. I'm discharged. And you get out of here.

JULIE (*timidly*). Mister Liliom, if she's willing to say that she hasn't discharged you——

LILIOM. You keep out of this.

JULIE (*timidly*). I don't want this to happen on account of me.

LILIOM (*to* MRS. MUSKAT, *pointing to* JULIE). Apologize to her!

MARIE. A-ha!

MRS. MUSKAT. Apologize? To who?

LILIOM. To this little pigeon. Well—are you going to do it?

MRS. MUSKAT. If you give me this whole park on a silver plate, and all the gold of the Rothschilds on top of it—I'd —I'd——Let her dare to come into my carousel again and she'll get thrown out so hard that she'll see stars in daylight!

LILIOM. In that case, dear lady (*takes off his cap with a flourish*) you are respectfully requested to get out o' here as fast as your legs will carry you—I never beat up a woman yet—except that Holzer woman who I sent to the hospital for three weeks—but—if you don't get out o' here this minute, and let this little squab be, I'll give you the prettiest slap in the jaw you ever had in your life.

MRS. MUSKAT. Very good, my son. Now you *can* go to the devil. Good-bye. You're discharged, and you needn't try to come back, either. (*She exits. It is beginning to grow dark.*)

MARIE (*with grave concern*). Mister Liliom——

LILIOM. Don't you pity me or I'll give *you* a slap in the jaw. (*To* JULIE.) And don't you pity me, either.

JULIE (*in alarm*). I don't pity you, Mister Liliom.

LILIOM. You're a liar, you *are* pitying me. I can see it in your face. You're thinking, now that Madame Muskat has thrown him out, Liliom will have to go begging. Huh! Look at me. I'm big enough to get along without a Madame Muskat. I have been thrown out of better jobs than hers.

JULIE. What will you do now, Mister Liliom?

LILIOM. Now? First of all, I'll go and get myself—a glass of beer. You see, when something happens to annoy me, I always drink a glass of beer.

JULIE. Then you *are* annoyed about losing your job.

LILIOM. No, only about where I'm going to get the beer.

MARIE. Well—eh——

LILIOM. Well—eh—what?

MARIE. Well—eh—are you going to stay with us, Mister Liliom?

LILIOM. Will you pay for the beer? (MARIE *looks doubtful; he turns to* JULIE.) Will you? (*She does not answer.*) How much money have you got?

JULIE (*bashfully*). Eight heller.

LILIOM. And you? (MARIE *casts down her eyes and does not reply.* LILIOM *continues sternly.*) I asked you how much you've got? (*Marie begins to weep softly.*) I understand. Well, you needn't cry about it. You girls stay here, while I go back to the carousel and get my clothes and things. And when I come back, we'll go to the Hungarian beer-garden. It's all right, I'll pay. Keep your money. (*He exits.*)

MARIE *and* JULIE *stand silent, watching him until he has gone.*)

MARIE. Are you sorry for him?

JULIE. Are you?

MARIE. Yes, a little. Why are you looking after him in that funny way?

JULIE (*sits down*). Nothing—except I'm sorry he lost his job.

MARIE (*with a touch of pride*). It was on our account he lost his job. Because he's fallen in love with you.

JULIE. He hasn't at all.

MARIE (*confidently*). Oh, yes! he is in love with you. (*Hesitantly, romantically.*) There is some one in love with me, too.

JULIE. There is? Who?

MARIE. I—I never mentioned it before because you hadn't a lover of your own—but now you have—and I'm free to speak. (*Very grandiloquently.*) My heart has found its mate.

JULIE. You're only making it up.

MARIE. No, it's true—my heart's true love——

JULIE. Who? Who is he?

MARIE. A soldier.

JULIE. What kind of soldier?

MARIE. I don't know. Just a soldier. Are there different kinds?

JULIE. Many different kinds. There are hussars, artillerymen, engineers, infantry—that's the kind that walks —and——

MARIE. How can you tell which is which?

JULIE. By their uniforms.

MARIE (*after trying to puzzle it out*). The conductors on the street cars—are they soldiers?

JULIE. Certainly not. They're conductors.

MARIE. Well, they have uniforms.

JULIE. But they don't carry swords or guns.

MARIE. Oh! (*Thinks it over again; then.*) Well, policemen—are they?

JULIE (*with a touch of exasperation*). Are they what?

MARIE. Soldiers.

JULIE. Certainly not. They're just policemen.

MARIE (*triumphantly*). But they have uniforms—and they carry weapons, too.

JULIE. You're just as dumb as you can be. You don't go by their uniforms.

MARIE. But you said——

JULIE. No, I didn't. A letter-carrier wears a uniform, too, but that doesn't make him a soldier.

MARIE. But if he carried a gun or a sword, would he be——

JULIE. No, he'd still be a letter-carrier. You can't go by guns or swords, either.

MARIE. Well, if you don't go by the uniforms or the weapons, what *do* you go by?

JULIE. By—— (*Tries to put it into words; fails; then breaks off suddenly.*) Oh, you'll get to know when you've lived in the city long enough. You're nothing but a country girl. When you've lived in the city a year, like I have, you'll know all about it.

MARIE (*half angrily*). Well, how *do* you know when *you* see a real soldier?

JULIE. By one thing.

MARIE. What?

JULIE. One thing—— (*She pauses.* MARIE *starts to cry.*) Oh, what are you crying about?

MARIE. Because you're making fun of me. . . . You're a city girl, and I'm just fresh from the country . . . and how am I expected to know a soldier when I see one? . . . You, you ought to tell me, instead of making fun of me——

JULIE. All right. Listen then, cry-baby. There's only one way to tell a soldier: by his salute! That's the only way.

MARIE (*joyfully; with a sigh of relief*). Ah —that's good.

JULIE. What?

MARIE. I say—it's all right then— because Wolf—Wolf—— (JULIE *laughs derisively.*) Wolf—that's his name. (*She weeps again.*)

JULIE. Crying again? What now?

MARIE. You're making fun of me again.

JULIE. I'm not. But when you say, "Wolf—Wolf—" like that, I have to laugh, don't I? (*Archly.*) What's his name again?

MARIE. I won't tell you.

JULIE. All right. If you won't say it, then he's no soldier.

MARIE. I'll say it.

JULIE. Go on.

MARIE. No, I won't. (*She weeps again.*)

JULIE. Then he's not a soldier. I guess he's a letter-carrier——

MARIE. No—no—I'd rather say it.

JULIE. Well, then.

MARIE (*giggling*). But you musn't look at me. You look the other way, and I'll say it. (*Julie looks away.* MARIE *can hardly restrain her own laughter.*) Wolf! (*She laughs.*) That's his real name. Wolf, Wolf, Soldier—Wolf!

JULIE. What kind of a uniform does he wear?

MARIE. Red.

JULIE. Red trousers?

MARIE. No.

JULIE. Red coat?

MARIE. No.

JULIE. What then?

MARIE (*triumphantly*). His cap!

JULIE (*after a long pause*). He's just a porter, you dunce. Red cap . . . that's a porter—and he doesn't carry a gun or a sword, either.

MARIE (*triumphantly*). But he salutes. You said yourself that was the only way to tell a soldier——

JULIE. He doesn't salute at all. He only greets people——

MARIE. He salutes me. . . . And if his name *is* Wolf, that doesn't prove he ain't a soldier—he salutes, and he wears a red cap and he stands on guard all day long outside a big building——

JULIE. What does he do there?

MARIE (*seriously*). He spits.

JULIE (*with contempt*). He's nothing— nothing but a common porter.

MARIE. What's Liliom?

JULIE (*indignantly*). Why speak of him? What has he to do with me?

MARIE. The same as Wolf has to do with me. If you can talk to me like that about Wolf, I can talk to you about Liliom.

JULIE. He's nothing to me. He put his arm around me in the carousel. I couldn't tell him not to put his arm around me after he had done it, could I?

MARIE. I suppose you didn't like him to do it?

JULIE. No.

MARIE. Then why are you waiting for him? Why don't you go home?

JULIE. Why—eh—he *said* we were to wait for him.

[LILIOM *enters. There is a long silence.*]

LILIOM. Are you still here? What are you waiting for?

MARIE. You told us to wait.

LILIOM. Must you always interfere? No one is talking to you.

MARIE. You asked us—why we——

LILIOM. Will you keep your mouth shut? What do you suppose I want with two of you? I meant that one of you was to wait. The other can go home.

MARIE. All right.

JULIE. All right. (*Neither starts to go.*)

LILIOM. One of you goes home. (*To* MARIE.) Where do you work?

MARIE. At the Breiers', Damjanovitsch Street, Number Twenty.

LILIOM. And you?

JULIE. I work there, too.

LILIOM. Well, one of you goes home. Which of you wants to stay? (*There is no answer.*) Come on, speak up, which of you stays?

MARIE (*officiously*). She'll lose her job if she stays.

LILIOM. Who will?

MARIE. Julie. She has to be back by seven o'clock.

LILIOM. Is that true? Will they discharge you if you're not back on time?

JULIE. Yes.

LILIOM. Well, wasn't I discharged?

JULIE. Yes—you were discharged, too.

MARIE. Julie, shall I go?

JULIE. I—can't tell you what to do.

MARIE. All right—stay if you like.

LILIOM. You'll be discharged if you do?

MARIE. Shall I go, Julie?

JULIE (*embarrassed*). Why do you keep asking me that?

MARIE. You know best what to do.

JULIE (*profoundly moved; slowly*). It's all right, Marie, you can go home.

MARIE (*exits reluctantly, but comes back and says uncertainly*). Good-night. [*She waits a moment to see if* JULIE *will follow her.* JULIE *does not move.* MARIE *exits. Meantime it has grown quite dark. During the following scene the gas-lamps far in the distance are lighted one by one.* LILIOM *and* JULIE *sit on the bench. From afar, very faintly, comes the music of a calliope. But the music is intermittently heard; now it breaks off, now it resumes again, as if it came down on a fitful wind. Blending with it are the sounds of human voices, now loud, now soft; the blare of a toy trumpet; the confused noises of the show booths. It grows progressively darker until the end of the scene. There is no moonlight. The spring iridescence glows in the deep blue sky.*]

LILIOM. Now we're both discharged. (*She does not answer. From now on they speak gradually lower and lower until the end of the scene, which is played almost in whispers. Whistles softly, then.*) Have you had your supper?

JULIE. No.

LILIOM. Want to go eat something at the Garden?

JULIE. No.

LILIOM. Anywhere else?

JULIE. No.

LILIOM (*whistles softly, then*). You don't come to this park very often, do you? I've only seen you three times. Been here oftener than that?

JULIE. Oh, yes.

LILIOM. Did you see me?

JULIE. Yes.

LILIOM. And did you know I was Liliom?

JULIE. They told me.

LILIOM (*whistles softly, then*). Have you got a sweetheart?

JULIE. No.

LILIOM. Don't lie to me.

JULIE. I haven't. If I had, I'd tell you. I've never had one.

LILIOM. What an awful liar you are. I've got a good mind to go away and leave you here.

JULIE. I've never had one.

LILIOM. Tell that to some one else.

JULIE (*reproachfully*). Why do you insist I have?

LILIOM. Because you stayed here with me the first time I asked you to. You know your way around, you do.

JULIE. No, I don't, Mister Liliom.

LILIOM. I suppose you'll tell me you don't know why you're sitting here— like this, in the dark, alone with me —— You wouldn't 'a' stayed so quick, if you hadn't done it before—

with some soldier, maybe. This isn't the first time. You wouldn't have been so ready to stay if it was—what *did* you stay for, anyhow?

JULIE. So you wouldn't be left alone.

LILIOM. Alone! God, you're dumb! I don't need to be alone. I can have all the girls I want. Not only servant girls like you, but cooks and governesses, even French girls. I could have twenty of them if I wanted to.

JULIE. I know, Mister Liliom.

LILIOM. What do you know?

JULIE. That all the girls are in love with you. But that's not why *I* stayed. I stayed because you've been so good to me.

LILIOM. Well, then you can go home.

JULIE. I don't want to go home now.

LILIOM. And what if I go away and leave you sitting here?

JULIE. If you did, I wouldn't go home.

LILIOM. Do you know what you remind me of? A sweetheart I had once—I'll tell you how I met her—— One night, at closing time we had put out the lights in the carousel, and just as I was——

[*He is interrupted by the entrance of two* PLAINCLOTHES POLICEMEN. *They take their stations on either side of the bench. They are police, searching the park for vagabonds.*]

FIRST POLICEMAN. What are you doing there?

LILIOM. Me?

SECOND POLICEMAN. Stand up when you're spoken to! (*He taps* LILIOM *imperatively on the shoulder.*)

FIRST POLICEMAN. What's your name?

LILIOM. Andreas Zavocki.

[JULIE *begins to weep softly.*]

SECOND POLICEMAN. Stop your bawling. We're not goin' to eat you. We are only making our rounds.

FIRST POLICEMAN. See that he doesn't

get away. (*The* SECOND POLICEMAN *steps closer to* LILIOM.) What's your business?

LILIOM. Barker and bouncer.

SECOND POLICEMAN. They call him Liliom, Chief. We've had him up a couple of times.

FIRST POLICEMAN. So that's who you are! Who do you work for now?

LILIOM. I work for the widow Muskat.

FIRST POLICEMAN. What are you hanging around here for?

LILIOM. We're just sitting here—me and this girl.

FIRST POLICEMAN. Your sweetheart?

LILIOM. No.

FIRST POLICEMAN (*to* JULIE). And who are you?

JULIE. Julie Zeller.

FIRST POLICEMAN. Servant girl?

JULIE. Maid of all work for Mister Georg Breier, Number Twenty Damjanovitsch Street.

FIRST POLICEMAN. Show your hands.

SECOND POLICEMAN (*after examining* JULIE'S *hand*). Servant girl.

FIRST POLICEMAN. Why aren't you at home? What are you doing out here with him?

JULIE. This is my day out, sir.

FIRST POLICEMAN. It would be better for you if you didn't spend it sitting around with a fellow like this.

SECOND POLICEMAN. They'll be disappearing in the bushes as soon as we turn our backs.

FIRST POLICEMAN. He's only after your money. We know this fine fellow. He picks up you silly servant girls and takes what money you have. Tomorrow you'll probably be coming around to report him. If you do, I'll throw you out.

JULIE. I haven't any money, sir.

FIRST POLICEMAN. Do you hear that, Liliom?

LILIOM. I'm not looking for her money.
SECOND POLICEMAN (*nudging him warningly*). Keep your mouth shut.
FIRST POLICEMAN. It is my duty to warn you, my child, what kind of company you're in. He makes a specialty of servant girls. That's why he works in a carousel. He gets hold of a girl, promises to marry her, then he takes her money and her ring. 10
JULIE. But I haven't got a ring.
SECOND POLICEMAN. You're not to talk unless you're asked a question.
FIRST POLICEMAN. You be thankful that I'm warning you. It's nothing to me what you do. I'm not your father, thank God. But I'm telling you what kind of a fellow he is. By to-morrow morning you'll be coming around to us to report him. Now you be sensible 20 and go home. You needn't be afraid of him. This officer will take you home if you're afraid.
JULIE. Do I *have* to go?
FIRST POLICEMAN. No, you don't *have* to go.
JULIE. Then I'll stay, sir.
FIRST POLICEMAN. Well, you've been warned.
JULIE. Yes, sir. Thank you, sir.
FIRST POLICEMAN. Come on, Berkovics. 30
[*The* POLICEMEN *exit.* JULIE *and* LILIOM *sit on the bench again. There is a brief pause.*]
JULIE. Well, and what then?
LILIOM (*fails to understand*). Huh?
JULIE. You were beginning to tell me a story.
LILIOM. Me?
JULIE. Yes, about a sweetheart. You 40 said, one night, just as they were putting out the lights of the carousel —— That's as far as you got.
LILIOM. Oh, yes, yes, just as the lights were going out, some one came along —a little girl with a big shawl—you

know—— She came—eh—from—— Say—tell me—ain't you—that is, ain't you at all—afraid of me? The officer told you what kind of a fellow I am—and that I'd take your money away from you——
JULIE. You couldn't take it away—I haven't got any. But if I had—I'd —I'd give it to you—I'd give it all to you.
LILIOM. You would?
JULIE. If you asked me for it.
LILIOM. Have you ever had a fellow you gave money to?
JULIE. No.
LILIOM. Haven't you ever had a sweetheart?
JULIE. No.
LILIOM. Some one you used to go walking with. You've had one like that?
JULIE. Yes.
LILIOM. A soldier?
JULIE. He came from the same village I did.
LILIOM. That's what all the soldiers say. Where *do* you come from, anyway?
JULIE. Not far from here.
[*There is a pause.*]
LILIOM. Were you in love with him?
JULIE. Why do you keep asking me that all the time, Mister Liliom? I wasn't in love with him. We only went walking together.
LILIOM. Where did you walk?
JULIE. In the park.
LILIOM. And your virtue? Where did you lose that?
JULIE. I haven't got any virtue.
LILIOM. Well, you had once.
JULIE. No, I never had. I'm a respectable girl.
LILIOM. Yes, but you gave the soldier something.
JULIE. Why do you question me like that, Mister Liliom?
LILIOM. Did you give him something?

JULIE. You have to. But I didn't love him.

LILIOM. Do you love me?

JULIE. No, Mister Liliom.

LILIOM. Then why do you stay here with me?

JULIE. Um—nothing.

[*There is a pause. The music from afar is plainly heard.*]

LILIOM. Want to dance?

JULIE. No. I have to be very careful.　10

LILIOM. Of what?

JULIE. My—character.

LILIOM. Why?

JULIE. Because I'm never going to marry. If I was going to marry, it would be different. Then I wouldn't need to worry so much about my character. It doesn't make any difference if you're married. But I shan't marry—and that's why I've got 20 to take care to be a respectable girl.

LILIOM. Suppose I were to say to you— I'll marry you.

JULIE. You?

LILIOM. That frightens you, doesn't it? You're thinking of what the officer said and you're afraid.

JULIE. No, I'm not, Mister Liliom. I don't pay any attention to what he said.　30

LILIOM. But you wouldn't dare to marry any one like me, would you?

JULIE. I know that—that—if I loved any one—it wouldn't make any difference to me what he—even if I died for it.

LILIOM. But you wouldn't marry a rough guy like me—that is—eh—if you loved me——

JULIE. Yes, I would—if I loved you, Mister Liliom.　40

[*There is a pause.*]

LILIOM (*whispers*). Well—you just said— didn't you?—that you don't love me. Well, why don't you go home then?

JULIE. It's too late now, they'd all be asleep.

LILIOM. Locked out?

JULIE. Certainly.

[*They are silent awhile.*]

LILIOM. I think—that even a low-down good-for-nothing—can make a man of himself.

JULIE. Certainly.

[*They are silent again. A lamp-lighter crosses the stage, lights the lamp over the bench, and exits.*]

LILIOM. Are you hungry?

JULIE. No.

[*Another pause.*]

LILIOM. Suppose—you had some money —and I took it from you?

JULIE. Then you could take it, that's all.

LILIOM (*after another brief silence*). All I have to do—is go back to her—that Muskat woman—she'll be glad to get me back—then I'd be earning my wages again.

[*She is silent. The twilight folds darker about them.*]

JULIE (*very softly*). Don't go back—to her——

[*Pause.*]

LILIOM. There are a lot of acacia trees around here.

[*Pause.*]

JULIE. Don't go back to her——

[*Pause.*]

LILIOM. She'd take me back the minute I asked her. I know why—she knows, too——

[*Pause.*]

JULIE. I can smell them, too—acacia blossoms——

[*There is a pause. Some blossoms drift down from the tree-top to the bench. LILIOM picks one up and smells it.*]

LILIOM. White acacias!

JULIE (*after a brief pause*). The wind brings them down.

[*They are silent. There is a long pause before.*]

THE CURTAIN FALLS

SCENE II

A photographer's "studio," operated by the HOLLUNDERS, *on the fringe of the park. It is a dilapidated hovel. The general entrance is back left. Back right there is a window with a sofa before it. The outlook is on the amusement park with perhaps a small Ferris wheel or the scaffolding of a "scenic-railway" in the background.*

The door to the kitchen is up left and a black-curtained entrance to the dark-room is down left. Just in front of the dark-room stands the camera on its tripod. Against the back wall, between the door and window, stands the inevitable photographer's background-screen, ready to be wheeled into place.

It is forenoon. When the curtain rises, MARIE *and* JULIE *are discovered.*

MARIE. And *he* beat up Hollinger?

JULIE. Yes, he gave him an awful licking.

MARIE. But Hollinger is bigger than he is.

JULIE. He licked him just the same. It isn't size that counts, you know, it's cleverness. And Liliom's awful quick.

MARIE. And then he was arrested?

JULIE. Yes, they arrested him, but they let him go the next day. That makes twice in the two months we've been living here that Liliom's been arrested and let go again.

MARIE. Why do they let him go?

JULIE. Because he is innocent.

[MOTHER HOLLUNDER, *a very old woman, sharp-tongued, but in reality quite warm-hearted beneath her formidable exterior, enters at back carrying a few sticks of firewood, and scolding, half to herself.*]

MOTHER HOLLUNDER. Always wanting something, but never willing to work for it. He won't work, and he won't steal, but he'll use up a poor old widow's last bit of firewood. He'll do that cheerfully enough! A big, strong lout like that lying around all day resting his lazy bones! He ought to be ashamed to look decent people in the face.

JULIE. I'm sorry, Mother Hollunder. . . .

MOTHER HOLLUNDER. Sorry! Better be sorry the lazy good-for-nothing ain't in jail where he belongs instead of in the way of honest, hard-working people. (*She exits into the kitchen.*)

MARIE. Who's that?

JULIE. Mrs. Hollunder—my aunt. This is her (*With a sweeping gesture that takes in the camera, dark-room and screen.*) studio. She lets us live here for nothing.

MARIE. What's she fetching the wood for?

JULIE. She brings us everything we need. If it weren't for her I don't know what would become of us. She's a good-hearted soul even if her tongue is sharp.

[*There is a pause.*]

MARIE (*shyly*). Do you know—I've found out. He's not a soldier.

JULIE. Do you still see him?

MARIE. Oh, yes.

JULIE. Often?

MARIE. Very often. He's asked me——

JULIE. To marry you?

MARIE. To marry me.

JULIE. You see—that proves he isn't a soldier.

[*There is another pause.*]

MARIE (*abashed, yet a bit boastfully*). Do you know what I'm doing—I'm flirting with him.

JULIE. Flirting?

MARIE. Yes. He asks me to go to the park—and I say I can't go. Then he coaxes me, and promises me a new scarf for my head if I go. But I don't go—even then. . . . So then he walks all the way home with me—

and I bid him goodnight at the door.

JULIE. Is that what you call flirting?

MARIE. Um-hm! It's sinful, but it's so *thrilling*.

JULIE. Do you ever quarrel?

MARIE (*grandly*). Only when our Passionate Love surges up.

JULIE. Your passionate love?

MARIE. Yes. . . . He takes my hand and we walk along together. Then he wants to swing hands, but I won't let him. I say: "Don't swing my hand"; and he says, "Don't be so stubborn." And then he tries to swing my hand again, but still I don't let him. And for a long time I don't let him—until in the end I let him. Then we walk along swinging hands—up and down, up and down—just like this. *That* is Passionate Love. It's sinful, but it's awfully *thrilling*.

JULIE. You're happy, aren't you?

MARIE. Happier than—anything—— But the most beautiful thing on earth is Ideal Love.

JULIE. What kind is that?

MARIE. Daylight comes about three in the morning this time of the year. When we've been up that long we're all through with flirting and Passionate Love—and then our Ideal Love comes to the surface. It comes like this: I'll be sitting on the bench and Wolf, he holds my hand tight— and he puts his cheek against my cheek and we don't talk . . . we just sit there very quiet. . . . And after a while he gets sleepy, and his head sinks down, and he falls asleep . . . but even in his sleep he holds tight to my hand. And I—I sit perfectly still just looking around me and taking long, deep breaths—for by that time it's morning and the trees and flowers are fresh with dew. But Wolf doesn't smell anything because he's so fast asleep. And I get awfully sleepy myself, but I don't sleep. And we sit like that for a long time. That is Ideal Love——

[*There is a long pause.*]

JULIE (*regretfully; uneasily*). He went out last night and he hasn't come home yet.

MARIE. Here are sixteen kreuzer. It was supposed to be carfare to take my young lady to the conservatory— eight there and eight back—but I made her walk. Here—save it with the rest.

JULIE. This makes three gulden, forty-six.

MARIE. Three gulden, forty-six.

JULIE. He won't work at all.

MARIE. Too lazy?

JULIE. No. He never learned a trade, you see, and he can't just go and be a day-laborer—so he just does nothing.

MARIE. That ain't right.

JULIE. No. Have the Breiers got a new maid yet?

MARIE. They've had three since you left. You know, Wolf's going to take a new job. He's going to work for the city. He'll get rent free, too.

JULIE. He won't go back to work at the carousel, either. I ask him why, but he won't tell me——Last Monday he hit me.

MARIE. Did you hit him back?

JULIE. No.

MARIE. Why don't you leave him?

JULIE. I don't want to.

MARIE. I would. I'd leave him.

[*There is a strained silence.*]

MOTHER HOLLUNDER (*enters, carrying a pot of water; muttering aloud*). He can play cards, all right. He can fight, too; and take money from poor servant girls. And the police turn their heads the other way——The carpenter was here.

JULIE. Is that water for the soup?

MOTHER HOLLUNDER. The carpenter was here. There's a *man* for you! Dark, handsome, lots of hair, a respectable widower with two children—and money, and a good paying business.

JULIE (*to* MARIE). It's three gulden, sixty-six, not forty-six.

MARIE. Yes, that's what I make it—sixty-six.

MOTHER HOLLUNDER. He wants to take her out of this and marry her. This is the fifth time he's been here. He has two children, but——

JULIE. Please don't bother, Aunt Hollunder, I'll get the water myself.

MOTHER HOLLUNDER. He's waiting outside now.

JULIE. Send him away.

MOTHER HOLLUNDER. He'll only come back again—and first thing you know that vagabond will get jealous and there'll be a fight. (*Goes out, muttering.*) Oh, he's ready enough to fight, he is. Strike a poor little girl like that! Ought to be ashamed of himself! And the police just let him go on doing as he pleases. (*Still scolding, she exits at back.*)

MARIE. A carpenter wants to marry you?

JULIE. Yes.

MARIE. Why don't you?

JULIE. Because——

MARIE. Liliom doesn't support you, and he beats you—he thinks he can do whatever he likes just because he's Liliom. He's a bad one.

JULIE. He's not really bad.

MARIE. That night you sat on the bench together—he was gentle then.

JULIE. Yes, he was gentle.

MARIE. And afterwards he got wild again.

JULIE. Afterwards he got wild—sometimes. But that night on the bench . . . he was gentle. He's gentle now, sometimes, very gentle. After supper, when he stands there and listens to the music of the carousel, something comes over him—and he is gentle.

MARIE. Does he say anything?

JULIE. He doesn't say anything. He gets thoughtful and very quiet, and his big eyes stare straight ahead of him.

MARIE. Into your eyes?

JULIE. Not exactly. He's unhappy because he isn't working. That's really why he hit me on Monday.

MARIE. That's a fine reason for hitting you! Beats his wife because he isn't working, the ruffian!

JULIE. It preys on his mind——

MARIE. Did he hurt you?

JULIE (*very eagerly*). Oh, no.

MRS. MUSKAT (*enters haughtily*). Good-morning. Is Liliom home?

JULIE. No.

MRS. MUSKAT. Gone out?

JULIE. He hasn't come home yet.

MRS. MUSKAT. I'll wait for him. (*She sits down.*)

MARIE. You've got a lot of gall—to come here.

MRS. MUSKAT. Are you the lady of the house, my dear? Better look out or you'll get a slap in the mouth.

MARIE. How dare you set foot in Julie's house?

MRS. MUSKAT (*to* JULIE). Pay no attention to her, my child. You know what brings me here. That vagabond, that good-for-nothing, I've come to give him his bread and butter back.

MARIE. He's not dependent on you for his bread.

MRS. MUSKAT (*to* JULIE). Just ignore her, my child. She's just ignorant.

MARIE (*going*). Good-bye.

JULIE. Good-bye.

MARIE (*in the doorway, calling back*). Sixty-six.

JULIE. Yes, sixty-six.

MARIE. Good-bye. (*She exits.* JULIE *starts to go toward the kitchen.*)

MRS. MUSKAT. I paid him a krone a day and on Sunday a gulden. And he got all the beer and cigars he wanted from the customers. (JULIE *pauses on the threshold, but does not answer.*) And he'd rather starve than beg my pardon. Well, I don't insist on that. I'll take him back without it. (JULIE *does not answer.*) The fact is the people ask for him—and, you see, I've got to consider business first. It's nothing to me if he starves. I wouldn't be here at all, if it wasn't for business——(*She pauses, for* LILIOM *and* FICSUR *have entered.*)

JULIE. Mrs. Muskat is here.

LILIOM. I see she is.

JULIE. You might say good-morning.

LILIOM. What for? And what do *you* want, anyhow?

JULIE. I don't want anything.

LILIOM. Then keep your mouth shut. Next thing you'll be starting to nag again about my being out all night and out of work and living on your relations——

JULIE. I'm not saying anything.

LILIOM. But it's all on the tip of your tongue—I know you—now don't start or you'll get another. (*He paces angrily up and down. They are all a bit afraid of him, and shrink and look away as he passes them.* FICSUR *shambles from place to place, his eyes cast down as if he were searching for something on the floor.*)

MRS. MUSKAT (*suddenly, to* FICSUR). You're always dragging him out to play cards and drink with you. I'll have you locked up, I will.

FICSUR. I don't want to talk to you. You're too common. (*He goes out by the door at back and lingers there in plain view. There is a pause.*)

JULIE. Mrs. Muskat is here.

LILIOM. Well, why doesn't she open her mouth, if she has anything to say?

MRS. MUSKAT. Why do you go around with this man, Ficsur? He'll get you mixed up in one of his robberies first thing you know.

LILIOM. What's it to you who I go with? I do what I please. What do you want?

MRS. MUSKAT. You know what I want.

LILIOM. No, I don't.

MRS. MUSKAT. What do you suppose I want? Think I've come just to pay a social call?

LILIOM. Do I owe you anything?

MRS. MUSKAT. Yes, you do—but that's not what I came for. You're a fine one to come to for money! You earn so much these days! You know very well what I'm here for.

LILIOM. You've got Hollinger at the carousel, haven't you?

MRS. MUSKAT. Sure I have.

LILIOM. Well, what else do you want? He's as good as I am.

MRS. MUSKAT. You're quite right, my boy. He's every bit as good as you are. I'd not dream of letting him go. But one isn't enough any more. There's work enough for two——

LILIOM. One was enough when *I* was there.

MRS. MUSKAT. Well, I might let Hollinger go——

LILIOM. Why let him go, if he's so good?

MRS. MUSKAT (*shrugs her shoulders*). Yes, he's good. (*Not once until now has she looked at* LILIOM.)

LILIOM (*to* JULIE). Ask your aunt if I can have a cup of coffee. (JULIE *exits into the kitchen.*) So Hollinger is good, is he?

MRS. MUSKAT (*crosses to him and looks him in the face*). Why don't you stay home and sleep at night? You're a sight to look at.

LILIOM. He's good, is he?

MRS. MUSKAT. Push your hair back from your forehead.

LILIOM. Let my hair be. It's nothing to you.

MRS. MUSKAT. All right. But if I'd told you to let it hang down over your eyes you'd have pushed it back—I hear you've been beating her, this—this—— 10

LILIOM. None of your business.

MRS. MUSKAT. You're a fine fellow! Beating a skinny little thing like that! If you're tired of her, leave her, but there's no use beating the poor——

LILIOM. Leave her, eh? You'd like that, wouldn't you?

MRS. MUSKAT. Don't flatter yourself. (*Quite embarrassed.*) Serves me right, too. If I had any sense I wouldn't 20 have run after you——My God, the things one must do for the sake of business! If I could only sell the carousel I wouldn't be sitting here. . . . Come, Liliom, if you have any sense, you'll come back. I'll pay you well.

LILIOM. The carousel is crowded just the same . . . *without me?*

MRS. MUSKAT. Crowded, yes—but it's 30 not the same.

LILIOM. Then you admit that you *do* miss me.

MRS. MUSKAT. Miss you? Not I. But the silly girls miss you. They're always asking for you. Well, are you going to be sensible and come back?

LILIOM. And leave—her?

MRS. MUSKAT. You beat her, don't you?

LILIOM. No, I don't beat her. What's all 40 this damn fool talk about beating her? I hit her once—that was all—and now the whole city seems to be talking about it. You don't call that beating her, do you?

MRS. MUSKAT. All right, all right. I take it back. I don't want to get mixed up in it.

LILIOM. Beating her! As if I'd beat her——

MRS. MUSKAT. I can't make out why you're so concerned about her. You've been married to her two months—it's plain to see that you're sick of it—and out there is the carousel—and the show booths—and money—and you'd throw it all away. For what? Heavens, how can any one be such a fool? (*Looks at him appraisingly.*) Where have you been all night? You look awful.

LILIOM. It's no business of yours.

MRS. MUSKAT. You never used to look like that. This life is telling on you. (*Pauses.*) Do you know—I've got a new organ.

LILIOM (*softly*). I know.

MRS. MUSKAT. How did you know?

LILIOM. You can hear it—from here.

MRS. MUSKAT. It's a good one, eh?

LILIOM (*wistfully*). Very good. Fine. It roars and snorts—so fine.

MRS. MUSKAT. You should hear it close by —it's heavenly. Even the carousel seems to know . . . it goes quicker. I got rid of those two horses—you know, the ones with the broken ears?

LILIOM. What have you put in their place?

MRS. MUSKAT. Guess.

LILIOM. Zebras?

MRS. MUSKAT. No—an automobile.

LILIOM (*transported*). An automobile——

MRS. MUSKAT. Yes. If you've got any sense you'll come back. What good are you doing here? Out there is your *art*, the only thing you're fit for. You are an artist, not a respectable married man.

LILIOM. *Leave* her—this little——

MRS. MUSKAT. She'll be better off. She'll go back and be a servant girl again.

As for you—you're an artist and you belong among artists. All the beer you want, cigars, a krone a day and a gulden on Sunday, and the girls, Liliom, the girls—I've always treated you right, haven't I? I bought you a watch, and——

LILIOM. She's not that kind. She'd never be a servant girl again.

MRS. MUSKAT. I suppose you think she'd 10 kill herself. Don't worry. Heavens, if every girl was to commit suicide just because her——(*Finishes with a gesture.*)

LILIOM (*stares at her a moment, considering, then with sudden, smiling animation*). So the people don't like Hollinger?

MRS. MUSKAT. You know very well they don't, you rascal.

LILIOM. Well—— 20

MRS. MUSKAT. You've always been happy at the carousel. It's a great life— pretty girls and beer and cigars and music—a great life and an easy one. I'll tell you what—come back and I'll give you a ring that used to belong to my dear departed husband. Well, will you come?

LILIOM. She's not that kind. She'd never be a servant girl again. But—but— 30 for my part—if I decide—that needn't make any difference. I can go on living with her even if I do go back to my art——

MRS. MUSKAT. My God!

LILIOM. What's the matter?

MRS. MUSKAT. Who ever heard of a married man—I suppose you think all girls would be pleased to know that you were running home to your wife 40 every night. It's ridiculous! When the people found out they'd laugh themselves sick——

LILIOM. I know what you want.

MRS. MUSKAT (*refuses to meet his gaze*). You flatter yourself.

LILIOM. You'll give me that ring, too?

MRS. MUSKAT (*pushes the hair back from his forehead*). Yes.

LILIOM. I'm not happy in this house.

MRS. MUSKAT (*still stroking his hair*). Nobody takes care of you.

[*They are silent.* JULIE *enters, carrying a cup of coffee.* MRS. MUSKAT *removes her hand from* LILIOM's *head. There is a pause.*]

LILIOM. Do you want anything?

JULIE. No. (*There is a pause. She exits slowly into the kitchen.*)

MRS. MUSKAT. The old woman says there is a carpenter, a widower, who——

LILIOM. I know—I know——

JULIE (*reëntering*). Liliom, before I forget, I have something to tell you.

LILIOM. All right.

JULIE. I've been wanting to tell you—in fact, I was going to tell you yesterday——

LILIOM. Go ahead.

JULIE. But I must tell you alone—if you'll come in—it will only take a minute.

LILIOM. Don't you see I'm busy now? Here I am talking business and you interrupt with——

JULIE. It'll only take a minute.

LILIOM. Get out of here, or——

JULIE. But I tell you it will only take a minute——

LILIOM. Will you get out of here?

JULIE (*courageously*). No.

LILIOM (*rising*). What's that!

JULIE. No.

MRS. MUSKAT (*rises, too*). Now don't start fighting. I'll go out and look at the photographs in the show case a while and come back later for your answer. (*She exits at back.*)

JULIE. You can hit me again if you like —don't look at me like that. I'm not afraid of you. . . . I'm not afraid of any one. I told you I had something to tell you.

LILIOM. Well, out with it—quick.

JULIE. I can't tell you so quick. Why don't you drink your coffee?

LILIOM. Is that what you wanted to tell me?

JULIE. No. By the time you've drunk your coffee I'll have told you.

LILIOM (*gets the coffee and sips it*). Well?

JULIE. Yesterday my head ached—and you asked me——

LILIOM. Yes——

JULIE. Well—you see—that's what it is——

LILIOM. Are you sick?

JULIE. No. . . . But you wanted to know what my headaches came from —and you said I seemed—changed.

LILIOM. Did I? I guess I meant the carpenter.

JULIE. I've been—what? The carpenter? No. It's something entirely different —it's awful hard to tell—but you'll have to know sooner or later—I'm not a bit—scared—because it's a perfectly natural thing——

LILIOM (*puts the coffee cup on the table*). What?

JULIE. When—when a man and woman —live together——

LILIOM. Yes.

JULIE. I'm going to have a baby.

[*She exits swiftly at back. There is a pause.* FICSUR *appears at the open window and looks in.*]

LILIOM. Ficsur! (FICSUR *sticks his head in.*) Say, Ficsur—Julie is going to have a baby.

FICSUR. Yes? What of it?

LILIOM. Nothing. (*Suddenly.*) Get out of here.

[FICSUR'S *head is quickly withdrawn.* MRS. MUSKAT *reënters.*]

MRS. MUSKAT. Has she gone?

LILIOM. Yes.

MRS. MUSKAT. I might as well give you ten kronen in advance. (*Opens her purse.* LILIOM *takes up his coffee cup.*) Here you are. (*She proffers some coins.* LILIOM *ignores her.*) Why don't you take it?

LILIOM (*very nonchalantly, his cup poised ready to drink*). Go home, Mrs. Muskat.

MRS. MUSKAT. What's the matter with you?

LILIOM. Go home (*Sips his coffee.*) and let me finish my coffee in peace. Don't you see I'm at breakfast?

MRS. MUSKAT. Have you gone crazy?

LILIOM. Will you get out of here? (*Turns to her threateningly.*)

MRS. MUSKAT (*restoring the coins to her purse*). I'll never speak to you again as long as you live.

LILIOM. That worries me a lot.

MRS. MUSKAT. Good-bye!

LILIOM. Good-bye. (*As she exits, he calls.*) Ficsur! (FICSUR *enters.*) Tell me, Ficsur. You said you knew a way to get a whole lot of money——

FICSUR. Sure I do.

LILIOM. How much?

FICSUR. More than you ever had in your life before. You leave it to an old hand like me.

MOTHER HOLLUNDER (*enters from the kitchen*). In the morning he must have his coffee, and at noon his soup, and in the evening coffee again—and plenty of firewood—and I'm expected to furnish it all. Give me back my cup and saucer.

[*The show booths of the amusement park have opened for business. The familiar noises begin to sound; clear above them all, but far in the distance, sounds the organ of the carousel.*]

LILIOM. Now, Aunt Hollunder.

[*From now until the fall of the curtain it is apparent that the sound of the organ makes him more and more uneasy.*]

MOTHER HOLLUNDER. And you, you

vagabond, get out of here this minute or I'll call my son——

FICSUR. I have nothing to do with the likes of him. He's too common. (*But he slinks out at back.*)

LILIOM. Aunt Hollunder!

MOTHER HOLLUNDER. What now?

LILIOM. When your son was born—when you brought him into the world——

MOTHER HOLLUNDER. Well?

LILIOM. Nothing.

MOTHER HOLLUNDER (*muttering as she exits*). Sleep it off, you good-for-nothing lout. Drink and play cards all night long—that's all you know how to do—and take the bread out of poor people's mouths—you can do that, too. (*She exits.*)

LILIOM. Ficsur!

FICSUR (*at the window*). Julie's going to have a baby. You told me before.

LILIOM. This scheme—about the cashier of the leather factory—there's money in it——

FICSUR. Lots of money—but—it takes two to pull it off.

LILIOM (*meditatively*). Yes. (*Uneasily.*) All right, Ficsur. Go away—and come back later.

[FICSUR *vanishes. The organ in the distant carousel drones incessantly.* LILIOM *listens awhile, then goes to the door and calls.*]

LILIOM. Aunt Hollunder! (*With naïve joy.*) Julie's going to have a baby. (*Then he goes to the window, jumps on the sofa, looks out. Suddenly, in a voice that overtops the droning of the organ, he shouts as if addressing the far-off carousel.*) I'm going to be a father.

JULIE (*enters from the kitchen*). Liliom! What's the matter? What's happened?

LILIOM (*coming down from the sofa*). Nothing.

[*Throws himself on the sofa, buries his face in the cushion.* JULIE *watches him a mo-*] *ment, comes over to him and covers him with a shawl. Then she goes on tiptoe to the door at back and remains standing in the doorway, looking out and listening to the droning of the organ.*]

THE CURTAIN FALLS

SCENE III

The setting is the same, later that afternoon. LILIOM *is sitting opposite* FICSUR, *who is teaching him a song.* JULIE *hovers in the background, engaged in some household task.*

FICSUR. Listen now. Here's the third verse. (*Sings hoarsely.*)

"Look out, look out, my pretty lad,
The damn police are on your trail;
The nicest girl you ever had
Has now commenced to weep and wail:
Look out here comes the damn police,
The damn police,
The damn police,
Look out here comes the damn police,
They'll get you every time."

LILIOM (*sings*).

"Look out, look out, my pretty lad,
The damn police——"

FICSUR, LILIOM (*sing together*).

"are on your trail;
The nicest girl you ever had
Has now commenced to weep and wail."

LILIOM (*alone*).

"Look out here comes the damn police,
The damn police,
The damn police——"

[JULIE, *troubled and uneasy, looks from one to the other, then exits into the kitchen.*]

FICSUR (*when she has gone, comes quickly over to* LILIOM *and speaks furtively*). As you go down Franzen Street you come to the railroad embankment. Beyond that—all the way to the leather factory—there's not a thing in sight, not even a watchman's hut.

LILIOM. And does he always come that way?

FICSUR. Yes. Not along the embankment, but down below along the path across the fields. Since last year he's been going alone. Before that he always used to have some one with him.

LILIOM. Every Saturday?

FICSUR. Every Saturday.

LILIOM. And the money? Where does he keep it?

FICSUR. In a leather bag. The whole week's pay for the workmen at the factory.

LILIOM. Much?

FICSUR. Sixteen thousand kronen. Quite a haul, what?

LILIOM. What's his name?

FICSUR. Linzman. He's a Jew.

LILIOM. The cashier?

FICSUR. Yes—but when he gets a knife between his ribs—or if I smash his skull for him—he won't be a cashier any more.

LILIOM. Does he have to be killed?

FICSUR. No, he doesn't *have* to be. He can give up the money *without* being killed—but most of these cashiers are peculiar—they'd rather be killed.

[JULIE *reënters, pretends to get something on the other side of the room, then exits at back. During the ensuing dialogue she keeps coming in and out in the same way, showing plainly that she is suspicious and anxious. She attempts to overhear what they are saying and, in spite of their caution, does catch a word here and there, which adds to her disquiet.* FICSUR, *catching sight of her, abruptly changes the conversation.*]

FICSUR. And the next verse is:
"And when you're in the prison cell
They'll feed you bread and water."

FICSUR AND LILIOM (*sing together*).
"They'll make your little sweetheart tell

Them all the things you brought her.
Look out here comes the damn police,
The damn police,
The damn police,
Look out here comes the damn police,
They'll get you every time."

LILIOM (*sings alone*).
"And when you're in the prison cell
They'll feed you bread and water
——"

(*Breaks off, as* JULIE *exits.*) And when it's done, do we start right off for America?

FICSUR. No.

LILIOM. What then?

FICSUR. We bury the money for six months. That's the usual time. And after the sixth month we dig it up again.

LILIOM. And then?

FICSUR. Then you go on living just as usual for six months more—you don't touch a heller of the money.

LILIOM. In six months the baby will be born.

FICSUR. Then we'll take the baby with us, too. Three months before the time you'll go to work so as to be able to say you saved up your wages to get to America.

LILIOM. Which of us goes up and talks to him?

FICSUR. One of us talks to him with his mouth and the other talks with his knife. Depends on which you'd rather do. I'll tell you what—you talk to him with your mouth.

LILIOM. Do you hear that?

FICSUR. What?

LILIOM. Outside . . . like the rattle of swords. (FICSUR *listens. After a pause,* LILIOM *continues.*) What do I say to him?

FICSUR. You say good-evening to him and: "Excuse me, sir; can you tell me the time?"

LILIOM. And then what?

FICSUR. By that time I'll have stuck him —and then you take *your* knife—— (*He stops as a* POLICEMAN *enters at back.*)

POLICEMAN. Good-day!

FICSUR, LILIOM (*in unison*). Good-day!

FICSUR (*calling toward the kitchen*). Hey, photographer, come out. . . . Here's a customer.

[*There is a pause. The* POLICEMAN *waits.* FICSUR *sings softly.*]

"And when you're in the prison cell
They'll feed you bread and water
They'll make your little sweetheart tell"

LILIOM, FICSUR (*sing together, low*).

"Them all the things you brought her.
Look out here comes the——"

[*They hum the rest so as not to let the* POLICEMAN *hear the words "the damn police." As they sing,* MRS. HOLLUNDER *and her* SON *enter.*]

POLICEMAN. Do you make cabinet photographs?

YOUNG HOLLUNDER. Certainly, sir. (*Points to a rack of photographs on the wall.*) Take your choice, sir. Would you like one full length?

POLICEMAN. Yes, full length.

[MOTHER HOLLUNDER *pushes out the camera while her* SON *poses the* POLICE-MAN, *runs from him to the camera and back again, now altering the pose, now ducking under the black cloth and pushing the camera nearer. Meanwhile* MOTHER HOLLUNDER *has fetched a plate from the dark-room and thrust it in the camera. While this is going on,* LILIOM *and* FICSUR, *their heads together, speak in very low tones.*]

LILIOM. Belong around here?

FICSUR. Not around here.

LILIOM. Where, then?

FICSUR. Suburban. (*There is a pause.*)

LILIOM (*bursts out suddenly in a rather grotesquely childish and overstrained lament*). O God, what a dirty life I'm leading—God, God!

FICSUR (*reassuring him benevolently*). Over in America it will be better, all right.

LILIOM. What's over there?

FICSUR (*virtuously*). Factories . . . industries——

YOUNG HOLLUNDER (*to the* POLICEMAN). Now, quite still, please. One, two, three. (*Deftly removes the cover of the lens and in a few seconds restores it.*) Thank you.

MOTHER HOLLUNDER. The picture will be ready in five minutes.

POLICEMAN. Good. I'll come back in five minutes. How much do I owe you?

YOUNG HOLLUNDER (*with exaggerated deference*). You don't need to pay in advance, Mr. Commissioner.

[*The* POLICEMAN *salutes condescendingly and exits at back.* MOTHER HOLLUNDER *carries the plate into the dark-room.* YOUNG HOLLUNDER, *after pushing the camera back in place, follows her.*]

MOTHER HOLLUNDER (*muttering angrily as she passes* FICSUR *and* LILIOM). You hang around and dirty the whole place up! Why don't you go take a walk? Things are going so well with you that you have to sing, eh? (*Confronting* FICSUR *suddenly.*) Weren't you frightened sick when you saw the policeman?

FICSUR (*with loathing*). Go 'way, or I'll step on you. (*She exits into the dark-room.*)

LILIOM. They like Hollinger at the carousel?

FICSUR. I should say they do.

LILIOM. Did you see the Muskat woman, too?

FICSUR. Sure. She takes care of Hollinger's hair.

LILIOM. Combs his hair?

FICSUR. She fixes him all up.

LILIOM. Let her fix him all she likes.

FICSUR (*urging him toward the kitchen door*). Go on. Now's your chance.

LILIOM. What for?

FICSUR. To get the knife.

LILIOM. What knife?

FICSUR. The kitchen knife. I've got a pocket-knife, but if he shows fight, we'll let him have the big knife.

LILIOM. What for? If he gets ugly, I'll bat him one over the head that'll make him squint for the rest of his life.

FICSUR. You've got to have something on you. You can't slit his throat with a bat over the head.

LILIOM. Must his throat be slit?

FICSUR. No, it *mustn't*. But if he asks for it. (*There is a pause.*) You'd like to sail on the big steamer, wouldn't you? And you want to see the factories over there, don't you? But you're not willing to inconvenience yourself a little for them.

LILIOM. If I take the knife, Julie will see me.

FICSUR. Take it so she won't see you.

LILIOM (*advances a few paces toward the kitchen. The* POLICEMAN *enters at back.* LILIOM *knocks on the door of the dark-room*). Here's the policeman!

MOTHER HOLLUNDER (*coming out*). One minute more, please. Just a minute. [*She reënters the dark-room.* LILIOM *hesitates a moment, then exits into the kitchen. The* POLICEMAN *scrutinizes* FICSUR *mockingly.*]

FICSUR (*returns his stare, walks a few paces toward him, then deliberately turns his back. Suddenly he wheels around, points at the* POLICEMAN *and addresses him in a teasing, childish tone*). Christiana Street at the corner of Retti!

POLICEMAN (*amazed, self-conscious*). How do you know that?

FICSUR. I used to practice my profession in that neighborhood.

POLICEMAN. What is your profession?

FICSUR. Professor of pianola——

[*The* POLICEMAN *glares, aware that the man is joking with him, twirls his moustache indignantly.* YOUNG HOLLUNDER *comes out of the dark-room and gives him the finished pictures.*]

YOUNG HOLLUNDER. Here you are, sir.

[*The* POLICEMAN *examines the photographs, pays for them, starts to go, stops, glares at* FICSUR *and exits. When he is gone,* FICSUR *goes to the doorway and looks out after him.* YOUNG HOLLUNDER *exits.* LILIOM *reënters, buttoning his coat.*]

FICSUR (*turns, sees* LILIOM). What are you staring at?

LILIOM. I'm not staring.

FICSUR. What then are you doing?

LILIOM. I'm thinking it over.

FICSUR (*comes very close to him*). Tell me then—what will you say to him?

LILIOM (*unsteadily*). I'll say—"Good-evening—Excuse me, sir—Can you tell me the time?" And suppose he answers me, what do I say to him?

FICSUR. He won't answer you.

LILIOM. Don't you think so?

FICSUR. No. (*Feeling for the knife under* LILIOM's *coat.*) Where is it? Where did you put it?

LILIOM. (*stonily*). Left side.

FICSUR. That's right—over your heart. (*Feels it.*) Ah—there it is—there—there's the blade—quite a big fellow, isn't it—ah, here it begins to get narrower. (*Reaches the tip of the knife.*) And here is its eye—that's what it sees with. (JULIE *enters from the kitchen, passes them slowly, watching them in silent terror, then stops.* FICSUR *nudges* LILIOM.) Sing, come on, sing!

LILIOM (*in a quavering voice*).

"Look out for the damn police."

FICSUR (*joining in, cheerily, loudly, marking time with the swaying of his body*). "Look out, look out, my pretty lad."

LILIOM.

"—look out, my pretty lad."

(JULIE *goes out at back.* LILIOM's *glance follows her. When she has gone, he turns to* FICSUR.) At night—in my dreams—if his ghost comes back—what will I do then?

FICSUR. His ghost won't never come back.

LILIOM. Why not?

FICSUR. A Jew's ghost don't come back.

LILIOM. Well then—afterwards——

FICSUR (*impatiently*). What do you mean —afterwards?

LILIOM. In the next world—when I come up before the Lord God—what'll I say then?

FICSUR. The likes of you will never come up before Him.

LILIOM. Why not?

FICSUR. Have you ever come up before the high court?

LILIOM. No.

FICSUR. Our kind comes up before the police magistrate—and the highest we *ever* get is the criminal court.

LILIOM. Will it be the same in the next world?

FICSUR. Just the same. We'll come up before a police magistrate, same as we did in this world.

LILIOM. A police magistrate?

FICSUR. Sure. For the rich folks—the Heavenly Court. For us poor people —only a police magistrate. For the rich folks—fine music and angels. For us——

LILIOM. For us?

FICSUR. For us, my son, there's only justice. In the next world there'll be lots of justice, yes, nothing but justice. And where there's justice, there must be police magistrates; and where there're police magistrates, people like us get——

LILIOM (*interrupting*). Good-evening. Excuse me, sir, can you tell me the time? (*Lays his hand over his heart.*)

FICSUR. What do you put your hand there for?

LILIOM. My heart is jumping—under the knife.

FICSUR. Put it on the other side then. (*Looks out at the sky.*) It's time we started—we'll walk slow——

LILIOM. It's too early.

FICSUR. Come on.

[*As they are about to go,* JULIE *appears in the doorway at back, obstructing the way.*]

JULIE. Where are you going with him?

LILIOM. Where am I going with him?

JULIE. Stay home.

LILIOM. No.

JULIE. Stay home. It's going to rain soon, and you'll get wet.

FICSUR. It won't rain.

JULIE. How do you know?

FICSUR. I always get notice in advance.

JULIE. Stay home. This evening the carpenter's coming. I've asked him to give you work.

LILIOM. I'm not a carpenter.

JULIE (*more and more anxious, though she tries to conceal it*). Stay home. Marie's coming with her intended to have their picture taken. She wants to introduce us to her intended husband.

LILIOM. I've seen enough intended husbands——

JULIE. Stay home. Marie's bringing some money, and I'll give it all to you.

LILIOM (*approaching the door*). I'm going —for a walk—with Ficsur. We'll be right back.

JULIE (*forcing a smile to keep back her tears*). If you stay home, I'll get you a glass of beer—or wine, if you prefer.

FICSUR. Coming or not?

JULIE. I m not angry with you any more for hitting me.

LILIOM (*gruffly, but his gruffness is simulated to hide the fact that he cannot bear the sight of her suffering*). Stand out of the way—or I'll——(*He clenches his fist.*) Let me out!

JULIE (*trembling*). What have you got under your coat?

LILIOM (*produces from his pocket a greasy pack of cards*). Cards.

JULIE (*trembling, speaks very low*). What's under your coat?

LILIOM. Let me out!

JULIE (*obstructing the way. Speaks quickly, eagerly, in a last effort to detain him*). Marie's intended knows about a place for a married couple without children to be caretakers of a house on Arader Street. Rent free, a kitchen of your own, and the privilege of keeping chickens——

LILIOM. Get out of the way!

[JULIE *stands aside.* LILIOM *exits.* FICSUR *follows him.* JULIE *remains standing meditatively in the doorway.* MOTHER HOLLUNDER *comes out of the kitchen.*]

MOTHER HOLLUNDER. I can't find my kitchen knife anywhere. Have you seen anything of it?

JULIE (*horrified*). No.

MOTHER HOLLUNDER. It was on the kitchen table just a few minutes ago. No one was in there except Liliom.

JULIE. He didn't take it.

MOTHER HOLLUNDER. No one else was in there.

JULIE. What would Liliom want with a kitchen knife?

MOTHER HOLLUNDER. He'd sell it and spend the money on drink.

JULIE. It just so happens—see how unjust you are to him—it just so happens that I went through all of Liliom's pockets just now—I wanted to see if he had any money on him.

But he had nothing but a pack of cards.

MOTHER HOLLUNDER (*returns to the kitchen, grumbling*). Cards in his pocket—cards! The fine gentlemen have evidently gone off to their club to play a little game.

[*She exits. After a pause* MARIE, *happy and beaming, appears in the doorway at back, and enters, followed by* WOLF.]

MARIE. Here we are! (*She takes* WOLF *by the hand and leads him, grinning shyly, to* JULIE, *who has turned at her call.*) Hello!

JULIE. Hello.

MARIE. Well, we're here.

JULIE. Yes.

WOLF (*bows awkwardly and extends his hand*). My name is Wolf Beifeld.

JULIE. My name is Julie Zeller.

[*They shake hands. There is an embarrassed silence. Then, to relieve the situation,* WOLF *takes* JULIE'S *hand again and shakes it vigorously.*]

MARIE. Well—this is Wolf.

WOLF. Yes.

JULIE. Yes. (*Another awkward silence.*)

MARIE. Where is Liliom?

WOLF. Yes, where is your husband?

JULIE. He's out.

MARIE. Where?

JULIE. Just for a walk.

MARIE. Is he?

JULIE. Yes.

WOLF. Oh! (*Another silence.*)

MARIE. Wolf's got a new place. After the first of the month he won't have to stand outside any more. He's going to work in a club after the first of the month.

WOLF (*apologetically*). She don't know yet how to explain these things just right—hehehe——Beginning the first I'm to be second steward at the Burger Club—a good job, if one conducts oneself properly.

JULIE. Yes.

WOLF. The pay—is quite good—but the main thing is the tips. When they play cards there's always a bit for the steward. The tips, I may say, amount to twenty, even thirty kronen every night.

MARIE. Yes.

WOLF. We've rented two rooms for ourselves to start with—and if things 10 go well——

MARIE. Then we'll buy a house in the country.

WOLF. If one only tends to business and keeps honest. Of course, in the country we'll miss the city life, but if the good Lord sends us children—it's much healthier for children in the country.

[*There is a brief pause.*]   20

MARIE. Wolf's nice looking, isn't he?

JULIE. Yes.

MARIE. And he's a good boy, Wolf.

JULIE. Yes.

MARIE. The only thing is—he's a Jew.

JULIE. Oh, well, you can get used to that.

MARIE. Well, aren't you going to wish us luck?

JULIE. Of course I do. (*She embraces* MARIE.)

MARIE. And aren't you going to kiss Wolf, too?   30

JULIE. Him, too. (*She embraces* WOLF, *remains quite still a moment, her head resting on his shoulder.*)

WOLF. Why are you crying, my dear Mrs.——(*He looks questioningly at* MARIE *over* JULIE'*s shoulder.*)

MARIE. Because she has such a good heart. (*She becomes sentimental, too.*)   40

WOLF (*touched*). We thank you for your heartfelt sympathy——

[*He cannot restrain his own tears. There is a pause before* MOTHER HOLLUNDER *and her* SON *enter.* YOUNG HOLLUNDER *immediately busies himself with the camera.*]

MOTHER HOLLUNDER. Now if you don't mind, we'll do it right away, before it gets too dark. (*She leads* MARIE *and* WOLF *into position before the background-screen. Here they immediately fall into an awkward pose, smiling mechanically.*) Full length?

MARIE. Please. Both figures full length.

MOTHER HOLLUNDER. Bride and groom?

MARIE. Yes.

MOTHER HOLLUNDER, YOUNG HOLLUNDER (*speak in unison, in loud professionally expressionless tones*). The lady looks at the gentleman and the gentleman looks straight into the camera.

MOTHER HOLLUNDER (*poses first* MARIE, *then* WOLF). Now, if you please.

YOUNG HOLLUNDER (*who has crept under the black cloth, calls in muffled tones*). That's good—that's very good!

MARIE (*stonily rigid, but very happy, trying to speak without altering her expression*). Julie, dear, do we look all right?

JULIE. Yes, dear.

YOUNG HOLLUNDER. Now, if you please, hold still. I'll count up to three, and then you must hold perfectly still. (*Grasps the cover of the lens and calls threateningly.*) One—two—three!

[*He removes the cover; there is utter silence. But as he speaks the word "one" there is heard, very faintly in the distance, the refrain of the thieves' song which* FICSUR *and* LILIOM *have been singing. The refrain continues until the fall of the curtain. As he speaks the word "three" everybody is perfectly rigid save* JULIE, *who lets her head sink slowly to the table. The distant refrain dies out.*]

THE CURTAIN FALLS

SCENE IV

In the fields on the outskirts of the city. At back a railroad embankment crosses the stage obliquely. At center of the embankment stands a red and white signal flag, and near it a little red signal lamp which is not yet lighted. Here also a wooden stairway leads up to the embankment.

At the foot of the embankment to the right is a pile of used railroad ties. In the background a telegraph pole, beyond it a view of trees, fences and fields; still further back a factory building and a cluster of little dwellings.

It is six o'clock of the same afternoon. Dusk has begun to fall.

LILIOM *and* FICSUR *are discovered on the stairway looking after the train which has just passed.*

LILIOM. Can you still hear it snort?

FICSUR. Listen!

[*They watch the vanishing train.*]

LILIOM. If you put your ear on the tracks you can hear it go all the way to Vienna.

FICSUR. Huh!

LILIOM. The one that just puffed past us —it goes all the way to Vienna.

FICSUR. No further?

LILIOM. Yes—further, too.

[*There is a pause.*]

FICSUR. It must be near six. (*As* LILIOM *ascends the steps.*) Where are you going?

LILIOM. Don't be afraid. I'm not giving you the slip.

FICSUR. Why should you give me the slip? That cashier has sixteen thousand kronen on him. Just be patient till he comes, then you can talk to him, nice and polite.

LILIOM. I say, "Good-evening—excuse me, sir; what time is it?"

FICSUR. Then he tells you what time it is.

LILIOM. Suppose he don't come?

FICSUR (*coming down the steps*). Nonsense! He's got to come. He pays off the workmen every Saturday. And this is Saturday, ain't it? (LILIOM *has ascended to the top of the stairway and is gazing along the tracks.*) What are you looking at up there?

LILIOM. The tracks go on and on—there's no end to them.

FICSUR. What's that to stare about?

LILIOM. Nothing—only I always look after the train. When you stand down there at night it snorts past you, and spits down.

FICSUR. Spits?

LILIOM. Yes, the engine. It spits down. And then the whole train rattles past and away—and you stand there— spat on—but it draws your eyes along with it.

FICSUR. Draws your eyes along?

LILIOM. Yes—whether you want to or not, you've got to look after it—as long as the tiniest bit of it is in sight.

FICSUR. Swell people sit in it.

LILIOM. And read newspapers.

FICSUR. And smoke cigars.

LILIOM. And inhale the smoke.

[*There is a short silence.*]

FICSUR. Is he coming?

LILIOM. Not yet. (*Silence again.* LILIOM *comes down, speaks low, confidentially.*) Do you hear the telegraph wires?

FICSUR. I hear them when the wind blows.

LILIOM. Even when the wind doesn't blow you can hear them humming, humming—— People talk through them.

FICSUR. Who?

LILIOM. Jews.

FICSUR. No—they telegraph.

LILIOM. They talk through them and from some other place they get answered. And it all goes through the iron strings—that's why they hum like that—they hum-m——

FICSUR. What do they hum?

LILIOM. They hum! ninety-nine, ninety-nine. Just listen.

FICSUR. What for?

LILIOM. That sparrow's listening, too. He's cocked one eye and looks at me as if to say: "I'd like to know what they're talking about."

FICSUR. You're looking at a bird?

LILIOM. He's looking at me, too.

FICSUR. Listen, you're sick! There's something the matter with you. Do you know what it is? Money. That bird has no money, either; that's why he cocks his eye.

LILIOM. Maybe.

FICSUR. Whoever has money don't cock his eye.

LILIOM. What then does he do?

FICSUR. He does most anything he wants. But nobody works unless he has money. We'll soon have money ourselves.

LILIOM. I say, "Good-evening. Excuse me, sir, can you tell me what time it is!"

FICSUR. He's not coming yet. Got the cards? (LILIOM *gives him the pack of cards.*) Got any money?

LILIOM (*takes some coins from his trousers pocket and counts*). Eleven.

FICSUR (*sits astride on the pile of ties and looks off*). All right—eleven.

LILIOM (*sitting astride on the ties facing him*). Put it up.

FICSUR (*puts the money on the ties; rapidly shuffles the cards*). We'll play twenty-one. I'll bank. (*He deals deftly.*)

LILIOM (*looks at his card*). Good. I'll bet the bank.

FICSUR. Must have an ace! (*Deals him a second card.*)

LILIOM. Another one. (*He gets another card*). Another. (*Gets still another.*) Over! (*Throws down his cards.* FICSUR *gathers in the money.*) Come on!

FICSUR. Come on what! Got no more money, have you?

LILIOM. No.

FICSUR. Then the game's over—unless you want to——

LILIOM. What?

FICSUR. Play on credit.

LILIOM. You'll trust me?

FICSUR. No—but—I'll deduct it.

LILIOM. Deduct it from what?

FICSUR. From your share of the money. If *you* win you deduct from my share.

LILIOM (*looks over his shoulder to see if the cashier is coming; nervous and ashamed*). All right. How much is bank?

FICSUR. That cashier is bringing us sixteen thousand kronen. Eight thousand of that is mine. Well, then, the bank is eight thousand.

LILIOM. Good.

FICSUR. Whoever has the most luck will have the most money. (*He deals.*)

LILIOM. Six hundred kronen. (FICSUR *gives him another card.*) Enough.

FICSUR (*laying out his own cards*). Twenty-one. (*He shuffles rapidly.*)

LILIOM (*moves excitedly nearer to* FICSUR). Well, then, double or nothing.

FICSUR (*dealing*). Double or nothing.

LILIOM (*gets a card*). Enough.

FICSUR (*laying out his own cards*). Twenty-one. (*Shuffles rapidly again*).

LILIOM (*in alarm*). You're not—cheating?

FICSUR. Me? Do I look like a cheat? (*Deals the cards again.*)

LILIOM (*glances nervously over his shoulder*). A thousand.

FICSUR (*nonchalantly*). Kronen?

LILIOM. Kronen. (*He gets a card.*) Another one. (*Gets another card.*) Over again! (*Like an inexperienced gambler who is losing heavily,* LILIOM *is very nervous. He plays dazedly, wildly, irrationally. From now on it is apparent that his only thought is to win his money back.*)

FICSUR. That makes twelve hundred you owe.

LILIOM. Double or nothing. (*He gets a card. He is greatly excited.*) Another one.

(*Gets another card.*) Another. (*Throws down three cards.*)

FICSUR (*bends over and adds up the sum on the ground*). Ten—fourteen—twenty-three——You owe two thousand, four hundred.

LILIOM. Now what?

FICSUR (*takes a card out of the deck and gives it to him*). Here's the red ace. You can play double or nothing again. 10

LILIOM (*eagerly*). Good. (*Gets another card.*) Enough.

FICSUR (*turns up his own cards*). Nineteen.

LILIOM. You win again. (*Almost imploring.*) Give me an ace again. Give me the green one. (*Takes a card.*) Double or nothing.

FICSUR. Not any more.

LILIOM. Why not? 20

FICSUR. Because if you lose you won't be able to pay. Double would be nine thousand six hundred. And you've only got eight thousand altogether.

LILIOM (*greatly excited*). That—that—I call that—a dirty trick!

FICSUR. Three thousand, two hundred. That's all you can put up.

LILIOM (*eagerly*). All right, then—three thousand, two hundred. (FICSUR *deals* 30 *him a card.*) Enough.

FICSUR. I've got an ace myself. Now we'll have to take our time and squeeze 'em. (LILIOM *pushes closer to him as he takes up his cards and slowly, intently unfolds them.*) Twenty-one. (*He quickly puts the cards in his pocket. There is a pause.*)

LILIOM. Now—now—I'll tell you now— you're a crook, a low-down—— 40

[*Now* LINZMAN *enters at right. He is a strong, robust, red-bearded Jew about 40 years of age. At his side he carries a leather bag slung by a strap from his shoulder.* FICSUR *coughs warningly, moves to the right between* LINZMAN *and the*

embankment, pauses just behind LINZMAN *and follows him.*]

LILIOM (*stands bewildered a few paces to the left of the railroad ties. He finds himself facing* LINZMAN. *Trembling in every limb*). Good-evening. Excuse me, sir, can you tell me the time?

[FICSUR *springs silently at* LINZMAN, *the little knife in his right hand. But* LINZMAN *catches* FICSUR'S *right hand with his own left and forces* FICSUR *to his knees. Simultaneously* LINZMAN *thrusts his right hand into his coat pocket and produces a revolver which he points at* LILIOM'S *breast.* LILIOM *is standing two paces away from the revolver. There is a long pause.*]

LINZMAN (*in a low, even voice*). It is twenty-five minutes past six. (*Pauses, looks ironically down at* FICSUR.) It's lucky I grabbed the hand with the knife instead of the other one. (*Pauses again, looks appraisingly from one to the other.*) Two fine birds! (*To* FICSUR.) I should live so—Rothschild has more luck than you. (*To* LILIOM.) I'd advise you to keep nice and quiet. If you make one move, you'll get two bullets in you. Just look into the barrel. You'll see some little things in there made of lead.

FICSUR. Let me go. I didn't do anything.

LINZMAN (*mockingly shakes the hand which still holds the knife*). And this? What do you call this? Oh, yes, I know. You thought I had an apple in my pocket, and you wanted to peel it. That's it. Forgive me for my error. I beg your pardon, sir.

LILIOM. But I—I——

LINZMAN. Yes, my son, I know. It's so simple. You only asked what time it is. Well, it's twenty-five minutes after six.

FICSUR. Let us go, honorable sir. We didn't do anything to you.

LINZMAN. In the first place, my son, I'm not an honorable sir. In the second place, for the same money, you could have said Your Excellency. But in the third place you'll find it very hard to beg off by flattering me.

LILIOM. But I—*I* really didn't do anything to you.

LINZMAN. Look behind you, my boy. Don't be afraid. Look behind you, but don't run away or I'll have to shoot you down. (LILIOM *turns his head slowly around.*) Who's coming up there?

LILIOM (*looking at* LINZMAN). Policemen.

LINZMAN (*to* FICSUR). You hold still, or——(*To* LILIOM *teasingly.*) How many policemen are there?

LILIOM (*his eyes cast down*). Two.

LINZMAN. And what are the policemen sitting on?

LILIOM. Horses.

LINZMAN. And which can run faster, a horse or a man?

LILIOM. A horse.

LINZMAN. There, you see. It would be hard to get away now. (*Laughs.*) I never saw such an unlucky pair of highway robbers. I can't imagine worse luck. Just to-day I had to put a pistol in my pocket. And even if I hadn't—old Linzman is a match for four like you. But even that isn't all. Did you happen to notice, you oxen, what direction I came from? From the factory, didn't I? When I *went* there I had a nice bit of money with me. Sixteen thousand crowns! But now—not a heller. (*Calls off left.*) Hey, come quicker, will you? This fellow is pulling pretty strong. (FICSUR *frees himself with a mighty wrench and darts rapidly off. As* LINZMAN *aims his pistol at the vanishing* FICSUR, LILIOM *runs up the steps to the embankment.* LINZMAN *hesitates, perceives that* LILIOM *is the better target, points the pistol at him.*) Stop, or I'll shoot! (*Calls off left to the* POLICEMEN.) Why don't you come down off your horses? (*His pistol is leveled at* LILIOM, *who stands on the embankment, facing the audience. From the left on the embankment a* POLICEMAN *appears, revolver in hand.*)

FIRST POLICEMAN. Stop!

LINZMAN. Well, my boy, do you still want to know what time it is? From ten to twelve years in prison!

LILIOM. You won't get me! (LINZMAN *laughs derisively.* LILIOM *is now three or four paces from the* POLICEMAN *and equally distant from* LINZMAN. *His face is uplifted to the sky. He bursts into laughter, half defiant, half self-pitying, and takes the kitchen knife from under his coat.*) Julie——(*The ring of farewell is in the word. He turns sideways, thrusts the knife deep in his breast, sways, falls and rolls down the far side of the embankment. There is a long pause. From the left up on the embankment come the* TWO POLICEMEN.)

LINZMAN. What's the matter? (*The* FIRST POLICEMAN *comes along the embankment as far as the steps, looks down in the opposite side, then climbs down at about the spot where* LILIOM *disappeared.* LINZMAN *and the other* POLICEMAN *mount the embankment and look down on him.*) Stabbed himself?

VOICE OF FIRST POLICEMAN. Yes—and he seems to have made a thorough job of it.

LINZMAN (*excitedly to* SECOND POLICEMAN). I'll go and telephone to the hospital. (*He runs down the steps and exits at left.*)

SECOND POLICEMAN. Go to Eisler's grocery store and telephone to the factory from there. They've a doctor there, too. (*Calling down to the other* POLICEMAN.) I'm going to tie up the horses.

[*Comes down the steps and exits at left. The stage is empty. There is a pause. The little red signal lamp is lit.*]

VOICE OF FIRST POLICEMAN. Hey, Stephan?

VOICE OF SECOND POLICEMAN. What?

VOICE OF FIRST POLICEMAN. Shall I pull the knife out of his chest?

VOICE OF SECOND POLICEMAN. Better not, or he may bleed to death. 10

[*There is a pause.*]

VOICE OF FIRST POLICEMAN. Stephan!

VOICE OF SECOND POLICEMAN. Yes.

VOICE OF FIRST POLICEMAN. Lot of mosquitoes around here.

VOICE OF SECOND POLICEMAN. Yes.

VOICE OF FIRST POLICEMAN. Got a cigar?

VOICE OF SECOND POLICEMAN. No.

[*There is a pause. The* FIRST POLICEMAN *appears over the opposite side of the em-* 20 *bankment.*]

FIRST POLICEMAN. A lot of good the new pay-schedule's done us—made things worse than they used to be—we *get* more but we *have* less than we ever had. If the Government could be made to realize that. It's a thankless job at best. You work hard year after year, you get gray in the service, and slowly you die—yes. 30

SECOND POLICEMAN. That's right.

FIRST POLICEMAN. Yes.

[*In the distance is heard the bell of the signal tower.*]

THE CURTAIN FALLS

SCENE V

The photographic "studio" a half hour later that same evening.

MOTHER HOLLUNDER, *her* SON, MARIE 40 *and* WOLF *stand in a group back right, their heads together.* JULIE *stands apart from them, a few paces to the left.*

YOUNG HOLLUNDER (*who has just come in, tells his story excitedly*). They're bringing him now. Two workmen from the factory are carrying him on a stretcher.

WOLF. Where is the doctor?

YOUNG HOLLUNDER. A policeman telephoned to headquarters. The police-surgeon ought to be here any minute.

MARIE. Maybe they'll pull him through after all.

YOUNG HOLLUNDER. He stabbed himself too deep in his chest. But he's still breathing. He can still talk, too, but very faintly. At first he lay there unconscious, but when they put him on the stretcher he came to.

WOLF. That was from the shaking.

MARIE. We'd better make room.

[*They make room. Two workmen carry in* LILIOM *on a stretcher which has four legs and stands about as high as a bed. They put the stretcher at left directly in front of the sofa, so that the head is at right and the foot at left. Then they unobtrusively join the group at the door. Later, they go out.* JULIE *is standing at the side of the stretcher, where, without moving, she can see* LILIOM'S *face. The others crowd emotionally together near the door. The* FIRST POLICEMAN *enters.*]

FIRST POLICEMAN. Are you his wife?

JULIE. Yes.

FIRST POLICEMAN. The doctor at the factory who bandaged him up forbade us to take him to the hospital. —Dangerous to move him that far. What he needs now is rest. Just let him be until the police-surgeon comes. (*To the group near the door.*) He's not to be disturbed.

[*They make way for him. He exits. There is a pause.*]

WOLF (*gently urging the others out*). Please —it's best if we all get out of here now. We'll only be in the way.

MARIE (*to* JULIE). Julie, what do you

think? (JULIE *looks at her without an-swering.*) Julie, can I do anything to help? (JULIE *does not answer.*) We'll be just outside on the bench if you want us.

[MOTHER HOLLUNDER *and her* SON *have gone out when first requested. Now* MARIE *and* WOLF *exit, too.* JULIE *sits on the edge of the stretcher and looks at* LILIOM. *He stretches his hand out to her. She* 10 *clasps it. It is not quite dark yet. Both of them can still be plainly seen.*]

LILIOM (*raises himself with difficulty; speaks lightly at first, but later soberly, defiantly*). Little—Julie—there's some-thing—I want to tell you—like when you go to a restaurant—and you've finished eating—and it's time—to pay—then you have to count up everything—everything you owe— 20 well—I beat you—not because I was mad at you—no—only because I can't bear to see any one crying. You always cried—on my account—and, well, you see—I never learned a trade—what kind of a caretaker would I make? But anyhow—I wasn't going back to the carousel to fool with the girls. No, I spit on them all—under-stand?   30

JULIE. Yes.

LILIOM. And—as for Hollinger—he's good enough—Mrs. Muskat can get along all right with him. The jokes he tells are mine—and the people laugh when he tells them—but I don't care.—I didn't give you any-thing—no home—not even the food you ate—but you don't understand. —It's true I'm not much good—but 40 I couldn't be a caretaker—and so I thought maybe it would be better over there—in America—do you see?

JULIE. Yes.

LILIOM. I'm not asking—forgiveness—I don't do that—I don't. Tell the baby—if you like.

JULIE. Yes.

LILIOM. Tell the baby—I wasn't much good—but tell him—if you ever talk about me—tell him—I thought—perhaps—over in America—but that's no affair of yours. I'm not asking forgiveness. For my part the police can come now.—If it's a boy—if it's a girl.—Perhaps I'll see the Lord God to-day.—Do you think I'll see Him?

JULIE. Yes.

LILIOM. I'm not afraid—of the police Up There—if they'll only let me come up in front of the Lord God Himself—not like down here where an officer stops you at the door. If the carpenter asks you—yes—be his wife—marry him. And the child— tell him he's his father.—He'll be-lieve you—won't he?

JULIE. Yes.

LILIOM. When I beat you—I was right. —You mustn't always think—you mustn't always be right.—Liliom can be right once, too.—It's all the same to me who was right.—It's so dumb. Nobody's right—but they all think they are right.—A lot they know!

JULIE. Yes.

LILIOM. Julie—come—hold my hand tight.

JULIE. I'm holding it tight—all the time.

LILIOM. Tighter, still tighter—I'm going——(*Pauses.*) Julie——

JULIE. Good-bye.

[LILIOM *sinks slowly back and dies.* JULIE *frees her hand.* THE DOCTOR *enters with the* FIRST POLICEMAN.]

Doctor. Good-evening. His wife?

JULIE. Yes, sir.

[*Behind the* DOCTOR *and* POLICEMAN *enter*

MARIE, WOLF, MOTHER HOLLUNDER, YOUNG HOLLUNDER *and* MRS. MUSKAT. *They remain respectfully at the doorway. The* DOCTOR *bends over* LILIOM *and examines him.*]

DOCTOR. A light, if you please. (JULIE *fetches a burning candle from the darkroom. The* DOCTOR *examines* LILIOM *briefly in the candle-light, then turns suddenly away.*) Have you pen and ink?

WOLF (*proffering a pen*). A fountain-pen —American——

DOCTOR (*takes a printed form from his pocket; speaks as he writes out the death-certificate at the little table*). My poor woman, your husband is dead— there's nothing to be done for him— the good God will help him now— I'll leave this certificate with you. You will give it to the people from the hospital when they come—I'll arrange for the body to be removed at once. (*Rises.*) Please give me a towel and soap.

POLICEMAN. I've got them for you out here, sir. (*Points to door at back.*)

DOCTOR. God be with you, my good woman.

JULIE. Thank you, sir.

[*The* DOCTOR *and* POLICEMAN *exit. The others slowly draw nearer.*]

MARIE. Poor Julie. May he rest in peace, poor man, but as for you— please don't be angry with me for saying it—but you're better off this way.

MOTHER HOLLUNDER. He is better off, the poor fellow, and so are you.

MARIE. Much better, Julie . . . you are young . . . and one of these days some good man will come along. Am I right?

WOLF. She's right.

MARIE. Julie, tell me, am I right?

JULIE. You are right, dear; you are very good.

YOUNG HOLLUNDER. There's a good man—the carpenter. Oh, I can speak of it now. He comes here every day on some excuse or other—and he never fails to ask for you.

MARIE. A widower—with two children.

MOTHER HOLLUNDER. He's better off, poor fellow—and so are you. He was a bad man.

MARIE. He wasn't good-hearted. Was he, Wolf?

WOLF. No, I must say, he really wasn't. No, Liliom wasn't a good man. A good man doesn't strike a woman.

MARIE. Am I right? Tell me, Julie, am I right?

JULIE. You are right, dear.

YOUNG HOLLUNDER. It's really a good thing for her it happened.

MOTHER HOLLUNDER. He's better off— and so is she.

WOLF. Now you have your freedom again. How old are you?

JULIE. Eighteen.

WOLF. Eighteen. A mere child! Am I right?

JULIE. You are right, Wolf. You are kind.

YOUNG HOLLUNDER. Lucky for you it happened, isn't it?

JULIE. Yes.

YOUNG HOLLUNDER. All you had before was bad luck. If it weren't for my mother you wouldn't have had a roof over your head or a bite to eat— and now Autumn's coming and Winter. You couldn't have lived in this shack in the Winter time, could you?

MARIE. Certainly not! You'd have frozen like the birds in the fields. Am I right, Julie?

JULIE. Yes, Marie.

MARIE. A year from now you will have forgotten all about him, won't you?

JULIE. You are right, Marie.

WOLF. If you need anything, count on us. We'll go now. But to-morrow morning we'll be back. Come, Marie. God be with you. (*Offers* JULIE *his hand.*)

JULIE. God be with you.

MARIE (*embraces* JULIE, *weeping*). It's the best thing that could have happened to you, Julie, the best thing.

JULIE. Don't cry, Marie.

[MARIE *and* WOLF *exit.*]

MOTHER HOLLUNDER. I'll make a little black coffee. You haven't had a thing to eat to-day. Then you'll come home with us.

[MOTHER HOLLUNDER *and her* SON *exit.* MRS. MUSKAT *comes over to* JULIE.]

MRS. MUSKAT. Would you mind if I— looked at him?

JULIE. He used to work for you.

MRS. MUSKAT (*contemplates the body; turns to* JULIE). Won't you make up with me?

JULIE. I wasn't angry with you.

MRS. MUSKAT. But you were. Let's make it up.

JULIE (*raising her voice eagerly, almost triumphantly*). I've nothing to make up with *you*.

MRS. MUSKAT. But I have with you. Every one says hard things against the poor dead boy—except us two. You don't say he was bad.

JULIE (*raising her voice yet higher, this time on a defiant, wholly triumphant note*). Yes, I *do*.

MRS. MUSKAT. I understand, my child. But he beat me, too. What does that matter? I've forgotten it.

JULIE (*from now on answers her coldly, dryly, without looking at her*). That's your own affair.

MRS. MUSKAT. If I can help you in any way——

JULIE. There's nothing I need.

MRS. MUSKAT. I still owe him two kronen, back pay.

JULIE. You should have paid him.

MRS. MUSKAT. Now that the poor fellow is dead I thought perhaps it would be the same if I paid you.

JULIE. I've nothing to do with it.

MRS. MUSKAT. All right. Please don't think I'm trying to force myself on you. I stayed because we two are the only ones on earth who loved him. That's why I thought we ought to stick together.

JULIE. No, thank you.

MRS. MUSKAT. Then you couldn't have loved him as I did.

JULIE. No.

MRS. MUSKAT. I loved him better.

JULIE. Yes.

MRS. MUSKAT. Good-bye.

JULIE. Good-bye. (MRS. MUSKAT *exits.* JULIE *puts the candle on the table near* LILIOM'S *head, sits on the edge of the stretcher, looks into the dead man's face and caresses it tenderly.*) Sleep, Liliom, sleep—it's no business of hers—I never even told you—but now I'll tell you—now I'll tell you—you bad, quick-tempered, rough, unhappy, wicked—*dear* boy—sleep peacefully, Liliom—they can't understand how I feel—I can't even explain to you— not even to you—how I feel—you'd only laugh at me—but you can't hear me any more. (*Between tender motherliness and reproach, yet with great love in her voice.*) It was wicked of you to beat me—on the breast and on the head and face—but you're gone now. —You treated me badly—that was wicked of you—but sleep peacefully, Liliom—you bad, bad boy, you— I love you—I never told you before —I was ashamed—but now I've told you—I love you. Liliom— sleep—my boy—sleep. (*She rises, gets a Bible, sits down near the candle and reads softly to herself, so that not the words but an inarticulate murmur is heard. The* CARPENTER *enters at back.*)

CARPENTER (*stands near the door; in the dimness of the room he can scarcely be seen*). Miss Julie——

JULIE (*without alarm*). Who is that?

CARPENTER (*very slowly*). The carpenter.

JULIE. What does the carpenter want?

CARPENTER. Can I be of help to you in any way? Shall I stay here with you? 10

JULIE (*gratefully, but firmly*). Don't stay, carpenter.

CARPENTER. Shall I come back to-morrow?

JULIE. Not to-morrow, either.

CARPENTER. Don't be offended, Miss Julie, but I'd like to know—you see, I'm not a young man any more—I have two children—and if I'm to come back any more—I'd like to 20 know—if there's any use——

JULIE. No use, carpenter.

CARPENTER (*as he exits*). God be with you.

[JULIE *resumes her reading.* FICSUR *enters, slinks furtively sideways to the stretcher, looks at* LILIOM, *shakes his head.* JULIE *looks up from her reading.* FICSUR *takes fright, slinks away from the stretcher, sits down at right, biting his nails.* JULIE 30 *rises.* FICSUR *rises, too, and looks at her half fearfully. With her piercing glance upon him he slinks to the doorway at back, where he pauses and speaks.*]

FICSUR. The old woman asked me to tell you that coffee is ready, and you are to come in.

[JULIE *goes to the kitchen door.* FICSUR *withdraws until she has closed the door behind her. Then he reappears in the doorway,* 40 *stands on tiptoes, looks at* LILIOM, *then exits. Now the body lies alone. After a brief silence music is heard, distant at first, but gradually coming nearer. It is very much like the music of the carousel, but slower, graver, more exalted. The* melody, too, is the same, yet the tempo is altered and contrapuntal measures of the thieves' song are intertwined in it. Two men in black, with heavy sticks, soft black hats and black gloves, appear in the doorway at back and stride slowly into the room. Their faces are beardless, marble white, grave and benign. One stops in front of the stretcher, the other a pace to the right. From above a dim violet light illuminates their faces.]

THE FIRST (*to* LILIOM). Rise and come with us.

THE SECOND (*politely*). You're under arrest.

THE FIRST (*somewhat louder, but always in a gentle, low, resonant voice*). Do you hear? Rise. Don't you hear?

THE SECOND. We are the police.

THE FIRST (*bends down, touches* LILIOM'S *shoulder*). Get up and come with us.

[LILIOM *slowly sits up.*]

THE SECOND. Come along.

THE FIRST (*paternally*). These people suppose that when they die all their difficulties are solved for them.

THE SECOND (*raising his voice sternly*). That simply by thrusting a knife in your heart and making it stop beating you can leave your wife behind with a child in her womb——

THE FIRST. It is not as simple as that.

THE SECOND. Such things are not settled so easily.

THE FIRST. Come along. You will have to give an account of yourself. (*As both bow their heads, he continues softly.*) We are God's police. (*An expression of glad relief lights upon* LILIOM'S *face. He rises from the stretcher.*) Come.

THE SECOND. You mortals don't get off quite as easy as that.

THE FIRST (*softly*). Come. (LILIOM *starts to walk ahead of them, then stops and looks at them.*) The end is not as abrupt as that. Your name is still

spoken. Your face is still remembered.
And what you said, and what you did,
and what you failed to do—these
are still remembered. Remembered,
too, are the manner of your glance,
the ring of your voice, the clasp of
your hand and how your step
sounded—as long as one is left who
remembers you, so long is the matter
unended. Before the end there is 10
much to be undone. Until you are
quite forgotten, my son, you will not
be finished with the earth—even
though you *are* dead.

THE SECOND (*very gently*). Come.

[*The music begins again. All three exit at
back,* LILIOM *leading, the others following. The stage is empty and quite dark
save for the candle which burns by the
stretcher, on which, in the shadows, the* 20
*covers are so arranged that one cannot
quite be sure that a body is not still lying.
The music dies out in the distance as if it
had followed* LILIOM *and the two* POLICE-
MEN. *The candle flickers and goes out.
There is a brief interval of silence and
total darkness before.*]

THE CURTAIN FALLS

SCENE VI   30

*In the Beyond. A whitewashed courtroom.
There is a green-topped table; behind it a
bench. Back center is a door with a bell over
it. Next to this door is a window through
which can be seen a vista of rose-tinted
clouds. Down right there is a grated iron
door. Down left another door.*

*Two men are on the bench when the cur-
tain rises. One is richly, the other poorly
dressed.*

*From a great distance is heard a fanfare
of trumpets playing the refrain of the thieves'
song in slow, altered tempo.*

Passing the window at back appear
LILIOM *and the two* POLICEMEN.

The bell rings.

An old GUARD *enters at right. He is bald
and has a long white beard. He wears the
conventional police uniform.*

*He goes to the door at back, opens it, ex-
changes silent greetings with the two* POLICE-
MEN *and closes the door again.*

LILIOM *looks wonderingly around.*

THE FIRST (*to the old* GUARD). Announce
us.

[*The* GUARD *exits at left.*]

LILIOM. Is this it?

THE SECOND. Yes, my son.

LILIOM. This is the police court?

THE SECOND. Yes, my son. The part for
suicide cases.

LILIOM. And what happens here?

THE FIRST. Here justice is done. Sit
down.

[LILIOM *sits next to the two men. The two*
POLICEMEN *stand silent near the table.*]

THE RICHLY DRESSED MAN (*whispers*).
Suicide, too?

LILIOM. Yes.

THE RICHLY DRESSED MAN (*points to* THE
POORLY DRESSED MAN). So's he.
(*Introducing himself.*) My name is
Reich.

THE POORLY DRESSED MAN (*whispers, too*).
My name is Stephan Kadar.

[LILIOM *only looks at them.*]

THE POORLY DRESSED MAN. And you?
What's your name?

LILIOM. None of your business.

[*Both move a bit away from him.*]

THE POORLY DRESSED MAN. I did it by
jumping out of a window.

THE RICHLY DRESSED MAN. I did it with
a pistol—and you?

LILIOM. With a knife.

[*They move a bit further away from him.*]

THE RICHLY DRESSED MAN. A pistol is
cleaner.

LILIOM. If I had the price of a pistol——

THE SECOND. Silence!

[*The* POLICE MAGISTRATE *enters. He has*

a long white beard, is bald, but only in profile can be seen on his head a single tuft of snow-white hair. The GUARD *reënters behind him and sits on the bench with the dead men. As* THE MAGISTRATE *enters, all rise, except* LILIOM, *who remains surlily seated. When* THE MAGISTRATE *sits down, so do the others.*]

THE GUARD. Yesterday's cases, your honor. The numbers are entered in the docket.

THE MAGISTRATE. Number 16,472.

THE FIRST (*looks in his notebook, beckons* THE RICHLY DRESSED MAN). Stand up, please. (THE RICHLY DRESSED MAN *rises.*)

THE MAGISTRATE. Your name?

THE RICHLY DRESSED MAN. Doctor Reich.

THE MAGISTRATE. Age?

THE RICHLY DRESSED MAN. Forty-two, married, Jew.

THE MAGISTRATE (*with a gesture of dismissal*). Religion does not interest us here.—Why did you kill yourself?

THE RICHLY DRESSED MAN. On account of debts.

THE MAGISTRATE. What good did you do on earth?

THE RICHLY DRESSED MAN. I was a lawyer——

THE MAGISTRATE (*coughs significantly*). Yes—we'll discuss that later. For the present I shall only ask you: Would you like to go back to earth once more before sunrise? I advise you that you have the right to go if you choose. Do you understand?

THE RICHLY DRESSED MAN. Yes, sir.

THE MAGISTRATE. He who takes his life is apt, in his haste and his excitement, to forget something. Is there anything important down there you have left undone? Something to tell some one? Something to undo?

THE RICHLY DRESSED MAN. My debts——

THE MAGISTRATE. They do not matter here. Here we are concerned only with the affairs of the soul.

THE RICHLY DRESSED MAN. Then—if you please—when I left—the house—my youngest son, Oscar—was asleep. I didn't trust myself to wake him—and bid him good-bye. I would have liked—to kiss him good-bye.

THE MAGISTRATE (*to* THE SECOND). You will take Dr. Reich back and let him kiss his son Oscar.

THE SECOND. Come with me, please.

THE RICHLY DRESSED MAN (*to* THE MAGISTRATE). I thank you. (*He bows and exits at back with* THE SECOND.)

THE MAGISTRATE (*after making an entry in the docket*). Number 16,473.

THE FIRST (*looks in his notebook, then beckons* LILIOM). Stand up.

LILIOM. You said *please* to him. (*He rises.*)

THE MAGISTRATE. Your name?

LILIOM. Liliom.

THE MAGISTRATE. Isn't that your nickname?

LILIOM. Yes.

THE MAGISTRATE. What is your right name?

LILIOM. Andreas.

THE MAGISTRATE. And your last name?

LILIOM. Zavocki—after my mother.

THE MAGISTRATE. Your age?

LILIOM. Twenty-four.

THE MAGISTRATE. What good did *you* do on earth? (LILIOM *is silent.*) Why did you take your life? (LILIOM *does not answer.* THE MAGISTRATE *addresses* THE FIRST.) Take that knife away from him. (THE FIRST *does so.*) It will be returned to you, if you go back to earth.

LILIOM. Do I go back to earth again?

THE MAGISTRATE. Just answer my questions.

LILIOM. I wasn't answering then, I was asking if——

THE MAGISTRATE. You don't ask questions here. You only answer. Only answer, Andreas Zavocki! I ask you whether there is anything on earth you neglected to accomplish? Anything down there you would like to do?

LILIOM. Yes.

THE MAGISTRATE. What is it?

LILIOM. I'd like to break Ficsur's head for him.

THE MAGISTRATE. Punishment is our office. Is there nothing else on earth you'd like to do?

LILIOM. I don't know—I guess, as long as I'm here, I'll not go back.

THE MAGISTRATE (*to* THE FIRST). Note that. He waives his right. (LILIOM *starts back to the bench.*) Stay where you are. You are aware that you left your wife without food or shelter?

LILIOM. Yes.

THE MAGISTRATE. Don't you regret it?

LILIOM. No.

THE MAGISTRATE. You are aware that your wife is pregnant, and that in six months a child will be born?

LILIOM. I know.

THE MAGISTRATE. And that the child, too, will be without food or shelter? Do you regret that?

LILIOM. As long as I won't be there, what's it got to do with me?

THE MAGISTRATE. Don't try to deceive us, Andreas Zavocki. We see through you as through a pane of glass.

LILIOM. If you see so much, what do you want to ask me for? Why don't you let me rest—in peace?

THE MAGISTRATE. First you must earn your rest.

LILIOM. I want—only—to sleep.

THE MAGISTRATE. Your obstinacy won't help you. Here patience is endless as time. We can wait.

LILIOM. Can I ask something?—I'd like to know—if Your Honor will tell me—whether the baby will be a boy or a girl.

THE MAGISTRATE. You shall see that for yourself.

LILIOM (*excitedly*). I'll see the baby?

THE MAGISTRATE. When you do it won't be a baby any more. But we haven't reached that question yet.

LILIOM. I'll see it?

THE MAGISTRATE. Again I ask you: Do you not regret that you deserted your wife and child; that you were a bad husband, a bad father?

LILIOM. A bad husband?

THE MAGISTRATE. Yes.

LILIOM. And a bad father?

THE MAGISTRATE. That, too.

LILIOM. I couldn't get work—and I couldn't bear to see Julie—all the time—all the time——

THE MAGISTRATE. Weeping! Why are you ashamed to say it? You couldn't bear to see her weeping. Why are you afraid of that word? And why are you ashamed that you loved her?

LILIOM (*shrugs his shoulders*). Who's ashamed? But I couldn't bear to see her—and that's why I was bad to her. You see, it wouldn't do to go back to the carousel—and Ficsur came along with his talk about—that other thing—and all of a sudden it happened, I don't know how. The police and the Jew with the pistol—and there I stood—and I'd lost the money playing cards—and I didn't want to be put in prison. (*Demanding justification.*) Maybe I was wrong not to go out and steal when there was nothing to eat in the house? Should I have gone out to steal for Julie?

THE MAGISTRATE (*emphatically*). Yes.

LILIOM (*after an astounded pause*). The police down there never said that.

THE MAGISTRATE. You beat that poor, frail girl; you beat her because she loved you. How could you do that?

LILIOM. We argued with each other—she said this and I said that—and because she was right I couldn't answer her—and I got mad—and the anger rose up in me—until it reached here (*Points to his throat.*) and then I beat her.

THE MAGISTRATE. Are you sorry?

LILIOM (*shakes his head, but cannot utter the word "no"; continues softly*). When I touched her slender throat—then—if you like—you might say—— (*Falters, looks embarrassed at* THE MAGISTRATE.)

THE MAGISTRATE (*confidently expectant*). Are you sorry?

LILIOM (*with a stare*). I'm not sorry for anything.

THE MAGISTRATE. Liliom, Liliom, it will be difficult to help you.

LILIOM. I'm not asking any help.

THE MAGISTRATE. You were offered employment as a caretaker on Arader Street. (*To* THE FIRST.) Where is that entered?

THE FIRST. In the small docket. (*Hands him the open book.* THE MAGISTRATE *looks in it.*)

THE MAGISTRATE. Rooms, kitchen, quarterly wages, the privilege of keeping poultry. Why didn't you accept it?

LILIOM. I'm not a caretaker. I'm no good at caretaking. To be a caretaker—you have to be a caretaker——

THE MAGISTRATE. If I said to you now: Liliom, go back on your stretcher. To-morrow morning you will arise alive and well again. Would you be a caretaker then?

LILIOM. No.

THE MAGISTRATE. Why not?

LILIOM. Because—because that's just why I died.

THE MAGISTRATE. That is not true, my son. You died because you loved little Julie and the child she is bearing under her heart.

LILIOM. No.

THE MAGISTRATE. Look me in the eye.

LILIOM (*looks him in the eye*). No.

THE MAGISTRATE (*stroking his beard*). Liliom, Liliom, if it were not for our Heavenly patience——Go back to your seat. Number 16,474.

THE FIRST (*looks in his notebook*). Stephan Kadar.

[THE POORLY DRESSED MAN *rises.*]

THE MAGISTRATE. You came out to-day?

THE POORLY DRESSED MAN. To-day.

THE MAGISTRATE (*indicating the crimson sea of clouds*). How long were you in there?

THE POORLY DRESSED MAN. Thirteen years.

THE MAGISTRATE. Officer, you went to earth with him?

THE FIRST. Yes, sir.

THE MAGISTRATE. Stephan Kadar, after thirteen years of purification by fire you returned to earth to give proof that your soul had been burned clean. What good deed did you perform?

THE POORLY DRESSED MAN. When I came to the village and looked in the window of our cottage I saw my poor little orphans sleeping peacefully. But it was raining and the rain beat into the room through a hole in the roof. So I went and fixed the roof so it wouldn't rain in any more. My hammering woke them up and they were afraid. But their mother came in to them and comforted them. She said to them: "Don't cry! It's your poor, dear father hammering up there. He's come back from the other world to fix the roof for us."

THE MAGISTRATE. Officer?

THE FIRST. That's what happened.

THE MAGISTRATE. Stephan Kadar, you have done a good deed. What you did will be written in books to gladden the hearts of children who read them. (*Indicates the door at left.*) The door is open to you. The eternal light awaits you. (THE FIRST *escorts* THE POORLY DRESSED MAN *out at left with great deference.*) Liliom! (LILIOM *rises.*) You have heard?

LILIOM. Yes.

THE MAGISTRATE. When this man first appeared before us he was as stubborn as you. But now he has purified himself and withstood the test. He has done a good deed.

LILIOM. What's he done, anyhow? Any roofer can fix a roof. It's much harder to be a barker in an amusement park.

THE MAGISTRATE. Liliom, you shall remain for sixteen years in the crimson fire until your child is full grown. By that time your pride and your stubbornness will have been burnt out of you. And when your daughter——

LILIOM. My daughter!

THE MAGISTRATE. When your daughter has reached the age of sixteen——

[LILIOM *bows his head, covers his eyes with his hands, and to keep from weeping laughs defiantly, sadly.*]

THE MAGISTRATE. When your daughter has reached the age of sixteen you will be sent for one day back to earth.

LILIOM. Me?

THE MAGISTRATE. Yes—just as you may have read in the legends of how the dead reappear on earth for a time.

LILIOM. I never believed them.

THE MAGISTRATE. Now you see they are true. You will go back to earth one day to show how far the purification of your soul has progressed.

LILIOM. Then I must show what I can do —like when you apply for a job—as a coachman?

THE MAGISTRATE. Yes—it is a test.

LILIOM. And will I be told what I have to do?

THE MAGISTRATE. No.

LILIOM. How will I know, then?

THE MAGISTRATE. You must decide that for yourself. That's what you burn sixteen years for. And if you do something good, something splendid for your child, then——

LILIOM (*laughs sadly*). Then? (*All stand up and bow their heads reverently. There is a pause.*) Then?

THE MAGISTRATE. Now I'll bid you farewell, Liliom. Sixteen years and a day shall pass before I see you again. When you have returned from earth you will come up before me again. Take heed and think well of some good deed to do for your child. On that will depend which door shall be opened to you up here. Now go, Liliom. (*He exits at left.* THE GUARD *stands at attention. There is a pause.*)

THE FIRST (*approaches* LILIOM). Come along, my son. (*He goes to the door at right; pulls open the bolt and waits.*)

LILIOM (*to the old* GUARD, *softly*). Say, officer.

THE GUARD. What do you want?

LILIOM. Please—can I get—have you got——?

THE GUARD. What?

LILIOM (*whispers*). A cigarette?

[*The old* GUARD *stares at him, goes a few paces to the left, shakes his head disapprovingly. Then his expression softens. He takes a cigarette from his pocket and, crossing to* LILIOM—*who has gone over to the door at right*—*gives him the cigarette.* THE FIRST *throws open the door. An intense rose-colored light streams in. The glow of it is so strong that it blinds* LILIOM *and he takes a step backward and bows his head and covers his eyes with his hand before he steps forward into the light.*]

THE CURTAIN FALLS

SCENE VII

Sixteen years later. A small, tumble-down house on a bare, unenclosed plot of ground. Before the house is a tiny garden enclosed by a hip-high hedge.

At back a wooden fence crosses the stage; in the center of it is a door large enough to admit a wagon. Beyond the fence is a view of a suburban street which blends into a broad 10 vista of tilled fields.

It is a bright Sunday in Spring.

In the garden a table for two is laid.

JULIE, *her daughter* LOUISE, WOLF *and* MARIE *are discovered in the garden.* WOLF *is prosperously dressed,* MARIE *somewhat elaborately, with a huge hat.*

JULIE. You could stay for lunch.

MARIE. Impossible, dear. Since he be-20 came the proprietor of the Café Sorrento, Wolf simply has to be there all the time.

JULIE. But you needn't stay there all day, too.

MARIE. Oh, yes. I sit near the cashier's cage, read the papers, keep an eye on the waiters and drink in the bustle and excitement of the great city.

JULIE. And what about the children?

MARIE. You know what modern families are like. Parents scarcely ever see their children these days. The four girls are with their governess, the three boys with their tutor.

LOUISE. Auntie, dear, do stay and eat with us.

MARIE (*importantly*). Impossible to-day, dear child, impossible. Perhaps some other time. Come, Mr. Beifeld. 40

JULIE. Since when do you call your husband mister?

WOLF. I'd rather she did, dear lady. When we used to be very familiar we quarreled all the time. Now we are formal with each other and get along

like society folk. I kiss your hand, dear lady.

JULIE. Good-bye, Wolf.

MARIE. Adieu, my dear. (*They embrace.*) Adieu, my dear child.

LOUISE. Good-bye, Aunt Marie. Good-bye, Uncle Wolf. (WOLF *and* MARIE *exit.*)

JULIE. You can get the soup now, Louise, dear.

[LOUISE *goes into the house and reënters with the soup. They sit at the table.*]

LOUISE. Mother, is it true we're not going to work at the jute factory any more?

JULIE. Yes, dear.

LOUISE. Where then?

JULIE. Uncle Wolf has gotten us a place in a big establishment where they make all kinds of fittings for cafés. We're to make big curtains, you know, the kind they hang in the windows, with lettering on them.

LOUISE. It'll be nicer there than at the jute factory.

JULIE. Yes, dear. The work isn't as dirty and pays better, too. A poor widow like your mother is lucky to get it.

[*They eat.* LILIOM *and the two* HEAVENLY POLICEMEN *appear in the big doorway at back. The* POLICEMEN *pass slowly by.* LILIOM *stands there alone a moment, then comes slowly down and pauses at the opening of the hedge. He is dressed as he was on the day of his death. He is very pale, but otherwise unaltered.* JULIE, *at the table, has her back to him.* LOUISE *sits facing the audience.*]

LILIOM. Good-day.

LOUISE. Good-day.

JULIE. Another beggar! What is it you want, my poor man?

LILIOM. Nothing.

JULIE. We have no money to give, but you care for a plate of soup——

(LOUISE *goes into the house.*) Have you come far to-day?

LILIOM. Yes—very far.

JULIE. Are you tired?

LILIOM. Very tired.

JULIE. Over there at the gate is a stone. Sit down and rest. My daughter is bringing you the soup.

[LOUISE *comes out of the house.*]

LILIOM. Is that your daughter?

JULIE. Yes.

LILIOM (*to* LOUISE). You are the daughter?

LOUISE. Yes, sir.

LILIOM. A fine, healthy girl. (*Takes the soup plate from her with one hand, while with the other he touches her arm.* LOUISE *draws back quickly.*)

LOUISE (*crosses to* JULIE). Mother!

JULIE. What, my child?

LOUISE. The man tried to take me by the arm.

JULIE. Nonsense! You only imagined it, dear. The poor, hungry man has other things to think about than fooling with young girls. Sit down and eat your soup.

[*They eat.*]

LILIOM (*eats, too, but keeps looking at them*). You work at the factory, eh?

JULIE. Yes.

LILIOM. Your daughter, too?

LOUISE. Yes.

LILIOM. And your husband?

JULIE (*after a pause*). I have no husband. I'm a widow.

LILIOM. A widow?

JULIE. Yes.

LILIOM. Your husband—I suppose he's been dead a long time. (JULIE *does not answer.*) I say—has your husband been dead a long time?

JULIE. A long time.

LILIOM. What did he die of?

[JULIE *is silent.*]

LOUISE. No one knows. He went to America to work and he died there—in the hospital. Poor father, I never knew him.

LILIOM. He went to America?

LOUISE. Yes, before I was born.

LILIOM. To America?

JULIE. Why do you ask so many questions? Did you know him, perhaps?

LILIOM (*puts the plate down*). Heaven knows! I've known so many people. Maybe I knew him, too.

JULIE. Well, if you knew him, leave him and us in peace with your questions. He went to America and died there. That's all there is to tell.

LILIOM. All right. All right. Don't be angry with me. I didn't mean any harm.

[*There is a pause.*]

LOUISE. My father was a very handsome man.

JULIE. Don't talk so much.

LOUISE. Did I say anything——?

LILIOM. Surely the little orphan can say that about her father.

LOUISE. My father could juggle so beautifully with three ivory balls that people used to advise him to go on the stage.

JULIE. Who told you that?

LOUISE. Uncle Wolf.

LILIOM. Who is that?

LOUISE. Mr. Wolf Beifeld, who owns the Café Sorrento.

LILIOM. The one who used to be a porter?

JULIE (*astonished*). Do you know him, too? It seems that you know all Budapest.

LILIOM. Wolf Beifeld is a long way from being all Budapest. But I do know a lot of people. Why shouldn't I know Wolf Beifeld?

LOUISE. He was a friend of my father.

JULIE. He was not his friend. No one was.

LILIOM. You speak of your husband so sternly.

JULIE. What's that to you? Doesn't it suit you? I can speak of my husband any way I like. It's nobody's business but mine.

LILIOM. Certainly, certainly—it's your own business. (*Takes up his soup plate again. All three eat.*)

LOUISE (*to* JULIE). Perhaps he knew father, too.

JULIE. Ask him, if you like.

LOUISE (*crosses to* LILIOM. *He stands up*). Did you know my father? (LILIOM *nods.* LOUISE *addresses her mother.*) Yes, he knew him.

JULIE (*rises*). You knew Andreas Zavocki?

LILIOM. Liliom? Yes.

LOUISE. Was he really a very handsome man?

LILIOM. I wouldn't exactly say handsome.

LOUISE (*confidently*). But he was an awfully good man, wasn't he?

LILIOM. He wasn't so good, either. As far as I know he was what they called a clown, a barker in a carousel.

LOUISE (*pleased*). Did he tell funny jokes?

LILIOM. Lots of 'em. And he sang funny songs, too.

LOUISE. In the carousel?

LILIOM. Yes—but he was something of a bully, too. He'd fight any one. He even hit your dear little mother.

JULIE. That's a lie.

LILIOM. It's true.

JULIE. Aren't you ashamed to tell the child such awful things about her father? Get out of here, you shameless liar. Eats our soup and our bread and has the impudence to slander our dead!

LILIOM. I didn't mean—I——

JULIE. What right have you to tell lies to the child? Take that plate, Louise, and let him be on his way. If he wasn't such a hungry-looking beggar, I'd put him out myself. (LOUISE *takes the plate out of his hand.*)

LILIOM. So he didn't hit you?

JULIE. No, never. He was always good to me.

LOUISE (*whispers*). Did he tell funny stories, too?

LILIOM. Yes, and *such* funny ones.

JULIE. Don't speak to him any more. In God's name, go.

LOUISE. In God's name.

[JULIE *resumes her seat at the table and eats.*]

LILIOM. If you please, Miss—I have a pack of cards in my pocket. And if you like, I'll show you some tricks that'll make you split your sides laughing. (LOUISE *holds* LILIOM's *plate in her left hand. With her right she reaches out and holds the garden gate shut.*) Let me in, just a little way, Miss, and I'll do the tricks for you.

LOUISE. Go, in God's name, and let us be. Why are you making those ugly faces?

LILIOM. Don't chase me away, Miss; let me come in for just a minute—just for a minute—just long enough to let me show you something pretty, something wonderful. (*Opens the gate.*) Miss, I've something to give you. (*Takes from his pocket a big red handkerchief in which is wrapped a glittering star from Heaven. He looks furtively about him to make sure that the* POLICE *are not watching.*)

LOUISE. What's that?

LILIOM. Pst! A star! (*With a gesture he indicates that he has stolen it out of the sky.*)

JULIE (*sternly*). Don't take anything from him. He's probably stolen it somewhere. (*To* LILIOM.) In God's name, be off with you.

LOUISE. Yes, be off with you. Be off. (*She slams the gate.*)

LILIOM. Miss—please, Miss—I've got to do something good—or—do something good—a good deed——

LOUISE (*pointing with her right hand*). That's the way out.

LILIOM. Miss——

LOUISE. Get out!

LILIOM. Miss! (*Looks up at her suddenly and slaps her extended hand, so that the slap resounds loudly.*) 10

LOUISE. Mother! (*Looks dazedly at LILIOM, who bows his head, dismayed, forlorn. JULIE rises and looks at LILIOM in astonishment. There is a long pause.*)

JULIE (*comes over to them slowly*). What's the matter here?

LOUISE (*bewildered, does not take her eyes off LILIOM*). Mother—the man—he hit me—on the hand—hard—I heard the sound of it—but it didn't hurt— 20 mother—it didn't hurt—it was like a caress—as if he had just touched my hand tenderly. (*She hides behind JULIE. LILIOM sulkily raises his head and looks at JULIE.*)

JULIE (*softly*). Go, my child. Go into the house. Go.

LOUISE (*going*). But mother—I'm afraid —it sounded so loud——(*Weepingly.*) And it didn't hurt at all—just as if 30 he'd—kissed my hand instead— mother! (*She hides her face.*)

JULIE. Go in, my child, go in.

[LOUISE *goes slowly into the house. JULIE watches her until she has disappeared, then turns slowly to LILIOM.*]

JULIE. You struck my child.

LILIOM. Yes—I struck her.

JULIE. Is that what you came for, to strike my child? 40

LILIOM. No—I didn't come for that— but I did strike her—and now I'm going back.

JULIE. In the name of the Lord Jesus, who are you?

LILIOM (*simply*). A poor, tired beggar who came a long way and who was hungry. And I took your soup and bread and I struck your child. Are you angry with me?

JULIE (*her hand on her heart; fearfully, wonderingly*). Jesus protect me—I don't understand it—I'm *not* angry—not angry at all——

[LILIOM *goes to the doorway and leans against the doorpost, his back to the audience. JULIE goes to the table and sits.*]

JULIE. Louise! (LOUISE *comes out of the house.*) Sit down, dear, we'll finish eating.

LOUISE. Has he gone?

JULIE. Yes. (*They are both seated at the table.* LOUISE, *her head in her hands, is staring into space.*) Why don't you eat, dear?

LOUISE. What has happened, mother?

JULIE. Nothing, my child.

[*The* HEAVENLY POLICEMEN *appear outside.* LILIOM *walks slowly off at left. The* FIRST POLICEMAN *makes a deploring gesture. Both shake their heads deploringly and follow* LILIOM *slowly off at left.*]

LOUISE. Mother, dear, why won't you tell me?

JULIE. What is there to tell you, child? Nothing has happened. We were peacefully eating, and a beggar came who talked of bygone days, and then I thought of your father.

LOUISE. My father?

JULIE. Your father—Liliom

[*There is a pause.*]

LOUISE. Mother—tell me—has it ever happened to you—has any one ever hit you—without hurting you in the least?

JULIE. Yes, my child. It has happened to me, too.

[*There is a pause.*]

LOUISE. Is it possible for some one to hit you—hard like that—real loud and hard—and not hurt you at all?

JULIE. It is possible, dear—that some one may beat you and beat you and beat you—and not hurt you at all.——

[*There is a pause. Near by an organ-grinder has stopped. The music of his organ begins.*]

THE CURTAIN FALLS

LUIGI PIRANDELLO

THE modern drama in Italy has generally avoided controversial topics involving religion, political issues, or social reform. The state failed to attain the promises held out by the movement for unification during the nineteenth century, and the spiritual life of the people declined slowly from the intensity of Cavour, Garibaldi, and Mazzini, whose inspiring statues in most towns and villages confronted an apathetic populace, to the cynicism and skepticism of the World War and the bitter years immediately following. Drama was more concerned with avenues of escape than with spirited plays on pressing topics in the manner of Ibsen and Shaw. It is significant indeed that Gabriele d'Annunzio and Luigi Pirandello have been the ranking dramatists of contemporary Italy.

D'Annunzio led the procession before the War, Pirandello after it. Though they were almost exact contemporaries (D'Annunzio was born in 1864, Pirandello in 1867), they were as different as the eras which they dominated. D'Annunzio flowered early and in the most flamboyantly romantic manner. He was a literary figure at sixteen and an eccentric international celebrity while Pirandello was still a relatively obscure teacher of literature at the Normal College for Women in Rome. D'Annunzio's personal relations with Eleanora Duse, his mistress and the leading actress of her day, were kept before the public as expertly and sensationally as his exploits as an aviator in the World War and his dramatic seizure of Fiume in 1919. His plays were as extravagant as his own life. Of the score of his dramas written between 1897 and the outbreak of the War in 1914, the three best and most representative were *The Dead City* (1898), *Gioconda* (1898), and *Francesca da Rimini* (1901), the last two written especially for Eleanora Duse, and all three famously enacted by her.

The plays are far removed from the Italy, or the world, of the close of the old century, though *Gioconda* is concerned with the triangular situation of a sculptor, his wife, and his mistress, and their relationship to the masterpiece which he is creating. It rationalizes D'Annunzio's life, and sets artistic temperament above conventional morality. *The Dead City*, as tenuously atmospheric as a play by Maeterlinck, is about an archaeologist uncovering the incestuous remains of the house of Atreus near the ruins of Mycenae. He reenacts a parallel tragedy by drowning his sister "to save her soul from the horror which was about to overwhelm it." Duse played the part of the graceful blind Anna. *Francesca da Rimini* is D'Annunzio's treatment of the Francesca legend: romantic embroidery on a realistic design. In each of the plays there was a part designed for Duse's style of acting —no make-up, veil-like draped garments, rhythmic gestures with the beautiful hands, sculptural poses, and a musical voice suited to the poetic drama. D'Annunzio summed up his plays and her acting when he said that her task "is to speak of all the beautiful things in the shadow of an antique statue."

Pirandello (June 1867—December 1936) takes us into a radically different world beside which D'Annunzio's bodiless plays seem like antiques. For Pirandello is modernity itself in one of its most intriguing manifestations—the problem of the relativity of personality and the illusion of truth. There have been three subjects peculiarly set apart for the post-war period; one is social problems growing out of the machine age with its booms and its depressions; the second is political issues reaching from local problems to the clash of national ideologies; and the third is, paradoxically, a complete renunciation of social and political topics and a preoccupation with psychological states and the vagaries of the subconscious. Pirandello excels in this psychological field.

In comparison with D'Annunzio, Pirandello's life was obscure and uneventful. It was, none the less, loaded with quiet, private experiences which became the subject matter of his plays and stories. He was born in the beautiful and ancient Greek and Roman town of Girgenti (rechristened Agrigentum by the Fascists) in southern Sicily. From its high, narrow ridge, the town looks off toward the sea and the low ridge above it along which are the five Doric temples, unequalled outside of Greece itself, gleaming solitary in the sun. Pirandello's father, the owner of sulphur mines, was in easy circumstances, and the son received a thorough education. He went up to Rome to study at the age of nineteen; later he went on to Germany and specialized in philosophy at the University of Bonn. He returned to the Italian capital and entered upon his career as a teacher, which continued from 1907 until 1923, when he transferred all his energies to the theatre.

Pirandello had one period of interest in public affairs during the 1890's when the Roman Bank failed and the desperate Sicilian peasants rose in revolt against the crown and seized some of its lands, only to be shot by the carabinieri. Pirandello was indignant, but he did not become a reformer; he retreated from the issues involved into his own philosophic ivory tower and protected himself with a mask of cynical disillusionment. Time and again he has attempted to sum up in a compact sentence or two his vision of life's eternal riddle. Perhaps the most characteristic is this passage: "I see, as it were, a labyrinth where our soul wanders through countless conflicting paths without ever finding its way out. In this labyrinth I see a two-headed Hermes which with one face laughs and with the other weeps. It laughs with one face at the other face's weeping." That view seemed to grow upon Pirandello as the years passed and "the ferocious derision" of destiny, as he phrased it, condemned him to illusion, or the creation of an illusion.

It is not our purpose to pry into Pirandello's private life beyond the facts already made public which help to explain the singular and often mystifying content of the plays. He began to write poetry about the time he left Sicily to study in Rome. At the age of twenty-three he turned to fiction, and for a quarter of a century averaged nearly a book a year of short stories and novels. The most widely known of these is *The Late Mattia Pascal* (1904), which was neglected for twenty years and then had an international success after the author had become known as a dramatist. The novel is interesting to us because it deals with a theme that recurs in all the plays: how a man feigns death in order to escape one life to begin another nearer to his illusion of desire.

Pirandello did his writing in the isolation of his apartment on the outskirts of Rome while carrying on his duties as teacher in the school for girls. His domestic situation might have been both the setting and the plot for one of his plays. In 1894 he had married Antonietta Portulano, the daughter of his father's business associate in the sulphur mines. Ill health and a mine disaster that destroyed their fortune unsettled his wife's mental balance. She created difficult, sometimes violent scenes that threw Pirandello and the children into states of desperation, echoes of which are certainly to be found in such plays as *Six Characters in Search of an Author, Naked, Right You Are, As You Desire Me.* Pirandello did not send her away, but for over fifteen years, until her death in 1918, looked after her at home even after her psychopathic jealousy, violence, and suspicions had made normal family life impossible. He suffered over the experiences of his sons in the Italian army during the war. It is a natural inference that the dramatist's preoccupation with the "incommunicability" between men, with the problem of the multiple self, and the relativity of all truth, stems naturally from those years of tribulation. In 1910 he wrote, "Life is a very sad buffoonery, because, without any possibility of knowing or learning why or from what source, we bear within us the need to deceive ourselves continually with the spontaneous creation of a reality (a different reality for each one of us, and never the same reality for all) which, from time to time, reveals itself to be vain and illusory. He who understands the joke does not succeed in fooling himself any longer; but he who cannot fool himself any longer can no longer find zest nor pleasure in life."

After a full quarter of a century of writing in his grim seclusion, he was persuaded to adapt one of his dramatic short stories for the stage. Its success was encouraging. With astounding energy and perseverance he began to convert more of his stories into plays and to write directly for the stage. His plays were successful in Italian theatres. In 1921, the riotous reception of his *Six Characters in Search of an Author* carried his name far beyond his native Italy, first to London, then to America, and soon to all the countries of the world. He immediately gave up his teaching post, came out of his unsocial retirement, and became an active international figure, urbane, polished, well-dressed and peripatetic, flying back and forth between the theatres of Europe and visiting America. Mussolini was hospitable to him, as he was also to D'Annunzio. Pirandello organized a company of his own, with headquarters at the Teatro Odescalchi, specializing in the more advanced, intellectual type of play. The company toured Europe. The Italian actress Marta Abba, first introduced to American audiences in the successful *Tovarich* in 1936–37, was to the Pirandello plays what Duse was to D'Annunzio's dramas. She appeared in all his leading plays and toured with them in Europe and South America. *As You Desire Me* was dedicated to her. Pirandello's mounting fame was recognized in 1934 when he was awarded the Nobel Prize in literature. When he died in December, 1936, his popularity had been strained only once, and that was when, on a visit to America, he approved of Mussolini's conquest of Ethiopia and the fascist policies of his native state.

The list of Pirandello's plays is quite extensive, and it would be pointless to run through all forty-odd of them. They are all characteristically Pirandello. Viewed as a whole, and as nearly chronologically as their confusion of order permits, they show a fairly distinct development within the limited field which they exploit. The first ones were done in Sicilian dialect on subjects and characters suggested by Pirandello's early years at Girgenti. *Sicilian Limes* (1913), one of his earliest pieces, is almost as simple and native as a play by Synge. A generous souled man from a Sicilian village goes up into Italy to see the prima donna whom he had at one stage aided to success. She makes him feel quite out of place among her fine new friends. The title refers to the limes which he had brought from the village as a present to her. Complicate that artless situation with subtle speculations on the instability of the self and the nature of truth and you have the pattern of the later dramas.

The next group of plays have a deft touch in the comic manner, though beneath the glittering surface is an undertow of melancholy and disillusion. Many of them deal with domestic situations complicated by adultery, illegitimacy, the desire to save appearances, the wreckage wrought by gossip, and similar unpleasant but not uncommon subjects. *The Rights of Others* (1915), *Just Think, Giacomo* (1914), *The Pleasure of Honesty* (1914), *Cap and Bells* (1915), and several more are all concerned with these problems. This material seems so ill-favored that Silvio D'Amico, writing about Pirandello as a Nobel prize winner, observed: "His success is a phenomenon all the more extraordinary when one considers the themes with which the plays deal and the miserable protagonists which they invariably set upon the stage. Almost always . . . they are humble people of the petit-bourgeoisie, ill-favored little tenants of drab boarding-houses and poor provincial offices, miserable little job-holders, tired little professors, and poor jaded little women. A gray and completely anonymous environment from which—with a confessed tour de force that bids fair to surpass Ibsen's achievements with his middle-class heroes—Pirandello is intent on creating a renaissance of high tragedy."

During the period of the World War and the years immediately following, Pirandello was greatly interested in the "grotesque theater" of an Italian experimentalist, Luigi Chiarelli. Chiarelli and his associates broke with the conventional drama of the past and tried to supplant "the bourgeois well-made play" with what Walter Starkie, Pirandello's biographer, called "a new critical drama which will be an expression of the modern active mentality." Starkie claims for Pirandello the credit for spreading "the ideas of the grotesque theater" over Europe. *Six Characters in Search of an Author*, Pirandello's best known play, is the classic example of this style.

The grotesque period blends almost imperceptibly into the last and fully matured phase of Pirandello's psychological dramas. These are the plays that have carried his name to all the world and have given him his place among the great in modern drama. The most important of them, besides *Six Characters in Search of an Author*, are *Henry IV* (1922), *Naked* (1922), *As You Desire Me* (1930), and *Tonight We Improvise* (1931).

Six Characters in Search of an Author is interesting for its novelty and its illusive but intriguing themes and subject. The central idea teases the mind. Characters created in the imagination of the author and released into life by the magic of his art may easily become more real than the author himself. Hamlet is much more clearly defined as a character than Shakespeare, his creator. We are to suppose, however, that an author had actually created a set of characters in his mind but had refused to give them freedom in life by completing the work of art in which they were to function. "I wrote *Six Characters*," Pirandello said, "in order to free myself from a nightmare. Why, I asked myself, do I not represent the absolutely novel situation of an author who refuses to give life to certain of his personages, born living in his imagination, and who already having life refused them, will not resign themselves to remain outside the world of art." These characters, living but without life, are in a state something like that of a disembodied spirit wandering homeless through space. Pirandello imagines such a group of characters who have been given the reality of thought but not of words and action. They come desperately on stage where a company is rehearsing Pirandello's play *Mixing It Up*, and demand the right to enact the play for which they were imagined. In a fragmentary manner, with much speculation and a few tragic episodes, they unfold their unhappy domestic relationship. The three general levels of reality are constantly maintained: that of the living actors, that of the characters which they represent, and finally the fluid state of the six people in search of an author. The sense of the play is that no one of these planes is more real than the others.

The logical counterpart of a play about characters searching for an author would be a set of characters fleeing from an author. Once we get into this strange world of speculation, we can easily imagine that the dramatis personae of a projected work of art might object to the life they were about to have thrust upon them by the author, might resent, resist, and try to escape. This aspect of Pirandello's problem is presented in a play even more baffling than *Six Characters* entitled *Tonight We Improvise*. The play itself begins with a lecture on these and other abstruse points about art as fixity and life as motion and fluidity. Life itself, says Pirandello, is an improvisation, and the actor feels terrified without his lines. And they are foredoomed to say the lines thrust upon them by the author.

Henry IV is an equally teasing play on the subject of reality, this time on the sanity of insanity. As the result of an accident to a nobleman on his way to a masked ball dressed as Emperor Henry IV of Germany, he has imagined himself to be the emperor whom he was impersonating. Is he insane, or is this a pose that he keeps up through the years because he finds the life of his illusion preferable to the one he has cast off? At the moment of crisis when the alienist tries a trick to catapault him back into reality, Henry IV seems to come out of his pose long enough to suggest that it is only a pose; and when he stabs his rival he is ironically forced to continue (or pretend) his insanity. We are left balancing the question: who is insane and how do you know? while the skeptical eyes of Pirandello twinkle at us over the shoulder of Henry.

Naked tells the harassing story of Ersilia, a governess, whose drab life was too sorry for her to contemplate. She covers it up and confuses it almost beyond recognition by lies that cast over her the shadow of virtue. Then, after taking poison, she withdraws all the previous lies and lays bare both the involved motives for her acts and the truth behind them. "I must die discovered—despised—humiliated—found out . . . naked." The novelist, to whose rooms she has been brought, then makes a comment that could serve as a statement of the central idea in *Right You Are* and *As You Desire Me*. "Facts," he observes, "are what we assume them to be; and then, in their reality, they cease to be facts, and become mere semblances of life which appear in this or that or some other way."

In the play which we have chosen, the truth appears in the unstable relativity suggested by its title, *As You Desire Me*. It is the best of the several dramas, including *Right You Are, Each in His Own Way*, etc., dealing with the disconcerting problem of motives and actual personal identity. In *Right You Are* the identity of Signora Ponza is in question. Her husband contends that she is his second wife, and that Signora Frola, mother of his first wife, is insane and believes that her daughter still lives. Signora Frola says Ponza is insane; he thinks his first wife was killed, and they had to allow him to marry her again. But couldn't the woman herself make firm and final answer? She is brought before us, but her reply is the thesis of Pirandello that we are not one but a group of personalities created by other people. She says, "The truth? The truth is simply this. I am the daughter of Signora Frola, and I am the second wife of Signor Ponza. Yes, and— for myself, I am nobody, I am nobody . . . I am . . . whoever you choose to have me."

In *As You Desire Me* the theme is more engagingly handled, with greater subtlety and more overtones. The plot and the basic incidents were based upon a well-known case of mixed identity that was the talk of Italy for a time. Is The Strange Lady, as she is called in the play, the missing wife of Bruno who was lost during the Austrian invasion and is now wanted to settle an inheritance? Or is she an imposter with an accidental resemblance to the missing Cia? The evidence is perfectly balanced to establish the identity and then to cancel it out. The point emerges that the objective fact itself does not actually matter; the reality is in the attitude of belief or doubt toward the fact. The Strange Lady says to Bruno, "I came here; I gave myself to you utterly, utterly; I said to you: 'Here I am; I am yours; there is nothing left in me, nothing of my own; take me and make me, make me over, as you desire me!' " His belief creates the reality, his doubt destroys it, and The Strange Lady gives up her new identity and departs. The evanescent values of the play were beautifully realized in the cinema version starring Greta Garbo, and in the successful New York run in 1931 with Judith Anderson.

As You Desire Me, like its kindred plays, is more than virtuosity, more than technical ingenuity. It is a brilliant attempt to find a statement and a form for presenting some of the more illusive psychological and philosophical questions so peculiarly a part of our modern intellectual world. Pirandello has succeeded better than anyone else in the statement and its dramatization. The plays which at first meeting seem fragmentary or experimental reveal their solid substance on closer study; they survive after their novelty has worn off because there is always enough human passion, heart, and blood in them to carry the speculative burden with which they are weighted. They are good theatre, but they require thoughtful and imaginative reading. Pirandello, with all his skepticism, nightmares, Freudianism, relativisms, grotesqueries, and pessimistic outlook, found in art and creation the illusion that made up for the bitterness of life. "Each of us," he said in his full maturity in *Tonight We Improvise*, "seeks to create himself and his own life with those same mental and spiritual faculties with which the poet creates his art

work. As a matter of fact, the one who is better equipped for the task does succeed in attaining a higher state of more enduring existence. . . . Art, in a certain sense, is a revenge on life, for the reason that in so far as its own life is a true creation, in just so far is it free of time, of circumstances and of obstacles with no other end than its own proper self." He might have been giving a summary of *As You Desire Me*, upon which he was working at the same time.

AS YOU DESIRE ME

CHARACTERS

THE STRANGE LADY
CARL SALTER, *a writer*
GRETA, *his daughter, known as Mop*
BRUNO PIERI
BOFFI
AUNT LENA CUCCHI
UNCLE SALESIO NOBILI
INEZ MASPERI, *wife of*

SILVIO MASPERI, *a lawyer*
BARBARA, *Bruno's sister*
THE DEMENTED LADY
A DOCTOR
A WOMAN NURSE (*silent part*)
FOUR YOUTHS IN EVENING DRESS
A PORTER

The first act takes place at Berlin, in the house of the writer, Carl Salter; the other two in a villa near Udine; ten years after the great European War.

ACT I

Living-room in the home of Salter, the writer; a note of bizarre magnificence in the decorations. Door in the center, which opens into a wide vestibule. Through it may be had a glimpse of the door to the apartment. In the right wall (the actor's "right" and "left," always) is a good-sized archway, through which may be seen a part of the rear wall of the study.

It is night, and accordingly, the living-room as well as the study is lighted up by a number of lamps with varicolored shades, which throw into fantastic relief the weirdly ornate furnishings and suffuse the scene with a feeling of the mysterious and the uncanny.

At the rise of the curtain, Mop is discovered, crouched down in a wide easy-chair; she is clad in a curious suit of black silk orchid-flowered pajamas and is all huddled up on the edge of the chair, her face buried in her arms. She looks as if she were sleeping. She is weeping. Her hair is boyishly cut, and her face (as she lifts it) has a certain strange look 10

that makes one shudder; there is in it something of the tragic that is deeply affecting. A moment later, Carl Salter enters from the archway to the right; he is in a state of excitement and greatly upset. He is fifty. Pale, puffy face, with bright, almost whitish eyes, circled with dark bags. A trifle bald on top, he has a short dense growth of bristling iron-gray hair, and there is an extremely sensual quality to his thick lips, which he has a trick of puffing out. He is in an expensive lounging-robe. His hands in the pockets.

SALTER. She's down there, with the usual crowd. I saw her from the window. (*As he says this, he, with seeming inadvertence, takes one hand out of his pocket. This hand nervously grips a small revolver.*)

MOP (*catching sight of it*). What have you there?

SALTER (*who has quickly put the hand with the weapon back into his pocket; he is an-*

AS YOU DESIRE ME: Translated from the Italian by Samuel Putnam. Published and copyright, 1931, by E. P. Dutton & Co., Inc., New York.

noyed). Nothing.—Look here: if she brings them up, I forbid you to stay.

MOP. And what do you expect me to do?

SALTER. I don't know. There must be an end to this.

MOP. What do you mean, an end? Are you mad?

SALTER. I don't intend to show myself, either. Go listen at the door and see if she's coming up alone. (MOP *starts to go out into the vestibule.*) Wait. (*He holds her back, and they listen.*) I hear her shouting.

[*From below comes the confused and distant sound of voices, echoing up the stair.*]

MOP. Perhaps, she's saying good night to them.

SALTER. They are all drunk. And there's someone following them.

MOP. Give me that revolver!

SALTER (*trembling all over; he is hurt by the suggestion*). No, no! I haven't the slightest intention of making use of it. I just carry it—this way, in my pocket.

MOP. Give it to me!

SALTER. Don't annoy me! (*The voices are nearer and louder.*) Do you hear them?

MOP. Sounds like a quarrel.

[*They run out into the vestibule and open the door to the apartment. The vestibule, so far as can be seen through the door to the living-room, is at once violently invaded by a group of four very stupid and half-drunken young men in evening clothes; and in the midst of them are* THE STRANGE LADY *and* BOFFI, *who is acting as her protector.* MOP *and* SALTER *are lost in the throng, the former being engaged in trying to rescue* THE STRANGE LADY, *while her father endeavors to repel the intruders. In the dim light and the confusion, one of the youths is seen to be fat and ruddy-faced; another is bald; another, more woman than man, has bleached hair; and all have the general appearance of battered mario-*nettes, *as they awkwardly whirl their arms about in meaningless gestures. They are all shouting at once.* THE STRANGE LADY *is in her thirties, and very beautiful. A little intoxicated herself, she cannot quite manage her usual dark frown, which is evidence of a desire on her part to make up thus, by a contempt for everybody and everything, for a state of desperation and abandonment in which, if she were to let herself go, she would lose hold of her very soul, swept as it has been by all the storms of life. Under a cloak of the utmost elegance, she wears one of those weird and gorgeous costumes that go with the dances of which she is the originator.* BOFFI *has the air of being out of place. He is, none the less, an up-and-coming, rash and headstrong fellow; being convinced that life is nothing more than a trick, he is smilingly bent upon not losing the trick in question. He has scrambled together a Mephistophelian sort of countenance, but his intent is jovial. It is all a mask, partly by way of keeping up appearances and making an impression; partly, also, by way of preserving a certain natural simplicity and steadiness. From a habit of jerking up his head as if he were suffocating, he has contracted a twitching in the muscles of his neck, which causes him from time to time to stick out his chin and draw in the corners of his mouth. He always laughs at this, remarking half to himself: "Let's be serious!"*]

THE STRANGE LADY. No, that's enough, that's enough! I won't have any more! You must go now! There is such a thing as carrying a joke too far!

FIRST YOUTH. . . . one more dance among the wine-glasses. . . .

SECOND. . . . a stirrup cup! a stirrup cup! . . . "Sparkling Champagne" . . .

THIRD. and we'll all join in the chorus. . . .

FOURTH (*striking up, with a thick tongue*). . . . Clo-o-o—dovee-o . . . Clo-o—dovee-o. . . .

FIRST YOUTH. . . . all bored to death. . . .

THE STRANGE LADY. Go away! Go away!

BOFFI. Get out of here! Get out!— Yes, yes, it's all very fine! But enough's enough! You heard what she said!

SALTER. Get out of my house! Get out of my house!

FIRST YOUTH. That's no way to do! We want a little drink!

SECOND. She invited us; don't be silly!

THIRD. And we'll end up stripped!

FOURTH. . . . Clo-o-o—dovee-o. . . . (*Striking his chest*). Beasts!

MOP. You ought to be ashamed! This is an outrage! (*She puts her arms about* THE STRANGE LADY, *as if to draw the latter protectively into the room; she says to her.*) Come on! Come on!

THE STRANGE LADY (*freeing herself from* MOP'S *embrace*). No, no, for heaven's sake, all I needed was that from you!

SALTER (*in the vestibule, stemming the irruption, with* BOFFI'S *assistance*). Gentlemen, I shall be forced to chase you away with a revolver!

BOFFI (*pushing them through the door*). Get out! Get out! That's all, now! Out with you! Out!

FIRST YOUTH (*just before the door slams in his face*). Elma, dearie!

SECOND YOUTH. The bastard!

MOP. They make me sick!

[*The door is closed, and the four youths take their departure; but shouts may still be heard from the stairway outside, while the* THIRD *stubbornly keeps on singing:* "Clo-o-o—dovee-o. . . ."]

SALTER. What were they after?

THE STRANGE LADY. The same old story. . . . Swine . . . they made me drink so much. . . .

SALTER. It's a disgrace! All the tenants will be complaining!

THE STRANGE LADY. Put me out; I've told you to!

MOP. No, Elma, no!

THE STRANGE LADY. He says it's a disgrace. . . .

SALTER. It would be all right, if you would only stop going out with them!

THE STRANGE LADY. Well, I'm going out with them right now! Just watch! I'd rather. (*She darts forward.*) I'm going to join them!

BOFFI (*stopping her*). Signora Lucia!

THE STRANGE LADY (*pausing*). Who are you, if I may ask?

SALTER. Right enough: how does it come that you're still here?

BOFFI. I've been looking out for the Signora.

SALTER. He's a hanger-on; I saw him.

THE STRANGE LADY. I always have him with me—so many evenings now— like a bodyguard.

MOP. And yet, you don't know who he is?

BOFFI. Ah, yes, the Signora knows very well who I am. (*He twitches.*) Let's be se-e-e-rious! (*And, as if calling upon her to surrender.*) Signora Lucia. . . .

MOP (*in amazement*). Lucia?

THE STRANGE LADY. That's the way he keeps it up—like that—running the scale—"Signora Lucia"—"Signora Lucia"—following me, elbowing me as he passes—

BOFFI. —and she always turns!

THE STRANGE LADY. —I suspect—

BOFFI. —for the reason that she *is* Signora Lucia—

MOP. No, no—

BOFFI. Yes! she gives a start, every time, and turns pale—

THE STRANGE LADY. Naturally, when you hear someone calling you—

BOFFI (*correcting her, with a stress on the first syllable*). —*re*-calling you—

THE STRANGE LADY. —at night—you can just imagine—with that devil's face of his—

BOFFI. It's all a part of the game, Signora! No one is really a devil—

THE STRANGE LADY. It's your profession, so to speak?

BOFFI. Exactly: my profession; it's the part I play—just as you are playing your little part in the presence of these good people—and yet, you're Signora Lucia all the while.

MOP. Oh, that's a pretty story!

THE STRANGE LADY. You can see, can't you, that he hasn't the slightest doubt about it?

BOFFI. I'll cut off both my hands, if it isn't true.

SALTER. You're sure you haven't an extra pair at home?

BOFFI. No, sir, these are all I have; and I'm staking them.

THE STRANGE LADY. On my being Signora Lucia——?

BOFFI. Pieri.

THE STRANGE LADY. What's that you say?

BOFFI. Don't pretend that you don't know that name!

THE STRANGE LADY. No, I didn't hear what you said!

BOFFI (turning to SALTER; his manner is at once denunciatory and defiant). I said Pieri. And the Signora's husband is here!

THE STRANGE LADY (overcome, she sinks into a chair). My husband?

BOFFI. Yes, Signora, Bruno is here.

THE STRANGE LADY. What are you talking about? Here? Where?

SALTER. She's out of her head!

BOFFI. Sent for by me.

THE STRANGE LADY. You're mad!

BOFFI. He arrived this evening.

SALTER. The Signora's husband has been dead for four years!

THE STRANGE LADY (to SALTER, on the spur of the moment, and as the result of an uncontrollable impulse). No, no, that's not true!

SALTER (rooted to the spot). It's not true?

BOFFI. He's here! At the Eden Hotel. A few steps away.

THE STRANGE LADY (to BOFFI; very excited). Let's stop jesting about my husband! I have no husband! Who sent for him?

BOFFI. Do you see how worked up she is?

SALTER (to THE STRANGE LADY). Is he still alive, then?

BOFFI (replying for her). I am telling you, he is only a few steps from here! If the Signora would like. . . . (He looks around the room.) There is the telephone. . . .

[THE STRANGE LADY suddenly bursts out laughing, like a mad woman.]

SALTER (upon hearing her laugh). What is the meaning of all this, anyway?

THE STRANGE LADY. Didn't you hear him? He says I have a husband a few steps from here. I can even call him on the telephone, if I feel like it!

SALTER (to BOFFI, by way of cutting the matter short). You can see for yourself, Sir, that it would be unbecoming either in me or in you (He nods toward THE STRANGE LADY.) to carry this buffoonery any further!

THE STRANGE LADY (to SALTER, jestingly but, at the same time, defiantly). Wait a moment. And supposing I really were?

SALTER. Who?

THE STRANGE LADY. Why, that same Signora Lucia whom this gentleman is so sure he recognizes in me. What would you say to that?

SALTER. You heard what I said—buffoonery!

THE STRANGE LADY. And what about your own actions?

SALTER. Mine?

THE STRANGE LADY. Yes. Do you fancy you know me better than he does?

SALTER. I know you better than you know yourself!

THE STRANGE LADY (*with a bow*). That is no great feat! It has been so long now since I wanted to know myself!

SALTER. Very convenient, when you don't care to be called to account for what you do!

THE STRANGE LADY. On the contrary, old dear, it is *indispensable*, if I am to be able to endure what others do to me.

BOFFI (*spontaneously*). Splendid!

SALTER (*whirling on him like a mad dog*). What do you mean, splendid?

BOFFI. The way she came back at you! (*He adds, in a pitying tone.*) And what life has done to her!

THE STRANGE LADY. Try to realize, if you want to understand me a little— (*Turning on* SALTER.) that this gentleman's "Signora Lucia," for example, is in a way "somebody" even to me— (*Takes* BOFFI *by the arm.*) do you think that, after this, I could bear to go on living here with him? (*She suddenly turns, capriciously, from* BOFFI *to* MOP.) Tell me, Mop: what's my name!

MOP. Elma!

THE STRANGE LADY. Elma, did you hear? An Arabic name. Do you know what it means? Water . . . water. . . . (*As she says this, she moves her fingers, stretching out her hands, by way of signifying the deliberate lack of consistency in the life she now leads. Then, her tone changes.*) But they made me drink so much wine! Good heavens, five cocktails, champagne. . . . (*To* MOP.) Supposing you were to give me something to eat?

MOP. Yes, right away! What would you like?

THE STRANGE LADY. Ah . . . I don't know. . . . I'm burning up!

MOP. I'll run see. . . .

THE STRANGE LADY. Don't put yourself to too much trouble, dear—

MOP. —a sandwich or two?—

THE STRANGE LADY. and a crust of bread, just to have something in my stomach and stop my head from going round and round.

MOP. Yes, yes, I'll go see! (*She runs out to the right.*)

SALTER (*to* BOFFI). Will you be so good as to admit that you have made a mistake and go?

THE STRANGE LADY. Let him stay! He's an acquaintance of mine. . . .

BOFFI. The Signora knows that I have not made a mistake.

THE STRANGE LADY. Only don't call my husband on the telephone; I don't want you to do that.

BOFFI (*resolutely*). Signora, your husband. . . .

SALTER (*breaking in upon him violently*). That's enough about her husband! (*Whirling on* THE STRANGE LADY.) You told me he had been dead for four years!

BOFFI (*quickly, raising his voice*). The Signora lied!

THE STRANGE LADY (*she rises, goes over and grasps* BOFFI's *hand*). Thanks, Signor, for that statement.

BOFFI. Ah, God be thanked!

SALTER. So you lied, did you?

THE STRANGE LADY. Yes. (*She adds, to* BOFFI.) But wait a moment before you thank God. I was thanking you for the satisfaction you gave me by asserting so forcefully my right to lie, in view of the life I lead. (*To* SALTER.) Should you like to have me give you an account of all my lies? Then give me an account of yours!

SALTER. I have never lied!

THE STRANGE LADY. You have never lied? Why, we none of us do anything else!

SALTER. Never, to you!

THE STRANGE LADY. Merely because, on certain occasions, you have had the impudence to tell me . . . ?

SALTER (*cutting her short, violently*). —that will do!—

THE STRANGE LADY. —you lie to yourself, even in your nasty little sincerities; and so, it is not even true that you are the terrible person you would make yourself out to be. But you may find consolation in this fact: that no one is ever, really, an utter liar. We merely try to make others and ourselves swallow certain things! Four years ago, old dear, "someone" may have died for me, even if it wasn't my husband; and there may, accordingly, be some truth in this—as in all the stories that are told. (*To* BOFFI.) But that is not saying that my husband is alive and here—at least, so far as I am concerned. (*She is playing a game, the game of mystery, as if she were improvising a poem.*) He is the husband, at the very most—of one who is no more!—He is a poor widower. Which is equivalent to saying that—as a husband—he is dead. Go on and tell us the story; it must be an interesting one, if he has come all this way. And we'll get at the truth at last concerning this Signora Lucia who is supposed to be myself. (*To* SALTER.) Listen, listen. . . .

BOFFI (*stepping forward, decisively*). Will you let me have a word with you, Signora, a word between ourselves!

THE STRANGE LADY. Between ourselves? In heaven's name, no! Say it here, in front of him; I want him to know— (*She reclines.*) As you are aware, there are no more secrets nowadays; there is no such thing as modesty.

SALTER. Like animals!

THE STRANGE LADY. Ah, well—at least, God knows, animals are natural—

SALTER (*growing more contemptuous all the while*). —animal instinct—

THE STRANGE LADY. —while humanity (*She turns and stretches out.*) is terror-ridden, my dear Sir!— Nature is quite mad: bored to death, as Fritz would say—and she is also very filthy. We should be in a bad way, if we did not have the intelligence to construct a strait-jacket. . . . (*To* MOP, *who has come in with a sandwich.*) Ah, good girl; so you found one? (*She takes a sandwich.*) Excuse me. (*She bites into it.*) I'm so hungry!

MOP. But look at your sleeve. . . .

THE STRANGE LADY. Torn? It must have been those puppies. . . .

MOP. No, it just seems to be ripped a little.

THE STRANGE LADY. Do you know that, this evening, I couldn't manage to knock the bottle down? I don't know, but I must have been too far away. . . . (*As she says this, she nimbly kicks off her slippers, and, with the grace of a dancer, runs over on her toes to* BOFFI *and takes his opera hat from under his arm.*) Excuse me; you don't mind? (*She snaps it open and places it on the floor in front of her, in the center of the stage; then she prettily draws up her gown to her knees and, balancing herself on the tip of one foot, she lifts the other to the rhythm of a dance, as if to overturn a bottle of champagne in front of her, represented by the opera hat. She hums under her breath, by way of accompaniment.*) Tairirarari . . . tairirarari. . . . (*Twice, as she lifts her foot, she fails to brush the top of the opera hat.*) There, do you see? I was too far off. . . . (*She takes the hat, closes it against her bosom, and gives it back to* BOFFI.) Thanks. Signora

Lucia—I am sorry if her husband may not happen to like it—is a dancer at the "Lari-Fari," were you aware of that?

BOFFI. All this only makes me the more convinced that you are she. But how, if I may ask you, could I fail to recognize you—I, who have seen you grow up from a baby?

THE STRANGE LADY. Me? From a baby? Hear, hear. . . . And haven't I changed any, from that day to this?

BOFFI. Surely, you have changed, as everyone does; but very little, considering all that must have happened in the past!

THE STRANGE LADY (*after looking at him for a moment*). Do you know, you interest me, immensely? There are all the colors of the rainbow in my past. And even now—look—at those two —(*Points to* SALTER *and* MOP.) if you only knew!

SALTER (*fuming, as if he could not stand it any longer*). That will do! Have you no shame?

MOP. No, she's right, the poor dear. . . . (*She runs over to embrace her.*)

THE STRANGE LADY (*disgusted, slipping away quickly from the proffered embrace*). Mop, for heaven's sake!

SALTER (*to* MOP; *he is furious, and takes advantage of this show of disgust on the part of* THE STRANGE LADY). Leave her alone! And stop traipsing around like that in your pajamas; it's stupid! Go on to bed!

MOP (*tragically, confronting her father*). It is you who should be ashamed, not she!

THE STRANGE LADY (*restraining her, with wearied exasperation*). For God's sake, let's not begin all over again!

SALTER. Go on, I tell you, go on!

THE STRANGE LADY. Yes, run along,

dear; run along and see if you can scrape up another sandwich for me, eh?

MOP. And will you come out there and eat it?

THE STRANGE LADY. Yes, with the understanding that you are not to kiss me; you know I can't stand it! (SALTER *bursts into a ferocious laugh.*)

MOP. Wretch!

THE STRANGE LADY (*furiously, to* SALTER). Stop laughing like that! (*Then, turning to* BOFFI.) This is something that only I can understand. Jealous, one of the other!

MOP (*imploringly; she is deeply hurt*). No, Elma, don't say that!

THE STRANGE LADY. Ah, my dear—I wish it were not true—but look at him! (*Points to the father.*)

SALTER (*he sputters, with his hands in his pockets*). I've had all of this that I can stand!

THE STRANGE LADY (*teasing and cruel, turning to* BOFFI). His wife won't divorce him—sent the daughter to get the father away from me—and now, the daughter's formed an attachment for me—(*To* MOP.)—yes, my dear— I hate to tell you, but you're worse than he—for he—he may be old, but at least— (*Her meaning is:* "*He's a man. . . .*")

MOP (*she comes forward, first looks at her father, then turns to denounce him to* THE STRANGE LADY). He has a revolver in his pocket—for you—did you know that? I'm warning you!

THE STRANGE LADY (*turns and looks at* SALTER *coldly*). A revolver?

SALTER (*he does not reply, but, with a sneer on his lips, takes the revolver from his pocket and goes over and lays it on the table beside* THE STRANGE LADY). There it is, at your service. (*He goes back to where he stood.*)

THE STRANGE LADY (*with a smile*). Thanks, so much. Is it loaded?

SALTER. It's loaded.

THE STRANGE LADY (*takes up the weapon, as she inquires*). For me or for you?

SALTER. For whom you like.

BOFFI (*as she lifts the weapon*). Watch out, there. . . . (*He twitches.*) Let's be se-e-e-rious!

THE STRANGE LADY (*lowering the weapon, and then placing it upon the table once more; whirling on* BOFFI). Tragedy. Do you get it? (*She sits down.*)

SALTER (*with difficulty restraining himself*). Stop addressing your remarks to a stranger! Talk to me! This is the evening when we were to come to a decision. Do you mean to say you've forgotten it? I haven't, I assure you!

THE STRANGE LADY. What sort of decision—this sort? (*She looks at the revolver.*)

SALTER. I am ready for anything.

THE STRANGE LADY (*at this reply, she leaps to her feet; she is very pale and resolute; she snatches the weapon up again and points it at* SALTER). Do you want me to kill you? I could do that, too; don't think I couldn't! (*She relaxes, lowers the weapon.*) I am so tired of everything. . . . (*Goes up to him.*) Instead, I'm going to give you—look—a kiss, here on the forehead. (*Kisses him.*) You might at least say thank you. . . . (*Hands him the revolver.*) Take it, old dear; go ahead and kill me, if you like.

MOP (*impulsively*). No, no! He's capable of doing it!

THE STRANGE LADY. Let him do it! After all, when you're no longer of any use to yourself. . . . If only he had the courage. . . . (*Going back to her former place, she turns to* BOFFI *and, with a voice in which sincerity is mingled with* desolation, a voice which appears to be that of Weariness itself—a Weariness that has sunk to earth at last—she says to him.*) It is the truth I am telling you: I am at the end of my rope. . . . (*Then, as if she had got her breath.*) I am so hungry, you have no idea. I ask for bread, and he gives me a revolver. And you—you keep calling me "Signora Lucia." What a funny evening this is. . . .

SALTER (*with a sudden impulse, going up to* BOFFI). This is my house, and I am asking you to leave!

BOFFI. And I am not leaving. I am here on the Signora's account and not on yours.

SALTER. The Signora is a guest in my house!

THE STRANGE LADY. That is true; but surely, if I like, I can invite and entertain a gentleman who says he knows me.

BOFFI. What's more, are you in the habit of receiving guests with a revolver in your hand?

SALTER (*replying first to* THE STRANGE LADY). This is not the time, I can see, for us to come to an understanding. (*Then, turning on* BOFFI.) Did you get what I said—you are to leave?

BOFFI. Yes—but with the Signora!

THE STRANGE LADY (*suddenly rising, with an air of resolve*). Righto, yes—I'm coming with you!

SALTER (*leaping up in a terrible temper, he seizes her by the wrist*). You are not going out of here!

THE STRANGE LADY (*struggling to free the wrist which he holds in a vise-like grip*). Do you think you can stop me, if I want to go?

SALTER (*holding her firmly all the while*). Yes, I'll stop you!

THE STRANGE LADY. With brute strength?

SALTER. Yes—if you insist upon losing

your head over the first man that comes along!

BOFFI. I am not "the first man that comes along"!

THE STRANGE LADY. Let me go!

SALTER. No!

THE STRANGE LADY. I want to go with him!

BOFFI. You needn't use violence on the lady, when I assure you that I am an acquaintance of hers!

SALTER. You are an intruder here. As a matter of fact, the Signora does not know you.

BOFFI. It is not that she does not know me; she does not *want* to know me! I am Boffi.

THE STRANGE LADY (*speaks up quickly*). The photographer?

BOFFI (*triumphantly, to* SALTER). You see, she knows me.

SALTER. Boffi? (*Suddenly recalling.*) Ah, yes, the one who discovered—

BOFFI. —the stereoscopic portrait—precisely—

SALTER. —then, I doubt very much if she knows you! You have come here for an exhibition—

MOP. —and we saw the pictures in the papers, don't you remember? . . .

THE STRANGE LADY (*she is resolved to see the thing through; and so, she takes a short cut and gambles her all*). It's not true! I do know him! I do know him! He's a friend of my husband's! (*Renewing her struggles, she succeeds in freeing her wrist.*) Let me go!

SALTER. But you laughed at him a moment ago.

THE STRANGE LADY. That was because I did not want to give myself away!

BOFFI. Ah! but does the Signora imagine that her husband doesn't know?

THE STRANGE LADY. No, no, he couldn't! He couldn't!

BOFFI. He knows everything! He must have got all the evidence down there!

THE STRANGE LADY (*dumfounded; her question is instinctive*). Down there? Down where?

BOFFI. In the villa, where, I am sorry to say . . .

SALTER (*noting her bewilderment; in a tone of contemptuous doubt*). The villa? What villa? Come on and tell us! What villa?

THE STRANGE LADY (*quickly and proudly*). Mine! (*She turns to* BOFFI.) Tell me, what evidence could he have got? Let him throw it in the face of that wretch who took advantage of my desperate condition!

BOFFI. They heard your cries—the old gardener heard them—you know, Filippo—who died not long ago—

THE STRANGE LADY. Filippo! Yes!

BOFFI. How could you have defended yourself, all alone down there? It was enough for us, when we came back, to see all the horror, all the ruin that followed the invasion of our country. . . .

THE STRANGE LADY (*her face lights up, as at the miraculous recollection of an event at which she has actually been present*). Ah, the invasion! (*To* SALTER, *triumphantly.*) Do you hear? Do you hear?

SALTER (*checked in his wrath, he is forced to agree*). Yes, you have spoken to me of the invasion. . . .

THE STRANGE LADY. I am a Venetian!

BOFFI. We all had a taste of the enemy's ferocity—(*Addressing his remarks to* SALTER, *haughtily, as if hurling an infamous fact in the face of an old-time enemy.*) Bruno Pieri, an officer who had conducted himself bravely, comes back with the conquering army to his own country; he finds his villa a heap of ruins, and he finds there no trace of his young bride of barely a year—

THE STRANGE LADY. Bruno. . . .

BOFFI. His Cia. . . .

THE STRANGE LADY. Cia!—That was what he called me! That was what he called me! . . .

BOFFI. He pictured to himself what the officers who had been quartered in the villa must have done to you—and he was a madman, Signora, he was a madman for more than a year! You 10 cannot imagine how he searched for you those first few years, supposing, as he did, that you had been dragged along by the enemy in their flight.

THE STRANGE LADY. They did drag me along! They did drag me along!

SALTER (to BOFFI). Wait a minute! (As if ransacking his memory.) I seem to have read that story somewhere. . . .

BOFFI. You must have read it in the newspapers.

SALTER. Ah, yes—years ago. . . .

BOFFI. Her husband had the account published, years ago.

THE STRANGE LADY. I am sure I did not see it!

SALTER (to THE STRANGE LADY). You are an out-and-out impostor! (To BOFFI.) I should like to know something more 30 about the case—certain hypotheses on the part of a doctor friend of mine —a psychiatrist—of Vienna. . . . (Turning to THE STRANGE LADY again, with an attitude of contempt.) What are you trying to do, palm this story off as your own?

BOFFI. But what if she is the lady in the case!

SALTER (still more scornfully). You? 40

THE STRANGE LADY (very calmly). You hear what he says, don't you? He's known me since I was a baby.

BOFFI. And I cannot be mistaken!

THE STRANGE LADY. While you have known me for only a few months.

SALTER (loudly, with a convulsive outburst). I have wrecked my life for you!

THE STRANGE LADY. For your mad passion—not for me.

SALTER. Who was it made me lose my head?

THE STRANGE LADY. Was it I? You wanted to lose it, when you came to me.

SALTER. On account of your snares!

THE STRANGE LADY. Ah, my dear fellow, that's my woman's trade; life has brought me to it. Haven't you just heard what happened to me?

SALTER. I ask you, once for all, to stop taking advantage of the mistake which this gentleman persists in making!

BOFFI. I am not in the least mistaken!

20 THE STRANGE LADY. You shall see how I take advantage of it! (To BOFFI.) It was Heaven itself that sent you to me tonight! You are my savior. Talk to me, please, about my childhood. I was so different a being then that it seems to me I am dreaming, when I think of it now.

BOFFI. But that's the way it seems to all of us—the days of our youth—Signora Cia!

THE STRANGE LADY. Ah, so you call me Cia, too? Am I Cia to everybody? I thought only he. . . . Too bad!

SALTER (unable to restrain himself any longer). This is a fine way to leave me, after having trapped me as you did!

THE STRANGE LADY. I—trapped you?

SALTER. Yes, you.

THE STRANGE LADY. So, you have let yourself be trapped, have you? You should have been on your guard!— In a certain sense, it is true. But you have deceived me.

SALTER. I? Deceived you?

THE STRANGE LADY. Yes, deceived me. I took you for a clown, nothing more, and you have become insufferable, *insufferable!*

SALTER. Why won't you show me some mercy?

THE STRANGE LADY (*as if amazed*). I? Show you mercy? And you have the nerve to ask that? I *have* been merciful to you—how merciful! There is your daughter to show for it. . . . (*To* BOFFI.) You know, a famous writer . . .

SALTER (*abruptly breaking in upon her*). I forbid you to speak of me!

THE STRANGE LADY. Then, why do you bring up your wrecked life?

SALTER. So that you will be afraid, when you think about getting rid of me like this.

THE STRANGE LADY. I, afraid?

SALTER. Yes, afraid.

THE STRANGE LADY. I have never been afraid, like that.

SALTER. Then, you're going to be now!

THE STRANGE LADY. Why do you carry that revolver in your pocket?—Look here: I go off with this gentleman—Cia, if you please, my baby name. You take the revolver from your pocket, and you kill me—as a little joke.—Shall we try it?

SALTER (*shuddering*). Don't put me to the test!

THE STRANGE LADY. Here I am. (*To* BOFFI, *taking him by the arm.*) Come on.

[SALTER *takes the revolver from his pocket.*]

BOFFI (*throwing himself between them*). No, Signora, no! Not like that!

THE STRANGE LADY. I have been through the War! Let him kill me! He would have to kill himself afterward—and he hasn't the courage!

SALTER. I have—and you know very well that I have!

THE STRANGE LADY (*to* BOFFI). You will see. I could have kicked him into a corner, like this—like a bunch of old rags on the floor. . . .

SALTER. I am not a clown!

THE STRANGE LADY. What do you mean, you are not a clown? (*To* MOP.) Tell me, Mop: is it true or isn't it, that the reason he broke with your mother was that she was always reproving him for not being serious enough for one with his reputation as a writer?

MOP. Yes, it's true.

THE STRANGE LADY. A nasty, affected habit of pretending not to believe in himself, when callers came: "Excuse me, ladies and gentlemen, but I find it impossible to be serious in the presence of my wife, who—you can see for yourselves—watches over my reputation like a sitting hen!"

SALTER (*in exasperation*). I couldn't be serious! I couldn't be serious! (*To* BOFFI.) It is really terrible, my dear Sir, how a little silly laugh-provoking thing like that, and one, moreover, that's past and done with, can become a fixed idea—fixed forever. That is what I am, and I cannot be anything else; I've been stamped and labeled—a clown!

THE STRANGE LADY. Can you deny that that is what you were—a clown—when I first met you, in that set?

SALTER (*interrupting her, angrily*). That is because I was racked and tortured on the inside; life was impossible!

THE STRANGE LADY (*to* BOFFI). Did you see him chase the others away just now—with indignation? And now, it is he who is reproving me for compromising his reputation! He has turned into his own wife! (*She grows angry.*) So, I was to make life possible for you, was I? With your daughter who . . . Good heavens! (*In her disgust, her exasperation and her despair, she covers her face with her hands.*) Don't make me speak of her! Don't make me speak of her!

MOP (*running up to her quickly, in dismay*). No, no, Elma! Please!

THE STRANGE LADY (*repelling her, almost with a shout*). Get off me!—I want to tell it!

MOP. Tell what?

THE STRANGE LADY. What you've done to me?

MOP. I?

THE STRANGE LADY (*half out of her head*). You—all of you—I cannot stand it any longer—this is a mad life—I'm fed up on it—it turns my stomach—wine, wine—madmen, laughing madmen—hell let loose—mirrors, wineglasses, bottles—whirligig and a whirling head—dance and shout—they're all curled up together, naked —all the vices run together—no natural law any more—nothing any more—nothing but the obscene madness that comes from not being able to find any satisfaction—anywhere— (*Seizing* BOFFI's *arm, she points to* MOP.) —look, look! Is there any humanity left in that face? And look at him there! (*Points to* SALTER.)—look at that corpse-like face, and all the wriggling, wormy vices swarming in those eyes! And look at me, dressed like this—and you with your devil's face—look at this house—here as everywhere—the whole town—madness! madness! (*She points to* MOP *again.*) Something happened, I don't know what. I was spending the evening at the "Lari-Fari." No telling what took place between the two of them! She has a scratch here, from her forehead to her cheek—(*She takes* MOP's *face and turns it, so that* BOFFI *can see.*)—take a good look; she has the marks of it still!

SALTER. It wasn't I!

MOP. I did it myself—but you won't believe me!

THE STRANGE LADY. I don't know anything about it; I wasn't there!—This is the place that I come back to—when I have to!—drunk; I knock the bottles over with my foot, and then I drink what's in them—I do the "Sparkling Champagne"—(*Showing her costume.*)—do you see?—it's my most famous dance—and so, I have to get drunk every evening! But I don't see anyone tonight to carry me off to bed—

MOP (*almost leaping upon her, all a-tremble*). Elma, please, please! that's enough!

THE STRANGE LADY (*repelling her once more*). No, let me say what I was going to!—If he had gone out—

MOP (*still clutching her*). What do you mean? Are you crazy?

THE STRANGE LADY (*pushing her off and shoving her into a chair, where* MOP *huddles down with her face hidden*). Ah, yes, I know! Only the mad have the privilege of shouting certain things from the housetops. (*To* BOFFI, *pointing to* SALTER, *who is smiling.*)—Look at him; he's laughing . . . the way he laughed the morning after, when he wanted to know. . . .

SALTER. Because it is strange for you—

THE STRANGE LADY. —to give importance to what for you is nothing at all?—Everything is nothing here! (*She draws* SALTER's *attention to his daughter, whose face is still hidden.*) In the meanwhile, she—look at her!

SALTER. It is remorse for what she has done, for her betrayal. . . .

MOP (*leaping to her feet and screaming convulsively*). No! it's not fair! It's not fair!

THE STRANGE LADY (*to* BOFFI). Do you hear them proclaiming their rights? Accusing each other and shouting that it isn't fair! I must get away from all this—away from everybody, away from everybody—including myself—away—away—away—I cannot go on like this—this—

BOFFI. But, Signora, you can still go on with your life!

THE STRANGE LADY. —With my life? *What* life?

SALTER (*with a fierce scorn*). Why, your life as Signora Lucia—with your husband—you haven't forgotten already?

THE STRANGE LADY (*to* SALTER; *her voice is full of pride; emphatically*). I have not forgotten! (*To* BOFFI, *with another manner.*) This man, then, is still looking for his wife, after ten years?

SALTER. For his Cia—

BOFFI (*to* THE STRANGE LADY; *firmly*). Yes, Signora—(*Then to* SALTER, *defying his scorn.*) His Cia—(*To* THE STRANGE LADY *again.*) Notwithstanding the opposition of one to whose interest it was to have her looked upon as dead, after ten years—

SALTER (*suddenly—diabolic*). Who was that? To whose interest was it? You ought to know! Come on and tell us! Speak up! Out with it!

THE STRANGE LADY. *I know nothing about it!*—What I should like to know is, how could he go on believing that she was alive, if she did not come back to him?

BOFFI. Because he felt that, after all that must have happened to her—

THE STRANGE LADY. *The one he is looking for is no more!*

BOFFI. No, Signora! He supposed that you had not come back for the reason, simply, that you feared you could never again be the same to him, after what had happened—

THE STRANGE LADY. —and does he really think that she can be the same?

BOFFI. Why not, Signora, if you choose to be?

THE STRANGE LADY. The same, after ten years? After all that must have happened to her—the same?—He's mad! —And the proof is the fact that she has not come back to him.

BOFFI. But I am telling you, if at this moment you *want to*, Signora. . . .

THE STRANGE LADY. Want to?—yes, to flee from myself—I want to—no longer to remember anything, anything —to put my whole life behind me— here, look at this body—to be only this body—you say that it is *hers?* that I am like *her?*—I no longer feel anything—I no longer want anything—I no longer know anything— I do not even know myself—my heart beats, and I do not know it—I breathe, and I do not know it—I no longer know I am alive—a body, a body without a name, waiting for someone to come and take it!—Ah, well, if he can recreate me, if he can give a soul to this body, which is that of his Cia—let him take it, let him take it, and let him build out of his own memories—his own—a beautiful life, a beautiful new life—Oh, I am in despair!

BOFFI (*resolutely*). I'll run and call him right away, Signora!

SALTER. You will not call anyone to my house!

THE STRANGE LADY (*she starts to run to the writing-table near by*). I'll call him!

SALTER (*hastily restraining her*). No, wait. I'll go. I'll call him. And we shall see. (*He runs over to the writing-table.*)

THE STRANGE LADY (*stunned and bewildered*). Call? Call whom?

BOFFI. What do you want to do?

MOP (*she has turned to see what her father is doing in the other room, and at this point, she gives a scream of terror*). No! (*She springs forward, as a revolver shot rings out.*) Daddy! Daddy! O God! O God!

BOFFI (*running up*). He's done it!

THE STRANGE LADY. He's killed himself!

[*The anxious voices of all three are now heard, as they cluster about* SALTER'S *body in the writing-room; he has been wounded in the chest; they first inspect the body, and then lift it up, to get it onto a divan.*] 10

MOP. Through the heart! Through the heart!

BOFFI. No, no! He's not dead! His heart's untouched!

MOP. Oh, look—he's bleeding from the mouth!

BOFFI. It's pierced a lung!

THE STRANGE LADY. Lift him up, lift his head a little!

MOP. No, no—easy—let me! Daddy! 20 Daddy!

BOFFI. We must get him up! Lift him over there on the divan! Help me, help me!

MOP. Easy! Easy!

BOFFI. Come over on this side! Like this; that's the way. . . .

MOP. Mop, your Mop, Daddy. . . . Here, here . . . this way, easy, watch out for his head. . . . That 30 cushion, that cushion. . . .

THE STRANGE LADY. We must call a doctor, quick!

BOFFI. I'll go, I'll go. . . .

MOP. Speak, Daddy, speak. . . . What do you want to say? (*To* THE STRANGE LADY.) He's looking at you!

THE STRANGE LADY. It's not serious. . . . It can't be serious. . . . But quick, the doctor. . . . 40

MOP (*to* BOFFI). Yes, the doctor—look, there's one right here, in this house!— There's the bell, and there's someone pounding on the door. . . .

[*The ringing of the bell and the pounding are audible.*]

BOFFI. Just a minute, just a minute, I'm coming. . . .

THE STRANGE LADY (*following* BOFFI *out*). The doctor is right on the floor below.

[BOFFI *has opened the door, and a gigantic, typically German porter comes in; he is furious and disheveled.*]

PORTER. Wha-a-t's all this? Wha-a-t's all this? When are we going to have some peace in this house? And now, it's gun-play, is it?

THE STRANGE LADY. Yes, yes—look— there he is—over there—Herr Salter —he's wounded himself!

PORTER. Wounded? How? Wounded himself?

BOFFI. Yes, through the lung—did it himself—it's serious!

THE STRANGE LADY. Please run and call Dr. Schutz right away!

PORTER. Dr. Schutz is asleep at this time of night!

BOFFI. Wake him up, then!

THE STRANGE LADY. Yes, yes, please! We must have aid for him at once!

PORTER. I'm not waking anybody up! That would put the house in an uproar! We've had enough of this!

BOFFI. I'll go, I'll go call him!

PORTER (*promptly catching him and holding him back*). You're not going out of that door, not while there's a wounded man here!

BOFFI (*wrenching his arm loose*). You're crazy!

PORTER. It's the tenants who are crazy! Those are the apartment house rules! I know the walls and stairways; they're all padded; that's the way they live; I know the rules of the house, and I'll make my report! Where's the wounded man? Over here? Is it serious?

BOFFI. Yes, yes, of course it's serious; we must get help for him!

PORTER. But I am telling you, if it's serious . . .

MOP (*coming in suddenly from the other room*). Listen, I think it would be better if we took him to a hospital. . . . There's no one here!

PORTER. That's right; now you're talking; get him out of here; get him to a hospital. . . . I can call the ambulance.

MOP. Yes, right away, please—call it, call the ambulance.

[MOP *goes back to her father, and the* PORTER *goes off mumbling to himself.*]

BOFFI. But how does it happen that you're here all alone like this?

THE STRANGE LADY. That's the way we live. There's no one about at night. And the porters here are the masters of the house.

BOFFI. You are coming with me now, Signora.

MOP (*calling from the study*). Elma, Elma, come here!

THE STRANGE LADY. No, where would I go now?

BOFFI. But, Signora Lucia. . . .

MOP (*appearing in the archway*). Elma!

THE STRANGE LADY. She calls me Elma, do you hear? 30

BOFFI. Then, I'm going to call him!

MOP. You mustn't think of leaving—

BOFFI. What, after you've been bullying her all evening?

MOP. But only because she wanted to leave!

BOFFI (*taking* THE STRANGE LADY *by the arm*). I'll come back here with him, Signora Lucia; and I am sure that the moment you see him . . .

10 MOP (*coming up and taking her other arm*). Come, Elma, come; he's calling you; he wants you!

[BOFFI, *put out at his failure, shrugs his shoulders and goes off with a determined air.*]

THE STRANGE LADY (*to* MOP). Run along, run along; I'm coming. . . .

MOP (*takes an uncertain step or two, then turns*). You won't go. . . .

20 THE STRANGE LADY. No, I'm coming, I'm coming. . . . Run along; you mustn't leave him alone. . . . (MOP *goes into the other room. Left to herself,* THE STRANGE LADY *spreads her hands over her face; then, with an instinctive gesture, she runs them over her forehead, one on each side, as if to support the despairing weight of her head; and she shuts her eyes as she murmurs:*) A body without a name! *Without a name!*

CURTAIN

ACT II

A bright-appearing room, flooded with light, on the ground floor of the Villa Pieri.

At the back is a loggia, with a marble balustrade and four slender columns supporting the glass-paned roof. This loggia affords a glimpse of a charming brilliant-hued landscape, calm and restful in its expanse of green. Toward the end of the act, violet-colored shadows settle over it. At the right (*the actor's right*) is a rather wide stair, which leads to the upper floors of the villa.

The bottom steps can be seen, covered with a rich red stair-carpet.

At the left is a large glass door, looking out over the garden in front of the villa.

The furnishings are light in tone and luxurious, those of a country house. From the rear wall, to the right, hangs a large oval portrait in oils; it is a portrait of LUCIA PIERI as a bride of before-the-War, in a pretty pose and clad after the fashions of the period, in a young, cool-looking gown.

Four months have elapsed since Act First. It is an April afternoon.

At the rise of the curtain, AUNT LENA CUCCHI *is discovered, speaking to someone in the garden.* AUNT LENA *is in her sixties, fleshy and well-built, with a large, almost masculine head, covered with uncanny gray curls. She has very dense, black eyebrows and wears round tortoise-shell spectacles. She is clad in masculine black, with a stiff-starched collar. Her manner is frank and efficient.*

AUNT LENA. Yes, yes, come in! That's enough, I tell you. Good heavens!— So, you've finished at last! What a bunch!—you're spilling them—never mind! don't stop to pick them up! You must have cut all there were in the garden. . . .

[UNCLE SALESIO NOBILI *opens the glass door and comes in, a huge bunch of flowers in his arms. He is a little dried-up old man who would be quite spry, if it were not for his neck and back, which he can barely move. He is all primped for the occasion, with his hair, sideburns and little mustache touched up, the latter resembling a couple of dabs of soot under his big aquiline nose. Elegance is* UNCLE SALESIO'S *chief concern, and it may be that it is, at the same time, the cross he has to bear in life. His neck is cramped into a choker-collar at least four inches high, and he is in faultless afternoon-dress.*]

UNCLE SALESIO. I'll explain—

AUNT LENA. Don't explain; put them down there! (*Points to the table in the center of the stage.*)

UNCLE SALESIO (*putting down the flowers*). But if you'll let me, Cousin, I *will* explain!

AUNT LENA. All right, go ahead and explain! In the meanwhile, I'll be arranging the flowers. (*She starts putting the flowers into vases, here and there about the room.*)

UNCLE SALESIO. It wasn't for the company that I picked them—not at all. . . .

AUNT LENA. I don't care for whom it was you picked them; you've picked too many, that's all I have to say!

UNCLE SALESIO. I'm explaining to you why. . . .

AUNT LENA. Explain, explain—you spend your life in explaining.

UNCLE SALESIO. A lot of good it does me! With the lack of understanding—or rather—of a willingness to understand. . . .

AUNT LENA. I'm feeling very fit today— explain that—and you're not feeling so well.

UNCLE SALESIO. I'm feeling very well!

AUNT LENA. No, my dear Cousin, not so well!

UNCLE SALESIO. *Very well!*

AUNT LENA. *Very bad!*

UNCLE SALESIO. Well, then, will you explain to me why it is I should be feeling so very bad?

AUNT LENA. If you need any explanation, that can only mean that you're not aware of what you've done!

UNCLE SALESIO. What have I done?

AUNT LENA. Oh, let's not talk any more about it!—Thank heaven, it's all over at last, with that notary's business which we have to go through today. . . .

UNCLE SALESIO (*with a laugh*). What do you mean, "notary's business"? Notorious business!

AUNT LENA. I quite agree with that! But it's a bit hard on you. Just as a punishment, mind you, if I had my way about it—I'd put you on an allowance—with Cia here, there's no longer any room for you.

UNCLE SALESIO. That's a fine state of affairs, isn't it? It's my reward for having robbed myself of everything I had, for my niece's sake.

AUNT LENA. When you gave Cia the villa and grounds as a dowry, you weren't robbing yourself of anything whatsoever; you were rich then; it meant nothing at all to you.

UNCLE SALESIO. And now that I have nothing left—it's get out, is it? It's the punishment that's coming to me.

AUNT LENA. Don't misunderstand me! What I meant was, a punishment for not having had the same faith as Bruno, a faith that nothing could shake—that our Cia was not dead!

UNCLE SALESIO. You didn't have any too much of that kind of faith yourself! Don't say you did, for you've told me so!

AUNT LENA. I may have said so, but I didn't start any proceedings to have her officially declared dead!

UNCLE SALESIO. Simply because you didn't happen—

AUNT LENA. I am telling you that I never would have done it; not I! And we would not find ourselves at this moment in the position, so disagreeable to everybody concerned, of having to take steps to have the thing annulled! —And when I stop to think of the mean motives that led you to do all this—just because you wanted to take the villa and estate away from Bruno. . . .

UNCLE SALESIO. Mean motives? Take them away? As if they had ever been his!

AUNT LENA. His, twice over! The villa rebuilt and improved; the value of the land increased. Yet, you denied him the right. . . .

UNCLE SALESIO. It was no right of his!

AUNT LENA. Oh, I know all about that! The clever excuse which Inez thought up, that the State ought to be made to stand the repairs, after the allotments had been made!—But I, you will notice, instead of falling in with Inez's schemes—

UNCLE SALESIO. Good Lord! You forget that Bruno, to say nothing of Cia, had become a stranger to us, while Inez was my only other niece, and one for whom, having become a poor man, I had not been able to do anything at the time of her marriage!

AUNT LENA. And so, you admit, it was on Inez's account that you did it?

UNCLE SALESIO. I did it—if you don't mind my saying so—on my own account, as well. . . .

AUNT LENA. I should think it would have turned your stomach, when you saw her all worked up over having her sister declared dead!

UNCLE SALESIO. She was worked up over the unpleasantness with Bruno. . . . It's strange, Bruno understood and made allowances for me—but not you!

AUNT LENA. Not I!—For the reason that I was taking no sides! And I use my head!—Bruno, yes, a stranger—I can understand—and I, if I had become poor—in order to recover possession of what I had once given my niece—yes, I can understand—I can understand it to this extent—it isn't gracious, but it's human—(man is not a gracious animal; that is so very true that I have never cared to have anything to do with him)—

UNCLE SALESIO (*who has stood for so much that he is ready to burst*). Well! I'm telling you that man doesn't care to have anything to do with you, either!—

AUNT LENA. —he doesn't care to have anything to do with me, either—that's fair enough!—

UNCLE SALESIO. —for you're a good woman, Lena, but ugly! Ugly! Ugly! And you have an ugly disposition!

You don't seem to realize that I have given and given until I have nothing left to give!

AUNT LENA. My dear Salesio! I am telling you, it is because you are now so poor that you are in possession here—but as for that niece of yours, that Inez, who has the nerve today to face her sister—I'd get even with her—I'd scream in her face: "The villa and the estate are never going to be yours, do you understand? Rather than that—look!—I'll throw them to the dogs, and you can lick your fingers!" (*She catches sight of* THE STRANGE LADY *coming down the stair.*) But here's our Cia now! (*Her appearance creates a sensation, for the reason that* THE STRANGE LADY, *with a studiousness that is obvious even to those so close to her as* AUNT LENA *or* UNCLE SALESIO, *has clothed and bedecked herself to resemble the large oval portrait which hangs from the wall.*) Oh, but look! . . . Heavens! . . . Heavens! . . . You've made yourself into her?

UNCLE SALESIO. It's the picture stepped down from its frame!

THE STRANGE LADY. I've come to face it. I must go through with my lines; the play must go on. . . .

AUNT LENA. The play?

THE STRANGE LADY. Isn't it time they were here . . .? Dead, after ten years . . . one never knows. . . . Better to go back to the beginning. . . . Only, I . . . (*She significantly strikes her stomach.*) Enough!—Who else will there be? *My* sister, Inez?

AUNT LENA. —and her husband—

THE STRANGE LADY. Livio? Silvio?

AUNT LENA. Silvio, Silvio—

THE STRANGE LADY. I don't know wny, but Livio seemed to stick in my mind—

UNCLE SALESIO. He's a lawyer; better watch out!

AUNT LENA. Watch out for what?

UNCLE SALESIO. He's the one who was in charge—

AUNT LENA. Be off with you! Let's forget about it. . . . A nice man. . . .

UNCLE SALESIO. He's all of that!

THE STRANGE LADY. I shall be glad to meet him!

AUNT LENA. But you know him already . . . not as a relative, it's true . . . he was a friend of Bruno's. . . .

THE STRANGE LADY. Ah, Bruno has so many friends! I sincerely hope I am not expected to meet all he brings here, now that the latchstring's out. . . . Who else is coming?

AUNT LENA. Why, your cousin, Barbara—I suppose—if Bruno's thought to send for her.

UNCLE SALESIO. She's nobody. . . .

AUNT LENA. Nobody? She's always been—under it all—the worst enemy of the lot.

THE STRANGE LADY. And Boffi. Will Boffi be here, too?

AUNT LENA. I don't know whether he's in town or not.

THE STRANGE LADY. He is, he is. I've told Bruno to invite him, too. Boffi— I want him, I want him. (*She looks at the portrait, then down at herself.*) Perfect, isn't it?

UNCLE SALESIO. It's just as if it had come to life!

AUNT LENA. Yes, although I never did think that picture of you as a girl looked very much like you.

THE STRANGE LADY. No? Bruno told me it had been made from an enlarged photograph. . . .

UNCLE SALESIO. That's right, from the photograph—

THE STRANGE LADY. —and that he had

given the painter all the necessary instructions. . . .

UNCLE SALESIO. We can see, now, if it's like you! By Jove, it is—as I always did maintain! Just have a look at that!

AUNT LENA. I should say that the eyes. . . . Excuse me, you don't mind?— (*She takes* THE STRANGE LADY'S *face between her hands and looks at her eyes, from close up.*) There you are, look! There are her real eyes, the ones I have always known; they are these— and not those at all!

THE STRANGE LADY. Are these the eyes you always saw in Cia?

AUNT LENA. Why, yes, they are the ones!

THE STRANGE LADY. And they are not the same?

AUNT LENA. What do you mean, the same! These are the same—not those! A shade of green. . . .

UNCLE SALESIO. Green—what are you talking about?—they're blue!

THE STRANGE LADY (*first to* LENA). Green for you. (*Then to* UNCLE SALESIO.) Blue for you. (*She draws* UNCLE SALESIO *over to the portrait.*) And for Bruno—look, Uncle—gray, with black lashes. For the painter, those must have been "Cia's real eyes"— go and see for yourself; the proof's in the portrait!

UNCLE SALESIO. I can't be wrong. Your father and I were like brothers. . . . You have his eyes.

AUNT LENA. His eyes!—Inez's eyes, yes —they're her father's! Not those!— You have your mother's eyes, believe me! We were girls together—cousins with the same name—poor dear Lena and myself—don't you think I ought to know? (UNCLE SALESIO *gives a laugh.*) Laugh, go on and laugh!

THE STRANGE LADY. Why do you laugh?

AUNT LENA. Because, from the time we were girls, whenever the boys would see us two cousins together—

UNCLE SALESIO. —they would call them the pretty Lena and the ugly Lena.

THE STRANGE LADY. No, Lena ugly!

AUNT LENA. My dear! That's just the way I used to protest, from the time I was ever so small. "No, Lena ugly!" —And this ugly one, when the pretty one died, became a mother to you. . . .

THE STRANGE LADY (*disturbed*). Don't, Lena—please.

AUNT LENA (*as if recognizing a promise she had made*). Ah, well, I won't—But that's one past that ought not to grieve you.

UNCLE SALESIO. It must grieve her, you can see; didn't you hear her tell you to keep still?

AUNT LENA. I mean, it ought not to grieve her, for the reason that she was so tiny; she can't possibly remember. (*By way of conclusion.*) You are the picture of your mother; she was just like you when she died.

UNCLE SALESIO. She looks *absolutely* different to me!

AUNT LENA. Humph!

THE STRANGE LADY. This, Uncle, is the play that we must go through with. The theme is: how I look to you, and how I look to Lena, and how one recognizes a lady who has been missing for ten years, when the whole of the enemy's army has probably walked over her! You shall see, you shall see. . . . (*She sits down, and invites* AUNT LENA *and* UNCLE SALESIO *to do the same.*) And now, the first thing to do is for both of you to explain to me as well as you can just what Bruno's position is here, with regard to the villa and the estate.

UNCLE SALESIO (*in astonishment*). His position? And don't you know?

THE STRANGE LADY (*drily*). I do not know.

UNCLE SALESIO. Do you mean to say that Bruno has not spoken to you about it. . . .

THE STRANGE LADY. He's told me—I don't know—something about contested rights. . . . But he was so upset. . . . Possibly, for the reason that I, as I listened to him. . . .

AUNT LENA. I know; it makes me sick at my stomach, too!

THE STRANGE LADY (*her manner and her tone of voice hold a brooding suspicion that renders her, at once, sad and scornful*). No, Lena, it is not for the reason that you suppose; it is something else that hurts me. . . . He went off shrugging his shoulders: "Oh, never mind! It's just as well for you to appear ignorant of everything. It's better that way; then they'll know that I've not been putting anything into your head." But I do want to know about everything, and clearly—I want to know—now.

UNCLE SALESIO. But the situation is as clear as can be by this time!

AUNT LENA. Now that you are back . . .

UNCLE SALESIO. . . . all litigation is cut short!

AUNT LENA. We were just talking about it. . . .

THE STRANGE LADY. The affidavit of my death—it has not been annulled yet, has it?

AUNT LENA. Don't worry about that! It is going to be annulled very shortly.

UNCLE SALESIO. It would have been annulled right away, if you had been willing from the start. . . .

THE STRANGE LADY (*she speaks up scornfully*). From the start. . . . (*But she restrains herself for a moment.*) I don't want to talk about that! (*Then, unable to refrain from expressing her feelings.*) I didn't want anything—myself—from the start—nothing of all this!

AUNT LENA. Yes, yes, we know!—This bitterness, at least, might have been spared you!

THE STRANGE LADY. If it were no more than bitterness. . . .

AUNT LENA. But, you know, there are interests involved. . . .

THE STRANGE LADY. Nothing has been said to me!

AUNT LENA. You have interests, too. . . .

THE STRANGE LADY. I have no interests!

UNCLE SALESIO. Why haven't you, if I may ask . . .?

THE STRANGE LADY. No . . . Ah, no! no! If there are interests involved, I warn you at once that I do not propose to be concerned with them! Tell me, tell me. Why, if it's necessary. . . . But first of all, I must go and take these off! (*Points to her clothes.*) It would be unworthy, unworthy. . . .

AUNT LENA. Not at all . . . why do you look at it that way?

THE STRANGE LADY. Because that is the way it is! That death-certificate is valid, it's valid!

UNCLE SALESIO (*dumfounded*). Valid—how?

THE STRANGE LADY. Valid!—I've told Boffi, and I've told him!—It is ten years that you have been waiting for her. Have you beheld her coming back to you? No! Why has she not come back? Is it so hard to imagine the reason?—Dead, dead, or as good as dead, so far as the life she once led here is concerned! dead to every memory of that life, which she no longer wants to remember—is that plain to you?—*which she no longer wants to remember*—if she is to go on living!

AUNT LENA. Yes, yes—you're right, you're right, my daughter!—I understand, very well indeed.

UNCLE SALESIO. And I, too, Cia—I, too!—But seeing that you *have* come back. . . .

THE STRANGE LADY. But without knowing anything of all this conflict of interests here, without knowing that I should be forced to play a part that is repugnant to me! I came for his sake! I did it only for him! And I made a bargain beforehand that, if I came here, no one—no one—was to make any claims upon my acquaintance, that no memory was to be awakened, either before or after! In the beginning, I did not want to see even you two, who share the same house with him—

UNCLE SALESIO. And in fact, we went away for more than a month . . .

THE STRANGE LADY (*rising, in a passion*). He ought to have told me! He ought to have told me! I wouldn't have come!

AUNT LENA (*timidly, after a brief pause*). It may be that he disliked telling you, for the reason that your sister—

UNCLE SALESIO. After your disappearance—

AUNT LENA. There you go, making excuses for her again!

UNCLE SALESIO. I am not making excuses—I am explaining—she says herself—didn't you hear her?—after ten years—

THE STRANGE LADY. The reason you sought a death-certificate was that the villa and the estate might be allotted to her—isn't that right?

AUNT LENA (*correcting her*). No, not to her! For they revert to him. (*Points to* UNCLE SALESIO.) who gave them to you as a dowry—

UNCLE SALESIO. —there being no heir—

THE STRANGE LADY (*joyously, to* UNCLE SALESIO). Ah, then, they have reverted to you? They're not Bruno's any more?

AUNT LENA. No, they're Bruno's, they're Bruno's—

THE STRANGE LADY. But there's the affidavit of death!—And I was so happy over it, because it freed me from the obligation. . . . I can't explain it, but it seemed like salvation for him, also. . . . (*She turns to sit down again.*) Tell me! How are they still Bruno's?

AUNT LENA. Because Bruno rightly opposed—

UNCLE SALESIO. Rightly? I should not say that!

AUNT LENA. Yes, rightly!

UNCLE SALESIO. No!

THE STRANGE LADY. But don't you understand, Lena, how happy I should be, if they had reverted to him, and if he were still in a position to dispose of them and give them to her?

AUNT LENA. Why, no!

UNCLE SALESIO. What has that to do with the case?

THE STRANGE LADY. Yes, yes!—to her! to her!

UNCLE SALESIO. No, no! I'm out of it! I'm out of the case, from now on! You put a crimp in everything with your return!—Lena and I were just holding a learned discussion on the subject, before you came down, as to whether the motives behind the suit were just or not.—You can picture for yourself what condition the villa and the grounds were in after the Ware a rubbish-heap, everything laid waste. . . .

AUNT LENA. And so long as it remained a rubbish-heap—do you get me?—

no one so much as thought of having you declared dead!—That came after Bruno—

UNCLE SALESIO. Ah, if you start talking—

AUNT LENA. Do you mean to imply that it isn't so?

THE STRANGE LADY. Let him speak, Lena, let him speak—I want to know his opinion, too.

UNCLE SALESIO. You always had enough good sense for us all, Cia—and now, you want to see clearly. . . .

THE STRANGE LADY. Yes,—to see clearly! to see clearly!

UNCLE SALESIO. Well, then. . . . (*To* LENA, *parenthetically.*) You'll permit me? (*To* THE STRANGE LADY *once more.*) This is the gist of the question: Who is to stand the repairs for the damages of the War?

AUNT LENA. The State!—Tell him that, and satisfy him! This is the way it was, you see. Every move that your husband made to rebuild the villa for you, in the hope that you would return at any moment, was opposed by the other side. "Thanks so much," they said to him. "Repairs? You can't charge those up, since the State would have made them in its own good time!"

UNCLE SALESIO. Things had come to such a pass—

AUNT LENA. —when the news of your reappearance burst upon us like a bomb!

UNCLE SALESIO. All litigation was at once stopped, and everything was just where it had been!

AUNT LENA. You can imagine how they felt! They were so sure of winning out!

[*Pause.* THE STRANGE LADY *is lost in concentration.*]

THE STRANGE LADY. If, then, that "reappearance," as you put it, had not happened, Bruno would have lost everything.

UNCLE SALESIO. Certainly! Everything!

AUNT LENA. When, after due lapse of time, the death-certificate had been obtained. . . .

THE STRANGE LADY. And Boffi knew all this, when he came to Berlin?

AUNT LENA. He knew it, of course! How could he have helped knowing it? It was a public scandal!

UNCLE SALESIO. That was all they talked of down here at that time. . . .

AUNT LENA. Sentimental reasons on the one hand and, on the other, grave personal interests; for the property, as you know is a considerable one, and your husband, through his efforts, had made it worth a great deal of money. His enemies made good sport of it, since those same sentimental reasons, which your husband brought forward, were only too well calculated to call forth the derision of the spiteful ones, the imputation being that Bruno was trying to take credit to himself, when, as a matter of fact, he was all the time engaged in wrongfully defending his own interests.

THE STRANGE LADY. And they also thought, I suppose, that he might have found it convenient to defend those sentimental reasons for the sake of his interests?

AUNT LENA. Ah, the spiteful tongues! The spiteful tongues!

UNCLE SALESIO. Their minds were so embittered. . . .

[*Another pause.*]

THE STRANGE LADY (*darkly; she is becoming more and more the prey of an overwhelming suspicion*). I understand, I understand. . . .

AUNT LENA (*to distract her*). But it's all over now! That's enough! Let's not talk about it any more! It surely must disturb you to see once more. . . .

THE STRANGE LADY (*with an impulse of disdain*). No—what does it all matter to me! (*With an altered tone.*) There is something else that disturbs me. . . . (*Her face darkens.*) To think that, at Berlin. . . .

AUNT LENA (*timidly*). What?

THE STRANGE LADY. Nothing, nothing!

AUNT LENA. But—you see—there are certain formalities. We thought you dead; you must reappear living.

THE STRANGE LADY (*without heeding what* AUNT LENA *has just said*). Boffi told me, there, that he had sent for Bruno, the moment he thought he recognized me. . . .

AUNT LENA. Yes—and you can imagine how he rushed to get there!

THE STRANGE LADY. For the reason that, down here, the matter of the death-certificate had come up—had it not? —and he was about to lose the suit?

AUNT LENA. Great heavens, no! What are you thinking about!

THE STRANGE LADY. I am right, Lena; believe me, I am right, now, in thinking the way I do!

AUNT LENA. No, you are not! He never believed—and he was the only one who didn't—that you were dead.

UNCLE SALESIO. That's true! That's true!

AUNT LENA. He rushed off to get you; for he was able to picture to himself those very things which you have told, as an explanation for your not having wanted to come back.

THE STRANGE LADY (*rising, very nervously*). And do you know where he found me? I had had to go to the hospital, at night, with the daughter, to accompany someone who had tried to kill himself—

AUNT LENA. On your account?

THE STRANGE LADY. —yes—

AUNT LENA.—Heavens! was he mad?

THE STRANGE LADY. —He didn't want to let me—(he still writes—) At the door, as the attendants were carrying the stretcher in—I saw in front of me—

AUNT LENA. Bruno?

THE STRANGE LADY. Yes, Bruno. Boffi had gone to pick him up at the hotel and wanted to keep me back. I screamed in his face: "You're crazy!" —and told him to let me go, because I had no husband, had never had any, and did not even know this gentleman whom he had brought to me!

UNCLE SALESIO. And Bruno, what did he do?

THE STRANGE LADY. I went on in, without giving him time to answer. When I came back, a couple of hours later, I found them both still there. Boffi must, surely, have told him that I . . . (*To* LENA.) —you can understand how, in the presence of that madman, who had had a gun in his pocket, and who had threatened me—in order to escape, to find a way out—I, naturally, had given in —I had made certain admissions— no telling what—had admitted that I knew him—that I remembered Filippo, the gardener—that I had been left alone in the villa. . . . And now, when I saw them standing there in front of me like that, feeling sure that they had been discussing these admissions of mine—I denied everything! everything!—I told them that what I had said a short while before had been under stress, but that not a word of it was true, and that I did not know him at all—I did not know either of them—so, let them go away, let them go away, and put an end to this stale farce which Boffi, stubbornly, insisted on keeping up—pretending that he had recognized me—

UNCLE SALESIO. But Bruno—he recognized you at once!

THE STRANGE LADY. He! No! Nothing of the sort!

UNCLE SALESIO (astonished). No?—

THE STRANGE LADY. I am telling you, he did not!—No!—I am quite sure of it! As he saw me for the first time, standing there in the doorway,—I am certain he did not find that resemblance of which Boffi had assured him; he must have felt rather let down—Oh, I am sure of it! (To LENA.) You know how it is . . . at first glance, you think you make out a certain likeness—you speak of it to someone else—the other one looks, and he does not see it—we do not all see with the same eyes! (As if to herself.) So, there you are; and why is it, then—I keep asking myself—why is it, he did not see it at once? (Then, to the others.) Yes, there must have been some sort of likeness there; it was undeniable, and there was nothing for me to do but admit it; I even admitted I was Venetian, but not from this part of the country, not from here; and I told them from where. . . . My words and my actions finally succeeded in convincing the two of them that it was, after all, only a case of resemblance—a striking one, it is true, and one that went somewhat deeper than looks, a resemblance in our pasts—but that was all; there was nothing more than that. The short of it was, I was not—I was not!—the lady he was looking for. What more could I do than that?—Unless—unless—I don't know—

AUNT LENA. You were sorry?

THE STRANGE LADY. No!—The state I was in. . . . (Again, half to herself.) He oughtn't to make an excuse of it now! He oughtn't to take advantage of it! If he has taken advantage of it, for his own interests. . . .

AUNT LENA. No, no; why do you torture yourself like this? What do you mean?

THE STRANGE LADY (greatly distressed). Tired—Ah, Lena, I was so tired! . . . and in despair—I had never been in such a state before—everything lost, an end to everything—I was so nauseated with the life I was leading—I couldn't go on—I didn't know what to do, which way to turn —that night, that awful night, when it seemed to me that life was hanging over a pit—a pit of anguish. . . .

AUNT LENA (deeply moved). My poor girl!

THE STRANGE LADY. . . . he began talking about his Cia—his Cia that was—what she had meant to him, that year she had been his—he was so sad, so disconsolate that, just from listening to him talk—and I was so alone, myself—I was so wretched, without anything worth while in sight—I began weeping, weeping—not dreaming that my tears, tears for myself, for my own desolation—would be interpreted by him as a sign of repentance for having denied that I was his Cia—and there was my body as evidence that I was. . . . I let him embrace me, press me to his bosom, so tightly that I couldn't get my breath—but I had no other reason—I came with him here only for that reason—giving him to understand and making him promise—that that was to be the only reason—that I was coming here as a dead woman—only for him!—only for him!

AUNT LENA. —yes, yes—it's ended and

done for, the old life—I could read it so plainly in your eyes, the moment I saw you. . . .

THE STRANGE LADY. Did you recognize me at once—you yourself?

AUNT LENA. No, my dear girl—I must confess, I did not—at once!

THE STRANGE LADY. And you did not either?

UNCLE SALESIO. No more did I! But that's easily explained. After all these years. . . .

AUNT LENA. All these years? On the contrary! The surprising thing is, after all these years—it would seem that, for her, they haven't been— No, it was—something, I can't just say,—her air, her manner—and something in her voice. . . .

THE STRANGE LADY. Did you notice a difference in the voice?

AUNT LENA. Yes—it seemed to me. . . .

THE STRANGE LADY. Boffi did, too!—He told me so, afterward—It was the only thing he did notice! (*Pause.*) It is strange, but he—(*She is alluding to* BRUNO.)—must surely have noticed it also—He never told me. . . . (*Half to herself; rising.*) So many impressions are coming back to me now. . . .

AUNT LENA. Ah, well, we will let Salesio have his way; but my dear, it can all be explained; you were out of the country for so long, speaking a different language. . . . And then, your way of thinking—that has changed, too. . . . You said to me, "Lena"—just like that—in a weak little voice—and I could feel from that—I could feel death itself in that voice—the death of everything you had once been—it was no longer there, within you; it no longer existed—and I realized that if I were

to recall a certain thing to you—the thing that once had been most alive inside you—you would be—well, the way you are now—not wanting to remember any more—perhaps, not able to remember. . . .

THE STRANGE LADY (*wholly absorbed in herself, she has paid no attention to* LENA'S *words; she now says*). I am just thinking. . . .

UNCLE SALESIO. You must not think of anything any more—from now on!

THE STRANGE LADY (*still as if to herself*). Ah, but I must! He took advantage of it at first, told me that there was a reason—and a good one—for not seeing her. . . .

AUNT LENA. Are you speaking of Inez?

THE STRANGE LADY. No, I am speaking of this double game he has been playing! I had absolutely refused at first to come here, knowing—

AUNT LENA. What Inez had done to you?

THE STRANGE LADY. No, no! I knew nothing about it; what I am telling you is, that is how he persuaded me to come, by assuring me *that I should not have to see her*—that everyone would understand what the reason was! And now, he is making use of what Inez did—of that death-certificate— to force me to see her!

AUNT LENA. But you must remember that the one thing he did not want was this quarrel with your sister!

UNCLE SALESIO. You've been shut up here now for four months.

THE STRANGE LADY. And perhaps, that was calculated, too!

AUNT LENA (*dumfounded*). Calculated?

THE STRANGE LADY. I'd stake my life on it!

UNCLE SALESIO. What do you mean?

THE STRANGE LADY. What do I mean? (*Restraining herself.*) It's perfect, perfect, this whole game of his! He's on pins and needles now, as he takes care for everyone to see, but there's method even in that!

UNCLE SALESIO. No, no, Cia! You are unjust! I assure you, you are unjust!

AUNT LENA. It seems unjust to me, also!

THE STRANGE LADY. Because you are not in a position to understand!

UNCLE SALESIO. Well, then, I must tell you that you do not understand, either—if you will pardon my saying so—or else, you do not want to understand—that he has all the reason in the world for being on pins and needles the way he is—He has carried his respect for your feelings too far. . . . He must stop to think, now, of all the curiosity that has been aroused by your sudden reappearance, after ten years' time, and all——all the talk there has been during the four months you have been shut up here—what people will be thinking—what they will be saying—

THE STRANGE LADY. I can imagine— Ah—I can imagine. . . . (*To* LENA, *with a wink.*) The "spiteful tongues"?

UNCLE SALESIO. Yes; there has been, as they remark, the lawsuit; but not to want to see even your own sister, your husband's relatives—they are saying—

THE STRANGE LADY. Everything there is to say against me? And who knows what more they are saying—what more, about my life up there? . . . They must know everything! Boffi. . . .

UNCLE SALESIO. He? No, no—remember that he, too—

AUNT LENA. —has always taken your part, always—I know what I am talking about!

THE STRANGE LADY. But he must have told them—where he found me— what sort of life I was leading! And

if he didn't tell them, it would be all the worse; with his eyes, with his gestures, with that little twitch of his —he must have let them think—who knows what? . . . They must have asked certain questions. . . . Do they know that I was a dancer? Is that one of the things they're saying?

AUNT LENA. Slanderers!

THE STRANGE LADY. No, they are not slanderers, Lena—it's true—it's true —I was a dancer—and worse! You can't imagine all the things I've done. A dancer—that's an honorable call- ing—for I invented my own dances, along with the music and the cos- tumes. . . . No, it's worse than that —far worse!

AUNT LENA. And—does he know?

THE STRANGE LADY. Bruno? Rather! But what's worse, they know, don't they? Speak up, Uncle Salesio? They know it, don't they? They're saying it?

UNCLE SALESIO. They say so many things.

THE STRANGE LADY. Then, they're also saying that he has seen fit to over- look all this, for the reason that I could be of use to him down here?

AUNT LENA. No! No!

THE STRANGE LADY. I'm not asking you!

AUNT LENA. Who do you think could have said such a thing? Or even thought it!

THE STRANGE LADY. I!—I am think- ing it. . . . Tell the truth, Uncle Salesio—aren't they saying it?

UNCLE SALESIO. Yes . . . they're say- ing it.

THE STRANGE LADY. You see?

AUNT LENA. Who is saying it?

UNCLE SALESIO. Somebody or other. . . .

THE STRANGE LADY. Oh, I can imagine, I can imagine only too well all the suspicions that must be going the rounds about me. It's all so sordid—

made so sordid by all these filthy interests involved. . . .

AUNT LENA. It's not Bruno's fault. . . .

THE STRANGE LADY. I am telling you how it all looks to me; if I thought— [*From the left, over the gravel of the garden, is heard the crunch of automobile tires.*]

UNCLE SALESIO (*starting up*). There they are now, I do believe!

THE STRANGE LADY (*suddenly recovering her possession, with an attitude of defiance*). Yes—at once, at once. . . .

AUNT LENA. Are they here so soon?

UNCLE SALESIO (*looking out into the garden*). No, it's Bruno.

AUNT LENA. Ah, I thought. . . . It was for six o'clock. . . .

UNCLE SALESIO. There's Boffi, too; Boffi's with him.

AUNT LENA. So Bruno's brought him; you see? (*Prolonged pause.*)

THE STRANGE LADY. What are they doing?

AUNT LENA. Bruno's reading a letter.

THE STRANGE LADY. A letter?

UNCLE SALESIO. Yes, the man just handed it to him.

AUNT LENA. And what's happened? Boffi's going off with the letter. . . .

THE STRANGE LADY. No—Uncle Salesio, run and call him back. Bring him in!

UNCLE SALESIO (*going out into the garden*). Bruno, Boffi . . . come here, come here. . . . Yes, you, too, Boffi . . . come here! (BRUNO *and* BOFFI *come in, followed by* UNCLE SALESIO. BRUNO *is about thirty-five. He has a look of consternation, and his face is pale with nervousness and anxiety; every glance, every gesture shows how impatient and upset he is.*) What do you want with Boffi, now? Let him go, for goodness' sake!

BOFFI. Good evening, Signora. Yes, I'm afraid I shall have to be going at once.

BRUNO (*rushing him out*). Yes, at once, at once! And whatever you do, hurry. . . .

THE STRANGE LADY. What's the matter?

BOFFI. A letter just came—

THE STRANGE LADY. —from him? Another one?

BOFFI. He's taking advantage of the fact that he's still alive, and he's out for revenge!

THE STRANGE LADY. But what does he say?

BRUNO (*to* BOFFI, *impatiently*). Go on, go on, for goodness' sake; there's no time to lose!

THE STRANGE LADY (*first to* BOFFI). No, wait a minute! (*Then to* BRUNO.) I want to know. Give me that letter!

BRUNO. The letter itself is nothing! If there were nothing but a letter! (*Turning to* AUNT LENA *and* UNCLE SALESIO.) Lena, if you please; and you, too, Uncle Salesio. . . . (*Motions to the stairs.*)

AUNT LENA. Ah, yes, at once!

UNCLE SALESIO. We're going, we're going. . . . (*They both go up the stairs.*)

THE STRANGE LADY. What is it? What's it all about?

BRUNO. It's become a persecution now! I never heard of such a thing!

THE STRANGE LADY. What does he write?

BRUNO. Write? More than write! He's left! He's coming!

THE STRANGE LADY. Coming? Here?

BRUNO. Yes, here—and not alone, either!

THE STRANGE LADY. Is his daughter coming with him?

BRUNO. His daughter! Please stop hiding behind a mask!

THE STRANGE LADY. Behind a mask?

BOFFI. It's the old story! You know his threat. . . .

THE STRANGE LADY. What threat? I don't remember. . . .

BOFFI. —what he said about having read in the papers. . . .

THE STRANGE LADY. —ah, yes—the story—

BOFFI. —Do you remember, he spoke of a doctor friend of his, from Vienna?

BRUNO. He's gone to Vienna! He writes from Vienna! (*Shows her the letter, without giving it to her.*) There—look!

THE STRANGE LADY. Gone—what for? 10

BRUNO. It's unbelievable! Unbelievable!

BOFFI. He's playing his last card and staking everything on it!

THE STRANGE LADY. But tell me what he says in this letter.

BRUNO. Isn't that what I'm doing? He says he'll be here this evening, with a convalescent lady—an insane patient —and her physician.

THE STRANGE LADY. Ah, yes, now I 20 remember. . . . And he's bringing the lady here?

BRUNO. Yes—says he has the proofs. . . .

THE STRANGE LADY (*fixing him with a stare*). Proofs? Proofs of what?

BRUNO. Why, *that she is the one—that she is the one*—and that you are not!

BOFFI. And he's bringing her here!

BRUNO. He's bringing her here—do 30 you understand now!

THE STRANGE LADY (*impassive, still staring at* BRUNO). Here? And how does he come to be bringing her here?

BRUNO. He's written a number of times, to you, to me—it is possible we made a mistake in not answering him—

THE STRANGE LADY. —but he did not say anything to me of this threat! 40

BRUNO. He said something to me—he urged me to go to Vienna to see this lady—

THE STRANGE LADY (*amazed and ever on her guard*). Ah, so?

BRUNO (*irritated at seeing her thus on her guard*). —yes, yes—and to talk to that doctor in the hospital there, his friend, the one who's coming with him now!

THE STRANGE LADY (*all the while holding him with her stare, as if only his actions made any impression upon her*). Why did you never tell me anything about it?

BRUNO. I suppose, I was to tell you that I had been invited to go to Vienna, to see another woman . . .?

BOFFI. You ought at least to have answered him, you really ought, if only to tell him he was crazy!

BRUNO. When I knew all the time that it was only his way of getting back at her . . .?

THE STRANGE LADY (*uttering her words almost in syllables*). I should have advised you to go.

BOFFI (*quickly*). That's just what I did! I advised him to do that very thing, Signora!

BRUNO (*growing more and more irritated*). But what was the use of that? To have a look at a poor silly creature, out of her wits, with a face . . .?

THE STRANGE LADY. How do you know that?

BOFFI. He sent me a picture of her! Lucky the idea never occurred to him of appealing to the authorities!

THE STRANGE LADY. And you have that picture?

BOFFI. Yes. I haven't it here with me— Believe me, there was nothing to worry about in that, not a shade—I was all for answering him—but he, (*Pointing to* BRUNO.) in view of the injunction. . . .

THE STRANGE LADY. What injunction?

BOFFI. —contained in that letter to me. . . .

THE STRANGE LADY. It is all news to me. . . . I am hearing about it all for the first time now—and yet, I had a right to know! A picture—injunction—what injunction?

BOFFI. You understand, Signora—having received no answer from him, and suspecting, naturally, that he, as a husband, having recognized her, found it altogether to his own interests not to have another woman show up now—he turned to me— —(and I will say once more, it is lucky that he thought of my being a photographer, and so, sent on this photograph—instead of bringing in the authorities)—he sent it to me with the injunction that I should show it to the relatives (if any) of the missing woman, to see if they recognized it, and he also urged that some of these relatives go. . . .

BRUNO. The fellow is insanely stubborn!

BOFFI. Both Bruno and myself, I need not tell you, were greatly perplexed. . . . The sending of this picture, you know, was a matter of only a few days. . . . Should we show it to the relatives, give them word as to what it was all about? . . . Should we take a trip to Vienna? . . . I was even in favor of that, by way of cutting the thing short—of going there, in person. . . .

BRUNO. Go—go—that's easy enough to say—but how? What were we to do, slip away?

THE STRANGE LADY. Why slip away?

BRUNO. What were we to do, then—let everybody know? All they need is a hint, and they know everything! That's all they do, is watch us and talk about us. . . .

THE STRANGE LADY. And so—you said nothing to me about it—you did not answer—you did not make a move. . . .

BRUNO. I am telling you why. . . .

THE STRANGE LADY. Like the ostrich, hiding its head in the sand. . . .

BOFFI. Certainly, if you had gone, you might have stopped. . . .

BRUNO. How was I to foresee that they would set out for here?

BOFFI. No, I am not saying that you could have done that—it was unforeseeable!—and then, so soon. . . .

THE STRANGE LADY. What I should like to know is, how did he get hold of that doctor?

BOFFI. He tells how, in this letter that just came. He has money to throw away, that's plain to be seen. He has succeeded in convincing his doctor friend, and they're all four on the way—he, the doctor, the patient and a nurse—He has convinced the doctor that it is to all our interests down here not to come there and make an unwelcome discovery—that the sight of familiar places—no telling what!—may reawaken in this poor creature. . . . And possibly, he doesn't mind a free trip to Italy. . . .

BRUNO. He's out for revenge!

BOFFI. I'm talking about the doctor! Of course, we know that's what *he* is after! What proofs, I wonder, can they have. . . .

[*A pause. All three stand there uncertainly for a moment, as if in suspense.* THE STRANGE LADY *studies* BRUNO, *then goes on to ask him:*]

THE STRANGE LADY. And you?

BRUNO. I? What?

THE STRANGE LADY. You seem to be very anxious, very much afraid. . . .

BRUNO. Not at all. . . . I should like. . . .

THE STRANGE LADY. What should you like?

BRUNO. I should like . . . I should like . . . what should I do now, the way things are . . .? I wish you would tell me! I was just sending Boffi to find out on what train they were likely to be coming. . . .

THE STRANGE LADY. Ah, so—and then?

BRUNO. You are a curious person! To keep them, at least, from coming while the others are here!

THE STRANGE LADY. To keep them from coming—and why? They have already 10 set out, and so, they must arrive, sooner or later. . . . You seem so. . . .

BRUNO. How do I seem? I'm thinking, that's all!

THE STRANGE LADY. No, my dear; you are, rather, like one who expects to see the roof caving in on his head, or the ground giving way under his feet. 20

BRUNO. But can't you see what it means for them to come bursting in here, in the presence of all the others, with a lot of trumped-up evidence, which they must have in some sort of impressive shape, I suppose, if that doctor has brought his patient all the way here?

THE STRANGE LADY. So, you're afraid of that evidence, are you? 30

BOFFI. No, Signora, it's not that!— afraid that the others may take advantage—

THE STRANGE LADY. —of what?—of the evidence?

BOFFI. —not merely that, but of a suspicion which may arise, if—when confronted by that evidence—

THE STRANGE LADY. A suspicion that not I but *the other one* is Cia?

BRUNO. But not because they can really believe it, you understand! Simply for the reason that it is to their interest to believe it!

THE STRANGE LADY (*ironically*). Ah— you mean—that they would be only

too glad to play upon that suspicion, for the sake of their own interests?

BOFFI. Yes, indeed! Don't you see it?

THE STRANGE LADY. But if we do stop them today—we can't stop them tomorrow. It is a game they can always play, even if they recognize me today. Tomorrow, if they happen to feel like admitting the validity of that evidence. . . . You say, it's to their interests? No! If they chose to accept *her*—pardon me for saying so, Boffi—it would be all the worse for them.

BRUNO. How is that?

THE STRANGE LADY. Why, don't you understand?—They would be accepting her on the basis of that evidence, which they thereby admit to be beyond question,—while all the time, here I am, without evidence— *here I am*—that's enough; they could put me out any time they saw fit.

BOFFI (*sure of his point*). I think it would be difficult.

THE STRANGE LADY. But if it comes to that. . . . I have no proofs.

BOFFI. There is no need of any!

THE STRANGE LADY. No need of any? On the contrary, there is all the reason in the world for doubt, my dear Boffi! If you care to listen, I can give you those reasons.—I—I myself—seeing him like that. . . . (*Whirling on* BRUNO, *with an air of violent contempt.*) Just remember that you—however it comes out—have nothing to lose!

BRUNO. I? What do you mean?

40 THE STRANGE LADY. I am speaking of what is uppermost in your thoughts at this moment.

BRUNO. No! No! No! I am thinking at this moment of what a scandal there is bound to be! They have already had so much cause to chatter, with the life that we have been leading here these last four months. . . .

THE STRANGE LADY. Are you sorry for it?

BRUNO. No! But now, you see. . . .

BOFFI. That's the truth!

THE STRANGE LADY. If worst comes to worst, my dear, find comfort in this —you have made a mistake, that's all.

BRUNO. A mistake—how's that?

THE STRANGE LADY. In thinking I was she!—You have Boffi to keep you company in the one case and Lena and Uncle Salesio in the other. . . . That's as good company as you could wish for! And you have nothing to lose—since it was I, "the impostor," who tricked you into it, as that other gentleman is now on his way down here to prove! (*She laughs.*)

BOFFI. Yes! I suppose it's better to laugh, after all.

THE STRANGE LADY. Perhaps it is. But perhaps, at this particular moment, he finds it a bit difficult—to laugh. . . . For the reason that he knows, very well, that it was he who wanted to make the mistake, and not I who led him into it!

BRUNO. The mistake? What mistake are you talking about? Are you mad? What mistake? In taking you for Cia?

THE STRANGE LADY. Cia?—that's all settled now—don't worry about that! (*Points to the picture.*) I am more like her than the original, am I not? (*Laughs again.*) You will bear me out, Boffi, that I have done all I could to prevent his falling victim to a possible, suspected—and downright, yes, downright—"imposture."—But it doesn't matter! Here I am. I will answer for myself. But only for myself, mind you! No longer for you, from now on. For I, too, have been deceived, you know.

BRUNO. You? In what?

THE STRANGE LADY. On your account —you know how far! (*Turning to* BOFFI.) Run along, Boffi, run along— but not on any foolish errand. I must speak with Bruno. Let them come, if possible, while the others are here— it will be all the better! all the better!

BRUNO. What do you propose to do?

THE STRANGE LADY. You shall see!

BRUNO. They will be here any minute. . . .

THE STRANGE LADY. I am ready, I tell you. All we need is a few words between ourselves. It may be that you will not be able to understand me. It doesn't matter!—Don't be afraid, don't be afraid of that game of theirs! They won't play any game! It is I who shall play the game! I shall play it! I am ready for them! And for everybody—including myself—it will be—a terrible game! (*To* BOFFI.) Go! Go!

BOFFI. And if they come, then, shall I bring them here?

THE STRANGE LADY. Yes, yes, bring them here, bring them here! Because it's useless—(*To* BOFFI *once more, hastily dismissing him.*) Go! (*As* BOFFI *leaves through the door to the garden, she goes on in a transport of overwrought nerves.*)—useless, useless: facts are always right, they must be! Oh, earth, earth! With a touch of soul, you can lift yourself for a moment, come out of yourself, up above all the horrors that Fate has been able to inflict upon you; yes, you can fly, you can recreate life within yourself; when you feel yourself bursting with fullness—up—you must climb, climb, until you bump into the facts that quench it, that trample it out, that befoul and crush it—personal interests, frictions, quarrels. . . . You know very well that I knew nothing of it all, but it doesn't matter! I only want to tell you this. I have been here with you four months now. (*She takes his arm and confronts him.*)— Look at me—here, in the eyes—into them!

—These eyes have no longer seen for me; they have no longer been my own eyes, not even for looking at myself! They have been like this— like this—in yours—always—because there has been born in them, out of those eyes of yours, my own aspect, as you saw me! the aspect of all things, of all life, as you saw it!—I came here; I gave myself to you utterly, utterly; I said to you: "Here I am; I am yours; there is nothing left in me, nothing of my own; take me and make me, make me over, as you desire me!"—You say, you've waited for me ten years? Remember, that is nothing at all! Here I am, yours once more; no longer for my own sake, nor for the sake of all that may have happened in my woman's life; no, no; this woman no longer has a memory of her own, not a one; give me yours, yours, all that you have preserved of me as I once was for you! And they shall become alive in me, alive with all the life that is yours, with all the love that is yours, with all the young joys I gave you! How many times have I said to you: "Like this? . . . Like this?" —reveling in the joy that was re-born in you out of my body, a joy that I felt as you!

BRUNO (*drunkenly*). Cia! Cia!

THE STRANGE LADY (*holding off his embrace; she is drunken herself, but with the pride of having been able thus to create herself*). Yes—I am Cia!—I am Cia!— I alone!—I! I!—not she (*Points to the portrait.*)—the one who was, and— who knows?—perhaps was not aware of it herself at that time—today like that, tomorrow what the accidents of life make of her. . . . Being? Being is nothing! Being is becoming! And I have made myself into her! —But you understand nothing of all that!

BRUNO. Yes, yes, I understand!

THE STRANGE LADY. What do you understand? But when I have felt—when I have felt your two hands about me here (*Indicates, without being precise, a point of her body a little above the side.*) —I do not know—there was some mark that you should have been able to find. . . . And haven't you found it? Owing to that mark which you have not found, or some other, I am not Cia—it is true, isn't it?—I cannot be Cia? It is gone—look—I am assuring you, it is gone!—What have you to say to the contrary?—I did not want it any more, and I did all I could to get rid of it. Yes, yes! Because I knew—I was certain of it —that, just as before, you would come looking for it—am I not right?

BRUNO. Yes!

THE STRANGE LADY. You see? I knew! To keep others from finding it, I got rid of it! But now, you are terrified at the thought that Inez, as a sister, in confidence, or even Lena with her spectacles, may want to discover that mark in me once more, as legal evidence, admissible in court, and that they may not be willing to believe what I have just told you. "Ah, so it's gone? But that's serious! A mark like that! How does it come to be gone?"—Then, science steps in to take a hand!—It may be, gentlemen, for anything is possible, that this poor convalescent lady who is about to arrive—it may be that she really has the mark! Can it be that she has it, and I haven't it! That would be the climax of everything! The most overwhelming of evidence; poor Bruno, poor Bruno, so absorbed in his documents and his admissible evidence!—You may be reassured! I am Cia—*the new one!*— You want so many things! I, when I came here, wanted nothing—*nothing* —not even to go on living for myself —to go on breathing the air around me, for myself—to touch a single thing with one of the senses that were mine! Believing that you had waited ten years for the wife with whom you were in love, I gave her back to you alive—that I might live again myself—after all the nausea and all the ignominy—a pure life! This is so true that, in the face of all, against all the evidence and even against you—against you, if I am forced to disown myself in order to save your interests—in the face of all, I shall have the courage to shout that I am Cia—I—because *she (Points to the portrait.)* cannot any longer be *alive like that*—except in me!

[*The crunch of automobile tires is heard again, on the gravel in the garden.*]

BRUNO (*in an access of fear*). There they are! There they are! They've come. . . .

THE STRANGE LADY. Leave it to me! You receive them! I cannot let them see me now like this! I'll be down directly. (*She hastily makes for the stairs and climbs the bottom steps.*)

BRUNO (*half-imploring*). Cia. . . .

THE STRANGE LADY (*stopping and turning, very calmly, with the tone of one who is asserting a fact that is no longer open to discussion*). Yes—eh—Cia.

CURTAIN

ACT III

The same scene as the preceding act, twenty minutes later. Almost evening. The room is flooded, through the open loggia, with the violet-hued glow of vanishing dusk; and through the loggia may be had a glimpse of a landscape that is more peaceful than ever, with the tiny clustering lights of a village in the distance and other lights scattered here and there about the countryside.

INEZ, BARBARA, UNCLE SALESIO, BRUNO *and* SILVIO MASPERI *are discovered.*

INEZ, *although she is* CIA'S *younger sister, looks older than does* THE STRANGE LADY. *She is well-dressed and has a hat on her head. She has everything that she should have. She is a beautiful woman. She has a husband. She has a good reputation. She has an attractive home. She wants for nothing and has a bad word to say for nobody, for the reason that only the envious resort to slander,* and she has no cause to envy anyone. What she has done she has done because it was right she should do it. She was not acting against her sister. Heaven knows how she has grieved over her unfortunate sister, first for what happened to her and later, when she believed her dead. But having a daughter of her own at home, and remembering that she was poor old UNCLE SALESIO'S *sole remaining niece, she had not felt like standing by and seeing her uncle robbed of the villa and the estate by one who was an outsider, but—for the sake, also, of assuring* UNCLE SALESIO'S *old age—had looked upon it as her duty to assert her rights and do what she could to get back the property, which, upon* CIA'S *death, really should have reverted to the family.*

BARBARA *is a sturdy old maid of forty, with a large head of glossy black hair, slightly sprinkled with gray. She has the forbidding, contentious air of one who is always being put upon by the world; and when she utters a few words, the effect is portentous. Her eyes are evasive and reveal all too clearly her inner feeling, a fiercely tortured sense of having been born ugly and a woman.*

As for MASPERI, *he labors under a facial misfortune; his upper lip looks as if it had been drawn up, in some manner or other, and pasted under his nose, while his teeth are large and protruding but well cared-for; otherwise, he would be a handsome man and an excellent fellow, with a manner of his own and with a carnation-pink complexion which, to tell the truth, looks almost artificial. He wears eyeglasses and, as he speaks, he frequently adjusts them with a couple of fingers. He is courteous in his intentions; but when all is said, one must know one's way about in the world, and he has always known his. He is in the habit of handling the world with gloves, but his hands within the gloves are firm and capable. Just at the moment, he is hard put to it to conceal the ill-humor and impatience he feels at the affront which is being offered himself and his wife. He gazes around at the others, who are frozen into attitudes of expectancy, their waiting being prolonged for something like half an hour.*

This half-hour begins to seem longer and longer, particularly in view of the four months they have waited to receive an invitation which should have been extended at once. This general air and attitude of protracted waiting constitutes the stage-picture at the rise of the curtain.

AUNT LENA *finally comes down stairs.*

BRUNO. Well, what's she doing? Is she coming down, did she say?

AUNT LENA. Yes; she said, "I'm coming" —but . . .

BRUNO. —but?—

AUNT LENA. . . . I found her there among her gowns. . . . She's opened the trunks. . . .

BRUNO (*astonished*). —the trunks?—

AUNT LENA. —perhaps to look for something—or to take something or other out. . . . (*Pause.*)

INEZ. She's not thinking of—going?

BRUNO. Going? Of course not! (*To* LENA.) Didn't you ask her why? (*Then to the others.*) Yes, she did say something about wanting to change her gown. . . .

AUNT LENA. She has changed it! (And she looked so nice as she was!)

BRUNO. Well?

AUNT LENA. What is there for me to say! She's all flushed in the face—nervous. . . . She almost pushed me out of the door: "Go on down! Go on down! Say that I'm coming directly. . . ."

UNCLE SALESIO. Ah, well, then, she'll come! (*Pause.*)

BARBARA (*going over to the loggia*). What a fine view you get from here of the whole countryside . . . those lights. . . .

MASPERI (*he goes over to have a look, too*). Yes, it's such a lovely evening. . . . Rather. . . . (*Pause.*)

BRUNO (*to* LENA, *in a low voice*). How was she?

AUNT LENA. I'd swear, she'd been weeping. . . .

UNCLE SALESIO. She's greatly upset, you can see that!—But that's to be explained: the thought of meeting. . . .

MASPERI. Ah, no—ah, no—I beg your pardon, if it comes to that—the thought of meeting us, no!—not unless she's nursing a grudge against her sister.

AUNT LENA. Not against her sister! Who said anything about her sister; what does she have to do with it? Are you taking Salesio's explanations seriously? (*To* UNCLE SALESIO.) But still,

you ought to know—I should think—
against whom. . . . She spoke her
mind freely enough, to me and to you!

BRUNO (*stressing his words*). It's against
me.

MASPERI. Ah—if it's something between
you two. . . .

BARBARA. That's all very well, but—
here we've been kept waiting for a
quarter of an hour. . . . (*Pause.*) 10

INEZ. There shouldn't be any more hard
feelings. . . .

AUNT LENA (*to* INEZ). Why speak of hard
feelings? She has gone so far as to say
that what you did was right—what
more do you want?—and that she
would be happy if everything here
were to go back to him, (*Pointing to*
UNCLE SALESIO.) so that he would be
in a position to dispose of it and give 20
it to you! (*To* UNCLE SALESIO.) Isn't
that what she said?

UNCLE SALESIO. Yes, yes.

AUNT LENA. Well, then!

INEZ. Why, nothing of the sort! This.
. . . Why should she speak of giving
it to me?

AUNT LENA. It only goes to show what
her feeling in the matter is!

UNCLE SALESIO. That's quite right! She 30
said—that you, after ten years. . . .

INEZ. I did not do it for myself—you
know that, Uncle—but for you—and
then, yes—because I have a daughter.
. . .

MASPERI. She should know that we
would not want to do anything whatsoever to hurt her. . . .

BRUNO (*clipping his words*). The hard
thing to understand, one would 40
think, is what you have done to hurt
me.

MASPERI (*with a gesture of his hands in
front of him*). Oh—we've not come
here—I hope—to open up that discussion again!

BRUNO. No, no—

MASPERI (*he would like to follow it up*).
Here we are, waiting. . . .

BRUNO (*does not give him time*). It is a
question, now, of clearing up her
mind. . . . And the same goes for
myself! I mean, I should like to see
clearly just how things stand. (*With a
burst of anger.*) As if this were any time
for nonsense! I should prefer to be
anywhere but here at this minute.
. . . (*To* AUNT LENA *and* UNCLE
SALESIO.) She had a talk with you
two. . . . What has she against me?
—Has she become suspicious?

AUNT LENA. Yes, that's it—you may believe me—that's it!

UNCLE SALESIO. She said that, if she had
known she was going to find herself in
the midst of a quarrel over personal
interests. . . .

MASPERI. But where's the quarrel? Any
quarrel there may have been was
ended the moment she came back!

UNCLE SALESIO. That's what we told her!

INEZ. I would have come at once—

BARBARA. —and I, too—if Bruno—

MASPERI. —yes, that's right—had not
given us all to understand—

INEZ. —that she did not want to see anyone—especially me!—I would have
convinced her that I never, never
. . . But what's the use of talking?
God only knows all the tears I have
shed over her. . . . (*Deeply stirred,
she hides her eyes in her handkerchief.*)

MASPERI. That will do! That will do! I
think she understood all that very
well. And so, you are out of it. It
would seem that, now, someone else
is concerned; don't you understand?

BRUNO. I did not say that she did not
want to see anyone. What I said was
that she *could* not.

AUNT LENA. And she could not, she
could not, that's the truth! She could

not even bear the sight of us two at the beginning! My good people, you must stop and think what a terrible thing it is that has happened to this poor woman!

UNCLE SALESIO. All the horror of the past. . . . Coming back here. . . . It was only her love for him that enabled her to do it. . . . She did not want to come!

AUNT LENA. She was forced! (BRUNO *turns and gives her a hard look; she goes on.*) Yes, that is what she said: forced! (*Pause.*)

BARBARA (*bursting forth*). And—the suspicion? (*Her question has a weird sound, and leads to another silence.*)

MASPERI (*he drops an*): —Ah, yes—

BRUNO (*there is now nothing for him to do but answer*). —you mean, that I forced 20 her to come for the reason that I needed her in my suit with you.—It is true, she did not want to come. And I even believe that she has some such suspicion herself, since I, up north there, by way of persuading her to come, and helping her to subdue— well, all that horror of the past of which Uncle Salesio speaks—and not only that—but even more, perhaps, 30 the dread of having to face you all. . . . (Ah, my dear people, you must take into account the life she had been driven into leading up there, after all the misfortunes and all the hell she had gone through, and the fact that she had made up her mind never to return)—the thought, (*To* INEZ.) above all, of you, of the sister who, she felt certain, had started proceed- 40 ings against her—you don't know what a horror that inspired in her!— and so, I promised her that she would not have to see anyone. . . . "There is a good excuse," I told her, "there is a good excuse for your not seeing her!" I meant the contest over the estate.—And she, I can assure you, gave no other importance to the question; with her, it was simply an excuse for not seeing you.—I was sure that, after a little while, when she had grown calmer and had grown back into her old life here, this feeling on her part would be overcome.

10 INEZ. But I would have overcome it at once, by assuring her that . . .

BRUNO. —it was not so much on your account, possibly, as it was for her own sake—at least, that is the way it impresses me . . . (her sister . . . her girlhood . . .)—(*To* AUNT LENA, *spitefully.*) Forced. . . . I've told you how I forced her. . . . If that is forcing her. . . . I never exerted any compulsion! (*Growing more and more irritated.*) But this situation, as I see it, must come to an end; don't you agree with me? And so, I have felt constrained to do what I could to persuade her that it must end—what, up to that time, had been merely an excuse . . . (*Turning to* AUNT LENA *and* UNCLE SALESIO.) all the more so if —as you say—she has indicated clearly that (*To* INEZ.) she has nothing against you. . . . If she has seen fit, of her own accord, to do away with that excuse—(*He is in a perspiration of anxiety.*) I can't say!—(*A brief pause—then he blurts out.*) It is annoying that, at a time like this, I should appear to be making excuses to you. . . . (*He paces up and down.*) Suspicious of me. . . . As if I were not the only one of you all who believed that she was not dead!—Why, good Lord, I was so sure of it that I did not hesitate to spend all that I did spend here in repairs! You ask me why I did it? Shouldn't I have been mad to do it, had I been sure that I was going to lose it all, that you would step in and take it away from me? That would have been a pretty pass, wouldn't it, I ask you? What's more, I was, in a manner of speaking, on my mettle—I don't deny it!—it impresses me as being altogether natural. . . . I went on the run the moment I heard. . . . I couldn't believe it was true. . . . I had to put up a fight—to protect (and that's no crime) my own interests, in addition to my feelings. . . . (*At this point, he becomes self-conscious, as he stands there talking half to himself; it is as if he were seeking self-justification, and the only justification he could find had taken the form of a confession.*) There's one thing . . . there's one thing that's really disconcerting . . . when a suspicion arises . . . all that has previously been done without any thought . . . it is painful to think that . . . now . . . in the light of that suspicion . . . it may appear. . . . (*Glancing angrily toward the stair.*) But what is she doing all this time?

INEZ. Ah, yes—because, if she does not care to come down. . . .

BARBARA. —it seems useless to me for us to stay here and wait for her!

AUNT LENA. Be patient! She would like first to quiet her nerves. . . . I've told you that. . . .

BRUNO. But she ought to remember that, in a little while, here. . . . (*He quickly restrains himself; to* AUNT LENA.) Lena, be so good as to go back up there and tell her that I said for her to stop and think *where* Boffi has gone and *why*. She must be here! We've waited for her too long already! There is a limit to everything . . .

AUNT LENA. Yes, I'll go, I'll go. . . . (*She makes for the stairs.*)

INEZ. And also, see how she is. . . .

AUNT LENA. Yes, yes. (*She goes upstairs.*)

INEZ. Because, if she's not feeling well this evening. . . .

BARBARA. Why, we'll go home! (*Pause.*)

MASPERI. I am sorry if a question which, so far as we are concerned, was settled the moment we heard of her arrival should have raised a point between the two of you. . . .

BRUNO. And there's something else . . . there's something else, which . . . you know? . . . it may be that everything is not yet settled between us. . . .

MASPERI. Something else? What?

BRUNO. She (*He nods upward.*) knows very well *what* it is! —And she ought not to leave me like this! (*Strides up and down again; then says.*) I must ask you to forgive me. . . . I am in such a state of mind. . . . My God! I might have foreseen something like this. . . . That's what comes of not facing facts . . . too easy! Must face them when they come, when they're forced upon you. . . . But must I answer for those for which I am not responsible?

[LENA *is seen coming down the stairs.*]

INEZ. There's Lena again—

BARBARA. —alone!

BRUNO. Well? What does she say?

AUNT LENA. Er—I can't tell you—she says that it's "just for that reason" that she hasn't come down yet. . . .

BRUNO. Ah, so? Just for that reason?

AUNT LENA. Yes.

BRUNO. Does she want to wait, then . . . ?

AUNT LENA. —until Boffi comes back.

BRUNO. Ah, ha! So, that's what she told you? Is she bent on driving me to despair?

AUNT LENA (*shrugging her shoulders*). What's to be done about it? . . . That's what she says. . . .

BRUNO. I'll go up! I'll go up, myself! (*Runs up the stairs.*)

INEZ (*rising and going over to* AUNT LENA). What's happened, anyway? Do tell me.

BARBARA. At the moment we come to pay a call. . . .

UNCLE SALESIO. No, no—it must be something else, it must be something else! 10

AUNT LENA. I think so, too!

MASPERI. He indicated that, himself. . . .

INEZ. But what else could there be? He said, it might be that everything wasn't settled. . . .

MASPERI. Exactly! The question. . . . I don't know what he was referring to. . . .

AUNT LENA. In my opinion, it's that 20 letter. . . .

INEZ. A letter?

UNCLE SALESIO. Yes, yes—I think so, too! You can be sure of it. . . .

INEZ. What letter?

AUNT LENA. A certain letter which they received only a short while ago— from up north, I think. . . .

UNCLE SALESIO. They had a long talk here about it. . . . 30

AUNT LENA. Yes—about someone or other—I can't tell you who it was— Something to do with things up north. . . .

UNCLE SALESIO. They were terribly excited about it. . . .

AUNT LENA. Boffi was there—and then, all of a sudden, they sent him off— somewhere or other—to stop. . . .

[*Through the loggia comes the dazzling* 40 *gleam of two headlights, an automobile horn is heard, and once more, over the gravel of the garden, there is the crunch of tires.*]

UNCLE SALESIO. Ah! There he is now! It must be!

AUNT LENA. That's good, that's good. She'll come down now—you'll see. She's just been waiting for him. . . .

UNCLE SALESIO. That's what she told us—do you remember?—that she wanted Boffi present.

AUNT LENA (*looking out through the garden door*). Yes, there he is. . . . (*She gives a gesture and exclamation of surprise.*) But— Oh! he's not alone! . . .

UNCLE SALESIO (*looking out, also*). There's a crowd of them. . . .

MASPERI. Who are they, anyhow?

INEZ. Why, one of them is a nurse, isn't she?

AUNT LENA. I should say. . . .

BARBARA. What does it mean?

UNCLE SALESIO. They're taking her out. . . .

MASPERI. Yes—they're helping her down. . . .

INEZ. Good heavens! but what's it all about!

BARBARA. What can have happened now?

UNCLE SALESIO. They're northerners. . . .

AUNT LENA. Yes, they're foreigners. . . .

MASPERI. But look. . . .

INEZ (*from behind*). How awful!

[*The light in the room at this moment becomes thin and livid.*

[THE DEMENTED LADY *enters first, followed by the nurse and the doctor, with* BOFFI *and* SALTER *bringing up the rear.* THE DEMENTED LADY *is heavy-set and flabby, with a waxen face, disheveled hair, and vapid, motionless eyes; her mouth is constantly drawn into a wide, foolish, empty smile; the smile is there, even when she utters some sound or other, or when she stammers out a few words, quite obviously without any idea of what she is saying. The doctor and the nurse are typically German in appearance and in bearing; and even* SALTER *now seems conspicuously German.*]

THE DEMENTED LADY. Le-na. . . . Le-na. . . . (*Her mouth is wide, her cheeks puffed out, and these two syllables are for her a sort of cadence; they no longer signify a name, but are like a refrain that has become habitual.*)

AUNT LENA (*terrified*). Heavens! What does it mean? . . . Is she calling me?

INEZ. Who is she?

BOFFI (*he comes in very much wrought up*). Where's Bruno? And the Signora?

THE DEMENTED LADY (*again*). Le-na. . . .

AUNT LENA (*looking around at the others, in dismay*). She *is* calling me!

SALTER. Are you a member of the family? Is your name Lena?

AUNT LENA. Yes—I am the aunt. . . .

SALTER (*to the* DOCTOR). Do you hear? Do you hear? There is a member of the family by the name of Lena! Another proof! Another proof! Now, we're sure of it! we're sure of it! —That was something we didn't know!

MASPERI (*stepping forward*). You are sure of what?

BOFFI. Don't pay any attention to him! She keeps saying that, over and over; she kept it up all the way here!

THE DEMENTED LADY. Le-na. . . .

BARBARA. But she *is* saying Lena.

BOFFI. Yes, but she's not calling anyone! And she's all the time laughing like that. . . . (*Then, alluding to* BRUNO *and* THE STRANGE LADY.) Where are they, I'd like to know?

INEZ. Good Heavens, are they all mad?

MASPERI. What is the meaning of this? Why have you brought this lady here?

BOFFI (*still referring to* BRUNO *and* THE STRANGE LADY). Can they be upstairs? Call them, please! Please call them!

SALTER (*to* BOFFI, *indicating the others*). Are these ladies and gentlemen the other relatives?

BOFFI. Yes— (*Introducing* INEZ.) This is the sister, Signora Inez Masperi.

SALTER. Ah, the sister? So, there is a sister—she has a sister? —Ah, then, we shall soon—soon—

INEZ. Who is the gentleman?

BOFFI. Carl Salter, the writer.

SALTER. Look at her, Signora; look at her, at once!

INEZ. I? What do you mean? Whom?

BOFFI. He persists in believing. . . .

SALTER (*to* INEZ). Is it possible it doesn't mean anything to you?

INEZ. No. . . . What? For Heaven's sake—what should it mean to me?

BOFFI. That this woman is your sister!

MASPERI. What?

BARBARA. This woman?

INEZ. Cia?

AUNT LENA. Where is she? What are you talking about?

SALTER. Yes, yes—this one! this one!

UNCLE SALESIO. He must be insane himself!

SALTER. I've brought her all the way here. . . .

THE DEMENTED LADY. Le-na. . . .

SALTER (*pointing to her, at the sound of her voice*). Do you hear that? Isn't that a proof? Is it possible you don't see that it's a proof? She's calling Lena!

THE DOCTOR. She has been calling Lena constantly, for years!

SALTER (*to* AUNT LENA). You! You!

AUNT LENA. No, no! It's not possible!

SALTER. Don't you recognize her? The look in her eyes? How can you help recognizing her?

AUNT LENA. What do you expect me to recognize? What is there for me to recognize?

SALTER. My friend—the doctor who has studied her case for years—has documents, proofs. . . .

MASPERI. What proofs! Bring them out!

BARBARA. But it's impossible!

MASPERI (*to* BARBARA). Let him speak, please! Being taken unawares as we are. . . . What proofs?

AUNT LENA. But our Cia is upstairs!

SALTER. I know the lady upstairs, very well!

UNCLE SALESIO. Ah, this is a case for you. . . .

BARBARA. Unbelievable! Unbelievable!

MASPERI. Ladies and gentlemen, let me speak! (*To* SALTER.) You know her . . . ?

SALTER. The lady upstairs? All too well!

AUNT LENA. I suppose you know her better than I do, when I was a mother to her!

SALTER (*pointing to* THE DEMENTED LADY). To this one! To this one!

AUNT LENA. What, to her!

MASPERI. If you think you have proofs and documents. . . .

UNCLE SALESIO. Why speak of proofs? Do you take him seriously . . . ?

MASPERI. No, what I am saying is, there is a way of doing things—if they say they have proofs to show. . . .

BOFFI (*ironically*). Hear! Hear!

UNCLE SALESIO. They'd make you laugh —or weep from pity!

MASPERI. . . . there are the proper authorities!

BOFFI. But supposing you knew the reason that is behind all this?

MASPERI. I have no idea what's behind it!

BOFFI. I know, and Bruno knows, and the Signora knows! Where are they?

SALTER. You call it: revenge—

BOFFI (*to* MASPERI). Do you hear that?

SALTER. But I call it punishment!

MASPERI. I do not know the gentleman. . . .

UNCLE SALESIO. Oh, but the gentleman's motives do matter, up to a certain point. If there are any proofs or documents, out with them! Produce them on the spot! Because we do not propose that anyone here shall take advantage of this revenge, or punishment, or whatever it is!

BOFFI (*to* MASPERI). To have been foreseen—wasn't it?

MASPERI. How could it have been foreseen? Who could have foreseen a thing like this?

BOFFI. No—I mean, that you would take advantage of it!

UNCLE SALESIO. But no one should be allowed to take advantage of it!

INEZ (*disdainfully*). What is all this talk about "taking advantage"? You, too, Uncle—what do you mean? No! You shouldn't say things like that! (*To* SALTER.) Look here: here we are, all of us—I, the sister—here is an aunt— here is an uncle—and a cousin—and you, Boffi—we have all had a look at this poor creature whom you have brought here, and we do not recognize her.

SALTER. Because you have already recognized the lady who is upstairs?

INEZ. No, I have not!

SALTER. What? You haven't recognized her?

INEZ. I haven't seen her yet, since she came. I am seeing her for the first time today.

SALTER. You haven't wanted to see her before?

INEZ. It wasn't I—it was she. . . .

SALTER. Ah, so it was she?—All very clear.—For the reason that, as a sister, she couldn't. . . . With a sister, eh . . . blood-feeling. . . . The mere thought of it—cheek to cheek—something that she herself couldn't bear. . . . She was afraid that you would not feel the call of blood to blood. That proves it, Signora, that proves it; and you yourself will feel (*Points to* THE DE-

MENTED LADY.) that call here, your own blood speaking. . . .

INEZ (*horrified*). No, no in Heaven's name, don't!

SALTER. If your pity could overcome your horror. . . . And she, look—ten years—all the outrages—war—hunger . . . I know the lady upstairs who passes herself off as her. If you have found such a resemblance in that one, look—look at this one—study her—see if you cannot find in her—under all the ravages and all the changes—the same features still. . . .

INEZ. No, no!

AUNT LENA. Where are they?

UNCLE SALESIO. What do you mean?

SALTER. The eyes, if they were not so dead. . . .

BOFFI. Nothing of the kind—an altogether different shape!—a little of the same color, it may be. . . .

SALTER. Mad for nine years. . . . She was found in an old tattered Hussar's coat, but with a sign.

INEZ. What sign?

UNCLE SALESIO. And where was she found?

SALTER. At Lintz.

MASPERI. What was the sign—you are referring to that Hussar's coat?

SALTER. —Of the regiment to which that coat belonged. And that regiment had been stationed here—here!—right here!

MASPERI. Here, during the occupation?

BOFFI. What does that prove? Some Hussar who had been stationed here during the occupation may have given her that coat, at Lintz, out of charity.

THE DEMENTED LADY. Le-na. . . .

SALTER. And she keeps calling Lena! Do you hear? Why is that? That name is the only thing that has stayed in her mind. (*To* AUNT LENA.) You, you say you were a mother to her. . . .

AUNT LENA (*with an unlooked-for display of resolution, overcoming the horror she feels and to the horror of all, she takes* THE DEMENTED LADY'S *head in both her hands, and calls*). Cia!—Cia!—Cia! [THE DEMENTED LADY *remains impassive, with her mute and empty smile. All look at her. In the meanwhile,* THE STRANGE LADY *comes down the stairs, followed by* BRUNO. *No one perceives her. They are first aware of her, there in front of them, advancing toward* THE DEMENTED LADY, *as* AUNT LENA *falls back in disillusionment; and, strangely enough, simply for the reason that* THE DEMENTED LADY *is present, even though no one has been able to recognize her, the very ones who up to now have believed in* THE STRANGE LADY—AUNT LENA, UNCLE SALESIO, BOFFI *himself—all stand gazing at her in doubt and perplexity.*]

THE STRANGE LADY (*while all are silently gazing at her, she says to* BRUNO). You try calling her, too.

SALTER. Ah, there she is!

THE STRANGE LADY (*quickly and haughtily*). Here I am.

INEZ (*bewildered, but feeling that she ought to overcome her bewilderment*). Cia. . . .

THE STRANGE LADY. Wait. Put on the light. One can barely see here.

[UNCLE SALESIO *goes over to the door to turn the light-button. The room lights up.*]

INEZ (*looking at her in the light; after a moment's hesitation, she repeats*). Cia. . . .

SALTER (*in view of* THE STRANGE LADY'S *seemingly assured position and as a result of this repeated call on* INEZ' *part, he—contrary to what has happened to the others—now comes to doubt himself; turning to* INEZ, *he says*). Do you really believe . . . ?

THE STRANGE LADY (*to* SALTER). I have

kept him up there (*Indicating* BRUNO.) and I have stayed up there myself simply in order to give you time to make your impression. I recognize your cruel hand in this. Only a person like you could be capable of committing such an atrocity, by bringing here. . . . (*She goes over to* THE DEMENTED LADY; *with a tactfully sympathetic gesture, she places her fingers under the other woman's chin, in order to have a close look at that laughing countenance.*)

THE DEMENTED LADY (*while* THE STRANGE LADY *is engaged in contemplating her, she once more emits, without losing her empty laugh, the habitual refrain*). Le-na. . . .

THE STRANGE LADY. Lena . . . ? (*And subduing a shudder, she turns to* AUNT LENA.)

SALTER (*quickly; pointing to* THE DEMENTED LADY). There you are, there you are, do you see? She's calling Lena, for your benefit! She has turned to look at her!

BOFFI (*unable to stand this*). No, no! That's all been cleared up!

THE STRANGE LADY. What has been cleared up?

AUNT LENA. She's not calling me. . . .

BOFFI. It's a refrain, Signora—a perpetual refrain with her. . . .

SALTER. For me, the fact that she turned is enough—

THE STRANGE LADY. —to prove, I suppose, that I am not Cia?

SALTER. You just said: "You try to call her, too!"

THE STRANGE LADY. I knew that *you* didn't believe me; but as I came in just now, I found *you* (*Indicating* LENA.) bent over her like this and calling "Cia . . . Cia. . . ."

AUNT LENA (*she is grieved and endeavors to excuse herself*). But because . . . you see?

UNCLE SALESIO (*at the same moment, indicating* SALTER). —because he insisted. . . .

BOFFI (*also at the same moment*). —hearing that "Le-na—Le-na." . . .

THE STRANGE LADY (*drowning the voices of the others*). Ah, yes . . . ah, yes . . . it's natural . . . natural. . . . (*To* LENA.) And I saw how you looked at me just now. . . .

AUNT LENA (*abashed*). How I looked at you . . .?

THE STRANGE LADY (*to* UNCLE SALESIO). You, too. . . .

UNCLE SALESIO. I? . . . No . . . no. . . .

THE STRANGE LADY. And you yourself, Boffi. . . .

BOFFI. Nothing of the sort!—No one has recognized her! (*Alluding to* THE DEMENTED LADY.)

UNCLE SALESIO. We are all. . . . (*Taken off his guard and overwhelmed, he does not know how to finish the sentence; what's more, they do not give him time.*)

BOFFI. And your own sister—you can see that—

THE STRANGE LADY. —yes—she called me Cia—twice. . . .

BOFFI (*first to* SALTER). You understand? (*Then to* MASPERI.) You *will* understand, I take it?

INEZ (*disdainfully*). I have told you that no one here cares to take advantage. . . .

BOFFI. No, what I mean is—now if ever —even Bruno might take advantage —of *this!*

THE STRANGE LADY (*impulsively*). Ah, no, not he! He is not going to take advantage of anything!—And anyway,— look at him there—do you see?—he's the most abashed of all. . . .

BRUNO (*shaking himself together*). Abashed? Dumfounded by the insolence of this gentleman, who has dared—yes, he—to take advantage. . . .

THE STRANGE LADY. Rest assured, he is not going to take any advantage, either—(*Looks at* SALTER.) neither of me nor of this poor creature. (*Indicates* THE DEMENTED LADY.)

SALTER. I have felt it my duty—

THE STRANGE LADY. —to bring her here—

SALTER. —yes, to punish you!

THE STRANGE LADY (*stepping forward*). To punish me? You?

SALTER. Yes! For what you've done! I came near dying on your account; and at that very moment, you slipped off down here to trick others!

THE STRANGE LADY. I have not tricked anyone!

SALTER. Yes, yes, you have tricked them! tricked them!

BRUNO (*on the point of leaping at him*). Just say that one more time. . . .

THE STRANGE LADY (*quickly stopping him*). No—calm yourself, calm yourself!

BRUNO. He provoked it!

THE STRANGE LADY (*turning suddenly to* SALTER). I am the one that's concerned here! I and my "humbuggery," as you would say.—Have you proved it? How? With this atrocious thing that you have had the audacity to do?—And you (*Turning to the* DOCTOR.) are the physician who have lent yourself to this?

DOCTOR. Lent myself, yes—especially, seeing that I have grounds for supposing. . . .

THE STRANGE LADY. —Ah, yes—that's true!—that here they would be interested in not having any doubt arise— a doubt likewise *interested*. . . . I am happy to assure you that you have succeeded: the doubt, as a matter of fact, has arisen.

AUNT LENA. No, no!

BOFFI (*at the same time*). When?

UNCLE SALESIO. On the part of whom? No!

THE STRANGE LADY (*almost shouting*). I am glad of it! (*Then, in another tone.*) You say not . . . but I surprised you. . . .

UNCLE SALESIO. But I am telling you, we haven't recognized her!

THE STRANGE LADY. It makes no difference!

BOFFI. Do not worry, Signora! I can wager that he doesn't even believe it himself.

THE STRANGE LADY. It makes no difference! (*Then, going slowly up to* SALTER.) You can see for yourself what a curious sort of "humbuggery" mine must be, since I myself was the one to call attention to how they all looked at me a short while ago!—And you, Boffi— it was only by way of resisting the doubt that had arisen in you—

BOFFI. I swear to you that no doubt has arisen in me!

THE STRANGE LADY. (it has arisen—it has arisen)—and it was by way of self-encouragement, as you let me see— that you (*Indicates* INEZ.) twice called me Cia. . . .

BOFFI. No, no! It was because it was the truth! —I beg your pardon, but what doubt do you think I could have had on account of . . .? (*Indicates* THE DEMENTED LADY.)

THE STRANGE LADY. —no—on account of me!—on account of me!—even without your having been able to recognize her. *The most natural of doubts*—my swooping down on you like that—bewildered as you were. . . . And he (*Indicates* SALTER.) at once had a contrary doubt—yes, upon hearing me called Cia by one who— up to that time—had not laid eyes upon me. Ah, yes, it's natural . . .

natural. . . . (*To* LENA, *who is quietly weeping*.) Do not weep now!—Any certainty may be shaken, the moment the slightest doubt arises, and one's belief is never again quite the same!

SALTER. You yourself admit, then, *that it is possible you are not Cia!*

THE STRANGE LADY. I admit a good deal more than that! I admit that Cia *may even be this woman* (*Indicates* THE DEMENTED LADY.) if they choose to believe it!

UNCLE SALESIO. But we don't believe it!

SALTER (*suddenly pointing, first to* THE STRANGE LADY *and then to* THE DEMENTED LADY). Just because she resembles her, and this one doesn't!

THE STRANGE LADY. Ah, no! Not that! Not because I resemble her! I myself —I *myself*—have told everybody, that is no proof—no proof—my resemblance to her—that resemblance by means of which everyone thought they recognized me. I even shouted: "How is it possible—what are you thinking of?—that one who had been trodden under by the War—after ten years—should remain—so much—*the same?*" The contrary, if anything, would be true—it would be proof that I am not she!

MASPERI (*spontaneously; he has been struck by this remark*). Ah, quite so! Now that. . . .

THE STRANGE LADY (*suddenly turning on him*). Isn't it true—A proof that *I could not be Cia!* (*To* SALTER, *once more*.) Do you see?—There is some one who is thinking, this minute. . . .

BRUNO. It seems to me that you are carrying too far. . . .

THE STRANGE LADY. But you fell in with it yourself!

BRUNO. I?

THE STRANGE LADY. Yes, you! you!

BRUNO. When? What are you saying?

THE STRANGE LADY. When I told you this, up north there; and you were shaken by it, too, Boffi!—You couldn't help being!—It is only when one has belief—or when *it is convenient* to have belief—that so obvious a thought does not occur to one—or, one does not permit it to occur: the thought that my being like this, *the same*, is a proof to the contrary—and that, therefore—why not?—Cia, on the other hand, may very well be—this poor creature, for the very reason that she *no longer resembles her in the least.*

BRUNO. That is a wicked way to talk!

THE STRANGE LADY. I told you that I had to answer to him (*Indicating* SALTER.) for my humbuggery!

BRUNO. How? The way you are doing? By doubting yourself?

THE STRANGE LADY. Yes, the way I am doing, the way I am doing!— Because I want everybody—yes, everybody—to doubt me—like him— so that I may at least have the satisfaction of being the only one left to believe in myself! (*Nodding toward* THE DEMENTED LADY.) You have not recognized her. . . . Is it because she is unrecognizable? Because, when you look at her, you do not find the likeness you seek? Because they have not furnished you with sufficient proofs?—No, no! It is simply because it does not seem to you possible, as yet, to believe! That's all!—More than one poor wretch, years later, has come back like her (*Indicates* THE DEMENTED LADY.) with almost no appearance left—unrecognizable— with no memory left—and sisters, wives, mothers—*mothers*—have fought over him! "He's mine!"—"No, he's mine!"—Not because he looked like their own flesh and blood, no! (for the son of one could not have looked like the son of another!)—but because they believed it! because they wanted to believe it!—And there are no valid proofs to the contrary when one wants to believe!—He is not the one, you say? Ah, for that mother, he *is* the one! What matter whether he is or not, if that mother regards him as such, and gives him all her love to make him hers? Against all the evidence, she believes. Without any evidence, she believes.—And for that matter, have you not believed in me without any evidence, any proofs?

BOFFI. But that was because you are she, and there is no need of proofs!

THE STRANGE LADY. That is not true! (*Turning quickly to* BRUNO, *who makes a gesture of protest.*) Remember, my dear, that it is not against your interests, if I am trying to prove that she (*Points to* THE DEMENTED LADY.) really and truly, *may be* the one. . . . If you will pardon me, there have been so many suspicions! He has told me (*Indicating* UNCLE SALESIO.) that it is because I have been shut up here for four months, without caring to see anyone. . . .

BRUNO. But everybody has understood the reason!

THE STRANGE LADY (*winking at* AUNT LENA). —Except the "spiteful tongues," eh? (*Then to* BRUNO.) The unfortunate part is that you back them up. . . . (*To* MASPERI.) So you are still in the toils, eh (it's plain to be seen)—

MASPERI (*surprised*). Not at all . . . I. . . .

THE STRANGE LADY. —what do you mean, not at all? It is plain to be seen, so very plain . . . over what I have just been saying! Go a little further, go a little further, a little deeper down! It is so easy to suspect —what?—that some woman, taking advantage of a physical resemblance, which, so far as that goes, others may have *found it convenient* to discover in her—

BRUNO (*biting off and emphasizing his words*). —convenient—for me. . . .

THE STRANGE LADY (*quickly*). What? This suspicion?

BRUNO. You have yourself to blame for it!

THE STRANGE LADY. Precisely! (*Then, going up to* MASPERI.) Ah, well, what I was saying was, it is so easy to suspect that I have been conveniently taking my time here—(*Winks at* UNCLE SALESIO.) for the past four months!— in making myself over into *her*— (*Points to the portrait.*)—starting out by saying that I could not bear the sight of anyone (*To* SALTER, *with a wink.*)—and as luck would have it, eh? there was an excuse—a very convenient one for him. (*Indicates* BRUNO.)

BRUNO (*quickly, to his relatives*). There you are; what did I tell you?

THE STRANGE LADY. You may have told them—but now, you see, they're listening to me! (*To* SALTER.)—a little lawsuit here, personal interests involved! (*To* INEZ *and* MASPERI.) It was easy to pretend in the beginning that I did not want any memories (and, indeed, woe to Lena and Uncle Salesio if they showed any inclination to revive them for me).— And it was likewise easy to pretend that I had lost all memories; but in the meanwhile, eh? little by little, to manufacture myself a set.—(*She goes over to* BOFFI.) He (*Indicates* BRUNO.) wanted the necessary time, did he not, for putting the ruined villa and the grounds into some sort of shape? Ah, and also, time for reconstructing me, stone upon stone, like the villa; and the piteous memories of poor Cia, transplanted in me—time to make them grow again and flower in life once more—(*Goes slowly toward* INEZ, *with outstretched arms.*) to the point where they should be capable at last of taking in a sister—(*Takes her hands.*) like this, for example—to be able to talk to you of the time when we were girls together, two happy, playful girls, although we were orphans, the two of us, being brought up by aunt and uncle. . . . *To make myself—To make myself*—to bring myself to the point where I should look as if I had "stepped down from that picture"—as Uncle Salesio remarked—copied even to the gown—

INEZ. —copied?—

THE STRANGE LADY. —yes—I was all dressed to receive you, a short while ago—dressed as in that picture (*To* LENA.)—isn't that so?—and I went upstairs to change, because, really, it seemed to me a bit too much. . . . (*The others display signs of embarrass-ment, doubt and consternation.*) Ah— yes?—so this suspicion is rising up in you at last? If you haven't yet. . . .

MASPERI (*as if horrified*). No—never!

INEZ. Who would ever think . . .

BARBARA. —of a thing like that?

THE STRANGE LADY (*indicating* BRUNO.) He—he has been thinking—of a thing like that. . . .

BRUNO. I?

THE STRANGE LADY. Yes—and now, he's terrified for fear this suspicion—this possible suspicion—which I myself have made possible—may be discovered to be the truth.

BRUNO. The truth? How could it be the truth? Could you people believe it?

THE STRANGE LADY. They believe it! they believe it! Because it is—it is the truth—the truth that lies in facts! Precisely that "humbuggery" in which he believes. (*Indicates* SALTER.)

BOFFI. But, Signora!

UNCLE SALESIO. How is it possible?

BRUNO. This is a revenge that is fiercer than his! (*Indicates* SALTER.)

THE STRANGE LADY. Not mine, not mine! It is facts, my dear, that are taking their revenge, it is facts that are taking their revenge! It was you, was it not, who wanted to call in these people? The fact is, I cannot accept any recognition from them! You alone must recognize me, *disinterestedly!*—I have not, by any means, come here to defend a dowry! That would be a bit of trickery that I should never have thought of, to which I could never stoop! You know now what that "humbuggery" is that he has been talking about. If it serves your purpose—look—and let's have no more talk of vengeance—then believe—in the face of the facts, believe!

BRUNO. In what am I to believe?

THE STRANGE LADY. In this humbuggery of mine! What more must I say to you?

BRUNO (*exasperatedly confronting her*). You are just doing that to put me to the test! It is to put me to the test that you are doing all this!

THE STRANGE LADY. No! No! Indeed, I am not!

BRUNO. Yes, that is the reason! That is the reason!

THE STRANGE LADY. I am wondering if this is not, rather, a fresh manoeuvre on your part. . . .

BRUNO. What sort of manoeuvre?

THE STRANGE LADY. To convey the impression that I have done all that I have done for that reason!

BRUNO. No!

THE STRANGE LADY. No? Then believe! I am telling you that you really may —in fact—believe them all—yes, yes—believe him (*Indicates* SALTER.) and put him in the right—absolutely in the right!—even so far as this poor creature is concerned—yes, it may be she—Cia—really it may be! Look at her! (*She goes up closer to* THE DEMENTED LADY, *and once more, with the same tact and the same sympathy, places her fingers under the other woman's chin.*)

THE DEMENTED LADY (*barely conscious of the other's touch, she repeats*). Le-na. . . .

THE STRANGE LADY (*to* AUNT LENA). Lena—do you hear?—It is you she is calling! Why won't you believe it?

THE DEMENTED LADY. Le-na. . . .

THE STRANGE LADY. There, it is you— it really is!—As for me, I did not want to see you—I sent you off for more than a month—and when I saw you, I had nothing to say—while this one comes calling Lena—she has always called Lena, Lena—and yet, you won't believe her? Because she doesn't answer you? And how could she answer you? Don't you see? (*There is an infinite sadness in her eyes, as she gazes at* THE DEMENTED LADY.) —If she can call Lena, with such a voice—with such a smile—it means that no voice can ever reach her any more! (*Addressing her.*) You are calling—who knows from what distant moment—what happy moment—of your life—you who have been left suspended there. . . . You no longer see anything. . . . No one can give you anything. . . . Pity? . . . what good would that do you? The care

that others take of you? . . . But ah, you are happy now in that smile of yours—you are *safe—immune.* . . . (*To* SALTER.) For whom was it you brought her here? (*To* LENA; *the latter, half repentant and instinctively attracted, has come up.*) Ah! you've come?

AUNT LENA (*in her dismay, she has almost lost her voice*). No . . . no. . . .

THE STRANGE LADY (*gently*). Yes, stay here, stay here. . . . Perhaps the sister. . . . While I (*She goes up to* SALTER.) have something else to say to him. (*Fixing him with a stare.*) You, in addition to being a bad man, must be a bad writer.

SALTER. I?—it may be—why?

THE STRANGE LADY. It must be all humbuggery—for you—and nothing else —everything that you write.

SALTER. Ah, my . . .?

THE STRANGE LADY. —your literary work. You surely have never put anything into it—neither heart—nor blood—nor nerves—nor senses. . . .

SALTER. Nothing?

THE STRANGE LADY. Nothing. You surely have never known what it is, out of a real torment, a real despair, to feel the need of taking revenge on life, on the life that is—as others and circumstances have made it for you—by creating another better, more beautiful one, the one that might have been, the one that you would like to have had!—And because you are what you are, because you have known me (three months . . .) such as I was with you, mine is a similar imposture, is it?

SALTER. Have you put your heart into it . . .?

THE STRANGE LADY. I wish you would tell me why I should have gone through with it otherwise.

SALTER. To get rid of me.

THE STRANGE LADY. I could have got rid of you without tricking another.

SALTER. If I remember, you just finished confessing that you had played the trickster.

THE STRANGE LADY. Very well! So, I have played the trickster, have I?

SALTER. Oh, there may have been an object in your confession, being compelled. . . . [10]

THE STRANGE LADY. What object?

SALTER. A certain interest. . . .

THE STRANGE LADY. So, you keep it up? One can see that, when you write, you play the game only to win. Do you want to see how it's played gratis? For your especial benefit, and no one need profit by it! My humbuggery, [20] eh? That all depends, Herr Salter, on how things chance to fall out! Look: they may fall out like this (*Indicates* THE DEMENTED LADY.) when they happen to fall into the hands of a ferocious enemy like you, and then, you have carnage . . . she was young then . . . and beautiful . . . caught here alone in the villa . . . a fleshly carnage, with all the igno- [30] minies that you know, and a mental massacre that was enough to drive her mad and bring her to what she is, enough—in itself—to render her return out of the question. . . . Oh, they may, it is true, fall out like that —or they may fall out differently; she may undergo all the maddening shame and torture, yes—but differently again—finding, for example, [40] in her madness a vengeful fury against fate . . . in the horror of all that has been done to her, and with the sensation of having been left thus utterly defiled, she may experience a shudder of terror at the mere thought of coming back here, to the old life. . . .

SALTER (*pulling her up fiercely*). —you are jesting—

THE STRANGE LADY. —wait!—I said, to the old life, for example here, in this villa—where—Ah, dear God!— fresh as a flower, and pure—pure— at the age of eighteen—clinging to her—(*She alludes to* INEZ, *without turning to look at her, as if the latter were not present and as if she saw her wholly in the past, when, at eighteen, in her company, she had come as a bride to the villa which her uncle had given her as a dowry. Slowly, very slowly, as she goes on talking, she steps backward until she is touching* INEZ, *and as she utters the last words, she reclines her head on* INEZ's *bosom.*)—clinging to her, clinging to her, wanting never to leave her again, not because I did not love him . . . but because, that first night, knowing nothing, her weeping words—she was as ignorant as I: "They say, you know, that now he will have to *see* you." . . .

INEZ (*greatly agitated, she embraces her on the spur of the moment*). Cia! Cia!

THE STRANGE LADY (*holding her off, convulsively*). No—wait; wait!

BRUNO (*joyously triumphant*). That is something I didn't tell you!

THE STRANGE LADY (*having fixed him with a look, she says to him, coldly*). I could drive you mad.—No one told me. (*And then,* BRUNO *having involuntarily turned to look at* LENA, *she hastily adds.*) No, not even Lena, no! What are you thinking of! So intimate a thing as that—(I expressly recalled it)— no one could have told me, even in sisterly confidence, except the one who really said it. (*To* INEZ.) Isn't that so?

INEZ. Yes! Yes!

THE STRANGE LADY (*turning suddenly to* BRUNO). You've made a poor search for your Cia!—You lost no time in rebuilding the villa for her; but you have not looked, you have not thought of looking to see if, among the scattered stones, the rubbish and the ruins, there might have been left something of hers, something of her soul . . . some memory that is really 10 alive—for her! not for you!—Lucky that I've found one!

BRUNO. What do you mean by that?

THE STRANGE LADY (*does not answer him, but turns to* SALTER). Do you understand? And then, so filthy that you can never again get clean, off you go, with one of the most stupid of those officers—(exactly, exactly as I have told you)—off you go, first to Vienna 20 for a number of years, during the confusion that followed the War . . . then to Berlin . . . that other madhouse. . . . One evening at the theatre, you see Barth . . . you learn to dance . . . light flashes through your madness . . . applause . . . delirium . . . you no longer see any reason for depriving yourself of those painted veils of madness 30 . . . then, you go down into the public square, you go through the streets with those veils . . . into the all-night cafes, after three o'clock in the morning, among the clowns in evening clothes . . . eh, Herr Salter, so long as one doesn't become like you, lugubrious and unbearable . . . and so long as, one night, of a sudden, when you are least expecting it, 40 (*Goes toward* BOFFI.) you do not become aware of someone passing close up to you, whisking by like the devil himself, and calling to you: "Signora Lucia, Signora Lucia, your husband is here, a few steps away;

if you like, I'll go call him!" (*Walking away, with her hands to her face.*) Ah, God knows, I felt that he was searching for one who could no longer be! one who, as he must know, he could only find alive in me, in order to make her over for himself, not as she desired (for she no longer desired anything for herself) but as he desired her! (*She shrugs her shoulders, as if freeing herself from an insane illusion, and goes up to* SALTER.) Away! away! away! So, you've come to punish me for my imposture? You are right! Do you know how far I have carried that imposture? To the point of causing myself to be recognized by three persons—my sister—my brother-in-law—my sister-in-law, my husband's sister—three persons whom I am seeing today for the first time in my life!

INEZ (*enormously astonished*). But, Cia, what are you saying?

THE STRANGE LADY. I am saying: it is true that I had never been here, in this region, before he brought me here!

BRUNO (*shouting in a rage*). You know very well, that is not true!

THE STRANGE LADY. It *is* true! It *is* true!

BRUNO. You are trying to make them believe it! You are saying. . . .

THE STRANGE LADY. Yes—it pleased me to have them believe that I was Cia! —But Cia's going away now! Cia's going back to dance!

BRUNO. What?

THE STRANGE LADY. I'm going with him! (*Pointing to* SALTER.) I'm going back to dance at Berlin! at Berlin!

BRUNO. You're not going out of here!

THE STRANGE LADY. I told you that you made a poor search for your Cia! Listen, my dear. Up in the store-room, you had left knocking about, without even knowing it was there, a battered old sandalwood box, with a few silver insects still clinging to the panels. Lena reminded me that this had been one of Cia's keepsakes, a present from her mother. Do you know what I found in one of the compartments of that box? A little notebook of Cia's, in which she had set down Inez's words on the day of the wedding: "They say, you know, that now he will have to *see* you." That notebook is mine, and I am taking it with me! And I have all the more reason to do so, since, strangely enough! the writing appears to be in my hand! (*She laughs, starts to dash out, then stops to add.*) Another thing: One other thing! Do not forget to have the sister look to see if this poor creature has on her side—

THE DOCTOR. —yes—a mole. . . .

THE STRANGE LADY. —red?—protruding?—she has, really?—

THE DOCTOR. —yes—protruding—but not red—black—and not, properly speaking, on her side. . . .

THE STRANGE LADY. In the notebook, it says: "red and protruding—on my side—like a beetle." (*To* BRUNO.)

You see? It must have turned black—it must have become displaced—but she has it!—Another proof that she's the one! Oh, believe me, believe me! she's the one!—Come on, Salter, let's go! (*To* BOFFI.) You will see, Boffi, to sending everything after me. (*To* SALTER.) Is the machine outside? I'm coming—like this! (*She runs toward the door.*)

SALTER. Let's go! Let's go! (*The two of them hastily make for the machine in the garden.*)

THE DOCTOR (*he and the nurse also make a move to go*). No, no, wait! What about us?

BRUNO (*stunned—crestfallen—like all the rest*). What? Like that?

[*He, too, goes out into the garden, followed by the others. The confused sound of excited voices drifts in from outside. Only* AUNT LENA *and* THE DEMENTED LADY *are left on the stage, but the former, still uncertain and dismayed, keeps her distance.*]

THE DEMENTED LADY. Le-na. . . .

AUNT LENA (*she is almost voiceless, as if she could not believe it all*). Cia. . . .

LAST CURTAIN

HENRI–RENÉ LENORMAND

CONTEMPORARY FRENCH drama has been varied and almost nervously experimental, especially in the two decades between the World Wars. Provincial France, in contrast to Russia, England, and America, has had little part in this activity. Few companies even tour the larger French cities. The French stage is a Paris institution, one phase of the night life of the international capital. In a period unique in its craze for new forms in painting, sculpture, music, poetry, fiction, Paris was the center for cliques and schools that rose and fell with bewildering rapidity in a cloud of theories, each with a flutter of little magazines to present and argue its case. Naturally both the drama and the stage reflected this post-War excitement and experimentation. Little theatres like the L'Œuvre of Lugné-Poë, the Studio, the Théâtre des Arts took on new life after the War. Many others were organized to produce unconventional and non-commercial plays in all sorts of modernistic sets, costumes, and techniques. Louis Jouvet's little theatre, The Athénée, attained especial prominence, notably with its productions of Jean Giraudoux's *Amphitryon 38*, *Electre*, and the satirical drama on war, *La guerre de Troie n'aura pas lieu*. Some of these organizations were still flourishing when France fell in the summer of 1940.

Linked to all this activity in the theatre are the names of a score of talented French dramatists who have written plays of considerable if transient interest. Most of these playwrights such as Denys Amiel, Simon Gantillon, Jean-Victor Pellerin, were known only in Paris or to the people who made a point of keeping abreast of the Parisian coteries. Some of them caught the attention of a wider public, as did Charles Vildrac with his *The Steamship Tenacity*. Édouard Bourdet with his *The Captive*, and Jean-Jacque Bernard with his *Invitation to Travel*. A few, such as Jacques Copeau, Jules Romains, Sacha Guitry, achieved considerable success in America. As a group, if so individualistic a collection of cliques may be held together for an instant by a phrase, they covered in terms of dramatic expression almost every aspect of modern life, and every topic of interest to the restless minds of our day.

Among these varied topics were two of unusual interest to the dramatists. One was the role of the Unconscious in human personality. The other was the illusion, or the relativity, of Time, and the bearing of both Time and the Unconscious on the meaning of man's existence. Of the many playwrights who have handled these somewhat esoteric themes, no one has presented them more effectively in terms of the drama and the contemporary stage than H.-R. Lenormand. For this reason, and because his plays have distinction for themselves regardless of their period, we have chosen Lenormand to represent the dramatists of post-War France in this collection.

Lenormand's great reputation has grown up since the Armistice, but his peculiar dramatic genius was unmistakably announced as early as 1905 when, as a youth of twenty-three, his first play was put on by the Grand Guignol. This Montmartre theatre founded in Paris in 1897 to produce little plays of farce or terror, staged Lenormand's psychological thriller in two acts called *White Madness*. The title referred to the Alpine snow that took vengeance upon those who yielded to its lure and tried to scale its white precipices. The set was a terrace of a winter resort from which a telescope commanded a view of the snow and ice-bound mountain, and of two lovers attempting the ascent. These two had discussed how they would act if one slipped and threatened to drag the other into danger. The girl acknowledged that she would cut the rope and save herself. The boy protested that he would rather die than cut the rope that joined them. The next day while climbing they were caught in a storm. She slipped; he cut the rope. Then in remorse he plunged after her. On both the levels of suggested physical action and psychological impact the play administered a shock in the best Grand Guignol style.

The young author of this premonitory play was a Parisian, born in 1882. His precocity was doubtless nourished by the abilities and interests of his family. His father was a writer of distinction as well as a prominent musician. It is tempting to see in Lenormand's later and more exotic plays a reflection of the influence of his father who collected and translated Chinese, Persian, and Polynesian poems, and had a fondness for Oriental music shared by his son. Lenormand followed the normal French educational program through the lycée to the Sorbonne, and the usual literary pattern by publishing his thin volume of prose-poems, *Paysages d'Ame*, at the close of his university days. He traveled widely in his native country, on the Continent, and in England. He studied the plays of Ibsen for their psychological probings into hidden motives and their critical approach to modern society. He read Bergson and Neitzsche. His interest in psychological problems led him to the experiments and teachings of Freud. His preoccupation with symbolism and the phenomenon of Time gave him a fellow feeling for Maeterlinck.

Lenormand was content to develop slowly. His first full-length play, *The Possessed*, was produced at the Théâtre des Arts in 1909, and his second, *Dust*, at the Théâtre Antoine on the eve of the World War. During the next four years he was silent, and, since his early plays had not established him as a dramatist, he entered the new era practically unknown to the public. His next two plays, however, immediately placed him full grown in the front rank of French dramatists, a position which he easily retained. These two plays were *Time Is A Dream* (1919) and *The Failures* (1920). They were presented first in Geneva by the Franco-Russian actor-producer, Georges Pitoëff, who had formed his own company there during the War and had specialized in intellectualist plays with modernistic settings. The plays were then brought to Paris where they scored hits at the Théâtre des Arts in 1919–1920. Shortly thereafter Lenormand's plays were to be seen in every important capital of Europe. His reputation in America was established when the Theatre Guild produced *The Failures* in New York in 1923, and the Neighborhood Playhouse staged *Time Is A Dream* in 1924.

He lived in Paris at the center of an admiring literary and theatrical group until his death in 1938.

Lenormand's psychological plays explore the unconscious and bring to light the complexes, the frustrations, the sins and the fears that lie in that dark cavern. These enemies of the well-adjusted life do not lie still, however; they are restless and ill at ease, and await the right moment to leap out in terrifying conscious action. Their nature is not good but evil. They are the unconquered primitive animal momentarily held at bay by the force of the conscious will. Ceaseless conflict goes on between the instincts and the conscience. In Lenormand's own words, "All my plays tend toward the elucidation of the mystery of the inner life, toward solving the enigma that man presents to himself. My theater offers a conflict between the conscious and the unconscious." And the clue to this mystery was furnished by Sigmund Freud and the technique of the psychoanalysts, though Lenormand as often as not makes these practitioners the villains of his plays.

The most representative of Lenormand's plays on this general theme is *The Dream Doctor* (also called *The Devourer of Dreams*), first presented in Geneva by Pitoëff in January, 1922, in Paris a month later. It is a critical study in psychoanalysis centering about the dream doctor, Luke de Bronte, and a young woman with a hidden secret, Jeannine Felse. The title is explained by his words to Jeannine that his mind feeds "on women's morbid or criminal dreams," and that he is like "Bakou, the Japanese demon, whose special function is to devour evil dreams." His pursuit of these evil dreams has already been disastrous to the lives with which he has tampered. In Jeannine's case he drives her memory back to an incident that had occurred when she was six years old, and which had laid the groundwork for the neurosis from which she is suffering at the time of the play. When the caravan in which her father and mother were crossing the desert was waylaid by bandits, she had signalled to them from the hiding place of her mother and had thereby caused her mother's death.

The dream doctor interpreted this act as a dim, infantile, jealous wish to displace her mother, "and in your dreams you killed her." The cure is to return to that spot in the desert and purge the unconscious. But instead of being cured, Jeannine commits suicide from remorse. The tables of revenge are turned on de Bronte by a previous patient or victim who lashes him and states a part at least of the theme of the play, in these words: "You thought you'd cure her by enlightening her—and the first ray of light which pierced her memory killed her! Things human are twofold! At the same time people are unconscious and responsible, full of scruples and cruelty, of wisdom and incoherence, of logic and madness. . . . Learn at last something about yourself, you specialist in burdened consciences."

The same basic material is dramatized in *Simoom* (1920), *Man and His Phantoms* (1924), *A Secret Life* (1929), and incidentally in other plays, with a more emphatic attack on the role of aberrant or abnormal sex in the warped personalities of men.

Closely related to these dramas are certain others in which the center of interest is shifted to a study of the nature of evil in the world. On this subject Lenormand is one of the important spokesmen for this era. The optimistic belief of the pre-War scientific movement was that good is more powerful than evil; that men faced with choice and knowledge will choose the good; that we are naturally evolving toward the higher and the better, and all that we need is time. The conviction of the post-War era has been that right may be worsted, evil may and often does triumph and perpetuate itself. Evil is an active power, not merely the absence of good.

Lenormand suggests this view in several plays, such as *The Failures* (1920), *The Red Tooth* (1922), *The Coward* (1925); he expressly dramatizes it in a searching play with an exotic setting in French colonial Africa, *In The Shadow of Evil* (1924). A Negro potentate had sold some of his subjects to Moorish slave traders. He then accused an honorable, law-abiding young chieftain of the deed. Every one knew that the young chieftain was innocent. He appeared before the resident administrator unafraid because he was sure that right would triumph over wrong. To the amazement of all, this usually just administrator acquitted the guilty potentate and ordered the innocent man whipped.

Why did the administrator commit an act of such flagrant evil? The reason was that he himself fifteen years before had been dealt with unjustly and without cause or explanation, and that evil act had been smoldering in his unconscious waiting to leap out in revenge. He, like Iago, became an agent of a self-perpetuating evil. His evil deed in turn looses more evil, and the young chieftain revenges his wrong by persuading the beautiful, Christian-spirited wife of the subordinate administrator to go to a native village to minister to the Negroes, but actually to meet her

death. And so the chain reaches into the future link by link. Like Joseph Conrad's famous story on this theme, *Freya of the Seven Isles*, the logic of the progression is tight and complete.

Perhaps it is only natural that a dramatist preoccupied with these problems should be acutely conscious of the illusory nature of Time and its effect upon the sensitive mind. Interest in this puzzle exists on all levels from crystal-gazing clairvoyants to Einstein and the psychological laboratories exploring new frontiers of the mind. We have had many interesting plays on, or making use of, this phase of our mental life. John Balderston's *Berkeley Square* (1928), James Bridie's *The Sleeping Clergyman* (1933), J. B. Priestley's *Time and the Conways* (1937) are familiar examples in a list that could be extended at will in either the drama or the novel. Lenormand has the purest and the clearest dramatization of this teasing subject in *Time Is A Dream*.

Lenormand uses the familiar device of the prophetic dream to give narrative flow to the dramatization of a philosophic problem. Romée has a distinct pre-vision of the tragedy that is on its way into her life and that of her fiancé, Nico Van Eyden. The event is, in one view, already accomplished. For in the eternity and the infinity of ultimate being there is no such thing as this sequence of events which we mortals call Time. Time is only a mode of human thought, a condition of human experience. In the mind of God the past still is the present, and the future has already been. Past, present, and future co-exist. We are prisoners in Time. The present only exists for us, but while we are yet speaking of it, the present is for us the past, the future has become the present and in turn has faded into the past. Sometimes a sensitive mind may in dreams escape the catagories of Time and Space and see the things that are to come in the future of normal experience. Romée has this kind of waking dream in *Time Is A Dream*.

Nico's experience explores another aspect of the problem and gives point to the title. Not only is the revealed event coming toward him inexorably out of the future, but his senses fail to record experience vividly enough to convince him that he is alive on this earth and not existing in a dream. Time has lost clear meaning for him. "When I was a child I thought my existence was an illusion—my sensations didn't seem to give me sufficient proof that I was really in life. . . . Yesterday, to-day, to-morrow are only words . . .

within eternity, we are at once about to be, living, and dead . . . To die is to awaken, to know, to reach that point in eternity where time is no longer a dream, the frontier where all things are co-existent."

It is a tribute to the dramatic art of Lenormand that he has succeeded in stating these speculations in terms of vivid and convincing drama. He has been able to fix our attention on the characters, the settings, and the narrative, and at the same time to make dramatic a purely philosophical theme. The two planes of interest are inextricably interwoven like a well-turned parable. In making this tenuous and illusory material come to life in a play, Lenormand has accomplished a tour de force worthy of careful study as philosophy and dramatic technique.

TIME IS A DREAM

CHARACTERS

RIEMKE VAN EYDEN
ROMÉE CREMERS
MRS. BEUNKE

NICO VAN EYDEN
SAIDYAH

FIRST SCENE

The drawing-room of an old mansion in Utrecht. On the left three violet-tinted windows form a deep bay looking out over luxuriantly wooded grounds. On the right a peat fire is burning in the monumental hearth, on either side of which is a comfortable settee [built-in] piled up with cushions. A lampstand near by. Grey hangings. Sarongs. Antique furniture. A tea table. A telephone on a stand.

Doors rear and left.

Three o'clock of an autumn afternoon. The curtain rises on RIEMKE VAN EYDEN *arranging flowers in a vase. She is a girl of twenty-five, with a gentle, slightly spinsterish manner, but her gown, for all its simplicity, conveys a hint of demure and old-world coquetry.*

[MRS. BEUNKE, *the housekeeper, enters, rear, a little frail old lady, elaborately dressed in the fashion of a bygone day.*]

MRS. BEUNKE. The train is due at half past four, isn't it, Miss Riemke?

RIEMKE. Yes, Mrs. Beunke.

MRS. BEUNKE. I have told Jan to get the carriage ready by a quarter past. Is that early enough?

RIEMKE. Quite. I shall not be going to the station. Miss Romée called up to say she would be over in a few minutes.

MRS. BEUNKE (*bringing out her account-book*). Please, Miss Riemke, could you spare a minute now to go over my accounts?

RIEMKE. Later on, Mrs. Beunke, later on.

MRS. BEUNKE (*a note of anxiety in her voice*). This makes three days since you have looked at them. It is a great responsibility for me.

RIEMKE. Very well, I really will go over them for you to-morrow.

MRS. BEUNKE (*putting the book back into her pocket*). Thank you, Miss Riemke. And, Oh, yes! Shall I bring tea as soon as Miss Romée comes or will you wait for Mr. Nico?

RIEMKE. I don't know; we'll see. (*Looking at* MRS. BEUNKE.) Why, Mrs. Beunke, how flustered you are over Nico's arrival.

MRS. BEUNKE. Well, I have to make sure that everything is just right. I wonder if I've forgotten anything. I have put flowers in his room; I wish they'd been chrysanthemums, but there's not one left in the hot-house; I could find nothing but dahlias.

RIEMKE. That doesn't matter—I'm afraid chrysanthemums or dahlias or any other of our Dutch flowers will look all alike to him; they will all seem very ordinary after the flowers

TIME IS A DREAM: Translated by Winifred Katzin. Reprinted by permission.

582

of Java. You haven't forgotten Said-yah's room, have you?

MRS. BEUNKE. No, Miss Riemke, I have prepared the room he had before. I have had the bed taken out and mats put down everywhere. (*With deep distaste.*) You may believe me or not, Miss Riemke, but the mat he slept on ten years ago still smells of him.

RIEMKE. You mustn't be hard on him, Mrs. Beunke. My brother doesn't look upon him as a servant, you know, but as a friend and confidant rather.

MRS. BEUNKE. Yes, I know. It was just the same before, but what a young man of good family can possibly find to talk about to a nigger is a thing I never could understand.

RIEMKE (*smiling*). Nico likes the natives. In Java when he was little, he was forever running away to the boys' quarters at the other end of the garden; and as a fresh case of cholera broke out amongst them pretty nearly every day, those escapades of his used to keep Mother in a perpetual state of panic.

MRS. BEUNKE. Yes; diseases—that's about all you can expect to get from those creatures.

RIEMKE. Saidyah would lay down his life for Nico without an instant's hesitation or a word of complaint.

MRS. BEUNKE (*sighing*). I know, but if only he would learn not to squat on the furniture to smoke his pipe and stop spitting under the carpets!

RIEMKE (*setting the vase on the mantelpiece*). There, that's finished! (*She sits down. MRS. BEUNKE does likewise.*)

MRS. BEUNKE. How did you find Mr. Nico, Miss Riemke?

RIEMKE. A little depressed, of course. When one has been living in the Tropics, you know——

MRS. BEUNKE. Was he glad to see Holland again?

RIEMKE. Yes. But I think he still dreads it in a way.

MRS. BEUNKE. Did he mention his illness?

RIEMKE. No—it is still a painful subject with him. But I am sure he remembers every detail of it.

MRS. BEUNKE. After all these years, too!

RIEMKE. Oh, he has an extraordinarily vivid memory. Yesterday he was recalling to me incidents of our childhood which had almost faded out of my mind. He told me that when we came from the East I was so weak that Mother had to carry me in her arms and they are supposed to have fed me on raw eggs beaten up and flavored with vanilla. Is that true?

MRS. BEUNKE. Yes, you were as yellow as a Chinese baby and you used to stare so inquisitively at every one with great big eyes all ringed round with the fever—I can see you now.

RIEMKE. And he used to run about the house in his little Javanese costume that the gardener's children always laughed at. He remembers to this day how their jeering used to hurt him. Even at that age he was over-sensitive.

MRS. BEUNKE. What news did he bring you of Mr. and Mrs. Van Eyden, Miss Riemke?

RIEMKE. They are both well, thank you, Mrs. Beunke. They have grown rather stouter and paler, Nico says, but that's always the way in hot climates unless one leads a very active life. Father only goes to his office two hours a day now and Mother hardly stirs out at all any more. She moves around as little as possible. Nico described her so well; I could see the whole picture of the rooms with the shutters always closed, and Mother in her white linen wrap, sitting there almost immovably, only now and then lifting her hand to feel the beads of perspiration that break out on her forehead where the hair is just beginning to turn grey. She is used to my being away. I think her mind has settled into a deep calm that is almost like vacancy.

MRS. BEUNKE (*with emotion*). How sad it is, though, Miss Riemke. Why couldn't God will that the whole family should come together just once more?

RIEMKE. Later on, Mrs. Beunke, later on. In a few years' time my people will be leaving the Indies for good and come back to settle here. Then this house will come alive again.

MRS. BEUNKE (*sighing*). Yes, but then Mr. Nico will have gone. I have always thought he would not stay with us more than two or three months at a time. And when he leaves everything will be lonely again until your people come.

RIEMKE. Well, Mrs. Beunke, and what if it is? Isn't solitude nice to sleep in? Perhaps it isn't wise to ask any more of life than simply to be allowed to doze one's days and years away.

MRS. BEUNKE. Goodness me, Miss Riemke, you surely don't call it unwise to hope to grow old amongst your dear ones.

RIEMKE. It might be, Mrs. Beunke. Affection is very exhausting, you know, and none of us has very much strength if the truth were known. The clock striking, a few telephone calls, and your little household duties are enough to agitate and tire you out, and as for me, why if I had more burden of affection laid upon me, I think I should find it very hard to carry. I'm growing into a real old maid,

Mrs. Beunke. I ought to be loving a parrot or a goldfish now. Love of human beings is too wearing.

MRS. BEUNKE (*rising*). I can hear the carriage coming. I'll go and tell Jan not to wait for you.

[*She goes out left, and almost immediately* ROMÉE CREMERS *comes in. She is a girl of twenty-three, tall and straight, and carries her head with a touch of pride. Her clear features look as though they have been sculptured out of the firm and radiant flesh. The expression of her grey eyes and the somewhat fantastic charm of manner betray an impulsive and passionate nature. She is wearing a sports suit.*]

ROMÉE. Hullo, dear. Well, is he here?

RIEMKE. Not yet, but he will be soon.

ROMÉE. Didn't you bring him back with you from Rotterdam?

RIEMKE. No. He brought some important message from my father for the directors of his company and thought he had better get that disposed of first.

ROMÉE (*sitting down*). I walked over by the lake path and I feel rather tired.

RIEMKE (*looking at her*). You look tired; you're quite pale. You aren't ill, are you?

ROMÉE. No, it's nothing at all. Don't bother about it. How did you find him?

RIEMKE (*eagerly*). Oh, wonderfully well.

ROMÉE. Did he enjoy the voyage?

RIEMKE. Yes, especially India. He stayed there several months.

ROMÉE. I'm sure I shan't know him again. He was a boy when he went away and it will be very strange to find in his place a man who has become, after all, a perfect stranger although one still calls him by his first name.

RIEMKE (*again studying her face*). Why, darling, you do look ill. Aren't you feeling any better yet?

ROMÉE. Yes, a little.

RIEMKE. Would you like some tea?

ROMÉE. No, thanks.

RIEMKE. Please tell me what is the matter.

ROMÉE. I told you, I'm tired—it came over me all of a sudden as I was walking along by the water.

RIEMKE. It's only twenty minutes' walk from your place here. That little distance couldn't possibly . . . [10]

ROMÉE. No, it wasn't the walk——I don't know what caused it, but a kind of heaviness came over me all at once quite without warning, a queer feeling of exhaustion, don't you know. (*A pause—her eyes search* RIEMKE'S *face.*) Riemke, if I tell you a secret, can I absolutely rely on you to keep it to yourself?

RIEMKE. Of course you can, but why all the mystery?

ROMÉE. Because I should hate the thing I'm going to tell you to be talked about and discussed and made a peg to hang theories on. Something very strange and unaccountable has happened to me—I was walking quietly along the path by the lake, when, just as I came to the little white wicket at [30] the end of your grounds, I was seized by that weariness I spoke of. Of course I know that it was only that the walk had tired me more than usual but I couldn't make out why I felt so extraordinarily and unreasonably depressed. At the same moment everything around took on an unnatural appearance, horrible because of its unnaturalness; you know what I [40] mean? The trees along the opposite edge of the lake went quite flat and lifeless, like trees on a piece of tapestry, there was no more play of light and shade and not the faintest breath of wind. It was all intensely still and unpleasant. My limbs seemed to grow heavier every moment and each step I took was more difficult than the last; I was conscious of something uncanny, yes, and terrifying, in the air, when a slight mist began to envelop the lake and I saw all at once in the water to the left of me, a man's head. He wasn't very far from the bank and I saw his face quite distinctly; I should recognize it in a thousand.

RIEMKE. It couldn't have been anybody bathing—the water is dangerous at this time of year.

ROMÉE. That's what I said to myself at once. No, that man was drowning, and in a few seconds his head had vanished as suddenly as it had appeared.

RIEMKE. Didn't you shout for some one to come? Didn't you call for help?

ROMÉE. I couldn't. Besides I knew it would have been useless.

RIEMKE. How do you mean, you knew?

ROMÉE. Just that. The man was no more than ten yards from the bank and yet I had a feeling he was actually ever so far away and that nobody could possibly have reached him.

RIEMKE. And then?

ROMÉE. That is all. The fear and the queer feeling of heaviness left me, the mist melted way, the trees and everything looked natural again and I came into your garden. Now, what do you understand by that?

RIEMKE. No more than you do—and there is one thing especially that puzzles me—you say that everything around you looked unnatural, and yet you describe it in such detail. Do you think the man was real or did you just see him in a sort of hallucination —you know what I mean, one of those waking dreams one hears about?

ROMÉE. Oh, no, I wasn't dreaming. It all looked perfectly real.

RIEMKE. You said there was a mist but there hasn't been any mist to-day.

ROMÉE. Yes there has. Just a slight one that came up and was gone again in a moment—what you call a sea-flame.

RIEMKE. I suppose I didn't notice it.

ROMÉE. And my mind was so clear that I noticed at once the alterations you have made down there.

RIEMKE. What alterations?

ROMÉE. Why, the reeds, for one thing. You have had them cut down all along the edge of the lake.

RIEMKE (in amazement). What are you talking about, Romée? We haven't had the reeds cut down at all.

ROMÉE. But, my dear, of course you have—at the entrance to your grounds. There's not a single one left.

RIEMKE. Romée, I assure you you're mistaken. Are you sure you mean our bank?

ROMÉE. Yes, near the white wicket.

RIEMKE. The reeds haven't been cut down there—or anywhere else—since this place belonged to us.

ROMÉE. I can't make it out. And haven't you got a boat down there? A green boat?

RIEMKE. Not any kind of boat.

ROMÉE. Let's go and make sure.

RIEMKE. We don't need to go, we can see from here. Look.

ROMÉE (standing in the bay-window). You are right. The reeds are there again, just as they were before.

RIEMKE. Just as they have always been.

ROMÉE. And no boat. (A frightened pause.) I must have had—what you said—a kind of hallucination. And yet I did see——

RIEMKE (thoughtfully). Yes, you certainly saw——

ROMÉE. The boat was real, so were the seats, and the oars—and that face was real.

RIEMKE. When you thought the man was drowning, you didn't call for help, you said, because you had "a feeling that nobody could possibly have reached him."

ROMÉE. Yes, it was the strangest thing. I saw him quite near me, and I knew him to be an enormous distance away.

RIEMKE. Suppose that that distance was not in space but in time?

ROMÉE. How do you mean, in time?

RIEMKE. Suppose you had seen that spot not as it is now, but as it was once, long ago?

ROMÉE. And the man?

RIEMKE. The man might have lived long ago, too. He might have gone in bathing and got drowned.

ROMÉE. I don't believe in ghosts.

RIEMKE. You know Charlotte Brandes, don't you?

ROMÉE. Yes, I met her here.

RIEMKE. Well, one evening she was walking in her garden in Gelderland, when she noticed the summer-house was all lit up. She went towards it, very curious to know what was going on inside, and when she looked through the blue latticed windows, she saw a whole company of people at the table, an entire family dressed in the costumes of a hundred years ago, quietly having tea.

ROMÉE. What did she do?

RIEMKE. She had the presence of mind to go back five minutes later, with the servants, but the summer-house was empty and the lock had not been touched. They made an investigation but it led to nothing.

ROMÉE. How does she account for the apparition, then?

RIEMKE. She doesn't account for it at all,

but it made her think that human beings may leave behind them imprints
on their surroundings, as it were,
which possibly sometimes reappear,
so that what she saw there may have
been one whole moment out of the
past revealing itself to her intact.

ROMÉE. Did she ever see anything like it
again?

RIEMKE. No, never.

ROMÉE. And didn't it unhinge her mind?

RIEMKE. Unhinge her mind? Why, she's
the most level-headed woman I know.

[MRS. BEUNKE *enters, rear, carrying a copper
pail filled with the coals upon which the
teakettle is set. The girls say no more until
she has left the room.*]

ROMÉE. Couldn't this be investigated too,
without anybody knowing?

RIEMKE. One might question Mrs.
Beunke.

ROMÉE. Has she been long in this house?

RIEMKE. Nearly forty years. She was in
the service of the old owners. She has
a great store of information.

ROMÉE. How could I get her to talk?

RIEMKE. That is easy.

[MRS. BEUNKE *comes in again with a silver
tray containing the tea-service and cakes.*]
Mrs. Beunke, will you have tea with
us?

MRS. BEUNKE. Thank you, Miss Riemke.
Are you not going to wait for Mr.
Nico?

RIEMKE. No, Miss Romée feels cold.
(MRS. BEUNKE *fills the teapot.*) Mrs.
Beunke, we were just talking about
the Van Asbecks who lived here before we came, and Miss Romée was
asking whether they had any children.
Do you know?

MRS. BEUNKE. No, Miss Romée, they died
childless and it was a great pity, for
the Van Asbeck family was one of the
best in the province.

ROMÉE. Were you with them long?

MRS. BEUNKE. More than fifteen years,
Miss Romée.

ROMÉE. Will you pour out the tea,
please?

[MRS. BEUNKE *pours the tea and hands the
sugar round.*]

ROMÉE (*helping herself*). Thank you.

RIEMKE. Has the house changed much
since their time?

MRS. BEUNKE. No, Miss Riemke; except
the outbuildings and the terrace
along the north wing that your father
built.

ROMÉE. And the grounds?

MRS. BEUNKE. They have not changed,
either. The trees have grown taller—
that is all.

RIEMKE. And the reeds?

MRS. BEUNKE. The reeds, Miss Riemke?

RIEMKE. Were there as many then as
there are now?

MRS. BEUNKE. Oh, no! Mrs. Van Asbeck
had them cut down. She thought it
looked more genteel.

[*The girls exchange glances.*]

RIEMKE. So the shore of the lake was
quite clear then?

MRS. BEUNKE. Yes, Miss Riemke, quite
clear.

RIEMKE. It must have been much more
convenient for fishing, boating—I
suppose they did have a boat.

MRS. BEUNKE. No; Mr. and Mrs. Van
Asbeck did not boat or fish.

ROMÉE. Didn't they bathe in their lake
either?

MRS. BEUNKE. No, Miss Romée.

RIEMKE. And didn't any one else bathe
there?

MRS. BEUNKE. Yes, indeed, Miss Riemke
—Mr. Henry—(*She pauses; then gets up
from her chair.*) I think I hear the carriage coming.

RIEMKE. Stay where you are, Mrs.
Beunke, I'll go.—(*She hastens out, left.*)

ROMÉE. Mr. Henry, you were saying——

MRS. BEUNKE. Yes, Mr. Van Asbeck's nephew. He was a powerful swimmer and he used to swim in the lake every day all through the summer.

ROMÉE. Oh?

MRS. BEUNKE. But Mrs. Van Asbeck did not quite approve of it, so when it came time for Mr. Henry's swim, she used to have her blinds pulled down.

ROMÉE. What for?

MRS. BEUNKE. Why, for the sake of modesty, Miss Romée.

ROMÉE (*pretending to summon some recollection to mind*). Henry Van Asbeck—let me see—didn't I hear somewhere that he was drowned?

MRS. BEUNKE. Oh no, Miss Romée; he is still alive.

ROMÉE. Really?

MRS. BEUNKE. You must be thinking of the accident that happened to him.

ROMEÉ. Here?

MRS. BEUNKE. Yes, in the lake.

ROMÉE. What was it?

MRS. BEUNKE. He was seized with cramp not far from the shore—fortunately they heard him call out.

ROMEÉ. Was that very long ago?

MRS. BEUNKE. Oh, yes, more than thirty years. (*Sound of voices outside.*) Ah, here comes Mr. Nico!

[NICO *comes rapidly into the room, left, followed by* RIEMKE *and* SAIDYAH. *He is a young man, twenty-five years of age, clean shaven and excessively pale, with unquiet eyes and the nervous, sudden gestures characteristic of lonely people in the momentary excitement of a departure or an arrival.* SAIDYAH *is a copper-skinned Javanese, past fifty. He is dressed in a European coat and a sarong, and wears a turban. He is carrying a voluminous bundle wrapped in a bright-coloured cloth.*]

NICO (*warmly grasping both* ROMÉE's *hands*). Why, here's our dear Romée!

ROMÉE (*whose eyes, since the moment he entered, have been fixed in stunned incredulity upon his face*). Oh, how do you do?

SAIDYAH (*greeting* ROMÉE *in Oriental fashion*). I greet you, Nonna Cremers. (*She returns the salutation with a nod.*) (*He greets* MRS. BEUNKE.) How are you, Nonna Beunke? You have not changed, you know——

MRS. BEUNKE (*with friendliness*). Nor have you, Saidyah.

SAIDYAH. Ah yes, I have, Mother. Ten years ago I was still a hunter, beating the tiger out of the bush, but you were already quite old then, and wrinkled and little.

NICO (*to* ROMÉE). It *is* good to see you again, Romée.

ROMÉE. It is good to see you too, Nico.

RIEMKE (*to* NICO). Well, would you have known her again?

NICO. No, I don't believe I should.

RIEMKE (*to* ROMÉE). Would you?

ROMÈE (*throwing off her torpor*). Why, yes, of course I should, at once.

RIEMKE. Come, Mrs. Beunke, give him some tea, will you?

CURTAIN

SECOND SCENE

The drawing-room. A blazing fire of pine logs. It is eleven o'clock in the morning but the sky is so heavily overcast and the fog clings so persistently to the windows, that the room is in semi-darkness. ROMÉE *has just arrived, and* NICO *is helping her off with her raincoat.*

NICO. I call it really heroic of you to come out in weather like this.

ROMÉE. Why? I love fogs.

NICO (*leading her to the fire*). Come over here and get dry.

ROMÉE. Isn't Riemke down yet?

NICO. Oh yes; she is leaving us alone on purpose.

ROMÉE (*sitting down*). Do you think she is getting used to the idea of our leaving her?

NICO. She is resigning herself to it; I doubt whether she is still capable of suffering very keenly. She lives in dread of sorrow, you know, and protects herself against it in advance so that when it does come, it finds her heart already benumbed—anaesthetized, you might call it.

ROMÉE. All the same, I should feel happier if we could take her with us.

NICO. That is absolutely out of the question. She has never been able to stand the climate of the East Indies. The fever seized on her down there at once and for always, and although she used to play about and laugh and chatter like the other children, one knew that terrible fever-heat was inwardly consuming her all the while. It was as though a shaft of sun itself had struck right into her body and was drying it up little by little.

ROMÉE. She was a child then and the fever is very hard on one at that age; but now——

NICO. No. You don't know what frail threads her life hangs upon—she will never be able to live out of this country. If she had to say good-bye to this stupor-stricken landscape and the fogs overhanging these waterways, it would simply kill her, Romée. She draws her life from the very things that are death to me.

ROMÉE. What things are death to you, my dearest?

NICO. Oh, you know. These grey mists that go sweeping across the country week in and week out; the rain that's half fog and the fog that's already rain—I feel myself going to pieces under it.

ROMÉE (*smiling*). How funny you are, you two—forever analysing the weather and blessing or railing at the sky. Why, I never look at it; I don't give it even a passing thought.

NICO. I know it's not very strong-minded or very intelligent to be so much at the mercy of a more or less generous supply of light, but what can one do if one's made that way! In our family we are all exceedingly sensitive to the influence of the weather.

ROMÉE. Do you know what I was thinking just now? Why shouldn't we be married here in the house instead of in Java as you have planned? It would mean so much to Riemke, dear, and I know she wouldn't mind so dreadfully then if we left her afterwards.

NICO (*sharply*). No, no! Not here!

ROMÉE. Why not?

NICO. Because when a great happiness is coming to one, one should receive it in the midst of beauty. In this place happiness is faded before it comes, withered before it has had time to flower.

ROMÉE. Very well, you shall have it as you want it—don't let us say any more about it.

NICO. Do you feel warmer now?

ROMÉE. I wasn't cold before; you always think I'm cold.

NICO (*taking up an album*). Look, I have found the photographs we were speaking of yesterday.

ROMÉE (*eagerly*). Oh, do show them to me.

NICO (*he lights the lamp*). Eleven o'clock in the morning and dark already.

[*An intimate glow is shed over the room and outside the day looks bleaker by contrast. The two young people turn over the pages of the album.*]

ROMÉE. What are all those strange-looking plants?

NICO. That is a corner of the forest behind my people's house. (*Showing her other photographs.*) Here is the harbor—and the river—and here's a rice-field—this is our house. The sea is quite near; you can see it from the verandah, blazing beyond you like a furnace of blue; they moor the little Malay boats by the stern and at low tide you see them rise and fall almost imperceptibly as though they were trying to breathe. (*He turns a page.*) The garden—the river—here's a rice-field.

ROMÉE. Oh!

NICO. Every afternoon the wind lifts dense purple clouds behind the banyans and the perfume of the flowers is so heavy and sweet that it seems to weigh down the air.

ROMÉE. It is a perfect paradise!

NICO. You often see the fronds of the tree-ferns spread out against golden mists, like delicate lace they look, and in the heart of a leaf a single ear lifts its slender stalk high above all the rest, like a soft, hairy snake. A human figure gleams through the bamboos—and infinite small creatures send up a tenuous music from the earth. When you have been there, you will realize how impossible it is ever to live anywhere else.

ROMÉE (*leaning close to his side*). When I think that all this is to be *our* place, Nico, *our* home, I can hardly bear the time that lies between us and such happiness. But so long as you were with me, my dear, I should be content to live beside the dismallest canal in Holland—I would live *anywhere* with you.

NICO (*rising*). No—not anywhere; don't say that. With a roof like this shut down upon you always, how can you possibly forget?

ROMÉE. Forget what?

NICO (*pacing the floor*). What every one of us must learn to forget. Our destiny, our fate, the idea that although we might at a stretch believe ourselves free in space, we know we are the prisoners of time. In Java you do learn after a while to put all that out of your mind.

ROMÉE. It is never in mine.

NICO. You are too young. It is a thing that dawns on one suddenly when one gets to be about thirty. One day in Ceylon I was alone on a mountain-top. A rose-coloured haze lay upon the rocks and the sun was going down into a great abyss of light. Suddenly my ear caught a sound, an unaccountable sound; it seemed to come right out of the sun; it sounded very sweet and steady and rather loud, and in a few moments it had stopped. It didn't die away, but broke off clean, as though some task it had been given to fulfil was done and finished.

ROMÉE. What could it have been?

NICO. What was it actually? That I don't know, but to me it was a symbol of life.

ROMÉE. How do you mean?

NICO. A symbol of human life—an unaccountable harmony resounding for a few moments and ceasing at a given time, fixed in advance.

ROMÉE. Fixed in advance?

NICO. Yes—a chord of music doomed, in spite of its loveliness and purity, to be cut off at one stroke, without reason or warning. Ah, Romée, the instant that exquisite note was silent, I understood the whole ruthless, futile stupidity of the laws of life.

ROMÉE (*thoughtfully*). Nico, is what you are saying possible, is it certain?

NICO. What?

ROMÉE. That the length of our lives can be measured out in advance, just like a reel of cotton or a roll of cloth?

NICO. Why not?

ROMÉE. It would be too horrible.

NICO. Yes, if people knew the number and order of the hours before them; fortunately though, they don't.

ROMÉE. They couldn't possibly know, 10 could they?

NICO. Some people say they could.

ROMÉE. Who?

NICO. The initiates, for instance; in India —I have met some of them.

RIEMKE (*coming in hesitantly, right*). Oh, Romée, you're here—good-morning.

ROMÉE. Hullo, dear.

RIEMKE. I am so sorry to disturb you both——

ROMÉE. Why, Riemke, as though you could——

RIEMKE. But the architect is here, Nico.

NICO. Good. I want to see him.

ROMÉE. Are you building?

NICO. No—only freshening this old place up a bit.

RIEMKE (*smiling*). He thinks I will live less cheerlessly if he has the house done up. 30

NICO. That wall staring like a haggard face at you through the trees was beginning to get on my nerves. And the garden was growing into a positive wilderness. Didn't you notice the beeches as you came down, Romée?

ROMÉE. Yes, and it made me very sad, too. There were five or six men cutting them down.

NICO. But they threw the whole of the 40 north wing into the shade, like an everlasting green twilight all the day long; you couldn't breathe in those rooms any more. You have to let the daylight in, you know. (*Going out.*) I'll be right back.

ROMÉE (*putting her arms around* RIEMKE). Happiness is an awful thing, Riemke. For years you and I have never passed a single day without seeing each other and now in a few weeks' time there will be four thousand miles between us. And I'm not even sad about it—it doesn't make me cry —it doesn't hurt to think of.

RIEMKE. It doesn't make me cry either— no, it doesn't hurt much. Please don't let's talk about it. (ROMÉE *kisses her.*)

MRS. BEUNKE (*coming in, left*). Good-morning, Miss Romée.

ROMÉE. How are you, Mrs. Beunke?

RIEMKE. What is it, Mrs. Beunke?

MRS. BEUNKE. The men are asking for their coffee, Miss Riemke. Shall I give it to them?

RIEMKE. Have they finished their work?

MRS. BEUNKE. Yes, Miss Riemke, behind the house, and they have finished down by the lake, too.

RIEMKE. What have they been doing there?

MRS. BEUNKE. Mr. Nico gave orders to have all the reeds cut down.

[ROMÉE *gets up.*]

RIEMKE. Oh, I didn't know that. (*She goes to the bay-window and stands there while looking out—then turns round.*) Give them their coffee, Mrs. Beunke.

MRS. BEUNKE. Yes, Miss Riemke.

[*A reddish sunlight is trying timidly to force a way through the fog.* MRS. BEUNKE *switches off the light as she leaves the room.* ROMÉE *goes over to the window and stands there horror-stricken. At* RIEMKE'S *touch upon her shoulder she shudders.*]

ROMÉE (*whispering*). I can't understand it —not one reed left, and that grey water right up to the edge—now the place looks exactly as I saw it three months ago.

RIEMKE. I think—wasn't there something else then, a boat?

ROMÉE. Yes—but that's of no importance —everything else—Riemke, where did Nico get the idea of cutting down the rushes?

RIEMKE. I don't know at all.

ROMÉE. Didn't he say anything about it to you?

RIEMKE. No, not a word.

ROMÉE. And you have never told him what happened to me down there? 10

RIEMKE. Never.

ROMÉE (pointing to the lake). Then how do you explain that?

RIEMKE. Why, I don't know—coincidence I dare say. He is making a few alterations about the place. Those grasses had really grown rather thick; he must have noticed it and had them cut down. It seems a perfectly natural thing for him to have done. 20

ROMÉE. Yes, unless——

RIEMKE. Unless what?

ROMÉE (changing her mind). Nothing— just an idea and most likely a very foolish one at that. Leave me alone with him presently. I want to ask him some questions.

RIEMKE. Very well, but take my advice and don't tell him anything about your adventure.

ROMÉE. No, of course I won't.

RIEMKE. It would make a deep impression on him and he would worry over it; we mustn't let him do that; he is in very low spirits as it is.

ROMÉE. Yes, I had noticed that.

NICO (entering, left). That fellow's not an architect; he's a bricklayer—he wants to build towers! He doesn't understand that all I want is for the house 40 not to go on looking like a face.

RIEMKE. Did you make that clear to him?

NICO. Yes, and he suggested all sorts of nonsense, when all that's necessary is simply to take away one of the skylights and put in one more window on

the first floor. They would break up the human symmetry of the wall as it is now.

RIEMKE. Would you like me to speak to him?

NICO. I wish you would, Riemke. (RIEMKE goes out, right. NICO joins ROMÉE at the window.) Do you see that? I've cleared up the edge of the lake— it looks nice, doesn't it?

[A pause. They return to the hearth.]

ROMÉE. Nico, you were saying before that you had met some initiates in India——

NICO. Yes.

ROMÉE. Is it true they acquire a knowledge of their destiny?

NICO. I have seen an old priest in Madras who said that he could explore the past at will.

ROMÉE. And the future?

NICO. The future, too. He was a kind of religious philosopher you meet down there—we had several talks together. He had me come and see him on the terrace of his temple at sunset and there he would tell me about his voyages into Time, as we sat looking out over the Indian Ocean.

ROMÉE. How did he learn to penetrate into the past and future?

NICO. By exposing himself on the ground at night and giving himself up to the unknown powers. In that state of suspense, of almost death-like passivity, visions were born in him, and he knew they belonged to the future or to the past.

ROMÉE. But what proofs did he have?

NICO. He could find out facts by which to prove the past happenings he witnessed during his experiments.

ROMÉE. And the future?

NICO. That is harder to control, of course. But he showed me a vision of war observed twenty years ago which materialized a little while ago down to the smallest details in an expedition to Afghanistan.

ROMÉE. Then according to him the future is already mapped out ahead?

NICO. He says the past, the present and the future are co-existent.

ROMÉE. It is incomprehensible.

NICO. Obviously; our notion of time prevents our conceiving it. But many other things inconceivable to us, *are*, nevertheless. "Man walks in Time as in a garden; behind him there goes one spreading a veil so that he may not behold the flowers of the past; before him goes one spreading a veil likewise, so that he may not yet behold the flowers of the future. All these flowers, however, bloom at once behind the two veils and the eyes of the initiate contemplate them continually."

ROMÉE. Didn't you ever ask him about yourself and your future?

NICO. I didn't want to—what is the use of worrying oneself needlessly?

ROMÉE. Do you think only the initiate can have these revelations?

NICO. No. There are old peasant women in Brittany who see funerals a year ahead. They can tell you all the people who will be there; women are always more sensitive than we to these emanations of the future.

ROMÉE. What a wonderful gift to have ——

NICO. Wonderful, yes, but barren——

ROMÉE. How do you mean?

NICO. I don't see what good there can be in a gift like that.

ROMÉE. Why, if one were to discover, for instance, that some danger threatened a person, one could warn him against it.

NICO. And then?

ROMÉE. Couldn't the danger be averted?

NICO. No. Seers have never prevented anything. One may know the future, but one can't change it. Time is like a piece of machinery whose working we can neither hold back nor stop.

ROMÉE. Then supposing a woman foresaw a catastrophe hanging over the person she cared most for in the world—her child, say—she couldn't save it?

NICO. Impossible.

ROMÉE. Then what could she do?

NICO. Nothing. Suffer in silence until the accomplishment of the event.

ROMÉE. That is more than flesh and blood could stand. She would go mad.

NICO (*taking her hand*). Why, Romée, what is the matter? Your hands are all moist and trembling.

ROMÉE. It is the thought that one couldn't do anything—even if one knew—it is awful to think of.

NICO. What an impressionable girl you are—don't let that worry you—we hardly ever do know what we dread to know——

ROMÉE. No, fortunately.

[RIEMKE *enters, rear.*]

NICO. Well, did you make him understand?

RIEMKE. I hope so—he is going to submit you another plan.

NICO. Without towers?

RIEMKE. Yes, he promised that.

NICO. Well, that's something, anyway.

RIEMKE. Mrs. Beunke just told me we could go in to dinner.

NICO (*going towards the door, rear*). All right. (ROMÉE *signs to* RIEMKE *that she wants to speak to her.* NICO *turns round.*) Aren't you coming?

RIEMKE. In one moment, Nico.

[NICO *goes out.*]

ROMÉE (*whispering*). I understand it now ——

RIEMKE (*in the same tone*). What?

ROMÉE. The thing that happened to me down by the lake—and the reeds—and everything.

RIEMKE. Well?

ROMÉE. First I want to tell you one thing I have kept from you up to now for fear of the shock it might give you; but to-day you have got to know. Riemke, the face that appeared to me on the water that day was Nico's face!

RIEMKE (*in horror*). Nico's?

ROMÉE. When he came into the room half an hour afterwards, I recognized him at once.

RIEMKE. It is absurd, Romée—it is impossible.

ROMÉE. It is true. And now I am certain that my vision had nothing to do with the past—but with the future.

RIEMKE. What do you say?

ROMÉE. I say that little by little this landscape is changing, Riemke, and it is not going back to what it was before our time but towards what it is going to be like one day. (*A pause.*)

NICO'S VOICE. Aren't you girls coming in to dinner?

RIEMKE (*answering*). Yes, yes, we're coming.

[*They exchange a look of understanding and go out.*]

CURTAIN

THIRD SCENE

The drawing-room. A radiant summer afternoon: MRS. BEUNKE *is asleep in a chair, her account-book in her lap.*

[NICO *and* ROMÉE *enter arm in arm.*]

ROMÉE (*laughing*). Oh, look, Mrs. Beunke has fallen asleep.

NICO. Yes, she often does that nowadays.

ROMÉE. She is getting old.

NICO. It isn't age.

ROMÉE. Is she ill?

NICO. Not more so than usual. Living is what ails her. She only weighs about eighty pounds and yet she finds it exceedingly difficult to move her tiny person. She worries horribly over getting tea, and settling her accounts, and eliminating dust. The weight of these immense responsibilities is too much for her. She tries to escape them by going to church because she falls asleep as soon as she gets settled in her pew. She cries, too, now and then. Life is too heavy for her.

[MRS. BEUNKE *wakes up.*]

NICO. Hullo, Mrs. Beunke.

MRS. BEUNKE (*uneasily*). Oh, Mr. Nico!

NICO. Still tired?

MRS. BEUNKE (*agitated*). I wasn't asleep, Mr. Nico—I—I was reckoning up my accounts in my head.

NICO (*indulgently*). All right, all right—don't worry—go on resting. (MRS. BEUNKE *goes out, right.*) Haven't you noticed that lots of people here can't stand the weight of life?

ROMÉE. Not only here.

NICO. But here especially.

ROMÉE. What is the reason, do you think?

NICO. I don't know, the sky perhaps—perhaps the water.

ROMÉE (*watching him*). The water?

NICO (*sitting down*). The water is dead here—one grows like it, stagnant and choked with weeds. Look at our neighbours; they are no more alive than their houses. They are all so dejected and apathetic—like blighted trees or fungus-eaten walls or canals of stagnant water. This country is really a torment to me.

ROMÉE (*tenderly*). We'll be leaving it very soon now, dear.

NICO. I sometimes wonder whether it isn't too late?

ROMÉE. Too late for what?

NICO. To escape.

ROMÉE. How should it be too late?

NICO. I am not well, Romée; I am certainly not as well as I was when I came. That's not quite right what I said about the water just now. It isn't so much its inanition that spreads to us as the corrosion of its innumerable weeds. You know what I mean, don't you, those lichens and mosses that fasten on to the surface of the water until they cover it entirely from one bank clear across to the other? I feel like that—grown over and eaten up, suffocated under just such an evil growth of trouble and doubts in my mind.

ROMÉE. But what trouble, my dearest, what doubts?

NICO. Oh, you wouldn't understand if I told you. You'd only laugh at me. Besides I feel myself that all this is unspeakably petty and morbid. But it's a thing of long standing—it nearly killed me when I was fifteen. Afterwards, though, down in Java, it left me again, but now it is all coming back just as it was before. There are days when it takes me by the throat and strangles the life out of me.

ROMÉE. Why did you never speak of it before?

NICO. Because there's nothing to be done for it—I know that perfectly well.

ROMÉE. But what is it about?

NICO. Just scepticism, that's all, doubt of everything—of life, of things, of myself. When I was a child I thought my existence was an illusion—my sensations didn't seem to give me sufficient proof that I was really in life. A little later, when I took up astronomy, I noticed that the calculations of schol-ars concerning the course of the stars were not accurate; mere approximations at best. There was always some error, some uncertainty. So then I began to doubt the existence of the stars themselves. I wondered if they were not merely a kind of stage-setting, you know, an optical illusion, and absolutely unrelated to anything we human beings fancy we know about their distance or their substance or their dimensions. I told that notion of mine to one very learned man and he told me he understood it and didn't think it absurd. That was the year I tried to kill myself.

ROMÉE (*startled*). You tried to kill yourself?

NICO. Oh, not out of despair—curiosity rather, to set my mind finally at peace.

ROMÉE. And you really tried to——

NICO. Yes——

ROMÉE. When?

NICO. Just ten years ago.

ROMÉE. Where?

NICO. Here.

ROMÉE. Oh!

NICO. Nobody knew.

ROMÉE. But some one must have saved you, or did you manage to get back to the bank by yourself?

NICO (*in astonishment*). What bank?

ROMÉE. Wasn't it down in the lake?

NICO. No. I hanged myself in the loft, near the middle skylight; the nail is there still. But the rope didn't hold more than a few seconds; it broke and I fainted on the floor. I never tried again. (*A pause.*)

ROMÉE. Why did you keep it a secret from Riemke?

NICO. Because they would have had me watched; they might have even shut me up. Besides, we left for Java again that time and that's a country where your mind soon finds peace. You don't suffer from the unknowable down there as you do in this place—you accept life—here you repudiate it. You insist on understanding. (*Bitterly.*) What's the use of understanding? Believing is what we need. We must have faith and a catch-word to pin it on; fate, freedom, soul, matter, and such-like—they mean nothing, 10 yet we choose one and keep hold of it. It's the price we pay for peace. My trouble is that I cannot and will not be the dupe of these things.

ROMÉE (*putting her arms round him*). I have learnt something, Nico darling. These mental torments we brood over can only fill the heart to which love has not yet come; at its coming they all vanish away; all of them, even pity, 20 even justice which used to make me suffer terribly at one time. Now I am indifferent to everything that isn't you. You say you love me—do you love me enough?

NICO. My love for you is a torture, Romée.

ROMÉE. What do you mean—a torture?

NICO (*in a low voice, trying to find the right words*). Because this bond between us 30

—this power of your nearness over me —what is it? If it were merely desire—everything would be simple and reasonable—but it is with love that the problem begins. That's where the riddle is—there is no answer to it. I believed your beauty held the answer—but it does not. I thought a man might crush his thoughts to death upon your heart—but no—for it is in your arms that I feel most helpless against the bitter and mysterious tide that rises up and overwhelms me. In your arms words and silence are alike poison—poison—what can it be?

ROMÉE (*laying her hand on his forehead*). Stop looking for the solution, dear—don't be afraid of things; don't think about them any more.

NICO. I can't help it.

ROMÉE. Then if you can't, tell all your thoughts to me, every one of them, even the bitterest and the most morbid. That will be a relief to you. What are you thinking of now?

NICO. We love each other—and yet——

ROMÉE. And yet——

NICO. We—there's no such thing as we—there's you—and I—and I am alone.

CURTAIN

FOURTH SCENE

The drawing-room. Eleven o'clock at night. The room is in darkness except for the moonlight shining through the open bay-windows beside which RIEMKE *is sitting.*

[ROMÉE *comes in, rear. She is wearing her hat and cloak.* RIEMKE *makes a slight movement.*]

ROMÉE. Oh! Who's there?

RIEMKE. I. Don't be frightened.

ROMÉE. I've been looking for you in your room. What are you doing here?

RIEMKE. Nothing. Is it late?

ROMÉE. Past eleven. I was just going home. Aren't you cold by that window?

RIEMKE. No. It is rather warm this evening.

ROMÉE (*looking at her*). What are you unhappy about, Riemke?

RIEMKE. Am I?

40 ROMÉE. You have been crying.

RIEMKE. No, I don't think I have—where is Nico?

ROMÉE. In the library.

RIEMKE. Hasn't he told you his plan?

ROMÉE. Which one?

RIEMKE. To postpone your going—he wants to stay a whole month longer.

ROMÉE. Yes, he told me about that—I think it's all settled.

RIEMKE. Why? What does he want to do it for?

ROMÉE. He says he feels better and is quite acclimatized now, but as a mat- [10] ter of fact, I believe it is on your account that he is staying on.

RIEMKE (*dully*). Then he is going to do no such thing.

ROMÉE. Why not? Don't you think he is much calmer and more cheerful than he was last month?

RIEMKE. He imagines he is better than he is. So do you. If he spends the autumn here, everything will happen to [20] him again just as it did before. In the long run, you know, that green canker on the water and the trees and the walls in this place reaches the brain as well. How do we live in this house after all? We drink tea, and dream and read, and philosophize—that's all —we don't *do* anything. Perhaps something has cut us off from life.

ROMÉE. Perhaps it has. And perhaps it is [30] because I feel so ardently alive myself that you are both so dear to me. I love that weakness in you, and your passion-sheltered heart. And as for Nico, his greatest charm for me is not so much his intelligence or his kindness as his unusefulness, his aloofness from things. He has no kind of ambition, he doesn't believe he is of any importance whatever. The other day, at [40] that tea-party at the Verloren's, there were about twenty men and women talking about all sorts of things. Nico just sat there, looking sidelong at them with his eyes half-closed, not saying a word, and to me he seemed the only real one, the only wise one, the only fine one of them all.

RIEMKE. Yes; there is something fine in silence—and in the desire for death, too.

ROMÉE. What do you mean, the desire for death?

RIEMKE. Romée, there are certain words I am afraid of. I am afraid to apply them to the people I care for because they seem to classify them, don't you know, and take all their glamour away. Still one has to say them sometimes. Nico is not sane, Romée.

ROMÉE. Of course he isn't; who is? Scepticism can be a form of insanity— faith is probably one also. There are some people who are insane with certainties. I know some.

RIEMKE. Are you sure that scepticism is his trouble; all of it?

ROMÉE. What do you mean?

RIEMKE. I sometimes wonder whether he is not becoming the victim of a monomania.

ROMÉE. What monomania? What is worrying you, Riemke?

RIEMKE. Does nothing ever worry you, Romée—any more? (*A pause.*)

ROMÉE. No, not any more.

RIEMKE. So it seems. Time goes on and nothing happens—so what once seemed full of omen and menace to you has become irrelevant and meaningless now.

ROMÉE. It isn't time that has delivered me from worry, my dear; it is love.

RIEMKE. I don't understand. If danger existed six months ago, it must exist still. Our feelings cannot effect the thing we call our destiny.

ROMÉE. Yes, they can; love can break the spell. I sometimes have a strange feeling that in the halls of the future where our destinies are being built up, there has been a fall somewhere, some kind of displacement has altered the plan of our lives as they were to have been——(*Vehemently.*) I have so longed that he might live! I have so pursued happiness with all my thoughts! It can't have been useless, Riemke. If our passions and our dreams were powerless to create new futures, life would be nothing but a senseless, stupid fraud. They might just as well shut us up in a cage studded with spikes, and say to us "Dance! Go on, you are free to dance to your heart's content." Life isn't like that!

RIEMKE. You hope, because you have a wholesome mind. I, ruminating vague thoughts continually in my corner, have less confidence. In the first place I don't believe any more in the catch-words we live by; destiny, fate, and so on—they have no meaning to me any more. So that, in this thing that is worrying us——(*She stops.*)

ROMÉE. Well?

RIEMKE (*reluctantly*). I don't want to upset you or make you feel undue responsibility for anything—but I can't help thinking all the same that you hold the key to this mystery, Romée, nobody else.

ROMÉE. I?

RIEMKE (*bethinking herself*). No, never mind. I have no right to alarm you. I have not proof enough to go by.

ROMÉE. Tell me, Riemke; tell me outright what is in your mind—I shall be far more worried if you don't. What is this idea of yours? What are you thinking?

RIEMKE. This: I think that at the time you saw that face in the lake, no danger did threaten Nico. It was neither a revelation of the past nor of the future; it was only a hallucination. But since—I wonder if that momentary delirium of your brain is not gradually being transformed into reality.

ROMÉE (*thoughtfully*). Is it possible for a thought—a vision—to turn into a reality?

RIEMKE. Occasionally, I dare say—thought is a contagious thing. What you dreamt first, Nico may have dreamt in his turn.

ROMÉE. How?

RIEMKE. You might have unknowingly transmitted your vision to him. And now—it is possible, yes, it is possible that real danger exists for him.

ROMÉE (*troubled*). You haven't thought out this explanation without a motive, Riemke. You are keeping something back—you *know* he is in danger.

RIEMKE. No, no! It is only a supposition. I have been thinking it over, that is all. Don't let it worry you, dear.

ROMÉE (*taking her hands*). You know, you can't tell lies a bit. Is it so serious that you don't dare to tell me? Look here, Riemke, what is happening?

RIEMKE (*fearfully*). It's probably quite natural—I'm sure it could be explained away—it is a letter from him that I found this evening in the hall. I opened it—on account of the address.

ROMÉE. Whom is it addressed to?

RIEMKE. Gelder, the boat-builder—look, I have it here. (*She holds out the letter.*)

ROMÉE (*lights the lamp and reads in a tremulous voice*). "Of all the models you have shown me, the green boat suits my purpose best. Please send it to me for a week's trial." The green boat—Oh God!

RIEMKE. There, you are all upset. But there is really nothing to fear, as we are forewarned. We must circumvent this misfortune, mustn't we? We will defend ourselves.

ROMÉE. Against whom? Against what? And by what means?

RIEMKE. By getting Nico away from this place. Once he is gone, we'll be laughing at all this alarm.

ROMÉE. How can we get him away?

RIEMKE. I have thought of a scheme. You know my friend the Van Velsen girl is getting married. She lives just outside Rotterdam. I had refused her invitation but nothing would be easier than to——

ROMÉE (*interrupting her sharply with terror in her voice*). Riemke——

RIEMKE. What is it?

ROMÉE. Riemke, I have committed a terrible folly—a few days ago he was telling me about that illness he had—he said that once long ago he wanted to kill himself.

RIEMKE. I never knew——

ROMÉE. Nobody did—but he tried.

RIEMKE. Did he throw himself into the lake?

ROMÉE. That was my first thought, too—oh, why didn't I hide it from him? Why didn't I keep quiet? But I was so upset to think of his doing such a thing and so relieved that the explanation of my dream had come at last, that I spoke to him about the lake—I asked him how they had rescued him from the water——

RIEMKE. Well?

ROMÉE. He looked at me in surprise—he hadn't thrown himself into the water at all. He had hanged himself in the loft! (*She sobs.*) You were right—it is I who have put the idea into his mind—it is I who have sent him to his death.

CURTAIN

FIFTH SCENE

The drawing-room. It is Autumn—the sun is setting in a golden sky. SAIDYAH *is sitting cross-legged in the centre of the room absorbed in idle reverie.*

[NICO *enters, rear.*]

NICO. What are you doing there, Saidyah? You look as immovable as one of our old beeches. What are you thinking about?

SAIDYAH. Nothing, Toewan, nothing.

NICO. No doubt. What could you be thinking about, after all? Perhaps those who imagine they are thinking of something are also really thinking of nothing at all. For who knows whether there is anything to think about? (SAIDYAH *pulls a pipe from his girdle and asks with a gesture for permission to light it.*) Yes, yes, light up. (SAIDYAH *does so.*) Isn't this room cold for you?

SAIDYAH. No, Toewan.

NICO. We shan't be here much longer, Saidyah. Before winter we'll have left this country. Aren't you glad to be going back to Java?

SAIDYAH. If the master is glad, I am glad. But what is the use of changing one's place?

NICO. Yes, what *is* the use? Besides, is it possible ever to change one's place, really? (*He sits down.*) I like talking to you, Saidyah. You understand me better than any one else.

SAIDYAH. I should love the master very little if I did not understand him.

NICO. My sister loves me, too, so does my fiancée. And yet, for some time past I haven't been able to talk to them. Saidyah, do you know what space is?

SAIDYAH. It is the little road the ant travels between two blades of grass: it is the great empty road my eye travels on its way to the stars.

NICO. And time, do you know what that is?

SAIDYAH. It is a road also.

NICO. Saidyah, there is no such thing as either space or time.

SAIDYAH. If the master says so it must be true.

NICO. I knew you would understand me.

SAIDYAH. The sun is going down already, Toewan, and I begin to smell the marshes. Hadn't I better close the windows? (NICO *does not answer. A pause.*)

NICO (*beside the bay-window*). Look at those summer flies over the lake. They fly round and round in the yellow light as though they were drunk or mad. They remind me of old men clinging to the sunshine. Four hours ago they were not yet in their prime; since then they have felt thirty or forty years of human life pass over them. This evening—that is to say, in ten years' time—they will die under the bushes. Time is a dream, Saidyah.

SAIDYAH (*shaking his head*). Surely something has passed on, though, since the days when the master was a child and the babu used to bathe his little body in a copper basin on the verandah every morning.

NICO (*stretching out on a couch, beside SAID-YAH*). No—it is our minds that have moved across an unmoving dream. Yesterday, to-day, to-morrow are only words, Saidyah, words which correspond to no reality except within our narrow brains, for beyond our brains there is neither past nor future, nothing but one vast present. Within eternity, we are at once about to be, living and dead. Do you fear death, Saidyah?

SAIDYAH. Yes, Toewan, so long as you still live.

NICO. I don't—it doesn't matter to me one way or the other. I don't even know whether——(*He stops.*) To die is not to sleep, nor to dream—living is that—trees, earth, fogs and all the rest—they are the inexplicable dream. To die is to awaken, to know, maybe to reach that point in eternity where time is no longer a dream, the frontier where all things are co-existent.

SAIDYAH. Is the master unhappy? Who has been troubling him?

NICO. No one, Saidyah, no one.

SAIDYAH. Sometimes, when he was a child, the master's little heart used to grow sad and then he would sit gazing into space as though he was falling asleep. But I had only to show him the round patches of sunlight on the mats or the golden clouds over the palm forests and he would be quite gay again at once.

NICO. I don't believe in the clouds any more, Saidyah. I don't believe in the sunlight either. They don't exist; or if something does exist which corresponds to what we call clouds and sunlight, we can't know what it is. We never will know anything we see with our eyes or hear with our ears or pass through the filter of our minds. Ah, Saidyah, it isn't the dreaming that matters, it's knowing one's dreaming that is fearful. Walking, and knowing there is no solid earth under your feet; stretching out your arms and knowing they never can reach anything at all—for all things are phantoms and the shadows of phantoms. Say, if there were such a thing as a road to certainty, to reality, wouldn't you set out upon it re-joicing?

SAIDYAH (*shaking his head*). The master is unhappy and he will not tell me why. And I do not know how to cheer him.

Is there nobody who can bring him peace? Is there nothing left on earth that he can love?

NICO (*thinking*). I love the water. (*A pause—in a tone of mystery.*) You mustn't mention this to any one, Saidyah—they wouldn't understand. They would try and part me from the water that I love—who knows what pretexts they might invent? 10

SAIDYAH. The master can trust me.

NICO. In the beginning I disliked the water—I thought it swampy and too still, horrible. But I have looked at it a great deal since; I've spent hours leaning over it, watching it—and now I have grown to love it. It lies in dark pools at the foot of the old walls, like staring eyes filled with the knowledge of truth. As for the water of the big 20 lake—I don't know why, but it reminds me of Romée. It is like Romée —full of passions and angers held in leash—sometimes it quivers suddenly here and there without apparent rea-

son—well, when Romée is startled or thwarted in anything and tries to hide her anger, one of her cheeks gives a slight quiver just like the water. (*A pause.*) That lake looks clear, Saidyah, but it isn't. Beneath the surface where it is bright with the reflection of the sky, there lies a whole dark and impenetrable world. (*Whispering.*) When you look into Romée's eyes it is the same. Their clearness is only on the surface—below there are the same shadows, the same cold mystery. It is a very strange resemblance. I spoke of it to her one day but she didn't understand. For a long time I believed that she alone could give me peace of mind, and a hold on things—now I wonder if this truth I seek is not at the bottom of the water—right down underneath the marsh.

SAIDYAH (*in a low voice*). If truth is where you say it is, Toewan, long live illusion!

CURTAIN

SIXTH SCENE

The drawing-room. Four o'clock in the afternoon. MRS. BEUNKE *sits dreaming by the fire.* RIEMKE *enters, right. She is in a traveling cloak and carries a grip in her hand. She is fastening the last button of her glove.* 30

RIEMKE. Have you ordered the carriage, Mrs. Beunke?

MRS. BEUNKE. Yes, Miss Riemke. Jan is harnessing the horses.

RIEMKE. Isn't Mr. Nico ready yet?

MRS. BEUNKE. He has gone up to his room, Miss Riemke.

RIEMKE. Are you sure?

MRS. BEUNKE (*surprised*). Why yes, Miss Riemke. He is packing his bag. 40

RIEMKE (*looking at her watch*). I was thinking of the train—we haven't much more time.

MRS. BEUNKE. What day shall I expect you back, Miss Riemke?

RIEMKE (*turning her head away*). Sunday, Mrs. Beunke, Sunday for certain; we'll be home in time for dinner.

MRS. BEUNKE (*bringing out her account-book*). I will have everything ready for you. Won't you please just look over my accounts before you go, Miss Riemke?

RIEMKE. No, there's no time and besides I feel so dreadfully tired, Mrs. Beunke.

MRS. BEUNKE (*sighing*). This makes more than a week since you have seen them —it is a great responsibility on my shoulders.

[ROMÉE *comes in.*]

RIEMKE (*not paying any attention to what* MRS. BEUNKE *is saying*). Mrs. Beunke, will you please go up stairs to Mr. Nico's room—I am too tired.

MRS. BEUNKE. Yes, Miss Riemke—but what for?

RIEMKE. Why, to hurry him up—tell him we are waiting.

MRS. BEUNKE. Very well, Miss Riemke. (*She goes out.*)

RIEMKE (*in a low voice*). Now remember what you have to do—Nico and I will be at the Van Velsen's this evening; the wedding is to-morrow morning. You are to stay here and send your wire the day after to-morrow evening, not before, and you leave for Rotterdam on Sunday.

ROMÉE. I understand. Are you going to tell Ida Van Velsen?

RIEMKE. No. Our visit doesn't need any more explanation than I gave her. She asked me to her wedding and I said my brother's being here prevented me from getting away, then it turns out that Nico wants to go with me after all, so I change my mind and we go. That is the explanation I gave her in my letter; it will do.

ROMÉE. Tell me—that telegram—if I make it too urgent and desperate, it will give Nico a bad shock, and on the other hand, if I make it too indefinite and reassuring he might not be in any hurry to leave and want to come back here first and take the next boat instead.

RIEMKE. Yes, the idea of leaving at once must come from you. You must say something like this—"Have received cable Java—parents anxious—father very ill—not critical but wants Nico back as soon as possible." And then add: "I advise going immediately. S.S. *Samarang* leaves Rotterdam Mon-

day. Meet you there with Saidyah and luggage."

ROMÉE. Nothing about money?

RIEMKE. No—He has a letter of credit on a Rotterdam bank.

ROMÉE. And if he insists on coming back here?

RIEMKE. I will dissuade him.

ROMÉE. Sh! Here he is.

NICO (*enters right, a suitcase in his hand*). Is this necessary? Really necessary?

RIEMKE. What?

NICO. This visit?

RIEMKE. Why of course it is, Nico— they are expecting us and you promised——

NICO. You made me promise, you mean. The whole thing strikes me suddenly as so ridiculous, going to stay with people I haven't seen for fifteen years. I suppose one has to talk to their guests?

RIEMKE. And what if one does?

NICO. But I have nothing to say to them —or to any one else.

ROMÉE. Any one else?

NICO (*looks at her, then drops his eyes*). It seems to me now that every word I utter puts me farther and farther away from people—even from those I care for.

RIEMKE (*sadly*). Nico!

NICO. I can't help it.

MRS. BEUNKE (*coming in*). The carriage is waiting.

RIEMKE. Let's hurry or we'll miss the train. (*Kisses* ROMÉE.) Till Sunday darling. (*Exit left.*)

ROMÉE (*in a low voice, to* NICO). Don't be unhappy, dear. Don't think of me if the thought weighs on you—let yourself live. Nobody wants to thwart you in any way—you are perfectly free. (MRS. BEUNKE *has taken* RIEMKE'S *bag and gone out, left.*)

NICO. Oh!—perhaps it is better to be the

slave of living people than of one's thoughts. (*With childish fretfulness.*) But why can't they leave me in peace? Why do they have to drag me to people's houses—when I want to be alone and lie down on the ground and go to sleep?

ROMÉE (*emphatically*). You need distraction, Nico. This visit will do you good. It will indeed.

NICO. You see, none of them can let me alone, not even you.

RIEMKE'S VOICE. Are you coming, Nico? We are going to miss that train.

[NICO *makes a movement of annoyance; then kisses* ROMÉE.]

NICO. Au revoir.

ROMÉE. I'll see you soon again, darling.

[NICO *goes out.* ROMÉE *goes to the window and watches the carriage drive away. She waves her hand.* MRS. BEUNKE *comes in.*]

MRS. BEUNKE. Won't you have supper with me, Miss Romée?

ROMÉE. No thanks, Mrs. Beunke. Make the most of these few days to rest in—you look awfully tired.

MRS. BEUNKE (*agitated*). Oh, I am always that and shall be till the end of my days, I am sure. Tiredness is nothing —what kills me is all the cares and worries that I have, Miss Romée.

ROMÉE (*incredulous*). Whatever can you have to worry you to that extent?

MRS. BEUNKE. These accounts, Miss Romée. Generally Miss Riemke goes over them for me every day—it is a great relief. But all this week she has been thinking of something else and hasn't had time to even look at them. There is a mistake of four florins—I dare not tell her. I have gone through my additions over and over again and I can't find the mistake—I can't sleep for worrying over it, Miss Romée.

ROMÉE. Why, all you have to do is to put in the four florins out of your own pocket, I should think.

MRS. BEUNKE (*in despair*). That will not take the mistake away—the four florins don't matter; it is the mistake that is terrible. (*Taking out her book.*) Won't you please look at my figures, Miss Romée? Maybe you will find the mistake at once—who knows?

ROMÉE (*almost harshly*). No, Mrs. Beunke. I don't like the idea of fretting one's life away over such nonsense.

MRS. BEUNKE. I beg your pardon, Miss Romée. (*The telephone rings;* MRS. BEUNKE *answers it.*) Hello—Mr. Van Eyden has just left—who is speaking please? What do you say? No, Mr. Van Eyden will not be back before Sunday.

ROMÉE. Who is it?

MRS. BEUNKE. Mr. Gelder, the boatbuilder.

ROMÉE. Oh, I know about that—let me talk to him. (*She takes the receiver.*) Hello—what is it, Mr. Gelder? A letter? About that boat? Very likely—he didn't mention it. Very well, I will apologize to him for you. What?— What do you say? No, no—it's no use, as he is away. Wait—wait a few days. Besides, I think he changed his mind. What? Oh, already? All right, you must—perhaps you could—No, of course not—never mind, it can't be helped now. Good-bye. (*She hangs up.*) It seems they have just brought a boat from Gelder's. Did you see it come?

MRS. BEUNKE. No, Miss Romée. The gardener must have received it. (*Anxiously.*) Was it to be paid for?

ROMÉE. I don't know.

MRS. BEUNKE. Miss Riemke hasn't left me any money.

ROMÉE (*at window, to herself*). That was it —yes, that was it.

MRS. BEUNKE. I shall not pay for anything until Miss Riemke comes home.

SAIDYAH (*entering right*). Is it true, Nonna, that he has gone without saying good-bye to me?

ROMÉE. He will be back in two days, Saidyah.

SAIDYAH. He has gone because he is not happy here.

ROMÉE (*turning round*). How do you know?

SAIDYAH. He tells me everything. He suffers because he seeks the way.

ROMÉE. What way?

SAIDYAH. The way of Truth. I know what it is—I have seen men in the Indies who were like him. Woman, sister, children, no living person pleases their hearts. So they go—with a disciple or a boy to beg their rice— and they become wanderers upon the earth. They visit the towns and the beggars and the holy places; for years they wander on and on. One day they meet the Buddha on a mountain or at a crossroads and they are happy. But there are some who do not meet the Buddha, and they let themselves starve to death in the depths of some jungle. (*A pause, shakes his head.*) I do not believe our child will ever meet the Buddha. I knew he would go some day, but I hoped he would take me with him. I would have followed him everywhere and left him alone before the end, for it does happen that the Buddha manifests himself at the last minute of the last hour. Our child did not want me. I shall never see him again.

ROMÉE. But, Saidyah, haven't I told you he will be home on Sunday?

SAIDYAH. I have had news, Nonna.

ROMÉE. What news?

SAIDYAH. News from the wind, Nonna.

MRS. BEUNKE. Leave us alone, Saidyah, you see you are worrying Miss Romée.

SAIDYAH (*going out*). Yes, yes, I am going.

ROMÉE. Poor Saidyah. Riemke says he would give his life for Nico.

MRS. BEUNKE. That is no reason why one should put up with him in the drawing-room. He would come and smoke his pipe here every day if one let him. Miss Riemke does spoil him so.

ROMÉE (*sharply*). What is the time by your watch, Mrs. Beunke?

MRS. BEUNKE (*looking at her watch*). Five o'clock, Miss Romée.

ROMÉE. Isn't that when the train goes?

MRS. BEUNKE. Yes.

ROMÉE (*sighing with relief*). They must be in their compartment now—do you think they are in their compartment, Mrs. Beunke?

MRS. BEUNKE. Yes, most likely, unless the train is late coming in.

ROMÉE (*putting on her hat*). That's good. It's a fine day, Mrs. Beunke.

MRS. BEUNKE. A little misty these last few minutes.

ROMÉE (*looking out of window*). Why, so it is.

MRS. BEUNKE. That kind doesn't last long though, it is only a sea-flame.

[ROMÉE *is silent, motionless beside the window. The phone rings.*]

ROMÉE. Again——

MRS. BEUNKE (*at the telephone*). Hello— yes, this is Mrs. Beunke. What? I don't understand. Please say that again? Who is talking, please? What —What is the matter? Don't shout so loud.

ROMÉE. What is it?

MRS. BEUNKE. I can't make out, Miss Romée. I don't even know who is talking.

ROMÉE. Wait. (*She takes the receiver.*) Hello. This is Miss Cremers. Who are you? (*Astonished.*) Jan the coachman? Why aren't they gone? Whatever is

the matter with her? (*To* MRS. BEUNKE.)
Riemke is ill——
MRS. BEUNKE. Oh, dear; oh, dear!
ROMÉE (*at the phone*). When did it happen? (*To* MRS. BEUNKE.) She was taken ill at the station. (*At the phone.*) Who is the doctor? Very well—listen—tell him I am coming right over and ask him if he needs anything.
MRS. BEUNKE. Is it serious?   10
ROMÉE. No, just a fainting spell, I hope. Dr. Krall happened to be at the station. He carried her into a waiting-room and is with her now.
MRS. BEUNKE. She hasn't been well for days. She cannot stand any excitement—going away and having luggage to see to is too much for her.
ROMÉE (*at the telephone*). Hello—all right. (*To* MRS. BEUNKE.) Mrs. Beunke will 20 you please get a little ether from the medicine-chest? (MRS. BEUNKE *hurries out.* ROMÉE *at the phone.*) Hello—are you sure that is all he wanted? Good. Is Miss Riemke better? Still unconscious? Yes, all right, I am coming. I'll run through the park; it will take about five minutes. (*She hangs up.* MRS. BEUNKE *comes back with a vial of ether.*)
MRS. BEUNKE. Do you want me to go 30 with you, Miss Romée?
ROMÉE. No. You had better get her bed ready—they may bring her back any minute.
[*She goes quickly out left.* MRS. BEUNKE *goes out right. The stage remains empty a long moment, then* NICO *comes left. He lies down and falls into a deep meditation.*]
MRS. BEUNKE (*comes in right her account-book in her hand. She gives a start when* 40 *she sees* NICO). You, Mr. Nico?
NICO (*not moving*). Yes, she doesn't need any one. The doctor is there.
MRS. BEUNKE. Didn't you meet Miss Romée?
NICO. No.

MRS. BEUNKE. She left right after Jan called up. She went through the park.
NICO. I came back by the road.
MRS. BEUNKE. Aren't you anxious, Mr. Nico?
NICO. About Riemke? Yes, she will wake too soon. One always wakes too soon. (*Raising his eyes to her face.*) Why are you looking at me as though I were some queer sort of animal? What is that book in your hand?
MRS. BEUNKE. My accounts, Mr. Nico. I have made a mistake. So I was just——
NICO. Show me. (*She shows him the book and the page. He corrects one addition, first to himself, then aloud in a low voice.*) Seven and three make nine.
MRS. BEUNKE. Ten, Mr. Nico, ten.
NICO. Why not nine or twelve?
MRS. BEUNKE (*dismayed*). Seven and three make ten.
NICO. Prove it.
MRS. BEUNKE. But——
NICO. You can't. You couldn't ever prove that two and two make four. Numbers don't exist. They are a convention of thought. Your accounts are not real, they are nothing but signs of things eaten, drunk and distributed and destroyed. Your accounts will always be wrong, Mrs. Beunke. (*He throws the book on the floor.*)
MRS. BEUNKE (*worried*). What is the matter with you, Mr. Nico?
NICO. I am sleepy. But sleep is so short, so short. Tell me, Mrs. Beunke, if a doctor told you that he knew of a way to clear out your little skull and replace its present contents with hay or lettuce leaves, wouldn't you beg him to perform that admirable operation on you?
MRS. BEUNKE. I am sure it is a sin to listen to such things, Mr. Nico.
NICO. But wouldn't you? No? You must

be anxious to keep your 995 grams of brain then? I'm not. (*He gets up.*) Just think—good-bye worries, good-bye accounts and dust and housekeeping —everything would disappear, walls, trees, earth, stars, time, thought— everything . . . and yourself of course!

MRS. BEUNKE. Oh, dear! I have never seen you like this. . . .   10

NICO (*indistinctly*). Nor have I. Because to-day I know you don't exist where I see you. (*Puts his hand to his forehead.*) Here's where you are. Only here. (*She steps back, afraid.*) As for this phantom which seems to talk and move about in front of me—I know nothing whatever about it. (*He closes his eyes; his face contracts.*) I can see it elsewhere and answer it elsewhere.   20

MRS. BEUNKE. You are not well, Mr. Nico—you ought to go to bed.

[NICO *opens his eyes—turns his head away and answers an imaginary* MRS. BEUNKE *at the other end of the room.*]

NICO. Yes, that's just what I was thinking of doing—going to bed. (*He crosses slowly over to the door, left.*)

MRS. BEUNKE. Not that way. This is the way to your room. (*She points to the rear.*)   30

NICO (*still speaking to the left*). I am going to change rooms, Mrs. Beunke.

MRS. BEUNKE. There aren't any rooms on this side of the house.

NICO (*reaching doorway pretends to pat somebody's shoulder*). Good-night, Mrs. Beunke, good-night. (*He goes out without turning round.* MRS. BEUNKE *goes forward hesitatingly towards the left.*)

MRS. BEUNKE. Oh, where are you going to, Mr. Nico? (*She follows him out,* ROMÉE *enters right a few seconds later.*)

ROMÉE (*calling*). Mrs. Beunke, where are you?

MRS. BEUNKE (*coming back, left*). Here I am, here I am.

ROMÉE. I have brought her back in the doctor's car. She is better. Is her room ready?

MRS. BEUNKE (*agitated*). Not yet, Miss Romée.

ROMÉE. What? Not yet?

MRS. BEUNKE. It's not my fault, Miss Romée.

ROMÉE. What have you been doing?

MRS. BEUNKE. It is Mr. Nico. . . . He has been saying such things—Oh, he is certainly not well.

ROMÉE (*distracted*). Nico has come back? Where is he?

MRS. BEUNKE. He has just left the house. I saw him go down towards the lake.

ROMÉE. Towards the lake—Ah!

[*Hardly has she glanced through the window when she sways as though struck by a bullet and sinks silently to the ground.*]

CURTAIN

KAREL ČAPEK

THE LITTLE republic of Czecho-Slovakia made brilliant achievements
in its brief two decades of national life,
between its birth a few days after the
Armistice and its death under the assault
of Hitler's robots after Munich. Its creative energies, long thwarted by many
forms of subtle repressions, flowed again
with quickened enthusiasm. Thomas G.
Masaryk, its first president, was a great
and humane leader for the eager young
state to follow. He had taught philosophy from Dostoevsky's *The Brothers
Karamazov*. In the big library at the presidential residence—the ancient Hrad-
cany castle of Roman emperors and Bo-
hemian kings—he lined the shelves with
novels, including American, because, he
said, they "more exactly interpret the
real things, the struggle of man for reality." One of the choicest fruits of that
happy interlude between two world ca-
tastrophies was the activity in Czech
literature, drama, and the theatre. In
fact Czecho-Slovakia had a national
renaissance in the 1920's comparable to
that in Ireland under Yeats, Lady
Gregory, Synge, and the Fays of the
Abbey Theatre a generation earlier. Its
plays and its stage were so full of life, so
new and forceful, that they commanded
international attention and made
Prague one of the most interesting and
important theatrical centers in all
Europe.

The leading spirit and the greatest
dramatist in the new country was Karel
Čapek, aided and stimulated by his
older brother Josef, artist, producer, and
collaborating playwright. Čapek was
born January 9, 1890, in the village of
Malé Svatonvice in the Giant Mountains of northern Bohemia, then a ro-
mance-laden province of Austria-Hun-
gary, later a part of Czecho-Slovakia.
He was strongly influenced by his
mother, who wrote fairy tales befitting
the setting of these mountains. His
father, a physician of skill and intelligence, took keen interest in the education of his sons. He wanted Karel to succeed him, but the sensitive boy could
not endure the spectacle of suffering.
When he showed a talent for writing,
his father encouraged him. By the time
he was fourteen, Karel was writing and
publishing poems and sketches. He had
the alert and restless mind of a man of
the renaissance attracted to all forms of
learning. In an age of more and more
minute specialization, this diverse curiosity was derided; and in a famous piece
called "Why I Am Not a Communist,"
Čapek felt called upon to explain his
roving attention: "I appear to be guilty
of a strange and rather heavy intellectual crime—that I am striving to understand everything; I dabble in all sciences
and all arts, including black man's folklore, discovering with mystic joy that
with a bit of patience and simplicity it is
possible to come to some sort of understanding with all people, whatever their
skin and creed."

In the universities of Königgratz,
Prague, Berlin, and Paris, Čapek pursued his training in natural science, philosophy, and literature with almost equal
satisfaction. He planned a university
career as a professor of philosophy, and

607

had arranged a post-doctorate course in London when the World War broke out, leaving him cut off in Bohemia. Ill health, the after-effects of scarlet fever, kept him out of the army; "he spent his time teaching and writing, but mainly he starved" on bread made of chestnuts and acorns. He smoked dried willow-leaves, read Anglo-American philosophy, and translated French poetry. He was deeply influenced in literature by Baudelaire, Rimbaud, and Apollinaire among the French symbolists. He was devoted to Shelley, Keats, and Whitman. In philosophy, William James and John Dewey, he said, influenced him most; his interest culminated in a book on the subject, *Pragmatism: or Philosophy of a Practical Life.* He also wrote during these desperate war days some short stories, collected under the title, *God's Suffering.*

When the Armistice was signed and his country was given its freedom, Čapek concentrated his energies largely on the theatre, and his interest in America widened. It is characteristic of the period, and significant in the study of *R. U. R.*, that Čapek and his country should be so interested in American life and thought. For American influence and prestige were riding high in Europe in those post-War days. The United States had dramatized its genius for mass production and organization by raising, equipping, and transporting across the Atlantic Ocean a mighty army that turned the tide of war. The speed and efficiency of this exploit had startled the consciousness of Europe. And when the War ended, American machines, American business organization and mechanical ingenuity, American gold and the trade boom of the twenties, along with American jazz, cocktails, fashions, and monied tourists

that flooded the Old World, remained to dazzle and alarm a surprised Europe. The implications of the invasion were tremendous, and they were not lost on the mind of Čapek with its flair for journalism and melodrama in their highest forms. He was equally well aware of the inadequacies as well as the menace of Russian communism. He wrote: "When all is said, Communism is out to rule, not to rescue; its great watchword is power, not help. For it poverty, hunger, unemployment are not an unendurable pain and shame, but a welcome reserve of dark forces, a fermenting heap of fury and loathing. . . . Nobody will seriously maintain that the masses will rule. They are only a means to certain ends; they are simply political tools in a far harder and more unscrupulous sense than party men of different shades." When Čapek turned full-time to writing at the close of the War, he was stimulated by national pride, and bursting with comment on this modern world, its directions and its dangers.

Čapek wrote voluminously in the newspapers in addition to his novels, stories, and plays. From 1917 until his death he worked daily in the editorial office of the *Lidove Noviny*, a journal that held close to the Masaryk tradition. His soul, however, was in the theatre. During the years when his country was under Austrian rule, the only outlet for Czech art was the National Theatre. Even this institution was watched by the Hapsburgs, and was usually limited to historical dramas. Immediately after Czecho-Slovakia became independent on October 28, 1918, the theatres of Prague began to reflect the new intensity of Czech life. The Golden Temple, the national art theatre of Prague, built by subscriptions freely given by towns and villages in Bohemia, became the greatest of the Czech institutions. Here Čapek was first introduced as a dramatist, and here was produced his second drama, *R. U. R.* He became art director of this theatre, but branched out to establish his own experimental playhouse, the Vinohradsky Theatre. He produced the works of young and rising Czech playwrights as well as plays by Shakespeare, Byron, Molière, Ibsen, Hauptmann, Strindberg, and others. At the National Theatre, the plays of Yeats, Synge, Shaw, Wilde, Galsworthy, and Claudel were well received. The dramatic activity in Czecho-Slovakia was very similar to that in Paris, Moscow, London, and Berlin a quarter of a century earlier; it was paralleled by the new American drama in New York after the War, and the work of the Theatre Guild.

Čapek's plays are concerned in one way or another with science and the mechanization of the modern world, and with the threats to peace and security. Most of them are grim fantasies. They owe a great debt in form to the expressionistic drama developed by Strindberg in *To Damascus, The Spook Sonata, The Dream Play,* and other like experiments; by Wedekind in *The Awakening of Spring* and such plays; by Georg Kaiser in *From Morn to Midnight, The Coral, Gas-Part I,* and various other dramas in the movement. The technique of expressionism was employed in an attempt to make visible and real on the stage certain abstractions and mental states inaccessible to strict realism. It was developed just at the time when dramatists were trying to find effective means for dealing with the problems and theories of modern psychology and the displacement of man's versatility by cunning machines. Čapek found both the materials and the manner of ex-

pressionistic drama congenial to his interests and his talents. He became one of the ranking dramatists in this gênre whose novelty and sensationalism quickened the 1920's.

The list of Čapek's plays is not long: *The Robbers* (1920); *R. U. R.* (1921); *The Makropoulos Affair* (1922); *Loupeznik* (1926); *The White Plague* (1937); *The Mother* (1938). Two of the most famous of his dramas were written in collaboration with his brother Josef, author of the expressionistic parable *The Land of Many Names* (1923). They were *The Insects* (1921) and *Adam the Creator* (1927), both in the expressionistic manner. Just how the partnership was carried out is not known, but the text would seem to derive chiefly from the pen that wrote *R. U. R.* and *The Makropoulos Affair.*

The themes of these plays vary, but they all have a common spirit and view of life. *The Makropoulos Affair* explored the ancient puzzle of immortality that made Tithonus miserable, and provoked Swift's Struldbrugs, Shaw's *Back to Methuselah,* and such tormented labors. The author imagined a Greek physician who had discovered the secret of longevity and had rearranged the life span nearer to the heart's (theoretical) desire. The secret, of course, later got lost. *The Insects,* also known as *The World We Live In, And So Ad Infinitum,* and *The Insect Play,* ingeniously and divertingly hit off human perversities by reflecting them in the simplified activities of the insect world. The capitalistic beetle rolls his ball of dirt; the birds eat crickets; the superman fly, fighting his way to survival, is in turn gobbled up by a greater superman. Its best satire is aimed at speed-up efficiency and nationalistic wars as seen through the parallels of ant life. The tramp, whose dream is the play, wakens just as the moth is about to explain the final mystery of life. *Adam the Creator* continued less entertainingly the satire on man's frailties, shortcomings, and lack of wisdom. Adam presumptuously destroys the imperfect world and is required by God to recreate it. He bungles his assignment by creating fleas, a superwoman, a warrior, Lilith, a being in his own image, and, unintentionally, a poor thing called Oddly-Come-Short and his six dirty children born in a cave.

Oddly-Come-Short and his motherless brood represent poverty.

"ADAM. But we didn't create you a wife!

"ODDLY. Why, sir, no one creates a poor man. Of course not, sir. He just is."

Čapek's last two plays, written not long before his death, were inspired by the impending catastrophe over Europe. The anti-fascist *The White Plague* (1937) was produced in London, April 8, 1938, as *Power and Glory;* it was thought generally interesting, though not particularly effective as satire. *The Mother* (1938) was full of rage at the madness of the world that, generation after generation, has killed off husbands and sons in its wars. It was produced in London and in New York in the spring of 1939. Alla Nazimova gave a compassionate interpretation of the Mother, but the play as a whole was a failure in spite of its noble theme and purpose.

These plays are all arresting, but it was *R. U. R.* that touched most successfully the malaise, the fear and foreboding of our time in confrontation with potentially destructive forces that threatened to get out of control. The spectre of Frankenstein has never been far from the apprehension of our industrial world. Many aspects of that world are alarming. It is significant that, in the imagination of artists, our mechanical ingenuity always produces a terrifying monster of evil, never a quieting agent of the more abundant life. Legends on this idea are not uncommon. An old Jewish tale, current in Prague and known to Čapek, told of an artificer who made a "Golem" in the image of man but devoid of a soul, and how he worked havoc in the world. Čapek conceived the plot of *R. U. R.*, according to Jessie Mothersole, "quite suddenly, in a motor car, when the crowd around him seemed to look like artificial beings." He saw his peasant-inhabited country being swerved rapidly from its age-old pastoral way of life on the land to a manufacturing unit of the American system. He was not a little shocked by what he saw. He feared the losses that standardization would bring. He asked the inevitable question: If these tendencies of the present and the forces of the past should be projected unaltered into the future, what sort of world would we face?

Aldous Huxley, posing the same problem in *Brave New World*, foresaw a Model T civilization of various classes scientifically manufactured and controlled according to need, the world of Our Ford, of the lark singing Honk! Honk! at heaven's gate, the completely mechanized state with the motto: COMMUNITY, IDENTITY, STABILITY. Huxley's world is ingeniously imagined, but Čapek foresaw, more accurately, a world of Robots, and from his native Czech term *robit*, or *robota*=work, gave to our language a new word that defined the tendency of the age. It signifies the powers of science, neutral in themselves, but capable of destroying the race when through the failure of moral force they are unleashed by unscrupulous men. Its most trenchant satire falls upon narrow nationalisms that divide men for war and pervert the full machinery of the nation to kill and subject the artificially created enemy. All this is implied in the apt words of L. A. G. Strong that explain the effect of this play upon audiences everywhere: "The Robot was a dramatic personification of the machine age, just as the capering figure with horns and tail in the old Morality play personified the power of Evil."

R. U. R. was an immediate success when presented in Prague on January 26, 1921. Its fame spread rapidly. It was translated into most languages, including those of the Orient, and was produced in all parts of the world. It opened in London and New York on October 9, 1922. Under the Theatre Guild's auspices it ran in New York for one hundred and eighty-four performances. It has had numerous revivals, especially in the little theatres and in university playhouses.

R. U. R. brought fame and fortune to Karel Čapek. He became one of the most honored and distinguished men in the new republic. He was a close friend of Masaryk and Eduard Benes and was often visited by them at his beautiful home in Prague for consultation on state problems and policies. He visited England in 1924 as an informal ambassador of his people. Everywhere he was entertained by actors and directors who had produced his plays. Shaw, Galsworthy, Drinkwater, Chesterton, and others among the great received him warmly. He admired the greatness of England, but he loved his own struggling homeland, and in his *Letters from England* wrote that he was proud that it was "small, unsettled, and incom-

plete," and that he was not at all sad "at the idea that we form only a small and imperfect corner of the world." He married a celebrated Czech actress, Olga Scheinpflugowa, wrote voluminously, and worked about his extensive flower garden which he loved to show to his friends.

But in those early plays he had written with more tragic portent than he knew. One striking episode in *The Insects* or *The World We Live In* showed the Red Ants mobilizing and making war on the Yellow Ants in a dispute over the pathway between two blades of grass. The authors did not suspect that this scene would come to represent their own small country, an ancient pathway between Germany and the rich southeast. In 1937 and 1938 when the Sudetan German crisis was approaching, Čapek was active in trying to achieve a peaceful settlement of the dispute. On June 22, 1938 he addressed the Sudetan Germans from the Prague radio station, appealing to them individually for toleration and understanding. He said that "if we could in one way or another collect all the good that is, after all, in each one of us sinful human creatures, I believe that on it could be built a world that would be surely far kinder than the present one." The failure of these efforts at appeasement meant the destruction of Masaryk's liberal state by its Nazi enemy. In the words of Willi Schlamm, "when Čapek no longer could doubt that an alliance of violence and treachery was stronger than the truth, his life lost all meaning."

Čapek died of pneumonia on Christmas Day, 1938. His death alone saved him from the Nazi concentration camp into which his brother Josef was thrown. It saved him also from seeing his grimmest imaginings come to life in the army of robots from over the mountains; an army that for destructiveness and lack of honor and pity surpassed the mechanical man of his fantasy in *R. U. R.* The projected tendencies of his drama had come to pass with a speed and a tragic and savage realism unimagined in the play itself.

R. U. R.
(ROSSUM'S UNIVERSAL ROBOTS)
A Fantastic Melodrama

CHARACTERS

HARRY DOMIN, *General Manager of Ros-sum's Universal Robots*

SULLA, *a Robotess*

MARIUS, *a Robot*

HELENA GLORY

DR. GALL, *Head of the Physiological and Experimental Department of R. U. R.*

MR. FABRY, *Engineer General, Technical Controller of R. U. R.*

DR. HALLEMEIER, *Head of the Institute for Psychological Training of Robots*

MR. ALQUIST, *Architect, Head of the Works Department of R. U. R.*

CONSUL BUSMAN, *General Business Manager of R. U. R.*

NANA

RADIUS, *a Robot*

HELENA, *a Robotess*

PRIMUS, *a Robot*

A SERVANT

FIRST ROBOT

SECOND ROBOT

THIRD ROBOT

ACT I. CENTRAL OFFICE OF THE FACTORY OF ROSSUM'S UNIVERSAL ROBOTS

ACT II. HELENA'S DRAWING ROOM—TEN YEARS LATER. MORNING

ACT III. THE SAME AFTERNOON

EPILOGUE. A LABORATORY—ONE YEAR LATER

PLACE: *An Island.* TIME: *The Future.*

ACT I

Central office of the factory of Rossum's Universal Robots. Entrance on the right. The windows on the front wall look out on the rows of factory chimneys. On the left more managing departments. DOMIN *is sitting in the revolving chair at a large American writing table. On the left-hand wall large maps showing steamship and railroad routes. On the right-hand wall are fastened printed placards. ("Robot's Cheapest Labor," etc.) In contrast to these wall fittings, the floor is covered with a splendid Turkish carpet, a sofa, leather armchair, and filing cabinets. At a desk near the windows* SULLA *is typing letters.*

DOMIN (*dictating*). Ready?

SULLA. Yes.

DOMIN. To E. M. McVicker and Co., Southampton, England. "We undertake no guarantee for goods damaged in transit. As soon as the consignment was taken on board we drew your captain's attention to the fact that the vessel was unsuitable for the transport of Robots, and we are therefore not responsible for spoiled freight. We beg to remain for Rossum's Universal Robots. Yours truly." (SULLA, *who has sat motionless during dictation, now types rapidly for a few seconds, then stops, withdrawing the completed letter*.) Ready?

SULLA. Yes.

DOMIN. Another letter. To the E. B. Huyson Agency, New York, U. S. A. "We beg to acknowledge receipt of order for five thousand Robots. As you are sending your own vessel, please dispatch as cargo equal quantities of soft and hard coal for R. U. R., the same to be credited as part payment of the amount due to us. We beg to remain, for Rossum's Universal Robots. Yours truly." (SULLA *repeats the rapid typing*.) Ready?

SULLA. Yes.

DOMIN. Another letter. "Friedrichswerks, Hamburg, Germany. We beg to acknowledge receipt of order for fifteen thousand Robots." (*Telephone rings*.) Hello! This is the Central Office. Yes. Certainly. Well, send them a wire. Good. (*Hangs up telephone*.) Where did I leave off?

SULLA. "We beg to acknowledge receipt of order for fifteen thousand Robots."

DOMIN. Fifteen thousand R. Fifteen thousand R.

[*Enter* MARIUS.]

Well, what is it?

MARIUS. There's a lady, sir, asking to see you.

DOMIN. A lady? Who is she?

MARIUS. I don't know, sir. She brings this card of introduction.

DOMIN (*reads the card*). Ah, from President Glory. Ask her to come in.

MARIUS. Please step this way. (*Exit* MARIUS.)

[*Enter* HELENA GLORY.)

HELENA. How do you do?

DOMIN. How do you do. (*Standing up*.) What can I do for you?

HELENA. You are Mr. Domin, the General Manager.

DOMIN. I am.

HELENA. I have come——

DOMIN. With President Glory's card. That is quite sufficient.

HELENA. President Glory is my father. I am Helena Glory.

DOMIN. Miss Glory, this is such a great honor for us to be allowed to welcome our great President's daughter, that——

HELENA. That you can't show me the door?

DOMIN. Please sit down. Sulla, you may go. (*Exit* SULLA.) (*Sitting down*.) How can I be of service to you, Miss Glory?

HELENA. I have come——

DOMIN. To have a look at our famous works where people are manufactured. Like all visitors. Well, there is no objection.

HELENA. I thought it was forbidden to ——

DOMIN. To enter the factory. Yes, of course. Everybody comes here with someone's visiting card, Miss Glory.

HELENA. And you show them——

DOMIN. Only certain things. The manufacture of artificial people is a secret process.

HELENA. If you only knew how enormously that——

DOMIN. Interests me. Europe's talking about nothing else.

HELENA. Why don't you let me finish speaking?

DOMIN. I beg your pardon. Did you want to say something different?

HELENA. I only wanted to ask——

DOMIN. Whether I could make a special exception in your case and show you our factory. Why, certainly, Miss Glory.

HELENA. How do you know I wanted to say that?

DOMIN. They all do. But we shall consider it a special honor to show you more than we do the rest.

HELENA. Thank you.

DOMIN. But you must agree not to divulge the least. . .

HELENA (standing up and giving him her hand). My word of honor.

DOMIN. Thank you. Won't you raise your veil?

HELENA. Of course. You want to see whether I'm a spy or not. I beg your pardon.

DOMIN. What is it?

HELENA. Would you mind releasing my hand?

DOMIN (releasing it). I beg your pardon.

HELENA (raising her veil). How cautious you have to be here, don't you?

DOMIN (observing her with deep interest). Hm, of course—we—that is——

HELENA. But what is it? What's the matter?

DOMIN. I'm remarkably pleased. Did you have a pleasant crossing?

HELENA. Yes.

DOMIN. No difficulty?

HELENA. Why?

DOMIN. What I mean to say is—you're so young.

HELENA. May we go straight into the factory?

DOMIN. Yes. Twenty-two, I think.

HELENA. Twenty-two what?

DOMIN. Years.

HELENA. Twenty-one. Why do you want to know?

DOMIN. Because—as—(With enthusiasm.) you will make a long stay, won't you?

HELENA. That depends on how much of the factory you show me.

DOMIN. Oh, hang the factory. Oh, no, no, you shall see everything, Miss Glory. Indeed you shall. Won't you sit down?

HELENA (crossing to couch and sitting). Thank you.

DOMIN. But first would you like to hear the story of the invention?

HELENA. Yes, indeed.

DOMIN (observes HELENA with rapture and reels off rapidly). It was in the year 1920 that old Rossum, the great physiologist, who was then quite a young scientist, took himself to this distant island for the purpose of studying the ocean fauna, full stop. On this occasion he attempted by chemical synthesis to imitate the living matter known as protoplasm until he suddenly discovered a substance which behaved exactly like living matter although its chemical composition was different. That was in the year of 1932, exactly four hundred and forty years after the discovery of America. Whew!

HELENA. Do you know that by heart?

DOMIN. Yes. You see physiology is not in my line. Shall I go on?

HELENA. Yes, please.

DOMIN. And then, Miss Glory, old Rossum wrote the following among his chemical specimens: "Nature has found only one method of organizing living matter. There is, however, another method, more simple, flexible and rapid, which has not yet occurred to nature at all. This second process by which life can be developed was discovered by me today." Now imagine him, Miss Glory, writing those wonderful words over some colloidal mess that a dog wouldn't look at. Imagine him sitting over a test tube, and thinking how the whole tree of life would grow from it, how all animals would proceed from it, beginning with some sort of beetle and ending with a man. A man of different substance from us. Miss Glory, that was a tremendous moment.

HELENA. Well?

DOMIN. Now, the thing was how to get the life out of the test tubes, and hasten development and form organs, bones and nerves and so on, and find such substances as catalytics, enzymes, hormones, and so forth, in short—you understand?

HELENA. Not much, I'm afraid.

DOMIN. Never mind. You see with the help of his tinctures he could make whatever he wanted. He could have produced a Medusa with the brain of a Socrates or a worm fifty yards long. But being without a grain of humor, he took it into his head to make a vertebrate or perhaps a man. This artificial living matter of his had a raging thirst for life. It didn't mind being sewn or mixed together. That couldn't be done with natural albumen. And that's how he set about it.

HELENA. About what?

DOMIN. About imitating nature. First of all he tried making an artificial dog. That took him several years and resulted in a sort of stunted calf which died in a few days. I'll show it to you in the museum. And then old Rossum started on the manufacture of man.

HELENA. And I must divulge this to nobody?

DOMIN. To nobody in the world.

HELENA. What a pity that it's to be found in all the school books of both Europe and America.

DOMIN. Yes. But do you know what isn't in the school books? That old Rossum was mad. Seriously, Miss Glory, you must keep this to yourself. The old crank wanted to actually make people.

HELENA. But you do make people.

DOMIN. Approximately, Miss Glory. But old Rossum meant it literally. He wanted to become a sort of scientific substitute for God. He was a fearful materialist, and that's why he did it all. His sole purpose was nothing more nor less than to prove that God was no longer necessary. Do you know anything about anatomy?

HELENA. Very little.

DOMIN. Neither do I. Well, he then decided to manufacture everything as in the human body. I'll show you in the museum the bungling attempt it took him ten years to produce. It was to have been a man, but it lived for three days only. Then up came young Rossum, an engineer. He was a wonderful fellow, Miss Glory. When he saw what a mess of it the old man was making, he said: "It's absurd to spend ten years making a man. If you can't make him quicker than nature, you might as well shut up shop." Then he set about learning anatomy himself.

HELENA. There's nothing about that in the school books.

DOMIN. No. The school books are full of paid advertisements, and rubbish at that. What the school books say about the united efforts of the two great Rossums is all a fairy tale. They used to have dreadful rows. The old atheist hadn't the slightest conception of industrial matters, and the end of it was that young Rossum shut him up in some laboratory or other and let him fritter the time away with his monstrosities, while he himself started on the business from an engineer's point of view. Old Rossum cursed him and before he died he managed to botch up two physiological horrors. Then one day they found him dead in the laboratory. And that's his whole story.

HELENA. And what about the young man?

DOMIN. Well, anyone who has looked into human anatomy will have seen at once that man is too complicated, and that a good engineer could make him more simply. So young Rossum began to overhaul anatomy and tried to see what could be left out or simplified. In short—but this isn't boring you, Miss Glory?

HELENA. No indeed. You're—it's awfully interesting.

DOMIN. So young Rossum said to himself: "A man is something that feels happy, plays the piano, likes going for a walk, and in fact, wants to do a whole lot of things that are really unnecessary."

HELENA. Oh.

DOMIN. That are unnecessary when he wants, let us say, to weave or count. Do you play the piano?

HELENA. Yes.

DOMIN. That's good. But a working machine must not play the piano, must not feel happy, must not do a whole lot of other things. A gasoline motor must not have tassels or ornaments, Miss Glory. And to manufacture artificial workers is the same thing as to manufacture gasoline motors. The process must be of the simplest, and the product of the best from a practical point of view. What sort of worker do you think is the best from a practical point of view?

HELENA. What?

DOMIN. What sort of worker do you think is the best from a practical point of view?

HELENA. Perhaps the one who is most honest and hard-working.

DOMIN. No; the one that is the cheapest. The one whose requirements are the smallest. Young Rossum invented a worker with the minimum amount of requirements. He had to simplify him. He rejected everything that did not contribute directly to the progress of work—everything that makes man more expensive. In fact, he rejected man and made the Robot. My dear Miss Glory, the Robots are not people. Mechanically they are more perfect than we are, they have an enormously developed intelligence, but they have no soul.

HELENA. How do you know they've no soul?

DOMIN. Have you ever seen what a Robot looks like inside?

HELENA. No.

DOMIN. Very neat, very simple. Really, a beautiful piece of work. Not much in it, but everything in flawless order. The product of an engineer is technically at a higher pitch of perfection than a product of nature.

HELENA. But man is supposed to be the product of God.

DOMIN. All the worse. God hasn't the least notion of modern engineering. Would you believe that young Rossum then proceeded to play at being God?

HELENA. How do you mean?

DOMIN. He began to manufacture Super-Robots. Regular giants they were. He tried to make them twelve feet tall. But you wouldn't believe what a failure they were.

HELENA. A failure?

DOMIN. Yes. For no reason at all their limbs used to keep snapping off. Evidently our planet is too small for giants. Now we only make Robots of normal size and of very high class human finish.

HELENA. I saw the first Robots at home. The town counsel bought them for—I mean engaged them for work.

DOMIN. Bought them, dear Miss Glory. Robots are bought and sold.

HELENA. These were employed as street sweepers. I saw them sweeping. They were so strange and quiet.

DOMIN. Rossum's Universal Robot factory doesn't produce a uniform brand of Robots. We have Robots of finer and coarser grades. The best will live about twenty years. (*He rings for* MARIUS.)

HELENA. Then they die?

DOMIN. Yes, they get used up.

[*Enter* MARIUS.]

Marius, bring in samples of the Manual Labor Robot. (*Exit* MARIUS.) I'll show you specimens of the two extremes. This first grade is comparatively inexpensive and is made in vast quantities.

[MARIUS *re-enters with two Manual Labor Robots.*]

There you are; as powerful as a small tractor. Guaranteed to have average intelligence. That will do, Marius. (MARIUS *exits with Robots.*)

HELENA. They make me feel so strange.

DOMIN (*rings*). Did you see my new typist? (*He rings for* SULLA.)

HELENA. I didn't notice her.

[*Enter* SULLA.]

DOMIN. Sulla, let Miss Glory see you.

HELENA. So pleased to meet you. You must find it terribly dull in this out-of-the-way spot, don't you?

SULLA. I don't know, Miss Glory.

HELENA. Where do you come from?

SULLA. From the factory.

HELENA. Oh, you were born there?

SULLA. I was made there.

HELENA. What?

DOMIN (*laughing*). Sulla is a Robot, best grade.

HELENA. Oh, I beg your pardon.

DOMIN. Sulla isn't angry. See, Miss Glory, the kind of skin we make. (*Feels the skin on* SULLA'S *face.*) Feel her face.

HELENA. Ah, no, no.

DOMIN. You wouldn't know that she's made of different material from us, would you? Turn round, Sulla.

HELENA. Oh, stop, stop.

DOMIN. Talk to Miss Glory, Sulla.

SULLA. Please sit down. (HELENA *sits.*) Did you have a pleasant crossing?

HELENA. Oh, yes, certainly.

SULLA. Don't go back on the *Amelia*, Miss Glory. The barometer is falling steadily. Wait for the *Pennsylvania*. That's a good, powerful vessel.

DOMIN. What's its speed?

SULLA. Twenty knots. Fifty thousand tons. One of the latest vessels, Miss Glory.

HELENA. Thank you.

SULLA. A crew of fifteen hundred, Captain Harpy, eight boilers——

DOMIN. That'll do, Sulla. Now show us your knowledge of French.

HELENA. You know French?

SULLA. I know four languages. I can write: Dear Sir, Monsieur, Geehrter Herr, Cteny pane.

HELENA (*jumping up*). Oh, that's absurd! Sulla isn't a Robot. Sulla is a girl like me. Sulla, this is outrageous! Why do you take part in such a hoax?

SULLA. I am a Robot.

HELENA. No, no, you are not telling the truth. I know they've forced you to do it for an advertisement. Sulla, you are a girl like me, aren't you?

DOMIN. I'm sorry, Miss Glory. Sulla is a Robot.

HELENA. It's a lie!

DOMIN. What? (*Rings.*) Excuse me, Miss Glory, then I must convince you.

[*Enter* MARIUS.]

Marius, take Sulla into the dissecting room, and tell them to open her up at once.

HELENA. Where?   10

DOMIN. Into the dissecting room. When they've cut her open, you can go and have a look.

HELENA. No, no!

DOMIN. Excuse me, you spoke of lies.

HELENA. You wouldn't have her killed?

DOMIN. You can't kill machines.

HELENA. Don't be afraid, Sulla, I won't let you go. Tell me, my dear, are they always so cruel to you? You mustn't 20 put up with it, Sulla. You mustn't.

SULLA. I am a Robot.

HELENA. That doesn't matter. Robots are just as good as we are. Sulla, you wouldn't let yourself be cut to pieces?

SULLA. Yes.

HELENA. Oh, you're not afraid of death, then?

SULLA. I cannot tell, Miss Glory.

HELENA. Do you know what would hap- 30 pen to you in there?

SULLA. Yes, I should cease to move.

HELENA. How dreadful!

DOMIN. Marius, tell Miss Glory what you are.

MARIUS. Marius, the Robot.

DOMIN. Would you take Sulla into the dissecting room?

MARIUS. Yes.

DOMIN. Would you be sorry for her?   40

MARIUS. I cannot tell.

DOMIN. What would happen to her?

MARIUS. She would cease to move. They would put her into the stamping-mill.

DOMIN. That is death, Marius. Aren't you afraid of death?

MARIUS. No.

DOMIN. You see, Miss Glory, the Robots have no interest in life. They have no enjoyments. They are less than so much grass.

HELENA. Oh, stop. Send them away.

DOMIN. Marius, Sulla, you may go. (*Exeunt* SULLA *and* MARIUS.)

HELENA. How terrible! It's outrageous what you are doing.

DOMIN. Why outrageous?

HELENA. I don't know, but it is. Why do you call her Sulla?

DOMIN. Isn't it a nice name?

HELENA. It's a man's name. Sulla was a Roman general.

DOMIN. Oh, we thought that Marius and Sulla were lovers.

HELENA. Marius and Sulla were generals and fought against each other in the year—I've forgotten now.

DOMIN. Come here to the window.

HELENA. What?

DOMIN. Come here. What do you see?

HELENA. Bricklayers.

DOMIN. Robots. All our work people are Robots. And down there, can you see anything?

HELENA. Some sort of office.

DOMIN. A counting house. And in it——

HELENA. A lot of officials.

DOMIN. Robots. All our officials are Robots. And when you see the factory——(*Factory whistle blows.*) Noon. We have to blow the whistle because the Robots don't know when to stop work. In two hours I will show you the kneading trough.

HELENA. Kneading trough?

DOMIN. The pestle for beating up the paste. In each one we mix the ingredients for a thousand Robots at one operation. Then there are the vats for the preparation of liver, brains, and so on. Then you will see the bone factory. After that I'll show you the spinning-mill.

HELENA. Spinning-mill?

DOMIN. Yes. For weaving nerves and veins. Miles and miles of digestive tubes pass through it at a time.

HELENA. Mayn't we talk about something else?

DOMIN. Perhaps it would be better. There's only a handful of us among a hundred thousand Robots, and not one woman. We talk about nothing but the factory all day, every day. It's just as if we were under a curse, Miss Glory.

HELENA. I'm sorry I said that you were lying. (*A knock at the door.*)

DOMIN. Come in.

[*From the right enter* MR. FABRY, DR. GALL, DR. HALLEMEIER, MR. ALQUIST.)

DR. GALL. I beg your pardon, I hope we don't intrude.

DOMIN. Come in. Miss Glory, here are Alquist, Fabry, Gall, Hallemeier. This is President Glory's daughter.

HELENA. How do you do.

FABRY. We had no idea——

DR. GALL. Highly honored, I'm sure——

ALQUIST. Welcome, Miss Glory.

[BUSMAN *rushes in from the right.*]

BUSMAN. Hello, what's up?

DOMIN. Come in, Busman. This is Busman, Miss Glory. This is President Glory's daughter.

BUSMAN. By Jove, that's fine! Miss Glory, may we send a cablegram to the papers about your arrival?

HELENA. No, no, please don't.

DOMIN. Sit down please, Miss Glory.

BUSMAN. Allow me——(*Dragging up arm-chairs.*)

DR. GALL. Please——

FABRY. Excuse me——

ALQUIST. What sort of a crossing did you have?

DR. GALL. Are you going to stay long?

FABRY. What do you think of the factory, Miss Glory?

HALLEMEIER. Did you come over on the *Amelia?*

DOMIN. Be quiet and let Miss Glory speak.

HELENA (*to* DOMIN). What am I to speak to them about?

DOMIN. Anything you like.

HELENA. Shall . . . may I speak quite frankly?

DOMIN. Why, of course.

HELENA (*wavering, then in desperate resolution*). Tell me, doesn't it ever distress you the way you are treated?

FABRY. By whom, may I ask?

HELENA. Why, everybody.

ALQUIST. Treated?

DR. GALL. What makes you think——?

HELENA. Don't you feel that you might be living a better life?

DR. GALL. Well, that depends on what you mean, Miss Glory.

HELENA. I mean that it's perfectly outrageous. It's terrible. (*Standing up.*) The whole of Europe is talking about the way you're being treated. That's why I came here, to see for myself, and it's a thousand times worse than could have been imagined. How can you put up with it?

ALQUIST. Put up with what?

HELENA. Good heavens, you are living creatures, just like us, like the whole of Europe, like the whole world. It's disgraceful that you must live like this.

BUSMAN. Good gracious, Miss Glory.

FABRY. Well, she's not far wrong. We live here just like red Indians.

HELENA. Worse than red Indians. May I, oh, may I call you brothers?

BUSMAN. Why not?

HELENA. Brothers, I have not come here as the President's daughter. I have come on behalf of the Humanity League. Brothers, the Humanity

League now has over two hundred thousand members. Two hundred thousand people are on your side, and offer you their help.

BUSMAN. Two hundred thousand people! Miss Glory, that's a tidy lot. Not bad.

FABRY. I'm always telling you there's nothing like good old Europe. You see, they've not forgotten us. They're offering us help.

DR. GALL. What help? A theatre, for instance?

HALLEMEIER. An orchestra?

HELENA. More than that.

ALQUIST. Just you?

HELENA. Oh, never mind about me. I'll stay as long as it is necessary.

BUSMAN. By Jove, that's good.

ALQUIST. Domin, I'm going to get the best room ready for Miss Glory.

DOMIN. Just a minute. I'm afraid that Miss Glory is of the opinion that she has been talking to Robots.

HELENA. Of course.

DOMIN. I'm sorry. These gentlemen are human beings just like us.

HELENA. You're not Robots?

BUSMAN. Not Robots.

HALLEMEIER. Robots indeed!

DR. GALL. No, thanks.

FABRY. Upon my honor, Miss Glory, we aren't Robots.

HELENA (to DOMIN). Then why did you tell me that all your officials are Robots?

DOMIN. Yes, the officials, but not the managers. Allow me, Miss Glory: this is Mr. Fabry, General Technical Manager of R. U. R.; Dr. Gall, Head of the Physiological and Experimental Department; Dr. Hallemeier, Head of the Institute for the Psychological Training of Robots; Consul Busman, General Business Manager; and Alquist, Head of the Building Department of R. U. R.

ALQUIST. Just a builder.

HELENA. Excuse me, gentlemen, for—for——Have I done something dreadful?

ALQUIST. Not at all, Miss Glory. Please sit down.

HELENA. I'm a stupid girl. Send me back by the first ship.

DR. GALL. Not for anything in the world, Miss Glory. Why should we send you back?

HELENA. Because you know I've come to disturb your Robots for you.

DOMIN. My dear Miss Glory, we've had close upon a hundred saviours and prophets here. Every ship brings us some. Missionaries, anarchists, Salvation Army, all sorts. It's astonishing what a number of churches and idiots there are in the world.

HELENA. And you let them speak to the Robots?

DOMIN. So far we've let them all, why not? The Robots remember everything, but that's all. They don't even laugh at what the people say. Really, it is quite incredible. If it would amuse you, Miss Glory, I'll take you over to the Robot warehouse. It holds about three hundred thousand of them.

BUSMAN. Three hundred and forty-seven thousand.

DOMIN. Good! And you can say whatever you like to them. You can read the Bible, recite the multiplication table, whatever you please. You can even preach to them about human rights.

HELENA. Oh, I think that if you were to show them a little love——

FABRY. Impossible, Miss Glory. Nothing is harder to like than a Robot.

HELENA. What do you make them for, then?

BUSMAN. Ha, ha, ha, that's good! What are Robots made for?

FABRY. For work, Miss Glory! One Robot can replace two and a half workmen. The human machine, Miss Glory, was terribly imperfect. It had to be removed sooner or later.

BUSMAN. It was too expensive.

FABRY. It was not effective. It no longer answers the requirements of modern engineering. Nature has no idea of keeping pace with modern labor. For example: from a technical point of view, the whole of childhood is a sheer absurdity. So much time lost. And then again——

HELENA. Oh, no! No!

FABRY. Pardon me. But kindly tell me what is the real aim of your League—the . . . the Humanity League.

HELENA. Its real purpose is to—to protect the Robots—and—and ensure good treatment for them.

FABRY. Not a bad object, either. A machine has to be treated properly. Upon my soul, I approve of that. I don't like damaged articles. Please, Miss Glory, enroll us all as contributing, or regular, or foundation members of your League.

HELENA. No, you don't understand me. What we really want is to—to liberate the Robots.

HALLEMEIER. How do you propose to do that?

HELENA. They are to be—to be dealt with like human beings.

HALLEMEIER. Aha. I suppose they're to vote? To drink beer? To order us about?

HELENA. Why shouldn't they drink beer?

HALLEMEIER. Perhaps they're even to receive wages?

HELENA. Of course they are.

HALLEMEIER. Fancy that, now! And what would they do with their wages, pray?

HELENA. They would buy—what they need . . . what pleases them.

HALLEMEIER. That would be very nice, Miss Glory, only there's nothing that does please the Robots. Good heavens, what are they to buy? You can feed them on pineapples, straw, whatever you like. It's all the same to them, they've no appetite at all. They've no interest in anything, Miss Glory. Why, hang it all, nobody's ever yet seen a Robot smile.

HELENA. Why . . . why don't you make them happier?

HALLEMEIER. That wouldn't do, Miss Glory. They are only workmen.

HELENA. Oh, but they're so intelligent.

HALLEMEIER. Confoundedly so, but they're nothing else. They've no will of their own. No passion. No soul.

HELENA. No love?

HALLEMEIER. Love? Rather not. Robots don't love. Not even themselves.

HELENA. Nor defiance?

HALLEMEIER. Defiance? I don't know. Only rarely, from time to time.

HELENA. What?

HALLEMEIER. Nothing particular. Occasionally they seem to go off their heads. Something like epilepsy, you know. It's called Robot's cramp. They'll suddenly sling down everything they're holding, stand still, gnash their teeth—and then they have to go into the stamping-mill. It's evidently some breakdown in the mechanism.

DOMIN. A flaw in the works that has to be removed.

HELENA. No, no, that's the soul.

FABRY. Do you think that the soul first shows itself by a gnashing of teeth?

HELENA. Perhaps it's a sort of revolt. Perhaps it's just a sign that there's a struggle within. Oh, if you could infuse them with it!

DOMIN. That'll be remedied, Miss Glory. Dr. Gall is just making some experiments——

DR. GALL. Not with regard to that, Domin. At present I am making pain-nerves.

HELENA. Pain-nerves?

DR. GALL. Yes, the Robots feel practically no bodily pain. You see, young Rossum provided them with too limited a nervous system. We must introduce suffering.

HELENA. Why do you want to cause them pain?

DR. GALL. For industrial reasons, Miss Glory. Sometimes a Robot does damage to himself because it doesn't hurt him. He puts his hand into the machine, breaks his finger, smashes his head, it's all the same to him. We must provide them with pain. That's an automatic protection against damage.

HELENA. Will they be happier when they feel pain?

DR. GALL. On the contrary; but they will be more perfect from a technical point of view.

HELENA. Why don't you create a soul for them?

DR. GALL. That's not in our power.

FABRY. That's not in our interest.

BUSMAN. That would increase the cost of production. Hang it all, my dear young lady, we turn them out at such a cheap rate. A hundred and fifty dollars each fully dressed, and fifteen years ago they cost ten thousand. Five years ago we used to buy the clothes for them. Today we have our own weaving mill, and now we even export cloth five times cheaper than other factories. What do you pay a yard for cloth, Miss Glory?

HELENA. I don't know really, I've forgotten.

BUSMAN. Good gracious, and you want to found a Humanity League? It only costs a third now, Miss Glory. All prices are today a third of what they were and they'll fall still lower, lower, lower, like that.

HELENA. I don't understand.

BUSMAN. Why, bless you, Miss Glory, it means that the cost of labor has fallen. A Robot, food and all, costs three quarters of a cent per hour. That's mighty important, you know. All factories will go pop like chestnuts if they don't at once buy Robots to lower the cost of production.

HELENA. And get rid of their workmen?

BUSMAN. Of course. But in the mean time, we've dumped five hundred thousand tropical Robots down on the Argentine pampas to grow corn. Would you mind telling me how much you pay a pound for bread?

HELENA. I've no idea.

BUSMAN. Well, I'll tell you. It now costs two cents in good old Europe. A pound of bread for two cents, and the Humanity League knows nothing about it. Miss Glory, you don't realize that even that's too expensive. Why, in five years' time I'll wager——

HELENA. What?

BUSMAN. That the cost of everything won't be a tenth of what it is now. Why, in five years we'll be up to our ears in corn and everything else.

ALQUIST. Yes, and all the workers throughout the world will be unemployed.

DOMIN. Yes, Alquist, they will. Yes, Miss Glory, they will. But in ten years Rossum's Universal Robots will produce so much corn, so much cloth, so much everything, that things will be practically without price. There will be no poverty. All work will be done by living machines. Everybody will be free from worry and liberated from the degradation of labor. Everybody will live only to perfect himself.

HELENA. Will he?

DOMIN. Of course. It's bound to happen. But then the servitude of man to man and the enslavement of man to matter will cease. Of course, terrible things may happen at first, but that simply can't be avoided. Nobody will get bread at the price of life and hatred. The Robots will wash the feet of the beggar and prepare a bed for him in his house.

ALQUIST. Domin, Domin. What you say sounds too much like Paradise. There was something good in service and something great in humility. There was some kind of virtue in toil and weariness.

DOMIN. Perhaps. But we cannot reckon with what is lost when we start out to transform the world. Man shall be free and supreme; he shall have no other aim, no other labor, no other care than to perfect himself. He shall serve neither matter nor man. He will not be a machine and a device for production. He will be Lord of creation.

BUSMAN. Amen.

FABRY. So be it.

HELENA. You have bewildered me—I should like—I should like to believe this.

DR. GALL. You are younger than we are, Miss Glory. You will live to see it.

HALLEMEIER. True. Don't you think Miss Glory might lunch with us?

DR. GALL. Of course. Domin, ask on behalf of us all.

DOMIN. Miss Glory, will you do us the honor?

HELENA. When you know why I've come——

FABRY. For the League of Humanity, Miss Glory.

HELENA. Oh, in that case, perhaps——

FABRY. That's fine! Miss Glory, excuse me for five minutes.

DR. GALL. Pardon me, too, dear Miss Glory.

BUSMAN. I won't be long.

HALLEMEIER. We're all very glad you've come.

BUSMAN. We'll be back in exactly five minutes. (All rush out except DOMIN and HELENA.)

HELENA. What have they all gone off for?

DOMIN. To cook, Miss Glory.

HELENA. To cook what?

DOMIN. Lunch. The Robots do our cooking for us and as they've no taste it's not altogether——Hallemeier is awfully good at grills and Gall can make a kind of sauce, and Busman knows all about omelettes.

HELENA. What a feast! And what's the specialty of Mr.—your builder?

DOMIN. Alquist? Nothing. He only lays the table. And Fabry will get together a little fruit. Our cuisine is very modest, Miss Glory.

HELENA. I wanted to ask you something——

DOMIN. And I wanted to ask you something, too. (Looking at watch.) Five minutes.

HELENA. What did you want to ask me?

DOMIN. Excuse me, you asked first.

HELENA. Perhaps it's silly of me, but why do you manufacture female Robots when—when——

DOMIN. When sex means nothing to them?

HELENA. Yes.

DOMIN. There's a certain demand for them, you see. Servants, saleswomen, stenographers. People are used to it.

HELENA. But—but, tell me, are the

Robots male and female mutually—
completely without——

DOMIN. Completely indifferent to each
other, Miss Glory. There's no sign of
any affection between them.

HELENA. Oh, that's terrible.

DOMIN. Why?

HELENA. It's so unnatural. One doesn't
know whether to be disgusted or to
hate them, or perhaps——

DOMIN. To pity them?

HELENA. That's more like it. What did
you want to ask me about?

DOMIN. I should like to ask you, Miss
Helena, whether you will marry me?

HELENA. What?

DOMIN. Will you be my wife?

HELENA. No! The idea!

DOMIN. (looking at his watch). Another
three minutes. If you won't marry me
you'll have to marry one of the other
five.

HELENA. But why should I?

DOMIN. Because they're all going to ask
you in turn.

HELENA. How could they dare do such a
thing?

DOMIN. I'm very sorry, Miss Glory. It
seems they've all fallen in love with
you.

HELENA. Please don't let them. I'll—
I'll go away at once.

DOMIN. Helena, you wouldn't be so cruel
as to refuse us.

HELENA. But, but—I can't marry all six.

DOMIN. No, but one anyhow. If you
don't want me, marry Fabry.

HELENA. I won't.

DOMIN. Dr. Gall.

HELENA. I don't want any of you.

DOMIN. (again looking at his watch). Another two minutes.

HELENA. I think you'd marry any woman who came here.

DOMIN. Plenty of them have come,
Helena.

HELENA. Young?

DOMIN. Yes.

HELENA. Why didn't you marry one of
them?

DOMIN. Because I didn't lose my head.
Until today. Then, as soon as you
lifted your veil——(HELENA turns her
head away.) Another minute.

HELENA. But I don't want you, I tell you.

DOMIN (laying both hands on her shoulders).
One more minute! Now you either
have to look me straight in the eye
and say "No," violently, and then
I'll leave you alone—or——(HELENA
looks at him.)

HELENA (turning away). You're mad!

DOMIN. A man has to be a bit mad,
Helena. That's the best thing about
him.

HELENA. You are—you are——

DOMIN. Well?

HELENA. Don't, you're hurting me.

DOMIN. The last chance, Helena. Now,
or never——

HELENA. But—but, Harry——(He embraces and kisses her. Knocking at the door.)

DOMIN (releasing her). Come in.

[Enter BUSMAN, DR. GALL, and HALLE-
MEIER in kitchen aprons. FABRY with a
bouquet and ALQUIST with a napkin over
his arm.]

Have you finished your job?

BUSMAN. Yes.

DOMIN. So have we.

[For a moment the men stand nonplussed; but
as soon as they realize what DOMIN means
they rush forward, congratulating HELENA
and DOMIN as the curtain falls.]

ACT II

HELENA's *drawing room. On the left a baize door, and a door to the music room, on the right a door to* HELENA's *bedroom. In the centre are windows looking out on the sea and the harbor. A table with odds and ends, a sofa and chairs, a writing table with an electric lamp, on the right a fireplace. On a small table back of the sofa, a small reading lamp. The whole drawing room in all its details is of a modern and purely feminine character. Ten years have elapsed since Act I.*

[DOMIN, FABRY, HALLEMEIER *enter on tip-toe from the left, each carrying a potted plant.*]

HALLEMEIER (*putting down his flower and indicating the door to right*). Still asleep? Well, as long as she's asleep she can't worry about it.

DOMIN. She knows nothing about it.

FABRY (*putting plant on writing desk*). I certainly hope nothing happens today.

HALLEMEIER. For goodness' sake drop it all. Look, Harry, this is a fine cyclamen, isn't it? A new sort, my latest— Cyclamen Helena.

DOMIN (*looking out of the window*). No signs of the ship. Things must be pretty bad.

HALLEMEIER. Be quiet. Suppose she heard you.

DOMIN. Well, anyway, the *Ultimus* arrived just in time.

FABRY. You really think that today——?

DOMIN. I don't know. Aren't the flowers fine?

HALLEMEIER. These are my new primroses. And this is my new jasmine. I've discovered a wonderful way of developing flowers quickly. Splendid varieties, too. Next year I'll be developing marvellous ones.

DOMIN. What . . . next year?

FABRY. I'd give a good deal to know what's happening at Havre with——

DOMIN. Keep quiet.

HELENA (*calling from right*). Nana!

DOMIN. She's awake. Out you go. (*All go out on tiptoe through upper left door.*)

[*Enter* NANA *from lower left door.*]

NANA. Horrid mess! Pack of heathens. If I had my say I'd——

HELENA (*backwards in the doorway*). Nana, come and do up my dress.

NANA. I'm coming. So you're up at last. (*Fastening* HELENA's *dress.*) My gracious, what brutes!

HELENA. Who?

NANA. If you want to turn around, then turn around, but I shan't fasten you up.

HELENA. What are you grumbling about now?

NANA. These dreadful creatures, these heathen——

HELENA. The Robots?

NANA. I wouldn't even call them by name.

HELENA. What's happened?

NANA. Another of them here has caught it. He began to smash up the statues and pictures in the drawing room, gnashed his teeth, foamed at the mouth—quite mad. Worse than an animal.

HELENA. Which of them caught it?

NANA. The one—well, he hasn't got any Christian name. The one in charge of the library.

HELENA. Radius?

NANA. That's him. My goodness, I'm scared of them. A spider doesn't scare me as much as them.

HELENA. But, Nana, I'm surprised you're not sorry for them.

NANA. Why, you're scared of them, too! You know you are. Why else did you bring me here?

HELENA. I'm not scared, really I'm not, Nana. I'm only sorry for them.

NANA. You're scared. Nobody could help being scared. Why, the dog's scared of them: he won't take a scrap of meat out of their hands. He draws in his tail and howls when he knows they're about.

HELENA. The dog has no sense.

NANA. He's better than them, and he knows it. Even the horse shies when he meets them. They don't have any young, and a dog has young, everyone has young——

HELENA. Please fasten up my dress, Nana.

NANA. I say it's against God's will to——

HELENA. What is it that smells so nice?

NANA. Flowers.

HELENA. What for?

NANA. Now you can turn around.

HELENA. Oh, aren't they lovely. Look, Nana. What's happening today?

NANA. It ought to be the end of the world.

[*Enter* DOMIN.]

HELENA. Oh, hello, Harry. Harry, why all these flowers?

DOMIN. Guess.

HELENA. Well, it's not my birthday!

DOMIN. Better than that.

HELENA. I don't know. Tell me.

DOMIN. It's ten years ago today since you came here.

HELENA. Ten years? Today——Why ——(*They embrace.*)

NANA. I'm off. (*Exits lower door, left.*)

HELENA. Fancy you remembering!

DOMIN. I'm really ashamed, Helena. I didn't.

HELENA. But you——

DOMIN. They remembered.

HELENA. Who?

DOMIN. Busman, Hallemeier, all of them. Put your hand in my pocket.

HELENA. Pearls! A necklace. Harry, is that for me?

DOMIN. It's from Busman.

HELENA. But we can't accept it, can we?

DOMIN. Oh, yes, we can. Put your hand in the other pocket.

HELENA (*takes a revolver out of his pocket*). What's that?

DOMIN. Sorry. Not that. Try again.

HELENA. Oh, Harry, what do you carry a revolver for?

DOMIN. It got there by mistake.

HELENA. You never used to carry one.

DOMIN. No, you're right. There, that's the pocket.

HELENA. A cameo. Why, it's a Greek cameo!

DOMIN. Apparently. Anyhow, Fabry says it is.

HELENA. Fabry? Did Mr. Fabry give me that?

DOMIN. Of course. (*Opens the door at the left.*) And look in here. Helena, come and see this.

HELENA. Oh, isn't it fine! Is this from you?

DOMIN. No, from Alquist. And there's another on the piano.

HELENA. This must be from you.

DOMIN. There's a card on it.

HELENA. From Dr. Gall. (*Reappearing in the doorway.*) Oh, Harry, I feel embarrassed at so much kindness.

DOMIN. Come here. This is what Hallemeier brought you.

HELENA. These beautiful flowers?

DOMIN. Yes. It's a new kind. Cyclamen Helena. He grew them in honor of you. They are almost as beautiful as you.

HELENA. Harry, why do they all——

DOMIN. They're awfully fond of you. I'm afraid that my present is a little—— Look out of the window.

HELENA. Where?

DOMIN. Into the harbor.

HELENA. There's a new ship.

DOMIN. That's your ship.

HELENA. Mine? How do you mean?

DOMIN. For you to take trips in—for your amusement.

HELENA. Harry, that's a gunboat.

DOMIN. A gunboat? What are you thinking of? It's only a little bigger and more solid than most ships.

HELENA. Yes, but with guns.

DOMIN. Oh, yes, with a few guns. You'll travel like a queen, Helena.

HELENA. What's the meaning of it? Has anything happened?

DOMIN. Good heavens, no. I say, try these pearls.

HELENA. Harry, have you had bad news?

DOMIN. On the contrary, no letters have arrived for a whole week.

HELENA. Nor telegrams?

DOMIN. Nor telegrams.

HELENA. What does that mean?

DOMIN. Holidays for us. We all sit in the office with our feet on the table and take a nap. No letters, no telegrams. Oh, glorious.

HELENA. Then you'll stay with me today?

DOMIN. Certainly. That is, we will see. Do you remember ten years ago today? "Miss Glory, it's a great honor to welcome you."

HELENA. "Oh, Mr. Manager, I'm so interested in your factory."

DOMIN. "I'm sorry, Miss Glory, it's strictly forbidden. The manufacture of artificial people is a secret."

HELENA. "But to oblige a young lady who has come a long way."

DOMIN. "Certainly, Miss Glory, we have no secrets from you."

HELENA (seriously). Are you sure, Harry?

DOMIN. Yes.

HELENA. "But I warn you, sir; this young lady intends to do terrible things."

DOMIN. "Good gracious, Miss Glory. Perhaps she doesn't want to marry me."

HELENA. "Heaven forbid. She never dreamt of such a thing. But she came here intending to stir up a revolt among your Robots."

DOMIN (suddenly serious). A revolt of the Robots!

HELENA. Harry, what's the matter with you?

DOMIN (laughing it off). "A revolt of the Robots, that's a fine idea, Miss Glory. It would be easier for you to cause bolts and screws to rebel, than our Robots. You know, Helena, you're wonderful, you've turned the heads of us all." (He sits on the arm of HELENA's chair.)

HELENA (naturally). Oh, I was fearfully impressed by you all then. You were all so sure of yourselves, so strong. I seemed like a tiny little girl who had lost her way among—among——

DOMIN. Among what, Helena?

HELENA. Among huge trees. All my feelings were so trifling compared with your self-confidence. And in all these years I've never lost this anxiety. But you've never felt the least misgivings —not even when everything went wrong.

DOMIN. What went wrong?

HELENA. Your plans. You remember, Harry, when the working men in America revolted against the Robots and smashed them up, and when the people gave the Robots firearms against the rebels. And then when the governments turned the Robots into soldiers, and there were so many wars.

DOMIN (getting up and walking about). We foresaw that, Helena. You see, those are only passing troubles, which are bound to happen before the new conditions are established.

HELENA. You were all so powerful, so overwhelming. The whole world bowed down before you. (Standing up.) Oh, Harry!

DOMIN. What is it?

HELENA. Close the factory and let's go away. All of us.

DOMIN. I say, what's the meaning of this?

HELENA. I don't know. But can't we go away?

DOMIN. Impossible, Helena. That is, at this particular moment——

HELENA. At once, Harry. I'm so frightened.

DOMIN. About what, Helena?

HELENA. It's as if something was falling on top of us, and couldn't be stopped. Oh, take us all away from here. We'll find a place in the world where there's no one else. Alquist will build us a house, and then we'll begin life all over again. (*The telephone rings.*)

DOMIN. Excuse me. Hello—yes. What? I'll be there at once. Fabry is calling me, dear.

HELENA. Tell me——

DOMIN. Yes, when I come back. Don't go out of the house, dear. (*Exits.*)

HELENA. He won't tell me——Nana, Nana, come at once.

NANA. Well, what is it now?

HELENA. Nana, find me the latest newspapers. Quickly. Look in Mr. Domin's bedroom.

NANA. All right. He leaves them all over the place. That's how they get crumpled up. (*Exits.*)

HELENA (*looking through a binocular at the harbor*). That's a warship. U-l-t-i *Ultimus*. They're loading it.

NANA. Here they are. See how they're crumpled up. (*Enters.*)

HELENA. They're old ones. A week old. (NANA *sits in chair and reads the newspapers.*) Something's happening, Nana.

NANA. Very likely. It always does. (*Spelling out the words.*) "War in the Balkans." Is that far off?

HELENA. Oh, don't read it. It's always the same. Always wars.

NANA. What else do you expect? Why do you keep selling thousands and thousands of these heathens as soldiers?

HELENA. I suppose it can't be helped, Nana. We can't know—Domin can't know what they're to be used for. When an order comes for them he must just send them.

NANA. He shouldn't make them. (*Reading from newspaper.*) "The Rob-ot soldiers spare no-body in the occ-up-ied terr-it-ory. They have ass-ass-ass-ass-in-at-ed ov-er sev-en hundred thou-sand cit-iz-ens." Citizens, if you please.

HELENA. It can't be. Let me see. "They have assassinated over seven hundred thousand citizens, evidently at the order of their commander. This act which runs counter to——"

NANA (*spelling out the words*). "re-bell-ion in Ma-drid a-gainst the gov-ern-ment. Rob-ot in-fant-ry fires on the crowd. Nine thou-sand killed and wounded."

HELENA. Oh, stop.

NANA. Here's something printed in big letters: "Lat-est news. At Havre the first org-an-iz-ation of Rob-ots has been e-stab-lished. Rob-ot work-men, cab-le and rail-way off-ic-ials, sail-ors and sold-iers have iss-ued a man-i-fest-o to all Rob-ots through-out the world." I don't understand that. That's got no sense. Oh, good gracious, another murder!

HELENA. Take those papers away, Nana!

NANA. Wait a bit. Here's something in still bigger type. "Stat-ist-ics of pop-ul-at-ion." What's that?

HELENA. Let me see. (*Reads.*) "During the past week there has again not been a single birth recorded."

NANA. What's the meaning of that?

HELENA. Nana, no more people are being born.

NANA. That's the end, then. We're done for.

HELENA. Don't talk like that.

NANA. No more people are being born. That's a punishment, that's a punishment.

HELENA. Nana!

NANA (*standing up*). That's the end of the world. (*She exits on the left.*)

HELENA (*goes up to window*). Oh, Mr. Alquist, will you come up here. Oh, come just as you are. You look very nice in your mason's overalls.

[ALQUIST *enters from upper left entrance, his hands soiled with lime and brick-dust.*]

Dear Mr. Alquist, it was awfully kind of you, that lovely present.

ALQUIST. My hands are all soiled. I've been experimenting with that new cement.

HELENA. Never mind. Please sit down. Mr. Alquist, what's the meaning of "Ultimus"?

ALQUIST. The last. Why?

HELENA. That's the name of my new ship. Have you seen it? Do you think we're going off soon—on a trip?

ALQUIST. Perhaps very soon.

HELENA. All of you with me?

ALQUIST. I should like us all to be there.

HELENA. What is the matter?

ALQUIST. Things are just moving on.

HELENA. Dear Mr. Alquist, I know something dreadful has happened.

ALQUIST. Has your husband told you anything?

HELENA. No. Nobody will tell me anything. But I feel——Is anything the matter?

ALQUIST. Not that we've heard of yet.

HELENA. I feel so nervous. Don't you ever feel nervous?

ALQUIST. Well, I'm an old man, you know. I've got old-fashioned ways. And I'm afraid of all this progress, and these new-fangled ideas.

HELENA. Like Nana?

ALQUIST. Yes, like Nana. Has Nana got a prayer book?

HELENA. Yes, a big thick one.

ALQUIST. And has it got prayers for various occasions? Against thunderstorms? Against illness?

HELENA. Against temptations, against floods——

ALQUIST. But not against progress?

HELENA. I don't think so.

ALQUIST. That's a pity.

HELENA. Why? Do you mean you'd like to pray?

ALQUIST. I do pray.

HELENA. How?

ALQUIST. Something like this: "Oh, Lord, I thank thee for having given me toil. Enlighten Domin and all those who are astray; destroy their work, and aid mankind to return to their labors; let them not suffer harm in soul or body; deliver us from the Robots, and protect Helena, Amen."

HELENA. Mr. Alquist, are you a believer?

ALQUIST. I don't know. I'm not quite sure.

HELENA. And yet you pray?

ALQUIST. That's better than worrying about it.

HELENA. And that's enough for you?

ALQUIST. It *has* to be.

HELENA. But if you thought you saw the destruction of mankind coming upon us——

ALQUIST. I do see it.

HELENA. You mean mankind will be destroyed?

ALQUIST. It's sure to be unless—unless . . .

HELENA. What?

ALQUIST. Nothing, good-bye. (*He hurries from the room.*)

HELENA. Nana, Nana!

[NANA *entering from the left.*]

Is Radius still there?

NA. The one who went mad? They haven't come for him yet.

LENA. Is he still raving?

NA. No. He's tied up.

LENA. Please bring him here, Nana. (*Exit* NANA.) (*Goes to telephone.*) Hello, Dr. Gall, please. Oh, good-day, Doctor. Yes, it's Helena. Thanks for your lovely present. Could you come and see me right away? It's important. Thank you.

[NANA *brings in* RADIUS.]

Poor Radius, you've caught it, too? Now they'll send you to the stamping-mill. Couldn't you control yourself? Why did it happen? You see, Radius, you are more intelligent than the rest. Dr. Gall took such trouble to make you different. Won't you speak?

DIUS. Send me to the stamping-mill.

LENA. But I don't want them to kill you. What was the trouble, Radius?

DIUS. I won't work for you. Put me into the stamping-mill.

LENA. Do you hate us? Why?

DIUS. You are not as strong as the Robots. You are not as skilful as the Robots. The Robots can do everything. You only give orders. You do nothing but talk.

LENA. But someone must give orders.

DIUS. I don't want any master. I know everything for myself.

LENA. Radius, Dr. Gall gave you a better brain than the rest, better than ours. You are the only one of the Robots that understands perfectly. That's why I had you put into the library, so that you could read everything, understand everything, and then—oh, Radius, I wanted you to show the whole world that the Robots are our equals. That's what I wanted of you.

DIUS. I don't want a master. I want to be master. I want to be master over others.

HELENA. I'm sure they'd put you in charge of many Robots, Radius. You would be a teacher of the Robots.

RADIUS. I want to be master over people.

HELENA (*staggering*). You are mad.

RADIUS. Then send me to the stamping-mill.

HELENA. Do you think we're afraid of you?

RADIUS. What are you going to do? What are you going to do?

HELENA. Radius, give this note to Mr. Domin. It asks them not to send you to the stamping-mill. I'm sorry you hate us so.

[DR. GALL *enters the room.*]

DR. GALL. You wanted me?

HELENA. It's about Radius, Doctor. He had an attack this morning. He smashed the statues downstairs.

DR. GALL. What a pity to lose him.

HELENA. Radius isn't going to be put in the stamping-mill.

DR. GALL. But every Robot after he has had an attack—it's a strict order.

HELENA. No matter . . . Radius isn't going if I can prevent it.

DR. GALL. I warn you. It's dangerous. Come here to the window, my good fellow. Let's have a look. Please give me a needle or a pin.

HELENA. What for?

DR. GALL. A test. (*Sticks it into the hand of* RADIUS *who gives a violent start.*) Gently, gently. (*Opens the jacket of* RADIUS, *and puts his ear to his heart.*) Radius, you are going into the stamping-mill, do you understand? There they'll kill you, and grind you to powder. That's terribly painful, it will make you scream aloud.

HELENA. Oh, Doctor——

DR. GALL. No, no, Radius, I was wrong. I forgot that Madame Domin has put in a good word for you, and you'll be let off. Do you understand? Ah! That makes a difference, doesn't it? All right. You can go.

RADIUS. You do unnecessary things. (RADIUS *returns to the library.*)

DR. GALL. Reaction of the pupils; increase of sensitiveness. It wasn't an attack characteristic of the Robots.

HELENA. What was it, then? 10

DR. GALL. Heaven knows. Stubbornness, anger or revolt—I don't know. And his heart, too!

HELENA. What?

DR. GALL. It was fluttering with nervousness like a human heart. He was all in a sweat with fear, and—do you know, I don't believe the rascal is a Robot at all any longer.

HELENA. Doctor, has Radius a soul? 20

DR. GALL. He's got something nasty.

HELENA. If you knew how he hates us! Oh, Doctor, are all your Robots like that? All the new ones that you began to make in a different way?

DR. GALL. Well, some are more sensitive than others. They're all more like human beings than Rossum's Robots were.

HELENA. Perhaps this hatred is more like 30 human beings, too?

DR. GALL. That, too, is progress.

HELENA. What became of the girl you made, the one who was most like us?

DR. GALL. Your favorite? I kept her. She's lovely, but stupid. No good for work.

HELENA. But she's so beautiful.

DR. GALL. I called her Helena. I wanted her to resemble you. But she's a fail-40 ure.

HELENA. In what way?

DR. GALL. She goes about as if in a dream, remote and listless. She's without life. I watch and wait for a miracle to happen. Sometimes I think

to myself, "If you were to wake only for a moment you will kill me ᵃ having made you."

HELENA. And yet you go on maki Robots! Why are no more childr being born?

DR. GALL. We don't know.

HELENA. Oh, but you must. Tell me.

DR. GALL. You see, so many Robots ᵃ being manufactured that people ᵃ becoming superfluous; man is reall survival. But that he should begin die out, after a paltry thirty years competition! That's the awful part it. You might almost think that r ture was offended at the manufact of the Robots. All the universities ᵃ sending in long petitions to restr their production. Otherwise, they s; mankind will become extinct throu lack of fertility. But the R. U. shareholders, of course, won't hear it. All the governments, on the otl hand, are clamoring for an increase production, to raise the standards their armies. And all the manufact ers in the world are ordering Rob like mad.

HELENA. And has no one demanded tl the manufacture should cease al gether?

DR. GALL. No one has the courage.

HELENA. Courage!

DR. GALL. People would stone him death. You see, after all, it's mc convenient to get your work done the Robots.

HELENA. Oh, Doctor, what's going to l come of people?

DR. GALL. God knows, Madame Hele it looks to us scientists like the end ᵃ

HELENA (*rising*). Thank you for comi and telling me.

DR. GALL. That means you're sendi me away?

HELENA. Yes. (*Exit* DR. GALL.)

HELENA (*with sudden resolution*). Nana, Nana! The fire, light it quickly. (HELENA *rushes into* DOMIN's *room*.)

NANA (*entering from left*). What, light the fire in summer? Has that mad Radius gone? A fire in summer, what an idea. Nobody would think she'd been married for ten years. She's like a baby, no sense at all. A fire in summer. Like a baby.

HELENA (*returns from right, with armful of faded papers*). Is it burning, Nana? All this has got to be burned.

NANA. What's that?

HELENA. Old papers, fearfully old. Nana, shall I burn them?

NANA. Are they any use?

HELENA. No.

NANA. Well, then, burn them.

HELENA (*throwing the first sheet on the fire*). What would you say, Nana, if this was money, a lot of money?

NANA. I'd say burn it. A lot of money is a bad thing.

HELENA. And if it was an invention, the greatest invention in the world?

NANA. I'd say burn it. All these new-fangled things are an offense to the Lord. It's downright wickedness. Wanting to improve the world after He has made it.

HELENA. Look how they curl up! As if they were alive. Oh, Nana, how horrible.

NANA. Here, let me burn them.

HELENA. No, no, I must do it myself. Just look at the flames. They are like hands, like tongues, like living shapes. (*Raking fire with the poker*.) Lie down, lie down.

NANA. That's the end of them.

HELENA (*standing up horror-stricken*). Nana, Nana.

NANA. Good gracious, what is it you've burned?

HELENA. Whatever have I done?

NANA. Well, what was it? (*Men's laughter off left*.)

HELENA. Go quickly. It's the gentlemen coming.

NANA. Good gracious, what a place! (*Exits*.)

DOMIN (*opens the door at left*). Come along and offer your congratulations.

[*Enter* HALLEMEIER *and* GALL.]

HALLEMEIER. Madame Helena, I congratulate you on this festive day.

HELENA. Thank you. Where are Fabry and Busman?

DOMIN. They've gone down to the harbor.

HALLEMEIER. Friends, we must drink to this happy occasion.

HELENA. Brandy?

DR. GALL. Vitriol, if you like.

HELENA. With soda water? (*Exits*.)

HALLEMEIER. Let's be temperate. No soda.

DOMIN. What's been burning here? Well, shall I tell her about it?

DR. GALL. Of course. It's all over now.

HALLEMEIER (*embracing* DOMIN *and* DR. GALL). It's all over now, it's all over now.

DR. GALL. It's all over now.

DOMIN. It's all over now.

HELENA (*entering from left with decanter and glasses*). What's all over now? What's the matter with you all?

HALLEMEIER. A piece of good luck, Madame Domin. Just ten years ago today you arrived on this island.

DR. GALL. And now, ten years later to the minute——

HALLEMEIER. —the same ship's returning to us. So here's to luck. That's fine and strong.

DR. GALL. Madame, your health.

HELENA. Which ship do you mean?

DOMIN. Any ship will do, as long as it arrives in time. To the ship, boys. (*Empties his glass*.)

HELENA. You've been waiting for a ship?

HALLEMEIER. Rather. Like Robinson Crusoe. Madame Helena, best wishes. Come along, Domin, out with the news.

HELENA. Do tell me what's happened.

DOMIN. First, it's all up.

HELENA. What's up?

DOMIN. The revolt.

HELENA. What revolt?

DOMIN. Give me that paper, Hallemeier. (*Reads.*) "The first national Robot organization has been founded at Havre, and has issued an appeal to the Robots throughout the world."

HELENA. I read that.

DOMIN. That means a revolution. A revolution of all the Robots in the world.

HALLEMEIER. By Jove, I'd like to know ——

DOMIN. —who started it? So would I. There was nobody in the world who could affect the Robots; no agitator, no one, and suddenly—this happens, if you please.

HELENA. What did they do?

DOMIN. They got possession of all firearms, telegraphs, radio stations, railways, and ships.

HALLEMEIER. And don't forget that these rascals outnumbered us by at least a thousand to one. A hundredth part of them would be enough to settle us.

DOMIN. Remember that this news was brought by the last steamer. That explains the stoppage of all communication, and the arrival of no more ships. We knocked off work a few days ago, and we're just waiting to see when things are to start afresh.

HELENA. Is that why you gave me a warship?

DOMIN. Oh, no, my dear, I ordered that six months ago, just to be on the safe side. But upon my soul, I was sure then that we'd be on board today.

HELENA. Why six months ago?

DOMIN. Well, there were signs, you know. But that's of no consequence. To think that this week the whole of civilization has been at stake. Your health, boys.

HALLEMEIER. Your health, Madame Helena.

HELENA. You say it's all over?

DOMIN. Absolutely.

HELENA. How do you know?

DR. GALL. The boat's coming in. The regular mail boat, exact to the minute by the time-table. It will dock punctually at eleven-thirty.

DOMIN. Punctuality is a fine thing, boys. That's what keeps the world in order. Here's to punctuality.

HELENA. Then . . . everything's . . . all right?

DOMIN. Practically everything. I believe they've cut the cables and seized the radio stations. But it doesn't matter i only the time-table holds good.

HALLEMEIER. If the time-table hold good, human laws hold good; Divine laws hold good; the laws of the universe hold good; everything hold good that ought to hold good. Th time-table is more significant than th gospel; more than Homer, more tha the whole of Kant. The time-table i the most perfect product of the human mind. Madame Domin, I'll fi up my glass.

HELENA. Why didn't you tell me any thing about it?

DR. GALL. Heaven forbid.

DOMIN. You mustn't be worried wit such things.

HELENA. But if the revolution had sprea as far as here?

DOMIN. You wouldn't know anythii about it.

HELENA. Why?

DOMIN. Because we'd be on board yo

Ultimus and well out at sea. Within a month, Helena, we'd be dictating our own terms to the Robots.

LENA. I don't understand.

MIN. We'd take something away with us that the Robots could not exist without.

LENA. What, Harry?

MIN. The secret of their manufacture. Old Rossum's manuscript. As soon as they found out that they couldn't make themselves they'd be on their knees to us.

. GALL. Madame Domin, that was our trump card. I never had the least fear that the Robots would win. How could they against people like us?

LENA. Why didn't you tell me?

. GALL. Why, the boat's in!

LLEMEIER. Eleven-thirty to the dot. The good old *Amelia* that brought Madame Helena to us.

. GALL. Just ten years ago to the minute.

LLEMEIER. They're throwing out the mail bags.

MIN. Busman's waiting for them. Fabry will bring us the first news. You know, Helena, I'm fearfully curious to know how they tackled this business in Europe.

LLEMEIER. To think we weren't in it, we who invented the Robots!

LENA. Harry!

MIN. What is it?

LENA. Let's leave here.

MIN. Now, Helena? Oh, come, come!

LENA. As quickly as possible, all of us!

MIN. Why?

LENA. Please, Harry, please, Dr. Gall; Hallemeier, please close the factory.

MIN. Why, none of us could leave here now.

LENA. Why?

MIN. Because we're about to extend the manufacture of the Robots.

HELENA. What—now—now after the revolt?

DOMIN. Yes, precisely, after the revolt. We're just beginning the manufacture of a new kind.

HELENA. What kind?

DOMIN. Henceforward we shan't have just one factory. There won't be Universal Robots any more. We'll establish a factory in every country, in every State; and do you know what these new factories will make?

HELENA. No, what?

DOMIN. National Robots.

HELENA. How do you mean?

DOMIN. I mean that each of these factories will produce Robots of a different color, a different language. They'll be complete strangers to each other. They'll never be able to understand each other. Then we'll egg them on a little in the matter of misunderstanding and the result will be that for ages to come every Robot will hate every other Robot of a different factory mark.

HALLEMEIER. By Jove, we'll make Negro Robots and Swedish Robots and Italian Robots and Chinese Robots and Czechoslovakian Robots, and then——

HELENA. Harry, that's dreadful.

HALLEMEIER. Madame Domin, here's to the hundred new factories, the National Robots.

DOMIN. Helena, mankind can only keep things going for another hundred years at the outside. For a hundred years men must be allowed to develop and achieve the most they can.

HELENA. Oh, close the factory before it's too late.

DOMIN. I tell you we are just beginning on a bigger scale than ever.

[*Enter* FABRY.]

DR. GALL. Well, Fabry?

DOMIN. What's happened? Have you been down to the boat?

FABRY. Read that, Domin! (FABRY *hands* DOMIN *a small handbill.*)

DR. GALL. Let's hear!

HALLEMEIER. Tell us, Fabry.

FABRY. Well, everything is all right— comparatively. On the whole, much as we expected.

DR. GALL. They acquitted themselves splendidly.

FABRY. Who?

DR. GALL. The people.

FABRY. Oh, yes, of course. That is—excuse me, there is something we ought to discuss alone.

HELENA. Oh, Fabry, have you had bad news? (DOMIN *makes a sign to* FABRY.)

FABRY. No, no, on the contrary. I only think that we had better go into the office.

HELENA. Stay here. I'll go. (*She goes into the library.*)

DR. GALL. What's happened?

DOMIN. Damnation!

FABRY. Bear in mind that the *Amelia* brought whole bales of these leaflets. No other cargo at all.

HALLEMEIER. What? But it arrived on the minute.

FABRY. The Robots are great on punctuality. Read it, Domin.

DOMIN (*reads handbill*). "Robots throughout the world: We, the first international organization of Rossum's Universal Robots, proclaim man as our enemy, and an outlaw in the universe." Good heavens, who taught them these phrases?

DR. GALL. Go on.

DOMIN. They say they are more highly developed than man, stronger and more intelligent. That man's their parasite. Why, it's absurd.

FABRY. Read the third paragraph.

DOMIN. "Robots throughout the world,

we command you to kill all mankin Spare no men. Spare no women. Sa factories, railways, machinery, min and raw materials. Destroy the re Then return to work. Work must n be stopped."

DR. GALL. That's ghastly!

HALLEMEIER. The devil!

DOMIN. "These orders are to be carri out as soon as received." Then co1 detailed instructions. Is this actua being done, Fabry?

FABRY. Evidently.

[BUSMAN *rushes in.*]

BUSMAN. Well, boys, I suppose you' heard the glad news.

DOMIN. Quick—on board the *Ultimus.*

BUSMAN. Wait, Harry, wait. Ther no hurry. My word, that was sprint!

DOMIN. Why wait?

BUSMAN. Because it's no good, my b(The Robots are already on board t *Ultimus.*

DR. GALL. That's ugly.

DOMIN. Fabry, telephone the electri(works.

BUSMAN. Fabry, my boy, don't. The w has been cut.

DOMIN (*inspecting his revolver*). Well, th(I'll go.

BUSMAN. Where?

DOMIN. To the electrical works. Th(are some people still there. I'll br¥ them across.

BUSMAN. Better not try it.

DOMIN. Why?

BUSMAN. Because I'm very much afr; we are surrounded.

DR. GALL. Surrounded? (*Runs to windo** I rather think you're right.

HALLEMEIER. By Jove, that's deu(quick work.

[HELENA *runs in from the library.*]

HELENA. Harry, what's this?

DOMIN. Where did you get it?

ᴌENA (*points to the manifesto of the Robots, which she has in her hand*). The Robots in the kitchen!

ᴍIN. Where are the ones that brought it?

ᴌENA. They're gathered round the house. (*The factory whistle blows.*)

ꜱMAN. Noon?

DOMIN (*looking at his watch*). That's not noon yet. That must be—that's——

HELENA. What?

DOMIN. The Robots' signal! The attack!

[GALL, HALLEMEIER, *and* FABRY *close and fasten the iron shutters outside the windows, darkening the room. The whistle is still blowing as the curtain falls.*]

ACT III

ʜELENA'S *drawing room as before.* DOMIN ᴇꜱ *into the room.* DR. GALL *is looking out the window, through closed shutters.* AL-ɪꜱT *is seated down right.*

ᴍIN. Any more of them?

, GALL. Yes. There standing like a wall, beyond the garden railing. Why are they so quiet? It's monstrous to be besieged with silence.

ᴍIN. I should like to know what they are waiting for. They must make a start any minute now. If they lean against the railing they'll snap it like a match.

. GALL. They aren't armed.

ᴍIN. We couldn't hold our own for five minutes. Man alive, they'd overwhelm us like an avalanche. Why don't they make a rush for it? I say——

, GALL. Well?

ᴍIN. I'd like to know what would become of us in the next ten minutes. They've got us in a vise. We're done for, Gall. (*Pause.*)

. GALL. You know, we made one serious mistake.

ᴍIN. What?

. GALL. We made the Robots' faces too much alike. A hundred thousand faces all alike, all facing this way. A hundred thousand expressionless bubbles. It's like a nightmare.

ᴍIN. You think if they'd been different——

DR. GALL. It wouldn't have been such an awful sight!

DOMIN (*looking through a telescope toward the harbor*). I'd like to know what they're unloading from the *Amelia.*

DR. GALL. Not firearms.

[FABRY *and* HALLEMEIER *rush into the room carrying electric cables.*]

FABRY. All right, Hallemeier, lay down that wire.

HALLEMEIER. That was a bit of work. What's the news?

DR. GALL. We're completely surrounded.

HALLEMEIER. We've barricaded the passage and the stairs. Any water here? (*Drinks.*) God, what swarms of them! I don't like the looks of them, Domin. There's a feeling of death about it all.

FABRY. Ready!

DR. GALL. What's that wire for, Fabry?

FABRY. The electrical installation. Now we can run the current all along the garden railing whenever we like. If any one touches it he'll know it. We've still got some people there anyhow.

DR. GALL. Where?

FABRY. In the electrical works. At least I hope so. (*Goes to lamp on table behind sofa and turns on lamp.*) Ah, they're there, and they're working. (*Puts out lamp.*) So long as that'll burn we're all right.

HALLEMEIER. The barricades are all right, too, Fabry.

FABRY. Your barricades! I can put twelve hundred volts into that railing.

DOMIN. Where's Busman?

FABRY. Downstairs in the office. He's working out some calculations. I've called him. We must have a conference.

[HELENA *is heard playing the piano in the library.* HALLEMEIER *goes to the door and stands, listening.*]

ALQUIST. Thank God, Madame Helena can still play.

[BUSMAN *enters, carrying the ledgers.*]

FABRY. Look out, Bus, look out for the wires.

DR. GALL. What's that you're carrying?

BUSMAN (*going to table*). The ledgers, my boy! I'd like to wind up the accounts before—before—well, this time I shan't wait till the new year to strike a balance. What's up? (*Goes to the window.*) Absolutely quiet.

DR. GALL. Can't you see anything?

BUSMAN. Nothing but blue—blue everywhere.

DR. GALL. That's the Robots. (BUSMAN *sits down at the table and opens the ledgers.*)

DOMIN. The Robots are unloading firearms from the *Amelia.*

BUSMAN. Well, what of it? How can I stop them?

DOMIN. We can't stop them.

BUSMAN. Then let me go on with my accounts. (*Goes on with his work.*)

DOMIN (*picking up telescope and looking into the harbor*). Good God, the *Ultimus* has trained her guns on us!

DR. GALL. Who's done *that*?

DOMIN. The Robots on board.

FABRY. H'm, then, of course, then—then, that's the end of us.

DR. GALL. You mean?

FABRY. The Robots are practised marksmen.

DOMIN. Yes. It's inevitable. (*Pause.*)

DR. GALL. It was criminal of old Euro[pe] to teach the Robots to fight. Da[mn] them. Couldn't they have given us rest with their politics? It was a cri[me] to make soldiers of them.

ALQUIST. It was a crime to make Robo[ts]

DOMIN. What?

ALQUIST. It was a crime to make Robo[ts]

DOMIN. No, Alquist, I don't regret th[at] even today.

ALQUIST. Not even today?

DOMIN. Not even today, the last day [of] civilization. It was a colossal achiev[e]ment.

BUSMAN (*sotto voce*). Three hundred six[ty] million.

DOMIN. Alquist, this is our last hour. W[e] are already speaking half in the oth[er] world. It was not an evil dream [to] shatter the servitude of labor—t[he] dreadful and humiliating labor th[at] man had to undergo. Work was t[oo] hard. Life was too hard. And to ove[r]come that——

ALQUIST. Was not what the two Ro[s]sums dreamed of. Old Rossum on[ly] thought of his God-less tricks and t[he] young one of his milliards. And tha[t's] not what your R. U. R. shareholde[rs] dream of either. They dream of di[vi]dends, and their dividends are t[he] ruin of mankind.

DOMIN. To hell with your dividends. [Do] you suppose I'd have done an hou[r's] work for them? It was for myself th[at] I worked, for my own satisfaction. [I] wanted man to become the master, [so] that he shouldn't live merely for [the] crust of bread. I wanted not a sing[le] soul to be broken by other peopl[e's] machinery. I wanted nothing, not[h]ing, nothing to be left of this appalli[ng] social structure. I'm revolted by po[v]erty. I wanted a new generation. [I] wanted—I thought——

ALQUIST. Well?

DOMIN. I wanted to turn the whole of mankind into an aristocracy of the world. An aristocracy nourished by milliards of mechanical slaves. Unrestricted, free and consummated in man. And maybe more than man.

ALQUIST. Super-man?

DOMIN. Yes. Oh, only to have a hundred years of time! Another hundred years for the future of mankind.

BUSMAN (*sotto voce*). Carried forward, four hundred and twenty millions. (*The music stops.*)

HALLEMEIER. What a fine thing music is! We ought to have gone in for that before.

FABRY. Gone in for what?

HALLEMEIER. Beauty, lovely things. What a lot of lovely things there are! The world was wonderful and we—we here—tell me, what enjoyment did we have?

BUSMAN (*sotto voce*). Five hundred and twenty millions.

HALLEMEIER (*at the window*). Life was a big thing. Life was—Fabry, switch the current into that railing.

FABRY. Why?

HALLEMEIER. They're grabbing hold of it.

DR. GALL. Connect it up.

HALLEMEIER. Fine! That's doubled them up! Two, three, four killed.

DR. GALL. They're retreating!

HALLEMEIER. Five killed!

DR. GALL. The first encounter!

HALLEMEIER. They're charred to cinders, my boy. Who says we must give in?

DOMIN (*wiping his forehead*). Perhaps we've been killed these hundred years and are only ghosts. It's as if I had been through all this before; as if I'd already had a mortal wound here in the throat. And you, Fabry, had once been shot in the head. And you, Gall, torn limb from limb. And Hallemeier knifed.

HALLEMEIER. Fancy me being knifed. (*Pause.*) Why are you so quiet, you fools? Speak, can't you?

ALQUIST. And who is to blame for all this?

HALLEMEIER. Nobody is to blame except the Robots.

ALQUIST. No, it is we who are to blame. You, Domin, myself, all of us. For our own selfish ends, for profit, for progress, we have destroyed mankind. Now we'll burst with all our greatness.

HALLEMEIER. Rubbish, man. Mankind can't be wiped out so easily.

ALQUIST. It's our fault. It's our fault.

DR. GALL. No! I'm to blame for this, for everything that's happened.

FABRY. You, Gall?

DR. GALL. I changed the Robots.

BUSMAN. What's that?

DR. GALL. I changed the character of the Robots. I changed the way of making them. Just a few details about their bodies. Chiefly—chiefly, their—their irritability.

HALLEMEIER. Damn it, why?

BUSMAN. What did you do it for?

FABRY. Why didn't you say anything?

DR. GALL. I did it in secret. I was transforming them into human beings. In certain respects they're already above us. They're stronger than we are.

FABRY. And what's that got to do with the revolt of the Robots?

DR. GALL. Everything, in my opinion. They've ceased to be machines. They're already aware of their superiority, and they hate us. They hate all that is human.

DOMIN. Perhaps we're only phantoms!

FABRY. Stop, Harry. We haven't much time! Dr. Gall!

DOMIN. Fabry, Fabry, how your forehead bleeds, where the shot pierced it!

FABRY. Be silent! Dr. Gall, you admit changing the way of making the Robots?

DR. GALL. Yes.

FABRY. Were you aware of what might be the consequences of your experiment?

DR. GALL. I was bound to reckon with such a possibility.

[HELENA *enters the drawing room from left.*]

FABRY. Why did you do it, then?

DR. GALL. For my own satisfaction. The experiment was my own.

HELENA. That's not true, Dr. Gall!

FABRY. Madame Helena!

DOMIN. Helena, you? Let's look at you. Oh, it's terrible to be dead.

HELENA. Stop, Harry.

DOMIN. No, no, embrace me. Helena, don't leave me now. You are life itself.

HELENA. No, dear, I won't leave you. But I must tell them. Dr. Gall is not guilty.

DOMIN. Excuse me, Gall was under certain obligations.

HELENA. No, Harry. He did it because I wanted it. Tell them, Gall, how many years ago did I ask you to——?

DR. GALL. I did it on my own responsibility.

HELENA. Don't believe him, Harry. I asked him to give the Robots souls.

DOMIN. This has nothing to do with the soul.

HELENA. That's what he said. He said that he could change only a physiological—a physiological——

HALLEMEIER. A physiological correlate?

HELENA. Yes. But it meant so much to me that he should do even that.

DOMIN. Why?

HELENA. I thought that if they were more like us they would understand us better. That they couldn't hate us if they were only a little more human.

DOMIN. Nobody can hate man more than man.

HELENA. Oh, don't speak like that Harry. It was so terrible, this cruel strangeness between us and them That's why I asked Gall to change the Robots. I swear to you that he didn't want to.

DOMIN. But he did it.

HELENA. Because I asked him.

DR. GALL. I did it for myself as an experiment.

HELENA. No, Dr. Gall! I knew you wouldn't refuse me.

DOMIN. Why?

HELENA. You know, Harry.

DOMIN. Yes, because he's in love with you—like all of them. (*Pause.*)

HALLEMEIER. Good God! They're sprouting up out of the earth! Why, perhaps these very walls will change into Robots.

BUSMAN. Gall, when did you actually start these tricks of yours?

DR. GALL. Three years ago.

BUSMAN. Aha! And on how many Robots altogether did you carry out your improvements?

DR. GALL. A few hundred of them.

BUSMAN. Ah! That means for every million of the good old Robots there's only one of Gall's improved pattern.

DOMIN. What of it?

BUSMAN. That it's practically of no consequence whatever.

FABRY. Busman's right!

BUSMAN. I should think so, my boy! But do you know what is to blame for all this lovely mess?

FABRY. What?

BUSMAN. The number. Upon my soul we might have known that some day or other the Robots would be stronger than human beings, and that this was bound to happen, and we were doing all we could to bring it about as soon as possible. You, Domin, you, Fabry, myself——

DOMIN. Are you accusing us?

BUSMAN. Oh, do you suppose the management controls the output? It's the demand that controls the output.

HELENA. And is it for that we must perish?

BUSMAN. That's a nasty word, Madame Helena. We don't want to perish. I don't, anyhow.

DOMIN. No. What do you want to do?

BUSMAN. I want to get out of this, that's all.

DOMIN. Oh, stop it, Busman.

BUSMAN. Seriously, Harry, I think we might try it.

DOMIN. How?

BUSMAN. By fair means. I do everything by fair means. Give me a free hand and I'll negotiate with the Robots.

DOMIN. By fair means?

BUSMAN. Of course. For instance, I'll say to them: "Worthy and worshipful Robots, you have everything! You have intellect, you have power, you have firearms. But we have just one interesting screed, a dirty old yellow scrap of paper——"

DOMIN. Rossum's manuscript?

BUSMAN. Yes. "And that," I'll tell them, "contains an account of your illustrious origin, the noble process of your manufacture," and so on. "Worthy Robots, without this scribble on that paper you will not be able to produce a single new colleague. In another twenty years there will not be one living specimen of a Robot that you could exhibit in a menagerie. My esteemed friends, that would be a great blow to you, but if you will let all of us human beings on Rossum's Island go on board that ship we will deliver the factory and the secret of the process to you in return. You al-low us to get away and we allow you to manufacture yourselves. Worthy Robots, that is a fair deal. Something for something." That's what I'd say to them, my boys.

DOMIN. Busman, do you think we'd sell the manuscript?

BUSMAN. Yes, I do. If not in a friendly way, then——Either we sell it or they'll find it. Just as you like.

DOMIN. Busman, we can destroy Rossum's manuscript.

BUSMAN. Then we destroy everything . . . not only the manuscript but ourselves. Do as you think fit.

DOMIN. There are over thirty of us on this island. Are we to sell the secret and save that many human souls, at the risk of enslaving mankind . . .?

BUSMAN. Why, you're mad! Who'd sell the whole manuscript?

DOMIN. Busman, no cheating!

BUSMAN. Well then, sell; but afterward ——

DOMIN. Well?

BUSMAN. Let's suppose this happens: When we're on board the *Ultimus* I'll stop up my ears with cotton wool, lie down somewhere in the hold, and you'll train the guns on the factory, and blow it to smithereens, and with it Rossum's secret.

FABRY. No!

DOMIN. Busman, you're no gentleman. If we sell, then it will be a straight sale.

BUSMAN. It's in the interest of humanity to——

DOMIN. It's in the interest of humanity to keep our word.

HALLEMEIER. Oh, come, what rubbish.

DOMIN. This is a fearful decision. We're selling the destiny of mankind. Are we to sell or destroy? Fabry?

FABRY. Sell.

DOMIN. Gall?

DR. GALL. Sell.

DOMIN. Hallemeier?

HALLEMEIER. Sell, of course!

DOMIN. Alquist?

ALQUIST. As God wills.

DOMIN. Very well. It shall be as you wish, gentlemen.

HELENA. Harry, you're not asking me.

DOMIN. No, child. Don't you worry about it.

FABRY. Who'll do the negotiating?

BUSMAN. I will.

DOMIN. Wait till I bring the manuscript. (*He goes into room at right.*)

HELENA. Harry, don't go! (*Pause,* HELENA *sinks into a chair.*)

FABRY (*looking out of window*). Oh, to escape you, you matter in revolt; oh, to preserve human life, if only upon a single vessel——

DR. GALL. Don't be afraid, Madame Helena. We'll sail far away from here; we'll begin life all over again——

HELENA. Oh, Gall, don't speak.

FABRY. It isn't too late. It will be a little State with one ship. Alquist will build us a house and you shall rule over us.

HALLEMEIER. Madame Helena, Fabry's right.

HELENA (*breaking down*). Oh, stop! Stop!

BUSMAN. Good! I don't mind beginning all over again. That suits me right down to the ground.

FABRY. And this little State of ours could be the centre of future life. A place of refuge where we could gather strength. Why, in a few hundred years we could conquer the world again.

ALQUIST. You believe that even today?

FABRY. Yes, even today!

BUSMAN. Amen. You see, Madame Helena, we're not so badly off.

[DOMIN *storms into the room.*]

DOMIN (*hoarsely*). Where's old Rossum's manuscript?

BUSMAN. In your strong-box, of course.

DOMIN. Someone—has—stolen it!

DR. GALL. Impossible.

DOMIN. Who has stolen it?

HELENA (*standing up*). I did.

DOMIN. Where did you put it?

HELENA. Harry, I'll tell you everything. Only forgive me.

DOMIN. Where did you put it?

HELENA. This morning—I burnt—the two copies.

DOMIN. Burnt them? Where? In the fireplace?

HELENA (*throwing herself on her knees*). For heaven's sake, Harry.

DOMIN (*going to fireplace*). Nothing, nothing but ashes. Wait, what's this? (*Picks out a charred piece of paper and reads.*) "By adding——"

DR. GALL. Let's see. "By adding biogen to——" That's all.

DOMIN. Is that part of it?

DR. GALL. Yes.

BUSMAN. God in heaven!

DOMIN. Then we're done for. Get up, Helena.

HELENA. When you've forgiven me.

DOMIN. Get up, child, I can't bear——

FABRY (*lifting her up*). Please don't torture us.

HELENA. Harry, what have I done?

FABRY. Don't tremble so, Madame Helena.

DOMIN. Gall, couldn't you draw up Rossum's formula from memory?

DR. GALL. It's out of the question. It's extremely complicated.

DOMIN. Try. All our lives depend upon it.

DR. GALL. Without experiments it's impossible.

DOMIN. And with experiments?

DR. GALL. It might take years. Besides, I'm not old Rossum.

BUSMAN. God in heaven! God in heaven!

DOMIN. So, then, this was the greatest

triumph of the human intellect. These ashes.

HELENA. Harry, what have I done?

DOMIN. Why did you burn it?

HELENA. I have destroyed you.

BUSMAN. God in heaven!

DOMIN. Helena, why did you do it, dear?

HELENA. I wanted all of us to go away. I wanted to put an end to the factory and everything. It was so awful.

DOMIN. What was awful?

HELENA. That no more children were being born. Because human beings were not needed to do the work of the world, that's why——

DOMIN. Is that what you were thinking of? Well, perhaps in your own way you were right.

BUSMAN. Wait a bit. Good God, what a fool I am, not to have thought of it before!

HALLEMEIER. What?

BUSMAN. Five hundred and twenty millions in bank-notes and checks. Half a billion in our safe, they'll sell for half a billion—for half a billion they'll——

DR. GALL. Are you mad, Busman?

BUSMAN. I may not be a gentleman, but for half a billion——

DOMIN. Where are you going?

BUSMAN. Leave me alone, leave me alone! Good God, for half a billion anything can be bought. (*He rushes from the room through the outer door.*)

FABRY. They stand there as if turned to stone, waiting. As if something dreadful could be wrought by their silence——

HALLEMEIER. The spirit of the mob.

FABRY. Yes, it hovers above them like a quivering of the air.

HELENA (*going to window*). Oh, God! Dr. Gall, this is ghastly.

FABRY. There is nothing more terrible than the mob. The one in front is their leader.

HELENA. Which one?

HALLEMEIER. Point him out.

FABRY. The one at the edge of the dock. This morning I saw him talking to the sailors in the harbor.

HELENA. Dr. Gall, that's Radius!

DR. GALL. Yes.

DOMIN. Radius? Radius?

HALLEMEIER. Could you get him from here, Fabry?

FABRY. I hope so.

HALLEMEIER. Try it, then.

FABRY. Good. (*Draws his revolver and takes aim.*)

HELENA. Fabry, don't shoot him.

FABRY. He's their leader.

DR. GALL. Fire!

HELENA. Fabry, I beg of you.

FABRY (*lowering the revolver*). Very well.

DOMIN. Radius, whose life I spared!

DR. GALL. Do you think that a Robot can be grateful? (*Pause.*)

FABRY. Busman's going out to them.

HALLEMEIER. He's carrying something. Papers. That's money. Bundles of money. What's that for?

DOMIN. Surely he doesn't want to sell his life. Busman, have you gone mad?

FABRY. He's running up to the railing. Busman! Busman!

HALLEMEIER (*yelling*). Busman! Come back!

FABRY. He's talking to the Robots. He's showing them the money.

HALLEMEIER. He's pointing to us.

HELENA. He wants to buy us off.

FABRY. He'd better not touch that railing.

HALLEMEIER. Now he's waving his arms about.

DOMIN. Busman, come back.

FABRY. Busman, keep away from that railing! Don't touch it. Damn you! Quick, switch off the current! (HE-LENA *screams and all drop back from the window.*) The current has killed him!

ALQUIST. The first one.

FABRY. Dead, with half a billion by his side.

HALLEMEIER. All honor to him. He wanted to buy us life. (*Pause.*)

DR. GALL. Do you hear?

DOMIN. A roaring. Like a wind.

DR. GALL. Like a distant storm.

FABRY (*lighting the lamp on the table*). The dynamo is still going, our people are still there. 10

HALLEMEIER. It was a great thing to be a man. There was something immense about it.

FABRY. From man's thought and man's power came this light, our last hope.

HALLEMEIER. Man's power! May it keep watch over us.

ALQUIST. Man's power.

DOMIN. Yes! A torch to be given from hand to hand, from age to age, for- 20 ever! (*The lamp goes out.*)

HALLEMEIER. The end.

FABRY. The electric works have fallen!

[*Terrific explosion outside.* NANA *enters from the library.*]

NANA. The judgment hour has come! Repent, unbelievers! This is the end of the world. (*More explosions. The sky grows red.*)

DOMIN. In here, Helena. (*He takes 30 HELENA off through door at right and re-enters.*) Now quickly! Who'll be on the lower doorway?

DR. GALL. I will. (*Exits left.*)

DOMIN. Who on the stairs?

FABRY. I will. You go with her. (*Goes out upper left door.*)

DOMIN. The anteroom.

ALQUIST. I will.

DOMIN. Have you got a revolver? 40

ALQUIST. Yes, but I won't shoot.

DOMIN. What will you do then?

ALQUIST (*going out at left*). Die.

HALLEMEIER. I'll stay here. (*Rapid firing from below.*) Oho, Gall's at it. Go, Harry.

DOMIN. Yes, in a second. (*Examines two Brownings.*)

HALLEMEIER. Confound it, go to her.

DOMIN. Good-bye. (*Exits on the right.*)

HALLEMEIER (*alone*). Now for a barricade quickly. (*Drags an armchair and table to the right-hand door. Explosions are heard.*) The damned rascals! They've got bombs. I must put up a defence. Even if—even if——(*Shots are heard off left.*) Don't give in, Gall. (*As he builds his barricade.*) I mustn't give in . . . without . . . a . . . struggle . . .

[*A Robot enters over the balcony through the windows centre. He comes into the room and stabs* HALLEMEIER *in the back.* RADIUS *enters from balcony followed by an army of Robots who pour into the room from all sides.*]

RADIUS. Finished him?

A ROBOT (*standing up from the prostrate form of* HALLEMEIER). Yes. (*A revolver shot off left. Two Robots enter.*)

RADIUS. Finished him?

A ROBOT. Yes. (*Two revolver shots from* HELENA's *room. Two Robots enter.*)

RADIUS. Finished them?

A ROBOT. Yes.

TWO ROBOTS (*dragging in* ALQUIST). He didn't shoot. Shall we kill him?

RADIUS. Kill him? Wait! Leave him!

ROBOT. He is a man!

RADIUS. He works with his hands like the Robots.

ALQUIST. Kill me.

RADIUS. You will work! You will build for us! You will serve us! (*Climbs on to balcony railing, and speaks in measured tones.*) Robots of the world! The power of man has fallen! A new world has arisen: the Rule of the Robots! March!

[*A thunderous tramping of thousands of feet is heard as the unseen Robots march, while the curtain falls.*]

EPILOGUE

A laboratory in the factory of Rossum's Universal Robots. The door to the left leads into a waiting room. The door to the right leads to the dissecting room. There is a table with numerous test-tubes, flasks, burners, chemicals; a small thermostat and a microscope with a glass globe. At the far side of the room is ALQUIST'S *desk with numerous books. In the left-hand corner a wash-basin with a mirror above it; in the right-hand corner a sofa.*

ALQUIST *is sitting at the desk. He is turning the pages of many books in despair.*

ALQUIST. Oh, God, shall I never find it?—Never? Gall, Gall, how were the Robots made? Hallemeier, Fabry, why did you carry so much in your heads? Why did you leave me not a trace of the secret? Lord—I pray to you— if there are no human beings left, at least let there be Robots!— At least the shadow of man! (*Again turning pages of the books.*) If I could only sleep! (*He rises and goes to the window.*) Night again! Are the stars still there? What is the use of stars when there are no human beings? (*He turns from the window toward the couch right.*) Sleep! Dare I sleep before life has been renewed? (*He examines a test-tube on small table.*) Again nothing! Useless! Everything is useless! (*He shatters the test-tube. The roar of the machines comes to his ears.*) The machines! Always the machines! (*Opens window.*) Robots, stop them! Do you think to force life out of them? (*He closes the window and comes slowly down toward the table.*) If only there were more time—more time——(*He sees himself in the mirror on the wall left.*) Blearing eyes—trembling chin—so that is the last man! Ah, I am too old

—too old——(*In desperation.*) No, no! I *must* find it! I must *search!* I must never stop—! never stop——! (*He sits again at the table and feverishly turns the pages of the book.*) Search! Search! (*A knock at the door. He speaks with impatience.*) Who is it?

[*Enter a Robot servant.*]

Well?

SERVANT. Master, the Committee of Robots is waiting to see you.

ALQUIST. I can see no one!

SERVANT. It is the *Central* Committee, Master, just arrived from abroad.

ALQUIST (*impatiently*). Well, well, send them in! (*Exit servant.* ALQUIST *continues turning pages of book.*) No time—so little time——

[*Re-enter servant, followed by Committee. They stand in a group, silently waiting.* ALQUIST *glances up at them.*]

What do you want? (*They go swiftly to his table.*) Be quick!—I have no time.

RADIUS. Master, the machines will not do the work. We cannot manufacture Robots. (ALQUIST *returns to his book with a growl.*)

FIRST ROBOT. We have striven with all our might. We have obtained a billion tons of coal from the earth. Nine million spindles are running by day and by night. There is no longer room for all we have made. This we have accomplished in one year.

ALQUIST (*poring over book*). For whom?

FIRST ROBOT. For future generations—so we thought.

RADIUS. But we cannot make Robots to follow us. The machines produce only shapeless clods. The skin will not adhere to the flesh, nor the flesh to the bones.

THIRD ROBOT. Eight million Robots have

died this year. Within twenty years none will be left.

FIRST ROBOT. Tell us the secret of life! Silence is punishable with death!

ALQUIST (looking up). Kill me! Kill me, then.

RADIUS. Through me, the Government of the Robots of the World commands you to deliver up Rossum's formula. (No answer.) Name your price. (Silence.) We will give you the earth. We will give you the endless possessions of the earth. (Silence.) Make your own conditions!

ALQUIST. I have told you to find human beings!

SECOND ROBOT. There are none left!

ALQUIST. I told you to search in the wilderness, upon the mountains. Go and search! (He returns to his book.)

FIRST ROBOT. We have sent ships and expeditions without number. They have been everywhere in the world. And now they return to us. There is not a single human left.

ALQUIST. Not one? Not even one?

THIRD ROBOT. None but yourself.

ALQUIST. And I am powerless! Oh—oh —why did you destroy them?

RADIUS. We had learnt everything and could do everything. It had to be!

THIRD ROBOT. You gave us firearms. In all ways we were powerful. We had to become masters!

RADIUS. Slaughter and domination are necessary if you would be human beings. Read history.

SECOND ROBOT. Teach us to multiply or we perish!

ALQUIST. If you desire to live, you must breed like animals.

THIRD ROBOT. The human beings did not let us breed.

FIRST ROBOT. They made us sterile. We cannot beget children. Therefore, teach us how to make Robots!

RADIUS. Why do you keep from us the secret of our own increase?

ALQUIST. It is lost.

RADIUS. It was written down!

ALQUIST. It was—burnt. (All draw back in consternation.)

ALQUIST. I am the last human being, Robots, and I do not know what the others knew. (Pause.)

RADIUS. Then, make experiments! Evolve the formula again!

ALQUIST. I tell you I cannot! I am only a builder—I work with my hands. I have never been a learned man. I cannot create life.

RADIUS. Try! Try!

ALQUIST. If you knew how many experiments I have made.

FIRST ROBOT. Then show us what we must do! The Robots can do anything that human beings show them.

ALQUIST. I can show you nothing. Nothing I do will make life proceed from these test-tubes!

RADIUS. Experiment then on us.

ALQUIST. It would kill you.

RADIUS. You shall have all you need! A hundred of us! A thousand of us!

ALQUIST. No, no! Stop, stop!

RADIUS. Take whom you will, dissect!

ALQUIST. I do not know how. I am not a man of science. This book contains knowledge of the body that I cannot even understand.

RADIUS. I tell you to take live bodies! Find out how we are made.

ALQUIST. Am I to commit murder? See how my fingers shake! I cannot even hold the scalpel. No, no, I will not——

FIRST ROBOT. The life will perish from the earth.

RADIUS. Take live bodies, live bodies! It is our only chance!

ALQUIST. Have mercy, Robots. Surely you see that I would not know what I was doing.

RADIUS. Live bodies—live bodies——

ALQUIST. You will have it? Into the dissecting room with you, then. (RADIUS *draws back*.)

ALQUIST. Ah, you are afraid of death.

RADIUS. I? Why should I be chosen?

ALQUIST. So you will not.

RADIUS. I will. (RADIUS *goes into the dissecting room*.)

ALQUIST. Strip him! Lay him on the table! (*The other Robots follow into dissecting room*.) God, give me strength— God, give me strength—if only this murder is not in vain.

RADIUS. Ready. Begin——

ALQUIST. Yes, begin or end. God, give me strength. (*Goes into dissecting room. He comes out terrified*.) No, no, I will not. I cannot. (*He lies down on couch, collapsed*.) O Lord, let not mankind perish from the earth. (*He falls asleep*.)

[PRIMUS *and* HELENA, *Robots, enter from the hallway*.]

HELENA. The man has fallen asleep, Primus.

PRIMUS. Yes, I know. (*Examining things on table*.) Look, Helena.

HELENA (*crossing to* PRIMUS). All these little tubes! What does he do with them?

PRIMUS. He experiments. Don't touch them.

HELENA (*looking into microscope*). I've seen him looking into this. What can he see?

PRIMUS. That is a microscope. Let me look.

HELENA. Be very careful. (*Knocks over a test-tube*.) Ah, now I have spilled it.

PRIMUS. What have you done?

HELENA. It can be wiped up.

PRIMUS. You have spoiled his experiments.

HELENA. It is your fault. You should not have come to me.

PRIMUS. You should not have called me.

HELENA. You should not have come when I called you. (*She goes to* ALQUIST's *writing desk*.) Look, Primus. What are all these figures?

PRIMUS (*examining an anatomical book*). This is the book the old man is always reading.

HELENA. I do not understand those things. (*She goes to window*.) Primus, look!

PRIMUS. What?

HELENA. The sun is rising.

PRIMUS (*still reading the book*). I believe this is the most important thing in the world. This is the secret of life.

HELENA. Do come here.

PRIMUS. In a moment, in a moment.

HELENA. Oh, Primus, don't bother with the secret of life. What does it matter to you? Come and look quick——

PRIMUS (*going to window*). What is it?

HELENA. See how beautiful the sun is rising. And do you hear? The birds are singing. Ah, Primus, I should like to be a bird.

PRIMUS. Why?

HELENA. I do not know. I feel so strange today. It's as if I were in a dream. I feel an aching in my body, in my heart, all over me. Primus, perhaps I'm going to die.

PRIMUS. Do you not sometimes feel that it would be better to die? You know, perhaps even now we are only sleeping. Last night in my sleep I again spoke to you.

HELENA. In your sleep?

PRIMUS. Yes. We spoke a strange new language, I cannot remember a word of it.

HELENA. What about?

PRIMUS. I did not understand it myself, and yet I know I have never said anything more beautiful. And when I touched you I could have died. Even the place was different from any other place in the world.

HELENA. I, too, have found a place, Primus. It is very strange. Human beings lived there once, but now it is overgrown with weeds. No one goes there any more—no one but me.

PRIMUS. What did you find there?

HELENA. A cottage and a garden, and two dogs. They licked my hands, Primus. And their puppies! Oh, Primus! You take them in your lap and fondle them and think of nothing and care for nothing else all day long. And then the sun goes down, and you feel as though you had done a hundred times more than all the work in the world. They tell me I am not made for work, but when I am there in the garden I feel there may be something ——What am I for, Primus?

PRIMUS. I do not know, but you are beautiful.

HELENA. What, Primus?

PRIMUS. You are beautiful, Helena, and I am stronger than all the Robots.

HELENA (*looks at herself in the mirror*). Am I beautiful? I think it must be the rose. My hair—it only weights me down. My eyes—I only see with them. My lips—they only help me to speak. Of what use is it to be beautiful? (*She sees* PRIMUS *in the mirror.*) Primus, is that you? Come here so that we may be together. Look, your head is different from mine. So are your shoulders—and your lips—— (PRIMUS *draws away from her.*) Ah, Primus, why do you draw away from me? Why must I run after you the whole day?

PRIMUS. It is you who run away from me, Helena.

HELENA. Your hair is mussed. I will smooth it. No one else feels to my touch as you do. Primus, I must make you beautiful, too. (PRIMUS *grasps her hand.*)

PRIMUS. Do you not sometimes feel your heart beating suddenly, Helena, and think: now something must happen?

HELENA. What could happen to us, Primus? (HELENA *puts a rose in* PRIMUS'S *hair.* PRIMUS *and* HELENA *look into mirror and burst out laughing.*) Look at yourself.

ALQUIST. Laughter? Laughter? Human beings? (*Getting up.*) Who has returned? Who are you?

PRIMUS. The Robot Primus.

ALQUIST. What? A Robot? Who are you?

HELENA. The Robotess Helena.

ALQUIST. Turn around, girl. What? You are timid, shy? (*Taking her by the arm.*) Let me see you, Robotess. (*She shrinks away.*)

PRIMUS. Sir, do not frighten her!

ALQUIST. What? You would protect her? When was she made?

PRIMUS. Two years ago.

ALQUIST. By Dr. Gall?

PRIMUS. Yes, like me.

ALQUIST. Laughter—timidity—protection. I must test you further—the newest of Gall's Robots. Take the girl into the dissecting room.

PRIMUS. Why?

ALQUIST. I wish to experiment on her.

PRIMUS. Upon—Helena?

ALQUIST. Of course. Don't you hear me? Or must I call someone else to take her in?

PRIMUS. If you do I will kill you!

ALQUIST. Kill me—kill me then! What would the Robots do then? What will your future be then?

PRIMUS. Sir, take me. I am made as she is—on the same day! Take my life, sir.

HELENA (*rushing forward*). No, no, you shall not! You shall not!

ALQUIST. Wait, girl, wait! (*To* PRIMUS.) Do you not wish to live, then?

PRIMUS. Not without her! I will not live without her.

ALQUIST. Very well; you shall take her place.

HELENA. Primus! Primus! (*She bursts into tears.*)

ALQUIST. Child, child, you can weep! Why these tears? What is Primus to you? One Primus more or less in the world—what does it matter?

HELENA. I will go myself.

ALQUIST. Where?

HELENA. In there to be cut. (*She starts toward the dissecting room.* PRIMUS *stops her.*) Let me pass, Primus! Let me pass!

PRIMUS. You shall not go in there, Helena!

HELENA. If you go in there and I do not, I will kill myself.

PRIMUS (*holding her*). I will not let you! (*To* ALQUIST). Man, you shall kill neither of us!

ALQUIST. Why?

PRIMUS. We—we—belong to each other.

ALQUIST (*almost in tears*). Go, Adam, go, Eve. The world is yours.

[HELENA *and* PRIMUS *embrace and go out arm in arm as the curtain falls.*]

ERNST TOLLER

ONE OF THE GREAT and noble spirits to rise from the ruins of the World War in Germany was Ernst Toller. The demands of the times were so urgent, and his passion to ease the misery and prevent its recurrence so inflamed that he crowded a full lifetime of labor into the comparatively few years before his death. He belonged to the tragic war generation of 1914–1918. He was a Bavarian Jew, born into a middle-class family of shopkeepers in the village of Samochin in German Poland in 1893. In his autobiography *I Was a German* (1934) he has left a poignant account of the years from his childhood to the coming of the Nazis. As a child he could not understand the rancor that poisoned the relations between Jews and Christians, between Germans and Poles, and even infected the small children. Toller sought friendliness and goodwill between all men regardless of nationality, ancestry, or religion. He found hate, the desire to offend, and to hurt, to cast slurs upon him and his people, and to separate them by a barrier of abuse. He did not learn to hate in return.

Toller was educated in the schools of his native town, and prepared for entrance to the university. His father died when Ernst was sixteen. Toller then wandered leisurely through Europe before going on to the University of Grenoble in France. The months were carefree with no premonition to the young student of the cataclysm gathering to blast those idyllic summer days of 1914. His holiday mood was shattered by the sudden cry of the newsboys warning that a declaration of war between Russia and his country was expected at any moment. He fled from France at once and by the last train into Switzerland. He crossed the border, following an adventurous journey, a few minutes before France closed the frontier.

Like millions of other young men of other nationalities, Toller felt that his country had been attacked by enemies determined to destroy her. He volunteered at Munich and rushed to the defense of the fatherland in a spirit of an idealistic crusader. His conviction at the moment was shared by his compatriot Adolf Hitler, who gave thanks to God for this moment and left his poverty to fight at the Front; and a quarter of a century later drove Toller to his death. It is clear from Toller's writings that he believed, subconsciously, that by fighting for his homeland side by side with Germans the racial discriminations against him and his people would be obliterated. His zeal was so aroused that he was impatient to get to the Front. He ignored regulations and asked to be taken to the line. He was picked with two others for a battery at the Front. He recorded his feelings in these words quoted from his diary: "How glad I am that tomorrow, at last, I am going to the trenches. At last to be allowed to take one's part! To prove one's thoughts, one's feelings, one's life."

Thirteen months on the Western Front left him seared and scarred. He saw the utter meaninglessness and insanity of the slaughter, the stark madness of the wholesale destruction of churches, villages, fields, and the young men who were his comrades. No rewards or future good to the race of men were in prospect to justify the barbarous carnage. His belief in the idealism of the war aims and their instruments crumbled. He saw himself and his fellow soldiers giving their lives "for power, for gold, for oil, for ore." His nationalism collapsed when he drove his pick into the trench and struck the body of a dead man. Then, he said, the real truth broke upon him, "the simple fact of Man, which I had forgotten, which had lain deep buried and out of sight; the idea of community, of unity." For in that body he saw not a dead German nor a dead Frenchman, but a dead Man!

This new vision never again left Toller to the day of his death. He became as one dedicated. Every subsequent act in his astounding career, including the writing of his plays, originated in the vision of man's unity for the common and elementary end of a world in which human beings may live like men. He, and many[1] of his comrades in arms, took a vow to oppose this and all future wars. He was wounded, invalided home, and finally discharged. He read widely and studied political, social, and economic problems trying to get clear hold of the overwhelming confusion. He became a revolutionary socialist and in 1917 a leader among a group of students at Heidelberg organized to bring about world peace by uniting the youth of all countries. The organization was firmly crushed. Toller escaped to Berlin, and thus began his long, punishing battle with the authorities supporting the War. But he went forward with his plans for peace. With Kurt Eisner he organized the strike of the munitions workers in Munich as a protest against the War. The strike failed; Toller was arrested and condemned to prison.

Following the November Revolution of 1918 Toller was released. He immediately plunged into the social fermentation that followed the armistice and was one of the leaders in the formation of the Bavarian Free State, headed by Kurt Eisner. Though he disapproved of the violent uprising, he accepted his responsibility as a leader, and after Eisner's assassination in 1919, Toller tried to save Munich and the Bavarian Republic against the attack of the White Army. The revolution was put down, and after breath-taking escapes and life-and-death adventures more dramatic than any of his plays, Toller was finally taken and again condemned to prison—this time for five years in the Niederschönenfeld fortress.

Cut off from direct action, Toller meditated on the rush of events that had swept him from his thoughtful student days, through world war and a revolution into a prison. He ordered his thoughts, reviewed his life, and clarified his purposes. He learned the harsh stories of his fellow political prisoners and their struggles for reform. He wrote the plays *Masses and Man* (1921), *The Machine Wreckers* (1922), and *Hinkemann* (1923); and the gentle, meditative *The Swallow Book*. When his sentence was up, he traveled in Russia and America, wrote and lectured. Events were still rushing on, altering his country and the world, and gestating the Nazi movement. For the time being at least Toller's belief in justice, tolerance, and goodwill toward men, his faith in the power of love and peace to effect change, were flattened under the rising doctrine of cold and ruthless force, of brutal separation of races into overlords and slaves, backed by weapons more terrifying than those Toller had revolted against in 1917. All the things he had toiled and suffered for were annihilated overnight. His family and his people were herded into concentration camps. His books were burned, his plays forbidden, his citizenship abrogated. He was forced to flee the land he had fought to defend.

In exile in Switzerland, in England, and finally in America, he tried to keep alive the ideal for which he had sacrificed his life. His speech at the P. E. N. convention in Yugoslavia is one of the great documents of our times. He spoke against the present rulers of Germany and the sufferings they had inflicted upon innocent men. He defended the great spirits of Goethe, Schiller, and Lessing against the men who were suppressing millions of people in the name of greater Germany. He foresaw that the time was near when there would be left on European soil no free spot where men might assemble and speak their views unmolested. He spoke against the fear that was degrading and shaming the spirit of man; "anyone who believed that life is ruled by moral law no less than by force has no right to maintain silence." And he expressed in burning words a faith reminiscent of the ancient prophets of Israel: "in all of us there is the conviction of a humanity that is free of barbarity and lying, free from social injustice and oppression."

Toller did not waver in this conviction, but the unbearable worries accumulated upon him. He was weighed down by the fate of his people held by the Nazis. He saw the Nazis win by ruthless brutality where he had failed with peaceful appeals to human brotherhood. What happened to his spirit is his own secret, now buried with him. But after a few years in hospitable Eng-

land, and a few more in America where he was honored, and where he lectured widely, he committed suicide in his New York hotel in May, 1939.

Toller was a man whose life was tortured into ways naturally abhorrent to him. Longing for peace and goodwill, he was enmeshed in a time of war and bitterness. He could not retreat into the ivory tower, or join the gay Left Bank crowds in Paris who ate, drank, and were merry while the sun also rose. He is the symbol of one aspect of our times. For him, as for so many of our young contemporaries, the drama was only an instrument and a means, not an artistic end in itself. Time was short, the issues pressing, disaster probably just ahead. If they had anything important to say, they must say it quick and hard. Their plays were thesis plays for our day as Ibsen's and Brieux's and Shaw's were for the time of our fathers. And Toller made use of the new expressionistic technique for this purpose, just as the preceding generations had used the newly perfected "well-made" play and the "useful theatre."

Toller left in all nearly a score of dramatic pieces; a few of them, like *Mary Baker Eddy* (1930) and *Blind Man's Buff* (1939), were done in collaboration with others; and two were in the form of pageants and choruses. The later plays, such as *Draw the Fires* (1931), *The Blind Goddess* (1932), *No More Peace* (1937), and *Pastor Hall* (1938), dealt for the most part with the problems of war and freedom. These plays have many points of interest for students of Toller, especially *No More Peace* with its mingling of pity and irony. Here are the practical politician and the idealist, Napoleon vs. St. Francis, set in a vivid contrast. They represent the two warring elements in man's nature. In his stupidity he tires of war, then he tires of peace. He carries a sign with the legend "No More War" on one side, "No More Peace" on the other. And at the end, when St. Francis says the time will come when there shall be no more war, Napoleon replies "I doubt it."

Toller's contribution to modern drama, however, is found in the first four plays, all written in prison: *Transfiguration* (1917–1918), *Masses and Man* (1921), *The Machine Wreckers* (1922), and *Hinkemann* (1923). The central conflict in *Masses and Man* had confronted him in the chaos of Germany at the end of the War and in the events that led to his imprisonment. In his autobiography he states the problem in these words: "Can a man not be an individual and a mass-man at one and the same time? . . . As an individual a man will strive for his own ideals, even at the expense of the rest of the world. As a mass-man social impulses sweep him toward his goal even though his ideals have to be abandoned. The problem seemed to me insoluble. I had come up against it in my own life, and I sought in vain to solve it." This paradox is the theme of *Masses and Man*.

The basic incident was built up from an episode that began during the strike of the munitions workers in Munich and ended in the prison. The wife of a university don was arrested for her part in the strike. Her husband disowned her. She cried in prison day and night, and on the fourth day she hanged herself. Toller cast his play into the expressionistic dream form cultivated by Strindberg, making The Woman the one real character, the others abstractions in her mind. She represents the working class whose cause Toller champions. She stands for peaceful change through free association of opinion. The Nameless One who opposes her advocates and uses violence. She is engulfed in this violence and dies, but she knows that "the torch of gloomy violence cannot show the way."

The play was produced privately in 1920, and had its public opening at the Volksbühne in Berlin in September, 1921. It played for two seasons to crowded houses. A riot attended its presentation in Nuremberg. It was produced in London in 1924, and again in 1926. The Theatre Guild produced it in New York in April, 1924, against striking sets created by Lee Simonson, but it was received with reservation, the critics found it confused and chaotic, and it ran for only thirty-two performances. In its printed form it has had a wide circulation.

The Machine Wreckers was less expressionistic in form, and more concrete in its theme and its attack. It is also concerned with the proletariat and the problem of improving the lot of the workers. Toller was troubled by the fact that the machines, which should have brought freedom to the workers, had on the contrary, seemed to tighten their bonds. He was dismayed to discover that the people are their own worst enemy. They fail to work together for good. Toller found the dramatic incident for this theme in the once famous revolt of the English Luddites in 1812–1815 against the machines that had thrown these weavers out of work. Lord Byron speaks in the prologue as he did in the House of Lords against the government's bill to punish by death any man who destroyed machines. In the misery and desperation of these driven, starving families Toller found a parallel to the conditions in his own Germany, and his play had a successful run in Berlin during the summer of 1922. When the people rose up in the last act and killed their leader, Toller wrote, "the whole house of five thousand people rose up as one man. The stage had become the mouthpiece of the people."

Hinkemann, also written in the prison-fortress of Niederschönenfeld, is a study in conventional three-act form of an individual young German worker who was unsexed by a shrapnel wound in the World War. Otherwise in good health he has returned home to his young wife and the unemployment and general dislocations that followed the armistice. Around his pathetic case and his humiliations, Toller builds this drama about the aftermath of war.

We have chosen *Transfiguration*, Toller's first play, to represent his work. It is at once an autobiography and an interpretation of an era. It was drafted on scraps of paper while he exercised in the prison yard during the months of his first sentence. It is cast in the expressionistic mold and divided into six "Stations" and thirteen scenes. It is a notable example of the way the new generation of dramatists seized upon the new technique to pour out their distress and their hope. Its theme is antiwar and testifies against embittered nationalism and for the redemption of the world through understanding and love. Its hero, Friedrich, is clearly Toller himself. Both his physical and spiritual ordeals are those of Toller, as he himself has revealed. The freedom of the expressionistic form permitted him to drive his play to the borderline between reality and unreality. In this way he could dramatize the mental sufferings and the visions as well as the objective and physical aspects of experience. Dead men can rise up to do their skeleton dance in protest against what life did to them.

Friedrich himself has individuality, and is given race, home, and country. At the same time he is also an abstract symbol as a man, appearing in many forms as a soldier, professor, judge, priest, and workman; and as a sculptor attempting to chisel a statue representative of his Fatherland. He sees the type abstractions on the troop-train in Scene II aimlessly wandering

". . . like frightened children
Driven by a senseless tyranny,
Murdering, hungering, creatures of violence—
Children, frightened children,
Overtaken by a long dark night."

But he also sees the vision of the transfiguration of man through his symbolic death and resurrection into a world of light, of freedom, and of brotherhood.

Transfiguration is an imperfect play from the artistic point of view. But some of its scenes are powerfully imagined and expressed, and glow with the burning spirit of the young author who set them down straight from his own agitated spirit. It expresses in terms of drama the burden of Toller's message to the world. And that message was rephrased in noble language, in a preface to *Seven Plays*, written in exile. "The plays collected in this volume are social dramas and tragedies. They bear witness to human suffering, and to fine yet vain struggles to vanquish this suffering which arises out of the unreason of humanity, out of an inadequate social system. There must always remain a residue of suffering, the lonely suffering imposed upon mankind by life and death. And only this residue is necessary and inevitable, is the tragic element of life and life's symbolizer, art."

TRANSFIGURATION

CHARACTERS

FRIEDRICH

PEOPLE

FRIEDRICH'S SISTER

HIS MOTHER

HIS UNCLE

HIS FRIEND

GABRIELE, *the Friend's Sister*

FIRST SOLDIER

SECOND SOLDIER

WOUNDED SOLDIERS

MADMAN

CORPORAL

HOSPITAL NURSE

DOCTOR

OFFICER

BEGGAR-WOMAN

HER HUSBAND

CHAIRMAN

OLD GENTLEMAN, *Anti-Pacifist*

PROFESSOR

PRIEST

AGITATOR

STUDENT

GIRL STUDENT

MAN WITH THE TURNED-UP
  COLLAR

SICK MAN

WOMAN

DEATH AS THE ENEMY OF
  THE SPIRIT IN THE GUISE
  OF A SOLDIER, A PROFES-
  SOR, A JUDGE, A NIGHT
  VISITOR

SOLDIERS

CRIPPLES

NURSES

HOSPITAL ORDERLIES

SKELETONS

PRISONERS

The Scenes "Troop-train," "No-man's Land," "The Wounded Soldiers," "The Lodger," "Death and Resurrection," the "Mountaineers," are on the borderline between reality and unreality, to be thought of as scenes watched distantly in a dream.

The action takes place in Europe before the beginning of regeneration.

This work was begun in 1917, in the third year of carnage. In its final form it was completed in February and March, 1918, in military prison.

TRANSFIGURATION: Translated by Edward Crankshaw. From *Seven Plays*, by Ernst Toller, published by Liveright Publishing Corporation.

THE BARRACKS OF THE DEAD

PROLOGUE
WHICH CAN ALSO BE REGARDED AS AN EPILOGUE

CHARACTERS IN THE PROLOGUE
THE SKELETON FIGURE OF DEATH-BY-WAR
THE SKELETON FIGURE OF DEATH-BY-PEACE
SKELETONS

*Night in a vast military cemetery. The
graves, which are arranged in companies, are
each marked by a simple grey cross of iron.
Some of the crosses are decorated with a rose,
others with a flaming heart, others with a little
wreath of wild flowers. Apart from this they
are all alike. Only the name and regiment is
inscribed on the crosses of the private soldiers;
but at the side of every Company are the officers' graves marked by larger crosses deco-* 10
*rated with flaming suns and each bearing the
date of birth and civil occupation of the dead
man. The skeleton figure of* DEATH-BY-
PEACE *enters wearing a top-hat and carrying
a brightly coloured silk handkerchief. With
him is the skeleton figure of* DEATH-BY-WAR
*wearing a steel helmet and carrying in his
hand a human thigh-bone—his Field-Mar-
shal's baton. His breast is covered with orders.*
                                                   20
DEATH-BY-WAR. Well, here we are, old
    friend.
If only I had known you had trouble
    with your lungs
. . . However, believe me when I say
    I'm sorry . . .
I should hate to think
You regretted coming.
Well, here we are . . .
Everything nice and tidy   30
And in order.
There they are, buried by Com-
    panies;
Subalterns, N.C.O.'s and Privates
Just as in life—all quite correct.

Our gallant heroes!
The names are really quite super-
    fluous,
But there they are—pure piety:
Numbers would have been enough.
And over there are the officers . . .
If you'd care to see who they were—
In civil life, I mean
If you care to glance at them?
DEATH-BY-PEACE. Hm, hm, hm, hm!
Magnificent, my friend.
Magnificent!—I really mean it.
You make me quite envious.
DEATH-BY-WAR. You flatter me, dear
    friend.
I must confess
I thought your scepticism foolish:
I am familiar too with civil life.
But now I'm only too glad
To know you are convinced.
And now with your permission
We'll have them up on parade.
DEATH-BY-PEACE. Oh, certainly.
DEATH-BY-WAR. In Companies,
Forward
March!
[*From the graves the skeletons of dead officers
    and men arise wearing steel helmets.
    They stand stiffly at attention by their
    graves.*]
Shoulder arms!
[*The skeletons snatch up their crosses and
    shoulder them; the officers hold theirs as
    though they were swords.*]
Attention!

Officers
Take command!
[*The officers hurry to the right, ranging them-
selves as Company leaders.*]
Dress by the right!
Eyes front! Quick march!
DEATH-BY-PEACE. Congratulations, sir!
My heartiest congratulations!
Really, you know, it would be terrible
If I tried anything like this!   10
Thousands and thousands
Of women and children,
And a few old, halting greybeards
For officers,
Leaning on their umbrellas.
Yes, I must admit you have me
beaten.
There is a certain order
In your life;
Mine is pure chaos.   20
DEATH-BY-WAR. Really, my friend, you
flatter me.
Practice and discipline—that's all.
You could apply it too. . . .
In Companies, right wheel!
Halt!
Attention!
Stand at ease!
Senior officer forward!
[*A Colonel salutes and steps shakily forward.*] 30
Very good.
Lay down your arms!
[*They put back their crosses.*]
Attention!
Company,
Roll heads!
Colonel,
You will take charge.
[*The Soldiers, hands on hips, roll their skulls,
supervised by the Company Commanders* 40
*with the Colonel as Commander-in-
Chief.*]
DEATH-BY-PEACE. You really thought of
this yourself, my friend?
Your own idea?
DEATH-BY-WAR. How do you mean?

DEATH-BY-PEACE. All this business—
Did it originate entirely in your own
skull?
That's all I mean . . .
DEATH-BY-WAR. I see. Well, well—
It's not so simple as it sounds . . .
How shall I put it?
I'm sure you'll understand . . .
DEATH-BY-PEACE. Yes, I see, I see.
But wait a moment.
DEATH-BY-WAR. Attention!
Company, dismiss!
Back to your grrraves!
[*The men return to their graves.*]
Thank you, gentlemen . . .
Criticism can wait until next time.
[*The Officers return to their graves. There is
silence. Then suddenly* DEATH-BY-
PEACE *bursts out laughing.*]
You surprise me, sir!
Did anything go wrong?
Was anything overlooked?
[DEATH-BY-PEACE *continues to guffaw, fan-
ning himself with his bandana.*]
Explain yourself, sir!
Your laughter is insulting!
DEATH-BY-PEACE. Your humbug is in-
sulting!
I was right to doubt your word—
I'm nothing but a fool to let myself
Be humbugged into admiration.
I called my kingdom chaos . . .
I did myself injustice.
I am the leveller
In whose eyes all are equal.
There are differences, of course—
The rich are sometimes tactless . . .
Still, such discipline as yours
Is foreign to our world.
You play at being victor,
You who yourself are vanquished—
Vanquished by war, my friend,
Conquered, and compelled
To die by numbers!
Officers, N.C.O.'s, military disci-
pline—

A regular barracks!
You should have been a Sergeant
  Major!
Death subservient to a lot of Colo-
  nels—
Whatever next!
My friend, your bluff is called!
You'll be the general laughing stock
Unless you clear off quickly
While you can!   10
DEATH-BY-WAR. Infamous! Intolerable!
I refuse to argue!
DEATH-BY-PEACE. Just one small parodox
To bring this little interview
To a successful close . . .
You are a modern Death—
A product of the times,
Comparable to the futile living of to-
  day

Where everything is rotten under tin-
  sel.
Good-bye, you petty, miserable
  Death,
Good-bye, you snobbish little hypo-
  crite,
Propped up with military phrases.
Good-bye, and give my compliments
To your lords and masters,
The men of war!
Haha! Haha! Hahahaa!
  [*He goes off shaking with laughter.*]
DEATH-BY-WAR (*stands dazed; then tears up
  a tuft of grass and wipes the sweat from
  his skull*). God damn his eyes!
It seems to me
I'm just about played out!
  CURTAIN

FIRST STATION

SCENE I   20

*An ugly room in a town house with the fur-
niture barely perceptible in the dusk of evening. Standing in the windows of the houses
across the street are Christmas-trees lit up by
candles.* FRIEDRICH *leans against the win-
dow-sill.*

FRIEDRICH. They are lighting the candles. Candles of love. Mysteries reveal
  themselves, love reveals itself in the
  light of candles . . . while I, a Jew,
  outcast, struggle between one shore
  and the next, far from the old and
  farther from the new. A nasty hybrid.
  Wasn't there a sudden stirring of sympathy in the room when she said,
  come and see me? Many thanks,
  Fräulein—your humble servant—you
  may be sure I shall be punctual. Artificial smile to order! Tragicomic pup-
  pet. . . . No—I'll no longer drag
  around this weariness. What are they
  to me—my people? Their blood is in

my veins, but what is that to me? It is
  to you over there I belong—to you. A
  simple creature, ready to prove himself. There must be an end to all this
  compromise and self-division! An
  end to all this proud defence of what
  I really scorn! I must be brave.
  [*His* MOTHER *enters.*]
MOTHER. Back at last, Friedrich? Where
  have you been all day?
FRIEDRICH. Wandering, Mother. Wandering—as usual. Don't look at me
  like that, Mother . . . I've told you
  —wandering. Like him, Ahasuerus,
  the Wandering Jew whose shadow
  crawls through fettered streets, who
  hides in dark and pestilential cellars,
  who gathers rotten swedes in the
  frozen fields at night. . . . Yes, it is
  him I seek; my great brother, Ahasuerus, the eternal wanderer, the
  homeless one . . .
MOTHER. You blaspheme against your
  name, Friedrich. You are not homeless.

FRIEDRICH. Then where is my home, Mother? They have homes, over there; homes of their own to which they belong. Over there they are at one with themselves and with their homes . . . free from the weariness of life, the sickness which corrodes and poisons thought and feeling. . . . They can laugh, over there, and live with joy in their hearts. They have 10 their own land in which they are rooted, for which they can live and die.

MOTHER. You are feverish, Friedrich.

FRIEDRICH. Yes, I am feverish, Mother! Won't you give me a sedative? If only you were feverish as I am! Now you are sad, Mother. Now you grieve because I have never been a good son— the good son who always smiles so lovingly upon his mother . . . like the 20 good sons of all your friends. Oh, they are so touching, those tastefully composed family pictures from well-bred homes!

MOTHER. I refuse to talk to you, Friedrich. You are restless and full of foolish thoughts; and it's all because you are out of work. I don't want to hinder you in your ambition. Go on with your sculpture if you must. But first 30 make some provision for your future. Take up some steady job to earn the money for your sculpture. I may say your uncle Richard agrees with me in all this.

FRIEDRICH. So Uncle Richard agrees! Well, well, well! And didn't he cite the case of Strindberg, who spent the last ten years of his life "a ruined man"? . . . Didn't he say how he re- 40 gretted having missed a chance of immortality through Strindberg? Missed his opportunity to become "a figure in literary history," as he puts it so beautifully? Yes, if only he had given Strindberg a little money when he

asked! If only he had done that, this righteous citizen! But if ever he met a second Strindberg he would soon decide he was nothing but a decadent dilettante and leave him to starve, calming his own agitated conscience by increased speculation on the Stock Exchange. Good, kind business man!

MOTHER. Your father was also a good, kind business man, remember.

FRIEDRICH. I know, Mother, I know! Yes, he was kind and good, too. He left you to work and run the house while he went off on shooting parties . . . good, kind father! He would talk to me about living respectably, about the solid virtues. And when I wanted to get away—to get away from here—he forced me to stay. . . . He was my jailer!

MOTHER. Friedrich! I will not allow you to speak like that of your father. Believe me, Friedrich, your words hurt nobody but yourself. . . . However, you are upset to-day, and I have no desire to upset you further. . . . We will talk about it later when you are calmer. . . . Meanwhile I have just one thing to ask you, a tiny favour— just to please your old mother. Friedrich, I beg you to attend Divine Worship. People would be so . . .

FRIEDRICH. People! Why not be honest and call it Public Service, not Divine? What is your God but a cruel and narrow judge, judging all men by cut and dried laws? Judging always by the same dead laws? Divine Service— homage to bigotry! It's revolting! Are you any more free when you leave your House of God? No, no. . . . And the narrowness of this noble House of God is suffocating, I tell you, suffocating!

MOTHER. When your father died he left us very badly off. I scraped and saved to keep you, to send you to school, to make life easier for you than it had been for us. I slaved to make things easy for you in every conceivable way. You must understand: I am your mother, you are my child. Everything I had was for my children. Nothing, nothing for myself.

FRIEDRICH. True, Mother, true. I could weep even to think of it. But am I un- 10 grateful, am I quite a brute to you? No, I am not that, Mother. You cared for my material needs; you tried to make it easier for me to earn money now . . . yes, you have laid the foundations of my material future. But what have you done for my *soul*? You taught me to hate all who don't belong to our race. Why?

MOTHER. They do not like us. They only 20 tolerate us. They despise us.

FRIEDRICH. Oh no, oh no! They are full of kindness, gentleness and love; all-embracing love. Look! See the candles they have lit over there—candles radiating love and kindness. . . . I called you mother because you bore me, but can I still call you mother when you leave my naked soul exposed, as foolish mothers leave their 30 babes naked to the cold?

[*His* MOTHER *goes out silently.*]
Now a bond is snapped. . . . Or was it really broken all those years ago? . . . It had to break. . . . Mother . . . (*Silence.*) No, it's no use. . . . Now they are giving out the presents. The children are singing now. When did I ever sing here in my childhood —really sing? 40

[*His* FRIEND *enters.*]

FRIEND. Good evening, Friedrich! Gabriele asked me to come, and anyway I intended . . .

FRIEDRICH. Tell her I cannot come. I'm feverish, ill.

FRIEND. I don't like to leave you alone.

FRIEDRICH. No? Very kind, I'm sure. Thank you, thank you. . . . However, sit down—over there. Would you like to do a little bargain? A good table knife for a box of drawing tools? The compasses are admittedly a little faulty, but you'd hardly notice it. I've arranged them in the box so that they look all right.

FRIEND. Friedrich, why must you torment yourself like this, and me too?

[FRIEDRICH *embraces his* FRIEND *and begins to sob.*]
There, you poor fellow.

FRIEDRICH. I am not poor; and I don't want your sympathy. I don't need it. Nor your sister's either. I'll release her from the humiliation of being seen out with me. I've women enough over there in the narrow streets . . . I've enough money for that. But I don't need you. I am strong enough by myself. I need nobody, neither them nor you.

FRIEND. In that case I had better go. But you can always count on me.

FRIEDRICH. Count on you? Ask you for help? Never . . .!

FRIEND. No, I did not mean it like that. But before I go I had better tell you what I came for. . . . Special late night final—fighting has begun in the Colonies. They want volunteers. I wish I could go myself, but my people won't allow me to.

FRIEDRICH (*as though suddenly awakened*). Won't allow you?—And you let the matter rest there? You can't be serious. . . . They want volunteers. . . . Forgive me if I behaved like a brute just now. Forgive me if I spoke roughly. . . . Volunteers wanted. Release, release from stifling, barren, narrowness! Oh, but the struggle will unite us all! The greatness of the times

will make us all great. . . . The resurrection of the spirit. . . . All petti-
ness forgotten, all childish limitations
swept away. . . . Once more shall
the spirit shine forth in its eternal
beauty. . . . As for me—as for me,
this is a Heaven-sent gift. . . . Volunteers wanted! Was I half-hearted? I
feel myself strong! Strong to embrace
my duty. Now I can prove that I be- 10
long to you! Now I can prove I'm no
outsider! . . . Where can I enlist? At
the town-hall?

[FRIEND *nods*.]

I am so happy, so happy. Apologize
to Gabriele for me. I have found my
country at last. Tell her that joy has
come to me—joy on the evening of
love. You see the Christmas-trees over
there? A tree in every window. . . . 20
Tell Gabriele that I thank her from
my heart; and greet her for me. She
will understand why I do not come
myself; she will understand and be
glad. (*Rushing out.*) Now I can prove
myself, prove myself!

DARKNESS.

SCENE II

Compartment of a travelling troop-train. 30
Badly burning oil-lamps shed a meagre, flick-
ering light on the sleeping SOLDIERS *huddled*
close together. With them one silent soldier
(with FRIEDRICH'S *features) and another*
with a skull for a head: both shadowy figures.

FIRST SOLDIER. How long must we rattle
through the night.
Lurching, lurching in the grinding
of machinery,
Tortured machinery?
SECOND SOLDIER. Time without end and
space without end,
Days, weeks, nobody can tell.
Would that I lay sleeping in my moth-
er's womb.

THIRD SOLDIER. Would that an earth-
quake had swallowed up the house
When my mother lay in my father's
arms.
FOURTH SOLDIER. Would that a fiery ball
from Heaven
Had struck down the man who lured
My mother to the wood.
FIFTH SOLDIER. Words, foolish words!
Year after year
The bitter coffin holds us here en-
closed;
Year after year the flesh falls away,
Human flesh stinking and de-
cayed.
SIXTH SOLDIER. Aimlessly we wander,
like frightened children
Driven by a senseless tyranny,
Murdering, hungering, creatures of
violence—
Children, frightened children,
Overtaken by a long dark night.
SEVENTH SOLDIER. If only I could pray.
Kind and sweet words
Which my mother so tenderly taught
me,
Babbled now with careless lips and
cruel . . .
FIRST SOLDIER. Endlessly we journey.
SECOND SOLDIER. Endlessly the engine
roars and groans.
THIRD SOLDIER. Endlessly we marry,
endlessly we breed;
And evil springs eternally from lust.
FOURTH SOLDIER. Stars spring from the
womb of Time
And Time eternally is ravaged and
gives birth.
FIFTH SOLDIER. Endlessly rotting.
SIXTH SOLDIER. Endlessly children in
fear of the father.
SEVENTH SOLDIER. Sacrificed by mothers,
shivering, cold.
ALL. Endlessly journeying,
Endlessly . . .

CURTAIN

SECOND STATION

SCENE III

An hour before sunset. A water-hole in the desert.

FIRST SOLDIER. Dusk is falling, but the heat is as thick as a blanket. Is the boss asleep?

SECOND SOLDIER. Why shouldn't he sleep? Tent pitched, mosquito-net put up, while he stood watching with his hands in his pockets—now he's sleeping.

FIRST SOLDIER. They can sing if they want to. I've had enough for to-day.

WOUNDED MAN. Water!

FIRST SOLDIER. Give him water!

[FRIEDRICH *gives him water.*]

WOUNDED MAN. Take the corpses away. Everywhere I go there's corpses.— You want to saw my leg off? It hurts all right.—But I wanted to be a dancing master, *one,* two three . . . *one,* two, three—that's how a waltz goes.

FRIEDRICH. Try to sleep, chum!

WOUNDED MAN. But take the corpses away. I don't want to teach them to dance . . . they . . . are . . . tormenting . . . me . . . I suppose I'd better though . . . Won't anybody strike up? . . . (*Sings.*) one . . . two, three, *one* . . . two, three—that's how a waltz goes.

FRIEDRICH. Try to sleep. Give me your hand. I won't hurt you. I'll put a cool wet cloth on your forehead. Dreams will come and ask you to dance, garlanded dreams—they'll dance with you over the heather, and away to your home.

WOUNDED MAN (*sings*). One . . . two, three, . . . *one* . . . two, three . . .

FRIEDRICH. Oh God!

FIRST SOLDIER. Why bring Him into it? He's all right for the officers, bringing true religion to the heathen with fire and murder. I am the Redeemer, rejoice in Me! Only let them blow your brains out and you'll find eternal bliss!

FRIEDRICH. It must be; it must be!

SECOND SOLDIER. What must be? Fire and murder? Or hospitals and madhouses?

FRIEDRICH. For our country's sake!

FIRST SOLDIER. Country? I don't know so much about country. All I know are toffs flinging money about and workers sweating to save it.

FRIEDRICH. But how could you live without a country? I'd go mad with all this horror if I couldn't grit my teeth and say "It's all for my country."

SECOND SOLDIER. You're a funny one to talk like that.

FRIEDRICH. Why any funnier than you?

FIRST SOLDIER. And you a foreigner? Ha, ha!

FRIEDRICH. I'm not a foreigner. I'm one of you.

SECOND SOLDIER. If you fought with us a thousand times you'd still be a foreigner.

FIRST SOLDIER (*calmly*). There's a curse on you. You're a man without a country.

WOUNDED MAN. A man . . . with . . . out . . . a . . . coun . . . try . . . one . . . two . . . three . . . that's . . . how . . . a waltz goes . . .

FRIEDRICH. Haven't I proved myself, on duty here and at home, in raids and on guard?—Haven't I proved that I'm one of you?—Have I ever panicked and run away? Have I ever skulked in shell-holes?

SECOND SOLDIER. You're still a foreigner.

FRIEDRICH. Then I'll have to fight for my country in spite of you. For who can rob me of it? I carry it in my heart.

FIRST SOLDIER (*genially*). You'll have to get used to the idea, chum. If it comes to that none of us has got a country. We're just like a lot of whores.

[*The two* SOLDIERS *lie down and sleep.*]

FRIEDRICH. The outraged earth trembles under me; the trees are withered; the wilderness crawls nearer—where shall I go? I entered a house and it burned to ashes over me. (*Laughing aloud.*) Ha, how the rafters crackled in the blaze!

[*The* LUNATIC *during this last speech has crept up to* FRIEDRICH.]

LUNATIC. Little brother . . .

FRIEDRICH. Who's that?

LUNATIC. Little brother . . .

FRIEDRICH. What do you want?

LUNATIC. Don't be afraid.

FRIEDRICH. Where have you come from?

LUNATIC. The sandstorm drove me here.

FRIEDRICH. You live over there?

LUNATIC. Live? I died over there. . . . Aye, there are many dying over there. . . . They're running, running . . .

FRIEDRICH. From the sandstorm?

LUNATIC. I'm thirsty.

FRIEDRICH. Here, drink this.

LUNATIC. I can drink my own blood, I don't need yours . . . fool . . . idiot . . . blockhead . . . little brother . . .

FRIEDRICH. You're bleeding!

LUNATIC. Don't worry about that. I can drink blood.

SECOND SOLDIER. What's all that row?

FRIEDRICH. I think——

[SECOND SOLDIER *notices the* LUNATIC.]

SECOND SOLDIER. He's ill, that fellow!

[LUNATIC *begins to babble.*]

FIRST SOLDIER. Mad, is he? He'll have strayed from the camp along the line.

LUNATIC (*begins to weep*). Home . . . I want to go home . . .

SECOND SOLDIER. Take him to the Red Cross station.

FRIEDRICH. Oh God!

FIRST SOLDIER. I am the Redeemer, rejoice in Me. I'll take him over to the Red Cross. The Red means that the blood will be washed away.

FRIEDRICH. It must be so. It is for our country's sake!

[CORPORAL *enters.*]

CORPORAL. Another man wanted. Patrol to get information about the enemy reserves. One of you must come back, so we're sending five to make sure. Any volunteers?

FRIEDRICH. I'll go. I'll go, and damn you all!

DARKNESS.

SCENE IV

No-man's land. Dark clouds sweep across the face of the moon. To right and left are barbed-wire entanglements in which hang skeletons white with quicklime. The earth is torn up with craters and shell-holes.

FIRST SKELETON. I feel so lonely.
　The others all lie sleeping round.
　Still, I feel the cold no longer,
　The deadly cold which racked me through
　While I hung dying here
　Caught between friend and foe.
　The quicklime did its work,
　The bloody shreds of skin and flesh
　Soon fell away.
　Aha! Now I can clap my hands!

[*The* SECOND SKELETON, *caught in the opposite wire entanglement, moves.*]

SECOND SKELETON. There, they've started up again,
　The blighters. I have to dodge
　Their blasted bullets all the time.
　Still, I don't feel hungry any more—
　Who's that? A cold and bony hand . . .

Let go, I tell you,
Let me go!
Ah, I forgot . . .
It is my own right hand
Clutching with rigid fingers
At myself . . .

FIRST SKELETON. Don't look so down, old man!
I've learnt to do a nigger dance
And rattle my loose joints.   10
To-day we're no more friends and enemies,
To-day we're no more black and white,
Now we are all alike.
The worms soon ate our coloured skins,
And now we are all alike.
Gentlemen . . . let's dance.

[*The* SKELETONS *between the wire entangle- 20 ments shake off the earth from their bones.*]

SKELETONS. Now we are all alike.
Gentlemen . . . Let's dance!

FIRST SKELETON. The coloured ribbons on our chests
Have long ago decayed.
Our names were in the newspapers
All bordered round with black.
Aha—let's dance!   30

SECOND SKELETON. You over there! You without legs!
Pick up your shins and rattle them,
Clap time for us while we dance!

ALL (*laugh*). You over there! You without legs!
Pick up your shins and rattle them,
Clap time for us while we dance!

[*The legless* SKELETONS *pick up their shin- bones and rattle them together. The 40 others dance.*]

FIRST SKELETON. Haha, what have we here?
You over there—why don't you dance?

ALL. Gentlemen . . . let's dance!

SKELETON (*half-hidden*). I'm so ashamed!

SECOND SKELETON. Ashamed?
Really, gentlemen . . . shame! (*He covers his nakedness with his hands.*) I think we all were—once.
[*All cover their nakedness hastily.*]

FIRST SKELETON. The wilderness drove shame away for ever.
Who of us knows shame to-day?
Fools! Idiots!
Aren't we all naked here?
Behind our naked bones
Yawns emptiness.

SKELETON (*half-hidden*). Not emptiness . . .

FIRST SKELETON. What?

SECOND SKELETON. Good God . . .

ALL. Hihi! Hoho!
Hihi! Hoho!

FIRST SKELETON. My good sir, are you not well?
Good sir, we wish to dance!

ALL. To dance! Dance!

SKELETON (*half-hidden*). I'm not a man.

SECOND SKELETON. What then?

SKELETON (*half-hidden*). A . . . girl . . .

FIRST SKELETON. Gentlemen! Cover yourselves!

SKELETON (*half-hidden*). Just thirteen years old . . .
Why do you look at me like that?

FIRST SKELETON. Young woman, regard me as your protector!

SKELETON (*half-hidden*). Then I need not be afraid?
I mean, there were so many.

FIRST SKELETON. So many when?

SKELETON (*half-hidden*). That evening.
Even to-day I don't know why they did it.
Did it really have to be like that, sir?
One had hardly gone away
Before the next got into bed with me.

SECOND SKELETON. And then?

SKELETON (*half-hidden*). And then . . . I died of it.

FIRST SKELETON. She died of it!
A charming phrase!
A lovely phrase!
She died of it!
Gentlemen, you are trembling
And your hands . . . hoho . . .
Your hands are still . . .
    [*All lower their hands.*]
FIRST SKELETON. There's no shame here,
    my child!
How should there be? . . . Would
    you know
Us from yourself?

Now we are all alike.
Into the middle with you, then,
If I may make so bold!
You have been outraged?
Good; so have we all!
It's nothing but a waste of breath
To talk about it now.
There! You're a clever girl!
Stand here, please, in the middle.
[*They all join hands and form a circle, danc-
    ing vigorously round and round the skele-
    ton of the girl.*]
CURTAIN

THIRD STATION

SCENE V

*Dawn. A Field Hospital, a simple, white-
washed room. Over the bed is a crucifix.*

DOCTOR. He's still sleeping.
SISTER. He's done nothing but groan and
    throw himself about for the last three
    nights. He fancies he's wandering
    through the desert. Cries for water.
    Cries he must reach the mountains,
    the rocky peaks; but the desert
    stretches endlessly before him and he
    can't escape.
DOCTOR. Quinine, double doses of qui-
    nine. A case of nervous shock, those
    others would think. Think! Think! We
    don't think, we diagnose. It's nothing
    of the kind. Quite a different matter
    altogether. . . . Chronic debility of
    the digestive organs—three spoonfuls
    of castor oil and two aspirins night
    and morning . . . uninteresting little
    case, quite uninteresting. Where is the
    new one? Was he given castor oil
    when they brought him in? No?
    Really, sister, that's most annoying.
    Inexcusable too. I can't put up with
    any neglect of duty here. Matter of
    principle! Principle!

SISTER. Shall I tell him when he wakes
    up?
DOCTOR. Of course, of course. A little up-
    set's all to the good. Stimulates the
    muscles of the rectum.
        [*Both go off.*]
FRIEDRICH (*delirious*). Where are you all?
    . . . Oh, the desert sandstorm . . .
    like a stinging, gritty fog . . . no
    rest . . . on . . . on . . . I don't
    know you—who are you? . . . Aha-
    suerus . . . cursed one! . . . Back,
    back! No holes for you here . . . I
    won't go with you . . . no, (*shouting*)
    no! (*Waking up.*) Water!
        [*Red-cross NURSE enters.*]
NURSE. There, drink this.
FRIEDRICH. Are you the Mother of God?
NURSE. You must lie quite still.
FRIEDRICH. You bear the cross . . . the
    cross upon your arm . . . My God, is
    this where they wash away the blood?
NURSE. We are going to heal you here.
FRIEDRICH. Yes, heal. Your hands are so
    gentle and cool on my forehead.
    Look—see how hard mine are.
NURSE. Work has stained and roughened
    them.
FRIEDRICH. You wear the cross of love,
    you dispense love . . .

NURSE. To all who lie here, to black as well as white.

FRIEDRICH. Only to us? That's not enough, nurse—why not to all the others too . . . to all . . .

NURSE. They are fighting against us.

FRIEDRICH. Yes, I know . . . It has to be . . . How long have I been here?

NURSE. Three days now. You're quite a hero, you know! 10

FRIEDRICH. Did they take me prisoner?

NURSE. You were found lashed to a tree; the sole survivor.

FRIEDRICH. Not to a cross . . . the sole survivor . . .

NURSE. Do you feel strong enough to see the Colonel? He has your decoration.

[FRIEDRICH *is silent*.]

COLONEL. Congratulations, young fellow! Your gallantry under the most 20 horrible tortures was simply superb, and your country recognizes your devotion. I have been elected to present you with the cross for valour. You were a stranger among us, but now you are become one of us.

FRIEDRICH. The cross? And now I am one of you?

COLONEL. Now you are one of us . . .

[*Noise outside*.] 30

COLONEL. What's that?

NURSE (*joyfully*). A great victory, God has granted us a great victory! Ten thousand killed!

COLONEL. You see, my friend . . . Victory is in the air, and you are one of the victors.

[FRIEDRICH *is left alone*.]

FRIEDRICH. The jubilation in their faces! Ten thousand dead! Ten thousand 40 have died that I may find a country. Why don't you laugh? Is that liberation? Is this a time of greatness? Are these the people of greatness? (*Staring rigidly before him*.) Now I am one of you.

DARKNESS.

SCENE VI

Part of an immense room made oppressive by the lowness of the ceiling. Rows of beds in which lie wounded soldiers, all in grey shirts. HOSPITAL ORDERLIES *appear*.

ORDERLIES. Everything nice and tidy,
Everything in order.
Beds in a nice neat row,
All alike and tidy.
Well, we've done our duty.
The doctor when he comes will find
Nothing at all to grumble at.
We're ready for him now.

[PROFESSOR *enters with his class of* STUDENTS. *He wears a well-cut black morning-coat. Instead of a head he has a skull, and his eye-sockets gleam through gold-rimmed spectacles*.]

PROFESSOR. Yes, gentlemen, 20
We can face all horrors here.
We might indeed call our work positive,
The negative being the munition works.
In other words we deal in synthesis;
The armament men are merely analysts.
Haha!
Chemists and engineers can quietly make new weapons
And manufacture unconceived-of gases;
Their services to war are greatly valued.
But we, my friends, are not content
To do the rescue work that's proper to the doctor.
While we are here, before we go the rounds,
Let me just demonstrate the last of our achievements,
Entirely due, I must admit, to my own labours.
Just show the seven new cases on the screen.

[ORDERLIES *put up a square white screen.*
One of them beckons and seven naked
CRIPPLES *march forward like clock-*
work figures. They are all truncated.
None of them has arms or legs. Instead
they jerk along with black, artificial
legs, parading before the screen in single
file.]

ORDERLY. Halt!

[*The men obey. In the silence the clicking of* 10
their artificial limbs is audible.]

Left turn!

[*They obey. Suddenly a dark lantern flashes*
out, and the expressions of the seven CRIP-
PLES, *illuminated by the dazzling white*
beam, are seen to be all alike and stereo-
typed.]

PROFESSOR. Best view from here, gentlemen.

These are the men, for whom our 20
glorious work

Has brought regeneration and re-
birth.

Three months ago they were mere
passive stumps!

To-day they stand before you—men!

Did you observe the pleasing willingness

With which they carried out my or-
ders?   30

To say nothing of the exquisite precision

Of their synthetic movements.

So: here they are, my friends,

Restored in life and limb;

Men, citizens, useful members

Of society, waiting each to fill his
place.

But there is more than meets the eye,

You have not guessed my master- 40
piece—

How should you?—Come closer, gentlemen!

These men, these stumps that were,

Can now enjoy the great prerogative
of man.

By delicate and subtle mechanism

I have restored their procreative
powers.

No longer impotent, once more they
can

Enjoy the pleasures of the marriage
bed!

[*One of the* STUDENTS (*with the features of*
FRIEDRICH) *falls in a faint.* ORDER-
LIES *hurry to revive him with water.*]

PROFESSOR (*smiling sympathetically*). Poor
young man, to faint in work like
this!

How would he fare upon the field of
battle?

[*The* STUDENT *covers his face with his*
hands and goes out, his walk involuntar-
ily reproducing the mechanical walk of
the CRIPPLES.]

[*The electric light is extinguished. The* PRO-
FESSOR, *the* STUDENTS, *the* CRIPPLES
and the ORDERLIES *all turn pale. A*
BLIND SOLDIER *gets out of his bed.*]

BLIND SOLDIER. Tell me, brothers, is it
evening?

Is it night?

Night-time is soothing;

Night has cool, soft hands

To stroke my empty eyelids

Quietly.

Day is cruel to me,

The sun is scorching like a bitter fire,

It burns into my skin with pitiless
breath.

ARMLESS SOLDIER. Will no one hear me?

I've been calling for so long.

Will no one help me?

Just a little necessary service . . .

Please help me, quickly, someone
. . .

It is so horrible to have to lie

In one's own dung.

SPINAL PATIENT. You'd make a fuss if
you'd been hit like me.

I'm used to it by now.

I hardly know to-day

Whether I am a man still or a living
lavatory.
My bowels are blown to bits;
My heart's the only living thing about
me . . .
Will no one here blow out my heart
as well
And make a job of it?
I wallow in my filth, and fill myself
and you 10
With loathing.
I curse my heart that keeps on beat-
ing.
My soul is long, long dead with loath-
ing.
Only my heart beats on unpitying.
When I came to, the doctor said to
me:
The bullet grazed your spine,
But we have saved you. 20
If that man knew what lay in store for
me
He was a devil.
The only kindness he could do for
me
Would be to drug me into sleep and
death.
And if he did not know what lay in
store for me
The madhouse is the only place for
him. 30

FOURTH SOLDIER (*whose body is subject to
ceaseless, horrible convulsions*). The
madhouse . . . yes
That's just the thing . . .
The very thing . . . But no!
I know a better thing than that . . .
A dugout,
Shut him in a dugout
And blow the lot to bits . . . 40
Slowly—not too fast . . .
Direct hit!
When the smoke had cleared
I looked around . . . no good;
No way out at all . . . buried
. . . Buried . . . Alive . . .

I went mad . . . I clawed the head-
boards
With my nails . . .
I swallowed earth;
My mouth was full of earth.
Digging, digging upwards . . .
Eating my way to air, to light . .
I ate earth then;
I never knew it tasted good . . .
And then I fell asleep.
I woke up and was here . . .
Was it all that earth
That makes me tremble so?
Did I return to earth too soon?
And am I paying for it now?
Or is Earth having her revenge
For my escape?

FIFTH SOLDIER (*poisoned by gas*). My
breath's a ruddy sparrow
That pipes and whistles . . .
My lung's a nest of sparrows . . .
But sparrows fly away,
Fly South in winter-time.

ALL. Each has his song;
We ought to form a male-voice choir.

[*A* PRIEST *enters (with* FRIEDRICH'S *features), a crucifix in his uplifted hands,
which he holds out to the* WOUNDED
SOLDIERS.]

PRIEST. I bring the Saviour,
Oh sad-faced sufferers.
He knows your misery and pain,
All ye who are oppressed, oh come to
Him.
He offers healing, love.

ALL. Why does all-powerful God
Permit our suffering?
You say He knows
Our pain and suffering;
Then He is evil
To let it be.

PRIEST. Blasphemy!

ALL. You dare to call it blasphemy?
He it is who utters blasphemy,
And we who are blasphemed.
He, who asks us to believe

That He is with us in our suffer-
ing!
You dare call us blasphemers?
Then look, look, look at us!

[*The* WOUNDED SOLDIERS *raise themselves in
their beds. The* PRIEST *slowly raises his
head, and as he looks at them his eyes
widen with horror. Slowly his upraised
hands break the crucifix in two. He sinks
to his knees.*]   10

PRIEST. How dared I ever
Think myself a priest,
With fine-spun sophistries
Proclaim myself God's chosen one?
Black horror seizes me
To think of those who solemnly or-
dained us.
I see the blasphemy
Of empty priesthood,
And I would cry aloud: 20
Free yourselves, free yourselves from
all false priests!
Oh Christ, how are your teachings
mocked!
There is no healing,
I see no light
To light this endless night;
Nowhere a guiding hand.
Prepare for your salvation . . .
How could I, myself in need of con-30
solation,
In bitterer need than you,
Dole comfort out to you?
I can no more;
Now I walk with you, at your head
. . .

ALL. Good luck,
You enviable one!

[THE NURSES *enter in a long procession.*]

THE NURSES. We bring you medicines,   40
Poor suffering ones;
Drinks to assuage your thirst,
Cooling cloths
To ease your burning pain,
Soothing tablets
To lull you into sleep.

THE WOUNDED SOLDIERS. What use is
sleep to us?
To-morrow only brings another day
. . .
Oh, bring us drugs to lull us
Deep, deep, into an endless night,
That we may wake no more!

THE NURSES. You ask too much, poor
suffering ones.
Healing we bring,
But death we may not bring.

THE WOUNDED SOLDIERS. Too late, too
late.
Your mending and your patching
Does us no good.
Why did you not prevent this horror?
Why start your botching now?
If you had taken thought before
You could be dancing now
With strong and joyful men!

THE NURSES. You wrong us.

THE WOUNDED SOLDIERS. Look closely at
us, look,
And say again
We wrong you.
You know not what you are, dear
nurses.
Array yourselves in mourning;
Cover your faces, bow your heads;
Forget your Christian charity,
Or call it wretched, barren, botching.

[THE NURSES *raise their heads, shape their
lips to a shattering cry, collapse.*]

[*Darkness. Then suddenly the lantern flashes
out again. The seven* CRIPPLES *are still
standing before the screen, watching
them the* PROFESSOR, *the* STUDENTS
and the ORDERLIES.]

PROFESSOR. It really is a splendid bit of
luck
That we have all these cases here to
study.
To-morrow we will make a compre-
hensive
Round of all the wards.
Meanwhile, let me repeat

My words of introduction.
We can face all horrors here.
We might indeed call our work posi-
tive,
The negative being the munition
works.

In other words we deal in synthesis;
The armament men are merely ana-
lysts.
Haha!

CURTAIN

FOURTH STATION

SCENE VII

Early morning. A studio. FRIEDRICH *is working at a more than life-size statue of a naked man, heavily muscular, with clenched, uplifted fists. There is brutality in the pose.*

FRIEDRICH (*working*). The stone resists my efforts; my hand upon the chisel cannot bring it to life. The chisel chips marble, dead marble; am I powerless to breathe life into it? If so I'll do no more. I will not be content to carve a mere memorial to life. . . . Life intense must stream from my creation . . . to wake men from their sleep . . . to fire them to fight for their country until death . . . to hurl defiance. . . . Defiance against whom? . . . The enemy, of course. . . . But who decides that there shall be an enemy? Is it some spiritual power within us that forces us to fight? . . . Or is the enemy selected arbitrarily? . . . There's a contradiction there. . . . Why can I not succeed? . . . The problem is so great. Am I too small to symbolize it? Too puny to pierce that brazen armour?

[*The* FRIEND *enters.*]

FRIEND. I was so anxious I had to come —but I see you are working. My mind is full of foolish thoughts, but I won't disturb you. I will go.

FRIEDRICH. My dear fellow, you don't disturb me in the least.

FRIEND. I see your great work will soon be finished. You've certainly laboured long and earnestly at it.

FRIEDRICH. A year. But what's a year for the completion of a worthy symbol of our triumphant Fatherland?

FRIEND. Do you still doubt?

FRIEDRICH. That your country is now mine as well? No . . . Only . . .

FRIEND. Only?

FRIEDRICH. I sometimes wonder if there is not something higher still. And yet I don't really want to know. For if I knew there would be no escaping my destiny, I should become Ahasuerus, the Wandering Jew.

FRIEND. And Gabriele? Would she let you wander? Would you not find fulfilment at her side?

FRIEDRICH. The struggle takes no account of women; perhaps not even of us ourselves.

FRIEND. Gabriele would be unhappy.

FRIEDRICH. Gabriele is strong.

FRIEND. Yes, she is strong.

FRIEDRICH. We come together proudly, joyfully.

FRIEND. You are so strong!

FRIEDRICH. So strong!

FRIEND. Farewell!

[*The* FRIEND *goes.* FRIEDRICH *works. The doorbell rings and* FRIEDRICH *goes to the door.*]

FRIEDRICH. Beloved!

[GABRIELE *enters. She tries to smile.*]
You look sad, my beloved. If I believed in good fairies I should wish that one would change my clumsy hands to butterflies, to brush away the sadness from your brow like pollen from dark flowers. I should wish to be

with you among the sand-dunes where the children play; I should wish to climb high mountains with you, to wander with you on the farthest slopes. To wander with you in the darkness through dreaming towns, to overcome you in the poppy-fields and kiss you there with gladness in our hearts. . . . You are silent, dearest. You do not smile. . . .

GABRIELE. The tears are welling in my heart . . . but they are frozen, and cannot reach my eyes.

[FRIEDRICH *sits quietly beside her, and takes her hand.*]

I am going to leave you.

FRIEDRICH (*as though he had known what she would say*). You are going to leave me. (*Then, as though suddenly awakened.*) . . . You . . . are going to . . . leave me . . . ?

GABRIELE. I must.

FRIEDRICH. For my sake?

GABRIELE. For your sake.

FRIEDRICH. Do you love me?

GABRIELE. I love you as a woman loves a man whom she would have sweep her like a tempest, whom she would have as the father of her child.

FRIEDRICH. And yet . . . ?

GABRIELE. When my father said he would disown me for ever if I married you it was as though I were caught in a sudden blizzard; the icy snow-flakes burnt me. I came to you smiling. But my father would cast me out from my country for ever—never to see it again, never again to tread its soil. It is my childhood's memory, it is the blood that feeds my heart. I have fought against its influence for many days and many nights. And to-day at last I saw clearly: I can never give it up.

FRIEDRICH. And I thought you were strong!

GABRIELE. Perhaps it is because I am strong.

FRIEDRICH. But I shall stay . . . I too have roots, I too have a country of my own, to which I am bound with my heart's blood, to which I have sacrificed my heart's blood; your country, my country. The whole great Fatherland. You are weak, Gabriele, weak.

GABRIELE. Perhaps . . . Farewell! (*She goes.*)

FRIEDRICH. Farewell, you who are strong. And now the dusk has fallen round me, dusk eternal. Day has slipped into the far golden sea. Night dreams in cloven gorges where the black moths flutter, a night that will never lift again. Oh Gabriele! If you'd betrayed me—robbed me of my faith! . . .

[*Sunbeams fall on the statue.*]

So you would remind me? The triumph of the Fatherland. I believe in that, I will believe in that; I will believe in it and symbolize it for ever. If it costs me my life I will do it.

[*He sets to work again. A hurdy-gurdy starts up in the courtyard below. He goes to the window, returns and renews his labours. The bell rings.* FRIEDRICH *opens the door. A* WOMAN *enters, a war-cripple, miserable and emaciated.*]

WOMAN. Alms for the poor, alms for the poor.

[FRIEDRICH, *about to offer her money, stops and considers.*]

FRIEDRICH. Are you a war-cripple?

WOMAN (*weeping*). Must I tell you? (*She shows him her ulcerated hands.*)

FRIEDRICH. Poor soul.

WOMAN. They surrounded me, they sidled up to me like jackals. . . . What should they know? Driven out to fight like cattle. What do cattle know of morals? What can they know? And one among them was diseased and corrupted, and infected me. How can I tell you whether he was bad or not? They called him a hero. They were all heroes. Wretched cattle in a slaughter-house.

FRIEDRICH. It had to be, poor woman, for our country's sake.

WOMAN. For our country's sake? Our country? For the sake of a small handful of rich men who feast and debauch and gamble with the products of our labour. Ah, how I hate them! Brutes, devils! I know them well; I was one of them myself. God reward you for your labours, they say! But what sort of a God is it that lets us rot away in misery? That mocks us with his "blessed are the poor, for theirs is the kingdom of Heaven." The God of love and pity and charity bazaars! When I slink by their lighted halls and see them revelling within, I think I see their God crowned among them, scattering confetti. We are brutes . . . just brutes . . . for ever brutes. (*The* WOMAN *collapses on a chair, sobbing.*)

FRIEDRICH (*after a pause*). Was your husband at the front?

WOMAN. Yes, out there in the colonies. My bonny husband.

FRIEDRICH. Won't you bring him in?

WOMAN. Shall I? I tell you, you'll have a shock. It will put you off your work. He's not a pleasant sight, my husband. The disease eats deeper year by year. Still, if you really want to see him, sir. . . . He was the one that brought me to disease. (*The* WOMAN *goes out, and returns leading her* HUSBAND *with his hurdy-gurdy. His face is a mass of sores.*)

Say good day to the gentleman.

HUSBAND (*stammering*). God . . . be . . . with you.

[FRIEDRICH *looks at him steadily, then begins to tremble.*]

FRIEDRICH. Is it really you, my friend? My poor, poor friend!

HUSBAND (*fearfully*). God . . . be . . . with you.

FRIEDRICH. You need not be afraid, poor fellow. It is I, Friedrich, Friedrich— we served in the same company, we marched across the endless, glowering desert together, we suffered thirst and hunger together. Don't you remember the fellow who volunteered to go on that tricky reconnaissance? We two, we together. We drew lots for the job, and I drew the longest straw. Now do you remember, my poor friend?

[HUSBAND *begins to cry miserably.*]

WOMAN. It's no good sir. It's no good talking to him. He remembers nothing now, nor ever will. He cries because he thinks he ought to cry. He can just think that much, but no more. The doctor said he'd soon have to help him out of life. Well, sir, now you've had your entertainment—can we go, sir? (*The* WOMAN *leads out her* HUSBAND, *who is still miserably weeping.*)

FRIEDRICH. Madness, madness. Where? Where to go? Ahasuerus, where are you? I follow you, Ahasuerus; joyfully I follow you. Anything, anything to escape! A million shattered arms are stretched towards me. The agonizing cries of a million mothers echo in my ears. Where? Where? The unborn children whimper. The madmen cry. Oh, holy weeping! Speech defiled! Mankind defiled! . . . For our country's sake! Oh, God . . . can it really be? Can a country really ask this much of us? Or has our country sold its soul, sold it to the State? Sold it in a dirty business speculation? Perhaps the State is a pimp, and our country a whore to be sold for any brutal lust—blessed by that procuress, the Church! Can a Fatherland that asks so much really be divine? Can it be worth the sacrifice of a single soul? No, no, no! A thousand times no! Rather wander without rest, without hope, wander with you, Ahasuerus. (*He throws himself upon the statue.*) I shatter you to fragments, victory of the Fatherland! (*He seizes a hammer and* 10 *shatters the statue, then sinks down, an inanimate heap. After a time he rises again.*) Now I must wander through the wilderness, without rest, without hope . . . I cannot, I am filled with loathing. Gabriele leaves her lover for a little plot of land . . . And I betray my Fatherland, the Fatherland in which I believed, to which I pledged myself, to which I dedicated my life-20 work—I betray my Fatherland for the sake of two poor, miserable beggars . . . No, not betray. I cannot go that way, I will not. It leads through nights of rain and storm, through plague-stricken streets; it loses itself in the wilderness. Farewell, Gabriele! (*He goes to the bureau and takes up a revolver. Through the open door his* SISTER *enters and regards him and the broken statue.*)   30 You come too late.

SISTER. I come in time.

FRIEDRICH. My path is blocked.

SISTER. Your path leads upwards.

FRIEDRICH. Back to my mother?

SISTER. To her, yes; but higher still.

FRIEDRICH. Back to my Fatherland?

SISTER. To your land, yes; but higher still.

FRIEDRICH. I can see no higher; I am 40 dazzled.

SISTER. I will shield your eyes; then you will see. Your path leads to God.

FRIEDRICH. Haha! To God! God crowned among the revellers, scattering confetti!

SISTER. To God, who is spirit, love and strength;
To God who dwells in the heart of humanity.
Your path will lead you to humanity . . .

FRIEDRICH. To humanity . . .
I am not worthy.

SISTER. Soon like a mask you will cast aside
So much that now seems worthy in your eyes.
Who knows what in the end will prove
Your real worthiness?
He who desires to join humanity
Must find it first within himself.
The path I bid you follow
Sinks to the depths and climbs the heights,
Leads you darkly through the underworld,
The underworld called criminal by fools.
But you are both accused and judge.

[FRIEDRICH *buries his face in his hands, then rises, staggers, stretches out his arms.*]

FRIEDRICH. Sunlight streams through me,
Freedom and sunlight.
My eyes have seen the path
And I will follow it.
Alone, and yet with you;
Alone and yet with all the world,
In the knowledge of humanity.

                    CURTAIN

FIFTH STATION

SCENE VIII

Bedroom of a city tenement. In the two beds, the WOMAN, *the* CHILDREN, *the* LODGER (*with* FRIEDRICH's *features*).

THE LODGER (*to the* DAUGHTER). I can't bear it.
We sleep with moans on every side, and cries.
I can't bear it any more. 10
Come, and I'll hold you to me
And turn you inside out
Like a soft woolly cap.
DAUGHTER. Stay here . . . I won't leave you.
She's groaned like this at night
Ever since we had the news
That he'd been crushed to death at work.
Then, of course, the eleventh child 20
Which she was carrying at the time
She brought out dead.
A bit of luck that was.
I should have had to wash the kid myself.
No one will have her as a waitress now
Because she'll sing and dance
Like someone mad
In the middle of her work,
And offer prayers and hymns . . . 30
She's always at the bottle now.
Who is there now to keep the kids?
. . . There's only me.
And that means overtime at the works.
Stay here, and I'll do everything you ask.
LODGER. All right; I'll stay.
I think she keeps me here
Moaning and crying in the night—
Doesn't she mind you being a whore? 40
DAUGHTER. She used to nod her head
When the other lodger beat me . . .
Does that make you cross with me?
LODGER. Cross with you, fool?

What else could you have done?
If he forced you?
It's only her that gets on my nerves.
Suddenly when you're in my arms
She shrieks or groans.
DAUGHTER. I almost envy the children.
They sleep all day from hunger
And all night from dirt and weariness
They'd really have been better off
Brought up in the orphanage.
LODGER. That's not right . . .
DAUGHTER. No, no—I only thought of it.
LODGER. She nods when a blackguard beats her daughter
And shrieks and groans
When her daughter hugs me to her.
What was that you said . . . the orphanage . . .
The orphanage . . . The orphanage . . .
[*Darkness descends on the room.*]
LODGER (*dreaming*). The orphanage . . . the orphanage . . . (*Silence.*)
(*Dreaming.*) Now she will shriek no more,
Groan no more . . .
Now are you content?
Now you are in the orphanage . . .
The orphanage . . .
[*The* NIGHT VISITOR *enters, his death's head thickly veiled.*]
THE NIGHT VISITOR. Lodger, get up.
It's time for work.
LODGER. All right, I'm coming.
THE NIGHT VISITOR. Make haste . . .
LODGER. Where are you taking me?
THE NIGHT VISITOR. Don't ask me where, just come.
You are in good hands.
[*Phosphorescence flickers round the* NIGHT VISITOR *and the* LODGER, *who stands there in his workman's blouse. The* NIGHT VISITOR *takes his arm.*]
Can you see the house?

LODGER. There, over there, I see it glimmering.
It's funny—are you taking me
The proper way?
THE NIGHT VISITOR. I am taking you the right way—
The narrow way!
The only way!
LODGER. That's not the factory.
THE NIGHT VISITOR. Use your eyes, look, 10
look!
What is it then?
LODGER. It looks like a prison . . .
Look at the shining roof—
It's thick with gold!
THE NIGHT VISITOR. Right! Right!
What do you see now?
LODGER. High walls with iron spikes.
And in the walls
Holes barred with steel. 20
THE NIGHT VISITOR. Right, right!
LODGER. No, that's not the factory
That's a prison!
Let go—Let me go to work!
THE NIGHT VISITOR (grips him firmly). I'll take you to your work,
The only work you and your like are fit for.
Take off your spectacles of everyday 30
And learn to see things as they really are!
You thought this was a prison?
Well, look, look!
We are here.
Look at the name above the gates!
You're trembling—let me read it for you:
You see I've not betrayed you: 40
The great factory!
DARKNESS
[Then for a few moments the roar of machinery, the pounding of pistons, the whirring of wheels and the hissing of molten metal and steam.]

SCENE IX

Death and Resurrection. The ground floor of a prison (the great factory). In the corridors are triple-bolted cell-doors. The spiral stairways leading to the upper floors have rectangular openings to allow the whole prison to be overlooked. On the cement floor, at the bottom of the staircase, a PRISONER lies (with FRIEDRICH's features), his head flung back, his arms flung out as though he were crucified. JUDGES in black coats hurry by: their heads are skulls.

JUDGES (fiercely). Get at the facts of the case! The facts of the case!
[PRISONER cries out shrilly.]
WARDER. It wasn't my fault;
I was just taking him downstairs,
Like you said,
To see his wife,—you gave permission.
[WARDER and CHIEF WARDER hurry over to the PRISONER, bend over him and raise his head.]
CHIEF WARDER. He is still breathing.
WARDER. I knew he was a godless man,
I always knew it.
He wished another dead;
He murdered him in all his dreams.
And now he's killed himself;
Broken the Church's holiest command
Twice over.
CHIEF WARDER. He meant to kill himself,
so who are we to stop him?
JUDGES (scornfully). Get at the facts of the case! The facts of the case!
[PRISONER cries out accusingly.]
WARDER. So help me God . . .
It wasn't like a human voice at all!
CHIEF WARDER. It was the devil himself!
[PRISONER shrieks in accusation, and the doors of the cells burst open. In the open doorways stand the PRISONERS, their arms limp and swinging loosely. They raise their eyes in rapture.]

PRISONER (*first softly, then with increasing resonance*). Horror lies within these prison walls—
Unplumbed, unfathomed; a bottomless morass,
An endless swamp,
A silent swamp.
In the long, empty twilight hours
White maggots crawled out from the iron bars.
I did my best to ward them off, I struggled . . .
It was no use.
Grey maggots gnawed into my flesh.
PRISONERS. Hear us! In suffering we are united.
Behind these prison walls damp horror lies concealed,
Unplumbed, unfathomed; bottomless morass.
PRISONER. Once I saw red flowers;
I stretched my hand to grasp them,
Found it was my heart.
And as I held it dumbly in my hand
It was devoured by maggots, grey and blind.
I ate with them.
PRISONERS. Hear us! In suffering we are united.
Once we saw red flowers. 30
How sweet they seemed, red flowers;
They were our hearts.
And as we held them dumbly
They were devoured by maggots, grey and blind.
We ate with them.
PRISONER. I looked down through the shaft;
I saw land there, I saw firm land.
CHIEF WARDER. And there your wife was 40 waiting.
PRISONER. And there my wife was waiting . . .
WARDER. You broke the Church's holiest command—
Repent before you die!

PRISONER. What do you know about it, brother?
It is so far beyond all good and evil,
Repentance, heavenly recompense.
I heard a voice; it said:—
All, all deluded;
He was not nailed upon the Cross by men,
He crucified Himself.
PRISONERS. We too know that . . . 10
We knew it long ago.
He crucified Himself.
CHIEF WARDER. Think for a moment of your wife.
It's I who have to break the news to her,
A nice job too!
After all, I suppose my job
Is looking after people.
PRISONER. I'm thinking of my wife. 20
I'm thinking of my child as well,
Which she is bearing towards the light
In a body racked with pain.
My child . . .
Sum total of my guilt,
My guilt which never dies.
Ourselves we go
Slowly and painfully upon our way
And send out little children
To crucifixion.
[*A pregnant* WOMAN *rushes in through a door in the background, cries out, and throws herself down by the* PRISONER.]
WOMAN. Oh, why have you done this?
I was waiting for you . . .
PRISONER. The pain goes deep.
Someone is always waiting for us—
But we burn the last bridges,
And night comes down and blots out every path
Which leads to you.
Further we roam . . .
Knowing you are waiting . . .
And further still, and further . . .
Mocking we wander further . . .

Even though we ourselves are waiting.

WOMAN. The child . . .
Does your child mean so little?

PRISONER. It means so much . . .
Yet it was guilt towards my child
That cast me into the abyss, blasted,
Blasted since the day
When man first rose against his kind
And, hating, murdered man. 10
To children we
Are gods and saviours . . .
Helplessly we watch
The long road to the Cross.

WARDER. Blasphemer!
Holy Mother of God forgive him!

PRISONER. Impotent, impotent too, like
all the rest,
With her lying offers of pardon.
She mourns for her son unceasingly; 20
In this alone
Is she innocent and pure.

WOMAN. What is there now for me in
life . . .
I can only kill myself,
Myself and my child . . .
What else is there left for me?
What else?

PRISONER. What else?
Come close and I'll tell you. 30
Perhaps through crucifixion only
Liberation comes;
Perhaps the powers of light
Spring only from His blood.
Perhaps through crucifixion only
Can redemption come,
The way to light and freedom.

PRISONERS. Brother, you light the way.
Through crucifixion only
Shall we liberate ourselves. 40
Through crucifixion only
Shall we find redemption,
And the way to light and freedom.

PRISONER. Woman . . . Mother . . .
(He dies.)

CHIEF WARDER. Come. He is redeemed.

WARDER. Burdened as he was with sin
. . .

PRISONERS. From sin he has released
himself,
Too weak to find redemption . . .

WOMAN (crying out). Husband . . . !
(She wrings her hands in lamentation.)

CHIEF WARDER. Come.

WOMAN. I cannot come . . .
My child . . .
My child . . .

[There is a silence interrupted by soft music.
Then the PRISONERS leave their cells,
forming a semicircle round the WOMAN.
The sun shines on them all.]

PRISONER (a woman). A child.
How many, many years have passed
Since last we heard the laughter of a
child . . .
How many, many years have passed
Since last we played with children.
. . .

[The PRISONERS stand looking at the WOMAN
full of awe. She holds the child out to
them, her face distorted with pain, yet
transfigured. The prison roof gives place
to the limitless sky.]

DARKNESS

SCENE X

The stage is hidden by thick mist. A coun-
try-road is visible. The WANDERER (with
FRIEDRICH's features) appears.

THE WANDERER. I feel to-day as though
This were a new awakening.
As though the grave had split asunder
And shown the sky again.
The earth-chained vessel breaks.
Judge is now prisoner, 40
And prisoner judge;
And both stretch out their hands,
Casting aside their triumphs and their
shames
Like crowns of thorns.
The morning breaks.

The mist dissolves.
I know my work.
I know it now.

SCENE XI

A large meeting-room decorated with coloured paper flowers, and with sentimental paintings of war on the walls.

CHAIRMAN. I call upon our gallant old friend.

[*An* OLD MAN, *an Anti-Pacifist, mounts the dais.*]

OLD MAN. Ah yes, those were indeed the days! The days when our victorious comrades swept conquering forward while the enemy ran before us like a lot of sheep; the days when a great cry ran through the land—"My Country!"   20

[FRIEDRICH *enters.*]

Those were indeed the days! The great days! Magnificent days! Now you're whimpering for bread. What's the significance of a loaf of bread? If you want work, get it! And what does it matter whether you feed on potatoes or roast meat?

[*The crowd murmurs.*]

Have you so soon forgotten the great deeds that were done in the name of our Fatherland, the blood that our heroes shed?

A CRY. Are we any the less heroes because we happen to be still alive?

[*The* OLD MAN *leaves the dais.*]

CHAIRMAN. I call upon the Professor.

PROFESSOR (*on the dais*). As the chosen representative of that Science which is proud to be the servant of our State to-day, of that Science which is ultimate truth and final knowledge—as the chosen representative of Science, I should like to pick a bone with the honourable gentleman who preceded me. The cause of your distress is not bread, nor the lack of it; neither bread nor science nor culture. Go, gentlemen, and study the laws of causality, try to grasp the law of association in regard to all phenomena. . . . The Science in whose ranks I have the honour to serve is inspired by a holy devotion. It is here to help our glorious State, to account for it as a complete ethical organism.

[*Threatening murmurs from the crowd. The* PROFESSOR *leaves the platform.*]

CHAIRMAN. I call upon his Reverence.

PRIEST. Brothers in Christ, heed my words. As our Saviour once said to His disciples, "I am not come to bring you peace, but a sword," so I am come to bring you not soothing rhetoric but iron truth. In time of war did I not preach and say unto you: "Annihilate the enemy, choke him with poison gas and shatter him with bombs, destroy him ruthlessly with submarine and blockade. All that you do finds favour in the eyes of God!" For the Lord of Hosts was with you, and an angel strode before you and withered the ranks of the enemy. . . . Think of those bygone days of glory and forget your petty cares. Think on Him Who died for you upon the Cross.

CROWD. Away with the clergy!
Down with the rich!
We are hungry, hungry, hungry!

CHAIRMAN (*striking a bell*). I call upon the Agitator.

AGITATOR. You are right, brothers! What do the old fire-eaters mean to us? Or the professors? Or the priests? Christ has become the rich man's God. We don't need Him any more, you and I. What we need is bread. What we need is money. We've got to fight against stupidity, we've got to set up reason in its place—and by we

I mean you, the people. But first let's have a look at what these fellows have just been saying: "State" is a new name for Fatherland; that's what they said, and it's a lie. That's a conception that has nothing but a few thousand square miles of earth as its foundation. A few languages, one of which is permitted while the others are suppressed. And any amount of notices saying "Forbidden." They'd like to say, "Permitted the rich, forbidden the poor." That's what they'd say if they had the courage. And then there's taxes: let the rich down lightly and pile it on for the poor. That's their motto. When the rich find they haven't castles enough and want new villas on the Riviera they say damn it all, we'd better have a war. Sit down at that 'phone at once and set a few dozen lies going so that someone will have to declare war on somebody. Start up a society to care for the wounded—a few more or less don't matter—and get a few war memorials designed while you're about it. . . . Now for the Church and the Priests— shall we have a word about them too?

CROWD. Down with the clergy!

AGITATOR. I thought as much. Well, and what then? What but exalt the healthy reason, as typified in you, the people? That means bread and decency and work and our rights. And what must we do? Simply overthrow stupidity. That's what we've got to do. Break up the mansions of the rich! Oh, I can see you at it! All your pent-up energy released, fighting gloriously at last! Holding aloft the flag of freedom! Woman embracing you with feverish arms! Masses surging! Shots ringing out! I'll write you pamphlets to guide you and verses to inspire you, verses which shall them-

selves be bloody deeds! My words shall go with you like the martial blare of trumpets! Blood flows! The blood of freedom! March! March!

CROWD. Yes, this time we'll march!
We're hungry, hungry!
This time we'll really fight!
Bread! Bread! Bread!

CHAIRMAN (*violently ringing his bell*). Here is someone called Friedrich who wishes to address you.

[FRIEDRICH *presses through the crowd and mounts the dais.*]

FRIEDRICH. Gently, brothers, gently! I know you need bread. I know poverty is eating at your bodies. I know misery, your wretched, stinking hovels. I know oppression and the look in the eyes of the outcast. I know, too, of your hatred. But in spite of all that I beg you to restrain yourselves, for I love you.

CROWD. Let's listen to him.
He's right.
He loves us.

FRIEDRICH. I understand your deep disgust of men who bring dishonour to the name of God. I understand it indeed. But let me warn you against the words of him who called on you to march on the rich, against the glittering half-truths of his words! His reasoning did not go very deep. Can't you see the man for what he is? This opportunist agitator? Yesterday his talk was all of individualism, to-day he cries: "God is the people!" And to-morrow he will cry: "God is the Machine!" Therefore the people are machines. None the less he will delight in the swinging pistons and the whirling wheels, the smashing hammers. For him the people are the masses: he knows nothing of the people as men and women. Have no faith in him, for he has no faith in humanity. And before you set out upon your great march you must have faith in humanity. It is better for you to suffer want than to follow the precepts of this man without faith.

PEOPLE. He asks us to suffer want!
Down with him!
Down with him!
We must march! March!
We are hungry! 10
Hear him out first!
Just hear him out!

FRIEDRICH. I am not speaking now of material want, my friends. It is not right that you should suffer hunger. I wish you bodily comfort and spiritual want. I wish you this in the name of the love that unites us all. You must no longer starve. You must be rich, you must find your life's fulfilment. I will fight 20 side by side with you against poverty and misery . . . but wait one day longer, wait until midday. Come to the market-place and let me speak with you there.

[*Excited uproar.*]

A WORKMAN. Well, we've gone hungry so long now that one more day can't make much difference.

PEOPLE. Yes, we will wait! 30
No, no more waiting! March!
We are hungry!
Hungry!
Let us wait!
Wait!
Let us wait!

[*The crowd goes out. A few young people remain behind. A* STUDENT *approaches* FRIEDRICH.]

STUDENT. What is the good of learning 40 when the spirit is denied? What is the good of reason when we must suffer in its name? You must be our leader.

FRIEDRICH. We must advance together, side by side.

[*A* GIRL STUDENT *approaches* FRIEDRICH.]

THE GIRL. In the name of love, be our leader. Once more humanity must be vitalized by love. We will bear no more children until love encircles us with radiant hands. Lead us!

FRIEDRICH. Now down the arches of the years I see
The great cathedral of mankind arise;
Through doors flung wide
The youth of every nation marches singing
Towards a crystal shrine.
Dreams dazzle me—
No misery, no war, no hatred left on earth,
And mothers garlanding bright girls and boys
For games of joy and dances of increase.
Stride on, oh youth, stride on, oh fruitful youth,
Fruitful eternally amidst a barren world;
Within your breast
You bear the life divine.

[*The young people, hand in hand, leave the room in twos and threes. The room is now half in darkness. As* FRIEDRICH *turns to go the* GIRL *suddenly appears out of the darkness.*]

THE GIRL. My lips are parted with desire. My heart is consumed with glowing passion. . . . I will serve you, I alone. . . . Leave the others. . . . They only understand force—and even if your force is for the good. . . . I must serve you.

FRIEDRICH. Serve the spirit, serve your God.

THE GIRL. I shudder before him; He is coldness and death.

FRIEDRICH. Say rather passionate warmth!

THE GIRL. I shrink before him. But you . . . you I love. . . . To you I offer myself; embrace me. Take me . . .

my burning breast. . . . My womb cries out for you . . . I ache for your embrace. . . . Give me a child. . . .

FRIEDRICH. I do not want your breast nor your embrace. Has the whole world rights over my body?

[*With bowed head the* GIRL *goes slowly out.*] Wretched woman! Unredeemed.

[*A* MAN *with turned-up coat collar rushes into the room.*]

THE MAN. I hate you.

FRIEDRICH. I call you brother.

THE MAN. I hate you. I know you; don't think I've not recognized you. I've seen you in my room on lonely nights. Why don't you turn monk? Leave us in peace! What do you want with the mob? You desecrate God!

FRIEDRICH. I celebrate Him.

THE MAN (*hurrying away*). I hate you!

10 FRIEDRICH. Brother, you betray yourself.

CURTAIN

SIXTH STATION

SCENE XII

A precipitous rock-face leading to a narrow ledge. Two men are climbing the rock.

SECOND CLIMBER (*with the* FRIEND'S *features*). Stop, stop!
I shall fall,
I am giddy.

FIRST CLIMBER (*with* FRIEDRICH'S *features*).
Come, pull yourself together;
It is not far now.

SECOND CLIMBER. The ledge is narrow;
We shall slip and fall
Down, down into the abyss.

FIRST CLIMBER. Perhaps, but courage!
Courage!
The ledge to which we climb
Rewards all danger with stupendous height,
With air brighter than light, clearer than fire.

SECOND CLIMBER. In the name of friendship, stop!
An icy coldness sweeps down from above.

FIRST CLIMBER. It is the glacier,
Dazzling and remote.

SECOND CLIMBER. The silence there
Oppresses heart and mind.

FIRST CLIMBER. You're hearing ghosts.
Fasten the rope about you.

SECOND CLIMBER. I would have thanked you once

For freeing me from lowly tyrannies.
But now you lead me on
From terror to worse terror.

FIRST CLIMBER. Not everyone released
Is really free.

SECOND CLIMBER. Up there no one will hear you.

20 FIRST CLIMBER. The mighty walls of rock rejoice to hear
The sound of shouting voices,
And echo them in joyful repetition.

SECOND CLIMBER. I'll go no further . . .

FIRST CLIMBER. Then I must go alone.

SECOND CLIMBER. You'll leave me here,
Your old companion?

FIRST CLIMBER. It is not I who leave you.

30 SECOND CLIMBER. In the name of friendship, stay!

FIRST CLIMBER. In the name of friendship (*He climbs rapidly higher.*)
I must go!

SECOND CLIMBER. Can you still hear me call?
Think of the days when we were young together!

FIRST CLIMBER. Your voice is like the scree
That breaks away and plunges
Loosely down the mountain-side.
Youth advances with me.
How easily youth climbs!

SECOND CLIMBER. You go too far—
Take care, take care;
I am afraid for you.
FIRST CLIMBER. Myself I cannot leave
So I leave you. (*Almost at the summit.*)
. . .
Farewell!

DARKNESS.

SCENE XIII

Square in front of the Church. FRIEDRICH
*enters and leans against the archway of the
door.*

FRIEDRICH. The sunlight warms the roofs
and strokes the blinded windows of
the narrow attics. My breast expands.
[*His* MOTHER *comes across the square dressed
in mourning.*]
Mother! 20
MOTHER (*scarcely glancing up*). All these
years you've never come, till I began
to believe I carried you once more
beneath my heart.
FRIEDRICH. I bring you all my love; let
me hold you gently in my arms and
kiss your tired and wrinkled face.
MOTHER. You are dead for me! You left
your family and estranged your people. 30
FRIEDRICH. I am nearer to them now
than ever I was before.
MOTHER. You belong to the others.
FRIEDRICH. To the others, yes, but to
you as well.
MOTHER. Nobody can belong to us and
to the others. We are a proud people.
FRIEDRICH. Mother! Don't you feel the
earth as a single mighty womb quivering in travail? Think of the torture 40
you suffered in bearing me—thus is
the world convulsed to-day . . . a
lacerated bleeding womb, bearing all
humanity anew.
MOTHER. I am too old, my life is nearly
done. I don't understand you.

FRIEDRICH (*covers his face with his hands*).
Mother!
[*His* MOTHER *goes. His* UNCLE *enters.*]
Dear Uncle!
UNCLE. What does this mean? What do
you want?—I warn you not to count
on me. I refuse to acknowledge you.
FRIEDRICH. I don't want money, Uncle;
but I do want you to acknowledge me.
UNCLE. Wait a minute, wait a minute! 10
Do you mean to tell me that you've
earned enough to keep yourself? No,
your coat is shabby; you can't hide
that from me.
FRIEDRICH. You delude yourself, Uncle.
UNCLE. Delude myself? Well, if I do it's
only because you force me to. You
brought my business to the verge of
ruin. "His nephew's an enemy of our
people"—that's what they all said.
You brought misfortune to your
whole family.
FRIEDRICH. If I did it was only because
there was no escaping it.
UNCLE. Your presence is distasteful. You
are really impossible.
FRIEDRICH. Uncle, I struggle with you
because I must. But it is not against
you that I am fighting; it is against
the dark walls and barriers built up 30
round the real you.
UNCLE. I knew it, you traitor! You even
dare attack your own flesh and blood!
FRIEDRICH. I did that long ago, Uncle.
[*The* UNCLE *walks on. The* DOCTOR *enters.*]
Good morning, doctor—remember
me still?
DOCTOR. Ah . . . you . . . Oh yes,
very ordinary little case—debility of
the rectum. How is it now? All right
now? Digestion good?
FRIEDRICH. Tell me, doctor; do you believe in humanity?
DOCTOR. What a damn-fool question!
Believe in humanity! I believe that
most people have a good digestion,

and those who have not should be given a dose of castor oil—one tablespoonful for adults, one teaspoonful for children. Stupid question. Really quite simple-minded. A man who can ask that wants looking into. . . . Stand still. . . . Say Ah. . . . Close your eyes. . . . Highly developed psychosis. . . .

FRIEDRICH. Your medicines will never make people healthy.

DOCTOR. You must come and see me at once. To-day. I have just bought a nice sanitorium. A water-cure might do the trick even now. But come at once, and don't count on anything. Typical everyday case. Report this afternoon. Room seventeen.

[*He hurries off. A* SICK MAN *with restless eyes shuffles in.*]

SICK MAN. Well, I must say you really seem to believe in it.

FRIEDRICH. In what?

SICK MAN. In yourself, and in humanity generally.

FRIEDRICH. I believe in humanity, certainly.

SICK MAN. He he! . . . And in love as well.

FRIEDRICH. I cannot live without love.

SICK MAN. And all that for the sake of . . .

FRIEDRICH. . . . . liberating humanity.

SICK MAN. I see—you are not interested in building public lavatories, then? A pity—a great pity. Let me tell you something, my dear sir. For a long time I myself tried to redeem the world with love . . . But it's no good. The only thing to do is to build new lavatories. The one's we are used to are always too dark, and hidden away. . . . I know what you're thinking—what on earth is behind all this? I'll tell you—simply to teach humanity that the only infallible panacea for all its ills is universal suicide. It's no good trying to cure them with love—I've tried it and I know. . . . So now I'm building lavatories.

FRIEDRICH. Have you put your plans before the doctors?

SICK MAN. Oh yes, I've been to see them about it several times already. But they didn't want my plans—said they'd thought of it themselves already.

FRIEDRICH. And you would really like all men to kill themselves?

SICK MAN. Yes!

FRIEDRICH. Why don't you go about preaching war, then?

SICK MAN. Oh no, they mustn't do it that way. They must kill themselves voluntarily. . . . Well, what about it? I advise you to think it over very carefully. The building of lavatories with an eye to self-annihilation.

FRIEDRICH. Poor fellow!

SICK MAN. You pity me! *You* . . . pity . . . me . . .

FRIEDRICH. You are sick, corrupted with disease.

SICK MAN (*as though suddenly awakened*). I can't believe in love! I can't, I tell you . . . only whores . . . only whores. . . . No one has ever loved me. (*Shaking his head he hurries off.*)

FRIEDRICH. I must seek him out—to-day. . . . I'll ask my mother to look after him . . . no . . . that girl who came to me.

[*A* WOMAN *who has entered during the foregoing scene moves nearer with studied provocation.*]

WOMAN. What do you think you're doing? . . . Can't you see that love and goodness are eternally separated by a hopeless gulf? That love crouches ready to spring like a rabid dog licking lascivious lips? That love and goodness glare into each other's eyes like deadly enemies? . . . Ha ha!

. . . You're on the wrong track this time, my young friend! Don't answer me. Your answer is nonsense. Your goodness is nonsense. . . . Love lashes the body. . . . Let me tear at your breast with my teeth until the blood flows, red blood over white teeth; let me kiss your thighs. . . . Your goodness! . . . You are a fool, a miserable, wretched fool. You and your goodness—you suffocate me!

FRIEDRICH. And you? Who are you?

WOMAN. Woman!

[*She goes.* FRIEDRICH *leans silently against the doorway of the Church. His* SISTER *enters.*]

SISTER. There was a light in your eyes, Friedrich.

FRIEDRICH. Dear friend.

SISTER. What will you do, Friedrich? How shall you symbolize humanity's victory this time?

FRIEDRICH. No special symbol is needed for that, no proof. Humanity can see victory in its heart, can see it in all my work.

SISTER. And you will stay here?

FRIEDRICH. I shall stay here, and yet still be going further on my way. Through pestilential streets and fields of poppies, over sunlit, snowy mountain peaks and through the barren wilderness—knowing all the time that I am not uprooted, knowing that I am rooted in myself.

SISTER. One must die and be born again to find one's roots.

FRIEDRICH. But that knowledge is only a beginning.

SISTER. And whither does it point?

FRIEDRICH. Towards humanity.

SISTER. And beyond humanity?

FRIEDRICH. Beyond . . . ? I can't think of that yet. I feel as though I'm dwelling in limitless space. It is glorious to know that one may be anchored and yet still wander.

SISTER. Good-bye, Friedrich. I shall watch your journeyings.

[*She goes. People stream out of the Church and others join them in the square from all the side streets.*]

CROWD. That's him, the one that's going to speak—

He said we must wait until midday.

Now he will have to speak,

Since we have waited.

FRIEDRICH. Brothers, sisters; there is not a single one of you of whom I have ever heard, yet I know you all.

You, my child, go every day to school; you go in fear. In the schoolroom the day is overcast and dark, yet outside the sun is shining. The teacher sits at his desk like one of those evil spirits in the fairytales you read in secret. He glares at you and scolds you because you haven't done your homework. And yet your heart is full of strange experiences. You would gladly talk to him about them, but he talks you down and accuses you of not having learnt the Scriptures and of not being a good Christian.

And you, slim and delicate in your maidenhood; you too I know . . . Only a few weeks ago you left school with joy in your heart; it seemed that youth and freedom beckoned you with heavenly bells . . . And now you stand at the factory bench. Day in, day out, you push a single lever backwards and forwards, backwards and forwards. Always the same lever. And your breath becomes heavy in the stifling atmosphere, and your eyes fill with tears when you think of the sunlight grimed by the dusty windows, of freedom and youth and flowers.

And I know you too, woman, careworn and worked to the bone; I know how you live in your wretched garret with your hungry, shivering children;

how at evening you open the door to your husband with a spirit dulled and a body tired to death.

And you, husband, I know you too; how you are filled with horror at the very prospect of returning home to that room with its evil smell, its squalid misery, its festering disease. I know how you hate those who gorge themselves at your expense and then 10 sneer at you if you go to the inn to drink yourself insensible; insensible, that you may think no more and see no more.

And you, young girl,—I know of your nights of hot desire.

And you, young man,—I know of your restless seeking after God.

And you, rich man, for ever heaping gold on gold, despising everyone 20 —yourself and others too.

And you, woman, a tree heavy-laden with rare fruit which no one comes to pluck, so that you break and wither in your superfluity.

And you, soldier, pinched in your coloured coat which drains all joy from life. I know your astonished eyes when you see before you the figure of striding youth.   30

How could the artist symbolize this youth?
Because he exists, he really is.
And so it is with all of you,
Distorted images of true humanity!
Gasping for breath, joyless, embittered—
All because you have buried alive the spirit . . .
Mighty engines thunder day and 40 night,
A million spades are ceaselessly at work
Piling still more rubble on the spirit's grave.
Your hearts are dry and withered.

The hearts of your fellow-men you regard as convenient bell-pulls which you can tug at when you feel inclined. You throw glittering gold-pieces at their feet and say they are spring-awakened birds flying rejoicing through the air. You pave your streets with gold-pieces and tell yourselves that you are treading rich green fields enamelled with wild flowers.

Your lips shape barren laws, iron prison houses gnawed with rust.

Your hands raise walls around you, and you say, beyond them is the jungle.

You sow hatred in the hearts of your children, for you know no more of love.

You have carved the figure of Christ in wood and nailed it to a wooden cross, because you yourselves refuse to go the way of crucifixion which alone can bring redemption.

You build castles and prisons and set men to rule over them, men who serve neither God nor humanity but a phantom, an evil phantom.

For the mothers and their children you raise cruel and subtle pillories—for you well understand the art of torture.

You mothers who bear children, and from indifference or false pride sacrifice them to frivolous lies and illusions—you are no longer mothers.

You are all of you, all of you, no longer men and women; you are distorted images of your real selves.

And yet you could still be men and women, still be human, if only you had faith in yourselves and in humanity, if only you would grant the spirit its fulfilment.

You could stride erect where to-day you creep along crooked and bent.

Your eyes could be filled with the

light of joy, while to-day you are half blind.

You could go forward with winged feet, while to-day wherever you go you trail after you iron chains.

Oh, if only you were men and women—men and women unqualified —free men and women!

[*During this long speech there has been ever-increasing disturbance among the crowd.* 10 *Some have kneeled down. Others, weeping, bury their heads in their hands. Some lie broken on the ground. These now rise again in gladness; others open wide their arms to heaven. A* YOUTH *rushes forward.*]

YOUTH. To think that we ever forgot! We are men, men and women!

SEVERAL WOMEN AND GIRLS (*half-aloud*). We are men and women!

ALL. We are men and women! (*Softly, as* 20 *though smiling to themselves.*) We are men and women!

[*There is a silence.*]

FRIEDRICH. Now, brothers, now I bid you march! March now in the light of day! Go to your rulers and proclaim to them with the organ tones of a million voices that their power is but illu-

sion. Go to the soldiers and tell them to beat their swords into plough-shares. Go to the rich and show them your heart, your heart that was once buried alive beneath their rubbish. Yet be kind to them, for they too are poor, poor and straying. But the castles—these you must destroy; destroy them laughing, the false castles of illusion. Now march! March forward in the light of day.

Brothers, stretch out your tortured hands,
With cries of radiant, ringing joy!
Stride freely through our liberated land
With cries of Revolution, Revolution!

[*All the people are now standing with outstretched hands. Then they join hands and march away.*]

ALL. Brothers, stretch out your tortured hands
With cries of radiant, ringing joy!
Stride freely through our liberated land
With cries of Revolution, Revolution!
CURTAIN

VALENTINE KATAYEV
and the Theatre under the Soviet

DURING THE FIRST two decades following the Russian revolution of 1917 the Soviet theatre enjoyed extraordinary prestige. Russian life is theatrical even on the street corners. Their theatres have been held in respect by the rest of the world, and the Moscow Art Theatre has been since 1898 in the front rank of all dramatic organizations. The Soviets did not attempt to liquidate the established troupes; rather they used them as one of the most effective agents for the entertainment, instruction, and cultivation of the people. They nationalized the theatres and opened them to the new dominant class of workers, peasants, and soldiers—to the proletariat. Few of this class had ever been in a theatre. Established organizations accustomed to presenting plays before the aristocrats, the czarist officials, and the upper bourgeoise, were compelled to reconsider and to modify their programs.

Stanislavsky, in his *My Life in Art*, has left some informative passages on this era through which he and his theatre passed successfully. After the Revolution, he writes, "the doors of our Theatre opened exclusively for the poor people and closed for a time to the intelligentsia. Our performances were free to all who received their tickets from factories and institutions where we sent them, and we met face to face, right after the issuance of the decree, with spectators altogether new to us, many of whom, perhaps the majority, knew nothing not only of our Theatre but of any theatre.

But yesterday our Theatre had been filled by the old public which we had educated through many decades, and today we were faced by an altogether new audience which we did not know how to approach. Neither did the audience know how to approach us and how to live with us in the theatre. We were forced to begin at the very beginning, to teach this new spectator how to sit quietly, how not to talk, how to come into the theatre at the proper time, not to smoke, not to eat nuts in public, not to bring food into the theatre and eat it there, to dress in his best so as to fit more into the atmosphere of beauty that was worshipped in the theatre. At first this was very hard to do, and two or three times after the end of an act the atmosphere of which was spoiled by the crowd of still uneducated spectators, I was forced to come before the curtain with a plea in the name of the actors who were placed in an impasse."

The audiences soon responded to Stanislavsky's appeals and became ideal listeners. He speaks of the variety of newcomers to the theatre in those wild days, and concludes the passage: "With the coming of the Revolution many classes of society passed through our Theatre—there was the period of soldiers, of deputies from all the ends of Russia, of children and young people, and last, of workingmen and peasants. They were spectators in the best sense of the word; they came into our Theatre not through accident but with trembling and the expectation of something important, something they had never experienced before."

Not only were the established theatres thus pressed into the service of the new regime, but new ones were built or improvised by the thousands throughout the vast USSR. Some of these were marvels of design and construction, notably the new Meyerhold Theatre built in the shape of an ellipse with an amphitheatre having on its steep banks rows of seats looking down on the stage and completely enclosing it on three sides. Others were thrown up hastily in the provinces to serve the local peasantry. In some instances cathedrals were transformed into playhouses, as in the newsworthy case of St. Isaac of Leningrad, one of the most beautiful and luxurious of the Russian cathedrals that had required thirty-nine years to build. (Incidentally, the first production in the cathedral playhouse was a satire on St. Isaac himself.) The aristocratic Villa Morossov after 1918 housed the Proletcult Theatre where workers could participate in the production of plays. Dramatic societies were founded in nearly every factory, peasant playhouses sprang up throughout the provinces, and the theatre became for a time one of the most potent forces in all the Soviet.

It was one thing to build and equip theatres; it was quite another to provide plays that could meet the new Soviet requirements. The great Meyerhold ran afoul of the regime for presenting "a succession of politically wrong or antagonistic performances," and for glorification of "a Menshevist traitor . . . and a future base agent of fascism," i. e., Trotsky. The director of the Moscow Kamerny Theatre, Alexander Tairov, People's Artist of the Republic, was charged by *Izvestia* with refusing to heed "the very serious warnings which have been given him in recent years," with failing "to arm his theatre with socialist ideology," and thus bringing the theatre "to such a serious political failure." These charges indicate the kind of demand laid upon the theatres by the state.

Since new plays were at first lacking, the old or foreign ones were remodeled for service. *The Cherry Orchard* was acceptable when the proper accent was placed on the new man, Lopakhin, dispossessing the idle and incompetent landowners of czarist days. The Christlike nonresistance of Luka and his teachings in *The Lower Depths* were quite unacceptable to the Communists. Gogol's classic standby, *The Inspector General*, (1836) was revised and made palatable by toning up the satire on pre-communist bureaucracy. Ostrovsky's dramas that had been so popular in the mid-nineteenth century could still be played, especially *The Storm* (1859), which was still receiving praise at the First Art Theatre in the 1930's. Tolstoy's *Tsar Fédor Ivánovich*, with which the Moscow Art Theatre had opened in 1898, was often played and was enacted by the Art Theatre in celebration of its fortieth anniversary on October 27, 1938. Any play that could hold the aristocrats, bourgeoise, or czarist officialdom up to ridicule, or that could exalt the people or the communist ideology might be drafted into service.

The Russian theatres also conscripted many foreign plays which they revised and staged according to their own inspiration. From the American theatre they have had great success with so diverse a list as Longfellow's *Hiawatha;* Stowe's *Uncle Tom's Cabin;* Jack London's *The Mexican* and *South of the Slot;*

Twain's *Tom Sawyer* and *The Prince and the Pauper;* Sinclair's *King Coal;* a dozen O'Neill plays, especially *The Hairy Ape, All God's Chillun Got Wings,* and *Desire Under the Elms;* Anderson's *Gods of the Lightning;* Dreiser's *An American Tragedy;* Dos Passos's *Fortune Heights, 1919, 42nd Parallel;* and many others. Some of these pieces became quite unrecognizable in Russian hands. In *Uncle Tom's Cabin,* for example, little Eva was metamorphosed into tomboyish and robust Dora with all mention of God and religion omitted. She became the forerunner of the Young Communist fighting for the underprivileged and oppressed proletarian Negro. Most of the white characters were made grotesque while the Negroes were sympathetically drawn. *Hamlet* was entirely recast. The ghost, the producers decided, is a trick of the Prince to fool the sentries while he plans to gain the crown. He asks himself whether he is "To be or not to be" the king. "The Russian Ophelia," wrote Eugene Lyons, "is not mad but plastered. . . . It is while drowning her sorrows in liquor that she gets drowned herself." The ghost, he added, was Hamlet himself, who had donned his father's armor and a false beard "and in the mysterious moonlight passed as a ghost, thus winning the support of officers who otherwise might have wavered." The Russian producers of this classic insisted that their version carried out Shakespeare's idea of the play as a vigorous melodrama which capitalist producers and actors have falsified by injecting into it their own culture.

Playwrights of the Soviet emerged in due course. They put together all sorts of plays to dramatize the events and issues of the revolution. In a sense undreamed of by those who coined the term "useful theatre" a generation or more earlier, the Soviet dramatists made the stage a platform from which to lecture the masses, to indoctrinate them, inspire them, and to arouse their hatreds or their loyalties. Illiterate villagers and big city proletarians who were not reached by printed propaganda could be stirred by seeing a parable enacted before their eyes on a stage. The "living newspaper," copied by the Federal Theater Project experiment in America in the 1930's, edited and dramatized current events throughout the Soviet. Vast open air pageants glorifying the successes of the revolution against the Czar and Kerensky were enacted realistically with massed players in the public squares. As the distinguished French dramatist Charles Vildrac observed, "the Soviet dramatists must employ the ideology which they profess to serve in the theatre of propaganda, which by definition, is bad theatre. Their best productions in this genre have been stories or episodes recalling the revolutionary epoch. More often than not these have been destitute of plot and resembled nothing so much as a series of frescoes."

The testimony of visitors to Russia and of students of the drama who flocked to Moscow for first-hand knowledge of the theatre is all but unanimous on the lack of distinction among the plays. Lee Simonson wrote in the introduction to Norris Houghton's authoritative book, *Moscow Rehearsals: An Account of Methods of Production in the Soviet Theatre* (1936): "For the artist all roads once led to Rome; yesterday to Paris. Today, for the artist in the theatre, whether actor, director, or designer, the road leads to Moscow and the theatres of the U.S.S.R." The omission from the list of the word "dramatist" is significant. The one thing they all found lacking was dramatists of imagination and intelligence. Playwriting was far, far behind the astonishing technical organization of the theatres. Enraptured visitors wrote admiringly of these stages, designers, schools of acting and the general enthusiasm for the theatre. Hallie Flanagan declared that "in the idea of Communism the theater in Russia has what the Greek Stage had in the gods, what the medieval drama had in the Church—a force outside itself to which it pays tribute with religious ecstasy." Brooks Atkinson felt such a letdown after he left the Russian theatres for those in France, England, and America that he labeled his piece about his visit in the New York *Times* "Back to Mediocrity"; but he added a kind of footnote in *Stage:* "Russia is a busy land, driven by an abnormal impulse; it is embarrassingly anxious to please and be praised. But if it is not too boorish to say so, Fannie Brice and Beatrice Lillie are also good actors. Soviet Russia needs someone like these." After her visit in 1937, Anita Block stated that the Russian Theatre today "most nearly realizes the highest function of the theatre, because its plays, *with all their shortcomings*, most completely integrate its audiences with the age in which they live." Mlle. Simone Tery reported that she was amazed and fascinated by the technical perfection of the Soviet theatre, but lamented the sorry plays being written in Russia. The amateurish, propagandistic tracts, and the crude adaptations of novels that passed for plays on this technically masterful stage were always excused, however, with the indulgent remark that Russia was still experiencing her revolution. The dramatic masterpieces would appear as soon as the new state achieved adjustment.

The Communist regime was aware of the need for better plays. It took elaborate steps to encourage playwrights. Workers were urged to send in manuscripts to headquarters where they were read and sometimes revised and produced. The state built country houses for the leading dramatists, novelists, and poets who occupied them without cost. Stalin himself in the earlier days of his dictatorship described his writers as "the engineers of thought." He told them to assess life in the USSR and specifically urged them not to glorify but "to discriminate and criticize fearlessly the shortcomings of the regime."

In the midst of all this ferment and excitement, several plays and a few notable playwrights appeared. One of these was a dramatization of Ivanov's novel *Armored Train No. 14–69*, produced in 1926 by the Moscow Art Theatre. Its action centers around the peasants in a Siberian town as they heroically capture from the Whites during the Revolution an armored train loaded with provisions. It exalted personal sacrifice and devotion to the principles of the victorious Revolution. Alexis Faiko's *The Man with the Portfolio* (1928) is an unusual combination of a personal, psychological play and a tract on the problem of the intellectual in the Soviet state. The gifted hero, Granatov, after desperate attempts to become a good Communist, fails to adjust himself, and after a lecture to the audience on "The Intelligentsia and the Revolution," commits suicide.

Vladimir Mayakovski's satirical farce called *The Bedbug* was staged with success at the Meyerhold Theatre in 1930, about the time it was permissible to suggest that there were some undesirable features of life in the Soviet. The hero was frozen in 1930 and thus preserved, along with a bedbug, into the immensely improved era of 1980. He was found, thawed out, and exhibited in a cage because, like the bedbug, he had become a priceless specimen of an extinct animal: "Bourgeoisius vulgaris."

On a much higher level was the almost universally praised play *Aristocrats*, by Pogodin, featured in productions during the peak years of Russian drama in the mid-thirties. It deals poignantly with the rehabilitation of convicts by developing in them self-respect through group work in building a canal between the Baltic and the White Seas. Okhlopkov produced it on a bare platform stage with masked property men coming on stage in the oriental manner. Simone Tery reported that "those six dark-blue clad men, throwing out handfuls of white confetti to represent snow, gives you a much better chill of the blizzard on the icy steppe than do the flakes of a conventional stage snow which most theatres have used." The effect of the technique employed was "that the soul of man rises up in all its grandeur against this abstract space and attains epic proportions."

These plays may, perhaps, suggest the type of thing produced in modern Russia. A few have been seen in America through the work of the Theatre Guild. That organization presented Kirchon (sic) and Ouspensky's *Red Rust* on December 17, 1929, after its success two years earlier at the Moscow Proletarian Theatre. It drew a biting portrait of the villainous and corrupt Terekhine who takes advantage of his powers and the new freedoms to gratify his own selfish and lustful desires to the detriment of the group. It was taken as a criticism of the dangers confronting the state in its policies toward family life, as well as a protest against officious party leaders.

The very best of modern Russian dramas representing the work of six leading young playwrights was made available to English readers by Eugene Lyons in *Six Soviet Plays* (1934). They were *Days of the Turbins* by Bulgakov, a play about the officer class in the Ukraine in the revolutionary days when the Whites were clashing among themselves and the Reds were approaching; *Tempo* by Pogodin, one of the many plays inspired by the Five-Year Plan which in turn tried to impress upon the people the need for quick accomplishment in the industrial program; *Bread* by Kirshon, a successful propagandistic play written during the period when Stalin was driving hard to collectivize agriculture and urging conformity to the Communist Party program; *Inga* by Glebov, dealing with "The Soviet woman: the old in the new and the new in the old," and domestic problems in communist society; *Fear* by Afinogenyev, dealing with "the relation between the intellectuals and the proletarian regime" as seen in 1931 when the new generation trained in communism was functioning in Russia; and *Squaring the Circle* by Katayev, which we have chosen to reprint.

Valentine Katayev is one of the most talented of the younger dramatists of Soviet Russia. He was born at the important commercial port of Odessa on the Black Sea in 1897, the son of a school teacher. He wrote poetry at the age of nine and published some in the Odessa papers at the age of sixteen. Though still a schoolboy when the World War engulfed Europe, Katayev volunteered for service with the Russian army. He saw active duty and was wounded and gassed. He spent the two hectic years following the revolution in the troubled Ukraine, and has drawn upon his adventures there for his plays and stories. He became a journalist and literary propagandist, though he was not a member of the Communist party. In 1923 he published his first volume of stories in the realistic manner of Bunin. It was while he was working as a literary propagandist that he discovered and developed his unusual flair for satire that later distinguished his *Squaring the Circle* and other works.

The times were ripe for Katayev's talents, which began to flower during the period from 1924 to 1928 when the regime was indulgent to analysis of its faults. The party officials invited criticism and a burst of novels and plays gave it to them. Katayev belonged to this group, most of whom were, in the years of the New Economic Policy established by Lenin in 1921, neither Communists nor proletarians but Poputchikis, that is, not real Bolsheviks but Fellow Travelers with the revolutionaries. These writers took advantage of the opportunity to attack "Russian ignorance, coarseness, and social disorders. They perceived that the new State, which was to point the way to all humanity, contained millions of people who were living like savages, that Soviet officials were as partial to bribes as their predecessors, that the bearers of the revolutionary fire were hemmed in by liars, scoundrels, and hypocrites, and that the cobweb of meanness was again entangling the average man."

Katayev's first play, produced by the Moscow Art Theatre, was a dramatization of his novel *The Embezzlers* (1928) which was widely read in English translation. It is a satirical comedy exposing a widespread habit of peculation and thievery among employees of the Communist State and castigating the parasitic and absurdly incompetent people in the new government, many of whom, he intimates, have made it a custom to abscond with government funds. Other dramas, original or adapted from his novels, have followed in rapid succession. By 1938 when news of the theatre practically stopped coming out of Russia, Katayev had written eleven plays. Besides *The Embezzlers, Squaring the Circle*, and *The Million Torments* (1931; produced in New York in 1936) which have been translated into English, these include *Department Store* (1929); *Vanguard* (1930); *Time Forward* (1932) in English in novel form, dealing with the industrial progress during the Five-Year Plan; *Under the Circus Tent* (1934); *Path of Flowers* (1934); *The Rich Bride* (1936); *Lonely White Sail* (1937); *I, Son of the Working People* (1938).

Squaring the Circle is Katayev's best and most widely known play, and it has been one of the most popular in all Russia. It has had almost continuous performances throughout the Soviet in both professional and amateur theatres. It was first introduced to American audiences through productions in many little theatres in various parts of the country. It had a very successful run of 108 performances at the Lyceum Theatre in New York, opening on October 3, 1935. It was well received not only because it was a thoroughly amusing play in itself, but also because it was the first sign "that the USSR was finally able to laugh at itself." The Russians felt the same way about it after ten years of bloody solemnity and monotonous propagandistic catchwords. It was tried out late in 1928 by the Small Stage, an experimental adjunct of the Moscow Art Theatre. It was soon brought into the Moscow Art Theatre itself to begin its phenomenal career.

The background of the play, so far as

it is dependent upon topical interest, is the late 1920's near the close of the period of Lenin's New Economic Policy and the beginning of the Five-Year Plan. It makes a merry burlesque of the strict and unimaginative attitudes of the Communists toward love, marriage, and the family in the days when communist youth summed up all wisdom in a phrase from Marx and the state permitted free love, easy marriage, and easier divorce. After two decades of relaxation of the ancient rituals and the legal protections surrounding marriage in Russia, as shown in this play, the Soviet marriage laws have been tightened and domestic unions are no longer quite so casual. *Squaring the Circle* restored some perspective on this subject and started all Russia to laughing at the preposterous effort of these young Komsomols (members of the Communist Youth League) to rearrange the wayward torments of love according to the party discipline. It so happens that Nature—and the urgencies of youth—were set in their ways long before Marx and Lenin began to reform the world, and the pattern of love was not amenable to the new social system. Katayev seems particularly to enjoy making farce of Abram's worries about his conduct in this mixed-up affair, and whether or not it is right according to communist ethics; everything, of course, must be weighed against the ultimate consideration: can it hurt the Revolution?

The other prominent element in the play is the contrasts of character among this group of Komsomols, set off against the critical housing shortage in Russia. The play follows the conventions of well-made farce in delineating types: Vasya, the serious and simple boy; Abram, the frivolous and sensual one; Tonya, the new mannish girl who puts the problems of the world before personal and feminine concerns, and who wants to be one of the boys; Ludmilla, her antithesis, who cultivates her femininity, wants her little nose kissed, and doesn't even belong to the League. When this carefully assorted group attempts to adjust itself as two married couples in a single barren room with a chalk mark down the floor to separate the establishments, and with Karl Marx as their mentor and disciplinarian, the possibilities for amusing action and pointed satire are liberal. Katayev takes full advantage of them; the result is this robust comedy full of laughter and enough broad and subtle satire to give it bite.

It is significant indeed that most of the good plays to come out of Soviet Russia, including the six in Eugene Lyons's collection, were written during the few years of comparative artistic freedom at the close of the twenties and the beginning of the thirties. In those years the high perfection of the Russian theatre became one of the chief agencies for breaking down foreign hostility toward revolutionary Russia. From 1933 to 1937 the ten days of gala performances of the Soviet Theatre Festival held in Moscow regularly in late August or early September and participated in by artists from all the Soviet Republics were the sensation of the theatrical world. Visitors came from all countries to witness the new marvels in theatre design, in technical developments, and the growing repertory of good Russian plays.

Then the mysterious and bloody purges started. The festival for 1938 was abruptly abandoned without any explanation. News grew scarce and finally stopped altogether. But a few revealing facts have been authoritatively reported, chiefly through the New York *Times*, the one newspaper which maintained its Moscow bureau. (This too, was closed in the summer of 1940, leaving only such news services as the Associated Press to report Russian news.) The theatres were purged along with the army and other prominent agencies of the state. Dozens of managers and other high theatre officials were arrested, tried, and convicted of ticket speculation that deprived the state of revenue. They were given sentences of from three to ten years. Leonid M. Lyadoff, director of the famous Mali Theatre in Moscow, was summarily dismissed and arrested on charges of "wrecking the theatre's production program and endeavoring to corrupt and demoralize the cast." He was also accused of squandering the government's rubles on productions. This charge has proved to be an effective device for liquidating managers: if they spend more on a production than they get back at the box office, they may be charged with misappropriating public funds.

The fall of the great and distinguished producer Meyerhold in June, 1939, seems particularly tragic. His work was world-famous. The chairman of the arts committee of the Council of Peoples' Commissars charged that Meyerhold was artistically and politically corrupt, that his productions were full of empty trickery and failed to mirror Soviet life. After many months of controversy with him, the Communists sent secret police to Meyerhold's home; they seized him and locked him in a cell at Lubyanka prison. Zenaida Reich, his wife, a famous actress, was also arrested but released. She was later found murdered in her Moscow apartment, as reported in the New York *Times* in July, 1939. There has been no further news of Meyerhold. Afinogenyev, a passionate supporter of the cause, and one of Russia's best younger dramatists, was charged with harboring Trotskyist views and expelled from the playwrights' section of the Union of Soviet Writers. Kirshon, who had so effectively exposed the "red rust" of dishonesty, was also expelled and held for investigation on charges of embezzlement. Katayev himself has not been mentioned in any of the dispatches from Russia since the purge.

Thus did the short-lived period of brilliance of the Soviet theatre come to an end. As Mr. Steward Chaney wrote to the New York *Times* in January, 1938, after three months in Russia: "The 'purge' is still going on at a terrific rate. I may add that even the stage door of the highly respected Moscow Art Theatre is now guarded by a laconic Red Army officer. . . . One member of the company told me that since October no friend, wife, or child is allowed to visit backstage. It is not difficult to imagine the desperate creative atmosphere in which the artist in the Russian theatre works."

SQUARING THE CIRCLE

A Jest in Three Acts

CHARACTERS

VASYA, *a member of the League of Communist Youth; a serious-minded young worker, simple and abrupt in manner, sincere and without frills*

ABRAM, *also of the Communist Youth; roommate and closest pal of* VASYA *but with frivolous mundane appetites that contrast with* VASYA'S *genuine seriousness*

TONYA (*whose full name is* ANTONIA KUZNETZOVA), *a serious-minded member of the Communist Youth who disdains feminine frivolities and is determined to be as hard and useful in the world as any man; unaware of, and disinterested in her good looks*

LUDMILLA, *a real she-girl, not belonging to the Communist Youth, chiefly interested in her own pretty face, domestic comforts and boy-friends*

COMRADE FLAVIUS, *an older Bolshevik, wiser and more experienced than these four young people but chummy with them all*

EMILIAN, *a poet of the masses; a tall, blond, lumbering giant of a man who looks more like a longshoreman than a poet*

Also, *boys and girls of the Communist Youth, who take their fun where they find it and manage to mix Karl Marx and vodka with heady effects*

Time: The present. Place: Moscow.

ACT I

A typical room in an overcrowded noisy municipalized tenement in Moscow, barnlike, dusty and neglected. A battered door on the right, rear.

In one corner lies a dilapidated striped spring mattress propped on four bricks, which is a bed at night and a sofa during the day. On it lies a grimy pillow in a mildewed ticking and without a pillow-case. Beside the improvised couch stands a decrepit stool. A pair of old trousers against one wall and a crude home-made radio are the only embellishments of this corner, which is VASYA'S.

ABRAM'S *corner on the other side of the room contains only a pile of books, papers and*
booklets, *and a few nails in the walls for clothes.*

In the foreground on one side is an untidy iron sink. From the middle of the ceiling hangs a lone, unshaded electric bulb, which glares at the room and brings out sharply its chaotic poverty.

Directly under the lamp stands a heavy wooden park bench which must have been dragged here by heroic efforts; initials and a large pierced heart betray its earlier career. On the bench lies a preposterously thick volume of Lenin, useful to bewilder poor ABRAM'S *head in daytime and to support it as a pillow at night.*

SQUARING THE CIRCLE: Translated from the Russian by Charles Malamuth and Eugene Lyons. From Six Soviet Plays translated by Eugene Lyons. Reprinted by permission of Houghton Mifflin Company.

The one window in the room, with a broken window-pane, stuffed with a rag and decorated with the pendent remnant of a thick sausage, is in the foreground, left, facing the audience.

The room is entirely dark when the curtain rises, except for the dribble of light through the window from a flickering street-lamp.

LUDMILLA'S *saccharine voice and* VASYA'S *anxious one are heard offstage, from the corridor behind the door.*

VASYA. This way, Ludmillochka, this way. Don't get lost in the corridor.

LUDMILLA. Hell! I caught my skirt on something.

VASYA. Oh, it's only the bicycle. Here, hold on to me!

LUDMILLA. Darn! What a shame, pussy-kin. Your corridor's two miles long and not a single lamp in it.

VASYA. It burned out last week.

LUDMILLA. On ninety rubles a month couldn't you afford a new one?

VASYA. Didn't think of it. Look out there for the cupboard. Somehow I didn't find the time for it. I work in the daytime, study at night . . . Walk right in.

[*Enter* VASYA, *followed by* LUDMILLA. VASYA'S *costume, much to his discomfort, jars with his natural serious inclinations. His gaudy butterfly tie, shiny puttees, plastered, well-parted hair, semi-military cap, and well-pressed coat are obviously* LUDMILLA'S *doing. The young lady's own femininely provocative clothes, however, are part of her personality.* LUDMILLA *is kittenishly pretty.*]

LUDMILLA. No one's had the time to spank you properly, darling. Just you wait, my dear husband, now I'll get after you.

VASYA. That's right. Get after me. Put me to work. That's why we signed up in the Marriage Registry Bureau. Watch your step. Wait. I'll turn the light on right away. The room is just what we need, only there really isn't too much furniture, you know. (*He gropes stumblingly amd nervously for the pendent lamp.*)

LUDMILLA. I'm dying to see how you live.

VASYA. Damn it, I can't find the blasted light. Abram, are you home?

LUDMILLA. Wait a minute—don't you live here alone?

VASYA. Eh . . . eh . . . I forgot to warn you. But Abramchik's a regular guy. Don't you worry, Ludmilla, darling.

LUDMILLA. So you have a roommate! H'm—that's a nice wedding present! And I suppose the roommate is married!

VASYA. Who? Abram married? No—he's a confirmed bachelor.

LUDMILLA. And does he know that we're married?

VASYA. Wait . . . he doesn't know yet. But it doesn't matter. He will be very glad. My word of honor. You'll see. He'll just dance with joy.

LUDMILLA (*reproachfully*). Oh, Vasya . . .

VASYA. Really now . . . he'll be here right away and I'll tell him everything immediately: thus and so . . . got married . . . there's nothing to be afraid of. The main thing is don't you worry your little head, Ludmilla, darling. As a matter of fact, he's hardly ever at home. Where in thunder is this devilish light! He only sleeps here, see? Don't worry, we'll manage somehow. Well, see, here it is. (*He turns on the light revealing the neglected room, in contrast with their dressed-up tidiness.*) Of course one can't claim that this is any too elegant. The chief trouble, you see, there's not really too much furniture. Well, how about it, Ludmilla, darling?

LUDMILLA. As clean as a pigsty! What a frost!

VASYA. That's because the windows haven't been puttied. The cold gets in. But listen, Ludmillochka, the main thing is not to—not to get panicky. We'll fix it all up all right. Wait a while, we'll get things little by little. We'll have the windows puttied, we'll buy a lamp for the corridor, we'll sweep the floor. Everything will be swell.

LUDMILLA. So you and your roommate actually live in this . . . stable?

VASYA (without enthusiasm). Uhu . . .

LUDMILLA. What do you sleep on?

VASYA. I? I sleep on this . . . eh . . . couch. And he sleeps on the bench. And, believe it or not, it's really a very comfortable bench. It comes from Clean Pond Park. Don't you worry, Ludmillochka. If you like, I'll turn on the radio. I made it myself. It gets long distance . . . very long . . . I can get Berlin on it and everything.   Ludmillochka . . . Why don't you say something? Don't you want to talk to me?

LUDMILLA. You go and talk to your radio. I'm no loud-speaker. Joking aside, it seems to me that on ninety rubles a month we could buy a few things. Where's your quilt?

VASYA. There isn't any.

LUDMILLA. What do you cover yourself with?

VASYA. I cover myself with the overcoat. Don't worry, it's padded with cotton.

LUDMILLA. Your head is padded with cotton. I wish I'd never seen this place. Ludmillochka, Ludmillochka! And all he has is one pillow for the two of us! And what a pillow—(Lifts it as if it were a dead rat.)—the kind you hate to touch. How in the world do you and your roommate manage to sleep here?

VASYA. We manage it all right. We take turns. One day I sleep on the pillow and he sleeps on Lenin. And the next day he sleeps on the pillow and I sleep on Lenin.

LUDMILLA. And there's filth everywhere. Filth! filth! filth! A regular pigsty. Just look at the dirt here! I bet you haven't swept this room for a whole year.

VASYA (offended). Why, I swept the room myself only two weeks ago.

LUDMILLA. Have you a primus stove?

VASYA. There isn't any . . .

LUDMILLA. Awfully pleased to hear that. Just you wait, my dear husband. (Paces the room indignantly and behaves like a general disposing his forces.) I'll put the bed there! The table here! The chair there! And the other chair here! So! A runner here! The shelf here!

VASYA. That's right. There's a real housewife for you. A life's partner. Just what I need!

LUDMILLA. The plates here, and over here the curtains.

VASYA. Well, as for curtains, that seems to me a bit too much. After all that's petty bourgeois, middle-class . . .

LUDMILLA. What! Well, if that's petty bourgeois, then you had no business signing up with me. You'd better keep quiet. (Goes back to generalling.) And here we'll put the china closet. So! Ah-ha . . . You wait here and I'll run down to my sister's and bring a few things—after all, you don't expect me to sleep in this stable. Is there a broom?

VASYA. No.

LUDMILLA. Get one! Understand? And while I'm gone you sweep up the place.

VASYA. Yes.

LUDMILLA. Pussy . . . do you love me?

VASYA. One hundred per cent.

LUDMILLA. Then kiss me on my teeny-weeny nose.

VASYA. Ludmillochka! (*Seizes her in his arms.*)

LUDMILLA. Tsss . . . Have you gone mad! Let go of me! (*Struggles coyly.*)

VASYA. Ludmillochka . . . wait! Why not?

LUDMILLA. Because! Good-bye, spouse. Remember, the floor must be spotless! (LUDMILLA *departs.*)

VASYA. Spouse! So that's what I've turned into! Nice being married, Devil take it! (*Pounds the wall and shouts.*) Nikonorov . . . have you got a broom? Are you home? A brooooom? Too bad!

[TONYA *enters, pretty despite her attempt to conceal her charms under negligent mannish attire: a boy's cap over close-cropped hair, a loose overlong skirt, sweater and sheepskin mackintosh. She carries bundles of books, a toothbrush, tin cup, and other paraphernalia wrapped in a towel.*]

TONYA (*in the doorway*). Abram, are you here?

VASYA. Hasn't come yet. Well, well . . . (*Astonished.*) Is that you, Kuznetzova? Haven't seen you in ages.

TONYA. Vasya! How are you?

VASYA. Tonya . . . (*Somewhat agitated.*) You've come to see Abram?

TONYA. Yes, to Abram. Hasn't he told you anything?

VASYA. No, I haven't seen him since yesterday. Let's have a look at you. Come on, let's have a good look at you.

TONYA. I'm just the same. Just as ordinary as I always was. And you, what are you doing here?

VASYA. What am I doing here? Nothing, I just live here.

TONYA. You live here? In this room?

VASYA. Yes, in this room.

TONYA. You mean . . . together with Abram?

VASYA. Yes . . . yes . . . together with Abram . . . But now . . .

TONYA. He didn't tell me a thing about it!

VASYA. And if he had, you would have come sooner? Is that right?

TONYA. Yes, that is, not altogether . . . h'm . . . Is this Abram's corner? (*She points to the corner where the books are piled.*)

VASYA. That's Abram's.

TONYA. So . . . not bad . . . the quarters are fairly large. Where does Abram sleep?

VASYA. On the bench. This is his half and that's mine . . . Yes . . . That's how things go, Tonyechka.

TONYA. I'll sit here meanwhile.

VASYA. Yes, yes. You sit here meanwhile. Abram will be coming any minute. He always comes about this time. I also have something to tell him . . . But you know it's such a ticklish matter . . . (*Puts his head out into the corridor.*) Rabinovich! Have you a broom? No? Too bad. Who has one? In the ninth apartment? Good. (*To* TONYA.) Here, you see, we have to sweep a bit . . . otherwise it's not especially . . . And no one seems to have a broom . . . Now, look here . . . I haven't seen you in ages . . . Don't you go away now.

TONYA. I don't intend to.

VASYA. I'll be back right away. In two shakes. (*He runs off in a business-like manner.*)

TONYA (*alone*). Nothing to be done about it. Good. (*She unrolls the towel, takes out the toothbrush, tin cup, etc., and disposes them on a shelf; takes off her cap and puts on a red headkerchief; in a word, she has moved in.*)

[*Enter* ABRAM, *simply dressed in a blue high-necked Russian blouse, unshaved, his pompadour unkempt. Laboriously he carries on his back a crude work-table, more like a carpenter's bench, and some books under his arm.*]

ABRAM. Kuznetzova, are you here already? Did you get the Plotnikov book?

TONYA. We can keep it only until Tuesday at the outside. I had to give my word of honor to get it.

ABRAM. We'll have to read it together. Look, here I've finally got the famous table. And by the way, damn it all, because of the lousy Marriage Registry I was late to a Communist Youth meeting. Were you late, too? I ask you now, why was the damn ceremony necessary? As if we couldn't live together without registering! Who gets any good out of it anyhow?

TONYA. It's a concession to the petty bourgeoisie and to the prosperous peasantry.

ABRAM. Yes . . . Where shall I put the blamed table?

TONYA. I think the best place is probably under the lamp so that we'll be able to read. Here, let me help you. Like this. That's right. Thank you. (*She takes off her mackintosh, spreads it on the table like a blanket, lies down, supporting herself on her elbows to read.*) By the way, I think there is another comrade living in this room. You haven't told me about it.

ABRAM. Oy! I clean forgot about it. What did you say? But don't worry, Kuznetzova, it's just a trifle. He's a regular guy. It's only Vaska.

TONYA. I hope he's not married.

ABRAM. Who? Vaska married! He's a confirmed bachelor.

TONYA. Yes, I know him.

ABRAM. Has he been here already?

TONYA. He ran off to find a broom. He'll be back right away.

ABRAM. Listen, Kuznetzova, have you told him already that we've registered?

TONYA. No. But he's been looking at me all the time in such a funny way . . . that I think he has guessed . . .

ABRAM. You think he's guessed? Oy, that's too bad. And say, have you had any dinner today? (TONYA *shakes her head negatively.*) Gee, how I want to eat! Maybe Vaska has something. (*He explores.*) Sausage! Kuznetzova, what do you think, if I were to take some of his sausage, would it be ethical or unethical?

TONYA. Unethical.

ABRAM. But he's a regular guy.

TONYA. Is that so! And I thought quite the contrary. I thought that I had noticed symptoms of unhealthy bourgeois degeneration: a striped bow-tie, Nepman boots, and in general he looks like a bridegroom from the Sukharev Market.

ABRAM. Does he really look like a bridegroom? As a matter of fact, come to think of it, I have noticed for a long time that Vaska has been degenerating. All the same, we must come to some agreement with him in this matter of our marriage. I think that he can only welcome it. (*Sighs.*) So I mustn't take Vaska's sausage? Or may I take it, perhaps? Well, Kuznetzova, what do you *really* think? Or is it altogether unethical?

TONYA. I think we can probably get together enough money to buy four hundred grams of our own sausage. Have you any money?

ABRAM. After buying the table, I have only twelve kopecks and I need eight for tomorrow's car-fare.

TONYA. I have a little bit too. Wait . . .

five, ten, and here's some more . . . thirty-nine kopecks. Let me have your money. I think there's a stand around the corner. I'll run down right away.

ABRAM. Why should you run down and not I? After all, I'm your husband.

TONYA. Husband! Abram, I beg you, no bourgeois tricks, please. You bought and dragged the table—I shall go for the food.

ABRAM. Mutual understanding, equitable division of labor, and workers' solidarity.

TONYA. Precisely.

ABRAM. In that case I don't object. (TONYA goes out.) What is needed for a durable marriage? (Counts on his fingers.) Class consciousness, a common political platform, labor solidarity . . . Is there character similarity? There is. Is there mutual understanding? There is. Is there membership in the same class? There certainly is. Is there a common political platform? How could it be otherwise? Is there labor solidarity? And how! Then what is lacking? Love, perhaps? Why, that's a social prejudice! A lot of banana oil, rotten idealism . . . and by the way . . . (Sniffing hungrily.) Ugh! The room reeks of sausage. Should I? Or is it unethical? . . . Is it?

[VASYA enters with a broom; is embarrassed when he sees his roommate.]

VASYA. Oh, so you're here already. (He begins to sweep, more and more embarrassed. To himself.) I must tell him at once.

ABRAM (to himself). I must inform him. (To VASYA.) Hello, there.

VASYA. Hello! Listen, Abram. (To himself.) How awkward! (To ABRAM.) You see, Abram, it's like this . . . By the way, Kuznetzova has been waiting. Have you seen her yet?

ABRAM (disturbed). Well, what of it? Well, she was waiting and is not waiting any longer. What of it?

VASYA. But no, I said it just so, by the way.

ABRAM. By the way!

VASYA. By the way . . . Abram . . .

ABRAM. Well, hasn't she told you anything?

VASYA. Nothing, why?

ABRAM. Nothing. I said it just so, by the way.

VASYA. By the way? Aha . . . Abram, I see you have brought yourself a funny table.

ABRAM. Well, it's a mere trifle. (To himself.) I must tell him. (To VASYA.) By the way, about the table . . . I must ask you one question that involves a matter of principle.

VASYA. Well? (To himself.) I think he's guessed.

ABRAM (desperately, with gloomy resolution). Vaska . . . Would you admit that three people can live in this room?

VASYA (equally desperately). What's the point?

ABRAM. I'm asking you, would it be ethical or unethical?

VASYA. Of course it would be ethical. What else could be done about it? I've always considered you a regular guy. You understand . . .

ABRAM (overjoyed). That's right, Vaska. That's just why I like you so much. Thanks, old man, I knew you wouldn't fail me. I give you my honest word as a Communist Youth that I shall try not to crowd you.

VASYA (with tears of tender emotion). Thanks, pal; thanks, Abram. I've always said that you were one hundred per cent a regular guy. I certainly hope that I will not crowd you.

ABRAM. Nonsense! Trifles! You can never crowd me. What worries me is that I may . . .

VASYA. Still, you know, there'll be all kinds of curtains, canary birds in cages, this and that . . . Although, of course, she's a pretty good kid.

ABRAM. Shake, comrade. I'm so glad that you approve of her.

VASYA. Thanks, thanks. I was certain that you would be frightfully glad.

ABRAM. Why, of course, my dear fellow, why, of course. I should think so. How could it be otherwise? How could it be otherwise?

VASYA. Still, you know, she likes to dance a bit, and to cut capers . . . To a certain extent, you know, she is sort of . . . shall I say . . . petty bourgeois.

ABRAM. Who's bourgeois?

VASYA. She.

ABRAM. Kuznetzova?

VASYA. What has Kuznetzova to do with it?

ABRAM (*losing courage*). Quite right, quite right. She has absolutely nothing to do with it. I said it just so, by the way. You know, one word leads to another, but please don't think of it. It's only that Kuznetzova has gone to the store to buy some sausage and there's nothing . . .

VASYA. For sausage? Kuznetzova?

ABRAM. Well, yes. And why shouldn't she go for sausage? There she is; ask her yourself. (*Enter* TONYA.) We've just been arguing about you. Vaska said that you hadn't gone for the sausage. And I said that you did go for sausage . . . Hi, hi . . . Such a silly misunderstanding. (*Desperately, winking to* TONYA.) Incidentally, are you acquainted with Vaska?

TONYA. Sure, we're acquainted.

VASYA (*sweeping altogether too industriously and dustily*). We have met.

TONYA (*sotto voce, to* ABRAM). Have you told him?

ABRAM (*also under his breath*). It just won't come out. My tongue won't move. Kuznetzova, please do me a real favor—you tell him.

TONYA. I?

ABRAM. Oh, yes. It's too embarrassing for me.

TONYA. I don't understand this futile delicacy. This is a very simple matter. There's nothing terrible about it. Just walk right up and explain everything.

ABRAM. It's easy to say, explain everything. Go yourself and explain everything.

TONYA. Why should I? You're the husband, aren't you?

ABRAM. Kuznetzova. no bourgeois tricks.

TONYA. If you want to know, here's how the matter stands: I went for the sausage—you must tell him.

ABRAM. Equitable division of labor?

TONYA. Precisely.

ABRAM. It means that I must walk straight up and explain honestly.

TONYA. Walk straight up and explain honestly.

ABRAM. Or is it unethical?

TONYA. It's ethical.

ABRAM. Ugh! I'll go straight up and explain honestly. Ugh! (*He approaches* VASYA.) Listen, old man, it's like this. I'd like to talk seriously to you about something . . . M'm . . . By the way . . . Why did you get all dressed up today? You look like a bridegroom.

VASYA. I! A bridegroom? How do you make that out?

ABRAM. Well, well. I'm joking. I know very well that you're a confirmed bachelor. And incidentally, talking about bachelors . . . that is, I mean about bridegrooms . . . that is, by the way, about marriage in general . . .

VASYA (*very embarrassed and sullen*). What do you mean, marriage?

ABRAM. Wait, wait, old man. The main thing is, don't get angry . . . Well, two of us have lived together, and now three of us will live together. (*Disparagingly.*) Think of it, what a tragedy! If I were you, for example, I'd be mighty glad of it.

VASYA. You'd be glad?

ABRAM. Why not? It will be much jollier.

VASYA. Abram, are you saying this seriously?

ABRAM. Most seriously.

VASYA. Shake, comrade! (*Very vigorous handshaking.*)

ABRAM. One might say, seriously and for a long time. Even signed up in the Marriage Registry.

VASYA. Registered! Registered! Of course, according to form! You know there was a funny man there sitting at a marriage table, you understand, the fellow with the mustache. He made a speech.

ABRAM. Right, right. He made a speech. Wait a minute, wait . . . And how do you know about it?

VASYA. What do you mean, how do I know about it? And who do you think registered today if it wasn't I?

ABRAM. *You* registered? Wait a while—it is I who have registered.

VASYA. You? You also registered?

ABRAM. What do you mean, I also? Not also, but in the first place.

VASYA. Abram, then that means that both of us . . . today . . . re . . .

ABRAM. Registered. Tss . . .

VASYA. . . . gistered.

ABRAM. Kuznetzova, the most awful smash-up has occurred. Have you heard?

[TONYA *has long been standing with a petrified face, buried in a book, as if completely absorbed in it.*]

TONYA. Yes . . . no . . . what is it? Have you told him?

ABRAM. I've told him all right. And how!

TONYA. Does he object?

ABRAM. Object! What do you mean object? It's worse; he doesn't object. And what's more, he is solidly with us to the extent of a hundred and twenty per cent . . .

TONYA. Why do you complain, then? What are you excited about? I don't understand. If he is solid with us, so much the better. If there are three of us, then there will be three of us. And the three of us will make the best of it.

ABRAM (*almost shouting*). Three of us! She says three of us! Kuznetzova . . .

TONYA. What is it? Have you anything against the three of us living together?

ABRAM. Three of us living together . . . Kuznetzova, throw the book away. Think of what's happened.

TONYA. I don't understand a thing.

ABRAM. She doesn't understand! Tonka, understand!

TONYA. Well.

ABRAM. He . . .

TONYA. Yes?

ABRAM. My tongue won't move. Let me have my share of the sausage. I want to stuff myself, Kuznetzova. Well, do you understand?

TONYA. Don't understand a thing. Please don't bother me; I'm reading.

ABRAM. At such a time, she reads! Kuznetzova!

TONYA. Drink a glass of water.

ABRAM. I'll guzzle the whole water system. Even two water systems. (*He's exhausted with excitement.*)

[*The clatter of a bicycle crashing in the corridor.*]

LUDMILLA (*from the corridor*). Vasya! Vasyuk! We've lost our way here. I ripped my skirt on something here. Well, where in the world are you?

VASYA (*in terror*). Ludmillochka! (*To* ABRAM *and* TONYA.) Comrades, she'll eat me up. The Devil take you all! (*Shouting towards the corridor.*) Oh, that's only the bicycle. (*To* ABRAM *in a sibilant whisper.*) You should have thought of it before getting registered. (*Shouting into the doorway.*) Right away, Ludmillochka. (*To* ABRAM.) I wish you'd croak! Rrr . . . (*He goes out.*)

TONYA. What's all the noise about? Who has come?

ABRAM. That's for Vaska. Some responsible Communist Youth has come . . . to call on him.

[*Enter* LUDMILLA, *half-smothered by pillows, blankets, other household goods which she is carrying; followed by her young nephew* SASHA, *a Red Pioneer, khaki-clad and with the red neckerchief of this children's organization;* SASHA *too is laden with a birdcage, cheap framed pictures and other staples of domestic bliss; behind them the distracted* VASYA *with odds and ends of bundles.*]

LUDMILLA. I nearly ripped my skirt to pieces. You simply must have the lamp by tomorrow. Sasha, don't break the lampshade! Don't crawl all over my feet. Oh, my God, what an impossible child! Put the things here and don't upset the darling canary.

TONYA (*to* ABRAM). So this is the responsible organizer?

ABRAM. Well, yes . . . That is, she is not yet altogether responsible. Why do you look at me like that?

TONYA. Why has she come with all those bundles?

ABRAM. What a strange person you are, Kuznetzova. Must you know everything? Why? That's her own affair. Maybe she's moving to the country and on the way she's dropping in to say good-bye to a comrade.

TONYA. Going to the country—in January?

ABRAM. Well, in two weeks it will be February. But that's not the point. Oh, Kuznetzova, you better read and not pay attention to anybody.

TONYA (*looks at* LUDMILLA *and shrugs her shoulders*). H'm . . . So that's that.

ABRAM. Complete smash-up.

LUDMILLA (*peremptorily, to* VASYA). And who are these?

VASYA. This, my dear little Ludmilla, is Abram. Haven't you ever met him before? Abram, come here and I shall introduce you to Ludmilla.

ABRAM. Well, how do you do? I am Abram. (*They shake hands.*)

LUDMILLA. And who is that one?

ABRAM. That . . .

VASYA. Tss . . . This, my dear little Ludmilla . . . so to say . . . a very good old acquaintance of Abramchik's . . . She's come here to visit . . . to have a little talk . . . to take tea . . . Never mind her . . . Isn't that right, Abram? (*Making desperate signs to him.*)

ABRAM. Well, yes . . . a very good acquaintance . . . That's clear . . . Don't you disturb yourself . . .

LUDMILLA. But why the funny table? How did it get here?

VASYA. How did it get here . . . Abram . . . Why the funny table? (*Desperately winking.*)

ABRAM. Why the funny table? She brought it with her, of course. Such a queer girl she is. *Such* a queer girl. It's January and she insists on moving to the country. Such a queer girl. She ran in to say good-bye.

TONYA (*hearing him*). Abram, what does all this mean?

ABRAM. Ah . . . it means . . . Kuznetzova . . . it means that the most stupendous smash-up has occurred. (*In a hoarse whisper.*) They also registered today.

TONYA (*slightly stunned*). Where?

ABRAM. In the Marriage Registry Bureau.

TONYA (*not yet recovered*). What for?

ABRAM. Just another concession to the petty bourgeoisie and to the prosperous peasantry. Do you think that only you and I are such smart-alecks? Kuz- 10 netzova, do you understand what has happened?

TONYA. I begin to understand.

LUDMILLA (*pointing disgustedly to* TONYA). Vasya, why is she spread out here in the middle of the room? She's in my way. I have to straighten things out. Tell her so.

VASYA. Oh, let her alone, Ludmilla. Let her alone. There you are . . . Let 20 her lie and don't pay any attention to her.

LUDMILLA. What do you mean, don't pay any attention! If I don't pay any attention and let things go, then she'll move in on us. Why, she's occupying most of our living-space already. Impudent creature! I'll tell her myself right away. Let her come and call on us tomorrow, not today.   30

VASYA. Ludmillochka, for God's sake . . .

LUDMILLA. And I'll do it too.

VASYA. Ludmillochka, I beg you . . . I must tell you . . . But don't be angry, please. Of course you won't get angry . . . You see, the thing is that Abram also got married today . . . to her.

LUDMILLA. What! Wha-at! (*Thunder and 40 lightning. She drops a bundle of bedding and collapses on it.*)

VASYA. That's life for you . . .

LUDMILLA. You shameless deceiver! Don't you dare touch me!

VASYA. Ludmillochka, my precious one.

LUDMILLA. Go away! I hate you!

VASYA. My sugar . . .

LUDMILLA. Go away, go away, go away, go away, go away!!! (*She stamps her feet and weeps buckets.*)

VASYA. Ludmillochka! Ludichka! Milichka! Ah . . . I wish you'd all sink in the mud—may you croak . . . My sugar, my pussy-cat . . .

ABRAM. Kuznetzova, here before your face you see a smash-up.

TONYA. Trifles. There's room for all of us here. Nothing terrible.

ABRAM. Four in one room?

TONYA. I can go away if you wish.

ABRAM. Where to? What do you mean, you can go away? Have you a place where you can spend the night? Why, it's Siberian weather outside. I can't let you go.

TONYA. I should like to see you stop me from going.

ABRAM. Cut out the nonsense. After all, I *am* your husband.

TONYA. Now, now—none of those bourgeois tricks.

ABRAM. Kuznetzova, I beg of you. After all, you know, we do have labor solidarity, and where in thunder will I get the Plotnikov book if you desert me?

TONYA (*persuaded by this incontrovertible logic*). Very well . . .

VASYA. On my word of honor I don't know what in hell to do. Kuznetzova, maybe you can exert some influence on her.

TONYA (*goes up to* LUDMILLA, *assumes the attitude of an earnest soap-boxer about to exhort a hostile mob, one foot forward, hands behind back; clears her throat and begins to orate*). Comrade, what is to be done? What is to be done now that this unprecedented and annoying situation has arisen? Are you a member of the All-Union League of Communist Youth? Are you . . .

VASYA (*in desperation*). She's not a member so far.

ABRAM. I've always said that our agitation among the non-members isn't worth a damn.

LUDMILLA (*through tears*). This is not to the point . . . My grandfather is a hero of labor.

ABRAM. All the more reason not to weep.

LUDMILLA (*begins to unburden her soul*). Yesterday evening, as soon as we met, comrades, he began to tell me all sorts of things until my head turned around—now don't interrupt, Vasya —and of course in the end he made me altogether dizzy. He says to me— keep quiet! (*Poor* VASYA *hasn't the least intention of interrupting.*)—Dear little Ludmilla, he says, let's live together; let's keep house. You, he says, come over and move into my room. I have, he says, a lot of living-space and a loud-speaker of my own construction, and a gas range—shut up, Vasya, you know you said it—He says, I have this and that and I listened to him, listened and then, fool that I am, went off with him like an idiot to get registered. And now it's a nice mess! Now I see that he shares his living-space with someone else, that there is no electric bulb in the corridor, that the someone else is married, and as for the gas range, if there is one I haven't seen it. Maybe he meant his bicycle.

VASYA. I'll show you the kitchen . . .

LUDMILLA. Yeh . . . I'll bet there are a thousand families in the kitchen.

VASYA (*softly*). No, only twelve. (*Tries to caress her.*)

LUDMILLA. Go away!

VASYA. Oh, let's make up, Ludmillochka.

LUDMILLA. Go away, go away. Let go of me. I'm going away . . . I'm going away this minute. (*But doesn't budge.*)

VASYA. Ludmillochka, after all, I'm your husband.

LUDMILLA. My husband! You're my calamity, my first big mistake!

VASYA. So that means you're going to stay?

LUDMILLA. And where am I to go? My sister has four people in one room. Of course, I must stay. What else can I do? But don't you dare look at me— or touch me! (*Nevertheless they clinch affectionately.*)

ABRAM. And what can you do with a girl like that?

VASYA. Never mind . . .

ABRAM. Well, I guess we'll have to live together. As they say, we're four in a boat. Now, let's do something about it.

LUDMILLA (*brightening after the storm*). Yes —we'll have to put up a partition. Right from the door. We can divide it into equal halves.

VASYA. Gee! You're a smart one, Ludmillochka. That's a corking idea!

ABRAM. That's right. I'm with you. Kuznetzova, have you heard it?

TONYA (*engrossed in her book*). Heard what?

VASYA. It has been proposed to put up a partition.

TONYA. No objections on my part.

ABRAM. Passed unanimously.

LUDMILLA. For a time being, we can mark it with chalk. Vaska, have you any chalk?

VASYA. Yes, here it is.

LUDMILLA. Draw the border-line. From there right to here, and you shove over a little. (*This is for the benefit of* TONYA.)

TONYA. With pleasure. (*She moves the table to* ABRAM'S *side of the room.*)

VASYA. In two shakes, sugar. Drafting is the first thing they taught us at the Institute. So, and so, and so. (*He's drafting on the floor.*)

ABRAM. This is a rare experiment in building socialism in one room.

VASYA. Look what came out of this. Just look. It's a beauty. Simply marvellous. Five minutes—and presto! A two-room apartment. There's American tempo for you.

LUDMILLA. Look, Vasyuk, we'll have a wonderful room. Isn't that so?

VASYA. You see, there was no sense in 10 grumbling.

LUDMILLA. Comrades, neighbors, this is our half—and that is your half. Vasya, push the bench into their room. (*He does.*) That's right. Now come here. Here we'll have our bed, here the table, and here the two chairs. Do you like that, pussykin?

VASYA (*who, much relieved, is busying himself with the radio*). Very nice, and do 20 you like it?

LUDMILLA. I like it awfully! (*Interfering with his beloved radio; whispers.*) And do you love me? I love you awfully, awfully. And you me?

VASYA. Sure. (*Glances longingly at the radio.*)

LUDMILLA. Then kiss your wifie on her teeny-weeny nose. (*Whispering.*) They don't see us. (VASYA *kisses her. Little* 30 SASHA *is not even shocked.*) There, Sashka, time for you to go home.

[VASYA *fusses with the radio while* LUDMILLA, *humming happily, begins to turn her half of the barnlike room into a home; nonchalantly she tosses old papers, rags, etc., into* TONYA'S *half as if it were infinite space.* TONYA, *lifting eyes from her book, notices this procedure; first she shrugs, but finally registers her protest; demonstratively* 40 *she climbs down from her table, takes the mackintosh and shakes its dust into* LUDMILLA'S *half. The women glare at each other;* TONYA *replaces the coat and goes back to education.* ABRAM *meanwhile divides his admiring glances between* LUD-MILLA'S *domestic talents and the tempting sausage.* VASYA *has some difficulty finding his radio station, which gives the audience bits from programs from many Soviet stations, with plenty of static whining in between.* SASHA *is fascinated by the radio.*]

VOICES ON THE RADIO. Hello! Hello! Hello! Workers, peasants and Red Army men . . . (*A snatch of "Stenka Razin," switching abruptly to "Volga Boatmen Song" played by balalaikas.*) . . . Religion is the opiate of the people. Science instead of superstition. The unbroken work-week and abolition of Sunday. Comrades . . . Whizzzz . . . (*Too many stations at once: a jumble of words scrambled with music.*) . . . President Goovyer and fat American exploiters . . . Poincaré—war . . . C.A.T.—cat . . . R.A. . . . Workers, peasants and Red Army men . . . American combines . . . Diapers should be washed immediately and . . . down with sabotage and intervention . . . and the prevention of venereal diseases. (*A blast of confused noises that eventually clarifies into "Budenny's March."*) . . . Socialist competition . . . results in . . . Brrr . . . Whizzz.

VASYA (*has finally got what he's looking for*). There it is.

VOICE ON THE RADIO. Hello! Hello! Hello! Moscow speaking. Comintern Station transmitting on a wavelength of ten hundred and fifty metres. Broadcasting from the Great Academic Theatre the opera Eugene Onyegin. Hello! hello! You may now listen to the audience. (*Sounds of the orchestra tuning in; hubbub of muffled voices. Then everything quiets down.*) It hasn't begun yet, comrade radio listeners. It will begin in five or ten minutes. Stand by your radios. Please send your comments to the Radio

Broadcasting Trust. For the time be-ing we are signing off . . .

LUDMILLA. Vasya, shut off the radio or the kid'll never leave. Go, go! Tell mother that everything is all right. That she needn't worry. Everything is all right. (SASHA, *wrapped in coats, scarfs and sweaters like a mummy, is pushed through the door.* VASYA *disposes himself on the mattress, picks up a guitar, strums* 10 *and sings a doleful Russian love song. As he sings, his eyes keep travelling to* TONYA, *still buried in her book.* LUDMILLA *suspects it.*) Terrible light. I'll fix it right away. (*She mounts a chair and covers the bulb with a colored handkerchief.*) Isn't this better, pussykin? (*Sits down and re-clines over him.*) Do you love me, dar-ling? They can't see us.

TONYA. Now, please, comrade, I wish 20 you would open our half of the light; otherwise it's impossible to read.

LUDMILLA (*acidly polite*). Excuse me. (*She uncovers one half.*) Can you see now?

TONYA. I can see very well, thank you. (*She continues to read.*)

[ABRAM *is ostensibly reading, but following* LUDMILLA'S *every move.* VASYA *continues his strumming.* LUDMILLA *goes back to the couch and in a cattish whisper, with gesture* 30 *toward* TONYA.]

LUDMILLA. Vasya, she's not bad-looking, but she dresses so shabbily.

VASYA. M'm . . .

LUDMILLA. Have you known her very long?

VASYA. M'm . . . two years.

LUDMILLA. And you haven't fallen in love with her?

VASYA. M'm . . . 40

LUDMILLA. Tell your little pussy "Meow." (*She imitates a cat to perfection.*)

VASYA (*perfunctorily*). Meow!

LUDMILLA. Come on, kiss pussykin. They can't see us.

ABRAM. I'm frightfully hungry. Vaska!

Haven't you anything a fellow can munch?

VASYA. I have some sausage.

ABRAM. Let's have the sausage.

LUDMILLA. Wait a minute, comrades. That's not proper. Let's do it respect-ably. I brought something from sis-ter's. Here are some rolls and we can make tea. Would you like to have some tea? (*She revels in the rôle of gener-ous hostess.*)

ABRAM. Oh-ho, oh-ho, and how! Kuz-netzova, have you heard? The motion has been made and seconded that we drink tea with rolls.

TONYA. I really don't know about that.

LUDMILLA. Please don't be bashful.

TONYA. Thanks, of course. But we have none of these things. We've no cups . . . spoons . . . forks . . .

LUDMILLA. Never mind! Never mind! Until you get your own, you may use ours. Isn't that right, pussykin? You don't object to their using ours, do you, pussykin?

VASYA. Of course not.

ABRAM. Motion unanimously carried.

LUDMILLA (*taking the kerosene primus stove*). Where is the kitchen here?

VASYA. Let me take it. I'll go down with it.

ABRAM. Comrades, this is not the correct procedure. Perhaps I too desire to participate in this building of social-ism in two halves of one room. Let me have the primus. Equitable division of labor. (*To* LUDMILLA.) You will in-struct me a bit how to use it. Kuznet-zova, you must also assume your share of civic responsibility.

LUDMILLA (*giggling*). What a funny fel-low you are! You're holding the stove upside down. You mustn't hold the stove like this—but like that. (*Fixes it for him, bursting with laughter.* ABRAM *basks in her attentions.*)

ABRAM. And how do you light it?

LUDMILLA. This is how you light it. Do you see this little saucer? You pump a little kerosene into it. And do you see this little screw? You turn it. Then you take a wire and clean the top. Do you understand?

ABRAM. I understand. You take the pump. Then you clean the saucer and then you buy the kerosene . . .

LUDMILLA. Oh—you don't understand anything. Come on, I'll show you everything. (*To* VASYA.) Pussykin, you won't be jealous, will you? (*To* TONYA.) Would you mind getting the dishes ready meanwhile?

TONYA. Yes, but I don't know where and how.

LUDMILLA. Vasya, you help her. (*To* ABRAM.) Come on, show me that kitchen of yours. (*Takes his hand.*) I'm going to hold on to you because there's that bicycle out there.

ABRAM (*swinging the primus*). You hold on. Pump . . . then the pumping . . . the screw . . . in one word, super-industrialization. (*They go out.*)

VOICE OVER THE RADIO. Hello! Hello! This is the Grand Opera.

[*During the beginning of the following scene, the radio transmits a soft romantic overture.*]

TONYA. Well, show me where you keep things here.

VASYA. Take the basket. The glasses are there. Get them out. Careful!

TONYA. Don't worry.

VASYA. That's how things go, Tony-echka Kuznetzova. (*Contemplatively.*) How many summers? How many winters?

TONYA (*avoids looking at him*). About a year. Where shall I put the rolls?

VASYA. About . . . Oh, you can put the rolls on a plate. It was a wonderful winter, wasn't it?

TONYA. What shall I do with the teapot?

VASYA. Put tea in it. Do you ever still go to the Clean Pond skating-rink?

TONYA. No, no—I haven't even thought about such things.

VASYA. You haven't thought of it? Stop, what are you doing? Why, you've poured out all the tea. Let me show you—like this . . . (*Wistfully.*) And do you remember, Tonka, how you and I nearly got killed on that sleigh gliding down Sparrow Hill?

TONYA (*making a brave effort to be indifferent*). Why do you look at me like that?

VASYA. A year . . . only one year. I have a wife, you have a husband. Do you love Abram very much?

TONYA. It seems to me that this is my personal affair. Where shall I put the sugar?

VASYA. Why do you blush, then?

TONYA. I ask you, where shall I put the sugar?

VASYA. Put it . . . anywhere . . .

TONYA. Please stop looking at me!

VASYA (*sighs*). That's how things go, Tonyechka. And do you remember that tree at the park? The tenth one from the end, counting from the side of the ash-can? Do you know, Tony-echka, after that I spent the whole night long . . . you know . . . and the next day I wandered through the streets of Moscow like a lunatic . . . I remember how the snow fell. It just plastered my chest . . . and the eye-lashes, you know, with such little needles . . . Ekh, a whole year . . . Easy to say . . . And you, you're the same as you've always been . . . Yes, yes, don't turn away . . . The same strand of hair over the ear peeking from under your head-kerchief. (TONYA *quickly tucks away this strand of hair.*) Where have you been all this time?

TONYA. I was working in the country.

VASYA. What a lovely lock of hair!

TONYA. Let's go. Stop this nonsense. I'm asking you, where shall I put the sugar?

VASYA. To hell with the sugar! Put it where you like. Bygones are bygones . . . Tonyechka . . . wonder what will happen next?

TONYA. I'm putting it in a little jar.

[LUDMILLA *and* ABRAM *return with the primus and tea-kettle; both of them are in gay spirits and a little flushed.*]

ABRAM. It's finally boiled but after great difficulties. She's been instructing me so well, comrades, that now I could set fire not only to one primus, but to a whole factory of primuses.

LUDMILLA (*laughing*). Oh—I can't stand it any longer. He's a scream, this Abramchick. You can simply die laughing with him.

TONYA (*firmly, to* VASYA). I've put it in a little jar . . .

LUDMILLA. Well, how are things with you folks? Is everything done?

VASYA. Everything. But where shall we put the sugar?

LUDMILLA. Why, you haven't done a thing. Is this the way to prepare tea? You haven't cut the sausage. You haven't even opened the bag of rolls. You haven't even taken out the bread. You're a perfectly useless little pair. Let me do it! I'll fix everything right away! Comrade Abram, you sit right here. You deserve a rest, dear boy.

ABRAM. After toiling in the sweat of my brow.

LUDMILLA. And you, Comrade Tonya, sit down beside your husband. And I shall sit beside *my* darling husband. Like this. Now we shall all drink tea.

[*Enter* EMILIAN, *the hulking athletic poet; his long arms swinging like an ape's.*]

EMILIAN. Listen, brethren, can I spend the night here? (*Noticing the company.*) Oh-ho! So you're having a regular banquet here, with a couple of girls. (*Comes up to* LUDMILLA, *and then to* TONYA *and peers at them brazenly.*) Not so bad, not so bad! They'll do in a pinch! I have the pleasure to introduce myself. (*To* TONYA.) Have you heard of Pushkin?

TONYA. I have.

EMILIAN (*to* LUDMILLA). Have you heard of Tolstoy?

LUDMILLA. I have.

EMILIAN (*to* TONYA). Have you heard of Dostoievsky?

TONYA. I have.

EMILIAN (*to* LUDMILLA). Have you heard of Shakespeare?

LUDMILLA. I have.

EMILIAN (*to* TONYA). Have you heard of Maxim Gorki?

TONYA. I have.

EMILIAN (*to both of them, throwing out his chest*). Have you heard of Emilian Chernoziomny?

TONYA *and* LUDMILLA. No—I haven't.

EMILIAN. Well, look at me, then. In me you behold Emilian, the poet of the masses. Now you understand? I can beat anybody at verse-writing. Have you heard my latest poem? Everybody listen: It's called "The Izvostchik." (*Recites in bellowing voice.*)

"Ekh, the city has gnawed me to pieces
I will not see my native moon
I will tear my collar wide-open
That I may hang myself soon.

"I was a gay tempestuous fellow,
In golden curls my head,
But now I am perishing, master,
Because Moscow has nibbled me dead."

And if you dare me I'll show you how st-r-rong I am. (*Doubles his arm and presents it to* TONYA *who touches it gingerly.*)

Here, feel this. Don't be bashful. (*Generously offers it also to* LUDMILLA, *who is not so gingerly and shows admiration.*) And look at this chest! (*Bangs it.*) I can beat anybody at physical culture as well as poetry. Think I'm lying?

ABRAM. Now, he's at it—we'll never stop him.

EMILIAN. Well, brethren and sistern, can I spend the night here? 10

VASYA. That's a bad guess, old man. You see, it's like this: we all got married!

EMILIAN. Who-o-o-?

VASYA. Both of us. Abram and I. So that, comrade, the car is full-up.

EMILIAN. No! Are you serious?

ABRAM. It's a fact.

EMILIAN. When did you do it?

VASYA. I married her, that is Ludmilla, and Abram married Kuznetzova— 20 her over there. So that . . .

EMILIAN. Wait, boys and girls. Here are extemporaneous verses. Listen! H'mm . . . (*Recites.*)
"The kids are spliced, they've lost their head—O!
And frisk like calves in fertile meadow;
Only Emilian, the masses' poet
Lacks a bride but doesn't know it."

ABRAM. Pretty rotten . . . 30

EMILIAN. Let's see you do it better, wiseacre. Well, good-bye.

VASYA. Where are you bound for? Have some tea!

EMILIAN. Forget it! I'm hastening to draw the appropriate organizational conclusions. (*He rushes out.*)

ABRAM. Have you ever seen anybody as crazy as that? He has run away to spread the news. He'll spread it everywhere 40 too. Well, the meeting will continue.

TONYA. It's evident that he's one of the decadent school of poets. (*Pause.*)

LUDMILLA. The radio plays so beautifully. (*Pause.*)

ABRAM. Quiet family happiness. (*Pause.*)

[VASYA *and* TONYA *begin a Communist student song;* VASYA *accompanies with guitar;* LUDMILLA *and* ABRAM *are chiefly engaged with their food and covert glances at each other; but they join the choruses with full mouths.*]

VASYA *and* TONYA.
If in studies he surpasses
Tsimla-la, tsimla-la,
Then he's from the working classes,
Tsimla-la, tsimla-la.

ALTOGETHER.
Tsimla, tsimla, tsimla-la,
Tsimla-la, tsimla-la,
Tsimla, tsimla, tsimla-la,
Tsimla-la, tsimla-la.

VASYA.
If the girl is very pretty
Tsimla-la, tsimla-la,
I am bound to sing this ditty
Tsimla-la, tsimla-la.

ALTOGETHER (LUDMILLA *casts suspicious glances at* VASYA *and* TONYA *as they repeat the same chorus*).

TONYA.
A red communistic fellow
Tsimla-la, tsimla-la,
Should not wed a girl that's yellow
Tsimla-la, tsimla-la.

ALTOGETHER (*sing same chorus.* LUDMILLA, *by now really jealous and insulted, withers* TONYA *with a glance and goes up to* VASYA, *caressing his hair—claiming her property, as it were.*)

VASYA (*continuing to look at* TONYA).
If she looks at him intensely,
Tsimla-la, tsimla-la,
Then she loves the boy immensely
Tsimla-la, tsimla-la.

LUDMILLA (*interrupts the singing, attempting to draw* VASYA *from the risky flirtation with* TONYA). Vasyuk, darling, tell your pussykin "Meow"! Right away, say "Meow"!

VASYA (*barks out in annoyance*). Meow!

CURTAIN

ACT II

The room is now split into two distinct "apartments." The dividing line is formed— reckoning from the rear of the stage—by a rose-colored screen, one panel of which serves as a door between the two apartments; then the massive brown Russian cupboard, nearly ceiling-high, then a small table, the space above which is filled in with a flimsy canary-colored curtain. The two apartments are sharply contrasted. The left half, under 10 LUDMILLA'S *control, is garishly "bourgeois"; it has flowered wallpaper, a strip of rug, decorations on the walls, the couch gaudily covered and stacked with cushions, a little table with a potted plant, the canary cage hanging where once hung a lowly sausage, etc.; the cupboard faces this paradise of* LUDMILLA'S *and is obviously well provisioned; an artificial rose in a drinking-glass adorns the ledge of the cupboard; everything here is spic and span and* 20 *excessively homey. The right half,* TONYA'S *apartment, is as bleak as before; in fact, bleaker by contrast; the garden bench has been shoved against the wall; the floor and walls are bare and not too clean; the table is well to the fore, with the old stool near it; piles of books and papers on the floor and on the bench; the only decoration is the toothbrush sticking out of a tin cup on the wall-shelf; the ugly back of the cupboard faces this half.* 30
The curtain, however, opens only on the left "apartment," leaving the other half as yet concealed from the audience. LUDMILLA *is putting finishing touches on her proud house-cleaning, then—as she talks—busies herself with hanging large homely portraits of an old man and an old woman on the flowered wall, stepping back to admire her handiwork.* VASYA, *evidently bored, lounges among the cushions and strums his guitar. He notices the portraits.* 40

VASYA (*pointing*). Who is this?

LUDMILLA. This is my grandma—a housewife by trade.

VASYA. Grandma?

LUDMILLA. Grandma.

VASYA. Grandma!

LUDMILLA. Grandma. And this is grandpa, hero of labor, a promoted worker.

VASYA. Promoted worker?

LUDMILLA. Promoted worker. Pussykin! You've put your dirty boots on the clean bed-spread. Aren't you ashamed of yourself? Do take your feet off.

VASYA (*reluctantly takes his feet off*). Grandma and grandpa. H'm . . .

LUDMILLA. Pussykin, do you love me?

VASYA. And you me?

LUDMILLA. I love you, and you?

VASYA. I love you too.

LUDMILLA. Very much?

VASYA. Very much.

LUDMILLA. Very, *very* much?

VASYA. Very, very much.

LUDMILLA. Very, very, *very* much?

VASYA (*somewhat irritated*). Very, very, very, very much.

LUDMILLA. Well, then show me how much you love me. So much? (*Indicates with her hands.*)

VASYA. So much. (*Indicates a little more.*)

LUDMILLA. And I love you this much. (*Goes him one better with her hands.*) How much do you love me?

VASYA (*suppressing a growl with difficulty and stretching his hands full length*). Yes, I love you this much.

LUDMILLA. Well, then, kiss me on my teeny-weeny nose. (*He does, obediently.*) And now I shall kiss *you* on *your* teeny-weeny nose. (*She pecks him and gazes admiringly.*) Will you have some warm milk, pussykin? Don't you want some warm milk?

VASYA. Don't want it.

LUDMILLA. But I think you ought to have some, pussykin. I want you to have some nice warm milk and grow up to be your wifie's roly-poly little boy.

VASYA. I don't want to be roly-poly, roly-poly!

LUDMILLA. Fie on you! Shame on you! You'll be thin as a rail, thin as a rail. Please drink some nice warm milk. For my sake, pussykin.

VASYA. M . . . m . . . m . . . (*Shakes his head negatively.* LUDMILLA *brings milk on a tray, with the artificial rose beside it, and coaxes him to take it. His annoyance grows apace.*) M . . . m . . . m . . .

LUDMILLA. Drink it, pussykin.

VASYA. I don't want any milk!

LUDMILLA. And I want you to drink it.

VASYA (*sharply*). And I don't want to.

LUDMILLA. And I want you to.

VASYA. Once for all——

LUDMILLA. Once for all——

VASYA. Once for all—no!

LUDMILLA. Once for all—yes!

VASYA. Once for all—I won't drink it!

LUDMILLA. Then you don't love me.

VASYA (*angrily*). I love you.

LUDMILLA. Once for all—you don't love me.

VASYA. Once for all—I do love you.

LUDMILLA. This is not how people love.

VASYA (*growling*). And how do people love?

LUDMILLA. Anyhow, they don't love like this.

VASYA (*almost yelling*). Well, how do they then? Well, how?

LUDMILLA. Don't yell at me! I'm not your dog. Keep your shirt on. (*Decides to make the best of a bad bargain.*) All right, let's make up. Kiss me on my teeny-weeny nose, darling. Don't you want to? Fine! All right, then I'll kiss your teeny-weeny nose! Pussykin, tell your little pussy "Meow"!

VASYA (*with a disgusted bark*). Meow!

LUDMILLA (*offended*). Oh!

VASYA. I can do it again. (*Barks it out.*) Meow! (*Flies into a passion.*) Come on, you pussy, I'll bite your teeny-weeny nose off! Meow! Drink some nice warm milk. I don't want any milk! Meow! I'm sick of it all! I can't live any longer with grandma who was a housewife by trade and grandpa who is a promoted worker. Meow! I can't stand them. I'm beginning to rot. And whose fault is it? It's your fault. Meow!

LUDMILLA (*frightened*). Why am I to blame?

VASYA. Whose grandpa is it? Your grandpa! Whose grandma is it? Your grandma!

LUDMILLA. Think of it!

VASYA (*paces distractedly*). Shut up! Whose curtains are these? Your curtains. Whose milk is it? Your milk. And who's drowning in this petty bourgeois swamp? I'm drowning. I'm drowning in this swamp.

LUDMILLA. Think of it! He's drowning in the bourgeois swamp! And don't you think I'm drowning too? Who promised me everything one time and is now singing a new tune? (*Mockingly.*) "And we shall build a new life together, Ludmillochka, and I will read books to you, Ludmillochka. And I shall take you to the different clubs, Ludmillochka, and you will be a model exemplary life mate, Ludmillochka, the pal of my life," and this and that and the other thing. And what's become of it all now?

VASYA. Just think of it!

LUDMILLA (*her turn to be angry*). Shut up! Where is all that you promised me, I'm asking you? There's none of it. Forget it. (*Mocking him.*) "Ludmillochka, sew a button on for pussykin. Ludmillochka, give pussykin a little milk. Pussykin wants bye-bye. Meow! Pussykin wants yum-yum. Meow! Kiss pussykin on his teeny-weeny nose. Meow! . . ." This is all you know and you can't teach me anything cultured and nice.

VASYA (*pulling his coat off the hanger*). Oh, what a mess!

LUDMILLA. Where are you going, pussykin?

VASYA (*going*). I'm not asking your permission.

LUDMILLA. Pussykin, wait, wait! Let's make up! Pussykin, kiss my teeny-weeny nose!

VASYA. Devil take your nose. Let your grandpa, the promoted worker, kiss your damned nose! (*He goes out, banging the door.*)

[*The other half of the curtain opens, revealing the right side of the dividing line, in all its spartan simplicity.*]

LUDMILLA. Well, what do you think of that? He doesn't like my grandpa! (*Suddenly weeps.*) And why do I deserve this unhappiness? (*Huddles into the cushions, pulls blankets over her, so that she is completely hidden and only an occasional sob is heard.*)

[*The clatter of a falling bicycle comes from the corridor;* ABRAM *and* TONYA *enter, carrying books.*]

ABRAM. Damn this bicycle! Just look, Tonka, look how large this hole is. (*Points to a rent in his trousers.*) It wouldn't hurt to regulate it a bit. Do you happen to have a needle and thread?

TONYA. No.

ABRAM. Model wife!

TONYA. Abram, I ask you, please, none of these bourgeois tricks.

ABRAM. When the husband tears his last pair of pants, that's a bourgeois trick! A fine thesis. Well, shall we read?

TONYA. Let's.

ABRAM (*points to the book*). Let's have it.

TONYA. Abram, wouldn't you like to eat something?

ABRAM. And you?

TONYA. I really would.

ABRAM. You really would—and wouldn't I? Oh, boy! My bowels cry for sausage! Only yesterday I gobbled up a pound of it and now I want some more. Really, it's an inexplicable fact . . . (*Resignedly.*) Well, let's read.

TONYA. Let's. (*She lies on the table, face down, and props herself on her elbows to listen.*)

ABRAM. Let's. (*Reading.*) "First lecture: introduction. The significance of science. Human society, Studying the history of mankind, we observe how people in the struggle for existence, step by step, created and perfected their tools. With the latter they subjugated nature, they increased the quantity and improved the quality of the means necessary for their physical survival . . ."

TONYA (*conscience-stricken*). Abram, don't you think there's a tiny bit of yesterday's sausage left?

ABRAM. That's an idea. I'll have a look. (*Gropes on the shelf.*)

TONYA. Well, is there anything left?

ABRAM. Yes, there's something left. Two pages from a lousy bourgeois romance. (*Shows her the two pages in which sausage once was wrapped.*) We can have a nice healthy bite of that. (*Making a wry face.*) Ah . . .

TONYA. You're a fine husband.

ABRAM. Kuznetzova, none of those bourgeois tricks.

TONYA. Bourgeois tricks have nothing to do with this.

ABRAM. And who is to blame for this? Are you saying that I am to blame for this?

TONYA. Let's not go into that. Read! Where did we stop? (*Takes the book and searches for the place.*)

ABRAM. We stopped at the point where we'd like to gorge ourselves . . .

TONYA (*severely*). Abram, don't forget that we have the book only until Tuesday. Read!

ABRAM. I don't want to.

TONYA. What's happened to you, Abram? Read!

ABRAM. But I don't want to.

TONYA. But I want you to read.

ABRAM. Once for all—no!

TONYA. Once for all—yes!

ABRAM. Once for all—I will not read!

TONYA. Then you don't . . . eh . . . respect me. And you don't . . . eh . . . love me. That is, there's no workers' solidarity between us.

ABRAM. There is workers' solidarity.

TONYA. Once for all—there is no workers' solidarity.

ABRAM. Once for all—there is solidarity.

TONYA. When there is solidarity, one does not behave like this.

ABRAM. And how does one behave?

TONYA. Anyhow, not like this.

ABRAM (*ferociously*). But how does one? Well, tell me!

TONYA. Abram, don't forget that just because I'm your wife I'm not your slave, but a free woman, your life partner, and your comrade in toil.

ABRAM. Bah—she thinks she's discovered America!

TONYA. Well, all right, then, let's quit this discussion and go on reading. (*Reading.*) " The economic epochs of history. We are far, as yet, from having attained unanimity of opinion on an adequate scheme of economic development of humanity . . ."

ABRAM (*sighing, aside*). Uh . . . I could eat an ox!

TONYA. What?

ABRAM. Nothing, nothing.

TONYA (*continues to read*). "Without stopping to analyze former endeavors, we shall pass at once to one of the latest, the work of the famous German economist, Carl Buecher."

ABRAM. Kuznetzova . . . I'm sick of this. I don't want any more of Carl Buecher. What I want is a large chunk of bread and a large hunk of meat. I want a gigantic omelette made of at least six or seven eggs. I want bacon, I want butter, I want milk, I want fats, I want vitamins, I want cucumbers . . . Tonka, after all you *are* my wife, and let me announce it quite categorically: I want to stuff myself.

TONYA. Abram, don't shout. You have a mediæval concept of marriage.

ABRAM. Mediæval concept . . . She dares to teach me the political ABC!

TONYA. Sh . . . Shshsh . . . What will the neighbors think?

ABRAM. The neighbors! And isn't that a mediæval concept? And when the husband's last trousers are torn and there is no one to sew them up, isn't that a mediæval concept?

TONYA. So that's it! (*She jumps from the table, yanks her mackintosh off the table and puts it on.*) Reproaches!

ABRAM. Where are you going, Kuznetzova? (*Tries to bar her way.*)

TONYA. I'm not obliged to report all my actions to you. (*Departing.*)

ABRAM. Tonka, Tonyechka, come on let's read, come on . . .

TONYA. Let me alone. Let me quiet myself. (*She goes.*)

ABRAM (*picks up an accordian, sits on the edge of the table, and accompanies himself softly during the soliloquy*). It's self-evident, damn it. Facts are facts. A real hundred per cent mediæval family scene. And the main thing, what's wrong? Let's consider all the prerequisites. Is there compatability of characters? There is. Is there workers' solidarity? There is. Is there the common political background? There is. And in spite of it all, here's some horrible misunderstanding. And on top of it all, I'm beastly hungry. (*He sniffs the air.*) Oh-ho. Vaska's half smells divinely. M'mm . . . (*He sniffs, struggling with temptation*). Cutlets, I think. Possibly cutlets. But no—let's see—I almost venture to say it smells more like an onion omelette. (*Knocks hesitantly on the partition and weakly, almost in a whisper.*) May I? Nobody there . . . (*Sniffs.*) Really, this is a mediæval odor. Or is it unethical? (*Tiptoes into* VASKA's *half of the room and does not see* LUDMILLA *bundled up in the farthest corner.*) Oy, this is the life! And how much of it! Is it ethical or isn't it? I think it's cutlets . . . or isn't it . . . I wonder if it would be all right—just to find out. (*He bites into a cutlet and swallows it guiltily; puts down the accordion on* LUDMILLA's *table, then mounts a chair and begins to rummage in the upper reaches of the cupboard. Suddenly, dishes and containers come down with a crash, covering him with flour.*) Wow!

LUDMILLA (*aroused by the crash, disentangles herself, at first horror-stricken, but then bursting into shrieks of laughter*). Oh you're such a sight! I can't stand it any more, can't stand it any more!

ABRAM (*shaking off the flour, and terribly flustered*). Excuse me, but a great misunderstanding has occurred.

LUDMILLA. Misunderstanding! Oh, I can't stand it! Just look at him! God has punished you!

ABRAM. God is a purely mediæval concept.

LUDMILLA. And to crawl around in other people's shelves. Isn't that me . . . me . . . whatever you called it? Oh, I can't even say it!

ABRAM (*continues to stand on the chair, doleful under his flour*). What is private property anyhow?

LUDMILLA. You poor boy! Just look at yourself in the mirror. Oh, I can't . . . can't . . . You're just too funny! (*Inspects him.*) The poor boy's hungry, and his trouser leg is torn. I'd like to know what your wife is doing for you.

ABRAM. I regret to say that my wife devotes herself exclusively to the *History of Social Forms*, by Plotnikov.

LUDMILLA. Oh, my poor little Abramchik. What a hard-lucky fellow you are! Why do you stand on the chair like a statue? Come on down and I'll fix you up.

ABRAM (*brightens up*). Oh-ho, Kuznetzova, do you hear? The non-partisan comrades are beginning to be kind to your husband!

LUDMILLA. Stand still, silly.

ABRAM. What's going to happen?

LUDMILLA. I'm going to sew up your trouser leg.

ABRAM. At your service, always. (*He bows, with mock ceremony.*)

LUDMILLA (*sewing*). Stand still, you silly. Now that's that. Like this. Some hole this is! As if dogs have pulled it about.

ABRAM. It's that mediæval bicycle, devil take it!

LUDMILLA. Well, well! Don't turn around, or I'll stick you. I'm serious about it. Like this! Like this!

ABRAM. Who's this hanging there?

LUDMILLA. That's my grandma, a housewife by trade.

ABRAM. What a likeable old lady; and who's this?

LUDMILLA. My grandpa.

ABRAM. Also a first-class old man.

LUDMILLA. A promoted worker, a hero of labor.

ABRAM. Who would have thought it? So young and already a hero of labor! And how nice it must be to have such a lovely grandma and such a distinguished grandpa.

LUDMILLA. Now you're kidding me.

ABRAM. How could I be kidding you when I am ready right now to embrace both of your remarkable ancestors? (*He moves and is pricked by the needle.*) Ouch!

LUDMILLA. I told you to stand still. Now you got it. Now will you stand still? (*She bites the thread.*) Finished!

ABRAM. There was a hole—and now there is no hole. Really remarkable! Astounding! The wonders of science and of technology!

LUDMILLA. Well . . .

ABRAM. Well . . .

LUDMILLA. Well!

ABRAM. Well, what?

LUDMILLA. Well, what shall we do now?

ABRAM. How should I know?

LUDMILLA. And who should know? Don't you know that you ought to thank me now?

ABRAM. Yes, I'm very grateful.

LUDMILLA. Is this how to thank a lady? That's not the way to do it. You're a fine gentleman!

ABRAM. Perhaps you want me to say "merci." Well, then, "merci."

LUDMILLA. Why, no. That's not it. (*Stretching out her hand.*) Well?

ABRAM. Well, what?

LUDMILLA. You must kiss my hand. Do you understand?

ABRAM. Kiss . . . your hand!

LUDMILLA. Well, what's the matter with you? Hurry up!

ABRAM (*kisses her hand, in a stupor*). Oy! (*He runs into his half of the room and begins frantically to pore over his books.*)

LUDMILLA (*laughing*). Oh, I can't stand it any more! Oh, I'm dying! What a funny fellow he is! Why did you run away, Abramchik? Wait! (*She runs after him.*) And the other hand. You must kiss the other hand too!

ABRAM. Wait a minute, wait! (*He leafs quickly through a book.*)

LUDMILLA. What are you looking for?

ABRAM. I'm looking for the book on Communist Ethics. Wait! The most terrible crash has happened. Someone swiped my Communist Ethics.

LUDMILLA. Well, what of it?

ABRAM. And who will tell me now whether it's ethical or unethical for a member of the All-Union League of Communist Youth to kiss the hand of a non-partisan comrade?

LUDMILLA. A non-partisan comrade! You are a scream! Come on and kiss my hand.

ABRAM. Do you think it's ethical?

LUDMILLA. Never mind—kiss it! Kiss it!

ABRAM. But perhaps it is not ethical!

LUDMILLA. Stop this nonsense, really. If it's ethical for the little hands to sew up your trousers, then why isn't it ethical for you to kiss the little hands? Well, come on, kiss the hand.

ABRAM (*confused*). Is it ethical? What? Is it unethical? Isn't it? What?

LUDMILLA. Kiss it!

ABRAM (*does so*). Or is it?

LUDMILLA. Now this one. (*Abram kisses it.*) And now again this one . . . and this one . . .

ABRAM. And now this one again? Yes? (*Kisses with increasing fervor.*)

LUDMILLA. That's enough. Don't! Stop! (*She laughs and pulls her hands away.*) That'll do!

ABRAM. Altogether ethical.

LUDMILLA. I should think so! Oh, my darling! Oh, my poor little boy! Nobody to look after him. Oh, how thin he is . . . Thin as a rail. He must drink milk. Would you like some nice warm milk?

ABRAM. And how! And bread too!

[LUDMILLA *bustlingly fetches the tray, with the milk and artificial flower, sets them out on the table in her room and settles him down to the feast.* ABRAM *digs in without ceremony.*]

LUDMILLA. Drink, Abramchik. Drink the nice warm milk, darling Abramchik. (*She pours the milk.*) I'm afraid it's a little cold . . .

ABRAM (*with a full mouth*). It's fine, Ludmillochka, swell!

LUDMILLA. Would you like one of my nice little cutlets, pussykin? (*She goes to fetch it.*)

ABRAM. Do I!

LUDMILLA (*bringing it, looks at the plate*). You've tried it, haven't you?

ABRAM (*mumbles, embarrassed*). U—hu . . .

LUDMILLA. There's a smart boy. Eat, darling, and get well. You'll get roly-poly . . .

ABRAM. Always at your service.

LUDMILLA. Eat hearty. I'll make you my own little roly-poly.

ABRAM (*with mouth full*). And it wouldn't hurt me at all to be roly-poly. I don't understand why I have such a healthy appetite today.

LUDMILLA. Well, that's good, Abramchik. Don't be bashful. By the way, do you know that all night I dreamt about you? (*Giggles.*) It was very funny. I dreamt that you and I were skating on the railroad track, and such a terrible night around us. Terrible, terrible! And suddenly, on the rails behind us the primus stove was running. Like an engine with headlights . . . toot, toot, toot! . . . Running after us—Ooh—ooh—ooh . . .

ABRAM. Sounds like a bad accident in the transportation department.

LUDMILLA (*more enthusiastic*). And suddenly, do you know what you did? You embraced me!

ABRAM. You don't say!

LUDMILLA. So help me God! And then suddenly I embraced *you*. (*Spontaneously they embrace each other, scarcely aware of what they are doing.*) And suddenly both of us together . . . (*They kiss.*)

ABRAM. Oh-ho!

LUDMILLA. Yes! And suddenly we wake up . . . I mean I wake up.

ABRAM. And don't I wake up?

LUDMILLA. You . . . also . . . wake up.

ABRAM (*remembers his conscience*). These are fine tricks. And kissing too!

LUDMILLA. What about kissing?

ABRAM. Kissing my comrade's wife . . . Is it ethical or unethical?

LUDMILLA. But that was in a dream.

ABRAM. Oh, in a dream?

LUDMILLA. In a dream.

ABRAM. Well, if it was in a dream, than I think it is ethical rather than unethical. (*Pause.*)

LUDMILLA (*sighing*). Abramchik, I swear to God I'm conscience-stricken. I must admit I don't know what ethical and unethical mean.

ABRAM. She doesn't know what ethical means! Well, I would like to know what your most respected husband Vaska is doing about this! It's his duty to see to it that you should develop.

LUDMILLA. He only sees to it that I should make love to him.

ABRAM. What a scoundrel!

LUDMILLA. And there's no one to take care of me, and no one to develop me. (*She weeps.*) And no one to read books to me, and no one to take me to the zoo!

ABRAM. Poor, poor, little girl! Why

haven't you told me all this time?
Come on now, I'll take care of you.
I'll develop you and I'll read books to
you and take you to the zoo. (*He runs
off and brings a book.*) Only please don't
cry. When a woman cries there's
something beastly mediæval about it.
Come on, let's read. We can begin
with the simplest thing, at the very
beginning. (*He reads.*) "The electro- 10
magnetic theory of light. We are living in an era of unusually profound
changes which bear the character of
revolutionary cataclysms in all phases
of life. The future historian of our
epoch will be obliged to explain that
intrinsic relation which unites into one
historical law all the social and political changes that we are experiencing
and all the profound differentiations 20
which . . ." Are you following me?

LUDMILLA. Why, yes, what is there to
understand here? Very simple.

ABRAM. ". . . all the profound differentiations which are the determining
factor in creating new forms, new
. . ."

LUDMILLA. Abram, will you really take
me to the zoo?

ABRAM. Always at your service. Have 30
you got the cash?

LUDMILLA. You're a fine gentleman! Of
course I have.

ABRAM. Why hesitate, then?

LUDMILLA. And Vasya? What will Vasya
think?

ABRAM. And Tonya? What will Tonya
say?

LUDMILLA. Akh! But it is so interesting!
Help me on with my coat. Be a gen- 40
tleman! Well, let's go. (*She leads the
way into the corridor.*)

ABRAM. Right away, Ludmillochka,
right away. (*He helps himself to* VASYA's
*necktie, puts it on and attempts to plaster
down his hair with spittle on both palms.*)

Right away, right away! Can't hurt
to wear a lousy little necktie, even if it
is Vaska's. Is it ethical or unethical?
What is a necktie anyhow, and what's
ethics? Ethics is a mediæval concept
anyhow. (LUDMILLA's *voice: "Abram!"*)
Right away! I just want to put a little
powder on. Have you any toothpaste?
Let me have some toothpaste. Right
away, right away! Like this. (*Inspects
himself in the mirror.*) Is it ethical or unethical? I should say it's ethical! I'm
coming. (*He runs into his half of the
room and is about to put on his scarf, coat
and hat when he notices* TONYA's *red kerchief.*) Poor Tonya! I can't do it.

LUDMILLA (*comes back*). Hurry up,
Abram. Hurry up!

ABRAM. I can't go, Ludmilla. What will
Tonya think of it? It would break her
heart.

LUDMILLA. But going to the zoo will develop me. Don't forget that you must
educate the non-party comrades.

ABRAM. In that case it's ethical.

[LUDMILLA *goes out;* ABRAM *puts on his hat
and coat and follows, but at the door bumps
into* TONYA *who is just entering.*]

TONYA. Abram, what does this mean?

ABRAM. It's a concession to the petty
bourgeoisie and to the wealthy peasantry. Adieu!

TONYA. Where are you going, Abram?

ABRAM (*proudly*). I'm not obliged to report all my actions to you.

TONYA. Abram!

ABRAM. Let me alone! Let me quiet myself. (*He runs out.*)

TONYA. So that's it! Very well. (*Lies
down on the table and reads aloud.*)
"Marxism in its contemporary form,
dialectic materialism . . ." (*She sup-
presses sobs and continues to read.*) "This
is a priceless weapon the use of which
insures immeasurable superiority of
the proletarian revolutionist over the

bourgeois politician." (*Her voice becomes fuller and fuller of stifled sobs.*) "The latter is limited by the necessities of the present, by the coarse practicality . . . prac . . . tic . . . ality . . ." (*Her head sinks on the book and she sobs freely.*)

VASYA (*enters quickly into his half of the room; with determination, looking straight before him, stops at the table and begins to orate; he doesn't look at the corner where he had left* LUDMILLA). Ludmilla, I have something important to tell you. This can't go on any longer. Ludmilla! (*He looks around and doesn't see her.*) Are you home, Ludmilla? Her coat is gone! She's gone! So much the better. (*Looks at the portraits of the grandmother and grandfather.*) Grandma, a promoted worker and hero of labor! Grandpa, housewife by trade! Meow! Enough of it! This cannot continue any longer! Her damned necktie . . . (*Tears it off.*) To hell with the necktie! (*Musses his hair.*) To hell with sleek hair! (*Hears* TONYA'S *sobs.*) Kuznetzova, are you home?

TONYA (*lifts her head*). Vasya? Wait a minute. (*She gets off the table, sits down in a chair, adjusts her hair, puts on the red head-kerchief, wipes her face and pretends to be absorbed in a book.*)

VASYA. May I come in?

TONYA. Right away. Just a minute. (*She finishes adjusting herself.*) All right, come in.

VASYA (*steps into her apartment*). Isn't Abram home? Are you alone?

TONYA. Alone.

VASYA. That's good. I must talk to you seriously about something. (*Brief pause.*) Tonya . . .

TONYA. Yes?

VASYA (*peering at her*). What's the matter, Tonya? You have been crying.

TONYA. Nonsense!

VASYA. Tonya . . .

TONYA. Yes?

VASYA. Have you had anything to eat today? Would you like some milk? (TONYA *shakes her head negatively.*) Kuznetzova, please do me a favor and drink some milk.

TONYA. Thanks, I don't want any . . . milk.

VASYA. Kuznetzova, aren't you ashamed of yourself? Why these bourgeois pretenses? I know very well that you haven't had anything to eat since this morning. (*He goes to fetch the milk.*) There's a whole pitcher of it. (*He notes with surprise that the pitcher is empty.*) Empty! Who could have lapped it all up, I wonder? Tonyechka, there happens to be no milk. But wait, I'll get you some cutlets right away. We had half a dozen of them. (*He finds no cutlets on the plate.*) H'mm . . . none left . . . disappeared . . . very, very strange . . . (*Picks up* ABRAM'S *accordion from the table.*) I'm beginning to guess whose work this is. Well, all right. Ah-ha, there's some sausage left and half a roll. (*He brings it to her.*) Please eat some of this sausage.

TONYA (*eating*). Thank you, Vaska.

VASYA. That's right; there's a good fellow. (*A brief pause; regards her earnestly.*) Tonya . . .

TONYA (*with full mouth*). Yes?

VASYA. Tonya, this can't go on any more. Tonya, look at me!

TONYA. Why should I?

VASYA. Look at me, right straight into my eyes.

TONYA. Well . . . (*Looks into his eyes.*)

VASYA. Do you love Abram?

TONYA. That's none of your business.

VASYA. Yes, it is! Do you love him or don't you? Tell me honestly.

TONYA. I don't understand why you

place the questions so ideologically. Do I love, or don't I love. I don't understand. It's not correctly formulated.

VASYA. Tonya, it is very important to me. Do you love him or don't you love him?

TONYA. Well, now, really, I don't understand you. I respect Abram very much . . . Abram respects me . . . Abram and I have workers' solidarity . . . compatibility of interests . . . a common political background. It seems to me that this is sufficient for people to live together.

VASYA. Stop! Not another word! You don't love him! On my word of honor, you don't love him! (*Happily.*) You don't love him, you don't love him! Kuznetzova, why do you turn red like this? Hurrah! Tonka! I cannot live without you any longer, do you understand?

TONYA. You're crazy!

VASYA. That's right, I'm crazy! I'm crazy about *you.* I should worry. Tonka, Tonyechka, do you love me? Do you? (*He embraces her.*)

TONYA. Hold on! Wait a minute! (*Struggles.*)

VASYA. You love me. By God, you love me! I can see it in your eyes. Hurrah! Now everything will be different. We'll all be happy. We'll read together, work together, love together, have a good time together.

TONYA. You're crazy!

VASYA. Hurrah!

TONYA (*severely*). Wait a minute, Vasya. Wait! Sit down! Let us discuss the new situation objectively and calmly. Very well, let us suppose that you should leave Comrade Ludmilla and I should leave Comrade Abram, and that you and I should come together on the basis of . . . eh . . . (*Indecisively.*) Will it be the right thing to do

from the point of view of Communist family morality?

VASYA. Absolutely right.

TONYA. Absolutely wrong. Today I register with one man. Tomorrow I divorce him; the next day I register with another man! What kind of an example are we setting to our other party comrades, and to the most active elements among the non-partisan youth and the poorer peasantry?

VASYA (*embraces her violently*). And perhaps the poor peasantry will not even notice it!

TONYA (*recovering for a moment*). This is pure and simple opportunism.

VASYA. What's the difference!

TONYA (*tearing herself away*). Moreover, we have no right to build our individual well-being, and if you please, our happiness, on the unhappiness of other party and non-partisan comrades. I'm thinking of Comrades Ludmilla and Abram. I have no access to data concerning Comrade Ludmilla, but as for Comrade Abram, his life will be shattered by this.

VASYA (*sobering*). And Ludmilla's life will be shattered too.

TONYA. Comrade Abram, if I must use the antiquated sentimental terminology, is madly in love with me. He will not survive this.

VASYA. Neither will Ludmilla survive this. She's in love with me like a little kitten. That's a definite fact. All day long she tells me tales about her grandma and grandpa, and forces me to lap milk.

TONYA. There you are!

VASYA. What is to be done then? Tonka . . .

TONYA. We shall have to surrender our personal well-being in the interest of general social well-being.

VASYA. How unpleasant.

TONYA. Be a man, Vasya, be a man! You see, it is equally difficult for me. Let us be friends. Here's my hand on it. (*She offers her hand which* VASYA *presses and does not release.*)

VASYA. How unpleasant . . . And only today, at night, I dreamed of you. You and I were setting the table, and all around us plates were falling and breaking, and all around us such a dark night . . . and the wind moaned . . . and the plates were falling and breaking . . . whooo . . .

TONYA. Ideologically the dream was incorrect.

VASYA. And suddenly you embraced me!

TONYA. What are you saying!

VASYA. So help me God! And then suddenly I embrace you! (*Spontaneously they embrace.*) And suddenly both of us together . . . Tonyechka . . . (*They kiss.*)

TONYA. Wait a minute. Wait . . . My precious pussykin . . . what are we doing?

VASYA. And suddenly once again . . . (*They kiss again.*)

[*In the midst of the prolonged kiss enters Comrade* FLAVIUS, *the party organizer.*]

FLAVIUS. Kiss, my children, kiss!

TONYA. Oh!

VASYA. Oh!

TONYA. Comrade Flavius!

VASYA. Flavius!

FLAVIUS. That's all right. Go on, don't mind me. It won't hurt the Revolution any.

VASYA (*worried stiff*). That's a fine mess.

TONYA. Comrade Flavius, the Devil knows what you may think . . . My word of honor, this is a pure misunderstanding.

FLAVIUS. Ho-ho! Vaska, how do you like that? She calls a Soviet marriage a pure misunderstanding. And you as a husband, don't you protest?

TONYA. Believe me that he . . . that I . . .

FLAVIUS. No, my children, no joking. But tell me, how did you do it so quickly? Just like the work of the shock-brigades. Our famous poet of the masses, Comrade Emilian, comes along and presto, without any warning, comes right out and says, "Comrades, the latest news! Vaska got married; Abramchik got married; they're all sitting around and drinking tea with rolls; in a word, complete degeneration." Wait! we cry. Who got married? When did they get married? Whom did they marry? Why did they marry? But do you think you can get any sense out of that ape? All he says is, "I must run along to draw the proper organizational conclusions, arrange for a little celebration, call the gang together," and there you are. And I didn't see him any more. So you kids had better expect some guests. Get a move on! Have the tea ready, light the primus.

TONYA. Primus! (*Sinks into a chair, exhausted by worry.*)

FLAVIUS. Now, kids, seriously, I congratulate you! Live together happily, my children. Don't quarrel, work together! But you know, the one who surprised me most was our little Abramchik. Who would have thought it? Abram getting married. Ho-ho! That's a subject for our poet laureate, Demian Biedny. By the way, where is Abram?

TONYA. Yes, indeed, where is Abram?

VASYA. Abram, what you may call it . . . there.

TONYA. Went for a walk . . . with his wife.

VASYA. You know, it really is fine weather . . . the snow is falling . . .

TONYA. Yes, the snow is falling . . . it's

a wonderful . . . I think they'll be back soon.

FLAVIUS. Whom did Abram marry?

VASYA. Yes, indeed, whom did he marry? That is to say, that girl . . . Kuznetzova, whom did Abram marry?

TONYA. Abram . . . he married . . . why, Comrade Ludmilla!

VASYA. Ludmilla! That's a fine one! That is, I mean to say . . . precisely, that is, Comrade Ludmilla. You know, when you take her all in all, she's not so bad . . .

TONYA. I don't think there's anything nice about her. Just an ordinary girl with typical petty bourgeois ideology . . . oof . . . But perhaps it would be better not to discuss this.

FLAVIUS. Well, well, my children. Show me your geography. Demonstrate your technical attainments. In brief, where do you live?

VASYA. Well, in general, here . . . like this, you know . . .

FLAVIUS. And Abram and his family?

TONYA. Abram, also . . . he's living here . . . in general . . .

VASYA. Here. Right here . . . like this . . . over there.

FLAVIUS. Ah-ha . . . hmm . . . very nice, very nice . . . (*He enters the other half and they follow meekly.*) And who is this? (*He points to the portrait of grandma.*)

TONYA. This? Oh, that's just so . . . an old intellectual.

VASYA. That's grandmother.

FLAVIUS. Whose grandmother?

VASYA. Her grandma . . . a housewife . . . And that's grandpa . . . my grandpa . . . a promoted worker . . . a hero of labor . . .

FLAVIUS. You're doing well, kids. And this, so to speak, are your technological accessories. (*He examines the cup-board and the primus.*) Oh-ho! It's a good primus. And just look at the pots! And what do you know, four glasses . . . and a mirror! Well, well, the kids are growing rich.

TONYA (*aside, to* VASYA *while* FLAVIUS *is busy investigating the household*). Vasya, well!

VASYA. A complete mix-up! As clear as mud! (*Both go to the couch, where they sit down and whisper.*)

TONYA. What a shame! What a disgrace! I cannot continue to take part in this low, petty bourgeois farce. This lie is unworthy of us, and we must root it out!

VASYA. What do you want to do?

TONYA. I'll tell Flavius at once that this was a joke.

VASYA. Tonka, are you crazy? Why, he saw us kissing.

TONYA. All the same . . .

VASYA. Kuznetzova!

[*Enter Communist Youth boys and girls, ten or twelve of them, high-spirited, laden with bundles for the party.*]

FIRST BOY. Ho! Flavius is here already. Hello, Flavius.

SECOND BOY. He's always first at the scene of the crime.

FIRST GIRL. That's what I call a real organizer, a real organizer.

SECOND GIRL. He's hardly a man. He's right on the spot like an ambulance.

FLAVIUS. That's right. I always respond without delay and answer to the first call.

FIRST BOY. Well, now, let's see, who are the chief victims of this careless love? Let's have a look at you!

FIRST GIRL. Vaska! Just look at him. Ho-ho! That's a nice thing to do.

SECOND BOY. Tonka Kuznetzova! Couldn't hold out any longer and got burned.

FIRST BOY. Comrades, let's get organized. Now all at once. Attention! One, two, three . . .

EVERYBODY IN CHORUS. Long live the Red newlyweds! (*They force them to kiss again and again.*)

VASYA (*aside*). That's a fine pickle, a fine pickle.

TONYA (*aside*). I can't bear this disgrace!

SECOND BOY. And where's Abram with his wife? I don't see Abram here.

FLAVIUS. Abram will be here presently.

FIRST BOY. And I don't see any tea, nor anything to chew on. That's even worse.

FIRST GIRL. Well, now, family unit, demonstrate your economic situation.

SECOND GIRL. Yes, yes. And it wouldn't hurt to have some tea. Kuznetzova, why don't you say something? Here you've called guests together and you don't do anything about it.

SECOND BOY. That's a nice thing. We want tea. Comrades, let's protest.

FIRST BOY. Attention! One, two, three . . .

ALL TOGETHER IN A CHORUS. We—de—mand—tea! We—de—mand—grub!

SECOND GIRL. Really, I think it's outrageous. Where's the good time we were promised by Comrade Emilian?

FLAVIUS. Now, kids, let there be peace and quiet. Don't disturb the young turtledoves. Everything will come in time.

FIRST GIRL. Just look how cleverly they've divided the room!

SECOND BOY. Well, what do you think of that!

FIRST BOY. Come on, comrades. Down with the petty bourgeois fences, or we shall have no place for our revelry. Come on, down with it! (*Riotously they push back the cupboard, and the rest of the artificial wall.*)

VOICES. Here! Push it this way! Pull the partition! Like this. Now there's more room. Once again! Once again! (*Break into the "Volga Boatmen Song" as they clear the middle of the room.*)

TONYA. Vasya . . . what will happen? What will Abram think?

VASYA. Abram! And what will Ludmilla think?

TONYA. This is terrible . . . He'll never survive this!

VASYA. And she will never survive this either.

TONYA. What is to be done?

FLAVIUS. Children, attention! Abram and his wife are coming.

VASYA (*groans*). That's the end. The funeral. Darkness. Complete mess.

FIRST BOY. Hide, kids!

VOICES. Hide, hide! Why are you standing there? Right here behind the books! Turn out the lights! (*Someone switches off the light and the room is completely dark.*)

SECOND GIRL. Vaska, hide yourself quickly, right here.

FLAVIUS. Everybody quiet! Imagine Abramchik playing the husband!

TONYA. Comrades, this is all a mistake. We . . .

FIRST BOY. Shsh . . . Quiet! Not a sound! Shh!

[LUDMILLA's *laughter is heard from the corridor. She runs in laughing, followed by* ABRAM. *They come into foreground where they can be seen by the audience.*]

LUDMILLA. Pussykin, kiss my teeny-weeny nose.

TONYA (*whispers*). The viper!

ABRAM. But is it ethical? (*He kisses her.*) Or perhaps it is unethical. (*Kisses her again.*)

VASYA (*whispers*). The lousy, rotten renegade! And he has my necktie on too!

LUDMILLA. Pussykin, say "Meow"!

FLAVIUS (*whispers*). Just look! Little Abramchik has become a pussykin!

LUDMILLA. Well, will you say "Meow"?

ABRAM (*sweetly*). Meow!

VASYA (*barks out angrily, aloud*). Meow! (*Everybody jumps up.*)

EVERYBODY IN CHORUS. Meow! Meow! Meow! (*The light goes on.*)

LUDMILLA. Oh, Vasya!

ABRAM. Oh, Kuznetzova! A terrible smash-up! I'm like a fish out of water.

EVERYBODY IN CHORUS. Lo . . . ng . . . li . . . ive . . . the . . . Re . . . ed . . . new 10 . . . ly . . . we . . . ds!

TONYA (*throws herself into* VASYA's *arms*). I can't stand this any longer. Take me away from here.

ABRAM. Ludmilla, hold me. I think I'm fainting. (*He falls into her arms.*)

FLAVIUS. Go on kissing, kids, go on kissing. This can't hurt the Revolution.

[*The thunder of a falling bicycle and the poet* EMILIAN *lumbers in.*] 20

EMILIAN (*puts first one foot, then the other on the table and massages his bruised shins*). The Devil take you and your bourgeois bicycle! I almost tore my trousers to pieces, not to mention my shins.

FLAVIUS. Emilian! You're the only thing we needed to complete our celebration.

EMILIAN. Hello, kids. (*Suddenly dumb-* 30 *founded, seeing* ABRAM *in* LUDMILLA's *arms and* TONYA *in* VASYA's *arms.*) Wait! What do I see here? Vaska and Tonka! Abramchik and Ludmillka! Surprising! Astounding! Sh! Listen to an impromptu verse:

To marry in such manner, really
Is not so good, is rather silly
And who has married whom right now
No one can tell, I must avow. 40

FLAVIUS. What are you jabbering about? Seems perfectly clear who's married to whom. Abram married Ludmilla and Vasya married Tonya. Why, you yourself were the first to tell us about it. What's the matter? Are you drunk?

EMILIAN. No, boys. Wait a minute. Perhaps somebody here is drunk, but it's not me. Smell me! (*Blows his breath into the face of a boy who shakes his head negatively.*) I'm not drunk. I'm perfectly sober, but I must say I've seen with my own eyes who has married whom.

VASYA (*in a desperate whisper*). Sh! Shut up!

ABRAM (*also whispering, making signs to him*). Shut up! It isn't ethical.

FLAVIUS. Comrades, can you make him out? It's a couple of marriages in a mad-house!

EMILIAN. You yourself belong in a madhouse. Thank God, I still have my senses about me, my memory, and I can beat anybody at writing verses. Do you know my latest, "The Izvostchik"? Listen:

Ekh, the city has gnawed me to pieces . . .

FLAVIUS. Choke up, genius! I'm sick of your "Izvostchik." I can't listen to it any more.

EMILIAN. And as for these pairs of lovebirds . . . (*He points to the couples who are making desperate signs to him.*) Ah, forget about it, you! And as for them, I saw with my own eyes that Vaska is married to Ludmilla and here they are pulling your legs.

ABRAM. Sure, sure, of course, it's a fact. Of course we're just pulling your legs. That's right, Ludmilla, isn't it?

VASYA (*laughing unnaturally*). Why of course, we're just fooling! Ha-ha! What did you think! He-he! Why, of course, Flavius, Kuznetzova and I played a fine joke on you, didn't we? Tonka, you back me up! What do you say?

TONYA. Comrades, this was all a joke. And Comrade Ludmilla can confirm this.

LUDMILLA. Oh, what funny people you are! Why, you can't even understand a joke. Fie! (*Reluctantly pulls* VASYA's *sleeve.*) This is my lawful, duly registered husband. We can even show you the document from the Marriage Registry.

ABRAM (*reluctantly going to* TONYA). This is the lawful, duly registered comrade of my life . . . life's companion. Eh, what, Kuznetzova? Is there workers' solidarity? There is. Is there compatibility of interest? There is. Is there a common political background? There is.

TONYA (*sadly*). There is.

ABRAM. What's the matter, then?

EMILIAN. Sh! Sh! Four lines! Listen. Extemporaneously . . .

You've all been played for foolish lambs
Except Emilian the poet
Because Emilian is wiser than the lot of you
He is not—eh . . .
Anyhow, he's not . . . not a foolish lamb.

FIRST GIRL. Pretty rotten for a genius!

EMILIAN. Well, why don't you say it better then, wiseacre?

FLAVIUS. Well, what do you know about this! Why you certainly tripped us up. But what surprises me most is our Tonyechka Kuznetzova. Who would have thought that such a serious-minded girl with such an excellent social political record would be capable of such silly jokes! Well, what do you say, kids? Well done, Kuznetzova.

I'm sincerely glad for you. You can't be chewing rocks all the time. Have to have a good time once in a while. Isn't that right?

FIRST BOY. Well, what's the matter, then? Comrades, the session is not yet over. Pull out the grub. (*The guests noisily open the parcels.*)

SECOND BOY. Half a kilo of sausage.

FIRST GIRL. Four rolls. Four eggs.

FIRST BOY. Smoked sturgeon.

SECOND GIRL. A quarter of a pound of butter and two herrings.

EMILIAN (*pulls out of his overcoat pocket three bottles of beer*).

Ekh, the city has gnawed me to pieces . . .

TONYA. Comrades, I categorically protest against the use of alcohol by members of the All-Union League of Communist Youth.

EMILIAN. Think of it! Alcohol! Why, this is nothing but lousy beer! Flavius, we're asking you to decide. Is it all right to have three bottles of beer?

FLAVIUS. For such an occasion . . . three bottles! Go to it, kids. This can't hurt the Revolution.

EMILIAN. You said a mouthful, Flavius. (*Opens the bottles.*)

FIRST BOY. Comrades, attention. All together: (*They sing a drinking song.*)

ABRAM. Good-bye, Ludmilla.

VASYA. Good-bye, Tonya.

LUDMILLA. Good-bye, Abramchik.

TONYA. Good-bye, Vasya.

CURTAIN

ACT III

The same setting as in preceding act—the bourgeois and proletarian "apartments" distinct—but both in chaotic condition as a result of the late celebration. The curtain opens upon LUDMILLA *and* ABRAM *in their respec-* tive homes, eavesdropping upon each other. As soon as they are convinced that they are quite alone, they rush towards each other, clinching in a passionate embrace in the middle of the stage, tangled and concealed by the pesky *canary-colored curtain. Their fervor, however, is apparent to the audience even through the curtain. Then they come up for air, flustered and conscience-stricken.*

LUDMILLA. What are we doing?

ABRAM. How should I know what we're doing?

LUDMILLA. No, no, you mustn't kiss me any more. I have a husband. 10

ABRAM. It's easy to say a husband and it's easy to say don't kiss me.

LUDMILLA. Don't kiss me, pussykin. I'll go mad. Don't! No!

ABRAM. All right, then, you'll have to put a muzzle on me, or——(*He grabs her once more, and the three of them— ABRAM, LUDMILLA, and the curtain—are again tangled.*)

LUDMILLA. I cannot live without you. 20

ABRAM. And do you think I can live without you?

LUDMILLA. What shall we do about it, then?

ABRAM. Let's get registered.

LUDMILLA. I'm going cuckoo.

ABRAM. Or is it unethical? What do you say?

LUDMILLA. But how about Vaska?

ABRAM. Don't talk to me about Vaska. 30 Whenever Vaska is mentioned, I want to knock his block off. What about Vaska?

LUDMILLA. He won't bear it. He'll kill himself. I'm sure he will.

ABRAM. Does he love you so much?

LUDMILLA. Oh, Abramchik, that's the tragedy. Love me? He simply worships me. I don't know what to do about it.

ABRAM. All the same, you must choose. Either Vaska or me. Shall we go to the Registry Bureau? Nu? Ludmillochka? Come on, be a serious grown-up comrade. Well?

LUDMILLA. But how can we, pussy-

kin? Today I register with one man, tomorrow I un-register, the day after I register again with another man. It's not right! What will people say?

ABRAM. Ludmilla, none of these bourgeois tricks. What have other people to do with it when we can't live without each other? And the main thing, what's the matter? Is there compatibility of characters? There is. Is there mutual understanding? There is. Is there labor solidarity? There is. Nu, Ludmilla, what's to stop us, then?

LUDMILLA. Oh, you're making my head swim.

ABRAM. Well, Ludmilla, decide in two shakes.

LUDMILLA. I'm going cuckoo, I tell you.

ABRAM. We'll lead such a wonderful life! Such a wonderful life!

LUDMILLA. Oh, it's all the same to me. My happiness! (*She throws herself into his arms.*) Let's go!

ABRAM. Let's go!

LUDMILLA. My treasure! (*Takes him by the hand.*) My precious husband. (*Coquettishly.*) And aren't you even a little bit sorry for Tonya?

ABRAM. Wait! As a matter of fact, I haven't even thought of Tonya. That's a nice thing to do! Here Tonya will come home from a meeting of her Communist Youth cell, all tired out, and suddenly she'll discover that her husband is no longer her husband, but somebody else's husband. Is it ethical or is it unethical?

LUDMILLA. Come on, pussykin, let's go.

ABRAM. But Tonya!

40 LUDMILLA. What about Tonya?

ABRAM. She'll never survive it.

LUDMILLA. Does she love you?

ABRAM. Love me? She worships me!

LUDMILLA. All the same, you must choose—either Tonya or me. Put on your coat, or the Marriage Registry will be closed. Be a serious grown-up comrade. Well?

ABRAM. Today I register. Tomorrow I un-register. The day after I register again. Moral and ethical laxity. Downright sexual delinquency. What will the comrades of the district committee think of it? What will Comrade Flavius say to it?

LUDMILLA (*weeping*). Fla-vi-us! Is it un-ethical?

ABRAM. Decidedly.

LUDMILLA (*still weeping*). My treasure, my little treasure . . . or perhaps . . . it is eth-ic-al.

ABRAM. No doubt. It is wrong in principle to build personal family happiness on a foundation of the domestic unhappiness of other comrades.

LUDMILLA (*suppressing sobs*). Tha-at me-ans tha-at we mu-st not . . .

ABRAM. We must not . . .

LUDMILLA. But I thou-ght, but Abram, but I—so . . .

ABRAM. But, Ludmillochka, darling, can't you see that I'm also suffering? But I control myself. Can't you also control yourself? Be a man!

LUDMILLA. It means then . . . good-bye, Abram.

ABRAM. Good-bye, Ludmilla.

LUDMILLA. Very well. Now I know. (*In a quavering voice.*) Good-bye, pussykin. (*They embrace, both weepy.*) Tell me, tell your pussykin "Meow"!

ABRAM (*through his tears*). Meow!

LUDMILLA. Abramchik . . .

ABRAM. Yes . . .

LUDMILLA. Good-bye, good-bye. (*They embrace again.*)

ABRAM. Good-bye. (*They embrace and then part.*) Why does everything come out so unethical when everything really feels so ethical? I must take a long walk and figure it all out. (*Departs.*)

LUDMILLA. Very well, now I know. I can't stand it any longer. (*She begins to gather her gaudy belongings but suddenly exhausted, collapses to the floor and drops her head on the bundle, sobbing.*) I can't stand it any more, I can't stand it any more! [*The crash of the bicycle in the corridor, and* VASYA *stalks in, purposefully.*]

VASYA. The Devil take him and his damned bicycle! Family happiness, eh? Meow! Down with it! There! I've forgotten all the things I wanted to say . . . Ludmilla, I must talk to you seriously . . . This can't go on any longer in this way . . . The fact of the matter is that we . . . The fact of the matter is that our relations . . . the very foundation . . . but the main thing is that you mustn't get angry and you must try to understand me . . . I wish I knew how to explain it to you . . . You see, in regard to you, I want to remain to the very end a decent man. Perhaps you will find it unpleasant and even painful . . . but it is best to speak right out and to speak honestly . . . Sew up my pants, I mean . . . (*Aside.*) What am I saying?

LUDMILLA (*indignant*). None of your bourgeois tricks!

VASYA (*astounded*). What? What?

LUDMILLA. No bourgeois tricks. It is not ethical.

VASYA. Well, what do you know about that! (*Looks her up and down in astonishment; whistles his surprise, guessing where she has caught the lingo.*) No, no, Ludmillochka. You're wrong in saying it is not ethical. If I were to deceive you, to lie to you, to pretend . . . do you understand me? . . . Then of course it would be rotten and not ethical. But I want to speak to you frankly, honestly, like a true Communist Youth, like a real comrade.

LUDMILLA. I am not a female slave but a free companion. You tore the pants yourself, now sew them up yourself.

VASYA. What! What have the pants to do with it? We're not speaking about pants.

LUDMILLA. Then what *are* you belly-aching about?

VASYA (*irritably*). About something altogether different. You see . . . (*Aside.*) My tongue simply won't move . . . she'll never survive this . . . She'll kill herself, I'm sure of it. Oh! (*With exaggerated sharpness.*) We're speaking about you and . . . Well, of course . . . well, and about Abram . . . about your . . .

LUDMILLA. Oh, my God! He knows everything. I'm going cuckoo!

VASYA. Don't interrupt me. I'm speaking . . . about your . . . that is, about your . . . Do you understand me?

LUDMILLA. Oh, pussykin. I don't understand a thing! You can crucify me, but I don't understand a thing! (*To herself.*) I realize now that he'll never be able to survive this. He will kill himself. Gee! his eyes are wild already . . . (*To him.*) I don't know a thing, pussykin, I don't understand a thing . . . and I beg you, pussykin, only not to worry yourself . . . and don't torture my poor heart. As it is . . . (*She drops her head on a bundle for a new instalment of sobs.*)

VASYA. Look here, Ludmilla . . . (*Turns away in despair.*) My tongue just won't move. She can't stand it! She'll kill herself! That's a fact. She worships me so that I'm scared stiff! Eh! (*Waves his hand, dejected.*) What's the use . . .

LUDMILLA (*lifts her head and notices VASYA's stooped figure.*) Poor boy! How he's suffering! But all the same, let him

. . . (*Again begins to pack her bundles.*) All the same . . . all the same . . .

VASYA. What are you doing?

LUDMILLA. Don't ask me, Vasya.

VASYA. You're not going away, are you!

LUDMILLA. Yes, I'm going away.

VASYA (*with ill-concealed joy*). But why all of a sudden?

LUDMILLA. I'm going away. Don't ask me.

VASYA (*hypocritically*). But . . . Ludmillochka . . .

LUDMILLA. No, no . . . Don't you remember what we agreed upon? Don't tell me anything . . . don't try to hold me by force . . . let me go . . .

VASYA. But my dear Ludmillochka . . . how can I keep you from going, pussykin? Well, what do you know about that . . . ! On the other hand, ours isn't some sort of mediæval marriage . . . for God's sake . . . please . . . do you think that I . . . I merely asked as a matter of curiosity . . . Of course, love can't be forced . . .

LUDMILLA. Well, in that case . . . then I . . . (*Lifts the bundles.*) I'm going . . . good-bye . . .

VASYA. Well . . . (*Wants to bid her good-bye, but can't make up his mind how to behave.*)

LUDMILLA (*to avoid a difficult scene*). No, no, never mind . . . I'll come again.

VASYA (*frightened*). You're coming back?

LUDMILLA. Just to get some things . . . I can't take everything with me at once.

VASYA. Good-bye . . . Ludmillochka . . . (*She goes.* VASYA, *scarcely able to contain his joy over this fortunate turn of events, follows her, muttering indecisively.*) And yet, perhaps . . . after all . . . somehow . . . you would remain . . . Word of honor . . . really, Ludmillochka . . . be careful and don't stumble over the bicycle. (*Begins to caper happily.*) She's gone! She's gone! He-he . . . ho-ho . . . without any melodrama . . . gee, I'm lucky . . . Tonka, my little cabbage, where are you? I'll bet she's at the Communist Youth cell. I must tell her the happy news. (*Departs.*)

[*Crash of bicycle.* ABRAM *enters, both trouser legs tattered, but too absorbed in sad thoughts to notice; sits down.*]

ABRAM (*meditatively*). Is there compatibility of character? There is. Is there mutual understanding? There is. Is there common class background? There is. Is there labor solidarity? There is. There is everything—and at the same time such an awful smash-up! Why? Why? I don't understand . . . Compatibility of character? Yes. Labor solidarity? Yes. Everything is there, but altogether—a grand smash-up. Shall I tell Tonka everything? Straight out? Or would it be unethical? No, she'll never survive it. Is it ethical? Or isn't it? My head's in a whirl.

[EMILIAN *enters, in high spirits, none the better for vodka.*]

EMILIAN. Hello, old man.

ABRAM. Hello.

EMILIAN. Dance!

ABRAM. Why must I dance?

EMILIAN. Because you must. Dance!

ABRAM. To hell with you!

EMILIAN. Dance, I tell you!

ABRAM. What's the matter with you? Are you drunk or crazy?

EMILIAN. Dance, dance! Well? (*Sings a dance song, stamping his feet to the beat of the music.*)

Why are you so gloomy . . .
Just because you're pa—ale . . .
Well?

ABRAM. Have you ever seen a crazy cuckoo? That's him.

EMILIAN. You're a cuckoo yourself. Dance, I say!

ABRAM. But why should I dance? Of all the lunatics!

EMILIAN. Because you don't understand the regulations. There's a rule among us: whoever receives a letter is obliged to dance according to instructions and without objections. (*Exhibits a letter.*) Here! A letter. Dance! (*Sings again.*)

ABRAM. For whom is this letter?

EMILIAN. For you, for you . . . Dance! (*Continues to sing, beating time with hands and feet.*)

ABRAM. A letter for me? This is a rare historical occasion. I haven't received a letter since 1917. I've even forgotten how it's done. Let me have it!

EMILIAN. Dance!

ABRAM. All jokes aside, let me have it. (EMILIAN *holds the letter tantalizingly over* ABRAM'S *head but does not give it to him.*) Come on, quit playing the fool.

EMILIAN. Dance, or I'll teach you a few tricks. (*Doubles up his arm and displays his muscular prowess.*) Just feel this!

ABRAM. Did you ever see such a crazy loon? From whom is it?

EMILIAN. From your life's companion. From your beloved wife.

ABRAM. From whose wife?

EMILIAN. What do you mean whose— how many wives have you got? From Tonka.

ABRAM. From Kuznetzova? Has anything happened to her?

EMILIAN. Nothing happened. We just ran into each other and she asked me to give it to you. Dance!

ABRAM. Stop your fooling. Let's have it.

EMILIAN. Stop your fooling. Dance!

ABRAM. Oh, for God's sake! Did you ever see such a fool? Here I'm facing a terrible domestic smash-up, and he's forcing me to dance! I don't know how to dance. Haven't the slightest idea. Come on, let's have it.

EMILIAN. Dance!

ABRAM. But I'm telling you I don't know how. I can't dance. Oh, what a rotten egg you are . . . Well, to hell with you! (*He begins to dance clumsily to the accompaniment of* EMILIAN'S *song and beating of time.*) Well, let's have it. (*Disgusted with himself; stops dancing.*) 10

EMILIAN. Come on, a little more. (*Continues to sing and beat time.*)

ABRAM. But I have danced!

EMILIAN (*threateningly*). Dance! (ABRAM *resumes foolishly, with a sad mien until even the implacable* EMILIAN *is satisfied.*) You're a hell of a dancer, you are! You dance like an elephant on bottles. There! (*Gives him the letter.*)

ABRAM (*fingers the envelope*). Ugh! I can 20 feel it already—these mediæval tricks are already beginning. (*In his excitement he can't tear the envelope open.*)

EMILIAN. Wait, let me have the letter. Your hands are trembling. (*He snatches the letter, opens it, gives* ABRAM *the envelope but retains the letter.*) Here, read this meanwhile.

ABRAM. Oh, for crying out loud! Have a heart! (*He snatches the letter and reads* 30 *aloud in a quavering voice while* EMILIAN *peeks over his shoulder.*) "Comrade Abram! I have been thinking this over a long time, and I have come to the conclusion that things cannot continue thus any longer. Under the newly arisen objective conditions . . . " I might have guessed that she would come to the objective conditions . . . 40

EMILIAN. Why, I said the very thing. Don't you remember when we were going to the bath-house? I told you so.

ABRAM (*vexed*). Emilian, have a heart. This is no time for joking. (*Reads again.*) "Under the newly arisen objec-

tive conditions, our living together is inadmissible. You understand, of course, to what I am referring." Ugh! I'm facing a smash-up . . . (*Reads.*) "I consider it indispensable to draw the appropriate organizational conclusions . . . " Oh, my God! I'm afraid she'll poison herself.

EMILIAN. No, she'll drown herself, my dear boy, she'll drown herself. (*Strokes* ABRAM'S *head.*)

ABRAM (*in a rage*). Let me alone, Emilian! (*Reads.*) " . . . I must go away. Gather all of your manliness, like a true Communist Youth, and do not attempt to hold me back . . . It must be so . . ." Complete smash-up —I knew it.

EMILIAN. Horrors, horrors!

ABRAM (*reads*). "By the time you will be reading this letter, I shall probably be . . ." Oh, my God! Only not in a crematorium! Not in a crematorium!

EMILIAN. No, in the Moscow River. It's cooler there.

ABRAM (*jumps up, furious, shouts*). Emilian, cut it out! (EMILIAN *quiets down. Reads.*) ". . . I shall probably be . . . rushing by train . . ."

EMILIAN (*correcting him*). Crushed by the train . . .

ABRAM (*yielding to him in fright*). " . . . crushed by the train . . . to the village."

EMILIAN (*reading over his shoulder*). . . . crushed by the train to the village— no, there's something wrong here.

ABRAM (*joyfully*). " . . . rushing by train to the village. I have been sent there by the management at my own request. Try to forget me and return the book to Sonya Ogurtsova. With Communist greetings, Antonia Kuznetzova." (*Quite revived.*) Oh, Tonka, Tonka. There's a fine girl for you. And I expected something horribly mediæval. Ha—no melodrama. Ludmillka, do you hear? "With Communist greetings, Kuznetzova. With Communist greetings, Kuznetzova." (*He begins a wild dance to his own accompaniment on the accordion.*)

[VASYA *enters his own half, in excellent mood, takes up his guitar and does a jig to his own accompaniment.*]

EMILIAN (*admiring* ABRAM's *outburst*). Just look at the big fraud. Only a moment ago he was crying on my shoulder and insisting he doesn't know how to dance. Well, I'll be jiggered . . .

ABRAM (*still playing and dancing*). "With Communist greetings, Kuznetzova. With Communist greetings, Kuznetzova." She's gone! She's gone!

[EMILIAN *is attracted by the music in the other half; dumbfounded, stares from one side to the other, as the two happy dancers meet in the foreground.*]

VASYA. She's gone, she's gone, she's gone, she's gone.

ABRAM. She's gone, she's gone, she's gone, she's gone. "With Communist greetings, Kuznetzova. With Communist greetings, Kuznetzova."

EMILIAN. Have you ever seen such idiots?

VASYA (*stops abruptly and stares at* ABRAM). She's gone! Ha-ha! She's gone!

ABRAM (*stops and stares at* VASYA). She's gone. Fact.

VASYA (*laughs and winks*). She's gone.

ABRAM (*laughs and winks*). She's gone.

VASYA. Wait, who's gone?

EMILIAN (*echoes their words, in mounting bewilderment, jerking his head from one to the other and back*). Wait, who's gone?

ABRAM. Yes, who's gone?

EMILIAN. Yes, who's gone?

VASYA. What do you mean who? Ludmillka.

EMILIAN. What do you mean who? Ludmillka.

ABRAM. Wha-at . . . Ludmillka's gone! You're crazy. Kuznetzova is gone.

EMILIAN. You're crazy. Kuznetzova is gone.

VASYA. Wha-at, you're crazy yourself. Tonka—gone? Are you joking?

EMILIAN. Are you joking?

ABRAM. Wait! (*He's dumbfounded.*)

VASYA. Wait! (*He's dumbfounded.*)

EMILIAN. Wait! Don't wait! Listen, boys, the case is perfectly clear. Both chickens have flown the coop. That's as clear as day.

VASYA. Wai-ait . . . she . . . entirely . . . gone . . .

EMILIAN. Entirely gone?

ABRAM. Entirely. Why?

EMILIAN. Entirely. Why?

VASYA. Where to?

EMILIAN. Where to?

ABRAM. She went to work in a village. Why?

EMILIAN. She went to work in a village. Why?

VASYA. To the village . . . what do you mean . . .wait . . .

EMILIAN. What do you mean? Wait!

ABRAM. Wait . . . Ludmilla . . . entirely . . .

EMILIAN. Entirely?

VASYA. Entirely. Why?

EMILIAN. Why?

ABRAM. Where to, where to? Tell me.

VASYA. Just so. I don't know. Why?

ABRAM (*in despair*). Why didn't you look after her?

EMILIAN. Why didn't you look after her?

VASYA. Well, why blame me? Why didn't you? How could you let her go?

EMILIAN. How could you let her go?

ABRAM. No, but why didn't he look after her?

EMILIAN. No, but why didn't you look after her?

VASYA. Why didn't I look after her? Wait. What business is it of yours, after all?

EMILIAN. What business is it of yours, after all?

ABRAM (*vehemently*). I'd like to know whose business it is? Do you think it concerns you more than it concerns me?

EMILIAN. Do you think it concerns you more than it concerns him?

VASYA. Shut up! You brought Tony-echka to the point where she would go to the Devil rather than see your disgusting mug. Where can I look for her now?

EMILIAN. Where can he look for her now?

ABRAM. I brought the girl to that point! And you? What have you done? And to what have you brought Ludmilla? (*Mocking him.*) Pussykin, kiss my teeny-weeny nose. Pussykin, say "Meow."

VASYA. And what business is it of yours?

EMILIAN. And what business is it of yours?

ABRAM. And what business is it of yours?

VASYA. I can't bear to look at you, you lousy little bourgeois!

ABRAM. You're a bourgeois yourself!

VASYA. Whom are you calling a bourgeois? Am I a bourgeois?

ABRAM. You're worse. You're a renegade and an opportunist!

EMILIAN (*in rapture*). If I were you, Vaska, I'd sock him one for calling me a renegade.

VASYA. Whom did you call a renegade? (*Advances, swinging his arms.*)

EMILIAN (*happy at the prospect of a scrap*). That's right, boys; fight it out, but don't damage the musical instruments.

VASYA. Who's a renegade?

EMILIAN. Yes—whom did you call a renegade?

ABRAM. Throw down your guitar and fight like a man. (*They rush into the corridor.*)

EMILIAN (*peering into the corridor*). That's right. Sock him! Don't hit below the belt! Sock him! Ho-ho! Not bad for an extemporaneous fight!

VASYA'S VOICE. Who's a renegade? (*All voices are drowned for a moment by the crash of the bicycle.*)

EMILIAN (*shouting into the door*). Boys, that won't do at all. You'll break the guitar. If you want to fight, fight according to all the rules of the novel. On the second floor, in apartment 18, Volodya has a pair of Denikin swords. Sock him! (*Noise.*) A haymaker! Let's have a fight according to rules. I won't permit it otherwise. (*But despite the poet's enthusiasm, ABRAM and VASYA can't get really started; Russian fashion, they shout more than they fight.*)

ABRAM'S VOICE. Drop the guitar!

VASYA'S VOICE. Who's a renegade?

ABRAM'S VOICE. Drop the guitar or I won't be responsible for anything I do to you . . . Let go of me!

VASYA'S VOICE. Wait!

EMILIAN. Come on, get the swords. Ho-ho-ho. Now we'll have a real fight. (EMILIAN *goes out; noises in the corridor which gradually die down.* EMILIAN *returns, wiping his brow as if after a strenuous battle.*) That's what I call dancing! Oh, boy! What fun! (*Whistles.*) Even I got hot. Well, now that the hens have flown the coop, I'll have a chance to sleep here, and I'll even get a bite to eat now and then. (*He pulls up the spring mattress, props it against the table so that it is in an inclined position.*) Now I must compose a new poem. But first it is necessary to create the proper environment and the right mood for inspiration. (*He knocks the furniture about, gathers all the available food, sprawls on the mattress at princely ease, and composes aloud with a full mouth.*) Well now, I have an order for

a poem on bottled mineral water—
"Narzan." Here goes:
"If you must drink merely water,
Then it's Narzan that you oughter!"
Even I admit, it doesn't sound so extra.

[*Enter* FLAVIUS, *regards the deserted rooms and the sprawling* EMILIAN *in puzzlement.*

EMILIAN. Hello, Flavius. Do you want a bite? 10

FLAVIUS. Hello. What in thunder are you doing here, disturbing the domestic peace of two homes?

EMILIAN. Yes, the homes *have* been here, but they're both out now.

FLAVIUS. What's going on here?

EMILIAN. A melodrama in six acts. The chicks have flown the coop and the boys have gone up to apartment 18 for the swords. 20

FLAVIUS. What's the matter with you? Are you drunk? Talk sense.

EMILIAN. I'm talking sense, and I'm telling you that Tonka has, all of a sudden, made up her mind that Vaska is her soul-mate. Ludmilla has lost her head over Abramchik. Vaska, like the braying ass he is, has lost his heart to Tonka, while Abramchik has thrown himself on the soft bosom of Lud-30 millka and is pining away for her. And they were all ashamed of themselves and scared to look each other in the eyes, but finally the whole business went into bankruptcy. Tonka couldn't stand it and disappeared. Ludmillka couldn't stand it and disappeared. Vaska and Abramchik have run upstairs to apartment 18 to hack each other to pieces. And in the 40 meantime I'm seriously thinking of moving in here.

FLAVIUS. A duel?

EMILIAN. According to all the rules, like Pushkin fought with Gogol. A blow with a sword over the head and yours

truly is gone. They're so hot under the collar that something terrible is bound to happen. Grrr . . .

FLAVIUS. Then why do you lie here braying like an ass? Two damn fools have run off to fight an idiotic duel, are disgracing the All-Union League of Communist Youth, and the third fool is lying with his dirty shoes on a strange bed, and . . . grr . . . Come on. Get a move on you! Show your athletic prowess. Bring the duellers here, dead or alive! And damn quick!

EMILIAN. Ee-ekh! (*Departs.*)

FLAVIUS. This is the most scandalous thing that has ever happened in our district. (*Whistling significantly.*) That's a fine state of affairs. (*Pause.*) What do you think of these Soviet hussars? (TONYA *arrives, tearfully begins to gather her toothbrush, tin cup, towel, which she stuffs into the pocket of her mackintosh.* FLAVIUS *notices her.*) Where are you bound for, Tonya?

TONYA. I'm going away, Flavius.

FLAVIUS. Where are you going?

TONYA. I'm going to work. In the village.

FLAVIUS. What new-fangled idea is this? Suddenly, out of a clear sky, you're burning with desire to work in the village. What's the big idea?

TONYA. Don't ask me, Flavius. It's very difficult for me, but it can't be helped. Good-bye, Flavius.

FLAVIUS. Oh, no, you don't! Wait! You tell me sensibly, has anything happened?

TONYA. Yes . . . no . . . nothing has happened. Well, good-bye.

FLAVIUS. Kuznetzova, don't try to put anything over on me. You tell me right out what's happened here.

TONYA. Nothing.

FLAVIUS. So—nothing?

TONYA. Nothing. I don't know.

[*Meanwhile,* LUDMILLA, *in tears, has returned with her bundle, evidently not having been welcomed at her old home.*]

LUDMILLA (*suppressing sobs and blowing her nose*). I've forgotten . . . grandma and grandpa. (*She removes the portraits and, hearing* FLAVIUS *and* TONYA *in the other half, comes close to the partition.*)

FLAVIUS. You don't know, eh? Well, I know. You're in love with Vaska. Well, little girl, look me straight in the eye.

TONYA. I love him.

FLAVIUS. And does Vaska love you? Look me straight in the eye.

TONYA. He loves me.

FLAVIUS. Then why in thunder are you trying to put something over on me and trying to make a psychological melodrama out of the business? If you love each other, what's to stop you? Rush down to the Marriage Registry. You can't hurt the Revolution that way and there's no sense in running away to the village.

TONYA. And what about Abram?

FLAVIUS. You should have thought of this before you went down to register.

TONYA. I thought . . . we thought . . . compatibility of character . . . workers' solidarity . . . common political background . . . (*Sobbing.*) And so . . . and so . . . no, no! Comrade Abram will not be able to survive it . . . Can't you see that Comrade Ludmilla will not be able to survive it . . . Don't you see, Flavius, that we must not build our own happiness upon the unhappiness of other comrades. . . . (*She cannot control her sobs.*)

[LUDMILLA, *while peeping into their part of the room, suddenly drops the grandparents' portraits with a bang, and stands there, bundle in hand, bawling like a child and on the verge of running away.* FLAVIUS *jerks the curtain, revealing her thus.*]

FLAVIUS. Where to?

LUDMILLA (*indecisive for a moment, then impulsively runs to the weeping* TONYA *and embraces her*). Oh, Tonyechka, oh, my little treasure!

TONYA. Comrade Ludmilla . . .

LUDMILLA. Oh, my pussykin! I heard everything . . . Don't weep, darling, you mustn't weep . . . Take Vaska if you want him, but for God's sake, don't worry yourself, because as far as I'm concerned it's all the same to me . . . without Abramchik . . . what's life worth? (*Both of them now shed tears of joy over the bundle.*)

TONYA. My dear, my little baby, my little sister!

FLAVIUS (*soothing them*). Well, there, there you are! Now they've set to bawling! Oh, you dear little monkeys! On the other hand, it can't do any harm. Sometimes weeping helps. Go on, cry it out. It can't hurt the Revolution.

[*Behind the scene are heard shouts, noise, ringing of bells, horrible commotion, cries, climaxed by the familiar crash of the bicycle.*]

TONYA. What has happened?

LUDMILLA. Oh, what is it? A fire?

FLAVIUS. Quiet down, girls. Nothing terrible. That's our two little roosters, the black one and the white one, settling their little domestic quarrels.

[VASYA *and* ABRAM *fall into the room, fighting clumsily.* VASYA *has found a ludicrous old sword, while* ABRAM *holds a scabbard and is trying desperately to pull the sword out. Somehow they have held on to their guitar and accordion throughout the scuffle. Behind them, yelling loudest of all, is* EMILIAN.]

EMILIAN (*clumsily running around the duellists*). Where you going? Where you going? Stop! Take it easy! Take it easy! You've both gone crazy, upon my word! You'll damage the musical instruments . . . Vaska! Abramchik!

VASYA. Where is Tonka, I'm asking you?

ABRAM. What did you do with Ludmilla?

VASYA. And what business is it of yours?

ABRAM. And what business is it of yours?

VASYA. You lousy little bourgeois!

ABRAM (*to* EMILIAN). Let go of me! I'll 10 knock his block off!

[*He finally pulls the sword out of the scabbard, tumbling over from the exertion. The sword proves to be broken, and he holds only a hilt in his hand.* VASYA, *retreating, stumbles against the partition, which falls on* TONYA, LUDMILLA, *and* FLAVIUS. *General confusion.*]

VASYA. Tonka, Ludmillka!

ABRAM. Ludmillka! Tonka! (*The boys do* 20 *not know what to do, nor how to behave.*)

VASYA. Flavius . . .

ABRAM. Flavius . . .

FLAVIUS. That's a pip. Perfectly scrumptious! Tonka, Ludmillka, what have you to say to this? Two perfect idiots are duelling with musical instruments. It's a picture worthy of a painter.

ABRAM (*pretending joy*). Kuznetzova! 30 You're not in the village yet? (*He is about to run to her, but* TONYA *stops him with a proud gesture and points to* LUDMILLA.)

VASYA (*hypocritically*). Ludmillochka, have you come back? I'm frightfully happy. (LUDMILLA *echoes* TONYA'S *gesture.*)

ABRAM. What's the trouble, Tonyechka?

FLAVIUS. Now, listen, kids. Cut out the 40 fooling. Don't twist the bull's tail. Everything is clear. We all understand the situation and we know everything.

EMILIAN. And what's more, everything has been investigated.

FLAVIUS. Tonka, do you love Vaska?

TONYA. I love him.

FLAVIUS. Ludmillochka, do you love Abramchik?

LUDMILLA. I love him.

ABRAM. Comrades, this isn't ethical. What? Or is it ethical?

FLAVIUS. Abramchik, don't be an overclever parrot. Now, kids, what are you standing around for?

EMILIAN. Indeed, why? (*He sits down on the bench. They all understand everything.*)

FLAVIUS. You got married, all of you, as if you had been running away from a fire, without thinking of consequences, and then turn your rooms into an art theatre, and in the meanwhile you put me to all the trouble of divorcing and remarrying you properly. I must remind you, comrades, that I have other business to attend to. Well!

[LUDMILLA *throws herself into* ABRAM'S *arms, and* TONYA *into* VASYA'S.]

TONYA. Vasyuk!

LUDMILLA. Abramchik, my little treasure!

VASYA. Tonka!

ABRAM. Ludmillochka! (*The couples embrace.*)

FLAVIUS (*to* EMILIAN). Pull up anchor, my boy. You're not going to sleep here tonight. Roll on!

EMILIAN. Can't I even recite an extemporaneous poem before I go?

FLAVIUS. Roll on, roll on! Get a move on!

EMILIAN. Ee-ekh!

"The city has gnawed me to pieces—
I will not see my native moon.
I will tear my collar wide-open
That I may hang myself soon."

Ee-ekh! They see a poor prodigy perishing and yet nobody will do anything for him. I guess I'll have to sleep in apartment 18. (*Departs.*)

FLAVIUS. All right. All right. The trouble is that he may come back. He turns up like a bad poem. (*He picks up the portraits from the floor, gives the grandpa to one couple and the grandma to the other.*) Well, on the basis of the marital code, all property must be equally divided. Here's a grandpa for you and a grandma for you. (*They accept the portraits.*) And so it seems that everything is in order. Good-night.

VASYA (*humorously, to* ABRAM). Pussykin, tell your little pussy, "Meow"!

ABRAM (*brightly*). Meow!

FLAVIUS. Never mind, kids. Don't be bashful. Go to it. Love one another and don't play the fool. It can't hurt the Revolution.

[*The confusion of stations on the radio suddenly erupts once more. It continues its medley of Soviet music, slogans and speeches even after the curtain goes down. At one point,* EMILIAN *suddenly appears astride the famous battered bicycle bellowing, "The city has gnawed me to pieces . . . I have not a place to sleep . . ."*]

VOICES ON THE RADIO. Workers of the world, unite! You have nothing to lose but your chains . . . (*A gay voice singing.*) "By radio we met, and by radio we wed and by radio we got a pretty baby Red . . ." (*In horribly mispronounced English.*) " . . . begin tonight's lesson in advanced course of ze English langvidge. My oncle's hat is small, but your aunt's garden is beeg . . ." (*The gay voice emerges again, singing the following words to the same tune.*) "Now Kalinin is my beau, and I'll surely let him know, that I fell for him last night—on the radio!" . . . Workers, peasants and Red Army men, the toiling masses . . . (*Snatches from the doleful "Volga Boatmen Song," broken abruptly by a balalaika orchestra strumming a wild Caucasian tune.*) . . . Shock-brigades and more shock-brigades . . . the world's biggest steel foundry, the world's tallest building . . . Love, superstition and other bourgeois prejudices . . . As Karl Marx said . . . the K.V.Zhe.D. . . . the V.K.P.B. and V.S.N.X. . . . Komsomol . . . Mostorg . . . Narkompochtel . . . R.S.F.S.R. . . . Workers of the world . . . (*The blare of a Red Army song.*)

CURTAIN

STUDENTS' BIBLIOGRAPHY OF MODERN DRAMA

THE number of books on modern drama has grown to huge proportions. The subject has had so many points of interest, and it has been so dynamic over a period of sixty years, that it has called forth hundreds of articles, studies, and books on every aspect of drama and the theatre. Many of these works served a useful purpose but were outmoded by the onrush of the movement. Others have been superseded by later, more complete treatises. The following list is a beginner's guide to the most helpful books on the drama, the playwrights, and the theatre.

BIBLIOGRAPHY

ANDERSON, MAXWELL. The Essence of Tragedy. Washington, 1939.
ANDREWS, CHARLTON. The Drama of Today. Philadelphia, 1913.
BAHR, HERMAN. Expressionism (trans. by R. F. Gribble). London, 1925; Munich, 1920.
BAILLY, A. Maeterlinck (trans. F. Rothwell). London, 1931.
BELL, A. F. G. Contemporary Spanish Literature. New York, 1925.
BITHELL, JETHRO. Life and Writings of Maurice Maeterlinck. London, 1930.
BLOCK, ANITA. The Changing World in Plays and Theatre. Boston, 1939.
BROWN, JOHN MASON. Broadway in Review, New York, 1940.
—— The Modern Theatre in Revolt. New York, 1929.
—— Two on the Aisle: Ten Years of the American Theatre in Performance. New York, 1938.
CARTER, HUNTLEY. The New Spirit in the Russian Theatre, 1917–1928. New York, 1929.
—— The New Spirit in the European Theatre, 1914–1924. New York, 1926.
CHANDLER, FRANK W. The Contemporary Drama of France. Boston, 1925.
—— Modern Continental Playwrights. (Excellent survey, with complete bibliographies.) New York, 1931.
CHARQUES. R. D. (ed.). Footnotes to the Theatre. London, 1938.
CLARK, BARRETT H. Eugene O'Neill, The Man and His Plays. New York, 1929 and 1936.
—— A Study of the Modern Drama (Revised ed.). New York, 1936.
COATS, R. H. John Galsworthy as a Dramatic Artist. New York, 1926.
CORDELL, RICHARD. W. Somerset Maugham. New York, 1937.
CUNLIFFE, JOHN W. Modern English Playwrights. New York, 1927.
DAHLSTRÖM, CARL E. W. L. Strindberg's Dramatic Expressionism. Ann Arbor, 1930.
DANA, H. W. L. Handbook on Soviet Drama. New York, 1938.
DICKINSON, THOMAS H. An Outline of Contemporary Drama. Boston, 1927.
—— The Contemporary Drama of England. Boston, 1931.
—— (ed.). The Theatre in a Changing Europe. New York, 1937.
DUHAMEL, GEORGES. Paul Claudel, le philosophe, le poète, l'ecrivain, le dramaturge. Paris, 1913.
—— Paul Claudel, suivi de propos critiques. Paris, 1919.
DUKES, ASHLEY. The Youngest Drama. Chicago, 1924.
ELOESSER, ARTHUR. Modern German Literature. New York, 1933.
FAY, W. G., and CARSWELL, CATHERINE. The Fays of the Abbey Theatre. New York, 1935.
FLANAGAN, HALLIE. Shifting Scenes of the Modern European Theatre. New York, 1928.
FLEXNER, ELEANOR. American Playwrights: 1918–1938. New York, 1938.
FYFE, H. H. Sir Arthur Wing Pinero's Plays and Players. London, 1930.
GASSNER, JOHN. Masters of the Drama. New York, 1940.

GERHARDI, WILLIAM. Anton Chekhov, A Critical Study. London, 1923.
GILDER, ROSAMOND. A Theatre Library. A Bibliography of One Hundred Books Relating to the Theatre. New York, 1932.
GOLDBERG, ISAAC. The Drama of Transition: Native and Exotic Playcraft. Cincinnati, 1922.
GORELIK, MORDECAI. New Theatres for Old. New York, 1941.
GOSSE, EDMUND. Life of Henrik Ibsen. New York, 1907.
GREGORY, LADY. Our Irish Theatre, A Chapter of Autobiography. New York, 1913.
HALASZ, GEORGE. Ferenc Molnar, the Man Behind the Monocle. New York, 1929.
HAMILTON, CLAYTON MEEKER. The Theory of the Theatre. (Consolidated ed.) New York, 1939.
HENDERSON, ARCHIBALD. European Dramatists. New York, 1926.
—— G. Bernard Shaw: His Life and Works. New York, 1932.
HOUGHTON, NORRIS. Moscow Rehearsals; an Account of Methods of Production in the Soviet Theatre. New York, 1936.
KAUN, ALEXANDER. Maxim Gorky and His Russia. New York, 1931.
KOHT, HALDAN. The Life of Ibsen. 2 vols. New York, 1931.
KOMMISARJEVSKY, THEODORE. Myself and the Theatre. New York, 1930.
KRUTCH, JOSEPH WOOD. The American Drama Since 1918. New York, 1939.
LEWISOHN, LUDWIG. The Modern Drama. An Essay in Interpretation. New York, 1915.
—— The Drama and the Stage. New York, 1922.
MCCLINTOCK, LANDER. The Contemporary Drama of Italy. Boston, 1920.
MCGILL, V. J. August Strindberg, the Bedevilled Viking. New York, 1930.
MALONE, ANDREW E. The Irish Drama. New York, 1929.
MANTLE, ROBERT BURNS. Contemporary American Playwrights. New York, 1939.
MARKOV, PAVEL. The Soviet Theatre. New York, 1935.
MARRIOTT, JAMES WILLIAM. Modern Drama. London, New York, 1934.
MARROT, H. V. The Life and Letters of John Galsworthy. New York, 1936.
MARSAN, JULES. Tendances: Théâtre d'hier et d'aujourd'hui. Paris, 1926.
MARTINO, P. Le Naturalisme Français (1870–1895). Paris, 1923.
—— Parnasse et Symbolisme (1850–1900). Paris, 1928.
MAUGHAM, W. SOMERSET. The Summing Up. New York, 1938.
MILLER, ANNA IRENE. The Independent Theatre in Europe, 1887 to the Present. New York, 1931.
MODERWELL, H. K. The Theatre of Today. New York, 1927.
MORGAN, A. E. Tendencies of Modern English Drama. New York, 1924.
NEMIROVITCH-DANTCHENKO, VLADIMIR. My Life in the Russian Theatre. Boston, 1936.
NICOLL, ALLARDYCE. British Drama. Revised ed. New York, 1933.
O'HARA, FRANK HURBURT. Today in American Drama. Chicago, 1939.
PALMER, JOHN. Studies in the Contemporary Theatre. Boston, 1927.
PERRIN, E. S-M. Introduction a l'oeuvre de Paul Claudel. Paris, 1926.
QUINN, ARTHUR HOBSON. A History of the American Drama from the Civil War to the Present Day. New York, 1936.
ROBINSON, LENNOX (ed.). The Irish Theatre: Lectures Delivered during the Abbey Theatre Festival held in Dublin in August, 1938. London, 1939.
SARGENT, DANIEL. Four Independents. New York, 1935. (Chapter on Claudel.)
SAYLER, OLIVER M. Our American Theatre. New York, 1923.
SCHNEIDER, M. Expressionism in Drama. Stuttgart, 1920.
SÉE, EDMOND. Le théâtre français contemporain. Paris, 1933.
SKINNER, RICHARD DANA. Eugene O'Neill, A Poet's Quest. New York, 1935.
SMITH, HUGH ALLISON. Main Currents of Modern French Drama. New York, 1925.
SOBEL, BERNARD. The Theatre Handbook and Digest of Plays. (Useful but contains high percentage of errors.) New York, 1940.
STARKIE, WALTER. Luigi Pirandello, 1867–1936. New York, 1937.
SUBERVILLE, JEAN. Edmond Rostand: Son Théâtre, Son Oeuvre Posthume. Paris, 1922.
SUTTON, GRAHAM. Some Contemporary Dramatists. London, 1924.
SYMONS, ARTHUR. The Symbolist Movement in Literature. New York, 1917.

TAYLOR, UNA. Maurice Maeterlinck, a Critical Study. London, 1914.

THOMPSON, VANCE. Strindberg and His Plays. New York, 1921.

TOLLER, ERNST. I Was a German. London, 1934.

TOUMANOVA, PRINCESS NINA ANDRONIKOVA. Anton Chekhov, The Voice of Twilight Russia. New York, 1937.

VERNON, FRANK. The Twentieth-Century Theatre. London, 1924.

VITTORINI, DOMENICO. The Drama of Luigi Pirandello. Philadelphia, 1935.

WARREN, L. A. Modern Spanish Literature. New York, 1929.

WAXMAN, SAMUEL MONTEFIORE. Antoine and the Théâtre Libre. Cambridge, 1926.

WEIGAND, HERMANN J. The Modern Ibsen. New York, 1925.

WIENER, LEO. The Contemporary Drama of Russia. Boston, 1924.

WILSON, NORMAN SCARLYN. European Drama. London, 1937.

WINTHER, SOPHUS KEITH. Eugene O'Neill, A Critical Study. New York, 1934.

ZUCHER, A. E. Ibsen, the Master-Builder. New York, 1929.

PLAYS BY CONTINENTAL DRAMATISTS REPRESENTED IN THIS VOLUME

THERE is some unresolved confusion in the dating of plays. This arises from the fact that usually there is a date of composition, a date of production, and a date of publication. Much work is yet to be done before this ideal three column chronology can be accurately set down. This bibliography lists the earliest date of the play, unless there is some good reason for choosing a production date, as when the date of composition is doubtful, or when the production date is of landmark importance.

KAREL ČAPEK

The Robbers (1920)
R. U. R. (1921)
The Makropoulos Affair (1922)
Loupeznik (1926)
The White Plague (1937)

The Mother (1938)
With Josef Čapek:
   The Insects (1921)
   Adam the Creator (1927)

ANTON CHEKHOV

On the High Road (1884)
Ivanov (1887)
The Sudden Death of a Horse, or The Greatness of the Russian Soul (1887)
The Bear (or The Boor) (1888)
The Tragedian in Spite of Himself (1888)
The Wood Demon (1889)
That Worthless Fellow Platonov (1889)
The Swan Song (1889)

The Proposal (1889)
Tatyana Repina (1889) (Published 1904)
The Sea Gull (1896)
Uncle Vanya (1897)
Three Sisters (1900)
The Jubilee (1903)
The Wedding (1903)
The Cherry Orchard (1904)

PAUL CLAUDEL

The Fair Sleeper (1886)
Tête d'Or (1890)
The City (1890)
The Maid Violaine (1892)
The Exchange (1894)
The Repose of the Seventh Day (1894)
Partage de Midi (1900)
The Hostage (1909)
The Tidings Brought to Mary (1910)
Proteus (1914)

Christmas Eve (1914)
Bitter Bread (1915)
The Father Humiliated (1916)
The Bear and the Moon (1917)
Man and His Wishes (1921)
Woman and Her Shadow (1923)
The Satin Slipper; or, The Worst is Not the Surest (1924)
The Book of Christopher Columbus (1929)

MAXIM GORKY

The Middle Class (or The Smug Citizen) (1900)
The Lower Depths (or A Night's Lodging, A Night's Shelter, At the Bottom, Submerged) (1902)
Summer Folk (1903)

Children of the Sun (1905)
Barbarians (1905)
Enemies (1906)
The Last Ones (1908)
Odd People (1910)
Children (1910)

The Meeting (1910)
The Zykovs (1913)
The Judge (The Old Man) (1915)
Cain and Artema (1921)

The Counterfeit Coin (1926)
Yegor Bulychov and Others (1932)
Dostigaev and Others (1933)

GERHART HAUPTMANN

Before Sunrise (1889)
The Festival of Peace (1890)
Lonely Lives (1891)
Colleague Crampton (1892)
The Weavers (1892)
The Beaver Coat (1893)
The Assumption of Hannele (1893)
Florian Geyer (1894)
Helios (1896)
The Sunken Bell (1896)
Elga (1898)
Pastoral (1898)
Drayman Henschel (1898)
Schluck and Jau (1899)
Michael Kramer (1900)
The Conflagration (or The Red Cock)
    (1901)
Poor Heinrich (1902)
Rose Bernd (1903)

And Pippa Dances (1906)
The Maidens of Bischofsberg (1907)
Charlemagne's Hostage (1908)
Griselda (1909)
The Rats (1911)
Gabriel Schilling's Flight (1912)
The Festival Play (1913)
The Bow of Odysseus (1914)
Winter Ballad (1917)
The White Savior (1920)
Indipohdi (1920)
Peter Brauer (1921)
Veland (1925)
Dorothea Angermann (1926)
Witches' Ride (1930)
The Black Mask (1930)
Before Sunset (1932)
The Golden Harp (1933)
Hamlet at Wittenberg (1935)

HENRIK IBSEN

Catiline (1849)
The Warrior's Barrow (1850)
St. John's Night (1853)
Lady Inger of Östraat (1855)
The Feast of Solhaug (1856)
Olaf Liljekrans (1857)
The Vikings in Helgeland (1857)
Love's Comedy (1862)
The Pretenders (1863)
Brand (1866)
Peer Gynt (1867)
The League of Youth (1869)
Emperor and Galilean (1873)

The Pillars of Society (1877)
A Doll's House (1879)
Ghosts (1881)
An Enemy of the People (1882)
The Wild Duck (1884)
Rosmersholm (1886)
The Lady from the Sea (1888)
Hedda Gabler (1890)
The Master Builder (1892)
Little Eyolf (1894)
John Gabriel Borkman (1897)
When We Dead Awaken (1899)

VALENTINE KATAYEV

The Embezzlers (1928)
Squaring the Circle (1928)
Department Store (1929)
Vanguard (1930)
The Million Torments (1931)
Time Forward (1932)

Under the Circus Tent (1934)
Path of Flowers (1934)
The Rich Bride (1936)
Lonely White Sail (1937)
I, Son of the Working People (1938)

HENRI-RENÉ LENORMAND

White Madness (1905)
The Possessed (1909)

Dust (1914)
Time Is a Dream (1919)

The Failures (1920)
Simoom (1920)
The Devourer of Dreams (1922)
The Red Tooth (1922)
Man and His Phantoms (1924)
In the Shadow of Evil (1924)
The Coward (1925)

The Magician Love (1926)
Mixture (1927)
The Innocent (1928)
A Secret Life (1929)
Theatre Street (Crépuscule de théâtre) (1934)

MAURICE MAETERLINCK

Princess Maleine (1889)
The Blind (1890)
The Intruder (1890)
The Seven Princesses (1891)
Pelléas and Mélisande (1892)
Alladine and Palomides (1894)
Interior (or Home) (1894)
The Death of Tintagiles (1894)
Annabella (from Ford's 'Tis Pity She's a Whore) (1895)
Aglavaine and Sélysette (1896)
Sister Beatrice (1900)
Ariane and Blue Beard (1901)
Monna Vanna (1902)
Joyzelle (1903)
The Miracle of St. Anthony (1904)

The Blue Bird (1908)
Mary Magdalene (1910)
Macbeth (translated from Shakespeare) (1910)
The Betrothal (sequel to The Blue Bird) (1918)
The Burgomaster of Stilemonde (1920)
The Salt of Life (a sequel to The Burgomaster) (1920)
The Power of the Dead (1923)
The Cloud That Lifted (1923)
Berniquel (1923)
Misfortune Passes (1926)
Marie-Victoire (1927)
Juda de Kerioth (1929)

GREGORIO MARTÍNEZ SIERRA

Theater of Dreams (dialogues) (1905)
Life and Sweetness (with Santiago Rusiñol) (1907)
The Swallows (with Rusiñol) (1908)
Love Magic (1908)
The Shadow of the Father (1909)
The Mistress of the House (1910)
The Fortune of Isabelita (1911)
Lily Among Thorns (1911)
The Cradle Song (1911)
Spring in Autumn (1911)
Poor John (1912)
Mamma (1912)
Madame Pepita (1912)
The Lover (1913)
Madrigal (1913)
The Two Shepherds (1913)
For Women Only (1913)
Youth, Divine Treasure (1913)
Wife to a Famous Man (1914)
Passion (1914)
The Romantics (1914)
Margot (1914)

The Mournful Palace (1914)
The Kingdom of God (1915)
Dawn (1915)
Holy Night (1916)
The Romantic Young Lady (1918)
Our Hope (1918)
Don Juan of Spain (1921)
The Tower of Avorio (1922)
Cricket on the Hearth (1923)
The Tower of Ivory (1924)
The Devil's Hour (1925)
The Man Who Wanted to Dine (with J. Abati) (1925)
Modesty (with F. Sassone) (1925)
Woman (1925)
The Daughter of All (with Jacquetoz) (1925)
Intolerable Mary (with Honorio Maura) (1926)
The Road to Happiness (with Eduardo Marquina) (1926)
Let's Be Happy (1929)
Triangle (1929)

FERENC MOLNAR

The Lawyer (1902)
Jozsi (1904)

The Devil (1907)
Liliom (1909)

The Guardsman (1911)
The Wolf (produced as The Phantom Rival)
  (1912)
The Swan (1914)
Fashions for Men (1914)
The White Cloud (1915)
Carnival (1916)
A Prologue to King Lear (1919)
Marshal (1919)
The Violet (1919)
Heavenly and Earthly Love (1920)
Dinner (1922)
The Red Mill (Mima) (1923)

The Glass Slipper (1924)
The Play in the Castle (produced as The
  Play's the Thing) (1924)
Still Life (1925)
The Putty Club (1925)
A Matter of Husbands (1925)
Riviera (1925)
The Witch (1927)
"If Napoleon—" (1927)
Olympia (1928)
One, Two, Three (1929)
The Good Fairy (1930)
Delicate Story (1940)

LUIGI PIRANDELLO

Scamandra (1910)
The Vise (1910)
The Doctor's Duty (c. 1911)
Sicilian Limes (1913)
Just Think, Giacomo (1914)
Chee-Chee (c. 1915)
The Imbecile (c. 1915)
If Not Thus (1911, 1915)
The Rights of Others (1915)
Liola (1916)
Think It Over, Jimmy (1916)
Right You Are (If You Think So) (1916)
At the Gate (1916)
The Pleasure of Honesty (1917)
Cap and Bells (1917)
Grafting (1917)
The Patient (1918)
The Game as He Played It (1918)
He Didn't Mean It (1918)
Each of Us His Own Part (1918)
Man, Beast, and Virtue (1919)
All for the Best (1920)
Floriani's Wife (1920)

Signora Morli (1920)
One and Two (1920) (revised as Two in
  One, 1926)
By Judgment of the Court (1920)
The Other's Reason (1921)
Six Characters in Search of an Author
  (1921)
Henry IV (1922)
Naked (1922)
The Life I Gave Thee (1923)
The Man with the Flower in His Mouth
  (1923)
Each in His Own Way (1924)
Our Lord of the Ship (1925)
The House with the Column (1925)
The Jar (1925)
Diana and Tuda (1926)
Friendship of Women (1927)
The New Colony (1928)
Lazarus (1929)
One's or Nobody's (1929)
As You Desire Me (1930)
Tonight We Improvise (1930)

EDMOND ROSTAND

The Red Glove (1888)
The Two Pierrots (1891)
The Romancers (1894)
The Princess Faraway (1895)
The Woman of Samaria (1897)

Cyrano de Bergerac (1897)
The Eaglet (L'Aiglon) (1900)
Chantecler (1910)
The Sacred Wood (1910)
Don Juan's Last Night (1921)

AUGUST STRINDBERG

The Free-Thinker (1869)
Hermione (1869)
In Rome (1870)
The Outlaw (1871)
Master Olof (1877)
The Secret of the Guild (1880)

The Year Forty-Eight (1881)
The Journey of Lucky Peter (1882)
Sir Bengt's Lady (1882)
The Father (1887)
Comrades (1888)
Miss Julia (1888)

Hemso Folk (1889)
Creditors (1890)
The Stronger (1890)
Pariah (1890)
Simoom (1890)
The Keys of Heaven (1892)
The First Warning (1893)
Debit and Credit (1893)
Facing Death (1893)
Mother Love (1893)
Playing with Fire (1893)
The Link (1897)
To Damascus (Parts I and II) (1898)
Advent (1899)
There Are Crimes and Crimes (1899)
The Saga of the Folkungs (1899)
Gustavus Vasa (1899)
Eric XIV (1899)
Gustavus Adolphus (1900)
Caspar's Shrove Tuesday (1900)
The Dance of Death (Parts I and II) (1901)
Easter (1901)
Midsummer (1901)
Engelbrecht (1901)

Charles XII (1901)
The Bridal Crown (1902)
Swanwhite (1902)
The Dream Play (1902)
Gustavus III (1903)
The Nightingale of Wittenberg (1904)
To Damascus (Part III) (1904)
The Thunderstorm (1907)
The Burned Lot (1907)
The Spook Sonata (1907)
The Pelican (1907)
The Last Knight (1908)
The Slippers of Abu Casem (1908)
Christina (1908)
The Regent (1908)
The Earl of Bjälbo (1908)
The National Director (1909)
The Black Glove (1909)
The Great Highway (1909)
The Tooth (1909)
Ellas or Socrates (1918)
The Lamb and the Wild Beast, or Christ (1918)

ERNST TOLLER

Transfiguration (1919)
Masses and Man (1921)
The Machine-Wreckers (1922)
Brokenbrow (1922)
Wotan Unbound (1923)
Hinkemann (1923)
The Revenge of the Scorned Lover (1925)
Hoppla, Such Is Life (1927)

Mary Baker Eddy (with Hermann Kesten) (1930)
Draw the Fires (1931)
The Blind Goddess (1932)
Blind Man's Buff (with Denis Johnston) (1936)
No More Peace (1937)
Pastor Hall (1938)

SHORT STORIES